P9-DNN-192

Reader's Digest Illustrated Guide to Gardening

Reader's Digest

Illustrated Guide to Gardening

The Reader's Digest Association, Inc.
Pleasantville, New York • Montreal

Illustrated Guide to Gardening

Editor: Carroll C. Calkins

Art Editor: Murray J. Miller

Research Associate and Assistant to the Editor: Georgea Pace

Associate Editors: Inge N. Dobelis, Ruth Goldeman, Susan J. Wernert

Art Associates: Dorothy R. Schmidt, Donald D. Spitzer

Copy Editors: Diana Marsh, Suzanne Weiss

Research Associates: Giza Braun, Laurel Gilbride, Patricia Selden

Assistant Artists: Janet G. Iannacone, Wendy B. Talve

Project Secretary: Dolores H. Damm

The acknowledgments and credits that appear on pages 5 and 672 are hereby made a part of this copyright page.

The original British edition of this book was published by The Reader's Digest Association Limited, London, in 1975.

Library of Congress Catalog Card Number 77-85145
ISBN 0-89577-046-6
Printed in the United States of America

Artists

Norman Barber
David Baxter
Howard Berelson
Leonora Box
George Buctel
Pam Carroll
Helen Cowcher
Cyril David
Brian Delf
Ian Garrard
Tony Graham, LSIA
Roy Grubb
Vana Haggerty
Nicolas Hall
Gary Hincks
David Hutter
Richard Jacobs
Gillian Kenny
Sarah Kensington
Patricia Ann Lenander
Richard Lewington
Donald A. Mackay
Edward Malsberg
Noel Malsberg
Constance Marshall
Sean Milne
Thea Nockels
Charles Pickard
Charles Raymond
Ken Rice
John Rignall
John Roberts
Allianora Rosse
Anne Savage
Jim Silks
Ray Skibinski
Kathleen Smith, MSIA
Les Smith
Joyce Tuhill
Joan Berg Victor
Michael Vivo
John Western
Michael J. Woods
Elsie Wrigley

Consultants and Advisers

General Consultants

Thomas H. Everett
Senior Horticulture Specialist
New York Botanical Garden

Roy Hay, MBE, VMH

Technical Adviser

Kenneth A. Beckett

Special Consultants

Cornelius Ackerson

Harvey E. Barké, Ph.D.
Professor and Chairman
Department of Biological Sciences
State University of New York
Agricultural and Technical College
at Farmingdale

Henry O. Beracha

Arthur Bing, Ph.D.
Professor of Floriculture and
Ornamental Horticulture
Cornell University

Norman F. Childers, Ph.D.
Blake Professor of Horticulture
Cook College, Rutgers University

August DeHertogh, Ph.D.
Professor of Horticulture
Michigan State University

Marjorie J. Dietz

James E. Dwyer

Jerome A. Eaton

Harold Epstein

Eleanor Brown Gambee

Myron Kimnach
Curator and Superintendent
Huntington Botanical Gardens
San Marino, California

A. H. Krezdorn, Ph.D.
Professor of Horticulture
University of Florida

Donald Maynard, Ph.D.
Professor of Plant Sciences
University of Massachusetts

John T. Mickel, Ph.D.
Curator of Ferns
New York Botanical Garden

Margaret C. Ohlander

Donald Richardson

Robert Schery, Ph.D.
Director, Lawn Institute
Marysville, Ohio

James S. Wells

Helen M. Whitman

Contents

The Climates in Your Garden

Only years of experience will reveal all the warm and cold spots in your garden. But, as a general climate guide, these maps can be useful.

The little (micro) climates in every garden are most obvious in Zones A, B, and C, where freezing weather is a fact of life, as indicated on the map on the facing page.

The cold pockets of frost will reveal themselves in the fall while south-facing slopes are still warm. In the spring the pattern of the snow as it melts clearly shows which spots are the first to warm up and which stay cold the longest.

As indicated in the text and plant lists in this book, the last date of frost in spring and the first frost date in the fall can be critical. While no dependable date can be given for any specific area in a given year, much less for a particular section of a garden, the average frost dates in spring and fall can be helpful in scheduling plantings.

By looking at the maps below, you can tell when, in an average year, it will be safe to set out tender plants in spring with reasonable assurance that they will not be killed by frost. By June 1 the entire country is freeze free, except at high elevations, such as in the Rocky Mountains and the Sierra Nevadas.

The maps below show how long the growing season can be reasonably expected to continue in the fall. By December 1 the whole country is susceptible to freezing weather, except the warmest parts of Florida, Texas, and the Pacific Coast.

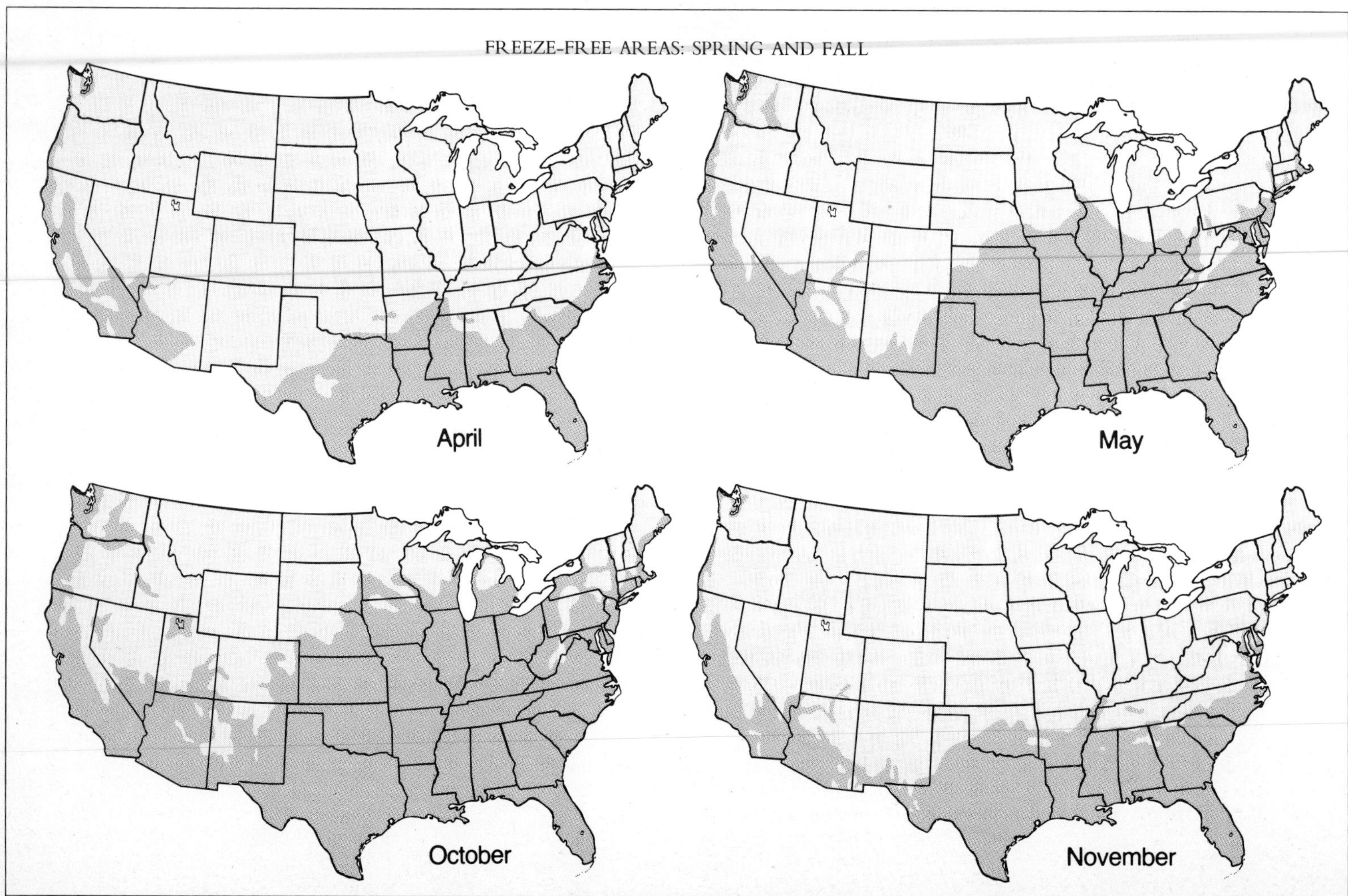

Temperature Zone Map

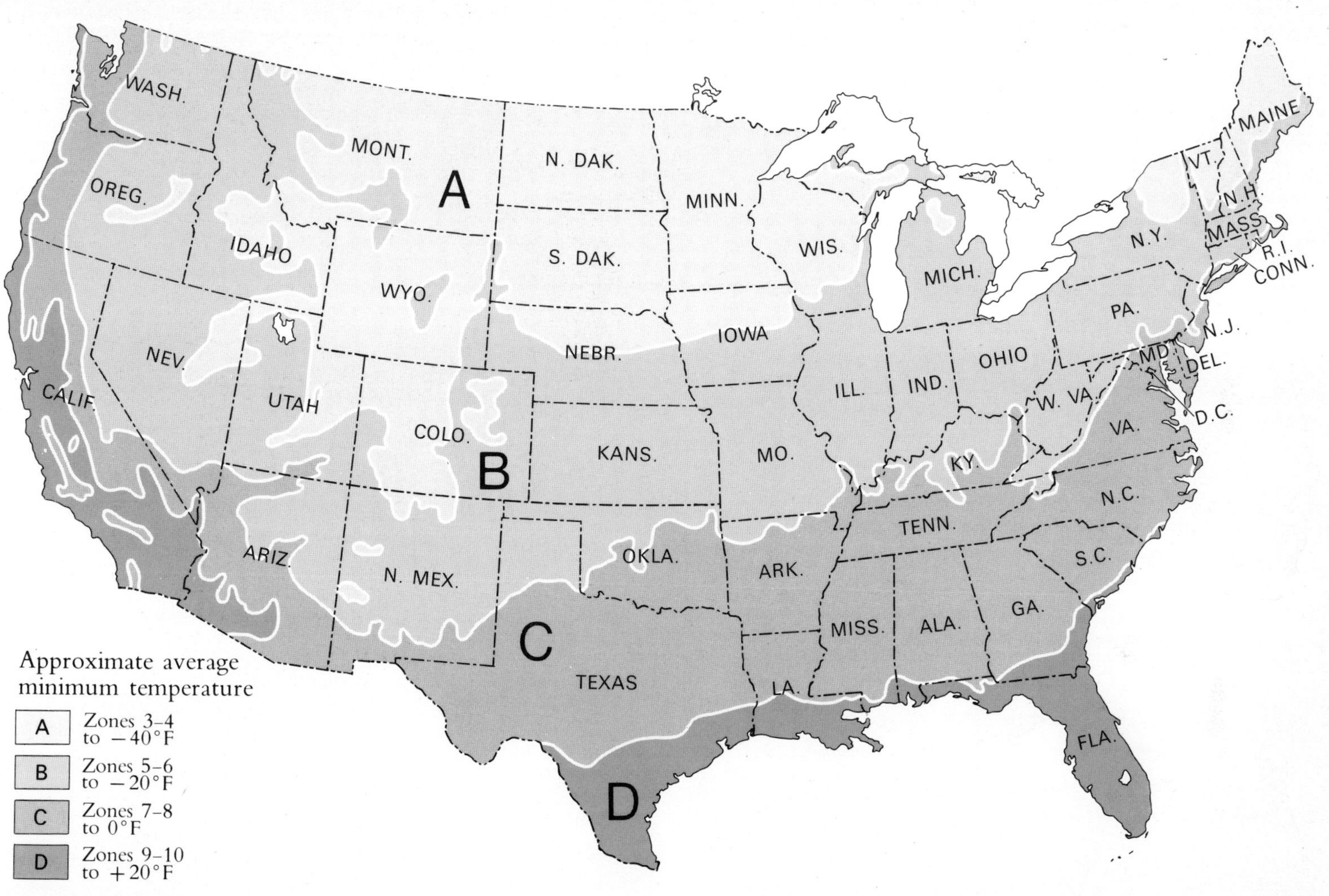

This map is a simplification of the standard U.S. Department of Agriculture Plant Hardiness Zone Map, which is widely used in garden literature and plant catalogs. Each of the four zones (A, B, C, and D) represents two USDA numbered zones, as indicated.

The letter designations accompany the plants listed in this book when the hardiness of the plant is of particular importance. A zonal designation indicates that the plant is hardy throughout that zone.

Climates tend to overlap, and the lines of separation are not as clear-cut as implied here. Many plants recommended for one zone will do well in the southern part of the adjoining colder zone, as well as in the next warmer zone. However, many tree and bush fruits, perennials, and bulbs require a cold-induced dormant season in order to set flowers or fruit.

Note that the indicated temperatures are an approximate average minimum. That is to say, some winters are colder and some warmer.

Temperature varies dramatically, of course, with elevation. It is colder at the top of a mountain in any zone than at the bottom. There are, of course, the microclimates to consider specifically. The temperature of a south-facing wall can be 10 degrees (or more) warmer than that of a north-facing wall. Areas sheltered from the wind will protect plants that are marginally hardy. While not perfect, the zone map of average minimum temperatures is the most useful single indicator of which plants are most likely to survive in your garden.

Using Plants to Best Advantage

A Guide to Plant Names

The Latinized botanical, or scientific, names of plants may seem unduly complex and sometimes difficult to pronounce, but they provide the best means of accurately identifying a plant. They also often describe some particular characteristic of a plant and reveal its relationship to other plants that might appear to be quite dissimilar.

All known plants have a botanical name, usually consisting of two or three words. The first word, always capitalized, is the name of a genus (a group marked by common characteristics or by one characteristic). This word, when used in conjunction with a second word, the specific epithet, provides the full botanical name of the species of the plant (a division of the genus). To designate subdivisions of species (subspecies and varieties), a third or fourth word is sometimes added to the name.

Magnolia, for example, is a familiar genus. *M. grandiflora* is a popular species (with, as you might deduce from the specific epithet, large, showy flowers). *M. g.* 'St. Mary' is an outstanding variety. In the case of magnolias, the genus name also serves as a common name (although *M. grandiflora* is called both Southern magnolia and bull bay).

One problem with the use of common names can be illustrated by the rose of Sharon. This is a hardy shrub that belongs to the genus *Hibiscus*—not, as might be assumed, to the rose genus (*Rosa*). The species is *H. syriacus*, and it has many handsome varieties, such as *H. s.* 'Bluebird' and *H. s.* 'Lady Stanley.' Rose of Sharon is related to a tropical plant, the Chinese hibiscus (*H. rosasinensis*), but one would never know this from its common name.

Another problem is that such common names as myrtle, laurel, bluebell, and daisy refer to one plant in some localities and other, quite different, plants elsewhere. Only botanical names can be depended upon everywhere. Botanical names, however, may be changed from time to time. In the process, both the old and new names are often used—for example, *"Franklinia,* or *Gordonia."*

Nevertheless, common names can be descriptive, colorful, and interesting; and in some places they are the only names listed. In the alphabetical plant listings in this book, common names are used first if they are widely known, followed by the botanical name.

A designation of variety may be Latinized, as in *Hibiscus rosasinensis totusalbus*, or appear in English as in *H. r.* 'American Beauty.' Note that in this book Anglicized varietal names appear within single quotation marks.

The word "variety" is used to indicate not only the variations in species that have developed in the wild but also those that have occurred naturally under cultivation or have been hybridized. In some catalogs and books, the word "cultivar" is used to distinguish horticultural selections and man-made hybrids from the natural varieties.

Gardens Start With Planning

To get the most from trees, shrubs, and flowers, you must first decide how you would like to use all the land that surrounds your house.

The purpose of a garden is to enrich the quality of life on the land that is under your control, be it a small backyard in the city or acres of space in the country. The ways to achieve this are many. Gardens offer color, fragrance, pleasing shapes, sound (from wind and birds), fresh tastes, and protection from the elements—in countless combinations. All of which helps to explain the endless fascination of gardening.

A garden, in its largest sense, includes the entire landscape as well as the relationship of plantings to the house. Ideally, both the planning of the garden and the siting of the home should be done at the same time, under the direction of a landscape architect. If the house is built before the garden, as is usually the case, the options are fewer. But the principles that concern the relation of the plantings to the house and the surrounding land remain the same.

The first thing to do in planning a garden is to make a rough sketch showing the relative size and position and the potential use of all major elements on your property, as illustrated on the facing page. In figuring out locations for flowering trees, showy shrubs, and colorful flower beds, consider putting them where they can easily be viewed through doors and windows. This will enable you to enjoy them from inside the house. Conversely, storage areas for tools and equipment, compost piles, and seasonal gardens for cut flowers and vegetables are best located where they are out of sight.

Now is also the time to decide whether the character of the garden will tend toward the formal or the informal. Formal design is essentially symmetrical; planting beds and single specimens of trees or shrubs (or groupings of plants) on one side of an axis or centerline, such as a walkway, are balanced with identical plantings on the other side. In a garden of this kind there is a definite sense of order and control; the edges are usually straight lines, and most plantings are likely to be neatly trimmed.

An informal garden is more asymmetrical in layout and likelier to have the curving lines found in nature. Plants are allowed to assume their natural form, and the hand of man is less obvious.

In the development of your garden design, all factors that can have an effect on the plants and people that will live on the land should be taken into account. You will want to know which places are sunny or shady, wet or dry, level or sloping, windy or protected from the breeze, fertile or poor in nutrients. Only if you have all this information can you choose the plants that are best adaptable to existing conditions.

Evaluating Existing Plants

In considering the plants already on the site, plan to keep as many of the better specimens as possible. Established trees and mature shrubs with interesting shapes will become important components of the garden.

Before any irrevocable decisions are made, existing plants should be evaluated for their potential contribution of leaves and flowers in each of the four seasons.

Even if a shrub is overgrown, it can often be pruned back and rejuvenated. This is much more rewarding than waiting years for a young plant to mature. In the chapter on shrubs and vines, you can find many that respond well to renovation.

Sometimes, however, it pays to be ruthless. No matter how handsome a plant may be, if it is obviously in the wrong place, it should be moved (if possible) or cut down. Do not hesitate to take out shrubs or trees that are too close to the house or are so crowded that they shade out—or otherwise encroach upon—more desirable plants.

Making New Plantings

Always consider the ultimate size of a shrub or tree before planting it.

This is more easily said than done, as you can readily see on almost any suburban street. In front of many houses are plants that have outgrown their allotted space. They darken rooms, obscure views, and even make it difficult to wash windows or paint trim. All of these problems can be avoided if the plants are chosen properly and set far enough away from the house in the first place.

It is usually better to select plants to suit a given situation than to try to change conditions to suit the plants. And, of course, some conditions, such as the weather, are beyond control.

A lawn, which is an essential element in most suburban gardens, will grow much more successfully if it has the amount of sunlight and kind of soil that suit it best. If there is not enough sunlight, something other than grass should be planted. But if the soil is not suitable, it can be improved without too much trouble.

It is more difficult to keep a lawn going in poor soil than it is to alter the soil before planting. Use a power tiller to mix into the topsoil the extra ingredients that may be required to meet the needs of a good lawn.

In laying out a lawn that will be cut with a riding mower, consider shaping the outline with curves that will accommodate the turning radius of the machine. This will eliminate the maneuvering required to get into corners.

Ideas for Saving Labor

A great boon to easy maintenance is a solid border around the lawn 6–8 inches wide and flush with the ground. This can be concrete, bricks set in concrete, or railroad ties. With one wheel of the lawn mower riding on this strip, hand trimming of the edge can be kept to a minimum.

Anything else that can be done in the design of a garden to reduce the time and effort it takes to keep the garden looking neat is all to the good. Hedges should be low enough to allow easy trimming; planting beds should be narrow enough to reach into for efficient weeding. High-maintenance areas, such as perennial borders and rock gardens, should not be larger than the available help can handle. Clean, crisp edges of masonry or wood for beds and planting areas can do wonders to improve the neatness of a garden and make the borders easier to maintain.

As an aid to maintenance, hard-surfaced paths throughout the garden area make it much easier to run a wheelbarrow or garden cart.

Also, if you intend to install a terrace or a swimming pool in the backyard, be sure that adequate access for trucks and heavy equipment is provided.

Give particular attention to your main entryway. Be sure it is clearly defined so that visitors can easily find their way to the door you want them to enter. Make walkways solid, well drained, and wide enough so that two people can walk comfortably side by side.

When it is time to buy the plants that will form the basic structure of your landscape, do not invest in anything of questionable hardiness for your climate. The trees and shrubs you plant are an investment that will grow for decades to increase the beauty—as well as the value—of your property.

If areas for outdoor living are to be included in the landscape, you may need to plan for fences, hedges, or informal mass plantings of trees and shrubs to provide privacy from (and for) people in nearby houses or on the street.

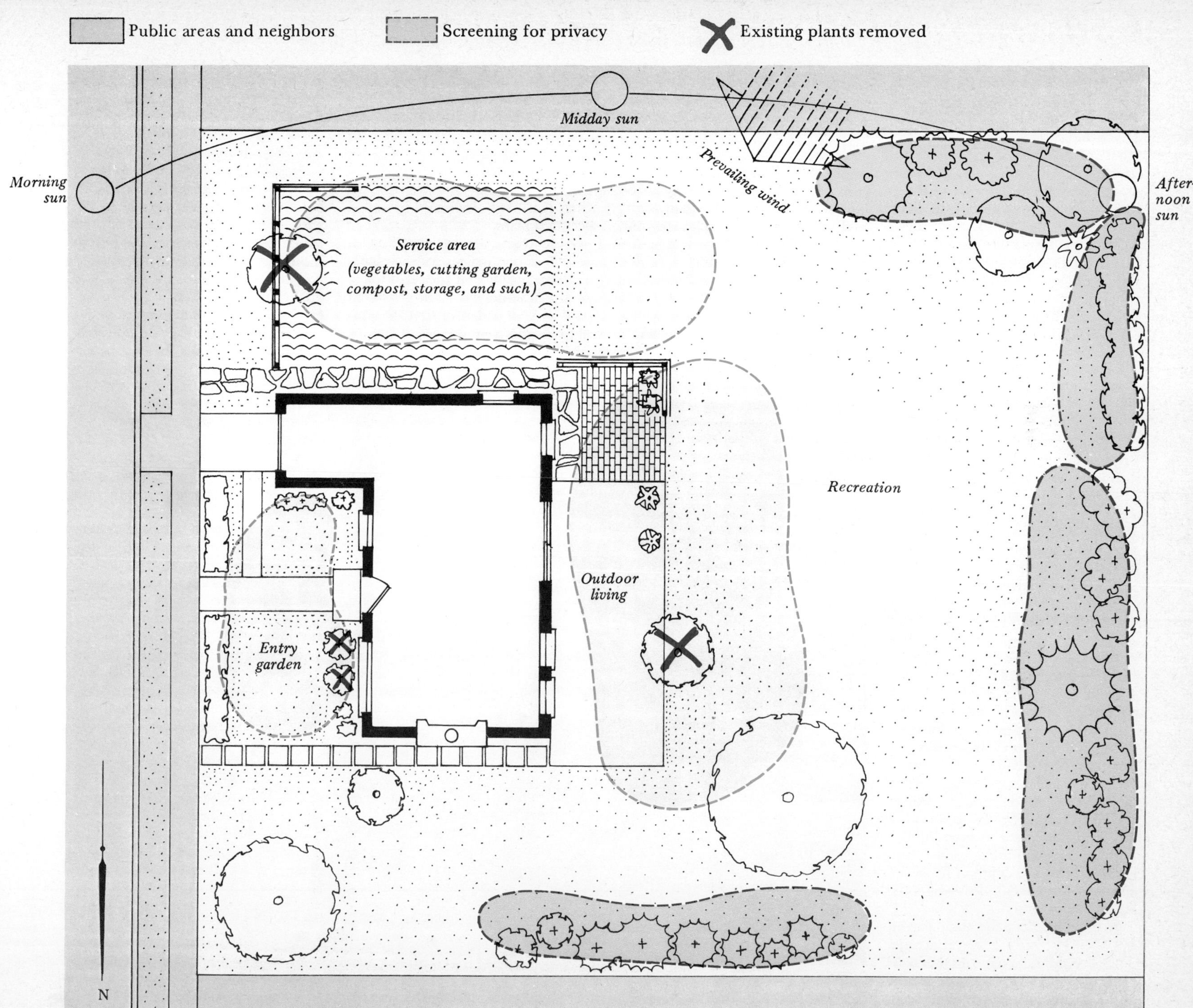

Begin planning with a scale drawing that shows existing shrubs, trees, and large features. Indicate special areas, and note such environmental factors as sun and wind.

Getting to Know the Plants

While the varied selection available in the world of plants is part of the pleasure of gardening, the number of possible choices can be a problem when it comes to planning. Even the basic categories can overlap. Some shrubs are larger than some trees, some trees are more colorful than some flowering plants, and some herbaceous plants are larger than shrubs. In the first stages of planning, therefore, it is best to simplify by considering the trees, shrubs, and flowers in their most typical forms.

Trees are dominant: because of the shade they cast, they have an influence on everything in their immediate vicinity. They must, therefore, be selected and planted with a thorough understanding of the size and shape they will eventually assume.

Of all the plant materials available, shrubs are the most versatile. They have the greatest range of sizes and shapes—from tall tree forms to low-growing subshrubs. Shrubs are also the most adaptable to various techniques of pruning and training.

Flowers offer the widest choice of colors and of blooming times. Many of them have the advantage of portability and can be used as needed to provide bright accents in any season except winter in cold climates.

Both trees and shrubs may be deciduous, which is to say that they drop their leaves in their dormant season; or they may be evergreen, retaining their foliage the entire year. They may also be broad-leaved or needle-leaved. Some broad-leaved trees and shrubs are deciduous, and some are evergreen; but with a few exceptions, such as the larch and the bald cypress (*Taxodium distichum*), the needle-leaved plants are all evergreens.

Evergreens do drop their leaves, but they lose only a few at a time. They are thus in a continual state of renewal but never without leaves. Some plants are called semi-evergreen, since in relatively mild climates they hold some leaves the year round. In colder climates they may drop all their foliage and still survive.

Some trees, shrubs, and flowers are said to have compound leaves. This means that they bear many leaflets on a common stalk. The texture of such a plant is likely to be lighter and airier than that of plants with simple leaves, which grow one to a stem. Familiar plants with compound leaves are the silk tree (*Albizia julibrissin*) and the rose acacia (*Robinia hispida*).

The needled evergreens, which include trees and shrubs, are generally the heaviest and darkest accents in the landscape. Too many in a small place can seem oppressive.

Both trees and shrubs are often grouped together for interesting mass plantings. On the other hand, a tree or shrub with a particularly interesting form can be quite effective when it is used alone as a so-called specimen plant.

Some trees, shrubs, and flowers are recommended for seaside planting. This means that they can tolerate the intense light and frequent wind and salt-laden air that are typical of locations by the ocean.

It pays in the long run to buy plants of the highest quality, even though they may be more expensive. Those you purchase from a nursery should have healthy foliage, free of any obvious discoloration, damage, pests, or diseases. It is best, when possible, to buy flowering plants in bloom so that you know exactly what you are getting. If they are sold balled and burlapped, the burlap should be tightly filled with soil.

The best assurance of dependable quality is to buy from a local nurseryman with a good reputation. If you buy by mail, order from a well-established supplier.

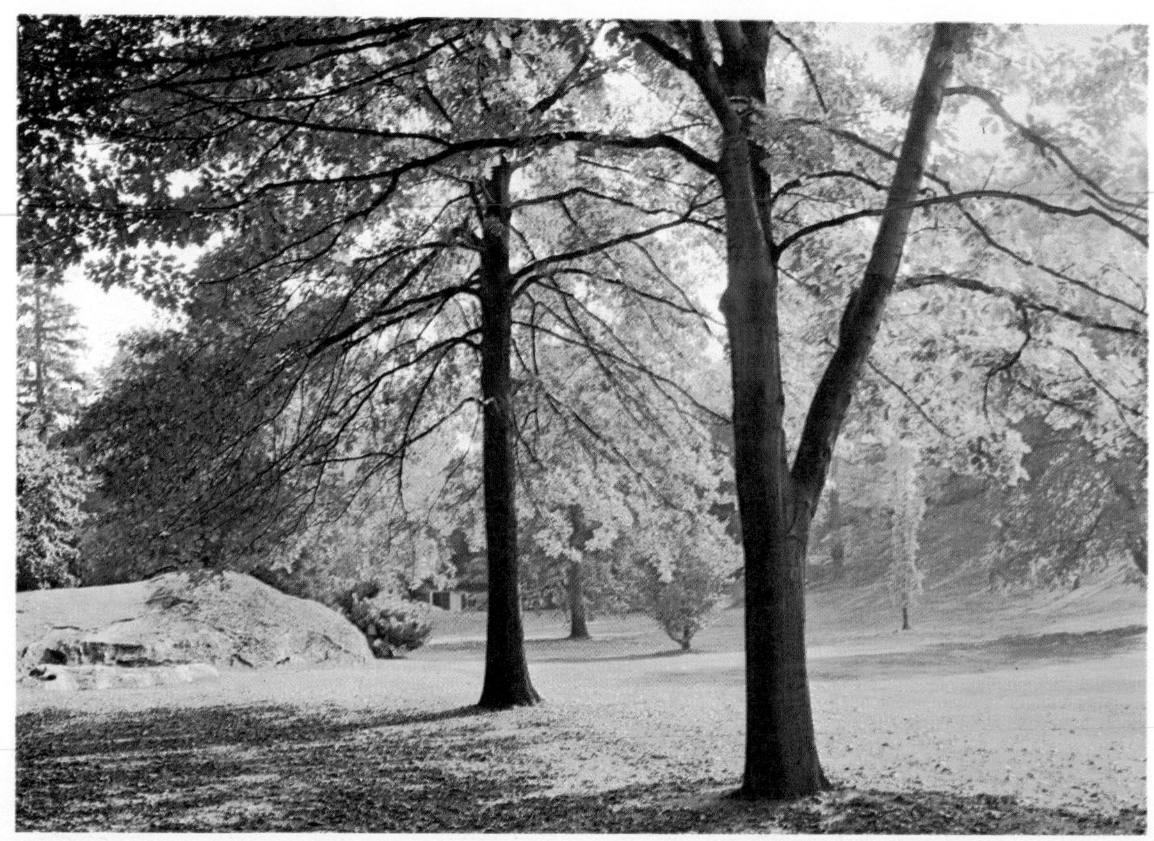

No other plant can match the dramatic impact of a tree, season after season, year after year, perhaps for many decades. To appreciate the extent to which a tree imposes its distinctive quality on the environment where it grows, try to envision this spacious parklike landscape without the dominant presence of the two large autumn-colored oaks.

Shrubs are versatile permanent plantings. They define space in a garden, serve as background for flowers and counterpoint for trees, and provide their own beauties. Here, a pink-flowered azalea highlights a flowering dogwood tree.

Flowers add excitement with their brilliant colors and seasonal changes. Perennials, such as the blue Japanese irises and the primroses surrounding them (above left), bloom year after year. Annuals grow fresh from seeds each year; many, such as poppies (above right), bloom all summer long. Tulips and grape hyacinths (below) are among the bulbs whose blossoms help make springtime joyous.

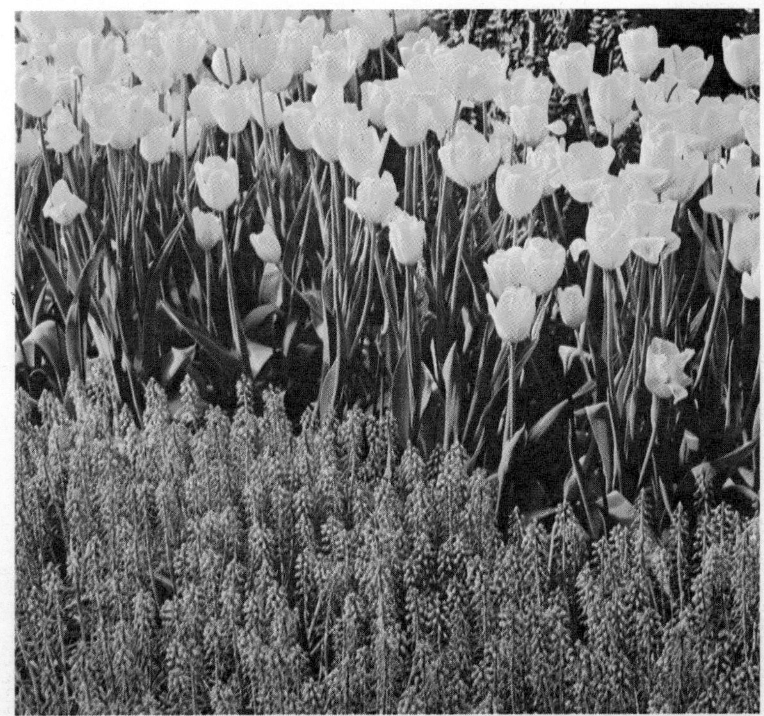

First, Consider the Trees

When the white ash (Fraxinus americana) *was originally planted behind this house, perhaps 30 to 40 years ago, it was a sapling only 5–6 ft. high. Had it been planted closer to the house then, it would be a problem now—its limbs threatening windows and roofing, its leaves clogging drainpipes—rather than the valuable landscape feature that it is.*

A successful plan for a garden area, a yard, or a complete landscape must begin with a comprehensive look at the trees—those that already exist and those yet to be planted—because trees dominate everything else around them.

Trees, more than any other plants, can significantly modify the environment. Their roots help to aerate and stabilize the soil. Their branches shield the ground from the brutal effects of hard rain, shade it from the heat of the sun, and give protection from the wind. Their foliage replenishes the air by taking in carbon dioxide and releasing oxygen, and helps to keep it clean by collecting soot and grime on leaf surfaces. Through the process called transpiration, trees give off water vapor and increase the humidity.

Trees will most likely outlive anything else you plant. When setting out a sapling, it is not unreasonable to expect that your grandchildren may one day play on a swing suspended from a sturdy limb or climb higher than the house among its branches.

Large shade trees are those with long, sturdy trunks and branches high enough to walk under. Considering their size and permanence, it is obviously unwise to plant them where they might outgrow the available space. Keep in mind that a shade tree, such as a plane tree or sugar maple, maintained in good health, will eventually become a spreading giant 75 feet or more in height. At that size the spread will be 50 feet or more (25 feet on each side of the trunk). Such a tree, therefore, should be planted at least 30 feet from the nearest structure. If it is too close to a house, it will darken the interior, its leaves will clog gutters, and its branches may damage upper windows or the roof.

In most gardens the typical shade tree is deciduous, and some such trees have the bonus of leaves that turn to bright colors before they drop in the fall. Some maples in particular are noted for the range and brilliance of their autumnal display. Then, in winter, their branching patterns provide a striking silhouette against the sky.

The large deciduous trees are excellent choices to plant on the south side of a house where they can cast shade on the wall and windows in summer. A well-shaded south wall can reduce considerably the amount of air conditioning needed and thus conserve energy. And, of course, in winter when the leaves are gone, the warming sun shining through bare branches cuts down on heating costs as well.

Trees can also help to conserve energy when used as windbreaks. Evergreens are generally best for this purpose, but even a dense planting of tall, hardy trees, such as the Berlin poplar, planted on the windward side of a house, can shield it effectively from the winter wind.

An outdoor living area is shaded by an evergreen weeping fig (Ficus benjamina). *This tree survives only in frost-free areas, but many deciduous trees can be trimmed as canopies in the North. The summer comfort is worth raking fallen leaves.*

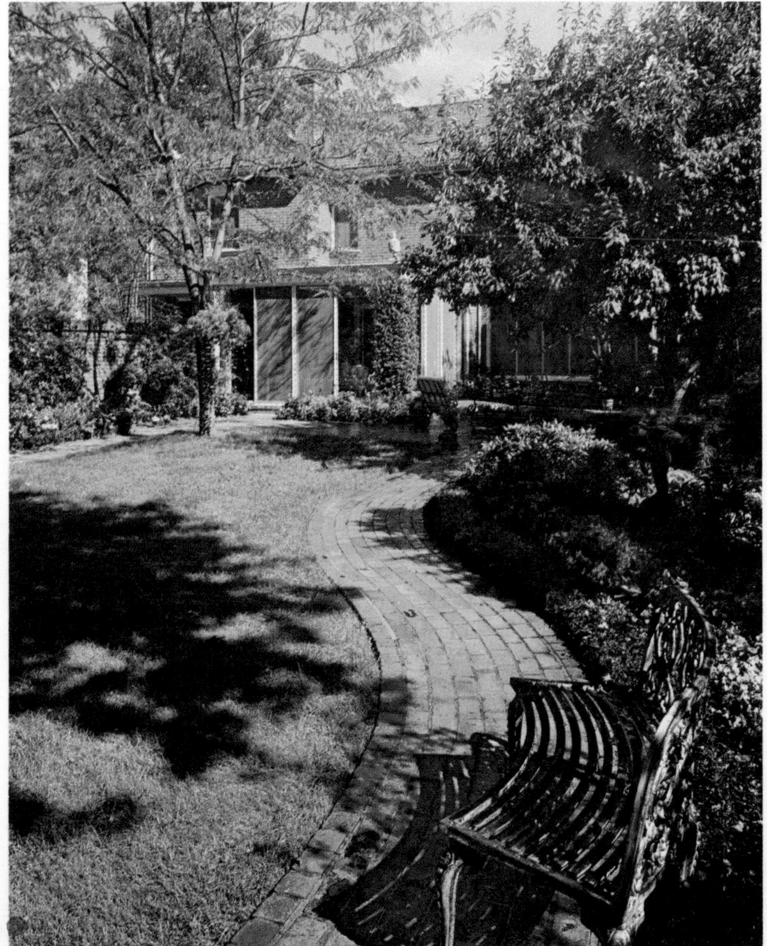

A black locust (Robinia pseudoacacia) *serves as a decorative energy saver. Its branches allow the warming sun to shine through in winter—even in late spring as shown—but in the heat of summer they provide welcome shade.*

Many trees are worth considering purely for their value as ornamentals. Flowering cherries, acacias, dogwoods, magnolias, and hawthorns produce flowers literally by the treeful. They are as colorful in their seasons as anything you can plant. Mountain ashes, hawthorns, hollies, and crab apples are noted for their colorful displays of fruit. And the bark of some trees, such as the plane trees and birches, is remarkably attractive.

Many of the upright hemlocks are excellent to use as screening and as background for flowering shrubs. Hemlocks can be allowed to grow freely for an informal effect, or they can be planted in rows and kept trimmed as formal hedges.

Fruit and nut trees, such as the apple, fig, walnut, and pecan, can do double duty as shade trees and food producers. One large fruit tree, well cared for, will produce ample fruit for a family of four for many years. If space is limited, consider dwarf fruit trees. Some thrive even in containers. Most dwarfs bear bright flowers as well as fruits.

Even if you live in a climate where it is difficult to maintain a garden, there are trees that you can grow. The Russian olive and the honey locust are outstanding among the attractive trees that do well in hot, dry places; various pines and junipers thrive in the salt-laden air of the seashore; in wet soil you can depend on the bald cypress, arborvitae, and willow. Even under the seemingly impossible conditions of city streets, where soot, grime, and traffic fumes prevail, such stalwart performers as the ginkgo, London plane, black locust, and white fir will survive.

Trees do not require a lot of maintenance, but dead, broken, or ill-placed branches must occasionally

Limited spaces seem less confining when small trees are planted in them. The trees in this enclosed outdoor living area have been standard trained—that is, they have been artificially dwarfed by pruning to keep their diminutive form with a minimum of maintenance. Other kinds of dwarf trees include those that have been genetically created by selective breeding and those that have been produced by grafting a normally large tree onto the rootstock of a smaller species.

be removed—preferably by professional tree surgeons. It is not wise for an inexperienced person to engage in pruning that involves leaving the ground; the risk of injury is not to be ignored. Nor is it a good idea to hire helpers for this kind of work who are not fully covered by insurance.

The Dutch elm disease. For generations, the American elm (*Ulmus americana*), with its graceful wineglass form, was a favorite large shade tree throughout much of the United States. But, because of the Dutch elm disease (DED), this stately tree may be doomed.

The DED is a fungous infection, nearly always fatal, carried by the larvae of a bark beetle. Efforts to combat it over the years have focused on protecting healthy trees with insecticides, controlling the beetle that acts as carrier, curing infected trees with fungicides, and, finally, if all else fails, destroying infected trees to retard the spread of the disease. Another approach to the problem has been to develop DED-resistant strains and hybrids of the American elm.

The insecticide methoxychlor is somewhat effective against the elm

A white-flowered wisteria, trained as a small tree, makes a striking single specimen, particularly in late spring when its thickly clustered blossoms set the tone for surrounding beds of tulips, English daisies, and forget-me-nots.

The pink-flowered crab apple (Malus) *is one of many ornamental trees that flourish in a variety of situations. It lends grace and fragrance to an intimate tea-for-two setting (left), or it can be a formal accent in a spruce-hedged front lawn.*

bark beetle. The systemic fungicides Benomyl and Lignasan, injected into the trunks of trees in fairly large doses, can protect them from DED infection for about a year.

Most promising are the resistant elms that are now becoming available. The most widely distributed of these, the urban elm, though highly resistant, is an elm in name only; it lacks the American elm's distinctive shape. DED-resistant strains of the American elm are now being distributed to selected nurseries. They may be the means of preserving this shapely tree for posterity.

The shrublike fringe tree (Chionanthus virginicus) *is among the last to leaf out in late spring. Its lacy bunches of flowers appear in early summer, sometimes even in midsummer, after most other flowering trees have finished blooming.*

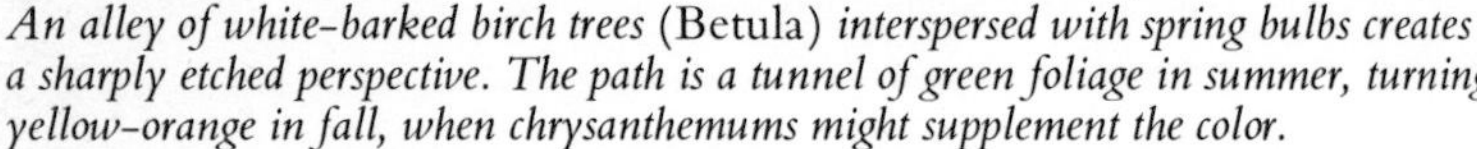

An alley of white-barked birch trees (Betula) *interspersed with spring bulbs creates a sharply etched perspective. The path is a tunnel of green foliage in summer, turning yellow-orange in fall, when chrysanthemums might supplement the color.*

Upper right: *Flowering dogwood trees* (Cornus) *shade a cozy garden nook with a cloud of pink and white blossoms in late spring. The lustrous green leaves will cast shade all summer. Red foliage will be joined by red berries in autumn.*

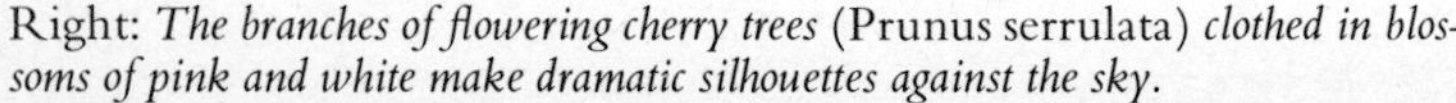

Right: *The branches of flowering cherry trees* (Prunus serrulata) *clothed in blossoms of pink and white make dramatic silhouettes against the sky.*

A shrublike maple tree (Acer), *its multiple trunks accented by sunlight, casts a canopy of green over a patio, supplementing the overhanging roof and softening the transition between the deep indoor shade and the open outdoors.*

A thick wall of mixed evergreens provides protection from the wind and privacy from neighbors and passersby in this suburban outdoor living area, creating the tranquil illusion of a secluded clearing in a forest.

The landscaping principle of dynamic tension is demonstrated in this Zen garden, where the fluid form of a line of scrub oaks (Quercus ilicifolia) *is heightened by the static repose of the rock arrangement that rests in front of it.*

Shrubs for Enhancement

If any one group of plants could be considered a staple in the landscape, it would have to be the shrubs. They range in height from ground-hugging prostrate junipers to lilacs that grow to 20 feet or more. They come in both deciduous and evergreen kinds, as well as in widely varying sizes and shapes.

Some shrubs, such as boxwoods and junipers, have magnificent foliage, while roses, rhododendrons, and camellias are famed for their flowers, and hollies and fire thorns are distinguished for their colorful berries. For every climate and condition of soil there are various shrubs that will thrive (see p. 119).

With such an imposing range of attributes, it is no wonder that shrubs sometimes get overused. This happens, for the most part, in front-yard planting, as a result of overcrowding or inappropriate placement. It fre-

A vine-covered terrace, with geraniums in urns and fuchsias hanging from above, opens onto an area made green by the judicious use of shrubs—including a magnolia (center), an evergreen oleander (left), and hydrangeas in large garden pots.

A low-growing shrubby pine augments the rustic feeling of this terrace while efficiently dividing the space without blocking communication. It masks the view from the steps below but does not obscure vision from the terrace itself.

quently comes about in the name of "foundation planting"—a familiar but unfortunate misnomer.

Foundation plantings first became popular in the days when most houses had full basements. To reduce the amount of excavation required, a high foundation wall was often built under the house. It was quite logical to screen this unsightly expanse of masonry with plants. Thus evolved the concept that a house should have plants around its foundation, particularly on the sides in public view.

In recent years basements have become more the exception than the rule. But the idea of a row of shrubs planted next to the house still prevails. And frequently, even in front of a relatively small house, the long-familiar assortment of foundation plants, such as privets, yews, and forsythias, are still used.

Planting in front of a house, to help relate the vertical structure to the horizontal plane of the land upon which it sits, is a valid concept. But restraint must be used. Do not use plants that will get too big to remain in proper scale with the wall against which they are seen and that will need heavy pruning to keep them within bounds. The pruning can be a tedious chore, and plants that have to be constantly cut back can never attain their attractive natural form. Do not put shrubs where they are likely to grow up to block the light that comes in a window.

Set all plants far enough from the wall of your house to allow easy access behind them, even after they are fully grown. This space is needed for painting and window washing, and the shrubs will look better if they are not pushed up tight against the wall of the house. Try to group the plants to achieve a natural effect; do not line

Rhododendrons in full bloom, soon to be joined by azaleas, flank a curving walk beneath an arbor, masking the window but not blocking the view from inside. Farther on, low-growing junipers separate the walk from a stand of yellow tree roses.

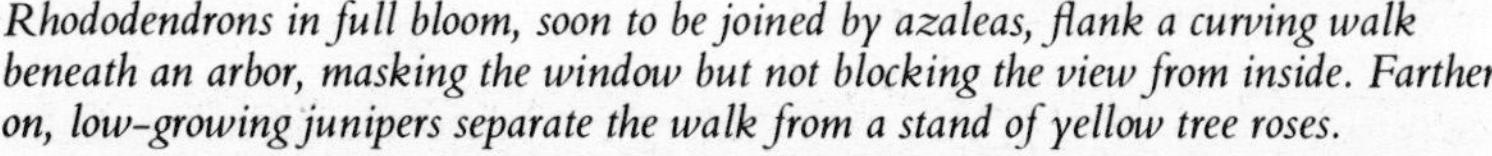

The beauty of a swimming pool is enhanced when the deck is screened by shrubs instead of a fence or wall. Here azaleas provide privacy while contributing the color and scent of their flowers to the pleasure of a swim.

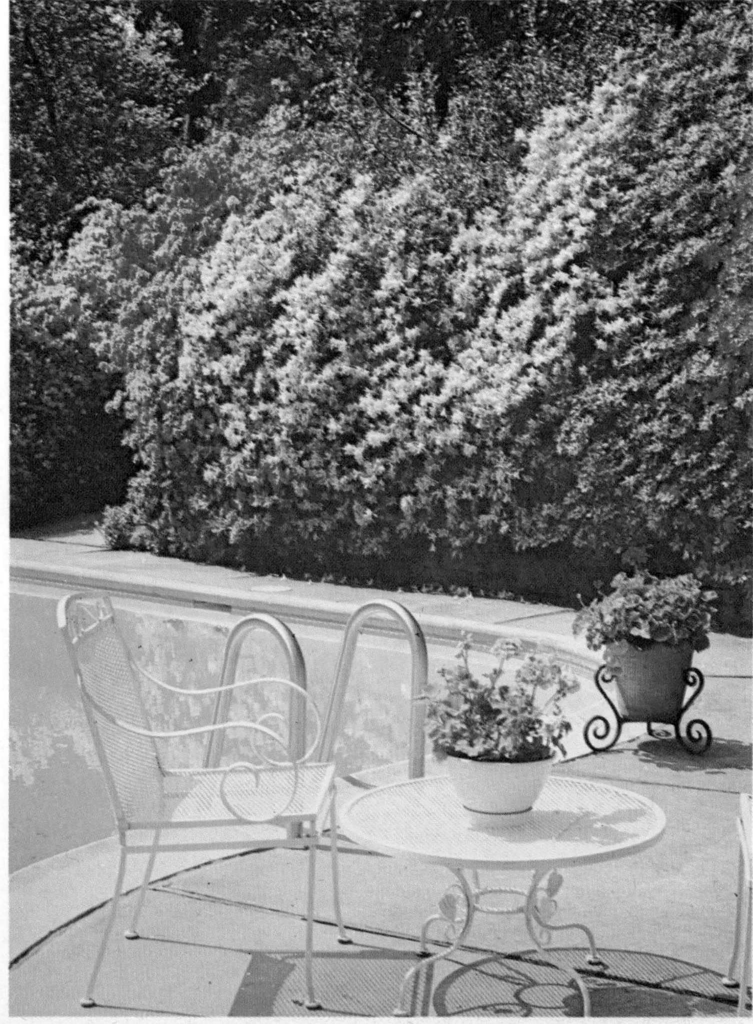

A wide variety of succulent shrubs can be grown around a desert home, including (from left) the ocotillo (Foquieria splendens), *with scarlet flowers borne on long, whiplike stems; the century plant* (Agave americana), *which bears its rare flowers on single stalks up to 40 ft. high; several kinds of yuccas; and cacti.*

A ficus tree and potted begonias are strikingly highlighted by succulent shrubs, including agaves, several cacti of the cereus type, a pink-flowered aloe (center), and a kalanchoe (right), its purplish flowers borne on long, spindly stems.

them up in straight rows. The shrubs planted under windows should be lower growing than those used between windows.

The tallest shrubs that are used for street-side plantings will look best if they are set adjacent to the corners of the house and combined with lower-growing plants to soften the outline of the whole. If the corner groupings are planted outward as an extension of the front of the house, the apparent size of the structure will be increased. Only for the most formal houses and gardens should the plants in front be placed in mirror-image symmetry and be trimmed to geometric shapes.

The shrubs that are best adapted to formal plantings are those that are relatively slow growing and reasonably symmetrical in their habit of growth. Formal plantings also need pruning—as do all of the plants most often used for hedges.

Hedges are usually composed of shrubs, but some trees are recommended. Shrubs can also be used as screens and dividers, either in trimmed hedges or in more informal groupings. They can, for example, block the view of a cutting garden, vegetable garden, play area, or other area that may occasionally seem unsightly from an outdoor sitting area.

Shrubs more often than not are grouped together for a mass effect. Such massed plantings of shrubbery can be ideal backgrounds for flowers. Some shrubs are of such striking character and habit of growth, however, that they can be used effectively as freestanding specimens. To qualify for this use, a plant should be attractive in all seasons. Plants grown for their foliage alone, such as boxwoods and Japanese hollies, easily qualify. Some of the larger rhododendrons, with their handsome leaves and showy flower clusters, are favorite specimen plants; so is the pieris, which has leaves that change color from season to season and pendent clusters of flowers followed by berries.

The mountain laurel makes a magnificent single planting, as does the bush form of the Japanese maple. The leaves of several small maples have unusually interesting shapes and colors, and the elegant open profile of these plants is revealed when the leaves drop in autumn. The plants remain points of sharp visual interest all through the winter.

Shrubs of specimen quality—and there are many—are the most useful as container plants. Planting in a container isolates and accentuates a plant and enables you to place it wherever you want it on the hard surface of a terrace or deck.

Succulents, such as cacti, yuccas, and kalanchoes, are sometimes overlooked as specimen shrubs, but their dramatic outlines make them excellent for decorative use. Because of their unusual form, they are particularly suitable for planting in containers. This also makes it easy to give them the well-drained soil that they must have.

Shrubs are also the basic material for topiary gardening, the ancient

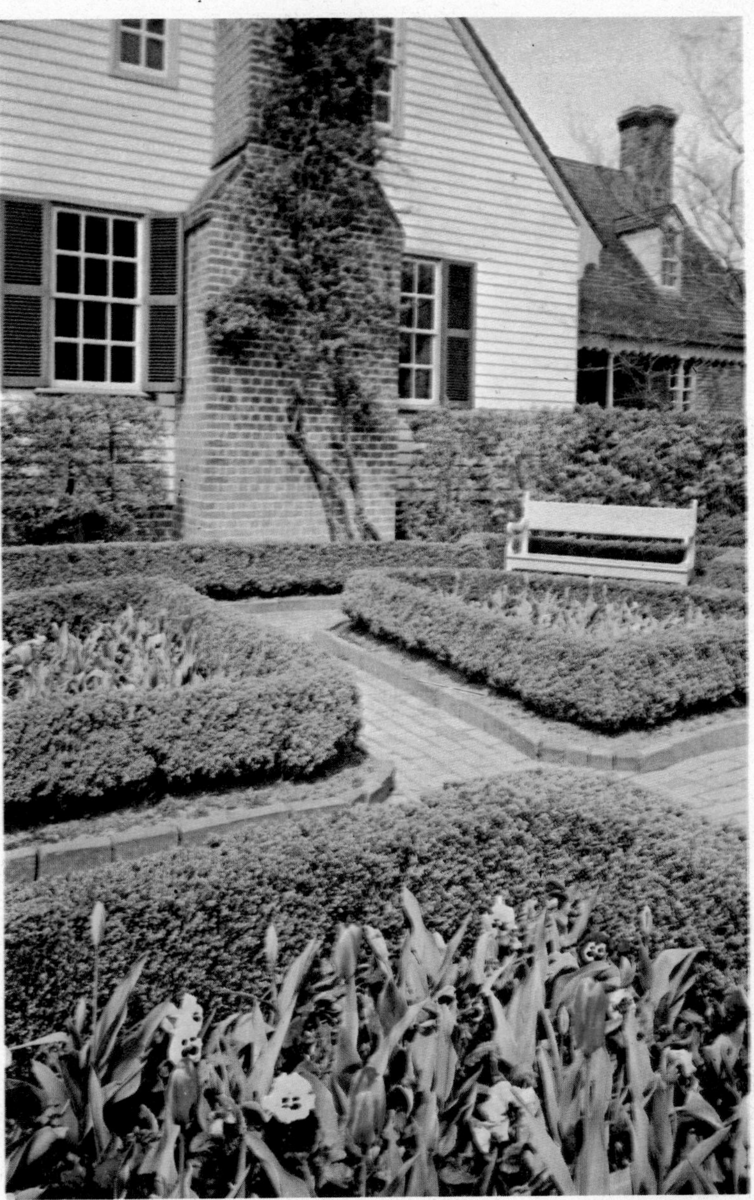

A mountain laurel hedge divides the house from the formal garden, where dwarf English boxwood (Buxus sempervirens suffruticosa) *edges tulip and pansy beds.*

Low-growing shrubs help prevent erosion on a steep hillside. Among the plants surrounding the upright ti tree (Cordyline terminalis) *are (from top) mirror plants* (Coprosma repens), *both green and variegated; a white-flowered* Lantana camara; *a variegated agave; a euphorbia; a cotoneaster; and sedum ground cover.*

practice of pruning plants to geometric or whimsical shapes. The boxwood, yew, and privet are most frequently used in this way. Another ancient practice handed down to us is that of espaliering—training a shrub to grow flat against a wall or trellis. Among the plants most used for this today are fire thorns and camellias.

Vines have their own distinctive place in the landscape. But they must be used with discretion. Some, such as the Boston ivy and Virginia creeper, have tendrils and disklike pads that will cling to almost any flat surface. They can cover the walls of a house and encroach on the windows. The wisteria is such a strong grower that, if given a chance, it can lift the roof of a porch right off its columns. Most other vines, however, are more tractable and can be easily trained and maintained on a framework of lath or wire.

A vine covering the south side of a house can, in hot climates, lower the temperature enough to make a significant reduction in the air-conditioning bill. And in climates where the warmth of the sun is beneficial in winter, a deciduous vine that will let the sunlight through is useful.

Most shrubs are container grown in a nursery and can be planted at any time of year. This means that you can buy them when they are in flower, fruit, or fall color and know exactly what you are getting before you plant them in the garden.

Fire thorns (Pyracantha) *are especially valued for their showy clusters of brightly colored berries, which appear in autumn and may last all winter.*

The mountain laurel (Kalmia latifolia), *a hardy broad-leaved evergreen, bears purple-trimmed blossoms of pink, white, or red in early summer.*

Rhododendrons, with their magnificent floral display in spring and early summer and their rich garment of glossy foliage, are among the most versatile of flowering shrubs—as long as they are grown in the acid soil they require.

The dense evergreen foliage of the lily-of-the-valley shrub (Pieris japonica), *often reddish or bronze colored in spring, turning green as it matures, makes it useful for screening or as a specimen plant.*

A huge azalea in blossom commands attention. After the gold and orange of its flowers fade, its handsome dark green leaves will stand out in sharp contrast to the delicate maidenhair ferns (Adiantum pedatum) *around it.*

The yellow-flowered forsythia, with its graceful fountainlike form, is frequently used as a freestanding specimen, either at the corner of a piece of property as shown or alone in its glory in a broad expanse of lawn.

Using Flowers for Accent

When we think of the charm of a garden, it is usually the flowers that come to mind first. Trees and shrubs establish the broad outlines of the landscape, but the flowers are invariably the highlights of a garden and provide color and fragrance for the longest period.

For every climate and growing season, there are flowering plants that will provide results far beyond the modest investment in time and trouble required to bring them into bloom. Even a beginner can plant with confidence, for there are some kinds that flourish readily—as well as others that are more challenging and, to the dedicated gardener, perhaps more interesting.

Annuals—plants that flower for one season and then fade forever—are among the most adaptable sources of garden color. Although many kinds, such as larkspurs, nasturtiums, and sweet alyssums, can be sown outdoors, some must (or may) be given an early start by sowing them indoors a few weeks before they are planted in the garden. Annuals can be used in flower beds or to fill in gaps in established borders. They can be grown in hanging baskets or in other containers. The taller kinds can be used for a temporary screen or background. And annuals, such as zinnias and marigolds, provide some of the loveliest cut flowers.

Biennials—plants that bloom the year after seeds are sown and die after flowering—are slightly more difficult to grow than most annuals and perennials. Favorite biennials are pansies, hollyhocks, Canterbury bells, and English daisies.

Flowering perennials—plants that live for two years or more—usually have shorter seasons of bloom than the majority of annuals. There are, however, some exceptions, such as day lilies. Certain perennials, including hostas, are valuable because of their attractive foliage.

Wisteria and blue-flowered clematis vines on the side of a house form part of a living window frame. The theme is carried through by an edging border of pink geraniums, hanging baskets of begonias, and a well-placed azalea bonsai.

Stone steps and the low evergreen shrubs flanking them are enlivened by beds of phlox and portable baskets of pink geraniums. Flowers that brighten the background include blue delphiniums, purple liatrises, and yellow day lilies.

A mass planting of a single kind of flower can have stunning impact, as shown by the forget-me-nots (Myosotis) *that surround this fountain with a cloudlike drift of delicate blue-violet.*

Bulbous plants, which are technically perennials, are an important source of garden color. Familiar hardy kinds include crocuses, daffodils or narcissi, hyacinths, tulips, and lilies, as well as snowdrops, scillas, and grape hyacinths. Nonhardy bulbous plants, such as tuberous begonias and gladioli, are magnificent for outdoor summer display, but in cold climates they must be stored indoors during the winter.

Less can be more when it comes to choosing colors for a garden. A relatively small area in which just one color is concentrated is more impressive and pleasing to the eye than a somewhat larger area planted with patches of various colors.

An attractive way to ensure an impressive effect from one kind of flower (or a grouping of plants that require the same conditions) is to group several plants together in a container or in a raised bed. The container or enclosure will serve as a frame to set the planting apart from its immediate surroundings.

A wooden tub in full sun, brimming with pink or red geraniums and cascading white petunias, will stand out in almost any setting. In very dry sunny locations the fleshy leaves of perennial sedums and sempervivums provide a welcome note of green, often with colorful flowers as well. Suitable container plants for shady locations are annual impatiens, lobelias, and tuberous begonias.

In the open garden similar color impact can be achieved with plantings of perennials, such as chrysanthemums, irises, or peonies, in either single-colored or multicolored groupings. For a green accent hostas or Solomon's seals are excellent.

A massed planting of annuals will provide months of color. In the sun marigolds, in shades of yellow and orange, bloom continuously. In shady places annual impatiens will flower all summer long and should

The harsh line of a garden wall is softened by a tall perennial border that includes red snapdragons (Antirrhinum majus) *and purple globe thistles* (Echinops ritro), *behind a low edging border of sweet alyssums* (Lobularia maritima).

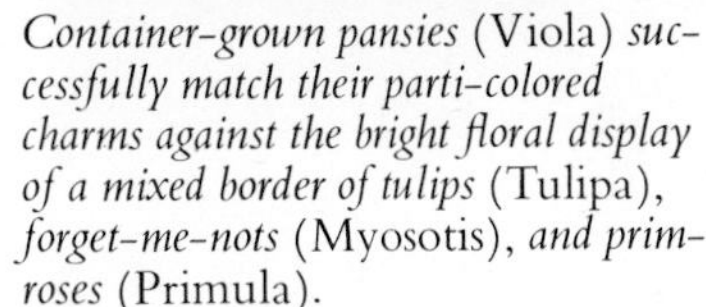

Container-grown pansies (Viola) *successfully match their parti-colored charms against the bright floral display of a mixed border of tulips* (Tulipa), *forget-me-nots* (Myosotis), *and primroses* (Primula).

A pink-flowered azalea, portable in its container, adds a splash of intense color to a terrace setting. Beside it grows a bed of white wax begonias (Begonia semperflorens) *and a honeysuckle vine* (Lonicera).

require no attention other than watering well during dry spells.

A mixed border can contribute to the garden a most interesting and colorful flower show. Such a planting traditionally includes some spring- and summer-flowering bulbs, a few other perennials, and a succession of annuals. A well-planned mixed border contains creative combinations of flower forms and colors that will bring pleasure to the eye throughout the flowering season.

A mixed planting of peonies, day lilies, and chrysanthemums would spread its bloom over a long season.

In a mixed border large groupings are best, with the tallest plants in the back, plants of intermediate heights toward the center, and lower-growing kinds in front. However, this order need not be followed too strictly. For an interesting contour, allow "promontories" of taller plants to reach forward and "bays" of lower ones to extend to the rear. But do not plant low-growing kinds directly behind tall growers.

For people who have ample space in their gardens and desire a bountiful supply of cut flowers, an out-of-the-way plot has many advantages. Here flowers can be grown in rows where they can be easily tended and picked, and no special consideration need be given to their relationship to one another. Asters, cosmos, snapdragons, and zinnias are some of the annuals favored for cutting; perennials include delphiniums, pyrethrums, and Shasta daisies.

Although roses have woody stems and thus are technically shrubs, they

The incomparable beauty of roses is emphasized when different kinds are grown together, such as red 'Blaze Climber' and soft pink 'Charlotte Armstrong.'

Fuchsia hybrida *is outstanding among the tender plants that are valuable for providing spots of outdoor color throughout the summer months.*

Hybrid tulips, available in a variety of forms and in all colors except true blue, are at their best in groups, providing masses of springtime color.

A garden pool provides the chance to add to your garden the unique charms of such flowers as fragrant night-blooming tropical water lilies.

serve many of the same purposes as hardy flowering perennials. Roses are among the best plants to grow for a supply of cut flowers. Some, such as floribundas, have a long season of continual bloom and produce enough flowers for both cutting and garden display. Although roses are magnificent while in bloom, they are generally not an asset to the landscape during their dormant season. They are, therefore, often planted together in a separate area that is screened from daily view.

In cold climates the indoor garden can extend the season of color by many months. Flowering bulbs, orchids, chrysanthemums, and African violets are but a few of the plants that can bring the pleasure of color and fragrance indoors when the outside world is dry and brown.

A greenhouse can be a valuable adjunct to a garden. Not only is it useful for growing such tropical specimens as the red-flowered anthurium (right), but it serves as a place in which to propagate and nurture many hardy and semi-hardy plants to be set outdoors in pots or planted in the ground in full flower. Thus, the garden's growing season is effectively lengthened and its variety increased.

The rich autumnal foliage of these cherry trees is echoed on the ground by a border of chrysanthemums in shades of orange, yellow, deep rose, and white.

Gardening Outdoors

Lawns and Ground Covers

A lawn is an ideal setting for a home. It also provides a pleasing background for ornamental plants and a useful area for leisure-time activities.

Lawns not only beautify an open space; they also freshen the air, insulate the ground in winter, and reduce temperatures in summer. In extremely hot weather they can be as much as 50 degrees cooler than artificial grass or paving. (Tall grass is somewhat cooler than short grass, short grass appreciably cooler than bare soil.)

It is for good reason that well-tended lawns along residential streets have become classics of the American landscape. The uniform color and texture, which so clearly reveal the underlying contours of the land, form the most practical and attractive setting for a house, as well as for trees and shrubs.

Wherever lawns are grown extensively there is a tendency to take them for granted. We expect them to perform consistently under all kinds of stress, to make a tight, mud-proof cover the year round, and to thrive on all types of soil, even though more than half of their food-making green foliage is regularly removed by mowing.

Lawn grasses are often not fertilized when they should be. They are frequently overwatered or underwatered. They may be cut too low, rolled when it is unnecessary, or subjected to other mistreatment.

It is a tribute to the flexibility of lawn grasses that in spite of such handling they are durable enough under average conditions to keep on growing and even to withstand games and foot traffic.

Grass. Grasses are ideal because they have meristematic (growing point) tissue nestled near the soil surface and at the base of expanding leaves. Because these growth points are so low to the ground, mowing does them no harm. By contrast, other plants tend to grow from the tip, and if cut, they require a longer time to recover.

Grass is basically a crop, whether it grows as a lawn or a meadow. The harvesting is the mowing, which must be done regularly. If this, the most important requirement of lawn maintenance, is neglected, weed grasses become dominant and can sometimes smother the finer grasses completely.

Experience has shown which grasses are especially suited for lawns. Mostly these grasses evolved as pasture species, and with few exceptions they came from the Old World. They have adapted to North American climatic peculiarities, and special strains have evolved from which many of our most useful varieties have been developed.

For lawns in the northern zone (see map on p. 42), only Old World species stay green into winter. In the milder parts of this region they hold their color under snow all winter.

Native prairie grasses turn brown after a frost, which is one of several reasons why they do not make satisfactory lawns.

Other ground covers can be used: pachysandra, vinca, and ivy are among the most popular. These and others are described on page 43.

Requirements for a lawn. Given reasonable attention to watering and feeding when the grass is obviously in need, lawns will almost take care of themselves. The major requirement on the part of the homeowner is, of course, consistent mowing, which helps to maintain a tight turf and eliminate tall-growing weeds. Regular mowing keeps the lawn usable and attractive. When cut frequently, the clippings are short and can be left on the lawn.

Sunlight. Most lawn grasses do best if they have from four to six hours of sunlight a day. One reason for this requirement is that shade is usually created by trees and, in shady situations, there is direct competition between the surface-feeding roots of the trees and the roots of lawn grass.

The grasses that do best in the shade, such as *Poa trivialis,* are deep rooted. Heavy fertilization in shady places is advisable to provide plant food for the tree roots and for those of the lawn grass as well.

Fertilizer. Except on naturally fertile soils, feeding a lawn is necessary to maintain its quality. Although lawns can survive without feeding, fertilized lawns wear better, fight weeds better, and look better. Many kinds of fertilizers are available, and new and more efficient ones are being developed. Rates of application are printed on the container.

Watering. Depending on where you live, watering may be needed. Grasses are equipped to endure some drought and actually may be healthier for it. But during long dry periods they will look better if irrigated regularly.

Weeds and pests. A consideration that cannot be overlooked is weed and pest control. Weeds can usually be controlled effectively with herbicides. Insects, fortunately, are a less prevalent problem. Suggested controls for weeds and pests are given on pages 40, 634, and 639.

Diseases. Diseases ebb and flow in response to weather, seasonal activity, and physiological changes. Controlling them is discussed on pages 40 and 634. The best way to approach the problem of disease is to plant disease-tolerant grasses (which most of the newer varieties are).

Other treatments. There may be an occasional need for soil aerifying, thatch removing, liming or acidifying the soil, or adding micronutrients, such as iron. Years usually elapse between such jobs. Details on these procedures are included on the pages that follow.

In most cases, however, a lawn will get along nicely with no more than regular mowing and well-planned fertilizing, supplemented when necessary by irrigation and weed control.

Types of lawn. Some homeowners want a perfect lawn, meticulously kept; others are contented with a weedy, coarse-textured sward. The former will devote much time and money to the lawn and may choose elegant grasses, such as those used for golf greens, which require a great deal of care. The latter may not object to coarser "hay grasses," so long as they require little attention.

Most homeowners choose a lawn somewhere in between. They want a nice-looking lawn that is serviceable and requires little care.

A wide selection to meet these requirements is available. For the North, the newly bred Kentucky bluegrasses, fine fescues, perennial ryegrasses, and colonial bent grasses are suitable; for the South, Bermuda, zoysia, centipede, St. Augustine, and Bahia grasses are favored. (Vegetative plantings of the improved varieties must be made, since they do not come true from seed.)

Traditionally, a distinction has been made between "show" lawns in front of the house and utility lawns in less conspicuous places. Although grass seed is packaged for both uses, there is often little difference; modern varieties serve well for either.

Seasonal differences. Northern lawns, which grow well in the long, cool fall season, benefit from planting, renovating, and fertilizing in autumn. Southern lawns are best treated in spring and summer. However, where they turn brown in winter, certain northern grasses (see p. 41) can be sown over them in fall to provide green all winter. In the transition zone between warm and cool areas neither warm northern nor cool southern grasses are easy to grow. However, a northern grass, such as a coarse fescue ('Kentucky-31'), can be used.

How to Make a New Lawn

New lawns can be started from seeds or from vegetative plantings of live stems (sprigs), biscuits of sod (plugs), or solid sod.

A modern trend, especially in new housing projects, is to buy sod, which has already been nursed through its juvenile stages by a professional. In this way a so-called instant lawn is produced.

Reputable sod growers offer choice varieties that are free of weeds and pests. Many buyers assume that sod is an easy (though expensive) road to success, needing little attention. However, sod laid on compact, infertile soil will be no more successful than a seeding would be.

Sodding avoids the early weeks of inconvenience in getting a new lawn laid down and established; but it does not diminish the requirements for maintaining the grass.

The Soil Bed

You can buy topsoil or mix in organic material such as peat moss, but the cost and effort are seldom justified, as grass will grow on almost any soil if it is properly watered and fertilized.

The many fine rootlets that grass develops each year in the top few inches of lawn will help to improve the structure of the soil.

Soil-Bed Preparation

Loosening compacted soil is essential. Remove all foreign materials. Do not bury them, since that may alter the chemical balance of the soil.

Cultivate to loosen the soil uniformly a few inches deep. Mix in a complete fertilizer that is relatively rich in phosphorus.

It is better to dig this fertilizer (such as a 12–12–12) containing at least 10–15 percent phosphorus into the ground. Or use superphosphate alone; then add nitrogen and potassium, the other basic ingredients.

Cultivation

Cultivate to break up large clods. Excessive cultivation, however, can cause soil-structure deterioration.

1. *To ensure good drainage, grade soil to slope slightly away from the house in all directions, if possible. If you add topsoil, spread it over the surface evenly. Eliminate bumps or high spots where a mower might cut the grass too short, and fill in any low spots where rainwater tends to collect or where a mower might miss.*

2. *Till the soil enough to loosen it, but do not whip it into a fine fluff. Pea-sized lumps and crevices should remain to catch the tiny seeds. Remove stones and other debris, and work in soil additions, such as peat moss, gypsum, or lime. Grade the soil once more; then wet it to firm it down.*

3. *Spread the grass seeds with a lawn spreader. The rate varies with the type of grass, but do not seed too thickly. The young plants need space to develop roots and leaves; if overcrowded, they may begin to fade in a few weeks. For bluegrass or fescue, use 1 or 2 lb. of top-quality seeds for 1,000 sq. ft.*

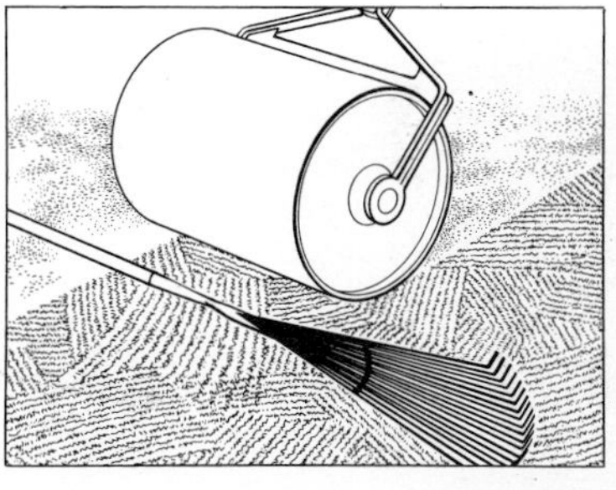

4. *Rake the seeds lightly with the back of a bamboo rake. Barely cover about half the total amount with soil, leaving the rest exposed. Then roll just once with an empty roller, to press seeds into contact with soil. Do not cover seeds completely; they must have light to sprout, as well as warmth, oxygen, and moisture.*

5. *Apply a complete fertilizer on the same day the seeds are spread. Use a fertilizer recommended for new lawns, in the amount suggested on the bag. Grass seeds themselves contain only enough nourishment to form the first sprout and roots; so added nutrients are necessary for further growth.*

6. *Keep the area thoroughly moist for at least two weeks, or until the grass is well established. Avoid light sprinklings: the moisture should penetrate the soil to a depth of several inches. If possible, the sprinklers should be set to cover the entire seeded area without having to be moved, so as not to disturb seeds.*

7. *Mow the grass as soon as it is about $2^{1}/_{2}$ in. high. (Mow only when the lawn is completely dry.) Cutting height is important. Do not cut shorter than 2 in. the first year, except for Bermuda and bent grass, which can be cut to 1 in. high. Rake up and remove the clippings, or attach a grass catcher to the mower.*

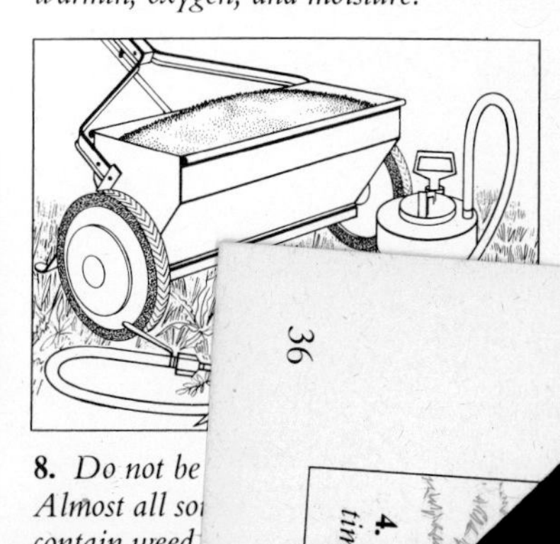

8. *Do not be*
Almost all so
contain weed
die off after u
Others can b
year with "u
prevented wi
emergent con

Do not whip the soil bed into a fluffy texture by repeated passes with a rotary tiller. This will break down the soil particles to such a small size that the surface will "melt" when heavily watered, sealing the pores of the soil and keeping the water from soaking in.

Lawn seeds are best situated for quick, effective sprouting if they sift into the crevices between soil lumps about as big as the tip of a finger.

Rolling

If the soil has not been unduly fluffed, rolling will not be needed. Rolling can undo the benefits of cultivation; and even if only lightly done, it can mash down the soil particles, making the surface less permeable.

Rolling will do no damage to sandy soils, and it may be necessary in order to reestablish capillary action that will transport water to deeper levels. It may also be necessary on heavy soils that have become unduly fluffy during preparation.

Planting

Vegetative planting—which is done with sod, plugs, sprigs, or runners—involves spacing and placement that differ for the various kinds of grass.

Special tools are available that lift out plugs of soil so that the vegetative material can be easily planted.

Sod, of course, is laid down in strips or squares like pieces of carpet. In all cases, the soil must be prepared as thoroughly as it would be for a new lawn.

Seeding

Usually approximately 3 pounds of seeds are used per 1,000 square feet (less with bent grass, more with perennial ryegrass). Use a lawn spreader to avoid possible misses. Spread half the seeds in one direction, the other half crosswise.

Spreaders that drop the seeds from a hopper have the advantage of cutting off the coverage exactly at borders. The centrifugal cyclone type, which throws seeds from a whirling disk, feathers the edges of the successive passes of seeds better and also covers the ground more quickly.

MAKING A CURVED EDGE

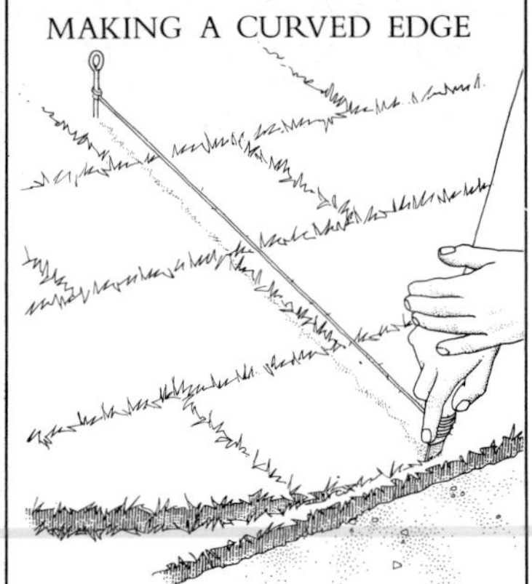

Lay the lawn beyond the point where a curved edge is required. Mark out the curve, using a piece of string attached to a stick. Hold the end of the string and a knife in one hand, and inscribe an arc. Use a half-moon edging tool to cut the turf.

LAYING TURF

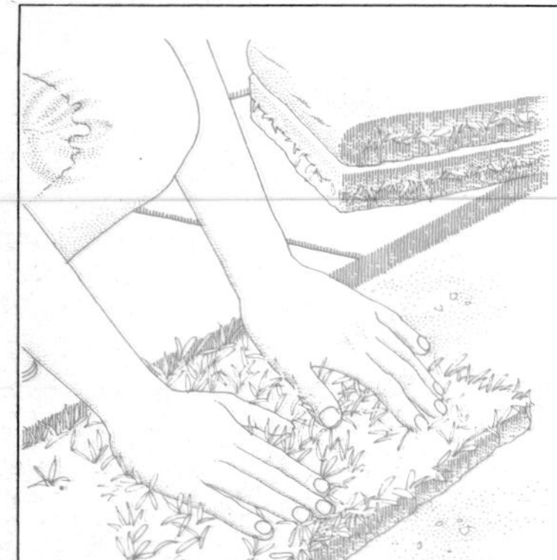

1. *Open out each turf and press it firmly into position.*

2. *Stand on a plank on the first row; lay the second, staggering the sections.*

3. *Roll the plank over onto the second row and lay the third row.*

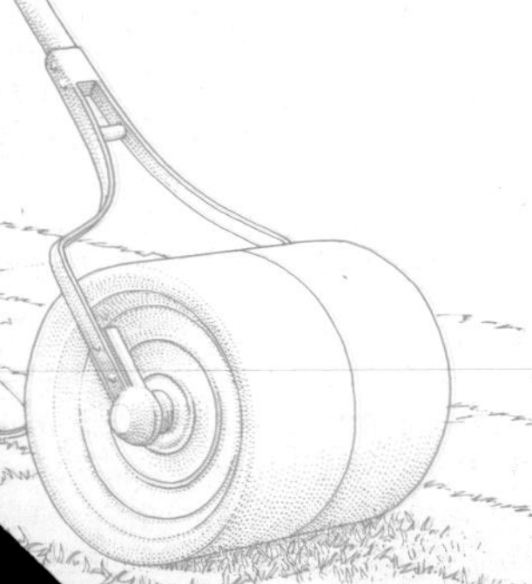

[illegible] lawn twice, the second [illegible] angles to the first.

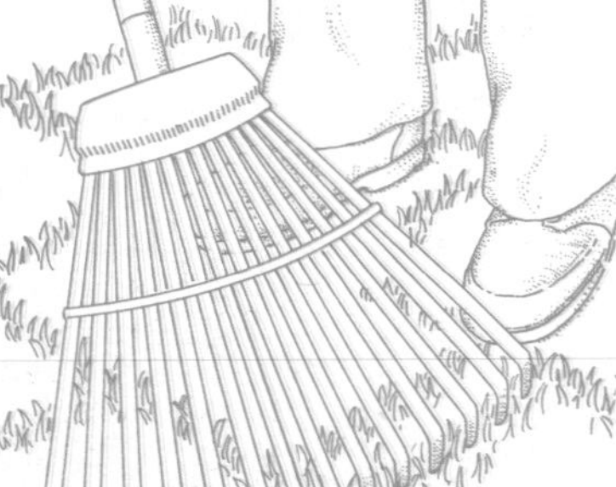

5. *Sweep the lawn to remove debris and to lift the flattened grass.*

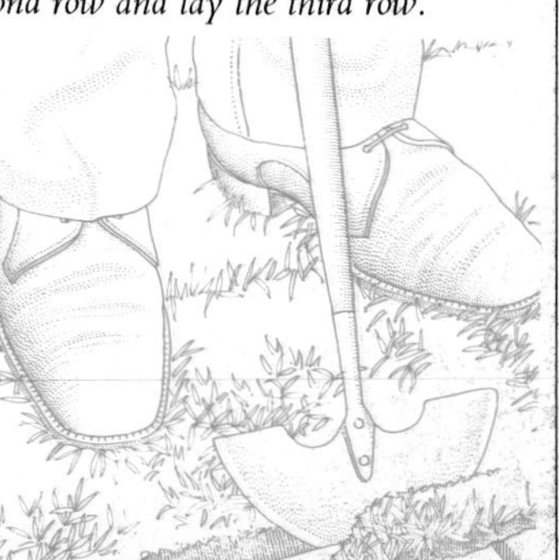

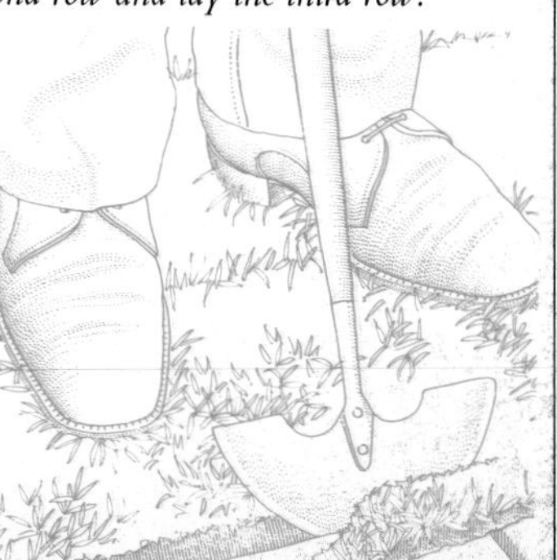

6. *Trim the edges with a half-moon edging tool, making a sloping cut.*

After seeds are sown, keep the soil bed moist. If it dries out, the seedlings will die. In warm weather ryegrass should sprout in one week, bluegrass and fescue in two weeks.

Mulching

A mulch over the seeding will help prevent rapid drying out. Even with a mulch, light watering daily, after an initial thorough soaking, is often necessary to encourage the quickest possible germination.

Mulch also helps protect a new seeding against heavy rains. As long as the soil surface remains somewhat rough, rain is likely to soak in rather than run off.

Possible kinds of mulch include straw (laid down no more than a few straws deep), excelsior, shredded twigs, pine boughs, crop or garden stems, and woven burlap. Twigs and other debris should be removed before the first mowing.

Maintaining the Lawn

Mowing

Plants require the green tissue that contains chlorophyll to manufacture the food they need for growth. Removal of the green leaves, as in mowing, can be counterproductive, particularly if the grass is suddenly cut too low. Cutting off green foliage can even kill the grass, especially in spring on lawns in northern climates

A rotary mower cuts with a propellerlike blade that revolves horizontally.

that have expended most of their accumulated reserves to provide a flush of new growth. Chronic partial defoliation can depress grass growth and its ability to recover quickly.

Rooting depth is related to the height of the foliage aboveground; thus, turf that is constantly cut too low becomes inhibited in its reach for moisture and nutrients in the soil. To avoid shallow rooting, cut away no more than half the foliage at a time.

As a general rule, lawn grasses do best when mowed to the highest level consistent with the homeowner's aesthetic requirements.

Mowing high is especially helpful under conditions of stress, such as shade, or if the soil and habitat are especially disadvantageous. But it can also create problems in the transition zone (see map on p. 42) when disease is prevalent.

Mowing height will vary with the kind of grass and its use. Golf-green grasses, especially creeping bent grasses in the North and select Bermuda grasses in the South, are mowed when about a quarter inch tall. When clipped this close, grass is often subject to unfavorable influences. Golf greens are mowed at least every second day and need constant professional attention.

Colonial bent grasses, which grow more erectly, are better suited for lawns, though they too are mowed fairly short—$^3/_4$–1 inch tall—about twice a week.

Other lawn grasses, including Kentucky bluegrasses, fine fescues, and most southern grasses, are generally mowed to a height of 1–2 inches, and weekly mowing is usually adequate.

Bermuda grass, however, is usually mowed somewhat shorter. Longer intervals between mowings may be appropriate for many types of grasses during the seasons of the year when growth slows down.

Mowers

Modern lawn-mowing equipment offers a wide choice, ranging from manual push mowers to self-propelled machines large enough to easily mow acres of grass. Gas-powered riding mowers have also become popular. They are either self-contained units or small garden tractors with attachments for mowing.

Reel mowers generally do a neater job of cutting than rotary mowers. When the sharp cutting blades of the spinning reel meet the stationary bed knife, they cut cleanly with a scissorslike action.

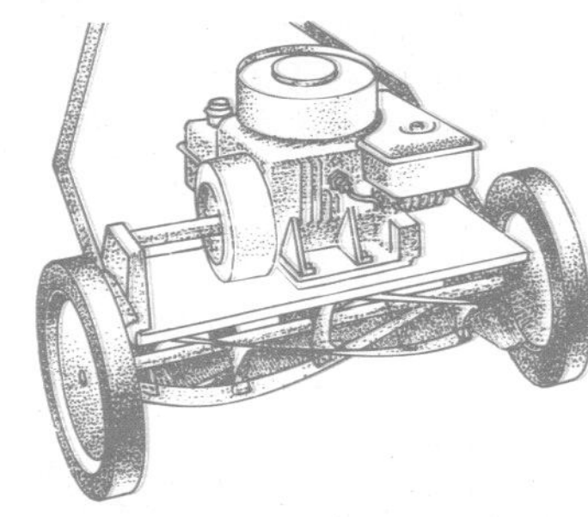

A reel mower cuts the lawn by means of a revolving reel of blades.

Rotaries and hammer knives cut by the impact of a fast-moving blade. This tends to fray the ends of the grass, especially if the blade is dull.

Reel mowers usually require professional attention for sharpening and adjustment. Rotary blades can be honed at home, but care must be taken when filing the cutting edge (as shown below) not to destroy the blade's balance. Before turning the machine over to remove the blade, be sure to disconnect the lead wire from the spark plug.

Reel machines are best used on lawns that are cut relatively low—on bent grass, Bermuda grass, zoysia, centipede grass, and some of the newer low-growing Kentucky bluegrasses and perennial ryegrasses.

The wheels are external to the blades; thus they cannot mow very close to borders and structures. The blades can be stopped and damaged where there are twigs, stones, or other debris.

For general use, especially when the grass can be cut fairly high, rotary mowers are more versatile, less expensive, and more easily maintained.

A heavy-duty mower is needed for some grasses. One of the toughest is zoysia. Ryegrasses often fray, due to tenacious strands of fibers in the leaf. Fescues bruise easily during hot, dry weather. Bluegrasses display tough seed-bearing stalks for two or three weeks in June. Bahia seed stalks are also hard to mow, and this grass is sometimes sprayed with a growth retardant to repress the formation of the seed stalks.

But on the whole a mower with its cutting edges in good condition and with an engine of sufficient power will handle these grasses.

SHARPENING A ROTARY CUTTER

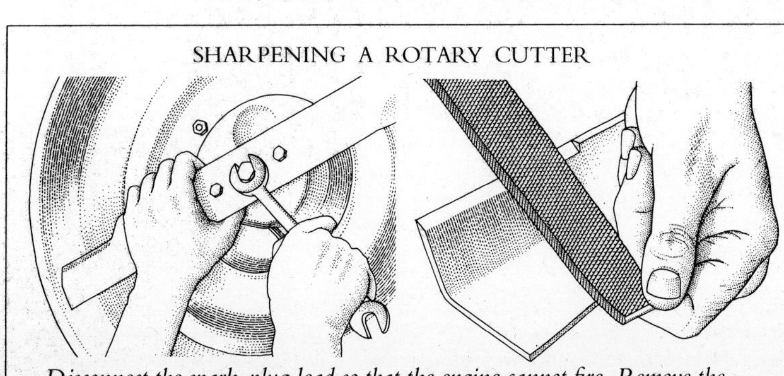

Disconnect the spark-plug lead so that the engine cannot fire. Remove the blade, put in a vise, and sharpen to the original cutting angle as shown. To keep the blade in balance, file equal amounts from each end.

Oscillating sprinklers spray back and forth in a rectangular pattern. They can also be set to spray in one direction.

Watering

Lawns use an inch or more of water per week in hot, dry weather. Where rain does not provide it, irrigation should. In arid climates, such as that in the Southwest, watering is, of course, essential.

Watering has a twofold purpose: it supplies moisture for the roots to take up and transpose to the plant, and it draws air into the pores of the soil so that the roots can breathe. As water percolates down through the soil, fresh air follows behind it. The water should be allowed to pass through before more is added so that oxygen can reach the deepest roots.

The more intensively managed lawn grasses, such as bent and Bermuda grasses, are adapted to humid conditions. Thus they need more watering than species that are not adversely affected by drought, such as fescue grasses, which in the North are often planted in sandy soils and under shade trees, where dryness is likely to develop.

Buffalo grasses in the South and wheat grasses in the North are native prairie grasses that have the endurance to withstand drought in arid climates. Other species of grasses require a more dependable supply of moisture, but they are able to survive short droughts.

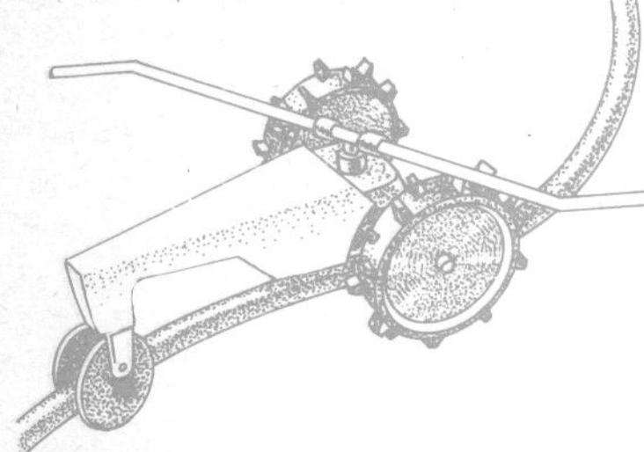

Rotating sprinklers cover a circular area. Some are stationary; others, such as this one, travel slowly, following the hose.

Heavy soils. Heavy soils, such as clays, are slow to soak up moisture but are also slow to dry out. This is because the structure of clay includes relatively few drainage pores but has many smaller capillary pores that retain moisture. Heavy soils must always be watered slowly for a fairly long time to soak the root zone. They can then go two weeks or more without watering.

Porosity and infiltration of dense or compacted soil can be increased by punching holes in (aerifying) the lawn with an engine-powered coring machine.

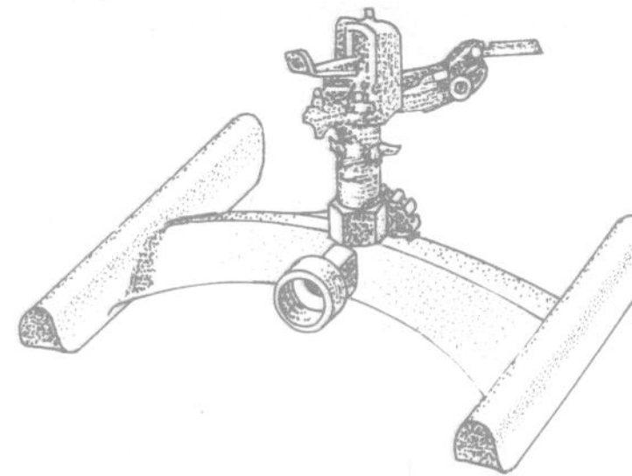

A pulsating sprinkler uses the force of the water to jog the spray head around in a full circle or a preset segment.

Sandy soils. Sandy soils tend, as a rule, to be overly porous and therefore have limited water-holding capacity. They soak up water quickly but drain it equally fast. For that reason they should be watered oftener than clays. They usually need watering about every three or four days in the absence of rain, but for shorter periods of time.

Sprinklers. The availability of water for lawns, as well as its quality and pressure, will vary with locality. These factors should be checked before installing an underground sprinkling system. The pressure will influence the distance that the spray heads can be set apart. As regards surface sprinklers, it is also a good idea to match the spray pattern to the shape of the area to be watered.

Wasteful runoff is caused when sprinklers apply water faster than it can soak into the ground. You can check your sprinkler by placing cans or jars within its spraying radius and noting whether all parts receive about the same amount of water in a given time.

Fertilization

Most lawns benefit from the addition of fertilizer. An adequately fed lawn is denser, more weed free, and more attractive. A well-fertilized lawn also withstands wear better and is more resistant to pests and diseases. Subsequent deep rooting improves soil structure, increases its water-holding capacity, and helps prevent erosion.

Fertilizers for lawns have a different formulation than those designed for gardens where the emphasis is on flowers and fruit rather than on foliage. Lawn fertilizers are also varied according to use.

Lawn seed beds need a high phosphate content. Lawn-maintenance fertilizer is rich in nitrogen, low in phosphorus, low to medium in potassium. On the western plains potassium may not be needed at all.

Nitrogen promotes leaf formation and a deep color. Some phosphorus and potassium should accompany it to maintain a proper balance and to avoid overstimulation that might encourage disease.

Suggested ratios. The three major nutrients of a complete fertilizer—nitrogen (N), phosphorus (P), and potassium (K)—can be in such ratios as 3–1–1, 5–2–3, and so on. The percentage of nutrients (calculated as elemental N and the oxides of P and K) would be 30–10–10, 20–8–12, and so on.

A centrifugal spreader throws seeds or granular fertilizer in a circle from a whirling plate.

Heavy feeders, such as 'Merion' bluegrass, Bermuda grasses, and the creeping bent grasses, can use the maximum amounts recommended on the bag, while fescues can get along well with half as much. Centipede grass also requires little. The fertilizer needs of other species rank in between.

The so-called ureaform fertilizers may not be as readily absorbed by the grass as a more soluble material like ammonium nitrate, but they do parcel out about one-third of their nutrients the first week or two, another one-third in the subsequent six or eight weeks. The last third is released slowly—even into the second and third year.

A gravity-drop spreader distributes seeds or granular fertilizer in a strip the same width as the hopper.

Thus a generous application constitutes a reservoir of nutrients, which is preferable to forcing a flush of growth all at once with soluble nitrogen. Fast growth requires too-frequent mowing and can upset the physiological balance in the grass, followed by quick exhaustion and a dearth of nutrients.

Nitrogen is the basis for fertilizer-rate recommendations—normally 1 pound of actual nitrogen per 1,000 square feet. Heavier applications are possible with gradual-release formulas that do not burn the grass. With these most of the nitrogen is ureaform.

The better lawn fertilizers contain at least some slowly available nitrogen, as well as phosphorus and potassium. Organic sources of nutrients, such as tankage or processed sewage, are nonburning and have a reasonably long release time.

Seasonal variants. In the South it is best to apply fertilizer in spring and summer. In the North most fertilizing should be done in autumn—at least 2 pounds per 1,000 square feet in the fall, with a lighter schedule in late spring and summer.

The rate at which organic fertilizers release nutrients depends on the weather. The organic molecules break down faster where the weather is warm and humid.

Spreaders. Fertilizing should be done with a spreader. The centrifugal (cyclone) design throws particles from a whirling plate; the gravity-drop type feeds them out at the exact width of the hopper.

The centrifugal spreader is easier to operate and covers a wide swath; the gravity spreader is more precise at boundaries.

Weeds

Most of those ubiquitous pests of lawns, weeds, can fortunately be controlled with herbicides. The one exception is grass weeds, which are so similar to the turf that they are hard to eliminate without injuring the desirable grass. For weed identification, see page 639.

Most undesirable annual grasses and some broad-leaved weeds can be controlled with preemergence herbicides—such as benefin, bensulide, DCPA, and siduron—which are granular or sprayable materials applied to the lawn before seed germination. They kill the sprouts as they come up. To be most effective, these materials must be spread uniformly at the proper time.

Crabgrass control. Preemergence application is also one of the best ways to control crabgrass. Crabgrass seeds germinate at about the time forsythias are in flower. The best controls to use are bensulide, siduron, and DCPA. Except for siduron, these chemicals also inhibit germination of desirable grasses for two or three months after application.

If crabgrass does come up, it can be controlled later with postemergents, such as DSMA, AMA, or MSMA. Two or three applications of a postemergent may be needed for complete control of crabgrass that has already become established.

Controlling other weeds. Broad-leaved weeds, such as plantain and other dicotyledons, can be eliminated with such selective weed killers as 2,4-D or controls including a similar material. These herbicides are absorbed by the foliage of broad-leaved weeds and are effective when applied according to instructions. They are most useful when weeds are young and growing vigorously, as in the warm, moist weather of spring. Heavier dosages may be needed as weeds mature or if the weather turns cold.

Sprays of systemic herbicides are ordinarily more effective than the granular form because they immediately coat the weed foliage and are more readily absorbed by the plant. Be careful, however, when spraying such chemical materials to make sure they do not drift over to other plants in the vicinity. Avoid spraying on windy days.

To avoid damage to centipede, St. Augustine, and Bahia grasses in the South, use special regional formulations.

Be careful when applying weed-killing chemicals. Herbicides can also harm ornamental plants, which may be unusually susceptible when they are newly budding in spring. Follow all the precautions that are indicated on the label.

Weed cleanup with herbicides is only temporary unless the adjacent grass is encouraged to fill the voids. Fertilizing is therefore an important adjunct of weed control. Weed-and-feed combinations that contain both fertilizer and herbicide are widely available. Do not use around trees or shrubs.

Controlling Moss and Algae

Moss and algae are seldom a problem on a healthy lawn. If they should appear, they can usually be controlled or eliminated by means of improved lawn culture.

Moss is most likely to develop in shady places, particularly on underfed grass or where the soil has been compacted. The best corrective measures are to add fertilizer, improve the surface drainage, and if necessary, aerate the soil.

Algae are infrequently encountered except where there is standing water. They can usually be eliminated by improving the drainage.

Thatch Removal

The dense mat of grass clippings that can accumulate on lawns may occasionally need to be removed. A certain amount of thatch is inevitable, and it is not necessarily harmful until it gets so thick that it impedes the fertilizer or the weed killers from reaching the root zone.

If thatch is too thick, engine-powered machines with vertically set blades are the simplest means of combing it out.

Thatch is partially removed when a lawn is aerified with a coring machine that removes plugs of soil. In all cases the debris should be raked up and disposed of. These machines are available for rent.

Renovation

A lawn may deteriorate so much that it needs some degree of renovation. Plowing it up and seeding or sodding it anew is a feasible but extreme measure. This may expose the soil to erosion and also expose buried weed seeds that may germinate.

Often a lawn can be renovated without using drastic measures. Fertilizing and weeding may be enough. If not, you can always sow new seeds.

This involves more than simply scattering seeds on top of a heavily

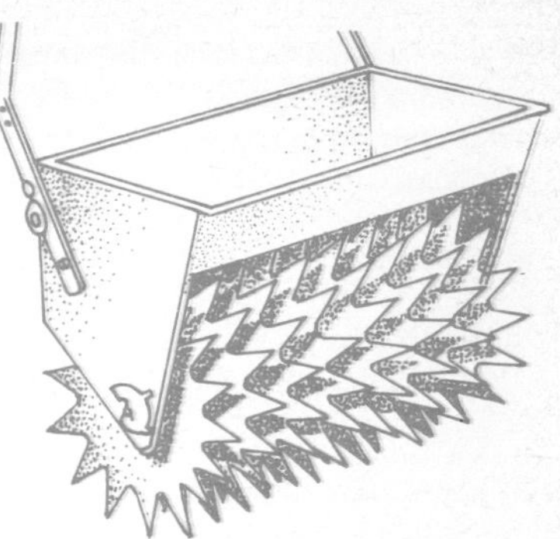

Combination cultivator-spiker has a weight pan on top. Added weight increases the depth of penetration.

thatched lawn. Renovation might begin with a close clipping almost to ground level. If there is too much thatch, it should be removed.

You can also help future seedlings by using a knockdown spray to slow the growth of the old vegetation and reduce competition. Materials such as paraquat are immediately inactivated in the soil and will not adversely affect a new seeding.

Scarify the surface with a thatch-removing machine set low enough for the blades to slice lightly into the soil. Go over the lawn as often as necessary to make grooves in the soil. When the soil is partially bared and the thatch is removed (so that the seeds can make good contact), sow a seed mixture containing the varieties you want.

Keep the lawn moist until the grass becomes established. Mulching will probably not be necessary, since stems of the chemically killed plants will serve the same purpose.

Once started, new varieties may eventually increase with proper care. Some success can be achieved without chemical treatment, but when the area is watered and fertilized, the old vegetation is likely to revive and compete for nutrients and water with the new varieties.

Renovation will not necessarily relieve the lawn of unwanted grasses. Weed controls can be used after the new grass is tall enough and has been mowed a few times.

After mowing, use a general fertilizer and in about two weeks a selective weed killer if necessary. Normal treatment with fertilizers and fungicides can then be resumed in the appropriate season.

Acid-Alkaline Balance

Lawn grasses tolerate a wide range of pH in the soil but respond best to the 5.5–7.5 span. This means moderately acid to mildly alkaline, 7 being neutral on the scale.

If a soil with an extreme pH was not limed or acidified before the lawn was planted, liming to increase alkalinity or sulfur treatment to lower it may be needed.

Repeated use of certain fertilizers may have an acidifying influence. A soil test will indicate the pH and whether it is changing. Kits are available for home use. Most state colleges offer a soil-testing service.

Centipede grass is less likely to develop chlorosis (yellowing of the leaves) in acid soil, but bent grasses thrive under moderately acid conditions. Bluegrasses and Bermuda grass generally do best under neutral or mildly acid conditions. Other species do well on mildly acid soils.

The amount of lime needed to reduce an acid condition depends on the kind of soil and the degree of acidity. From 20–50 pounds of ground limestone per 1,000 square feet will bring a mildly acid soil close to neutral. Strongly acid soils (especially heavy types) may need 100 pounds per 1,000 square feet annually for several years.

Acidifying alkaline soils, such as those on the High Plains, may require the application of 10–50 pounds of elemental sulfur per 1,000 square feet, depending on the degree of alkalinity.

What Can Go Wrong With Lawns

A healthy, well-tended lawn will be resistant to most of the ills listed here, particularly if disease-resistant varieties are used. It also pays to plant a mixture of grasses instead of just one strain. The lawn will thus show less damage should one strain succumb.

For information on symptoms not included here and for illustrations of some of the problems that are listed, see the section "Plant Disorders" on page 600. To find trade names of chemicals that have been mentioned in the book, refer to the chart on page 635. *Note:* Apply all chemicals carefully, and observe all precautions listed on the label.

Symptoms and signs	Cause	Control
Mounds of sand and soil on lawn.	Ants	Chlordane or Diazinon should be applied to holes.
Tiny (¼ in.) pests suck juices from leaves and crowns. Patches of grass are discolored. Several generations each year.	Chinch bugs	Dusting is effective; use ASP-51 (Aspon), carbaryl, chlorpyrifos, or Diazinon. Granulars or sprays can also be used.
Grubs chew roots off grass plants; grass is yellowed and often can be rolled up like carpet. Moles, which damage lawns, eat grubs, but once grubs are controlled chemically, moles will go elsewhere.	Grubs (larvae of chafers and Japanese, Oriental, Asiatic, and June beetles)	Apply chlordane as dust, spray, or granules. One treatment will last 5 yr. Use milky disease spore dust as biological control (for Japanese beetle grubs only), applying 1 tsp. at 5-ft. intervals in rows 5 ft. apart.

Symptoms and signs	Cause	Control
Holes in leaves; chewed shoots; some entire plants destroyed.	Armyworms, cutworms, or sod webworms	Spray with chlorpyrifos, Diazinon, or methoxychlor.
Large heaps of loose soil; tunnels under turf.	Moles	Use mole trap, or place smoke pellets in runs. Control grubs.
Slippery gelatinous layer develops over grass.	Algae or gelatinous lichens	Drain and spike soil. Apply sulfate of iron (4 rounded tbsp. to 1 gal. of water) or copper sulfate (1 rounded tsp. to 10 gal. of water). Top-dress and feed.
Leaf blades with orange-red spots on pustules. Leaves often pale yellow.	Bluegrass rust	At 10-da. intervals from midsummer to early fall, spray lawns with carbamate fungicide, such as ferbam, maneb, or thiram.
In summer, very dark green circular areas, 2–4 ft. in diameter, appear on lawn. Later, these areas turn lighter in color; small mushrooms appear.	Fairy ring (mushrooms)	Apply dolomitic limestone in spring or fall. Mow lawn closely where mushrooms are found. Mix 2–3 tsp. of copper sulfate with 10 gal. of water, and water mixture in.
Patches of yellow, dying grass, which later become brown or covered with cottony white mold. Often seen after long-lasting snow cover has melted or when nitrogen has been applied later than August.	Fusarium snow mold	Apply anilazine, Benomyl, quintozene, or thiram. Keep lawn well aerated. Spray after ground freezes and before snow falls. Repeat if there is significant thaw.
Small straw-colored spots on lawn. Later, large crusty mats. Mats can suffocate and kill grass. Fungus may develop when snow cover is more than 4 in. deep; shows up as snow melts.	Gray snow mold (*Typhula*)	Break up crusty masses with rake. Spray with anilazine, Benomyl-thiram combination spray, cadmium fungicide, or quintozene. For prevention, apply before ground freezes; repeat after January thaw.
Oval to round brown spots on foliage.	Helminthosporium leaf spots	Spray lawn with anilazine, chlorothalonil, mancozeb, or thiram.
Leaves show white powdery deposit in early summer or late summer and fall.	Powdery mildew	Apply foliar sprays of cycloheximide or dinocap.
Pink or reddish gelatinous growths, particularly on fine-leaved grasses.	Red thread	Apply anilazine, chlorothalonil, or mancozeb. Aerate lawn regularly and apply sulfate of ammonia at 1 tbsp. per sq. yd., but not in late autumn or winter. Plant resistant varieties such as 'Fylking.'
Black stripes of fungous spores along grass blades, splitting them open.	Striped smut	Benomyl spray should be applied in spring and fall.

Modern Turf Grasses

Many improved kinds of lawn grasses are now available. Some were discovered as superior clones in established turf and were isolated and perpetuated by means of vegetative propagation as pure lines.

Others were synthesized from several select lines. Still others are the result of highly involved breeding procedures, such as the crossing of select parental lines in the greenhouse (the method used to develop the Rutgers bluegrass hybrids).

The most convenient way to buy seeds is in mixtures developed for specific uses, such as show lawns, play lawns, or lawns in shady areas. There are also many varieties developed for specific climates and uses.

Northern Species

Kentucky bluegrass (*Poa pratensis*). Kentucky bluegrass and its many varieties are the outstanding lawn grasses for the North. They are often somewhat slow to develop and cover the ground, but once established, they grow well and are easily cared for. Bluegrass spreads by underground stems (rhizomes), takes well to mowing, and is generally an excellent choice for all situations, except where the soil is very poor.

'Merion' bluegrass began the age of special turf-grass varieties and is still excellent except where virulent diseases have built up. The varieties 'Baron,' 'Enmundi,' 'Fylking,' 'Pennstar,' and 'Sydsport' stem from European ancestors. Most of the other introductions—such as 'Adelphi,' 'Glade,' and 'Plush,' developed at Rutgers University—tend to be low, dark green, resistant to many diseases, and outstanding in winter.

Perennial ryegrass (*Lolium perenne*). Improved ryegrasses are as attractive as bluegrass, although they do not spread, do not mow quite so neatly, and do not tolerate extreme climates as well as the bluegrasses. They do, however, have one definite advantage: no other fine turf grass establishes itself so fast, which makes them ideal for quick cover.

Many of the best varieties derive from the Rutgers University breeding program. Of these 'Manhattan' was the earliest. It was so named because it was derived from a hardy composite of more than a dozen selections taken chiefly from Central Park in New York City.

'Pennfine' was developed at Pennsylvania State University. 'Game' and 'NK-100' have partially European ancestors. Other excellent domestic varieties include 'Citation,' 'Derby,' 'Diplomat,' 'NK-200,' 'Omega,' and 'Yorktown.' Each variety has some unique characteristics. Local turf-grass specialists can tell you which ones might best fit your particular conditions.

Fescues (*Festuca rubra*). Fine fescues are adapted to dry habitats, poor soils, and shade. They are wirier and finer textured than bluegrass and are especially attractive in the cooler months. Chewings fescue varieties, which include 'Highlight,' 'Jamestown,' and 'Koket,' are prized for density. Spreading and creeping varieties, such as 'Ruby,' are used for coverage where the development of their rhizomes is important to stabilize the soil. Coarse fescues, such as 'Kentucky-31,' make rugged lawns. They are also sown over southern grasses to provide winter green.

Bent grass (*Agrostis* species). Bent grasses are among the most elegant turf grasses; but they have exacting requirements, especially in their need for frequent mowing. They do well in humid climates, such as the western slopes of the Pacific states, around the Great Lakes, and in the misty Appalachian uplands.

Colonial bent grass, such as 'Highland,' is well suited for lawns that cannot receive the special care that is required for creeping bent grasses, such as 'Emerald.'

Southern Species

Bermuda grass (*Cynodon dactylon*). Bermuda grass is attractive and aggressive. It spreads rampantly by runners, needs frequent mowing, and requires exposure to full sun. Unselected common Bermuda grass can be grown from seeds.

Crosses (with *C. transvaalensis*) produce sterile hybrids whose particular characteristics can only be propagated vegetatively. These include the outstanding Tifton varieties: 'Tiffine,' 'Tifway,' 'Tifgreen,' 'Tifdwarf,' and others that have the same prefix. 'Santa Ana' was bred in California to resist smog. Many other varieties have been bred for specific local conditions throughout the South.

Zoysia (*Z. matrella*). A slow-growing, tough grass that makes an excellent lawn once established, zoysia spreads by horizontal stems called stolons as well as by fleshy underground parts called rhizomes. Zoysia does not come true from seed and is therefore generally planted vegetatively. It will grow well in either sun or partial shade.

'Emerald' is a favorite in the South. 'Meyer,' more tolerant of cold weather, is sometimes planted in the North, but it has such a short growing season there that northern grasses are generally preferred. It is somewhat more useful in the transitional zone.

Centipede (*Eremochloa ophiuroides*). Centipede is a low-maintenance grass that does not need a high level of fertility and does best in acid soil. It can be started from seeds or, more effectively, by vegetative starts.

Centipede grass spreads by stolons, forms attractive medium-textured turf, and is well adapted to the southeastern coastal plains. 'Oaklawn' and 'Tennessee' are popular varieties.

St. Augustine (*Stenotaphrum secundatum*). St. Augustine grass is perhaps the most used ground cover in Florida and along the Gulf Coast. It has a number of insect and disease problems, but it is inexpensive and can be grown in partial shade.

St. Augustine is fairly coarse, spreads by stolons, and in time tends to thatch. There is an improved selection, 'Floratine,' and a still newer variety, 'Floratum,' which is noted for its resistance to the SAD virus—a problem in eastern Texas.

Bahia grass (*Paspalum notatum*). Initially a pasture species, Bahia grass has gained favor especially in Florida because of its modest maintenance requirements and availability as seed. The Argentine strain, darker green and somewhat velvety, is usually planted in lawns.

Not as attractive as select Bermuda grasses and zoysias, Bahia grows in sun or partial shade and is useful in the Deep South, where other grasses may not be at their best.

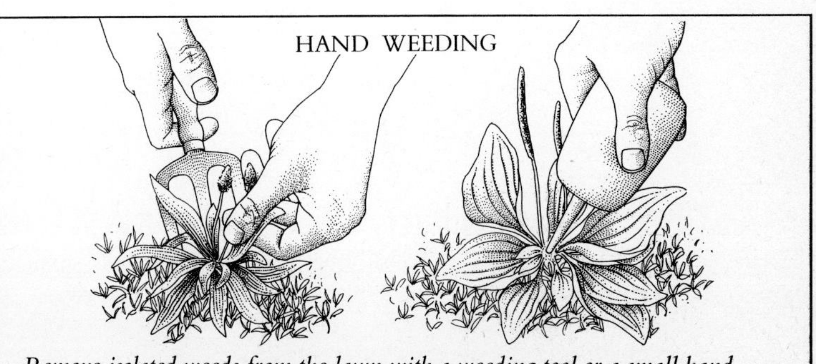

Remove isolated weeds from the lawn with a weeding tool or a small hand fork, or treat them individually with a spot weed killer.

Lawn Grass Zone Map

Lawn grasses for the United States can be divided into two groups: northern grasses, such as bluegrass, bent grass, ryegrass, and fescue; and southern grasses, including zoysia, Bermuda, Bahia, St. Augustine, and centipede.

The key to the two zones indicated on this map is the soil temperature, particularly at night. The southern grasses survive temperatures into the 90's but do not grow well in cold ground and may not withstand freezing. The northern grasses thrive in cooler climates and can take high daytime temperatures if the nights are cool. These grasses are at their best where the temperature during the day is about 70° F and 10–20 degrees cooler at night. Between the two areas lies a transitional zone, where northern grasses can be used in northerly exposures, at higher elevations, and on shaded ground; and southern grasses can be used in warmer, southerly and westerly exposures and full sun.

Bear in mind that this map is intended to serve only as a general guide in determining what kinds of grass are best suited to your locale. There are many local climates within any area, and their temperatures may vary considerably from the norm. These microclimates may be due to elevation, nearby bodies of water, prevailing winds, sheltering landscape features, or other factors.

Moreover, such variables as humidity, amount of precipitation, and general soil quality all affect the success of a lawn. There are many varieties of each type of grass, and most of them were developed over the years to flourish under conditions far more specific than can be indicated on a map of this size. There are also hundreds of seed mixtures and blends devised by lawn specialists for customers in various areas.

The most reliable guide to what will grow in your area is what is already growing there. Consult your county extension agent, an established local seedsman, or ask a neighbor with a thriving lawn.

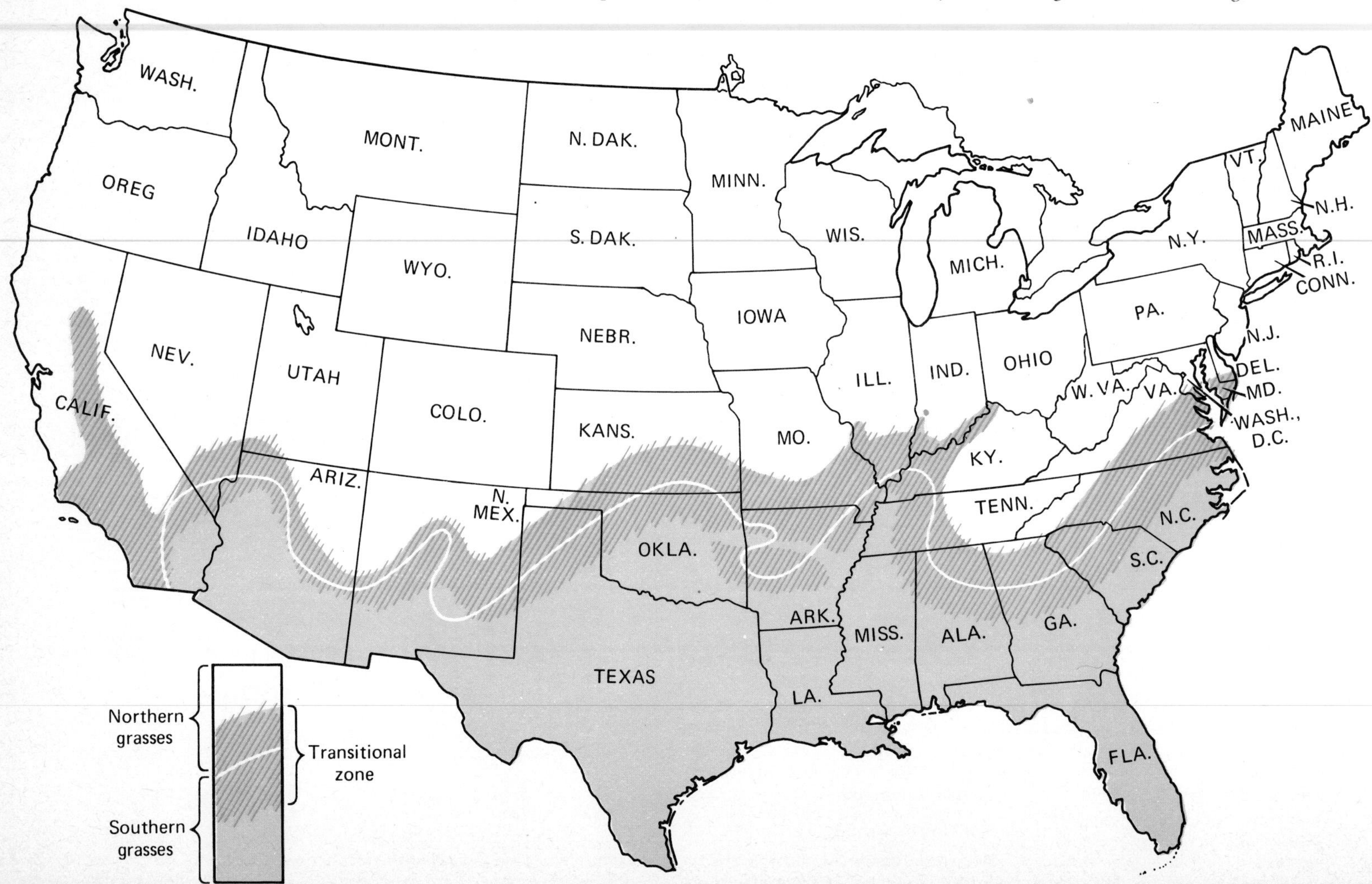

Ground Covers

Plants suitable for ground covers are listed here alphabetically according to their best known common names. Others are noted in the chapters on shrubs, rock plants, and perennials.

These plants are all particularly adaptable to steep slopes or rocky terrains, where a lawn is not practical; some thrive in deep shade and can be used under trees. Established ground covers shade out most weeds.

To determine whether a plant will survive the lowest average temperatures in your area, check the zone in the Hardiness column. Then refer to the Temperature Zone Map on page 9 as indicated.

The methods of propagation recommended here are described in the chapter on perennials (see p. 234).

Ajuga
Cotoneaster
Crown vetch
Euonymus
Goutweed
Ivy
Juniper
Lilyturf
Pachysandra
Periwinkle
Wild strawberry

Common and botanical names	Hardiness *(Map, p. 9)*	Decorative characteristics, special requirements, and remarks	Propagation
Ajuga, or Bugleweed *(Ajuga)* Carpet bugleweed *(A. reptans)*	A	Shiny leaves form tight mat. From late spring into early summer small spikes of blue blooms appear. Foliage may die back to crowns in cold winters, but plants recover in spring. Grow in sun or shade.	Divide clumps in spring or fall.
Cotoneaster *(Cotoneaster)* Bearberry *(C. dammeri)*	B	Evergreen leaves are about 1 in. long. Fruits are bright red. A useful prostrate plant. Grow in sun and moist soil. Susceptible to fire blight.	Take semi-hard-shoot cuttings in summer.
Crown vetch *(Coronilla)* *C. varia*	A	Fast-growing shoots bear compound leaves. Pealike blooms are pale pink. Excellent for sunny slopes. Spreads rapidly. Deciduous.	Make root divisions in spring or fall.
Euonymus *(Euonymus)* Wintercreeper *(E. fortunei* varieties)	B	Leaves on mature specimens assume several different shapes. The 1-in. evergreen leaves are dark purple from fall through winter. Oval leaves are handsomely highlighted by rounded light pink fruits. Runners will cling to rough surfaces. Grow in sun.	Take semi-hard-shoot cuttings in summer or firm-shoot cuttings in late summer.
Goutweed, or Bishop's-weed *(Aegopodium)* *A. podagraria*	A	A deciduous plant that grows to about 1 ft. in height. Small white blossoms open in early summer. A rapid spreader that does best in partial shade, it can be controlled by up to 3 mowings each year.	Make root divisions in spring or fall.
Ivy *(Hedera)* English *(H. helix* varieties)	B	Evergreen leaves form dense carpet. Runners climb rough masonry surfaces. Grow in sun or deep shade.	Take semi-hard-shoot cuttings in summer or late summer.
Juniper *(Juniperus)* Creeping *(J. procumbens nana)*	A	Bluish-green needles are borne on branches that seldom grow taller than 1 ft. Branches grow in horizontal tiers. Plant slowly develops tight, rounded profile. Grow in sun. Evergreen.	Make soil layers or take firm-shoot cuttings in late summer.
Lilyturf *(Ophiopogon)* Dwarf *(O. japonicus)*	C	Deep green, grassy leaves are evergreen. Purplish flowers are followed by small blue fruits. Grow in sun or shade.	Divide and transplant.
Pachysandra *(Pachysandra)* *P. terminalis*	B	Has handsome, shiny, evergreen foliage. Creamy white blooms open in late spring. Initial close planting encourages rapid coverage. Useful in shade, especially under maples, where little else will grow.	Transplant clumps. Take semi-hard-shoot cuttings in summer.
Periwinkle *(Vinca)* Common *(V. minor)*	B	Shiny ovate leaves are up to 2 in. long. In midspring lilac-blue blossoms appear. Varieties are available with white or pink blooms. A rapid spreader, this evergreen thrives in sun or shade.	Make root divisions in spring and fall.
Strawberry, wild *(Fragaria)* *F. chiloensis*	B	Evergreen leaves are shiny above, bluish-white beneath. Large dark red fruits form after white blossoms fade. Grow in partial shade.	Transplant rooted runners.

Trees

Birch trees, with their distinctive white bark, are effective in group plantings.

Few plants provide as much personal pleasure, or make such a useful contribution to the immediate environment, as the trees you plant in your garden.

Trees give an air of maturity and permanence to a garden. They add height and depth to even simple garden designs and provide shelter and privacy. Deciduous trees give shade in summer, while in winter the naked branches have a stark beauty outlined against the sky. Evergreen trees, be they broad-leaved or coniferous, will maintain their attraction throughout the year and are especially appreciated in colder climates during the drab months when there is little garden color.

Trees condition the air by taking in carbon dioxide and giving off oxygen. They also give off water. A large tree releases thousands of gallons a day through its leaves by the process of transpiration.

Most people select trees for their foliage, flowers, and forms, or for a specific purpose, such as to provide a windbreak. Since trees have to be lived with for many years, it is particularly important to choose, at the start, the right tree for the right purpose and place. In suburban residential areas, in particular, it is important for a tree planted in a garden to be in keeping with the surrounding area.

This does not mean that your choice must be limited. But, if your neighbor has a weeping willow, rewarding as it is to grow, one is probably enough in that immediate area. And, while it is best not to follow the local pattern slavishly, it is not recommended that you seek out the most unusual or impressive tree you can possibly find. Study the setting to see which tree would best fit in.

The imposing beech tree, for example, equally attractive for its shape, leaves, and autumn colors, is as out of proportion in the small suburban garden as is an isolated crab apple in parkland. However, there are settings in the suburbs where good-size trees are appropriate and a tulip tree or one of the large flowering cherries would be an excellent addition to the landscape.

One reason for planting trees is to create a shelterbelt against the wind. Dense evergreen or coniferous trees are best for this.

If shade is desired, do not plant erect and columnar trees, such as the incense cedar. Instead, grow wide-spreading or weeping trees, such as the maple, birch, and willow. If a tree is to be planted in the foreground, open shapes, such as the paper birch and honey locust, provide a frame for the rest of the garden. For a boundary the solid shape of a plane tree or an oak or the dark, pyramidal shape of a fir will give a feeling of privacy by obscuring the houses beyond.

The different shapes and sizes of the various leaves can also be chosen for specific effects. The fernlike leaves of honey locusts produce attractive patterns, and the small leaves of birches and many Japanese maples have interesting shapes.

Today's gardens are generally small, and nearly all the maintenance is carried out by the owner. The amount of work necessary can be greatly reduced by adopting informal layouts for the ornamental part of the garden. Once planted, trees and shrubs require little attention. They make an ideal setting for perennial and annual flowers and can often be used to provide the partial shade and shelter that some of these plants require.

If you intend to plant a single specimen tree—on a lawn, at the back of a wide border, or near a boundary—consider carefully the merits and disadvantages of your choice. If the prime consideration when choosing a tree is its shape—

such as spreading, columnar, or weeping—only the soil, position, and eventual size need be evaluated.

On the other hand, if you choose a tree for a seasonal characteristic, such as its flowers or autumn colors, try to ascertain its appearance at other times of the year. When the massed display of blossoms in spring fades away, you may have a tree of no particular beauty for the rest of the year. Bear in mind that the vivid autumn color of the foliage of most trees is effective for little more than one month.

Evergreen trees are popular, not only for their screening and hedging value but also for their beautiful shapes. Many evergreens, and especially conifers, are both wind and drought resistant, once established. They are ideal as specimen trees on lawns, and even the smallest garden can accommodate a dwarf conifer. It is during winter in northern gardens that evergreens are at their most impressive. The green foliage brings welcome color to a drab scene, and this can be made even more interesting by selecting evergreens with golden, silver, or blue-green foliage. A mixed grouping that includes plantings of all-green and variegated evergreens is particularly effective.

Fitting the tree to the site. As a general rule it is not advisable to plant trees close to your house. Not only can the roots eventually injure the foundation and drains but fast-growing trees can also quickly exclude light and air from the house. Avoid planting anything but dwarf evergreens or medium-size deciduous trees, such as Japanese cherries or dwarf crab apples, in small front gardens. Trees should be in harmony with the house; they should not overshadow it. A wide-spreading or tall tree on a small front lawn can be quite out of proportion. Where trees overhang paths and driveways, there is both a nuisance and a danger from broken branches and, in autumn, from fallen leaves that are slippery underfoot in wet weather. For such small areas, narrow, columnar conifers or similar types of deciduous trees fulfill the aesthetic as well as the practical needs.

Where space allows, a group planting of three or five trees is usually more effective than a single specimen. The best effects come from letting one shape dominate the group—one tall tree, one thin tree, and one triangular-shaped tree will look awkward. No set pattern can be specified, but the trees should belong to the same genus and have roughly the same dimensions and shapes. Three hawthorns, for example, or three crab apples, with different-colored flowers and fruit, make a handsome group, as do several Japanese maples of various leaf shapes and autumn tints. A group of variegated and green hollies is striking in winter, especially if the trees have berries of different hues. Conifers with silver or golden leaves are other obvious choices, while the blue-gray spruces are best as single specimens.

The spacing between trees in a group depends on the varieties to be planted. The idea is to put them close enough together so that they are obviously a grouping—but not so close that they touch or shade one another when they mature. The nurseryman from whom you buy the trees can give you a good estimate as to their ultimate spread in your climate. Some judicious pruning can also be done if they tend to overgrow.

Trees for screens and shelterbelts should be planted close together, but the initial spacing could well allow for the removal of every other tree as they grow larger.

Such screens in their early stages are often made up of fast-growing deciduous trees and slower-growing conifers. As the conifers become effective, the deciduous trees are then removed, providing this was the ultimate goal when you set out. Most nurseries and garden centers will give advice on suitable trees.

The trees described and illustrated in the chart beginning on page 51 provide a varied basis for selection. However, the choice is so vast that it is worth checking catalogs or, ideally, inspecting the trees at nurseries before making a decision.

Trees, more than anything else in the garden, can create a particular atmosphere. For example, trees that have a formal appearance include the fir, horse chestnut, cedar, and yew; for a pastoral feeling choose a birch, oak, or weeping willow; more romantic are the magnolia, maple, or beech; and to complement an urban landscape, there are the flowering cherry, linden, honey locust, and some of the firs.

Popular trees are relatively inexpensive, but buying rare types can call for a substantial outlay. In such a case it is even more important to inspect the tree of your choice in a local nursery or an arboretum, and ideally at the time of year when it is at its best—either in flower, fruit, or autumn color.

It is possible to plant trees of almost any size; but after they get to be 15 feet or so high, the problems and costs increase considerably, and the chances of success diminish. So it is usually best to buy a tree when it is small. There is also pleasure to be derived from watching it grow through its most vigorous, formative period, when you can enjoy the foliage at eye level.

Tree surgery. The wise gardener should check the condition of his established trees once a year, and if heavy pruning or repair is necessary, he should call for professional help. Overhanging branches can be a safety hazard—and a homeowner can be liable for any damage sustained by passersby. Treatment of splitting trunks, top pruning of tall trees, and felling of diseased or unwanted trees are best left to professional tree surgeons, who have both the knowledge and equipment to deal most efficiently and safely with such difficult and potentially dangerous garden problems.

The householder and the law. A householder may be held responsible for any destruction of neighboring land by encroaching roots and overhanging branches. He may also be required to pay compensation for any damage to plants on adjoining land that is caused by spraying.

Prevent roots from harming your own and neighboring property by planting trees well away from buildings and walls. The main cause of cracks in walls can be traced to trees extracting moisture from the soil, especially in heavy clay; the dry soil subsides and brings about a settlement of the foundations. The poplar and ash are the worst offenders and should never be planted near houses. Roots of large maple trees can literally raise a concrete sidewalk. The distance to which roots will spread is assumed to equal the eventual height of the tree, although some extend much farther.

Roots cannot penetrate into the main drains of houses because the socketed joints are sealed, but they do sometimes find their way into the open joints of drainage tiles. If an area of the garden tends to become waterlogged after rain, any land drains should be examined and invading roots removed. There are professionals who do this job.

Overgrown hedges and trees that may be a hazard are yet another responsibility where they border on neighboring land or public roads. The householder may be required to trim the hedge back properly or remove any trees that are potential dangers. When damage has actually occurred, the person who owns the land on which the offending plant grows may have to pay for it.

These few restrictions, however, are minor when compared to the beauty of foliage and flowers, the bounty of dappled shade, and th striking sculptural forms that o trees can bring.

How to Plant a Tree

When, Where, and How to Dig the Hole

The ideal planting time for deciduous trees is midautumn to early spring, when the ground is neither waterlogged nor frozen solid. Broad-leaved evergreens are best planted earlier in the fall or later in spring, when the soil is warm and moist. Conifers are planted in mid-spring or early fall. Keep roots moist to prevent foliage from shedding.

Trees ordered from a nursery will probably arrive either bare rooted or with roots contained in a ball of soil wrapped in burlap. If you pick the tree up from the nursery, it may already be growing in a container. In that case it can be planted at any time except in midwinter; but if you plant in summer, be sure to keep the tree well watered until autumn.

Poor growth among newly planted trees is most commonly caused by inadequate drainage. Therefore, to ensure good drainage is a prime consideration. The first step is proper selection of the planting site. A spot that is swampy or where water tends to collect after a rainfall is not a good place to plant most trees.

For the average young tree, the planting hole should be about 3 feet across and 18 inches deep—large enough to give the roots plenty of room to spread in all directions.

If you are planting in grass, mark out a circle, remove the sod as shown below, break it up, and save it to incorporate with the soil you put around the roots. Begin digging from the center of the circle, saving the topsoil as you go. When you see the soil becoming more yellowish or lighter colored, it means you have reached the less organic subsoil. Keep digging, but put this in a separate pile.

When the hole is dug, fill it with water to test drainage. If it takes longer than an hour or so to empty, you have a problem that might be easily solved or might require the installation of a whole drainage system (see "What You Should Know About the Soil," p. 592). Sometimes a layer of impermeable clay will be fairly thin, and you can break through by thrusting your garden fork deeply into the bottom of the hole. If so, break up the base of the hole and proceed. If not, you might be well advised to pick another site.

All trees should be staked during their first two or three years. If one stake is used, place it before the tree is planted. Stout wooden stakes treated with wood preservative are obtainable from most nurseries. They should be long enough to reach just below the point where the trunk begins to branch out. With a bare-rooted tree, use a single stake in the center of the hole; with a balled-and-burlapped tree, drive in two stakes after planting, one on either side of the root ball.

Make starting holes for the sharpened stakes, insert them, and hammer them in with a sledge.

Place a layer of rubble in the bottom of the hole to increase aeration. This is of value only if the hole already drains; it will not solve the problem of poor drainage.

Add sod and fertilizing matter as shown below. Mix the subsoil you have taken out with an equal amount of topsoil, and use the mix to fill the hole halfway. Tread firmly, fill with water, and let drain.

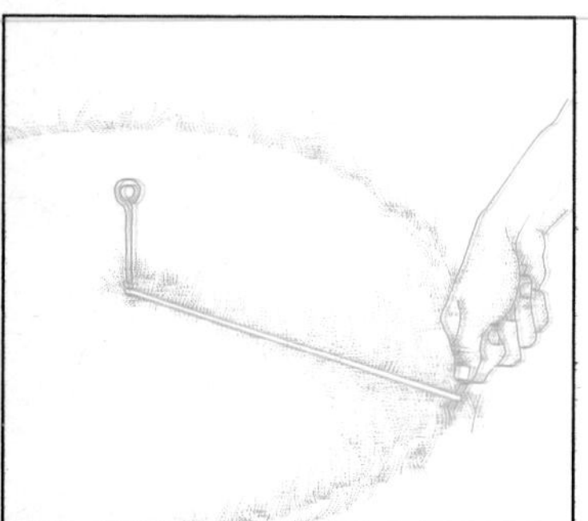

1. *Use a peg, a knife, and a piece of string to mark a 3-ft. circle in the grass.*

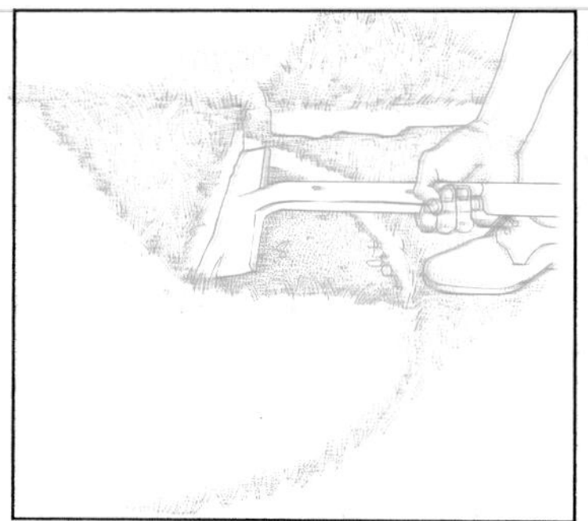

2. *Remove the sod from within the circle, and stack it on one side for future use.*

3. *Dig the hole 18 in. deep; loosen the bottom soil with a fork. Test drainage.*

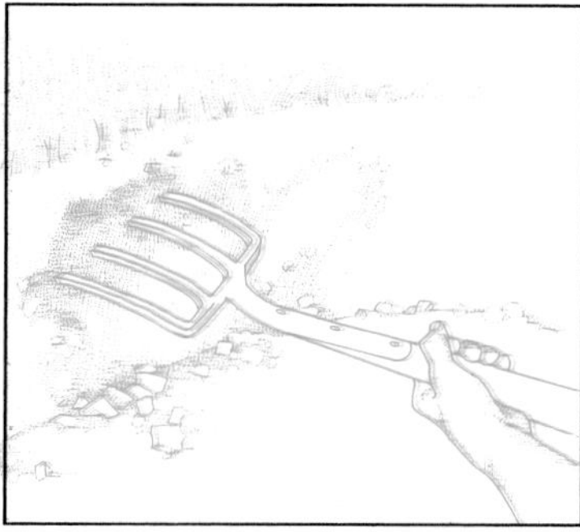

4. *With heavy soils, use a garden fork to break down the sides of the hole.*

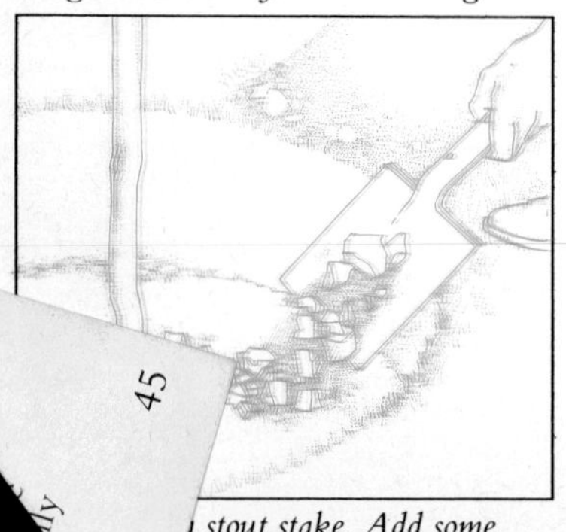

stout stake. Add some or rubble to help aeration.

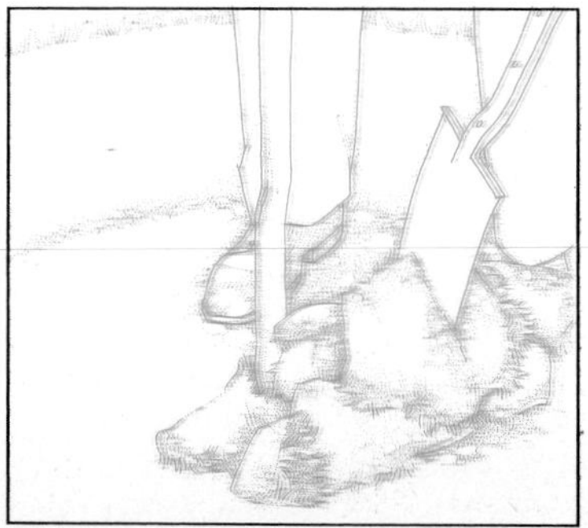

6. *Chop the sod into 3- to 4-in. pieces; put them into the hole, grass side down.*

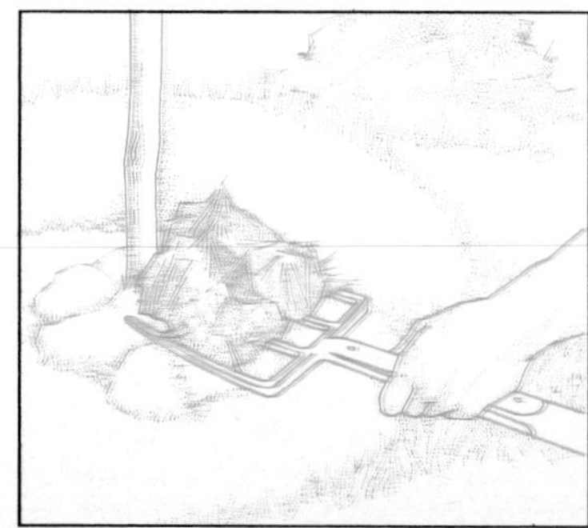

7. *Add well-rotted manure, leaf mold, or compost to act as a slow fertilizer.*

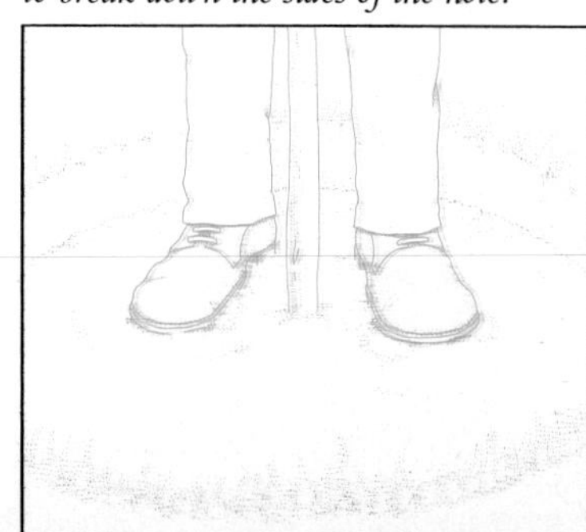

8. *Half-fill the hole with subsoil and topsoil. Tread firmly and water.*

Planting and Staking a Young Tree

Before planting a tree the top branches, and the roots if they are exposed, should be trimmed as shown. Remove container-grown trees from their containers, gently shake loose a little of the soil, and prune the roots. Remove roots that have grown around the circumference of the pot or they will continue to engird the tree; in effect the tree will still be pot-bound.

Mix the remaining topsoil with peat moss, well-rotted compost, or manure at a ratio of two parts soil to one part additive. Crumble this mixture well, to avoid air pockets.

Planting is easier if done by two people. Let one hold the tree in position while the other places a flat piece of wood across the hole. The old soil mark on the stem should be level with the piece of wood; remove or add soil accordingly. If the tree is bare rooted, make a mound over which to spread the roots.

With a balled-root tree, now is the time to loosen the top of the burlap, but do not remove it. While one person holds the tree upright—or against the stake with a bare-rooted tree—the other should start filling the hole with the soil mix. Shake a bare-rooted tree from time to time to make sure that the soil is settling around the roots, and if the soil is sandy, tread it down as you go. In heavier soil, when the roots are covered, soak the area with water to settle the soil before filling the hole.

Fill in the hole and firm the soil down until it is level with the surrounding ground. The old soil mark on the trunk should be just visible.

Surround the bare-soil area with a small mound to form a kind of basin to catch and hold water in the root area. Keep the surface free of grass and weeds for two or three years so that the young roots will not have to compete for nourishment.

The tree must now be firmly tied to the stakes. The best ties are strong plastic or webbing straps with rubber buffers. With a bare-rooted tree, attach the tie about 4 inches below the lowest branch, or use burlap wrapped in a figure eight and secured with strong cord as shown below right. If there is a crook in the trunk that is likely to rub against the stake, put another tie near it.

The reason for using two stakes with a balled-root tree is to prevent the tree from rocking back and forth in the wind. Stretch rope or wire from the padded trunk to strong stakes on either side of the tree.

Inspect ties periodically, especially after strong winds, and retie if necessary. As the tree grows, loosen ties to prevent strangulation.

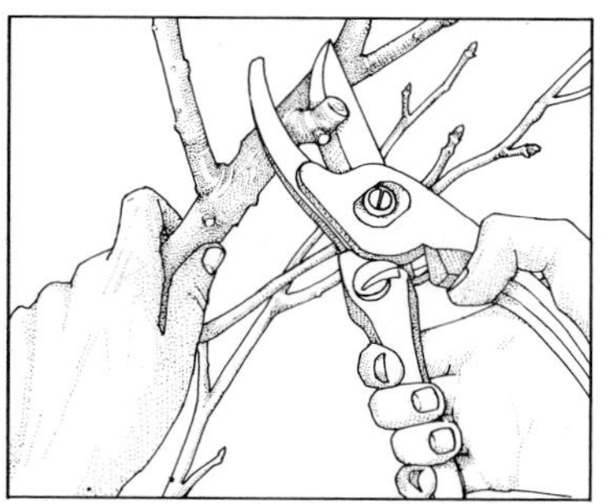

1. *On top branches, cut off any dead stumps of wood, flush with branch.*

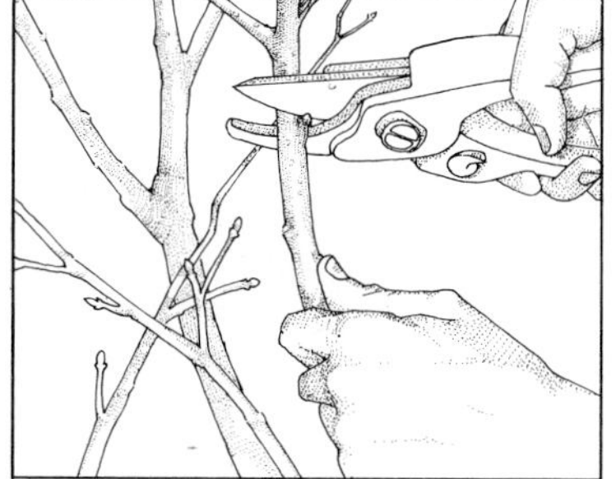

2. *Trim any branches with damaged tips back to an outward-facing bud.*

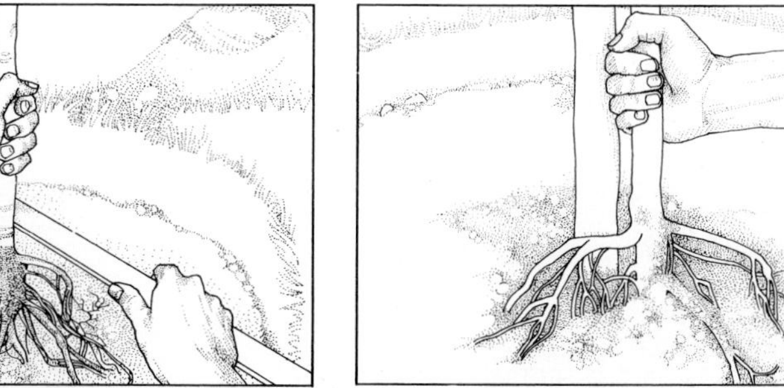

3. *Line up the old soil mark on the trunk level with surrounding surface.*

4. *Begin filling in hole with enriched topsoil. Shake tree to avoid air pockets.*

5. *Continue to fill, firming soil down often, until the hole is filled in.*

6. *Level with a fork. Water well and let drain. Leave bare two or three years.*

REMOVE DAMAGED ROOTS

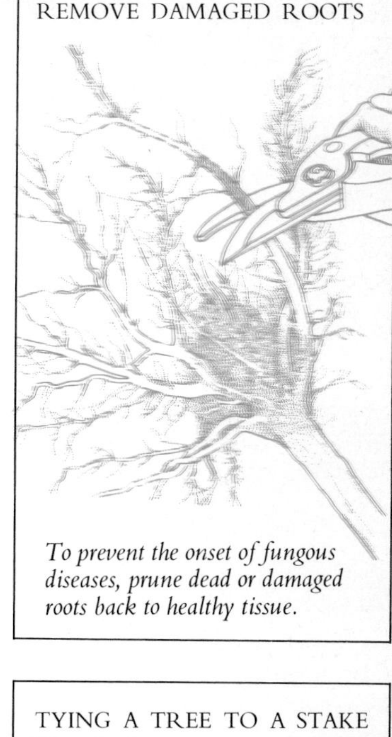

To prevent the onset of fungous diseases, prune dead or damaged roots back to healthy tissue.

TYING A TREE TO A STAKE

Tree ties. *Fix strap around stem, buckle around stake, with the rubber buffer in between.*

Burlap. *Wrap around stake, then around stem, and stake.*

Taking Care of Trees

Mulching and Feeding After Planting

Mulching holds in moisture, inhibits weeds, and encourages organisms that aerate and enrich the soil. It also protects against overheating in summer and freezing and thawing in winter. As time passes, it will also provide a little nourishment.

Peat moss (mixed with soil), leaf mold, bark chips, peanut hulls, and other useful mulches can be bought from garden centers or nurseries. Apply in early autumn or spring when soil is moist and warm, mulching 3–4 inches deep over the root area.

Feeding is generally not needed for trees in their formative years. Later on, small discolored leaves and premature leaf fall may indicate a lack of nourishment.

Make nutrients available to the tiny feeder roots by boring a number of holes in the soil around the perimeter of the root area (roughly the same spread as the branches) and filling them with fertilizer as shown. There are a number of good slow-release fertilizers on the market that provide their nutrients gradually over a period of a year or more.

An alternative to boring holes is to use slow-release tree-food spikes that can be hammered into the soil. If the root area is paved over or otherwise inaccessible, it is also possible to inject liquid fertilizer into holes bored in the trunk; but this entails considerable risk of introducing disease; so it pays to consult an expert.

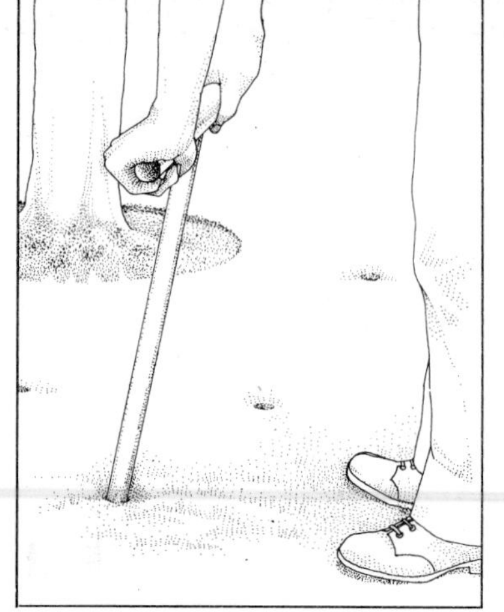

1. *Use a soil auger to bore holes 12 in. deep, 18–24 in. apart over root area.*

2. *Funnel granular fertilizer into the holes. Fill with soil; tamp down.*

Preventing a Young Tree From Drying Out

Established trees seldom need watering except in times of extreme drought. The foliage of young trees, however, may wilt; and evergreens, particularly conifers, may turn brown and scorched looking within a few weeks after planting. This condition may be caused by a lack of water or by drying winds.

Soak the soil thoroughly, providing at least 3 gallons at a time once a week. An antidesiccant spray also helps to prevent water from being lost through the foliage.

Trees grown in containers must be watered regularly and thoroughly. This may be necessary even in winter, especially if the containers are sheltered from the rain.

If a young tree is being scorched by drying wind, which in some climates can happen in winter, make a shelter of burlap or thick sheet plastic around it as high as the tree. To make the shelter, insert three or four stakes around the tree and secure the material to them. Leave the top of this windbreak open to the rain.

Removing Suckers From Grafted and Budded Trees

A sucker is a shoot that appears near the base of a main stem. It diverts energy and must be removed—particularly from trees that have been grafted or budded onto the rootstocks of related species. With these trees, suckers develop from below the graft, and if not removed, they will subvert the graft.

Trace the sucker to its point of origin belowground, grasp it firmly, and pull it cleanly away. Cutting encourages more suckers.

Never cut suckers off; always pull them away cleanly.

Selecting a New Leading Shoot After Damage

Trees that grow in columnar or pyramidal shapes can be damaged when young by strong winds. They may be deformed, or the upright stem from which side branches radiate may be snapped off. If this happens, reestablish new growth by training another leading shoot, selecting one that is growing upright, as near as possible to the damaged point of the old leader.

Use a bamboo cane long enough to reach from the top of the supporting stake to 2 feet above the tip of the new leader. Loosen the tree tie at the top of the stake, insert the cane between stake and tie, and refasten. Secure the base of the cane with strong, cord or a twist tie. Attach the new leader to the cane in several places, and cut off the old leader flush with the stem. Leave the cane in place for about two years, or until the new leading shoot has become self-supporting. Check the ties from time to time to be sure they are not hampering the young shoot's growth.

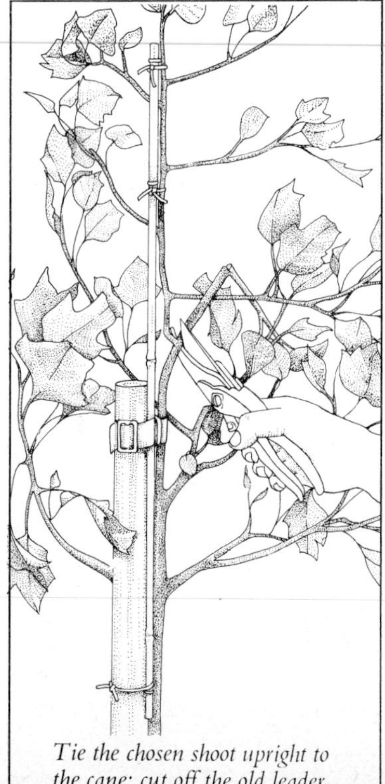

Tie the chosen shoot upright to the cane; cut off the old leader.

Removing a Competing Leader From a Young Tree

Some trees, especially those with erect, conical, or pyramidal growth habits, will occasionally fork at the tip of the leading shoot. If allowed to grow, this secondary leader will spoil the tree's symmetrical shape.

A competing leader on a single-stemmed tree—commonest on conifers—must be completely removed at its point of origin. On trees that form side shoots, prune the second leader back to half its length, cutting diagonally just above an outward-facing bud. This will induce the competing leader to put out horizontal side shoots.

In mild climates this pruning can be done at any time the plant is not actively growing. Where winters are severe, trim in early spring.

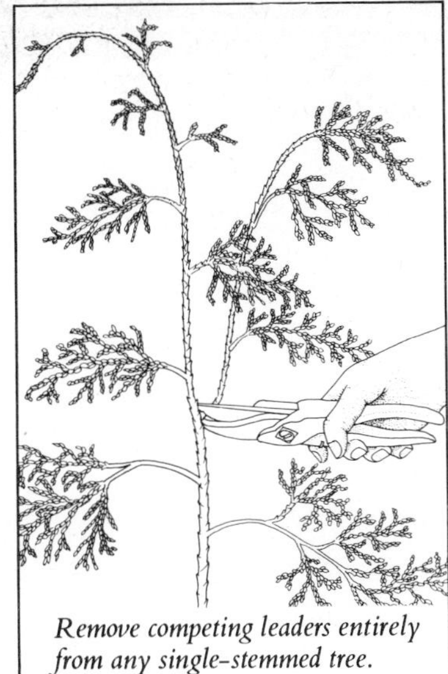

Remove competing leaders entirely from any single-stemmed tree.

Cutting a Long Branch to Shape

In most cases a tree will produce its branches to conform with its natural shape. Sometimes, however, one branch will grow too vigorously in a quest for light or in response to other conditions. The result may be a lop-sided appearance and perhaps overall weakened growth.

You can restore symmetry by pruning such branches during the tree's dormant period to about one-third of their length. Cut back to a side shoot growing in the same direction. If the branch is more than an inch thick, seal the wound.

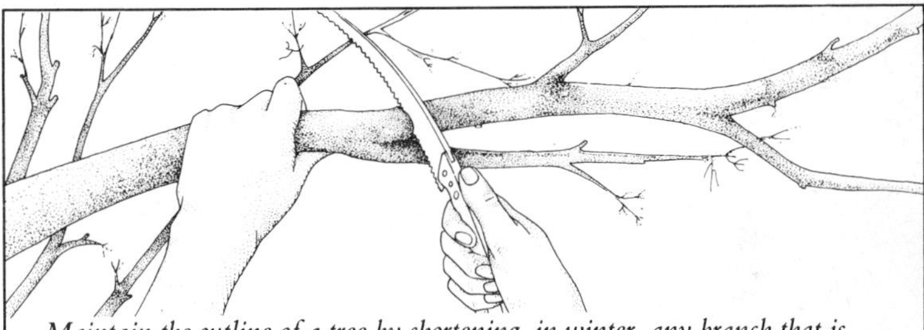

Maintain the outline of a tree by shortening, in winter, any branch that is growing too strongly. Cut to a side shoot about two-thirds of the way back.

Removing Water Sprouts From Tree Trunks

Two types of side shoots may develop on the trunk of a tree. Where a large branch has been removed, straight, thin shoots, known as water sprouts, may appear. These should be cut off flush with the trunk.

On untrained young trees, side shoots will grow from the trunk. Prune, but do not remove until the trunk has reached the height you want; then cut them off.

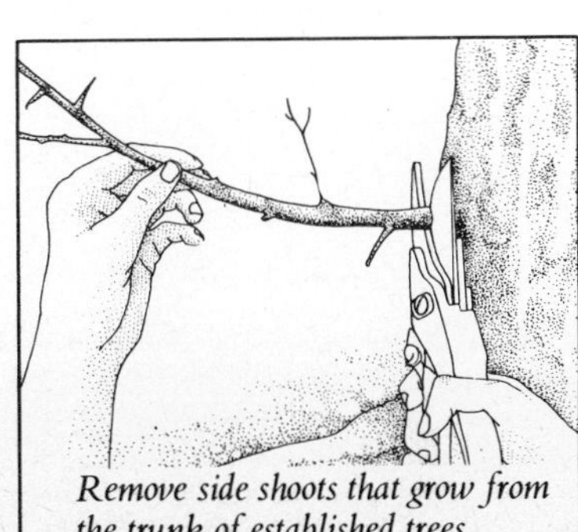

Remove side shoots that grow from the trunk of established trees.

Cutting Off Unwanted Thick Branches

It may occasionally be necessary to remove a large, thick branch, either because it has been damaged or because it is growing at an awkward angle or over a neighbor's land. The danger here is that the weight of the branch may cause it to break away before the cut has been cleanly finished, thereby damaging the trunk.

To prevent this, first use a pruning saw to reduce the long branch to a convenient length, leaving about 18 inches to be dealt with in the final cut. (If this is impossible, support the offending branch by tying it to a higher one while you saw it off at the 18-inch mark.) Then saw the remaining stump about one-third of the way through from the underside, flush with the trunk, before finishing the cut from the top.

Finally, trim the cut with a sharp knife and seal with compound. This helps the wound to heal and prevents fungous spores and other diseases from entering the tree.

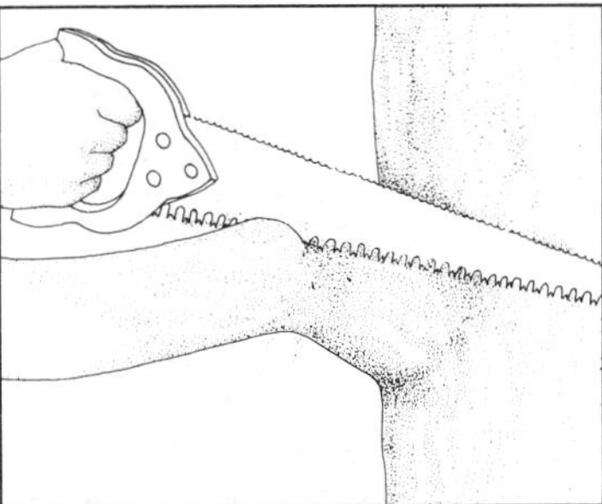

1. *Shorten an unwanted branch, leaving a section about 18 in. long.*

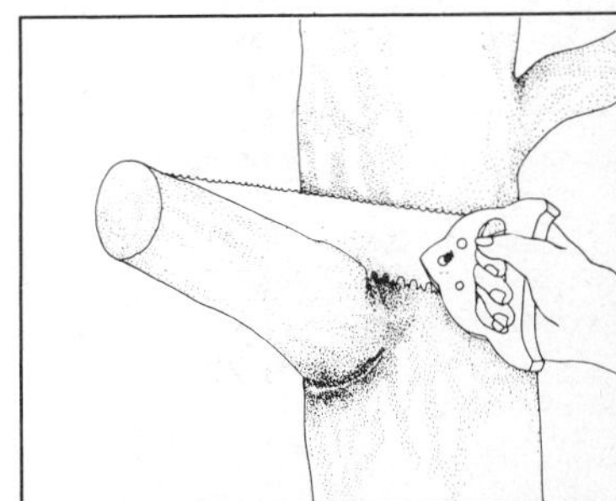

2. *Undercut the stump close against the trunk; then saw through from above.*

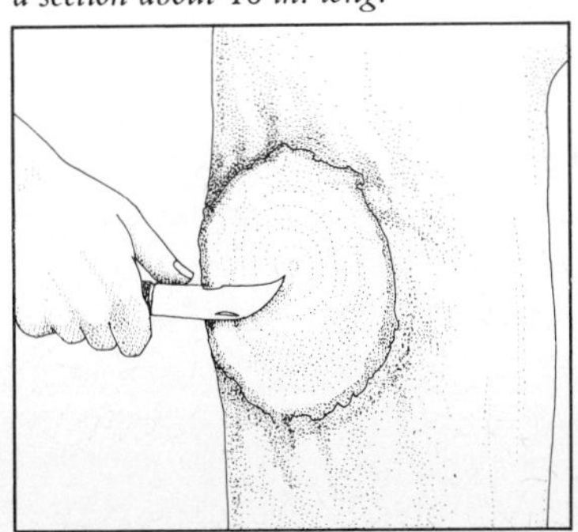

3. *Smooth the surface of the cut by paring off all ragged edges with a knife.*

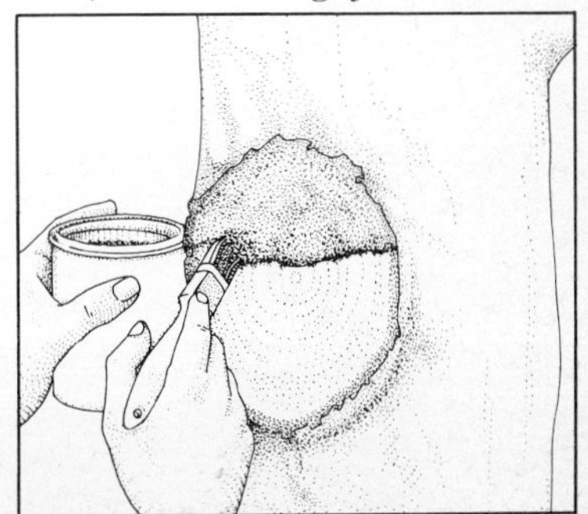

4. *Cover all cuts larger than 1 in. with tree-wound paint to prevent disease.*

What Can Go Wrong With Trees

If your tree shows symptoms that are not described below, turn to the full-color identification section for pests and diseases starting on page 600. To find the trade names of chemicals given in the chart, see the list beginning on page 635.

Symptoms and signs	Cause	Control
Needled evergreens		
Needles sticky or deformed; may show sooty mold. Pests may be visible.	Aphids, mealy-bugs, or spittlebugs	Use chlorpyrifos, Diazinon, malathion, or dormant spray of miscible oil or oil emulsion.
	Mites	Apply dicofol, endosulfan, or tetradifon.
Needles have chewed edges or holes. Pests are visible.	Bagworms, gall midges, gypsy moth larvae, leaf miners, or sawfly larvae	Apply *Bacillus thuringiensis,* carbaryl, Diazinon, malathion, or methoxychlor.
Needles have holes. Shoots and stems show borer damage.	Nantucket tip or pine shoot moths, pitch pine borers, or weevils	Apply carbaryl, Diazinon, dimethoate, lindane, or methoxychlor.
Needles and stems have crusty, sticky, or waxy accumulations.	Scale insects	Use dormant spray of miscible oil or oil emulsion. In late spring or early summer apply Diazinon or malathion.
Cankers or branches exude resin. Yellow masses may ooze from cankers.	Cytospora canker (fungus)	Remove and destroy infected branches; treat cuts with wound dressing. Fertilize trees.
Shoots die back. Needles show tiny black fruiting bodies. Twigs and cones are also attacked.	Needle-and-twig blight (fungus)	Spray with Benomyl or copper fungicide as new growth appears. Treat twice more at 10-da. intervals. Fertilize regularly.
Needles develop yellow spots; entire needle eventually browns and falls.	Needle cast (fungus)	Spray 2 or 3 times at 14-da. intervals with Bordeaux mixture or maneb.
Needles and twigs show orange jelly. Cankers may develop.	Rust (fungus)	Remove and destroy infected material. Spray with carbamate 4 or 5 times at 10-da. intervals.
Broad-leaved trees		
Tree is disfigured. Insects, honeydew, and sooty mold fungus may be visible.	Aphids, boxelder or lace bugs, leafhoppers, psyllids, or whiteflies	Apply dormant spray of miscible oil or oil emulsion. Or use cover spray of Diazinon, malathion, or methoxychlor.
	Mites	Apply dicofol or endosulfan.

Symptoms and signs	Cause	Control
Leaves have silvery white dots; may curl and dry up. Pests, honeydew or sooty mold fungus may be visible.	Aphids, lace bugs, psyllids, thrips, or whiteflies	Use chlorpyrifos, Diazinon, malathion, or dormant spray of miscible oil or oil emulsion.
	Mites	Apply dicofol, endosulfan, or dormant spray of miscible oil or oil emulsion.
Stems or branches have holes. Galls may occur.	Bark beetles, birch borers, giant hornets, Japanese weevils, lilac borers, pod galls, stem galls, or twig pruners	Apply carbaryl, Diazinon, dimethoate, lindane, or methoxychlor.
Leaves have holes or ragged edges.	Inchworms, leaf beetles, leaf galls, leaf miners, leaf rollers, rose chafers, sawfly larvae, or tent caterpillars	Apply *Bacillus thuringiensis,* carbaryl, Diazinon, malathion, methoxychlor, or dormant spray of miscible oil or oil emulsion.
Branches, stems, and leaves have accretions of scale. Tree appears weakened.	Scale insects	Apply dormant spray of miscible oil or oil emulsion. Spray with chlorpyrifos, Diazinon, or malathion in late spring or early summer.
Leaves may brown or spot. Shoots may blacken. Cankers may grow.	Anthracnose (fungus)	Spray with copper, dodine, ferbam, or maneb. Prune off infected material.
Leaves, twigs, and flowers may suddenly wilt, turn brown, and then blacken.	Bacterial fire blight	Spray with antibiotic or Bordeaux mixture as blooms are opening.
Swellings occur on roots, twigs, and trunks, especially on plants in rose family.	Crown gall (bacteria)	If possible, remove galls; or apply a .92% Bacticin paste to galls.
Branches weaken or wilt. Leaf drop follows. Eventually entire tree dies.	Dutch elm disease (fungus)	Dormant spray of methoxychlor may kill fungus-carrying beetles.
Brown, black, or purple spots, with yellow halos.	Leaf spot (fungus)	Spray with Benomyl, Captan, dodine, or maneb.
Bark has water-soaked areas that crack open; pinkish spots develop in spring.	Nectria canker (fungus)	Destroy infected material. Spray in spring with Bordeaux mixture.
Leaves have rusty orange spots.	Rust (fungus)	Spray with chlorothalonil, mancozeb, or thiram.
Leaves and young fruits have green mold, which turns black and scablike.	Scab (fungus)	In late spring and early summer, spray with Benomyl, dodine, or mancozeb.
Leaves on upper branches may droop and fall.	Wilt (fungus)	Remove infected plants. Apply terrazole soil drench.

Deciduous Trees

Deciduous trees are those that drop their leaves in the dormant season. In the chart that follows, they are listed alphabetically according to their best known common names. Recommended species and varieties are also listed.

Although many factors influence a deciduous tree's survival, the most dependable indicator of its hardiness is the lowest temperature that it can endure in winter. To determine whether a specific tree can reasonably be expected to survive the lowest average temperature in your particular area, check the zone designation for that tree in the Hardiness column. Then refer to the Temperature Zone Map on page 9.

The figures at the far right indicate the height each tree can be expected to attain—contingent, of course, upon growing conditions and the care it receives. Some trees grow taller in the wild; in such cases, the figure in parentheses is the maximum probable height for that tree at maturity.

Flowering almond

Flowering apricot (*P. armeniaca* 'Ansu')

White ash

European beech

Common and botanical names	Hardiness *(Map, p. 9)*	Decorative characteristics, special requirements, and remarks	Approximate height when mature
Almond, flowering *(Prunus)*			
P. amygdalus alboplena	□□C□	Double white flowers appear in late winter or early spring.	15-25 ft.
P. a. roseoplena	□□C□	Bears double pink blooms at same time as *P. a. alboplena.*	15-25 ft.
Apricot, flowering *(Prunus)*			
Japanese *(P. mume)*	□□C□	Fragrant pale pink flowers in late spring. Large green or yellow fruit.	20-30 ft.
P. armeniaca 'Ansu'	□B□□	In midspring pale pink flowers appear. Fall foliage is sometimes red.	20-25 ft.
P. a. 'Charles Abraham'	□B□□	Dark red buds open into long-lasting double pink flowers.	20-30 ft.
Ash *(Fraxinus)*			
Arizona *(F. velutina)*	□B□□	Distinguishable by gray down on young twigs and undersides of leaves.	40-45 ft.
Modesto *(F. v.* 'Modesto')	□B□□	Will tolerate drier conditions than other ashes.	40-50 ft.
European weeping *(F. excelsior pendula)*	A□□□	Branches droop to form umbrella shape.	40-60 ft.
Flowering *(F. ornus)*	□B□□	In late spring fragrant whitish flowers develop in terminal clusters.	40-50 ft. (60 max.)
Green *(F. pennsylvanica lanceolata)*	A□□□	Bright green foliage turns vivid yellow in fall. This is excellent choice for windy sites. Seedless variety is available.	40-50 ft. (60 max.)
White *(F. americana)*	A□□□	In autumn its compound leaves turn to colors ranging from yellow to purple. Seedless varieties that do not leave unsightly litter on ground are available.	50-75 ft. (120 max.)
Aspen, see Poplar			
Beech *(Fagus)*			
American *(F. grandifolia)*	A□□□	Attractive light gray bark and foliage that turns yellow-bronze in fall add distinction to this large tree. Casts dense shade. Requires space around it.	60-80 ft. (120 max.)
European *(F. sylvatica)*	□B□□	Dark green leaves are slightly toothed.	50-70 ft. (120 max.)
Copper, or purple *(F. s. atropunicea)*	□B□□	Leaves are rich purple to copper color. Branches sweep close to ground. One of handsomest large trees.	40-50 ft. (65 max.)
Dawyck *(F. s. fastigiata)*	□B□□	Upright habit of growth produces narrow profile.	40-50 ft. (80 max.)
Fernleaf *(F. s. laciniata)*	□B□□	Similar to *F. sylvatica,* but edges of leaves are deeply cut.	40-50 ft. (80 max.)
Rivers purple *(F. s. riversii)*	□B□□	Young leaves open clear purplish pink in spring, then change to purple.	50-70 ft.
Weeping *(F. s. pendula)*	□B□□	Plant where pendulous spreading branches can touch ground unhindered.	50-70 ft.

DECIDUOUS TREES *(continued)*

European white birch  — Higan flowering cherry  — Chinese chestnut  — Chinese scholar tree  — Kaffirboom coral tree

Common and botanical names	Hardiness *(Map, p. 9)*	Decorative characteristics, special requirements, and remarks	Approximate height when mature
Birch *(Betula)*			
European white *(B. pendula)*	A	Bark is white, and older branches are gracefully pendulous. Most attractive when planted near evergreens. Easily grown but not long-lived. Like most birches, this is best transplanted while small.	30-40 ft. (60 max.)
Weeping *(B. p. gracilis)*	A	Recognizable by thin, pendulous branches and deeply cut leaves.	30-40 ft.
Gray *(B. populifolia)*	B	White bark with black spots. Good choice for poor soils.	15-30 ft.
Paper *(B. papyrifera)*	A	Bark is whitest of all birches, and leaves turn brilliant yellow in fall. Provides more shade and is less susceptible to borers than *B. pendula*.	50-70 ft. (120 max.)
Sweet, or cherry *(B. lenta)*	A	Dark reddish-brown bark resembles that of cherry tree. Drooping catkins in spring and yellow foliage in fall are among assets. Plant in rich, moist soil.	40-50 ft. (75 max.)
Box elder, see Maple			
Buckeye, see Horse chestnut			
Cherry, flowering *(Prunus)*			
Higan *(P. subhirtella)*	B	Pale pink blossoms cover tree in midspring; blue-black fruits develop in summer. Leaves are less than 2 in. long.	20-30 ft.
Mazzard *(P. avium plena)*	A	Double white flowers open in late spring. Very hardy tall tree.	40-50 ft. (70 max.)
Oriental *(P. serrulata* 'Amanogawa')	B	Semi-double flowers are pale pink.	15-20 ft.
P. s. 'Fugenzo'	B	Large double flowers are dark pink, fade to lighter shades when open.	20-25 ft.
P. s. 'Sekiyama'	B	Also known as *P. s.* 'Kwanzan,' this variety has dark pink double blossoms that hang downward. Young leaves bronze, turn green during summer.	20-25 ft.
P. s. 'Shirotae'	B	Excellent semi-double or double variety with pleasing fragrance.	20-25 ft.
Yoshina *(P. yedoensis)*	B	Grows fast and provides white flowers tinged with pink that have faint aroma. Can be seen in profusion around Tidal Basin, Washington, D.C.	20-25 ft.
Chestnut, Chinese *(Castanea)*			
C. mollissima	B	Least susceptible to chestnut blight. Set 2 trees, preferably different varieties, about 100 ft. apart for best cross-pollination, more nuts.	40-50 ft. (60 max.)
Chinaberry, see Melia			
Chinese scholar tree, or Japanese pagoda tree *(Sophora)*			
S. japonica	B	Ascending and spreading branches form neat canopy of dark green leaves. Small, creamy white, pealike flowers appear in early summer. Good city tree.	30-40 ft. (75 max.)
Coral tree *(Erythrina)*			
Kaffirboom *(E. caffra)*	D*	Wide-spreading with sculptural branching. Showy orange-red tubular flowers appear in midwinter, before new leaves appear. Poisonous seeds.	25-40 ft.
Naked *(E. coralloides)*	D*	Bright red flowers in early spring are followed by foliage that grows to 10 in. across and turns yellow before dropping in fall. Poisonous seeds.	20-30 ft.
Natal *(E. humeana)*	D*	Brilliant orange flowers, rich green leaves. Poisonous seeds.	20-30 ft.

*Not hardy below 30° F

Cork tree

Cornelian cherry

Carmine flowering crab apple

Crape myrtle *(L. indica)*

Common and botanical names	Hardiness *(Map, p. 9)*	Decorative characteristics, special requirements, and remarks	Approximate height when mature
Cork tree *(Phellodendron)*			
P. amurense	A	Heavy-textured, soft, porous bark and shapely, wide-spreading form. Small ¼-in. black berries, borne only on female trees, may be a nuisance when they fall. Leaves and berries emit scent of turpentine when crushed. Grass grows easily beneath, as leaves cast light shade. Adapts to almost any soil. Resistant to pests and diseases. Withstands pollution well. In spite of common name, this is not the source of cork, which is *Quercus suber*	30-45 ft. (50 max.)
Cornelian cherry *(Cornus)*			
C. mas	B	Small, rounded tree with dense, dark green leaves and clusters of little yellow flowers in early spring. Foliage turns soft red in autumn. Useful as windbreak or screen. Tolerates shade and city conditions.	15-20 ft. (25 max.)
Crab apple, flowering *(Malus)*			
Arnold *(M. arnoldiana)*	B	Flower buds are rose-red. Once open, blossoms are pink outside, white inside. In autumn yellow fruits add to the beauty of this wide-spreading tree.	20-25 ft.
Carmine *(M. atrosanguinea)*	B	Lustrous leaves, rose-purple flowers, and deep red fruits. Resistant to apple scab.	18-20 ft.
Japanese *(M. floribunda)*	B	In late spring this rounded tree has fragrant rose-red flowers that later fade to white. Fruits are red and yellow, showy each year from late summer to midfall. A leader among the ornamental crab apples.	25-30 ft.
M. 'Barbara Ann'	B	Large flowers in late spring are dark purplish pink. Autumn fruits are purple.	20-30 ft.
M. 'Dolgo'	A	Aromatic white flowers appear in abundance only every other year, in late spring. Red fruits in late summer are good for jelly. This wide-spreading tree is very hardy and resistant to scab.	35-40 ft.
M. 'Dorothea'	B	Among the few crab apples with semi-double flowers that set colorful fruit. Semi-double dark pink blossoms open in late spring, even on very young trees. Produces abundance of yellow fruits. Resists scab.	20-25 ft.
M. 'Katherine'	B	Double pink and white flowers blossom in late spring. Tiny, dull red fruits.	15-20 ft.
M. 'Red Jade'	B	Pendulous branches. Single white flowers and persistent vivid red fruits.	15-20 ft.
Parkman *(M. halliana parkmanii)*	B	Pea-sized red fruits follow double pink blossoms in late spring. Shiny, leathery leaves. Tree develops vase shape as it matures.	12-15 ft.
Tea *(M. hupehensis)*	B	Small fan-shaped tree with graceful, pendulous branches. Dark pink buds develop into white blossoms in late spring. In alternate years flower production is sparse. Greenish-yellow fruits are tinged with red.	18-25 ft.
Crape myrtle *(Lagerstroemia)*			
L. indica	C	Tree or tall shrub with showy crinkled flowers up to 1½ in. across. Colors range from white to pink to purple. Peeling light brown or gray bark reveals pinkish inner bark. Leaves show yellow, orange, and red in autumn.	10-20 ft.
Queen *(L. speciosa)*	D*	Flowers, 3½ in. across, are lavender to pink, with at least 6 petals and yellow stamens. Thick, leathery leaves grow to about 12 in. long.	15-25 ft. (80 max.)

Cypress, bald, see p. 72

*Not hardy below 30° F

DECIDUOUS TREES *(continued)*

Flowering dogwood *(C. florida)*  — Dove tree  — Franklin tree  — American fringe tree  — Ginkgo  — Golden chain

Common and botanical names	Hardiness *(Map, p. 9)*	Decorative characteristics, special requirements, and remarks	Approximate height when mature
Dogwood, flowering *(Cornus)*			
C. florida	□B□□	In late spring tiny greenish flowers are surrounded by white or pink bracts that resemble the petals of a large flower. Leaves turn red in fall, and scarlet fruits attract birds. In winter large flower buds and twiggy horizontal branches make this tree attractive in the landscape.	10-20 ft. (40 max.)
Red-flowered *(C. f. rubra)*	□B□□	Bracts range from pink to red. Not quite so hardy as *C. florida.*	10-20 ft.
C. nuttallii	□□□D	Blooms in midspring and often again in autumn. Showy bracts are white or pink, appearing in midspring; fruits are orange or red. Thrives in Pacific states but seldom survives on East Coast.	40-50 ft. (75 max.)
Japanese *(C. kousa)*	□B□□	Blooms in midsummer; more compact than *C. florida.* Showy, long-lasting, pointed bracts change from green to white to pink. Red fruits in autumn, which last several weeks, resemble large raspberries.	15-20 ft.
Dove tree *(Davidia)*			
D. involucrata	□B□□	This choice tree has showy creamy white bracts (resembling doves in flight) that accompany inconspicuous flowers. It may take a few years before this tree blossoms for the first time. Leaves remain green in autumn.	25-40 ft. (60 max.)
Empress tree, see Paulownia			
Flame tree, see Poinciana, royal			
Franklin tree *(Franklinia,* or *Gordonia)*			
F. alatamaha	□B□□	Blooms in fall after most other trees. White, 3-in., camellialike flowers are enhanced by shiny 6-in. leaves that turn orange-red in fall. Slow-growing in northern range; may not survive sustained sub-zero temperatures.	18-20 ft. (30 max.)
Fringe tree *(Chionanthus)*			
American *(C. virginicus)*	□B□□	White flower panicles appear in early summer, just after late-developing leaves. These are followed by blue berries in grapelike clusters on female trees. In fall leaves turn yellow. Susceptible to scale infestations.	12-20 ft. (30 max.)
Chinese *(C. retusus)*	□B□□	White flowers cover tree from early to mid summer. Leaves and flower clusters are about half as large as those of *C. virginicus.* Excellent small tree.	15-20 ft.
Ginkgo, or Maidenhair tree *(Ginkgo)*			
G. biloba	□B□□	Fan-shaped leaves turn yellow in fall. Plant only male trees, since fruit on female trees is unsightly and foul smelling when it falls. Although gawky when young, tree becomes handsome, shapely specimen. Virtually immune to diseases and pests and withstands city conditions.	35-60 ft. (120 max.)
Golden chain *(Laburnum)*			
L. watereri	□B□□	In late spring yellow pealike flowers develop in long, hanging clusters, followed by 2-in. brown seedpods lasting into winter and containing seeds that are poisonous if eaten. Leaves like clover. Good small garden tree.	15-20 ft. (30 max.)

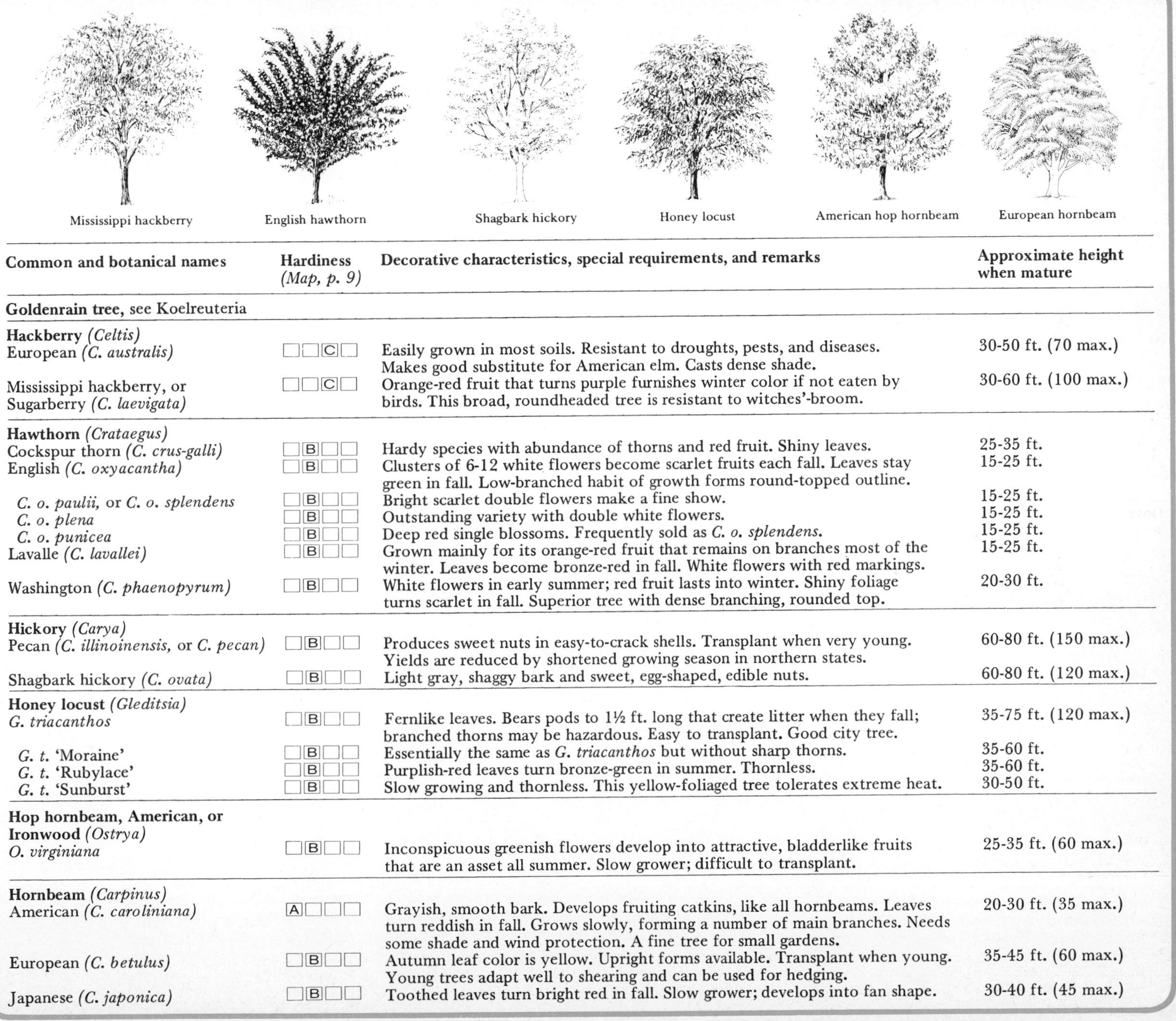

Mississippi hackberry — English hawthorn — Shagbark hickory — Honey locust — American hop hornbeam — European hornbeam

Common and botanical names	Hardiness *(Map, p. 9)*	Decorative characteristics, special requirements, and remarks	Approximate height when mature
Goldenrain tree, see Koelreuteria			
Hackberry *(Celtis)*			
European *(C. australis)*	C	Easily grown in most soils. Resistant to droughts, pests, and diseases. Makes good substitute for American elm. Casts dense shade.	30-50 ft. (70 max.)
Mississippi hackberry, or Sugarberry *(C. laevigata)*	C	Orange-red fruit that turns purple furnishes winter color if not eaten by birds. This broad, roundheaded tree is resistant to witches'-broom.	30-60 ft. (100 max.)
Hawthorn *(Crataegus)*			
Cockspur thorn *(C. crus-galli)*	B	Hardy species with abundance of thorns and red fruit. Shiny leaves.	25-35 ft.
English *(C. oxyacantha)*	B	Clusters of 6-12 white flowers become scarlet fruits each fall. Leaves stay green in fall. Low-branched habit of growth forms round-topped outline.	15-25 ft.
C. o. paulii, or *C. o. splendens*	B	Bright scarlet double flowers make a fine show.	15-25 ft.
C. o. plena	B	Outstanding variety with double white flowers.	15-25 ft.
C. o. punicea	B	Deep red single blossoms. Frequently sold as *C. o. splendens.*	15-25 ft.
Lavalle *(C. lavallei)*	B	Grown mainly for its orange-red fruit that remains on branches most of the winter. Leaves become bronze-red in fall. White flowers with red markings.	15-25 ft.
Washington *(C. phaenopyrum)*	B	White flowers in early summer; red fruit lasts into winter. Shiny foliage turns scarlet in fall. Superior tree with dense branching, rounded top.	20-30 ft.
Hickory *(Carya)*			
Pecan *(C. illinoinensis,* or *C. pecan)*	B	Produces sweet nuts in easy-to-crack shells. Transplant when very young. Yields are reduced by shortened growing season in northern states.	60-80 ft. (150 max.)
Shagbark hickory *(C. ovata)*	B	Light gray, shaggy bark and sweet, egg-shaped, edible nuts.	60-80 ft. (120 max.)
Honey locust *(Gleditsia)*			
G. triacanthos	B	Fernlike leaves. Bears pods to 1½ ft. long that create litter when they fall; branched thorns may be hazardous. Easy to transplant. Good city tree.	35-75 ft. (120 max.)
G. t. 'Moraine'	B	Essentially the same as *G. triacanthos* but without sharp thorns.	35-60 ft.
G. t. 'Rubylace'	B	Purplish-red leaves turn bronze-green in summer. Thornless.	35-60 ft.
G. t. 'Sunburst'	B	Slow growing and thornless. This yellow-foliaged tree tolerates extreme heat.	30-50 ft.
Hop hornbeam, American, or Ironwood *(Ostrya)*			
O. virginiana	B	Inconspicuous greenish flowers develop into attractive, bladderlike fruits that are an asset all summer. Slow grower; difficult to transplant.	25-35 ft. (60 max.)
Hornbeam *(Carpinus)*			
American *(C. caroliniana)*	A	Grayish, smooth bark. Develops fruiting catkins, like all hornbeams. Leaves turn reddish in fall. Grows slowly, forming a number of main branches. Needs some shade and wind protection. A fine tree for small gardens.	20-30 ft. (35 max.)
European *(C. betulus)*	B	Autumn leaf color is yellow. Upright forms available. Transplant when young. Young trees adapt well to shearing and can be used for hedging.	35-45 ft. (60 max.)
Japanese *(C. japonica)*	B	Toothed leaves turn bright red in fall. Slow grower; develops into fan shape.	30-40 ft. (45 max.)

DECIDUOUS TREES *(continued)*

Common horse chestnut — Jacaranda — Katsura tree — Kentucky coffee tree — *Koelreuteria paniculata* (goldenrain tree)

Common and botanical names	Hardiness *(Map, p. 9)*	Decorative characteristics, special requirements, and remarks	Approximate height when mature
Horse chestnut, or Buckeye *(Aesculus)*			
Common *(A. hippocastanum)*	A	Clusters of large, red-spotted white flowers in late spring. Large leaves in uneven star pattern of 5-7 leaflets are poisonous in early spring and do not change color in autumn. Late summer blight may disfigure them. Chestnuts, poisonous unless processed, abundantly produced.	45-60 ft. (75 max.)
Double-flowered *(A. h. baumannii)*	A	Since its double white flowers are sterile, it does not produce nuts. This eliminates considerable cleaning up under tree.	45-60 ft.
Indian *(A. indica)*	C	Long clusters of white flowers are marked with yellow at top, tinged rose at bottom. Lance-shaped leaflets grow as long as 9 in.	40-50 ft. (60 max.)
Ohio buckeye *(A. glabra)*	A	Rounded shape, orange fall color. Young leaves and seeds poisonous.	20-25 ft. (30 max.)
Red *(A. carnea)*	A	Pink to red flowers and reddish leaves. Although similar to *A. hippocastanum,* this hybrid is considered more ornamental.	30-50 ft. (80 max.)
Yellow, or sweet, buckeye *(A. octandra)*	A	Yellow flowers grow in upright clusters 4-6 in. long and bloom in late spring and early summer. Young leaves and fruits poisonous if eaten.	40-50 ft. (60 max.)
Ironwood, see Hop hornbeam, American			
Jacaranda *(Jacaranda)* *J. acutifolia,* or *J. mimosifolia*	D*	Has fragrant, funnel-shaped violet flowers in 8-in. clusters from midspring to early summer. Feathery leaves cast broken shadows. Fast grower that tolerates most conditions. Grows best in sandy soil. Good street tree.	25-40 ft. (60 max.)
Judas tree, see Redbud			
Katsura tree *(Cercidiphyllum)* *C. japonicum*	B	Often forms several trunks at base and has spreading branches. Makes columnar specimen if grown with a single trunk. Blue-green leaves turn yellow to scarlet in fall. Requires considerable moisture.	25-40 ft. (100 max.)
Kentucky coffee tree *(Gymnocladus)* *G. dioica*	B	Coarse tree with 1½- to 3-ft. compound leaves that remain green in fall. Bears flat reddish-brown pods 8 in. long. Winter profile is picturesque.	40-50 ft. (90 max.)
Koelreuteria *(Koelreuteria)*			
Goldenrain tree *(K. paniculata)*	B	In summer tan or yellow seedpods form after small, bright yellow blooms fade. No autumn color change. Grows in most soils. Does best in full sun.	20-30 ft. (35 max.)
K. formosana	D	Flowers and foliage similar to those of *K. paniculata,* but pods are orange and red. Plant in full sun. Both are relatively free of pests and diseases.	20-30 ft. (40 max.)
Larch, see p. 74			
Larch, golden, see p. 74			

*Not hardy below 30° F

Crimean linden

Black locust

Saucer magnolia

Common and botanical names	Hardiness *(Map, p. 9)*	Decorative characteristics, special requirements, and remarks	Approximate height when mature
Linden *(Tilia)*			
American *(T. americana)*	A	Coarse-textured leaves are often up to 8 in. long. In early summer small aromatic flowers attract bees. Leaves turn brown in late summer.	40-60 ft. (120 max.)
Crimean *(T. euchlora)*	B	Glossy heart-shaped leaves produce abundant shade. A rapid grower with slightly pendulous habit.	25-40 ft. (65 max.)
Silver *(T. tomentosa)*	A	Leaf undersides are covered with whitish down, hence common name. Upright branches produce pleasing pyramidal shape. Less suitable for city planting than other lindens because soot adheres to leaves.	40-60 ft. (100 max.)
Small-leaved *(T. cordata)*	A	Grows slowly, developing pyramidal form. Good street and city tree.	30-50 ft. (100 max.)
T. c. 'Greenspire'	A	Leaves are about 3 in. long. Branches grow radially from straight trunk. An excellent, fast-growing street and city tree.	30-50 ft.
T. c. 'Handsworth'	A	Young twigs, vivid light yellowish green, are especially attractive in winter. Good city tree.	30-50 ft.
Liquidambar, see Sweet gum			
Locust *(Robinia)*			
Black locust, or False acacia *(R. pseudoacacia)*	A	This tree has large compound leaves and aromatic white flowers in pendulous racemes. Reddish-brown pods, up to 4 in. long, stay on tree through winter.	50-60 ft. (75 max.)
R. p. decaisneana	A	Same general appearance as *R. pseudoacacia* except that flowers are pale rose.	50-60 ft.
Idaho *(R.* 'Idaho')	B	Blossoms are deep reddish purple. Survives in poor soil and hot, dry climates where other trees might fail.	35-40 ft.
Magnolia *(Magnolia)*			
Anise *(M. salicifolia)*	B	In late spring soft hairy buds open into fragrant, handsome white blossoms. Leaves appear later and turn yellowish in fall. When crushed, they exude anise aroma. In winter watch out for magnolia scale on all species and varieties. Treat scale as recommended on p. 601.	18-30 ft.
Cucumber tree *(M. acuminata)*	B	Flowers in late spring are small, greenish yellow, and not very noticeable. Fruits, 3-4 in. long, are pink to red in autumn and very showy. Attractive leaves have pale green downy undersides. Fast-growing, handsome tree.	50-70 ft. (90 max.)
M. kobus	B	White lily-shaped blossoms have pale purple line at base. They appear in midspring but do not last long.	20-30 ft.
M. loebneri 'Merrill'	B	Will bloom at younger age than other magnolias with fragrant 4-in. white flowers in mid to late spring before leaves appear.	50 ft.
Saucer *(M. soulangeana)*	B	Showy, large purplish flowers even on young trees. Many varieties available, with flowers ranging from white to pink. Tree may have one or more trunks.	15-25 ft.
Yulan *(M. denudata,* or *M. conspicua)*	B	Cup-shaped blossoms are creamy white and aromatic. They open in late spring before pale green leaves come out.	35-50 ft.
Maidenhair tree, see Ginkgo			

DECIDUOUS TREES *(continued)*

Sugar maple

Melia azedarach (chinaberry)

European mountain ash

White mulberry

Common and botanical names	Hardiness *(Map, p. 9)*	Decorative characteristics, special requirements, and remarks	Approximate height when mature
Maple *(Acer)*			
A. davidii	□ B □ □	This tree has interesting white-striped, glossy green bark. In spring 8-in.-long leaves are red but soon change to green, and yellow-green flowers put on a fine display. In autumn leaves turn to shades of yellow and purple.	20-35 ft. (45 max.)
Amur *(A. ginnala)*	□ B □ □	In late summer winged fruits turn red, while leaves remain green. In fall foliage becomes brilliant scarlet. A hardy species attracting few pests.	15-20 ft.
Box elder *(A. negundo)*	A □ □ □	No autumn color changes. Fast growing, weak wooded, prolific seeder. Good where summer drought and winter cold prohibit growing better maples.	30-50 ft. (70 max.)
Full-moon *(A. japonicum)*	□ B □ □	Lobed leaves turn crimson in fall.	20-30 ft.
Japanese *(A. palmatum)*	□ B □ □	Somewhat similar to *A. japonicum* but with more intricately lobed leaves, which turn vivid red in autumn. Needs good soil. Does best in partial shade.	15-20 ft.
Norway *(A. platanoides)*	□ B □ □	Branches covered with tiny yellow blossoms before leaves open in spring. Autumn foliage is yellow. As with many maples, greedy surface roots cause shrubs to do poorly if planted beneath them, but ground covers will survive.	50-60 ft. (90 max.)
A. p. 'Crimson King'	□ B □ □	Leaves are dark red all summer.	50-60 ft.
A. p. 'Summershade'	□ B □ □	An upright, heat-resistant variety with somewhat leathery leaves.	50-60 ft.
Paperbark *(A. griseum)*	□ B □ □	Attractive reddish-brown bark peels like that of paper birch.	20-25 ft.
Sugar *(A. saccharum)*	□ B □ □	Bright green leaves have whitish undersides and turn bright yellow in fall. Branches arch and are often pendulous. Prone to structural damage during winter. Sap is used for maple sugar.	50-75 ft. (120 max.)
Sycamore *(A. pseudoplatanus)*	□ B □ □	No color change in fall. A useful species for seacoast plantings.	50-60 ft. (100 max.)
Trident *(A. buergerianum)*	□ B □ □	Outstanding shade tree for small gardens. Holds up well in dry spells.	20-25 ft.
Melia *(Melia)*			
Chinaberry *(M. azedarach)*	□ □ C □	Fragrant lilac flowers appear in clusters in spring. In autumn birds enjoy its yellow berries.	30-40 ft. (50 max.)
Texas umbrella tree *(M. a. umbraculiformis)*	□ □ C □	Early spring flowers are lilac colored. Berries are yellow. Spreading, fast-growing tree with pendent foliage that casts dense shade.	25-30 ft.
Mimosa, see Silk tree			
Mountain ash *(Sorbus)*			
American *(S. americana)*	A □ □ □	Up to 15 leaflets form compound leaves. Late spring flowers are white. Bright red berries appear in autumn. Does best in acid soil.	20-30 ft.
European, or rowan tree *(S. aucuparia)*	A □ □ □	Reddish leaves and vivid red fruit clusters in fall make this a handsome specimen for lawns.	20-30 ft. (50 max.)
Korean *(S. alnifolia)*	□ B □ □	Produces many flowers that measure up to 1 in. across. In fall leaves turn orange to scarlet; berry clusters assume same colors. Bark is dark gray and smooth.	25-35 ft. (60 max.)
Mulberry *(Morus)*			
White *(M. alba)*	□ B □ □	White, pink, or purple fruit. Fast growing. Withstands poor soil and drought. Attracts birds. Ripened fruits tend to drop and cause stains.	20-45 ft. (60 max.)

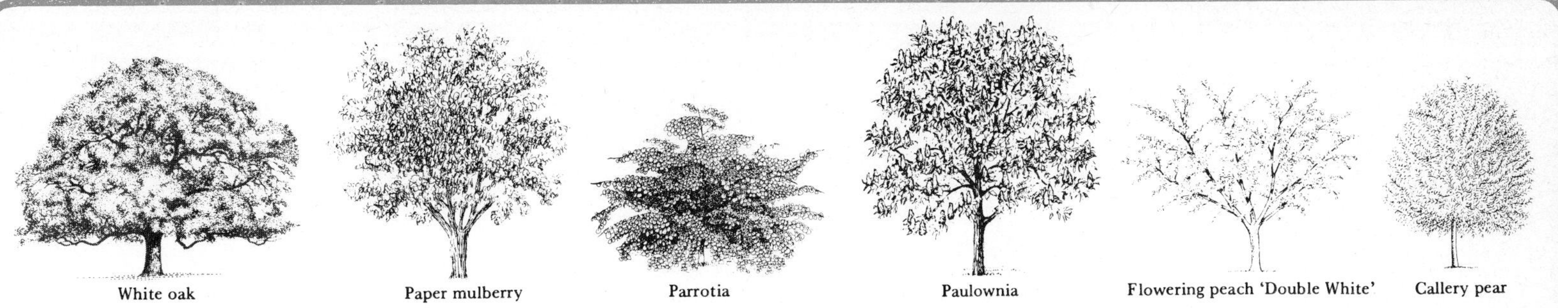

White oak — Paper mulberry — Parrotia — Paulownia — Flowering peach 'Double White' — Callery pear

Common and botanical names	Hardiness *(Map, p. 9)*	Decorative characteristics, special requirements, and remarks	Approximate height when mature
Oak *(Quercus)*			
Pin *(Q. palustris)*	B	Lower branches droop downward. Leaves turn red in fall. Needs acid soil.	50-75 ft. (120 max.)
Red *(Q. borealis,* or *Q. rubra)*	B	Rich red leaves in fall. Easily transplanted; a rapid grower.	50-60 ft. (80 max.)
Scarlet *(Q. coccinea)*	A	Shiny green leaves become vivid scarlet in autumn. Habit of growth is open. Not an easy species to transplant.	50-60 ft. (80 max.)
Shingle *(Q. imbricaria)*	B	Shiny deep green leaves turn russet in fall. If allowed to grow freely, these trees will assume rounded shape with age. A row planting can be clipped to form high hedge or windbreak.	40-50 ft. (80 max.)
Shumard *(Q. shumardii)*	B	Imposing hardwood similar in characteristics to *Q. coccinea.*	50-75 ft. (120 max.)
White *(Q. alba)*	A	Spreading branches form stately, rounded head. In autumn foliage turns purplish red and clings to tree until late winter. This is a slow-growing species and extremely long-lived; transplants best when small.	50-75 ft. (100 max.)
Willow *(Q. phellos)*	B	Thin willowlike leaves, pointed at both ends, turn dull yellow in fall.	40-60 ft. (90 max.)
Paper mulberry *(Broussonetia)*			
B. papyrifera	B	Irregularly lobed leaves. Female catkins that develop in late spring turn into orange to red fruits in mid to late summer. Trunk gnarled on old trees.	35-45 ft. (50 max.)
Parrotia *(Parrotia)*			
P. persica	C	Flowers with showy red stamens appear in spring before leaves. In fall foliage turns bright yellow, orange, or scarlet. Horizontal, wide-spreading branches. Attractive, flaking bark. Few pests or diseases attack this tree. Not easy to transplant.	15-20 ft. (30 max.)
Paulownia, or Empress tree *(Paulownia)*			
P. tomentosa	C	Coarse, large, hairy leaves appear after fragrant pale violet flowers open in late spring. Dry seedpods hang on tree for a year or more. Provide soil rich in humus in sheltered place. A good lawn specimen that grows quickly when young. Has deep taproot that makes transplanting difficult.	40-50 ft.
Peach, flowering *(Prunus)*			
P. persica 'Double Red'	B	Flowers appear earlier than those of other ornamental peaches.	18-25 ft.
P. p. 'Double White'	B	Covered with double white flowers in midspring.	18-25 ft.
P. p. 'Helen Borchers'	B	Bright pink flowers measure up to 2½ in. across.	18-25 ft.
P. p. 'Iceberg'	B	Handsome white-flowered variety.	18-25 ft.
P. p. 'Weeping Double Pink'	B	Has pendulous branches and double pink flowers.	18-25 ft.
P. p. 'Weeping Double Red'	B	Branches droop gracefully downward.	18-25 ft.
Pear *(Pyrus)*			
Callery (*P. calleryana* 'Bradford')	B	Clusters of white flowers open in late spring, followed by inedible, small rust-colored fruits that birds consume. Good street tree with glossy foliage that turns bright crimson in autumn.	15-25 ft. (30 max.)

DECIDUOUS TREES *(continued)*

Chinese pistachio · London plane tree · Purple-leaved flowering plum · Poinciana · Royal poinciana · Poplar *(P. candicans)*

Common and botanical names	Hardiness *(Map, p. 9)*	Decorative characteristics, special requirements, and remarks	Approximate height when mature
Pecan, see Hickory			
Pistachio *(Pistacia)*			
Chinese *(P. chinensis)*	□B□□	Leaves resemble those of sumac. Colorful foliage in fall, which is unusual in hot climates. Grows rapidly and tolerates heat, drought, and alkaline soil.	45-50 ft. (65 max.)
Plane tree, or Sycamore *(Platanus)*			
London *(P. acerifolia)*	□B□□	Cream-colored bark flakes to reveal yellow inner bark. Similar to *P. racemosa.* Usually produces fruits in clusters of 2. Good for urban gardens.	50-75 ft. (100 max.)
Western *(P. racemosa,* or *P. californica)*	□□□D	Flaking bark and large, coarse leaves. Clusters of up to 7 ball-like fruits. Protect against anthracnose blight (p. 610).	50-75 ft. (100 max.)
Plum, flowering *(Prunus)*			
P. blireiana	□B□□	In spring leaves open with copper color that lasts into summer. Double flowers are light pink. Needs considerable pruning to thrive.	20-30 ft.
Purple-leaved *(P. cerasifera atropurpurea)*	A□□□	Reddish-purple leaf coloration, enhanced by full sun, lasts all summer. Light pink flowers survive only a few days. Purple autumn fruits, 1 in. in diameter, are edible.	20-25 ft.
Poinciana *(Caesalpinia)*			
Bird-of-paradise bush *(C. gilliesii)*	□□C□	Feathery greenish-blue foliage is borne on angular branches. Yellow flowers with prominent red stamens stay in bloom all summer long. Wide-spreading small tree or shrub.	10-20 ft.
Poinciana, royal, or Flame tree *(Delonix)*			
D. regia	□□□D *	Feathery foliage and scarlet and yellow flower clusters in summer. A showy addition wherever climate is frost free.	25-40 ft.
Poplar, Aspen, or Cottonwood *(Populus)*			
Balm of Gilead *(P. candicans)*	A□□□	Toothed leaves with hairy undersides are often more than 6 in. long.	50-70 ft. (100 max.)
Berlin poplar *(P. berolinensis)*	A□□□	A hardy species. Useful for windbreaks in severe climates in Midwest.	40-50 ft. (75 max.)
Carolina poplar *(P. canadensis eugenei)*	□B□□	Has shiny, coarse leaves and narrow, pyramidal shape. Do not plant near pipes or drains—roots are invasive.	60-85 ft. (135 max.)
Cottonwood *(P. deltoides)*	A□□□	Capsules discharge annoying cotton. Cottonless kinds available.	60-80 ft. (90 max.)
Japanese poplar *(P. maximowiczii)*	□B□□	Spreading branches bear thick, coarse leaves earlier in spring than any other poplar. Protect against poplar canker (p. 619).	50-70 ft. (100 max.)
Quaking aspen *(P. tremuloides)*	A□□□	The 3-in. leaves stir in even gentlest breezes. In fall leaf color is dazzling yellow. Plant in groups for most striking effect.	50-70 ft. (100 max.)
Silver poplar *(P. alba nivea)*	A□□□	Whitish-gray bark and silver-white undersides of leaves. Needs adequate space.	50-70 ft. (100 max.)
Prunus, see Almond; Apricot; Cherry; Peach; Plum			

*Not hardy below 30° F

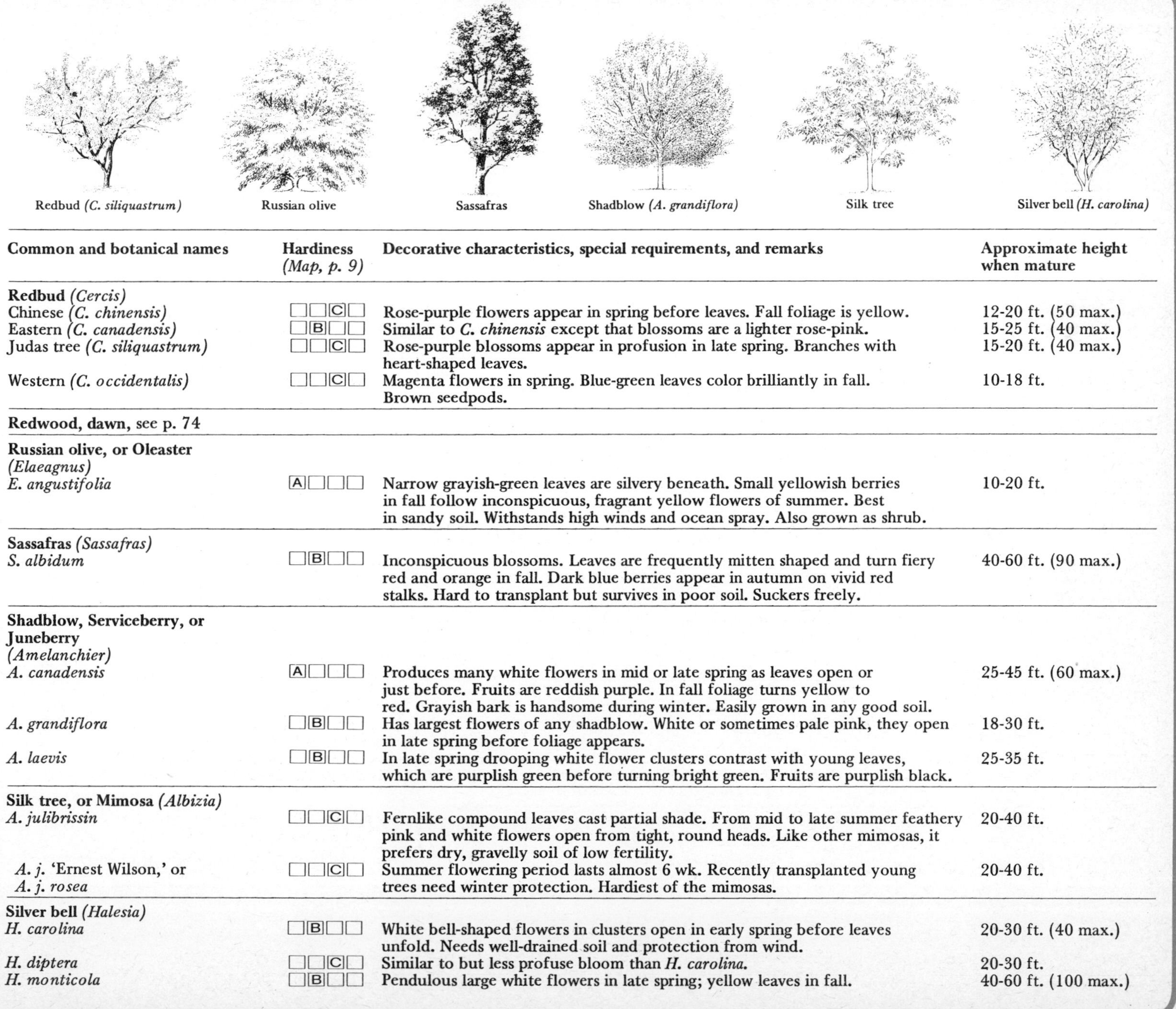

Redbud *(C. siliquastrum)* · Russian olive · Sassafras · Shadblow *(A. grandiflora)* · Silk tree · Silver bell *(H. carolina)*

Common and botanical names	Hardiness *(Map, p. 9)*	Decorative characteristics, special requirements, and remarks	Approximate height when mature
Redbud *(Cercis)*			
Chinese *(C. chinensis)*	C	Rose-purple flowers appear in spring before leaves. Fall foliage is yellow.	12-20 ft. (50 max.)
Eastern *(C. canadensis)*	B	Similar to *C. chinensis* except that blossoms are a lighter rose-pink.	15-25 ft. (40 max.)
Judas tree *(C. siliquastrum)*	C	Rose-purple blossoms appear in profusion in late spring. Branches with heart-shaped leaves.	15-20 ft. (40 max.)
Western *(C. occidentalis)*	C	Magenta flowers in spring. Blue-green leaves color brilliantly in fall. Brown seedpods.	10-18 ft.
Redwood, dawn, see p. 74			
Russian olive, or Oleaster *(Elaeagnus)*			
E. angustifolia	A	Narrow grayish-green leaves are silvery beneath. Small yellowish berries in fall follow inconspicuous, fragrant yellow flowers of summer. Best in sandy soil. Withstands high winds and ocean spray. Also grown as shrub.	10-20 ft.
Sassafras *(Sassafras)*			
S. albidum	B	Inconspicuous blossoms. Leaves are frequently mitten shaped and turn fiery red and orange in fall. Dark blue berries appear in autumn on vivid red stalks. Hard to transplant but survives in poor soil. Suckers freely.	40-60 ft. (90 max.)
Shadblow, Serviceberry, or Juneberry *(Amelanchier)*			
A. canadensis	A	Produces many white flowers in mid or late spring as leaves open or just before. Fruits are reddish purple. In fall foliage turns yellow to red. Grayish bark is handsome during winter. Easily grown in any good soil.	25-45 ft. (60 max.)
A. grandiflora	B	Has largest flowers of any shadblow. White or sometimes pale pink, they open in late spring before foliage appears.	18-30 ft.
A. laevis	B	In late spring drooping white flower clusters contrast with young leaves, which are purplish green before turning bright green. Fruits are purplish black.	25-35 ft.
Silk tree, or Mimosa *(Albizia)*			
A. julibrissin	C	Fernlike compound leaves cast partial shade. From mid to late summer feathery pink and white flowers open from tight, round heads. Like other mimosas, it prefers dry, gravelly soil of low fertility.	20-40 ft.
A. j. 'Ernest Wilson,' or *A. j. rosea*	C	Summer flowering period lasts almost 6 wk. Recently transplanted young trees need winter protection. Hardiest of the mimosas.	20-40 ft.
Silver bell *(Halesia)*			
H. carolina	B	White bell-shaped flowers in clusters open in early spring before leaves unfold. Needs well-drained soil and protection from wind.	20-30 ft. (40 max.)
H. diptera	C	Similar to but less profuse bloom than *H. carolina.*	20-30 ft.
H. monticola	B	Pendulous large white flowers in late spring; yellow leaves in fall.	40-60 ft. (100 max.)

DECIDUOUS TREES *(continued)*

Smoke tree | Snowbell *(S. obassia)* | Sour gum | Sourwood | *Stewartia koreana* | American sweet gum

Common and botanical names	Hardiness *(Map, p. 9)*	Decorative characteristics, special requirements, and remarks	Approximate height when mature
Smoke tree *(Cotinus)* *C. coggygria purpureus*	B	Fluffy purplish flower clusters appear in summer. When they fade, hairy flower stalks continue "smoky" effect that gives this tree its common name. Rounded leaves, up to 3 in. long, are blue-green in summer, changing to yellow to orange-red in autumn. Named varieties are female, and these give best display. Newly transplanted trees need frequent watering for first 2-3 yr.	12-15 ft. (25 max.)
Snowbell *(Styrax)*			
S. japonica	B	In early and mid summer fragrant, white bell-shaped flowers appear in profusion on undersides of branches. Good lawn tree. Few insect or disease problems.	20-30 ft.
S. obassia	B	Large oval or almost round leaves have hairy undersides. White flowers open in early summer and are partly hidden by leaves. Flowers are followed by egg-shaped seedpods up to 1 in. long. Grows rapidly but does poorly in dry soil.	20-30 ft.
Sour gum, Tupelo, or **Pepperidge** *(Nyssa)* *N. sylvatica*	B	Horizontal branches that droop at ends bear leathery, dark green leaves. Foliage turns vivid orange to scarlet in fall. Grows well even in very moist soil—for instance, bordering swamps and streams.	30-60 ft. (90 max.)
Sourwood, or **Sorrel tree** *(Oxydendrum)* *O. arboreum*	B	Glossy, leathery leaves on drooping branches are dark green, turning to brilliant red in autumn. Hanging 6- to 8-in. clusters of fragrant, white bell-shaped flowers resemble lilies of the valley and are followed by gray fruits. Does best in acid soil.	15-35 ft. (75 max.)
Stewartia *(Stewartia)*			
S. koreana	B	White camellialike flowers appear in mid to late summer. Attractive flaking bark; fall leaf color ranges from purple to bright red-orange. Not an easy tree to transplant; add humus, and water often.	20-30 ft. (50 max.)
S. ovata grandiflora	C	Four-in.-wide white flowers with purple stamens open in midsummer. Leaves in fall are orange-scarlet.	15 ft.
S. pseudocamellia	C	Handsome red bark peels off in large pieces. White flowers and bright crimson leaves are attractive in autumn.	40-50 ft. (60 max.)
Sweet gum *(Liquidambar)*			
L. formosana	D	Three-lobed leaves turn from orange-red to bright scarlet in fall.	40-60 ft. (120 max.)
American *(L. styraciflua)*	D	Same autumn display as *L. formosana*. Leaves are star shaped. A fragrant gum exudes from crevices in trunk. Not easy to transplant. Requires ample space to develop its beautiful symmetry.	50-70 ft. (135 max.)
Sycamore, see Plane tree			

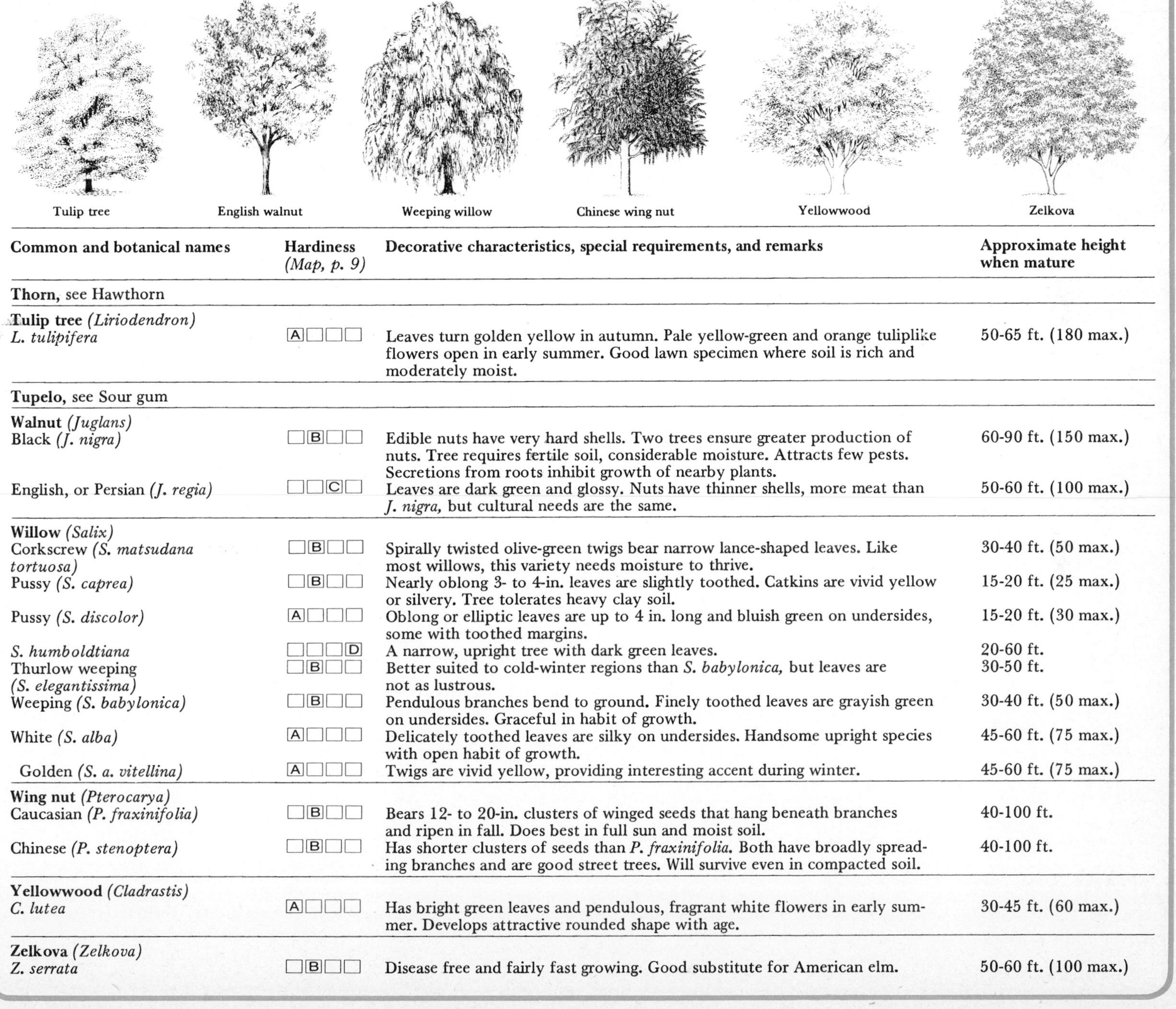

Tulip tree | English walnut | Weeping willow | Chinese wing nut | Yellowwood | Zelkova

Common and botanical names	Hardiness (*Map, p. 9*)	Decorative characteristics, special requirements, and remarks	Approximate height when mature
Thorn, see Hawthorn			
Tulip tree *(Liriodendron)*			
L. tulipifera	A	Leaves turn golden yellow in autumn. Pale yellow-green and orange tuliplike flowers open in early summer. Good lawn specimen where soil is rich and moderately moist.	50-65 ft. (180 max.)
Tupelo, see Sour gum			
Walnut *(Juglans)*			
Black *(J. nigra)*	B	Edible nuts have very hard shells. Two trees ensure greater production of nuts. Tree requires fertile soil, considerable moisture. Attracts few pests. Secretions from roots inhibit growth of nearby plants.	60-90 ft. (150 max.)
English, or Persian *(J. regia)*	C	Leaves are dark green and glossy. Nuts have thinner shells, more meat than *J. nigra,* but cultural needs are the same.	50-60 ft. (100 max.)
Willow *(Salix)*			
Corkscrew *(S. matsudana tortuosa)*	B	Spirally twisted olive-green twigs bear narrow lance-shaped leaves. Like most willows, this variety needs moisture to thrive.	30-40 ft. (50 max.)
Pussy *(S. caprea)*	B	Nearly oblong 3- to 4-in. leaves are slightly toothed. Catkins are vivid yellow or silvery. Tree tolerates heavy clay soil.	15-20 ft. (25 max.)
Pussy *(S. discolor)*	A	Oblong or elliptic leaves are up to 4 in. long and bluish green on undersides, some with toothed margins.	15-20 ft. (30 max.)
S. humboldtiana	D	A narrow, upright tree with dark green leaves.	20-60 ft.
Thurlow weeping *(S. elegantissima)*	B	Better suited to cold-winter regions than *S. babylonica,* but leaves are not as lustrous.	30-50 ft.
Weeping *(S. babylonica)*	B	Pendulous branches bend to ground. Finely toothed leaves are grayish green on undersides. Graceful in habit of growth.	30-40 ft. (50 max.)
White *(S. alba)*	A	Delicately toothed leaves are silky on undersides. Handsome upright species with open habit of growth.	45-60 ft. (75 max.)
Golden *(S. a. vitellina)*	A	Twigs are vivid yellow, providing interesting accent during winter.	45-60 ft. (75 max.)
Wing nut *(Pterocarya)*			
Caucasian *(P. fraxinifolia)*	B	Bears 12- to 20-in. clusters of winged seeds that hang beneath branches and ripen in fall. Does best in full sun and moist soil.	40-100 ft.
Chinese *(P. stenoptera)*	B	Has shorter clusters of seeds than *P. fraxinifolia.* Both have broadly spreading branches and are good street trees. Will survive even in compacted soil.	40-100 ft.
Yellowwood *(Cladrastis)*			
C. lutea	A	Has bright green leaves and pendulous, fragrant white flowers in early summer. Develops attractive rounded shape with age.	30-45 ft. (60 max.)
Zelkova *(Zelkova)*			
Z. serrata	B	Disease free and fairly fast growing. Good substitute for American elm.	50-60 ft. (100 max.)

Broad-leaved Evergreen Trees

Most broad-leaved evergreens have wide leaves like those of most deciduous trees, but they do not drop their leaves in the fall. In the chart that follows, they are listed alphabetically, according to their best known common names. The generic name of each appears next, in parentheses and in italics. Recommended species and varieties are also listed.

Although many factors influence a tree's chance of survival, the most dependable indicator of its hardiness is the lowest temperature that it can endure in winter. To determine whether a specific tree may reasonably be expected to survive the lowest average temperature in the area where you live, check the zone designation for that tree in the Hardiness column. Then refer to the Temperature Zone Map on page 9.

The figures at the far right indicate the height each tree can be expected to attain. Some trees grow taller in the wild; in such cases, the figure in parentheses is the maximum probable height for that tree.

Acacia baileyana (silver wattle)

Agonis flexuosa (willow myrtle)

Evergreen ash

Lemon bottlebrush

Kurrajong bottle tree

Brisbane box

Common and botanical names	Hardiness (*Map, p. 9*)	Decorative characteristics, special requirements, and remarks	Approximate height when mature
Acacia (*Acacia*)			
Everblooming (*A. retinodes*)	□□C□	Narrow leaves can be longer than 5 in. Tiny flowers bloom most of year.	20-30 ft.
Silver-green wattle (*A. decurrens dealbata*)	□□□D	Silver-gray bipinnate leaves. Aromatic, dark yellow flower clusters in early to mid spring are followed by 4-in. pods.	50-60 ft.
Silver wattle (*A. baileyana*)	□□□D*	Bipinnate leaves are bluish gray. Rounded, pale yellow flower heads open in clusters in mid and late winter. A fast grower.	20-30 ft.
Sweet (*A. farnesiana*)	□□□D	Bipinnate leaves develop on heavily thorned branches. Aromatic, vivid yellow blooms are attractive in late winter and early spring.	10-15 ft.
Weeping (*A. pendula*)	□□□D*	Thin blue-gray leaves up to 3 in. long. Yellow flower clusters. Drooping habit.	25-30 ft.
Agonis (*Agonis*)			
Willow myrtle (*A. flexuosa*)	□□□D*	Willowlike leaves are 6 in. long. White blossoms open in clusters.	20-30 ft. (40 max.)
Ash, evergreen, or shamel (*Fraxinus*)			
F. uhdei	□□□D	Foliage is shiny and brilliant green. Occasional pruning helps maintain naturally rounded shape. Loses leaves in colder climates. A fast grower.	20-30 ft.
Bottlebrush (*Callistemon*)			
Lemon (*C. citrinus*, or *C. lanceolatus*)	□□□D*	Narrow leaves up to 3 in. long turn from copper to green. Grown for showy, bright red flower spikes about 6 in. long, shaped remarkably like bottlebrush. Plant is sun loving and drought resistant.	20-25 ft.
Weeping (*C. viminalis*)	□□□D*	Pendulous branches. Tree requires staking and pruning. Needs ample water.	20-30 ft.
Bottle tree (*Brachychiton*, or *Sterculia*)			
Flame (*B. acerifolium*)	□□□D*	Leaves are shiny, generally lobed, and up to 10 in. wide. Flowers in mid to late summer are bright scarlet. Fruits are black and up to 4 in. long.	40-60 ft.
Kurrajong (*B. populneum*)	□□□D	Poplarlike oval leaves up to 3 in. long can be either lobed or lobeless. Yellowish or greenish blossoms are tinted red on inside.	50-60 ft.
Brisbane box (*Tristania*)			
T. conferta	□□□D*	Leathery leaves are 3-6 in. long, oval shaped, and usually clustered at ends of twigs. White blooms in clusters in leaf axils. Bark is reddish brown.	50-60 ft.

*Not hardy below 30° F

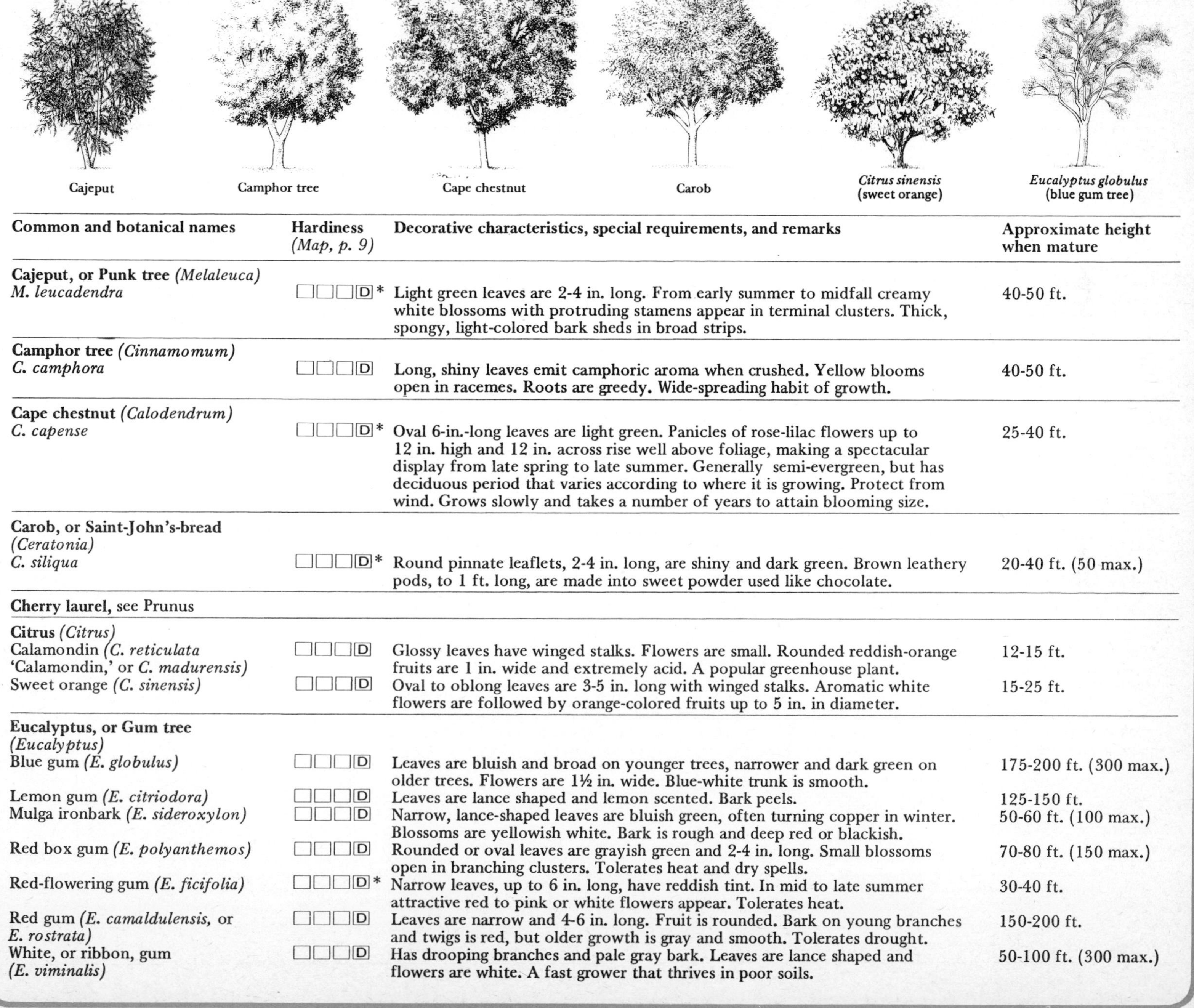

Cajeput — Camphor tree — Cape chestnut — Carob — *Citrus sinensis* (sweet orange) — *Eucalyptus globulus* (blue gum tree)

Common and botanical names	Hardiness *(Map, p. 9)*	Decorative characteristics, special requirements, and remarks	Approximate height when mature
Cajeput, or Punk tree *(Melaleuca)* *M. leucadendra*	□□□D*	Light green leaves are 2-4 in. long. From early summer to midfall creamy white blossoms with protruding stamens appear in terminal clusters. Thick, spongy, light-colored bark sheds in broad strips.	40-50 ft.
Camphor tree *(Cinnamomum)* *C. camphora*	□□□D	Long, shiny leaves emit camphoric aroma when crushed. Yellow blooms open in racemes. Roots are greedy. Wide-spreading habit of growth.	40-50 ft.
Cape chestnut *(Calodendrum)* *C. capense*	□□□D*	Oval 6-in.-long leaves are light green. Panicles of rose-lilac flowers up to 12 in. high and 12 in. across rise well above foliage, making a spectacular display from late spring to late summer. Generally semi-evergreen, but has deciduous period that varies according to where it is growing. Protect from wind. Grows slowly and takes a number of years to attain blooming size.	25-40 ft.
Carob, or Saint-John's-bread *(Ceratonia)* *C. siliqua*	□□□D*	Round pinnate leaflets, 2-4 in. long, are shiny and dark green. Brown leathery pods, to 1 ft. long, are made into sweet powder used like chocolate.	20-40 ft. (50 max.)
Cherry laurel, see Prunus			
Citrus *(Citrus)*			
Calamondin *(C. reticulata* 'Calamondin,' or *C. madurensis)*	□□□D	Glossy leaves have winged stalks. Flowers are small. Rounded reddish-orange fruits are 1 in. wide and extremely acid. A popular greenhouse plant.	12-15 ft.
Sweet orange *(C. sinensis)*	□□□D	Oval to oblong leaves are 3-5 in. long with winged stalks. Aromatic white flowers are followed by orange-colored fruits up to 5 in. in diameter.	15-25 ft.
Eucalyptus, or Gum tree *(Eucalyptus)*			
Blue gum *(E. globulus)*	□□□D	Leaves are bluish and broad on younger trees, narrower and dark green on older trees. Flowers are 1½ in. wide. Blue-white trunk is smooth.	175-200 ft. (300 max.)
Lemon gum *(E. citriodora)*	□□□D	Leaves are lance shaped and lemon scented. Bark peels.	125-150 ft.
Mulga ironbark *(E. sideroxylon)*	□□□D	Narrow, lance-shaped leaves are bluish green, often turning copper in winter. Blossoms are yellowish white. Bark is rough and deep red or blackish.	50-60 ft. (100 max.)
Red box gum *(E. polyanthemos)*	□□□D	Rounded or oval leaves are grayish green and 2-4 in. long. Small blossoms open in branching clusters. Tolerates heat and dry spells.	70-80 ft. (150 max.)
Red-flowering gum *(E. ficifolia)*	□□□D*	Narrow leaves, up to 6 in. long, have reddish tint. In mid to late summer attractive red to pink or white flowers appear. Tolerates heat.	30-40 ft.
Red gum *(E. camaldulensis,* or *E. rostrata)*	□□□D	Leaves are narrow and 4-6 in. long. Fruit is rounded. Bark on young branches and twigs is red, but older growth is gray and smooth. Tolerates drought.	150-200 ft.
White, or ribbon, gum *(E. viminalis)*	□□□D	Has drooping branches and pale gray bark. Leaves are lance shaped and flowers are white. A fast grower that thrives in poor soils.	50-100 ft. (300 max.)

*Not hardy below 30° F

BROAD-LEAVED EVERGREENS *(continued)*

Ficus retusa nitida (Indian laurel) | Fire wheel tree | English holly (*I. altaclarensis*) | Toyon holly | Jerusalem thorn | Kaffir plum

Common and botanical names	Hardiness (*Map, p. 9*)	Decorative characteristics, special requirements, and remarks	Approximate height when mature
Ficus, or Fig tree *(Ficus)*			
Indian laurel *(F. retusa nitida)*	□□□D*	Small waxy leaves are 2-4 in. long, dense on upright branches. Tolerates trimming to pyramid or standard. Often seen with several aerial roots.	60-75 ft.
Moreton Bay fig *(F. macrophylla)*	□□□D*	Shiny oblong leaves are up to 10 in. long and 4 in. wide; undersides are brown. Fruits are 1 in. wide and purple with white markings. Bark is gray.	60-75 ft.
Rusty-leaf fig *(F. rubiginosa)*	□□□D*	Leathery oval leaves, dark green and 3-6 in. long, have rusty fuzz on undersides. Can be grown in pots when young. Flourishes near ocean.	50-100 ft.
Weeping fig *(F. benjamina)*	□□□D*	Leathery deep green leaves 2-4 in. long densely cover graceful, drooping branches. Fruits are reddish orange.	20-30 ft.
Fire wheel tree *(Stenocarpus)*			
S. sinuatus	□□□D*	Oaklike foliage is glossy and leathery. Large, wheel-shaped blooms are fiery red with yellow stamens and have unpleasant odor. Does best in acid soil.	40-50 ft.
Holly *(Ilex)*			
American *(I. opaca)*	□B□□	Elliptic, spiny leaves up to 3 in. long are yellowish green on undersides. Dull-colored foliage compared with English holly. Fruits are usually red, but in some varieties, yellow. Needs well-drained, acid soil.	35-45 ft.
English *(I. altaclárensis)*	□□C□	A hybrid with attractive leaves that are shiny, more than 4 in. long, and have regularly arranged teeth on margins. Red berries.	35-45 ft.
English *(I. aquifolium)*	□□C□	Oblong to oval leaves are up to 4 in. long, upper surfaces are shiny, margins bear teeth. Fruits are usually bright red, but in some varieties, yellow. Branches of varieties with variegated foliage are used as Christmas decorations.	30-40 ft. (70 max.)
I. a. argenteamarginata	□□C□	Leaves have silvery white edges.	20-30 ft.
I. a. aureomarginata	□□C□	Edges of leaves are golden yellow.	20-30 ft.
I. pedunculosa	□B□□	Glossy green leaves, up to 3 in. long with smooth margins, are oval shaped and turn coppery in winter. Cherrylike fruits are brilliant scarlet color and form on long branches. Habit of growth is upright.	10-20 ft.
Yaupon *(I. vomitoria)*	□□C□	Oblong or elliptic leaves are more than 1 in. long with wavy-toothed margins. Tiny scarlet fruits form abundantly on gray stems, either singly or in groups of 3. Good as clipped hedge.	15-25 ft.
Holly, toyon, or California *(Heteromeles)*			
H. arbutifolia	□□□D	Leaves are leathery, have many teeth, and are pointed. White flowers open in clusters in early to mid summer. Red fruits are hollylike. Attracts bees.	6-15 ft.
Jerusalem thorn *(Parkinsonia)*			
P. aculeata	□□□D	Drooping thorny branches bear thin, feathery leaves up to 1 ft. long. Fragrant yellow blooms open in early spring. Makes good sheared hedge.	25-30 ft.
Kaffir plum *(Harpephyllum)*			
H. caffrum	□□□D*	Alternate leaves are shiny and leathery. Fruits are deep red. A rapid grower.	30-35 ft.

*Not hardy below 30° F

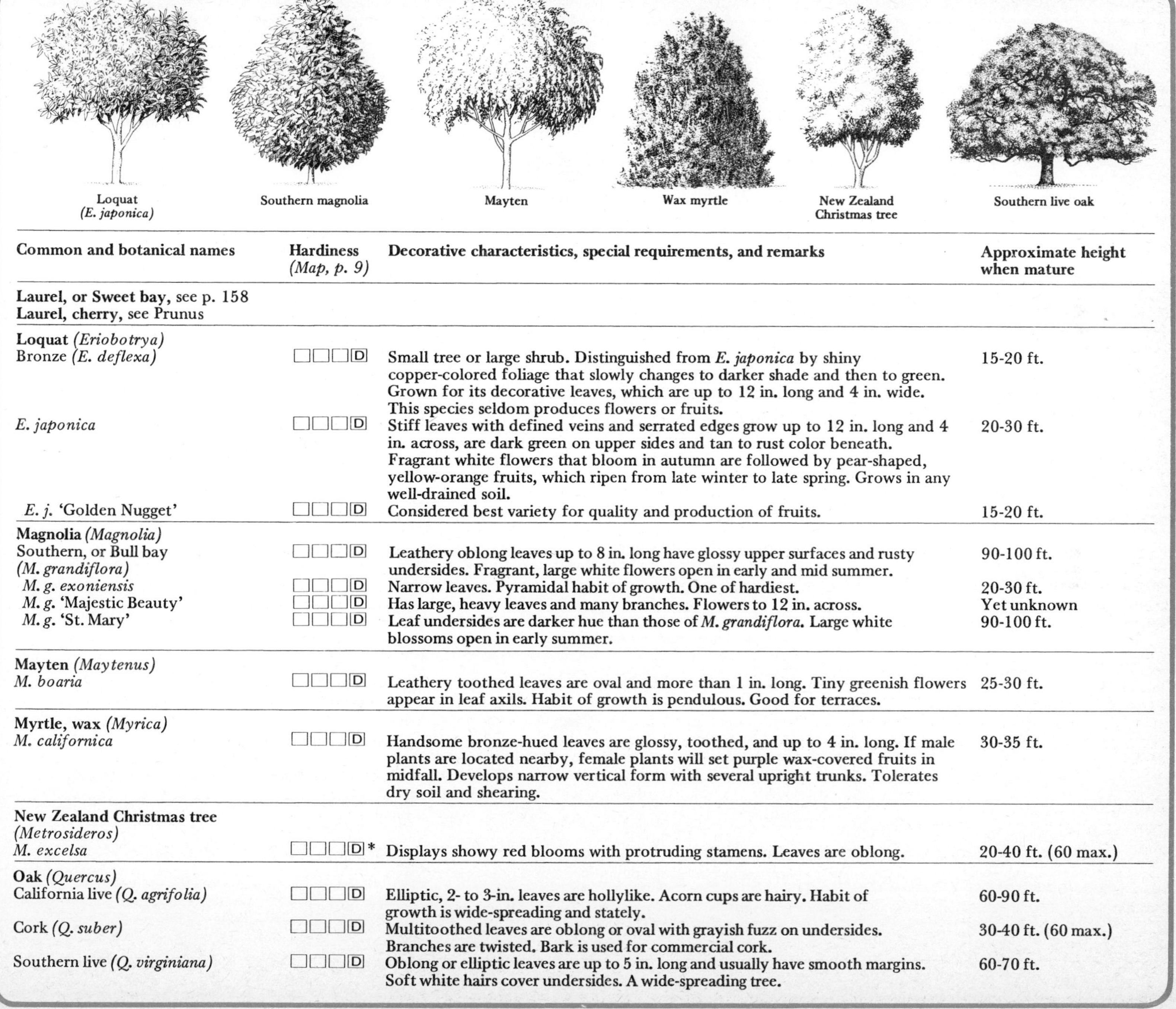

Loquat (*E. japonica*) · Southern magnolia · Mayten · Wax myrtle · New Zealand Christmas tree · Southern live oak

Common and botanical names	Hardiness *(Map, p. 9)*	Decorative characteristics, special requirements, and remarks	Approximate height when mature
Laurel, or Sweet bay, see p. 158			
Laurel, cherry, see Prunus			
Loquat *(Eriobotrya)*			
Bronze *(E. deflexa)*	□□□D	Small tree or large shrub. Distinguished from *E. japonica* by shiny copper-colored foliage that slowly changes to darker shade and then to green. Grown for its decorative leaves, which are up to 12 in. long and 4 in. wide. This species seldom produces flowers or fruits.	15-20 ft.
E. japonica	□□□D	Stiff leaves with defined veins and serrated edges grow up to 12 in. long and 4 in. across, are dark green on upper sides and tan to rust color beneath. Fragrant white flowers that bloom in autumn are followed by pear-shaped, yellow-orange fruits, which ripen from late winter to late spring. Grows in any well-drained soil.	20-30 ft.
E. j. 'Golden Nugget'	□□□D	Considered best variety for quality and production of fruits.	15-20 ft.
Magnolia *(Magnolia)*			
Southern, or Bull bay *(M. grandiflora)*	□□□D	Leathery oblong leaves up to 8 in. long have glossy upper surfaces and rusty undersides. Fragrant, large white flowers open in early and mid summer.	90-100 ft.
M. g. exoniensis	□□□D	Narrow leaves. Pyramidal habit of growth. One of hardiest.	20-30 ft.
M. g. 'Majestic Beauty'	□□□D	Has large, heavy leaves and many branches. Flowers to 12 in. across.	Yet unknown
M. g. 'St. Mary'	□□□D	Leaf undersides are darker hue than those of *M. grandiflora*. Large white blossoms open in early summer.	90-100 ft.
Mayten *(Maytenus)*			
M. boaria	□□□D	Leathery toothed leaves are oval and more than 1 in. long. Tiny greenish flowers appear in leaf axils. Habit of growth is pendulous. Good for terraces.	25-30 ft.
Myrtle, wax *(Myrica)*			
M. californica	□□□D	Handsome bronze-hued leaves are glossy, toothed, and up to 4 in. long. If male plants are located nearby, female plants will set purple wax-covered fruits in midfall. Develops narrow vertical form with several upright trunks. Tolerates dry soil and shearing.	30-35 ft.
New Zealand Christmas tree *(Metrosideros)*			
M. excelsa	□□□D*	Displays showy red blooms with protruding stamens. Leaves are oblong.	20-40 ft. (60 max.)
Oak *(Quercus)*			
California live *(Q. agrifolia)*	□□□D	Elliptic, 2- to 3-in. leaves are hollylike. Acorn cups are hairy. Habit of growth is wide-spreading and stately.	60-90 ft.
Cork *(Q. suber)*	□□□D	Multitoothed leaves are oblong or oval with grayish fuzz on undersides. Branches are twisted. Bark is used for commercial cork.	30-40 ft. (60 max.)
Southern live *(Q. virginiana)*	□□□D	Oblong or elliptic leaves are up to 5 in. long and usually have smooth margins. Soft white hairs cover undersides. A wide-spreading tree.	60-70 ft.

*Not hardy below 30° F

BROAD-LEAVED EVERGREENS *(continued)*

Olive
(O. europea)

Orchid tree
(B. variegata)

Canary Island
date palm

Evergreen pear

California pepper tree

Persea borbonia
(red bay)

Common and botanical names	Hardiness *(Map, p. 9)*	Decorative characteristics, special requirements, and remarks	Approximate height when mature
Olive *(Olea)*			
O. europea	□□□D	Leaves 1-3 in. long, with silvery undersides. Aromatic blossoms and fruits form if exposed to 12- to 15-wk. period of fluctuating day temperatures (35°-60° F) in winter. Produces the true olive, which is inedible without special processing and usually a nuisance on ornamentals. Semi-fruitless varieties available. Mature trees have contorted branches.	20-25 ft. (70 max.)
O. e. 'Manzanillo'	□□□D	Large fruits. Picturesque, low-spreading habit. Good for landscaping.	15-20 ft.
O. 'Swan Hill'	□□□D	Like *O. e.* 'Manzanillo,' but has all male flowers. Remains fruitless.	15-20 ft.
Orchid tree *(Bauhinia)*			
B. purpurea	□□□D*	Purplish narrow-petaled flowers look somewhat like orchids. They appear from midwinter until early spring. An impressive sight, frequently used as street tree in warm climates.	20-30 ft.
B. variegata	□□□D*	Light green leaves have 2 lobes. Handsome light pink to lavender, broad-petaled flowers with prominent white stamens open in leaf axils during early spring. Sets 1-ft. pods. Often confused with and sold as *B. purpurea.*	15-25 ft.
B. v. candida	□□□D*	White blossoms are delicately streaked with light green veins.	15-25 ft.
Palms (several genera)			
California fan *(Washingtonia filifera)*	□□□D	Erect, grayish-green, fan-shaped leaves have spined stalks 3-5 ft. long. Dead leaves often remain on upper trunk. Good choice where soil is dry.	60-80 ft.
Canary Island date *(Phoenix canariensis)*	□□□D*	Arching featherlike leaves are up to 20 ft. long. Yellowish-red, ¾-in.-long fruits often hang in clusters. Trunk is up to 3 ft. thick.	30-40 ft. (60 max.)
Coconut *(Cocos nucifera)*	□□□D*	Feathery leaves up to 18 ft. long form near top of trunk, which is often curved. Coconuts begin to develop when trees are still young. Good near sea.	70-90 ft.
Mexican blue *(Erythea armata)*	□□□D*	Fan-shaped tree with shiny blue-green leaves. Fleshy, yellow, rounded fruits and white flowers. Tolerates drought.	20-40 ft.
Mexican fan *(Washingtonia robusta)*	□□□D*	Coarse, fan-shaped leaves develop only near top of trunk. Old leafstalks extend through band of fibrous matter covering trunk.	80-90 ft.
Pear, evergreen *(Pyrus)*			
P. kawakamii	□□□D	Foliage is shiny. Scented white flowers bloom from winter until early spring. Fruits are about 1/3 in. in diameter. Fine for espaliering.	20-30 ft.
Pepper tree *(Schinus)*			
California *(S. molle)*	□□□D	Light green, much-divided leaves hang down from gnarled branches. Flowers are yellowish. Rose-colored fruits last into midwinter.	30-40 ft.
Persea *(Persea)*			
P. indica	□□□D	Leathery oblong leaves are 4-6 in. long. Tiny blossoms open in clusters at leaf axils. Fruits are ¾ in. long.	15-20 ft.
Red bay *(P. borbonia)*	□□□D	Bluish-green oblong leaves are up to 6 in. Bluish-black fruits are ½ in. long and have red stalks. Needs constant moisture in root area.	30-40 ft.

*Not hardy below 30° F

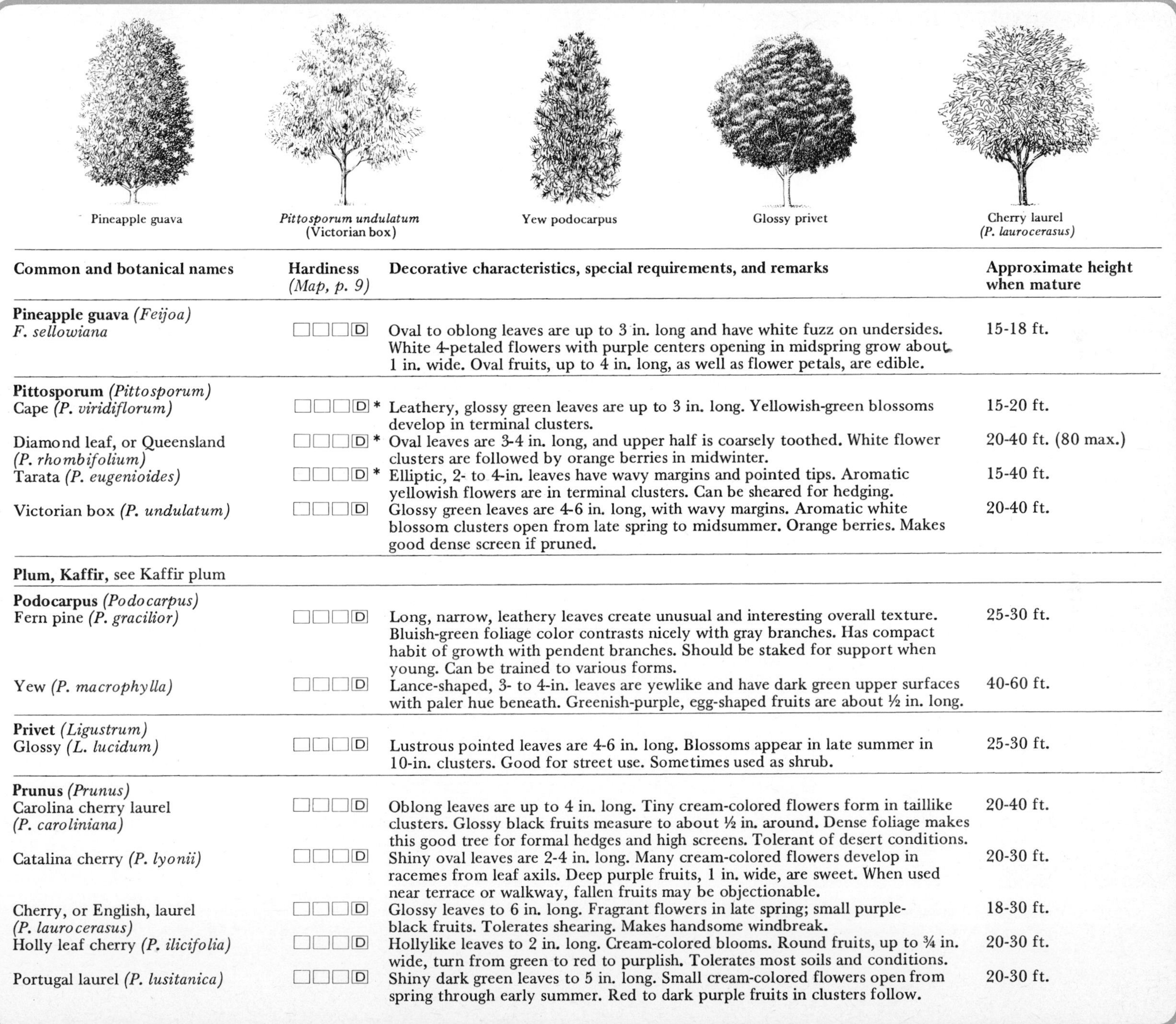

Pineapple guava — *Pittosporum undulatum* (Victorian box) — Yew podocarpus — Glossy privet — Cherry laurel (*P. laurocerasus*)

Common and botanical names	Hardiness *(Map, p. 9)*	Decorative characteristics, special requirements, and remarks	Approximate height when mature
Pineapple guava *(Feijoa)*			
F. sellowiana	□□□D	Oval to oblong leaves are up to 3 in. long and have white fuzz on undersides. White 4-petaled flowers with purple centers opening in midspring grow about 1 in. wide. Oval fruits, up to 4 in. long, as well as flower petals, are edible.	15-18 ft.
Pittosporum *(Pittosporum)*			
Cape *(P. viridiflorum)*	□□□D *	Leathery, glossy green leaves are up to 3 in. long. Yellowish-green blossoms develop in terminal clusters.	15-20 ft.
Diamond leaf, or Queensland *(P. rhombifolium)*	□□□D *	Oval leaves are 3-4 in. long, and upper half is coarsely toothed. White flower clusters are followed by orange berries in midwinter.	20-40 ft. (80 max.)
Tarata *(P. eugenioides)*	□□□D *	Elliptic, 2- to 4-in. leaves have wavy margins and pointed tips. Aromatic yellowish flowers are in terminal clusters. Can be sheared for hedging.	15-40 ft.
Victorian box *(P. undulatum)*	□□□D	Glossy green leaves are 4-6 in. long, with wavy margins. Aromatic white blossom clusters open from late spring to midsummer. Orange berries. Makes good dense screen if pruned.	20-40 ft.
Plum, Kaffir, see Kaffir plum			
Podocarpus *(Podocarpus)*			
Fern pine *(P. gracilior)*	□□□D	Long, narrow, leathery leaves create unusual and interesting overall texture. Bluish-green foliage color contrasts nicely with gray branches. Has compact habit of growth with pendent branches. Should be staked for support when young. Can be trained to various forms.	25-30 ft.
Yew *(P. macrophylla)*	□□□D	Lance-shaped, 3- to 4-in. leaves are yewlike and have dark green upper surfaces with paler hue beneath. Greenish-purple, egg-shaped fruits are about ½ in. long.	40-60 ft.
Privet *(Ligustrum)*			
Glossy *(L. lucidum)*	□□□D	Lustrous pointed leaves are 4-6 in. long. Blossoms appear in late summer in 10-in. clusters. Good for street use. Sometimes used as shrub.	25-30 ft.
Prunus *(Prunus)*			
Carolina cherry laurel *(P. caroliniana)*	□□□D	Oblong leaves are up to 4 in. long. Tiny cream-colored flowers form in taillike clusters. Glossy black fruits measure to about ½ in. around. Dense foliage makes this good tree for formal hedges and high screens. Tolerant of desert conditions.	20-40 ft.
Catalina cherry *(P. lyonii)*	□□□D	Shiny oval leaves are 2-4 in. long. Many cream-colored flowers develop in racemes from leaf axils. Deep purple fruits, 1 in. wide, are sweet. When used near terrace or walkway, fallen fruits may be objectionable.	20-30 ft.
Cherry, or English, laurel *(P. laurocerasus)*	□□□D	Glossy leaves to 6 in. long. Fragrant flowers in late spring; small purple-black fruits. Tolerates shearing. Makes handsome windbreak.	18-30 ft.
Holly leaf cherry *(P. ilicifolia)*	□□□D	Hollylike leaves to 2 in. long. Cream-colored blooms. Round fruits, up to ¾ in. wide, turn from green to red to purplish. Tolerates most soils and conditions.	20-30 ft.
Portugal laurel *(P. lusitanica)*	□□□D	Shiny dark green leaves to 5 in. long. Small cream-colored flowers open from spring through early summer. Red to dark purple fruits in clusters follow.	20-30 ft.

*Not hardy below 30° F

BROAD-LEAVED EVERGREENS *(continued)*

Sea urchin tree 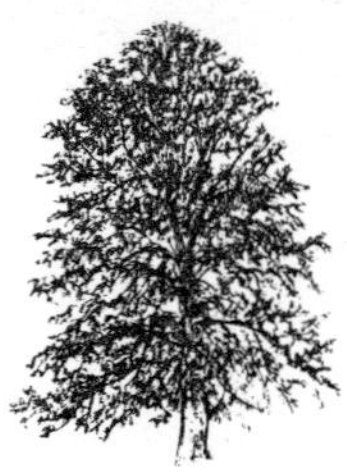 | Silk oak 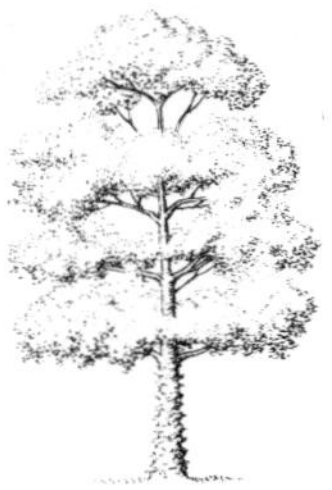 | Floss silk tree  | Soapbark tree  | Strawberry tree  | Australian tea tree

Common and botanical names	Hardiness *(Map, p. 9)*	Decorative characteristics, special requirements, and remarks	Approximate height when mature
Sea urchin tree *(Hakea)* *H. laurina*	□□□D *	Gray-green leaves are narrow and elliptic in shape, growing up to 6 in. long. Crimson florets in rounded clusters have long, thin, yellow stamens. Blooms appear in winter or occasionally in late autumn. Does well even in poor soil and is usually pest free. Will tolerate an occasional light frost.	20-25 ft.
Silk oak *(Grevillea)* *G. robusta*	□□□D *	Leaves, a rich green on upper sides, silver tones underneath, fall from time to time year round in sufficient quantity to necessitate raking. Masses of brilliant yellow-orange flowers bloom in midspring on 4- to 10-in. racemes. Branches are brittle; so tree needs protection from wind. Large and fast growing. New trees are pyramidal in shape. Stake when young. Grows well in hot, sunny climates and will tolerate poor but well-drained soil and drought. Good desert tree. Often seen as 2- to 4-ft. greenhouse plant.	80-100 ft. (150 max.)
Silk tree, floss *(Chorisia)* *C. speciosa*	□□□D *	Fanlike leaflets in groupings of 5-7 fall just when flowers open in late autumn or winter or whenever temperature drops below 27° F. Flowers make spectacular show ranging in color from white to yellowish and pink to rose-purple, the petal bases shading to cream or white and often spotted.	30-60 ft.
Soapbark tree *(Quillaja)* *Q. saponaria*	□□C□	Leaves are lustrous, thick, and leathery. White ½-in.-wide blooms appear in clusters of 3-5 during spring. Attractive star-shaped fruits. Bark has soapy quality. Young trees are narrow, with pendulous branches.	25-30 ft. (60 max.)
Strawberry tree *(Arbutus)* *A. unedo*	□□C□	Toothed leaves on sticky, hairy branches are a glossy dark green with red stems and grow 3-4 in. long. White blooms, tinted pink or greenish, hang in 2-in. clusters. Strawberrylike fruits, ¾ in. in diameter and red-orange in color, are edible but not very tasty. Both blooms and fruits appear in autumn. Reddish inner bark makes attractive display when outside cover peels and cracks. Branches become contorted on mature trees. Survives in very poor soils and extreme climates.	10-25 ft.
Tea tree, Australian *(Leptospermum)* *L. laevigatum*	□□□D *	Teardrop-shaped leaves up to 1 in. long are gray-green. Single white flowers with ½-in.-wide petals form around cup-shaped cones along stems in spring. Attractive curved trunk with peeling bark; umbrellalike branches. Lives longest in well-drained acid soil in hot coastal regions.	20-30 ft.
Thorn, Jerusalem, see Jerusalem thorn			
Wax myrtle, see Myrtle, wax			

*Not hardy below 30° F

Coniferous Trees

Conifers are cone-bearing plants; most are evergreen with needlelike leaves. In the chart that follows, the trees are listed in alphabetical order, according to their best known common names. The generic name of each appears next, in parentheses and in italics. Recommended species and varieties are also listed.

Although many factors influence a tree's chances of survival, the most dependable indicator of its hardiness is the lowest temperature it can endure. To determine whether a conifer can reasonably be expected to survive the lowest average temperature in your area, check the zone designation for that conifer in the Hardiness column. Then refer to the Temperature Zone Map on page 9.

The figures at the far right indicate the height each tree can be expected to attain—contingent, of course, upon growing conditions and the care it receives. Some trees grow taller in the wild; in such cases, the figure in parentheses is the maximum probable height for that tree.

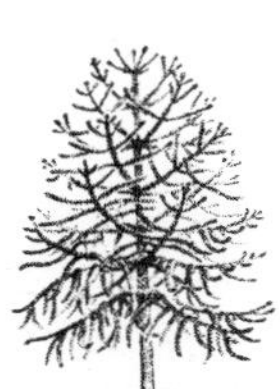
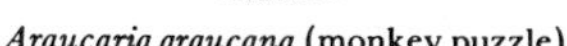
Araucaria araucana (monkey puzzle)

American arborvitae

Hiba arborvitae

Blue Atlas cedar

Common and botanical names	Hardiness *(Map, p. 9)*	Decorative characteristics, special requirements, and remarks	Approximate height when mature
Araucaria *(Araucaria)*			
Bunya bunya *(A. bidwillii)*	D *	Sharp-pointed oblong leaves are green and glossy. Cones resemble pineapples.	80-125 ft.
Hoop pine *(A. cunninghamii)*	D *	Needlelike leaves. A stately tree.	100-165 ft.
Monkey puzzle *(A. araucana)*	C	Tiers of branches produce intricate, open tree that casts little shade. Flat oval leaves tightly clothing branches are stiff and long lasting.	70-90 ft.
Norfolk Island pine *(A. excelsa)*	D *	Branches grow in horizontal tiers. Leaves are sharp and pointed.	150-200 ft.
Arborvitae *(Thuja)*			
American *(T. occidentalis)*	A	Dark green to yellow-green foliage. Cones to ½ in. long. Varieties of different heights and shapes, some with yellow, blue-green, or variegated leaves. Reddish bark. Needs more than average moisture.	60-65 ft.
Giant *(T. plicata,* or *T. lobbii)*	B	Flat sprays of shiny green leaves with white marks beneath are handsome bronze from late fall through winter.	150-200 ft.
Oriental *(T. orientalis,* or *Platycladus orientalis)*	B	Densely branched trees with bright green foliage. Egg-shaped cones have scales with hooklike tips. Varieties include pyramidal kinds and those with yellow, blue, and variegated foliage.	50-100 ft.
Arborvitae, hiba, or false *(Thujopsis)*			
T. dolabrata	C	Similar in appearance to the common yew. Leaves, white banded beneath, grow in flat sprays. Bears small woody cones. Needs moisture.	50-100 ft.
Bunya bunya, see Araucaria			
Cedar *(Cedrus)*			
Atlas *(C. atlantica)*	C	Light green leaves less than 1 in. long have silvery sheen. Pale brown cones are often 3 in. long. Forms flat top at maturity. Like all cedars, it needs plenty of room and does best in moist but very well drained soil.	70-80 ft. (100 max.)
Blue Atlas *(C. a. glauca)*	C	Foliage is beautiful bluish shade.	80-100 ft.
C. a. fastigiata	C	Bluish-gray needlelike leaves have silvery hue. Narrow upright form.	50-70 ft.
Cedar of Lebanon *(C. libani)*	B	Dark to bright green 1-in.-long leaves and brown cones up to 4 in. long.	70-80 ft. (100 max.)
Deodar *(C. deodara)*	C	Branches with pendulous ends are characteristic of this species. Deep blue-green leaves are about 2 in. long. Red-brown cones are up to 5 in. long.	70-80 ft. (150 max.)
C. d. glauca	C	Much like *C. deodara,* but foliage has silvery cast.	75-100 ft.

*Not hardy below 30° F

CONIFERS *(continued)*

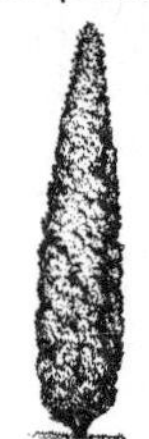
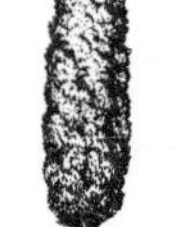
Incense cedar

Cryptomeria japonica

Monterey cypress

Bald cypress *(T. distichum)*

Lawson false cypress

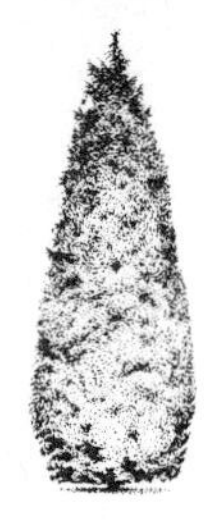
Leyland cypress

Common and botanical names	Hardiness *(Map, p. 9)*	Decorative characteristics, special requirements, and remarks	Approximate height when mature
Cedar, incense *(Calocedrus)*			
C. decurrens	B	Small, shiny scalelike leaves are aromatic when crushed. Bark is reddish brown and furrowed. Few insects bother this tree.	60-100 ft. (135 max.)
Cryptomeria *(Cryptomeria)*			
C. japonica	C	Abundant small leaves that curve inward at their ends, small cones, and shredding, reddish-brown bark make this an attractive tree. Foliage becomes brownish in winter. Cannot tolerate prolonged heat, drought, cold winter wind.	80-100 ft. (180 max.)
C. j. lobbii	B	Similar to *C. japonica* but somewhat hardier.	50-70 ft.
Cypress *(Cupressus)*			
Italian *(C. sempervirens)*	C	Horizontal or erect branches bear branchlets with 4 rows of deep green scalelike leaves. Cones are somewhat spherical.	50-80 ft. (150 max.)
C. s. stricta	C	Profile is narrow and decidedly upright.	50-60 ft.
Monterey *(C. macrocarpa)*	C	Scalelike leaves are in 4 rows. Female cones are longer than they are wide. When young, tree has pyramidal form; develops wide top with age. Shear to form hedges and windbreaks. Fine along seacoast. A fast grower.	40-75 ft. (90 max.)
Mourning *(C. funebris)*	C	Flattened branchlets are on pendulous branches. Sometimes called *Chamaecyparis funebris.*	60-65 ft.
Cypress, bald, or swamp *(Taxodium)*			
Montezuma *(T. mucronatum)*	C	Similar to *T. distichum* except for wider top, larger cones, shorter leaves. Partially deciduous toward northern limits of its hardiness zone.	40-75 ft. (150 max.)
T. distichum	B	Feathery, light green, deciduous foliage turns orange in fall. Bark is pale brown and scaly. Mature trees develop unique upright "knees" near base of trunk. Grows best in ordinary wet or damp soil.	100-120 ft.
Cypress, false *(Chamaecyparis)*			
Hinoki *(C. obtusa)*	B	Scalelike leaves on branchlets hanging in flat sprays are shiny green and have pale white lines on undersides. Cones, 3/8 in. wide, are orange-brown. Bark is red-brown. Many varieties are slow growing. Some reach only 3-10 ft. Some have rich yellow foliage. Needs moist soil.	70-80 ft. (120 max.)
Lawson *(C. lawsoniana)*	B	Pendulous branches have reddish-brown bark. Scalelike leaves in sprays are usually green or blue-green, but there are varieties with silver, blue, yellow, and white-tipped leaves. Male cones are reddish; mature female cones, brown. Needs considerable moisture.	80-200 ft. (200 max.)
Sawara *(C. pisifera)*	B	Horizontal branches form narrow pyramidal shape. Brownish-red bark peels in older specimens. Some varieties have yellow branch tips or leaves that are pale blue or silver-gray. Has open habit of growth.	150-165 ft.
Cypress, Leyland *(Cupressocyparis)*			
C. leylandii	A	Flat sprays of gray-green scalelike leaves. Adaptable to either dry or moist situations. Takes pruning well. Good hedge or screen plant. A fast grower.	40-60 ft.

White fir

Douglas fir

Western hemlock

Chinese juniper

Common and botanical names	Hardiness *(Map, p. 9)*	Decorative characteristics, special requirements, and remarks	Approximate height when mature
Fir *(Abies)*			
Cilician *(A. cilicica)*	[ ] [B] [ ] [ ]	Bright green leaves with white bands on their undersides, large reddish-brown cones, ash-gray bark, and pyramidal habit make an appealing species.	40-60 ft. (100 max.)
Greek *(A. cephalonica)*	[ ] [B] [ ] [ ]	Sharp-pointed needles, up to 1 in. long, spread widely around shoots.	75-90 ft. (120 max.)
Momi *(A. firma)*	[ ] [B] [ ] [ ]	Shiny green needles, notched at tips, in 2 rows. Cones up to 5 in. long.	75-100 ft. (150 max.)
Nikko *(A. homolepis)*	[ ] [B] [ ] [ ]	Evenly spaced branches. Needles that are 1 in. long with white bands beneath and purplish cones up to 4 in. long. Outstanding.	60-80 ft. (120 max.)
Veitch *(A. veitchii)*	[A] [ ] [ ] [ ]	Needles point forward, curve upward, have white undersides. Blue-purple cones over 2 in. long. Good in East but not in drier parts of Midwest.	50-70 ft.
White *(A. concolor)*	[A] [ ] [ ] [ ]	Needles are bluish or green, and large cones are greenish purple. Reasonably resistant to drought and heat. Best fir for city gardens.	60-80 ft. (120 max.)
Fir, Douglas *(Pseudotsuga)*			
P. menziesii, or *P. taxifolia*	[ ] [B] [ ] [ ]	Short flat needles have 2 light-colored bands on undersides. Egg-shaped cones are often over 4 in. long and hang down. Handsome tree.	90-100 ft. (300 max.)
P. m. glauca	[A] [ ] [ ] [ ]	Soft needles are blue-green. Grow in sheltered spot. Has shallow roots, can blow over in windstorm.	80-90 ft. (150 max.)
P. m. pendula	[ ] [B] [ ] [ ]	Resembles *P. menziesii* except that branches droop.	70-80 ft.
Gingko, see p. 54			
Hemlock *(Tsuga)*			
Canada *(T. canadensis)*	[A] [ ] [ ] [ ]	Leaves are shiny, dark green on upper sides, with 2 whitish lines underneath. Shallow rooted and easy to transplant in many soil types but may fail on windy sites and in city smog. Can be sheared to form hedges.	75-100 ft.
Carolina *(T. caroliniana)*	[ ] [B] [ ] [ ]	Resembles *T. canadensis,* but does better in city conditions.	60-70 ft.
Japanese *(T. diversifolia)*	[ ] [B] [ ] [ ]	Needles that cling to branches for up to 10 yr. produce dense effect.	70-80 ft.
Siebold *(T. sieboldii)*	[ ] [B] [ ] [ ]	Slender horizontal branches with shiny, dark green leaves.	80-100 ft.
Western *(T. heterophylla)*	[ ] [ ] [C] [ ]	Energy goes mainly into height, since side branches are pendulous and short. Thrives in moist summer environment. Not good choice for eastern gardens.	90-120 ft. (200 max.)
Hoop pine, see Araucaria			
Juniper *(Juniperus)*			
Chinese *(J. chinensis)*	[A] [ ] [ ] [ ]	Numerous varieties available, some with blue-green to steel-blue foliage.	20-35 ft. (65 max.)
J. c. stricta	[ ] [B] [ ] [ ]	This narrow, erect form is often sold as *J. excelsa stricta.*	20-35 ft.
Eastern red cedar *(J. virginiana)*	[A] [ ] [ ] [ ]	Like many junipers, this species has needlelike foliage on young branches and scalelike leaves on older wood. Fruit is dark blue. Reddish-brown bark peels off in strips. Grows well in rocky soil. Yellow-tipped and grayish-green-needled varieties are widely available.	50-75 ft. (100 max.)
Needle *(J. rigida)*	[ ] [B] [ ] [ ]	An excellent evergreen with drooping branches. Needlelike leaves.	25-35 ft.
Rocky Mountain *(J. scopulorum)*	[A] [ ] [ ] [ ]	Often forks near base like *J. virginiana.* Blue fruit ripens during second year.	25-35 ft. (50 max.)

CONIFERS *(continued)*

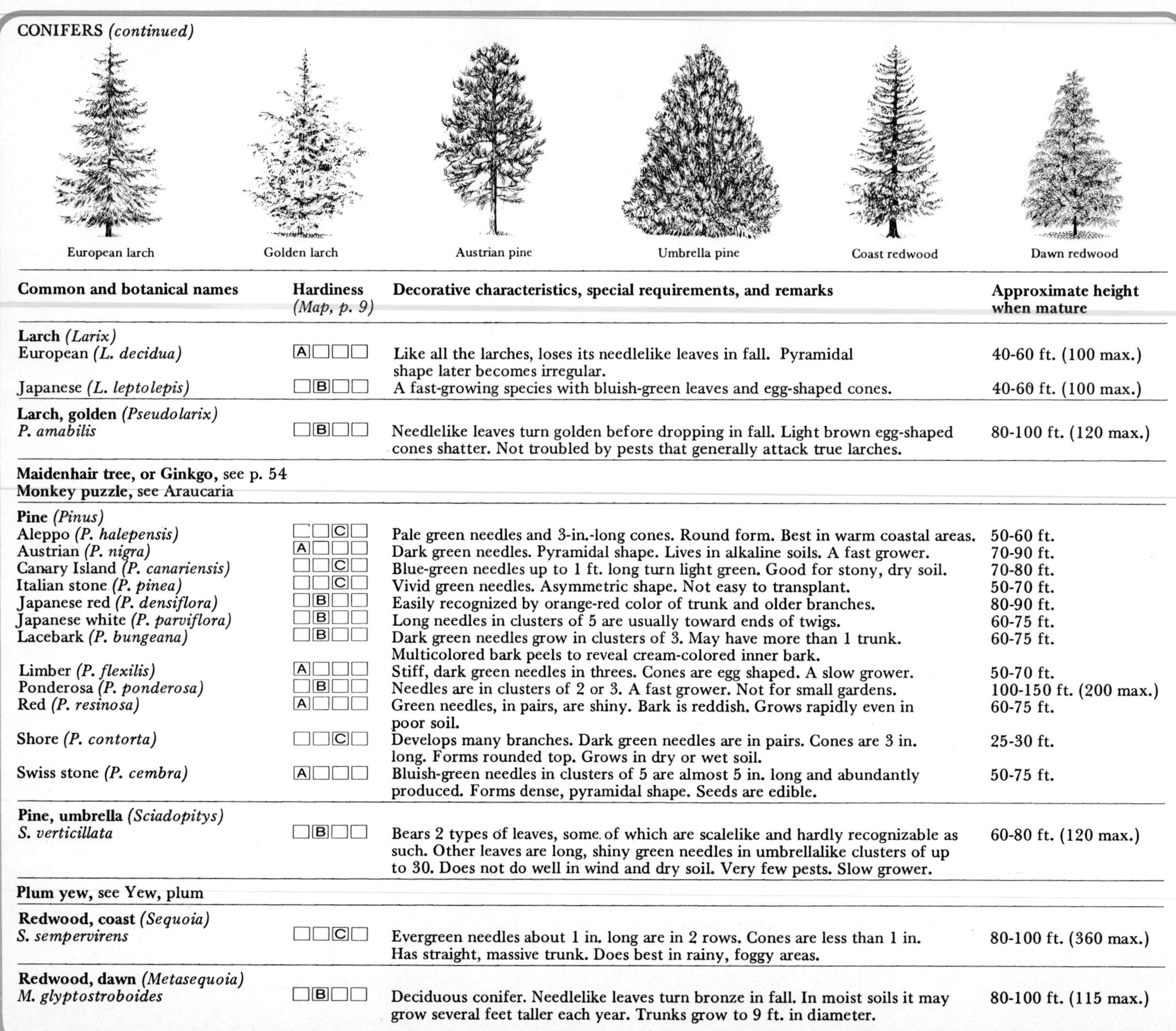

European larch — Golden larch — Austrian pine — Umbrella pine — Coast redwood — Dawn redwood

Common and botanical names	Hardiness *(Map, p. 9)*	Decorative characteristics, special requirements, and remarks	Approximate height when mature
Larch *(Larix)*			
European *(L. decidua)*	A	Like all the larches, loses its needlelike leaves in fall. Pyramidal shape later becomes irregular.	40-60 ft. (100 max.)
Japanese *(L. leptolepis)*	B	A fast-growing species with bluish-green leaves and egg-shaped cones.	40-60 ft. (100 max.)
Larch, golden *(Pseudolarix)*			
P. amabilis	B	Needlelike leaves turn golden before dropping in fall. Light brown egg-shaped cones shatter. Not troubled by pests that generally attack true larches.	80-100 ft. (120 max.)
Maidenhair tree, or Ginkgo, see p. 54			
Monkey puzzle, see Araucaria			
Pine *(Pinus)*			
Aleppo *(P. halepensis)*	C	Pale green needles and 3-in.-long cones. Round form. Best in warm coastal areas.	50-60 ft.
Austrian *(P. nigra)*	A	Dark green needles. Pyramidal shape. Lives in alkaline soils. A fast grower.	70-90 ft.
Canary Island *(P. canariensis)*	C	Blue-green needles up to 1 ft. long turn light green. Good for stony, dry soil.	70-80 ft.
Italian stone *(P. pinea)*	C	Vivid green needles. Asymmetric shape. Not easy to transplant.	50-70 ft.
Japanese red *(P. densiflora)*	B	Easily recognized by orange-red color of trunk and older branches.	80-90 ft.
Japanese white *(P. parviflora)*	B	Long needles in clusters of 5 are usually toward ends of twigs.	60-75 ft.
Lacebark *(P. bungeana)*	B	Dark green needles grow in clusters of 3. May have more than 1 trunk. Multicolored bark peels to reveal cream-colored inner bark.	60-75 ft.
Limber *(P. flexilis)*	A	Stiff, dark green needles in threes. Cones are egg shaped. A slow grower.	50-70 ft.
Ponderosa *(P. ponderosa)*	B	Needles are in clusters of 2 or 3. A fast grower. Not for small gardens.	100-150 ft. (200 max.)
Red *(P. resinosa)*	A	Green needles, in pairs, are shiny. Bark is reddish. Grows rapidly even in poor soil.	60-75 ft.
Shore *(P. contorta)*	C	Develops many branches. Dark green needles are in pairs. Cones are 3 in. long. Forms rounded top. Grows in dry or wet soil.	25-30 ft.
Swiss stone *(P. cembra)*	A	Bluish-green needles in clusters of 5 are almost 5 in. long and abundantly produced. Forms dense, pyramidal shape. Seeds are edible.	50-75 ft.
Pine, umbrella *(Sciadopitys)*			
S. verticillata	B	Bears 2 types of leaves, some of which are scalelike and hardly recognizable as such. Other leaves are long, shiny green needles in umbrellalike clusters of up to 30. Does not do well in wind and dry soil. Very few pests. Slow grower.	60-80 ft. (120 max.)
Plum yew, see Yew, plum			
Redwood, coast *(Sequoia)*			
S. sempervirens	C	Evergreen needles about 1 in. long are in 2 rows. Cones are less than 1 in. Has straight, massive trunk. Does best in rainy, foggy areas.	80-100 ft. (360 max.)
Redwood, dawn *(Metasequoia)*			
M. glyptostroboides	B	Deciduous conifer. Needlelike leaves turn bronze in fall. In moist soils it may grow several feet taller each year. Trunks grow to 9 ft. in diameter.	80-100 ft. (115 max.)

Giant sequoia

Serbian spruce

Torreya californica (California nutmeg)

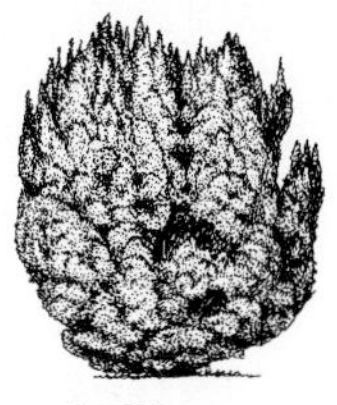
English yew

Chinese plum yew

Common and botanical names	Hardiness *(Map, p. 9)*	Decorative characteristics, special requirements, and remarks	Approximate height when mature
Sequoia, giant, or Big tree *(Sequoiadendron)*			
S. giganteum	□□[C]□	Among tallest and most massive-trunked trees known; some are up to 40 ft. in diameter. Has short scalelike needles and cones 2-3 in. long. Needs considerable rain and fog for proper growth.	100-150 ft. (300 max.)
Spruce *(Picea)*			
Colorado *(P. pungens)*	[A]□□□	Extremely hardy evergreen with sharp, bluish-green needles. Some varieties have silvery white or bluish-white needles. Susceptible to spruce gall aphid attacks. One of few spruces that can survive city conditions.	70-100 ft.
Dragon *(P. asperata)*	□[B]□□	Pale green to bluish needles stay on branches as long as 7 yr., making attractively dense form. Grayish-brown bark peels off.	60-75 ft.
Engelmann *(P. engelmannii)*	[A]□□□	Retains lower branches longer than many other spruces. Has bluish-green foliage. Needs great amount of room. Fine-looking, extremely hardy tree.	75-150 ft.
Norway *(P. abies,* or *P. excelsa)*	[A]□□□	Branches are pendulous at ends. Foliage is handsome deep green. Numerous varieties exist, including a few dwarf forms and one with dark yellow foliage. Grows rapidly when young.	150-165 ft.
Serbian *(P. omorika)*	[A]□□□	Branches become pendulous with age. Shiny green needles are flat and have 2 white stripes on undersides.	90-115 ft.
White *(P. glauca)*	[A]□□□	Moderately attractive evergreen with bluish-green foliage on ascending branches that droop at tips. Tolerates considerable drought and heat. Varieties encompass 1 dwarf and several compact growers.	70-90 ft.
Torreya *(Torreya)*			
California nutmeg *(T. californica)*	□[B]□□	Glossy green 2½-in.-long leaves are evergreen except in northernmost range, where they may drop in autumn. Green and purple fruits. Fissured bark.	50-75 ft.
Japanese *(T. nucifera)*	□[B]□□	Similar to *T. californica,* but thin evergreen leaves are only about half as long. Assumes pleasing pyramidal shape.	50-75 ft.
Yew *(Taxus)*			
English *(T. baccata)*	□□[C]□	Wide, rounded top. Will grow in shade or sun and can be sheared. Like all yews, susceptible to black vine weevils and other pests. Foliage and berries of all yews are poisonous if eaten.	20-40 ft. (60 max.)
Irish *(T. b. stricta,* or *T. b. fastigiata)*	□[B]□□	Many upright branches and dark green leaves spreading in all directions around the shoots distinguish this variety.	20-40 ft.
Japanese *(T. cuspidata capitata)*	□[B]□□	Female bears bright scarlet berries. Faster growing and hardier than *T. baccata.* Some forms of *T. cuspidata* are also denser and spread more.	30-40 ft. (50 max.)
Yew, plum *(Cephalotaxus)*			
Chinese *(C. fortunei)*	□□[C]□	Green needlelike leaves are borne on branches that are pendulous at tips. Fleshy egg-shaped fruits are purple, ripening in second season. Not for use where summers are hot and dry. Good choice near seacoast.	15-20 ft. (30 max.)

Dwarf Conifers for Borders and Rock Gardens

Many conifers are available in dwarf forms, ranging from a few inches to 2 feet or more in height, making them ideal for rock gardens, foundation plantings, containers, and other areas where space is limited.

Actually, with a few exceptions, such as the prostrate juniper, the term "dwarf" does not relate to ultimate height but to an extremely slow rate of growth. If purchased when they are a few inches high, these conifers can be counted on to remain miniatures for many years.

To determine whether a dwarf conifer can reasonably be expected to survive the lowest average temperature in your area, check the zone designation for that conifer in the Hardiness column. Then refer to the Temperature Zone Map on page 9.

The special needs of dwarf conifers are the same as for large conifers except where otherwise stated.

Arborvitae (*Thuja occidentalis caespitosa*)

Hiba arborvitae (***Thujopsis dolabrata nana***)

Cedar (***Cedrus deodara aurea pendula***)

Cryptomeria japonica vilmoriniana

False cypress (*Chamaecyparis lawsoniana minima aurea*)

Fir (***Abies balsamea hudsonia***)

Common and botanical names	Hardiness (*Map, p. 9*)	Decorative characteristics, special requirements, and remarks
Arborvitae (*Thuja*)		
T. occidentalis caespitosa	A	This is a true miniature with rounded shape and drooping green to yellow leaves. Excellent rock-garden plant.
T. o. 'Hetz Midget'	A	Although similar to *T. o. caespitosa,* this variety has golden foliage.
T. o. 'Rheingold'	A	Yellow-green foliage in summer, turning coppery in winter. After 30 yr. 6 ft. high. Pyramidal habit of growth.
T. orientalis aurea nana	B	Yellow-green leaves are borne on vertical sprays. Rounded shape. Dense branching habit of growth. Fine rock-garden plant.
T. plicata cuprea	B	Golden new growth changes to green. Conical shape. Less than 2 ft. high.
Arborvitae, hiba, or false (*Thujopsis*)		
T. dolabrata nana	B	This slow grower bears shiny 1/8-in. leaves on narrow branches. After 50 yr. it may not be taller than 2 ft. or wider than 8 ft.
Cedar (*Cedrus*)		
C. atlantica glauca pendula	B	Handsome bluish-green foliage hangs from gracefully drooping branches.
C. deodara aurea pendula	C	Foliage is light yellow in spring, turning golden later in season. Almost prostrate. New shoots with upright habit of growth should be pruned out.
Cryptomeria (*Cryptomeria*)		
C. japonica compressa	B	A mounded plant with dense, ascending branches and branchlets. Leaves in juvenile form are small and quite fine; in adult form they are long and recurved. At 30 yr. less than 2 ft. high, 2½ ft. wide.
C. j. cristata	B	Tips of new growth are contorted with thickly clustered leaves. Rounded cones are about 1 in. in diameter.
C. j. globosa nana	B	Foliage is light green. When young, plant is cone shaped, but with maturity shape becomes more rounded.
C. j. vilmoriniana	B	During winter foliage turns an attractive dark reddish bronze. A slow grower that develops a dense, rounded shape.
Cypress, false (*Chamaecyparis*)		
C. lawsoniana minima aurea	B	Tips of new growth are bright yellow but turn yellowish green to green the following year. Branches are twisted. With age shape changes from rounded to conical.
C. l. m. glauca	B	Leaves are gray-green to bluish, and twisted branches form rounded shape.
C. pisifera nana	B	Leaves form in small fanned clusters. Plant is rounded when young, spreading at base and rising to form dome at center as it matures.
Fir (*Abies*)		
A. balsamea hudsonia	A	Rounded leaves are dark green, scented, and nearly 1 in. long. Horizontal growth of young branches produces flat-topped profile. This variety can be planted where soil is somewhat alkaline.
A. koreana prostrata	B	Leaves are a glossy gray-green above, silvery beneath. This is low-spreading form of Korean fir. At 14 yr. 2 ft. high, 4 ft. wide.
A. lasiocarpa compacta	B	Silver-blue leaves are 1½ in. long. Pale grayish branches are corky. Symmetrical branching forms wide conical profile.
A. procera prostrata	A	Bluish foliage displays waxy sheen. Branches spread horizontally in asymmetrical pattern, producing pleasing informal effect.

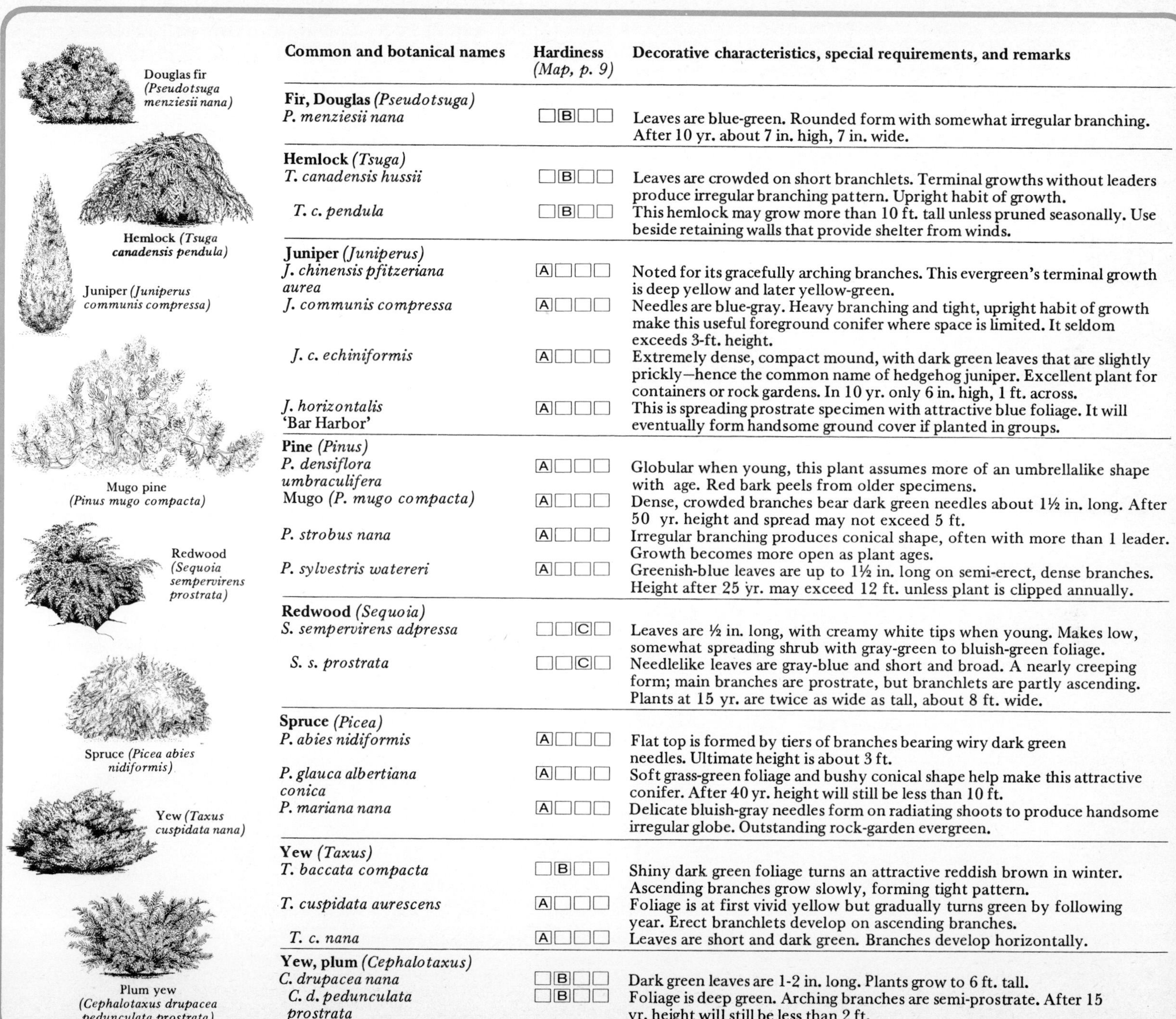

Douglas fir (*Pseudotsuga menziesii nana*)

Hemlock (*Tsuga canadensis pendula*)

Juniper (*Juniperus communis compressa*)

Mugo pine (*Pinus mugo compacta*)

Redwood (*Sequoia sempervirens prostrata*)

Spruce (*Picea abies nidiformis*)

Yew (*Taxus cuspidata nana*)

Plum yew (*Cephalotaxus drupacea pedunculata prostrata*)

Common and botanical names	Hardiness (*Map, p. 9*)	Decorative characteristics, special requirements, and remarks
Fir, Douglas (*Pseudotsuga*)		
P. menziesii nana	B	Leaves are blue-green. Rounded form with somewhat irregular branching. After 10 yr. about 7 in. high, 7 in. wide.
Hemlock (*Tsuga*)		
T. canadensis hussii	B	Leaves are crowded on short branchlets. Terminal growths without leaders produce irregular branching pattern. Upright habit of growth.
T. c. pendula	B	This hemlock may grow more than 10 ft. tall unless pruned seasonally. Use beside retaining walls that provide shelter from winds.
Juniper (*Juniperus*)		
J. chinensis pfitzeriana aurea	A	Noted for its gracefully arching branches. This evergreen's terminal growth is deep yellow and later yellow-green.
J. communis compressa	A	Needles are blue-gray. Heavy branching and tight, upright habit of growth make this useful foreground conifer where space is limited. It seldom exceeds 3-ft. height.
J. c. echiniformis	A	Extremely dense, compact mound, with dark green leaves that are slightly prickly—hence the common name of hedgehog juniper. Excellent plant for containers or rock gardens. In 10 yr. only 6 in. high, 1 ft. across.
J. horizontalis 'Bar Harbor'	A	This is spreading prostrate specimen with attractive blue foliage. It will eventually form handsome ground cover if planted in groups.
Pine (*Pinus*)		
P. densiflora umbraculifera	A	Globular when young, this plant assumes more of an umbrellalike shape with age. Red bark peels from older specimens.
Mugo (*P. mugo compacta*)	A	Dense, crowded branches bear dark green needles about 1½ in. long. After 50 yr. height and spread may not exceed 5 ft.
P. strobus nana	A	Irregular branching produces conical shape, often with more than 1 leader. Growth becomes more open as plant ages.
P. sylvestris watereri	A	Greenish-blue leaves are up to 1½ in. long on semi-erect, dense branches. Height after 25 yr. may exceed 12 ft. unless plant is clipped annually.
Redwood (*Sequoia*)		
S. sempervirens adpressa	C	Leaves are ½ in. long, with creamy white tips when young. Makes low, somewhat spreading shrub with gray-green to bluish-green foliage.
S. s. prostrata	C	Needlelike leaves are gray-blue and short and broad. A nearly creeping form; main branches are prostrate, but branchlets are partly ascending. Plants at 15 yr. are twice as wide as tall, about 8 ft. wide.
Spruce (*Picea*)		
P. abies nidiformis	A	Flat top is formed by tiers of branches bearing wiry dark green needles. Ultimate height is about 3 ft.
P. glauca albertiana conica	A	Soft grass-green foliage and bushy conical shape help make this attractive conifer. After 40 yr. height will still be less than 10 ft.
P. mariana nana	A	Delicate bluish-gray needles form on radiating shoots to produce handsome irregular globe. Outstanding rock-garden evergreen.
Yew (*Taxus*)		
T. baccata compacta	B	Shiny dark green foliage turns an attractive reddish brown in winter. Ascending branches grow slowly, forming tight pattern.
T. cuspidata aurescens	A	Foliage is at first vivid yellow but gradually turns green by following year. Erect branchlets develop on ascending branches.
T. c. nana	A	Leaves are short and dark green. Branches develop horizontally.
Yew, plum (*Cephalotaxus*)		
C. drupacea nana	B	Dark green leaves are 1-2 in. long. Plants grow to 6 ft. tall.
C. d. pedunculata prostrata	B	Foliage is deep green. Arching branches are semi-prostrate. After 15 yr. height will still be less than 2 ft.

Shrubs and Vines

Shrubs are among the garden's most versatile plants, not only serving as a background to other displays but providing their own varying colors and textures.

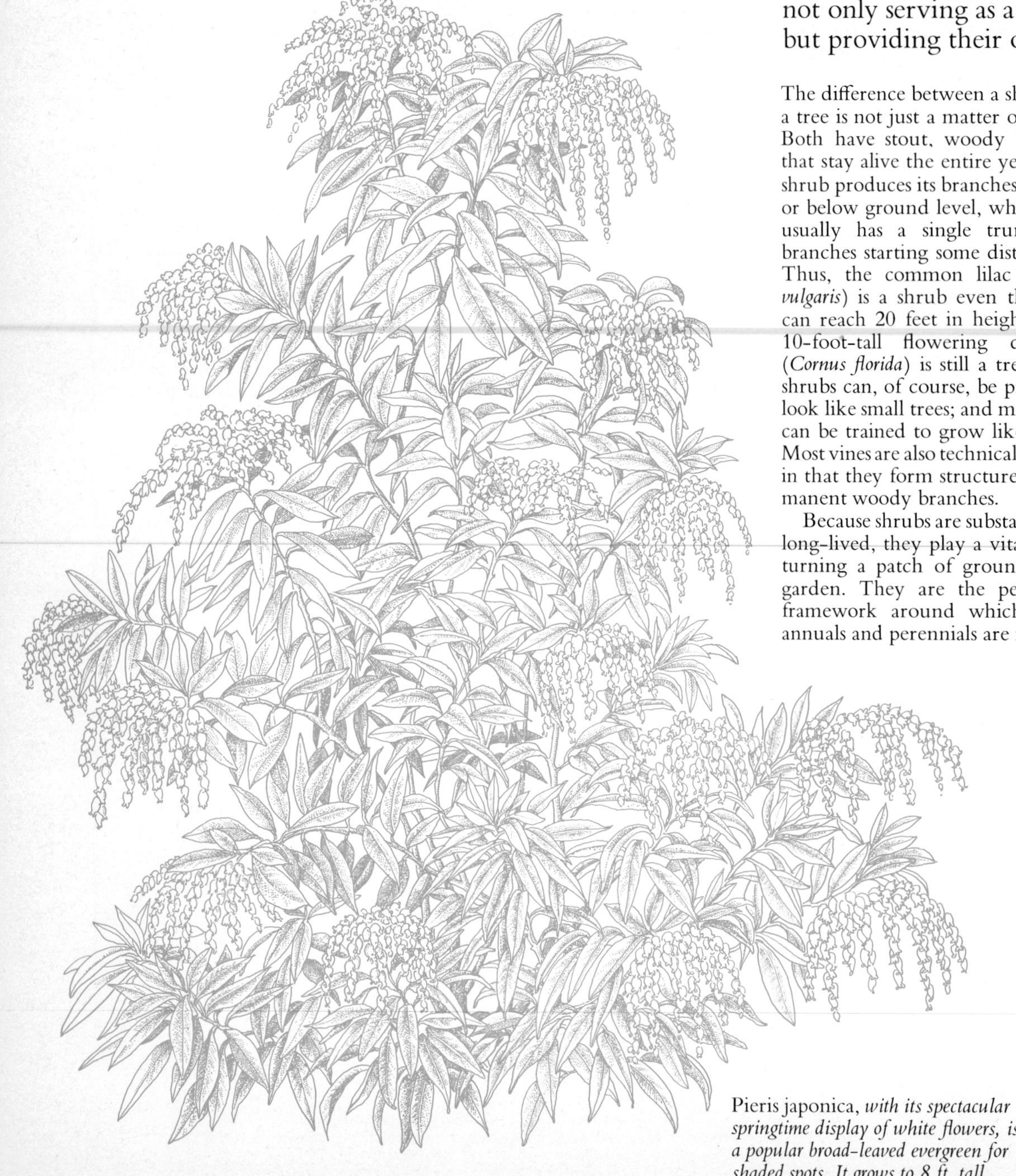

Pieris japonica, *with its spectacular springtime display of white flowers, is a popular broad-leaved evergreen for shaded spots. It grows to 8 ft. tall.*

The difference between a shrub and a tree is not just a matter of height. Both have stout, woody branches that stay alive the entire year, but a shrub produces its branches at, near, or below ground level, while a tree usually has a single trunk with branches starting some distance up. Thus, the common lilac (*Syringa vulgaris*) is a shrub even though it can reach 20 feet in height, and a 10-foot-tall flowering dogwood (*Cornus florida*) is still a tree. Large shrubs can, of course, be pruned to look like small trees; and many trees can be trained to grow like shrubs. Most vines are also technically shrubs in that they form structures of permanent woody branches.

Because shrubs are substantial and long-lived, they play a vital role in turning a patch of ground into a garden. They are the permanent framework around which showy annuals and perennials are interwoven year by year. A garden without them lacks emphasis and variety, and in the winter is reduced to a flat and lifeless plain. With their leaves, flowers, berries—and sometimes even with brightly colored bark—shrubs and vines provide visual interest in all seasons.

Deciduous or evergreen. A deciduous plant drops its leaves in the fall or, in warm and semi-desert areas, at the beginning of the dry season; it spends the winter in bare-framed dormancy and leafs out again each spring. Compared with evergreens, which retain their foliage all winter, many deciduous shrubs make up for their wintry drabness with a spectacular spring or summer show of flowers, and perhaps with an autumnal display of colored leaves as well. Many gardeners value deciduous shrubs because they *do* change with the seasons. Also, most deciduous shrubs are less expensive than evergreens and grow more rapidly.

Evergreens provide winter color, of course, and offer certain other advantages: many kinds thrive in shady places; the tone and texture of their foliage make an interesting contrast to the more flamboyant deciduous shrubs and flowering annuals; and they give the landscape year-round stability.

There are broad-leaved evergreens, and there are those with needles. Generally speaking, the farther south you go, the wider choice of broad-leaved evergreens you will have. Most tropical and subtropical shrubs are evergreen, and in the country's Sun Belt of the Deep South, Southwest, and Pacific Coast, they constitute the majority of garden shrubbery. Some kinds, like the magnolias, are represented in the South by evergreens but have deciduous species that grow well in the

North. Others, such as the California privet (*Ligustrum ovalifolium*), lose their foliage only in regions where bitter winter storms denude their branches. And some, like the mountain laurel (*Kalmia latifolia*) and *Rhododendron maximum,* stay green almost everywhere.

Most needle evergreens tend to flourish in more northerly climates, although there are several exceptions to this rule. Such evergreen plants as the creeping juniper (*Juniperus horizontalis*) are common in the South.

The zone map on page 9 is a guide to choosing shrubs that will be winter hardy in your locale.

Other variables will affect your choice: the composition of the soil—sandy, loamy, or clayey; its acid-alkaline balance; the degree of humidity and amount of precipitation where you live; the amount of sun the plant will receive; elevation; and if you live by the sea, the special problems posed by salt spray. For help with these questions, turn to the chart on page 119, which describes the characteristics and requirements of the commonest shrubs. For more specific information, consult a reputable nurseryman in your area, or get in touch with the county extension agent of the U.S. Department of Agriculture.

Uses of shrubs. A shrub may be upright, rounded, weeping, or spreading. The shape you choose depends largely on the use you plan to make of the plant in your garden.

If, for example, you need a hedge to act as a windbreak, the tough, upright bayberry (*Myrica pensylvanica*) makes sense. The English boxwood (*Buxus sempervirens*), rounded and quite tolerant of pruning, is a good choice for a low boundary hedge. If yours is a small garden and you want a shrub to brighten a corner, there is no point in planting a rounded viburnum, which will have outgrown its elbowroom long before it reaches a respectable height. If you have space and you want to mask a compost heap or some such eyesore, look for a large evergreen, such as a myrtle (*Myrtus communis*), rhododendron, mountain laurel (*Kalmia latifolia*), holly (*Ilex*), yew (*Taxus*), or an upright form of juniper. Deciduous shrubs might do the job in the summer but would be considerably less effective in other seasons, when their branches are bare.

Ideally used, shrubs serve to define and delineate space in a garden. They guide the eye toward what the gardener wants highlighted, and they guide the feet along the paths he wants followed. In a small garden they can create the illusion of depth, and in an open space they can form cozy nooks. The effects depend on the imagination and skill with which the shrubs are planted.

Many shrubs, ground covers, and vines can be useful for disguising unattractive parts of a garden or home. A prostrate juniper will spread over a manhole cover and still allow for removal of the cover. A chain-link fence will seem to disappear under a covering of *Wisteria floribunda*. Various climbing varieties of evergreen English ivy (*Hedera helix*) will do the same job in mild climates or will turn a dull cement-block wall into a living green backdrop for plants with flowers. An evergreen honeysuckle (*Lonicera nitida*) that is fan trained on a trellis will hide trash cans, a compost heap, tool shed, or

Wisteria, a hardy and long-lived deciduous vine, can grow to 100 ft. and has fragrant flower clusters in late spring, early summer.

whatever, and it will fill the air with its fragrance as well.

Many shrubs have this bonus of sweet-scented flowers; beneath or around your windows is, therefore, a good place for them. Lilacs, mock oranges, and some viburnums are all good for this purpose. They will also do a great deal to add to the pleasure of your terrace, patio, or swimming-pool area.

Shady parts of a garden are no problem for shrubs if you use the right ones. Witch hazel (*Hamamelis virginiana*) and hydrangea are two that actually prefer partial shade. Many others, such as the daphne, magnolia, skimmia, and many viburnums, do very well without the benefit of full sun.

Designing for color. Shrubs are a major part of a garden's color scheme, and because they are permanent fixtures, their placement must be carefully planned.

You must decide before planting whether adjacent shrubs should be in flower at the same time, and if so, how well the colors of their blossoms will combine. You must choose among the constant evergreens, sparked by occasional flowers and berries, and the ever-changing deciduous shrubs; and you must decide whether or not the two types should be blended or planted in separate groupings.

The possible color combinations of shrubs in a garden are nearly infinite, and in choosing one over another the gardener comes into his own as a landscape artist.

Your choice of color is obviously a question of your own taste. Still, certain combinations will always work and are worth considering. The association of gray foliage and white flowers, for instance, is particularly effective near water. Gray-foliaged shrubs are also useful for separating brightly colored ones that might otherwise clash. One of the finest of these is *Elaeagnus commutata,* whose silvery foliage seems to shimmer in the sun.

The combination of blue- and white-flowered shrubs against a brick wall makes a pleasant contrast. This effect could easily be achieved by grouping together one or more plants each of a blue- and a white-flowered variety of butterfly bush (*Buddleja davidii*), which blooms in late summer.

Rather than grouping shrubs in strong color contrasts, it is often better to choose a toning sequence of colors, using shades of silver, gray, and pink, or perhaps a blending of blue, mauve, rose, purple, and white.

However, bright effects should not be dismissed, and there is at least one such effect that only the right shrubs can provide. The combination of the spring heath (*Erica carnea*), with its flowers of bright purple or red, used as a ground cover beneath a witch hazel, with its bright yellow flowers, makes a spectacular splash of color late in the fall and even into winter, when there is little other color in the garden.

Clever use of color can mean more than appealing visual effects, however. It can also alter the perspective of your garden. Using soft colors near the end of the garden, for example, tends to disguise the boundary limits and to give the illusion of depth. This effect is heightened by using brighter-colored foliage in the foreground and middle distance.

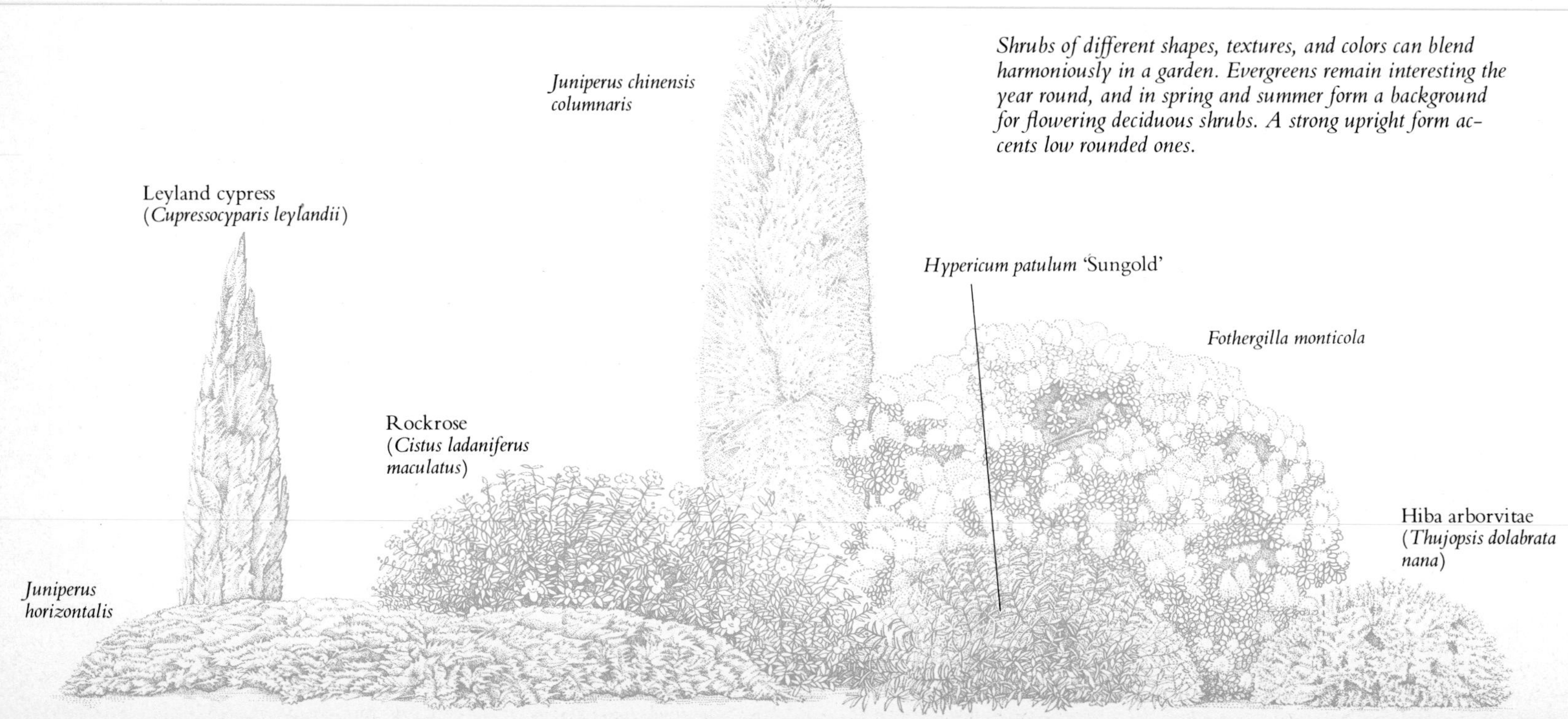

Shrubs of different shapes, textures, and colors can blend harmoniously in a garden. Evergreens remain interesting the year round, and in spring and summer form a background for flowering deciduous shrubs. A strong upright form accents low rounded ones.

Planting and Supporting Shrubs

How to Space and Plant Freestanding Shrubs

Shrubs are supplied by nurseries in three forms: container grown, with balled roots, or with bare roots.

Container shrubs are established plants growing in pots of soil or soil substitute. They can be planted outdoors at any time of year except in the dead of winter. If you plant in summer, keep the soil well watered until autumn. Newly planted shrubs may die if the soil dries out.

Balled-root shrubs have some soil around the roots, kept in place by burlap. Plants that have difficulty establishing themselves are sold this way to keep the root systems intact. Shrubs that can develop easily after transplanting are often sold with bare roots.

Bare-root and balled-root shrubs are best planted in autumn or early winter after dormancy has set in but before the ground is frozen, or early in the spring. Evergreens can be set out earlier in the fall or later in the spring than can deciduous shrubs. The latter, if they are not fully dormant, can have their seasonal cycle upset by the shock of transplanting and put forth easily damaged new growth at the wrong time.

First, you must prepare the soil. Remove perennial weeds from the bed with a garden fork. Dig over the soil to one spade's depth, and if possible, let it settle for about two weeks. If you must plant immediately, firm the whole bed thoroughly by treading it down.

If you are planting more than one shrub, work out the spacing beforehand and mark the planting positions. The space between shrubs should be at least half the total of their combined ultimate spread. For example, two shrubs expected to spread 4 feet and 6 feet, respectively, should be planted about 5 feet apart.

Remove the marker. Dig a hole as deep as and slightly wider than the shrub's container or root ball. If the plant is bare rooted, allow room for its roots to spread comfortably.

Measure for depth against the plant itself. With a container-grown shrub, the surface of the soil in the pot should be level with the surrounding soil. With balled- or bare-root shrubs, use the mark on the stem that indicates the former soil level. Do not cut away the burlap around a balled-root shrub.

Mix the soil from the hole with well-rotted compost, manure, or peat moss—2 parts of the soil to 1 part of the organic material. Break up the soil at the bottom of the hole. Trim the top growth of the shrub as illustrated below.

If the shrub is container grown, water it well before removing the container. Make sure that the plant has an extensive root system. If it does not, return it to the nursery.

If your shrub is bare rooted, look for damaged or diseased roots and cut them back to healthy growth. Before putting the plant in the hole, make a small mound on the bottom over which to spread the roots.

When you set the shrub in the hole, hold it firmly by the base of the stem to keep it vertical while you fill in the hole with the prepared soil. With a container-grown or balled-root shrub, fill the hole about halfway; then water thoroughly and let the water settle before filling to the top. Tread the soil firmly. Top with more soil and tread again. Then soak well all around the base of the plant.

With a bare-root shrub, lift the plant up and down as you fill the hole, gently shaking the roots so that the soil will settle around them. Firm the soil with your feet several times to eliminate air pockets.

1. *Check hole for depth. The base of the stem should be at soil level.*

2. *Add peat moss or manure to the excavated soil. Loosen soil at bottom.*

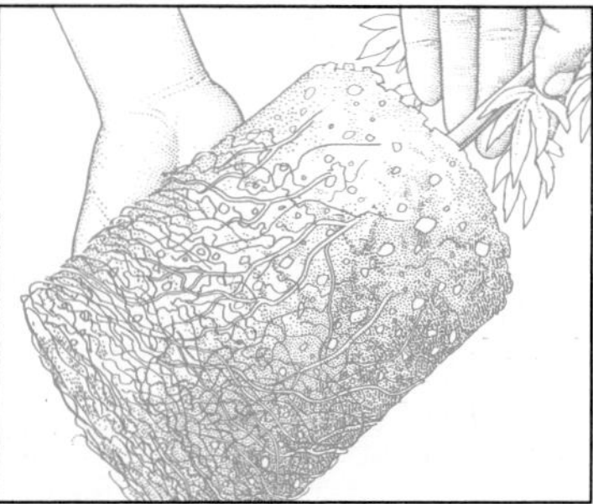

3. *Water well and remove container. Make sure roots are well developed.*

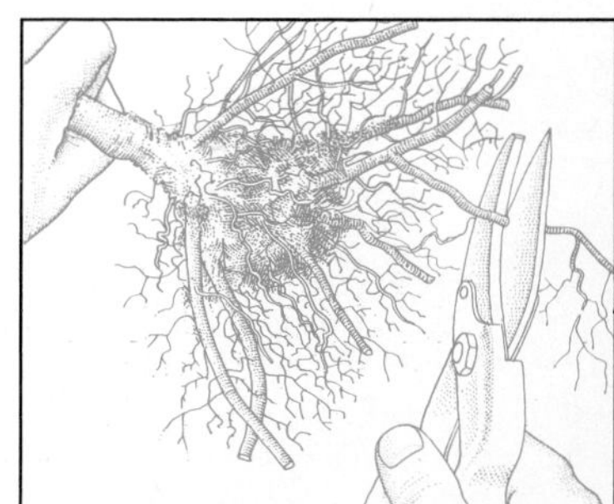

4. *With a bare-root shrub, cut back all damaged and diseased roots.*

5. *Hold plant firmly in place. Fill in the hole, eliminating air pockets.*

6. *Tread the soil and add more until it is level all around. Soak thoroughly.*

7. *With all shrubs, prune stumps of old wood flush with the stem.*

8. *Remove damaged or diseased wood. Always cut just above a bud.*

Planting a Climbing Vine Against a Wall or Fence

The soil at the foot of a wall or fence is often too dry for planting without preparation. This is particularly true if the structure serves as a shield against prevailing winds, since the leeward side gets less rain. And because semi-hardy vines should never be planted in cold, exposed positions, the leeward side of a wall or fence is the best location for them.

Plant self-supporting vines about 3 inches from the wall, supported vines about 6 inches. The soil may need to be made more moisture retentive by the addition of organic matter. Mulch plants to conserve moisture.

Most ivies, Virginia creepers, and climbing hydrangeas fasten themselves to walls with little or no assistance. Other vines may need the support of a trellis or horizontal wires.

Rigid plastic netting with mesh sizes of 4–6 inches provides a good support. The large mesh simplifies training and tying, and the plastic surface reduces the risk of damage to young growth from chafing.

Put supports in place before planting—about an inch from the wall so that the growing vine can twine around them.

Most plants tend to grow away from a wall; so attach young shoots to their supports as soon as possible after planting. Use string, strips of cloth, twist ties, or plant rings. Do not use bare wire, as it can cut and bruise stems. After this, shoots should start to twine themselves around the support without further help.

1. *Dig the hole 12 in. from base of wall, and spread the roots outward.*

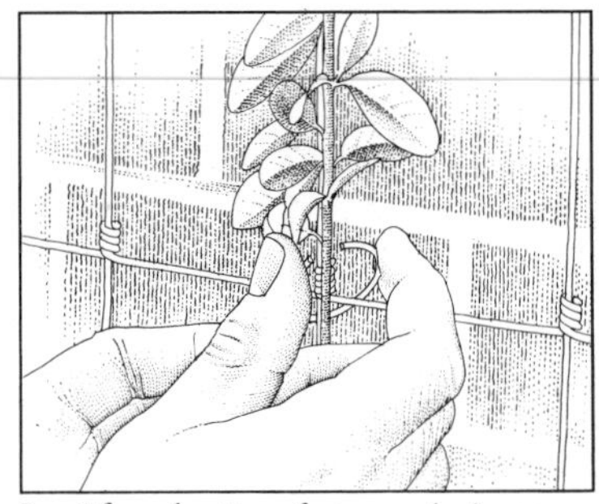

2. *After planting, fasten each shoot to supports with string or plant rings.*

Staking Shrubs Vulnerable to Wind Damage

If a columnar shrub more than 3 feet tall is growing in an exposed, wind-buffeted position, it may require staking after planting.

The stake should be stout and long enough to reach just below the head of the shrub. You can buy stakes from nurseries or garden centers; they are usually treated with preservatives before sale. Do not use untreated stakes, which may rot.

Drive the stake in close to the base of the shrub, taking care to minimize root damage. Then, fasten the shrub, either with a tree tie, sold for the purpose, or a strip of strong cloth.

Tree ties have built-in pads of plastic or hard rubber to keep the stake from damaging the stem of the shrub through abrasion. You can accomplish the same purpose with cloth strips tied in a figure-eight pattern—around the stem, around the stake, and back again—until the tie is both firm and cushioned.

One tie at the top should be enough for a shrub less than 6 feet tall. Taller plants need another tie about halfway down the stake.

Inspect the stem in midsummer and again every autumn to see if the ties have become constrictive. If they are too tight, retie them.

TWO WAYS TO TIE A SHRUB

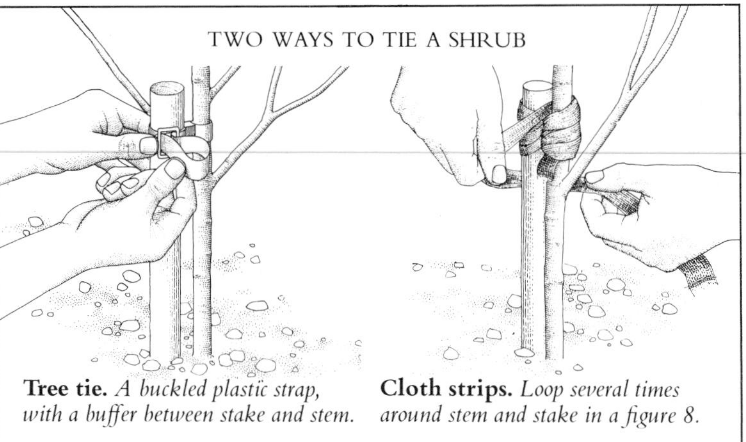

Tree tie. *A buckled plastic strap, with a buffer between stake and stem.*

Cloth strips. *Loop several times around stem and stake in a figure 8.*

Planting a Shrub in a Lawn

A shrub grown in a lawn looks best if its bed is cut neatly out of the turf. You can do this job by making a sort of compass out of a small bamboo or dowel stake, a piece of string, and a sharp knife.

Insert the stake into the grass at the center of the proposed bed, tie the string to it, mark off the radius of the bed on the string, and tie the knife at that point. Then, holding the string taut, score the circumference of the bed on the lawn. Reinforce the scoring by chopping it further with a spade. Slice the sod into sections and remove it, stacking it to one side for later use in planting.

Dig the bed, and plant the shrub in the normal way. The sections of sod, placed grass-side-down in the bottom of the planting hole, add valuable humus to the soil.

The size of the bed should finally be about equal to the spread of the fully grown shrub, but you can start with a small bed and enlarge it a little at a time as the shrub grows.

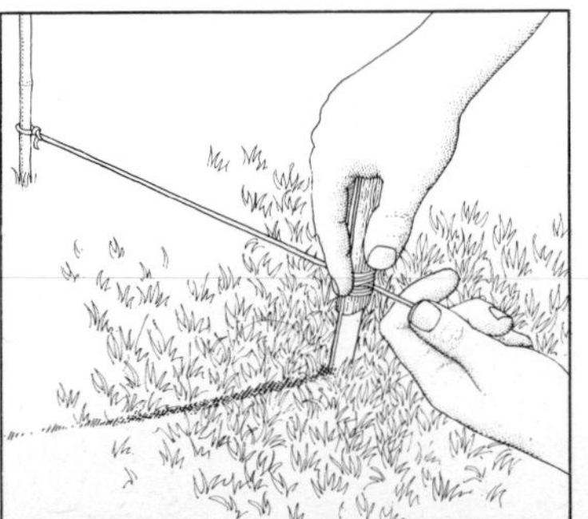

1. *Mark out a circular bed, using a knife on a string attached to a peg.*

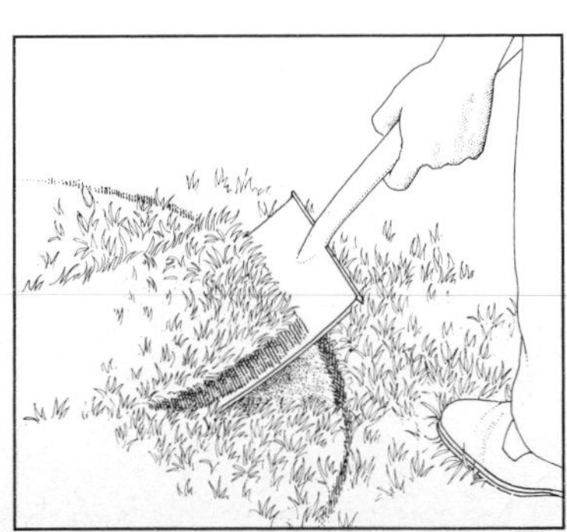

2. *Slice out the sod with a spade. Save sod for its value as plant food.*

Growing Shrubs in Containers

False cypress (*Chamaecyparis lawsoniana minima aurea*)

Lavender (*Lavandula officinalis*)

Hypericum calycinum

Mexican orange (*Choisya ternata*)

Rhododendron 'Mary Fleming'

Many of the most decorative shrubs can be grown in large pots or tubs to adorn your patio or terrace. The fact that the roots are restricted may actually improve flowering.

Not all shrubs respond well to container culture, however; the magnolia and large forms of daphne, for example, do not. In general avoid kinds with thick, fleshy roots.

Some shrubs that grow particularly well in containers include the aucuba, barberry, bluebeard, camellia, clematis, smaller forms of cotoneaster, deutzia, escallonia, euonymus, fire thorn, flowering currant, forsythia, hebe, honeysuckle, hypericum, jasmine, kerria, lilac, mahonia, Mexican orange, passionflower, prunus, rockrose, spirea, tamarix, weigela, and wisteria.

Planting. A shrub expected to grow 4–5 feet tall and 3–4 feet wide will need a tub at least $2\frac{1}{2}$ feet wide by $1\frac{1}{2}$ feet deep. If there are no drainage holes in the bottom, you can make them with a drill.

Begin with a layer of drainage material 1–$1\frac{1}{2}$ inches deep. Broken clay pots, large pebbles, or coarse gravel are frequently used.

Add a layer of potting soil or soil substitute deep enough so that when the plant is placed on it the base of the stem will be level with the rim of the tub. You can mix your own soil from 3 parts peat moss to 1 part coarse sand. Add about 4 tablespoons of all-purpose fertilizer per bushel.

Make sure that the root ball is moist and the root system is good before setting the shrub in the container. Fill in around the shrub with more of the prepared planting mix.

Firm it down well; then fill with more soil mix to $\frac{1}{2}$ inch below the rim. Water thoroughly, let the water settle, and soak the soil again.

Care and feeding. Confined roots cannot seek out water; so you must bring it to them. Water well whenever the soil surface dries out.

A year after planting—and again monthly or if the leaves seem small and discolored or when growth is meager—apply a liquid fertilizer.

Shrubs that tend to grow large can be kept small and healthy by annual or biannual root pruning. In any case, maintaining a healthy shrub requires pruning both the top growth and the roots in autumn or early spring every four to six years. Remove the shrub and strip about 4 inches of roots and soil from the root ball. Scrub the container and repot with fresh soil mix.

PLANTING IN A TUB

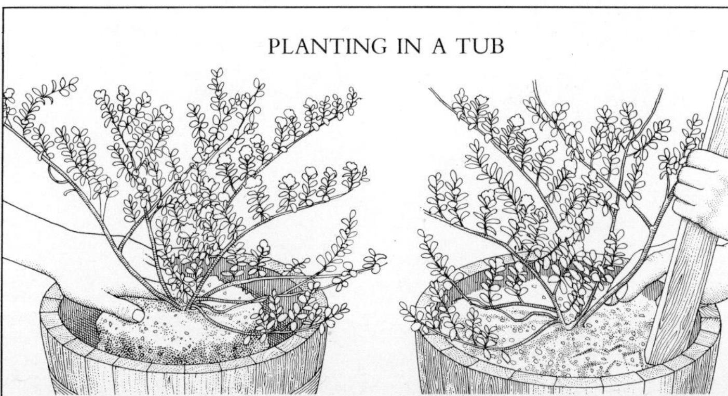

1. *Plant in a large tub. Set the base of the stem level with the rim.*

2. *Firm the soil down thoroughly with a piece of wood. Water well.*

PRUNING THE SHRUB

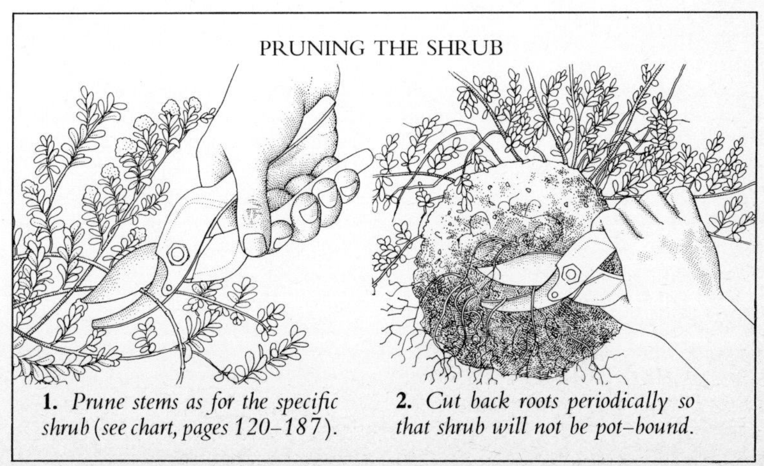

1. *Prune stems as for the specific shrub (see chart, pages 120–187).*

2. *Cut back roots periodically so that shrub will not be pot-bound.*

Care and Protection of Shrubs All Year Round

Mulching, Watering, and Feeding New Shrubs

Soon after planting, while the soil is still moist, spread mulch about 2 inches thick between and around the shrubs. This will retain moisture in the soil and help to keep down weeds. If you use an organic mulch, such as leaf mold, straw, or bark chips, it will feed the plants in later years also, as it breaks down and is absorbed into the soil. Spread a thick, fresh layer of mulch each spring.

If a shrub is planted in autumn, winter, or early spring, watering after the first watering-in will probably be unnecessary—unless, of course, the plant starts to wilt during a long dry spell. If you plant in late spring or summer, however, the shrub will probably need to be watered frequently during the first few weeks to help it get established.

Late winter or very early in the spring is the time to add nutrition to the soil in the form of an all-purpose granulated fertilizer. Clear away any remaining mulch, and sprinkle the fertilizer around the plant at the rate of about 1 cup per square yard or less, depending on the quality of the soil. Work the granules into the soil with a hoe.

After planting and whenever pests appear, spray with the appropriate pesticide. Do this on a dry day but not in bright sun.

MULCHING

Spread peat moss, leaf mold, or similar material to retain moisture after planting.

Always water thoroughly after planting. Use a nozzle to break the flow of water.

Protecting Tender Shrubs in Winter

The zone map on page 9 defines four regions in terms of average low temperatures. You can extend the effective range of some shrubs by sheltering them from extreme cold, especially from freezing winds, which do the most damage.

The first consideration is to choose a sheltered position at planting time—on the south side of a high wall or fence, for example, or behind a dense evergreen hedge. Shade-tolerant shrubs will also be protected from the worst winds if they are planted among trees.

But shelter is not always enough. During severe cold spells, tender shrubs will need to be blanketed with a material that will offer additional protection from wind and cold. Straw serves the purpose, as do boughs of needle evergreens; evergreen boughs from discarded Christmas trees can also be used.

With a large shrub, wrap the material around the branches, and bind with sheets of burlap tied with twine. Plants, like fuchsias, that regularly produce shoots from the base must also be protected in this vital area. Put a 6- to 9-inch layer of straw, peat moss, or even coarse sand around the base of the plant in late autumn, and leave it there until spring.

Wall shrubs and vines can be protected by removable mats made of chicken wire and straw. Simply sandwich the straw tightly in a 4- to 5-inch layer between two sheets of the chicken wire; then join the edges of the sheets by twisting the wires together. In bad weather hang the mats in front of the plants.

The same device can be used for small freestanding shrubs. Shape each mat into a cylinder, and stand it on end like a collar around the shrub. You can also top the cylinder with a lid of similar construction.

An alternative is to make a tepee from about six bamboo canes tied together at the top. Loop string around the tepee halfway down, and stuff this framework with evergreen boughs or straw; or simply cover the tepee with a sheet of burlap.

A fair amount of protection can be given evergreens by spraying in fall and winter with an antidesiccant to prevent excessive moisture loss.

Strong slatted wooden frames over evergreens protect them from any snow that may slide off a roof.

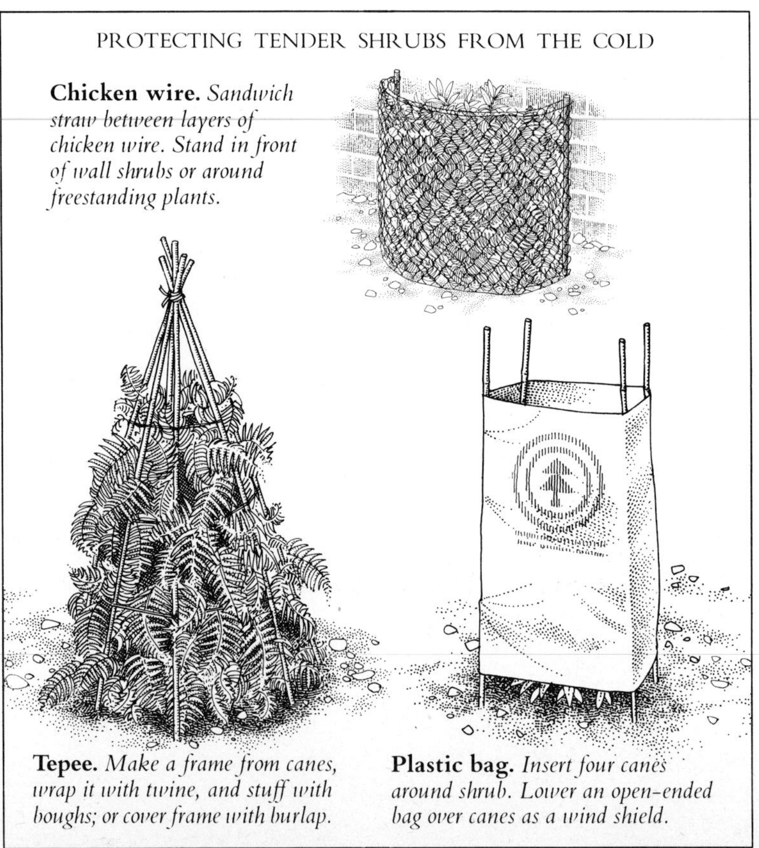

PROTECTING TENDER SHRUBS FROM THE COLD

Chicken wire. *Sandwich straw between layers of chicken wire. Stand in front of wall shrubs or around freestanding plants.*

Tepee. *Make a frame from canes, wrap it with twine, and stuff with boughs; or cover frame with burlap.*

Plastic bag. *Insert four canes around shrub. Lower an open-ended bag over canes as a wind shield.*

Removing Unwanted Suckers From Shrubs

A sucker is a shoot that grows from the plant base or belowground.

On most shrubs suckers are simply part of the plant and can be left in place. But a shrub that has been grafted onto a different rootstock can be weakened by the growth of suckers, and they should be removed. Shrubs likely to produce this sort of sucker include hollies, magnolias, camellias, rhododendrons, and lilacs.

An unwanted sucker is put forth by the rootstock; so it always appears below the union, the point where the graft has been made. With shrubs the union is usually planted below the surface; so suckers spring from belowground.

In all cases trace the sucker to its point of origin and wrench it off by hand. Do not cut it off aboveground, as this will simply encourage the growth of more suckers.

REMOVING SUCKERS

Dig to where the sucker joins the plant; then wrench it off.

Improving Your Berry Crop

Many shrubs and some trees are grown primarily for the colored berries or fruit they produce in autumn or winter. Poor crops can be caused by various factors.

In the first place, some varieties produce more abundant crops than others of the same species. Check with your nurseryman when you buy. (And buy only from well-established sources.)

The right growing conditions are also important. A sun-loving shrub, such as the fire thorn, can grow in the shade, but it will flower and fruit poorly. A shrub's affinity for acid or alkaline soil should also be noted.

Some shrubs are dioecious—that is, the male and female flowers grow on separate plants—and cross-pollination has to occur before fruit will form. Plant dioecious shrubs—such as hollies, skimmias, and aucubas—in groups of three or more females, with a male plant in the center of the group to ensure pollination.

Weather conditions can affect each year's crop. If a plant suffers drought at flowering time or as its berries are forming, either flowers or fruits can drop prematurely. Frost at flowering time can prevent the formation of fruit altogether. Even dreary and chilly weather at flowering time can make bees and other pollinating insects sluggish, thus damaging the crop.

Birds, too, can damage berry crops severely. In the winter finches may eat buds that would flower the following year. Thrushes and mourning doves may eat ripening fruits. If birds are a problem, about the only method of control is to cover shrubs with netting or black cotton.

The cotoneaster is particularly valued for its showy bunches of berries, which are bright red in most species and persist from autumn well into winter.

Transplanting a Healthy, Established Shrub

An established shrub can be transplanted from early autumn to late spring provided the soil is neither frozen nor waterlogged.

The main danger in transplanting is that the roots can be badly damaged. To avoid this, dig deeply all the way around the shrub near the perimeter of the foliage. It is better to take too much soil than not enough.

Lever the shrub out with a shovel; then crumble away the surplus soil to lighten the load and reduce the size of the new planting hole.

Plant as though you were putting in a new balled-root shrub (see p. 81). Water thoroughly.

1. *Dig a trench around the shrub to avoid root damage, and pry it out.*

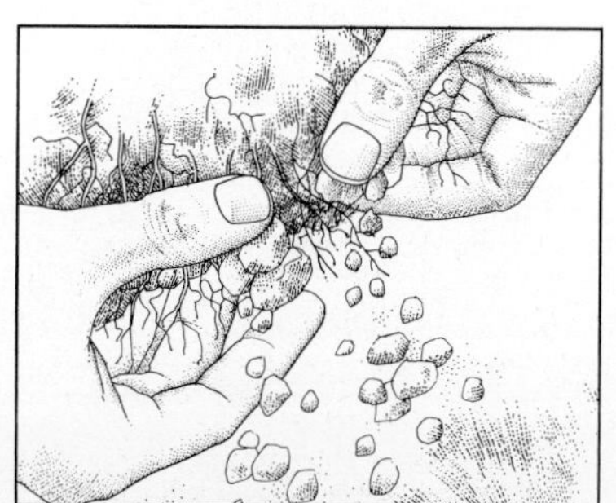

2. *Expose some of the roots by crumbling soil before replanting.*

Growing Evergreens Successfully

Evergreen shrubs are often less tolerant of intense cold and drought than are deciduous shrubs; therefore, they need to be carefully sited.

Unless a species is known to be wind tolerant, plant evergreens in sheltered places. Make sure that they are kept moist. If they are exposed to drying winds, spray with an anti-desiccant or erect a burlap screen.

Watering is particularly important for both needle and broad-leaved evergreen shrubs grown in containers. Lack of water shows first in the browning of the lower branches of a shrub. As a rule of thumb, water an evergreen shrub whenever the surface of the soil in the container shows signs of drying out.

Container-grown specimens can also suffer from starvation. This usually shows as a general slowing down of growth, with smaller, often paler, yellow-green leaves. To maintain healthy growth, apply liquid or solid plant food at monthly intervals from midspring until late in the summer.

Keeping Weeds Down With Hoe and Herbicides

Once a shrub has grown, it will probably cast too much shade for weeds to be much of a problem beneath its branches. Until then, however, any weeds that do appear must be regularly removed.

The first weapon against them, while they are still very small, is the old-fashioned hoe. But use it with care; many shrubs have shallow roots spreading near the surface.

Weed killers can be used between shrubs, but be careful not to splash the foliage. Use a piece of cardboard, a sheet of plywood, or something of the sort to protect the leaves of shrubs as you apply the herbicide. A paraquat weed killer becomes inactive on contact with the soil; so it will not damage shrub roots.

Smother annual weeds with a 1- to 2-inch mulch layer in spring.

Weeds can be defined as plants that grow where you do not want them. The ultimate solution is to choke them out with plants that you do want, such as grass.

What Can Go Wrong With Shrubs

The most common problems that occur in the growing of shrubs are described below. If your plants show symptoms not described here, turn to the section on plant disorders on page 600. Trade names for chemicals are listed on page 635.

Symptoms and signs	Cause	Control
Shrub is disfigured. Pests may be visible.	Aphids, lace bugs, leafhoppers, psyllids, or whiteflies	Use dormant oil spray or Diazinon, malathion, or methoxychlor cover spray.
	Clover, gall, or spider mites	Apply dicofol, endosulfan, or tetradifon.
Leaves curled or dried, with silvery dots.	Aphids, lace bugs, psyllids, thrips, or whiteflies	Apply chlorpyrifos, Diazinon, malathion, miscible oil, or oil emulsion.
Sooty mold and insects may be visible.	Rust or spider mites	Apply dicofol, endosulfan, miscible oil, oil emulsion, or tetradifon.
Leaves have holes or ragged edges.	Inchworms, leaf beetles, leaf galls, leaf miners, leaf rollers, rose chafers, sawfly larvae, or tent caterpillars	Apply *Bacillus thuringiensis,* carbaryl, Diazinon, malathion, miscible oil, or oil emulsion.
Leaves are chewed or rolled up.	Leaf miners or leaf rollers	Apply *Bacillus thuringiensis,* carbaryl, Diazinon, malathion, or methoxychlor.
Leaves may be chewed, stems or roots eaten.	Root weevils	Apply carbaryl, Diazinon, dimethoate, lindane, or methoxychlor.
Branches, leaves, and stems have accretions of scale.	Scale insects	Apply dormant spray of miscible oil or oil emulsion; in late spring or early summer, use chlorpyrifos, Diazinon, or malathion.

Symptoms and signs	Cause	Control
Leaves may develop spots or turn brown. Shoots may blacken. Stems may have cankers.	Anthracnose (fungus)	Spray with copper, dodine, or maneb. Prune and destroy infected material.
Flowers, young leaves, and twigs suddenly wilt, brown, and then turn black.	Bacterial fire blight	As blooms open, spray with antibiotic (streptomycin) or Bordeaux mixture.
Leaves, buds, and flowers show gray mold.	Botrytis (fungus)	Spray with chlorothalonil or dichloran.
Swellings develop on roots, twigs, and trunk. Rose family is especially vulnerable.	Crown gall (bacteria)	If possible, remove galls; or apply .92% Bacticin paste to galls. If galls are large and at soil level, destroy shrubs.
Leaves have brown, purple, or jet-black spots, usually with yellow haloes.	Leafspot	Spray with Benomyl, Captan, dodine, folpet, or maneb.
Bark has water-soaked areas that crack open; pinkish spots develop in spring.	Nectria canker (fungus)	Remove and destroy infected material. Spray in spring with Bordeaux mixture or liquid lime sulfur.
Tiny spots on undersides of petals enlarge and bleach out. Flowers wilt. Primarily attacks rhododendrons and azaleas.	Petal blight (fungus)	Spray with Benomyl every 5 da. during bloom season.
Leaves have white powder, become black and distorted.	Powdery mildew (fungus)	Spray with cycloheximide, dinocap, or sulfur.
Leaves have rusty orange spots.	Rust (fungus)	Spray with chlorothalonil, mancozeb, or thiram.
Leaves and young fruits have green mold, which turns black and scablike. All leaves may fall.	Scab (fungus)	Spray in late spring or early summer with Benomyl, dodine, folpet, or mancozeb.

How to Grow New Shrubs From Cuttings

Hardwood Cuttings From Deciduous Shrubs

The simplest way to propagate many hardy deciduous shrubs is by taking hardwood cuttings in late fall or early winter. These are taken from vigorous stems that have just completed their first season's growth.

Hardwood cuttings are taken after the shrubs have dropped their leaves and begun a period of dormancy. See details under Propagation on charts starting on page 120.

In mild regions, where the ground does not freeze to a depth of more than an inch or two, choose a site sheltered from winds and spade it thoroughly. In heavy soil incorporate coarse sand or perlite with compost or peat moss. The proportions are not critical, but use enough to lighten the soil, usually about two parts soil to one part of the mixture.

Make a narrow trench by pushing in a spade to its full blade depth and wiggling it back and forth for several inches. Place a 1- to 2-inch layer of sand or perlite in the bottom.

Choose a pencil-thick stem of the current season's growth and cut near the base. Trim to 9–12 inches long—a long shoot will make two or more cuttings, but avoid using the soft tip as a cutting, since it is harder to root and may produce weak growth.

Sever each cutting cleanly; cut just below a bud at the base and just above a bud at the top end.

Where frost may be a problem, cuttings are inserted vertically 3–4 inches apart in a trench, as shown; the lower half or two-thirds of the cutting is belowground when the trench is filled in. Fill in soil and firm it with your foot.

Vertically placed cuttings that become loosened by frost action should be pushed down until the base is imbedded in the sand. Except for regular weeding and watering, this is the only care needed.

In still colder regions bury the cuttings horizontally under 6–8 inches of sand or sandy soil after first tying them together in bundles of six or more. In early spring dig up the cuttings, separate, and insert vertically in a trench as shown in Fig. 2.

The second spring the easily rooted cuttings will be ready to be moved to their permanent quarters. Shrubs that are slower to root or grow should be left for another year.

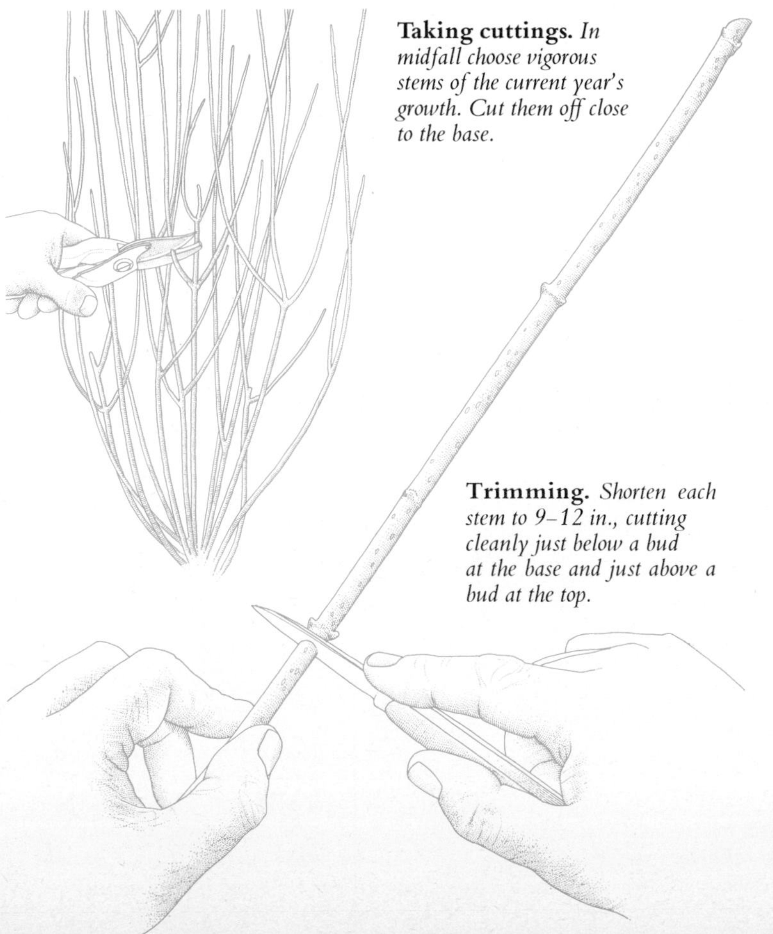

Taking cuttings. *In midfall choose vigorous stems of the current year's growth. Cut them off close to the base.*

Trimming. *Shorten each stem to 9–12 in., cutting cleanly just below a bud at the base and just above a bud at the top.*

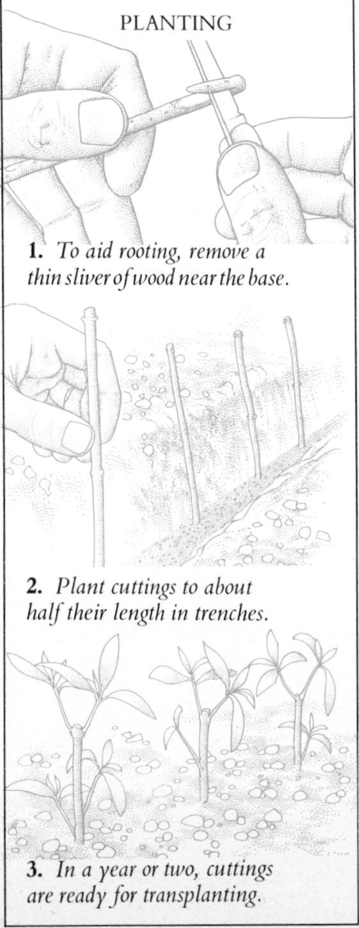

PLANTING

1. *To aid rooting, remove a thin sliver of wood near the base.*

2. *Plant cuttings to about half their length in trenches.*

3. *In a year or two, cuttings are ready for transplanting.*

Firm-Shoot Cuttings From Evergreens

The best time for taking firm-shoot cuttings of many broad-leaved evergreens and conifers is in early to mid fall when new growth has hardened. For broad-leaved evergreens, make terminal cuttings 4–6 inches long. Trim the leaves from the lowest inch, and insert the cutting in a rooting mix—either sand or equal parts peat moss and perlite. In mild climates set directly into nursery rows when rooted; in cold climates leave in a cold frame the first winter.

Few conifers root readily from cuttings. In late summer take firm-shoot cuttings from short side growths, with a heel (see p. 88) or without. Root in a greenhouse or cold frame.

Some shrubs, particularly among the broad-leaved evergreens and the conifers (needle evergreens), are difficult to root. Such cuttings often respond to wounding prior to rooting. To do this, remove a thin sliver of bark from one side or opposite sides near the base of the cutting.

Protecting with antidesiccant. Evergreen cuttings are subject to water loss from the leaves, which may retard rooting or even be fatal. This can be averted by spraying with a liquid antidesiccant, available from most garden centers.

Semi-Hard-Shoot Cuttings—Taking Them in Summer

There are some shrubs—the aucuba, bluebeard, and Mexican orange among them—that root poorly from hardwood cuttings but respond well if semi-hard material is used instead.

Semi-hard cuttings are from the current year's growth; they have become somewhat firm and woody toward the base but are still growing. The best time to take them is during the heat of mid to late summer; in a very hot year, however, they may be ready a bit earlier.

Semi-hard cuttings require some attention from the time they are taken until they have become well rooted. The essentials are: some sort of propagating frame (with or without bottom heat), regular watering, and shading from direct sun.

When the young plants have rooted but are not yet established, they can either be potted or set outside in a nursery bed. Either way, it will be a year or two before they are ready for planting in their permanent locations.

Take the cuttings by severing 6- to 8-inch side shoots from the current season's growth. These will be easy to identify—leaves will be growing on them. Cut each shoot off close to the main stem.

Strip the leaves from the bottom part of a shoot; then cut it straight across just below the lowest leaf node. Trim off the soft tip, cutting just above a leaf, to make a cutting that is 2–4 inches long.

Heeled cuttings. Semi-hard cuttings may root more surely if they include at the base a small wedge of the parent stem, known as a heel. This encourages roots to form by preventing the sap, as it flows down from the leaves, from draining away into the soil. Some shrubs, such as the fire thorn and ceanothus, will root very poorly—or more likely not at all—if the heel is missing from a semi-hard cutting.

First, clip off a main shoot that carries several side shoots, preferably without flowers. At the spots where the side shoots join the main stem, remove shoots by making V-shaped incisions into the wood of the parent. Use a sharp knife to cut just deep enough to include some of the cambium layer (the tissue just beneath the bark).

Trim the tip back to make cuttings 2–3 inches long. Care for them as illustrated on the next page for all semi-hard cuttings.

Taking the cuttings. *Late in the summer choose 6- to 8-in. side shoots of the current season's wood—any shoots with leaves on them. Cut them off close to the main stem.*

Trimming. *Remove the lower leaves and sever the shoots just below the lowest leaf nodes, cutting straight across. Trim off the soft tips of the shoots so that the cuttings are 2–4 in. long.*

TAKING HEELED CUTTINGS

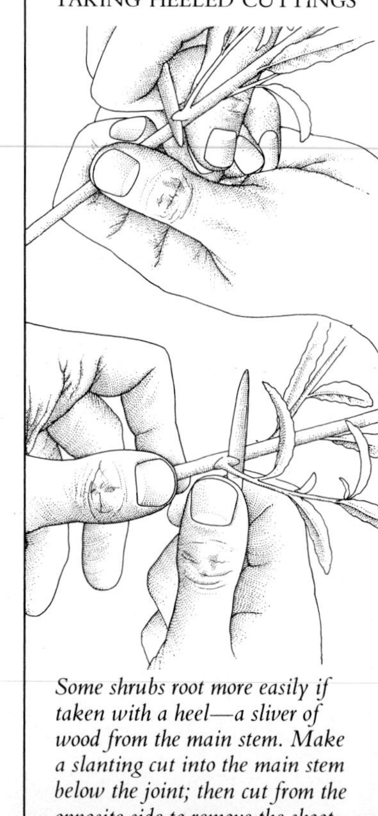

Some shrubs root more easily if taken with a heel—a sliver of wood from the main stem. Make a slanting cut into the main stem below the joint; then cut from the opposite side to remove the shoot and its V-shaped heel.

Planting and Care of Semi-Hard-Shoot Cuttings

Once the cuttings have been taken, fill a pot to just below its rim with a light soil mix meant for starting seeds, or mix your own from equal parts of peat moss and coarse sand.

The size of the pot used will depend on the length and number of cuttings. A 3-inch pot should be large enough for up to 5 cuttings, a 5-inch pot for as many as 10. For a really large number, a box is best.

You may lose a few cuttings; it is therefore wise to start with more than you need so that you can select the strongest for repotting later on.

Make a hole in the soil about one-third the length of a cutting. Insert the cutting and firm the soil gently around it. Plant the other cuttings in the same way, spaced evenly, and water well with a fine spray from a mister or hose.

At this stage three things are critical to successful rooting: humidity, warmth, and partial shade.

You can provide the first of these by turning the pot into a small greenhouse. All it takes is a clear plastic bag and two pieces of galvanized wire about 12–15 inches long. Bend the wires (coat-hanger wire will do nicely) into arcs and insert the ends into the soil so that the two arcs form a cross-shaped support. Slip the bag over this framework and secure it below the rim of the pot with string, tape, or a rubber band. The same device can be adapted for starting cuttings in a box.

Place the propagating container in a shaded greenhouse or cold frame. Beware of direct sunlight; it will cause rapid overheating in the closed atmosphere.

Ideal rooting conditions exist for most hardy plants when the soil temperature is maintained at a steady 60°–65° F. Although it is not absolutely essential, supplying the heat from beneath hastens the rooting of most plants. This can be done by placing the container on the greenhouse heating pipes or by using soil-warming cables. Propagating frames or units with similar cables built into them are also available.

If all the suggested steps are taken properly—the cuttings taken at the right time and in the right way, suitable soil used, temperature and humidity maintained—and if no fungus or other disease intervenes, rooting should occur in two or three weeks. But the work is not over.

Hardening off. After cuttings have rooted, they need to be acclimatized slowly to the harsher conditions they will face outside their plastic tents. Keep them in the greenhouse or frame and raise the plastic half an inch or so, or poke a few holes in it to let in air. Keep the cuttings away from strong light. After a week, raise the plastic higher or increase the number of holes in it.

After yet another week, remove the covering. Water the cuttings, wait one more week, and they will be ready to go into individual pots.

Repotting. Shake rooted cuttings from the pot and gently separate them. Prepare a $3\frac{1}{2}$-inch pot for each cutting by putting a little drainage material in the bottom and covering with a layer of potting mix. Stand the young plant on this and fill it with the mix to just below the lowest pair of leaves.

Firm the soil to about $\frac{1}{2}$ inch below the rim of the pot. Water generously. Keep the plant in a greenhouse or cold frame. Never let the soil dry out.

It should take the roots about three weeks to reach the limits of the pot. If the shrub is hardy in your climate, it can now be planted in the open, in a prepared bed, to become established. Tender plants should first go into larger pots and be protected until spring.

1. *Insert cutting one-third of its length into a pot of peat moss and sand.*

2. *Water generously with sprayer or a watering can with a fine head.*

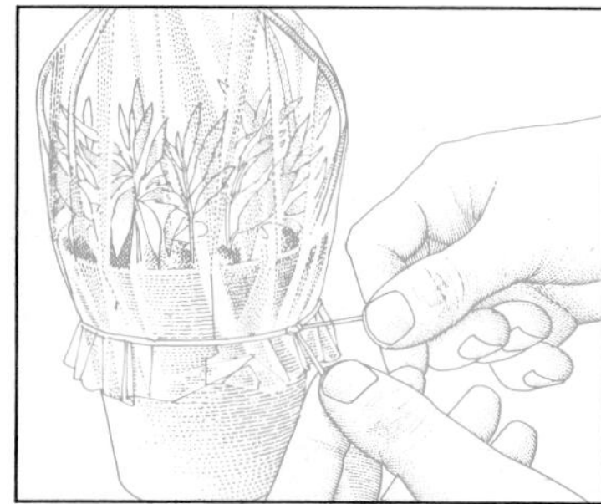

3. *Make a frame of galvanized wire; plastic cover retains humidity.*

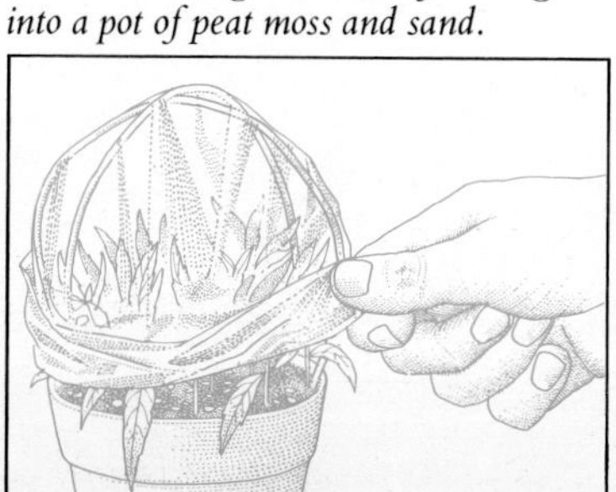

4. *After rooting, harden off by raising the plastic a little at a time.*

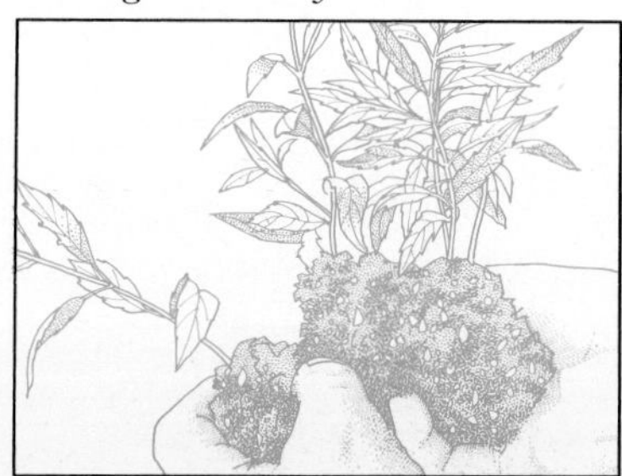

5. *After about three weeks shake out and gently separate the cuttings.*

6. *Plant rooted cuttings singly in $3\frac{1}{2}$-in. pots of potting soil.*

7. *When plant is established, it is ready for planting in the garden.*

Softwood Cuttings Taken From Shoot Tips

Softwood cuttings are immature, soft-shoot tips, taken before they have become hard. Although commonly used to grow hardy herbaceous perennials and house plants, they provide the least convenient method of propagating trees and shrubs. Still, if you wish to take cuttings in early summer, this is the method to use. But from the time of insertion until rooting and potting have taken place, the cuttings will require constant care.

A warm propagating case, preferably with heating cables in the bottom, is required. Watering, shading, and attentive care are critical. A mist propagation unit will help to simplify the procedure (see p. 454). The cuttings will not be ready to be set out in the garden for one or two years.

Soft-shoot cuttings should be young and nonflowering, firm but not hard, and 2–4 inches long. Take them no later than midsummer.

First, cut off a shoot that has four or five pairs of leaves. Using a sharp knife or razor blade, and cutting cleanly and diagonally, sever the shoot just beneath the pair of leaves closest to the main stem. Now remove the first two pairs of leaves nearest the bottom, taking care to avoid tearing the shoot.

Take about 10 cuttings for planting in a 5-inch pot. Fill the pot to just below its rim with a light soil mix or with a mixture of equal parts peat moss and coarse sand.

Make holes in the soil about one-third the length of the cuttings. Insert the cuttings and firm the soil. Continue propagation as for semi-hard cuttings, but allow more time for each step.

Growing Shrubs From Pieces of Root

Some plants, both herbaceous and woody, readily produce shoots directly from their roots, particularly at a point where damage has occurred. Consequently, pieces of root can be used as cuttings. Some shrubs that are likely to grow well from root cuttings are spireas, cotoneasters, and sumacs. One feature of root cuttings to keep in mind is that they require less attention than semi-hard or soft-shoot cuttings.

In autumn, winter, or early spring, lift the plant with a garden fork or, with a large plant, unearth part of the root system. Cut off some thick roots close to the main stem.

With a sharp knife, cut pieces about 1½ inches long from these roots. (Thinner roots can be used, but they should be 2–3 inches long and planted horizontally about ½ inch deep.) Cut each piece of root straight across at the end nearest the stem, diagonally at the other end.

Fill a pot to just below its rim with a light soil mix or with equal parts peat moss and coarse sand.

Make a hole in the soil mix to accommodate the full length of the cutting, using a dibble.

Insert the cutting, flat end uppermost, so that its top is flush with the soil surface. A 5-inch pot will hold about six cuttings comfortably.

Cover with ¼ inch of coarse sand and spray with water. Keep cuttings in a greenhouse or cold frame, and maintain warmth and moisture.

Six months later shake out the rooted cuttings from their pots and separate them gently. Pot them separately and give them the same care as recommended for semi-hard-shoot cuttings (see p. 89).

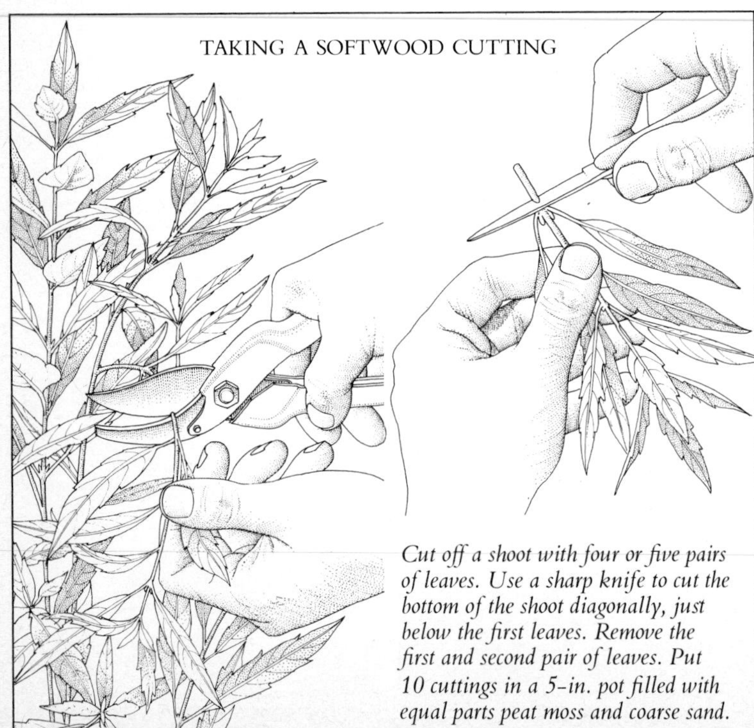

Cut off a shoot with four or five pairs of leaves. Use a sharp knife to cut the bottom of the shoot diagonally, just below the first leaves. Remove the first and second pair of leaves. Put 10 cuttings in a 5-in. pot filled with equal parts peat moss and coarse sand.

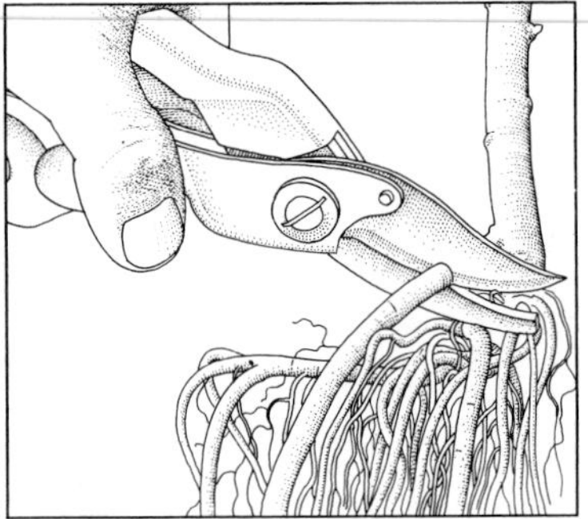

1. *Use pruning shears to cut off a thick root close to the main stem of the shrub.*

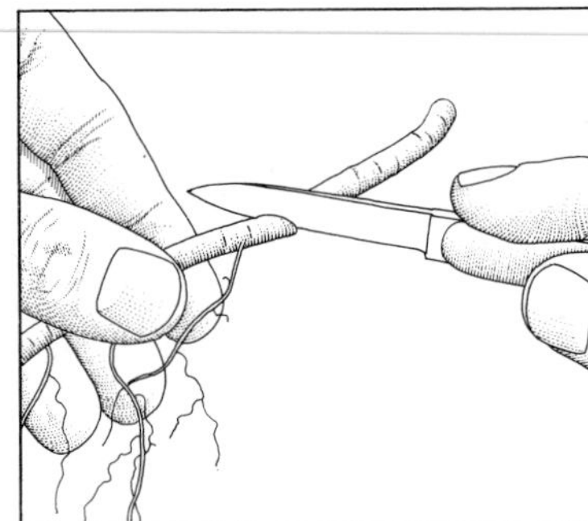

2. *Cut into 1½-in. pieces, straight across at the top, angled at the base.*

3. *Plant in mixture of peat moss and sand, the top flush with the surface.*

4. *In six months plants should be ready to move to 3½-in. pots.*

Leaf-Bud Cuttings for Quantity and Speed

If you want to propagate many plants from a limited amount of parent material, leaf-bud cuttings may be the best way to do it. If you take these cuttings at the right time, they can root and break into growth more quickly than other types of cuttings. (But note that a year after rooting, hardwood or semi-hard cuttings will probably have grown into larger plants.)

In late summer or early fall, clip off some semi-hard lateral shoots—shoots that began growing the previous spring. Each shoot will have several leaves, and at the axil of each leaf—the spot where the leaf joins the stem—will be a growth bud.

About $^{3}/_{4}$ inch below the lowest leaf, cut through the shoot at an angle with a sharp knife. Then sever the shoot straight across just above the bud in the leaf axil. Do the same with the next leaf. You should get three or four cuttings from each shoot in this way.

Wound each cutting by scraping some bark off the $^{3}/_{4}$-inch stub. Dip the end, including the wounded part, in rooting hormone.

Fill a pot to just below its rim with a light sandy soil or with equal parts peat moss and coarse sand or perlite. Insert the cuttings so that each bud barely shows above the surface. A 6- to 7-inch pot should hold about a dozen cuttings.

Water lightly with a small hand sprayer or by shaking water onto the buds with your fingertips. Cover the pot with a wire-and-plastic tent, as with semi-hard cuttings (see p. 89). Place it in a greenhouse or cold frame, and make sure that it is protected from direct sun.

In six months cuttings should be ready for hardening off and repotting in individual containers. Shake them from the pot and gently separate them.

Place drainage material, covered with a layer of porous soil, in the bottom of some $3^{1}/_{2}$-inch pots. Stand a rooted cutting in each pot and fill with soil until the cutting is covered to just below the original leaf.

Firm the soil to about $^{1}/_{2}$ inch below the rim of the pot. Water generously. Keep the pots in a greenhouse or cold frame. Never allow the soil to dry out.

In three to six weeks the roots should have spread to the outside of the soil. If the shrub is hardy, it can then be planted out in the open, in a prepared bed. Tender plants should go into a larger pot and spend a year in a greenhouse or cold frame before being planted outdoors.

Gray Mold—The Main Enemy of Cuttings

The greatest threat to cuttings is Botrytis, or gray mold. It is a fungus that appears as a fluffy, grayish-white coating on stems, leaves, or flower buds and is most troublesome from autumn to early spring.

Gray mold thrives in cool, moist conditions and requires dead or dying plant tissue to grow on. If it appears on a cutting, the plant is lost and should be destroyed—not composted. Getting rid of the infected plants is necessary because once it gets established, Botrytis will kill the rest of the cuttings as well.

The best way to prevent mold is attentive care. Look carefully at your cuttings at least weekly, and remove dying or dead leaves. A fungicide, such as Benomyl or Captan, can also be effective (see p. 617).

Using Rooting Hormones to Promote Growth

Rooting powders and rooting liquids contain hormones that, when applied to the base of a cutting, stimulate root formation.

These hormones are present in the plants themselves, but often in such minute quantities that natural rooting takes place very slowly. The application of hormones can either speed up rooting or make it more certain for plants like winter sweet (*Chimonanthus*) that are difficult to root. However, with English ivy (*Hedera helix*), which roots quickly and easily on its own, hormone treatment can have a negative effect.

Rooting powders and liquids come in various strengths: weaker for softwood, stronger for hardwood cuttings. There are also general-purpose formulations. For large-scale propagation, use the specific strength for the job. For only a few cuttings, an all-purpose formula is probably the best.

1. *Late in the summer cut off a shoot that has several leaves on it.*

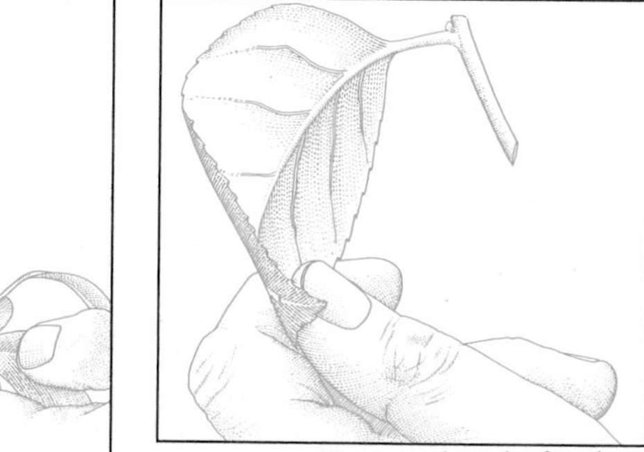

2. *Cut straight across above leaf axils, and at an angle $^{3}/_{4}$ in. below them.*

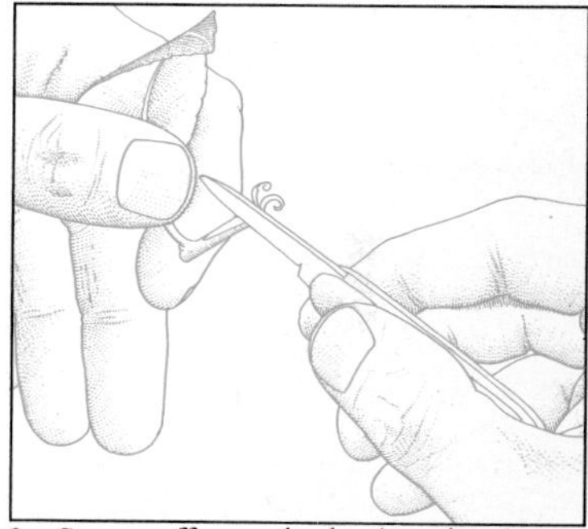

3. *Scrape off some bark; then dip the wounded part in rooting hormone.*

4. *Plant cuttings so that the leaf axil just shows. Maintain humidity.*

5. *About six months later plant the cuttings in separate $3^{1}/_{2}$-in. pots.*

Layering—New Plants From a Growing Shoot

Ordinary Soil Layering—The Basic Method

Soil layering is a simple method of propagating shrubs without using a greenhouse or cold frame. It takes advantage of the fact that a plant that has been cut, lacerated, or fractured is likely to produce roots when the wound is in contact with the soil.

The best branches for soil layering are nonflowering ones that have grown in the current year. They provide the freshest shoots.

Deciduous plants are best layered in autumn or winter. Layer evergreens in autumn or spring.

First, fork over the surface of the soil around the plant. Then, choose a flexible branch and bend it down until it reaches the ground 9–12 inches from its tip. Strip the leaves from the branch as shown in the illustration.

Wound the underside with a knife by cutting a shallow tongue in the direction of the growing tip; or injure the surface tissue by twisting.

Dig a 3- to 4-inch hole at the spot where the wound touches the ground, and partly fill it with equal parts peat moss and coarse sand. Push the branch into the hole, forming a sharp angle at the wound.

Peg the branch to the ground with a bent piece of galvanized wire 6–8 inches long. Stake the upright tip. Fill the hole with the soil mix.

Repeat the process with other branches. Water the whole area thoroughly, and make sure that it never dries out.

Most plants will have rooted 12 months later. You can determine whether they have done so by carefully scraping away the soil.

If roots are well established, sever the new plant from the parent branch, lift it out with a good root ball, and plant it where you want it.

If the roots have not grown well but the top growth seems healthy, replace the soil and wait a few more months before checking again.

Each branch of the current year's growth of a shrub can produce a rooted plant without first being severed from the parent plant.

1. *First, bend the branch to the ground. Then, at a spot 9–12 in. from its tip, dig a hole 3–4 in. deep.*

2. *Strip the leaves from the part of the branch that is over the hole.*

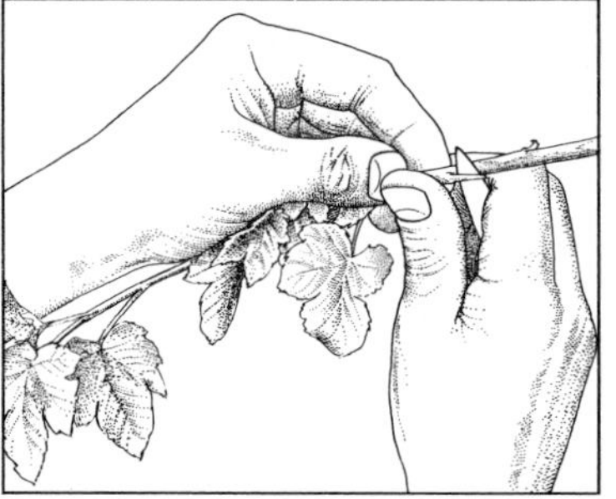

3. *Cut a shallow tongue into the underside of the branch, cutting toward the growing tip. Alternatively, twist the branch sharply to break the surface tissue.*

4. *Bend branch upward at the wound, and peg into the hole with wire.*

5. *Stake the upright tip and fill in the hole with soil. Water well.*

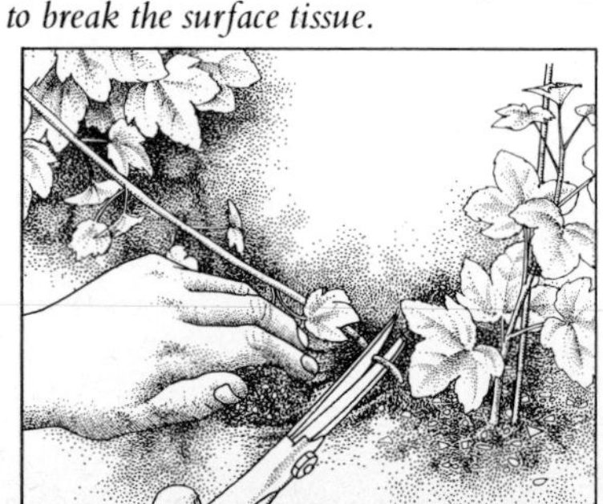

6. *A year later, if roots have grown, sever and transplant the young shrub.*

Serpentine Soil Layering for Vines

Serpentine soil layering is a handy method of propagating vines and many shrubs with long, vinelike stems, such as honeysuckle and jasmine. It should be done at the same time as ordinary soil layering, using the long, trailing shoots that have grown during the current year.

Bend a shoot carefully to the ground and, where it touches, dig a hole 2 inches deep.

Wound the shoot on the underside, as with ordinary layering, and peg it into the hole with a bent piece of wire. A hairpin or paper clip can serve the purpose.

Fill the hole with equal parts peat moss and coarse sand. Cover with soil and firm down with your fingers.

Leave the next two pairs of leaves aboveground; then repeat the layering operation. Continue along the entire length of the shoot. Water well and do not allow to dry out.

A year later each buried point should have rooted. (Check by scraping the soil away.) If roots are established, sever the sections between the exposed leaf pairs, and plant in the normal way. If not, rebury the shoot for a few months longer; then check again.

There is a technique that makes transplanting easier, although it involves more trouble at the beginning. Instead of pegging the shoots directly into the ground, prepare small pots of light soil mix, sink them into the ground, and peg into them. The layers can then be moved without disturbing the new roots.

1. *Bend down a shoot, peg into a 2-in. hole, and fill hole with light soil.*

2. *Repeat the operation, leaving two pairs of leaves above the ground.*

Air Layering for Stiff or Upright Branches

Branches that cannot be layered at soil level can be layered in the air. This can be done anytime between late spring and midsummer.

Select a healthy branch of the current year's growth, and strip the leaves from the middle. Wound it by taking a slice of wood about an inch long, cutting well into the cambium layer. Apply rooting hormone.

Wrap a strip of plastic 4–5 inches wide around the cut, and tie it at the bottom as shown at right. Fill with a moist mixture of equal parts peat moss, coarse sand, and sphagnum moss, and tie at the top.

In about 10 weeks you should be able to see or feel roots. Remove the covering and cut off the branch below the layer. Put the new plant into a 4- to 6-inch pot of light soil, and keep it moist in a closed cold frame for about two weeks.

Harden the plant by gradually opening the frame, a little more each day, until the plant is fully exposed. Plant in the open in spring.

1. *Select a branch of the current year's growth and strip off a pair of leaves.*

2. *Cut off a 1-in. slice of wood and dab rooting hormone onto the area.*

3. *Wrap cut area with plastic, tie at the bottom, and stuff with soil mix.*

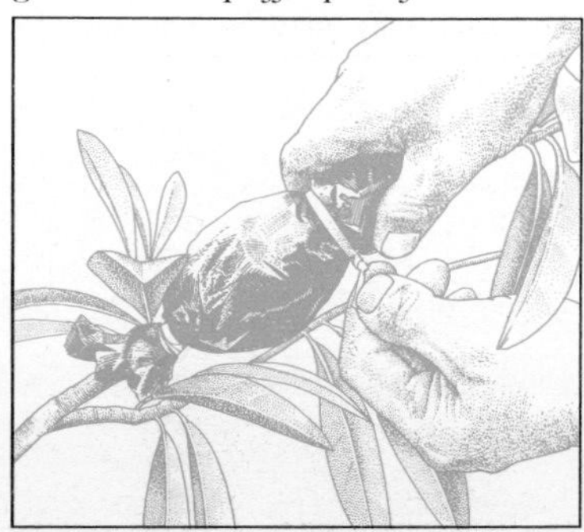

4. *Tie the plastic tube at the top and leave it for at least 10 weeks.*

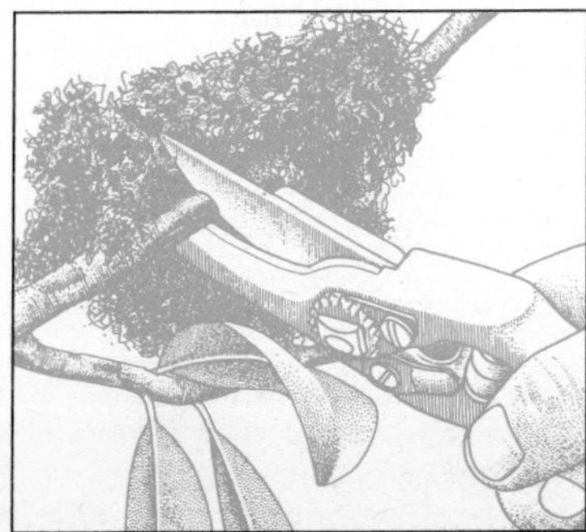

5. *When roots have formed, remove plastic and cut off the new plant.*

6. *Plant in a 4- to 6-in. pot. Keep moist and protected for two weeks.*

New Shrubs From Seeds, Suckers, and Division

Collecting and Preparing Seeds for Sowing

Shrub seeds ripen at different times of year. Since birds seem to know just when certain seeds are ripe, their appearance is a fairly reliable signal as to when to harvest. However, one must get there before the birds and before the dry seeds spill out. Most shrub seeds ripen in the fall, but even in cold climates, seeds of a few, such as honeysuckle, are collected in late spring, and beauty bush ripens in late summer. Many kinds of rhododendron produce seeds in midfall.

The seeds of some shrubs will germinate without special treatment. Among these are the azalea, rhododendron, pieris, mountain laurel, buddleja, sweet pepper bush, deutzia, enkianthus, hypericum, hydrangea, potentilla, beauty bush, mock orange, spirea, and weigela.

Other seeds, such as those of the barberry, common lilac, arborvitae, and most of the spruces and pines, have a single dormant period requiring two or three months of cold to break dormancy and induce germination. This can be accomplished in cold climates by sowing seeds outdoors in the fall in a cold frame, where they will germinate the following spring. These seeds can also be enclosed in a plastic bag with barely moist peat moss and stored in a household refrigerator (40° F) for two or three months prior to sowing.

A few shrubs, such as the cotoneaster, holly, and juniper, have double dormancy, which requires a warm period followed by a cold period before germination can occur.

If the seeds are sown outdoors, they can take two years to germinate. However, this time can be considerably shortened by putting the seeds in a plastic bag with slightly moist peat moss. Keep the bags at room temperature for about five months to break the first dormant period. Then store them in the same bags in a household refrigerator for three months to break the second period of dormancy. Following this cold treatment, sow the seeds.

Pulpy seeds, such as yew seeds, should have the pulp removed before storing or sowing. This can be done by soaking them in water to soften the pulp. The good seeds will sink and the bad ones will float.

Nonpulpy seeds should be cleaned of chaff (bits of the seed capsule or other extraneous material that could cause rot after sowing). All seeds should be dusted with rotenone to kill weevils and other insects.

A few seeds, including those of genistas and wisterias, have the problem of seed-coat dormancy. This must be overcome mechanically or with hot water or acid. The hard covering of seeds large enough to hold can be broken through with a file or by scraping with a knife.

If hot water is used to soften the dormant coating, it should be at least 190° F. Pour it over the seeds and let them soak overnight. For the acid treatment, immerse the seeds in sulfuric acid (which is dangerous and highly corrosive). Remove them periodically with wooden tweezers to observe the degree of corrosion of the seed coat; the point is to make the seed more permeable to water. After treatment, rinse the seeds in water and sow them immediately in a cold frame or in pots indoors or in a greenhouse. If seeds are sown in the fall in a cold frame, protect them from rodents, which find them inviting in winter when there is little other food. The most practical protection is to put fine wire mesh, such as household screening, over the pots or the soil in the cold frame. For more on sowing seeds, see page 238.

Growing New Shrubs From Suckers

Several kinds of trees and shrubs propagate naturally by means of shoots from beneath the ground. Known as suckers, these shoots offer an easy way to grow new plants.

The method is useful only with plants growing from their own roots. Suckers from grafted plants, such as some roses, rhododendrons, lilacs, viburnums, and witch hazels, will reproduce the rootstock, not the top plant. Shrubs that produce true suckers include the deutzia, forsythia, mock orange, species roses, spirea, sumac, and some *Prunus* species.

Between midfall and early spring remove soil from the base of a sucker to see if roots have formed. If so, trace the sucker to its point of origin (a stem or root), cut it off, and carefully lift it out.

Well-rooted plants can go into permanent sites. Put poorly rooted ones in special beds to develop.

PROPAGATION BY SUCKERS

In autumn or winter uncover the base of a sucker to check for roots. If any have formed, cut off the sucker near its point of origin, lift out, and plant.

Producing Large New Plants From Simple Division

Many shrubs produce their main branches from underground buds. The buried bases of these branches, therefore, produce roots. These shrubs resemble woody herbaceous perennials, and can be divided in the same way, providing an easy method of getting large new plants instantly.

Shrubs that can be propagated by this method include the glory-bower, indigo, kerria, and ruscus.

Simply lift an existing shrub and divide it at its base into two or more equal-size pieces, each with plenty of healthy roots attached. The separate pieces can be planted immediately.

This method works best when carried out in the spring, but it can be used with likelihood of success at any time between midautumn and midspring. A shrub should be at least three years old before being divided.

1. *Plants that produce main branches from belowground can be divided.*

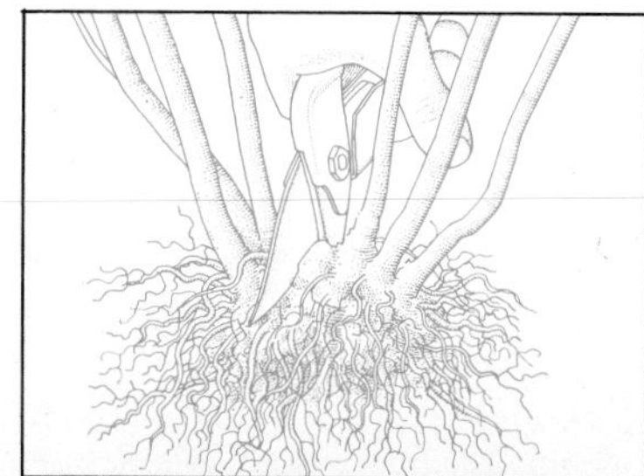

2. *Divide the plant into equal-size pieces with roots; then replant them.*

Basic Methods of Pruning Shrubs and Vines

A shrub will rarely die if it is left unpruned. However, it is often desirable to control its size, to improve the overall shape, or to remove dead or diseased branches. Such pruning is basic for all shrubs. On some shrubs growth may be improved if light is let into the center by cutting away old branches. And some shrubs will bear larger—but generally fewer—flowers if they are pruned each year. To sum up, prune selectively.

Three tools are used for pruning: pruning shears for removing shoots and small stems; long-handled lopping shears for larger stems; and a pruning saw for large branches. A sharp knife may also be needed for trimming around large wounds.

When shortening branches, cut just above an outward-facing bud or shoot. Cut diagonally, parallel with the angle of the bud or shoot and never straight across.

When removing entire branches, cut flush with the trunk or main branch. Then trim the raw area with a sharp knife, and paint it with a tree-wound paint or any oil-base household paint. This will help prevent disease spores from entering the shrub through the wound, and although not absolutely essential, it is a worthwhile precaution.

Shrubs that have been heavily pruned—especially those that receive such treatment annually—benefit from a 2-inch-thick mulch after pruning, plus a cupful per square yard of a complete fertilizer.

Removing Dead, Straggly, and Weak Wood

Most shrubs need only to have their dead, straggly, and weak wood pruned as a matter of general upkeep. This can be done at any time of year. You will probably do it when a shrub develops a long straggly branch or to remove a branch that has been damaged by a storm or some other mishap. It is a good idea to examine all the shrubs in the garden each spring to determine their pruning needs.

Remove any dead or damaged wood, cutting back to a healthy, outward-facing shoot or bud facing outward. Then remove shoots that are obviously weak, cutting right back to a main branch. Prune any straggly branches by half to a strong shoot or bud facing outward.

Do not remove any well-formed, healthy wood, or you are likely to do away with buds that would produce flowers later.

Some shrubs that should have only their damaged wood pruned include the daphne, euonymus, hebe, potentilla, rockrose, *Viburnum burkwoodii,* and *V. carlesii.*

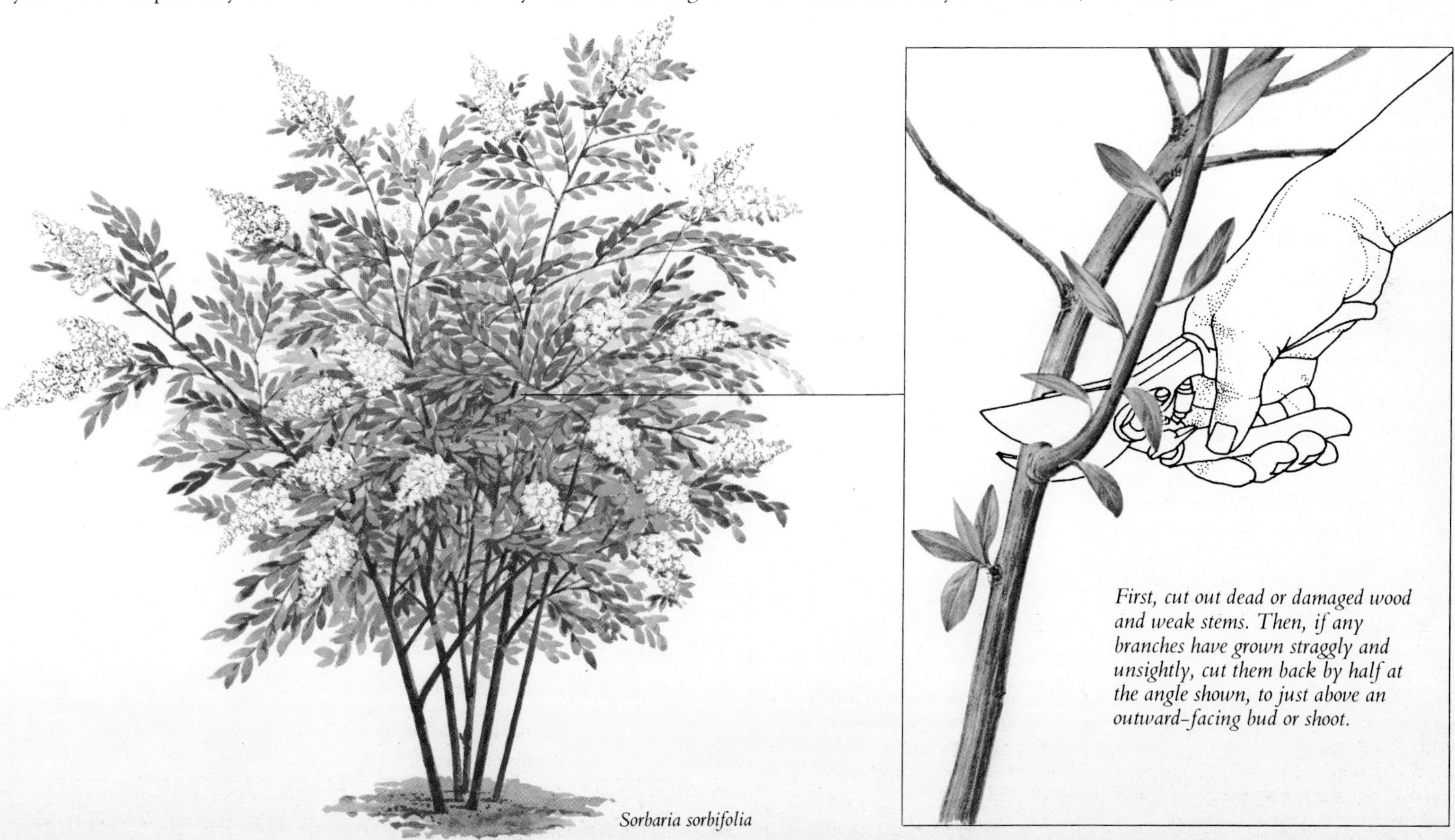

Sorbaria sorbifolia

First, cut out dead or damaged wood and weak stems. Then, if any branches have grown straggly and unsightly, cut them back by half at the angle shown, to just above an outward-facing bud or shoot.

Pruning Shrubs That Flower on Last Year's Wood

Some shrubs, as they mature, have a tendency to lose their shape, to become too dense overall, and to produce fewer flowers than before.

The shrubs that do this and produce their flowers on shoots that were formed during the previous season can be pruned to good advantage immediately after blooming—each year if necessary.

First, cut out or shorten some of the oldest branches. Then, if the shrub is still crowded, thin out the weakest of the new shoots. Always cut just above a vigorous side branch.

SOME SHRUBS THAT CAN BE PRUNED BY THIS METHOD	
Acacia	*Hydrangea macrophylla*
Beauty bush	Kerria
Bottlebrush	Mock orange
Buddleja alternifolia	*Prunus glandulosa albiplena, P. triloba*
Currant, flowering	Stephanandra
Deutzia	Weigela
Forsythia	

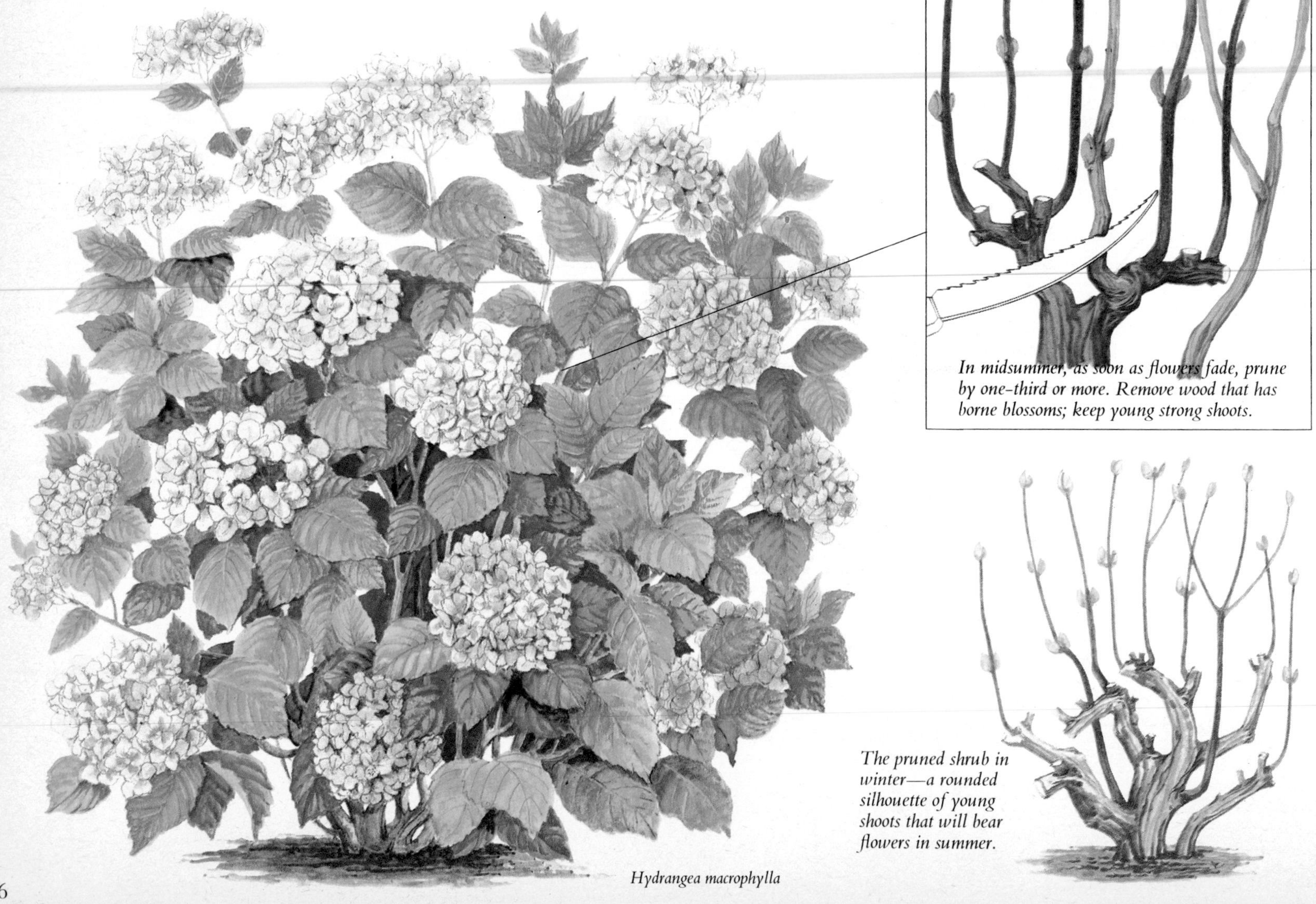

In midsummer, as soon as flowers fade, prune by one-third or more. Remove wood that has borne blossoms; keep young strong shoots.

The pruned shrub in winter—a rounded silhouette of young shoots that will bear flowers in summer.

Hydrangea macrophylla

Pruning Shrubs That Flower on New Shoots

Some shrubs flower on long shoots that have grown in the current season. To restrict their size or to encourage larger but fewer flowers, the shrubs can be pruned in late winter or spring as growth begins.

Cut all of last year's shoots back to two or three buds or shoots from their base. Unless you want to thin out or reduce the size of the permanent framework, do not cut back into the older wood.

After pruning, fortify the shrub by applying a cupful of a complete fertilizer per square yard. Mulch with a 2-inch layer of peat moss, compost, or well-rotted manure.

SOME SHRUBS AND VINES THAT CAN BE PRUNED BY THIS METHOD

- Bluebeard
- Broom, Spanish
- *Buddleja davidii*
- Ceanothus (deciduous kinds)
- Crape myrtle
- *Fuchsia magellanica*
- *Hydrangea arborescens grandiflora, H. paniculata grandiflora*
- Indigo
- Lippia
- Passionflower
- Solanum
- *Spiraea bumalda, S. japonica*
- Spirea, false
- *Tamarix pentandra*
- Vitex

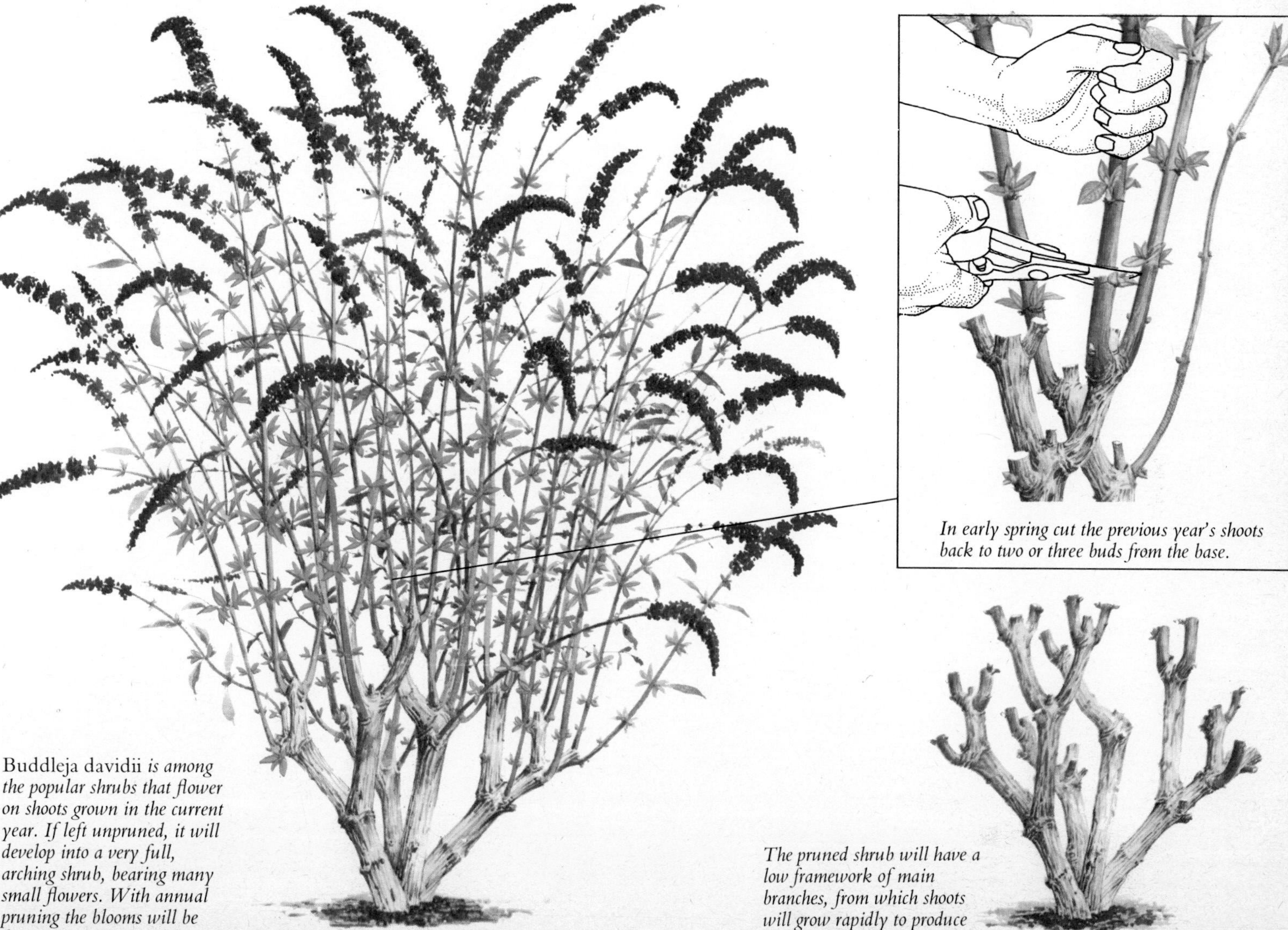

In early spring cut the previous year's shoots back to two or three buds from the base.

Buddleja davidii *is among the popular shrubs that flower on shoots grown in the current year. If left unpruned, it will develop into a very full, arching shrub, bearing many small flowers. With annual pruning the blooms will be fewer, but much larger.*

The pruned shrub will have a low framework of main branches, from which shoots will grow rapidly to produce flowers in summer.

Cutting Down Large, Overgrown Plants

Some shrubs, particularly evergreens, seldom need pruning unless they become overgrown or bare at the base, after many years. In spring use a pruning saw to cut down all the main branches to within a few inches of the ground. Apply a cupful of a complete fertilizer per square yard. Apply a mulch, and water deeply during prolonged dry spells. The shrub will not flower the following summer, but within a few years its appearance should be improved.

SOME SHRUBS THAT MAY REQUIRE THIS TREATMENT

Aucuba	Pieris
Bayberry	Privet
Daisybush	*Prunus laurocerasus* varieties
Elaeagnus	Viburnum
Mahonia	Yew (*Taxus*)

Begin in spring by clearing away top growth with long-handled lopping shears.

Saw off branches a few inches from the ground. Apply tree-wound paint to prevent disease.

Prunus laurocerasus schipkaensis

Rejuvenating an Aging Specimen

Sometimes an old shrub will become so overgrown, ungainly, and crowded with branches that you may be tempted to cut it down entirely. But a program of rejuvenation can usually give new life to old plants. This approach to pruning is less drastic than that recommended on the opposite page for cutting down overgrown plants.

In spring, before leaf growth starts, cut back all old branches to various heights, ranging from 2 to 6 feet. Remove excessively thin, wispy branches and all suckers (if any) from around the base. Apply a complete fertilizer, and mulch.

SOME SHRUBS THAT MAY REQUIRE THIS TREATMENT

- Aucuba
- Bottlebrush
- Cotoneaster
- Elaeagnus
- Fothergilla
- *Hibiscus syriacus*
- Lilac (*Syringa*)
- Mock orange
- Orange, Mexican
- Privet
- Viburnum

In very early spring, before leaves appear, cut back old branches to 2–6 ft. high.

A lilac (Syringa) *will eventually become scraggly, its flowers sparse and discolored. Suckers will arise from the rootstock and will sap its energy. Prune in winter to renew it.*

Remove all suckers below ground level with a pruning saw or the sharp edge of a spade.

Restricting the Size of Climbing Plants

Leave most climbers and vines unpruned until they get too large; then prune them after they flower. Prune those grown for foliage, rather than for flowers, in spring or summer.

Self-clinging climbers, such as the climbing hydrangea or English ivy, can be trimmed on the wall.

Climbers on supports, such as the honeysuckle, should first be detached. Then remove lateral growths, leaving only main stems.

If the main stems look old and woody, remove some of them and keep some of the younger ones—either the shoots growing at ground level or those low on the old stems.

For clematis, see page 104; for wisteria, see page 118.

SOME VINES THAT CAN BE PRUNED BY THIS METHOD

Actinidia	Hydrangea, climbing
Bougainvillea	Silver-lace vine
Clematis montana	Trumpet creeper
Honeysuckle	Virginia creeper

Having taken the climber down from its supports, see if the main stems are very old. If so, cut them back to the vigorous young shoots near the bases of the stems. If the main stems are still only a few years old, retain them and remove all their lateral growth.

A vine that clings by suckers can be trimmed after flowering as though it were a hedge; if it bears no flowers, trim in spring. Vines like this honeysuckle (Lonicera) *that need support should be taken down before pruning.*

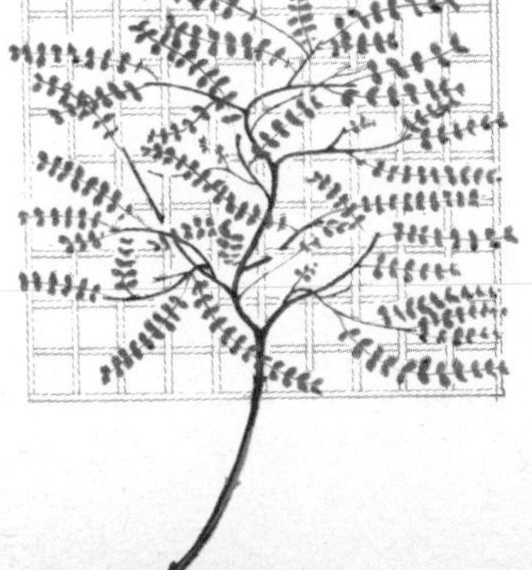

Then tie the pruned vine back into position on its supports. Flowering vines can be expected to bloom again the next year.

Pruning Shrubs Trained As Espaliers

Some shrubs that have particularly attractive foliage, flowers, or berries lend themselves to espaliering against fences or walls. During the formative years prune to develop a framework of well-placed, permanent branches. This is done by shortening the leader shoots that you have selected to make the basic framework. Cut them back to one-third or one-half their lengths each spring. When the shrub has filled its allotted space, cut back the leaders to within an inch or so of their established length every year. At the same time, cut back all of the shoots that grow outward from the wall.

On shrubs that bear flowers on growth that has developed within the current year, do all necessary pruning in early spring. If flowers are borne on the previous year's growth, prune immediately after they bloom.

SOME SHRUBS THAT CAN BE PRUNED BY THIS METHOD	
Ceanothus (evergreen kinds)	Fremontodendron
Cotoneaster	Jasmine
Fire thorn	Quince, flowering
Forsythia	Viburnum
	Yew (*Taxus*)

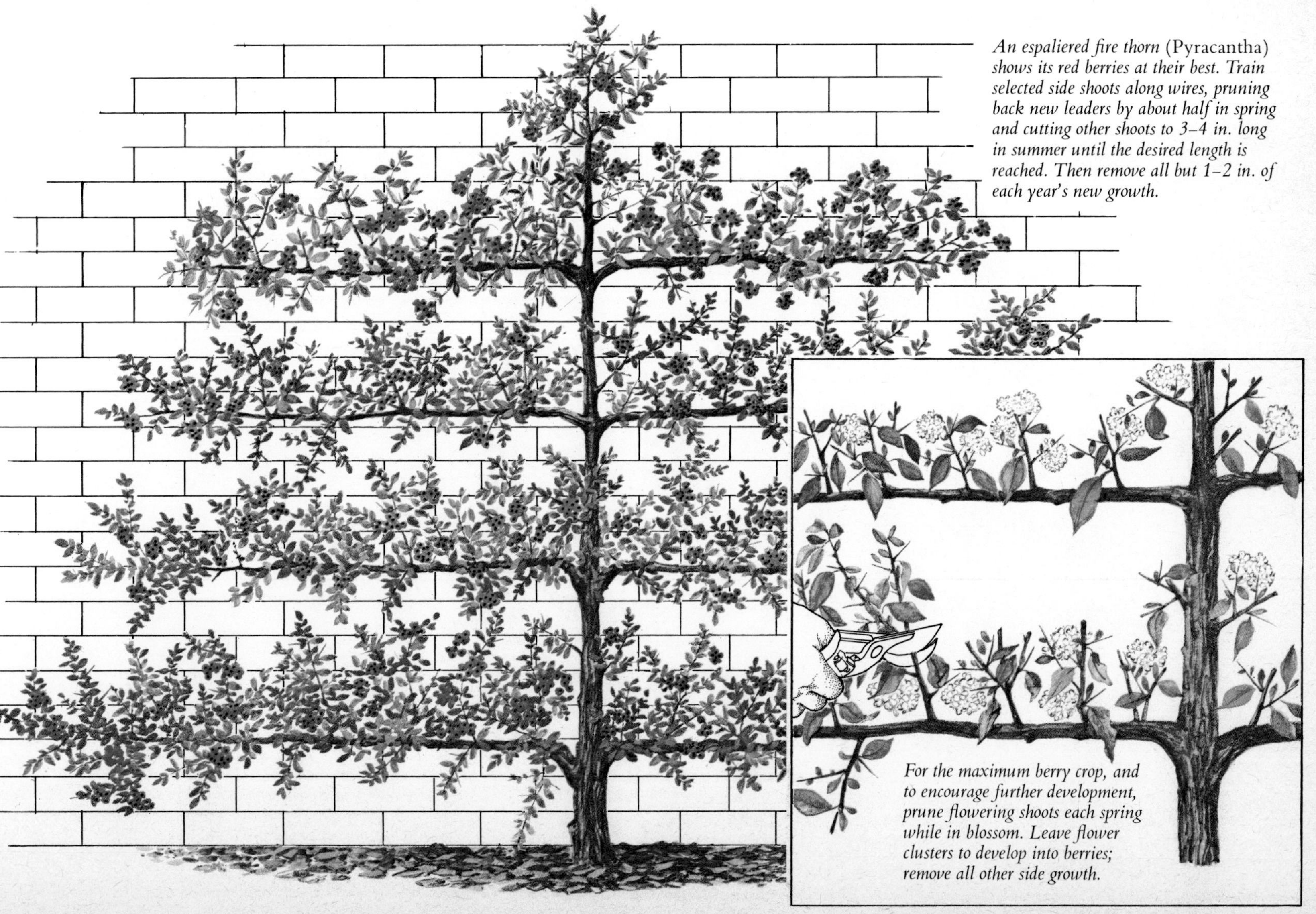

An espaliered fire thorn (Pyracantha) *shows its red berries at their best. Train selected side shoots along wires, pruning back new leaders by about half in spring and cutting other shoots to 3–4 in. long in summer until the desired length is reached. Then remove all but 1–2 in. of each year's new growth.*

For the maximum berry crop, and to encourage further development, prune flowering shoots each spring while in blossom. Leave flower clusters to develop into berries; remove all other side growth.

Pruning 34 Popular Shrubs, in Close-up

Bluebeard (*Caryopteris*). Unless it is pruned each spring, the bush becomes twiggy and bears small flowers.

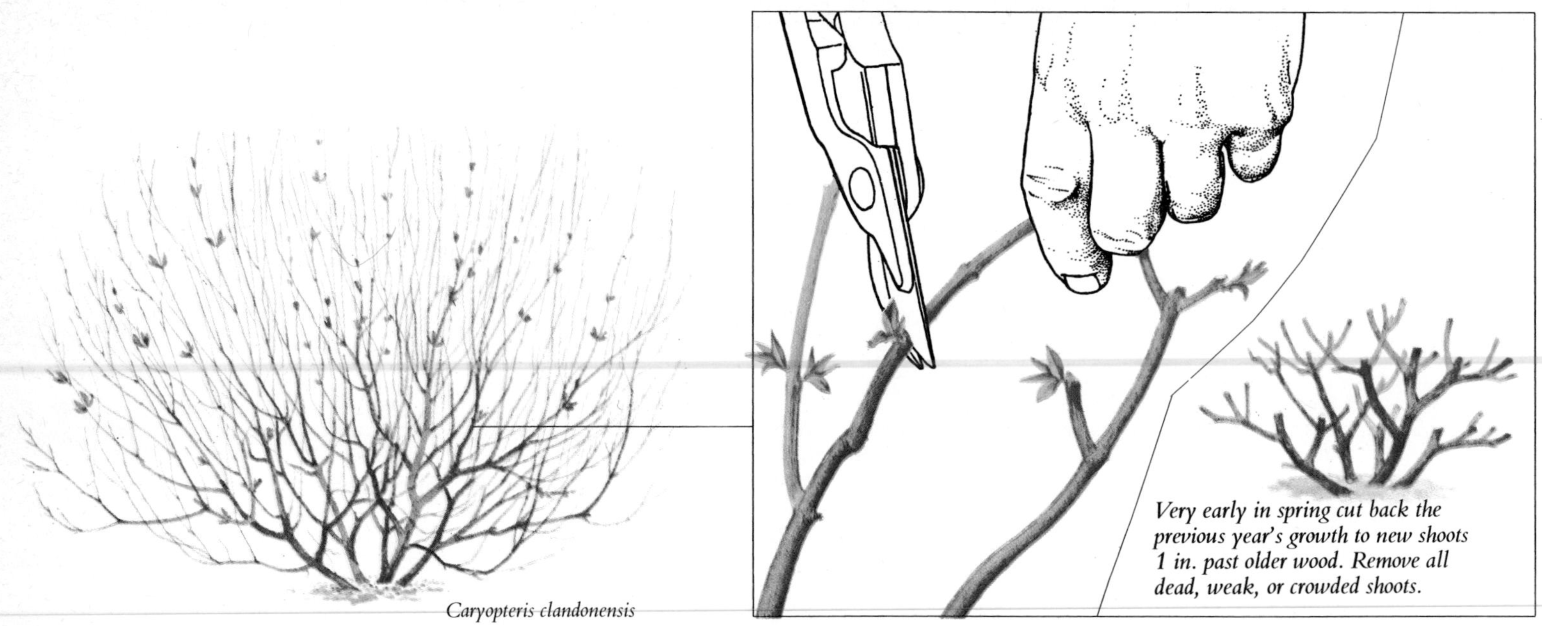

Caryopteris clandonensis

Very early in spring cut back the previous year's growth to new shoots 1 in. past older wood. Remove all dead, weak, or crowded shoots.

Broom, Scotch (*Cytisus scoparius*). Prune after the flowers fade to prevent the shrub from becoming leggy.

Cytisus scoparius

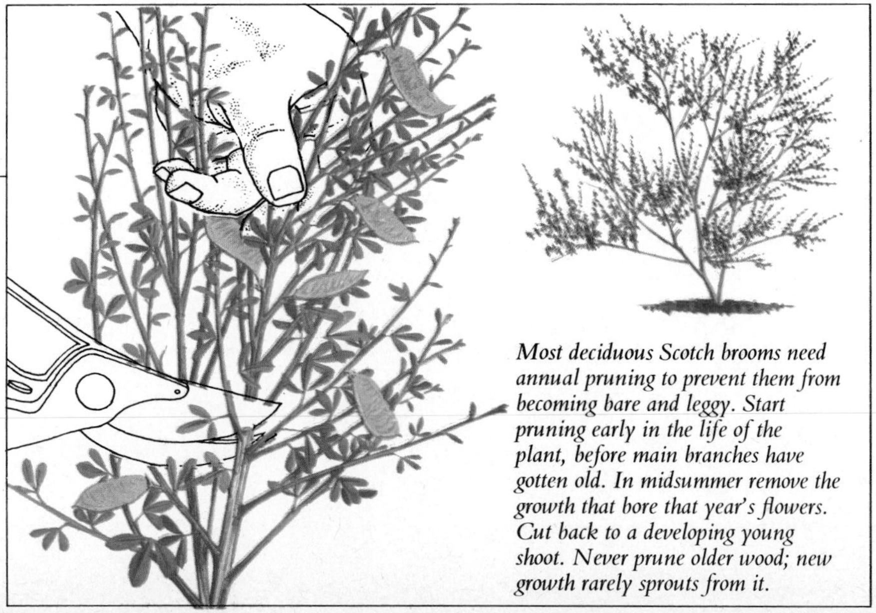

Most deciduous Scotch brooms need annual pruning to prevent them from becoming bare and leggy. Start pruning early in the life of the plant, before main branches have gotten old. In midsummer remove the growth that bore that year's flowers. Cut back to a developing young shoot. Never prune older wood; new growth rarely sprouts from it.

Broom, Spanish (*Spartium*). Cut back untidy old plants as hard as you like; trim young ones by about half.

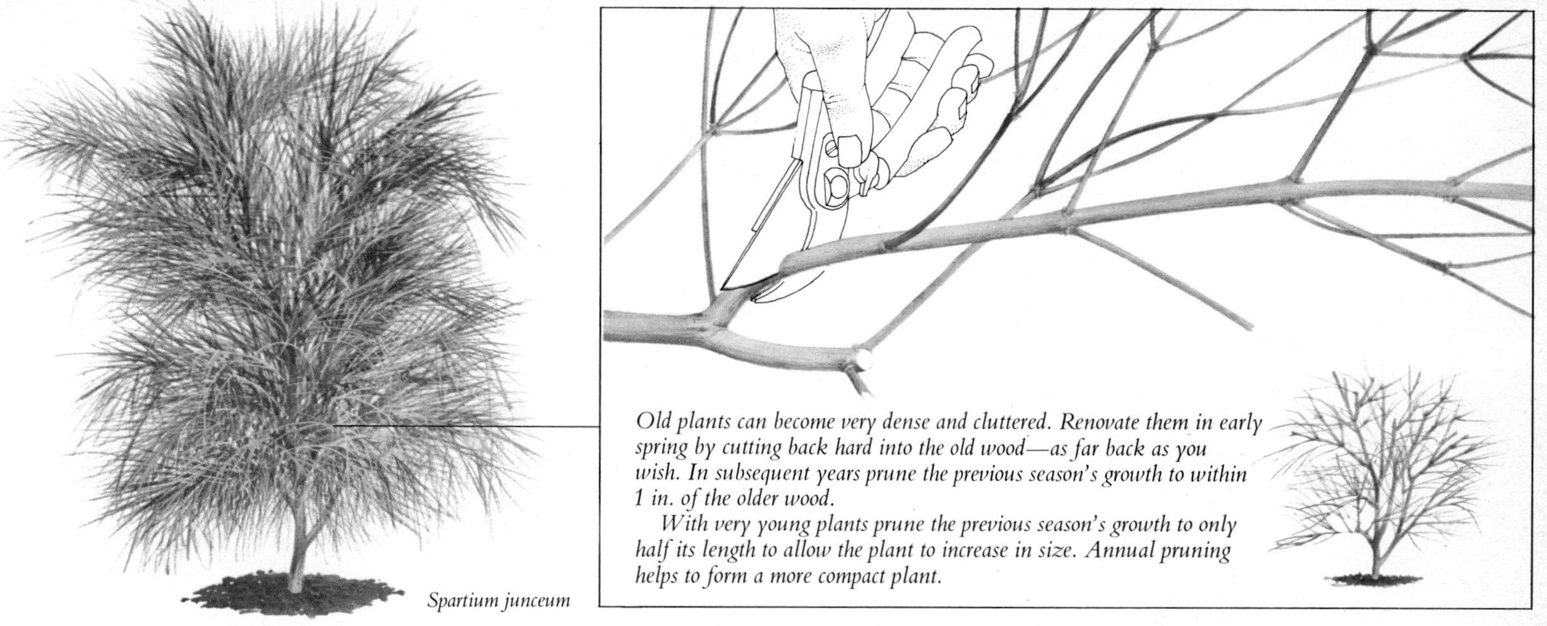

Old plants can become very dense and cluttered. Renovate them in early spring by cutting back hard into the old wood—as far back as you wish. In subsequent years prune the previous season's growth to within 1 in. of the older wood.

With very young plants prune the previous season's growth to only half its length to allow the plant to increase in size. Annual pruning helps to form a more compact plant.

Spartium junceum

Buddleja (*Buddleja alternifolia*). After flowering, remove old shoots to encourage the growth of new ones.

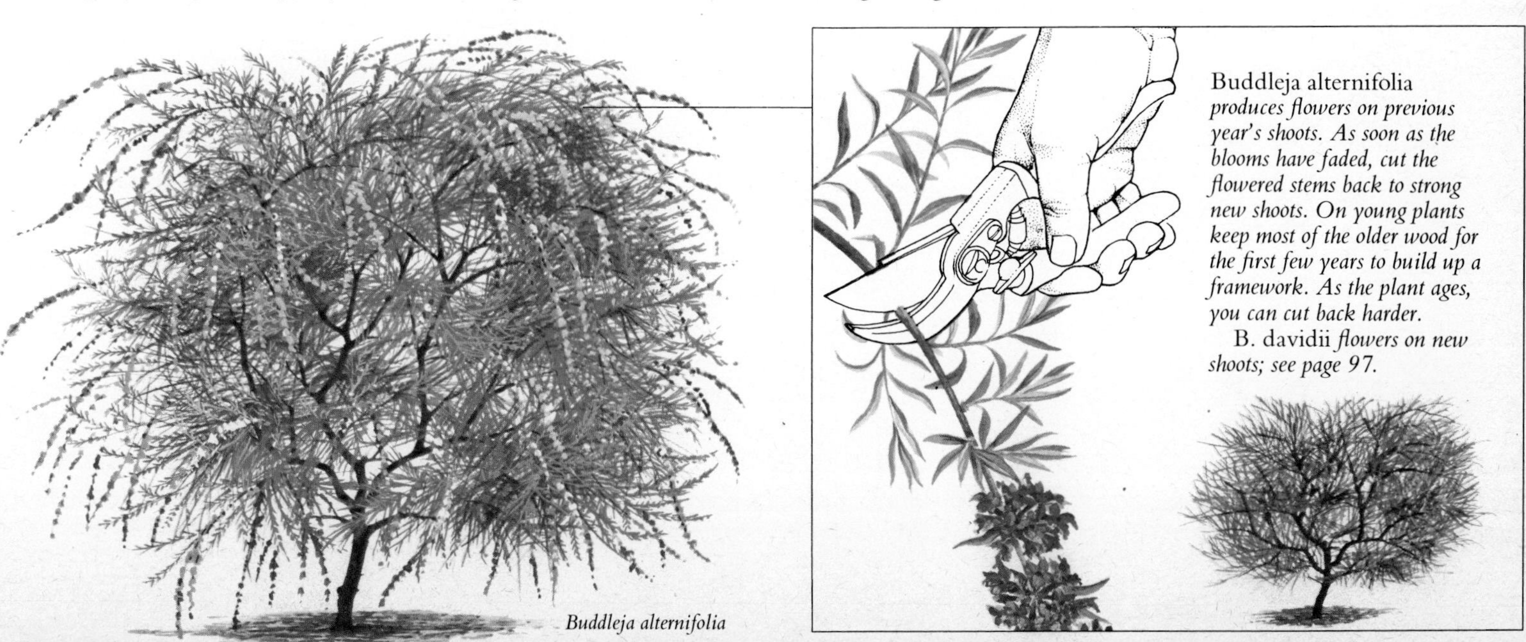

Buddleja alternifolia *produces flowers on previous year's shoots. As soon as the blooms have faded, cut the flowered stems back to strong new shoots. On young plants keep most of the older wood for the first few years to build up a framework. As the plant ages, you can cut back harder.*

B. davidii *flowers on new shoots;* *see page 97.*

Buddleja alternifolia

Ceanothus (*Ceanothus delilianus*). Prune deciduous ceanothus in midspring; new shoots will flower in late summer.

Ceanothus delilianus
'Gloire de Versailles'

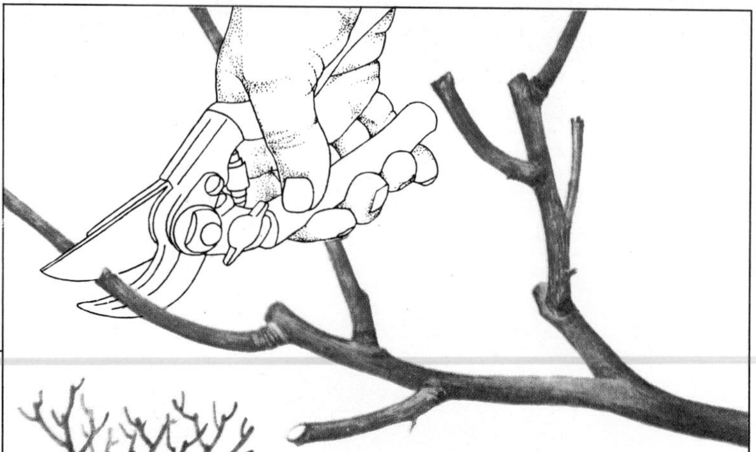

Each spring cut previous year's shoots back to two or three pairs of buds from the base. Prune young plants more lightly until a strong framework has been built up. With evergreen species just shorten leggy stems by half after the shrub has flowered.

Clematis. For the greatest show of flowers, no pruning is necessary, but eventually the tangled shoots may need to be cut back.

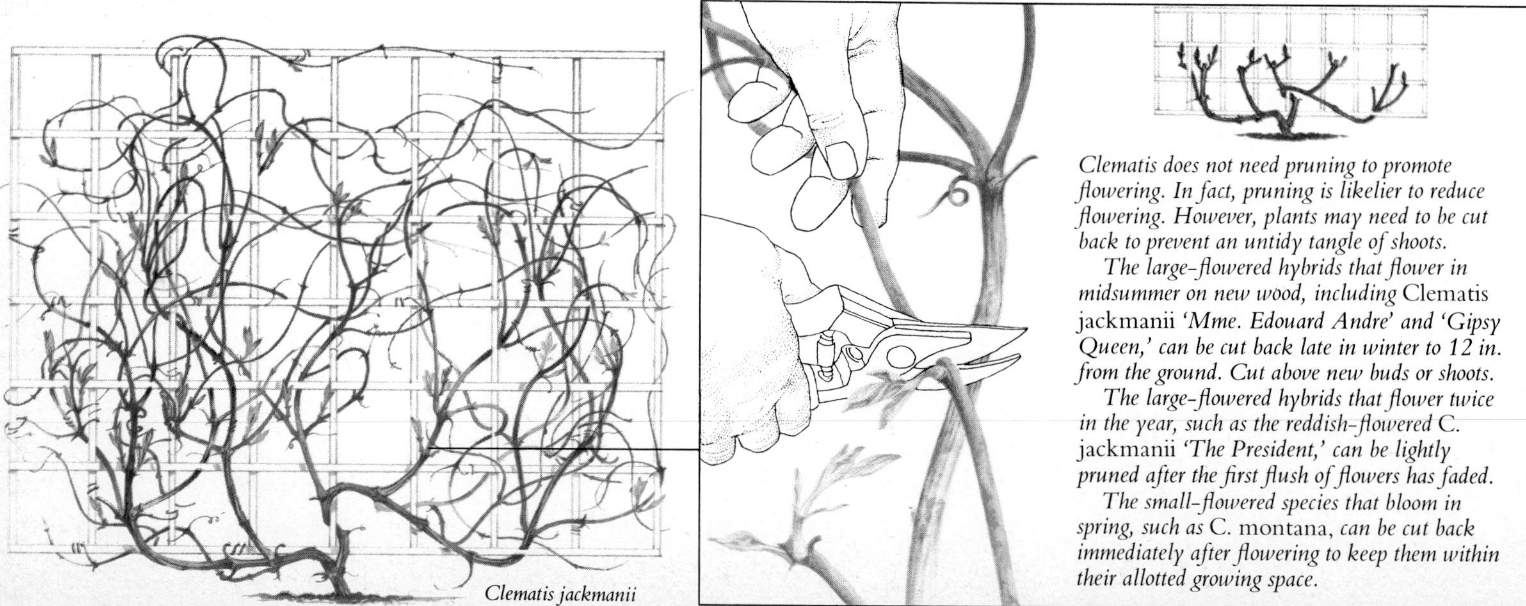

Clematis jackmanii

Clematis does not need pruning to promote flowering. In fact, pruning is likelier to reduce flowering. However, plants may need to be cut back to prevent an untidy tangle of shoots.

The large-flowered hybrids that flower in midsummer on new wood, including Clematis jackmanii *'Mme. Edouard Andre' and 'Gipsy Queen,' can be cut back late in winter to 12 in. from the ground. Cut above new buds or shoots.*

The large-flowered hybrids that flower twice in the year, such as the reddish-flowered C. jackmanii *'The President,' can be lightly pruned after the first flush of flowers has faded.*

The small-flowered species that bloom in spring, such as C. montana, *can be cut back immediately after flowering to keep them within their allotted growing space.*

Currant, flowering (*Ribes*). Regularly replace old wood with new by pruning after the flowers fade.

Deutzia. Remove the flowered stems in midsummer to prevent the shrub from becoming cluttered.

Dogwood (*Cornus alba* and *C. stolonifera*). For colored stems in winter, prune hard early the previous spring.

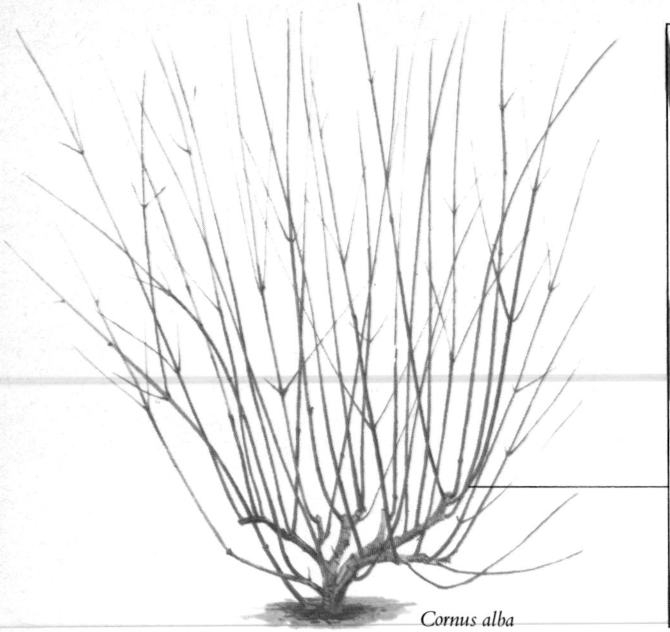

Cornus alba

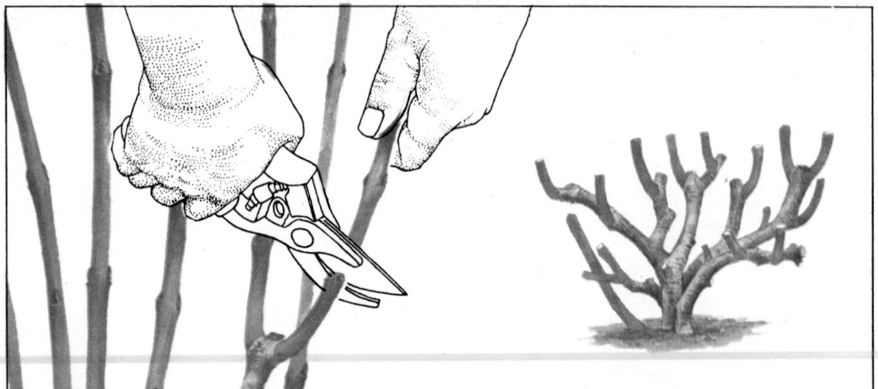

Cornus alba, *with its bright red bark, and* C. stolonifera flaviramea, *with its yellow bark, are valued for their colored stems in fall and winter. Young shoots are the brightest; so very early in the spring cut back the previous year's growth to a few inches tall.*

To renovate an old bush, as shown at left, cut strong shoots back hard and remove dead or weak shoots completely, producing a framework about 12 in. high.

Forsythia. Encourage fresh new wood by cutting out poor-flowering old wood regularly after spring flowers fade.

Forsythia intermedia

Most forsythias produce new branches from near the base. These will replace older wood, which flowers poorly. Do not prune a young bush; when it has been fully grown for two or three years, take out the oldest branches every year or two after the flowers fade. Cut low on the branch, just above a young shoot.

On Forsythia suspensa fortunei *prune the flowered shoots after blossoming to two buds from their bases.*

Fuchsia, hardy (*Fuchsia magellanica*). Cut back hard early in spring to encourage strong new shoots.

Fuchsia magellanica

In the North, growth may be damaged or killed to near ground level during winter. In spring, as soon as new growth appears, remove all dead shoots, cutting just above fresh new shoots near the base. Where main branches survive the winter, prune the laterals to one or two buds from the base, and remove the weak shoots.

Hydrangea, peegee (*Hydrangea paniculata grandiflora*). Prune the tall, white-flowered shrub back hard in spring.

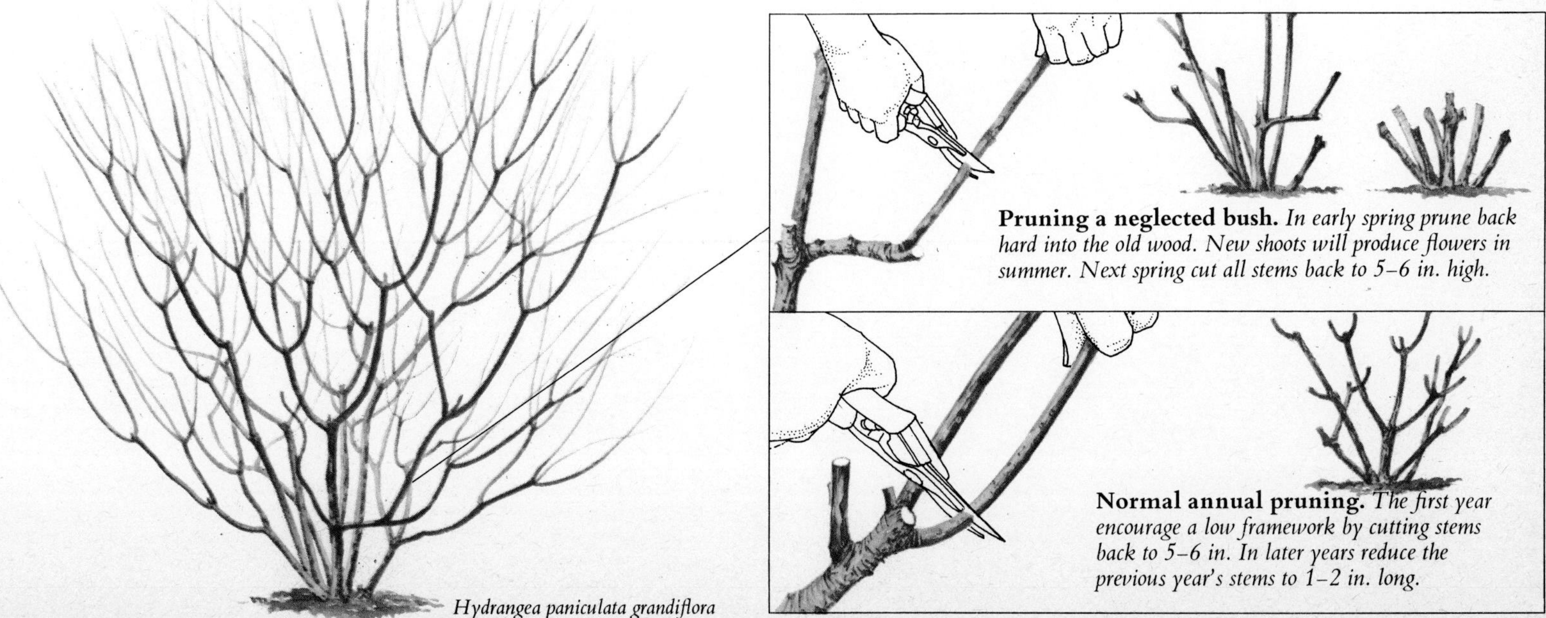

Hydrangea paniculata grandiflora

Pruning a neglected bush. *In early spring prune back hard into the old wood. New shoots will produce flowers in summer. Next spring cut all stems back to 5–6 in. high.*

Normal annual pruning. *The first year encourage a low framework by cutting stems back to 5–6 in. In later years reduce the previous year's stems to 1–2 in. long.*

Hypericum, low-growing (*Hypericum calycinum*). Cut back with shears in early spring for a dense, low cover.

Hypericum calycinum

Early in spring use garden shears to cut the old shoots back to within 2–3 in. of the base. At the same time clear away dead leaves and garden debris. Young shoots will develop quickly, and they will flower during the summer.

Hypericum, shrubby (*Hypericum patulum*). In early spring remove dead and spindly wood from the tall-growing hypericums.

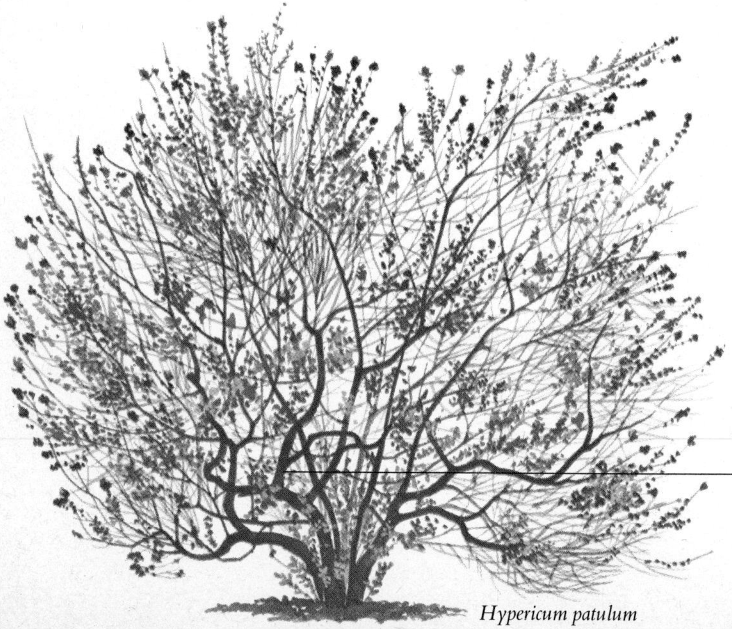

Hypericum patulum

Keep the bush the desired size by regularly cutting out all dead or weak growth in spring and by cutting back other growth to the point where new shoots arise. If the shrub has grown too large, dense, or straggly, cut it back hard in spring to where the young shoots are appearing. They will form a new framework. The shrub will not flower well until the following year.

Indigo (*Indigofera*). Winter frosts may do the pruning for you; if not, cut back hard in early spring.

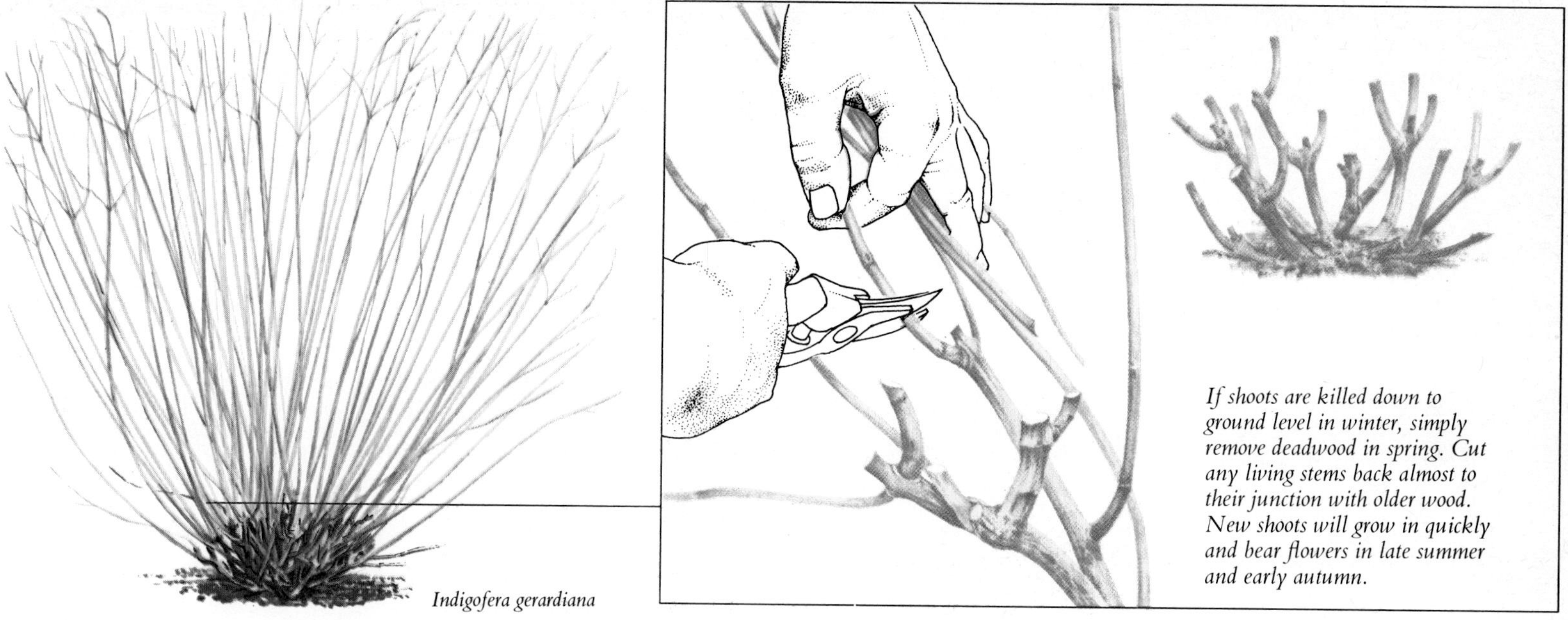

Indigofera gerardiana

If shoots are killed down to ground level in winter, simply remove deadwood in spring. Cut any living stems back almost to their junction with older wood. New shoots will grow in quickly and bear flowers in late summer and early autumn.

Jasmine, winter (*Jasminum nudiflorum*). After the shrub has flowered, cut back flowering shoots, and thin out weak stems.

Jasminum nudiflorum

If it is simply left to itself, the winter jasmine will soon become a dense tangle of scrubby-looking growth. To prevent this, early each spring cut back the shoots that have borne flowers to two or three buds from their junctions with the main branches. Cut away deadwood and weak growth to allow air to circulate. The white jasmine vine (J. officinale grandiflorum*) needs no such shortening. Simply remove any dead or overcrowded stems.*

Kerria. The best flowers appear on the young shoots; prune in late spring after the flowers have faded.

Kerria japonica

Kerrias produce new shoots each year near ground level, which flower the following season and then often die back. Encourage this habit by removing the flowering stems after the flowers have faded at the end of spring. Cut right back to the ground or, on stronger stems, to where new shoots are developing. Kerria japonica pleniflora *may need to have all its stems cut to the ground.*

Lavender (*Lavandula*). Prune in midspring to prevent this shrub from becoming leggy and sparse.

Without pruning, lavender will become leggy and bare stemmed. In midspring cut down the dead flower spikes from the year before, plus about 1 in. of top growth. Flowers can be removed in autumn if you wish to tidy the plant for winter, but trim in spring anyway. When plants are young, prune hard to encourage a bushy shape; but do not cut into the old wood of older plants, or the trimmed branches may die back.

Lippia (*Aloysia*). If the branches survive winter, hard-prune in midspring for larger flowers.

Aloysia triphylla

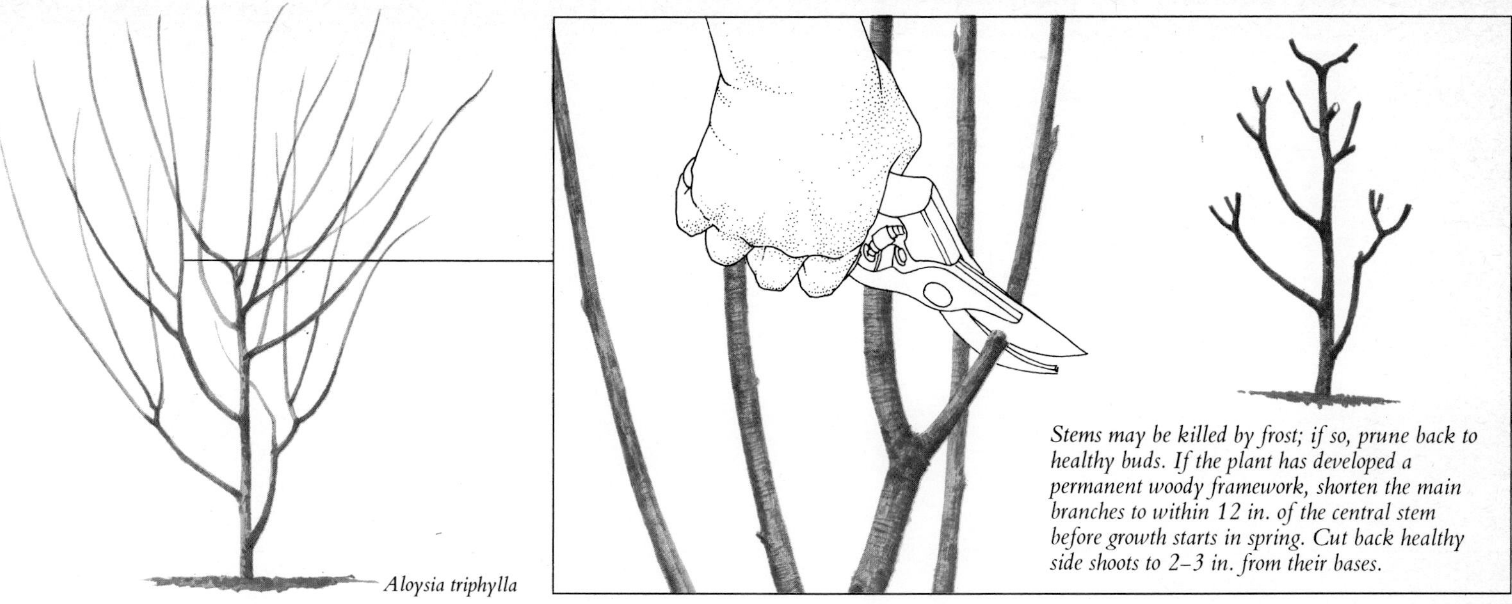

Stems may be killed by frost; if so, prune back to healthy buds. If the plant has developed a permanent woody framework, shorten the main branches to within 12 in. of the central stem before growth starts in spring. Cut back healthy side shoots to 2–3 in. from their bases.

Mock orange (*Philadelphus*). Rejuvenate an aging plant by cutting out the oldest branches to make room for young ones.

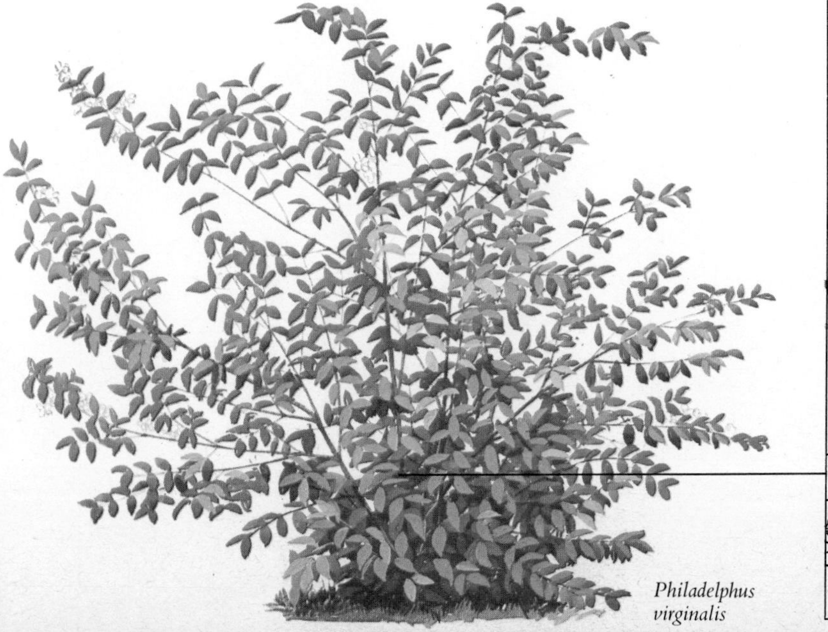

Philadelphus virginalis

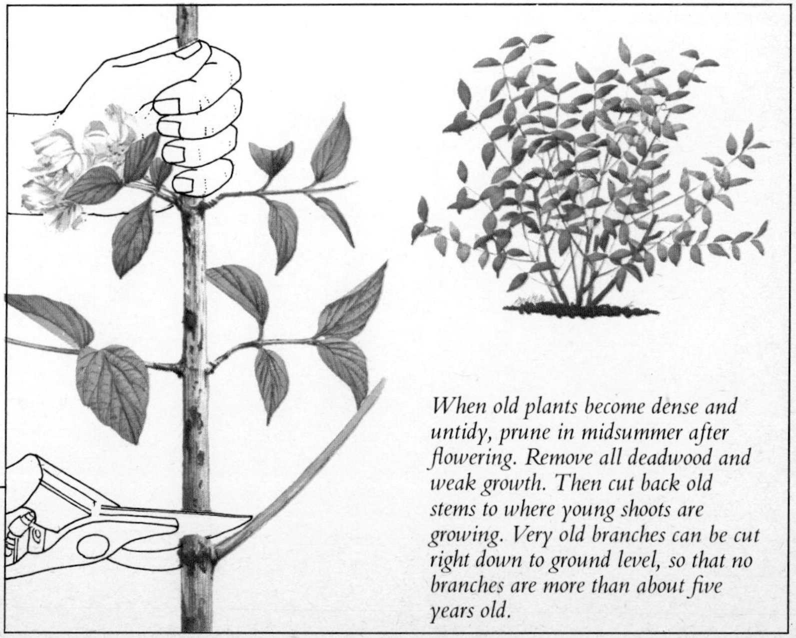

When old plants become dense and untidy, prune in midsummer after flowering. Remove all deadwood and weak growth. Then cut back old stems to where young shoots are growing. Very old branches can be cut right down to ground level, so that no branches are more than about five years old.

Plumbago (*Ceratostigma*). Cut to the ground in early spring for flowers on the new season's wood.

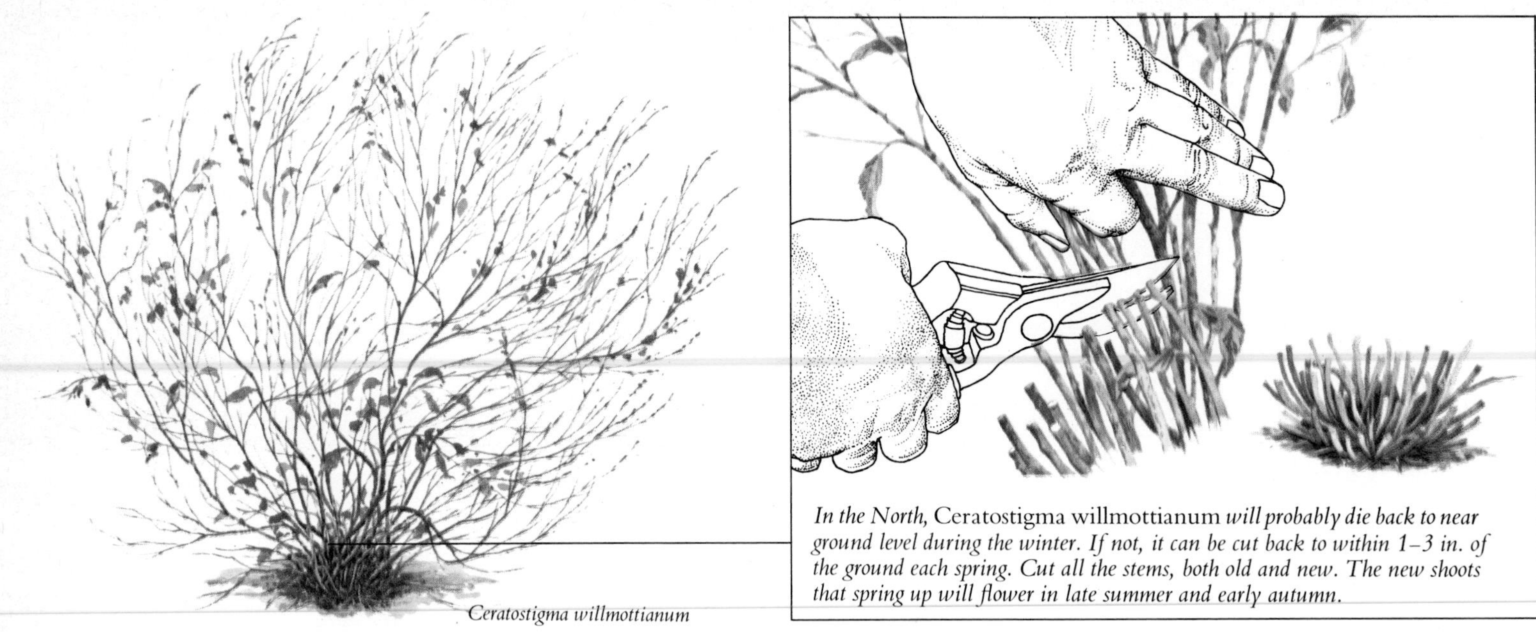

Ceratostigma willmottianum

In the North, Ceratostigma willmottianum *will probably die back to near ground level during the winter. If not, it can be cut back to within 1–3 in. of the ground each spring. Cut all the stems, both old and new. The new shoots that spring up will flower in late summer and early autumn.*

Quince, flowering (*Chaenomeles*). Keep a wall-trained shrub within bounds by pruning in the early part of summer.

Grown as a freestanding shrub, the flowering quince needs no pruning except to limit its size. When it is trained against a wall, tie in the leaders each year until the space is filled. In early to mid summer cut back young shoots not wanted for training to four or five leaves.

Chaenomeles speciosa

Rubus (*Rubus cockburnianus*). Cut out old stems after flowering to encourage new shoots to grow up from the base.

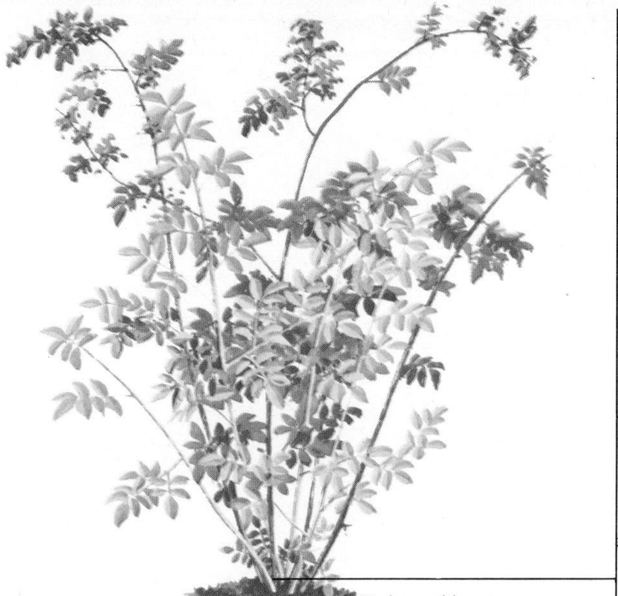

Rubus cockburnianus

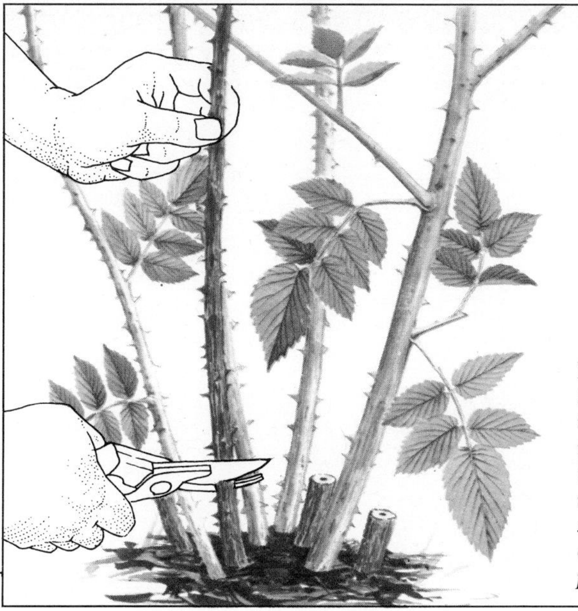

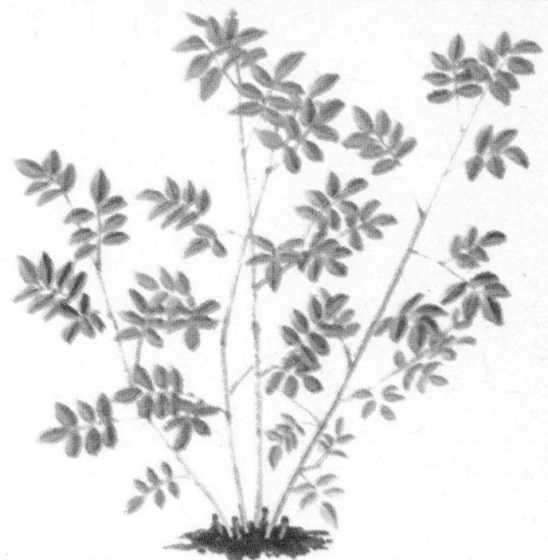

Rubus cockburnianus *is a raspberry that is grown for its white stems in winter. After the shrub has flowered in midsummer, cut out the stems that have borne flowers. Those that remain will be white in winter and will flower the next summer. Or you can forego flowers and ensure a good show of white stems by pruning the shrub back in late winter.*

Santolina. Prune in midspring to produce larger flowers and to prevent the plant from becoming straggly and unkempt.

Santolina chamaecyparissus

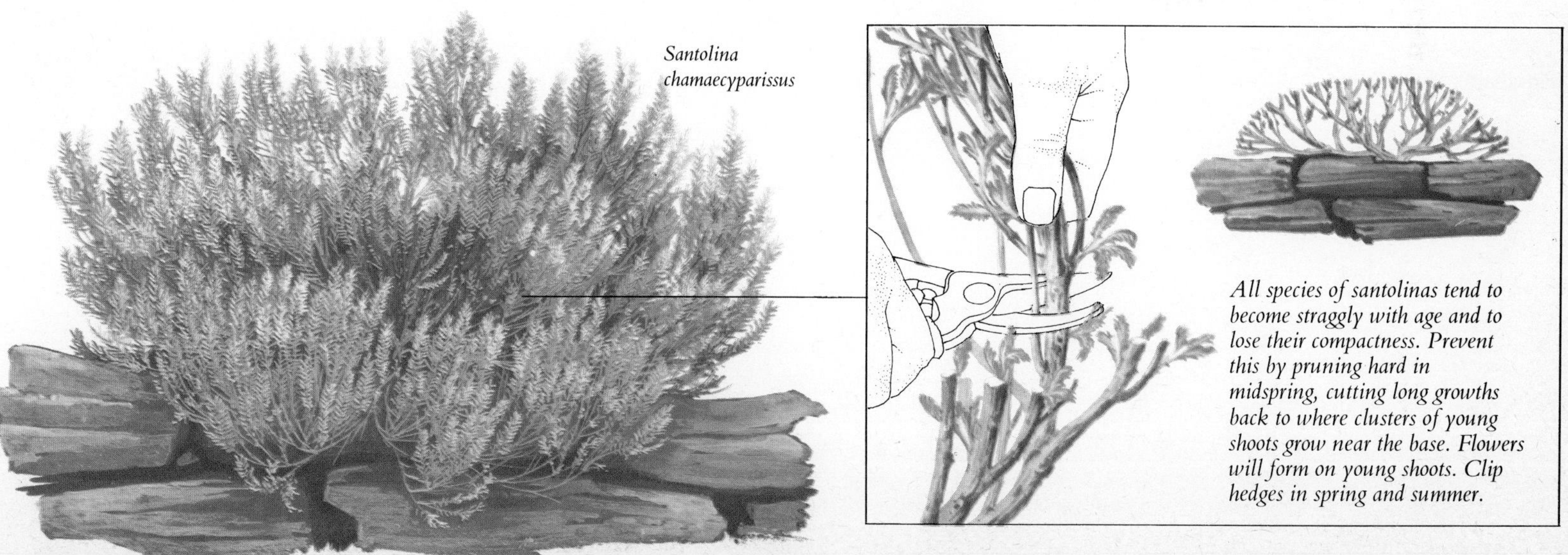

All species of santolinas tend to become straggly with age and to lose their compactness. Prevent this by pruning hard in midspring, cutting long growths back to where clusters of young shoots grow near the base. Flowers will form on young shoots. Clip hedges in spring and summer.

Spirea (*Spiraea arguta*). When the plant has become overgrown, renovate it by cutting back the old stems after the flowers have faded.

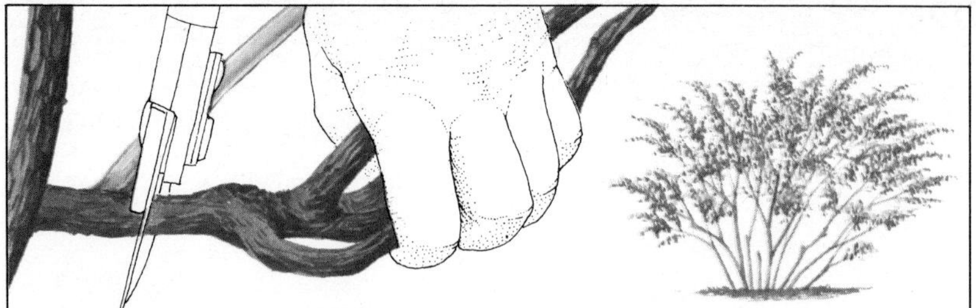

Some spireas, including Spiraea arguta *and* S. thunbergii, *produce their flowers on stems that grew the previous year. An old, overcrowded plant can be renovated late in spring, immediately after the flowers have faded. Cut back old stems to the point where younger shoots are growing.*

Both old and young plants require that their flowering shoots be shortened every year. Simply cut away the section of the stem that has borne flowers. The young lateral shoots already growing below that point will flower the following year.

Spiraea arguta

Spirea (*Spiraea japonica*). Prune almost to the ground in spring, and flat heads of pink flowers will develop in late summer.

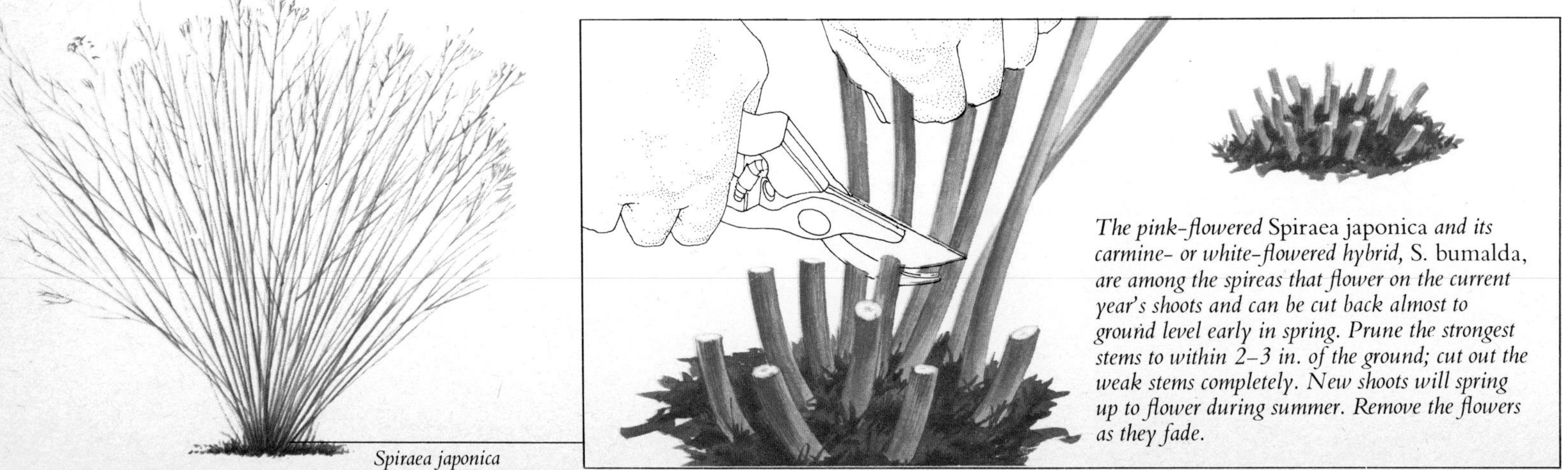

The pink-flowered Spiraea japonica *and its carmine- or white-flowered hybrid,* S. bumalda, *are among the spireas that flower on the current year's shoots and can be cut back almost to ground level early in spring. Prune the strongest stems to within 2–3 in. of the ground; cut out the weak stems completely. New shoots will spring up to flower during summer. Remove the flowers as they fade.*

Spirea, false (*Sorbaria*). For better foliage and larger flowers, cut down all the stems every winter.

Sorbaria aitchisonii

Stephanandra. Prune hard after flowering in summer to encourage attractive colored leaves and stems.

Stephanandra tanakae

Sumac (*Rhus*). Prune back previous year's growth in winter to produce large, attractive foliage for autumn display.

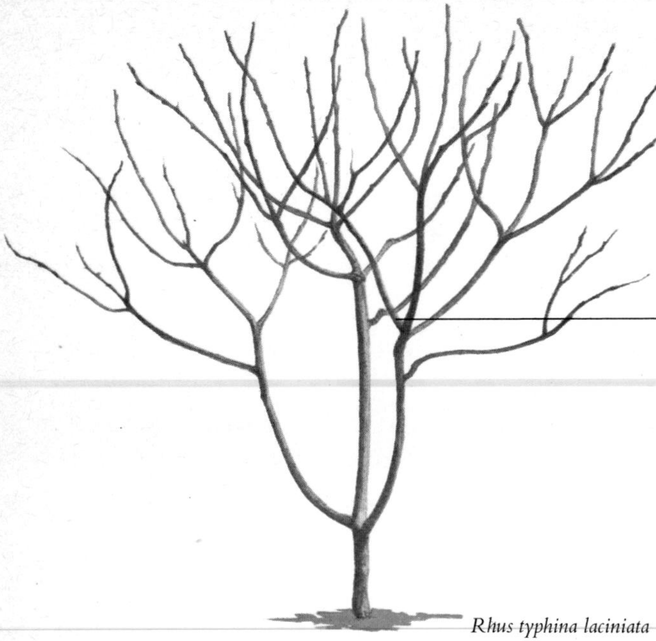

Rhus typhina laciniata

Many sumac species are valued for the fiery red and orange coloration of the autumn foliage. To get a good display, with extralarge leaves, cut the previous year's growth back to about 4 in. from the old wood near the end of winter. In this way a strong, low framework will be built up gradually.

Sweet pepper bush (*Clethra*). To restrict the size of an old shrub, prune out the oldest stems in early spring.

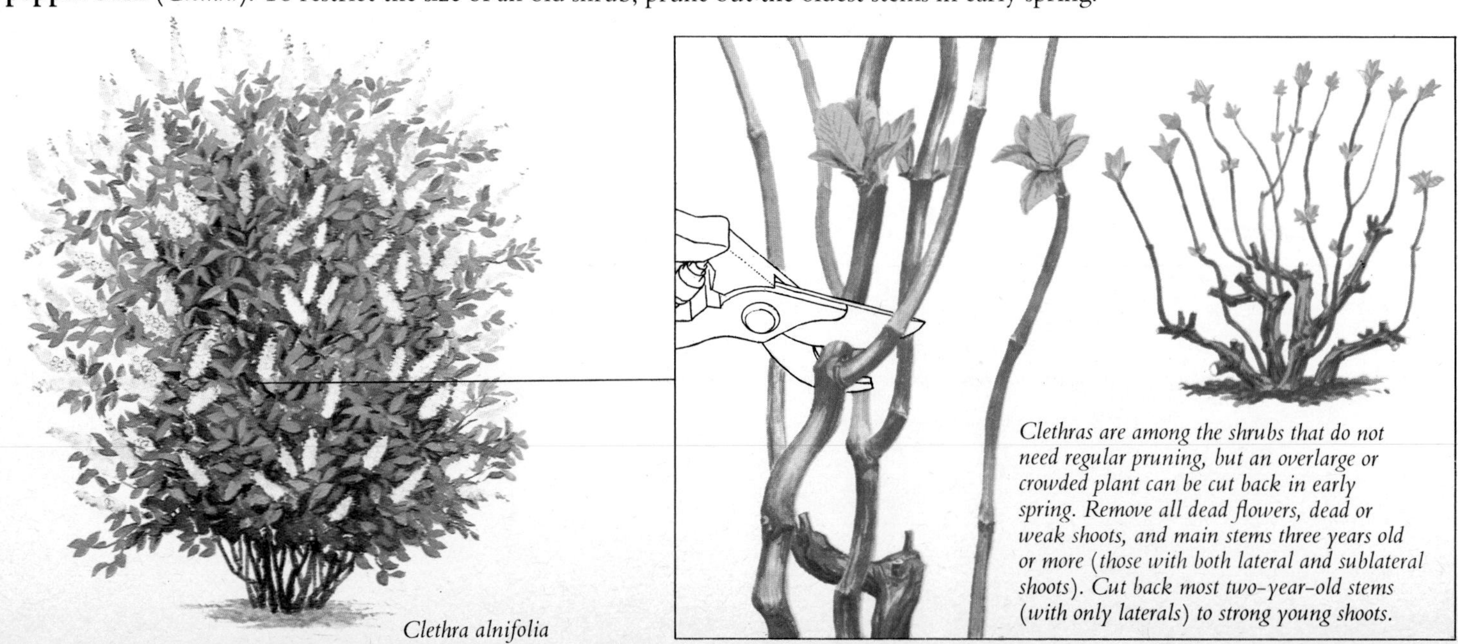

Clethra alnifolia

Clethras are among the shrubs that do not need regular pruning, but an overlarge or crowded plant can be cut back in early spring. Remove all dead flowers, dead or weak shoots, and main stems three years old or more (those with both lateral and sublateral shoots). Cut back most two-year-old stems (with only laterals) to strong young shoots.

Tamarix. To keep the plants compact, prune summer-flowering species hard late in winter, spring bloomers after flowering.

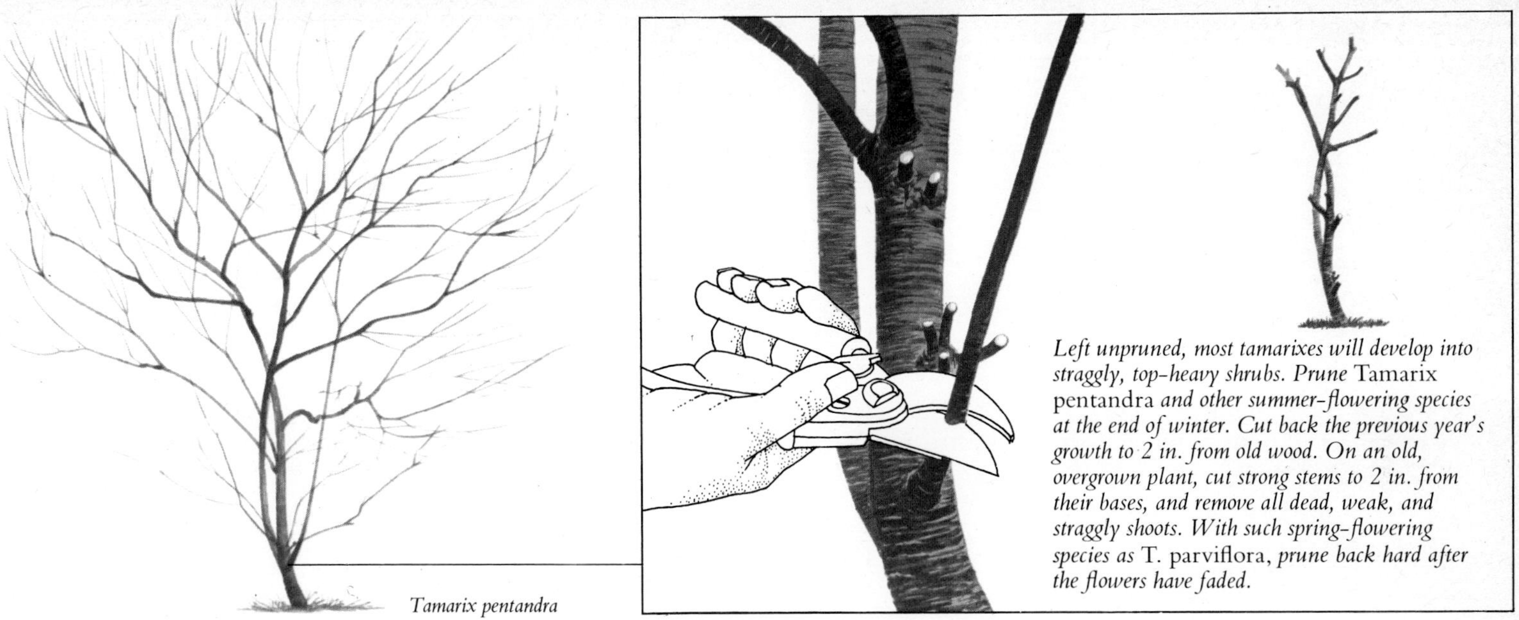

Tamarix pentandra

Left unpruned, most tamarixes will develop into straggly, top-heavy shrubs. Prune Tamarix pentandra *and other summer-flowering species at the end of winter. Cut back the previous year's growth to 2 in. from old wood. On an old, overgrown plant, cut strong stems to 2 in. from their bases, and remove all dead, weak, and straggly shoots. With such spring-flowering species as* T. parviflora, *prune back hard after the flowers have faded.*

Vitex. Cut the stems right down in winter for late summer flowers and large, aromatic leaves.

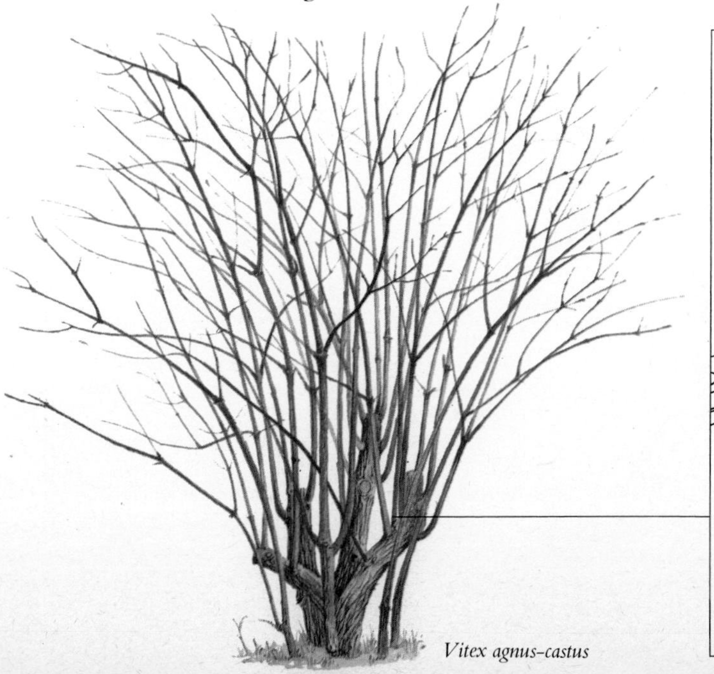

Vitex agnus-castus

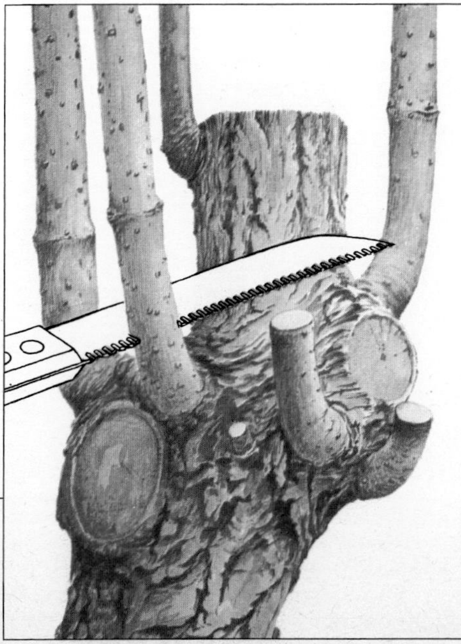

The vitex, or the chaste tree, can be cut back hard late every winter. To keep a shrub small, remove all stems to within 2–3 in. of the ground. For a larger specimen allow a framework of trunk and main branches to build up over several years; then cut each year's new growth to within 2–3 in. of its base in midwinter. Cut out all weak shoots completely. For thicker shoots use a pruning saw, not loppers, and apply tree-wound paint.

Weigela. To prevent plants from becoming overcrowded, prune away the flowered shoots after they have bloomed in summer.

Weigela florida

Weigelas can quickly become dense and crowded, with fewer flowers. To prevent this, cut out dead and weak shoots after flowering in summer, and prune the flowered stems just above a point where young shoots are developing. With an old, neglected shrub, cut the oldest branches down to a few inches from the ground. If pure green leaves appear on Weigela florida variegata, *remove the whole shoot.*

Wisteria. To promote good flower clusters on this vine, cut back the fast-growing shoots in summer.

Wisteria sinensis

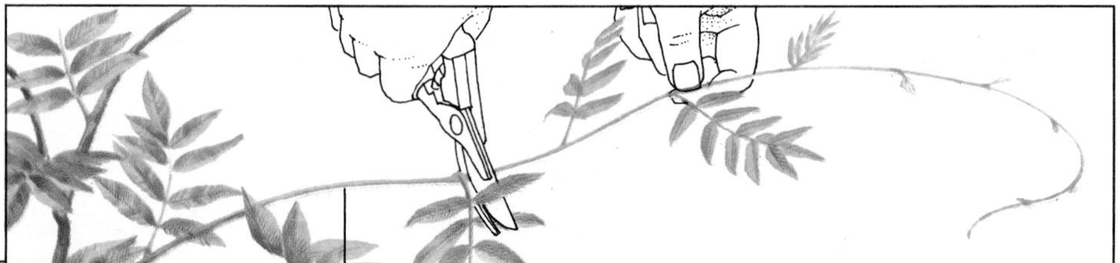

Winter pruning

In summer train the long leaders in the direction you want the plant to spread. To encourage flowering spurs, pinch or cut back unwanted shoots to a length of 6–12 in. In midwinter shorten these shoots further—to two or three buds from their base.

An alternative method, for more flower buds, is to work the plant over every couple of weeks during summer, pinching back all growth not needed to extend the plant. Pinch back shoots to about 4 in., and later pinch back any extension growth to two leaves. In this way each shoot will be pinched back about three times during the season. No winter pruning will be needed.

Shrubs for Your Garden

On the following pages you will find descriptions of and basic information about more than 170 different shrubs that will grow in various parts of the United States. This information is presented in chart form to facilitate your finding what you need to know to keep your shrubs healthy and productive. Vines are listed separately at the end of the section.

Names and characteristics. Botanists classify all plants according to genus (general groupings of plants with similar characteristics) and species (specific plants within the genus). In the first column of each left-hand page that follows, you will find shrubs listed by genus, arranged alphabetically according to their best known common names. In many cases, such as the fuchsia and magnolia, the common name is also the name of the genus. With others, like the dogwood, it is not. In either case, the name of the genus (*Cornus* for dogwood) appears in italics in parentheses immediately following the common name.

Some shrubs are valued for their flowers, some for their foliage, some for their habit of growth. The characteristics described in this column, and all information on the left-hand pages of the chart, apply to shrubs specifically included in the chart that are in the mentioned genus.

On the right-hand chart pages, shrubs of each genus mentioned are subdivided into species, varieties, and hybrids. The illustration that accompanies each generic heading shows one of the species within that genus; it does not portray the genus as a whole.

Uses and requirements. Each shrub has its advantages and its limitations. Some are ideal for hedges; others make good windbreaks; still others need protection from the wind. In addition, many shrubs have rather specific needs in terms of soil characteristics, sunlight, water, drainage, pruning, feeding, general care, and pest control. To find the recommended treatment for control of pests or diseases, look up specific plant disorders in the Index.

Insofar as this information applies to the genus as a whole, it is incorporated under the heading Uses and Requirements on the chart. Further details on planting and care of shrubs appear on pages 81–86. For pruning methods see pages 95–118.

Propagation. An economical and satisfying way to obtain more shrubs is to propagate those you already have. With most shrubs the simplest propagation methods are to take hardwood cuttings or to soil-layer branches. But several other techniques are workable. The methods are illustrated on pages 87–94.

Under the heading Propagation on the following pages, you will find the appropriate method, or methods, for propagating each kind of shrub.

Species and varieties. On the right-hand pages of the chart, you will find a selection of some widely planted shrubs. Each one's species name consists of the name of its genus, plus a second word (called a specific epithet). A third word indicates a subspecies or variety. The genus name is always written out and capitalized the first time it appears; for the related plants that follow, the genus name (and in many cases, the specific epithet) is abbreviated.

Both the genus name and the specific epithet (including any subspecies) are always italicized. Also italicized in the system followed here is a varietal name if it is in Latinized form, such as *veitchii* (*Gardenia jasminoides veitchii,* for example). All Anglicized varietal names appear in roman type and in single quotation marks—*G. j.* 'August Beauty,' for example.

A shrub that is listed by genus and species can be reproduced from seeds. The vast majority of varieties, however—whether they came into existence through hybridization or as chance deviate seedlings, or "sports"—can be duplicated only by vegetative propagation: via cuttings, division, layers, or grafts. There are a very few exceptions to this rule, but unfortunately, varietal names do not indicate which varieties of shrubs will indeed "come true" from seeds.

In buying a shrub, it is important to ask for it by its full botanical name. There are wide differences among the species (and even among the varieties) in any genus, including whether they are evergreen or deciduous, as well as their size, hardiness, flower color, flowering time, and special requirements.

Hardiness. Before buying a shrub, your first consideration should be whether or not it will survive in the climate where you live. As a general guide, the U.S. Department of Agriculture regularly prepares and distributes a *Plant Hardiness Zone Map.* On this map the continental United States is divided into eight major zones, based on average minimum temperatures. On page 9 you will find a simplification of this map, divided for convenience into four major zones; each zone represents a difference of about 20° F in average wintertime low-temperature readings. Beside the name of each species or variety, under the heading Hardiness, the coldest zone in which the shrub can reasonably be expected to grow has been indicated.

Bear in mind that the map is at best only a general indication of the climate where you are located. Higher altitudes in each area are likely to be colder than the zone map indicates; other topographical features create additional microclimates that can vary greatly from the average minimum temperatures listed.

Nor is the minimum wintertime temperature the only consideration affecting plant hardiness. Cold winds can do more damage than mere low temperatures. Therefore, a shrub that could be killed in an exposed location might well survive unscathed on the lee side of a hedge or wall on the same premises. The dates of the first and last frost are also important, as are the relative humidity and the amount of sunlight the shrub receives. The lowest temperature that a shrub can be expected to tolerate is still, however, the most useful and dependable single indicator of its likelihood of survival. In addition, some hardy plants *require* cold winters and cannot survive in southern zones. Your local nurseryman will know which these are.

On the other hand, some plants will not survive temperatures below 30° F, and these are marked with an asterisk following the hardiness-zone indication on the charts.

Characteristics and remarks. In this column on the chart, you will find a description of special qualities, most of which set a species or variety apart from other members of its genus. Such qualities may be decorative characteristics, such as the kind of foliage a shrub bears; its time of flowering; the size, color, or fragrance of its blossoms; or the nature of its fruit.

Some shrub species require special growing conditions. Certain kinds cannot tolerate dry heat in summer; others are endangered by extreme humidity. Some must be planted in the sun, others in shade.

Soil requirements often vary among species. If a plant requires acid or alkaline soil, rapid drainage, or swampy conditions, the need is indicated here. If a species is tolerant of such special conditions as urban pollution or ocean salt spray, this, too, is noted.

Height and spread. The dimensions given are those that the particular species, variety, or hybrid is known to reach after several years in good growing conditions. The ultimate size, however, will vary according to the local climate, the degree of shelter, the amount of sunlight, the soil, the care the shrub receives—particularly during its formative years—and the frequency and manner of pruning.

Common and botanical names, general characteristics	Uses and requirements	Propagation (*See also p. 87*)
Abelia *(Abelia)* Characterized by small tubular or bell-shaped summer flowers that range in color from white to shades of rosy pink. Leaves are small and on some kinds an interesting bronze-green color. Branches arch gracefully.	Some kinds have dense habit of growth and can be used for hedges. They are all strong growers and can be pruned in spring to any extent required for their specific situation in garden. Likes well-drained, humusy soil. Will grow in sun or partial shade.	Take soft-shoot cuttings in late spring or semi-hard-shoot cuttings in summer; with deciduous sort take leafless hardwood cuttings in fall. Can be soil-layered in spring. Ripe seeds can be kept in closed containers for up to 1 yr. prior to planting.
Acacia *(Acacia)* Quick grower but relatively short-lived—20-30 yr. Tiny, yellow, finger-shaped flowers (sometimes fragrant), crowded in globular clusters or spikes, have prominent stamens. Flowers open in early to mid spring.	Well suited to tub culture. Plant in full sun in any good garden soil. Transplant only young specimens, since taproot makes moving established plants difficult or impossible. Water transplants thoroughly until well adjusted to new location.	Seeds should be soaked in hot water for a few minutes and then soaked in cold water for about 2 da. to soften coatings. Plant while wet. Germination often takes up to 5 wk. Take semi-hard-shoot cuttings in summer.
Acacia, rose *(Robinia)* Pea-shaped flowers in late spring or early summer open in hanging racemes. Compound alternate leaves made up of 12 or 13 rounded leaflets that give plant interesting texture.	Useful in poor, rocky soils where few other plants will grow. Helps prevent erosion on steep banks. Can be trained as a standard (single stem). Spreads rapidly by suckers and needs plenty of room. In some locations it could become nuisance.	Sow seeds when ripe, or store in a cool, dry place for up to 1 yr. Soak seeds overnight in water at 90° F; then plant. Take root cuttings or remove and plant suckers.
Almond, see Prunus		
Anemone, bush *(Carpenteria)* Clusters of saucer-shaped flowers are white, fragrant, and up to 3 in. across. Shiny leaves 3-4 in. long.	Grows best in sun or partial shade and light, well-drained soil. Intolerant of wet winters and must be screened from strong, cold winds. Not easy to transplant.	Increased by seeds or soil layers. Take semi-hard-shoot cuttings in summer.
Aralia, five-leaved *(Acanthopanax)* Grown primarily for its handsome foliage. Inconspicuous summer flowers develop in multibranched clusters. Only 1 species generally grown.	Excellent as border plant or as accent on lawns. Suitable for city use because it can tolerate soot and grime. Takes well to trimming and is sometimes used for hedges. Spines at base of leaves make it effective barrier plant. It will grow in shade in any good soil and is generally free of pests.	Sow seeds after stratifying or take root cuttings. Leafy semi-hard-shoot cuttings can also be taken in summer.

Abelia floribunda

Acacia podalyraefolia

Robinia hispida

Carpenteria californica

Acanthopanax sieboldianus

Species and varieties	Hardiness (Map, p. 9)	Decorative characteristics and remarks	Height and spread when mature
Deciduous *Abelia schumannii*	☐☐C☐	Oval-shaped, slightly toothed leaves are about 1 in. long. Dark pink to lavender-pink flowers bloom from midsummer to early fall.	H 6 ft.–S 6 ft.
Evergreen or semi-evergreen *A.* 'Edward Goucher' (pink)	☐B☐☐	Leaves are semi-evergreen. Lavender-pink blossoms open from midsummer to early fall. Even if killed to ground, usually recovers.	H 5 ft.–S 5 ft.
A. floribunda (Mexican)	☐☐☐D	Leaves are slightly toothed, more than 1 in. long. Has rust-colored twigs and pendulous red flowers in summer; occasionally blooms early—in late winter.	H 6 ft.–S 5 ft.
A. grandiflora (glossy)	☐B☐☐	Leaves that are semi-evergreen, or deciduous in cold climates, turn bronze-purple in fall. Pink flowers open in clusters of up to 4 from late summer until late fall and bloom until frost. A good hedge plant.	H 5 ft.–S 5 ft.
Evergreen *Acacia armata* (kangaroo thorn)	☐☐C☐	A spiny species with numerous rounded flower heads and small waxy leaves. Will live in dry, sandy soil and is suitable for hedges.	H 10 ft.–S 12 ft.
A. decora (graceful wattle)	☐☐☐D	Narrow, curved, bluish leaves; yellow ball-shaped flower heads in clusters in midspring. Drought resistant. Can be trimmed as hedge.	H 6-8 ft.–S 6-8 ft.
A. glandulicarpa	☐☐☐D	Tiny, waxy green leaves and profuse ball-shaped yellow flowers that are fragrant. A compact, low-branching shrub.	H 8 ft.–S 8 ft.
A. podalyraefolia	☐☐☐D	Blue-gray foliage is hairy and displays silvery cast. Its rounded flower heads develop in racemes. One of the first acacias to bloom.	H 8-15 ft.–S 15 ft.
A. verticillata	☐☐C☐	Thin, whorled, dark green leaves are almost 1 in. long and needlelike. Flower spikes are 1 in. long.	H 6-15 ft.–S 8-15 ft.
Deciduous *Robinia hispida*	☐B☐☐	Clusters of pink to purplish-pink blossoms have attractive character of wisteria. It is often trained upright as a standard to show blossoms to best effect. Fruits and brittle twigs are covered with bright red bristles. Seedpods are up to 3 in. long.	H 4 ft.–S 3-6 ft.
Evergreen *Carpenteria californica*	☐☐C☐	Leaves are oblong. Flowers develop individually or in clusters of 2-7.	H 8-10 ft.–S 8 ft.
Deciduous *Acanthopanax sieboldianus*	☐B☐☐	Glossy leaves are composed of up to 7 somewhat wedge-shaped leaflets that spread in finger fashion from tip of stalk on arching branches. They are an attractive dark green and turn yellow before dropping in fall. Plant blooms rather sparsely with greenish-white flowers; but lack of bloom not a disadvantage for plant with such handsome leaves. Fruits are seldom seen in cultivation, since male and female plants are rarely planted in close proximity in home gardens.	H 9 ft.–S 6-10 ft.

	Common and botanical names, general characteristics	Uses and requirements	Propagation *(See also p. 87)*
 *Fatsia japonica*	**Aralia, Japanese** *(Fatsia)* Leathery, glossy leaves up to 15 in. wide have 8- to 12-in. stalks and blades with as many as 9 pointed oval lobes. Small whitish flowers are followed by blue-black berrylike fruits hanging in heavy trusses.	Grown as house plant in cold climates. Makes good tub plant. Will live in full sun or considerable shade. Does best in sandy soil mixed with peat moss or other organic material. Older plants often sucker; allow to grow or sever with sharp spade. Thin yearly to expose attractive branch structure.	Sow seeds when ripe. Transplant suckers in early or mid spring. Take leafy semi-hard-shoot cuttings in summer or air-layer.
 *Aucuba japonica*	**Aucuba** *(Aucuba)* A handsome, densely leaved plant, with shiny, often variegated leaves. Minute male and female blossoms are on separate plants. Fruit (female plants only) is red or creamy white berry, showy on some kinds.	Useful in seacoast gardens, since it tolerates salt spray. Withstands smog. Lives in sun or shade, although foliage sometimes burns in sun. Needs a great deal of water. For optimum berry production, plant at least 4 female specimens to every male.	Sow seeds when ripe. Layer a branch into soil in spring. Take semi-hard-shoot cuttings in summer.
	Azalea, see p. 222		
 *Azara microphylla*	**Azara** *(Azara)* Has leathery foliage. Vanilla-scented blossoms have sepals but no petals, and the many stamens are usually showy.	Needs shade and considerable moisture for best results.	Plant seeds or take hardwood cuttings in fall.
 *Bambusa multiplex*	**Bamboo** (several genera) These members of the grass family usually have hollow jointed stems. There are several closely related genera, all with attractive, feathery foliage and slender, arching stems that often develop in clusters. Bamboos are classified as running or clump, depending on how rhizomes (underground stems) grow. If rhizomes are fast spreading and produce numerous vertical stems that may cover sizable areas, they are called running. If rhizomes are not spreading and vertical stems form close to parent plant, they are called clump bamboos. All plants mentioned here are running types except for *Bambusa multiplex*. Most genera produce flowers only at long intervals, and most are rapid growing.	Plant in full sun in any good garden soil. Running bamboos, which spread by underground rhizomes, frequently overwhelm their surroundings unless planted in tubs sunk 3 ft. into ground. Top growth should be cut back severely every 2 yr. Clump bamboos are less aggressive and slower growing.	Increase running bamboos by root cuttings taken from midwinter to early spring. Make root divisions of clump bamboos. Take shoot cuttings or make soil layers when weather is warm.
	Bamboo, heavenly, see Heavenly bamboo		

Species and varieties	Hardiness (Map, p. 9)	Decorative characteristics and remarks	Height and spread when mature
Evergreen *Fatsia japonica*	□□□D	Flowers appear in mid to late fall in distinctive branching clusters. Berries last into winter. Occasional pruning prevents leggy growth.	H 15 ft.–S 15 ft.
F. j. moseri	□□□D	Lower and more compact than *F. japonica.*	H 6 ft.–S 6 ft.
F. j. variegata	□□□D	Leaves are edged with creamy white. Needs some shade from strong sun.	H 10 ft.–S 10 ft.
Evergreen *Aucuba japonica*	□□C□	Shiny oval leaves are deep green and up to 8 in. long. Panicles, 2-5 in. long, have small olive-colored blossoms in early spring. Bright red fruits (female only) last until spring. Both male and female plants available.	H 12 ft.–S 7 ft.
A. j. crotonifolia	□□C□	Much the same as *A. japonica,* but foliage has golden yellow spots.	H 12 ft.–S 7 ft.
A. j. fructualbo	□□C□	Sparsely spotted leaves. This female variety bears creamy white berries.	H 12 ft.–S 7 ft.
A. j. longifolia	□□C□	Leaves are green, narrow, and willowlike. Scarlet berries are numerous.	H 12 ft.–S 7 ft.
A. j. picturata	□□C□	Center of leaf bears large yellow blotch. Female plants available.	H 12 ft.–S 7 ft.
A. j. variegata (gold-dust plant)	□□C□	Yellow spots on leaves create interesting effect. Bright red berries on female plants only, but male plants available.	H 12 ft.–S 7 ft.
Evergreen *Azara microphylla* (box leaf)	□□□D	Shiny, dark green leaves to 1 in. long. Fragrant greenish-yellow flowers open in late winter and early spring. Orange-red berries. General habit of growth is spreading, but branches are erect. Good for espaliering. Slow growing when young.	H 12-18 ft. S 8-12 ft.
Evergreen *Arundinaria variegata*	□□C□	Leaves show handsome white striping. Slender stems die in cold winter areas and should be cut back to ground in spring to stimulate new growth. Needs restraint, especially in fertile soil. Spreads by suckers.	H 3 ft.–S 3-6 ft.
Bambusa multiplex	□□□D *	Reddish-green leaves to 6 in. long have silvery undersides. Among varieties are one with yellow- and green-striped shoots and another with white-striped leaves. A clump-forming species. A slow grower, good for hedging.	H 25 ft.–S 4-10 ft.
Phyllostachys aurea	□□C□	Upright, rigid, straw-colored stems are edible when young. Narrow, densely growing leaves to 5 in. long look best when watered regularly.	H 20 ft.–S 4-10 ft.
Phyllostachys niger	□□C□	Leaves are up to 5 in. long and faintly toothed at edges. Undersides are bluish green. Green stems turn black as they mature, displaying white bands beneath each joint. Needs restraint. Young shoots are edible.	H 20 ft.–S 4-10 ft.
Pseudosasa japonica	□□C□	Glossy leaves 4-12 in. long have whitish, slightly hairy undersides. Not aggressive spreader. Used as tub plant. In cold winter areas stems die back to ground, but plants produce new growth each spring.	H 15 ft.–S 3-6 ft.
Sasa palmata	□□C□	Green 4- to 15-in.-long leaves have silvery undersides. In North foliage may stay green in mild winters. Spreads by suckers.	H 8 ft.–S 3-6 ft.

*Not hardy below 30° F

	Common and botanical names, general characteristics	Uses and requirements	Propagation (*See also p. 87*)
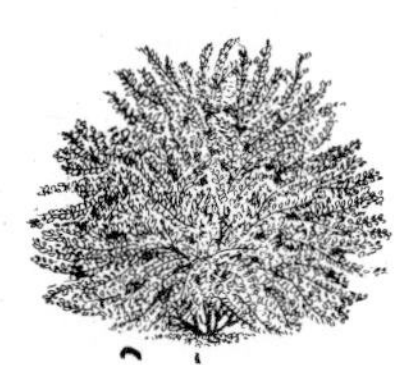 *Berberis thunbergii*	**Barberry** *(Berberis)* Most barberries are known for yellow spring blooms. Branches are thorned. Foliage of some deciduous kinds turns attractive bright colors in fall. Some types also have re-markably showy display of berries in fall. Wide range of sizes makes these plants useful for many places in landscape.	The dense thorny kinds, of which there are a considerable number, make excellent barrier plantings in full sun or partial shade. Some of smaller kinds are useful for rock gardens, and those with showiest berries make interesting container plants for fall and early winter display. Will grow in any good soil. Deciduous types withstand poor, dry soil conditions. Barberries are seldom attacked by insects.	Seeds can be sown when ripe or stored in cool place for up to 1 yr. Seeds can also be stratified for 2 mo. at 40° F. Root divisions can be made. Take leafy semi-hard-shoot cuttings in summer or hardwood cuttings in autumn.
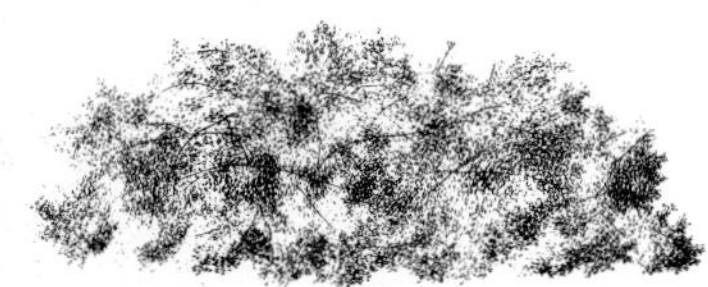 *Bauhinia galpinii*	**Bauhinia** *(Bauhinia)* Handsome twin-lobed leaves and spectacular flowers that resemble orchids, which bloom in winter and early spring. Forms pods in fall.	Can be trained as espalier. Plant only in well-drained soils. A slow grower.	Easily raised from seeds.
	Bay, sweet, see Laurel		
 *Myrica pensylvanica*	**Bayberry** *(Myrica)* Aromatic leaves are alternate. Small green flowers are inconspicuous, but female plants produce waxy fruit.	Attractive and useful along seashore. Grows well in dry, sandy soils of low fertility. Transplant with large soil ball to reduce shock. Stands shearing.	Soak seeds in warm water to remove wax. Stratify for 3 mo. at 40° F and plant.

Species and varieties	Hardiness *(Map, p. 9)*	Decorative characteristics and remarks	Height and spread when mature
Deciduous			
Berberis circumserrata	□ B □ □	Flowers are yellow and bloom in clusters of 2 or 3 in late spring. In fall foliage is brilliant red and persistent fruits are yellowish red.	H 3 ft.–S 3 ft.
B. koreana	□ B □ □	Large leaves color well in fall. Flowers in drooping clusters. Young twigs grooved and reddish but turn dark brown later in season. Vivid red berries.	H 6 ft.–S 5 ft.
B. mentorensis	□ B □ □	Faintly toothed leaves up to 2 in. long are evergreen in warmer regions. Produces many thorns. Survives in city gardens and dry summers.	H 6 ft.–S 5 ft.
B. thunbergii (Japanese)	□ B □ □	Dense, thorny, and a profuse bloomer. Red fruit often lasts through winter. Grows well in poor soil. Will live in shade.	H 6 ft.–S 6 ft.
B. t. atropurpurea	□ B □ □	Leaves are reddish purple from spring through autumn.	H 5 ft.–S 4 ft.
B. t. erecta	□ B □ □	An erect, compact grower. Makes good low-maintenance hedge.	H 5 ft.–S 3 ft.
B. t. variegata	□ B □ □	Leaves have interesting pale gray, yellow, and white blotches.	H 5 ft.–S 4 ft.
Evergreen			
B. buxifolia nana	□ B □ □	Handsome foliage. Leaves about 1 in. long. Good for low hedging.	H 1½ ft.–S 1½ ft.
B. candidula	□ B □ □	Leaves are deep green above, white beneath. Fruit is pale gray. Dense habit of growth makes this especially useful in rock garden.	H 3 ft.–S 3 ft.
B. darwinii	□ □ □ D	Oblong, 3-pointed, glossy green leaves. Densely blooming yellow-orange flowers and purple fruits. One of the most beautiful.	H 8 ft.–S 9 ft.
B. gagnepainii (black)	□ B □ □	Narrow wavy leaves and bluish-black fruit. Do not plant in wheat-growing areas, since it may act as alternate host to black stem rust disease.	H 6 ft.–S 5 ft.
B. julianae	□ B □ □	Narrow toothed leaves are deep green on top, light green beneath. Berries are bluish black. Develops heavy growth. One of hardiest evergreen barberries.	H 6 ft.–S 4 ft.
B. sargentiana	□ □ C □	Elliptic toothed leaves are dark green, 2-4 in. long. Thorns are often 1 in. long. Fruit is small, bluish black.	H 5 ft.–S 5 ft.
B. stenophylla (rosemary)	□ B □ □	Hybrid with dark green, lance-shaped leaves often more than 1 in. long. Undersides are whitish. Berries are black. Makes fine sheared hedge.	H 8 ft.–S 12 ft.
B. verruculosa (warty)	□ B □ □	Oval leathery leaves are shiny green above and whitish beneath. Foliage turns bronze in fall. Has very large flowers. Purplish-black fruit.	H 4 ft.–S 4 ft.
Semi-deciduous			
Bauhinia galpinii (red)	□ □ □ D *	In summer or autumn up to 10 bright red flowers appear in each long, showy cluster. Pods are about 5 in. long. Somewhat sprawling or semi-vining.	H 15 ft.–S 15 ft.
Deciduous			
Myrica pensylvanica	□ B □ □	Oblongish leaves are 3-4 in. long and remain on plant through part of winter. Small, waxy, light gray berries are borne abundantly along stem and are used in candle making. Gives off pleasant aroma if crushed.	H 9 ft.–S 8 ft.

*Not hardy below 30° F

	Common and botanical names, general characteristics	Uses and requirements	Propagation *(See also p. 87)*
Callicarpa dichotoma	**Beauty-berry** *(Callicarpa)* Tiny tubular flowers in clusters open during summer, but most are obscured by toothed foliage. In fall berry clusters put on good display after leaves turn yellow and drop.	Does best in full sun and needs fertile soil. In North plants may be killed to ground in winter, but new growth will appear in spring, flower, and bear fruit.	Seeds can be sown when ripe or can be stored in a dry, cool place for later use. Root divisions are easily made. Leafy semi-hard-shoot cuttings should be taken in summer, or leafless hardwood cuttings in fall.
Kolkwitzia amabilis	**Beauty bush** *(Kolkwitzia)* Produces good show of flowers in early summer. Oval leaves, up to 3 in. long, turn reddish in fall. Brown, hairy fruits last into winter. Bark is brown and peels off in strips. There is only one species in this genus.	A popular accent plant that does best in dry, sandy soil but is very tolerant of most soils.	Can be raised from seeds planted when ripe, but a particularly good shade of pink is best perpetuated by leafy semi-hard-shoot cuttings taken in summer.
Caryopteris clandonensis	**Bluebeard** *(Caryopteris)* Heavy production of blue flowers with protruding stamens, borne in tight clusters. It develops winged nutlike fruits.	Effective because of its unusual cool blue flower color and season of bloom, which extends from late summer until frost sets in. Requires the good drainage of sandy soils. Needs full sun. Mulch root area heavily after soil freezes. In its northernmost range top growth is often killed by frost, but new branches will form in spring if all old growth is cut back to soil line.	Take firm-shoot cuttings in late summer or leafless hardwood cuttings in autumn.
Callistemon viminalis 'Captain Cook'	**Bottlebrush** *(Callistemon)* Dense, brushlike spikes of flowers reveal handsome, protruding stamens. Small, narrow leaves provide attractive, feathery effect. Woody seed capsules often persist for years.	Good shrub for seacoast gardens. Plant in full sun in well-drained, humusy soil. Protect from cold winds. Fast growing and easily trained.	Sow ripened seeds in spring; or take firm-shoot cuttings in late summer.

Species and varieties	Hardiness (*Map, p. 9*)	Decorative characteristics and remarks	Height and spread when mature
Deciduous *Callicarpa americana*	C	Leaves, 4-6 in. long, have rust-colored undersides. Distinguished by its tiny bluish blossoms and bright purple berries that are produced in abundance. Chief ornamental value comes from berries.	H 6 ft.–S 5 ft.
C. bodinieri giraldii	B	Elliptic leaves are 4 in. long and turn pink or purple before falling. Clusters of very small lilac-colored flowers are followed by attractive bluish-violet berries that last well into winter. Habit of growth is upright.	H 8 ft.–S 6 ft.
C. dichotoma	B	Leaves are coarsely toothed and 1-3 in. long. The little berries that follow the pink flowers, which measure only ½ in. across, are lilac to violet in color. In fall stems take on purplish color.	H 4 ft.–S 4 ft.
C. japonica	B	Leaves faintly toothed and up to 5 in. long. Many minute pink or white blooms in midsummer are followed by showy violet-colored fruits, which persist until leaves have turned yellow and fallen in midfall.	H 4 ft.–S 4 ft.
Deciduous *Kolkwitzia amabilis*	B	Bell-shaped blossoms are light pink to lavender-pink with yellow throats. They are in clusters on erect branches that arch gracefully at ends. Since poor, washed-out pinks are sometimes sold, it is best to select and buy plants while they are in bloom.	H 8 ft.–S 8 ft.
Deciduous *Caryopteris clandonensis*	B	Vivid blue flowers open in late summer. This is hybrid between *C. incana* and *C. mongholica.*	H 4 ft.–S 4 ft.
C. c. 'Blue Mist'	B	Blossoms in autumn more profusely than *C. clandonensis.* Well suited to smaller gardens.	H 2 ft.–S 3 ft.
C. c. 'Heavenly Blue'	B	Autumn flowers are darker blue than those of *C. c.* 'Blue Mist.' A single, well-established specimen often produces more than 30 clusters. Good where space is limited.	H 2 ft.–S 1½ ft.
C. incana	C	Oval leaves are toothed, up to 3 in. long; undersides are thickly covered with gray hairs. Bluish-purple flowers open in juncture between upper leaves and their stems in early to mid fall. Considered less ornamental than *C. clandonensis* varieties but valued for late-season bloom.	H 5 ft.–S 4 ft.
Evergreen *Callistemon linearis* (narrow-leaf)	D	Bright red flowers adorn this species in midsummer.	H 5 ft.–S 4 ft.
C. phoeniceus	D	Narrow leaves and rather loose spikes of reddish-purple flowers in early spring, again in fall.	H 6-8 ft.–S 6 ft.
C. viminalis 'Captain Cook'	D *	Light green narrow leaves on pendulous branches and bright red flowers in summer. Makes excellent low screen. This variety does not grow as tall as *C. viminalis.* Requires frequent watering.	H 6-8 ft.–S 6 ft.
C. violaceus, or *C. lilacinus*	D *	Dense, rounded bush with light green foliage and 2-in.-long spikes of dark red flowers in early spring.	H 10-12 ft.–S 10 ft.

*Not hardy below 30° F

	Common and botanical names, general characteristics	Uses and requirements	Propagation *(See also p. 87)*
 *Buxus sempervirens suffruticosa*	**Boxwood** *(Buxus)* Grown mainly for pungent, deep green foliage that forms dense screen on mature plants. Tiny, inconspicuous flowers open in midspring.	Outstanding for hedges and topiary gardens. Generally does best in alkaline to neutral soils. Protect from wind and sun in cold winter areas, as these may burn leaves.	As soon as seeds ripen, they can be sown, stratified, or stored in cool, dry place for up to 1 yr. Root divisions can also be made. Take leafy semi-hard-shoot cuttings in spring or autumn, or leafless hardwood cuttings in fall.
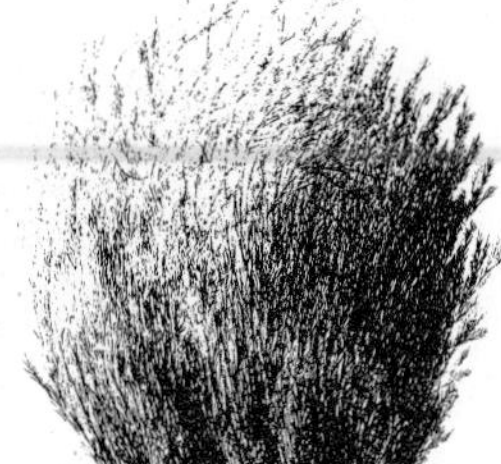 *Coleonema pulchrum*	**Breath of heaven** *(Coleonema,* or *Diosma)* Long, thin shoots bear very narrow leaves that emit fragrance when bruised or torn. Blossoms appear singly in winter and early spring.	Plant in sun in sandy soil containing plenty of leaf mold or peat moss. Must have good drainage. Sometimes grown in greenhouses in pots.	Take leafy semi-hard-shoot cuttings in summer.
 *Cytisus praecox*	**Broom** *(Cytisus)* Purple or white pealike blossoms are sometimes aromatic and always showy. Compound leaves consist of 3 leaflets. Green twigs are interesting feature in winter, especially in northern regions where color is scarce. The word "broom" probably derives from a name given centuries ago. It was descriptive of the upright dense growth of the Scotch broom, which was used for making brooms.	Good for borders, rock gardens, and informal plantings. Requires only average fertility but must have good drainage. Prefers acid soil conditions but will tolerate some alkalinity. Plant in full sun or partial shade. Transplant young specimens only. Older plants are difficult to move. Needs judicious pruning after flowers fade. Has no particular disease or insect problems.	Seeds can be planted when ripe or stored in cool, dry place for up to 1 yr. prior to sowing. Soak in sulfuric-acid concentrate for ½ hr., rinse carefully, then plant. Use glass container and avoid getting acid on skin, as it is highly corrosive. Take leafy semi-hard-shoot cuttings in early summer or firm-shoot cuttings in late summer.
	Broom, butcher's, see Ruscus		

Species and varieties	Hardiness (*Map, p. 9*)	Decorative characteristics and remarks	Height and spread when mature
Evergreen *Buxus microphylla japonica*	B	Young branches winged. Leaves are less than 1 in. long. Habit of growth is open.	H 6 ft.–S 6 ft.
B. m. koreana	A	One of hardiest varieties, although leaves may turn brownish during winter. Stands clipping especially well.	H 2 ft.–S 2 ft.
B. sempervirens (English)	B	Shiny green leaves are rounded and paler green on undersides than tops.	H 20 ft.–S 10 ft.
B. s. handsworthii	B	Leaves are deep green. Upright in habit, this variety is vigorous grower and well suited to hedging.	H 6 ft.–S 4 ft.
B. s. suffruticosa (dwarf English)	B	Low habit of growth makes this a good candidate for edging, particularly in formal plantings.	H 3 ft.–S 3 ft.
Evergreen *Coleonema album*	D	Heatherlike, with small white blossoms. Leaves are ¼-½ in. long and very slightly toothed.	H 2-3 ft.–S 3 ft.
C. pulchrum	D	Flowers, ¾ in. across, are rose-pink. Leaves to 1½ in. long.	H 2-3 ft.–S 3 ft.
Deciduous *Cytisus battandieri* (Atlas)	D	Silky, whitish hairs cover leaflets, which often grow more than 3 in. long. Cone-shaped racemes of pineapple-scented yellow flowers develop at ends of young shoots in early summer.	H 15 ft.–S 8 ft.
C. beanii	B	In late spring vivid yellow flowers open in clusters of 1 to 5, often completely covering foliage. This is an outstanding semi-prostrate species.	H 2 ft.–S 3 ft.
C. leucanthus, or *C. albus* (Portuguese)	B	White or yellow-white flowers open in early summer. Leaflets are about 3 in. long.	H 1 ft.–S 2 ft.
C. multiflorus (white Spanish)	B	White blossom clusters appear in late spring on this upright species.	H 8 ft.–S 4 ft.
C. praecox (Warminster, or moonlight)	B	Noted for light yellow or yellowish-white flowers in spring. Its winter twig display is especially effective. Do not prune heavily.	H 6 ft.–S 5 ft.
C. purpureus (purple)	B	Low, sprawling habit of growth and heavy production of pale purple flowers in late spring make this a desirable species.	H 2 ft.–S 3 ft.
C. scoparius (Scotch)	B	Blossoms open a brilliant yellow in late spring. Twigs are particularly decorative in winter. There are several varieties, including one with red flowers and another with double blooms.	H 8 ft.–S 8 ft.
Evergreen *C. canariensis* (Canary Island)	D *	Leaves are wedge shaped. Aromatic yellow blossoms appear in late spring and early summer. Develops many branches. Sometimes sold as *Genista canariensis.*	H 6 ft.–S 5 ft.
C. racemosus (Easter broom)	D *	Deep yellow flowers are displayed on delicate 2- to 4-in.-long racemes. Also sold as *Genista racemosa.*	H 12 ft.–S 8 ft.

*Not hardy below 30° F

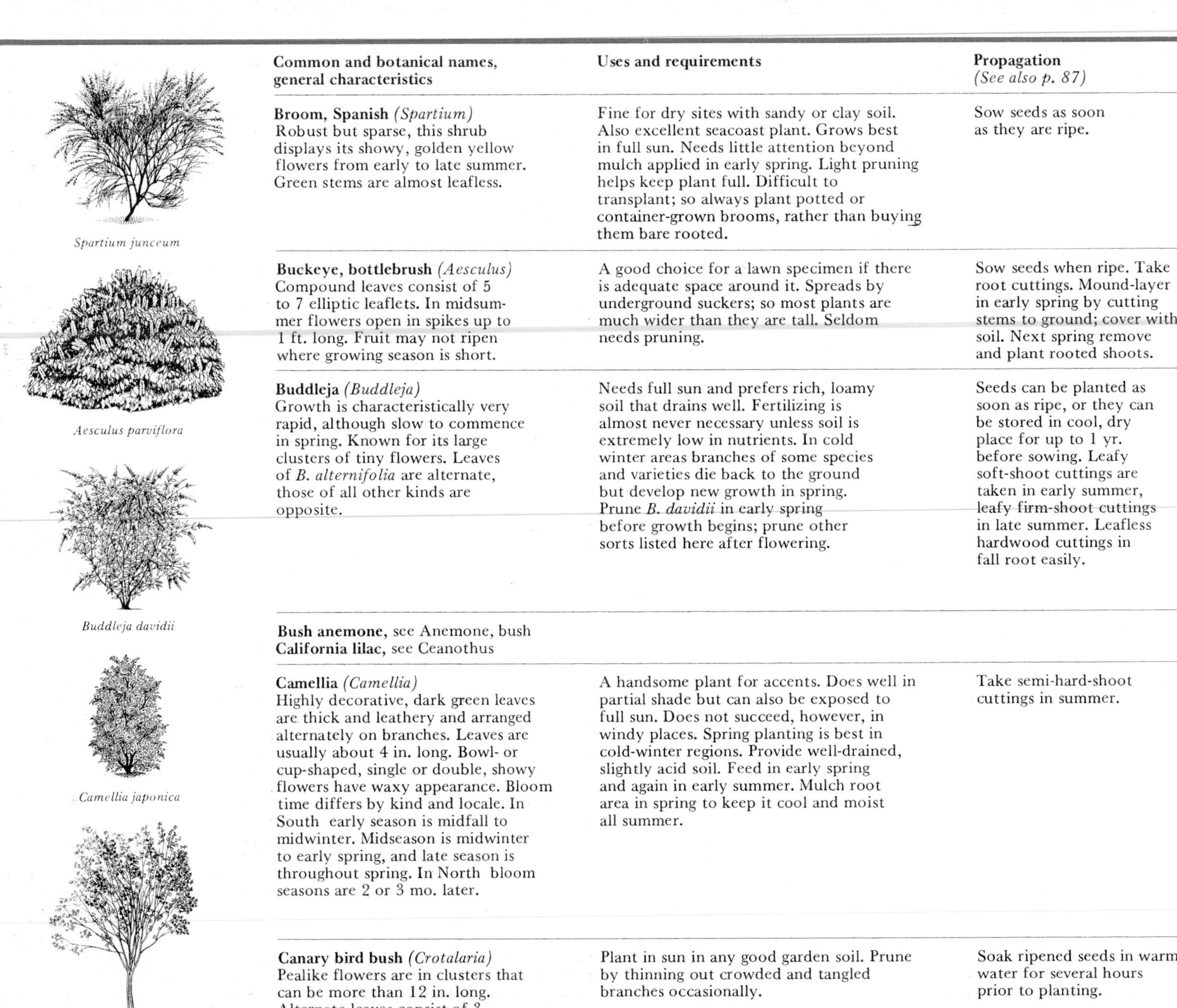

Common and botanical names, general characteristics	Uses and requirements	Propagation *(See also p. 87)*
Broom, Spanish *(Spartium)* Robust but sparse, this shrub displays its showy, golden yellow flowers from early to late summer. Green stems are almost leafless.	Fine for dry sites with sandy or clay soil. Also excellent seacoast plant. Grows best in full sun. Needs little attention beyond mulch applied in early spring. Light pruning helps keep plant full. Difficult to transplant; so always plant potted or container-grown brooms, rather than buying them bare rooted.	Sow seeds as soon as they are ripe.
Buckeye, bottlebrush *(Aesculus)* Compound leaves consist of 5 to 7 elliptic leaflets. In midsummer flowers open in spikes up to 1 ft. long. Fruit may not ripen where growing season is short.	A good choice for a lawn specimen if there is adequate space around it. Spreads by underground suckers; so most plants are much wider than they are tall. Seldom needs pruning.	Sow seeds when ripe. Take root cuttings. Mound-layer in early spring by cutting stems to ground; cover with soil. Next spring remove and plant rooted shoots.
Buddleja *(Buddleja)* Growth is characteristically very rapid, although slow to commence in spring. Known for its large clusters of tiny flowers. Leaves of *B. alternifolia* are alternate, those of all other kinds are opposite.	Needs full sun and prefers rich, loamy soil that drains well. Fertilizing is almost never necessary unless soil is extremely low in nutrients. In cold winter areas branches of some species and varieties die back to the ground but develop new growth in spring. Prune *B. davidii* in early spring before growth begins; prune other sorts listed here after flowering.	Seeds can be planted as soon as ripe, or they can be stored in cool, dry place for up to 1 yr. before sowing. Leafy soft-shoot cuttings are taken in early summer, leafy firm-shoot cuttings in late summer. Leafless hardwood cuttings in fall root easily.
Bush anemone, see Anemone, bush **California lilac,** see Ceanothus		
Camellia *(Camellia)* Highly decorative, dark green leaves are thick and leathery and arranged alternately on branches. Leaves are usually about 4 in. long. Bowl- or cup-shaped, single or double, showy flowers have waxy appearance. Bloom time differs by kind and locale. In South early season is midfall to midwinter. Midseason is midwinter to early spring, and late season is throughout spring. In North bloom seasons are 2 or 3 mo. later.	A handsome plant for accents. Does well in partial shade but can also be exposed to full sun. Does not succeed, however, in windy places. Spring planting is best in cold-winter regions. Provide well-drained, slightly acid soil. Feed in early spring and again in early summer. Mulch root area in spring to keep it cool and moist all summer.	Take semi-hard-shoot cuttings in summer.
Canary bird bush *(Crotalaria)* Pealike flowers are in clusters that can be more than 12 in. long. Alternate leaves consist of 3 leaflets. Pods, 2 in. long, contain loose seeds that rattle.	Plant in sun in any good garden soil. Prune by thinning out crowded and tangled branches occasionally.	Soak ripened seeds in warm water for several hours prior to planting.

Spartium junceum

Aesculus parviflora

Buddleja davidii

Camellia japonica

Crotalaria agatiflora

Species and varieties	Hardiness (*Map, p. 9*)	Decorative characteristics and remarks	Height and spread when mature
Deciduous *Spartium junceum*	C	Has slender green branches and few or no small, bluish-green, narrow leaves. Fragrant pealike blossoms grow in terminal clusters that are often more than 1 ft. long.	H 8 ft.–S 7 ft.
Deciduous *Aesculus parviflora*	B	Ornate pink stamens protrude from white flowers to make this a very showy plant when in bloom.	H 12 ft.–S 36 ft.
Deciduous *Buddleja alternifolia* (fountain)	B	Lance-shaped leaves have green undersides. The earliest buddleja to flower, its long garlands of tiny lavender-blue blossoms open in early summer on last year's wood. Branches are pendulous. A particularly hardy species.	H 10 ft.–S 15 ft.
B. asiatica	D	Fragrant white flowers in 5-in. panicles appear in mid to late spring.	H 2-6 ft.–S 3-8 ft.
B. davidii (butterfly bush)	B	Fragrant, pale purple flowers with orange throats develop on long, arching, spikelike clusters from late summer until frost. Many varieties are available, with colors ranging from white to purple and crimson. They attract butterflies.	H 12 ft.–S 8 ft.
B. globosa	D	Semi-evergreen elliptic leaves have rust-colored, hairy undersides. Globular heads of fragrant yellow flowers open in 4- to 8-in. panicles in late spring.	H 15 ft.–S 10 ft.
Evergreen *Camellia japonica*	C	Bloom time differs by variety and climate. Varieties include several double and semi-double forms with white, red, or pink flowers.	H 30 ft.–S 15 ft.
C. j. 'C. M. Wilson'	C	Large, light pink anemone form blooms in midseason.	H 30 ft.–S 12 ft.
C. j. 'Colonel Firey'	C	Large, formal, dark red flowers bloom mid to late season.	H 30 ft.–S 12 ft.
C. sasanqua	C	Leaves are only about 2 in. long, and flowers open earlier than those of *C. japonica* and its varieties. Flowers in white, pink, or purple; single, semi-double, and double. General habit of growth is open and willowy.	H 20 ft.–S 10 ft.
C. s. 'Cleopatra'	C	Rose-pink semi-double flowers on very compact plant.	H 20 ft.–S 10 ft.
C. s. 'Yuletide'	C	Fiery-red single flower centered with yellow stamens. Bushy habit of growth.	H 20 ft.–S 10 ft.
Evergreen *Crotalaria agatiflora*	D *	Greenish-yellow flowers attract hummingbirds and orioles. Flowers are also useful for cutting for arrangements. Main bloom period is late summer, but in frost-free regions plant blooms intermittently for many months.	H 6-12 ft.–S 3-8 ft.

*Not hardy below 30° F

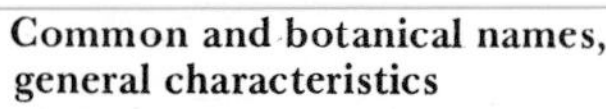

Common and botanical names, general characteristics	Uses and requirements	Propagation *(See also p. 87)*
Candle bush, see Senna **Carpenteria**, see Anemone, bush **Caryopteris**, see Bluebeard **Cassia**, see Senna		
Catha, or Khat *(Catha)* Bears bronze-green 4-in. leaves, small white flowers, and unusual fruits. Stems, bark, and leaves in fall and winter are reddish.	Plant in full sun in any good garden soil. Does well even in poor-quality soils.	Propagate from leafy firm-shoot cuttings in late summer.
Ceanothus *(Ceanothus)* Bears small flowers in attractive upright, branching, spikelike clusters. When ripe, fruit opens into 3 separate segments.	Locate in sun and provide a light, well-drained soil of moderate acidity. Water well during first year after transplanting. Plants are generally drought resistant; overwatering should be avoided. Plants often have short life span.	Soak seeds overnight in hot water, and stratify for 3 mo. at 40° F. Take soft-shoot cuttings in spring or semi-hard-shoot cuttings in summer. Can also be soil-layered.
Cestrum *(Cestrum)* Handsome blossoms open in abundance in junctures of leaves and stems or at branch tips. Flowers of most kinds are fragrant. In fall it bears tiny berrylike fruits.	Does best in quick-draining, sandy soil that is well fortified with humus or leaf mold. Prune to thin out old and poorly located branches in spring. Plants may freeze in heavy frost but recover quickly.	Root leafy soft-shoot cuttings in spring, semi-hard-shoot cuttings in summer, or hardwood cuttings in fall. Or when attainable, sow seeds in sandy soil.
Chaste tree, see Vitex **Cherry**, see Prunus		

Catha edulis

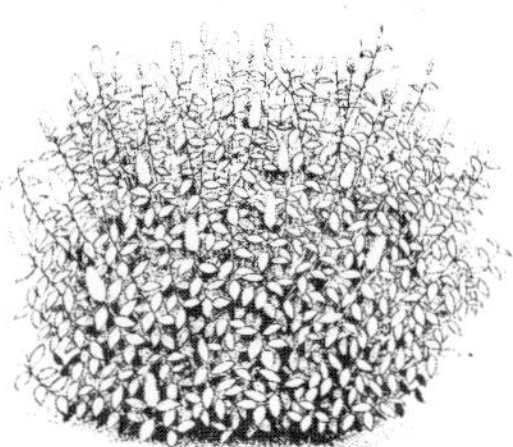

Ceanothus delilianus

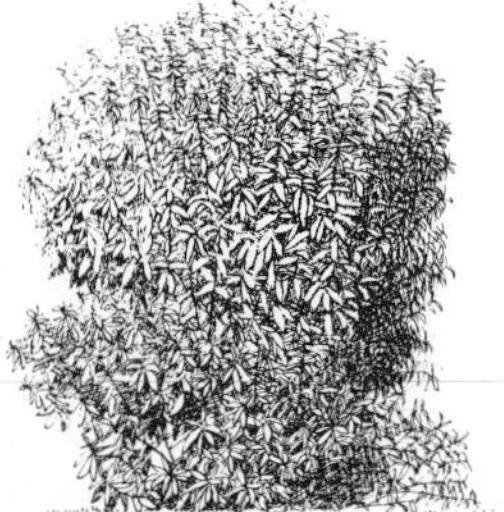

Cestrum aurantiacum

Species and varieties	Hardiness *(Map, p. 9)*	Decorative characteristics and remarks	Height and spread when mature
Evergreen *Catha edulis*	□□□D *	Fruit capsules cling to plant throughout winter and then split to display their decorative, bright red seeds. Most leaves are opposite, but a few are alternate. Likes heat.	H 10 ft.–S 8 ft.
Deciduous *Ceanothus delilianus*	□□C□	Leaves to 3 in. long. This hybrid has very tiny blue flowers that appear in great numbers in midspring.	H 6 ft.–S 3 ft.
C. d. 'Autumn Blue'	□□C□	Its pale to deep blue flowers create an unusual accent.	H 3 ft.–S 3 ft.
C. d. 'Gloire de Plantieres'	□□C□	Flowers are deep blue.	H 3 ft.–S 3 ft.
C. d. 'Gloire de Versailles'	□□C□	Fragrant powder-blue blossoms. Fine for espaliering. One of most popular varieties of *C. delilianus.*	H 8 ft.–S 8 ft.
Evergreen *C. arboreus* 'Ray Hartman'	□□C□	Pale to bright blue flowers in early spring. Can be grown as shrub or small tree.	H 10-20 ft.–S 15 ft.
C. cyaneus 'Sierra Blue'	□□C□	Dense, rich, and glossy green foliage to base of plant. Deep blue flowers bloom in spring. Can be sheared to form hedge or trimmed to make informal screen.	H 6-12 ft.–S 5-8 ft.
C. griseus (carmel)	□□C□	Dark green leaves to 2 in. long. Hairy undersides. Violet-blue flowers.	H 2-8 ft.–S 3-6 ft.
C. g. 'Santa Ana'	□□C□	Similar to *C. griseus* but with pure blue flowers.	H 4-8 ft.–S 20 ft.
C. impressus 'Mountain Haze'	□□C□	Somewhat spreading, with broad elliptic to nearly round leaves and blue flowers.	H 5 ft.–S 3-5 ft.
C. thyrsiflorus (blue blossom)	□□C□	Glossy leaves 2 in. long or more. Blossoms ranging in color from dark blue to nearly white appear in early spring. Sometimes grown as small tree.	H 8-25 ft.–S 6-10 ft.
C. veitchianus	□□C□	Small glossy leaves. Bright blue flowers in dense clusters on 1- to 2-in. stems in late spring and early summer.	H 12 ft.–S 12 ft.
Evergreen *Cestrum aurantiacum*	□□□D *	Oval leaves are almost 3 in. long. Orange-yellow 1-in. flowers in late spring.	H 12 ft.–S 6-8 ft.
C. nocturnum (night-blooming jasmine)	□□□D *	Glossy leaves are thin, leathery, and up to 9 in. long. Clusters of aromatic blooms in shades of pale green-white to cream open at night.	H 10 ft.–S 7 ft.
C. parqui (willow-leaved jasmine)	□□□D *	Flowers in clusters in junctures of leaf and stem and at branch ends are green-yellow and about 1 in. long. Blooms open at night.	H 8 ft.–S 5-6 ft.
C. purpureum	□□□D *	Red-purple flowers in nodding clusters at branch ends. Red fruits.	H 12 ft.–S 6-8 ft.

*Not hardy below 30° F

Cocculus laurifolius

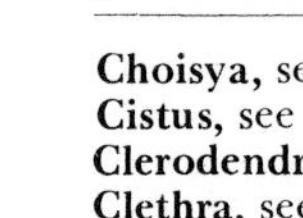

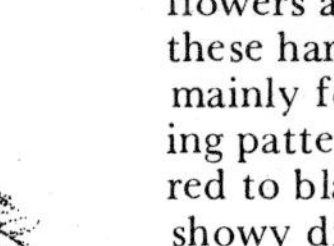

Cotoneaster horizontalis

Common and botanical names, general characteristics	Uses and requirements	Propagation *(See also p. 87)*
Choisya, see Orange, Mexican **Cistus,** see Rockrose **Clerodendrum,** see Glory-bower **Clethra,** see Sweet pepper bush		
Cocculus *(Cocculus)* Alternate leaves are arranged in finger fashion. Tiny male and female flowers appear on separate plants.	Does well in any good garden soil but should have considerable moisture in dry climates or periods of drought.	Plant seeds or take leafy semi-hard-shoot cuttings in early summer.
Coralberry, Chenault, see Symphoricarpos **Cornus,** see Dogwood		
Cotoneaster *(Cotoneaster)* Although small white or pinkish flowers appear in spring or summer, these hardy shrubs are grown mainly for their attractive branching pattern, foliage, and small red to black fruit that makes a showy display in fall and, in most types, remains through winter.	The lower-growing, more restrained kinds make fine additions to rock gardens. Plant in full sun or partial shade in any good soil. Borers (spray with lindane) and lace bugs (see p. 605) sometimes attack plants. Susceptible to fire blight (see p. 619), which causes cankers to form at base of shoots that have died back.	Seeds can be sown when ripe or stored for up to 1 yr. in cool, dry place and then planted. In some cases, germination may take 2 yr. All kinds can be soil-layered. Some can be increased by semi-hard-shoot cuttings in summer, others by leafless hardwood cuttings in fall.
Crape myrtle, see p. 53		
Creambush, or Ocean spray *(Holodiscus)* The 2- to 4-in. deeply toothed alternate leaves are grayish green. Tiny cup-shaped flowers with showy protruding stamens are displayed in large panicles.	Excellent as background plant for perennial beds. Will develop most growth in rich soil in partial shade but will also grow in dry soil and sun.	Sow seeds or increase by soil layers.

Holodiscus discolor

Species and varieties	Hardiness *(Map, p. 9)*	Decorative characteristics and remarks	Height and spread when mature
Evergreen *Cocculus laurifolius* (laurel leaf)	☐☐☐D	Leathery elliptic leaves are shiny and about 6 in. long, and have yellowish-green veins. Flowers are in stout racemes. Small berrylike fruits, on female plants only, are black and fleshy.	H 15 ft.–S 8-10 ft.
Deciduous *Cotoneaster adpressa* (creeping)	☐B☐☐	Pinkish flowers open in early summer. Fruits are red. A prostrate species that grows slowly and is excellent for rock gardens.	H 6 in.–S 2-3 ft.
C. apiculata (cranberry)	☐B☐☐	Leaves have pointed tips. A handsome species with pink blooms and scarlet fruits.	H 4 ft.–S 3-4 ft.
C. horizontalis (rock)	☐B☐☐	Its forked, wide-spreading branches bear rounded leaves; semi-evergreen in mild climates, deciduous in cold ones. Early summer flowers are pinkish, and fruits are brilliant red. It can easily be espaliered.	H 2 ft.–S 3-5 ft.
C. h. perpusilla	A☐☐☐	Has smaller leaves and is shorter than *C. horizontalis.*	H 1½ ft.–S 2-3 ft.
Evergreen *C. congesta* (Pyrenees)	☐☐C☐	Short branches encourage low profile. Oval leaves have whitish undersides. Flowers are pinkish, opening in early summer. Pea-size fruits are vivid red.	H 3 ft.–S 2-3 ft.
C. dammeri (bearberry)	A☐☐☐	Flowers are white and fruits are red. If soil is loose, the prostrate branches of this species will root at joints, making it useful on slopes.	H 1 ft.–S 1-2 ft.
C. henryana	☐☐C☐	Pendulous branches bear grayish, semi-evergreen leaves with fuzzy undersides. Flowers develop in hairy clusters, and berries are deep red.	H 12 ft.–S 6-8 ft.
C. lactea	☐☐C☐	Twigs are covered with whitish hairs. Creamy white blossoms in early to mid summer are followed by red berries. An excellent plant for hedges.	H 12 ft.–S 10 ft.
C. microphylla (rock spray)	☐☐C☐	Glossy leaves, white flowers, and profusion of scarlet berries make this an outstanding candidate for planting in foregrounds.	H 2 ft.–S 15 ft.
C. m. thymifolia	A☐☐☐	Similar to *C. microphylla,* but with smaller leaves, flowers, and fruits.	H 1-1½ ft.–S 6-10 ft.
C. salicifolia repandens	☐B☐☐	Semi-evergreen leaves are veined, and stalks are often reddish. Flowers are white and fruits are red. Low and spreading.	H 1-1½ ft.–S 2-4 ft.
Deciduous *Holodiscus discolor*	☐B☐☐	Branches are gracefully arching or pendulous. Undersides of oval leaves are fuzzy and whitish. White to creamy flowers open in midsummer in 9-in. clusters. As flowers fade, they turn golden brown and remain effective for many weeks. However, if bloom is desired the following summer, shrub should be pruned immediately after flowering. This will also prevent seed formation.	H 10-18 ft.–S 8-12 ft.

	Common and botanical names, general characteristics	Uses and requirements	Propagation (*See also p. 87)*
  *Ribes sanguineum*	**Currant, flowering** *(Ribes)* Once prized for their edible berries, plants are now grown mainly for decorative effects. Flowers are generally yellow or greenish yellow, but those of some kinds are red. They open early in spring and are followed by fruit in midsummer.	Good for coastal gardens. Can be sheared for hedges. Plant in full sun or partial shade in ordinary soil. Tolerates alkalinity. Must have water in dry spells. If growth is slow, feed in spring and summer. Alternate host to white pine blister rust; so never plant within 1,000 feet of white pines. Aphids can cripple shoots. Spray with systemic insecticide. Leaf spot fungus can cause foliage to become blotchy. Spray with Captan, maneb, or zineb at first sign of outbreak.	Increase by seeds, soil layers, or leafless hardwood cuttings taken in fall.
	Currant, Indian, see Symphoricarpos **Cytisus,** see Broom		
 *Olearia haastii*	**Daisybush** *(Olearia)* Bears white or violet daisylike blossoms in summer. Leaves are usually alternate, and those of most kinds are covered on undersides with whitish fuzz.	Plant in good loamy soil, adding lots of leaf mold if soil is sandy. Will grow in full sun or partial shade and stands up well in long periods of heat.	Sow seeds or take semi-hard-shoot cuttings in summer.
 *Daphne burkwoodii* 'Somerset'	**Daphne** *(Daphne)* Clusters of tiny flowers are handsome, and those of some kinds are fragrant. Although they resemble lilac blooms, they are not as large. Colorful fruit is fleshy or leathery. Leaves, fruit, and bark are poisonous.	An excellent choice for borders and rock gardens. Select a position in full sun or partial shade that is well protected from wind. Does best in light, easily worked soil with considerable humus. Most kinds prefer slightly alkaline to neutral conditions. Often hard to transplant. Move only young specimens. Aphids can cripple shoot tips by sucking sap from tissues. Spray with systemic insecticide. Virus diseases can stunt growth. There is no cure; dig up and destroy affected plants.	Can be increased by soil layers or root cuttings. Leafy semi-hard-shoot cuttings can also be taken in summer, or leafless hardwood cuttings in fall. Seeds should be stratified for 3 mo. at 40° F before planting.

Species and varieties	Hardiness (*Map, p. 9*)	Decorative characteristics and remarks	Height and spread when mature
Deciduous *Ribes aureum* (golden)	[A][ ][ ][ ]	Yellow flowers in spreading or drooping clusters. Fruits are purplish to black.	H 8 ft.–S 4-6 ft.
R. odoratum	[ ][B][ ][ ]	Deeply toothed lobed leaves turn scarlet in fall. Aromatic yellow flowers grow in drooping clusters. Fruits are black. Plant is susceptible to wheat stem rust.	H 6 ft.–S 3-5 ft.
R. sanguineum (pink winter)	[ ][B][ ][ ]	Lobes of leaves are unevenly toothed. Pink or red flowers grow in showy hanging clusters. Fruits are bluish black. A good companion for forsythia.	H 10 ft.–S 7 ft.
Evergreen *Olearia haastii* (New Zealand)	[ ][ ][C][ ]	Glossy grayish-green leaves are about 1 in. long. Fragrant white flowers open in clusters. Dense habit of growth makes this a valuable windbreak. It also survives under seaside conditions and where smog is present.	H 8 ft.–S 15 ft.
Deciduous *Daphne burkwoodii* 'Somerset'	[ ][ ][C][ ]	Deep green foliage resembles boxwood and is semi-evergreen in mild climates. Pink blossoms are star shaped and very fragrant. They open in late spring and early summer. Does best in partial shade.	H 5 ft.–S 4 ft.
D. genkwa (lilac)	[ ][B][ ][ ]	Scentless lilac-blue flowers open along slender branches in spring before opposite leaves unfold. A slow spreader, its young twigs have a silky sheen.	H 3 ft.–S 3 ft.
D. giraldii	[ ][B][ ][ ]	Faintly aromatic yellow blossoms in early summer. Scarlet berries follow.	H 2 ft.–S 1-2 ft.
D. mezereum	[ ][B][ ][ ]	Highly scented rose-purple flower clusters unfold in early spring before alternate leaves open. In summer its scarlet berries attract birds. An upright grower, it prefers partial shade.	H 3 ft.–S 2 ft.
D. m. alba	[ ][B][ ][ ]	Handsome variety. Has white blossoms and yellow fruits. Fine for limited space.	H 3 ft.–S 2 ft.
Evergreen *D. cneorum*	[ ][B][ ][ ]	Oblong leaves to 1 in. long. Sweetly fragrant rose-pink flowers open in spring. Fruits are yellowish brown. Mulch in summer and protect from frost.	H 6 in.-1 ft.–S 2 ft.
D. collina	[ ][ ][C][ ]	Terminal clusters of 10-15 sweetly scented, rose-purple blossoms in late spring.	H 3 ft.–S 3 ft.
D. laureola (spurge)	[ ][ ][C][ ]	Leaves are 2-3 in. long. Yellowish-green blossoms open in early spring in short-stalked racemes and are usually scentless. Fruits are bluish black. Does best in partial shade and slightly acid soil.	H 2 ft.–S 1½-2 ft.
D. odora	[ ][ ][C][ ]	Purplish-rose blossoms are very fragrant and abundantly produced in tight terminal clusters. It flowers in spring. Feed and prune lightly.	H 5 ft.–S 2-3 ft.
D. o. marginata	[ ][ ][C][ ]	Similar to *D. odora,* but leaves have yellow borders.	H 4-6 ft.–S 3-4 ft.
D. retusa	[ ][ ][C][ ]	Terminal clusters of fragrant, purplish-white flower clusters appear in late spring. Fruits are red. A tidy, compact species.	H 3 ft.–S 2-3 ft.

	Common and botanical names, general characteristics	Uses and requirements	Propagation (*See also p. 87*)
 *Deutzia scabra candidissima*	**Deutzia** *(Deutzia)* Growth rate is rapid. Blossoms when plants are still quite young. Flowers are usually white and develop in abundance on previous year's wood. Leaves are toothed. In winter bark shreds on most kinds.	Grow in full sun or partial shade. Plant in any good soil. Mulch in spring. Flowers at times do not develop well due to poor light, lack of nutrients in soil, or too little water. Feed with general fertilizer, water more in dry spells. Prune just after blooming by thinning out old branches. Generally free of insects and diseases; tolerates polluted air.	Sow seeds when ripe, or store them for up to 1 yr. in cool, dry place prior to planting. Root divisions can be made in spring. Take semi-hard-shoot cuttings in summer or leafless hardwood cuttings in fall.
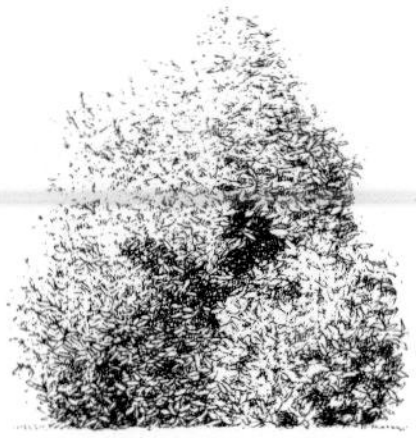 *Duranta erecta*	**Dewdrop, golden, or Sky-flower** *(Duranta)* Tubular flowers on drooping branches.	Plant in full sun in any good garden soil.	Sow seeds or take semi-hard-shoot cuttings in summer.
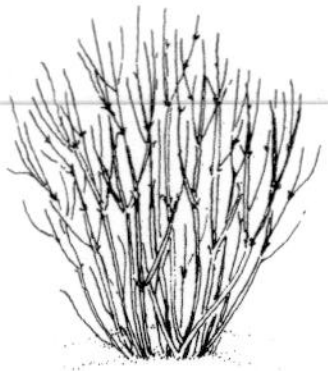 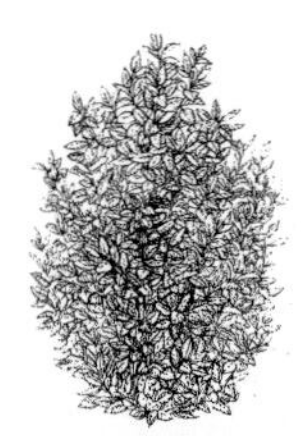 *Cornus alba sibirica*	**Dogwood** *(Cornus)* Berries are decorative in fall. Some kinds have colorful twigs, which are particularly striking in cold climates where they can be seen against background of snow as illustrated at left.	Most kinds grow equally well in full sun or partial shade. They need rich soil and plenty of water in periods of heat and drought. Most dogwoods are resistant to pests and diseases. Easily grown and hardy.	Take semi-hard-shoot cuttings in summer or leafless hardwood cuttings in fall.
Elaeagnus pungens	**Elaeagnus** *(Elaeagnus)* Leaves are alternate, leathery, and often decorative. The deciduous kinds often have colorful fruits.	Can be used singly as a specimen plant or in a row as a hedge. Ability to resist wind and survive in dry soil makes this especially good selection for many areas of Midwest and along seacoast. Plant in full sun or very light shade. Give new transplants a great amount of water during their first summer.	Stratify seeds for 3 mo. at 40° F, or store them for up to 1 yr. in cool, dry place before stratifying. Take root cuttings in spring. Also soil-layer for new plants. Take leafy semi-hard-shoot cuttings in summer. Propagate deciduous kinds by leafless hardwood cuttings in fall, or plant suckers.

Species and varieties	Hardiness (*Map, p. 9*)	Decorative characteristics and remarks	Height and spread when mature
Deciduous *Deutzia gracilis*	□B□□	Oblong leaves are often more than 2 in. long. Flowers in upright clusters up to 4 in. long in late spring. Yellowish-gray bark shreds slightly.	H 5 ft.–S 3-4 ft.
D. lemoinei	A□□□	Leaves are often as long as 4 in. Flowers in late spring in flattened or pyramidal upright clusters up to 4 in. long. A hardy hybrid.	H 7 ft.–S 5-7 ft.
D. rosea eximia	□B□□	Flowers are pale pink and in clusters 2 in. across that are handsome in late spring or early summer.	H 6 ft.–S 4-6 ft.
D. scabra candidissima	□B□□	A fine variety with attractive double pure white blossoms.	H 8 ft.–S 5-8 ft.
D. s. 'Pride of Rochester'	□B□□	Double blush-pink flowers that are pure white inside and about 1 in. across appear in large clusters in early summer.	H 8 ft.–S 5-8 ft.
Evergreen *Duranta erecta,* or *D. repens*	□□□D	Leaves are oval. Small light blue to lilac-colored flowers are borne on 6-in. racemes. Fleshy golden yellow berries grow in clusters.	H 18 ft.–S 6-10 ft.
Deciduous *Cornus alba* (Tatarian)	A□□□	Oval leaves with bluish-green undersides turn red in fall. Vivid red twigs are spectacular in winter. Flowers appear in early summer. Pale blue fruits.	H 9 ft.–S 4-8 ft.
C. a. sibirica (Siberian)	A□□□	Autumn leaf color is red. Has creamy blossoms in late spring and tiny blue berries. Prune in early spring to show off red twigs in winter. Tolerates moisture.	H 8 ft.–S 4-8 ft.
C. sanguinea (bloodtwig)	A□□□	Resembles *C. alba,* but twigs are usually darker red. Fruits are dark purple.	H 12 ft.–S 4-8 ft.
C. stolonifera (red osier)	A□□□	Underground stems produce heavy clumps. White flowers open in late spring or early summer. Ripe seeds of this species should be stratified for 3 mo. at 40° F before planting. Suckers removed and planted in autumn will root readily.	H 6 ft.–S 4-8 ft.
C. s. flaviramea	A□□□	Twigs are greenish yellow. Needs moisture.	H 6 ft.–S 4-8 ft.
Deciduous *Elaeagnus commutata*	A□□□	Has erect habit of growth with oblong to oval silvery leaves up to 4 in. long. Yellow blossoms are tiny but heavily scented, appearing in late spring. Silvery fruits are egg shaped.	H 12 ft.–S 4-6 ft.
E. umbellata	A□□□	Elliptic or ovalish leaves with silvery undersides are borne on spreading branches with scaly bark. Aromatic flowers are yellowish white and open in late spring or early summer. Fruits are silvery, turning red with age.	H 15 ft.–S 6-10 ft.
Evergreen *E. pungens* (thorny elaeagnus, or silverberry)	□□C□	Small pendulous blossoms are silvery white with aroma similar to that of gardenia. They open in midfall on plant with leaves up to 5 in. long. Brown fruits turn red at maturity. Tolerates shearing.	H 12 ft.–S 8-12 ft.
E. p. fruitlandii	□□C□	Similar to *E. pungens,* but leaves are more rounded.	H 12 ft.–S 8-12 ft.
E. p. maculata	□□C□	Variegated leaves have large golden spot in center. Effective during winter.	H 12 ft.–S 8-12 ft.
E. p. marginata	□□C□	Edges of leaves are silvery.	H 12 ft.–S 8-12 ft.
E. p. variegata	□□C□	Leaves have yellow-white or white margins.	H 12 ft.–S 12 ft.

Common and botanical names, general characteristics	Uses and requirements	Propagation *(See also p. 87)*
 *Enkianthus perulatus* **Enkianthus** *(Enkianthus)* Most leaves are bunched at ends of twigs. Fall leaf color is showy. Heathlike flowers grow in terminal clusters, opening in late spring.	Useful in borders and attractive when planted with azaleas and rhododendrons. Does best in sheltered spot in partial shade with well-drained soil of medium acidity. Insect and disease resistant.	Sow seeds when ripe. Responds well to soil layering. In summer take semi-hard-shoot cuttings.
Erica, see Heath		
Escallonia franciscana **Escallonia** *(Escallonia)* Arching branches bear flower clusters at terminals and sometimes in junctures of leaves and stems. Blossoms open in summer and often intermittently until fall. Flowers nearly all year in mild climates.	Good addition to seaside gardens, since its thick stems screen more sensitive plants from salt spray. Does best in full sun and fertile, well-drained soil. Avoid highly alkaline soils. Feed in early spring.	Take firm-shoot cuttings in late summer.
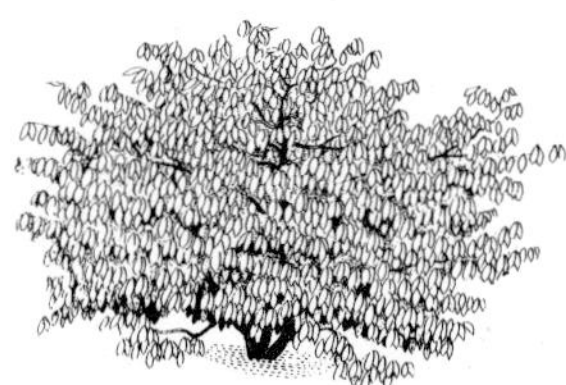 *Euonymus alatus* **Euonymus** *(Euonymus)* Tiny flowers in late spring and early summer are inconspicuous, but fruit and autumn leaf coloration is often attractive and sometimes spectacular. Fruits appear in midsummer and last until frost in cold climates.	The wide range of forms within the genus makes these useful plants for many garden situations. Plant in full sun or partial shade in any good soil. Give young transplants a great amount of water in dry spells. Young stems of almost all kinds are subject to attack by euonymus scale and aphids. Spray with contact insecticide. If powdery mildew causes white patches on leaves, spray with dinocap or use a sulfur dust or spray.	Stratify seeds at 40°F for 4 mo. prior to planting. Germination is often poor. Evergreens can be increased by semi-hard-shoot cuttings in summer or hardwood cuttings in fall. Deciduous forms respond to soft-shoot cuttings in spring.

Species and varieties	Hardiness *(Map, p. 9)*	Decorative characteristics and remarks	Height and spread when mature
Deciduous *Enkianthus campanulatus*	B	Marginally toothed leaves are 1-3 in. long. Autumn leaf color is bright scarlet. Nodding bronze-yellow flowers have red veins. In fall small green pods develop, turning rust colored when mature.	H 25 ft.–S 4-12 ft.
E. cernuus rubens	C	Leaves are less than 1 in. long and turn scarlet in fall. Clusters of dark red bell-shaped flowers have up to 12 blooms.	H 15 ft.–S 4-10 ft.
E. perulatus	B	Oblong or elliptic leaves are often more than 2 in. long. Spectacular scarlet and yellow leaves in fall. Flowers are white.	H 5 ft.–S 4 ft.
Evergreen *Escallonia exoniensis*	C	Leaves ½-1½ in. long are lustrous green above, paler beneath. White or pink-tinged flowers about ½ in. long grow in terminal clusters. This is a hybrid.	H 10 ft.–S 6-8 ft.
E. franciscana	C	Hybrid with sticky new shoots, broad leaves to 1 in. long, pink flowers.	H 10 ft.–S 6-8 ft.
E. organensis	D	Young branches are angled and resinous. Toothed oblong leaves to 3 in. long often have red margins. Small red flowers are fragrant.	H 6 ft.–S 4-6 ft.
E. rubra	D	Branches are reddish brown. Lance-shaped leaves are up to 2 in. long and sticky. Flowers are red.	H 12 ft.–S 5-7 ft.
E. virgata	D	Erect or arching branches; broad leaves almost 1 in. long. Flowers have wide-spreading white petals. Sometimes semi-evergreen.	H 8 ft.–S 4-6 ft.
Deciduous *Euonymus alatus* (winged)	A	Young branches have interesting corklike fins. When 3-in. leaves turn fiery red in fall, this becomes one of showiest plants in garden.	H 8 ft.–S 6-8 ft.
Evergreen *E. fortunei* (wintercreeper)	B	Mature plants often bear shiny leaves with several different shapes. Fruit is light pink. Spreading, vinelike habit of growth makes this useful species for rock gardens or near rough-surfaced walls, which it will readily climb.	H 6 in.-1 ft.–S 2-6 ft.
E. f. carrierei	B	Variegated leaves may develop on several branches. Produces many berries.	H 2-3 ft.–S 2-3 ft.
E. f. coloratus (purple leaf)	B	One-in. leaves have purplish cast from autumn through winter.	H 6 in.-1 ft.–S 3-6 ft.
E. f. radicans	B	Same habit of growth characteristics as *E. fortunei,* but leaves are often shorter and not quite so shiny.	H 6 in.-1 ft.–S 2-6 ft.
E. f. 'Sarcoxie'	B	Shiny semi-evergreen leaves are 1 in. long. Upright habit of growth.	H 4 ft.–S 2-3 ft.
E. f. vegetus	B	Similar to *E. fortunei,* but less trailing in habit of growth.	H 2-4 ft.–S 3-5 ft.
E. japonicus	D	Glossy elliptic leaves are about 3 in. long. Rounded fruits are light pink. Several varieties have leaves with yellow or white margins. Suitable for hedges and for seacoast gardens.	H 15 ft.–S 6-10 ft.
E. kiautschovica, or *E. patens*	C	Slightly toothed leaves to 4 in. are often semi-evergreen in northern climates. Short growing season may prevent pinkish fruits from developing.	H 8 ft.–S 4-6 ft.

	Common and botanical names, general characteristics	Uses and requirements	Propagation *(See also p. 87)*
	False spirea, see Spirea, false		
Corylus avellana contorta	**Filbert, or Hazelnut** *(Corylus)* Alternate, usually hairy, double toothed leaves. Minute flowers appear before leaves, the male flowers in catkins, the females in clusters, both on same plant. Edible egg-shaped nuts have smooth, hard shells covered by leafy growth.	Thrives in partial shade and in any well-drained soil. Will also live in heavy, wet clay. Grow several specimens for adequate cross-pollination and good nut crop.	Remove rooted suckers, and plant. Seeds usually should be stratified at 40° F for 3 mo. and then planted. Branches can be soil-layered. Take semi-hard-shoot cuttings in early summer.
Pyracantha coccinea	**Fire thorn** *(Pyracantha)* Valuable shrub from several standpoints. Foliage is attractive, and small white flower clusters provide fragrance. Highly ornamental fruit clusters in autumn are red, orange, or yellow and remain on plants well into winter and sometimes until spring.	Thorns help make this a useful barrier. It can be clipped or left unsheared. Also fine for espaliering. Needs sun or partial shade, thriving in wide range of soils. Mulch roots in spring and water freely in dry spells.	Ripened seeds can be stratified at once or stored for up to 1 yr. in cool, dry place prior to stratifying. Take semi-hard-shoot cuttings in summer or firm-shoot cuttings in late summer.
Chorizema ilicifolium	**Flame pea** *(Chorizema)* Noted for shape of its attractive leaves and handsome pealike blossoms that form profusely in terminal racemes. Develops short pods after flowers fade.	Good on trellises, since thin stems often require some support. Does best in sunny location with ample moisture, but drainage must be good.	Take semi-hard-shoot cuttings in summer.
Forsythia 'Beatrix Farrand'	**Forsythia, or Golden bell** *(Forsythia)* Yellow flowers in clusters of up to 6 produce outstanding effect in early to mid spring, when few other shrubs are in bloom. Branches are often arching or pendulous, and in some kinds tips root where they touch ground.	Strong, fast grower that looks especially attractive when located in clumps in front of evergreens. As hedges, they can be sheared or left to develop natural informal shapes. Withstands air pollution and is suitable for city gardens. Plant in full sun or partial shade in any good garden soil. Mulch roots and water well during hot, dry spells. Prune after flowering, removing old wood low down to encourage formation of vigorous new shoots.	Stratify seeds for 2 mo. at 40° F. Separate rooted pieces from old plants. Many kinds respond readily to soil layering. Take semi-hard-shoot cuttings in summer or leafless hardwood cuttings in fall.

Species and varieties	Hardiness (Map, p. 9)	Decorative characteristics and remarks	Height and spread when mature
Deciduous *Corylus americana* (American)	B	Alternate leaves, 2-5 in. long, have hairy undersides. Bears round nuts about ½ in. in diameter, which grow in clusters of 2-6. A woodland shrub with little landscape value.	H 10 ft.–S 6-10 ft.
C. avellana aurea (European)	A	Yellowish leaves are about 3-4 in. long and heart shaped at base. Tips of nuts sometimes protrude through husks.	H 15 ft.–S 15 ft.
C. a. contorta	A	Curiously twisted branches give this variety unusual gnarled look. Its bare branches are prized by flower arrangers.	H 15 ft.–S 15 ft.
Evergreen *Pyracantha angustifolia*	C	Occasionally seen with prostrate branches, this species flowers in late spring. Its fruit is vivid orange to brick-red and frequently clings to plant until early spring.	H 12 ft.–S 8 ft.
P. coccinea	C	Toothed ovalish leaves are almost 2 in. long. Blossom clusters are coated with soft hairs. Produces heavy crop of brilliant red berries.	H 15 ft.–S 15 ft.
P. c. 'Kasan'	C	Berries are orange-red. Hardier than *P. coccinea.*	H 15 ft.–S 15 ft.
P. c. lalandii	C	Fruit is orange. Excellent choice for training on walls.	H 15 ft.–S 15 ft.
P. c. 'Lowboy'	C	Has lush green leaves, which grow on low and wide-spreading branches. Berries are brilliant orange.	H 2-4 ft.–S 2-5 ft.
P. crenulata rogersiana	C	Twigs are covered with rust-colored hairs, and glossy leaves are less than 2 in. long. This variety sets an enormous amount of red-orange fruits.	H 10 ft.–S 10 ft.
P. koidzumii, or *P. formosana*	D	Clusters of large scarlet fruits.	H 10 ft.–S 8 ft.
Evergreen *Chorizema cordatum*	D*	Oval or rounded heart-shaped leaves have faintly toothed margins. Upright scarlet and purple blooms provide stunning show in early spring.	H 9 ft.–S 5-8 ft.
C. ilicifolium	D*	Differs from *C. cordatum* in being lower and having pricklier, hollylike leaves.	H 2-4 ft.–S 2-3 ft.
C. varium (bush)	D*	Erect, downy shoots. Prickly toothed, somewhat heart-shaped leaves. Orange-red and crimson blooms.	H 6 ft.–S 4-5 ft.
Deciduous *Forsythia* 'Beatrix Farrand'	B	Abundant display of vivid yellow blossoms, which are more than 2 in. wide. Habit of growth is generally upright, although outer branches are sometimes arching.	H 9 ft.–S 8 ft.
F. intermedia 'Spring Glory'	B	Two-in. flowers are lighter yellow than those of *F.* 'Beatrix Farrand.'	H 9 ft.–S 8 ft.
F. suspensa fortunei	B	Bright yellow flowers are more than 1 in. wide, opening on mainly upright branches that arch at ends.	H 12 ft.–S 9 ft.
F. viridissima bronxensis	B	Although restrained in habit of growth, this variety has masses of light yellow flowers that appear in midspring, even on young specimens.	H 2 ft.–S 2 ft.

*Not hardy below 30° F

	Common and botanical names, general characteristics	Uses and requirements	Propagation (*See also p. 87*)
 *Abeliophyllum distichum*	**Forsythia, white** (*Abeliophyllum*) Resembles forsythia in habit of growth and prolific bloom, but flowers are smaller. They open on fingerlike racemes in midspring, showing pale pink coloration but quickly turn to white. Oval leaves are 1-2 in. long.	A single specimen adds interesting emphasis when planted in front of evergreen background. Thrives in full sun or partial shade and average garden soil with good drainage.	Sow seeds as soon as they ripen. Take leafy semi-hard-shoot cuttings in summer or leafless hardwood cuttings in fall.
 *Fothergilla major*	**Fothergilla** (*Fothergilla*) A neat, low grower noted for bottlebrushlike white flower spikes in mid to late spring that sometimes open before foliage appears. Alternate leaves are toothed and coarse. In autumn they turn into spectacular combinations of red, orange, and yellow. Fruit is a dried capsule.	Does best in partial shade and cool, moist location with somewhat acid, peaty soil.	Stratify seeds for 5 mo. at room temperature, and continue for another 3 mo. at 40° F prior to sowing. Take semi-hard-shoot cuttings in summer, or remove and plant suckers. Responds well to soil layering.
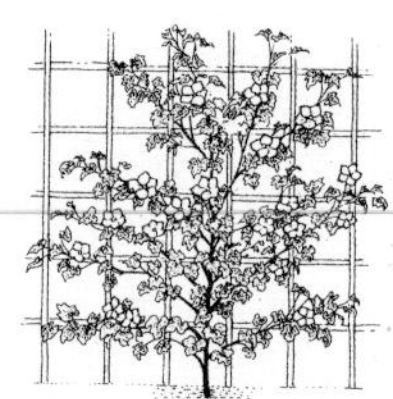 *Fremontodendron californicum*	**Fremontodendron, or Flannelbush** (*Fremontodendron,* or *Fremontia*) Alternate leaves are about 1 in. long. Two-in.-wide hollyhock-shaped blossoms are borne singly and in junctures formed between leaves and stems. Blooms in early spring, often lasting into midfall.	Fine for training against wall. Suitable for coastal gardens if protected from strong winds. Plant in full sun and in rich, well-drained, sandy soil.	Sow seeds when ripe. Take semi-hard-shoot cuttings in summer.
 *Fuchsia magellanica*	**Fuchsia** (*Fuchsia*) Striking flowers begin to open in early to late summer in shades of purple, red, white, or blue, as well as in combinations of these colors. Often hanging, blossoms form individually or in small clusters in junctures of leaves and stems. Stamens usually protrude and are very decorative.	Excellent as shrub, bedding plant, or trained in tree form; also good in hanging baskets and window boxes. Easy to grow in any good soil if drainage is adequate. Plant in partial shade. In mild climates after flowers fade, cut back branches to stimulate development of shoots that will bear next season's blossoms. In cold climates delay pruning until spring.	Sow seeds as soon as they are ripe, or store in cool, dry place for up to 1 yr. prior to sowing. Take soft-shoot cuttings in spring or semi-hard-shoot cuttings in summer. Roots can be divided in spring or autumn.
 *Gardenia jasminoides* 'August Beauty'	**Gardenia** (*Gardenia*) Leathery leaves are opposite and up to 4 in. long; upper surfaces have glossy, waxy sheen. Elegant large white flowers are fragrant, developing singly in junctures of leaves and stems from spring into fall.	Can be used in containers, as a hedge, or as single specimen plants. Plant in sandy, slightly acid, well-drained soil fortified with peat moss. Does best in full sun but will live in slightly shady location. Provide roots with heavy mulch throughout summer. Avoid cultivation, as roots are near soil surface.	Take semi-hard-shoot cuttings in early summer or hardwood cuttings in fall or winter.

Species and varieties	Hardiness *(Map, p. 9)*	Decorative characteristics and remarks	Height and spread when mature
Deciduous *Abeliophyllum distichum*	□B□□	Foliage is blue-green. Leaves are opposite and have short hairs on both sides. In cold winter regions dark purple flower buds may be damaged by frost unless plants are protected.	H 4 ft.–S 4 ft.
Deciduous *Fothergilla gardenii*	□B□□	Leaves are up to 2 in. long and wedge shaped. Their undersides are bluish white and covered with hairs. One-in.-long spikes of small white flowers are borne at ends of branches.	H 3 ft.–S 2½ ft.
F. major	□B□□	Oval or rounded leaves are 2-5 in. long and somewhat hairy underneath. Flowers are fragrant. Habit of growth is upright.	H 9 ft.–S 6 ft.
F. monticola	□B□□	Oval leaves are up to 4 in. long. Spikes of fragrant blossoms are almost 3 in. long. More spreading than *F. major.* A good shrub that blends well with evergreens in open woodlands.	H 6 ft.–S 6 ft.
Evergreen *Fremontodendron* 'California Glory'	□□C□	Lemon-yellow flowers with red-tinted exteriors are about 1½-2½ in. wide. A vigorous, free-flowering hybrid.	H 15 ft.–S 6-10 ft.
F. californicum	□□□D	Lobed leaves up to 4 in. long have fuzzy undersides. Flowers are yellow.	H 10-30 ft.–S 8-12 ft.
F. c. napensis	□□C□	Shoots are slender. Leaves are 1 in. long or less. Yellow flowers are not more than 1½ in. across.	H 10-20 ft.–S 8-10 ft.
F. mexicanum	□□□D	Flowers, somewhat hidden by leaves, are yellow, often tinged with orange.	H 18 ft.–S 8-10 ft.
Evergreen *Fuchsia hybrida*	□□□D *	Single to double flowers in wide range and combinations of colors. Shape of flowers varies considerably, as does size–from about ½ in. to about 3 in. Often grown in containers. In cold climates treat as annuals or grow in greenhouse.	H 3-12 ft.–S 3-6 ft.
F. magellanica	□B□□	Lance-shaped leaves are up to 2 in. long, light green, and toothed. Flowers are red with splashes of blue or pale purple. May ramble for up to 20 ft. when trained on wall or trellis. Sometimes deciduous.	H 3 ft.–S 3 ft.
F. m. riccartonii	□B□□	Abundant bloom of crimson blossoms. Although top growth may winter-kill, plant will recover in spring.	H 10 ft.–S 4 ft.
Evergreen *Gardenia jasminoides* 'August Beauty'	□□□D	Has thick array of lush green leaves that grow up to 4 in. long. Produces fair number of fragrant, frequently double, white flowers, which are often 2-3 in. in diameter and bloom from late spring through fall.	H 6 ft.–S 3-5 ft.
G. j. 'Mystery'	□□□D	Lustrous green leaves on compact plant. Double, creamy-colored flowers, which grow as large as 5 in. across, bloom during summer.	H 6 ft.–S 3-5 ft.
G. j. veitchii	□□□D	Displays large double flowers, which bloom from late spring to late fall. Often grown in greenhouses.	H 6 ft.–S 3-5 ft.

*Not hardy below 30° F

	Common and botanical names, general characteristics	Uses and requirements	Propagation *(See also p. 87)*
 *Genista pilosa*	**Genista** *(Genista)* Tiny leaves are sparsely produced, and plants carry on photosynthesis of foods with their green chlorophyll-containing stems. Pealike blossoms are usually yellow but sometimes white. They generally appear in racemes. Flat pods form later in season after flowering.	Will grow in poor, sandy soil. Does best in hot, dry place. Needs sun. Not easy to transplant. Plant with plenty of peat moss. After blooms fade, cut back flowering branches to prevent seed formation.	Sow seeds as soon as they are ripe, or store in cool, dry spot for up to 1 yr. before planting. Soak in hot water for 12 hr. prior to sowing. Take leafy semi-hard-shoot cuttings in summer or leafless hardwood cuttings in fall. Can also be soil-layered.
	Geraldton waxflower, see Waxflower, Geraldton		
 *Clerodendrum trichotomum*	**Glory-bower** *(Clerodendrum)* Leaves are opposite and frequently lobed. Decorative blossoms develop in clusters and include calyxes that often display more color than tubelike corollas. Stamens protrude. Fleshy fruits develop in autumn.	Plant in full sun in fertile, well-drained soil. Do not cultivate around roots, or many suckers will develop, spoiling overall contour.	Stratify seeds for 3 mo. at 40°F or store for up to 1 yr. in cool, dry place before stratifying. Take semi-hard-shoot cuttings in summer. After leaves drop in fall, suckers should be pulled off, not cut, and planted in easily worked soil.
	Golden dewdrop, see Dewdrop, golden		
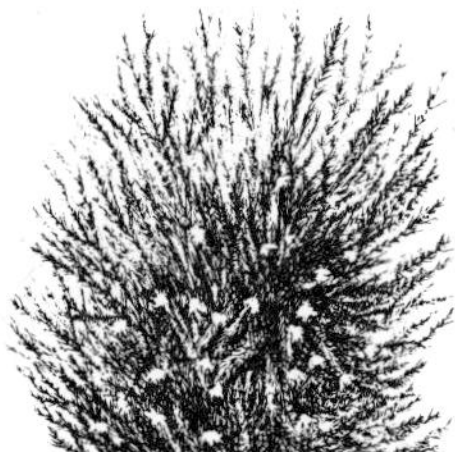 *Grevillea thelemanniana*	**Grevillea** *(Grevillea)* Leaves are alternate, with size and shape varying by kind. Flowers in pairs develop in tight panicles or racemes with long, often brightly colored styles that project from the centers of the flowers.	Plant in sun in any good garden soil. Survives extended dry spells.	Sow ripened seeds in moist sand. Keep sand warm until germination occurs.
 *Halimium ocymoides*	**Halimium** *(Halimium,* or *Helianthemum)* Golden yellow, roselike flowers bloom in loose clusters in late spring and early summer. They are not long lasting but create striking contrast to opposite grayish-green, oblong leaves.	Ideal for rock gardens and seacoast settings. Most effective when grown in groups. Plant in full sun. Does best in sandy soil and alkaline conditions. Spreads rapidly. Prune lightly after flowering to maintain compact form.	Take semi-hard-shoot cuttings in summer.

Species and varieties	Hardiness (Map, p. 9)	Decorative characteristics and remarks	Height and spread when mature
Deciduous *Genista aethnensis*	☐☐☐D	Golden yellow flowers open in mid to late summer. Pods are curved and covered with hairs when young. This species tolerates alkaline soils.	H 15 ft.–S 15 ft.
G. germanica	☐B☐☐	Has oblong or elliptic leaves and twigs covered with hairs. Small yellow flowers appear abundantly in midsummer. Short pods have silky hairs.	H 1½-2 ft.–S 1-2 ft.
G. hispanica	☐☐C☐	Golden yellow blossoms cover this species in late spring to early summer. Pods are hairy. In winter big green spines and green twigs make plant look like an evergreen.	H 1-2 ft.–S 6 ft.
G. monosperma	☐☐☐D	Very narrow and delicate grayish branches have practically no leaves. Aromatic white flowers bloom in late winter and spring.	H 20 ft.–S 10 ft.
G. pilosa	☐B☐☐	In late spring yellow flowers grow in junctures of leaves and stems. Pods more than 1 in. long. Prostrate habit of growth.	H 1 ft.–S 7 ft.
Deciduous *Clerodendrum trichotomum* (harlequin)	☐B☐☐	Elliptic or oval leaves are often lobed and frequently up to 7 in. long. Ornate pale pink flower clusters are aromatic and have protruding stamens. Blue berries and prominent red calyxes put on handsome show in late summer and early fall, lasting through midfall or longer.	H 20 ft.–S 15 ft.
Evergreen *C. bungei* (Kashmir bouquet)	☐☐☐D	Rapid-growing shrub with toothed heart-shaped leaves up to 1 ft. long, which give off unpleasant smell when crushed. Dense clusters of fragrant rose-red flowers in summer. Prune severely in spring; remove suckers. In some winters it may die back to ground level but should recover.	H 6 ft.–S 4-6 ft.
Evergreen *Grevillea lanigera*	☐☐☐D *	Has slender, ½-inch-long, hairy leaves. Reddish flowers grow in crowded, terminal, spikelike racemes.	H 3-6 ft.–S 6-10 ft.
G. noelii	☐☐☐D *	Has thin needlelike leaves, about 1 in. long, which densely cover its fine branches. In spring white and rose-red clusters of flowers make lovely display. Habit of growth is spreading.	H 4 ft.–S 5 ft.
G. rosmarinifolia (rosemary)	☐☐☐D *	Rosemarylike leaves with silvery undersides are more than 1 in. long. Flowers that appear are reddish.	H 6 ft.–S 6 ft.
G. thelemanniana (hummingbird bush)	☐☐☐D *	Dark green leaves are 1-2 in. long and considerably segmented and narrow. Pinkish blooms have yellow-green tips and may appear at any time on 2-in.-long by 2-in.-wide terminal racemes.	H 5 ft.– S 5 ft.
Evergreen *Halimium lasianthum*	☐☐C☐	Leaves are thin and from ½-1½ in. long. Brilliant 1½-in.-wide yellow flowers have purple-tinged petal bases. Habit of growth is spreading.	H 3 ft.–S 2-3 ft.
H. ocymoides	☐☐C☐	Leaves on nonflowering shoots are gray, and leaves on flowering shoots are green. Flowers more than 1 in. wide have yellow petals, which display dark purple spots at their bases. This species tolerates salt spray well.	H 3 ft.–S 4 ft.

*Not hardy below 30° F

	Common and botanical names, general characteristics	Uses and requirements	Propagation (*See also p. 87*)
 *Erica carnea*	**Heath** *(Erica)* Various heights, from small trees to ground covers. Many needlelike leaves develop in clusters of up to 6. Small white, pink to dark rose, or orange blossoms usually form in clusters and are sometimes nodding. Fruits are capsule shaped.	Low types are a handsome sight when grown in large groups. Plant in full sun or in slightly shady area, and in great amount of peat moss. Most kinds prefer acidity. Prune occasionally to stimulate side shoots and prevent plants from developing leggy look.	Seeds can be sown when ripe. Take semi-hard-shoot cuttings in summer. Root divisions can also be made.
 *Daboecia cantabrica*	**Heath, Irish** *(Daboecia)* Closely resembles heath. Its alternate, elliptic leaves are about ½ in. long. Urn-shaped flowers open in nodding terminal clusters.	Makes fine rock-garden plant. Does best in full sun but will tolerate partial shade. Requires moist, sandy soil fortified with great amount of peat moss.	Sow ripened seeds at once, or store them in dry place for up to 1 yr. prior to sowing. Take semi-hard-shoot cuttings in early summer, firm-shoot cuttings in late summer.
 *Calluna vulgaris*	**Heather, Scotch** *(Calluna)* Small, opposite leaves are so numerous that twigs are almost completely hidden. Small, nodding flowers are borne profusely in terminal clusters.	Good as ground cover on slopes where soil is reasonably moist, sandy, and acid. Not for fertile conditions, which stimulate leggy growth. Flowers best in full sun but tolerates very slight shade. Occasional pruning in early spring maintains low profile.	Sow seeds when ripe or make root divisions. Take semi-hard-shoot cuttings in summer or firm-shoot cuttings in late summer.

Species and varieties	Hardiness (Map, p. 9)	Decorative characteristics and remarks	Height and spread when mature
Evergreen *Erica arborea*	C	Hairy twigs support leaves in threes. Tiny white blooms are fragrant.	H 15 ft.–S 6-10 ft.
E. canaliculata	D	Has densely hairy shoots and ¼-in.-long leaves in threes. White or pink flowers, clustered near ends of branches, have prominent black stamens.	H 6 ft.–S 3-4 ft.
E. c. boscaweniana	D	Leaves are in threes. Rose-red blossoms that generally develop at ends of branches appear in early winter.	H 3 ft.–S 2-3 ft.
E. carnea (spring)	B	Rose-pink blossoms open from midwinter to late spring, depending on location and exposure. Stands slightly alkaline soil. Good for rock gardens.	H 1 ft.–S 6 in.-1 ft.
E. ciliaris (Dorset)	C	Leaves are grayish with hairy edges. Five-in. terminal clusters bear small red blooms in early summer.	H 1 ft.–S 6 in.-1 ft.
E. cinerea (bell heather)	B	Glossy green leaves in threes turn copper in fall. Rose-purple flowers appear from early summer to early fall. After they fade, prune heavily to stimulate branching. Tolerates alkaline soil.	H 1½ ft.–S 6 in.-1 ft.
E. darleyensis	B	Tiny leaves are rolled at edges and grow in fours. Pale purplish-pink blooms are often seen from early winter into spring. Tolerates alkalinity.	H 2 ft.–S 1-2 ft.
E. lusitanica	C	Leaves in threes or fives are ¼ in. long. White flowers with pink stamens clothe branches in midwinter to early spring. Dense habit of growth.	H 12 ft.–S 6-8 ft.
E. mammosa	D	Leaves are scattered or in fours. Drooping dark red to pink or orange flowers grow in dense spikes. Stiff, upright habit of growth.	H 4 ft.–S 3-4 ft.
E. mediterranea	C	Leaves form in fours or fives on upright branches. Small dark red blossoms with protruding stamens open in midspring.	H 6 ft.–S 3-5 ft.
E. tetralix (cross-leaved)	A	Grayish hairy-edged leaves grow in fours. Small rose-red blooms put on display from early summer to midfall. Grows best in moist soil with great amount of peat moss. Habit of growth is generally prostrate.	H 2 ft.–S 1-1½ ft.
E. vagans (Cornish)	C	Leaves in groups of 4 to 5. Pinkish-purple blossoms grow in clusters to 6 in. from midsummer to midfall. Varieties have white, dark pink, or red flowers. Spreading habit of growth.	H 1 ft.–S 6 in.-1 ft.
Evergreen *Daboecia cantabrica*	C	Sets numerous rose-purple blossoms to ½ in. long, from early summer to midfall. Its habit of growth is upright and neat.	H 1½ ft.–S 6 in.-1 ft.
D. c. alba	C	Similar to *D. cantabrica,* but with white flowers.	H 1½ ft.–S 6 in.-1 ft.
D. c. praegerae	C	Has deep rose-pink flowers that are somewhat larger than *D. cantabrica.*	H 1 ft.–S 6 in.-1 ft.
Evergreen *Calluna vulgaris*	B	The true Scotch heather with rose-pink flowers that bloom from midsummer to midfall. In varieties offered, leaves vary from yellow-green to dark green or sometimes gray. Single or double flowers may be red, pink, white, or purple. Flowering season varies with variety, from midsummer to midfall. Habit of growth may be low and spreading or rounded and bushy.	H 1½ ft.–S 6 in.-1 ft.

Nandina domestica

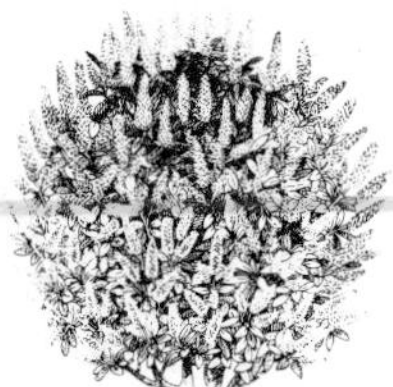

Hebe speciosa

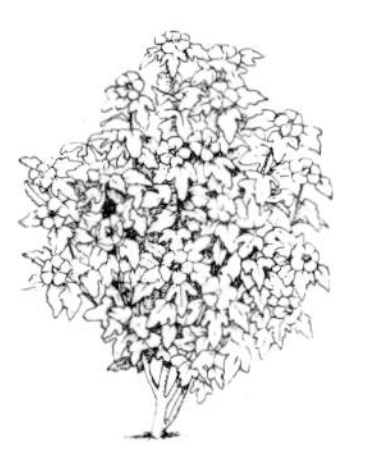

Hibiscus syriacus 'Admiral Dewey'

Common and botanical names, general characteristics	Uses and requirements	Propagation *(See also p. 87)*
Heavenly bamboo *(Nandina)* Not a bamboo, but related to barberries. Leaves have thin 1- to 2-in. leaflets. Small flowers borne in terminal clusters.	Plant in full sun. Will grow in almost any type of soil but must have sufficient moisture.	Ripened seeds should be kept moist before planting. Germination usually takes several months.
Hebe *(Hebe,* or *Veronica)* Leaves are opposite and leathery. Flowers are usually white or pinkish, developing in clusters at terminals or sometimes in junctures of leaves and stems.	Some kinds can be sheared to create informal hedges. Plant in full sun or partial shade in any well-drained, sandy soil.	Sow seeds when ripe. Take firm-shoot cuttings in late summer.
Hibiscus *(Hibiscus)* Showy flowers are several inches across, either single or double, sometimes frilled or laciniated, in many colors, often with contrasting throat color. Deciduous forms, suited to cold climates as well as the Gulf states, flower when blooms on other shrubs are scarce—midsummer to early fall. Evergreen forms limited to frost-free subtropical climates. Their lustrous leaves are almost as great an asset as flowers that appear throughout summer. Hundreds of varieties are grown.	Grow in full sun in any well-drained soil. Young plants of deciduous forms need protection during first few winters in very cold regions. Protect evergreen forms from frost and strong coastal winds; often grown as annuals where subject to winter damage. Prune established plants in early spring by removing about one-third of old wood. Often used as hedge, espalier, container plant, or even small tree.	Ripened seeds can be sown at once or stored in cool, dry place for up to 1 yr. and then planted. Lower branches can be soil-layered. Take soft-shoot cuttings in spring or firm-shoot cuttings in late summer. Deciduous kinds also respond to leafless hardwood cuttings taken in autumn.

Species and varieties	Hardiness (Map, p. 9)	Decorative characteristics and remarks	Height and spread when mature
Evergreen *Nandina domestica*	D	New leaflets, bronze in spring, turn red in fall. Clusters of white flowers are up to 1 ft. long in midsummer. Red fruits attractive into early winter.	H 8 ft.–S 4-6 ft.
N. d. alba	D	Much like *N. domestica* except that fruits are white.	H 8 ft.–S 4-6 ft.
Evergreen *Hebe andersonii*	D *	Numerous branches hold 4- to 5-in.-long fleshy leaves. Displays tiny white flowers with pale purple tips in late summer and early fall.	H 8 ft.–S 4-6 ft.
H. buxifolia	D	Glossy deep green leaves less than 1 in. long overlap for dense effect. One-in. spikes bear white blooms in midsummer.	H 5 ft.–S 2-4 ft.
H. cupressoides	D	Scalelike leaves and tiny, pale blue or purple flowers in early summer.	H 6 ft.–S 4 ft.
H. speciosa	D *	Angled twigs bear 2- to 4-in.-long hairy leaves. Red-purple or blue-purple blooms in 4-in.-long clusters from midsummer to early fall.	H 5 ft.–S 5 ft.
H. traversii	D	Heavily branched, with 1-in.-long leaves. White flower clusters in midsummer.	H 6 ft.–S 3-5 ft.
Deciduous *Hibiscus syriacus* (rose of Sharon, or althaea)	B	Single or double flowers are rose or purple to white. Hybrid forms preferable.	H 12 ft.–S 6-8 ft.
H. s. 'Admiral Dewey'	B	Double pure white flowers are more than 2 in. in diameter.	H 12 ft.–S 6-8 ft.
H. s. 'Bluebird'	B	Late-blooming, single blue blossoms are almost 4 in. wide.	H 12 ft.–S 6-8 ft.
H. s. 'Boule de Feu'	B	Double purplish-red blossoms are more than 2 in. across.	H 12 ft.–S 6-8 ft.
H. s. coelestis	B	Violet blooms to 3 in. wide have red streaks from base to middle of each petal.	H 12 ft.–S 6-8 ft.
H. s. 'Hamabo'	B	Single light pink flowers have reddish lines along half length of petals.	H 12 ft.–S 6-8 ft.
H. s. 'Lady Stanley'	B	Three-in.-wide flowers are white with red stripes from base to mid petal.	H 12 ft.–S 6-8 ft.
H. s. totusalbus	B	Single brilliant white blossoms are almost 4 in. wide.	H 12 ft.–S 6-8 ft.
Evergreen *H. huegelii*	D *	Deeply lobed leaves are toothed. Lilac or purple flowers are spotted at base.	H 4-5 ft.–S 6-8 ft.
H. rosasinensis (rose of China)	D *	Rose-red to white flowers are sometimes double. Hybrid forms preferable.	H 30 ft.–S 6-8 ft.
H. r. 'Agnes Gault'	D *	Solitary rose-pink blossoms are sometimes 6 in. wide.	H 30 ft.–S 10-12 ft.
H. r. 'American Beauty'	D *	Similar to *H. r.* 'Agnes Gault' except that its single flowers are pink.	H 20 ft.–S 8-10 ft.
H. r. 'Butterfly'	D *	Single blossoms are vivid yellow.	H 20 ft.–S 8-10 ft.
H. r. 'Ecstasy'	D *	Dark rich red flowers are single and have white rays from base of each petal.	H 20 ft.–S 8-10 ft.
H. r. 'Full Moon'	D *	Double flowers are brilliant lemon-yellow.	H 20 ft.–S 8-10 ft.
H. r. 'White Wings'	D *	Single white blossoms have splash of red at centers.	H 20 ft.–S 8-10 ft.

*Not hardy below 30° F

	Common and botanical names, general characteristics	Uses and requirements	Propagation *(See also p. 87)*
 *Ilex crenata*	**Holly** *(Ilex)* A handsome, valuable addition to any garden. Alternate leaves are often attractive. Greenish or white flowers that grow in juncture of leaf and stem are seldom noticeable. Berrylike fruits are frequently spectacular, but are borne only on female plants; so in order to assure fruits, both male and female plants must be planted in close proximity.	Excellent choice for hedges. Plant in sun or partial shade. Add plenty of peat moss or compost to planting holes. Prune heavily after transplanting to lessen shock. A slow grower and not easy to establish. Water well during first year. When plants achieve good size, they can be selectively pruned in winter to provide indoor decoration. Lower branches on older shrubs have tendency to bend to ground and root, assuming unruly appearance. To avoid this, trim off lowest branches.	Prior to planting, seeds should be stratified at room temperature for 3 to 5 mo. and then given temperature of 40° F for another 3 mo. Germination often takes from 2-5 yr. Take semi-hard-shoot cuttings in summer. Can also be soil-layered.
 *Lonicera tatarica*	**Honeysuckle** *(Lonicera)* Leaves are opposite. Bell-shaped or tubular blossoms develop in terminal clusters or in pairs at junctures of leaves and stems. Often aromatic flowers are white, pink, red, or yellow. Fleshy berries in white, red, yellow, blue, or black attract and are quickly devoured by birds.	Makes excellent addition to any shrub border. Grows in moist, loamy soil. Lives in full sun or partial shade. Extremely easy shrub to grow and one that is seldom troubled by insects or diseases. Prune after flowering to shape plant. In winter cut back some of older stems at ground level to encourage vigorous young growth.	Seeds can be stratified at once or stored in a cool, dry place for up to 1 yr. and then stratified for 3 mo. at 40° F. If germination does not occur within 4 mo., stratify for another 3 mo. at 40° F. Responds to soil layering and root division. Take semi-hard-shoot cuttings in summer or hardwood cuttings in fall. Increase deciduous kinds by taking leafless hardwood cuttings in autumn.
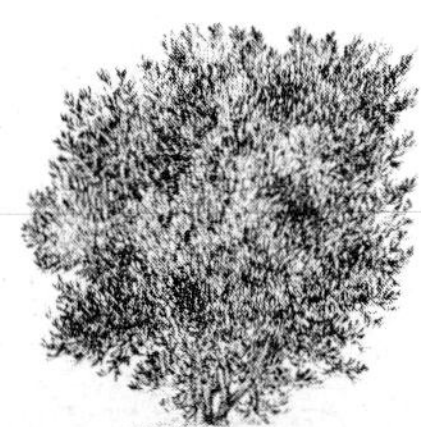 *Dodonaea viscosa purpurea*	**Hopbush** *(Dodonaea)* Alternate narrow leaves in various colors are 3 in. or more long and have resinous dots. Inconspicuous green flowers grow in short racemes.	Excellent choice for screens. Does best in full sun to retain full color of leaves; turns green if in shade. Will grow in any soil with medium moisture. Withstands city smog.	Take semi-hard-shoot cuttings in summer or firm-shoot cuttings in late summer, or can be grown from seeds.

Species and varieties	Hardiness (*Map, p. 9*)	Decorative characteristics and remarks	Height and spread when mature
Evergreen *Ilex cornuta* (Chinese)	C	Glossy oblong leaves bear 3 spines at tips and often 2 more on sides. They are sometimes up to 5 in. long. Bisexual plant sets red fruit clusters without need for separate male and female specimens planted close together.	H 9 ft.–S 5-8 ft.
I. c. burfordii	C	Wedge-shaped leaves are brilliant green and have only 1 spine at tip. Forms abundance of fruit.	H 9 ft.–S 5-8 ft.
I. c. 'Dazzler'	C	Showy large clusters of bright red berries against very shiny foliage.	H 9 ft.–S 5-8 ft.
I. c. rotunda (dwarf)	C	An excellent dwarf variety that withstands drought and considerable heat.	H 2-3 ft.–S 2-3 ft.
I. crenata (Japanese)	B	A highly popular species with oblong 1- to 2-in. deep green leaves resembling those of boxwood. Fruits are black and not especially noticeable. Develops dense growth that responds well to shearing.	H 15 ft.–S 4-8 ft.
I. c. convexa	B	Leaves are convex on upper sides and concave underneath. Handsome when sheared. Spreading habit of growth.	H 5 ft.–S 10 ft.
I. c. 'Green Island'	C	More open branching habit than many *I. c.* varieties. Leaves are flat topped. A fast grower.	H 4 ft.–S 6 ft.
I. c. helleri	B	Attractive dark green leaves are about ½ in. long. Slow grower. Compact.	H 4 ft.–S 5 ft.
Deciduous *Lonicera fragrantissima*	B	Thick oval leaves are deep green and up to 2 in. long; upper surfaces are deeper green than undersides. Creamy white blossoms from midwinter to midspring offer intense aroma. Red fruits appear in late spring. Semi-evergreen where winters are mild. Tolerates clay soil.	H 6 ft.–S 6 ft.
L. korolkowii	B	Oval leaves are 1 in. long, pointed, and hairy on undersides. Their color is handsome bluish green. Pale pink flowers in late spring and early summer are followed by red fruits in late summer.	H 12 ft.–S 6-8 ft.
L. tatarica	B	Pointed oval leaves are more than 2 in. long. Pink to white blossoms provide fine aroma in late spring and early summer. Yellow or red fruits appear in mid to late summer. Habit of growth is erect and tidy.	H 9 ft.–S 6-8 ft.
Evergreen *L. nitida* (box)	C	Dark green oval leaves are about ½ in. long. Creamy white blossoms in late spring are aromatic but not especially noticeable. Bluish-purple fruits can be seen in early to mid fall. Makes handsome hedge and withstands salt spray and wind.	H 6 ft.–S 6 ft.
L. pileata (privet)	B	Oblong or ovate, semi-evergreen leaves are shiny and usually more than 1 in. long. Fragrant white flowers in mid to late spring and purple fruits in midfall are its assets. Good choice for rock gardens along coast.	H 2 ft.–S 2-4 ft.
Evergreen *Dodonaea viscosa purpurea* (purple)	D *	Bronze-green leaves that are lance shaped and to 5 in. long turn attractive reddish purple in midfall. Seedlings vary somewhat in coloration.	H 10-15 ft.–S 12 ft.
D. v. 'Saratoga'	D *	Lance-shaped leaves are rich purple all year.	H 10-15 ft.–S 12 ft.

*Not hardy below 30° F

	Common and botanical names, general characteristics	Uses and requirements	Propagation *(See also p. 87)*
 *Hydrangea arborescens grandiflora*	**Hydrangea** *(Hydrangea)* Large leaves are usually toothed and opposite. Small- to medium-sized, normally 5-petaled flowers open in large round or oblong clusters. Flowers are generally of 2 kinds: showy sterile ray flowers without stamens or pistils, and less conspicuous fertile flowers.	Plant in average to rich soil in full sun if near coast or partial shade if inland. Protect from strong winds. Watch out for powdery mildew on foliage of *H. macrophylla.* If it occurs, treat as recommended on p. 607. Blue-flowered type of *H. macrophylla* may turn pink in alkaline soil. Color can be restored by watering with aluminum sulfate at rate of 3 oz. per gal. of water. This makes soil acid.	Seeds can be sown when ripe or stored for up to 1 yr. in cool, dry place prior to sowing. Take firm-shoot cuttings in late summer or leafless hardwood cuttings in fall.
 *Hypericum* 'Rowallane'	**Hypericum, or Saint-John's-wort** *(Hypericum)* Long-lasting, cup-shaped flowers appear in clusters in shades of pale to bright yellow. Leaves generally have no marginal teeth or lobes.	Makes outstanding addition to borders or rock gardens. Most kinds grow in sun or shade and will live in dry, sandy soil.	Ripened seeds can be planted at once or stored in cool, dry place for up to 1 yr. prior to sowing. Take semi-hard-shoot cuttings in summer or firm-shoot cuttings in late summer. Also responds to root division.
	Ilex, see Holly		
 *Indigofera gerardiana*	**Indigo** *(Indigofera)* Alternate compound leaves and pealike blossoms develop in racemes in angles formed between leaves and stems. Tiny dry pods form in autumn.	Grows in any soil that drains well but must have exposure to full sun.	Immerse ripened seeds in very hot water, and soak for 8 hr. prior to planting. Make root divisions in early spring. Take semi-hard-shoot cuttings in summer, or root cuttings in late winter or early spring.
 *Jasminum nudiflorum*	**Jasmine** *(Jasminum)* Branches are viny. Opposite leaves consist of 3 leaflets 1-3 in. long. Yellow flowers are solitary and single, occasionally double. A plant commonly called jasmine, or star jasmine, is *Trachelospermum jasminoides,* grown as vine (p. 191).	Useful for covering walls or unsightly tree stumps. Can be planted in greenhouses in cool climates. Plant in sun in soil fortified with plenty of humus or peat moss.	Plant seeds as soon as ripe, or store in cool, dry place for up to 1 yr. prior to sowing. Make soil layers. Take semi-hard-shoot cuttings in summer or firm-shoot cuttings in late summer.

Species and varieties	Hardiness (Map, p. 9)	Decorative characteristics and remarks	Height and spread when mature
Deciduous *Hydrangea arborescens grandiflora*	A	White flowers open in early summer in semi-flattened clusters. Habit of growth is open and rounded. Root divisions of this variety are easily made.	H 4 ft.–S 4 ft.
H. macrophylla (hortensia)	B	Blue, purple, pink, or white flower clusters are rounded and often up to 10 in. wide; they begin opening in midsummer. Its several varieties offer same color options as species. Withstands partial shade. A good seacoast plant.	H 12 ft.–S 6-10 ft.
H. paniculata grandiflora (peegee)	A	Huge white flower clusters, appearing in late summer, are long lasting and turn pink and purple as they age. A vigorous, dependable variety.	H 25 ft.–S 6-10 ft.
H. quercifolia (oak leaf)	B	Reddish twigs. Red leaves in fall. Erect clusters of white blossoms in summer turn purple later. Tolerates dry soil and sun but also does well in shade.	H 6 ft.–S 4-6 ft.
Evergreen *Hypericum calycinum*	B	Foliage turns purplish in autumn. Flowers are somewhat sparse but up to 2 in. across; blooms from midsummer to early fall. This species makes useful and highly decorative ground cover.	H 1 ft.–S 1-2 ft.
H. patulum 'Sungold'	B	Semi-evergreen leaves are more than 2 in. long. Three-in. blossoms in early fall are striking golden yellow. In its northernmost range, top growth may winter-kill. Requires full sun. Tolerates heavy clay soil.	H 5 ft.–S 6 ft.
H. 'Rowallane'	C	From midsummer numerous deep golden yellow blossoms are produced at tips of shoots. Dense growth assumes oval outline.	H 2 ft.–S 3 ft.
Deciduous *Indigofera gerardiana* (Himalayan)	D	Has many branches. Each leaf consists of up to 21 leaflets measuring about ½ in. each in length. Reddish-purple blooms appear in abundance in midsummer in up to 6-in.-long racemes.	H 4 ft.–S 3-4 ft.
I. incarnata	B	In midsummer white flowers form on 5- to 10-in. spikes. A useful ground cover, especially on slopes, where its roots prevent erosion.	H 1½ ft.–S 1-3 ft.
I. kirilowii	B	Leaflets are up to 1½ in. long. Rose-colored blossoms open in early summer on 5-in. spikes. Excellent ground cover that suckers rapidly.	H 3 ft.–S 2-3 ft.
I. potaninii	B	Lilac-pink flowers open in early summer and last for weeks.	H 4 ft.–S 2-4 ft.
I. tinctoria	D *	Reddish-orange blooms appear in early summer. Plant is commercial source of blue dye.	H 2 ft.–S 1-2 ft.
Deciduous *Jasminum nudiflorum* (winter)	B	Deep green leaves are made up of 3 oval leaflets. Vivid yellow blooms open in midspring and reach width of up to 1 in. Habit of growth is upright, although branches droop. Tolerates partial shade and heavy clay soil. Needs winter protection in northernmost range. Prune occasionally to maintain shape.	H 10 ft.–S 10 ft.
Semi-evergreen *J. mesnyi* (primrose)	C	Dark green leaves consist of 3 leaflets 2-3 in. long. Large yellow flowers to 1½ in. wide bloom from late fall to midspring in mild climates, from late winter to midspring in colder areas.	H 8-10 ft.–S 3-4 ft.

*Not hardy below 30° F

	Common and botanical names, general characteristics	Uses and requirements	Propagation (*See also p. 87*)
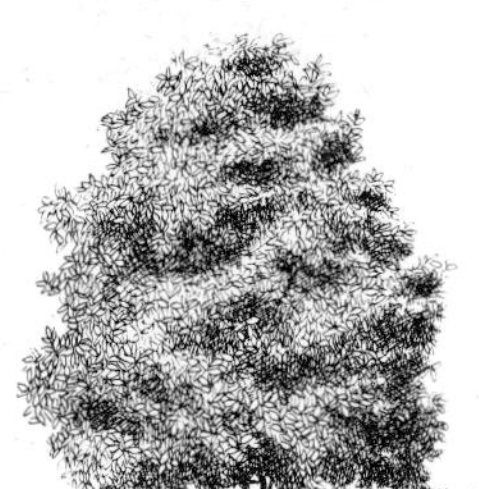 *Murraya paniculata*	**Jessamine, orange** *(Murraya)* Attractive compound leaves consist of 3-9 glossy oval leaflets. Heavily perfumed, bell-shaped flowers open in clusters several times each year. Fruits are egg shaped.	Plant in sun or partial shade in any good garden soil. Water regularly and feed frequently.	Propagates readily by seeds or cuttings.
 *Juniperus chinensis columnaris*	**Juniper** *(Juniperus)* Handsome foliage is of 2 distinct types: needle shaped and scalelike. Young vigorous branches usually bear the former, while both are generally seen on older plants. Females set small blue berrylike fruits that may take up to 3 yr. to mature. A particularly valuable group of plants in wide range of heights and shapes.	Good choice near buildings. Takes pruning well and can be sheared for formal hedges. Does best in hot, dry places in full sun. Plant in any good garden soil enriched with compost or humus. Will live in slightly acid to slightly alkaline conditions. Withstands smog.	Ripened seeds should be stratified for 3-5 mo. at room temperature and then left another 3 mo. at 40°F prior to sowing. Make soil layers. Take firm-shoot cuttings in late summer.
	Kalmia, see Laurel, mountain		
 *Kerria japonica*	**Kerria** *(Kerria)* Single or double yellow flowers are handsome in late spring. Semi-pendulous branches are attractive green and show to particular advantage in winter. Its bright green leaves are heavily veined and turn yellow in autumn. There is only one species in this genus.	Useful for espaliering on walls, arches, and fences; also good selection for foundation plantings and borders. Grows in sun or shade and tolerates poor soil. Mulch roots in spring, and water thoroughly in dry weather. Prune out older wood occasionally to maintain vigor. Top growth may winter-kill in cold climates, but plants often recover.	Divide root clumps in spring before growth resumes. Take soft-shoot cuttings in spring or leafless hardwood cuttings in autumn.
	Kolkwitzia, see Beauty bush		
 *Lantana camara*	**Lantana** *(Lantana)* Stems are generally hairy and sometimes prickly. Leaves have rough upper surfaces. When crushed, foliage emits unpleasant odor. Masses of tiny flowers in dense heads form at ends of branches or in junctures of leaves and stems.	Grown outdoors as shrub in climates where little or no frost occurs. In cold climates grown as annual and then discarded. Can be trained into tree (standard) form and grown in container. Occasionally they are stored over winter in frost-free room or greenhouse and planted out again in summer.	Take soft-shoot cuttings in spring or early summer.

Species and varieties	Hardiness (Map, p. 9)	Decorative characteristics and remarks	Height and spread when mature
Evergreen *Murraya paniculata,* or *M. exotica*	D *	Leaflets are up to 2 in. long. Waxy white blossoms are almost 1 in. wide. Treelike in habit of growth. Can be pruned as hedge.	H 10 ft.–S 5-8 ft.
M. p. 'Dwarf'	D *	Very similar to *M. paniculata* but with clusters that contain more blooms, although total number of clusters may be fewer.	H 6 ft.–S 4 ft.
Evergreen *Juniperus chinensis* 'Ames'	A	Steel-blue foliage. Pyramidal shape. A slow grower.	H 7 ft.–S 3 ft.
J. c. blaauwii	A	Feathery blue foliage. Irregular, dense habit of growth; vase shaped.	H 4 ft.–S 3 ft.
J. c. columnaris	A	Narrow and columnar with dense gray-green foliage.	H 12-15 ft.–S 2 ft.
J. c. pfitzeriana	A	Gray-green foliage on nodding branchlets. Spreading habit of growth.	H 5 ft.–S 10 ft.
J. horizontalis	A	Grayish-blue or bluish-green foliage forms on spreading branches. Fruit is blue. Some varieties show purplish coloration in fall. Shapes and sizes vary widely. Varieties include several handsome creepers.	H 1-2 ft.–S 4-10 ft.
J. procumbens	A	Greenish-blue needles, each bearing 2 white spots close to base. Creeping habit of growth makes it fine ground cover, especially on banks. There are varieties of *J. procumbens* that are more compact.	H 2 ft.–S 4-10 ft.
J. sabina	A	Deep green foliage grows on spreading or ascending branches. Needles on generally low-growing varieties range in color from pale green to grayish green. Brown fruit shows a delicate blue powdery coating.	H 8 ft.–S 3-4 ft.
J. squamata	B	Spreading branches turn up gracefully at tips. Bluish-green needles show whitish hue on upper surfaces. Oval fruits are purplish black. Varieties include bluish-needled specimens that are excellent in rock gardens.	H 3 ft.–S 2-3 ft.
Deciduous *Kerria japonica*	B	Alternate leaves are up to 4 in. long, oval and toothed. Single yellow blossoms are more than 1 in. wide and form along ends of branches.	H 6 ft.–S 6 ft.
K. j. pleniflora	B	Rounded double flowers are brilliant yellow and long lasting. They bloom abundantly and make pleasing sight, causing branches to bend gracefully beneath their weight. An outstanding variety.	H 8 ft.–S 6 ft.
Evergreen *Lantana camara*	C	Opposite leaves are toothed, heart shaped or oval, and 2-4½ in. long; undersides are hairy. Flower clusters change from yellow to red and orange as they age. Shiny fruits are blue-black.	H 8 ft.–S 8 ft.
L. montevidensis	D *	Ovalish leaves are 1 in. long with clearly defined veins. Small rose-pink blossoms are about 1 in. wide and appear on plants during most of year. A good trailing species that responds to soil layering.	H 2 ft.–S 4-5 ft.

*Not hardy below 30° F

Common and botanical names, general characteristics	Uses and requirements	Propagation (*See also p. 87*)
Laurel, or Sweet bay *(Laurus)* Has aromatic leaves that are used to flavor stews, roasts, and sauces. Small, hardly noticeable flowers and tiny berries. This is highly desirable foliage plant.	Well suited to coastal gardens. Excellent choice for tubs. Takes shearing especially well and can be used for topiaries. Vigorous grower. Plant in full sun or partial shade in well-drained soil, and water freely in dry weather.	Sow seeds as soon as they ripen. Take firm-shoot cuttings in late summer.
Laurel, cherry, see p. 69		
Laurel, mountain *(Kalmia)* A handsome ornamental, especially when its flowers open in early summer. Blossoms are flat or cup shaped and form on lateral or terminal clusters. Leaves are poisonous to livestock.	Excellent companion for other evergreens and attractive when planted under tall oaks. Does best in partial shade and acid, peaty soil that retains some moisture but also drains well.	Ripened seeds can be planted immediately or stored in cool, dry place for up to 1 yr. before sowing. Germination rate is frequently higher when seeds are stratified at 40° F for 3 mo. and then planted. Also responds to soil layering.
Lavender, see Perennials, p. 253 **Lavender cotton**, see Santolina		
Leadplant *(Amorpha)* Dependable but sometimes invasive plant. Its leaves are compound, and tiny, pealike blossoms form in terminal clusters that often branch. Slightly sticky pods follow flowers.	Use as single specimen plant or in borders, particularly where soil is poor and dry. Grow in full sun. May spread out of bounds unless restrained.	Seeds can be sown when ripe. Take leafy semi-hard-shoot cuttings in summer or leafless hard-wood cuttings in fall. Can also be increased by soil layering and suckers.
Lemon verbena, see Lippia		
Leucothoe *(Leucothoe)* Displays handsome alternate leaves and small white urn-shaped flowers. Its stems assume graceful arching habit. In late fall foliage turns red or bronze.	Blends in nicely with many other evergreens. Grows best in semi-shade found in open woodlands. Soil should be consistently moist, acid, and rich in organic matter. Occasional removal of older wood at soil level helps maintain vigor and graceful shape.	Seeds can be sown when ripe or stored in cool, dry place for up to 1 yr. prior to planting. Take semi-hard-shoot cuttings in summer or firm-shoot cuttings in late summer. Can also be increased easily by root divisions made in early spring.
Lilac *(Syringa)* Small tubular flowers are often intensely fragrant and appear in handsome clusters. Flower color varies with kind but includes blooms of pale violet, blue-violet to deep purple, pink-violet.	Fine as single specimen plant or informal, unclipped hedge. Withstands smog in city gardens. Plant in full sun or partial shade in well-drained alkaline soil. Mulch roots in midspring. Water thoroughly during dry spells.	Ripened seeds should be stratified for 2 mo. at 40° F prior to planting. Take semi-hard-shoot cuttings in summer.

Laurus nobilis

Kalmia latifolia

Amorpha canescens

Leucothoe fontanesiana

Syringa vulgaris

Lilac *(Syringa)*—continued

Species and varieties	Hardiness *(Map, p. 9)*	Decorative characteristics and remarks	Height and spread when mature
Evergreen *Laurus nobilis*	D	This good-looking species has fragrant oblong leaves up to 4 in. long and greenish-black fruits. The laurel of ancient Greece.	H 20 ft.–S 20 ft.
Evergreen *Kalmia latifolia* (mountain laurel)	B	Moderately glossy oval leaves are up to 4 in. long. Flowers are white to rose and extremely showy. Selections with deep red buds often available.	H 15 ft.–S 8 ft.
K. polifolia (pale, or bog, laurel)	A	Leaves, opposite or in threes, are 1½ in. long, glossy green above, powdery white beneath. Rose-purple flowers appear in late spring and early summer. Suitable only for bog areas.	H 8 in.-2 ft. S 1-1½ ft.
Deciduous *Amorpha canescens*	B	Densely hairy gray leaves often are made up of from 15 to more than 40 leaflets up to ¾ in. long; they remain attractive throughout growing season. In midsummer blue blossoms open on 4- to 6-in. spikes.	H 4 ft.–S 3-4 ft.
Evergreen *Leucothoe axillaris*	C	Leathery leaves are somewhat lance shaped and 2-4 in. long. Flower clusters in mid to late spring are up to 3 in. long, developing in junctures of leaves and stems.	H 6 ft.–S 3-5 ft.
L. fontanesiana, or *L. catesbaei*	B	Glossy, dark green leaves show fine bronzy hue throughout winter. This attractive species bears waxy flower clusters in early summer. Generally semi-evergreen in coldest parts of Zone B.	H 6 ft.–S 3-5 ft.
Deciduous *Syringa amurensis japonica* (Japanese tree)	B	Leaves are hairy and 6 in. long. Yellowish-white flowers open in early summer. A late bloomer among lilacs. Habit of growth is treelike.	H 30 ft.–S 8-10 ft.
S. chinensis (Chinese)	A	A hybrid with smooth oval leaves that grow 2 in. long. Flowers are pale purple.	H 10 ft.–S 6-8 ft.
S. josikaea (Hungarian)	A	Violet flowers unfold in late spring or early summer.	H 12 ft.–S 12 ft.

Lilac *(Syringa)*—continued

	Common and botanical names, general characteristics	Uses and requirements	Propagation (*See also p. 87*)
 *Syringa vulgaris*	**Lilac** *(Syringa)*—continued Flowers may also be in shades of cream to yellow-white. Bloom period for lilacs may last up to 6 wk. or longer in zones where assortment of species and varieties can be grown. Leaves are opposite, quite variable in size and shape, and usually not lobed.	Remove most flowers from recent transplants during first year to give them good start. For optimum flowering, apply dried cow manure every second spring; remove dead blossoms to prevent seed formation. Cut back to first node where new buds can be seen. If cut beyond this point, next year's flowers will be lost. Every second or third year, prune out most suckers from base of shrub.	On plants grown on their own roots (not grafted), rooted suckers can be dug up from around base and replanted.
	Lilac, California, see Ceanothus		
 *Aloysia triphylla*	**Lippia, or Lemon verbena** *(Aloysia,* or *Lippia)* Small blossoms are borne in clusters. Nutlets develop after blossoms fade but have no decorative value.	Makes good cool-room house plant where cold winters prevent its use outdoors. Also excellent for tubs on terraces. Plant in sun in any good garden soil. Water well during dry periods.	Take semi-hard-shoot cuttings in summer. Divide root clumps in early spring or fall.
 *Magnolia stellata* 'Waterlily'	**Magnolia** *(Magnolia)* Elegant flowers make this a valuable shrub in climates where it will grow. Blossoms are large and have 6 -15 petals. They open before or at same time as alternate leaves that have smooth margins. In late summer or early fall conelike fruits split open to reveal handsome bright red seeds.	Plant in full sun or partial shade in lime-free, well-drained soil containing plenty of peat moss or other organic matter. In northern gardens transplanting is best done in spring. Fleshy root system makes transplanting difficult. Buy only balled and burlapped specimens. Mulch roots in midspring and water freely in dry weather. Apply complete fertilizer around roots every 2 or 3 yr. if grown in infertile soil.	Ripened seeds should be stratified for 4 mo. at 40° F prior to planting. Take soft-shoot cuttings in spring. Can also be soil-layered in spring.
 *Mahonia lomarifolia*	**Mahonia** *(Mahonia)* Alternate, compound, green to blue-green leaves are decorative all year. In fall leaflets of some species and varieties turn purplish or bronze. One common name, holly grape, alludes to resemblance of its spiny-toothed leaves to those of holly. Small, yellow, bell-shaped blooms are aromatic and develop in terminal clusters, or panicles. Fruits are dark blue or bluish-black berries.	Attractive in foundation plantings and shrub borders. Does best in partial shade and fertile soil and in a place with protection from winter sun and wind. Water well during droughts.	Ripened seeds should be stratified for 3 mo. at 40° F prior to planting. Take semi-hard-shoot cuttings in early summer or firm-shoot cuttings in late summer. Remove and plant suckers; soil-layer lower branches; or divide root clumps.

Species and varieties	Hardiness (*Map, p. 9*)	Decorative characteristics and remarks	Height and spread when mature
Deciduous *Syringa laciniata* (cut-leaf)	B	Leaves are deeply cleft into prominent lobes. In late spring dozens of light purple blossoms open along branches of this species.	H 6 ft.–S 4-5 ft.
S. microphylla (littleleaf)	A	Length of ovate leaves is always less than 2 in. and often under ½ in.; undersides are hairy. In late spring or early summer small, aromatic, lilac-colored blooms open.	H 5-7 ft.–S 10-12 ft.
S. persica (Persian)	B	Leaves are less than 3 in. long, lance shaped, and often lobed. A tidy grower that produces many perfumed, pale lilac blossoms in late spring.	H 6 ft.–S 4-5 ft.
S. vulgaris (common)	A	A strong, sometimes treelike species with oval- and heart-shaped leaves up to 6 in. long. Lilac-colored flowers open in late spring and are intensely fragrant. Widely grown are those varieties, often called French lilacs, having single or double flowers in white and shades of pink, blue, or purple.	H 20 ft.–S 12 ft.
Evergreen *Aloysia triphylla,* or *Lippia citriodora*	D	Narrow, lance-shaped, 3-in.-long leaves often grow in circles of threes or fours around stems. They emit lemony fragrance, especially when crushed. Very small flowers in spikes open in midsummer. Often grown in herb gardens. Leaves used in potpourris, as garnish in iced drinks, or brewed like tea.	H 8 ft.–S 4-6 ft.
Deciduous *Magnolia liliflora*	C	Leaves are large, up to 7 in. long. The 6-petaled flowers appear before leaves and are white inside, purple outside.	H 12 ft.–S 6-8 ft.
M. stellata (star)	B	Fragrant, double, white, star-shaped blossoms about 3 in. wide bloom in midspring before leaves appear. Sensitive to extreme cold or heat. Fine lawn specimen.	H 18 ft.–S 12 ft.
M. s. 'Waterlily'	B	Pink flower buds turn into striking white blossoms. Habit of growth is bushier and more upright than *M. stellata.*	H 18 ft.–S 15 ft.
M. thompsoniana	C	Hybrid with fragrant, 6-in.-wide creamy white flowers.	H 10-20 ft.–S 10 ft.
M. t. 'Urbana'	C	Resembles *M. thompsoniana* but is somewhat hardier.	H 10-20 ft.–S 10 ft.
Evergreen *Mahonia aquifolia* (Oregon grape)	B	Oblong or oval leaflets are leathery and often shiny. Erect flower clusters about 3 in. long open in late spring. Fruit is edible. Restrict height to about 3 ft. to prevent branches from bending.	H 3-4 ft.–S 3-4 ft.
M. a. compacta	B	An improvement over *M. aquifolia,* since leaves have higher sheen and good bronze coloration in autumn. Also is shorter and more compact.	H 2-3 ft.–S 2-3 ft.
M. a. 'Golden Abundance'	B	Vigorous grower with brilliant green leaves and spectacular clusters of yellow flowers in spring and blue-purple fruits in fall. Excellent hedge or screen.	H 3-5 ft.–S 3-5 ft.
M. bealei (leatherleaf)	C	Leathery leaflets with marginal teeth retain their bluish-green color all winter. Upright flower clusters are up to 6 in. long and generally open around midspring. Pruning discourages top-heaviness.	H 8 ft.–S 4-5 ft.
M. lomarifolia	C	Individual leaves consisting of 12-20 leaflets are about 3 in. long and toothed. Its 3- to 7-in. flower clusters provide a pleasing sight in late fall and early winter.	H 9-12 ft.–S 8 ft.

	Common and botanical names, general characteristics	Uses and requirements	Propagation (See also p. 87)
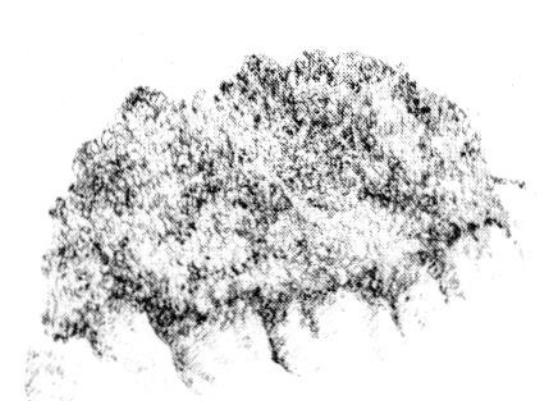 *Arctostaphylos densiflora* 'Howard McMinn'	**Manzanita** *(Arctostaphylos)* Attractive alternate leaves have smooth margins. Small, frequently nodding, waxy, bell- or urn-shaped blossoms open in racemes. Red or brownish fruits resemble small apples. Most types have crooked branches and smooth red to purple bark.	Not easy to transplant. Pot-grown plants from nursery are safest. Locate in sun in well-drained, sandy soil. Protect from wind. Water during dry spells. Pinch tips during growing season to control growth.	Ripened seeds can be stored in cool, dry place for up to 1 yr. prior to planting. Germination rate is often higher if seeds are stratified for 3 mo. at 40°F and then planted. Take semi-hard-shoot cuttings in early summer or firm-shoot cuttings in late summer. Soil-layer lower branches.
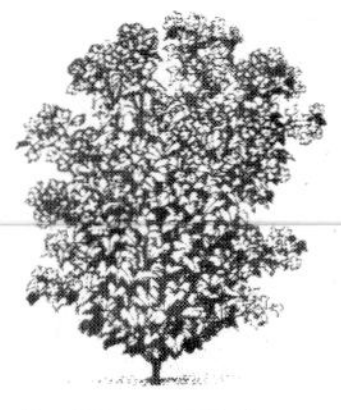 *Abutilon vitifolium*	**Maple, flowering** *(Abutilon)* Leaves of some kinds resemble those of maple trees. Early summer flowers that develop in junctures of leaves and stems are usually nodding and often trumpet or bell shaped.	Provide with full sun and protection from strong winds. Water well during dry periods, especially in first year after transplanting. If scale insects attack plants, spray with malathion.	Take semi-hard-shoot cuttings in summer.
Coprosma repens	**Mirror plant** *(Coprosma)* Leaves are opposite. Dense heads contain tiny greenish-white blossoms. Male and female flowers appear on separate plants. Berrylike fruits.	Makes good hedge and grows well near sea. Does best in partial shade. Plant in sandy soil; mix in plenty of peat moss. For fruiting, plant a male and female plant in close proximity. Stands clipping and shearing well.	Take semi-hard-shoot cuttings in summer or firm-shoot cuttings in late summer.
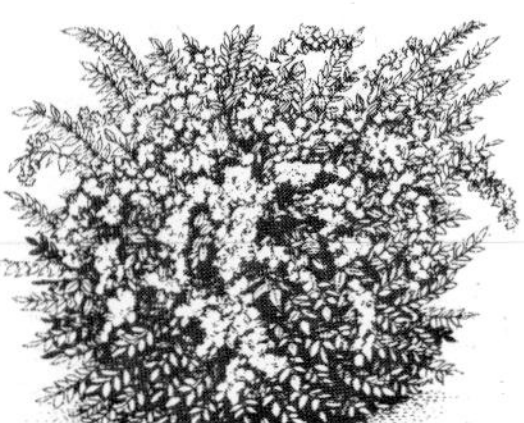 *Philadelphus lemoinei* 'Avalanche'	**Mock orange** *(Philadelphus)* Habit of growth is generally upright, but branches curve or droop. Opposite leaves sometimes have marginal teeth. Attractive single or double flowers are often fragrant and make fine showing from late spring to early summer.	Excellent for borders. Plant in full sun or partial shade in any well-drained garden soil. Prune as soon as possible after flowering, since blooms grow from wood that develops during preceding year.	Sow ripened seeds at once, or store in cool, dry place for up to 1 yr. prior to planting. Make root divisions in early spring. Lower branches can be soil-layered. Take semi-hard-shoot cuttings in summer or leafless hardwood cuttings in fall.

Species and varieties	Hardiness (*Map, p. 9*)	Decorative characteristics and remarks	Height and spread when mature
Evergreen *Arctostaphylos columbiana* (hairy)	C	Open form with strong, red-barked branches; hairy leaves and branches. White flowers from early to mid spring are followed by red fruits in summer.	H 3-15 ft.–S 1½-10 ft.
A. densiflora (Sonoma)	D	Branches are low and spreading; root where they contact soil. Glossy leaves, white or pink flowers, red-black bark.	H 1-1½ ft.–S 2-4 ft.
A. d. 'Howard McMinn'	D	Dense, widely spreading plant with glossy, bright green pointed leaves on red branches. Rose-pink bell-like flowers from early to mid spring.	H 2½ ft.–S 3-7 ft.
A. d. 'Sentinel'	D	Stiff, upright plant with downy, light green leaves. Can be trained as small tree.	H 6 ft.–S 3 ft.
A. edmundsii (Little Sur)	C	Pink flowers in early to mid winter on red stems with light green, roundish leaves. Needs excellent drainage. Often used as ground cover.	H ½-2 ft.–S 12 ft.
A. manzanita (common)	D	Twisted branches turn red-brown with age. Oval leaves of 1-3 in. have small single prickles at leaf tips. In mid to late spring wealth of pink or white blossoms appears. Fruits are dull red.	H 12 ft.–S 6-8 ft.
A. stanfordiana	D	Glossy leaves are more than 1 in. long. In early and mid spring bright pink flowers put on fine display. Berries in shades of red to brown appear in autumn. Bark is red.	H 6 ft.–S 4-5 ft.
Evergreen *Abutilon megapotamicum*	D	Leaves are up to 3 in. long and are toothed and sometimes slightly lobed. Features attractive pendent red blossoms with bright yellow stamens. Will grow in alkaline soils. Has interesting drooping shape that makes it good for growing in containers and hanging baskets.	H 6 ft.–S 6 ft.
A. vitifolium	D *	This is semi-evergreen species with twigs and leaves covered with whitish hairs. Large flowers are pale violet, blue, or white. Tolerates alkaline soil and salt spray. Good outdoors in mild, relatively frost-free climates.	H 12 ft.–S 10 ft.
Evergreen *Coprosma repens,* or *C. baueri*	D	Ovalish leaves are highly glossy and up to 3 in. long. Fleshy fruits are orange-red. Varieties with variegated foliage are also grown. Dwarf forms are available. In its northernmost range, foliage is often semi-evergreen.	H 3-25 ft.–S 3-10 ft.
Deciduous *Philadelphus lemoinei* 'Avalanche'	B	Outstanding variety, with gracefully arching branches. Extremely fragrant single blossoms are 1 in. wide.	H 4 ft.–S 3-4 ft.
P. l. 'Belle Etoile'	B	Branches droop. Single flowers are more than 2 in. wide and aromatic.	H 4 ft.–S 3-4 ft.
P. l. 'Boule d'Argent'	B	Double 2-in.-wide blooms are only mildly fragrant.	H 3-4 ft.–S 3-4 ft.
P. virginalis 'Minnesota Snowflake'	B	Branches are decidedly drooping. From 3 to 7 fragrant double flowers open in each cluster and are more than 1 in. wide. Very hardy and well suited to northern gardens.	H 6 ft.–S 4-5 ft.
P. v. 'Natchez'	B	Spectacular white flowers bloom singly and grow up to 2 in. across.	H 4-5 ft.–S 4-5 ft.
P. v. 'Virginal'	B	Double 2-in. blossoms are intensely fragrant.	H 4-5 ft.–S 5 ft.

*Not hardy below 30° F

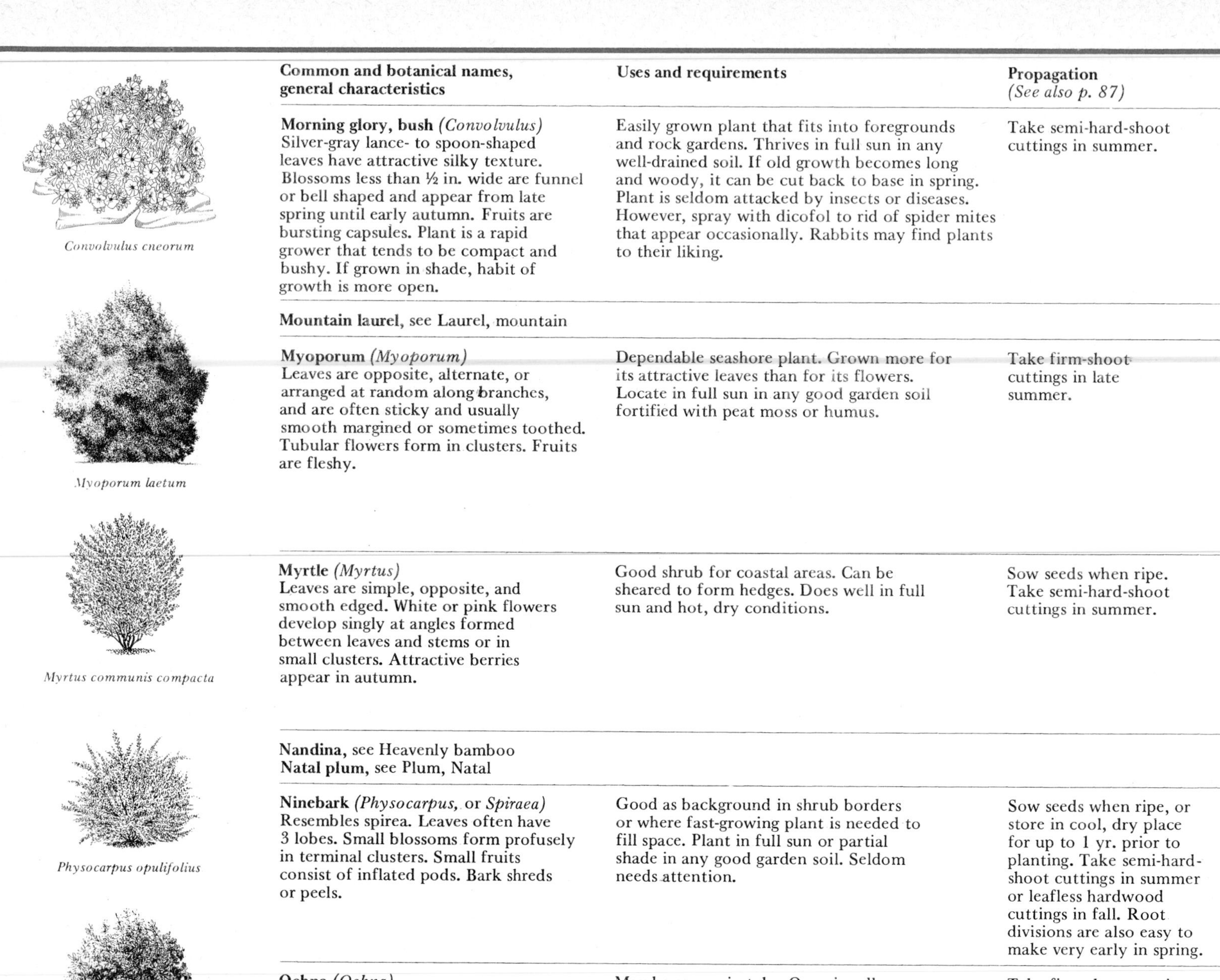

	Common and botanical names, general characteristics	Uses and requirements	Propagation *(See also p. 87)*
Convolvulus cneorum	**Morning glory, bush** *(Convolvulus)* Silver-gray lance- to spoon-shaped leaves have attractive silky texture. Blossoms less than ½ in. wide are funnel or bell shaped and appear from late spring until early autumn. Fruits are bursting capsules. Plant is a rapid grower that tends to be compact and bushy. If grown in shade, habit of growth is more open.	Easily grown plant that fits into foregrounds and rock gardens. Thrives in full sun in any well-drained soil. If old growth becomes long and woody, it can be cut back to base in spring. Plant is seldom attacked by insects or diseases. However, spray with dicofol to rid of spider mites that appear occasionally. Rabbits may find plants to their liking.	Take semi-hard-shoot cuttings in summer.
	Mountain laurel, see Laurel, mountain		
Myoporum laetum	**Myoporum** *(Myoporum)* Leaves are opposite, alternate, or arranged at random along branches, and are often sticky and usually smooth margined or sometimes toothed. Tubular flowers form in clusters. Fruits are fleshy.	Dependable seashore plant. Grown more for its attractive leaves than for its flowers. Locate in full sun in any good garden soil fortified with peat moss or humus.	Take firm-shoot cuttings in late summer.
Myrtus communis compacta	**Myrtle** *(Myrtus)* Leaves are simple, opposite, and smooth edged. White or pink flowers develop singly at angles formed between leaves and stems or in small clusters. Attractive berries appear in autumn.	Good shrub for coastal areas. Can be sheared to form hedges. Does well in full sun and hot, dry conditions.	Sow seeds when ripe. Take semi-hard-shoot cuttings in summer.
	Nandina, see Heavenly bamboo **Natal plum**, see Plum, Natal		
Physocarpus opulifolius	**Ninebark** *(Physocarpus,* or *Spiraea)* Resembles spirea. Leaves often have 3 lobes. Small blossoms form profusely in terminal clusters. Small fruits consist of inflated pods. Bark shreds or peels.	Good as background in shrub borders or where fast-growing plant is needed to fill space. Plant in full sun or partial shade in any good garden soil. Seldom needs attention.	Sow seeds when ripe, or store in cool, dry place for up to 1 yr. prior to planting. Take semi-hard-shoot cuttings in summer or leafless hardwood cuttings in fall. Root divisions are also easy to make very early in spring.
Ochna serrulata	**Ochna** *(Ochna)* Leathery leaves are toothed, oblong, bronze colored in spring; they later turn dark green. Leaf veins are conspicuous. Small flowers that appear in early summer are followed by fleshy fruits.	May be grown in tubs. Occasionally grown indoors. Thrives in full sun or partial shade in any good soil. Needs good amount of nutrients and water.	Take firm-shoot cuttings in late summer or hardwood cuttings in autumn. Also propagated by seeds.

Species and varieties	Hardiness *(Map, p. 9)*	Decorative characteristics and remarks	Height and spread when mature
Evergreen *Convolvulus cneorum*	□□□D	Leaves are up to 2½ in. long. Flowers are pink or whitish with yellow throats and appear singly or in clusters of up to 6; outer edges of petals are hairy. When grown in full sun, flowers open fully.	H 2-4 ft.—S 3 ft.
Evergreen *Myoporum debile*	□□□D *	Has trailing branches and lance-shaped leaves that are slightly toothed and up to 4 in. long. Pink flowers are solitary or in pairs. Rose-pink fruits, to ½ in. in diameter, are edible.	H 3 ft.—S 4 ft.
M. laetum	□□□D	Often treelike, with alternate, brilliant green leaves that are glossy and up to 4 in. long. Blossoms are white and purple-spotted. Fruits are reddish purple. Young shoots are sticky.	H 15 ft.—S 6-8 ft.
M. l. carsonii	□□□D	Leaves are quite broad and large and darker green than *M. laetum*. Foliage clothes plant to ground. A fast grower.	H 10-15 ft.—S 6-8 ft.
Evergreen *Myrtus communis* (common)	□□□D	Glossy lance-shaped or oval leaves are 1-2 in. long and pleasantly fragrant when bruised or crushed. White or pinkish blooms almost 1 in. wide that open in midsummer display many protruding fluffy stamens. Berries are blue-black.	H 9 ft.—S 6-8 ft.
M. c. compacta (dwarf)	□□□D	Creamy white flowers open in midspring. Useful as low edging plant or as formal hedge because of small leaves that grow densely. This dwarf variety is slow growing and quite compact.	H 2-4 ft.—S 2-4 ft.
Deciduous *Physocarpus opulifolius*	A□□□	Rounded or ovalish leaves are more than 3 in. long. In early summer white or pinkish flowers up to ¼ in. wide make a nice showing. In autumn clustered dried capsules turn from reddish to brown and cling to plant throughout winter. Habit of growth is upright or sometimes arching.	H 8-10 ft.—S 6-8 ft.
P. o. nanus	A□□□	This dwarf variety has smaller and less lobed leaves than *P. opulifolius*. Makes good hedge because of its dense habit of growth.	H 2 ft.—S 1-2 ft.
Evergreen *Ochna serrulata,* or *O. multiflora* (bird's-eye bush)	□□□D *	Alternate leaves are 3-5 in. long. Petals on yellow flowers are slightly twisted. Long-lasting shiny black berrylike fruits are attached to striking red receptacles, which are revealed after flower petals fall. Common name of bird's-eye bush is derived from its appearance at this stage.	H 5 ft.—S 4 ft.

*Not hardy below 30° F

	Common and botanical names, general characteristics	Uses and requirements	Propagation (*See also p. 87*)
 *Nerium oleander*	**Oleander** *(Nerium)* Narrow, oblong, leathery leaves are up to 8 in. long. White, yellowish, pink, or red flowers in showy clusters in summer are single or double. All parts are poisonous if eaten. Contact with foliage can result in dermatitis.	Good as summer tub plant and as house plant or as valuable addition to border backgrounds. Does best in full sun and tolerates heat, salt spray, high wind, and smog. Prefers moist, well-drained soil with plenty of humus. As growth becomes dense or untidy, remove older growth at soil line.	Take semi-hard-shoot cuttings in summer or firm-shoot cuttings in late summer.
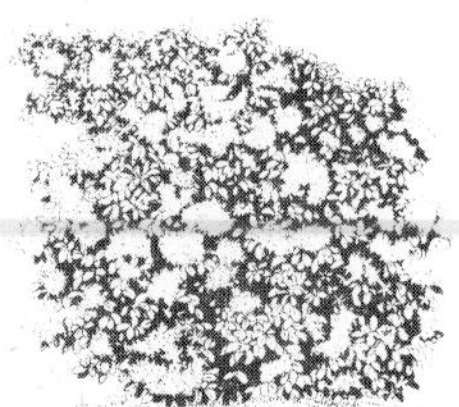 *Choisya ternata*	**Orange, Mexican** *(Choisya)* Compound leaves are opposite. Flowers are displayed in clusters of up to 6.	Good border plant. Grow in full sun or partial shade. Plant in sandy soil that drains well, and water thoroughly in dry weather. Prune occasionally to maintain good outline.	Take semi-hard-shoot cuttings in summer.
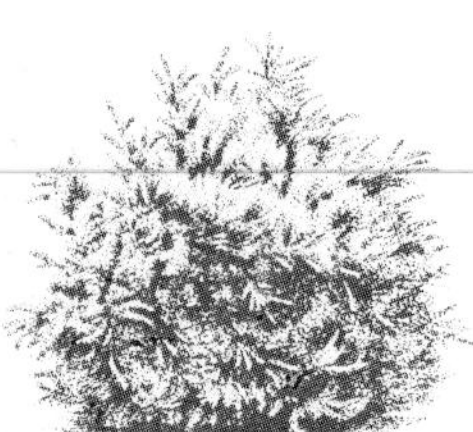 *Osmanthus delavayi*	**Osmanthus** *(Osmanthus)* Opposite leaves may be hollylike, finely toothed or smooth edged. Small blossoms are intensely fragrant and develop in junctures of leaves and stems or in terminal clusters. Fruits are egg shaped and fleshy.	Ideal for planting beside a window to scent indoors. Does well in full sun or partial shade in any good garden soil.	Seeds can be sown when ripe but often take 2 yr. to germinate. Take firm-shoot cuttings in late summer.
 *Exochorda macrantha* 'The Bride'	**Pearlbush** *(Exochorda)* Ovalish 1- to 3-in.-long leaves have smooth margins. Showy white flowers to 2 in. wide form profusely in racemes.	Does best in full sun in any good garden soil. After flowers fade, prune out all old, weak wood to reduce crowding and maintain vigorous growth.	Seeds can be sown as soon as ripe or stored in cool, dry place for up to 1 yr. prior to planting. Take leafy soft-shoot cuttings in spring. Responds well to root divisions; lower branches can be soil-layered as well.
	Pepper bush, sweet, see Sweet pepper bush **Philadelphus,** see Mock orange		
 *Photinia villosa*	**Photinia** *(Photinia)* Leaves are oblong to elliptic. Attractive shrubs, some with leathery evergreen foliage, abundant white flower clusters, and handsome red fruits.	Plant in full sun in any well-drained soil enriched with plenty of organic matter.	Seeds should be stratified at 40° F for 3 mo. prior to sowing. In early summer take semi-hard-shoot cuttings of evergreen and deciduous forms. Deciduous types can be propagated by leafless hardwood cuttings taken in fall.

Species and varieties	Hardiness (Map, p. 9)	Decorative characteristics and remarks	Height and spread when mature
Evergreen *Nerium oleander*	D	Narrow leaves are 4-8 in. long. Upper surfaces are deep green; undersides are lighter in hue and display conspicuous midrib. Yellow, white, purple, red, or pink blossoms appear in midspring and last through late summer.	H 10-20 ft.–S 4-10 ft.
N. o. 'Petite Pink'	D	This low-growing variety displays flowers in handsome shade of pink.	H 2½ ft.–S 1-2 ft.
Evergreen *Choisya ternata*	D	Fragrant leaflets are 3 in. long and have smooth edges. Orange-scented white flowers are up to 1 in. wide.	H 8 ft.–S 6 ft.
Evergreen *Osmanthus delavayi,* or *Siphonosmanthus delavayi*	C	Starry white flowers bloom from early to mid spring, and blue-black fruits appear in late summer. Tolerates heavy clay soils if soil is aerated with humus or peat moss and coarse sand.	H 8 ft.–S 8 ft.
O. fortunei	D	Oval leaves on this hybrid are 3-4 in. long. They resemble those of English holly. Flowers open in junctures of leaves and stems in early summer. Bluish-black berries are attractive in early fall.	H 8 ft.–S 8 ft.
O. fragrans (sweet olive)	D	Oblong or oval leaves are 2-4 in. long and sometimes faintly toothed. White flowers appear in midspring. Often grown in greenhouses.	H 10-25 ft.–S 6-10 ft.
O. heterophyllus, or *O. aquifolium,* or *O. ilicifolius*	C	Glossy oval or oblong leaves are more than 2 in. long. Greenish-white blooms in early and mid summer are followed in early fall by bluish-black fruits. Tolerates clipping; so it makes good hedge.	H 18 ft.–S 6-10 ft.
O. h. variegatus	C	Similar to *O. heterophyllus* but leaves have cream-colored edges.	H 18 ft.–S 6-10 ft.
Deciduous *Exochorda macrantha* 'The Bride'	A	In midspring tight, shiny, pearl-colored buds expand into handsome blossoms that last through late spring. Bushy and compact, this outstanding variety is good in limited space where accent is needed.	H 4 ft.–S 4 ft.
E. racemosa	B	Blooms less profusely than *E. macrantha* 'The Bride,' but its flowers are larger, almost 2 in. wide; they open in mid to late spring.	H 10-12 ft.–S 6-10 ft.
Deciduous *Photinia villosa*	B	Leaves have pointed tips and hairy undersides. In fall they turn red-bronze. In late spring and early summer flowers open in flat 2-in. clusters.	H 15 ft.–S 8-10 ft.
Evergreen *P. glabra*	C	Shiny leaves grow to about 3 in. long. Flower clusters are up to 4 in. long and last from late spring to midsummer.	H 10 ft.–S 6-8 ft.
P. serrulata	C	Glossy leaves to 8 in. long open with reddish hue, then turn green. Blooming from late spring to midsummer, flower clusters are often 6 in. wide.	H 15-35 ft.–S 6-12 ft.

	Common and botanical names, general characteristics	Uses and requirements	Propagation (See also p. 87)
 *Pieris formosa*	**Pieris** *(Pieris,* or *Andromeda)* Generally alternate leaves are toothed. Flower buds are attractive all winter. In mid to late spring white blossoms resembling lilies of the valley and of considerable beauty are borne in terminal panicles. All kinds grow slowly.	Does best in partial shade and needs sandy soil fortified with peat moss or humus that provides some acidity. Mulch roots with rotted oak leaves or pine needles.	Ripened seeds can be sown at once or stored in cool, dry place for up to 1 yr. prior to planting. Lower branches can be soil-layered. Take semi-hard-shoot cuttings in early summer or firm-shoot cuttings in late summer.
 *Pittosporum tobira*	**Pittosporum** *(Pittosporum)* Alternate leaves are thick. Aromatic flowers appear singly or in clusters, generally terminal but occasionally in junctures of leaves and stems. Fruits are capsules.	Good for hedges; has attractive outline that does not require shearing. Plant in full sun or partial shade in any good soil.	Sow seeds when ripe. Take semi-hard-shoot cuttings in early summer or leafy firm-shoot cuttings in late summer.
 *Carissa grandiflora* 'Boxwood Beauty'	**Plum, Natal** *(Carissa)* A spiny shrub with glossy leathery leaves that grow up to 3 in. long. Large white or pink flowers develop in clusters and appear all year round. Fruits are fleshy berries varying in sweetness with different types; can be used for preserves. Habit of growth may be upright or spreading.	Good for seacoast gardens. Can be used singly as specimen plant. Also suitable for hedges, since it stands shearing and its spines help create effective barrier. Grows best in full sun but will tolerate fair amount of shade. Does well in most types of soil.	Propagate by seeds and semi-hard-shoot cuttings in early summer or firm-shoot cuttings in late summer.
 *Ceratostigma willmottianum*	**Plumbago** *(Ceratostigma)* Alternate, sometimes semi-evergreen leaves have hairs along margins. Oval clusters of blue flowers.	Does best in full sun but will tolerate partial shade. Plant in any type of soil. Usually best cut back to ground each fall.	Divide roots in midspring. Take semi-hard-shoot cuttings in summer.
	Plum yew, see Yew, plum		
 *Potentilla fruticosa* 'Katherine Dykes'	**Potentilla** *(Potentilla)* Erect branched stems support compound leaves with at least 3 and sometimes 5 slightly hairy leaflets. Single roselike flowers in many clusters from early summer to midfall.	A fine coastal plant. Suitable for hedges. Does best in full sun but tolerates shade. Grows well in any soil and will live even in heavy clays. Except for watering in dry spells, it needs little care once established.	Sow seeds when ripe. Make root divisions in early to mid spring or early fall. Take semi-hard-shoot cuttings in early summer or firm-shoot cuttings in late summer. The latter cuttings root especially well.

Species and varieties	Hardiness *(Map, p. 9)*	Decorative characteristics and remarks	Height and spread when mature
Evergreen *Pieris floribunda* (mountain)	□ B □ □	Faintly toothed, ovalish or elliptic leaves are 1-3 in. long. Masses of semi-pendulous flowers grow in upright 2- to 4-in. panicles. Makes striking hedge.	H 6 ft.–S 6 ft.
P. formosa (Himalayan)	□ □ □ D	Both leaves and blossom racemes are up to 6 in. long.	H 12 ft.–S 12 ft.
P. f. forrestii (Chinese)	□ □ □ D	In early spring new leaves are handsome scarlet, turning green before they reach mature length of 2-4 in. Flowers are fragrant.	H 8 ft.–S 8 ft.
P. japonica (lily-of-the-valley shrub)	□ B □ □	Young leaves show handsome coppery color in early spring. Mature leaves are dark green, glossy, and more than 3 in. long. Flowers droop on 5-in. panicles. Outstanding ornamental shrub with dense habit of growth.	H 8 ft.–S 8 ft.
Evergreen *Pittosporum tobira*	□ □ C □	Ovalish leaves are leathery and up to 4 in. long. White or yellow-white blossoms are borne in terminal clusters in late spring. Fruits are hairy. Good along seacoast. Often grown as house plant.	H 10 ft.–S 6-8 ft.
P. t. variegata	□ □ C □	Very similar to *P. tobira* but leaves bear attractive white markings. Lemon-scented foliage; branches somewhat brittle.	H 10 ft.–S 6-8 ft.
Evergreen *Carissa grandiflora*	□ □ □ D	Branches have 1½-in. spines. Dark green leaves are ovalish. Waxy white blossoms are 2 in. wide and appear in late spring or early summer. Egg-shaped fruits are red and up to 2 in. long. Grows rapidly and has rounded habit of growth.	H 10-15 ft.–S 4-10 ft.
C. g. 'Boxwood Beauty'	□ □ □ D	Very dark green leaves are densely set on short compact branches. Has mounding habit of growth and is semi-upright.	H 2 ft.–S 2 ft.
C. g. 'Fancy'	□ □ □ D	Displays rich green leaves, profuse show of aromatic white flowers, and very large red-orange fruits. Upright habit of growth.	H 6 ft.–S 4-5 ft.
C. g. tuttlei	□ □ □ D	Red fruits follow abundant white blossoms. This variety is spreading but has comparatively compact habit of growth. Used also as ground cover.	H 2-3 ft.–S 3-5 ft.
Evergreen or semi-evergreen *Ceratostigma willmottianum* (Chinese)	□ □ □ D	Multiflowered clusters are colorful from midsummer to midfall. Blossoms have blue petals with pink tubes and often measure 1 in. across. May drop its leaves after frost.	H 2-4 ft.–S 2-4 ft.
Deciduous *Potentilla fruticosa* 'Gold Drop'	A □ □ □	Lacy foliage and brilliant primrose-yellow blossoms are showy. Fine for border backgrounds.	H 2½ ft.–S 2½ ft.
P. f. 'Katherine Dykes'	A □ □ □	Silvery green foliage on arching branches combines with light yellow flowers. Outstanding where space is limited and border accent is needed.	H 2½ ft.–S 3 ft.
P. f. 'Klondike'	A □ □ □	Similar to *P. f.* 'Gold Drop' but with larger blooms.	H 2½ ft.–S 2½ ft.
P. f. 'Moonlight'	A □ □ □	Pale yellow blooms. Low growing. Called *P. f.* 'Maanelys' in Sweden, where native.	H 2½ ft.–S 2½ ft.
P. f. 'Tangerine'	A □ □ □	Plants grown in sun produce yellow blooms; in shade, orange.	H 2½ ft.–S 2½ ft.

	Common and botanical names, general characteristics	Uses and requirements	Propagation *(See also p. 87)*
 *Ligustrum ovalifolium*	**Privet** *(Ligustrum)* Privet leaves are generally oval. White blossoms are considered by some to have unpleasant odor. Blue or black fruits are berrylike and sometimes inconspicuous.	Tolerates sand and thrives in salt spray. Withstands dust, smog, high wind, and frequent shearing. Deciduous kinds are among the least expensive plants to use as hedge. The evergreens often serve as single specimen plants in borders. Plant in full sun or partial shade in any good garden soil.	Seeds can be stratified when ripe or stored in cool, dry place for up to 1 yr. prior to stratifying for 3 mo. at 40° F. Take soft-shoot cuttings in spring or firm-shoot cuttings in late summer.
 *Prunus laurocerasus* 'Otto Luykens'	**Prunus** *(Prunus)* A vast and valuable genus with both evergreen and deciduous plants. All the flowers have 5 petals and are bisexual. Leaves are simple, alternate, and usually toothed. Deciduous kinds are grown mostly for spring flowers, and a few have edible fruits. Evergreen kinds valued for attractive foliage, flowers, and small ornamental fruits.	Plant in full sun or partial shade in any good garden soil. Protect evergreen forms from strong wind during winter and keep roots moist.	Take semi-hard-shoot cuttings in summer, or grow from stratified seeds.
	Pyracantha, see Fire thorn		
 *Chaenomeles speciosa*	**Quince, flowering** *(Chaenomeles,* or *Cydonia)* Slightly angular branches. Flowers open before or just after leaves unfold. Aromatic green or yellow fruits used in preserves.	Grows best in full sun and average soil; tolerates both dry and wet conditions. In alkaline soil leaves may turn yellow (p. 608). Needs only occasional pruning. Protect against scale (p. 615) and fire blight (p. 619).	Divide roots or soil-layer lower branches. Take semi-hard-shoot cuttings in summer or leafless hardwood cuttings in fall.

Species and varieties	Hardiness (*Map, p. 9*)	Decorative characteristics and remarks	Height and spread when mature
Deciduous *Ligustrum amurense* (Amur)	A	Flowers in early to mid summer. Good choice for northern gardens. May be semi-evergreen in temperate areas.	H 15 ft.—S 8-10 ft.
L. obtusifolium regelianum (Regel)	A	Horizontal branches gracefully support oblong or elliptic leaves that are more than 2 in. long. Nodding spikes of blossoms open in midsummer.	H 5 ft.—S 3-4 ft.
L. ovalifolium, or *L. californicum*	B	Semi-evergreen with glossy leaves. Ill-smelling flowers open in midsummer. Most widely used privet for hedges.	H 15 ft.—S 15 ft.
L. o. aureum	B	Resembles *L. ovalifolium,* but leaves are yellow with green spot in centers.	H 15 ft.—S 15 ft.
L. sinense	C	Showy midsummer flowers. Very graceful habit of growth.	H 12 ft.—S 9 ft.
L. vicaryi	A	Outer leaves are yellow but yellowish green if grown in shade.	H 12 ft.—S 9 ft.
L. vulgare lodense	B	Compact variety with large clusters of glossy black fruits.	H 4 ft.—S 6 ft.
Evergreen *L. japonicum*	C	Glossy, deep green, leathery foliage. Blossom panicles to 6 in. long.	H 12 ft.—S 6-10 ft.
L. j. rotundifolium	A	Shiny dark green leaves in greater abundance than *L. japonicum.* Superb hedge.	H 6 ft.—S 3-5 ft.
L. 'Suwannee River'	A	Handsome and hardy, this hybrid makes excellent low hedge.	H 3-4 ft.—S 3 ft.
Deciduous *Prunus glandulosa albiplena* (dwarf flowering almond)	A	Handsome in bloom with double white flowers in late spring.	H 4 ft.—S 4 ft.
P. g. sinensis	A	This variety has dark green lance-shaped leaves and double pink flowers.	H 4 ft.—S 4 ft.
P. tomentosa (Manchu, or Nanking, cherry)	A	Sometimes treelike with small white flowers in midspring followed by edible vivid red fruits in early and mid summer. Makes good lawn specimen or hedge.	H 9 ft.—S 4-6 ft.
P. triloba (flowering almond)	B	Small double pink flowers bloom in midspring before foliage appears.	H 12 ft.—S 10 ft.
Evergreen *P. laurocerasus* 'Otto Luykens'	C	Shiny dark green leaves with white flower spikes in spring, followed by purple to black fruits. Growth is compact, and spreading.	H 10-20 ft.—S 10-20 ft.
P. l. schipkaensis	B	Leaves are 2-4½ in. long. An especially hardy and attractive variety.	H 9 ft.—S 2-3 ft.
P. l. zabeliana	A	Smaller leaves than *P. l. schipkaensis* develop on horizontal branches. Not good in restricted areas.	H 5 ft.—S 10 ft.
Deciduous *Chaenomeles japonica*	B	Brick-red flowers are followed by yellow fruits almost 2 in. long. Low growing.	H 3 ft.—S 2-3 ft.
C. speciosa, or *C. lagenaria*	B	Single, semi-double, or double flowers range from white to pink, red, or orange. Fruits are pear shaped to rounded, 2- 2½ in. long, and aromatic. Spreading habit of growth. Numerous varieties.	H 6-10 ft.—S 6 ft.

	Common and botanical names, general characteristics	Uses and requirements	Propagation *(See also p. 87)*
 *Raphiolepis indica*	**Raphiolepis** *(Raphiolepis)* Leaves are thick and fleshy. Pink or white blossoms develop in terminal clusters, and fruits are bluish black or purplish black.	Plant in full sun or partial shade in any good garden soil fortified with peat moss or humus.	Sow ripened seeds. Take firm-shoot cuttings in late summer.
	Rhododendron, see p. 222		
 *Cistus purpureus*	**Rockrose** *(Cistus)* Leaves have smooth margins and are usually hairy. Large paper-thin blossoms look somewhat like single roses.	Good choice for larger rock gardens and protected areas along seacoast. Looks best when planted in groupings. Must have full sun and well-drained, sandy soil. Does not tolerate acidity and strong wind. Not easy to transplant.	Soil-layer lower branches. Take firm-shoot cuttings in late summer from nonflowering side growth.
	Rose, see p. 204 **Rose of Sharon,** see *Hibiscus syriacus*		
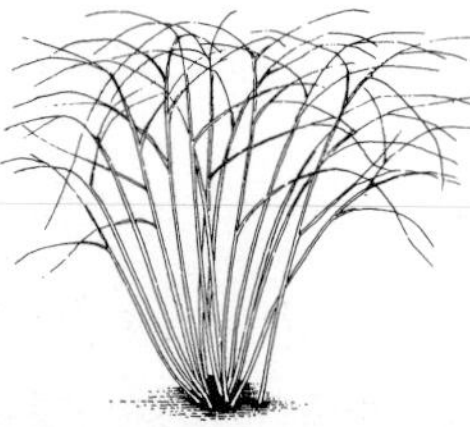 *Rubus cockburnianus*	**Rubus** *(Rubus)* Usually has thorny canes and alternate leaves. Composed of several leaflets with smoothed edges. Flowers of some kinds are followed by red berries, sometimes called ornamental raspberries. This genus also includes blackberries and dewberries.	Ornamentals of this group, according to kind, are used for their foliage, flowers, and colorful stems; grown also for berry crop. Makes useful barrier. Does well in full sun or partial shade in any well-drained soil.	Stratify seeds at 70° F for 3 mo.; then expose to 40° F for 3 mo. before planting. Make root divisions or take root cuttings in early spring. Take semi-hard-shoot cuttings in summer or leafless hardwood cuttings in fall. Often soil-layers naturally.

Species and varieties	Hardiness (*Map, p. 9*)	Decorative characteristics and remarks	Height and spread when mature
Evergreen *Raphiolepis delacouri*	□□□D	Toothed leaves and pink blossoms form on this decorative compact hybrid. Makes attractive terrace plant.	H 6 ft.–S 3-4 ft.
R. indica (Indian hawthorn)	□□□D	Glossy leathery leaves are toothed and up to 3 in. long. Pinkish or white flowers are about ½ in. wide.	H 5 ft.–S 4-5 ft.
R. i. 'Apple Blossom'	□□□D	Flowers are pink and white.	H 5 ft.–S 4-5 ft.
R. i. 'Enchantress'	□□□D	This dwarf variety has shiny green leaves. Large rose-pink flowers form in dense clusters from late winter to early summer.	H 3 ft.–S 4 ft.
R. i. 'Fascination'	□□□D	Flowers, deep rose with white centers, make showy display in late spring.	H 5 ft.–S 4-5 ft.
R. i. 'Jack Evans'	□□□D	Dense green leaves, occasionally tinted purple, have silvery sheen. Masses of flowers are brilliant pink. Habit of growth is low and compact.	H 4 ft.–S 5 ft.
R. umbellata	□□C□	Thick leathery leaves are up to 3 in. long and slightly toothed. Aromatic white blossoms are attractive in late spring.	H 10 ft.–S 4-8 ft.
Evergreen *Cistus albidus*	□□□D	Elliptic or oblong leaves are sometimes more than 2 in. long. Rose-lilac blooms are up to 2 in. wide, and centers are marked with yellow.	H 6 ft.–S 4-5 ft.
C. hybridus, or *C. corbariensis*	□□□D	Pure white flowers are striking in midsummer.	H 3 ft.–S 2-3 ft.
C. ladaniferus maculatus	□□□D	Branches and leaves are sticky. Leaves have whitish hairs on undersides and grow up to 4 in. long. In early and mid summer, showy white blossoms with dark red centers sometimes measure 4 in. wide.	H 4 ft.–S 3-4 ft.
C. laurifolius	□□□D	Undersides of leaves are sticky and very hairy. White flowers with yellow centers begin to appear in midsummer and continue to open until early fall. Prune after flowering to promote compactness.	H 6 ft.–S 3-5 ft.
C. purpureus	□□□D	Oblong, 2-in.-long leaves grow on sticky, hairy twigs. Rose-crimson petals bear dark maroon basal blotch. Blossoms open in early and mid summer, often measuring up to 3 in. across.	H 4 ft.–S 4 ft.
Deciduous *Rubus cockburnianus*	□□C□	Admired in winter for its stems that are coated with an interesting white, waxy powder. Leaves, also white coated, consist of 7-9 oblong- to lance-shaped leaflets. Flowers are small and purplish in thin, 4-to 6-in.-long terminal panicles. Fruits are not palatable.	H 5-7 ft.–S 4-6 ft.
R. odoratus	A□□□	Stems are almost thornless, hairy when young. Leaves are 3-5 lobed and are 4 in.-1 ft. wide, with finely toothed margins. Undersides of leaves are hairy. Fragrant rose-purple to whitish blooms 1½-2 in. across are displayed abundantly in loose clusters in summer. Flat red fruits are not palatable. Bark peels and shreds. Habit of growth is erect.	H 5-9 ft.–S 4-6 ft.

	Common and botanical names, general characteristics	Uses and requirements	Propagation (*See also p. 87*)
 *Ruscus aculeatus*	**Ruscus** *(Ruscus)* Foliage and berries make grand display in winter. Has flat, leathery, leaflike branches. Spreads quickly by means of suckering shoots. Often used in dried arrangements.	Plant in groups of 3-5; be sure 1 or 2 are males if fruit is desired. Thrives in full sun or shade in almost any soil. Needs seasonal thinning to remain vigorous.	Sow seeds when ripe. Divide well-established clumps in early spring or fall. Also propagated from individual suckers.
	Saint-John's-wort, see Hypericum		
 *Gaultheria shallon*	**Salal** *(Gaultheria)* Low-growing shrub with toothed leaves and berrylike fruits. White flowers are bell shaped. Branches are often used in flower arrangements and are called lemon leaves by florists.	Good choice for rock gardens or woodland settings. Difficult to transplant. Grows in full sun or partial shade. Must have acid soil. In poor soil plants grow to 1½ ft., but in fertile soil and shade they may reach 5 ft. or more.	Sow ripened seeds in peat moss and sand. Take semi-hard-shoot cuttings in summer. Responds to soil layering and to root division.
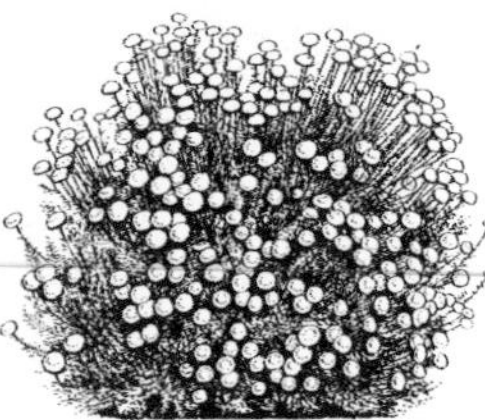 *Santolina virens*	**Santolina, or Lavender cotton** *(Santolina)* Alternate leaves are aromatic. Rounded heads of blooms are yellow, cream colored, or white.	Plant in full sun in any well-drained soil.	Take soft-shoot cuttings in spring.
 *Sarcococca confusa*	**Sarcococca** *(Sarcococca)* Leaves are stalked and quite leathery. Aromatic, small whitish blossoms have no petals, and separate male and female flowers form on each plant. Berrylike fruits are dark red or black.	Does best in shade and will thrive in wide range of soils if moisture is adequate. Difficult to transplant; water well after doing so.	Sow ripened seeds.
 *Cassia artemisioides*	**Senna** *(Cassia)* Cultivated primarily for its decorative yellow blossoms, generally in spikelike clusters, which may appear throughout year and may bloom intermittently for some time. Large compound leaves composed of several leaflets. Fruit is long, round or flat pod.	Plant in full sun in any good garden soil that is well drained. Water deeply but infrequently. Prune hard immediately after flowering except for *C. artemisioides,* whieh requires less pruning.	Sow seeds when ripe. Take semi-hard-shoot cuttings in summer.

Species and varieties	Hardiness (Map, p. 9)	Decorative characteristics and remarks	Height and spread when mature
Evergreen *Ruscus aculeatus* (butcher's-broom)	☐☐C☐	Stems are branched. Branches have spiny tips. Berries are yellow or red. When cut and dried, branches are used as Christmas decorations.	H 3 ft.–S 3 ft.
R. hypoglossum	☐☐C☐	Faster spreading than *R. aculeatus*. Good ground cover.	H 1-1½ ft.–S 3 ft.
Evergreen *Gaultheria shallon*	☐B☐☐	Leathery leaves are oval or round and up to 5 in. long. Small waxy flowers with white or pink corollas develop in 3- to 5-in. terminal clusters; they open in early summer. Purplish-black fruits are edible.	H 1½-5 ft.–S 2-3 ft.
Evergreen *Santolina chamaecyparissus*	☐☐C☐	Fuzzy silver-gray leaves are almost 1 in. long. Flowers appear in mid to late summer on 6-in. stalks. For neatness cut back each year after blooms fade.	H 2 ft.–S 2-3 ft.
S. pinnata	☐☐C☐	Slightly hairy green leaves are up to 1½ in. long. Flowers are dull white.	H 2 ft.–S 2-3 ft.
S. virens, or *S. viridis*	☐☐☐D	Narrow deep green leaves are up to 2 in. long and have toothed edges. Dwarf habit of growth makes this suitable edging plant.	H 1½ ft.–S 1½-2 ft.
Evergreen *Sarcococca confusa*	☐☐C☐	Dark green lance-shaped to elliptic leaves are up to 2½ in. long and 1 in. wide. Fruits are black. Dense habit of growth.	H 6 ft.–S 3-4 ft.
S. hookeriana humilis	☐☐C☐	Leaves are glossy and dark green. Flowers bloom in midspring. Fruits are black. Makes good ground cover.	H 2 ft.–S 1½-2 ft.
S. ruscifolia	☐☐C☐	Glossy, elliptic or ovalish leaves are up to 3 in. long. Flowers open from early fall to late winter. Berries are dark red.	H 6 ft.–S 4-5 ft.
S. saligna	☐☐C☐	Resembles *S. ruscifolia,* but its berries are purple.	H 6 ft.–S 4-5 ft.
Deciduous *Cassia alata* (candle bush)	☐☐C☐	Leaflets have blunt tips. Long-lasting yellow flowers are 1 in. wide and bloom from late fall to midwinter. Needs infrequent but thorough watering.	H 8-10 ft.–S 6-8 ft.
Evergreen *C. artemisioides* (feathery)	☐☐☐D *	Silky grayish leaflets. Pale yellow blossoms form in junctures of leaves and stems from midwinter to midspring, often into summer.	H 4 ft.–S 3-4 ft.
C. bicapsularis	☐☐☐D	Leaves are composed of 3-5 pairs of leaflets. Flowers bloom from midfall to late winter.	H 12 ft.–S 6-8 ft.
C. corymbosa (flowery)	☐☐C☐	Oblongish leaves usually consist of 3 pairs of leaflets. A profuse bloomer from spring to fall. Fine for greenhouse culture.	H 10 ft.–S 5-6 ft.
C. glauca	☐☐☐D	Leaflets are oblongish. Flat pods are green. Blooms nearly all year.	H 15 ft.–S 8-10 ft.
C. splendida (golden wonder)	☐☐☐D	Leaves consist of 4 leaflets, each about 3 in. long. Flowers are bright yellow and bloom from late fall to midwinter.	H 10 ft.–S 6-8 ft.

*Not hardy below 30° F

	Common and botanical names, general characteristics	Uses and requirements	Propagation *(See also p. 87)*
 *Garrya elliptica*	**Silk tassel** *(Garrya)* Grown mainly for its silver-gray catkins that form in midwinter on male plants; those of female specimens are less attractive.	Locate in full sun or partial shade. Does best in well-drained, loamy soil but will tolerate sandy or rocky conditions. It is necessary to plant female and male plants near one another if silky purple-green fruits are to develop.	Take semi-hard-shoot cuttings in summer. Soil-layer lower branches.
	Siphonosmanthus, see Osmanthus		
 *Skimmia japonica*	**Skimmia** *(Skimmia)* Short-stalked leaves are aromatic when crushed. Has small clusters of creamy white flowers. Male and female flowers of some kinds on separate plants; male blossoms scented. Red fruit is like that of holly.	Does best in partial shade. Leaf discoloration may result if planted in hot, dry places. For good fruit production, plant 3 or 4 females in close proximity to every male.	Sow seeds when ripe. Take semi-hard-shoot cuttings in summer.
	Snowberry, see Symphoricarpos		
 *Spiraea japonica*	**Spirea** *(Spiraea)* Leaves are usually toothed or lobed. Bears attractive flattish clusters or plumelike panicles of white, pinkish-purple, or red flowers. Fruit is a dry capsule.	Excellent for informal hedges and for coastal areas. Easy to transplant and requires little care. Does best in full sun and average moisture but will live in almost any soil.	Sow seeds when ripe. Take semi-hard-shoot cuttings in summer or firm-shoot cuttings in late summer. Root divisions are easy to make.
 *Sorbaria aitchisonii*	**Spirea, false** *(Sorbaria)* Handsome shrub with elegant, feathery, ashlike leaves. Lance-shaped leaflets with toothed margins make up its long compound leaves. Creamy white flower plumes are up to 1 ft. long.	Use at back of borders. Thrives in full sun as well as partial or deep shade. Does best if peat moss or other humus-forming material is mixed into soil. Rapid growth increased by fertilizing in spring and summer. Water well in dry spells. Prune in late winter to promote strong, new stems.	Sow seeds when ripe, or store in cool, dry place for up to 1 yr. before planting. Make root divisions in early spring. Leafy semi-hard-shoot cuttings may be taken in summer, or hardwood cuttings in autumn.

Species and varieties	Hardiness *(Map, p. 9)*	Decorative characteristics and remarks	Height and spread when mature
Evergreen *Garrya elliptica*	□□C□	Has leathery oblong or elliptic leaves with hairy undersides. Male catkins up to 10 in. long, females up to 4 in., are seen from early to late winter. Sometimes a small tree.	H 8-20 ft.—S 6 ft.
G. fremontii	□□C□	Shiny deep green leaves are up to 3 in. long. Catkins start to appear in midspring; males are up to 8 in. long, females up to 2 in.	H 6-15 ft.—S 6-7 ft.
Evergreen *Skimmia foremanii*	□□C□	A bisexual hybrid that produces an abundance of flowers and fruits.	H 4 ft.—S 4 ft.
S. japonica	□□C□	Produces numerous branches. Yellowish-green, oblong or elliptic leaves up to 5 in. long are generally bunched near ends of twigs. Usually has male and female blooms on separate plants.	H 4 ft.—S 4 ft.
S. reevesiana	□□C□	Leaves are smaller and duller green than *S. japonica*. Since its flowers include both stamens and pistils, each specimen sets dull red fruits.	H 6 ft.—S 4-5 ft.
Deciduous *Spiraea arguta*	□B□□	In late spring this hybrid blooms more abundantly than any other white-flowering kind. It makes a striking single specimen plant.	H 6 ft.—S 6 ft.
S. bumalda	□B□□	Doubly toothed leaves are lance shaped or ovalish. White or deep pink blossoms appear in midsummer on this hybrid. A good choice for limited space.	H 3 ft.—S 4 ft.
S. b. 'Anthony Waterer'	□B□□	Leaves have pinkish hue when young but turn green when they reach full size. Rose-red blossom clusters sometimes measure 6 in. across. This variety flowers in summer.	H 3 ft.—S 3 ft.
S. japonica	□B□□	Oblong or oval leaves have wedge-shaped bases; their undersides are pale, and veins are covered with hairs. Pink blossoms form in loose, flat clusters in summer. Habit of growth is upright.	H 5 ft.—S 6 ft.
S. thunbergii	□B□□	Lance-shaped leaves are brilliant green, turning orange-red in autumn. White flowers open in abundance in mid or late spring on this highly attractive species. In New England late winter frosts sometimes damage flower buds. Plant in sheltered location in its northernmost range.	H 5 ft.—S 4-5 ft.
S. vanhouttei	□B□□	A hybrid with oval leaves. Pure white blossoms in late spring or early summer are borne on branches that arch gracefully. Fine as clipped or unclipped hedge and well suited to city gardens, since it tolerates smog.	H 6 ft.—S 4-5 ft.
Deciduous *Sorbaria aitchisonii*	□B□□	Young branches are vivid red. Bright green leaves consist of up to 21 leaflets. Flowers are borne in erect panicles up to 10 in. long during mid and late summer.	H 10 ft.—S 9 ft.
S. sorbifolia	A□□□	Branches arch gracefully. Pinnately compound leaves consist of 13-23 coarsely textured leaflets; they are among the first to appear in spring but have no significant fall color. Very showy in midsummer when tiny white flowers open in pyramidal clusters up to 10 in. long.	H 6 ft.—S 5-7 ft.

	Common and botanical names, general characteristics	Uses and requirements	Propagation *(See also p. 87)*
 *Stachyurus praecox*	**Stachyurus** *(Stachyurus)* Chains of tiny, yellow, waxy, cup-shaped flowers open in early spring before leaves develop. Buds hang from branches in fall and winter. Leaves change color in fall but are not brilliant.	Useful wherever late winter and early spring accent is needed. Plant in full sun or partial shade in any good garden soil fortified with peat moss or leaf mold.	Take semi-hard-shoot cuttings in summer. Lower branches are easily soil-layered.
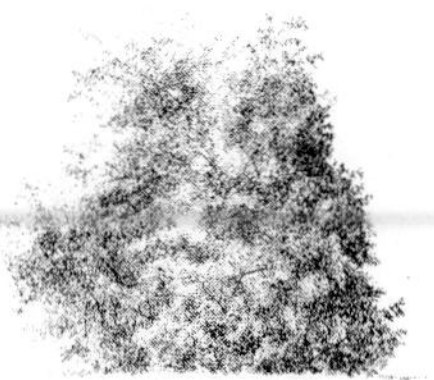 *Grewia occidentalis*	**Starflower, lavender** *(Grewia)* A fast-growing plant, it has many semi-climbing stems and pale green to grayish-green leaves that are faintly toothed and up to 3 in. long. Blossoms produce a fine display from late spring into late fall.	Fine for espaliering and for use near sunny walls. Plant in full sun.	Sow ripened seeds or take cuttings.
 *Stephanandra incisa*	**Stephanandra** *(Stephanandra)* Main assets include somewhat fernlike leaves that are faintly toothed or lobed; they turn yellow, orange, or purplish in fall. Although its small whitish flower clusters somewhat resemble those of spirea, they are much less decorative. In winter bark is a handsome light brown.	Plant in full sun or partial shade. Easily grown in any soil. Once established, it produces abundance of suckers close to its base.	Sow ripened seeds or make root divisions. Take semi-hard-shoot cuttings in summer. Arching branches sometimes root where they touch ground.
 *Rhus typhina laciniata*	**Sumac** *(Rhus)* Grown for its leaves, which in autumn turn fiery red, sometimes with orange undertones. Flowers are generally greenish yellow. Also of decorative value are its brilliant red fruits, which are hairy and appear in tight vertical clusters. Plants usually bear either male or female flowers, occasionally both. If unisexual, male and female plants should be grown near each other to ensure formation of fruit that sets on female plants only.	A strong grower that spreads by underground roots; so it is best limited to informal settings with plenty of room. Thrives in any soil. Autumn leaf coloration is best on plants placed in light, sandy loam and exposed to full sun.	As soon as seeds ripen, stratify them for 5 mo. at room temperature and then at 40° F for another 3 mo. prior to sowing. Make root cuttings in early spring. Remove and plant rooted suckers in spring or fall.
 *Clethra alnifolia*	**Sweet bay**, see Laurel **Sweet olive**, see Osmanthus		
	Sweet pepper bush, or **Summer sweet** *(Clethra)* Short-stalked, toothed leaves. Fragrant white flowers grow in terminal spikes.	Looks attractive on fringe of woodlands. Needs full sun and neutral or acid soil.	Take firm-shoot cuttings in late summer. Responds well to root division and soil layering. Remove and plant rooted suckers in fall.

Species and varieties	Hardiness (Map, p. 9)	Decorative characteristics and remarks	Height and spread when mature
Deciduous or semi-evergreen *Stachyurus chinensis*	C	Yellow bell-shaped flowers form in catkinlike racemes.	H 8 ft.–S 9 ft.
S. praecox	C	Leaves are almost 6 in. long with toothed margins and pointed tips. Foliage turns soft red and yellow in fall. During winter twigs are a handsome red-brown. In its northernmost range this shrub needs protection from late winter frosts that can damage primrose-yellow catkins.	H 12 ft.–S 10 ft.
Evergreen *Grewia occidentalis*	D *	Has oblong leaves and purple-pink to mauve flowers that are starlike and have yellow centers. These grow singly, in pairs, or in threes, forming in junctures of leaves and stems. Its fruits are red-purple, 4-lobed, and up to 1 in. wide. Frequently misidentified and sold as *G. caffra.*	H 10 ft.–S 6-9 ft.
Deciduous *Stephanandra incisa* (lace shrub)	B	In autumn leaves turn reddish purple. Small greenish-white blossoms are seen in early summer on arching branches. Good for border backgrounds.	H 7 ft.–S 6 ft.
S. i. crispa	B	Inconspicuous flowers are greenish white. Dense habit of growth makes this useful hedge plant that needs almost no pruning.	H 3 ft.–S 3 ft.
S. tanakae	B	In fall 2- to 4-in. leaves turn red, orange, or yellow. Greenish-brown twigs support white blossoms in early and mid summer.	H 6 ft.–S 6 ft.
Deciduous *Rhus aromatica* (fragrant)	B	Roughly toothed compound leaves emit pleasant scent. Yellowish flowers appear in early to mid spring before leaflets unfold. This species can be propagated by semi-hard-shoot cuttings taken in summer.	H 3-7 ft.–S 2-5 ft.
R. copallina (shining)	B	Oblong leaflets up to 4 in. long are a handsome glossy green and have smooth margins. Greenish blooms appear in mid to late summer.	H 10-18 ft.–S 6-10 ft.
R. glabra laciniata	A	This is an extremely hardy variety with deeply cut leaves and attractive bright red fruits. Flowers are green and form in dense panicles.	H 10-20 ft.–S 6-10 ft.
R. integrifolia (lemonade berry)	D *	A shrub or tree with simple, smooth-margined, elliptic leaves. Pinkish-white blossoms.	H 30 ft.–S 6-12 ft.
R. typhina laciniata (staghorn)	A	Has delicately segmented leaves and greenish flower clusters in early or mid summer. It also forms handsome spires of rich red fruits.	H 10-30 ft.–S 8-12 ft.
Deciduous *Clethra alnifolia*	B	Oblong leaves with pointed tips are up to 5 in. long. Foliage colors well in fall. Small blossoms begin to open in midsummer.	H 9 ft.–S 9 ft.
C. a. rosea	B	In autumn foliage turns to shades of orange and yellow. Flowers are light pink. Needs moisture. A good variety for seacoast settings.	H 9 ft.–S 9 ft.

*Not hardy below 30° F

	Common and botanical names, general characteristics	Uses and requirements	Propagation *(See also p. 87)*
 *Symphoricarpos albus laevigatus*	**Symphoricarpos** *(Symphoricarpos)* Vigorously branching shrub that is grown primarily for its clusters of showy, fleshy fruits in fall.	Good shrub for city use, since it withstands smog. Plant in full sun or partial shade in any garden soil. Tolerates alkalinity.	**Take semi-hard-shoot cuttings in summer, hardwood cuttings in fall. Also propagated by root cuttings, root division, soil layering, and transplanting of rooted suckers. Difficult to grow from seeds.**
	Syringa, see Lilac		
 *Tamarix pentandra*	**Tamarix** *(Tamarix)* Twigs on supple, slender branches bear tiny scalelike leaves. In autumn both twigs and foliage drop. Small pink blossoms are displayed in conspicuous spraylike panicles or racemes.	Good for hedges or screens. Since branches bend easily in winds, it will tolerate seacoast conditions, taking salt spray in stride. Thrives in sandy, lime-free soil.	**Ripened seeds can be sown at once or stored in cool, dry place for up to 1 yr. and then planted. Take semi-hard-shoot cuttings in summer or leafless hardwood cuttings in autumn. Both usually root readily.**
	Taxus, see Yew		
 *Vaccinium corymbosum*	**Vaccinium** *(Vaccinium)* Short-stalked, alternate leaves frequently have tiny hairs on margins. Autumn leaf coloration is often vivid scarlet and crimson. Small flowers are relatively inconspicuous. Fruit is a berry and is sometimes edible. This genus includes blueberries, huckleberries, and cranberries.	Not easy to transplant. Buy only balled and burlapped specimens. Plant in full sun or partial shade in peaty, acid soil with pH of 4-5. Must have constant moisture. Restrain weeds with mulch of wood chips or hardwood sawdust. Covering plants with cheesecloth, netting, or wire enclosure is sometimes necessary to keep birds from berries.	**Sow seeds when ripe. Low-growing kinds respond to root division in early spring. Take semi-hard-shoot cuttings in summer. Take leafless hardwood cuttings of nonevergreen kinds in fall. Shoots can be soil-layered in spring or fall.**
	Verbena, lemon, see Lippia		
 *Viburnum opulus roseum*	**Viburnum** *(Viburnum)* Leaves are opposite and often show handsome fall coloration. Small flowers are usually white and develop in attractive flat or ball-like terminal clusters. Fruits are frequently colorful.	Grows well in full sun or partial shade in acid or alkaline soil with moderate moisture. In warm climates evergreen kinds may need some shade. Deciduous kinds grow rapidly, and old plants benefit from removal of some of oldest wood at ground level every few years.	**Ripened seeds can be stored for up to 1 yr. in cool, dry place and then stratified for 5 mo. at room temperature. Stratify another 3 mo. at 40° F before planting.**

Viburnum *(Viburnum)*—continued

Species and varieties	Hardiness *(Map, p. 9)*	Decorative characteristics and remarks	Height and spread when mature
Deciduous *Symphoricarpos albus laevigatus* (snowberry)	A	Leaves are oblong or oval. Very small blossoms appear in early summer. White berries form in abundance in early fall, bending branches to ground. Fungus may turn berries brown. For control, see anthracnose, p. 603.	H 3-4 ft.–S 6 ft.
S. chenaultii (Chenault coralberry)	B	Leaves have hairy undersides. Bears pink berries that are white on shaded side. This hybrid makes a good low hedge.	H 3 ft.–S 8 ft.
S. orbiculatus (Indian currant)	A	Leaves turn a striking crimson in autumn. Inconspicuous white or yellowish-white flowers are followed by masses of bright reddish-purple berries that last well into winter. Suckers freely; so it is useful on slopes.	H 6 ft.–S 4-5 ft.
Deciduous *Tamarix hispida*	C	Twigs are hairy. Fluffy flowers open in late summer and early fall. Prune in early spring.	H 4 ft.–S 3-4 ft.
T. parviflora	A	Flowers appear in spring. Displays dark brown to purple bark. Prune immediately after flowers fade. Often sold as *T. tetrandra.*	H 15 ft.–S 15 ft.
T. pentandra	A	Leaves are purplish. Similar to *T. hispida,* with flowers appearing at same time. Prune in early spring. An especially hardy species.	H 15 ft.–S 15 ft.
Deciduous *Vaccinium corymbosum* (highbush blueberry)	A	Pale green twigs are warty. Elliptic leaves are 2-3 in. long; in autumn they turn a striking scarlet. Pinkish or white blossoms are urn shaped. They appear in late spring and are followed by profusion of edible bluish-black fruits. Makes an effective hedge.	H 12 ft.–S 10 ft.
V. parvifolium	A	Flowers are pinkish. Red berries are about ¼ in. wide.	H 10 ft.–S 6-8 ft.
Evergreen *V. ovatum* (California huckleberry)	D	Twigs are hairy. Slightly toothed leaves have glossy bright green upper surfaces. Pink or white bell-shaped blossoms open in summer. Berries are black.	H 10 ft.–S 6-8 ft.
V. vitis-idaea (cowberry, or cranberry)	B	Glossy green oval leaves develop on erect shoots. Urn- or bell-shaped flowers are pink or white and open in late spring or early summer. Fruits are bright red. Once established, this creeping species makes a fine ground cover, especially for wild-flower gardens.	H ½ ft.–S 1½ ft.
Deciduous *Viburnum bodnantense*	C	This hybrid has red fall foliage and fragrant pink flowers that turn white.	H 10 ft.–S 10 ft.
V. b. 'Dawn'	C	Aromatic blossoms are rose with a white flush. Tolerates heavy clay soils.	H 10 ft.–S 10 ft.
V. burkwoodii (Burkwood)	B	This hybrid has shiny foliage that is semi to fully evergreen in frost-free climates. Aromatic blossoms are white.	H 6 ft.–S 4-5 ft.

Viburnum *(Viburnum)*—continued

	Common and botanical names, general characteristics	Uses and requirements	Propagation *(See also p. 87)*
 *Viburnum opulus roseum*	**Viburnum** *(Viburnum)*—continued In some kinds these fruits remain on plants into winter. Birds are attracted to fruits of other kinds and quickly devour them. A very valuable and extensive group of landscape plants.	Evergreen kinds need less pruning except to shape and remove weak wood. If grown as hedge, prune to maintain desired height and form. When planting kinds with ornamental fruits, to ensure fruiting, it is advisable to plant nearby individuals of 2 or more clones (plants raised from different seeds or propagated from different seedlings). Earliest-flowering kinds may fail to set fruit some years if weather at blossoming time is cold, rainy, or even windless. Insects—particularly aphids, but also thrips, two-spotted mites, and scale—may need to be controlled, and in some regions powdery mildew may occur in late summer (see section on plant disorders, p. 600).	Root divisions and soil layers can be made. Take semi-hard-shoot cuttings in late summer. Deciduous kinds respond to leafless hardwood cuttings taken in fall.
 *Vitex agnus-castus*			
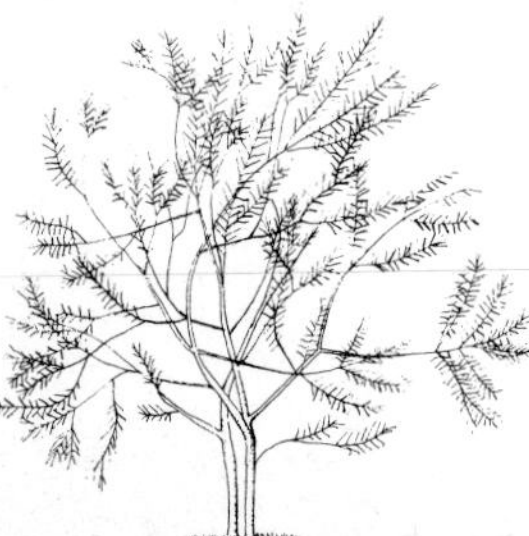	**Vitex** *(Vitex)* Opposite long-stalked leaves consist of 3-7 leaflets with hairy undersides. Tiny fragrant blossoms form in terminal spikes and are followed by very small fruits.	Plant in full sun in any well-drained soil.	Stratify seeds for 3 mo. at 40° F prior to planting. Branches can be soil-layered. Take semi-hard-shoot cuttings in summer or leafless hardwood cuttings in fall.
Chamaelaucium uncinatum	**Waxflower, Geraldton** *(Chamaelaucium)* Small narrow leaves are vivid green and usually opposite. An upright grower with many branches.	Plant in full sun in any good garden soil.	Sow seeds when ripe. Plant semi-hard-shoot cuttings in sand and peat moss mixture in summer.

Species and varieties	Hardiness (*Map, p. 9*)	Decorative characteristics and remarks	Height and spread when mature
Deciduous *Viburnum carlcephalum* (fragrant)	B	Leaves are glossy. In mid to late spring aromatic rounded flower clusters cover this hybrid. Fruits are deep blue.	H 7 ft.–S 7 ft.
V. carlesii (Korean spice)	A	Very fragrant pink buds open white. Parent of improved hybrids.	H 4-5 ft.–S 5 ft.
V. macrocephalum sterile (Chinese snowball)	B	Leaves to 5 in. long are often semi-evergreen where winters are mild. Flat flower clusters make fine show in late spring and early summer.	H 10 ft.–S 6-9 ft.
V. opulus roseum, or *V. o. sterile* (snowball)	A	Maplelike leaves turn red in fall. Flower clusters open in late spring and early summer. Does not set fruit, since flowers are sterile. Susceptible to attacks by aphids.	H 12 ft.–S 12 ft.
V. plicatum tomentosum (double file)	B	Branching habit is horizontal. Outer flowers in each cluster are sterile; fertile flowers at centers produce red fruits that later turn blue-black. Flowering period is from late spring to early summer.	H 10 ft.–S 8 ft.
V. sieboldii	B	Glossy, oval, wrinkled leaves are up to 6 in. long. Ill-scented flowers in late spring or early summer. Deep pink or red fruits turn blue-black.	H 30 ft.–S 10-15 ft.
V. tomentosum sterile, or *V. plicatum*	B	Three-in.-round flower clusters appear in late spring. All flowers are sterile; therefore plant does not set fruit.	H 9 ft.–S 6-9 ft.
Evergreen *V. davidii*	C	Shiny leathery leaves are 2-6 in. long. White blossoms in early summer are followed by light blue fruits in early and mid fall.	H 3 ft.–S 5 ft.
V. dilatatum (linden)	B	In late spring and early summer flowers open in clusters up to 5 in. wide. Reddish-brown leaves and scarlet fruits appear in fall.	H 9 ft.–S 6-9 ft.
V. japonicum	C	Shiny leaves. Fragrant blossoms in early summer followed by red fruits.	H 6 ft.–S 4-5 ft.
V. odoratissimum	C	Has glossy leaves. Fragrant flowers show in late spring. Red fruits turn black.	H 10 ft.–S 5-6 ft.
V. rhytidophyllum	B	Handsome crinkled leaves are up to 7 in. long; semi-evergreen in cold-winter regions. Creamy white blossoms appear in early summer. Red fruits turn black.	H 10 ft.–S 10-15 ft.
V. tinus (laurustinus)	C	Shiny deep green leaves are 2-3 in. long. Flowers in mid to late summer often show a pink hue. Fruits are blue-black. Makes good sheared hedge. Needs winter protection in its northernmost range.	H 10 ft.–S 8-10 ft.
Deciduous *Vitex agnus-castus* (chaste tree)	C	Green lance-shaped leaves are grayish beneath and exude pleasant odor when crushed. Small, fragrant, light purple to bluish blossoms in 7-in. spikes open from midsummer to early fall.	H 10 ft.–S 6-8 ft.
V. negundo	B	Leaflets usually display toothed edges. Dark bluish-lavender flowers are attractive to bees.	H 15 ft.–S 8-12 ft.
Evergreen *Chamaelaucium uncinatum*	D*	Leaves slightly over 1 in. long are curved on top. Small lilac, pink, or white blooms open in groups of 2-4 in midspring in leaf axils, or some in terminal clusters. In older plants trunks become twisted and bark is shaggy. Good cut flower. Often sold as *C. ciliatum.*	H 6 ft.–S 4-5 ft.

*Not hardy below 30° F

	Common and botanical names, general characteristics	Uses and requirements	Propagation (See also p. 87)
 *Weigela florida*	**Weigela** *(Weigela)* Leaves are opposite. Blossoms are usually funnel shaped and more than 1 in. long in clusters of up to 3, appearing in late spring and early summer.	Easily grown in full sun or partial shade in any good garden soil that drains well. If pruning becomes necessary, it should be done as soon as flowers fade, since blooms develop on short shoots from previous year's growth.	Sow seeds when ripe. Take soft-shoot cuttings in spring or leafless hardwood cuttings in fall.
	Wild lilac, see Ceanothus		
 *Salix humilis*	**Willow** *(Salix)* Rapid grower with brittle branches. Alternate leaves are generally lance shaped and narrow. Erect catkins, of great ornamental value on some kinds, appear before or just as leaves unfold.	Grow in full sun or partial shade in any good garden soil. Many species and varieties do best in moist soil. A few, however, grow better in poor, dry soil.	Seeds must be sown as soon as they are ripe, due to brief viability. Take semi-hard-shoot cuttings in summer or leafless hardwood cuttings in fall.
 *Corylopsis pauciflora*	**Winter hazel** *(Corylopsis)* Lime-green leaves are toothed and display prominent veins. Yellow flowers open so early in spring that in northern gardens they may be damaged by late frosts, and in some years they may be killed by winter cold. Tiny and aromatic, they develop in hanging racemes. Plants have somewhat open habit of growth and delicate pattern of branching.	Attractive in a woodland setting or with an evergreen background. Grow in full sun or partial shade. Plant in sandy soil with generous amounts of peat moss. Does not tolerate alkalinity. Provide protection from cold winds.	Seeds should be stratified for 5 mo. at room temperature and then for another 3 mo. at 40° F prior to sowing. Take semi-hard-shoot cuttings in summer.
 *Chimonanthus praecox*	**Winter sweet** *(Chimonanthus)* Opposite leaves have smooth margins. Honey-scented blossoms open in early to mid spring before leaves unfold. They have no petals, but overlapping yellow sepals are prominent.	Prefers full sun but will tolerate partial shade. Grows in any soil, including heavy clay, but does best where drainage is good. Water well in hot, dry weather.	Sow seeds when ripe. Make soil layers in autumn.

Species and varieties	Hardiness (Map, p. 9)	Decorative characteristics and remarks	Height and spread when mature
Deciduous *Weigela* 'Bristol Ruby'	☐B☐☐	Masses of blossoms open ruby-red and turn yellowish crimson as they mature. This hybrid flowers in late spring and again heavily in summer and lasts throughout fall. Established plants assume handsome rounded shape.	H 7 ft.–S 4-5 ft.
W. candida	☐B☐☐	Unlike other white-flowered weigelas, blossoms on this hybrid hold their color and do not turn pink.	H 5-9 ft.–S 3-5 ft.
W. florida, or *W. rosea*	☐B☐☐	Elliptic leaves are 3-4 in. long; their underside veins are hairy. Rose-pink flowers develop on spreading branches. Tolerates alkaline soil.	H 10 ft.–S 8 ft.
W. f. foliis purpuriis	☐B☐☐	Pink blooms make attractive sight on this variety. Habit of growth is more restrained than that of *W. florida.*	H 5 ft.–S 4 ft.
W. f. variegata	☐B☐☐	Pink blossoms are especially handsome in combination with leaves that have pale yellow edges.	H 5 ft.–S 4 ft.
W. vanicekii, or *W.* 'Newport Red'	☐B☐☐	A fine red bloomer with good resistance to cold winters.	H 5-6 ft.–S 3-4 ft.
Deciduous *Salix gracilistyla* (rose-gold pussy)	☐B☐☐	Bluish-green leaves are 2-4 in. long and have hairy undersides; they form on gray hairy twigs. Reddish catkins are seen in early to mid spring.	H 6 ft.–S 6 ft.
S. humilis	A☐☐☐	Wandlike stems bear "pussies" (catkins) in early spring. Open habit of growth.	H 3 ft.–S 3-6 ft.
S. purpurea (purple osier)	☐B☐☐	Young twigs are purplish, changing to gray with age. Leaves are 2-4 in. long; upper surfaces are darker colored than undersides. Good where soil is moist.	H 8 ft.–S 4-5 ft.
S. p. nana	☐B☐☐	Bluish-green to grayish leaves provide fine accent. Tolerates shearing and heavy, wet soil. Makes striking hedge with interesting feathery effect.	H 4 ft.–S 4 ft.
S. sachalinense sekka (fantail)	☐B☐☐	Young flattened branches assume twisted shapes, giving this variety unusual profile, particularly in winter. Catkins are silvery and up to 2 in. long.	H 30 ft.–S 10-12 ft.
Deciduous *Corylopsis pauciflora* (buttercup)	☐☐C☐	Oval 2- to 3-in.-long leaves have heart-shaped bases. Racemes contain 2 or 3 blossoms.	H 6 ft.–S 10 ft.
C. spicata (spike)	☐B☐☐	Resembles *C. pauciflora* in outline, but leaves are 3-5 in. long. As many as 12 flowers develop in each raceme.	H 6 ft.–S 10 ft.
Deciduous *Chimonanthus praecox*	☐☐☐D	Extremely aromatic, cup-shaped blossoms are about 1 in. wide. Insides of sepals reveal purplish-brown stripes.	H 9 ft.–S 9 ft.
C. p. grandiflorus	☐☐☐D	Very similar to *C. praecox,* but with less fragrant flowers.	H 9 ft.–S 9 ft.

	Common and botanical names, general characteristics	Uses and requirements	Propagation (See also p. 87)
 *Hamamelis mollis*	**Witch hazel** *(Hamamelis)* Short-stalked leaves are alternate and generally turn yellow or sometimes red in autumn. Spidery-looking flowers are produced in shades of yellow or copper-red, or sometimes yellow with reddish centers. Most kinds bloom from late winter to early spring. Fruit capsules explode when ripe, propelling 2 glossy black seeds many feet.	Red-flowering kinds are more conspicuous than those that produce yellow flowers; so better suited for gardens to be viewed from distance. Easily grown in full sun or partial shade in any soil. Needs moisture. Tolerates smog.	Seeds should be stratified for 5 mo. at room temperature and then for another 3 mo. at 40° F. prior to sowing. Germination may take 2 yr. Responds well to soil layering. Take semi-hard-shoot cuttings in summer.
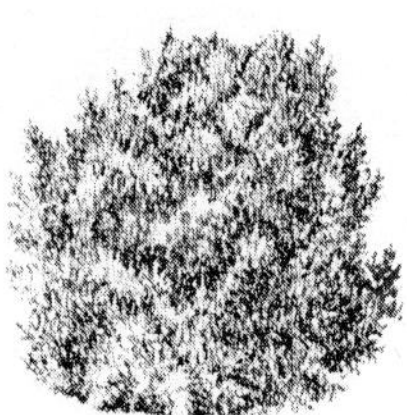 *Taxus media hicksii*	**Yew** *(Taxus)* Handsome deep green leaves are about 1 in. long and needlelike but fairly soft; undersides bear 2 parallel grayish-green or pale yellow lines. Male and female blossoms form on separate plants, but only females set red or brownish berries, which are fleshy and open at 1 end, revealing seeds. Mature plants display scaling, reddish-brown bark. All kinds are slow growing. Seeds and leaves are poisonous.	Many kinds make beautiful hedges and topiaries, since they stand shearing. Grow in full sun or partial shade in any good garden soil. Plants of both sexes must be grown near each other if females are to produce berries in fall.	Ripened seeds can be stratified at once, or they can be stored for up to 1 yr. in cool, dry place prior to stratifying, which should be done for first 5 mo. at room temperature. Follow with another 3 mo. of stratifying at 40° F and then sow. Take semi-hard-shoot cuttings in summer or firm-shoot cuttings in late summer.
 *Cephalotaxus harringtonia*	**Yew, plum** *(Cephalotaxus)* Resembles yew, but its handsome leaves are longer and show 2 bluish-gray lines on undersides. Male and female blossoms are produced on separate plants in fall. Fleshy fruits are about 1 in. long and plumlike, maturing during 2nd yr.	Excellent choice for coastal gardens. Good screen or hedge. Can also be grown for some time in containers. Plant in full sun or partial shade in any good garden soil. Protect from high temperatures and dry conditions.	Ripened seeds can be stratified at 40° F for 3 mo., or store in cool, dry place for up to 1 yr. and then stratify prior to planting. Take firm-shoot cuttings in late summer.
 *Yucca aloifolia*	**Yucca** *(Yucca)* Valued for its handsome spikes of flowers. Blooms are generally white or yellowish and cup shaped.	Good tub plant. Grow in full sun in coarse, sandy soil. Seldom needs water.	Sow seeds when ripe. Make root cuttings or remove rooted offshoots from base of plant.

Species and varieties	Hardiness (*Map, p. 9*)	Decorative characteristics and remarks	Height and spread when mature
Deciduous			
Hamamelis intermedia	□B□□	Flowers are a fine copper-red shade. Many good flowering varieties have been derived from this hybrid.	H 30 ft.–S 15-18 ft.
H. i. 'Arnold Promise'	□B□□	Large, fragrant golden yellow flowers bloom late winter to early spring. Fall leaf color is bright red and yellow.	H 20 ft.–S 20 ft.
H. japonica	□B□□	Three- to 4-in. oval or rounded leaves turn red in autumn. Vivid yellow blossoms sometimes have reddish or purplish centers.	H 25 ft.–S 15-18 ft.
H. mollis (Chinese)	□B□□	Slightly toothed leaves are 3-7 in. long; undersides are covered with grayish hairs. Aromatic golden yellow blossoms have reddish centers more than 1 in. wide.	H 25 ft.–S 15-18 ft.
H. m. brevipetala	□B□□	Large aromatic flowers are orange-yellow in late winter and early spring.	H 12 ft.–S 10 ft.
H. vernalis	□B□□	Three- to 5-in. leaves are generally oblong and toothed around tips. Fragrant deep yellow flowers occasionally have reddish centers. Petals close during very cold weather.	H 6 ft.–S 5 ft.
H. virginiana	□B□□	Many toothed, elliptic leaves are 4-6 in. long. Brilliant yellow flowers do not appear until mid to late fall. Mature specimens assume attractive vaselike profile.	H 15 ft.–S 8-10 ft.
Evergreen			
Taxus canadensis	A□□□	Foliage may brown in winter if exposed to full sun. Berries are scarlet. Tolerates shade but protect from exposure to high wind. Semi-prostrate habit of growth makes this species useful as ground cover beneath tall evergreens.	H 3 ft.–S 3-6 ft.
T. cuspidata expansa	□B□□	Berries are scarlet. Low and spreading in habit of growth, this form is particularly valuable for hedging.	H 3-4 ft.–S 15-20 ft.
T. media	□B□□	As branches mature, they turn reddish green. This hybrid has pyramidal shape. Many varieties offered, some much lower growing than *T. media.*	H 5-15 ft.–S 15-20 ft.
T. m. hatfieldii	□B□□	Conical habit of growth; dense foliage. No berries.	H 20 ft.–S 6-10 ft.
T. m. hicksii	□B□□	Good berry bearer. Columnar habit of growth.	H 12 ft.–S 10 ft.
Evergreen			
Cephalotaxus harringtonia	□B□□	Leaves are needlelike and frequently from 1 in. to almost 2 in. long. These ordinarily form in 2 planes along branches and last for 3-4 yr. Large red egg-shaped fruits are more than 1 in. long. It is necessary to plant male and female specimens near each other in order to have fruits develop on females. A very slow grower and has rather wide-spreading habit of growth.	H 10-12 ft.–S 8-10 ft.
Evergreen			
Yucca aloifolia (Spanish bayonet)	□□□D	Trunk is sparsely branched. Branches are narrow and grow upright. Sharply pointed leaves are more than 2 ft. long. White blossoms are often 4 in. wide and appear in 2-ft. clusters in late summer; occasionally, they show purple shading.	H 25 ft.–S 6-8 ft.
Y. gloriosa (Spanish dagger)	□□□D	Pointed soft-tipped leaves are gray-green, smooth at edges, and reach length of more than 2 ft. Four-in.-wide flowers that are greenish white, or sometimes reddish, bloom in late summer.	H 8 ft.–S 3-4 ft.

Useful Vines to Grow

Vining plants have the advantage of flexible stems that can be trained to provide the maximum display of foliage, flowers, or fruits. Also, vines take up very little ground area.

Some vines are climbers that attach themselves to their support by twining tendrils, rootlets, or clinging disks. Others must be tied up in order to climb. Whether or not they are self-supporting is indicated in the first column on the charts.

Vines are listed here alphabetically according to their best-known common names. Note, too, that the deciduous and evergreen plants have been grouped on separate charts.

To determine whether a vine can reasonably be expected to survive the lowest average temperature in your area, check the zone designation for that vine in the Hardiness column. Then refer to the Temperature Zone Map on page 9.

Most vines can be cut back lightly at any time to keep them in bounds. For details on pruning those that are overgrown, see page 100.

Serpentine soil layering, a method of propagating vines, is illustrated on page 93. For specific information on planting vines, see page 82.

DECIDUOUS VINES

Actinidia kolomikta

Blueberry climber
(Ampelopsis brevipedunculata)

Aristolochia durior

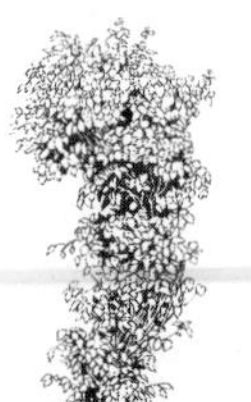
Oriental bittersweet
(Celastrus orbiculatus)

Anemone clematis
(Clematis montana)

Common and botanical names, general characteristics	Species and varieties	Hardiness *(Map, p. 9)*	Decorative characteristics, special requirements, and remarks
Actinidia *(Actinidia)* Robust plant with twining stems, numerous alternate leaves, and edible fruits. Since male and female blossoms form on separate plants, individual specimens of both sexes should be grown near each other to ensure fruiting.	*A. arguta* (bower actinidia, or tara vine)	□ B □ □	Oval leaves are up to 5 in. long. Small greenish-white flowers open in midsummer. Greenish-yellow fruits are sweet. Fast growth forms dense cover.
	A. chinensis (Chinese gooseberry, or kiwi vine)	□ □ C □	Velvety red hairs on new shoots; leaves to 8 in. long. White to yellow blooms appear in early summer.
	A. kolomikta	□ B □ □	Male plant often has large white to pinkish mark at end of 5-in. leaf. Flowers, in early spring, are white and aromatic. Fruits are greenish yellow.
Ampelopsis *(Ampelopsis)* Small berries appear in fall. Once established, plant tendrils attach themselves to walls.	*A. brevipedunculata,* or *A. heterophylla amurensis* (blueberry climber)	□ B □ □	Leaves of this fast grower are simple and noticeably lobed. Fruit clusters turn from light purple to yellow to dark blue.
Aristolochia *(Aristolochia)* Has twining stems and large, handsome leaves. Can be used as a screen.	*A. durior* (Dutchman's pipe)	□ B □ □	Foul-smelling yellowish-brown flowers resemble small tobacco pipes. Rounded leaves are up to 1 ft. long.
Bittersweet *(Celastrus)* Has twining stems, alternate stalked leaves, which are usually deciduous. Tiny greenish blooms. Colorful fruits split to show red-to-orange-coated seeds.	*C. orbiculatus* (Oriental)	□ B □ □	Rounded leaves are 3-5 in. long. Orange-yellow fruits develop in junctures of leaves and stems.
	C. scandens (American)	A □ □ □	Oblong leaves are up to 5 in. long. Yellow fruits poisonous. Rampant grower that needs plenty of room but is useful for covering tops of low stone walls.
Clematis *(Clematis)* Opposite leaves are compound. Twining leaf stalks cling to supports. Vine needs partial shade, alkaline soil, and loose mulch to help keep roots cool and moist.	*C. chrysocoma*	□ □ □ D	Pale pink flowers are almost 2 in. in diameter.
	C. jackmanii	□ B □ □	Purple blooms as wide as 6 in. appear from midsummer to midfall. Hybrid has many large-flowering varieties.
	C. j. 'Gipsy Queen'	□ B □ □	Purple flowers.
	C. j. 'Madame Edouard Andre'	□ B □ □	Outstanding red blossoms.
	C. j. 'The President'	□ B □ □	Reddish-brown flowers.
	C. montana (anemone clematis)	□ □ C □	Leaves are prominently toothed. White 1- to 3-in. blossoms open in late spring.
	C. m. rubens (pink anemone)	□ B □ □	Young leaves are purplish bronze. Deep pink blooms.
	C. texensis (scarlet clematis)	□ B □ □	Ovalish leaves are bluish green. Vine displays scarlet, urn-shaped blooms from midsummer to early fall.

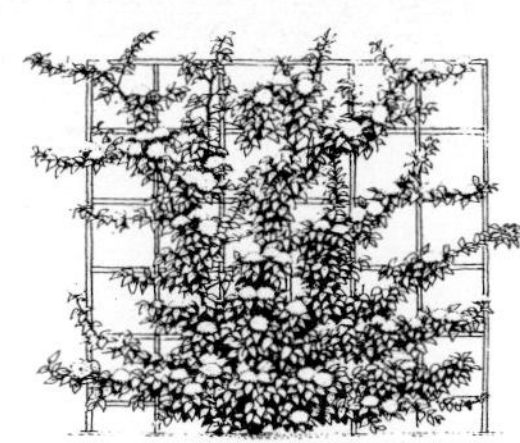

Hydrangea anomala petiolaris

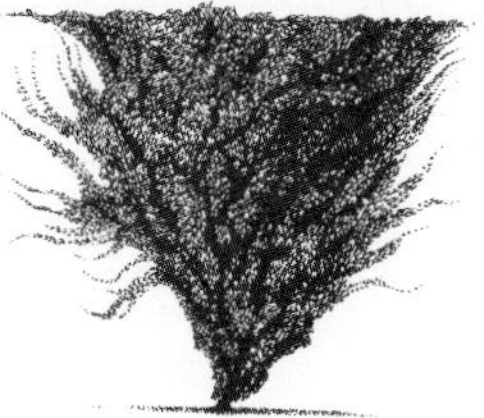

Boston ivy (*Parthenocissus tricuspidata*)

Silver-lace vine (*Polygonum aubertii*)

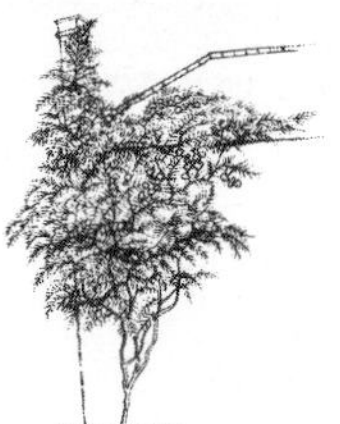

Trumpet creeper (*Campsis radicans*)

Virginia creeper (*Parthenocissus quinquefolia*)

Chinese wisteria (*Wisteria sinensis*)

Common and botanical names, general characteristics	Species and varieties	Hardiness (*Map, p. 9*)	Decorative characteristics, special requirements, and remarks
Grapevine *(Vitis),* see p. 526			
Hydrangea, climbing *(Hydrangea)* Flower clusters are white. Leaves, usually toothed, are opposite. Rootlike growth on stem clings to support.	*H. anomala petiolaris*	□B□□	Side growth may reach as far as 3 ft. from main stem, forming dense screen that is useful for masking service yards or other work areas.
Ivy, Boston *(Parthenocissus,* or *Ampelopsis)* Compound leaves, in 3 parts, turn bright red in fall. Inconspicuous flowers are followed by dark blue to black berries. Rootlike tendrils cling to unpainted masonry surfaces with disklike pads; vines climb trees if bark is sufficiently rough.	*P. tricuspidata*	□B□□	Shiny green leaves are up to 8 in. across. May be semi-evergreen in mild climates.
	P. t. lowii	□B□□	Leaves are up to 1½ in. wide. New growth is often purplish.
	P. t. veitchii	□B□□	Young leaves are purplish. Ultimate width is ½-¾ in.
Silver-lace vine, or Chinese fleece vine *(Polygonum)* Bees are attracted to small flowers that form in racemes or terminal clusters. This vine has twining stems.	*P. aubertii*	□B□□	Lance-shaped leaves are up to 2½ in. long. Aromatic greenish-white blossoms open in late summer. Requires little care except for some pruning after blossoms fade. Can be trained on trellis.
Trumpet creeper *(Campsis,* or *Bignonia)* Fast grower has compound leaves, vivid trumpetlike blooms (which attract hummingbirds), and long seedpods. Rootlets along stems attach to supports, but vine may also require tying. Not a good choice where space is limited, but ideal for growing over roof, toolshed, or similar structure.	*C. grandiflora* (Chinese)	□□C□	Leaves consist of up to 9 leaflets. Bright red flowers in late summer are 3 in. wide.
	C. radicans	□B□□	Orange to red blossoms, 2 in. in diameter, appear in midsummer.
	C. tagliabuana 'Madame Galen'	□B□□	Although nearly identical to *C. radicans,* blooms of this vine are slightly larger.
Virginia creeper *(Parthenocissus,* or *Ampelopsis)* Leaves of this high climber have 5 leaflets, which grow as long as 6 in. and radiate outward like spokes of a wheel. Twining stems attach themselves to supports by disklike pads.	*P. quinquefolia*	A□□□	Large leaves turn fiery red in fall. Birds seek out deep blue to black berries. Should not be allowed to grow into treetops, since twining stems can smother them within a few seasons.
	P. q. englemannii	A□□□	Vine is similar to *P. quinquefolia* but has smaller leaflets.
Wisteria *(Wisteria)* This genus has large compound leaves and pealike flowers in handsome pendent clusters. Long velvety seedpods develop in autumn. Wisterias are climbers with twining stems that have been known to break flimsy structures; they require sturdy support. There are two groups: one, the Chinese, twines from left to right; the other, Japanese, from right to left.	*W. floribunda* (Japanese)	□B□□	In late spring dark blue or violet blooms form clusters up to 18 in. long. Flowers may smell sweet.
	W. f. longissima	□B□□	Blossom color is violet to reddish violet.
	W. f. l. alba	□B□□	White flowers have a rich perfume.
	W. f. rosea	□B□□	Pale pink blooms are heavily scented.
	W. f. 'Royal Purple'	□B□□	Deep purple flowers make a showy display.
	W. sinensis (Chinese)	□B□□	Aromatic bluish-violet flowers open in late spring and hang in clusters up to 1 ft. long.
	W. s. alba	□B□□	Pure white blooms are attractive, especially when planted together with colored wisterias.

EVERGREEN VINES

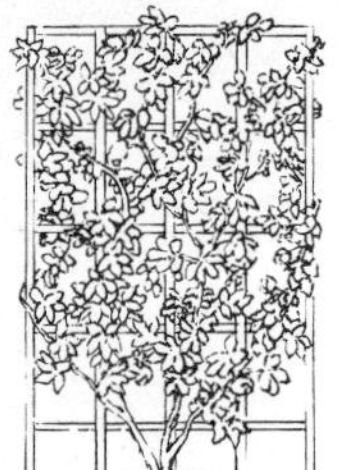
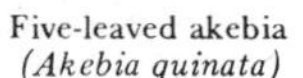
Five-leaved akebia (*Akebia quinata*)

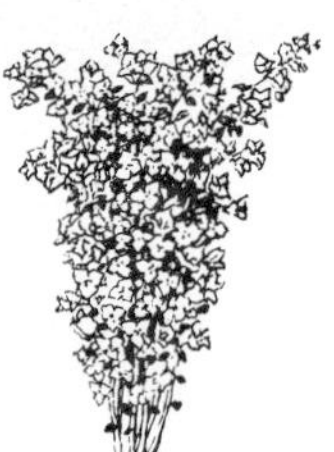
Bougainvillea glabra

Clock vine (*Thunbergia grandiflora*)

Cross vine (*Bignonia capreolata*)

Fatshedera lizei

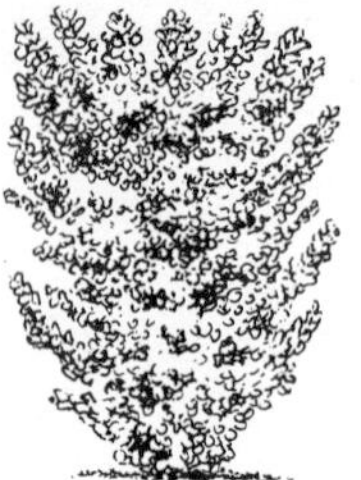
Creeping fig (*Ficus pumila*)

Mexican flame vine (*Senecio confusus*)

Common and botanical names, general characteristics	Species and varieties	Hardiness (*Map, p. 9*)	Decorative characteristics, special requirements, and remarks
Akebia (*Akebia*) Compound leaves on twining stems are deciduous in cold climates but evergreen in the South. Male flowers are purplish brown; female flowers are tan. This twiner needs shade. Some kinds are invasive and need plenty of space.	*A. quinata* (five-leaved)	□ B □ □	Leaves consist of 5 leaflets. Inconspicuous but aromatic flowers open at night in late spring. Purple pods up to 3 in. long are edible.
	A. trifoliata (three-leaved)	□ B □ □	Leaves consist of 3 leaflets that are 2-3 in. long. Their tips are notched, and edges are wavy. This fast grower flowers in mid to late spring.
Bougainvillea (*Bougainvillea*) Small blossoms have handsome bracts. Woody twiner with awkwardly climbing stems that need tying to trellises. Good for softening contours. Vine resists drought.	*B. glabra*	□ □ □ D *	Red to purple 1-in. bracts appear on drooping branchlets in midsummer.
	B. spectabilis	□ □ □ D *	This species grows more rapidly than *B. glabra,* but its reddish bracts last a shorter time. Stems are completely covered with hairs.
Clock vine (*Thunbergia*) Rapid growth and attractive flowers make this woody climber with twining stems good for use on porch or trellis. Leaves often have arrow-shaped base.	*T. fragrans*	□ □ □ D *	White blossoms to 3 in. wide are aromatic. Opposite, slightly lobed leaves borne on square stems.
	T. grandiflora (blue sky vine, or sky-flower)	□ □ □ D	Ovalish leaves up to 8 in. long have toothed edges. Blue or white 3-in.-wide blossoms form handsome 3-ft. drooping clusters. Flowering occurs almost all year but is most profuse in midspring.
	T. laurifolia	□ □ □ D *	Leaves are 5 in. long. Pale blue to purple blooms with yellow throats are 3 in. wide.
Cross vine (*Bignonia,* or *Anisostichus*) Compound leaves consist of 2 leaflets. Handsome blooms form in groups in junctures of leaves and stems. Pods appearing in fall are up to 8 in. long. This striking vine climbs with tendrils.	*B. capreolata,* or *A. capreolatus*	□ □ C □	Leaves are 4-6 in. long. Reddish-orange, trumpet-like, 2-in.-wide flowers appear in late spring. Vine is outstanding for use as screen.
	B. chamberlaynii, or *Anemopaegma chamberlaynii*	□ □ □ D *	Ovalish leaves have glossy upper surfaces that are deeper green than undersides. Yellow flower clusters appear in late summer and early fall.
Fatshedera (*Fatshedera*) Leaves resemble English ivy's but are larger. Needs tying to supports or trellises.	*F. lizei*	□ □ C □	Shiny leaves grow to 7 in. long and 10 in. wide. Clusters of tiny light green flowers opening in early and mid fall are up to 10 in. long.
Fig, creeping, or climbing (*Ficus*) Excellent screening plant that has dense growth of leaves. Lies flat against support. Young rootlets grip support tightly.	*F. pumila,* or *F. repens*	□ □ □ D	Oval or heart-shaped leaves are up to 4 in. long on branches that bear fruit, less than 1 in. long on other parts of plant. Has inedible yellow fruits about 2 in. long.
Flame vine, Mexican (*Senecio*) Leaves resemble those of ivy but are fleshier. Flowers form in terminal clusters and will bloom all year where winters are mild. Vines seldom grow taller than 8 ft. Thin stems need tying to supports or trellises.	*S. confusus*	□ □ □ D	Leaves to 2 in. long are deciduous in cooler areas. Flowers are first orange, then orange-red.
	S. scandens	□ □ □ D	Hairy, grayish-green leaves are lance shaped or ovalish, sometimes lobed at base. Yellow blossoms develop in open clusters.

*Not hardy below 30° F

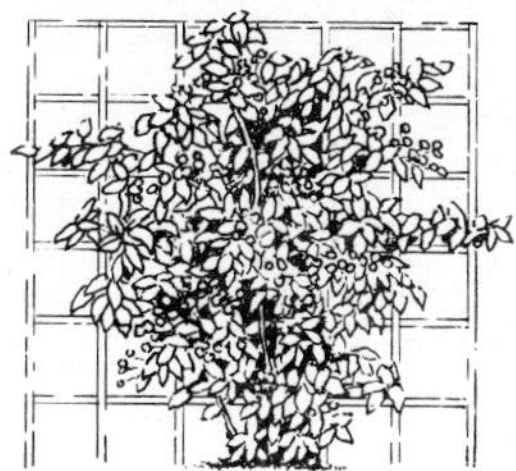
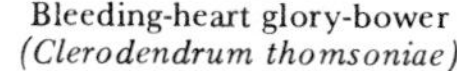
Bleeding-heart glory-bower
(Clerodendrum thomsoniae)

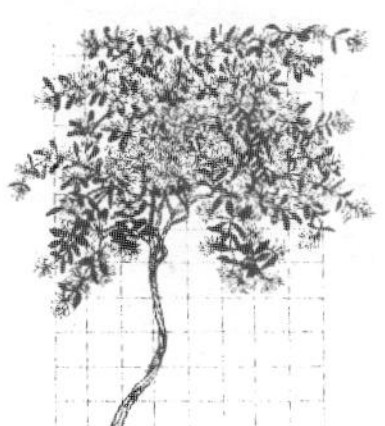
Giant Burmese honeysuckle
(Lonicera hildebrandiana)

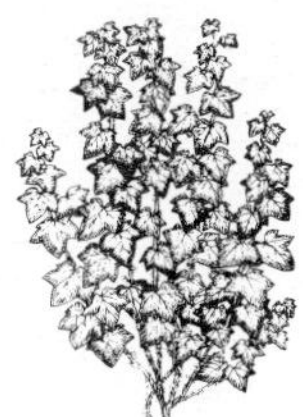
English ivy
(Hedera helix)

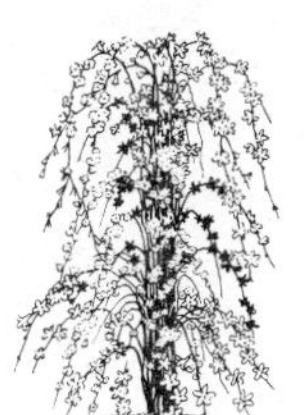
Primrose jasmine
(Jasminum mesnyi)

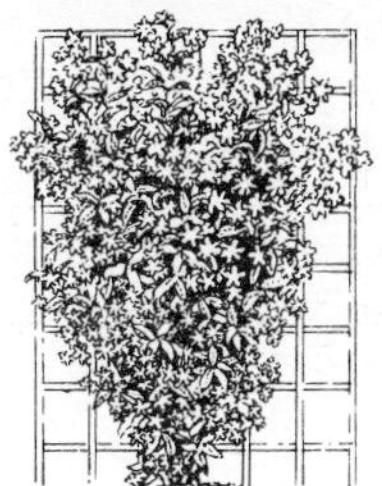
Star jasmine
(Trachelospermum jasminoides)

Common and botanical names, general characteristics	Species and varieties	Hardiness *(Map, p. 9)*	Decorative characteristics, special requirements, and remarks
Glory-bower *(Clerodendrum)* This shrubby vine has twining stems and attractive flower clusters.	*C. thomsoniae,* or *C. balfouri* (bleeding-heart glory-bower)	D	Opposite ovalish leaves up to 5 in. long. Cream and crimson blossoms form at different times in different regions.
Honeysuckle *(Lonicera)* Attaches by twining stems with small disklike pods. Tubular flowers that form in clusters at ends of side shoots or in pairs in junctures of leaves and stems. Attractive berries, in wide range of colors, are favorite food of birds. Grows best in moist, well-drained, slightly alkaline soil.	*L. heckrottii* (coral, or goldflame)	B	In early summer purplish-pink outer blossoms with yellow tubular-shaped inner sections appear and last throughout summer. May be semi-deciduous or deciduous in cooler parts of hardiness zone.
	L. henryi	B	Leaves are up to 4 in. long. Purplish-red, ¾-in.-long flowers open at juncture of leaves and stems in early summer. Fruits are black. Vine may be semi-evergreen in colder parts of hardiness zone.
	L. hildebrandiana (giant Burmese)	D	Scented white blooms change to orange.
	L. sempervirens (trumpet)	A	Ovalish leaves have bluish-green undersides. Red to yellow blossoms in late spring to late summer.
Ivy *(Hedera)* Leaves are alternate, stalked, and toothed or lobed. This genus, popular for its decorative foliage, produces tiny greenish flowers and black fruits. Rootlets along stems cling to rough surfaces.	*H. canariensis* (Algerian)	C	Six-in.-long leaves. Dark red twigs and leaf stalks.
	H. c. variegata (variegated)	C	Leaf margins are cream colored.
	H. colchica	C	Dark green, rather coarse leaves are occasionally lobed; width ranges from 4 to 10 in.
	H. helix (English)	B	Leaves are 2-5 in. long, with 3-5 lobes; tops are deep green, undersides yellowish green. Some varieties have purplish or yellow leaves.
	H. h. baltica	B	This small-leaved variety is especially hardy.
Jasmine *(Jasminum)* This easily grown genus has white, yellow, or pink flower clusters that are usually fragrant. Compound leaves are either alternate or opposite. Its awkwardly climbing stems need tying to supports or walls. Most kinds are evergreen or semi-evergreen to deciduous.	*J. floridum* (showy)	C	Semi-evergreen leaves; yellow blossoms in midsummer.
	J. humile (Italian)	C	Leaves are sometimes semi-evergreen. Sweet-scented blossoms are golden yellow.
	J. mesnyi, or *J. primulinum* (primrose)	C	Glossy leaves are up to 2 in. long. In midspring this semi-evergreen vine bears yellow blossoms.
	J. multiflorum (pinwheel)	D	Leaves are about 2 in. long. Blossoms are white.
	J. nitidum (angel-wing)	D *	Glossy, leathery green leaves are elliptical to lance shaped and up to 3 in. long. Flower buds are reddish purple. White flowers are very fragrant.
	J. officinale grandiflorum (white)	D	Glossy leaves are semi-evergreen or deciduous. White 2-in.-wide flowers open in midsummer.
Jasmine, star *(Trachelospermum,* or *Rhynchospermum)* This twiner clings by rootlets or can be tied to supports. Has oval 3-in.-long leaves. Pairs of thin pods follow fragrant blossom clusters.	*T. asiaticum*	D	New leaves are reddish bronze. Creamy white flowers last from midspring into midsummer.
	T. jasminoides (star, or Confederate)	D	Pure white blossoms appear at same time as those of *T. asiaticum.* Each cluster is about 1 in. wide. Vine needs shade and considerable moisture.

*Not hardy below 30° F

EVERGREEN VINES *(continued)*

Carolina jessamine (*Gelsemium sempervirens*)

Parrot's-beak (*Clianthus puniceus*)

Passionflower (*Passiflora caerulea*)

Solanum jasminoides

Orange trumpet vine (*Pyrostegia ignea*)

Violet trumpet vine (*Clytostoma callistegioides*)

Common and botanical names, general characteristics	Species and varieties	Hardiness (*Map, p. 9*)	Decorative characteristics, special requirements, and remarks
Jessamine, Carolina (*Gelsemium*) Handsome climber with twining stems has glossy leaves up to 4 in. long and aromatic flowers. All parts are poisonous.	*G. sempervirens*	□□□D	Yellow blossom clusters open from early to late spring. Pods are almost 1 in. long.
	G. s. plena (double-flowered)	□□□D	Has double long-blooming flowers.
Parrot's-beak (*Clianthus*) Compound leaves are grayish when young. Pealike blooms are drooping. Has clambering stems that should be tied to supports.	*C. puniceus*	□□□D	Crimson 3-in.-wide flowers have faint white marks at bases of petals. Flowers fade to paler shade of red. Smooth-surfaced pods develop in autumn.
Passionflower (*Passiflora*) Vine has alternate leaves, decorative flowers, and many-seeded fruits. Vine climbs with tendrils. Most kinds are semi-evergreen in cooler parts of hardiness zone.	*P. alatocaerulea,* or *P. pfordtii*	□□□D *	Three-lobed leaves are sometimes semi-evergreen. Profuse, fragrant blooms, almost 4 in. wide, are in combination of white, blue, purple, and pink.
	P. caerulea	□□□D *	Leaves, with 5 lobes, may be semi-evergreen. Large, fragrant flowers are white, purple, and pink. Yellow pods are 1½ in. long.
	P. edulis (passion fruit, or purple granadilla)	□□□D *	Semi-evergreen leaves are toothed, 3-lobed, and 4-6 in. long. Purple and white blossoms are about 2 in. across. Deep purple, 3-in.-long fruits are edible.
	P. racemosa, or *P. princeps*	□□□D	Ovalish leaves may be unlobed or have up to 3 lobes. Four-in.-wide flowers, formed in racemes, are purple to dark red, with white bands. Leathery-skinned, egg-shaped fruits are up to 3 in. long.
Solanum (*Solanum*) Flowers usually develop at or near junctures of leaves and stems. Stems are clambering and need tying to supports or interlacing. Plants may be evergreen or deciduous in cooler parts of hardiness zone. Berries are edible in certain kinds, poisonous in others. Juice in wilted leaves is deadly poison in all kinds.	*S. jasminoides* (jasmine nightshade, or potato vine)	□□□D *	Leaves sometimes deciduous. Branching clusters of white starlike flowers, with faint blue markings, open in late summer and early fall. Climber is attractive and fast growing.
	S. rantonnetii (Paraguay nightshade, or blue potato bush)	□□□D	Vine is usually deciduous. Deep lavender blossoms appear in midsummer and are long lasting. Drooping fruits are vivid red.
	S. wendlandii (Costa Rican nightshade, or giant potato creeper)	□□□D *	Compound, deciduous leaves have glossy sheen. Blue or pale purple flowers appear in branched, hanging clusters; each flower is 2½ in. wide.
Trumpet vine, orange (*Pyrostegia,* or *Bignonia*) Woody vine has compound leaves and clusters of tubular flowers. Narrow seedpods are up to 1 ft. long. Rapid grower climbs with tendrils.	*P. ignea,* or *P. venusta*	□□□D *	Leaves consist of ovalish leaflets that are up to 1 in. long. Bright reddish-orange 3-in. blossoms open for 2-3 wk. during midwinter; vine flowers again in midsummer but not as abundantly.
Trumpet vine, violet (*Clytostoma,* or *Bignonia*) Compound leaves, with 2 leaflets, have tendrils at ends of main stalks. Bell-shaped blossoms form in pairs. Fruits have prickly coats.	*C. callistegioides,* or *B. callistegioides,* or *B. speciosa,* or *B. violacea*	□□□D	Glossy oblong leaves are 2½-3 in. long. Pale purple flowers form at terminals and open in mid to late spring.

*Not hardy below 30° F

Hedges

Hedges are an essential part of most gardens. They can be clipped and formal, or they can be loosely informal, with arching branches clothed with flowers in season.

Hedges are used to provide privacy, to screen one part of the garden from another, to serve as backgrounds for flower borders and other plantings, and as windbreaks.

Evergreens can be ideal as hedging plants because they stay dense and green all winter long. Among the best are yews, hollies, and boxwoods, all of which grow densely and need clipping only once a year. Where climate permits, fast-growing evergreen privets are also used; but to keep them tidy and to promote bushy growth, they must be clipped two or even three times a year.

Hedges of conifers, most of which are evergreen, are often dark green and rather somber, but there are lighter-colored conifers, such as the Leyland cypress (probably the fastest growing), which forms new shoots 2½–3 feet long each year. This, like the hemlock (a longtime favorite for hedges), can be clipped without fear of shoots dying back. To create a thick, interwoven shield of branches, plant young conifers at intervals of about 2 feet.

Where the hedge is not employed as a boundary, informal flowering or berrying shrubs, such as *Fuchsia magellanica,* the lilac, rose of Sharon (*Hibiscus syriacus*), buckthorn, and hawthorn, can be allowed to develop their individual characteristics more than clipped formal hedges can.

Several kinds of barberries, the commonest of which is the deciduous Japanese barberry (*Berberis thunbergii* and its numerous varieties), also make good informal hedges. They have yellow or orange flowers and attractive, usually red berries.

Trees are often grown as giant hedges to create windbreaks. They are more effective in protecting a garden from wind than a fence or wall because they allow the air to filter through, slowing it down gradually. A wall stops the wind completely but produces strong downdrafts. In coastal areas Austrian pines that are planted a few yards apart make ideal windbreaks, since they are resistant to salt spray. Hedges of linden trees afford good shelter for inland gardens.

On the following pages are illustrated listings of the deciduous and evergreen plants most frequently used for hedges. Included with each is information about height, location, and hardiness. The height indicates the sizes to which they are usually trimmed. Most of them will grow taller if allowed to.

Location indicates whether the plant takes sun or shade. Those with flowers will, of course, be more floriferous in full sun.

To find out whether a plant can reasonably be expected to survive the lowest average temperatures in your area, check the zone designations under Hardiness and refer to the temperature zone map on page 9.

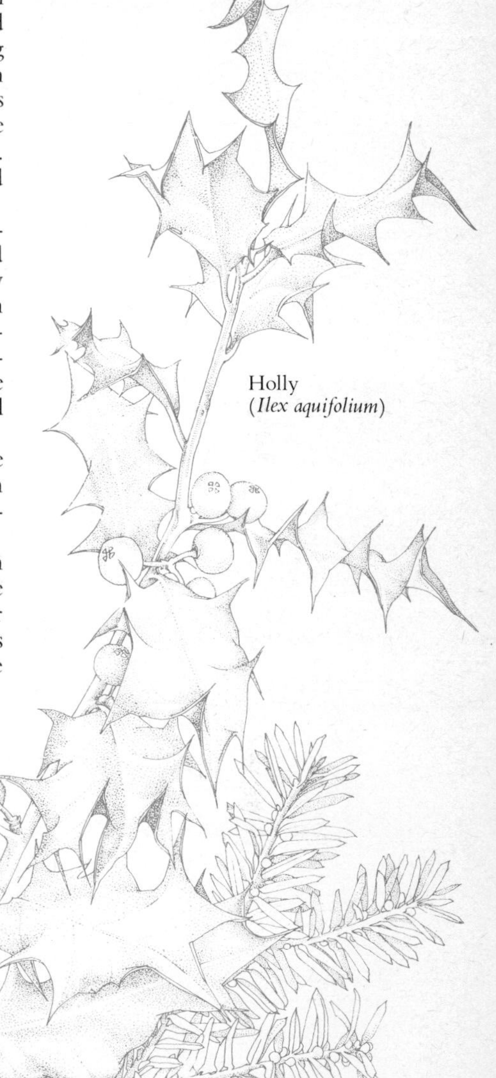

Holly (*Ilex aquifolium*)

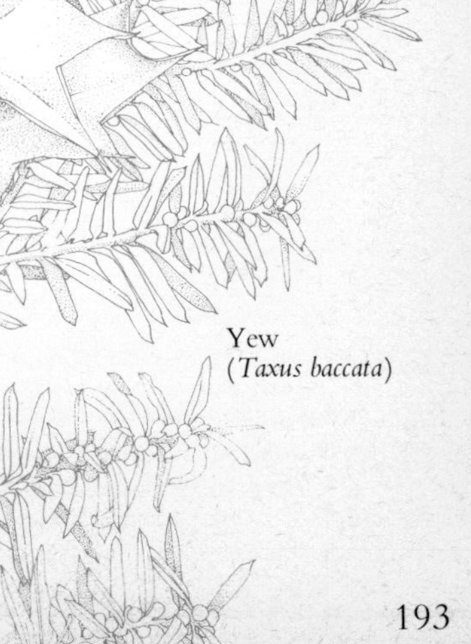

Forsythia intermedia

Yew (*Taxus baccata*)

Deciduous Hedge Plants

Barberry

Brilliant red berries often cling to *Berberis thunbergii* all winter. An outstanding selection for problem spots, it thrives where other plants fail. In fall its leaves turn to shades of orange-red. *B. t. atropurpurea* has reddish foliage throughout the growing season.
Height: 2–4 ft.
Location: sun or shade.
Hardiness: Zone B.

Beech

Fagus sylvatica, the European beech, and its copper and purple varieties are useful as windbreaks. They retain their red-brown autumn leaves throughout winter and early spring. Beeches grow well in all but wet, heavy soils. Branches are a handsome gray.
Height: 6–15 ft. or more.
Location: sun or partial shade.
Hardiness: Zone B.

Buckthorn

Rhamnus frangula 'Tallhedge' combines shiny, deep green leaves with a natural columnar habit for a handsome effect. Small fruits begin to appear while summer blooms are still on the plants. Fruits that the birds do not eat last well into fall.
Height: 3–15 ft.
Location: sun or partial shade.
Hardiness: Zone A.

Buckthorn, sea

Hippophae rhamnoides bears narrow leaves with grayish-green upper surfaces and silvery-green undersides. Orange berries appear in autumn if both male and female plants are grown together. It makes a good seaside hedge, as it tolerates salt spray.
Height: 3–15 ft.
Location: sun or partial shade.
Hardiness: Zone A.

Elaeagnus

E. angustifolia, the Russian olive, has straplike leaves up to 5 in. long, which are silvery beneath. The small flowers in early summer have a fragrance similar to gardenias, and are succeeded by yellow and silvery fruits that are relished by birds. Plants withstand dry climates, sandy soils, and salt-laden ocean breezes.
Height: 3–15 ft.
Location: sun or partial shade.
Hardiness: Zone A.

Forsythia

F. intermedia has the largest flowers of the forsythias. In early or mid spring it is a mass of yellow blooms. Like almost all other forsythia species, it can easily be trained to form a dense hedge. Excellent varieties include 'Lynwood,' 'Spring Glory,' and 'Karl Sax.'
Height: 3–8 ft.
Location: sun or shade.
Hardiness: varies with kind.

Fuchsia

Hedges of *F. magellanica riccartonii* are common where winters are mild. The bright red blooms are delightful in summer. *F. magellanica* flourishes near the sea. Its generally solitary purple and red flowers open in early summer.
Height: 2–6 ft.
Location: sun or partial shade.
Hardiness: Zone C.

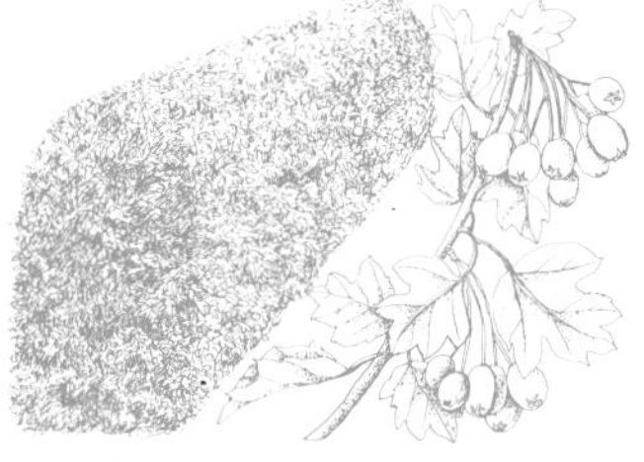

Hawthorn

Crataegus monogyna, the English hawthorn, is a good hedge plant, as its heavy branching habit and thorns make a nearly impregnable barrier. White blooms are followed by red berries. The foliage remains on the shrub until late fall.
Height: 3–5 ft. or more.
Location: sun or partial shade.
Hardiness: Zone B.

Hornbeam

Carpinus betulus, the European hornbeam, is a small, robust tree with leaves up to 5 in. long. Catkins appear in mid and late spring and are followed by pendulous clusters of winged nutlets (but not if the hedge is clipped).
Height: 3–5 ft. or more.
Location: sun or partial shade.
Hardiness: Zone B.

Mock orange

Many species and varieties of *Philadelphus* are suitable for hedging. All have fragrant white blossoms in midsummer. *P. coronarius* offers flowers up to $1\frac{1}{2}$ in. across. *P. lemoinei* is a hybrid with an upright habit of growth.
Height: *P. coronarius,* 6–8 ft. *P. lemoinei,* 4–6 ft.
Location: sun.
Hardiness: varies with kind.

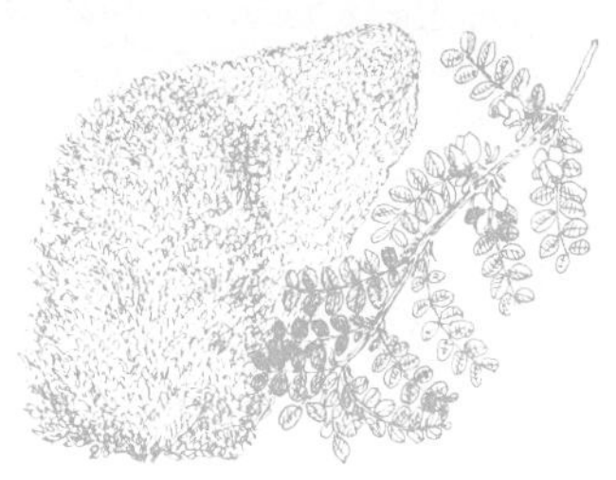

Pea tree, Siberian

Bright yellow, pealike blossoms appear on *Caragana arborescens* in late spring. A vigorous shrub with leaves up to 3 in. long, it makes a fine windbreak that requires little maintenance. In fall 2-in. pods develop.
Height: 4–15 ft.
Location: sun.
Hardiness: Zone A.

Plum, flowering

Prunus cerasifera, the cherry, or myrobalan, plum, which has dark green leaves, makes a very colorful hedge if interplanted with *P. c. atropurpurea,* the purple-leaved plum. Both types have clusters of small white flowers in early spring, which are sometimes followed by striking red or yellow "cherry plums."
Height: 6–15 ft.
Location: sun.
Hardiness: Zone A.

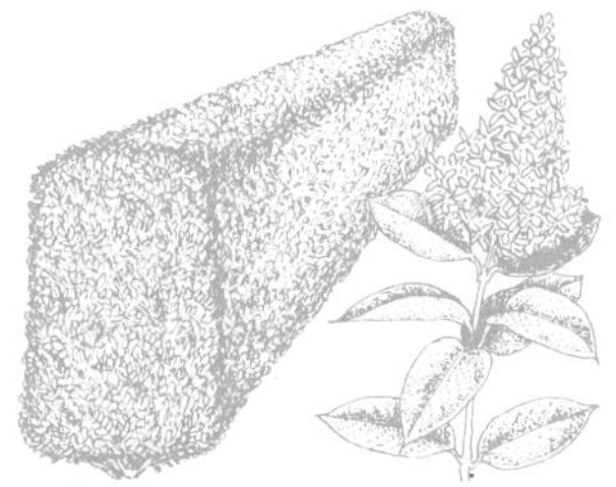

Privet

Many species of *Ligustrum* make excellent hedges. All are rapid growers with glossy leaves. *L. amurense* withstands severe cold. *L. obtusifolium* bears black berries in fall. *L. ovalifolium,* or *L. californicum,* is a semievergreen. *L. vulgare* grows in almost any soil; its black fruits develop in heavy clusters.
Height: 2–12 ft.
Location: sun.
Hardiness: varies with kind.

Quince, flowering

Chaenomeles japonica, or *Cydonia japonica,* is an outstanding dwarf with red blooms that open in late spring before the leaves unfold. *C. speciosa,* or *C. lagenaria,* has bright red flowers in early to mid spring. Varieties are available with white or pink blossoms.
Height: *C. japonica,* 3 ft. *C. lagenaria,* 6 ft.
Location: sun or shade.
Hardiness: Zone B.

Rose

Rosa in any shrub form can be used as a hedge. Outstanding species include *R. hugonis,* with vivid yellow blooms, and *R. multiflora,* which produces many white flowers in early summer and bright red fruits in fall. *R. rugosa* is an excellent seacoast plant. Its flowers are white or red. Floribundas also make good hedges.
Height: 3–6 ft.
Location: sun.
Hardiness: varies with kind.

Willow

Salix purpurea nana has attractive, soft, gray to blue-green leaves, borne on slender branches. This is not an effective barrier plant but has considerable value wherever soil is heavy and wet.
Height: 2–3 ft.
Location: sun.
Hardiness: Zone B.

Evergreen Plants for Hedges

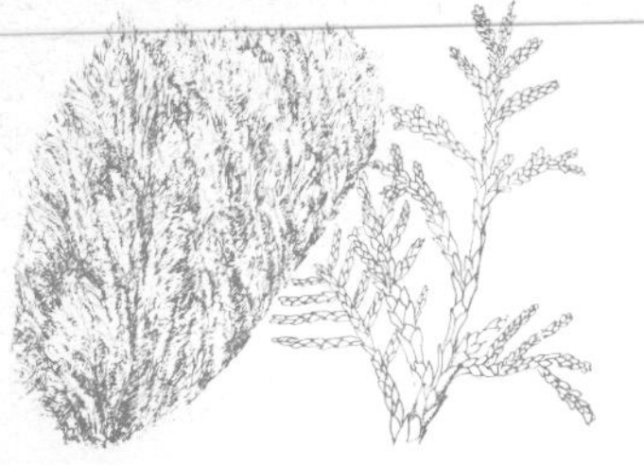

Arborvitae, giant, or western red cedar

Thuja plicata, or *T. lobbii,* is a fast grower with handsome deep green leaves. In its northernmost range its leaves turn bronze from fall through winter. This tree needs moist soil and considerable humidity.
Height: 6–15 ft. or more.
Location: sun.
Hardiness: Zone B.

Barberry

Berberis stenophylla has arching branches with clusters of golden flowers in spring. In fall purplish-black berries appear. Its leaves are up to 1 in. long. This plant stands up well to shearing. One of the hardiest, *B. julianae,* has spiny 3-in. leaves.
Height: 3–6 ft.
Location: sun or partial shade.
Hardiness: Zone B.

Boxwood

Most boxwoods can be used as hedges. *Buxus sempervirens* has dark green leaves up to $1\frac{1}{4}$ in. long. This plant assumes a treelike habit of growth if it is not clipped. It is a fine choice for privacy screens.
Height: 1–2 ft. or more.
Location: sun or partial shade.
Hardiness: varies with kind.

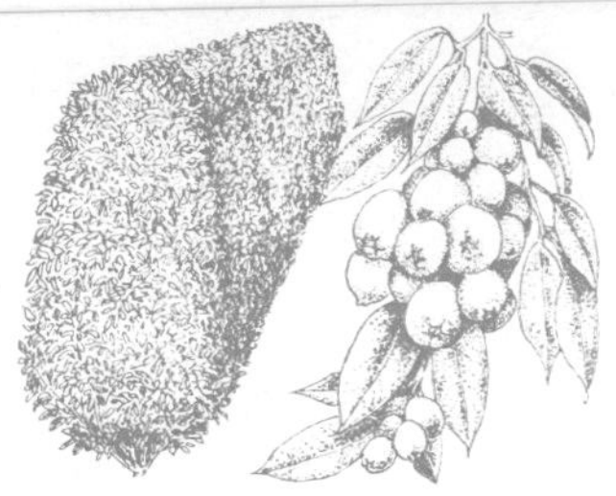

Bush Cherry

Syzygium paniculatum, or *Eugenia paniculata,* has white flowers in small, $\frac{1}{2}$-in. clusters. The new leaves have an attractive reddish hue. The fruit, a rose-purple color, is sometimes used for making jelly. This is a useful plant in California and Florida but does not do well in salt spray.
Height: 3–15 ft. or more.
Location: sun.
Hardiness: Zone D. Not hardy below 30° F.

Camellia

Almost any ca… es can be … a is avail- … ith large … nk, red, … ppearing … raplike, … n. long.

Cotoneaster

C. lactea has gracefully arching branches with twigs that bear whitish hairs. Specimens of this shrub form a dark-green-leaved hedge of imposing character. White flowers develop in late spring, and clusters of red berries last from fall into winter.
Height: 6–12 ft.
Location: sun or partial shade.
Hardiness: Zone C.

Cypress, false

Any upright form of this genus makes a suitable hedge. *Chamaecyparis lawsoniana* has soft leaves and grows compactly. It needs a great amount of moisture. *C. thyoides* has light green, scalelike leaves and reddish-brown bark. This is a good plant for wet-soil areas.
Height: 4–15 ft. or more.
Location: sun.
Hardiness: varies with kind.

Cypress, Leyland

Cupressocyparis leylandii, the Leyland cypress, is an extremely vigorous conifer, ideal for tall hedges. A hybrid, it grows very fast and has a distinct columnar habit. Its leaves are small and scalelike. This is a good selection where rapid screening is desired.
Height: 3–15 ft. or more.
Location: sun or partial shade.
Hardiness: Zone B.

Escallonia

E. rubra is identified by its reddish twigs that are up to 2 in. long. The leaves are lance shaped and have sticky surfaces. In midsummer small red blossoms form in loose, hanging clusters. Several of its varieties also make excellent hedges.
Height: 3–12 ft.
Location: sun.
Hardiness: Zone C.

Euonymus

E. japonicus has glossy green leaves, handsomely variegated in many varieties, yellow flowers in spring so small as to be insignificant, and pink berries in fall. It grows in any soil with good drainage and tolerates shearing very well.
Height: 2–12 ft.
Location: sun or partial shade.
Hardiness: Zone C.

Fire thorn

Noted for its fruit clusters that appear in fall in vivid colors, *Pyracantha* is available in several fine species, all of which have thorns and small white blossoms. *P. coccinea lalandii* has ovalish leaves up to $1\frac{1}{2}$ in. long. The leaves of *P. crenulata* are often 3 in. long. Both species bear orange-red berries.
Height: 3–12 ft.
Location: sun.
Hardiness: varies with kind.

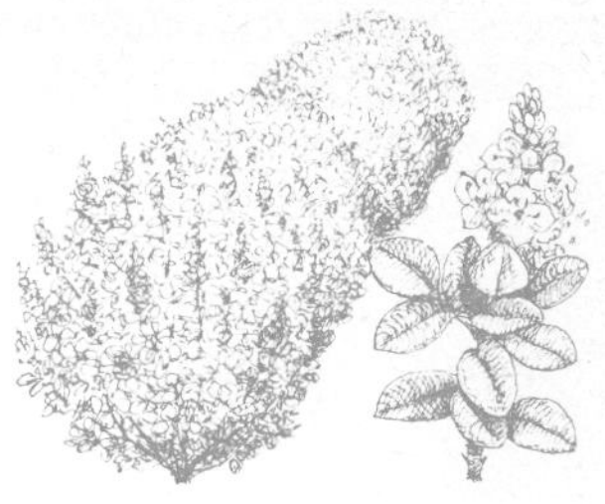

Hebe

The overlapping 1-in. leaves of *H. buxifolia,* or *Veronica buxifolia,* produce an interesting overall texture. In midsummer white flowers open in 1-in. spikes. This is a popular plant in West Coast gardens. It does well in sandy soil and grows best with infrequent watering and feeding.
Height: 2–4 ft.
Location: sun.
Hardiness: Zone C.

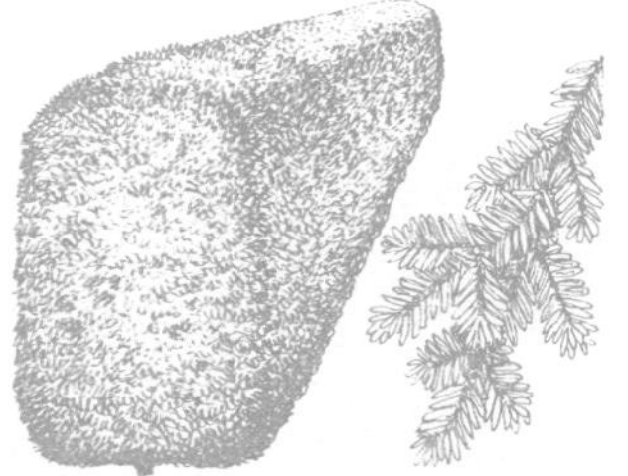

Hemlock

The upper surfaces of the needles on *Tsuga canadensis* are green, and the undersides are light gray. This conifer is a forest tree with an upright habit of growth. It requires moderate moisture and shelter from high winds. It will not thrive in heat or city conditions. Other upright-growing hemlock species also make good hedges.
Height: 6–15 ft. or more.
Location: sun or partial shade.
Hardiness: varies with kind.

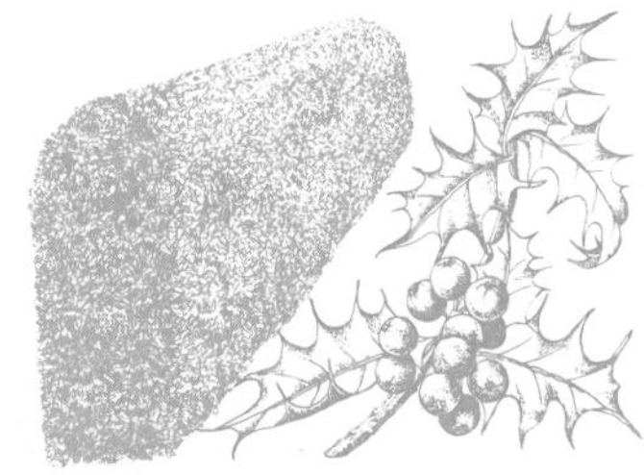

Holly

The foliage of *Ilex aquifolium,* the English holly, has long been a favorite Christmas decoration. The glossy, dark evergreen leaves and thick growth of this species make it an attractive hedge. The vivid red fruit clings to the plants well into winter. *I. opaca,* the American holly, has dull upper-leaf surfaces and yellow-green undersides. Its fruit is also red.
Height: 4–15 ft. or more.
Location: sun or partial shade.
Hardiness: varies with kind.

Honeysuckle

Lonicera nitida, the shrubby honeysuckle, is grown mainly for its small foliage, which forms a dense barrier. Although fragrant whitish or yellowish-green flowers open in mid and late spring, they are sparse and relatively inconspicuous. This species resists salt spray in shore gardens.
Height: 2–4 ft.
Location: sun or partial shade.
Hardiness: Zone C.

Mahonia

M. aquifolia, also known as Oregon grape, is noted for its erect clusters of deep yellow blossoms that open in late winter or early spring. They are followed by edible blue-black fruits. The hollylike leaves are glossy green. All tall *Mahonia* species can be used as hedges.
Height: 2–3 ft.
Location: partial shade.
Hardiness: varies with kind.

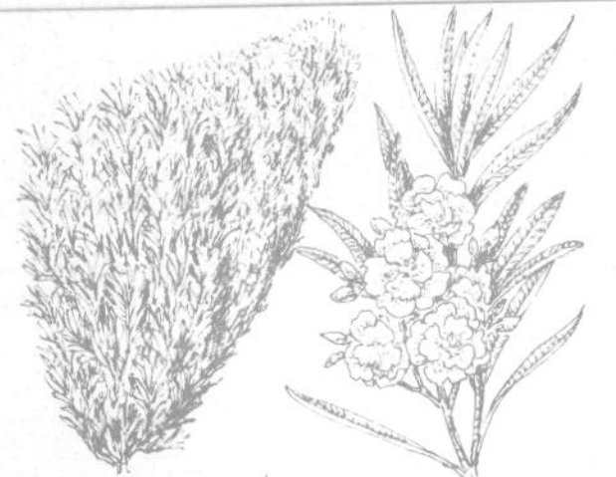

Oleander

Nerium oleander has large white, yellow, pink, red, or purple flowers from midspring through late summer. Bamboolike leaves are up to 8 in. long. It needs little care and does well in dry, hot southern areas. It also withstands salt spray, wind, and smog. All parts are poisonous.
Height: 3–12 ft.
Location: sun.
Hardiness: All warmer parts of Zone C; also Zone D. Not hardy below 30° F.

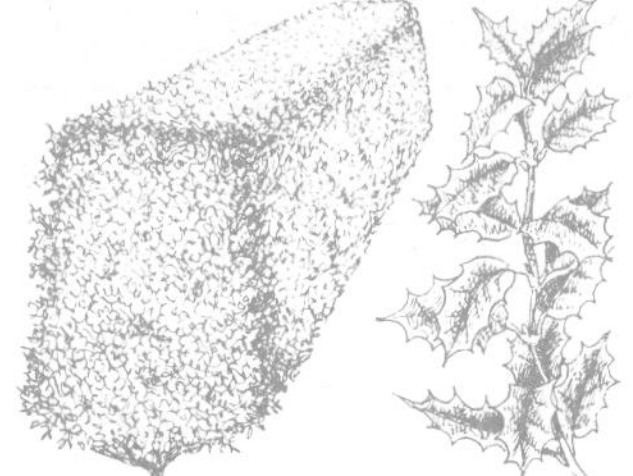

Osmanthus

Most species of osmanthus make suitable hedges. *O. heterophyllus ilicifolius* offers aromatic, greenish-white flowers throughout the summer. Blue-black berries develop in early fall. Glossy oblong to oval leaves grow to 2 in. or more. This plant stands shearing well.
Height: 3–15 ft.
Location: sun or partial shade.
Hardiness: varies with kind.

Pittosporum, Japanese

P. tobira has striking deep green leaves that may grow up to 4 in. long. Creamy-white flower clusters open in late spring. Although inconspicuous, they are intensely fragrant. Ideal for West Coast and southern gardens, this is an especially useful shrub in seashore settings.
Height: 3–12 ft.
Location: sun or partial shade.
Hardiness: Zone C.

Plum, Natal

Carissa grandiflora has forked spines and oval leaves that are up to 2½ in. long. Its aromatic, 2-in. waxy white flowers open in late spring or early summer. Edible, 2-in. red fruits are egg shaped. This is a good choice for coastal gardens in southern Florida or California.
Height: 3–12 ft.
Location: sun.
Hardiness: Zone D. Not hardy below 30° F.

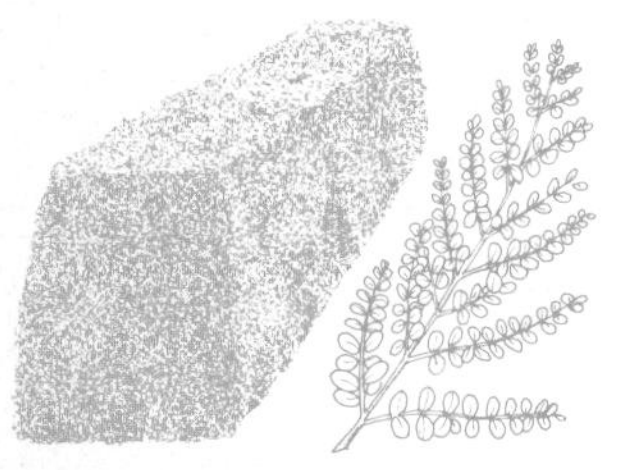

Privet

Ligustrum japonicum has shiny, deep green leaves that grow up to 4 in. long. Unless plants are clipped, 4- to 6-in. blossom clusters develop from midsummer to early fall. *L. lucidum* has longer leaves than *L. japonicum,* and its flower clusters grow to almost 10 in. long.
Height: 3–15 ft.
Location: sun or partial shade.
Hardiness: Zone C.

Prunus

The Portugal laurel (*Prunus lusitanica*) and the cherry laurel (*P. laurocerasus*) are fine hedging plants that grow into small- or medium-sized trees if allowed to develop naturally. The leaves are shiny, toothed, and up to 5 in. long. Fragrant white flowers are followed by purplish fruits.
Height: 4–15 ft.
Location: sun.
Hardiness: Zone C.

Santolina

Lavender cotton (*S. chaemaecyparissus*) is a handsome dwarf shrub with silvery, dissected, fernlike leaves. In midsummer bright lemon-yellow, rounded flowers help make it a delightful hedge. This is a useful plant that requires no shearing. In its northernmost range it should be given a heavy winter mulch.
Height: 1–2 ft.
Location: sun.
Hardiness: Zone C.

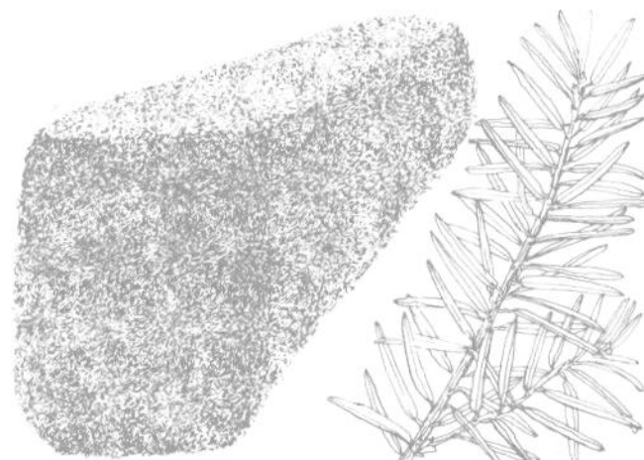

Yew

All species of yew that attain sufficient height can be used as hedges. *Taxus baccata,* the English yew, is a slow-growing, broad-shaped conifer with dark green foliage and brownish-green fruit. The red berries on *T. cuspidata* produce an attractive contrast to the dark green leaves. *T. media,* a fine hybrid, combines good looks with extreme hardiness.
Height: 2–15 ft.
Location: sun or shade.
Hardiness: varies with kind.

How to Grow a Successful Hedge

Hedges can be planted either as a single row or as a double, staggered row. The double row will make a stronger, denser hedge.

Deciduous hedges can be planted any time in fall, late winter, or spring when the ground is not frozen. In mild regions hedges can be planted throughout the winter as well. But it is best to plant evergreens in early fall or in spring.

If bare-root plants are delivered before you are ready to plant them, set them in a shallow trench, and cover their roots with soil.

To plant, dig a trench about 2 feet wide and 1 foot deep along the length of the proposed hedge. The trench, of course, should be larger if the size of the root balls requires it.

Fork peat moss or compost into the bottom of the trench. Put in about a wheelbarrowful for every 6 feet. When replacing the topsoil, mix in some compost, peat moss, or other suitable organic material to lighten the texture of the soil. Also mix in superphosphate—2–3 ounces (2–3 rounded tablespoons) for every 6 feet of trench.

Use a length of cord to define the location of the row or rows.

For a double row of hedging shrubs, establish the rows 18 inches apart, and stagger the plants so that no two are growing directly opposite each other.

Dig the holes big enough to give the roots plenty of space when spread out or to receive the soil ball around the roots. If you are up to it, double digging is especially useful (see p. 597). Set each shrub so that the nursery soil-mark on the stem (where the light- and dark-colored barks meet) is at ground level. Carefully work the soil into the spaces between the roots of bare-root specimens, and gently shake the stem up and down to get rid of air pockets. Fill in the rest of the hole.

Finally, firm the soil by treading lightly. Then water thoroughly to settle soil about the roots.

To prevent the wind from loosening the newly set plant, firmly fix posts at the end of each row. Run a wire tightly between the posts, and tie each plant to the wire. Alternatively, individual stakes can be used to support each plant, but drive them into the ground before planting to avoid root damage.

Newly planted hedges require a few weeks to recover from transplanting. In exposed locations recently planted evergreens may be scorched by the wind. To prevent this, use a screen of burlap netting or brushwood.

To prevent excessive water loss through the leaves of evergreens after planting, spray the foliage with an antidesiccant.

If the weather is dry during the first several months after planting, water the newly established hedge thoroughly at least once a week.

Pruning a new hedge. For informal hedges it is usually enough to clip back the newly set out plants by one-third after planting.

Formal hedges require a dense base and thick, uniform growth. To encourage this, shorten the plants, except most conifers, by one-third to one-half their height after planting.

Continue cutting back by one-half or one-third of the new growth every year until the required height is reached. Maintain it at this level by shearing back the new growth almost to its base every year.

Use a line between two stakes to mark the height, and cut to this level. Taper the sides of the hedge toward the top to encourage a thick base.

Formal hedges that grow moderately to rapidly should be pruned two or three times a year, in spring and summer. Informal hedges that bloom on the previous season's shoots should be pruned after flowering; those that bloom on the current season's shoots should be pruned in spring.

Use hedge shears to clip small-leaved shrubs, such as privet, box, or shrubby honeysuckle. Pruning shears are better for cutting back long-leaved shrubs to prevent the leaves from being cut in half.

Power trimmers work well on young, short green shoots, but they may lacerate woody branches if they are not powerful enough for the job.

Fertilize established hedges in spring, top-dressing the roots with any complete garden fertilizer. Repeat in early summer, watering after the application of fertilizer if the soil is dry; then mulch. Mulching hedges helps to keep the soil evenly moist.

PLANTING AND TRAINING A NEW HEDGE

1. *Dig a 2-ft.-wide trench; put peat moss at bottom; refill with soil.*

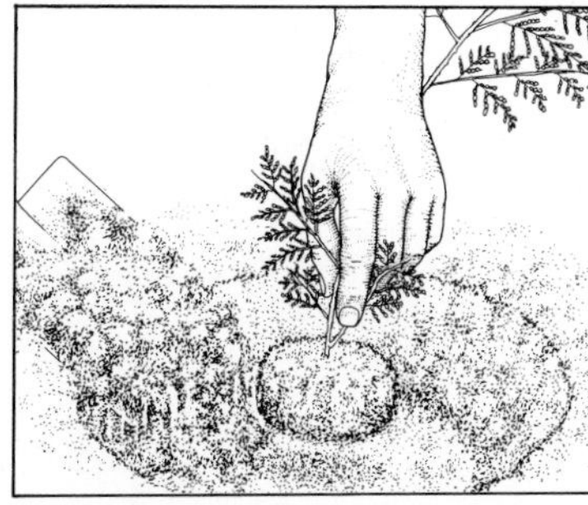

2. *Dig individual holes at the proper spacing, and set the plants in place.*

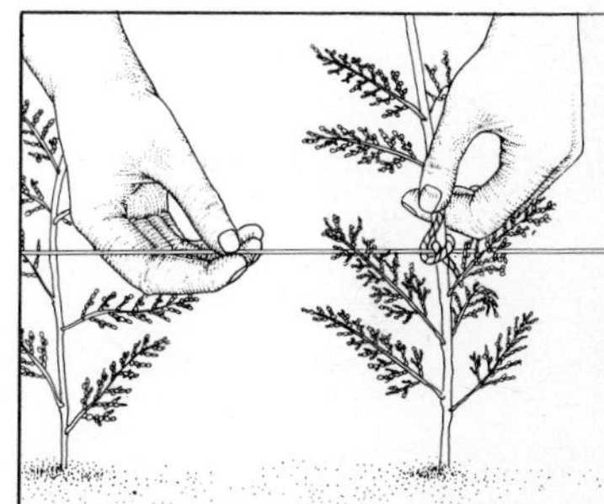

3. *Prevent wind damage to plants by tying them to a horizontal wire.*

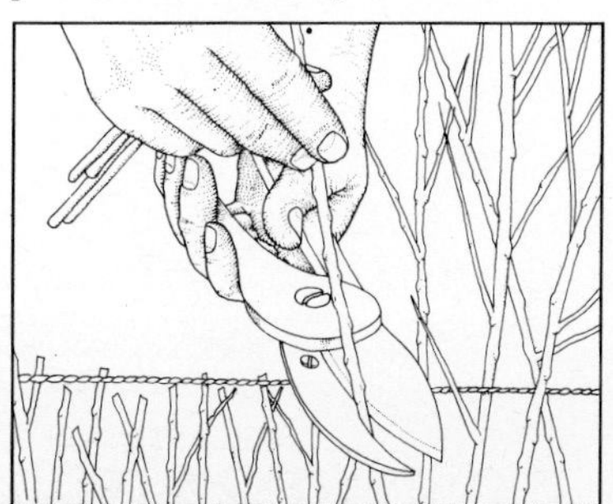

4. *For a formal hedge shorten newly planted shrubs by half after planting.*

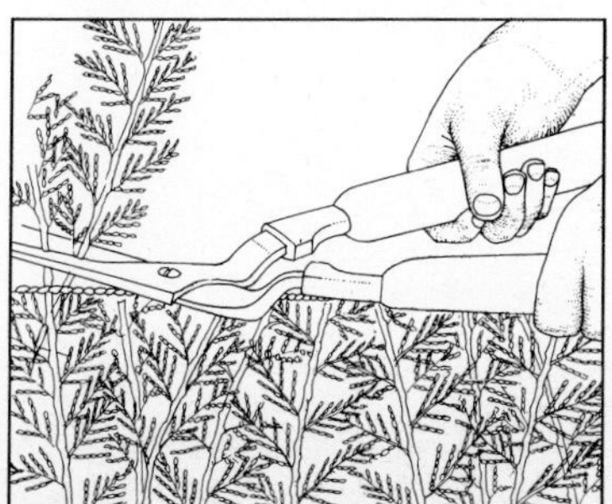

5. *Cut new growth by half annually until the hedge is required height.*

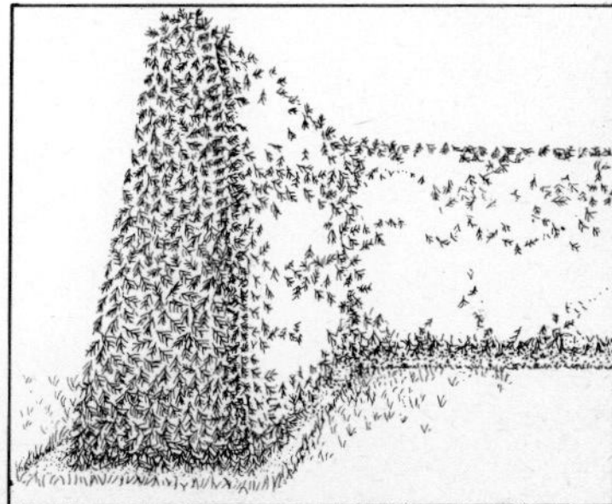

6. *Trim the mature hedge so that it tapers from the base toward the top.*

Bonsai

Bonsai (pronounced "bone-sigh"), an ancient Oriental art form, has become part of Western culture. It combines creative impulse with sound horticultural practice.

There is a mystique surrounding the art of bonsai. Encouraged if not actually engendered by tales of small specimens several centuries in the making, ritualistically tended to by generation after generation of meticulous Oriental root pruners, this mystique tends to frighten people away. And, in fact, in the Imperial Garden of Japan, there are several living bonsai that are reputed to be more than 500 years old. But to be deterred from the art by these masterpieces is like not taking up a paintbrush because the "Mona Lisa" hangs in the Louvre.

The essential fact about bonsai is that it *is* an art form, one in which the raw material and the finished product are alive and growing. Like any art, bonsai can require considerable time and energy if the gardener aims for perfection; yet it can offer deep satisfaction to the enthusiastic weekend amateur as well.

The art is practiced by training young trees to acquire and display the characteristics of maturity while remaining small. A finished bonsai is not a miniature replica of a full-size tree but a sort of line sketch meant to bring an image to mind. It is less important what a bonsai plant *is* than what it suggests. The viewer's response is the measure of success.

A five-needled white pine can be trained to convey the image of a gnarled Monterey cypress enduring high on a windswept ocean-side cliff. From the line of the branches and the twist of the trunk, you can sense the force of a stiff salt wind. Or a zelkova might express the upright form of an American elm, straight and serene, fully at peace with its environment. In either case, an emotion is evoked. Therein lies the art.

To create an evocative image requires a knowledge that is not necessary in caring for ordinary potted plants. You need an appreciation of how a maturing tree is shaped by its environment as well as an understanding of the principles of growth by which bonsai is similarly formed.

Youth and maturity. It matters less how old a bonsai is than how old it *seems* to be. One young tree looks very much like another. The main stem grows straight and slender; the branches are evenly balanced and clothed in foliage as they reach for the light; the roots probe deep underground for nourishment.

As a tree matures, its main stem thickens into a trunk, tapering toward the top. The center of the tree becomes a skeletal framework, supporting twiggy growth and thick foliage at the top and around the outside edges. Lower branches of the tree, shaded by this dense top growth, either die back or must reach for the light, growing heavy as they do so and therefore drooping down. Roots increase in girth, and the soil around them erodes.

Each kind of tree experiences this growth process in its own way, responding to temperature, growing conditions, and the force of the elements. All trees specialize in surviving under the conditions in which they have evolved—that is what evolution means. The bald cypress (*Taxodium distichum*) develops a massive trunk and great knobby roots that rise above the water of its native southern swamps. The lower branches of the redwood (*Sequoia sempervirens*) die back as its huge trunk thrusts the foliage high above the surrounding vegetation and stands firm against the wind. The bristlecone pine (*Pinus aristata*) squats gnarled and thick as a gnome to survive the brutal winter blasts at timberline in the Rockies. Thus time reveals the specific character and life history of each tree.

Principles of form. The idea of bonsai originated in ancient China (the word comes from two Chinese characters that mean, roughly, "to plant in a tray") and was adopted by the Japanese sometime during the 11th or 12th century. By the early 1500's the practice had been refined into a precise art form with well-defined standards.

A bonsai always has a front and a back side. From the front the line of the trunk should be clearly visible nearly to the top of the tree.

The triangle (heaven, man, and earth) is basic to bonsai composition: one branch to the right, one to the left, a third between or just above them to the rear. Prune to avoid both parallel branches and opposite branches.

In upright trees the top should lean slightly forward.

There should be no signs of human handiwork. Pruning scars that do not heal over and cannot be covered by foliage should be carved to suggest natural injury.

A bonsai five-needled pine about 8 in. high and 350 years old. The trunk bends in four directions, expressing endurance in the face of hardship. It continues to grow and develop, yet remains small through the techniques of this rewarding ancient art.

Japanese Classifications and Styles of Bonsai

In the centuries that bonsai has been practiced in Japan, a complex classification system has developed.

The first categories are by size. The large size (*dai bonsai*) measures 26–40 inches from the base of the trunk to the top of the tree. The medium size (*chiu bonsai*), the most popular in Japan, is 12–26 inches. The small size (*ko bonsai*), generally the easiest to handle and the commonest in the United States, is 7–12 inches tall. Those less than 7 inches tall are known as *mame bonsai,* the most difficult to maintain.

Next come the five basic styles of training: formal upright, informal upright, leaning, cascade, and semi-cascade (illustrated at right).

Beyond this, bonsai trees are divided into such categories as trees with one trunk (*tankan*), two trunks (*sokan*), or multiple trunks (*kabudachi*); a clump of trees from one root (*ikada buki*) or from separate roots (*yama yori*); trees with twisted trunks (*nejikan*); windswept trees (*fuki na gashi*); trees clinging to rocks (*ishi tsuki*); trees whose roots grow over rocks into the soil below (*seki joju*); or octopus-style trees (*tako zukuri*).

Further classifications often refer to seasonal qualities: the color or fragrance of spring flowers, autumn fruit or colored foliage, attractive or unusual bark in the winter, or large or small leaves in summer.

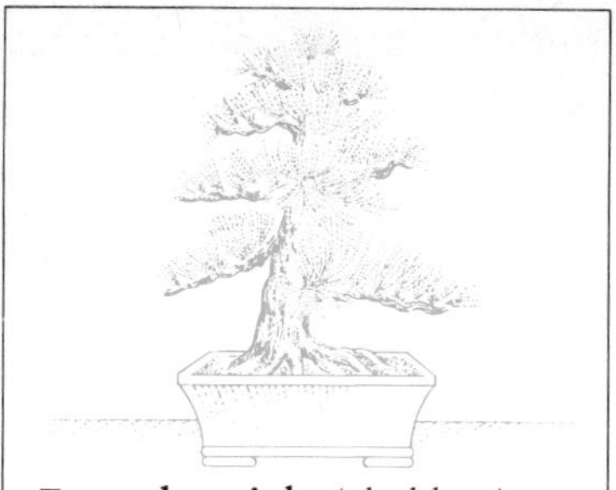
Formal upright (chokkan). *Trunk is straight, top erect.*

Informal upright (moyo gi). *Trunk is curved, top slightly bent.*

Leaning (shakan). *Trunk leans one way, lowest branch the other.*

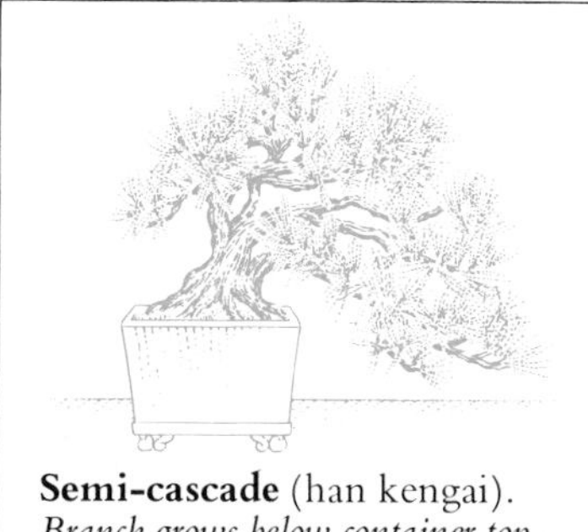
Semi-cascade (han kengai). *Branch grows below container top.*

Cascade (kengai). *Trunk curves to 1 ft. or more below the container.*

Buying and Caring for a Finished Bonsai

To call a bonsai finished is misleading. Its training may be completed, but a bonsai—unlike a painting or sculpture—is never truly finished. It will continue to grow and evolve.

To buy a bonsai is to become a collaborator with the artist who created it. You can pay thousands of dollars for a bonsai masterpiece, but unless you too have mastered the art, it is unwise to do so. Fortunately, plants of good quality can be bought for modest prices. To care for one is a way to develop basic skills.

Location. A bonsai is not a house plant. It needs fresh air, sunshine, and a seasonal growth cycle. Pick a plant that is adapted to your climate. Place it where it will get good air circulation and light from all sides. It can be brought indoors for display for a week or two at a time; but when you take it back outside, the change must be made gradually, over a period of days. In climates where the roots might freeze, place the bonsai in a deep cold frame for the winter.

Water and food. A bonsai must never be allowed to dry out. Using a mister or a syringe, water daily in spring and summer, and whenever needed the rest of the year. During hot, dry weather, spray the branches and foliage even oftener.

Feeding is important, but use restraint. As a rule of thumb, dilute liquid plant food to one-quarter the recommended strength; apply four or five times each growing season.

Pruning. As a living thing, a bonsai cannot remain static; it must be allowed to grow. Pruning for size, therefore, is a matter either of encouraging new growth and then cutting it back or, as with most conifers, of controlling the new growth.

Regular Root Pruning to Maintain Health

Root pruning and soil replacement keep a bonsai healthy. Both should be done yearly with fruiting and flowering trees and all *mame bonsai,* every two to three years with most deciduous species, and every three to five years with evergreens.

Remove and save any moss or soil covering. Then turn the container upside down, holding one hand on the soil, and tap the bottom of the container to free the root mass. Loosen the soil around the roots so that they hang down freely. Prune away about one-third of the roots around the edges and about half on the bottom, cutting parallel with the bottom of the container. Repot in fresh soil (see p. 203).

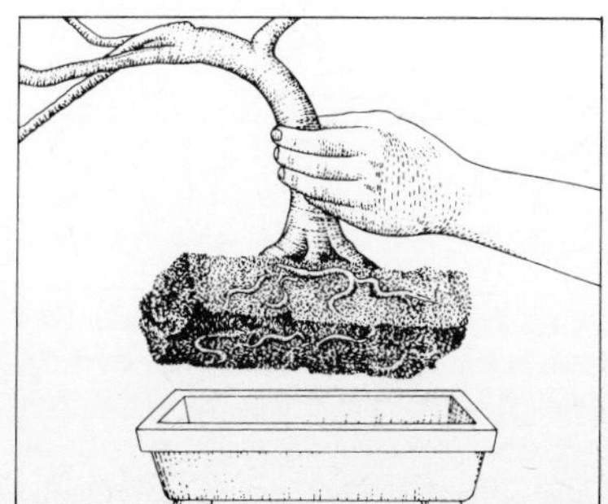
Lift out the entire root mass.

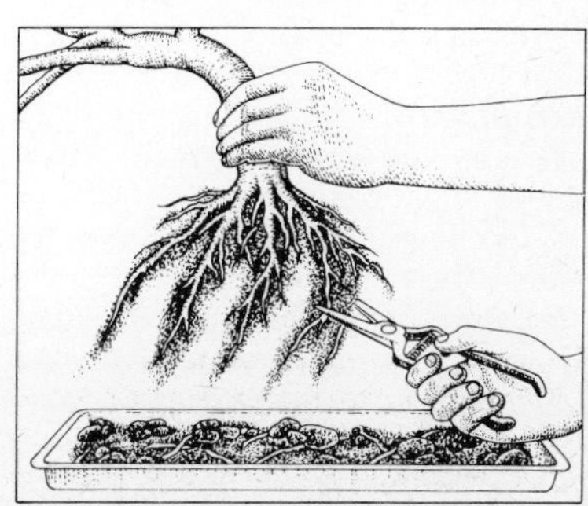
Loosen soil; trim roots straight across.

Creating Your Own Bonsai

A bonsai can be created from any woody or semi-woody plant, though some—pines, spruces, junipers, maples, hornbeams, flowering quinces, azaleas, and hollies—are grown more often than others.

There are several ways to obtain plant material for creating bonsai. Plants can be propagated from seeds, cuttings, or layers; they can be collected from the wild, or they can be purchased from a nursery in various stages of growth. Each method has advantages; and each presents some challenges:

Propagating. The only way to obtain an uncommon species may be by propagation. It is certainly the best way to produce *mame bonsai.* It can, however, be a lengthy and often difficult process. Follow the instructions for propagating woody plants (see pp. 87–94). Begin bonsai training just as soon as the roots have become established.

Collecting. Naturally dwarfed plants provide the best start for an eloquent form. Collecting them can become an engrossing hobby in itself. But such plants tend to transplant poorly and must be coddled for a year or two before training can begin—if, indeed, they survive at all.

Buying. Nursery stock is probably the best source of material for a beginner. You can buy a plant with roots already somewhat conditioned to a reduced environment and with branches already formed but still supple enough for shaping. Do not overlook the nursery's trash pile, where good bonsai candidates may have been consigned because of their asymmetrical growth—called "deformity" by the nurseryman, "character" by the bonsai hunter.

In choosing a plant, first look for one with small leaves. Then appraise the trunk for its tapering and potentially interesting form. Consider the branch placement, looking for particularly vigorous branches low on the trunk. Finally, look for well-developed roots, evenly spread out.

Initial Training

During the first stages of conversion to a bonsai, when a plant undergoes drastic change, it will develop better if it grows outside in a garden bed. If this is difficult, use a tub or large pot of enriched potting soil outside. Allowing the root system to develop encourages the trunk and branches to add girth quickly. When, after a season or two, the plants are potted in their bonsai containers, growth will be much slower.

The Soil

Ordinary potting soil, designed to encourage rapid growth in potted plants, is not suitable for bonsai. The environment in the bonsai container must approximate the natural conditions that support shallow root growth for the species involved. In most cases, you must prepare your own soil from a combination of garden loam, clay subsoil, sand, and humus. This means grading it into strata, just as earth is stratified: first a drainage layer, covered by heavy subsoil to hold moisture, and finally a thin layer of rich topsoil. And frequently, as in nature, there will be a covering of moss on the soil.

Some Japanese bonsai growers use as many as a dozen nested wire sieves, with mesh sizes ranging from 3 to 36 wires to the inch, for this purpose. First, the soil is dried and crumbled; then it is passed through the nested sieves, the coarsest sieve on the top and the finest at the bottom. Soil from the bottom sieve is discarded as too fine—it will pack into solid clay when wet.

The basic requirement can be met by three sieves: a coarse one, with 3 or 4 wires to the inch; a medium model, with 8 wires to the inch; and ordinary window screening, with 14 or 15 wires per inch. Dry and sift separately garden loam, clay subsoil, and humus (peat moss or leaf mold). For the drainage layer, use half coarse sand and half an equal blend of loam, clay, and humus from the coarse sieve. For the basic potting mixture, to pack around the roots, use 1 part medium-grade humus, 2 parts sand (3 parts with conifers), 1 part medium-grade clay, and 2 parts medium-grade loam. For the topsoil, mix equal parts of fine loam, clay, and humus.

These formulations are not rigid. They are a standard from which to vary, depending on climate and the needs of your plants. More clay will mean better moisture retention; more sand, faster drying. Flowering and fruiting trees need extra nourishment; so add more humus and loam to the mixture.

The Container

Like the frame around a painting, a bonsai container must complement the plant without competing with it. Ideally, it should be flat and shallow, producing a kind of horizon to help achieve the illusion of size. Leaning and cascade styles require deeper pots for balance, from both an aesthetic and a practical point of view.

A bonsai container must have good drainage. Most have two large and several small holes in the bottom for this purpose. For the same reason, bonsai pots should have feet to elevate the container slightly.

Tradition provides some guidance in choosing colors for bonsai containers. For conifers and plants with dark foliage, use muted earth colors—dark red, gray, brown, or even deep purple. Light green foliage or silvery trunks call for lighter tones. Use muted greens or blues for colorful autumn foliage, white or off-white for red or yellow flowers and fruits. For trees that have white flowers or berries or variegated leaves, black is the favored color. The Japanese most often use unglazed containers. But in dry climates it is easier to keep a plant's roots moist in a glazed container.

Pruning Guidelines: The Rules of Growth

To control a bonsai's growth by pruning is to play the role of the environment in developing the tree's nature. Awareness of the following principles of growth, by which trees develop the characteristics of age, will help to shorten this years-long process to a matter of months.

Plants must produce some new growth each season to stay healthy.

Trees grow in two ways: branches and twigs are lengthened by buds; girth is increased by a new cambium layer each season (annual rings), which is formed even if bud growth is continually cut back.

Terminal, or end, buds grow first. If they are removed, the nearest buds, dormant at the base of leaves or hidden within stems, will become terminal buds.

The branch with the most foliage that gets good light grows the fastest.

Although a bonsai requires constant pruning to achieve and keep its form, the trimming must be done in a way that will direct growth, not inhibit it entirely. Sometimes a plant will seem to be almost dormant for a year after being pruned for a bonsai container; more likely it will respond by putting forth vigorous upright branches. The upper branches will probably flourish at the expense of the lower ones. Trim most of these upper branches off, and limit the others to one or two leaves, while permitting more leafage on the lower branches, to counter the natural superiority of upper branches. This will also encourage shorter, closer-set twigs in the crown—a characteristic of age.

To develop a tapering trunk, trim the leader back; then use wiring to make one of the resultant shoots into a new leader. When it has grown for a time, repeat the process. Control the direction in which new branches grow by pruning just ahead of buds that face the way you wish.

Steps in Making a Bonsai From a Nursery Specimen

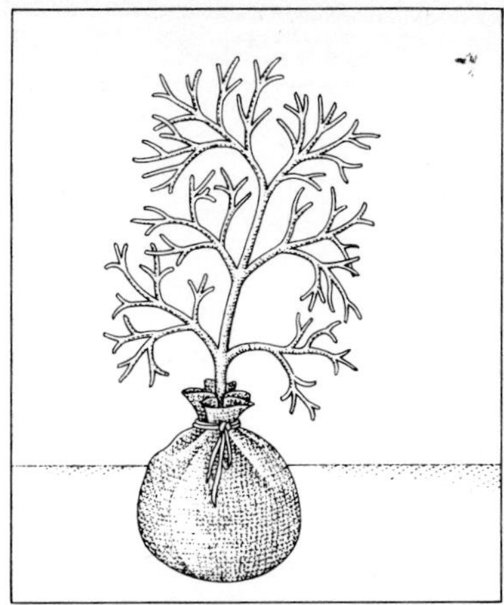

Selection. *Choose a young dormant tree that suggests an interesting form. Set it at eye level, and study development and branching habit for promising aspects. Study it from all angles, and decide as to front and back. Carefully remove a little soil from the base of the trunk to expose and evaluate the sculptural form of the main roots.*

Pruning for form. *Eliminate opposite branches and cut back long ones. The two lowest branches should face in opposite directions; the third should extend toward the rear. Uncover root ball and cut it back by one-third to one-half without disturbing the main roots near the trunk or the threadlike feeders growing from them.*

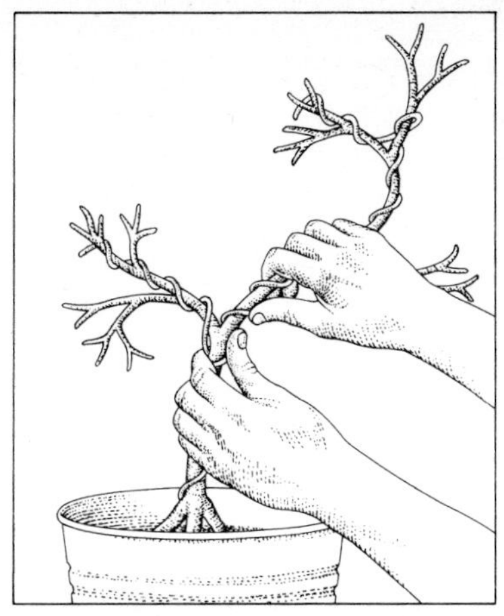

Early training. *Plant the tree in a garden bed, tub, or large pot. When new growth develops, wrap annealed copper wire in a spiral up the trunk and out around the main branches, gently bending them to the desired shape. Do not wrap too tightly or the bark may be scarred. Rewire the tree from time to time as its girth increases.*

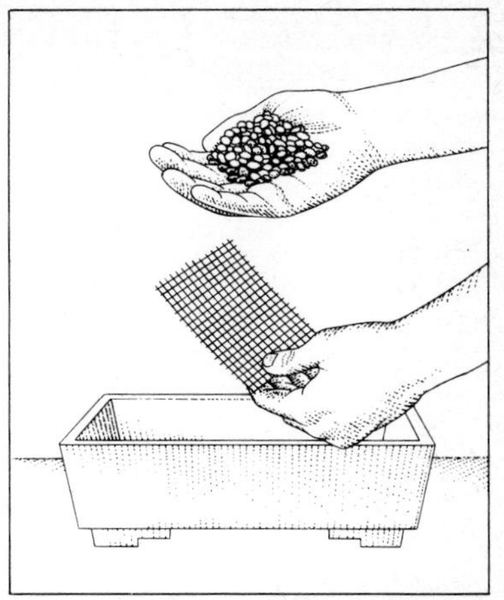

Preparing the container. *After about a year it should be time to "pot down" to a shallow bonsai container. Cover the bottom of the container with galvanized wire screening and then with a layer of sifted drainage material. Add a thin layer of peat moss, then sifted coarse potting soil (see opposite page for proportions and instructions).*

Root pruning. *About a week before transplanting, prune back most new top growth. Then, after the container has been prepared, remove the plant from the ground or its pot. Loosen soil from around the roots. Cut roots back to the main horizontal members and feeder roots. Work quickly so that the roots do not dry out as you cut.*

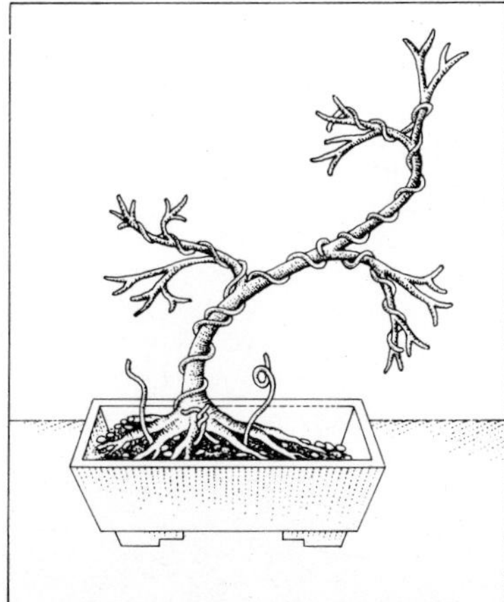

Wiring in place. *Position the plant attractively in the bonsai container. Spread roots evenly, adding soil if necessary to reach the desired level. If you are using a rock or other complementary feature, put it in place. Pass insulated electrical wire over roots and through the small holes in the bottom of the container to hold the plant firmly.*

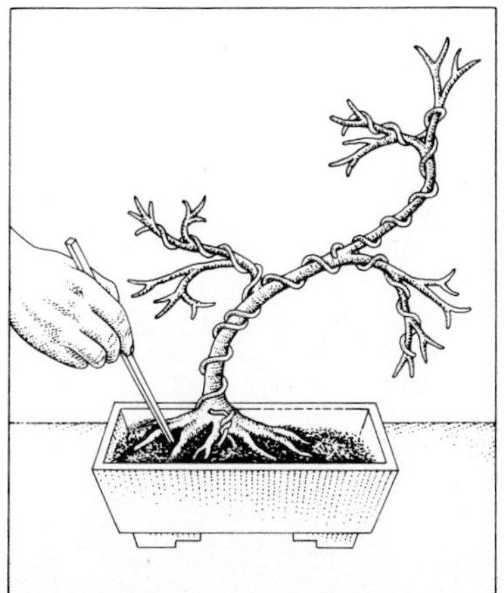

Adding soil. *Hold the tree in place with one hand while firming potting soil around the roots with a wooden chopstick. Finally, add a thin layer of fine soil, and top the planting with a ground cover of moss. Saturate with water and place the bonsai in a protected spot for two or three weeks, or until new growth appears.*

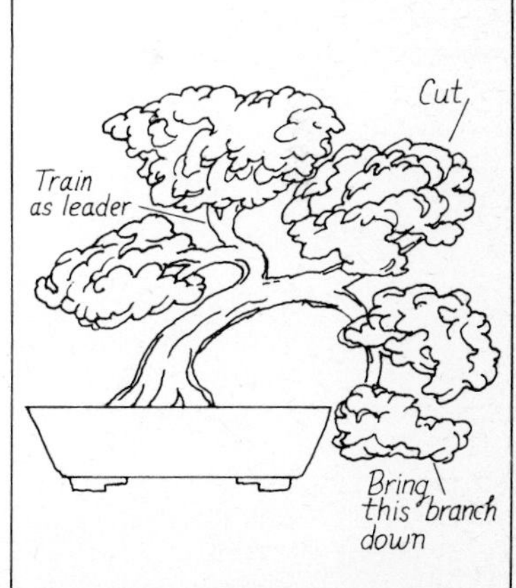

Visualizing future growth. *To provide guidance for future training of the bonsai, make a sketch of how you envision it to be. But remember, the sketch is only one possibility; the growth of the plant may suggest better ones. Control form by pruning, more wiring, and other training devices, such as soft string to tie down branches.*

Roses

Probably more than any other flower, the rose has captured the imagination of humankind and has been celebrated in song and legend since ancient times.

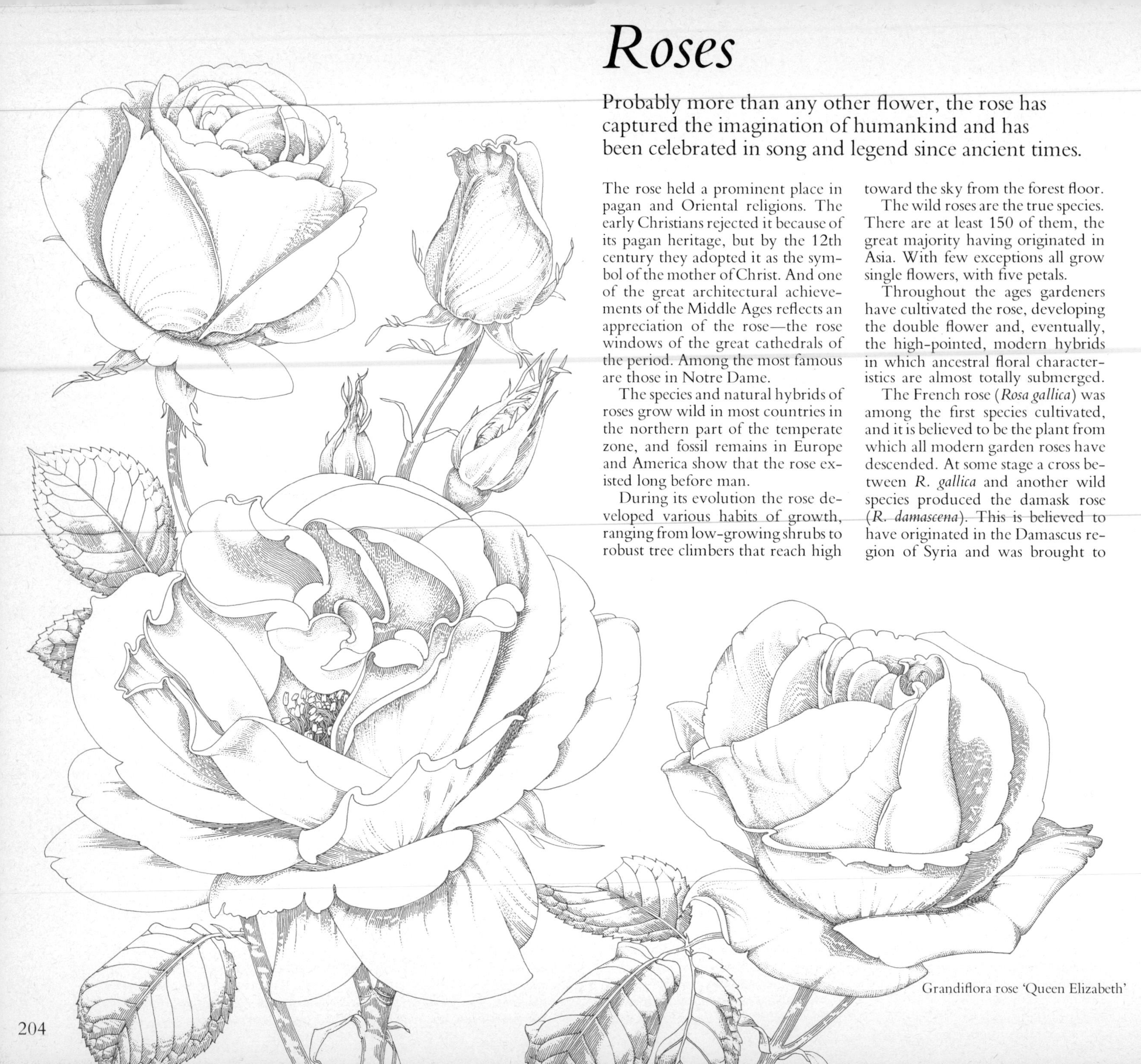

The rose held a prominent place in pagan and Oriental religions. The early Christians rejected it because of its pagan heritage, but by the 12th century they adopted it as the symbol of the mother of Christ. And one of the great architectural achievements of the Middle Ages reflects an appreciation of the rose—the rose windows of the great cathedrals of the period. Among the most famous are those in Notre Dame.

The species and natural hybrids of roses grow wild in most countries in the northern part of the temperate zone, and fossil remains in Europe and America show that the rose existed long before man.

During its evolution the rose developed various habits of growth, ranging from low-growing shrubs to robust tree climbers that reach high toward the sky from the forest floor.

The wild roses are the true species. There are at least 150 of them, the great majority having originated in Asia. With few exceptions all grow single flowers, with five petals.

Throughout the ages gardeners have cultivated the rose, developing the double flower and, eventually, the high-pointed, modern hybrids in which ancestral floral characteristics are almost totally submerged.

The French rose (*Rosa gallica*) was among the first species cultivated, and it is believed to be the plant from which all modern garden roses have descended. At some stage a cross between *R. gallica* and another wild species produced the damask rose (*R. damascena*). This is believed to have originated in the Damascus region of Syria and was brought to

Grandiflora rose 'Queen Elizabeth'

western Europe by the Crusaders.

The earliest varieties of the original species probably started as "sports"—chance offshoots that differ from the plant on which they arose. For example, a pink flower might appear on a plant that usually bears white blooms. These sports have been propagated by grafting, budding, or taking cuttings—all are ancient skills—to establish new varieties.

It was the arrival in Europe of the China rose (*R. chinensis*) at the close of the 18th century that changed the course of rose history. By then gardeners had learned how to breed roses, and by crossing the old with the new, tea roses and hybrid perpetuals were developed. These were the most popular kinds until the end of the 19th century.

Much of the early hybridizing took place in France. Empress Josephine made roses fashionable with a garden of all the species and varieties available at the time.

The hybrid tea roses, probably the most popular with today's gardeners—largely because they are hardier than many of their precursors—are relatively recent. They were developed in France at the end of the 19th century by crossing tea roses with hybrid perpetuals.

A little later came the polyanthas, with clusters of small roses. These were produced by hybridizing the Japanese *R. multiflora* with *R. chinensis.* Further crossbreeding in Denmark and the United States led to the popular floribundas. These in turn were crossed with hybrid teas to produce the grandifloras.

As roses became more highly bred, their use in gardens became more formal. During the 19th century it was fashionable to grow roses by themselves in geometric beds. Often, only roses of one variety would be grown in each bed. This practice is still followed in some estate and exhibition gardens.

Nowadays roses are often grown in a more casual manner and mingled with other plants. There are probably two main reasons for this. The segregated rose bed is dead space for several months of the year and contributes nothing to the garden when the roses are not in bloom. And in today's more limited garden spaces, the average gardener usually wants to grow a variety of plants.

Mixing roses and other plants. Roses can be combined with other shrubs or herbaceous perennials, placed individually in a particular position, or used to fill a corner, flank a doorway, or adorn a house wall. For instance, tall, arching, modern shrub roses, such as 'Nevada,' 'Frühlingsgold,' and the species *R. moyesii,* look splendid behind a bank of low evergreens or other shrubs of moderate size or behind some of the lower-growing hybrid teas or floribundas.

When combining roses of different varieties, or growing them among other plants, keep in mind the size and flowering seasons of all the plants. Also, be certain to allow at least 2 feet of space between the plants to provide air circulation. Make sure that short varieties of hybrid teas and floribundas will not be hidden by tall grandifloras, such as 'Queen Elizabeth,' 'Mount Shasta,' 'Camelot,' or 'Arizona.' Some nursery catalogs indicate the height to which each variety may grow.

Floribundas are ideal roses to mix with other plants to create an interesting visual effect or to prolong the flowering season. In general, they are hardier than hybrid teas. They combine well with dwarf azaleas, which they follow in flowering, or with any small shrubs. Floribundas are the best roses to include in a perennial border to cover gaps after the spring and early summer bloomers have faded or to fill blank spaces before the autumn display.

Dedicated rose growers usually prefer not to mix hybrid teas with any other kind of plant. However, many gardeners will find the appearance of the garden greatly improved if they conceal the rather leggy structure of the hybrid teas by planting various other low-growing perennials or annuals.

Edgings for rose beds. Miniature roses are a good choice to use as edgings. Also suitable are the low-growing annuals with a long flowering season, such as ageratums, wax begonias, and sweet alyssums. Perennials often used include iberises and santolinas.

Roses for hedges. Several types of roses make handsome floral hedges, although they are leafless in winter. Except for the floribundas, they take up more space laterally than the usual hedging plants. Good results can be obtained by planting them only slightly closer together than they would be planted in the garden and by pruning them lightly.

The best all-round hedging roses are the rugosas, because of their dense foliage. Most rugosas also have a long flowering period. The royal purple 'Roseraie de l'Hay,' the white 'Blanc Double de Coubert,' and the double, soft lavender 'Delicata' grow fairly tall. The hybrid white 'Snow Dwarf' makes a good 4-foot hedge.

For lower hedges (but with a shorter flowering period), the most dramatic color patterns are made by

Rose beds may be edged with low-growing annuals, such as ageratums (shown here), sweet alyssums, and wax begonias. All flower over a long period.

a few of the very old gallica roses—especially the popular crimson- and white-streaked 'Rosa Mundi' (*R. gallica* 'Versicolor').

The thorny Scotch rose, *R. spinosissima,* makes a highly efficient barrier against animals and also tolerates poor soil. The 'Stanwell Perpetual' variety bears masses of scented, double light pink flowers over a long blooming period.

Another vigorous variety, with large, double white flowers is 'Karl Forster.' It has good green foliage and blooms intermittently during the season. The flowers carry only a slight scent.

Among climbing roses, 'New Dawn' makes an excellent dense hedge or screen. When regularly pruned, it behaves as a shrub rose. It is well branched and strong, and is covered almost continuously with sweetly scented blush-pink flowers.

The bright red-flowered 'Blaze,' although not suited to making a thick, free-standing hedge, can be trained along a fence by tying its branches horizontally.

The scented white floribunda 'Iceberg' makes a fine hedge, 5 feet or more in height. 'Betty Prior,' with its single pink flowers, blooms constantly through the growing season. Lower and not quite so vigorous, but beautiful, is the red-blooming 'Frensham,' with semi-double flowers.

The grandiflora 'Queen Elizabeth' makes a lovely prickly-stemmed hedge, which in season has pink blossoms. Planted at 2-foot intervals and trimmed in winter or early spring, it will grow 6 feet high. For a shorter, thicker hedge, cut the plants back severely in early spring.

Roses to provide ground cover. A few roses that hug the ground closely are excellent for covering the bare soil and, when established, for suppressing weeds. They can also be used to cover steep banks.

The best roses for ground cover include 'Max Graf,' a rugosa hybrid with scented, single pink flowers and crimped petals. It flowers in midsummer and spreads widely, taking root as it goes. *R. wichuraiana,* called the memorial rose, grows 1–1½ feet tall and makes good cover on banks. It produces its scented, small, creamy white flowers in late summer and grows even in poor soil.

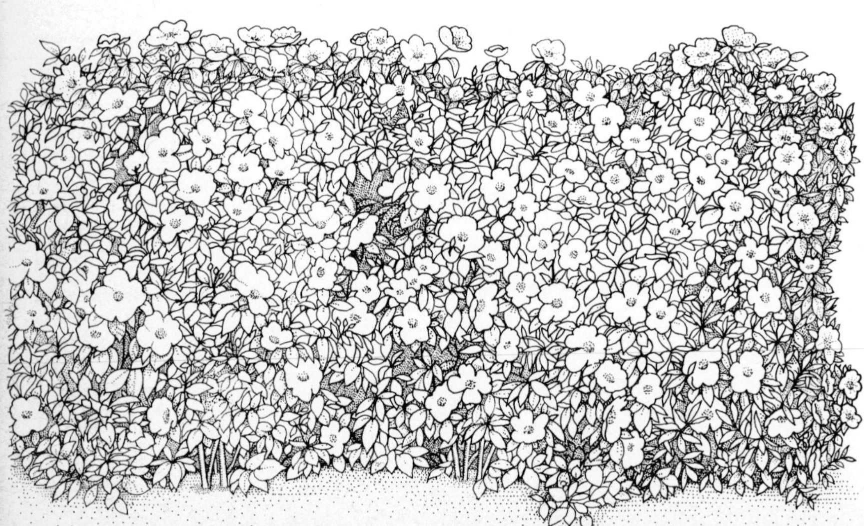

The white rugosa rose 'Snow Dwarf' makes a good 4-ft. hedge.

Roses in containers. For terrace decoration, roses in tubs, pots, or boxes are a good choice. Containers about 20 by 20 by 20 inches are best. But miniature roses can go in a 1- by 1- by 1-foot container. Floribundas, polyanthas, and miniatures make bushy plants with many flowers.

The soil must be well drained and moisture retentive. Mix garden soil with about one-third peat moss and one-third perlite or coarse sand.

Never let plants dry out completely. Control insects and fungi with regular spraying, and apply a dry or liquid fertilizer monthly. In cold climates put the containers in a protected garage for the winter.

All-America roses. In buying rose plants, one sooner or later encounters certain bushes with attached green and white tags bearing the initials AARS plus the name of the variety of rose. Or, when ordering by catalog, one sees that some varieties are designated as AARS—All-America Rose Selections. What does this mean to the home gardener?

The story behind All-America Rose Selections is interesting. Many years ago, before the Plant Patent Act was enacted, roses were named and often renamed indiscriminately by unscrupulous dealers, with the result that one variety might be sold under half a dozen names.

When the Plant Patent Act became effective, it was hoped that this situation would improve. The act was designed to protect developers of new varieties of roses and to partially compensate them for their efforts. Unfortunately, because the law required only that a patented plant be different in some respect from plants already in existence, the ultimate result was that the market was soon flooded with patented varieties, many of them inferior to varieties already available.

This uncontrolled situation led some of the leading rose growers to organize All-America Rose Selections in 1938. The purpose of the nonprofit organization was to test new varieties of roses to determine which ones were worthy of recommendation to the buying public.

'King's Ransom' is a yellow hybrid tea rose grown as a tree (standard).

Candidates for the All-America award are grown outdoors for two years at 26 testing stations throughout the United States.

During the testing period roses receive the normal care that would be given them by an average gardener. The roses are evaluated by official AARS judges according to a prescribed point system. They are scored on vigor, hardiness, disease resistance, foliage, flower production, bud and flower form, opening and final color, fragrance, stem, and overall value and novelty.

Only the top-scoring roses in each category are considered for the AARS designation. Some years no roses qualify.

The Most Popular Classes of Roses

Hybrid tea. More roses of the hybrid tea class are sold than of any other. Most of the hybrid teas produce double flowers with long-pointed buds borne one to a stem. They flower intermittently and have a wider color range than the older tea roses.

Popular varieties include 'Chrysler Imperial' (red); 'Tropicana' (reddish orange); 'Tiffany' (pink); 'King's Ransom' (yellow); 'John F. Kennedy' (white); 'Gypsy' (orange-red); and 'Hawaii' (coral).

Floribunda. Flowers in clusters are borne continuously and in profusion on floribunda plants. When they were introduced early in the 20th century, the flowers were borne in large clusters, and most were single or semi-double. Many of the newer varieties, however, have blossoms much like the hybrid teas, although they are smaller and may be single, semi-double, or double.

Popular varieties include 'Sarabande' (red); 'Rosenelfe' (pink); 'Iceberg' (white); 'Red Gold' (bicolor); 'Circus' (yellow, red, pink blend); and 'Fashion' (coral).

Grandiflora. The grandiflora is a tall, stately bush with great vigor, whose overall appearance is somewhere between that of the hybrid tea and the floribunda. Individual flowers resemble those of the hybrid tea, but they appear several to a stem like the floribunda.

Favorites are 'Queen Elizabeth' (pink); 'Camelot' (salmon-coral); 'Arizona' (copper); 'Carousel' (red); and 'John Armstrong' (dark red).

Polyantha. A few stalwart representatives of the once-popular polyantha class are still represented in catalogs. They are distinguished by clusters of small flowers on low plants that bloom intermittently.

Commonly grown are 'The Fairy' (semi-double pink); 'Cecile Brunner' (light pink with hybrid tea flower form); and 'Margo Koster' (coral-orange with almost round buds and cup-shaped flowers).

Miniature. The miniature plants are small in stature, generally 10–15 inches tall, with proportionately sized flowers that are mostly semi-double or double. Some bear flowers that are almost identical in form to the hybrid teas. Miniatures are particularly suitable for growing in containers. Some favorites are 'Red Imp' (deep crimson); 'Pixie Rose' (rose-pink); 'Baby Gold Star' (yellow); 'Shooting Star' (red-gold); and 'Cinderella' (white).

Tree, or standard. The tree form has a slim, erect, bare stem on top of which the desired variety—usually a hybrid tea or floribunda—is grafted (budded). Tree roses have a formal elegance, and they provide an attractive vertical accent.

Tree roses (also called standard roses) are trained on stems about $3\frac{1}{2}$ feet high. Half standards, or dwarf trees, are trained on stems about 2 feet high; miniatures, $1\frac{1}{2}$ feet.

Weeping trees are taller, with stems up to 5 or 6 feet. The budded top is a rambler with flexible canes that hang down to the ground.

Climbers. The large-blossomed climber rose plants that are repeat blooming or everblooming have mostly replaced the older climbers that have only one period of bloom. Most climbers have flowers quite similar to the hybrid tea, although some look more like the clustered floribundas.

Popular varieties are 'Coral Dawn' (coral-pink); 'High Noon' (yellow); 'Blaze' (crimson); 'New Dawn' (pink); and 'White Dawn' (white).

Shrub roses. For informal landscape use and as hedges, shrub rose plants are of particular value. They are not widely available in nurseries but are often listed in catalogs of rose specialists. Included here are the true species, the hybrids between the wild species and their natural sports, and the man-made hybrids. The plants tend to be shrublike, and many grow 4–5 feet high and equally wide.

Among the more recent hybrids are 'Will Scarlet' (scarlet); 'Nevada' (white); 'Belinda' (pink); and 'Cornelia' (coral).

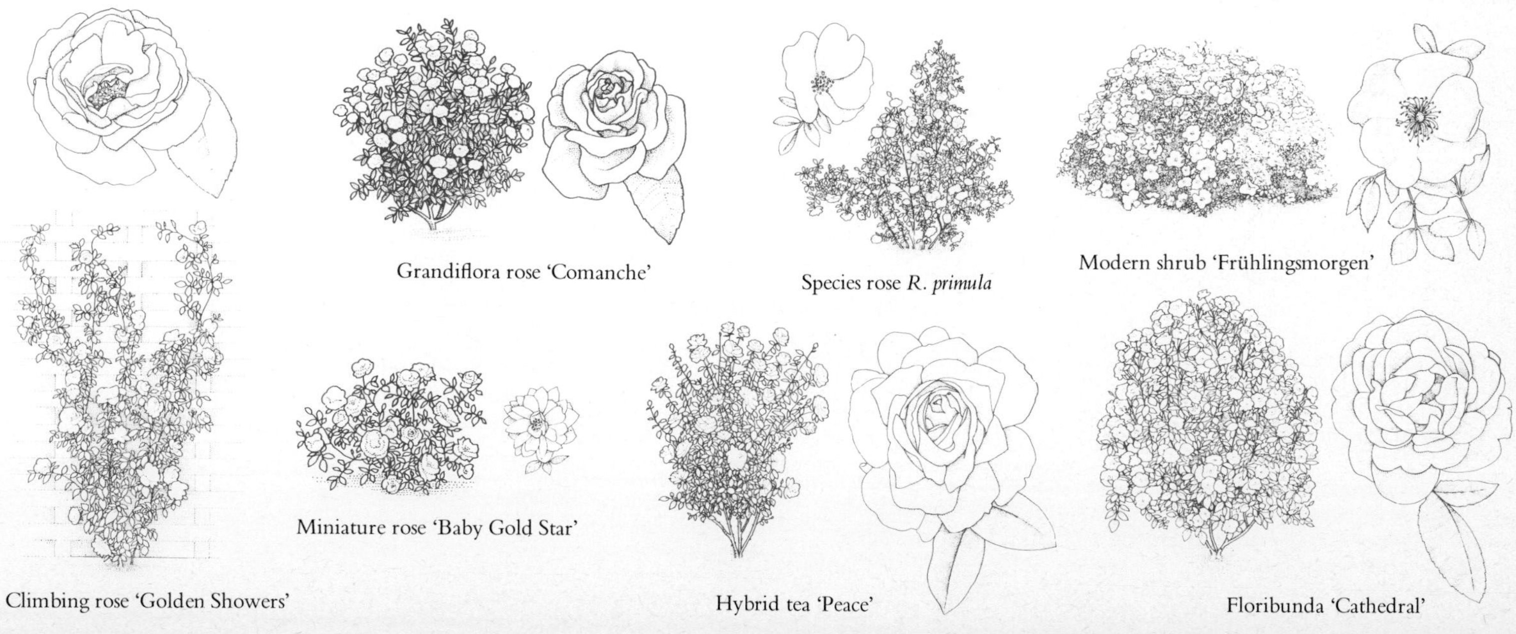

Grandiflora rose 'Comanche'

Species rose *R. primula*

Modern shrub 'Frühlingsmorgen'

Miniature rose 'Baby Gold Star'

Climbing rose 'Golden Showers'

Hybrid tea 'Peace'

Floribunda 'Cathedral'

Step-by-step Guide to Rose Planting

Creating the Best Conditions for Roses

Roses will grow in a wide variety of soils and situations, and will survive with relatively little attention. But they do best in an open, sunny location that has a fairly rich, slightly acid soil. If humus is added, clay is excellent. Good drainage is essential, although roses need ample watering in the absence of rain. Once planted, roses will survive in the same bed for many years if the ground is regularly mulched and fed.

Moisture retention in the soil is of utmost importance. A month before planting, dig the ground to the depth of a spade, and work in about one-third by volume of humusy material, such as compost, peat moss, leaf mold, or well-rotted manure. No commercial fertilizer need be added at this time. Leave the topsoil untrampled so that it is loose and air can circulate. Level the soil for the sake of appearance if so desired.

Heavy clay and sandy soils will need even more organic matter, often as much as one-half by volume. In addition to those materials mentioned above, chopped-up turf is excellent when available, since it breaks down into humus quickly and its nutrients will not leach out of the soil rapidly. After this initial improvement of the planting site, roses in clay and sandy soils benefit greatly from yearly application of a top-dressing of well-rotted manure or garden compost.

If the soil is alkaline, spread 2 buckets of peat moss and 2 handfuls of slow-release acid fertilizer, such as cottonseed meal, per square yard, and mix it into the top 6–10 inches of soil. Powdered sulfur at the rate of 1–2 pounds per 100 square feet is an alternative. If the soil is too acid (below a pH of 5.5), apply ground limestone at a rate of 3–5 pounds per 100 square feet.

In areas where it is difficult to provide proper drainage, you may want to consider planting your roses in raised beds.

When to plant. The best time to plant bare-root roses in cold sections of the country is in early spring. This gives the roots time to become established before top growth begins. Fall planting is slightly riskier, and the plants must be protected through the winter. In mild regions where the soil does not freeze for long periods, roses are best planted in late fall or late winter.

If bare-root plants are purchased from a gardening center or ordered by mail and arrive during a spell of hard frost, they can be kept in a garage or shed, wrapped in their packing—usually a plastic bag with damp sphagnum moss around the roots. Open the plastic to allow air to get to the roots so that they do not mold. Keep the packing damp (not soggy), and occasionally water the stems as well. If the roots are not wrapped, cover them with burlap, peat moss, newspapers, or any material that will keep them moist.

It is best to plant roses as soon as possible. If it is necessary to store the plants more than a few days, bury the roots in a shallow, slant-sided trench in a shaded spot and water them well.

Container-grown plants can be set out just about any time they are available. However, most northern nurseries pot bare-root plants in very early spring, and it is preferable to purchase them in spring or early summer before they get too pot-bound. Roots that are confined in a container often grow so tightly together that they have trouble establishing themselves when planted in the garden. Also, if a nursery forces its potted roses into early growth and bloom, care must be taken not to set such plants in the garden until the danger of frost no longer remains, as the young growth will be very tender and more subject to damage than plants already acclimated to the outdoors.

Planting distances. Plant each rose at least 15 inches from any path or lawn. The following distances between plants are recommended for the indicated varieties.

Miniature—12 inches. Tree, or standard—at least 3 feet. Hybrid tea, floribunda, hybrid perpetual, polyantha, bushes of moderate growth—at least 18 inches; bushes of stronger growth—2 feet or more. Grandiflora—minimum of 2–4 feet. Shrub—5 feet. Climber and rambler—at least 7 feet.

Preparing the Roses Before Planting

When planting, bring the roses to the garden a few at a time. Ideally, a windless, overcast day is the best time to plant. While waiting for such conditions, keep the plants shaded and the roots damp.

If bare-root plants arrive with dry, shriveled stems, immerse them in water completely for a few hours. If they do not plump up, return them to the nursery for replacement.

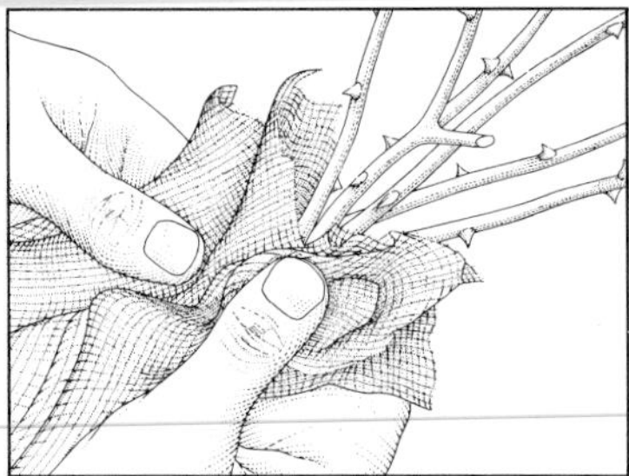

1. *To prevent drying prior to planting, keep roots covered or standing in water.*

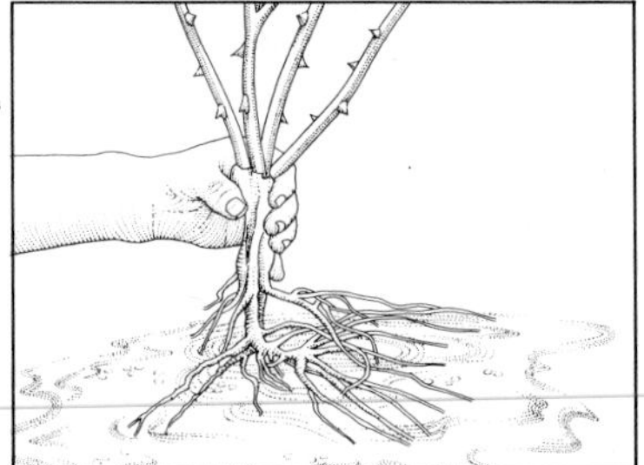

2. *If roots seem dry, make a mud puddle; swirl roots in it before planting.*

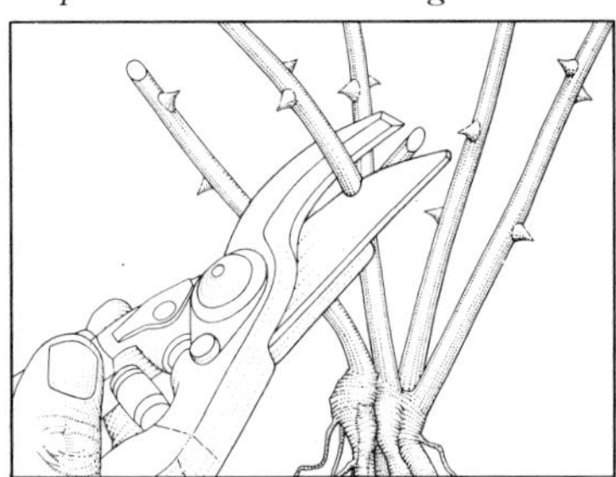

3. *Cut back any dead or damaged canes to wood that is firm and live.*

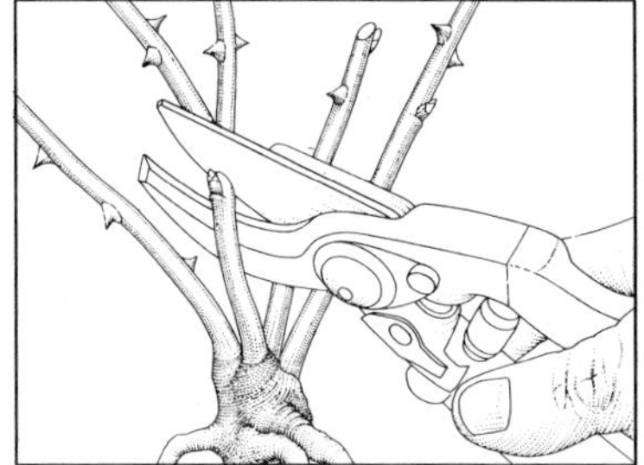

4. *Always cut back canes on an angle and just above an outward-facing bud.*

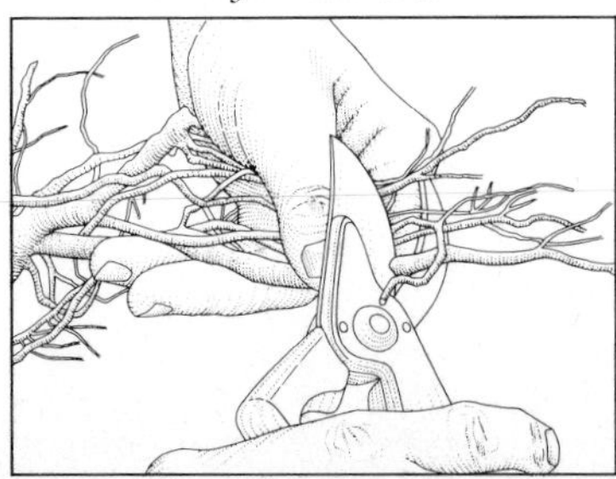

5. *Trim back damaged roots and roots that are too long to fit the hole.*

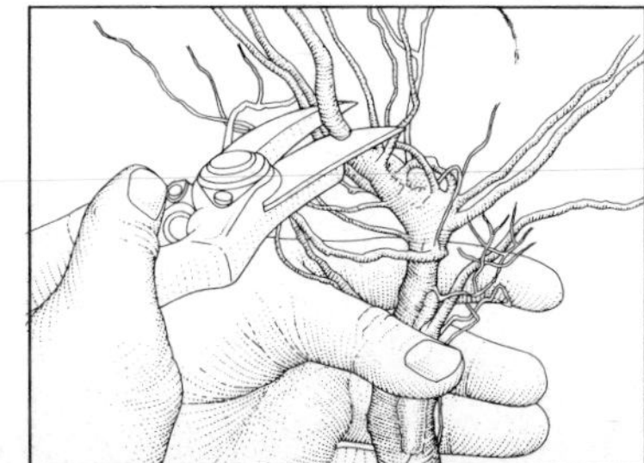

6. *Cut out any coarse, thickened root that appears to be an old taproot.*

Shaping the Hole to Fit the Roots

Dig a hole deep and wide enough to accommodate the roots without crowding them when they are spread out in the natural position in which they have been growing. Some roots grow toward one side. Instructions often call for planting the roses on a mound of soil with the roots spread down the sides. Unless done carefully, however, this procedure can lead to planting at an improper depth.

Spread out the roots, and comb them out with the fingers to keep them from crossing. They should not be coiled around the circumference of the hole.

Lay a stake across the hole to mark the prospective level of the soil in the bed, and use this to establish the correct planting depth.

DIGGING THE HOLE TO SUIT THE ROOTS

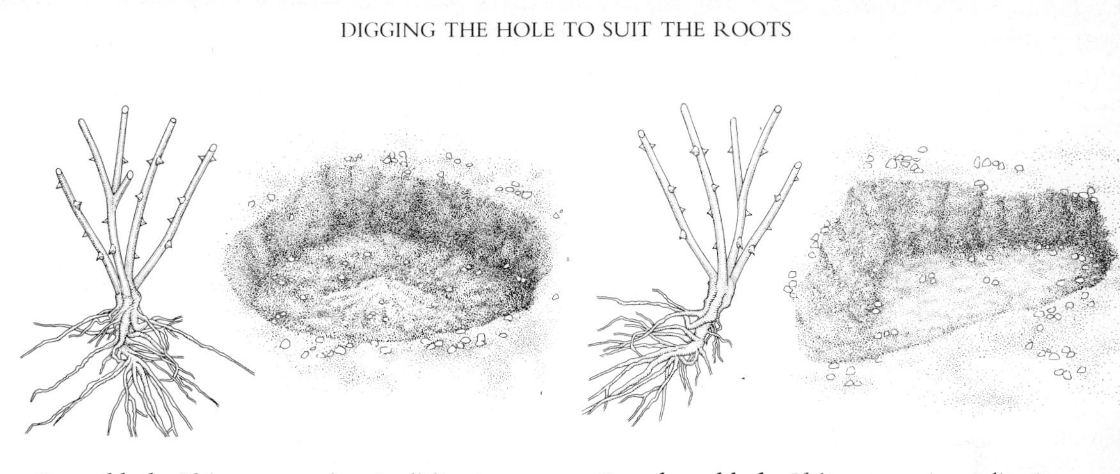

Round hole. *If the roots spread out in all directions from the main stem, dig a round hole about 2 ft. in diameter and 1 ft. or more in depth. Spread the planting mixture 1 in. deep in the hole before spreading out the roots.*

Fan-shaped hole. *If the roots run in one direction, make the hole fan shaped. Slant the hole if necessary to accommodate the longest roots, and at the same time keep the bud union at the proper depth for your climate.*

Planting Bush Roses at the Proper Depth

When deciding how deep to plant a rose, it is important to understand the reasons behind what often appears to be conflicting information. The controversy has to do with the bud union and the distance above or below the ground that it should be set. The bud union is the point at which the hybrid variety has been budded to the rootstock, and this union is essential to the growth of the hybrid. In cold climates it affects the survival of the plant.

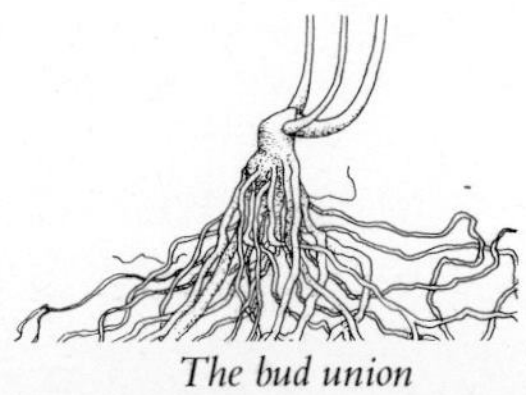

The bud union

When the bud union is above the soil level, new canes are produced more freely from the base. This is highly desirable. Therefore, in mild climates roses are always set with the union about an inch above the soil level. In climates where temperatures drop below 20° F for much of the winter, the traditional recommendation has been to set the union 1–2 inches below the soil level to protect it from cold injury. But recently many cold-climate gardeners have found it preferable to set the union above the soil level and then to protect it with a thick mulch in winter.

All roses require firm planting. When the hole is about two-thirds filled, tread the soil around the perimeter of the roots. Then slowly add water to fill the hole, and let it soak in before adding more soil. This helps to eliminate the air pockets. Finish filling the hole, and make a catch basin around the edge of the hole to hold water in the root area. After watering again, mound 6 inches of soil over the canes for a few weeks to prevent drying. Remove the extra soil before the buds begin to swell in spring.

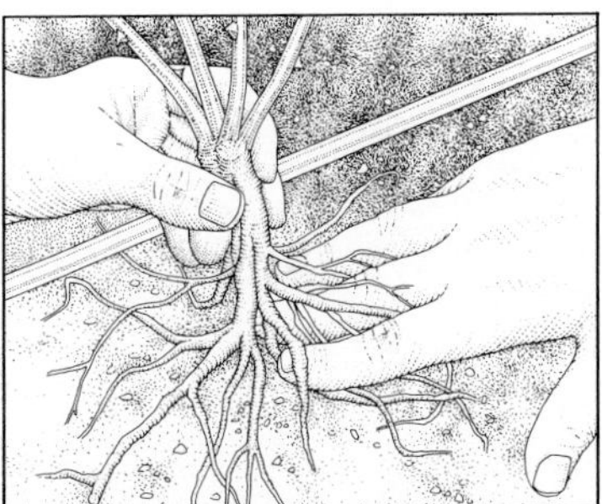

1. *Mark the soil level with a cane. Hold the rose with bud union at proper level.*

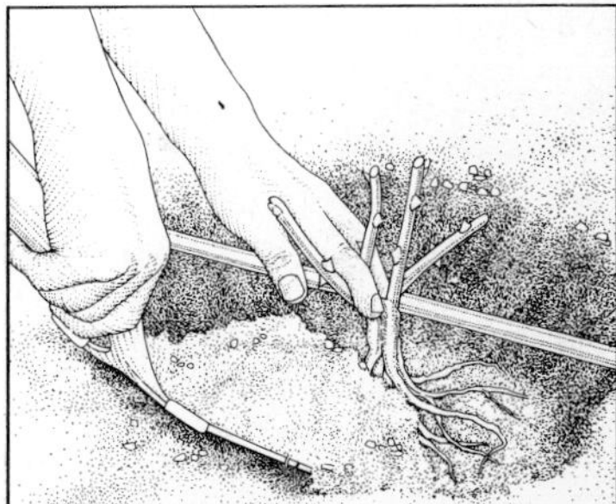

2. *Add some planting mixture over the roots, and fill about two-thirds of hole.*

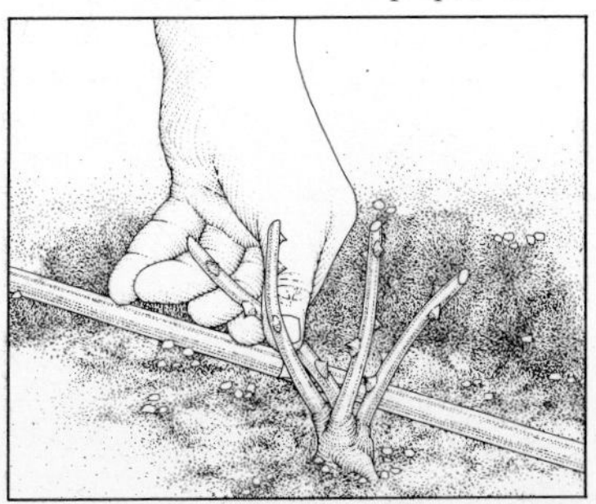

3. *Jiggle the plant up and down to make sure the soil fills spaces between roots.*

4. *Tread the soil and water thoroughly. Add the rest of the soil, tread, and water.*

Planting and Staking a Tree (Standard) Rose

Although tree roses are planted in much the same way as others, there are a few special considerations.

Because a standard is quite tall and is supported by a single cane, it must be firmly staked. This is best done at planting time. Use a 1- by 1-inch stake or a strong metal rod or pipe. It should be long enough to extend 2 feet into the ground and several inches into the foliage. If wood is used, sharpen the stake, and paint the underground portion with a wood preservative (such as pentachlorophenol). Do not use creosote, which is toxic to plants.

After digging, set the stake in the center of the hole. Since the trunk of a standard rose often suffers from sunscald, especially in hot climates, shade it by putting the stake on its south side. Alternatively, the trunk may be wrapped with burlap.

Set the rose close to the stake and as nearly vertical as possible. Most gardeners believe in using the same planting depth for all climates. The bud union, where the main cane joins the roots, is set at soil level; avoid deeper planting. (The practice of burying the entire plant over the winter in cold climates makes it unnecessary to set the bud union below soil level when planting.)

Hold, or temporarily tie, the standard firmly in position against the stake while covering the roots. Wiggle the plant slightly to settle it in. Tread the soil over the roots when the hole is half full. Fill the hole with water, and let it soak in. Finish filling the hole, firm the soil again, and water. Form a catch basin with earth mounded around the plant to help hold the water.

The standard should be secured to the stake with at least two ties. Place one securely at the top, just beneath the head of the plant, and another midway down the main stem. Do not hesitate to use a third tie if it seems necessary. Plastic ties are available and convenient to use, but garden twine can also be used if the stem is well wrapped with burlap. (The burlap wrapping is often applied for protection against sun or cold.)

Keep the plant well watered. In cold climates dig up the plant in late autumn, lay horizontally, and cover with soil. Replant in early spring.

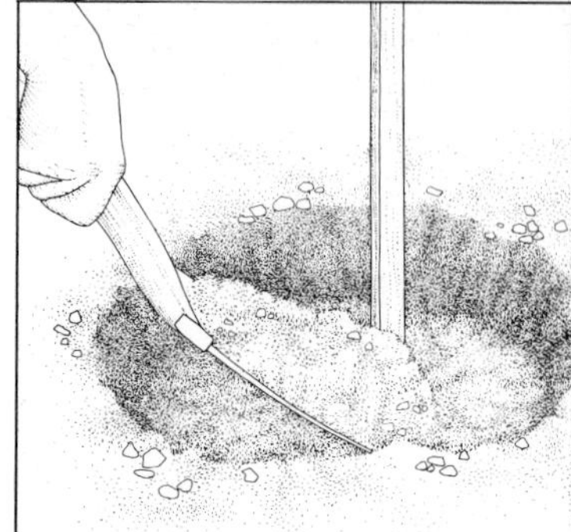

1. *Dig hole 12–15 in. wide, and then hammer in stake. Add planting mixture.*

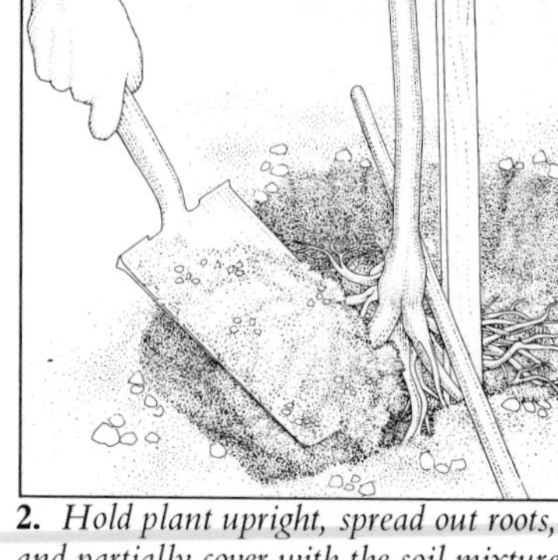

2. *Hold plant upright, spread out roots, and partially cover with the soil mixture.*

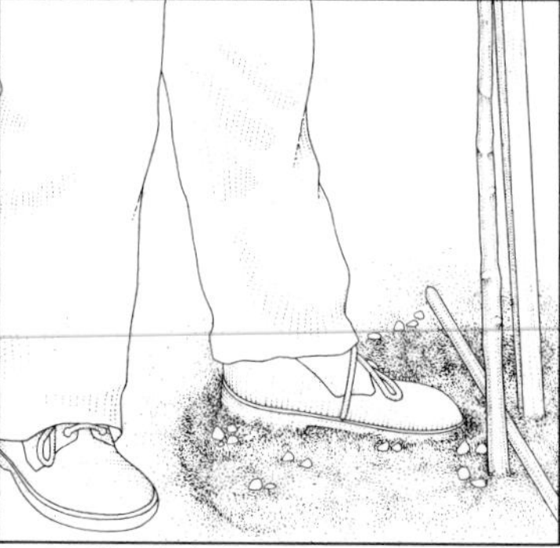

3. *Half-fill hole with mixture, firm, and water. Then fill in to ground level.*

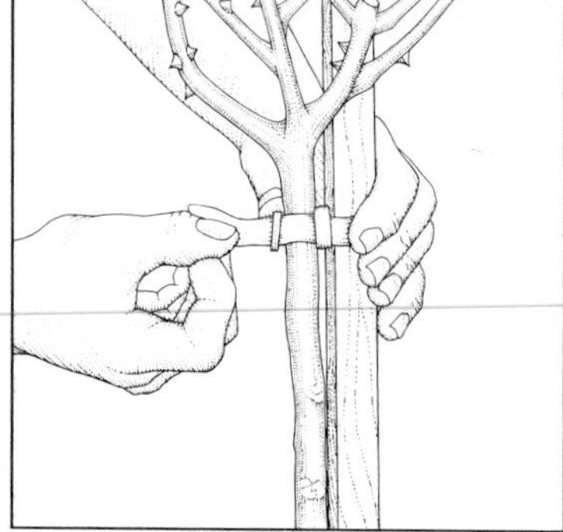

4. *Secure the standard to the stake with several rubber or plastic ties.*

Planting Climbers Against a Wall

The basic planting method for climbers is the same as for bush roses.

Before training the rose against a wall, stretch plastic-coated wire between two screw eyes, and tighten with a turn buckle. The wire should be 4–6 inches from the wall to allow air to circulate behind the stems.

In tying the rose canes to the wire, train the main canes to a horizontal position. Most of the large-flowered climbers produce more blooms when they are trained in this way.

There is usually more deadwood on young climbers than on bush or standard roses. This should be cut back to just above a live bud.

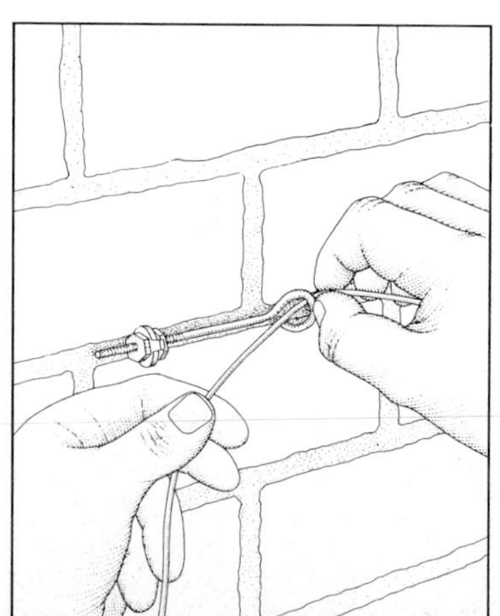

1. *Fix plastic-coated wire horizontally on the wall at 15-in. intervals.*

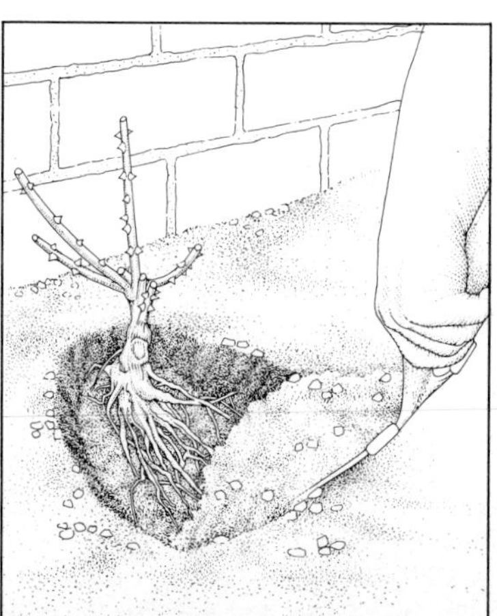

2. *Plant the rose 12 in. from the wall, with the roots pointing away from it.*

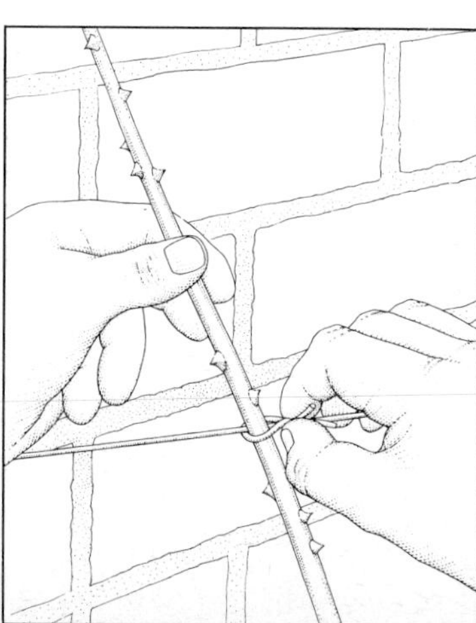

3. *As the canes grow, spread them out in a fan shape and attach to wires.*

Caring for Roses Throughout the Year

How to Identify and Remove Suckers

Always be on the watch for shoots that come from below ground level and from the stems of standard roses. These suckers grow from the rootstock below the point of union and can usually be identified by their leaves and thorns, which are different from those of the top growth. The sucker leaflets are narrower than those of the garden rose, and the thorns are needlelike. It is commonly thought that suckers have seven leaflets on each leaf and that the growth above the point of union has only five leaflets, but this is not always the case.

The surest test is to trace the suspect growth to its point of origin, which will be below the union of rootstock and branches if the growth is a sucker. Wrench the sucker off at its point of origin; do not cut it, because this is merely a form of pruning that will encourage additional suckers to grow.

Deadheading Roses to Encourage More Flowers

As soon as hybrid tea blooms wither, cut them off with pruning shears to a point just above a strong shoot or an outward-facing leaf bud. This will encourage a second flowering.

Many rose growers simply cut back to the first leaf with five leaflets. But this may result in the loss of several potential flowering stems.

Toward the end of the season, deadhead more lightly—to the first leaf bud below the flower—as young growth that will not harden before winter should be discouraged.

In fall in cold climates, cut the flower off with a short stem.

With floribundas deadheading must be ruthless. There are no leaf buds on the blossom stems; so the whole flower truss must be cut back to the first leaf bud below it. Seed heads should not be allowed to form unless they are wanted for decoration or seeds and, even then, not until the rose is two years old.

Bush roses. *Dig away soil, find junction, and wrench sucker off.*

Tree roses. *Remove all shoots on stem below bud union.*

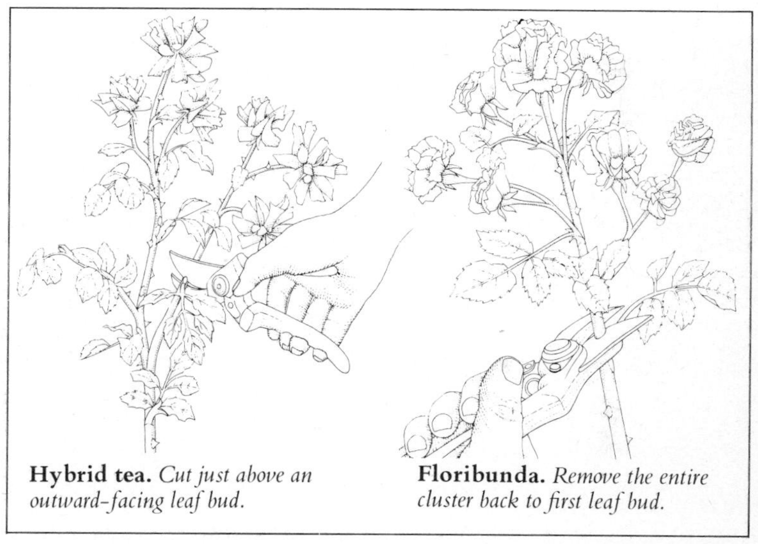

Hybrid tea. *Cut just above an outward-facing leaf bud.*

Floribunda. *Remove the entire cluster back to first leaf bud.*

Encouraging Larger Blooms by Disbudding

If some of the flower buds are removed from hybrid teas, the remaining flowers will grow larger.

As new stems develop on hybrid teas, one or more side buds appear just below the central terminal bud. While they are still tiny, nip off the side buds with your fingers at a point 6 inches below the terminal bud.

Some rose exhibitors remove the larger center buds and the smallest buds from each cluster on floribunda roses to achieve the same results.

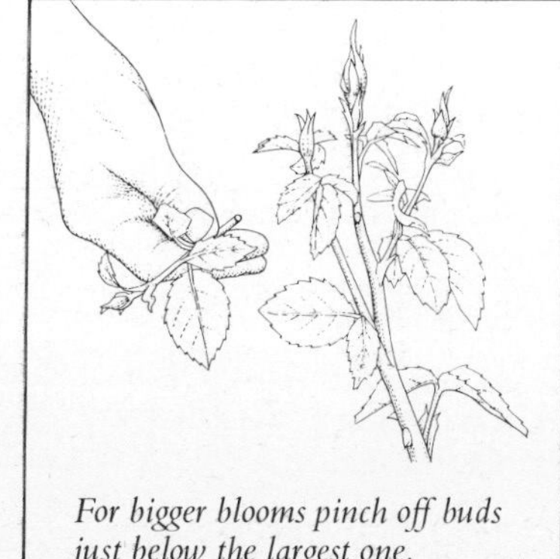

For bigger blooms pinch off buds just below the largest one.

When to Water and Spray Roses

The weather and the nature of the soil dictate when to water. Sandy soils need abundant water. In other kinds most roses, other than newly planted ones, will tolerate even a two- or three-week drought.

Ideally, it is best to water roses with a canvas soaker or some other device that provides water only around the roots. Overhead watering can damage roses in full flower.

When the plants are not in bloom, a sprinkler that gives a fine mistlike spray can be used. To prevent mildew, water early in the day so that the plants will be dry by nightfall. Do not use a coarse stream of water that will splash soil on the leaves, since this can spread soil-borne diseases. A gentle soaking is most desirable.

Also, spray with a general-purpose insecticide-fungicide sold for use on roses. Use a sprayer (the tank-type pressure sprayer is best) that gives a fine mist. Begin to spray early in the growing season, and repeat regularly according to package instructions. Cover the upper- and lower-leaf surfaces, as well as surrounding soil.

A Simple Feeding and Mulching Routine

In the first year after planting, roses should not be fed. In subsequent years feeding can begin as early as February in mild climates and as new growth begins in colder areas. Additional feedings should be given as one blooming period ends, to stimulate the next one. In cold areas roses should not be fed after August. Superphosphate, with cottonseed or blood meal, or a commercial rose fertilizer, should be scratched lightly into the soil around the plants.

As soon as the ground warms up in spring, apply a 2- to 4-inch cover of mulch (water first if the soil is dry) to conserve moisture, improve the soil, and keep weeds down. Well-rotted cow or horse manure is a good mulch and also adds nutrients, but it contains weed seeds and is scarce.

Good mulches include compost, ground corncobs, shredded leaves, sawdust, salt hay, straw, peanut shells, shredded bark, buckwheat hulls, and cocoa hulls.

Rake the mulch aside when applying fertilizer. Liquid fertilizers can be applied directly through the mulch. Replace mulch annually to minimize pests and diseases.

FEEDING

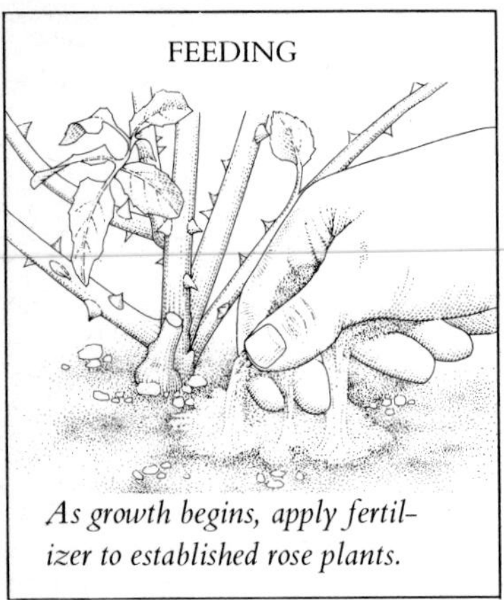

As growth begins, apply fertilizer to established rose plants.

MULCHING

After fertilizing, apply a mulch to conserve moisture.

What Can Go Wrong With Roses

For the best results, roses require regular attention to their needs. If your plants show symptoms that are not described below, consult the section on plant disorders on page 600. Look up chemicals on page 635 to find trade names.

Symptoms and signs	Cause	Control
Shoots and flower buds are covered with greenish insects. Severe attacks cause malformation of stems, leaves, and buds.	Aphids	Spray with Diazinon, dimethoate, endosulfan, or malathion.
Leaves are eaten, sometimes also rolled.	Caterpillars and sawfly larvae	Spray with carbaryl, methoxychlor, rotenone, or trichlorphon.
Leaves show pale mottling, may yellow and fall prematurely. Small jumping and flying insects on plant.	Leafhoppers	Spray with carbaryl, malathion, or nicotine.
Leaves and flower buds may be severely distorted. Leaves often have tattered or spotted appearance.	Plant bugs	Spray with Diazinon, malathion, methoxychlor, or nicotine.
Flowers are malformed, or buds turn brown and fail to open. Tiny insects scurry among petals.	Thrips	Spray with dimethoate, formothion, malathion, or rotenone.
Leaves are off-color, often bronzed, with fine silver-white dots. Leaves may be webbed.	Two-spotted mites (red spider mites)	Once a week spray top and bottom of leaves with chlorobenzilate, dicofol, malathion, or tetradifon. Or use a systemic, such as dimethoate.
Knotted galls on roots. Plants are sickly, stunted, off-color.	Root-knot nematodes	Buy plants certified free of nematodes. Treat soil with metam-sodium before planting.
Leaves have black rounded spots and may fall prematurely.	Black spot (fungus)	Spray with Captan, dodine, maneb, or zineb.
Stems and crowns are attacked, causing dieback and purplish-black to brown cankers.	Cankers (fungus)	Prune affected stems back to at least 1 in. below any discolored area on stems. Do this after spring growth begins. After each cut dip knives and pruners in half-strength liquid chlorine bleach. Spray with dinoseb or lime sulfur.
Plants are attacked at soil line, causing large knotty growths.	Crown galls (bacteria)	Remove and destroy badly affected plants. Treat galls with Bacticin when discovered. Difficult to control.
Leaves and young shoots have whitish coating. They may be distorted.	Powdery mildew (fungus)	Spray with Benomyl, cycloheximide, or dinocap.
Shoots are twisted or malformed; covered with orange powder. Small yellow spots are visible on undersides of leaves, which may fall prematurely.	Rust (primarily on West Coast)	Not always easy to control, but spray with maneb or zineb at first sign of attack. Cut out and destroy affected shoots.
Shoot tips are blackened or purplish. Slightly discolored patches may occur on young leaves.	Frost or cold winds	If this happens regularly, make sure final pruning is delayed until spring so that young shoots are produced later.
Leaves yellow and fall early. Flowers are few and short-lived. General growth is thin and poor.	Starvation, drought, or combination of both	Usually occurs when roses are grown in thin, gravelly soil or against walls that block rain. Make sure that soil does not dry out. Mulch annually with well-decayed manure or garden compost, plus rose fertilizer.

Growing Better Roses by Good Pruning

When to Prune and How to Do It

The best time to prune most roses is at the end of the dormant season in your area, just before new growth begins and as the buds begin to swell. In mild climates this may be as early as December or January; in colder climates it may be as late as April. Wait until you are sure that all danger of hard frost is past, or newly pruned tips may be killed.

This rule does not apply to climbers, ramblers, and weeping standards. Climbers are best given a light pruning when they finish flowering and again in the spring. Ramblers are best pruned after flowering, as are weeping standards (which are ramblers grafted onto tall stems).

Terms used in pruning roses. A stem or branch of the current year's growth is called new wood. Hybrid teas, floribundas, and other modern roses flower on these stems.

"Old wood" is a stem of some previous year's growth. Ramblers and most climbers (except the climbing sports) flower on old wood. The shoots grow one year and bear flowers the next.

An "eye" is a young or incipient growth bud, found in the axil of a leaf. In winter an eye appears as a mere pinhead on a stem, from which a shoot may grow.

There are two types of bud. One is a growth bud (or eye, as above), from which a stem will form. The other is a flower bud.

The shoots by which the main stems of roses extend themselves are known as leaders. "Laterals" are stems that grow from a leader.

A "snag" is a dead stump resulting from a pruning cut made too far above a bud or too far from the junction of one cane with another.

How to make a pruning cut. To make a pruning cut, use strong, sharp pruning shears to cut the stem cleanly, leaving no ragged edges. Cut no more than a quarter inch above an eye or a growth bud. Angle the cut so that it slopes slightly back and away from the bud. This angle will allow moisture to drain away.

Correct cut (left); the others are wrong.

The bud should face outward to allow growth to spread from the center and keep the bush uncrowded. This applies to all roses except ramblers and climbers, which must be encouraged to grow along a support, and prostrate types, which are trained along the ground.

To prevent damage, do not cut too close to the bud. Alternatively, if the cut is made too high above the bud, the stem may die back.

If two growth buds develop at the same point after pruning, pinch out the weaker one. This must be done carefully with your thumbnail or the point of a clean, sharp knife.

When removing a complete stem, cut as close as possible to the parent stem with pruning shears; then trim the stump flush with the stem, using a sharp knife.

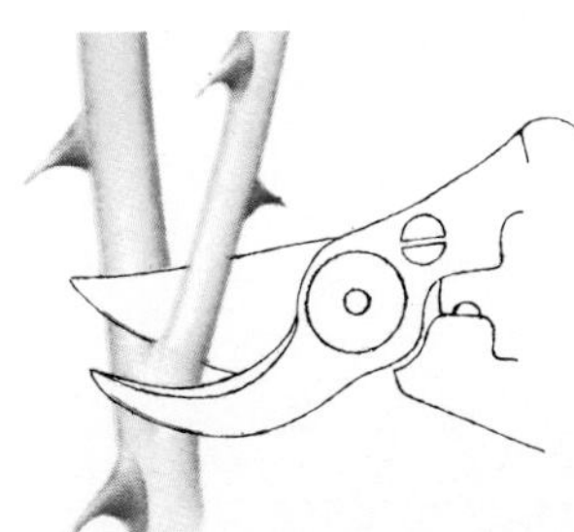

Remove stem flush with adjoining one.

Do not try to cut thick stems with pruning shears. Instead, use long-handled loppers for a good, clean cut. For old hardwood use a narrow-bladed pruning saw. Saw cuts should be pared clean with a knife.

Pruning Newly Planted Roses

Any necessary pruning of bush and tree roses that are planted in spring must be done immediately. If they are planted in fall however, prune them in spring.

The basic steps of pruning (essentially, removing dead or weak wood and stems that cross and rub) apply to all types of roses. Treat each rose according to its type, and prune as recommended.

Newly planted hybrid teas and grandifloras are pruned hard to about 4 inches from the ground.

Floribundas are pruned in the same way except that they should be cut a little higher—about 5–6 inches from the ground. Cut short varieties, such as 'All Gold,' somewhat lower.

Moderately prune newly planted species roses. They bloom on the wood produced in the previous season, and the more stems, the greater the next crop of flowers.

Climbing and rambling roses need moderate cutting back in order to compensate for the inevitable loss of roots when they are transplanted. Both old and modern shrub roses should be treated the same way.

Cut polyanthas back by one-third, and prune miniature roses back to within 2 inches of the ground.

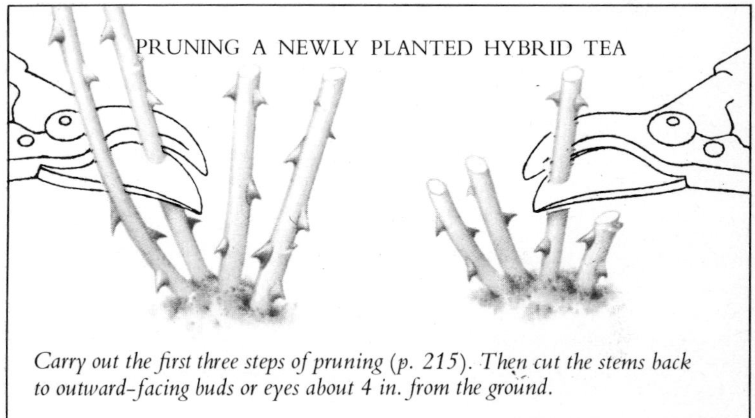

PRUNING A NEWLY PLANTED HYBRID TEA

Carry out the first three steps of pruning (p. 215). Then cut the stems back to outward-facing buds or eyes about 4 in. from the ground.

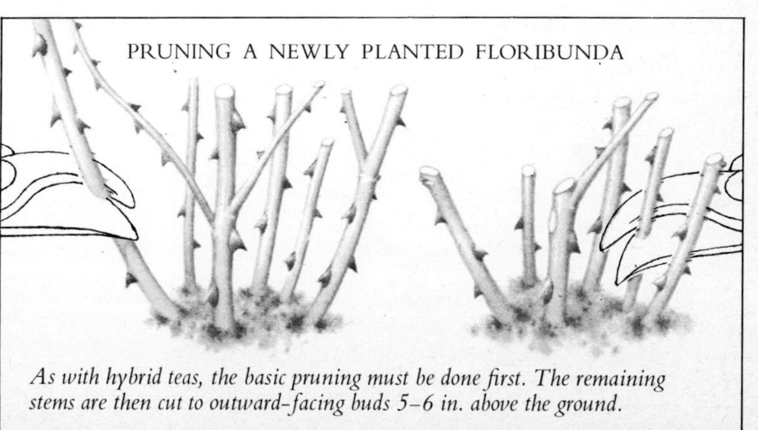

PRUNING A NEWLY PLANTED FLORIBUNDA

As with hybrid teas, the basic pruning must be done first. The remaining stems are then cut to outward-facing buds 5–6 in. above the ground.

How to Prune Bush and Tree Roses

Basically, the object of all rose pruning is to remove deadwood and crossed canes, to shape and thin for better circulation of air, and to encourage the production of the largest or the greatest number of flowers. Suckers—shoots that originate below the bud union and have different foliage—should also be removed whenever seen (p. 211).

Make all pruning cuts just above an outward-facing bud in order that new shoots will grow away from the center of the bush and minimize crowding. Begin with the three basic pruning steps described on the opposite page; then prune each one according to its type.

Hybrid teas, floribundas, and grandifloras should have their tops cut back by about one-third each year in spring, when the buds begin to grow and there is no danger of hard frost. This is moderate pruning for garden display. Larger, but fewer, flowers of exhibition quality can be produced with harder pruning—as far back as three buds above the base of the stem.

Grandifloras and floribundas often develop new shoots more freely than do hybrid teas; so somewhat less pruning is needed to stimulate growth.

Hybrid perpetuals bloom best on one-year-old wood. Each spring remove some three- to four-year-old wood at soil level, and trim new growth back to about 3 or 4 feet. Light pruning should be done when flowers are cut for indoor use or when dead flowers are removed.

Miniatures and polyanthas need little pruning beyond trimming their tips back in spring, thinning, and removing weak shoots. In summer miniatures often send up some shoots much taller than the others; thin these back to maintain symmetry.

Tree, or standard, roses, either hybrid teas or floribundas, should be pruned in the same way as bush roses, but more severely. Shape each plant to provide a rounded head.

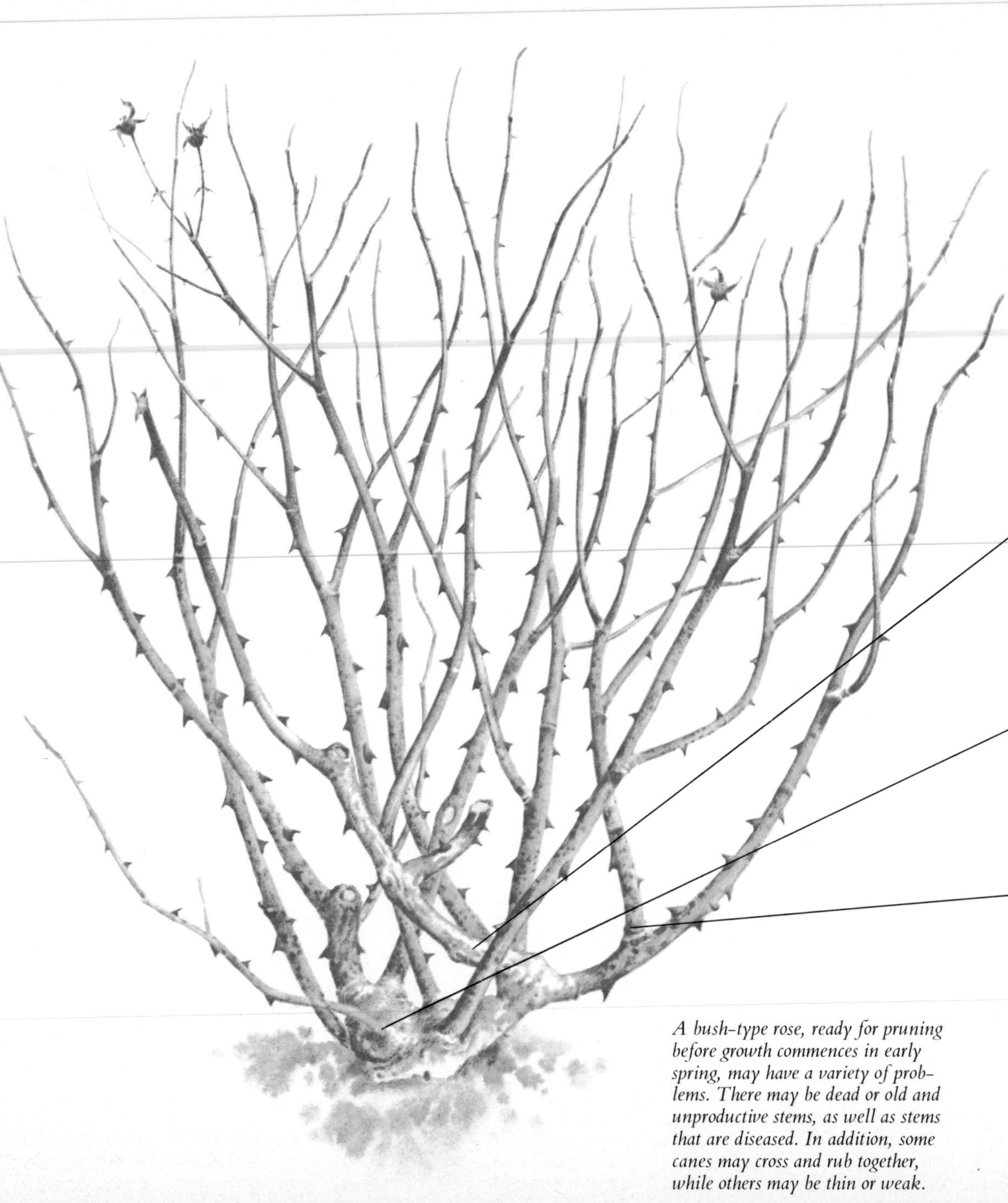

A bush-type rose, ready for pruning before growth commences in early spring, may have a variety of problems. There may be dead or old and unproductive stems, as well as stems that are diseased. In addition, some canes may cross and rub together, while others may be thin or weak.

THE THREE BASIC PRUNING STEPS

1. Cut back dead stems. *Cut back any dead stem to the point where it meets a healthy stem, or, if necessary, cut it all the way back to the union between budwood and rootstock. Cut back any part of a stem that is diseased to just above an outward-facing bud on healthy wood.*

2. Cut out thin or weak stems. *To allow more nourishment to reach vigorous wood, cut out completely all very thin or weak stems. Cut them back to their point of union with a strong stem or with the rootstock. Feeble wood will merely waste the plant's strength and probably produce no flowers.*

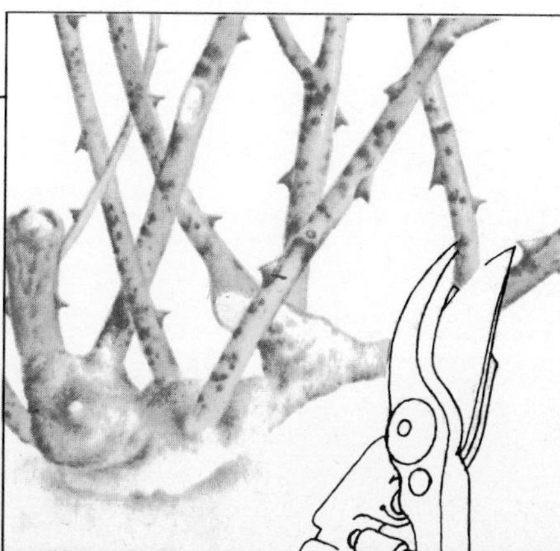

3. Cut stems that cross or rub. *When two stems cross, cut back the weaker of the two to a growth bud below the point where they cross. This prevents overcrowding of new growth and allows air and light to penetrate. With climbers and ramblers this is not practical. Simply train stems so that they do not rub.*

HOW MUCH SHOULD YOU PRUNE?

Weak varieties and thin shoots should always be cut back harder than vigorous varieties and strong shoots. Prune tree roses harder than bushes, and hybrid teas harder than grandifloras and floribundas.

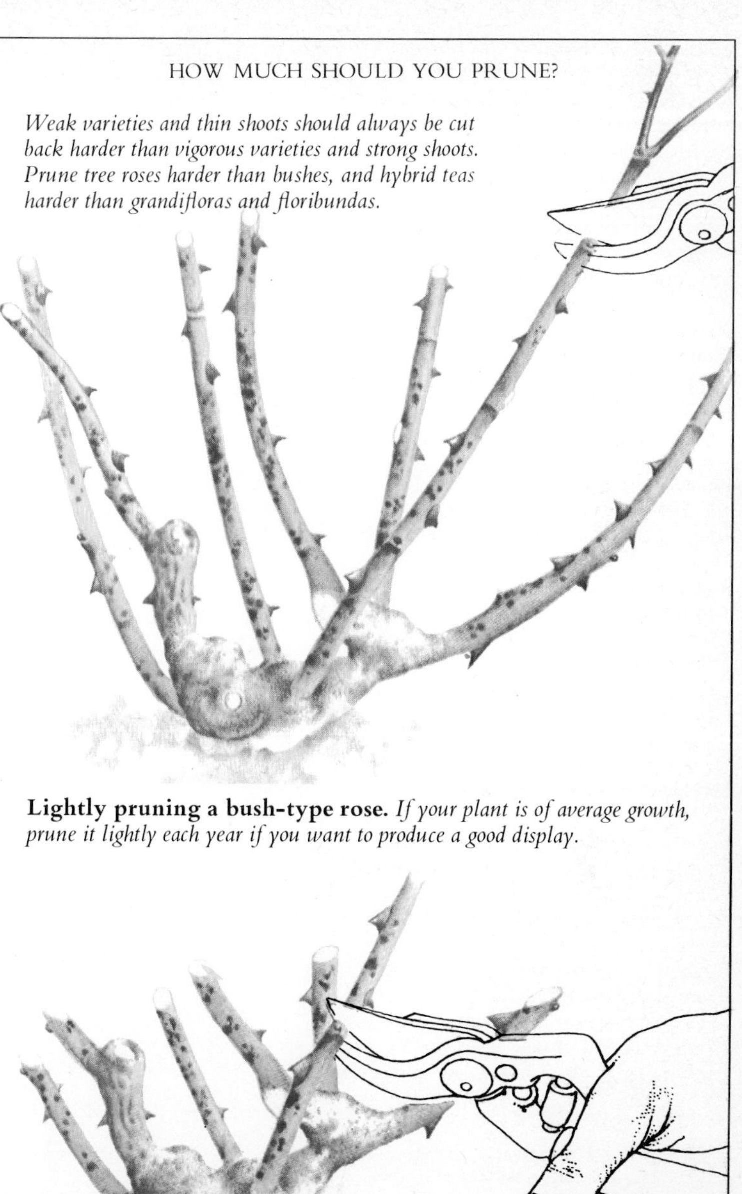

Lightly pruning a bush-type rose. *If your plant is of average growth, prune it lightly each year if you want to produce a good display.*

Hard pruning a bush-type rose. *If you want to grow large, well-formed roses, though few in number, prune your plant back hard annually.*

Pruning Climbing Roses

One of the most important points to keep in mind if you have climbing roses is not to delay pruning—it will only become more difficult. Yearly attention pays dividends in improved appearance, better flowering, and easier maintenance.

Some climbers naturally produce more new canes than do others and thus will require heavier pruning to prevent undisciplined growth. But basically, all dead or weak wood should be removed in spring. In summer, as soon as the flowers have faded, cut back the laterals on which they were borne to within two or three buds of the main canes. On varieties that bloom just once, such as the 'Dr. Van Fleet,' some of the older canes can be cut back to the base each spring. On all other climbers remove old canes only when necessary to shape the plant or to prevent overcrowding.

New leaders, which are obviously larger in diameter than the laterals, frequently appear higher up on old canes. In such cases, cut back these canes to just above the new growth.

Tips of laterals that are too long can be pruned back at any time.

As new leaders develop, be sure to tie them to the supports. Later on they will be less supple.

SUMMER PRUNING

After a climber has bloomed, trim back the flowered stems to selected new buds. Do not let seedpods form, as these will deprive the rose of energy, which will be better used to produce new growth and more flowers. Discard prunings; do not add them to the compost pile. The thorns could cause injury.

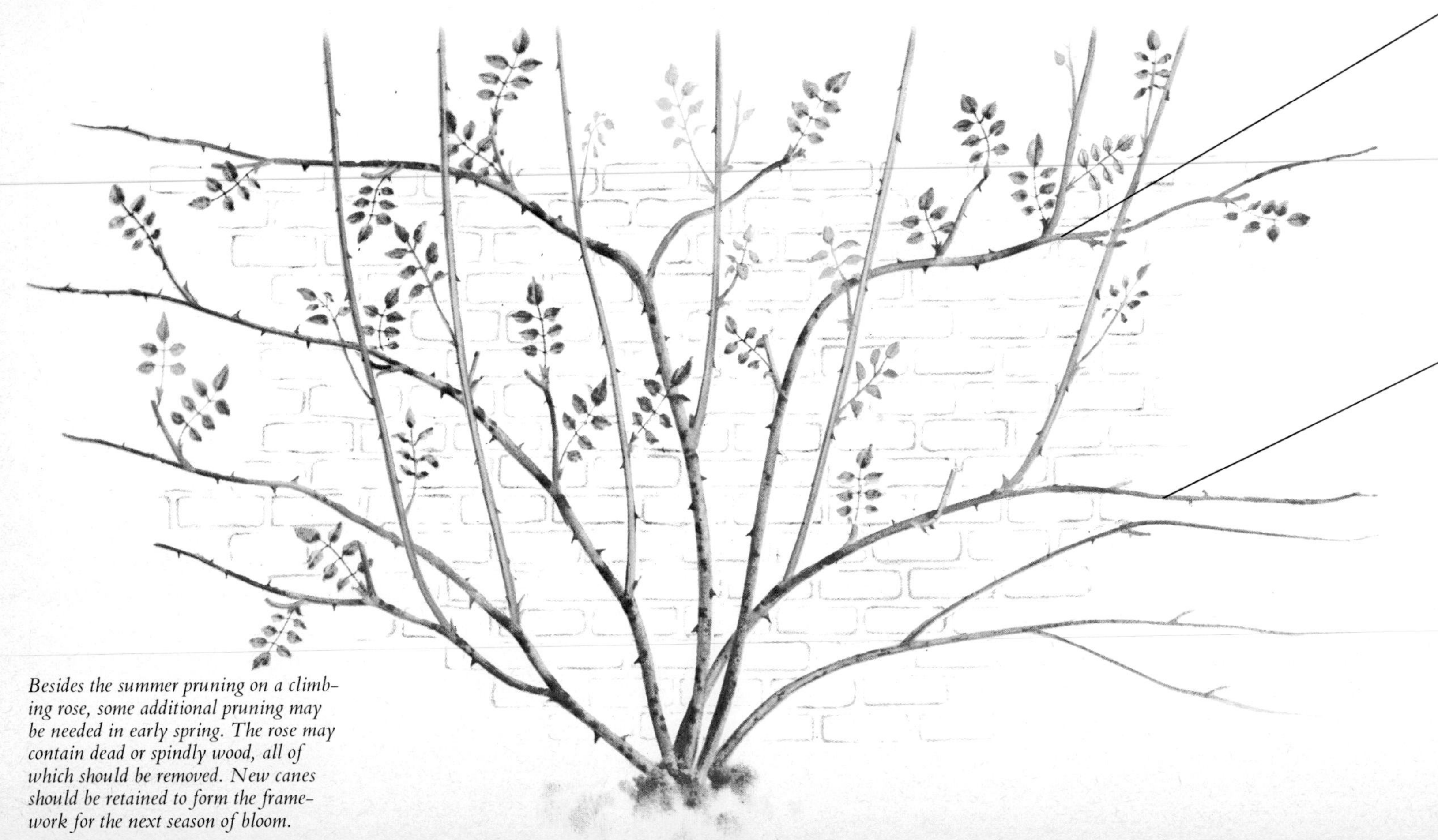

Besides the summer pruning on a climbing rose, some additional pruning may be needed in early spring. The rose may contain dead or spindly wood, all of which should be removed. New canes should be retained to form the framework for the next season of bloom.

Pruning Ramblers

True ramblers develop long, flexible canes from the base of the plant. These canes do not produce flowers until their second year.

It is best to prune ramblers soon after they have flowered. At that time it is usually much easier to tell which are the canes that have just borne the flowers and should therefore be removed.

Most rambler varieties develop new canes in abundance. For each new cane remove an old one at ground level. If too many new ones come up, remove the weaker ones.

Some varieties, however, produce new canes above the base, and old ones can only be cut back to that point. When there is little new basal growth, retain the strongest old canes, and cut the side shoots back to two or three buds in early spring.

Ramblers are best trained on supports that allow the air to move freely. When they are grown against a wall, the reflected heat may invite red spider mites and thrips.

Weeping standards, which are ramblers budded on an upright stem, are pruned like ramblers.

SPRING PRUNING

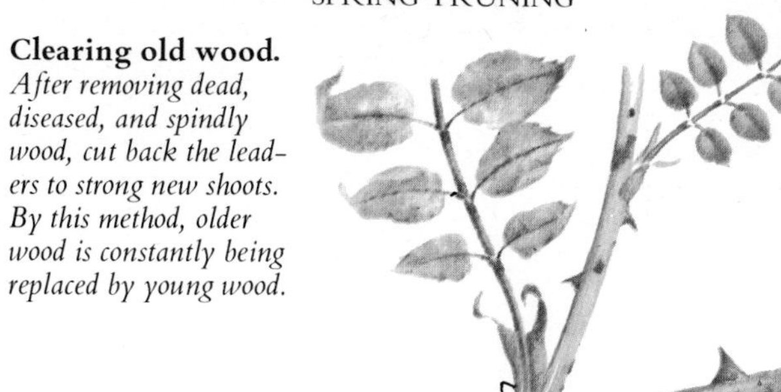

Clearing old wood. *After removing dead, diseased, and spindly wood, cut back the leaders to strong new shoots. By this method, older wood is constantly being replaced by young wood.*

Encouraging new wood. *If no new shoots have grown from a leader, prune it and its laterals by about half. When an old stem ceases to throw out new shoots, cut it out completely to encourage new growth from the base.*

TRAINING A CLIMBING ROSE

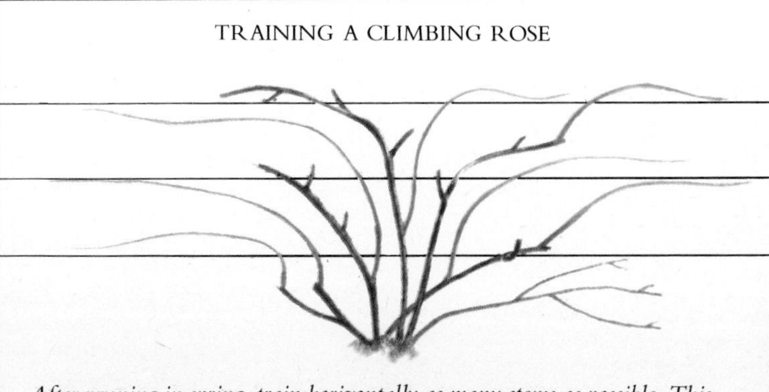

After pruning in spring, train horizontally as many stems as possible. This will help new flowering shoots to break from the stems.

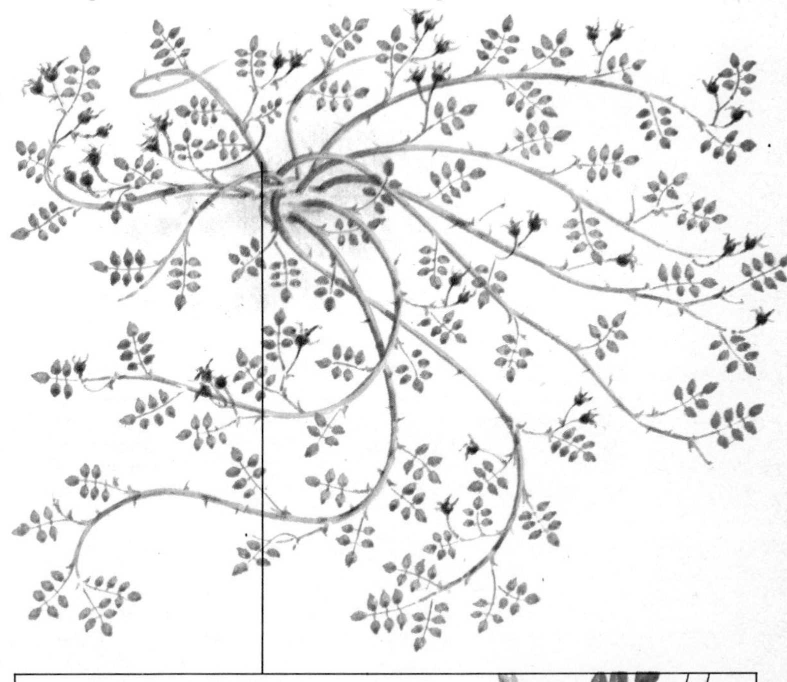

Where new growth sprouts liberally from the base of a rambler, cut the old flowered canes right down to the ground. Trim the cuts with a knife and leave no snags.

Pruning Shrub Roses—Species and Hybrids

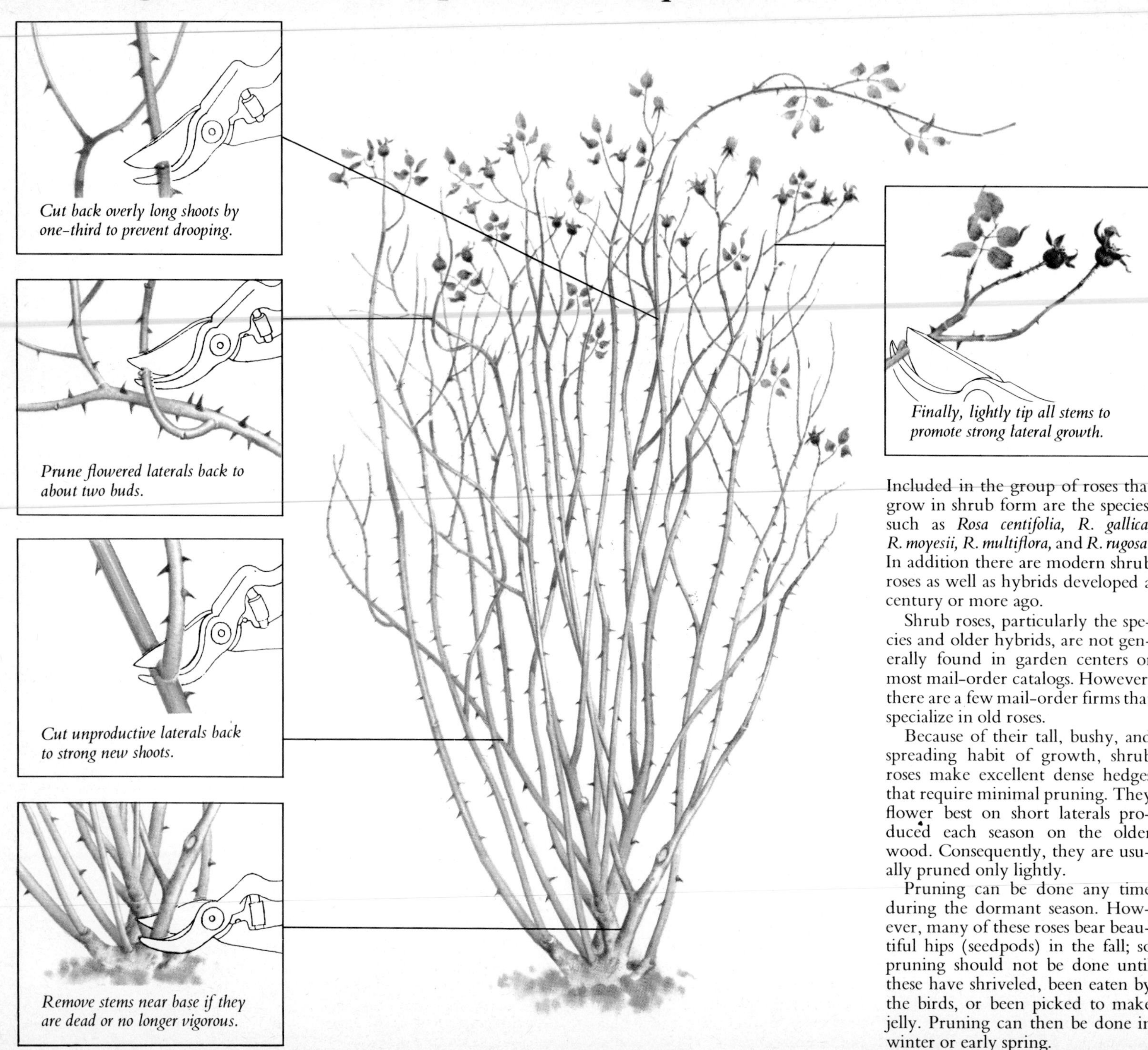

Cut back overly long shoots by one-third to prevent drooping.

Prune flowered laterals back to about two buds.

Cut unproductive laterals back to strong new shoots.

Remove stems near base if they are dead or no longer vigorous.

Finally, lightly tip all stems to promote strong lateral growth.

Included in the group of roses that grow in shrub form are the species, such as *Rosa centifolia, R. gallica, R. moyesii, R. multiflora,* and *R. rugosa.* In addition there are modern shrub roses as well as hybrids developed a century or more ago.

Shrub roses, particularly the species and older hybrids, are not generally found in garden centers or most mail-order catalogs. However, there are a few mail-order firms that specialize in old roses.

Because of their tall, bushy, and spreading habit of growth, shrub roses make excellent dense hedges that require minimal pruning. They flower best on short laterals produced each season on the older wood. Consequently, they are usually pruned only lightly.

Pruning can be done any time during the dormant season. However, many of these roses bear beautiful hips (seedpods) in the fall; so pruning should not be done until these have shriveled, been eaten by the birds, or been picked to make jelly. Pruning can then be done in winter or early spring.

Growing New Roses From Cuttings

Growing roses from cuttings is an inexpensive although not always a successful way to propagate them. At best, it takes two to four years to obtain a good-sized plant.

The commonest method is to take cuttings from a flowering shoot just as the buds on that shoot are beginning to open. Make the cuttings 5 inches long, ensuring that each has three to five leaves. Make the bottom end of each cutting just below a node, and remove the lower leaf. Dip this bottom end in a hormone rooting powder, and insert the cutting 1 inch deep in a shady place.

Cover each cutting with a large glass jar or plastic container. Keep the soil moist, and inspect the cuttings after about six weeks. If new growth is visible, remove the jar.

Leave the cuttings in place until the following spring, when they can be set in their permanent positions. In cold climates completely cover the cuttings with a mound of soil in late fall and leave until spring; then gradually remove the soil. Cuttings can also be protected in a cold frame.

If you wish to take hardwood cuttings in the fall, select strong side shoots, about as thick as a pencil, from the current year's growth. Two kinds of cuttings can be made at this time. Heel cuttings are taken where the side shoot is attached to the main stem. Hold the side shoot firmly in a gloved hand, and remove it from the main stem with a quick downward twist. Or cut the side shoot close to the main stem with a sharp knife.

The second method is to sever a stem down low, just above a bud. Then trim the base of the cutting just below a bud.

Both types of hardwood cuttings should be treated in the same way. If the cutting is longer than 1 foot, shorten it from the top, severing just above a bud.

In mild climates cut off all but the top pair of leaves. Using a sharp knife, nick out the buds in all the leaf axils except for the pair of leaves.

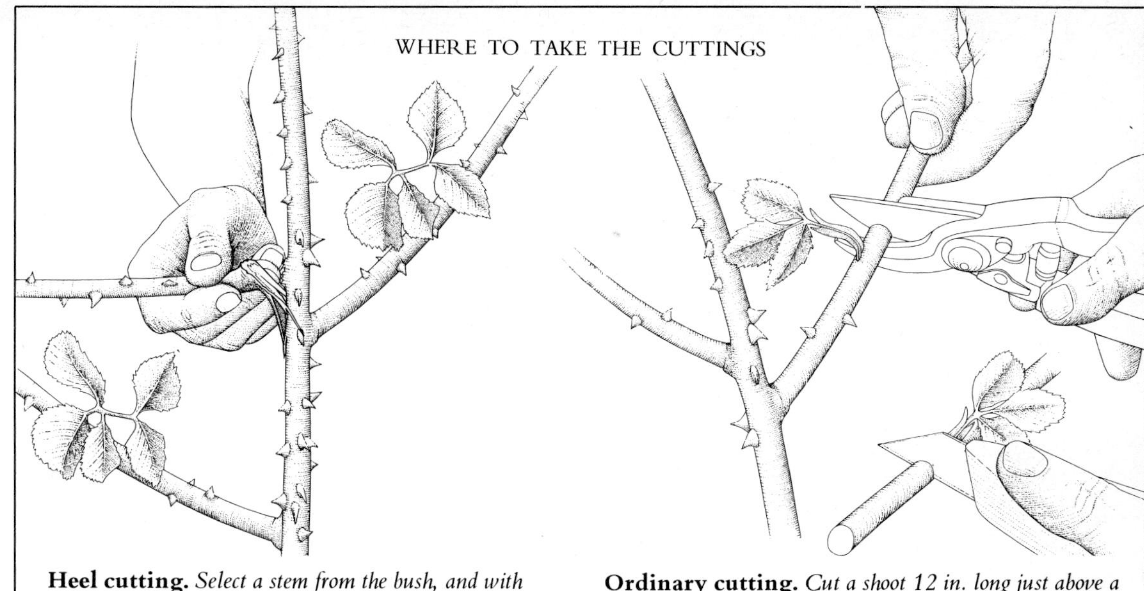

Heel cutting. *Select a stem from the bush, and with a sharp downward twist, pull it off with heel attached.*

Ordinary cutting. *Cut a shoot 12 in. long just above a bud. Trim the base of the shoot, cutting just below a bud.*

In a shady part of your garden, make a narrow, V-shaped trench, 9 inches deep, and sprinkle about 1 inch of coarse sand or perlite in it. Dip the base of each cutting in a hormone rooting powder.

Lay the cuttings almost vertically on the side of the trench. Space them 6 inches apart, with the base of each resting on the sand. Firm the soil around the cuttings and water thoroughly. Leave them in place until the fall of the following year, and then plant them in their final location.

In cold climates only leafless hardwood stem cuttings should be used. Make them in fall, shortly before hard-freezing weather sets in. Lay them horizontally in an 8-inch-deep trench, and cover with sand or soil. After the ground freezes, apply a mulch over the area. In spring dig up the cuttings, and set them in a trench as shown in the illustrations. In fall put them in permanent positions where they can be protected through the winter with a mound of soil.

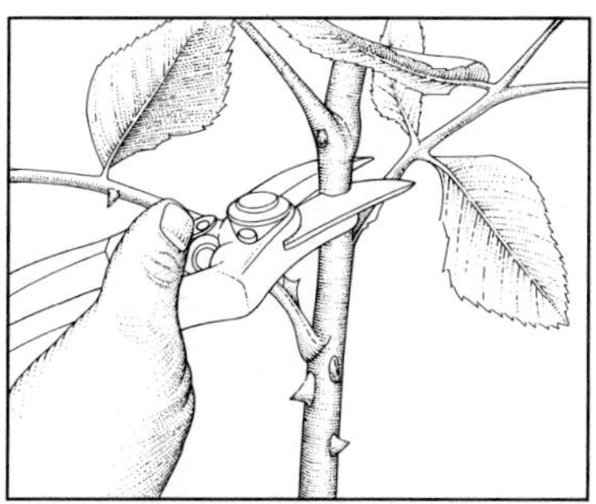

1. *Shorten the cutting from the top if it is more than 12 in. long.*

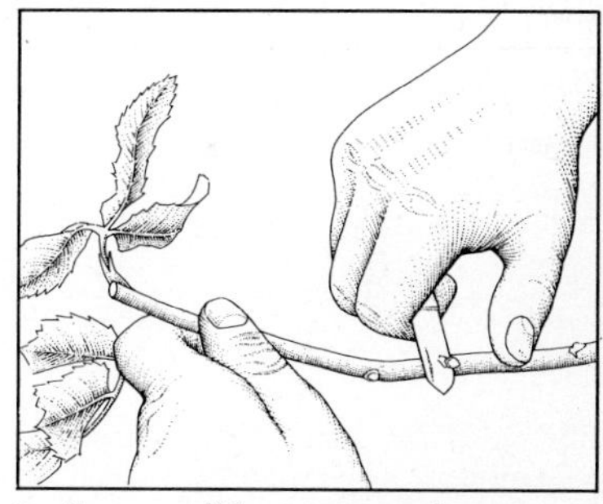

2. *Remove all leaves except the top two; nick out buds in the other leaf axils.*

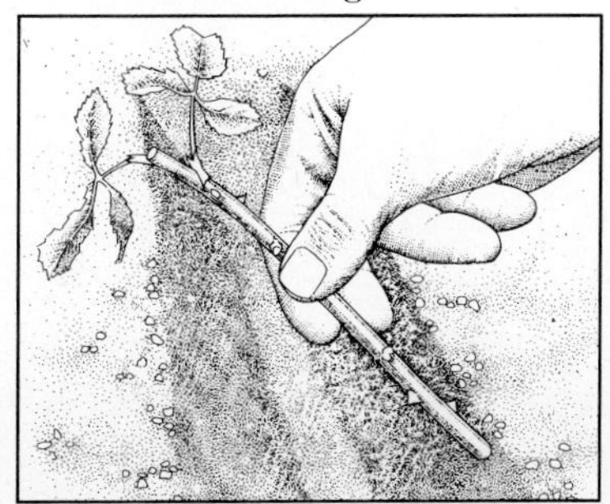

3. *Lay the cuttings 6 in. apart on one side of a narrow, 9-in.-deep trench.*

4. *Fill in the trench, tread the soil fairly firmly, and water thoroughly.*

Propagating Hybrid Teas by Budding

Preparing Rootstock and Budwood

The best way to propagate hybrid tea roses is by budding—that is, cutting a dormant growth bud, or "eye," from the desired variety and grafting it onto a vigorous rootstock.

Rootstocks can be raised from seeds (a slow process), from cuttings, or bought in nurseries that specialize in roses. Many kinds of roses can be used as rootstocks, including *R. multiflora, R. canina* (dog rose), and the climbing 'Dorothy Perkins.'

Before the grafts can be made, rootstocks must be well established. In late autumn or early spring plant the desired number 12 inches apart. Cover the roots and the lowest inch or so of stem with soil; water well.

The next summer cut the budwood (the stem that will provide the bud) from the variety that you want to propagate. Select a strong 12-inch length of stem on which the flowers have just faded. The dormant growth buds lie within the leaf axils.

To make the stem easier to handle, remove all thorns. Next, cut off the leaves, retaining half an inch of leaf stalk. Remove the faded flowers, severing the stem just above a bud or leaf axil. Submerge the budwood in water.

Hold the stem of the rootstock to one side with your foot. Carefully dig out the soil on the other side, making sure that the top roots are completely exposed. Remove any soil from the stem and wipe it dry.

Using a budding knife or other sharp tool, make a T-shaped cut in the bark close to the roots. Cut the top of the T first, making it about half an inch long. Do not cut into the woody tissue below the bark.

With an upward stroke, cut a slightly longer "tail" that meets the top cut. Using the blunt edge of the knife blade (or the quill of the budding knife), gently pry apart the bark and fold it outward. The rootstock is now ready for grafting.

PLANTING THE ROOTSTOCK

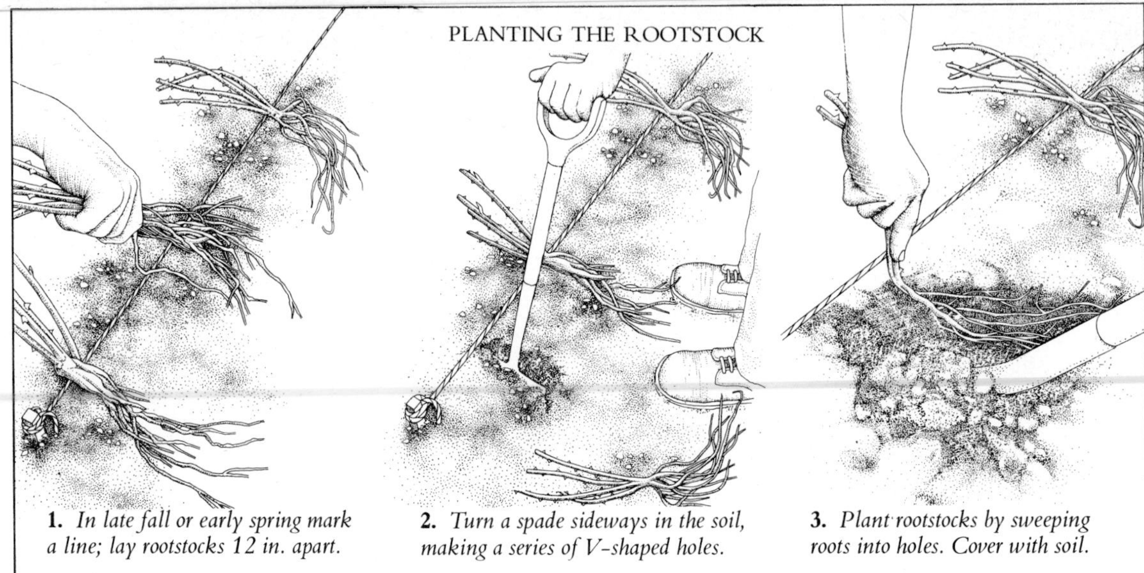

1. *In late fall or early spring mark a line; lay rootstocks 12 in. apart.*

2. *Turn a spade sideways in the soil, making a series of V-shaped holes.*

3. *Plant rootstocks by sweeping roots into holes. Cover with soil.*

HOW TO PREPARE BUDWOOD AND ROOTSTOCK

1. *In midsummer cut a 12-in. length of stem from the plant to be propagated.*

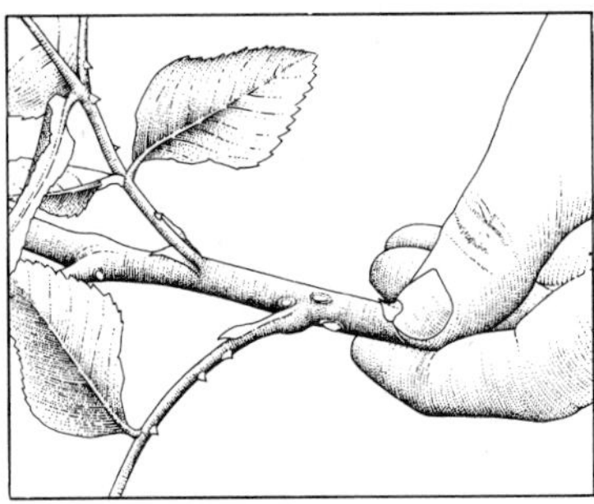

2. *Remove thorns from the stem, or budwood, by pressing thumb sideways.*

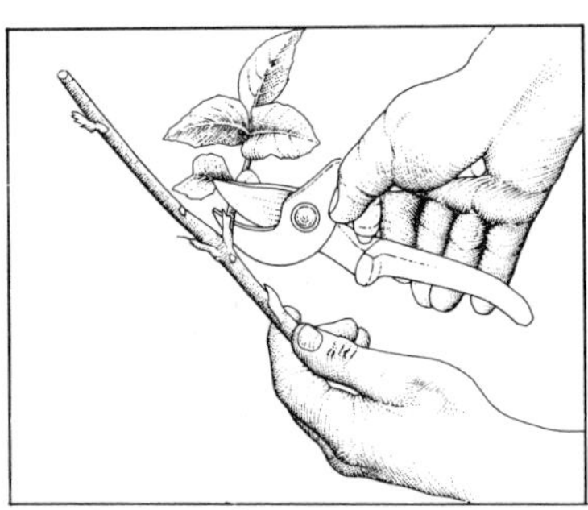

3. *Clip leaves from the budwood, retaining $^1/_2$ in. of leaf stalk.*

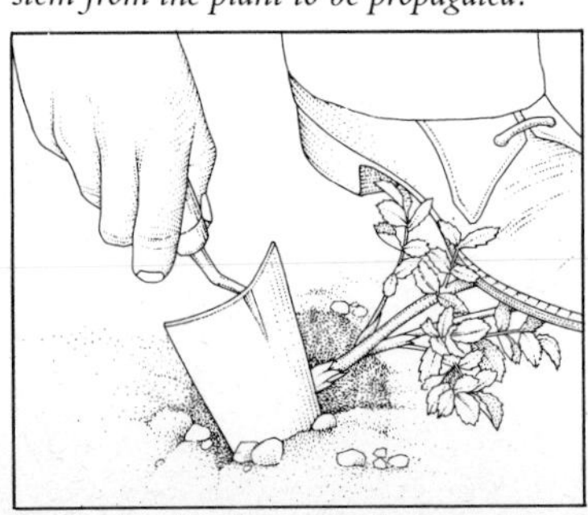

4. *Push aside the rootstock stem with your foot. Remove soil with a trowel.*

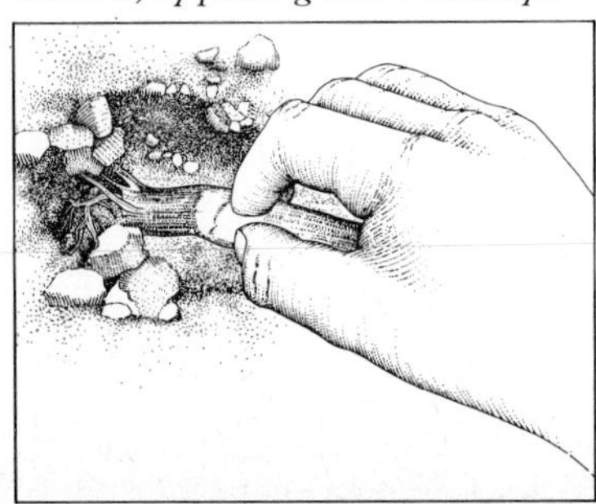

5. *With your fingers or a cloth, clean rootstock just above the roots.*

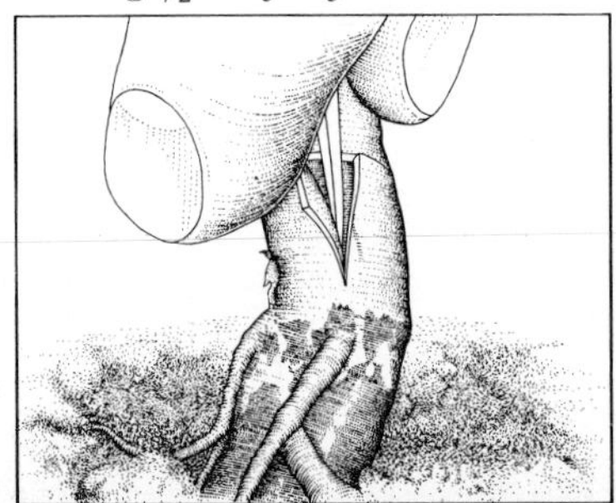

6. *Make a T-shaped cut in the bark of the rootstock and open the flaps.*

Combining Bud and Rootstock

After preparing the rootstock, remove the budwood from the water. Then slice out one of the dormant growth buds.

To do this, begin the cut half an inch above the bud. Draw the blade behind the bud, coming out half an inch below. Use a shallow scooping motion, so that a sliver of wood behind the bark is also removed. The piece produced is called the shield.

Hold the shield with one hand, and peel back the strip of bark until the sliver of wood is exposed. Hold the sliver between your thumb and index finger. With a slight twist, ease it out smoothly from the bark and then discard. If the sliver of wood has been satisfactorily removed, the dormant bud will be visible as a tiny bump on the inner side of the remaining piece of shield.

Hold the shield by the stump of leafstalk, and slide it into the T cut on the rootstock. Trim off any portion of the shield that protrudes above the top of the cut. Close the flaps around the shield.

With damp raffia, soft twine, or budding rubber (which can be purchased from horticultural supply houses), tie the insert in place firmly but not too tightly. Make two turns below the stub of the leafstalk and three turns above. Do not cover the bud. Carefully replace the soil around the rootstock until the soil is level with the base of the grafted bud.

Inspect the bud several weeks after grafting. If it is plump and green, budding has been successful, and the twine can be removed. (Budding rubber need not be removed.) If the bud has shriveled, insert and tie a second shield in a fresh T cut made on the same rootstock.

Winter treatment for budded plants is the same as for other roses, with one exception: late in the season all of the plant above the graft should be cut off.

Generally, a bud will not grow until the first spring after grafting. When the new growth is several inches long, pinch it back to two buds above the grafting point. This will encourage growth. In autumn transplant to a permanent site.

Buds can be grafted onto the main stems of established rose plants, rather than onto rootstocks. To make a graft onto a plant growing in a hedge, insert buds in the upper sides of the young side shoots, as close to the main stem as possible. Make two or three grafts on each brier.

BUDDING A STANDARD

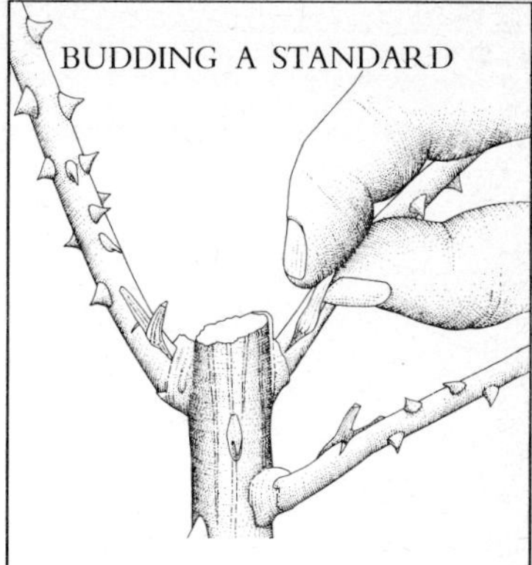

To make a standard (tree) rose, grow a rootstock until it reaches the desired height. In summer, bud onto the main stem or, preferably, onto the upper surfaces of three shoots at the top.

GRAFTING THE BUD ONTO THE ROOTSTOCK

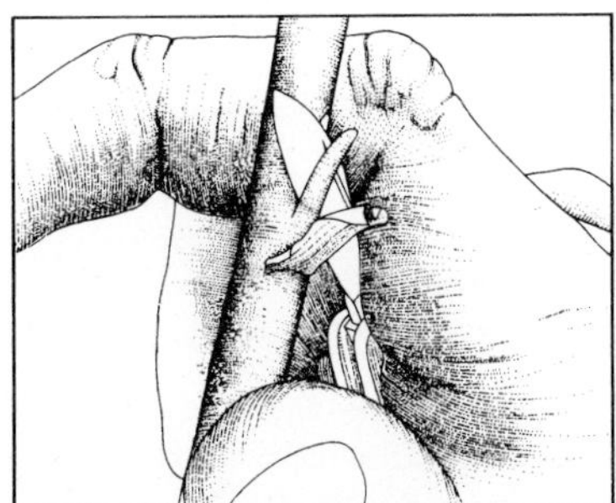

1. *Scoop a bud ("eye") from the budwood, cutting $^1/_2$ in. above and below.*

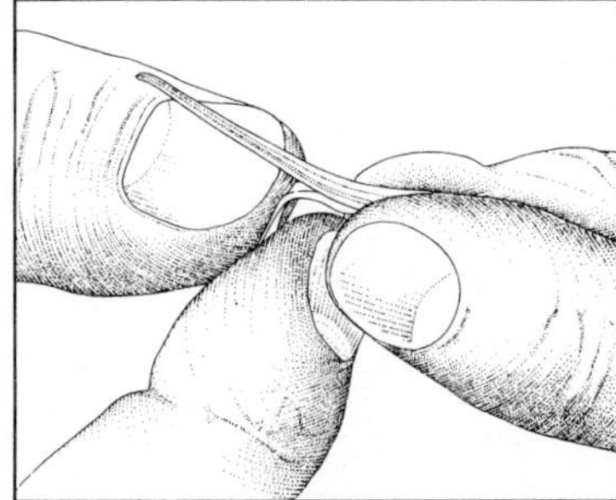

2. *Peel and retain the bark from the piece of budwood (shield).*

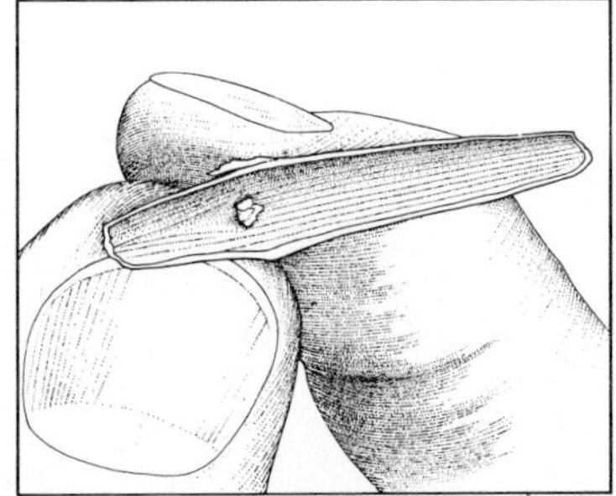

3. *The growth bud is visible as a small bump on the inside of the shield.*

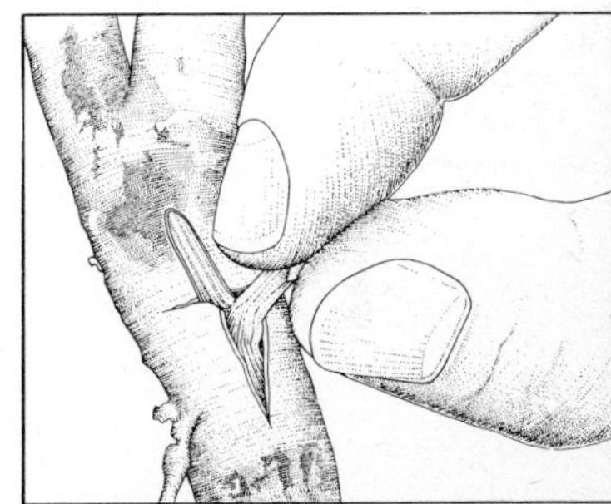

4. *Using the stump of leafstalk as a handle, slide the shield into the T cut.*

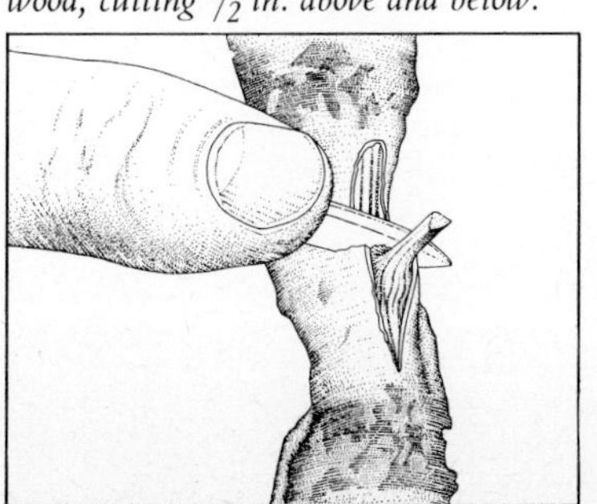

5. *Carefully cut off the upper end of the shield and close the bark flaps.*

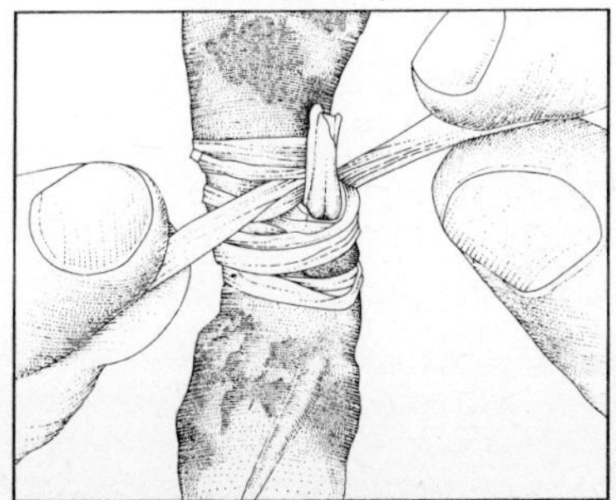

6. *Tie shield to stem. Raffia or twine should be removed several weeks later.*

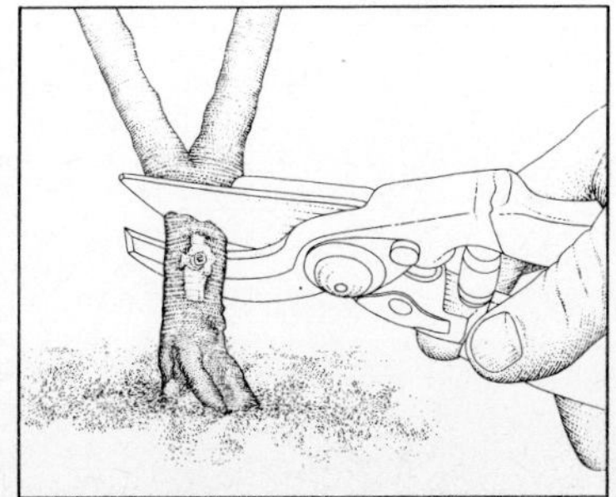

7. *In late winter clip the top growth (above the bud) from the rootstock.*

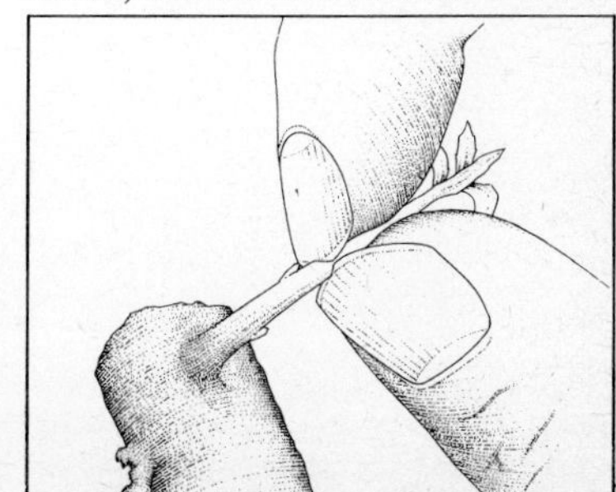

8. *When new growth is several inches long, pinch it back above the second bud.*

Rhododendrons and Azaleas

The vivid displays produced by rhododendrons and azaleas can last from spring into summer. There are plants to fit any size of garden, but the soil must be right.

The value of this group of plants for the home landscape can hardly be overestimated. Ranging from mat-like dwarf shrubs only a few inches high to trees more than 40 feet tall, rhododendrons and azaleas offer a remarkable variety of sizes and shapes.

Most rhododendrons have magnificent foliage, and the flowers of many varieties are among the most beautiful in the world of shrubs. The flowers' colors are white, lavender, violet, purple, pink, crimson, scarlet, orange, and yellow. Their shapes are tubular, starry, funnel- or bowl-shaped, and bell-like, varying in size from 3/4 to 6 inches wide and from 3/4 to 4 inches long. The flowers are usually produced in rounded trusses with as many as 15 individual blossoms on each one.

Rhododendrons and azaleas grow beautifully in dappled sunlight or partial shade and in moist, acid soil. They also do quite well in full sunlight, but flowers last longer with some shade. They will not survive in alkaline soil or in hot, dry situations.

Rhododendrons and azaleas have a remarkable range of hardiness. Gardeners in even the coldest climates can enjoy at least a few of these attractive shrubs.

The word "rhododendron" is derived from the Greek words *rhodon* ("rose") and *dendron* ("tree"). When the traditional large-leaved rhododendrons are in bloom, they fully live up to the promise of their name.

The first species made available for garden use, in the mid 1600's, was *Rhododendron hirsutum,* native to the mountains of Europe. In 1753 the Swedish botanist Linnaeus officially established and named the genus *Rhododendron.* At the same time he created the separate genus *Azalea.* Then, in the 19th century, another botanist, George Don, discovered that there was little botanical difference between the two, and they were both classified as the genus *Rhododendron,* which they remain to this day. Gardeners, however, still prefer to talk of rhododendrons and azaleas as separate kinds of plants, and they are so identified in nurseries and catalogs. In the variety listings starting on page 225, they will be discussed under their separate names, but the information in the following text refers to both.

There are deciduous and evergreen species of both kinds. The evergreens are the most popular, but there is an increasing interest in deciduous azaleas. Few deciduous rhododendrons are grown. Rhododendrons occur in the wild all over the world. Most hybrids have been developed from species native to Burma, China, and northern India. Many of these were crossed with native American species, particularly *R. catawbiense,* which grows wild in the mountains from Virginia to Georgia. The varieties developed from these crosses are remarkably hardy. Most *R. catawbiense* hybrids will survive winter temperatures as low as −25° F. The flower buds, however, may be killed at −15° F.

Since the flowers are the major glory of the rhododendron, the degree of bud hardiness is a critical factor. The hardiness ratings given on pages 225–226 are based on bud hardiness. The plants themselves will survive temperatures 10–15 degrees lower. This is a valuable safety margin for the harder-than-average winters that come along every 10 years or so in most cold climates.

The more resistant a rhododendron is to cold weather, the more resistant it will also be to heat. Therefore, to grow rhododendrons in a warmer climate than is usually recommended, it is best to choose the hardiest varieties.

Rhododendron 'Scarlet King' is an evergreen that grows 4–8 ft. tall. Its large clusters of scarlet blossoms are borne in the spring.

Growing Healthy Rhododendrons and Azaleas

All rhododendrons must have a well-drained soil that is rich in humus and definitely on the acid side. A pH of 4.5–5.5 is best. (Neutral is 7. For more information about the acid-alkaline balance and how to control it, see p. 594.)

Azaleas are more adaptable than rhododendrons. The deciduous varieties do well in soils with a pH below 4 and as high as 6. The optimum for evergreen azaleas is about pH 5.

The soil must contain sufficient humus to hold moisture long enough for the roots to take it up. But the soil should not be soggy, or roots will die. To test drainage, dig a hole about 18 inches deep, and fill it with water. If it takes more than 10 or 15 minutes to soak in, there is not sufficient drainage.

Sometimes drainage in a planting hole can be improved by breaking the ground to a greater depth. If this does not work, spade up an area the size of the root ball, and put the plant on the surface. Then mound up around the root ball with a soil mixture that has the necessary humus and acidity. You may need three or four wheelbarrows of soil to cover the root area with a gently sloping mound that will not wash away.

These plants also lend themselves to being grown in raised beds and large containers, where the structure of the soil and the pH can be precisely controlled.

All rhododendrons and azaleas should be mulched with coarse organic material immediately after planting. The mulch should be heavy enough to stay in place and open enough to admit air and water. Wood or bark chips, pine needles, salt hay, or oak leaves are excellent. Peat moss is not; when it dries, it becomes almost impervious to water and can be blown away.

When a plant is firmly set in the planting hole, fill the hole with garden soil in the recommended pH range, to which some humus has been added—about 10 percent by volume. The humus can be peat moss, compost, rotted sawdust, or similar material available locally. The shrub should be planted at the same depth at which it grew in the nursery (you will see the soil line on the trunk). Cover the top of the root ball with about 1 inch of soil.

In setting out plants that were grown in containers in a nursery, it is essential to break up the root ball before planting. The shape of the soil around the roots, as formed by the container, must be thoroughly broken, and the outer roots should be well loosened. If this is not done, the feeder roots may never grow out into the surrounding soil; the plant will become root-bound and die within two or three years.

As for fertilizer, the common practice of putting it directly in the bottom of a planting hole can be fatal to rhododendrons and azaleas. Always bear in mind that these plants should be fertilized only moderately. Rhododendrons and azaleas respond best to moderation in all aspects of cultivation: moderate light, moderate water, and moderate pruning.

During planting, it is safe to add bone meal, but no more than one handful for each plant. Mix it thoroughly with the soil in the top 9–12 inches of the hole, which is where most of the roots will grow.

After the plant is well rooted, it is safe to fertilize once early each spring and again in midfall. Scatter no more than one handful of 10–10–10 dry fertilizer evenly over the root area of each plant, and water it in. As a general rule, give rhododendrons and azaleas only one-fourth to one-half the amount of any fertilizer recommended for shrubs.

If you prefer to use a soluble fertilizer, such as 20–20–20, mix 1 teaspoonful with a gallon of water, and sprinkle this amount into the soil around each plant. The feeding can be repeated every two or three weeks during the season of active growth.

Growing Rhododendrons in Alkaline Soil

Although you may live where the soil and water are alkaline, you can grow rhododendrons by providing the acid conditions they require. Plant them in a raised bed at least 18 inches high, containing a specially prepared growing medium.

The sides of the raised bed should be made of masonry or rot-resistant wood, such as redwood, cedar, or cypress. Other woods should first be treated with a preservative containing copper naphthenates.

The growing medium should have a pH of 5, and certainly no higher than 5.5. It can be made up of peat moss, leaf mold, composted oak leaves, well-rotted wood chips, or rotted sawdust, plus some of your best topsoil—about 10 percent by volume. Mix thoroughly; then check the pH with a soil-test kit. If the pH is too high, acidity can be increased by adding flowers of sulfur (see p. 594). Spread about half a cup over a circle 4 feet in diameter. Repeat six months later as needed.

How and When to Prune Rhododendrons

Rhododendrons seldom need pruning except to control their size and shape. Any required pruning should be done as soon as they have finished blooming. The plant grows vigorously at that time, and it is wise to keep this energy from going into unwanted growth. Simply cut the branches to the shape and size you want, making clean cuts with sharp tools. The pruning of both young and old plants is illustrated below.

If a plant outgrows its site, it can be relocated. Because of their relatively shallow and fibrous root systems, rhododendrons are among the easiest of all plants to move.

SPINDLY YOUNG PLANTS

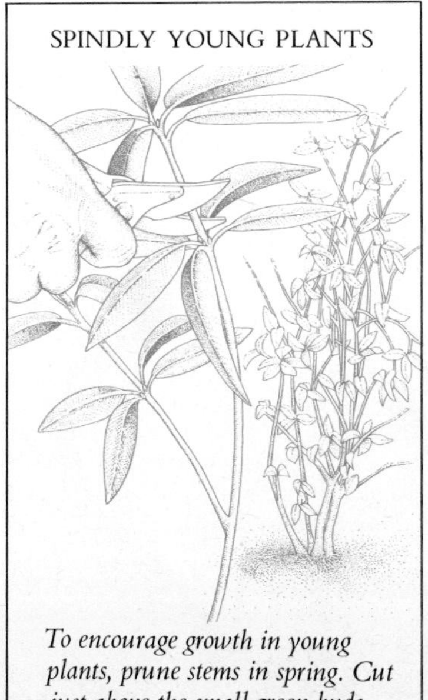

To encourage growth in young plants, prune stems in spring. Cut just above the small green buds.

STRAGGLY OLD SHRUBS

For renewal, use a saw to cut back old shrubs in early spring to within 3 ft. from the ground.

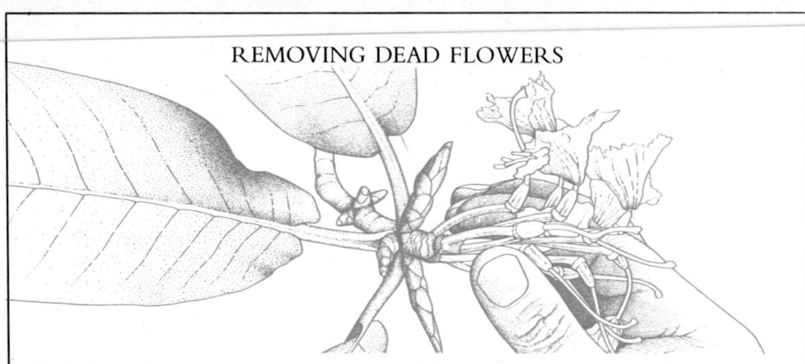

To help produce the maximum number of flowers each year, carefully break off the entire flower heads as soon as rhododendrons have finished blooming.

Caring for Greenhouse-Grown Azaleas

The greenhouse-grown azaleas that florists sell in full bloom for Easter and other occasions can be planted outside, where they will continue to grow and flower each year if given proper care. When they have finished flowering indoors and the danger of frost is past, plant them in the garden. Care for them as you would any rhododendron.

Break up the sides of the root ball thoroughly, or the roots may never expand beyond the size and shape of the container and the plant will fade away after a year or two.

In frost-free climates most azaleas can be left outside all year. If you live in a part of the country where it freezes in winter, dig the plants up in autumn and pot them. Store them in a light, cool, frost-free place. Water just enough to keep the soil from drying out. In spring plant the azaleas in the garden as soon as there is no further danger of frost.

Encouraging Rhododendrons to Flower

It is not unusual to buy a heavily budded rhododendron in early spring, to plant it and enjoy a magnificent show of flowers, only to be disappointed the following year when it is seen that few if any flower buds have developed.

In most such cases the problem is too little light. Although these plants will grow well in dappled shade, and even survive in deep shade, unless they get at least three or four hours of high-intensity light every day, they will not set many flower buds.

Flower production is also affected by feeding. Phosphate, in particular, increases the number of buds. For plants 3–5 feet across, sprinkle two or three large handfuls of superphosphate or twice that amount of bone meal around each plant, and scratch it lightly into the soil. It may take a year or so for the effects to show. This topdressing can be applied for two or three successive years. Giving phosphate at this rate is safe; the same amount of a 10–10–10 complete fertilizer would be harmful.

Some plants will establish a pattern of blooming heavily only every second year. This rhythm of alternate flowering can be broken by removing some of the buds after they are fully formed in the fall if they seem to be too crowded.

What Can Go Wrong With Rhododendrons and Azaleas

Some of the problems that are likely to occur in growing rhododendrons and azaleas are discussed in the chart below. If your plant should show symptoms that are not described in this chart, turn to the full-color identification section on plant disorders and diseases beginning on page 600. This illustrates symptoms that may occur on different parts of a plant—leaves, flowers, stems, or roots. To find trade names of recommended chemicals, turn to page 635.

Symptoms and signs	Cause	Control
Leaves have rusty brown mottling and may fall.	Lace bugs	Spray with malathion at first sign of attack.
Leaves lose luster and turn grayish green. Symptoms of mite damage occur primarily during hot summer and on evergreen azaleas. Lace bug damage appears in early to mid summer.	Lace bugs	Spray with malathion at first sign of attack; be certain to spray leaf undersides. Repeat 3 times at 10-da. intervals.
	Red spider mites	Spray with dicofol or other miticide. To prevent infestation, spray leaves regularly with water.
Older branches at center of shrub may have small holes. Some branches may die.	Rhododendron borers	Spray with lindane or malathion twice in late spring; allow 2 wk. between applications. Check with local experts for specific timing, which is critical for control. Borers can be killed by inserting wire into their tunnels.
Leaf edges have semi-circular notches. Leaves may have poor color, indicating that weevil larvae are feeding on roots or main stem.	Vine weevils	In late spring or early fall, spray at 10-da. intervals with chlordane or methoxychlor, or apply 14% granular Diazinon.
Leaves have round, dark red or brown spots late in summer.	Leaf spot (fungus)	Spray with zineb or other fungicide before spots appear in late spring. Later applications are not effective.
Tiny spots on undersides of petals enlarge and bleach out. Flowers wilt.	Petal blight (fungus)	Spray with Benomyl every 5 da. during bloom season.
Young shoots on single branch wilt in midsummer, or entire shrub may wilt. Diseased branches show brown stain under bark just below soil level.	Wilt (fungus)	Remove and destroy diseased branches; in severe cases destroy entire shrub. To prevent disease, use soil drench such as Terrazole. To prevent spread, take care not to splash spores from soil surface onto shrub.
Leaves show yellow patches between veins or are flushed all over; may wither.	Chlorosis	Treat with chelated compounds (sequestered iron), and mulch with peat moss.

Varieties of Rhododendrons and Azaleas to Grow

There are scores of rhododendron and azalea hybrids, and among them are attractive plants suitable for a wide range of climates. The zone ratings given here relate to bud hardiness of the particular plant keyed to the Temperature Zone Map on page 9. Notice that in some cases the zone letter is supplemented with a plus or minus symbol. A plus means that the plant will tolerate a temperature 5–10 degrees colder than that given on the zone map. For example, B+ indicates that the plant is hardy through Zone B (to a minimum temperature of −20° F) and will also survive in the warmer areas of Zone A (to −25° or −30° F). On the other hand, a B− rating indicates that the plant will be safe only in the warmer areas of Zone B.

Most hardiness problems can be avoided if you buy plants at established local nurseries. It seldom pays to buy from itinerant plant peddlers, who are usually misinformed about the plants they sell. In addition, the plants are likely to be of poor quality if not actually diseased.

The rating column on the charts has two numbers that have been assigned by the American Rhododendron Society to indicate the overall quality of the plant. The first number refers to the flower and truss (flower cluster); the second refers to the rest of the plant. The highest rating is a 5/5. A rating of 2/5 indicates a relatively poor flower on an excellent plant; a 5/2 reveals that the flowers are exceptional but the plant is less than ideally full and vigorous. In a few cases where the A.R.S. ratings have not yet been established, a panel of experts has made the evaluation.

Although azaleas belong to the genus *Rhododendron,* they are quite different in appearance and garden use from plants commonly called rhododendrons. They are therefore considered separately on the following charts.

Names	Color	Hardiness (*Map, p. 9*)	Rating	Height
The hardiest				
'Album Elegans'	Pale lilac fading to white	Zone B+	2/2	6–8 ft.
'America'	Dark red	Zone B	2/2	4–5 ft.
'Boule de Neige'	Clear white	Zone B+	3/4	5–6 ft.
'Catalode,' or 'County of York'	Creamy white	Zone C+	3/3 (fragrant)	5–6 ft.
'Catawbiense Album' (*R. catawbiense album*)	White with yellow spots	Zone B	3/3	8–9 ft.
'Catawbiense Boursault'	Mauve or rosy lilac	Zone B+	2/3	4–5 ft.
'Chionoides'	Clear white	Zone C	2/4	3–4 ft.
'English Roseum'	Pink	Zone B+	2/3	5–6 ft.
'E. S. Rand'	Crimson-red	Zone B−	2/2	4–5 ft.
'Katherine Dalton'	Clear, light pink	Zone A	3/3 (fragrant)	4–5 ft.
'Maximum Roseum'	Clear pink	Zone B−	2/2	6–8 ft.
'Nova Zembla'	Dark red	Zone B	3/3	4–5½ ft.
'Parsons Grandiflorum'	Pale lilac	Zone B	1/3	6–7 ft.
'Purpureum Elegans'	Purple-blue	Zone B+	2/3	5–6 ft.
'Roseum Elegans'	Mauve	Zone B+	2/4	5–6½ ft.
'Roseum Pink'	Clear pink	Zone B	2/3	5–7 ft.
Not quite so hardy				
'A. Bedford'	Lavender-blue, dark blotch	Zone C−	4/3	5–6½ ft.
'Blue Peter'	Light blue, purple blotch	Zone C	4/3	5–6 ft.
'Dr. V. H. Rutgers'	Aniline-red, fringed	Zone B−	2/3	4–5 ft.
'Fatuosum Flore-pleno'	Lavender-blue	Zone C+	3/3	5–6 ft.
'Goldworth Yellow'	Apricot to yellow	Zone C	1/2	3–4 ft.
'Gomer Waterer'	Rose tinged to bluish white	Zone C	3/4	5–6 ft.
'John Walter'	Crimson-red	Zone C	2/3	3–4 ft.
'John Wister,' or 'Janet Blair'	Pale pink with bronze	Zone B−	4/3	4–5 ft.
'Mars'	Deep red	Zone C−	4/3	4–4½ ft.
'Professor F. Bettex'	Brilliant red	Zone C	3/2	5–5½ ft.
'Purple Splendor'	Pale purple, ruffled	Zone C−	4/3	4–5½ ft.
'Scintillation'	Light pink, bronze throat	Zone C+	4/4	6–8 ft.
'Trilby'	Deep crimson	Zone C−	2/2	3–4 ft.
'Vivacious'	Bright, clear red	Zone C	4/4	3–4½ ft.

Names	Color	Hardiness (*Map, p. 9*)	Rating	Height
Semi-dwarf and dwarf rhododendrons				
'Anna Baldsiefen'	Bright rose	Zone B	2/3	2–2½ ft.
'Dora Amateis'	White-spotted green	Zone B	4/4	3–4 ft.
'Mary Fleming'	Peach-pink to yellow	Zone C	3/2	1½–2 ft.
'P. J. Mezitt'	Light lavender-purple	Zone A	3/4	3–4 ft.
'Purple Gem'	Light purple	Zone B	3/4	1½–2 ft.
'Purple Imp'	Pale blue	Zone B	2/4	1–1½ ft.
'Racemosum' (*R. racemosum*)	Pink	Zone B	2/3	2–2½ ft.
'Ramapo'	Bright pink-tinged violet	Zone B	3/4	1½–2 ft.
'Windbeam'	Pale pink	Zone B+	4/3	3–4 ft.
Evergreen azaleas (Kurume)				
'Addy Wery'	Blood-red	Zone C–	4/3	2–3 ft.
'Coral Bells'	Pink	Zone C–	3/2	1½–2 ft.
'Hino-Crimson'	Bright crimson-red	Zone B–	4/4	1½–2 ft.
'Red Progress'	Bright red	Zone C	5/4	2½–3 ft.
'Salmon Beauty'	Salmon-red	Zone C–	3/3	2–2½ ft.
'Sherwood Orchid'	Orchid-purple	Zone C	3/3	2½–3 ft.
'Sherwood Red'	Bright red	Zone C	4/3	2½–3 ft.
'Snow'	White	Zone C–	3/3	2½–3 ft.
Evergreen azaleas (Gable)				
'Herbert'	Purple	Zone B+	3/3	2½–3 ft.
'Lorna'	Dark pink, double flowered	Zone B	3/3	1½–2 ft.
'Louise Gable'	Salmon, double flowered	Zone B–	5/4	2–2½ ft.
'Polaris'	White, semi-double	Zone B–	4/3	2–2½ ft.
'Rosebud'	Pink	Zone B–	5/3	1½–2 ft.

Names	Color	Hardiness (*Map, p. 9*)	Rating	Height
'Rose Greely'	White	Zone B	4/3	2–2½ ft.
'Stewartstonian'	Bright red	Zone B	4/4	2½–3 ft.
Evergreen azaleas (Glen Dale)				
'Buccaneer'	Red	Zone C–	3/3	3–3½ ft.
'Gaiety'	Bright pink	Zone C–	4/4	3–3½ ft.
'Geisha'	Striped color	Zone C+	5/4	2½–3 ft.
'Suwanee'	Lavender	Zone C–	3/3	3–3½ ft.
'Treasure'	White	Zone C–	4/3	3½–4 ft.
Evergreen azaleas (Kaempferi)				
'Atalanta'	Lavender-purple	Zone B–	3/3	3½–4 ft.
'Fedora'	Pink	Zone B–	3/3	4–4½ ft.
'Mikado'	Crimson	Zone B–	3/3	3–3½ ft.
'Othello'	Brick-red	Zone B–	3/4	3½–4 ft.
'Wilhelmina Vuyk,' or 'Palestrina'	White	Zone B–	3/3	3½–4 ft.
Deciduous azaleas				
'Gibraltar'	Brilliant orange, frilled	Zone B+	4/3	4½–5 ft.
'Homebush'	Bright pink, double	Zone B+	3/2	5–5½ ft.
'Klondyke'	Deep yellow	Zone B+	3/3	4–4½ ft.
'Peachy Keen'	Light pink, suffused red	Zone B+	4/3	2½–3 ft. (semi-dwarf)
'Pink William'	Silvery pink	Zone B	4/3 (fragrant)	3½–4 ft.
'Primrose'	Pale yellow	Zone B+	4/2	4½–5 ft.
'Red Letter'	Brilliant red	Zone B+	4/3	4½–5 ft.
'Rufus'	Deep red	Zone B+	4/2	3½–4 ft.
'Tintoretto'	Orange and pink, frilled	Zone B	3/2	4½–5 ft.
'White Swan'	White	Zone B+	2/2	4½–5 ft.

Perennials

Many of our best-loved flowers are herbaceous perennials that spring up afresh year after year and make outstanding features in borders.

Whether your garden is a cramped backyard or a generous plot of land around a country house, there are always places to use perennials for the varied color and character of their flowers and foliage.

The terms "perennial" and "herbaceous perennial" are often used interchangeably to mean a plant that comes up year after year and in most cases dies down to dormant roots each winter, leaving only lifeless stems. The lupine, delphinium, phlox, and monarda are popular examples. A few, such as the yucca and dianthus, are termed and treated as herbaceous plants even though their leaves remain green all year. Tolerance to cold depends on the kind.

Some perennials, such as the hollyhock, centranthus, delphinium, and linum, have short lives of only four or five summers—something overlooked by gardeners who never think of plants growing old. Yet others, such as the aster, coreopsis, and anthemis, live longer but bloom with greater freedom if dug up and divided every few years. And a small number, such as the peony and the thalictrum, may outlast one's lifetime without attention.

In the days when estate gardens were common, life more leisurely, and gardening help more readily available and affordable, herbaceous borders were popular. Generally they were 10 feet wide and at least 30 feet long, with a background of sheared evergreens.

While the border was magnificent for many months, it required considerable space and experienced workmen—two factors that led to its demise in this country, although one can still see elaborate borders in a few

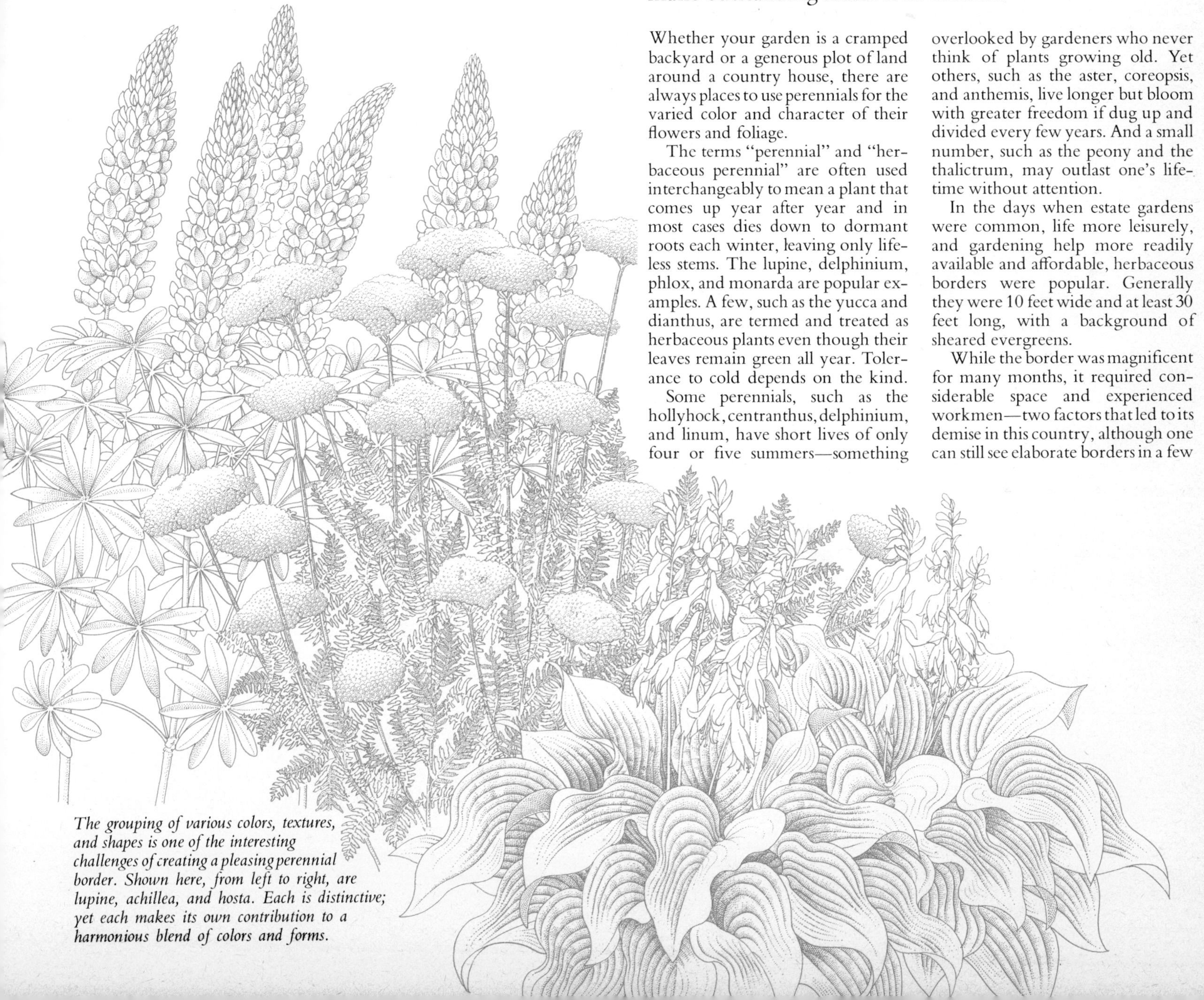

The grouping of various colors, textures, and shapes is one of the interesting challenges of creating a pleasing perennial border. Shown here, from left to right, are lupine, achillea, and hosta. Each is distinctive; yet each makes its own contribution to a harmonious blend of colors and forms.

public, botanical, or estate gardens.

Today, in our smaller suburban gardens, perennials are regaining popularity. One reason is the development of the mixed border in which perennials are grown with other types of plants—annuals, biennials, roses, bulbs, and shrubs—to provide a display over a considerably longer period.

The island bed has also become popular in gardens where long borders do not fit conveniently into the design or maintenance program. An island garden, accessible from all sides, is far easier to plant, cultivate, and weed than a wide, one-sided border. The taller plants should be set toward the center, with the shorter ones toward the edges. Free-form shapes are usually more effective than circles or ovals. Star or diamond shapes should be avoided because their angles are awkward to plant and difficult to maintain.

Another popular style of perennial garden is one in which three to five different perennials make up the entire border. The perennials are carefully chosen according to color and blooming time to provide the longest possible period of color. For example, by selecting the early-, mid-season-, and late-blooming varieties from among irises, day lilies, peonies, and chrysanthemums, there will be flowers for many months with minimal care.

Perennials can also be used to good advantage as ground cover, in which vigorous, spreading, and fairly short types are planted close together to form a dense, continuous mass, concealing the bare ground. Such plantings are useful for covering banks or, if the plants are shade lovers, for carpeting the ground beneath shrubs, perhaps interplanted with naturalized bulbs (planted informally). Theoretically, ground-cover plants smother weeds, but in the initial stages careful weeding is required, and afterward some hand weeding is always needed, because hoeing is not practical. For a list of ground-cover plants, see page 43.

A pleasing variation of a solid planting is a checkerboard area of pavement and soil, with the open squares planted with specimens chosen for both foliage and flowers, such as the bergenia and day lily. This can often be done on a terrace with as few as one or two planted squares.

Herbaceous perennials look well planted informally in a great variety of places. Around the edges of garden pools and streams they complement aquatic plants. On the edges of woodlands and in open fields, they can be planted in drifts. Beside steps and over the edges of paths, wispy or spreading plants, such as the baby's breath or dianthus, spill out to soften straight edges. And as single accents in strategic places—by a lamppost, a garden gate, or a birdbath—just one handsome perennial, such as a day lily, peony, or achillea, which will retain its good looks even when not in bloom, will add interest.

On balconies and roofs of apartments favorite perennials can be grown in containers.

Lately plants with good foliage have become much appreciated for their textural qualities and long-season effect—among them the ornamental grasses, artemisias, hostas, pulmonarias, sedums, and yuccas. Silver-, gold-, and purple-leaved types are particularly interesting, not only to gardeners but to flower arrangers who make considerable use of hardy perennials. The seed heads of the Chinese lantern and Oriental poppy and the flowers of the achillea, echinops, and sea lavender are often dried for indoor decoration.

Achieving an attractive border greatly depends upon how the plants are arranged. Late-flowering or foliage plants should conceal gaps left by earlier flowers; colors should be pleasing, and all plants should be in scale. Carefully kept notes can be an asset. No book or catalog will provide the exact flowering dates for your garden. However, if you record your own bloom dates, you can recombine plants that flower at the same time.

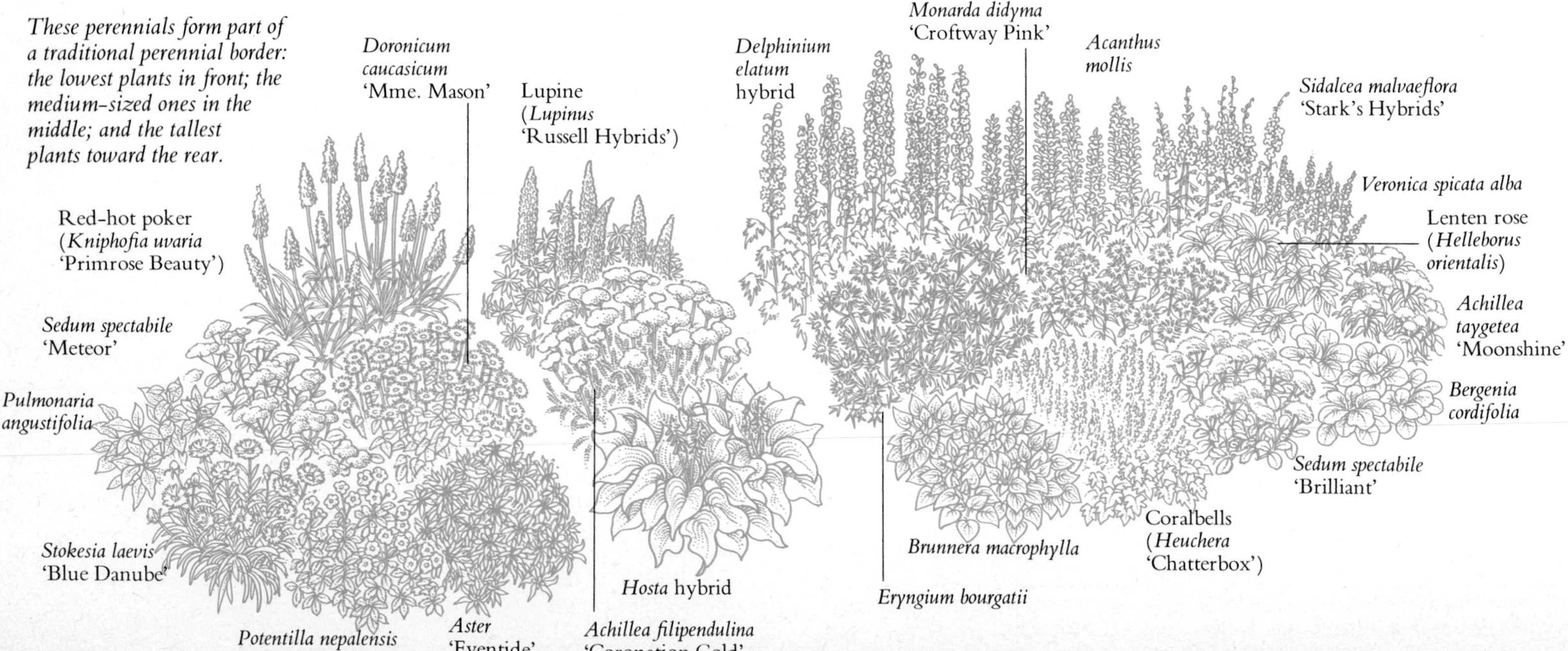

These perennials form part of a traditional perennial border: the lowest plants in front; the medium-sized ones in the middle; and the tallest plants toward the rear.

Giving Perennials the Right Start

Preparing the Perennial Border for Planting

Spade or rototill the bed two or three weeks prior to planting to give the soil time to settle. In addition, incorporate a bucketful of peat moss or compost per square yard, or spread about 1–3 inches of this material over the entire area before spading. Also, sprinkle a complete general-purpose garden fertilizer (such as a 5–10–5) over the area prior to spading. Use fertilizer in amounts specified on the package.

Just before planting, rake the area to break up any large clumps of soil and to level the surface.

Drawing a plan to show the approximate location of each perennial is a good idea. A large piece of graph paper works well for this. Outdoors, use label stakes to mark the location of plants before setting them out.

1. *Spade peat moss and fertilizer into soil a few weeks before planting.*

2. *Level the soil surface with a rake just prior to setting out plants.*

Setting Out the New Perennials

Perennials can be planted almost any time the soil can be worked. Spring is the most popular season, but fall is also excellent. In cold regions spring planting is probably safer; fall planting must be done early so that plants become established before winter. Apply mulch after the ground has frozen, to prevent alternate freezing and thawing, which heaves plants up out of the soil and exposes roots to the air and the hazards of drying.

Container-grown plants establish themselves readily even when in bloom and can be planted in summer if they are kept well watered.

Dormant perennials, either bare rooted or in small pots, may arrive by mail several days before it is convenient to plant them. Open the package, water if necessary, and keep in a cool place indoors or in a shaded place outdoors away from drying winds. The sooner they are planted, the better are their chances of survival. Always water well after planting.

Take care to set the plants at the proper depth. In most cases this means that the point at which roots and stems meet should be at the established soil level. If planted too shallowly, the roots will be exposed; if too deeply, the crowns can rot.

Following the planting plan, draw guidelines on the bed with the corner of a hoe. In a large bed the guidelines are easier to follow if they are marked out with sand. These will remain even if rain should postpone planting. Work on one section at a time; or do the back first, and work toward the front. Space the plants to allow for the eventual spread of the foliage. The best effects are obtained when three or more of one kind of plant are set together.

For plants with small root systems, use a trowel to make holes; for large root systems, use a spade. Make holes large enough to accommodate the spread-out roots. Set the plant upright in the center. Firm the soil around each plant and water.

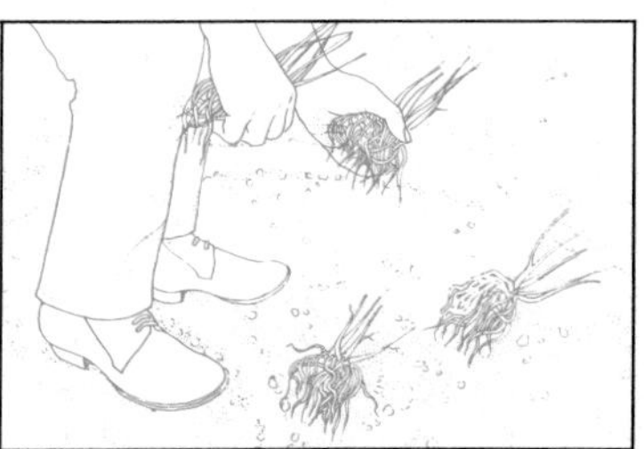

1. *Space out a few plants at a time within a marked-off section of bed.*

2. *Use a trowel to dig planting holes deep and wide enough for the roots.*

3. *Set the plant in the center of the hole, spread the roots, and return soil.*

4. *Firm in the plant with your fingers and the back of a trowel.*

PLANTING BIG ROOTS

Large-rooted plants. *Use a spade to dig out a deep hole wide enough to accommodate roots. Set the root ball in the center, and fill the hole with soil. Firm in with your heel.*

PLANTING DIVISIONS

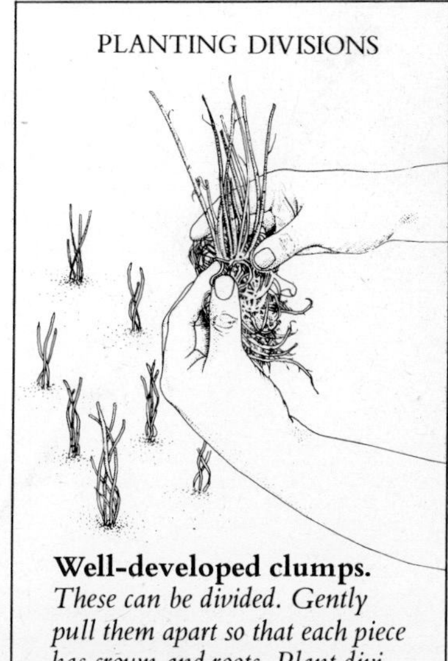

Well-developed clumps. *These can be divided. Gently pull them apart so that each piece has crown and roots. Plant divisions immediately to keep them from drying out.*

Jobs to Be Done When Spring Arrives

Keeping the Ground Clear of Weeds

Begin weeding as soon as growth appears. Neglecting the job only leads to more work later on if the weeds are allowed to mature and disperse their seeds. Also, weeds flourish in well-prepared soil and deprive the perennials of both nutrients and moisture. Keep a basket nearby, and drop weeds into it as you remove them. If left on moist soil, many of them will reroot. Add the weeds to the compost pile. Once the ground has been cleared of weeds, a mulch can be applied to deter further growth. Another benefit of a mulch is that it conserves soil moisture during dry spells.

In small beds weeding can be done with a short-handled cultivator. But for larger areas, to eliminate prolonged stooping, a long-handled tool is preferable.

To remove weeds with a standard hoe, cut them off with a chopping motion, drawing the hoe toward you and taking care not to injure any of the desirable plants. The flat side of a Warren hoe is used the same way; the two-pronged side is used for larger weeds.

The scuffle, or Dutch, hoe is pushed backward and forward through the soil, just below the surface, to cut off the weeds.

Cultivators break up the surface soil and uproot weeds at the same time. When such persistent, deep-rooted weeds as quack grass are growing around the base of a plant, it may be necessary to dig up the plant, split it apart, and replant it in order to remove weeds in the center of the clump or entangled with the roots.

REMOVING SURFACE AND DEEP-ROOTED WEEDS

Around plants. *Chop off weeds among close-growing plants with a short-handled cultivator.*

Between rows. *For surface weeding and between rows of plants, a long-handled scuffle hoe can be used.*

In matted clumps. *Use a spading fork to loosen matted weeds growing amid clumps of perennials.*

Loosening the Soil in Established Beds

At the start of the growing season, and again in late autumn, the soil in established beds should be loosened. This is particularly important on heavy or unmulched soil that has become compacted. Loosening allows air and moisture to penetrate to the roots of plants and at the same time exposes weeds. A fork can be used, but a long-handled, tined cultivator is ideal.

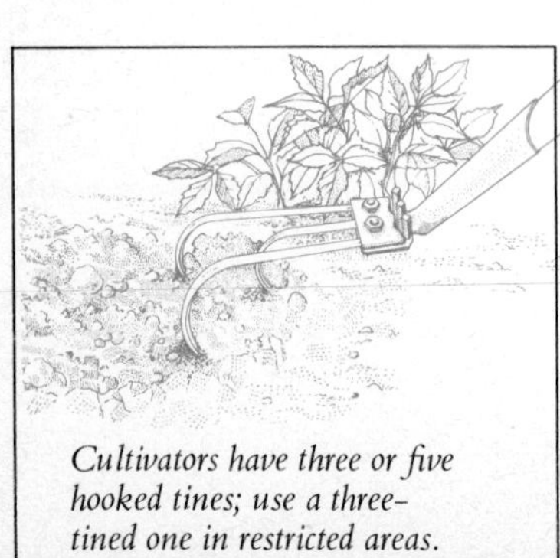

Cultivators have three or five hooked tines; use a three-tined one in restricted areas.

Supplying Plant Food and Constant Moisture

The health of plants can be maintained or improved, and their growth encouraged, by the application of a complete fertilizer containing the three most important plant nutrients—nitrogen, phosphorus, and potash—in varying proportions.

Organic or slow-release fertilizers are particularly suited to perennials, since the nutrients are released slowly over the full period of growth. In early spring, just as growth becomes apparent and before mulching, apply fertilizer by hand. Avoid letting it come in contact with foliage. Alternatively, use a complete inorganic fertilizer with an analysis such as 4–12–4. Always apply fertilizers according to directions.

From late spring to early summer the plants can be fed every three or four weeks with a fast-acting liquid foliar spray.

Watering should not be necessary if the bed has been mulched, except during prolonged dry spells. The mulch, which is a layer of organic material over the soil, conserves moisture by reducing evaporation. If watering is needed, use a sprinkler that gives a steady and even spray, so that the water penetrates deeply.

Clay soils, which compact under heavy rain, should have their surfaces loosened before watering, feeding, or mulching. A mulch also serves some other worthwhile purposes. It prevents compacting. It improves the quality of both clay and sandy soils. It helps to keep water from spattering the undersides of leaves and thus lessens the spread of soil-borne fungous disease. It helps to suppress weed seedlings. And as the organic materials break down, they add nutrients to the soil.

Apply mulch in late spring after the ground has been weeded but before growth is advanced. In dry weather soak soil before mulching.

It is best to cover the planting bed completely. But if this is not possible, it is better to apply a thick mulch around the plants than to spread it thinly over the whole bed.

MULCHING

Spread mulch, 2–3 in. deep, over the root area of the plants. Use rotted garden compost or manure, leaf mold, cocoa shells, or other materials. Level with the back of a rake. In dry weather always water soil before applying mulch.

How to Support Top-heavy Perennials

Perennials need support if they have a floppy habit of growth, are top-heavy when in flower, or are likely to suffer from wind or storm damage. Use bamboo stakes, galvanized wire hoops or mesh, or twiggy brushwood. Lightweight individual plants and clumps can be supported by brushwood, but heavier plants are best staked with canes or wire mesh. Put supports in place before growth has become too advanced and difficult to handle.

The supports should reach to just below the flower spikes; so one must know in advance the eventual approximate height of a plant (p. 239).

Plants supported by brushwood, hoops, or wire mesh need no tying in, but tall stems should be attached to their cane supports with strong raffia or garden twine or with one of the commercially available ties. These are usually made of thin wire covered with plastic or paper, cut to length or in rolls.

Wire-Mesh Supports for Tall-Growing Plants

A plant that grows exceptionally tall (5–6 feet)—such as certain filipendulas, some sorts of heliopsis, rudbeckias, Solomon's seals, and the tall delphinium—can be supported with wire-mesh cylinders. Once the support is in position, no tying in is necessary. Use 4-inch-square galvanized mesh (also available in green) to make a cylinder that is wide enough to just enclose the whole group of plants. If the cylinder is smaller than the diameter of the mature plants, it will not show.

Insert three tall bamboo canes upright in the ground inside the cylinder. Tie each cane to the wire mesh, first just above ground level, then halfway up, and again at the top.

For taller plants it may be necessary to fit a second cylinder on top of the first. Overlap the two cylinders, and tie them together with twine.

1. *Push canes into the soil inside the mesh, and tie together with soft twine.*

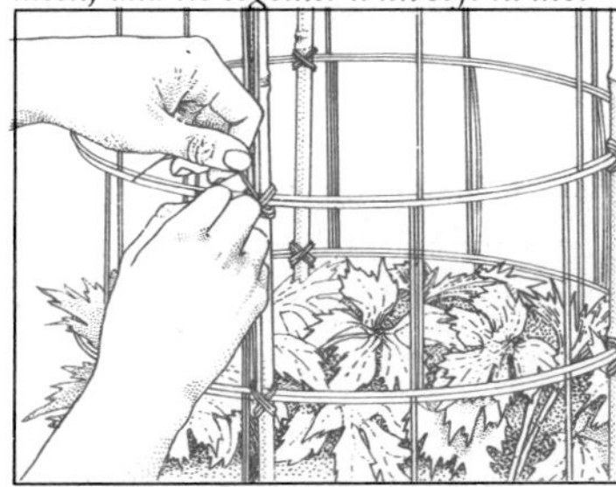

2. *For taller plants, overlap mesh cylinder with another one above.*

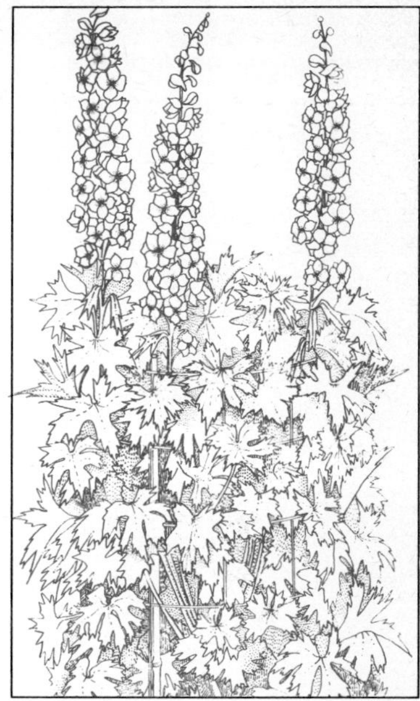

3. *As the plants grow, the stems are held securely within the framework.*

Supporting Plants With Stakes and Twine

Use bamboo cane stakes or other available slender wood or metal stakes to support single stems or groups of plants, such as delphiniums, phlox, and thalictrums, that are more than 2 feet and up to 4–5 feet in height.

For a single-stemmed plant firmly insert one bamboo cane in the ground close to the plant, and attach the stem with raffia, twine, or plastic-covered wire. As the stem grows, add more ties at approximately 1-foot intervals or as needed.

For a group of plants or a large clump, firmly insert three stakes in the ground close to the plant at equidistant intervals. These will be hidden when the plant fills out.

Knot the twine to one cane, 6–9 inches aboveground; then loop the twine around the other two canes and secure. Tie again as plant grows.

1. *Support a clump of delphiniums with bamboo canes and twine.*

2. *As the plants grow, add another piece of twine, 9 in. above the first.*

3. *When mature, plants will be supported by several circles of twine.*

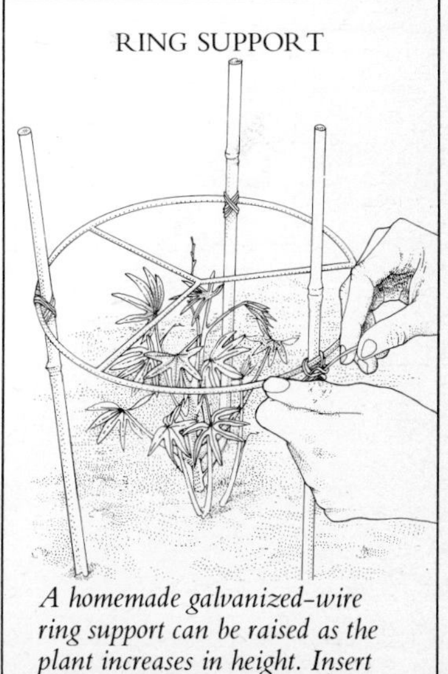

RING SUPPORT

A homemade galvanized-wire ring support can be raised as the plant increases in height. Insert three bamboo canes around the plant, and place the ring over them, tying it to each of the canes.

Seasonal Care of Perennials

Keeping Floppy Plants Up With Twiggy Brushwood

To support plants up to 2 feet in height that tend to become floppy, use strong twiggy brushwood similar to what is sometimes used for peas to climb on.

When pruning small trees or trimming hedges, save little twiggy branches (sometimes called pea-sticks) for this purpose. Almost any tree or shrub provides good material, particularly the spirea, vitex, birch, and oak.

Before inserting the brushwood in the ground, sharpen the lower ends, and make sure that the soil is soft and easily permeable. Because it is branched, brushwood cannot be pounded into the ground, and too much pressure will break it. If the soil is compacted, prepare a hole by first inserting a metal rod.

Push in each piece of brushwood deeply enough so that it will hold firmly under the weight of the growing plant. Two or three pieces for each group of plants are usually sufficient. If the plants are of a kind known to sprawl badly after heavy rains or storms, however, or to form especially large spreading clumps, insert additional brushwood.

1. *Push twiggy brushwood into the center of a clump of plants.*

2. *Break the tops of the sticks, turning them to the center of the plants.*

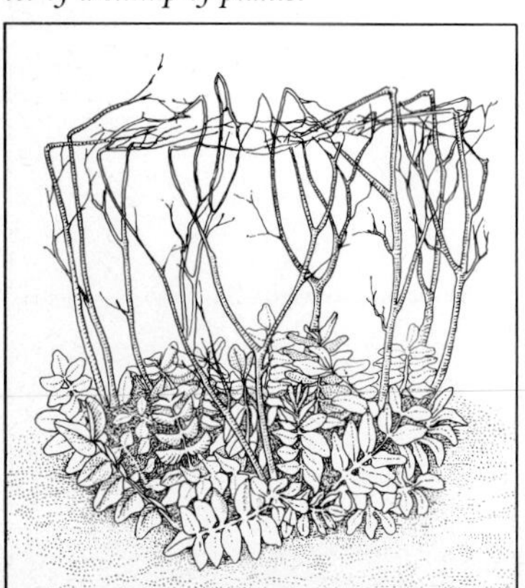

3. *Interlace the tops so that they form a close framework over the plants.*

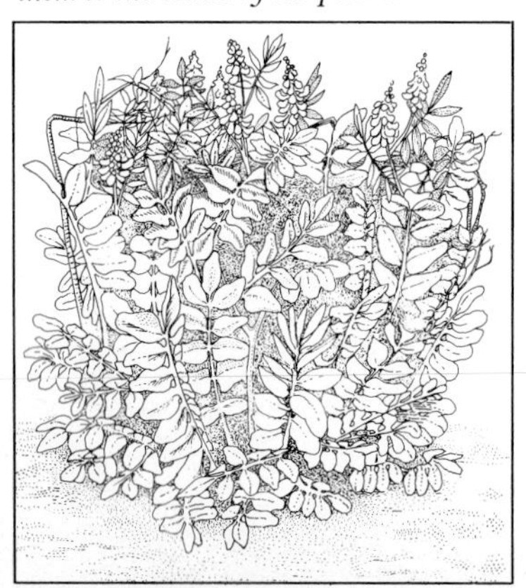

4. *As the plants grow, stems and leaves will hide the supports.*

Removing Faded Flowers and Stems

As soon as the early spring and summer flowers have faded, cut them back. On some plants, such as the delphinium, the phlox, and the low-growing achillea, you can then get the benefit of a second period of bloom. Continue to remove all faded flowers into the fall. This procedure, known as deadheading, improves appearance and prevents self-sowing of seeds, which often produces undesirable plants.

Cut back plants with single, bare flower stems—for example, the red-hot poker—as close as possible to the base, at ground level.

On plants where the lower parts of flower stems have leaves growing on them, cut off the stems just below the top leaves.

The heads of some plants—for instance, achilleas—often dry on the plant and remain attractive into fall.

Bare flower stems should be cut to ground level (left). Trim stems with foliage to just below the top leaves (right).

Cutting Back Straggly Plants After Flowering

Many mat-forming rock-garden plants (p. 352), which are often used as edging in perennial borders, grow straggly after blooming. Such plants, the aubrieta and candytuft, for example, need hard pruning with scissors or hedge shears. Cut back to about one-half to two-thirds of their original height. This hard pruning promotes new growth and sometimes encourages reblooming. If not pruned, plants grow woody, bloom less, and become straggly.

Some plants, such as the anthemis and pyrethrum, that have one profuse bloom, make little new growth. To keep them tidy, cut back by about one-third after they flower.

MAT-FORMING PLANTS

Mat-forming rock-garden plants are cut back hard.

Lifting Tender Tubers; Interplanting Hardy Bulbs

In cold regions, if tender bulbs or tubers, such as tigridias or dahlias, have been interplanted among the perennials for summer color, they should be lifted in late fall and stored until spring in a cool, dry place.

At the same time spring-flowering bulbs, such as daffodils and tulips, can be interplanted among the perennials. These bulbs will provide the garden with considerable color in spring, a time when most perennial borders are short on color. Daffodils will continue to flower for many years without any attention, but tulips are best replenished each year or at least every two or three years. When planting, remember that bulb foliage must be left to ripen after flowering. However, it can be well hidden by taller perennials.

In fall spring-flowering bulbs can be planted in spaces between perennials, which will help hide bulbs' faded foliage after they finish blooming.

Tending to Perennials Before Winter

Perennial borders should be tidied up when growth ceases in the fall. Continue flower removal as necessary, and in cold regions remove the foliage of plants that normally die down to the ground.

Divide and replant overgrown clumps (see p. 234). Before replanting, fork over the soil; then rake in bone meal or superphosphate.

In very cold areas mulch perennials after the ground freezes to prevent alternate freezing and thawing of soil, which can tear roots and lift crowns above soil level, resulting in the death of plants. Use a light mulch that will not smother plants: pine branches, oak leaves, salt hay. Remove the mulch gradually in spring.

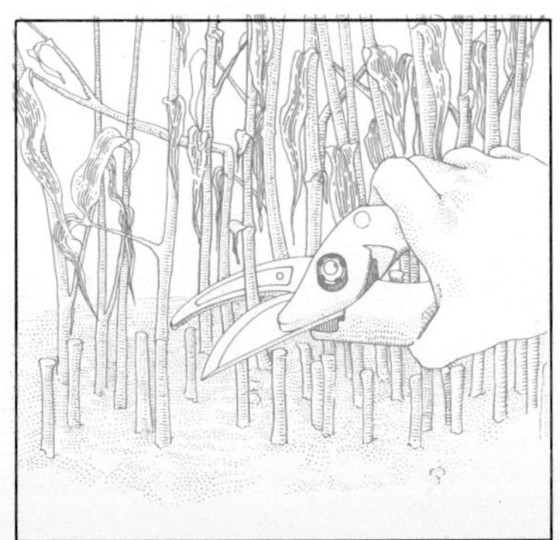
1. *Cut the dead stems of perennials to just above ground level.*

2. *Cover the plant with a layer of salt hay or evergreen boughs.*

What Can Go Wrong With Perennials

If your plants show symptoms that are not described here, turn to the full-color identification drawings of pests and diseases on page 600.

For a comprehensive selection of the trade names of recommended chemicals, turn to page 635.

Symptoms and signs	Cause	Control
Stem tips and flower spikes are covered with sticky insects. In severe cases growth may be distorted, flowers fail to open.	Aphids	Spray with carbaryl, Diazinon, endosulfan, or malathion.
Leaves are chewed.	Caterpillars	Spray with carbaryl, methoxychlor, or rotenone.
Young stems, chewed through below ground level, wilt and fall over.	Cutworms	Soak crowns of affected plants with malathion, or rake lindane into soil.
Leaves have silvery spots. Leaves, buds, and flowers are webbed together or severely distorted.	Mites (two-spotted or cyclamen)	Spray or dust with dicofol, endosulfan, or tetradifon; or apply dimethoate or oxydemeton-methyl as foliar spray or soil drench.
Young leaves, flower buds, or stem tips are distorted. Leaves may have small, irregular holes.	Plant bugs (four-lined, harlequin, phlox, or tarnished)	Spray with Diazinon or methoxychlor.
Young shoots are eaten and slime trails present.	Slugs or snails	Use pellets of metaldehyde, methiocarb, or mexacarbate.
Leaves, young shoots, and sometimes flowers are covered with waxy white powder; may become withered or distorted.	Powdery mildew (fungus)	Spray with Benomyl, dinocap, or sulfur.
Leaves (occasionally young stems) have brown or red pustules, which erupt and show powdery spores. Leaves may yellow and die.	Rust (fungus)	Spray with a carbamate (ferbam, maneb, thiram, or zineb). May be difficult to control.
Leaves and soft stem tips wither, yellow, and hang down; entire plant may be infected (particularly Michaelmas daisies).	Verticillium wilt (fungus)	Remove infected shoots and spray with Benomyl or thiram.
Flower buds fail to develop properly, withering or dropping before they open.	Drought	Soak with 2 gal. of water per sq. yd.; repeat at least weekly during dry spells. Mulch with peat, garden compost, or wood chips.
Stems are thin and often crowded; flowers are small. Leaves wilt, especially on hot days; lower ones yellow and die prematurely.	Starvation or drought	Spray plants with foliar feed, soak thoroughly with water, and mulch with decayed manure or garden compost. Divide clumps as required.

Increasing Your Stock by Dividing Perennials

Lifting Overgrown Plants From the Soil

An overgrown perennial is either one that has outgrown its allotted space in the garden or one that does not produce as much bloom as it did formerly. Some plants, the phlox and iris, for example, reach this state in a few years. Others, such as the helenium and day lily, take five or more years. Yet others seldom require division, the gas plant being a notable example.

Lifting of overgrown perennials for division (the methods are described here and on the next page) should be done before growth begins or when it slows, after flowering. Plants that flower very early are best divided in autumn, while those that flower very late are best tended to in spring. Most others can be divided in spring or fall. However, these rules are flexible, and division can often be done when it is most convenient if special aftercare is given.

Since perennials remain in the same spot for many years, it pays to improve the soil prior to replanting. Incorporate peat moss or compost, plus bone meal or superphosphate.

Choose a day for lifting when the soil is neither frozen nor sticky. In very cold regions division in late summer or fall should be done well in advance of very cold weather to allow roots to become established before the ground freezes. Also keep in mind that the sooner the plants are divided and reset after lifting, the less setback will occur. Always protect lifted plants from sun or drying winds while they await your attention, and water if unavoidable delays occur. Plants divided in fall should first have their foliage cut back to make division easier.

Dividing Rhizomatous-Rooted Plants

Plants that grow from rhizomes are easily lifted, since the rootstock (which is really a swollen underground stem) grows at, or just below, the surface of the soil. The bergenia, bearded iris, and Solomon's seal are all rhizomatous, and each plant can be separated into several new ones. Ideally, this should be done in the early spring, just as the new growth buds begin to emerge. For iris division, see page 341.

After lifting the plant, carefully remove all the soil, so that the old rhizomes can be seen, together with the younger rhizomes growing from it. If the soil clings, making it difficult to see all the rhizomes, wash it away with a stream of water.

In separating the side growths from the old rhizomes, cut the new divisions off with a sharp knife to avoid damaging the tissues. To prevent drying, plant the young rhizomes at once.

In planting, make sure that the rhizomes are completely covered and well anchored in the soil and are at about the same depth as the original plant. Rhizomes of bearded irises are an exception and are generally planted horizontally with the upper third of the rhizome above soil level (see p. 341). Deeper planting may rot the rhizome.

If you are unable to plant the divisions immediately, do not let them dry out. Store them in a box, and cover them with moist sand or peat moss. Never leave them unplanted for more than a day or two.

1. *The bergenia may need dividing every three years, preferably just as growth commences in spring. Choose healthy young rhizomes growing from an old one. Make sure that each rhizome contains at least two growth buds or young shoots and that the thin fibrous roots on the rhizome are undamaged. After selecting new growths, which should be 2–3 in. long, carefully cut them off.*

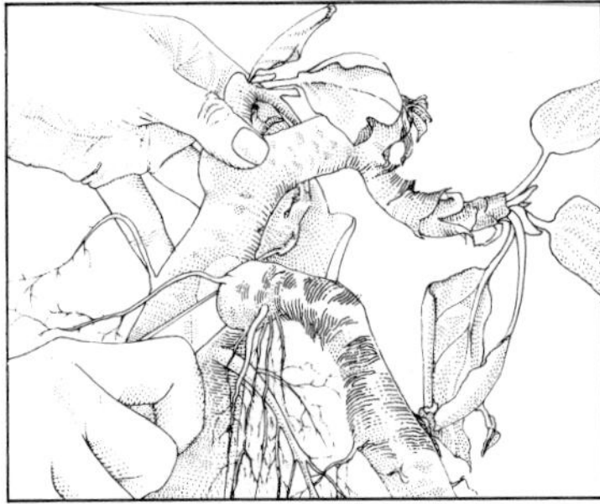

2. *Cut off the side growths flush with the old rhizome, which can be discarded.*

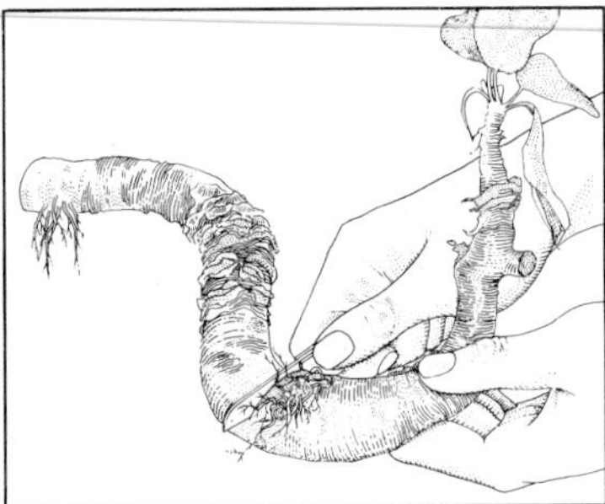

3. *Trim cut pieces to just below a cluster of fine, healthy roots.*

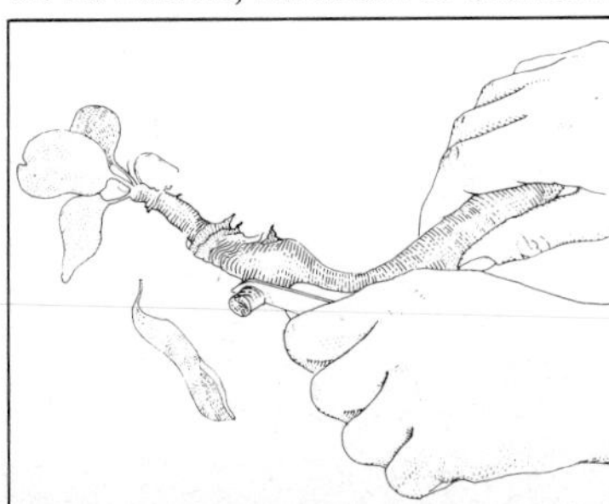

4. *Remove any stumps or pieces of rotten stem and any dead leaves.*

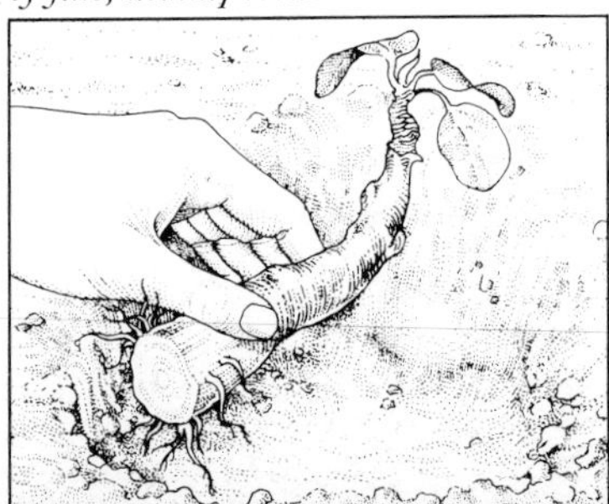

5. *The young trimmed rhizome is now ready for planting in the garden.*

Division of Young Perennials

Two- or three-year-old perennials that have fibrous roots, such as the helenium, rudbeckia, and the perennial aster, are easily divided in spring if more plants are needed.

The larger divisions—those with three or more shoots—can be set out immediately in their permanent locations, where they can be expected to make a good show of bloom that same season. Smaller divisions are best planted in an out-of-the-way bed until the following autumn or spring, when they can be moved to their permanent places.

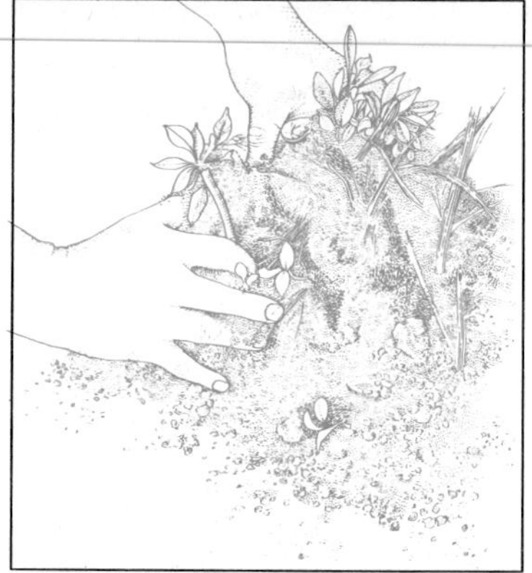

1. *Divide plants with small root systems by gently pulling them apart.*

2. *Trim off with a knife any roots that are rotten, dead, or damaged.*

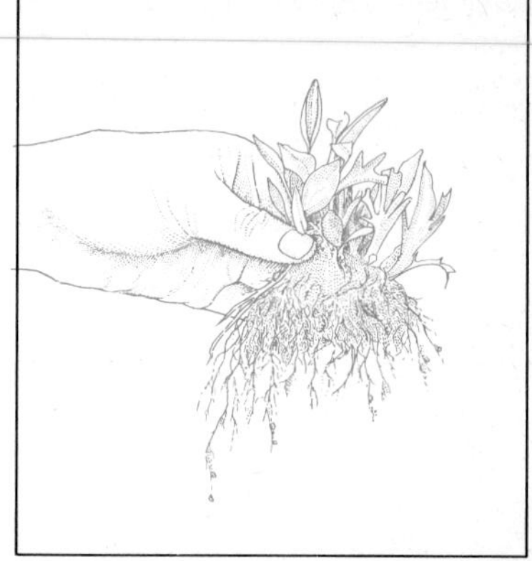

3. *Plant pieces with several shoots in the border, smaller ones in an unused area.*

Division of Old Fibrous- and Fleshy-Rooted Perennials

Large, overgrown, fibrous-rooted perennials, such as the helenium and phlox, are sometimes difficult to divide, since both the crowns and the shoots form a solid mass. After lifting the clump, force the prongs of two garden forks, back to back, into the center of the clump, and pry apart as shown at right.

After making the major divisions, use a sharp knife to cut away the older, woodier portions toward the center. Then separate the pieces into sections. Try to have at least six buds or shoots on each. When planting, be sure to firm the soil around the roots; then water thoroughly to settle the soil and eliminate air pockets.

Plants that have extremely tough, woody crowns—for instance, baptisias—cannot usually be split with forks. In such cases, cut through the crown with a strong, sharp knife, so that each severed portion has both roots and growth buds. Replant the divisions at once and water them.

Fleshy-rooted plants, such as the hosta, also are best divided by prying apart with two garden forks. Work carefully to avoid damaging the fleshy roots.

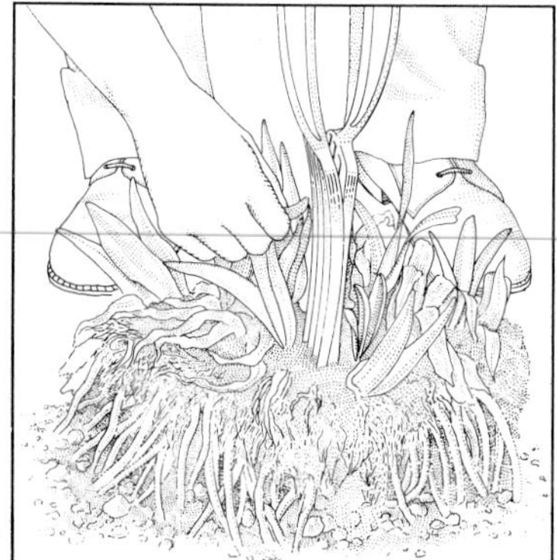

1. *Separate overgrown matted plants with two forks, back to back.*

2. *Press handles of the forks together; then force them apart to lever and split the clump in two. Split the two sections in half in the same way.*

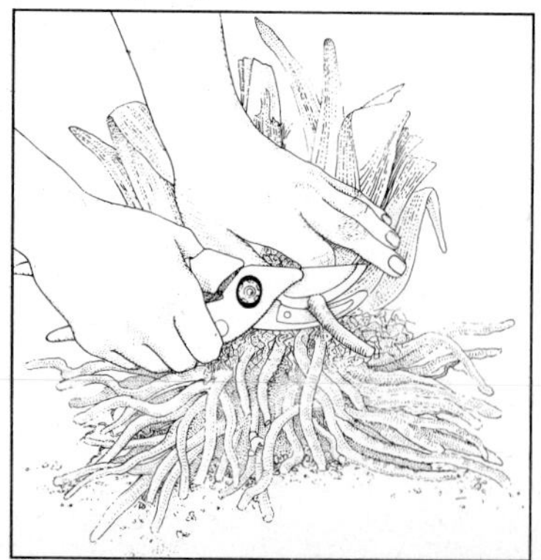

3. *Cut away any woody shoots and dead roots from the divisions.*

4. *On fleshy-rooted plants trim rotten or damaged roots back to healthy tissue.*

5. *Plant out divisions at once in their permanent flowering positions.*

How to Grow New Perennials From Cuttings

Division of Plants With Tuberous Roots

The method of dividing tuberous-rooted plants varies according to the type of tuber.

Dig up the clump, and carefully remove the soil without breaking the tubers. If necessary, wash the tubers in a bucket of water so that the growth buds are clearly visible.

Tuberous roots, such as those of the herbaceous peony, have growth buds in the crown, where tubers join together. Slice through the clump, from crown downward, to divide the plant into several pieces, each complete with tubers and several growth buds. Plant the divisions at once. Pieces of a single tuber with only one bud generally take longer to become established than do sections with three or four tubers and buds. In extremely cold regions the new divisions should be mulched after the ground freezes.

Peonies resent being disturbed and seldom require division; so only dig and divide when necessary and only in early autumn.

Day lilies have slender tubers and form dense clumps that are best pried apart with garden forks. Replant with several leaf "fans" in a group if a quick display is desired; otherwise, one fan is sufficient.

DIVIDING A PEONY

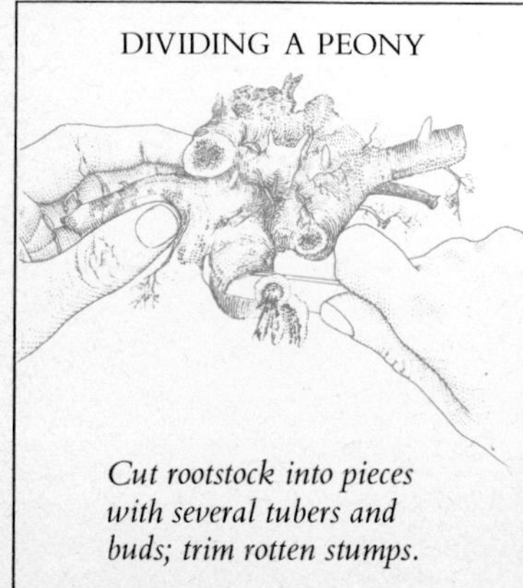

Cut rootstock into pieces with several tubers and buds; trim rotten stumps.

Taking Tip Cuttings in Summer and Autumn

Some perennials, notably low-growing shrubby plants—the phlox, penstemon, and sedum—and foliage perennials—the anthemis and rue—are best increased from tip cuttings.

Take tip cuttings from the ends of nonflowering lateral shoots. This can be done whenever the stems are semi-firm. In cold areas rooted cuttings are best protected by a cold frame during their first winter.

Take the cuttings, 3–4 inches long, from the tips of healthy, leafy stems, ensuring that each cutting has at least three leaf joints (nodes).

Fill a pot to just below its rim with equal parts of peat moss and coarse sand or perlite, or use a commercial seed-starter mixture. A 4-inch pot will hold about six cuttings, but avoid overcrowding.

Trim each cutting just below the lowest leaf node, using a sharp knife or a razor blade. Pull off or cut away the lowest pair of leaves.

Make shallow holes in the rooting mixture with a pencil. Insert each cutting so that the base of its stem touches the bottom of the hole without burying any of the leaves. Firm in with the fingers.

Water the pot thoroughly and label. Cover the pot with a plastic bag with a few small holes for ventilation; secure with a rubber band. To keep the bag from touching the cuttings, make a framework of sticks or wires before putting on the plastic. Set pots of cuttings in a shaded spot or cold frame to root.

If cuttings are taken in cool weather, a propagating case with bottom heat of 60° F will hasten rooting.

To check to see if the cuttings have rooted, tug them gently. If they do not yield, they have rooted and can be removed from the plastic covering or propagator. Leave the pot of cuttings uncovered for four or five days. Then remove the cuttings by turning the pot upside down and dislodging the contents all in one piece. The cuttings can also be pried out, but be careful not to break off any of the roots.

Separate the cuttings gently, and pot again as shown. Firm the soil, water thoroughly, and drain.

In mild regions put the pots in a shaded spot or cold frame for about a week before setting them out in the garden. Pinching out the growing tip at this time will encourage the plants to develop strong roots before making top growth.

In cold regions winter the cuttings in a closed cold frame. Plunge pots in sand or peat moss. Plant outside where you want them in spring after there is no danger of frost.

1. *Snip off nonflowering side shoots 3–4 in. long when semi-firm.*

2. *Trim the cuttings straight across the stem, just below a leaf node.*

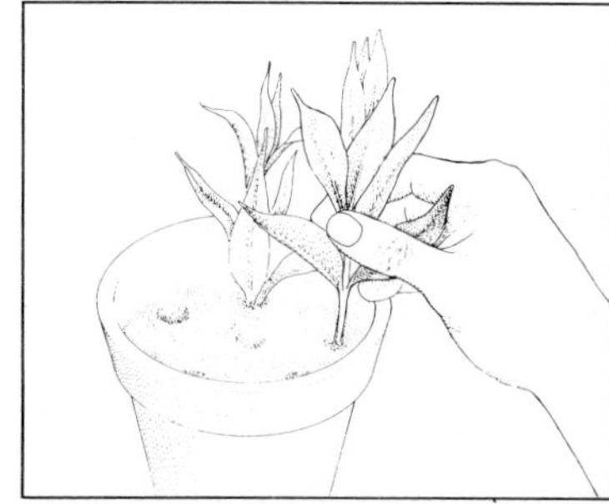

3. *Make planting holes in a 4-in. pot of rooting mixture; insert the cuttings.*

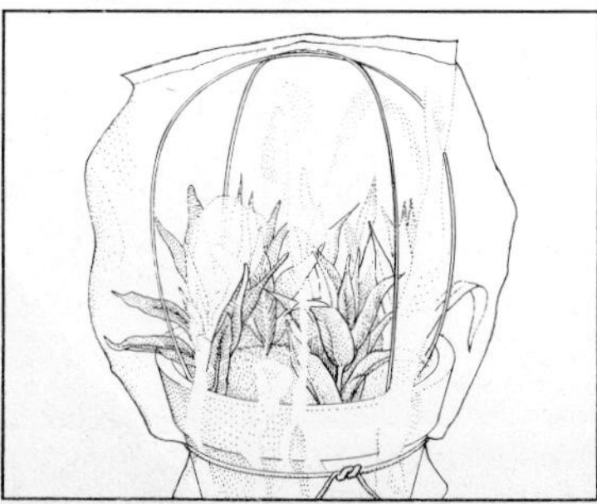

4. *Crisscross two wire loops to make a framework, and cover with plastic.*

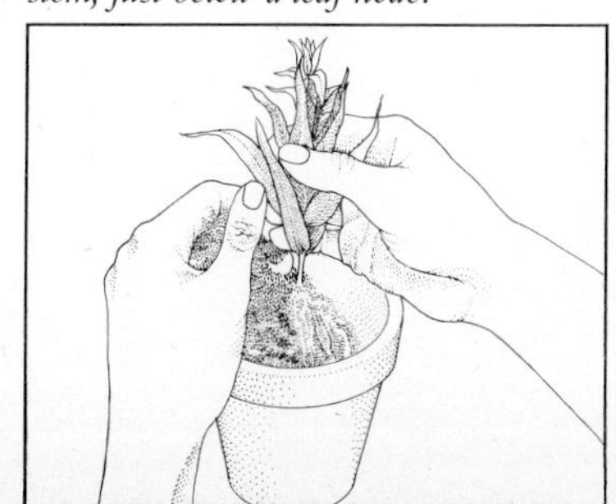

5. *After five or six weeks plant each rooted cutting in a 3-in. pot of soil.*

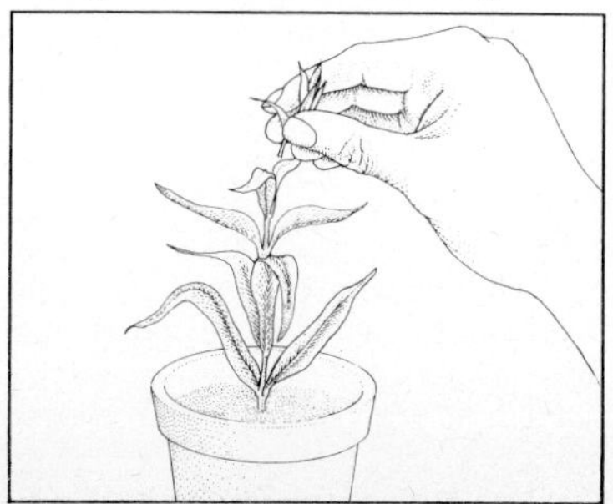

6. *Pinch out the tip of each cutting. In cold areas winter in a cold frame.*

Taking Basal Cuttings in Spring

Most clump-forming perennials, such as the anchusa, achillea, delphinium, baptisia, scabiosa, and many others, are propagated not only by division but also from the young shoots that appear at the base of the plants in spring.

Cut off some of these basal shoots when they are 3–4 inches long, at crown level or just below. Use a sharp knife to make a clean cut.

Insert cuttings into porous soil in a cold frame; or put them in 4- to 5-inch pots filled with equal parts of peat moss and sand (or perlite). Then put the pots into a cold frame. The advantage of putting cuttings into pots in a shaded cold frame, rather than directly into the soil, is that it allows them to be moved from the frame at any time, perhaps for hardening off after rooting, without transplanting. Water cuttings well by spraying them from overhead, and keep the frame closed. As new growth starts to show, increase ventilation by gradually opening the frame during the warmer hours.

After six weeks set the cuttings singly in 3- or 4-inch pots of soil. Plant them outside in summer as soon as they are rooted, or hold them over the winter in a cold frame.

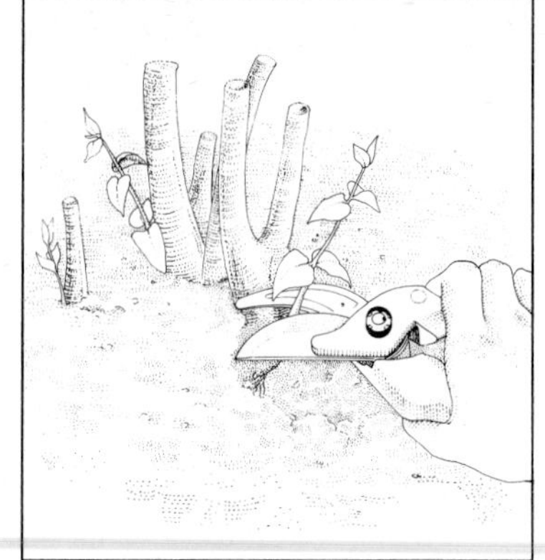

1. *Scrape soil from crown of clump-forming perennial; sever young shoots.*

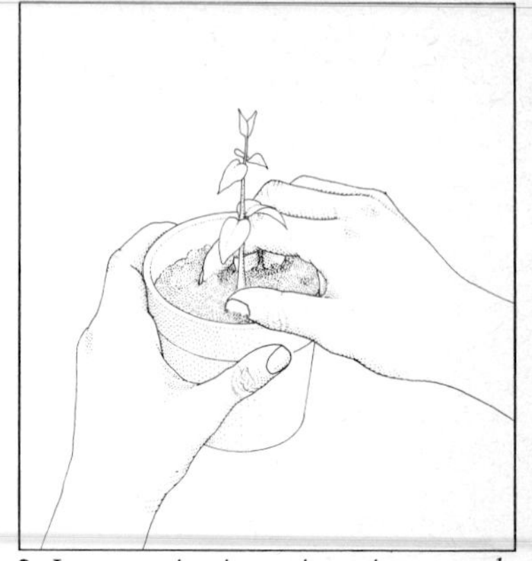

2. *Insert cutting in rooting mixture, and place in a cold frame.*

Growing Perennials From Pieces of Root

Many perennials with fleshy roots lend themselves to rapid multiplication via root cuttings. When a plant has no well-defined vegetative shoots—the Oriental poppy, for instance—this is the most practical means of propagation to perpetuate a plant.

Root cuttings can be taken from mature plants at any time but are most often made during periods of less active growth—as in the late summer, fall, or very early spring.

Cut thick or fleshy roots, such as those of the dicentra and the Oriental poppy, into 2- to 3-inch pieces. Cut thin roots, such as those of the phlox, to about 2 inches.

Fill large pots or flats with equal parts of peat moss and sand (or perlite). Make holes 2 inches apart, 2–3 inches deep. Insert thick cuttings vertically, and cover their tops with $\frac{1}{4}$ inch of the mixture. Place thin roots horizontally and cover as above. Keep moist.

When cuttings have two or three sets of leaves, transplant them to individual pots, and later into the garden. In cold regions keep the plants over the winter in a cold frame.

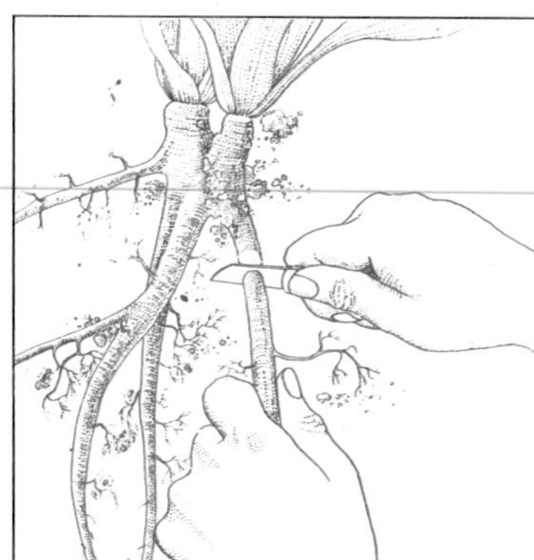

1. *In late summer, fall, or early spring, cut thick roots into 2- to 3-in. lengths.*

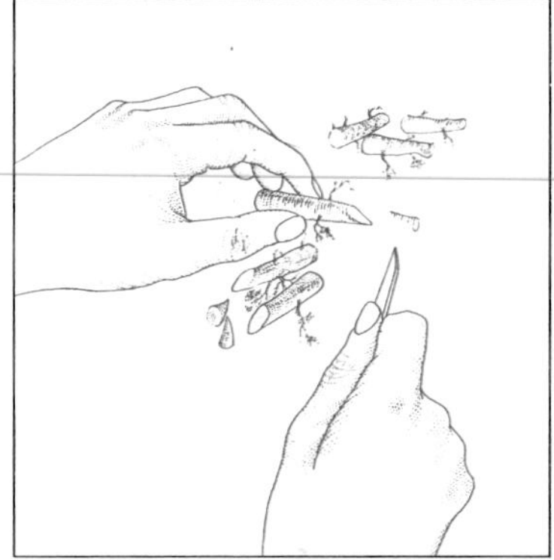

2. *Cut lower end of cutting at a slant to distinguish base from top.*

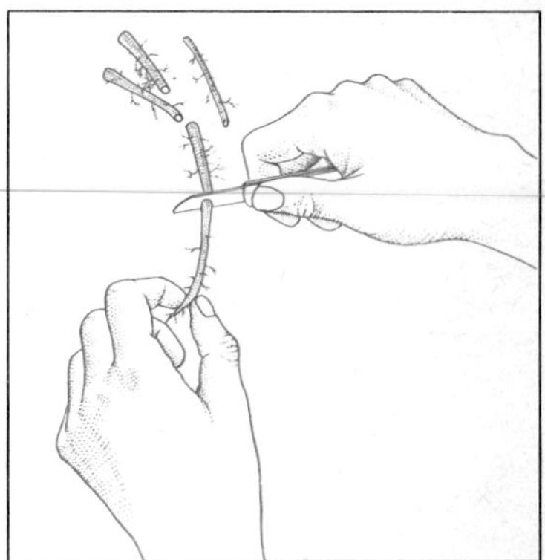

3. *Cut thin roots into 2-in. pieces, slicing them straight across.*

4. *Insert thick roots in mixture, slanted side down; cover tops $\frac{1}{4}$ in.*

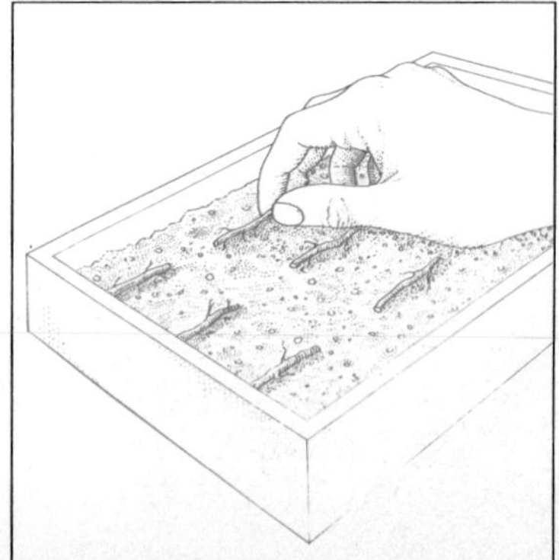

5. *Lay thin root cuttings flat on the rooting mixture, and cover $\frac{1}{4}$ in.*

6. *When cuttings have formed leaves, plant them singly in pots of soil.*

Growing New Plants From Seeds

Buying Versus Gathering Seeds

In nature all flowering plants reproduce themselves from seeds that fall to the ground when ripe. These seeds usually spend time under the cover of dead leaves and germinate when conditions are suitable.

Cultivated plants can also be propagated from seeds, but the offspring often vary. Although most of our garden plants originated from species growing in the wild, they have been hybridized to produce different and often improved forms. When seeds from these hybrids are collected and sown, the plants will differ and will usually be inferior to the parent. Always store collected seeds in a closed container kept in a cool place until they are sown.

Consider growing seedlings in an unused piece of ground, saving only the most attractive ones. In order to perpetuate a seed-raised strain, subsequent plants must be propagated by cuttings or division.

Packaged seeds can usually be relied upon to produce true to type seedlings (or variable seedlings having desirable characteristics), and they provide an inexpensive means of raising plants.

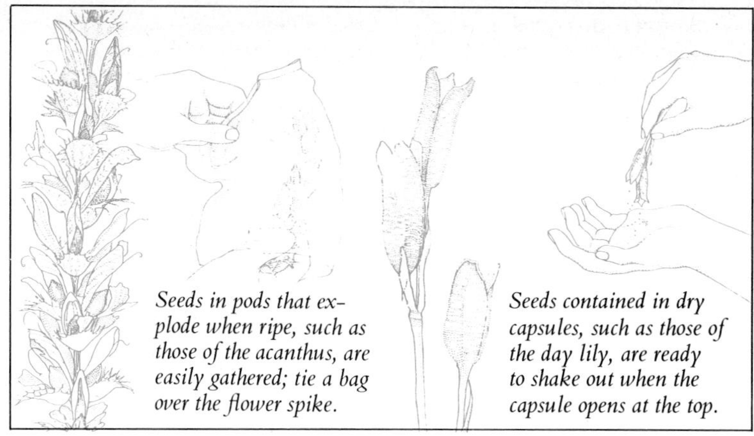

Seeds in pods that explode when ripe, such as those of the acanthus, are easily gathered; tie a bag over the flower spike.

Seeds contained in dry capsules, such as those of the day lily, are ready to shake out when the capsule opens at the top.

Sowing Seeds and Transplanting Seedlings

Sow seeds in mid to late winter in a greenhouse (p. 451) or under lights elsewhere (p. 408). Window light is seldom adequate. When the weather warms up, sow seeds in a cold frame or sheltered bed.

When sowing small quantities of seeds indoors, the simplest method is to plant only one kind in a pot. Fill the pot to about ½ inch below its rim with a commercial seed-starting mixture or your own sterilized formula (equal parts of soil, peat moss, and perlite). Level, firm gently, water with a fine spray, and let drain.

Sprinkle the seeds evenly but thinly over the surface; cover with ⅛-inch layer of starting medium. Leave fine seeds uncovered.

Cover the seed container with a pane of glass or a plastic bag to retain necessary moisture and warmth for germination. Keep the container out of the sun to avoid excessive heat. Most seeds germinate at 65°–70° F. Depending on the kind, seedlings should appear in about one to three weeks. When they do, remove the glass or plastic covering.

When seedlings are large enough to handle easily, transplant to a flat or pot filled with sterilized soil, and space 1–2 inches apart. Give them all the sun and light available to prevent weak, spindly growth. As seedlings become crowded, pot individually.

Before setting the seedlings out, acclimate them to outdoor conditions by putting them in a cold frame or sheltered spot in the garden. Set pots or flats on the surface of the soil, and lightly shade for a few days; then gradually admit more air and light. Later transplant to an out-of-the-way bed for further growth. In late summer of the same year, plant in permanent positions, or wait until the following spring.

For an early start in cold climates, outdoor seed sowing is best done in a heated frame. A soil-heating cable set for 65° F is satisfactory. In an unheated frame, sow about six weeks prior to the last spring frost. Prepare soil in frame by adding peat moss or perlite, so that it will not crust over and deter the emergence of the seedlings. Sow seeds shallowly in rows or in pots as previously described. Shade the frame with burlap until seeds germinate; then give full light, ventilation, and moisture. Transplant as needed into well-spaced rows or pots in the cold frame, and then later to the garden.

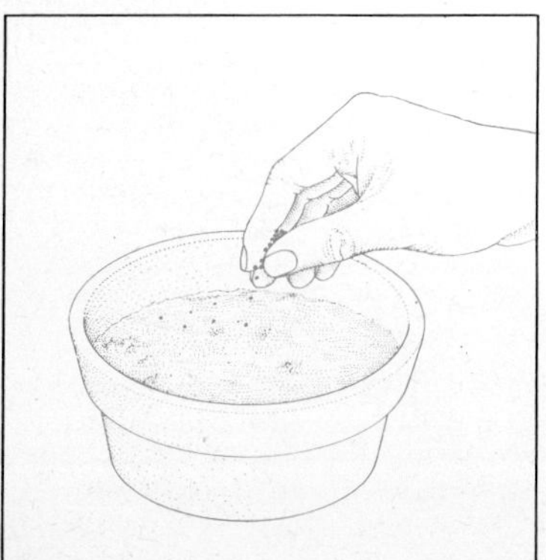

1. *In late winter sprinkle seeds on moist potting mixture; cover them thinly.*

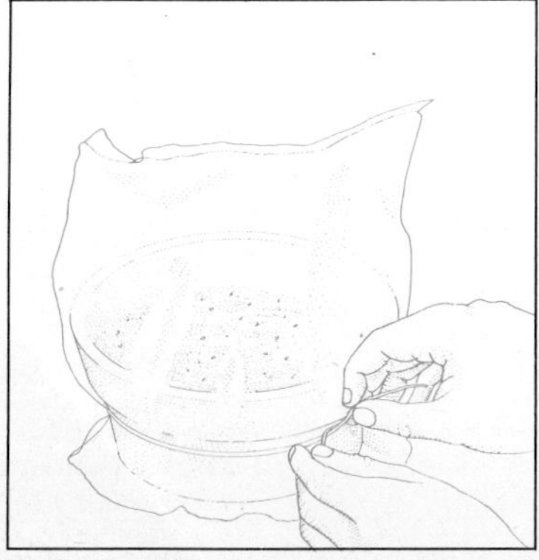

2. *Cover with a plastic bag, which must be removed when seedlings appear.*

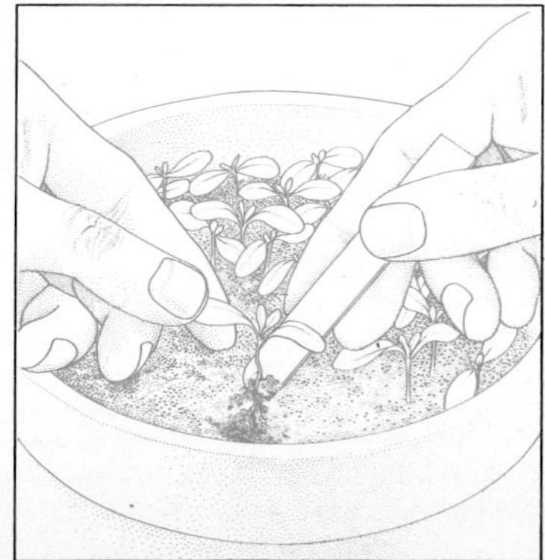

3. *When seedlings have two pairs of leaves, space out in another container.*

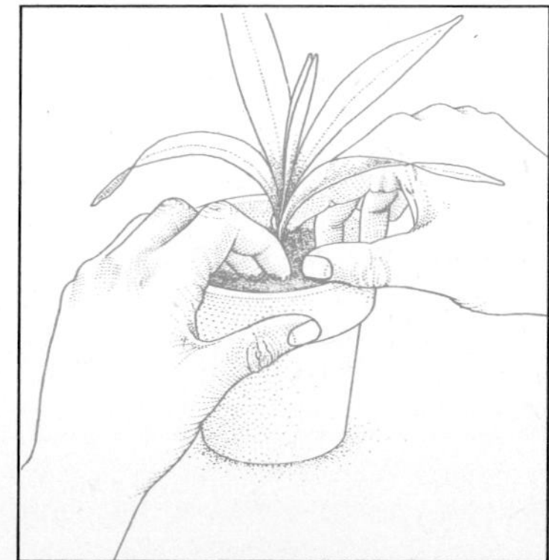

4. *One or two months later move vigorous plants to individual pots.*

Perennials for Your Garden

Most of the plants described in the chart that follows are long-lived and suitable for growing in herbaceous borders or with other plants. The plants are listed according to their best known common names. Also included are recommended species and varieties. New varieties are constantly being introduced, and the older ones dropped, but the generic characteristics remain much the same, as indicated in the first column.

Height (H) is measured to the tip of the flower stem; spread (S) applies to the horizontal area covered by the foliage after several years. The range of height and spread for the genus appears in the first column; the height of each species is in the next column. Size, of course, is influenced by soil and climate.

Almost all plants listed here have a wide range of adaptability, and so many climatic, cultural, and varietal differences affect hardiness that zone designations often prove misleading. Therefore, few specifics are included here. Check hardiness locally.

Acanthus mollis

Achillea filipendulina 'Gold Plate'

Aconite (*Aconitum napellus*)

Agapanthus africanus

Common and botanical names, general characteristics	Species and varieties	Special requirements and remarks	Propagation (*See p. 234*)
Acanthus, or Bear's-breech (*Acanthus*) Basal clusters of handsome, deeply lobed, shiny leaves often 2 ft. long and 1 ft. wide; spikes of tubular flowers open in early summer. Can be grown only in mild climates. H 2-3 ft.; S 2½ ft. or more.	*A. mollis,* whitish, lilac, or rose, 2-3 ft. *A. m. latifolius,* as above, larger leaves, 2-3 ft.	Locate in shade except in coastal areas where it will withstand sun. Plants can be cut back to ground after bloom for complete renewal of growth. In summer wash leaves with stream from hose to keep clean. Roots are invasive, plants difficult to eradicate.	Divide plants in spring; take root cuttings in spring; sow seeds in spring.
Achillea, or Yarrow (*Achillea*) Showy plants, some with attractive, pungent, fernlike leaves. Flowers in broad flat heads or loose clusters; all can be dried. H 1½-3 ft.; S 1-3 ft.	*A. filipendulina* 'Gold Plate,' mustard-yellow, 3-4 ft. *A. f.* 'Coronation Gold,' bright yellow, 4 ft. *A. millefolium* 'Fire King,' deep rose-red, 1-1½ ft. *A. ptarmica* 'Perry's Giant White,' double, white, 1½ ft. *A. taygetea* 'Moonshine,' yellow, 1½ ft.	Does best in full sun and average to poor soil. Very hardy, withstands drought well. *A. ptarmica* may be invasive but can be dug out easily. Mature clump of *A. filipendulina* often has 100 or more flower heads that last many weeks in dry weather. All are virtually trouble free.	Divide in early fall; or sow seeds of *A. millefolium* and *A. ptarmica* in spring.
Aconite, or Monkshood (*Aconitum*) Long spikes of hooded flowers in late summer above deeply cut leaves. Poisonous if eaten. H 2½-8 ft.; S 1-2 ft.	*A. fischeri,* or *A. carmichaelii,* pale blue, 2½-3½ ft. *A. f. wilsonii,* violet-blue, 6-8 ft. *A. f. w.* 'Barker's Variety,' violet-blue, 4-5 ft. *A. napellus,* blue to violet, earliest, 3½-4 ft. *A. n. sparksii,* deep violet-blue, 3-4 ft.	Grows best in partial shade and in soil enriched with compost. Tall varieties may need staking. Plants never invasive. Excellent for cut flowers and good substitute for delphinium; blooms late in season when few other perennials bloom. Tuberous roots.	Divide in early spring or sow seeds in spring. Do not disturb unless crowding reduces bloom.
Agapanthus, or African lily (*Agapanthus*) Evergreen and deciduous tuberous-rooted plants with handsome strap-shaped leaves, clusters of blue or white funnel-shaped flowers. H 1½-2 ft.; S 1-2 ft.	*A. africanus* (lily of the Nile), blue, 3 ft. *A. a. albus,* white, 3 ft. *A. a. mooreanus,* blue, grassy leaves, quite hardy, 1½ ft. *A. a.* 'Rancho Dwarf,' white, 2 ft. *A. inapertus,* blue, quite hardy, 4 ft.	In mild climates grow in beds or tubs. In North does best in tubs; store in light, frost-free place over winter. Give light shade to full sun outdoors and rich sandy soil. Fertilizing and watering increase bloom.	Divide evergreen forms in spring or fall, deciduous in fall; or sow seeds in spring to bloom in 3-4 yr.

Alchemilla vulgaris

Willow amsonia (*Amsonia tabernaemontana)*

Anchusa azurea 'Dropmore'

Anemone hybrid

Anthemis tinctoria 'Moonlight'

Common and botanical names, general characteristics	Species and varieties	Special requirements and remarks	Propagation *(See p. 234)*
Alchemilla, or Lady's mantle *(Alchemilla)* Distinguished but not spectacular, with fluffy flower sprays in midsummer above handsome, rounded, lobed, plaited leaves. H 6 in.-1½ ft.; S 1 ft. or more.	*A. alpina* (mountain lady's mantle), sulfur-yellow, grayish leaves, 6 in. *A. vulgaris* (common lady's mantle), yellow-green, 1½ ft.	Grows well in sun or partial shade. Undemanding as to soil, provided it is well drained. Its leaves are favorite subject of photographers, as edges hold beads of dew. Flowers last up to 2 wk. in water. An especially handsome plant for all-green border, wild-flower garden, or shaded rock garden.	Divide plants in early spring; or sow seeds.
Amsonia, or Bluestar *(Amsonia)* Clusters of small soft blue flowers in late spring and shiny willowlike leaves that cover the entire stem. Long tapering seedpods also add interest. H 2-3 ft.; S 1-2 ft.	*A. tabernaemontana* (willow amsonia), light blue, 2-3 ft.	Prefers partial shade and ample moisture. Generally trouble free. Clumps grow in beauty and seldom require division. A rather late starter in spring; so take care not to injure when cultivating. For all-season good looks this rates high. Not widely available.	Divide deeply rooted plants in spring; or sow seeds in spring. Plants often self-sow but are not invasive.
Anchusa, or Alkanet *(Anchusa)* Clusters of small blue flowers like forget-me-nots in early to mid summer. For *A. myosotidiflora,* see Brunnera. H 1-5 ft.; S 1-1½ ft.	*A. azurea* 'Dropmore,' blue, 4-5 ft. *A. a.* 'Little John,' brilliant blue, 1 ft. *A. a.* 'Pride of Dover,' dark sky-blue, 4 ft. *A. a.* 'Royal Blue,' royal blue in pyramidal clusters, 3 ft. (similar to, and often listed as, 'Loddon Royalist').	Best in sun with ample water. Plants may bloom again if they are cut back after flowering. Tall varieties may require staking. Their self-sowing habit can be nuisance in small garden, but plants can be pulled easily. Somewhat coarse foliage.	Divide plants or sow seeds in spring. Often self-sows in garden. Take root cuttings.
Anemone *(Anemone)* Fall blooming except spring for *A. pulsatilla.* Single to double flowers up to 3 in. across above foliage that is similar to grape leaves (ferny in *A. pulsatilla).* H 8 in.-3 ft.; S 1-2 ft.	*A.* hybrids, mainly *A. hupehensis japonica* selections (Japanese anemone), including single-flowered white or pink and the semi-double 'Queen Charlotte,' deep pink, 2½-3 ft. *A. pulsatilla,* or *Pulsatilla vulgaris* (pasqueflower) in various shades of lavender to red and white, 8 in. *A. vitifolia robustissima,* single, silver-pink, 2½ ft.	Main requirement is rich well-drained soil and in cold regions light mulch over winter. Partial shade desirable. Plants take several years to become established and multiply slowly. *A. vitifolia robustissima* hardier than *A.* hybrid forms.	Divide plants or sow seeds in spring. No need for division for many years.
Anthemis, or Chamomile *(Anthemis)* Deeply cut leaves and 2½-in. yellow daisylike flowers from midsummer until early fall. Flowers are long lasting when cut for indoor decoration. H 1-3 ft.; S 1 ft.	*A. biebersteiniana,* bright yellow, 1 ft. *A. nobilis,* or *Chamaemelum nobile* (garden chamomile), white and yellow, 1 ft., grown as ground cover or as herb. *A. tinctoria* (golden Marguerite), yellow or gold, 2-3 ft. *A. t.* 'Beauty of Grallagh,' deep yellow. *A. t.* 'E. C. Buxton,' lemon-yellow. *A. t. kelwayi,* dark yellow. *A. t.* 'Moonlight,' pale yellow.	Excellent choice for hot, dry areas with sandy soil. Since somewhat weak stemmed, plants may need staking. Divide frequently to avoid dead centers in plants, and remove faded flowers to extend period of bloom and prevent self-sowing. The foliage is aromatic when it is bruised.	Divide in early spring or fall; take cuttings of basal shoots in same season. Seeds of *A. t. kelwayi* sometimes available.

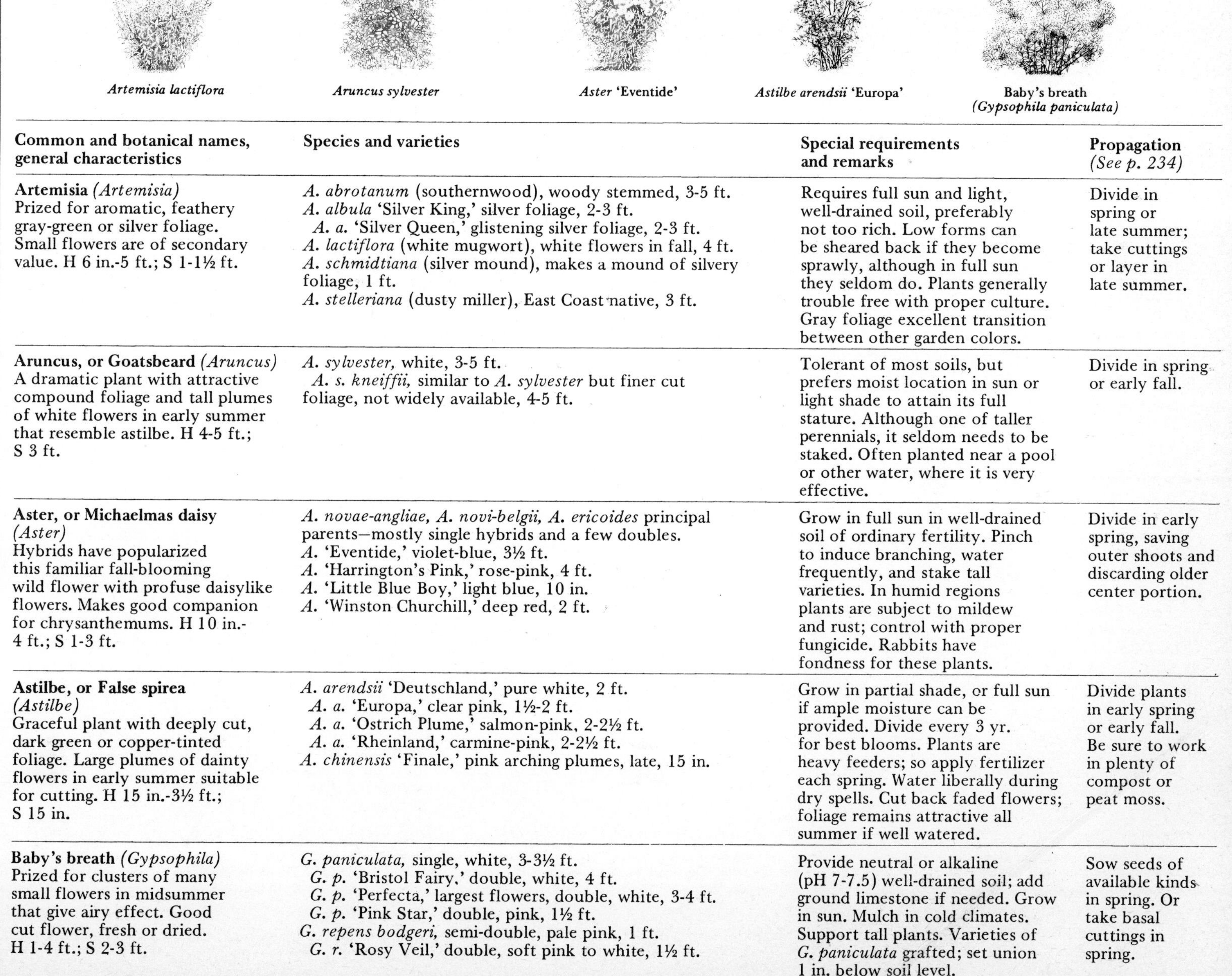

Artemisia lactiflora — *Aruncus sylvester* — *Aster* 'Eventide' — *Astilbe arendsii* 'Europa' — Baby's breath (*Gypsophila paniculata*)

Common and botanical names, general characteristics	Species and varieties	Special requirements and remarks	Propagation (*See p. 234*)
Artemisia (*Artemisia*) Prized for aromatic, feathery gray-green or silver foliage. Small flowers are of secondary value. H 6 in.-5 ft.; S 1-1½ ft.	*A. abrotanum* (southernwood), woody stemmed, 3-5 ft. *A. albula* 'Silver King,' silver foliage, 2-3 ft. *A. a.* 'Silver Queen,' glistening silver foliage, 2-3 ft. *A. lactiflora* (white mugwort), white flowers in fall, 4 ft. *A. schmidtiana* (silver mound), makes a mound of silvery foliage, 1 ft. *A. stelleriana* (dusty miller), East Coast native, 3 ft.	Requires full sun and light, well-drained soil, preferably not too rich. Low forms can be sheared back if they become sprawly, although in full sun they seldom do. Plants generally trouble free with proper culture. Gray foliage excellent transition between other garden colors.	Divide in spring or late summer; take cuttings or layer in late summer.
Aruncus, or Goatsbeard (*Aruncus*) A dramatic plant with attractive compound foliage and tall plumes of white flowers in early summer that resemble astilbe. H 4-5 ft.; S 3 ft.	*A. sylvester,* white, 3-5 ft. *A. s. kneiffii,* similar to *A. sylvester* but finer cut foliage, not widely available, 4-5 ft.	Tolerant of most soils, but prefers moist location in sun or light shade to attain its full stature. Although one of taller perennials, it seldom needs to be staked. Often planted near a pool or other water, where it is very effective.	Divide in spring or early fall.
Aster, or Michaelmas daisy (*Aster*) Hybrids have popularized this familiar fall-blooming wild flower with profuse daisylike flowers. Makes good companion for chrysanthemums. H 10 in.-4 ft.; S 1-3 ft.	*A. novae-angliae, A. novi-belgii, A. ericoides* principal parents—mostly single hybrids and a few doubles. *A.* 'Eventide,' violet-blue, 3½ ft. *A.* 'Harrington's Pink,' rose-pink, 4 ft. *A.* 'Little Blue Boy,' light blue, 10 in. *A.* 'Winston Churchill,' deep red, 2 ft.	Grow in full sun in well-drained soil of ordinary fertility. Pinch to induce branching, water frequently, and stake tall varieties. In humid regions plants are subject to mildew and rust; control with proper fungicide. Rabbits have fondness for these plants.	Divide in early spring, saving outer shoots and discarding older center portion.
Astilbe, or False spirea (*Astilbe*) Graceful plant with deeply cut, dark green or copper-tinted foliage. Large plumes of dainty flowers in early summer suitable for cutting. H 15 in.-3½ ft.; S 15 in.	*A. arendsii* 'Deutschland,' pure white, 2 ft. *A. a.* 'Europa,' clear pink, 1½-2 ft. *A. a.* 'Ostrich Plume,' salmon-pink, 2-2½ ft. *A. a.* 'Rheinland,' carmine-pink, 2-2½ ft. *A. chinensis* 'Finale,' pink arching plumes, late, 15 in.	Grow in partial shade, or full sun if ample moisture can be provided. Divide every 3 yr. for best blooms. Plants are heavy feeders; so apply fertilizer each spring. Water liberally during dry spells. Cut back faded flowers; foliage remains attractive all summer if well watered.	Divide plants in early spring or early fall. Be sure to work in plenty of compost or peat moss.
Baby's breath (*Gypsophila*) Prized for clusters of many small flowers in midsummer that give airy effect. Good cut flower, fresh or dried. H 1-4 ft.; S 2-3 ft.	*G. paniculata,* single, white, 3-3½ ft. *G. p.* 'Bristol Fairy,' double, white, 4 ft. *G. p.* 'Perfecta,' largest flowers, double, white, 3-4 ft. *G. p.* 'Pink Star,' double, pink, 1½ ft. *G. repens bodgeri,* semi-double, pale pink, 1 ft. *G. r.* 'Rosy Veil,' double, soft pink to white, 1½ ft.	Provide neutral or alkaline (pH 7-7.5) well-drained soil; add ground limestone if needed. Grow in sun. Mulch in cold climates. Support tall plants. Varieties of *G. paniculata* grafted; set union 1 in. below soil level.	Sow seeds of available kinds in spring. Or take basal cuttings in spring.

Balloonflower
(*Platycodon grandiflorum*)

Baptisia australis

Bergenia crassifolia orbicularis

Boltonia latisquama

Brunnera macrophylla

Common and botanical names, general characteristics	Species and varieties	Special requirements and remarks	Propagation (*See p. 234*)
Balloonflower (*Platycodon*) Spikes of large, cup-shaped flowers open from inflated balloonlike buds in midsummer and bloom for many weeks. Attractive leaves. Long lasting when cut. H 1½-3 ft.; S 1 ft.	*P. grandiflorum,* blue, 2-3 ft. *P. g. album,* white, 2-3 ft. *P. g.* 'Double Blue,' deep blue, 2 ft. *P. g. mariesii,* bright blue, 1½ ft. *P. g. m. album,* white, 1½ ft. *P. g.* 'Shell Pink,' light pink, 1½-2 ft.	Long-lived, provided soil drains well. Grow in sun or partial shade (pink varieties fade in sun). Plant appears in late spring. Cut flowers in evening; put in deep water. Next day strip lower leaves; cut ½ in. off stems before arranging.	Sow seeds in spring. Divide in spring (difficult due to fleshy taproot; resents disturbance).
Baptisia, or Wild indigo (*Baptisia*) Grown for its deep blue flowers that bloom on tall spikes in early summer, followed by attractive black seedpods that can be used effectively in dried arrangements. Flowers make attractive fresh bouquets. H 3-4 ft.; S 2-4 ft.	*B. australis,* deep blue, 3-4 ft.	Easily grown in average soil and in sun or partial shade. Vigorous plants grow very large and must be pried from soil to be divided. However, they are not invasive. Birds are fond of seeds if stems are left uncut over winter. Plants are very winter hardy.	Divide thick roots in early fall or very early spring; or sow seeds in early spring.
Bergenia (*Bergenia,* or *Megasea*) Grown primarily for striking, 8- to 10-in., glossy green, round leaves that are evergreen, reddish in winter. Flowers in midspring on short stems. H 10 in.-1½ ft.; S 1½ ft.	*B. cordifolia,* reddish pink, most readily available, 1 ft. *B. c. alba,* white, 10 in. *B. crassifolia orbicularis,* rose, large flowers, 1½ ft. New hybrids are beginning to appear but are not yet widely available.	Care-free plants for sun or shade, moist or dry soil. Foliar feeding tends to increase vigor. In cold regions flowers may not appear. Most effective planted in groups. Spreading but not invasive.	Divide creeping rhizomes after flowering or in early fall. Frequent division prevents dead centers.
Betony, see Stachys			
Boltonia (*Boltonia*) Mostly tall-growing plants bearing in mid to late summer small starlike flowers that resemble wild asters. Found wild in many regions. H 2-6 ft.; S 2-3 ft.	*B. asteroides,* white and shades of purple, 4-6 ft. *B. latisquama,* pink to purple, 4-6 ft. *B. l. nana,* pink, 2 ft.	Requires full sun and average garden soil. Useful for wild-flower garden or as background plant in perennial border. Not widely offered in garden catalogs but often listed by wild-flower specialists.	Divide plants in spring; or sow seeds in spring.
Brunnera, or Siberian bugloss (*Brunnera,* or *Anchusa*) In mid to late spring loose clusters of blue, starlike flowers rise above large, dark green, heart-shaped leaves. H 1-1½ ft.; S 1½ ft.	*B. macrophylla* (often listed as *Anchusa myosotidiflora*), blue flowers, ¼ in. across, 1-1½ ft.	Does best in partly shaded area with moist soil. Multiplies slowly and needs to be divided only when centers of clumps look vacant. Effective with spring-flowering bulbs in informal plantings. Makes interesting ground cover during summer.	Divide in early spring; or take root cuttings in late summer.

Bugbane
(*Cimicifuga simplex*)

Butterfly weed
(*Asclepias tuberosa*)

Campanula persicifolia

Cassia marilandica

Catananche caerulea

Common and botanical names, general characteristics	Species and varieties	Special requirements and remarks	Propagation (*See p. 234*)
Bugbane (*Cimicifuga*) Tall plumelike flower spikes top a basal cluster of fernlike leaves in early to mid fall. Useful at back of border or in wild-flower garden. H 3-5 ft.; S 1½-2 ft.	*C. dahurica* (dahurian bugbane), white, late summer, 5 ft. *C. racemosa* (black snakeroot), white, midsummer, 5-8 ft. *C. simplex,* early to mid fall, 4-4½ ft. *C. s.* 'White Pearl,' white, early to mid fall, 3-4 ft.	Best in semi-shade but will grow in deep shade or full sun. When grown in sun, it is especially important to mix plenty of compost or peat moss into soil to help retain moisture. Flower spikes make excellent cut flowers, although some people find aroma objectionable.	Divide in early spring. Plants not generally invasive.
Butterfly weed (*Asclepias*) Familiar wild flower, but its clusters of orange flowers in midsummer make it choice plant for perennial garden. Attractive foliage and seedpods. H 2 ft.; S 1 ft.	*A. tuberosa,* brilliant orange, 2 ft.	A notably trouble-free perennial that can remain in same place for years and not outgrow its allotted space. Shoots are very slow to appear in spring; so mark plant's location. Attractive before, during, and after bloom.	Sow seeds in spring. Division not recommended, as plant has easily broken taproot.
Campanula, or Bellflower (*Campanula*) Diverse group of plants with small, neat foliage and mostly cup-shaped flowers. Taller varieties listed here; for shorter forms, see p. 356. H 2-3 ft.; S 1-2 ft.	*C. glomerata* (clustered bellflower), blue, white, 2 ft. *C. lactiflora* 'Pritchard's Variety,' blue, 3 ft. *C. latifolia* (great bellflower), violet, 3 ft. *C. l.* 'Brantwood,' deep violet, 3 ft. *C. persicifolia* and hybrids (peach-leaved bellflower), in various shades of blue or white, 2-2½ ft.	Grow in full sun or partial shade in soil of average fertility. Tall varieties seldom need staking. Removing faded flower spikes helps to prolong flowering. Valuable border plants suitable for cutting.	Divide or take basal cuttings in spring; or sow seeds in spring.
Carnation, garden, see Dianthus			
Cassia, or Wild senna (*Cassia*) A most impressive shrublike plant with fine-textured leaves and clusters of yellow flowers that bloom in late summer. Good-looking all summer. H 3-4 ft.; S 3-5 ft.	*C. marilandica,* bright yellow, 3-in. flower clusters, 3-4 ft.	Large plant that stands on its own without staking and is generally free of insects and diseases. Grows best in full sun or very light shade. Soil must be well drained. Division seldom necessary. Although native American plant, it is not widely available.	Divide plants in early spring; or sow seeds in spring.
Catananche, or Cupid's dart (*Catananche*) Blue or white flowers resembling wild chicory appear in midsummer on slender-stemmed plants with narrow, silvery leaves. Good for cutting. H 2 ft.; S 1 ft.	*C. caerulea,* blue with deeper blue center, 2 ft. *C. c. alba,* white, 2 ft.	Avoid soggy soil and grow in full sun. Plants must be divided frequently to ensure survival. Not reliably hardy in Zone A. Grow in groups for best effect. Flowers dry well for winter use.	Sow seeds in spring or divide plants; take root cuttings in early summer.

Centaurea montana

Centranthus ruber

Chelone obliqua

Chinese lantern
(Physalis alkekengi)

Clematis heracleaefolia davidiana

Common and botanical names, general characteristics	**Species and varieties**	**Special requirements and remarks**	**Propagation** *(See p. 234)*
Centaurea *(Centaurea)* Tufted flowers on long stems bloom in mid to late summer, some with rather coarse leaves. The blue ones are particularly valued. H 2-4 ft.; S 1-2 ft.	*C. dealbata* (Persian centaurea), lilac to purple, 2 ft. *C. d.* 'John Coutts,' bright pink, 2 ft. *C. d. steenbergii,* bright purple, 2 ft. *C. macrocephala* (globe centaurea), yellow, thistlelike, 4 ft. *C. montana* (mountain bluet), blue, one of the best, 2 ft. *C. ruthenica,* similar to *C. macrocephala,* less coarse, 3 ft.	Easily grown. Requires very well-drained soil in sunny location. Plants withstand drought. *C. montana* most commonly seen; a rapid spreader. It self-sows, which in some gardens may prove a nuisance. All hardy if soil is well drained.	Divide plants in very early spring. Seeds can be sown in spring but are rarely available.
Centranthus *(Centranthus)* Bushy plants with 3- to 4-in. gray-green leaves, fragrant crimson or white flowers in dense clusters along stems. Blooms early to mid summer. H 2-3 ft.; S 1-2 ft.	*C. ruber* (red valerian), crimson, 2-3 ft. Not to be confused with valerian, *Valeriana officinalis,* p. 262. *C. r. albus,* white, 2-3 ft.	Grow in full sun and ordinary garden soil. Plants multiply rapidly, less so in poor soil. Plant attractive over long period.	Sow seeds in spring; or divide plants in spring.
Chelone, or Turtlehead *(Chelone)* Short spikes of flowers like penstemon are borne in late summer on tall, unbranched stems. Alternate dark green leaves are broad and strongly veined. H 2-4 ft.; S 2-4 ft.	*C. glabra,* white or tinged pink, 2 ft. *C. lyonii,* pink to rose-purple, 3-4 ft. *C. obliqua,* rose-pink, 2 ft.	Plant in partial shade in rich, moisture-retentive soil. Plants spread rapidly; so will need to be divided every few years. Generally insect free. Most often listed in wild-flower catalogs, as plants usually grow in moist woodland.	Divide plants in early spring. Plants spread by underground runners.
Chinese lantern *(Physalis)* Valued primarily for colorful, papery, inflated calyx (lantern) that is dried and used for winter decoration. Flowers not ornamental. H 8 in.-2½ ft.; S 1-3 ft.	*P. alkekengi,* or *P. franchetii,* obscure small white flowers, fruit surrounded by inflated orange-red calyx, 2-2½ ft. *P. a.* 'Pygmy,' flowers and fruit as above, 8 in. (Often grown as pot plant.)	Select a location in sun or very light shade; any average soil is suitable. Plants spread by creeping rhizomes. To control spread, cut off with sharp spade and remove. To dry flowers, pick when they show color, strip leaves, hang in dark, airy location.	Sow seeds in spring (often grown as annual); divide or take root cuttings in spring.
Chrysanthemum, see Daisy, Shasta, and p. 264			
Clematis *(Clematis)* Not as well known as clematis vines, these herbaceous forms make interesting border plants. Long blooming. Some are fragrant. H 2-4 ft.; S 2-3 ft.	*C. heracleaefolia davidiana,* deep blue, late summer, 3 ft. *C. integrifolia caerulea,* blue, early to late summer, 2 ft. *C. recta,* white, early to mid summer, 3-4 ft. *C. r. grandiflora,* white, early to mid summer, 3 ft. *C. r. mandshurica,* white, early to mid summer, 3-4 ft.	Provide well-drained, humus-rich soil, preferably on alkaline side; grow in sun or partial shade. Mulch to keep soil cool. Avoid cultivating around plants; roots are shallow. Support plants with wire-mesh cylinders or twiggy brush in spring. Fluffy seedpods add interest and remain on plants for some time.	Take stem cuttings in midsummer for bloom following year. Protect over first winter.

Columbine
(*Aquilegia* 'Spring Song')

Purple coneflower
(*Echinacea purpurea* hybrid)

Coralbells
(*Heuchera* hybrid)

Coreopsis lanceolata 'Sunburst'

Common and botanical names, general characteristics	Species and varieties	Special requirements and remarks	Propagation (*See p. 234*)
Columbine (*Aquilegia*) Graceful plant that in late spring bears funnel-shaped flowers with prominent spurs above basal cluster of segmented leaves. Many varieties available. H 15 in.-3 ft.; S 6 in.-1 ft.	*A. caerulea* (Colorado columbine), blue and white, 2½ ft. *A. chrysantha* 'Silver Queen,' white, long blooming, 2-2½ ft. *A.* 'Dragonfly Hybrids,' lavender, red, yellow, white, 18 in. *A.* 'McKanna's Giant Hybrids,' mixed colors, long spurs, 3 ft. *A.* 'Spring Song,' mixed colors, extrapetaled, early, 2½ ft.	Grow in sun or partial shade, in moist, well-drained soil. Remove faded flowers to prevent self-sowing, which may produce inferior colors and blooms. Leaf miners may disfigure leaves with white streaks; control with late-spring spraying of Diazinon or malathion. Old clumps tend to die; so renew occasionally.	Propagated by seeds sown in early spring; occasionally by division in very early spring.
Coneflower, see Coneflower, purple, and Rudbeckia			
Coneflower, purple (*Echinacea*) Long-lasting, large daisylike flowers with rounded cone-shaped centers on long stiff stems bloom in mid to late summer. Excellent for cutting. H 2½-3 ft.; S 1-1½ ft.	*E. purpurea* is undoubtedly one parent of following hybrids, but other parent uncertain. *E.* 'Bright Star,' rose-red, maroon center, 2½-3 ft. *E.* 'Robert Bloom,' carmine-purple, orange center, 2½-3 ft. *E.* 'The King,' coral-crimson, maroon-brown center, 3 ft. *E.* 'White Lustre,' white, drooping petals, 3 ft.	Care-free plant with stiff stems that make staking unnecessary. Grows best in well-drained sandy soil. Locate plants in full sun for best results. Favorite of Japanese beetles where they are prevalent. Spray to control. Flowers are long lasting, well suited for drying.	Divide plants in early spring. 'Bright Star' seeds are available and can be sown in spring.
Coralbells (*Heuchera*) Slender stems carry small bell-shaped flowers in early summer and often again later. Attractive evergreen leaves. Dainty cut flower. H 1-2 ft.; S 1-1½ ft.	Hybrids of *H. sanguinea.* *H.* 'Bressingham Hybrids,' mixed in white, pink, red, 2 ft. *H.* 'Chatterbox,' deep rose-pink, 1½ ft. *H.* 'Pluie de Feu,' cherry-red, 1½ ft. *H.* 'Rosamundi,' coral-pink, 1½ ft. *H.* 'White Cloud,' white to cream, 1½ ft.	Plant in spring in sun or partial shade. Provide well-drained soil with ample humus. Set crowns 1 in. below soil level. In spring remove any damaged leaves. Remove faded flower stems to encourage later bloom. In Zones A and B, light mulch helps keep plants from heaving out of the soil in very early spring.	Divide in spring; root leaf cutting with small piece of leaf stalk attached in summer; sow seeds in spring.
Coreopsis, or Tickseed (*Coreopsis*) Daisylike flowers bloom in profusion over long period in summer. Leaves are neat and unobtrusive, broader in some kinds than in others. Excellent cut flower. H 1-3 ft.; S 1-2 ft.	*C. auriculata nana* (dwarf-eared), orange-yellow, 6 in. *C.* 'Baby Sun,' hybrid usually raised from seeds, yellow, 20 in. *C. lanceolata,* yellow, 2 ft. *C. l.* 'Sunburst,' semi-double, bright yellow, 2 ft. *C.* 'Mayfield Giant,' yellow, 3 ft. *C.* 'New Gold,' double, yellow, 2½ ft. *C. verticillata* 'Golden Shower,' yellow, 2 ft.	Locate plants in full sun. Provide well-drained sandy soil. Keep flowers or seed heads picked to prolong flowering. *C. verticillata* withstands drought particularly well and has very narrow, almost threadlike leaves. All benefit from division every few years except *C. lanceolata,* the commonest form, which seldom needs this.	Divide plants in spring; or sow seeds of available varieties in spring.

Cynoglossum nervosum

Shasta daisy
(*Chrysanthemum maximum* 'Alaska')

Day lily
(*Hemerocallis* hybrid)

Delphinium elatum hybrid

Common and botanical names, general characteristics	Species and varieties	Special requirements and remarks	Propagation (*See p. 234*)
Cynoglossum, or Chinese forget-me-not (*Cynoglossum*) Small flowers like forget-me-nots borne on branching stems above rough, hairy leaves for several weeks in mid to late summer. H 2-3 ft.; S 1-1½ ft.	*C. grande,* blue or purple, 2-3 ft. *C. nervosum,* gentian-blue, 2½ ft. Not to be confused with annual cynoglossum, p. 295.	Very hardy plant that does well in dry soil and in sun or partial shade. May need staking. Spreads rapidly; so best divided every 2 or 3 yr. Plants branch well and are covered with small blue flowers.	Divide in very early spring or early fall; or sow seeds in early spring. Plants usually self-sow.
Daisy, Shasta (*Chrysanthemum*) Single or double flowers grow on long stems, bloom in early summer and intermittently thereafter, especially when picked. Neat foliage. Suitable for cutting. H 1-2 ft.; S 1-2½ ft.	*C. maximum* 'Aglaya,' double, white, fringed petals, 2 ft. *C. m.* 'Alaska,' single, white with yellow center, 2 ft. *C. m.* 'Esther Read,' double, white, 1½ ft. *C. m.* 'Little Miss Muffet,' semi-double, white, 14 in. *C. m.* 'Majestic,' very large single, white, 2 ft. *C. m.* 'Thomas Killin,' double, white, crested center, 2 ft.	Best grown in full sun, although doubles may do better in partial shade. Soil should be rich and moist but well drained. Soggy winter soil can cause death of plant. Treat for aphids and plant bugs in spring.	Divide plants or make basal cuttings in spring; or sow seeds in spring.
Day lily (*Hemerocallis*) Large, mostly single, funnel-shaped flowers, usually with broad petals and sepals, often fragrant. Blooms midspring to fall, according to variety. Handsome, narrow, sword-shaped evergreen or deciduous leaves curve gracefully. H 15 in.-4 ft.; S 2-4 ft.	Hundreds of hybrids with mixed parentage, in all colors except blue and pure white, and in many patterns. Select according to early, midseason, or late bloom, and height according to need. Evening bloomers open toward evening and stay open through following day or longer. Triploids have thick petals, are very weather resistant. The common lemon lily (*H. flava*) and the tawny orange day lily (*H. fulva*) are forerunners of the hybrids.	Grow in full sun or partial shade. Although minimal care is needed, plants have more blooms of superior quality if grown in soil with ample humus, fertilized in spring, and watered when actively growing in spring and summer. Mulch in summer to conserve moisture. Avoid deep cultivation, as fleshy roots grow near surface. Remove dead leaves in spring. Divide every 4-5 yr. for best bloom. Plant in spring, summer, or early fall.	Divide in midspring or late summer. Sow seeds in spring or late summer. Root leafy proliferations, which often form on stem, in late summer.
Delphinium (*Delphinium*) Tall spikes of closely spaced flowers (*D. elatum* types) or shorter spikes of loosely spaced flowers (*D. belladonna*) bloom in early to late summer. Each of the flowers consists of 5 showy sepals, 1 with a spur. True petals are smaller, often crowded in throat, and are called the "eye" or "bee." Flowers that are bicolored are the showiest. H 2½-6 ft.; S 1-3 ft.	*D. belladonna* hybrids, white and shades of blue, 3-5 ft. *D.* 'Connecticut Yankee,' blue, purple, lavender, white, 2½ ft. *D. elatum* hybrids (including 'Pacific ' and 'Blackmore and Langdon' hybrids), shades of blue, purple, pink, and white, often with contrasting "eye" or "bee."	Locate in sun in soil well mixed with humus and preferably slightly alkaline. Fertilize heavily, supply ample water, and stake tall varieties early, before they topple. Spray to control mildew, cyclamen mites, and black spot. Mulch over winter in cold regions, or carry them over in cold frame.	Divide in early spring; or take basal cuttings; sow seeds early indoors for bloom same season.

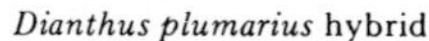
Dianthus plumarius hybrid

Dicentra spectabilis

Doronicum caucasicum magnificum

Echinops ritro

Common and botanical names, general characteristics	Species and varieties	Special requirements and remarks	Propagation *(See p. 234)*
Dianthus, Pink, or Garden carnation *(Dianthus)* Single to double flowers—some fringed, most fragrant—bloom over long period. Narrow leaves. Colors: pink, red, salmon, yellow, or white, often with contrasting borders around central "eyes." H 1-2 ft.; S 1 ft.	*D. allwoodii* hybrids, double or single, 1-1½ ft. *D. caryophyllus* hybrids (garden carnation), 1½-2 ft. (Here belong the grenadin carnations and related large-flowered florist types listed in catalogs.) *D. plumarius* hybrids (cottage or grass pink), single or double, 1-1½ ft.	Dianthuses bloom best in cool weather and should be planted in full sun. They prefer slightly alkaline soil that is extremely well drained. *D. caryophyllus* hybrids need richer soil than others. Keep faded flowers picked to prolong bloom. Remove side buds as soon as they appear on *D. caryophyllus* types to obtain larger flowers.	Sow seeds in spring; take cuttings of vigorous nonflowering side shoots in midsummer.
Dicentra, or Bleeding heart *(Dicentra)* Graceful plants with pendulous heart-shaped flowers blooming on arching stems in late spring, some intermittently all summer. Fernlike leaves for all or part of season. *D. formosa* everblooming. H 1-2½ ft.; S 1-2 ft.	*D. eximia,* (fringed bleeding heart), pink, 1 ft. (Many hybrids of *D. eximia* with *D. formosa* or *D. oregana* range from pink to red, bloom off and on all summer.) *D. formosa* (western bleeding heart), rose-lavender, 15 in. *D. f.* 'Sweetheart,' white, 15 in. *D. spectabilis* (common bleeding heart), large, pink, 2½ ft.	All bleeding hearts like humus-rich soil in sun or shade. *D. formosa* and *D. eximia* self-sow freely. Locate *D. spectabilis* so that bare spaces left after leaves die back in late summer will be hidden by other foliage. Be sure to mark spot with a label so that area will not be disturbed during fall or spring cleanup.	Divide brittle fleshy roots in very early spring; or take root cuttings of *D. spectabilis* in spring. *D. eximia* self-sows freely.
Doronicum, or Leopard's-bane *(Doronicum)* Mid- to late-spring flowering with single, large, yellow daisy-like flowers above mass of rich green heart-shaped leaves. Makes a good cut flower. H 1½-2 ft.; S 1-1½ ft.	*D. caucasicum magnificum,* yellow, 2 ft. *D. c.* 'Finesse,' cactus flowered, yellow, 1½ ft. *D. c.* 'Mme. Mason,' yellow, 2 ft. *D. plantagineum,* very large, yellow, 2½ ft., not widely available.	Will thrive in partial shade or full sun. Plants may require staking. They go dormant in summer (except 'Mme. Mason'), and foliage disappears; so plan to have other plants hide them.	Sow seeds in spring; or divide plants in late summer. Germination may be erratic.
Echinops, or Globe thistle *(Echinops)* Globular flower heads are borne in late summer above dark green thistlelike foliage that is whitish beneath. Flowers excellent for drying. H 3-5 ft.; S 1½-2 ft.	*E. ritro* (steel globe thistle), shades of blue, 3-5 ft. *E. sphaerocephalus* (common globe thistle), silver-gray, 5 ft. *E.* 'Taplow Blue,' deep blue, 4 ft.	Long-lived, easy-care plants that withstand considerable drought. Do best in full sun. Avoid wet or soggy soils. Plants somewhat difficult to divide, as roots extend a foot or more deep. Small pieces of root left in ground when digging will generally sprout and make new plant. Wear gloves when picking flowers because of prickly leaves.	Divide plants or take root cuttings in spring; sow seeds in spring.

Erigeron speciosus

Eryngium bourgatii

Euphorbia epithymoides

Filipendula hexapetala

Allegheny foamflower (*Tiarella cordifolia*)

Common and botanical names, general characteristics	Species and varieties	Special requirements and remarks	Propagation (*See p. 234*)
Erigeron, or Fleabane (*Erigeron*) Daisylike flowers with narrow petals are borne in clusters from early to late summer. Less showy than many other plants. H 9 in.-2 ft.; S 1-1½ ft.	*E. aurantiacus,* semi-double, orange, 9 in. *E. speciosus,* single, blue, 1½-2 ft. *E. s.* 'Azure Fairy,' semi-double, lavender, 2½ ft. *E. s.* 'Foerster's Darling,' semi-double, pink, 1½-2 ft. *E. s.* 'Pink Jewel,' single, baby-pink, 2 ft. *E. s.* 'Red Beauty,' single, bright rose, 1½ ft.	Select location in full sun where soil is well drained and of average fertility; plants tolerate dry soil. Remove faded blooms to encourage more flowering. Plants spread slowly.	Divide plants in spring; sow seeds in spring.
Eryngium, or Sea holly (*Eryngium*) Effective plant with steel-gray to blue thistlelike flowers blooming in mid to late summer. Foliage is also thistlelike and prickly. H 1½-3 ft.; S 1-2 ft.	*E. alpinum* (blue-top eryngo), silvery blue, 1½ ft. *E. amethystinum* (amethyst sea holly), grayish blue, 2 ft. *E. bourgatii* (Mediterranean sea holly), steel-blue, 1½ ft. *E. planum,* blue, best in wild-flower garden, 3 ft. *E.* 'Violetta,' violet-blue, 2 ft.	Since plant is very long-lived and resents disturbance, locate in full sun and well-drained soil that is not soggy in winter. Generally trouble free. Flowers retain their color when dried if picked when fully open.	Divide fleshy roots or take root cuttings in spring; sow seeds in spring.
Euphorbia, or Spurge (*Euphorbia*) Relatively inconspicuous flowers are surrounded by showy petal-like white or yellow bracts in late spring or midsummer. H 1½-2 ft.; S 1½-2 ft.	*E. corollata* (flowering spurge), white, midsummer, 2 ft. *E. epithymoides,* or *E. polychroma,* chartreuse-yellow, 1½ ft.	Long-lived plants that resent disturbance. Locate in full sun and well-drained and not very rich soil. All euphorbias have milky sap that can cause irritation. If used as cut flowers, sear bottom of stems in flame before putting in water.	Divide plants or take basal cuttings in spring.
Fern, see p. 384			
Filipendula, or Meadowsweet (*Filipendula*) Feathery terminal clusters of small flowers bloom in early or mid summer. Some have finely divided fernlike foliage; others are coarser. Roots of *F. hexapetala* are tuberous. H 1½-4 ft.; S 1-1½ ft.	*F. hexapetala,* single, white, early summer, 1½ ft. *F. h. florepleno,* double, white, early summer, 1½ ft. *F. purpurea elegans,* or *F. palmata elegans,* double, white, red stamens, early summer, 15 in. *F. rubra,* pink, early to mid summer, 4-6 ft. *F. ulmaria plena,* double, white, midsummer, 4 ft.	Tall types especially well suited for back of border, along stream, or in woodland planting. *F. hexapetala* and its double form prefer moist soil; others tolerate more dryness. All are long-lived plants that seldom require division.	Divide plants in spring; sow seeds in spring.
Foamflower (*Tiarella*) Basal heart-shaped leaves with slender spikes of small white flowers blooming in late spring. H 8-12 in.; S 12 in.	*T. cordifolia* (Allegheny foamflower), white, 1 ft. *T. wherryi,* white, more compact than above, 1 ft.	Grow in partial shade and in slightly acid soil that is moisture retentive. Particularly good ground cover in wild-flower garden and rock garden. Also suitable for shaded portions of perennial border, where its spread will need to be controlled. *T. wherryi* least invasive.	Divide plants in spring or early fall.

  *Gaillardia aristata*	 *Galega officinalis*	 Gas plant *(Dictamnus albus)*	 *Gazania* hybrid	 *Geranium grandiflorum*

Common and botanical names, general characteristics	**Species and varieties**	**Special requirements and remarks**	**Propagation** *(See p. 234)*
Gaillardia, or Blanketflower *(Gaillardia)* Large, single, daisylike flowers with varied contrasting markings on petal tips or near center bloom from midsummer to early fall or hard frost. For annual gaillardias, see p. 297. H 6 in.-3 ft.; S 6 in.-1½ ft.	*G. aristata,* yellow, often with purple or red, 2 ft. *G.* 'Baby Cole,' red with yellow petal tips, 6 in. *G.* 'Burgundy,' wine-red, 2½ ft. *G.* 'Dazzler,' yellow with maroon center, 2-3 ft. *G.* 'Goblin,' red with yellow petal tips, 1 ft. *G.* 'Portola,' combinations of red and yellow, 2½ ft.	Sun-loving plants that require very well-drained soil if they are to survive cold winters. Often need staking, as plants tend to sprawl. Remove faded blooms for further flowering. Good cut flower.	Divide plants or sow seeds in spring; make root cuttings in summer.
Galega, or Goat's rue *(Galega)* Short spikes of pealike flowers bloom from early summer to fall above bushy, vigorous plants with graceful bluish-green leaves. H 3 ft.; S 1½-2 ft.	*G. officinalis,* purplish blue, 3 ft. *G. o. alba,* white, 3 ft. *G. o. carnea,* rose-pink, 3 ft.	Vigorous perennials that grow well in full sun and almost any soil, performing best when it is relatively moist and rich. Plants seldom need to be staked. Division necessary only after many years.	Divide plants in spring; or sow seeds in spring when available.
Gas plant, or Burning bush *(Dictamnus)* Handsome, usually long-lived plant with pink or white flower spikes, blooming in early to mid summer. Aromatic, leathery, rich green leaves and attractive, persistent seedpods good for drying. H 2-3 ft.; S 2-2½ ft.	*D. albus* (often listed as *D. fraxinella*), white, 2-3 ft. *D. a. purpureus,* pink with darker veins, 2-3 ft.	Grow in sun or partial shade, in moderately rich soil. Staking not necessary. Common name derives from resin on leaves and upper part of stems, which is said to ignite if lighted after still, warm day, though this is easier said than done. Leaves and pods poisonous, can cause dermatitis.	Plants best left undisturbed. Sow seeds where plants are to grow, as they resent transplanting.
Gazania *(Gazania)* Daisylike flowers with striking markings on petals in contrasting colors. Evergreen in mild climates; flowers all summer. H 6-15 in.; S 1 ft.	Hybrids derived from *G. longiscapa* and *G. rigens.* Many varieties are available. Colors include yellow, gold, cream, white, and red, with varied markings. Height varies according to variety.	A perennial often grown as an annual, especially in colder regions where plants are not hardy. Locate in full sun, in light, sandy soil. Tolerates drought. Flowers close during cloudy weather and at night; so they do not make good cut flowers.	Sow seeds in spring. Needs early start to bloom in cool climates before frost. Cuttings can be rooted and wintered in greenhouse.
Geranium, or Cranesbill *(Geranium)* These dainty, mostly single-flowered plants bloom from early to late summer. Not to be confused with the common geranium *(Pelargonium),* p. 297. H 1-3 ft.; S 1-2 ft.	Only taller types listed here. For low forms, see p. 360. *G. endressii,* light rose with darker veins, 1½ ft. *G. e.* 'Johnson's Blue,' light blue, 1½ ft. *G. e.* 'Wargrave Pink,' clear pink, 1½ ft. *G. grandiflorum,* magenta with red veins, 1-1½ ft. *G. pratense,* blue with red veins, 3 ft.	Grow in full sun or partial shade, in soil of average fertility. Overly rich soil may produce rampant growth. Plants seldom need division unless flowering is poor. Not good cut flower.	Divide plants in spring; or sow seeds of available kinds.

Gerbera jamesonii

Geum hybrid

Globeflower (*Trollius ledebouri*)

Goldenrod (*Solidago* hybrid)

Pampas grass (*Cortaderia selloana*)

Common and botanical names, general characteristics	Species and varieties	Special requirements and remarks	Propagation (*See p. 234*)
Gerbera, or Transvaal daisy (*Gerbera*) Large daisylike flowers with very long, graceful petals; single and double forms. Blooms all summer. Excellent cut flower. H 1-1½ ft.; S 1-1½ ft.	*G. jamesonii,* white through cream, yellow, orange, pink, salmon, rose to red, 1-1½ ft.	Locate in full sun except in very hot regions. Add compost or peat moss to soil, and make sure soil is well drained. Plants respond well to periodic fertilizing during summer. In colder regions lift in fall; keep in greenhouse or sunny window for winter bloom.	Sow seeds in early spring; divide plants in spring.
Geum, or Avens (*Geum*) Mostly double flowers up to 3 in. across. Attractive basal leaves are evergreen in South. Blooms late spring to midsummer. Good cut flower. Generally short-lived. H 1-2 ft.; S 1-1½ ft.	Hybrids derived mostly from *G. chiloense.* *G. heldreichii,* double, orange, 1½ ft. *G.* 'Lady Stratheden,' semi-double, yellow, 2 ft. *G.* 'Mrs. Bradshaw,' semi-double, scarlet, 2 ft. *G.* 'Princess Juliana,' semi-double, bronzy orange, 2 ft. *G.* 'Starker's Magnificent,' double, apricot-orange, 1 ft.	Select sunny or partially shaded location. Soil should be well drained but moisture retentive. May need support. Cut flower stems back after flowering. Not reliably hardy in Zone A and northern Zone B.	Divide plants in spring; sow seeds in spring. Fresh seeds germinate best.
Globeflower (*Trollius*) Divided, shiny dark green leaves set off large single or double flowers like buttercups that bloom in late spring. Long-lasting cut flower. H 2-3 ft.; S 1-1½ ft.	Plants are not widely offered in U.S.A. Some sources offer a number of hybrids of *T. europaeus* in shades of yellow and orange. The most widely available globeflower is *T. ledebouri,* orange-gold, 2-2½ ft.	Grows best where soil is very moist, even swampy; so usually does best in partial shade and where soil contains plenty of peat moss or compost. Plants will multiply, but division not generally necessary for at least 5 or 6 yr.	Divide plants in spring. Sow seeds in spring or fall. May take more than a year to germinate.
Gloriosa daisy, see Rudbeckia, p. 305			
Goldenrod (*Solidago*) Good for late summer color. The hybrids of the common goldenrod have improved compact form. Goldenrod pollen does not cause hay fever. H 2½-3 ft.; S 1-2 ft.	Most garden varieties are hybrids derived from *S. canadensis* and *S. virgaurea.* *S.* 'Cloth of Gold,' soft primrose-yellow, 1½ ft. *S.* 'Golden Mosa,' dark yellow, 3 ft. *S.* 'Leraft,' golden yellow, 3 ft. *S.* 'Peter Pan,' canary-yellow, 2½ ft.	Like their counterpart, the wild goldenrod, the hybrids require sun and average well-drained garden soil. Divide every 3 or 4 yr. Remove faded flowers to prevent self-sown seedlings, which usually revert to less desirable forms.	Divide plants in spring.
Grasses, ornamental (several genera) Popular evergreen or deciduous plants grown for decorative leaves and graceful spikes or panicles of tiny flowers that bloom in summer. Weedy types should be avoided. H 6 in.-9 ft.; S 1-4 ft.	*Avena sempervirens,* blue-gray, evergreen, 3 ft. *Cortaderia selloana* (pampas grass), feathery plumes, 6-9 ft. *Festuca ovina glauca,* blue-green, evergreen, 10 in. *Miscanthus sinensis gracillimus,* gray-green, 4-5 ft. *Pennisetum alopecuroides,* purplish flower spikes, 4 ft. *Uniola latifolia,* drooping flower panicles, 2-2½ ft.	Most grow best in sun and in average soil. Many are very vigorous and require frequent division. Excellent accent or background plants when used with taste and in moderation. Some good in arrangements, used either fresh or dried.	Divide plants in spring; or sow seeds in spring.

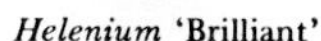
Helenium 'Brilliant'

Helianthus decapetalus multiflorus

Heliopsis 'Golden Plume'

Heucherella tiarelloides

Hibiscus hybrid

Common and botanical names, general characteristics	Species and varieties	Special requirements and remarks	Propagation *(See p. 234)*
Helenium, or Sneezeweed *(Helenium)* Prized for its mostly late summer to fall bloom of long-lasting daisylike single flowers and neat foliage. A good cut flower. H 1½-4 ft.; S 1-2 ft.	Most varieties are hybrids of *H. autumnale* and *H. bigelovii.* *H. a. pumilum magnificum,* deep yellow, 1-1½ ft. *H.* 'Brilliant,' coppery orange, red, yellow tones, 3 ft. *H.* 'Butterpat,' yellow, 3-4 ft. *H. hoopesii,* orange, blooms earlier than others, 2 ft. *H.* 'Moerheim Beauty,' deep bronze-red, 2½ ft.	Add peat moss or compost to soil before planting, and position plants in full sun; rich soil is not necessary. Plants respond to ample moisture with improved growth. Most need no support. Rabbit proof.	Divide plants in spring. Seeds can be sown in spring.
Helianthus, or Sunflower *(Helianthus)* Showy but somewhat coarse plants. Multitude of single or double flowers resembling dahlias bloom in late summer or early fall. H 4 ft.; S 2-3 ft.	Hybrids mostly derived from *H. decapetalus multiflorus.* Origin seldom indicated. *H. d. m. florepleno,* large, double, yellow, 4 ft. *H. d. m. f.* 'Loddon Gold,' double, yellow, 4 ft. *H.* 'Golden Pyramid,' single, yellow, fine needlelike leaves, 4 ft.	Grow in full sun and average soil. Plants multiply rapidly and will need frequent division. If not divided, they may "sport" back to single. Generally trouble free. Not to be confused with annual sunflowers.	Divide plants in spring. Seeds not widely available but can be sown in spring.
Heliopsis, or Golden sunflower *(Heliopsis)* Valued for late summer bloom. Double or semi-double flowers 3-4 in. across with long stems are excellent for cutting. H 2-5 ft.; S 1½-2 ft.	*H. helianthoides pitcheriana,* double, deep yellow, 5 ft. *H. scabra incomparabilis,* semi-double, yellow, 3 ft. Following hybrids derived mostly from *H. scabra:* *H.* 'Golden Plume,' double, yellow, greenish center, 3-3½ ft. *H.* 'Gold Greenheart,' double, yellow, green center, 3 ft. *H.* 'Hohlspiegel,' semi-double, yellow, serrated tips, 3 ft. *H.* 'Summer Sun,' double, bright yellow, 3 ft.	Grow in average garden soil in full sun. Plants will perform better when moisture can be supplied during dry spells, but excessive periods of rain may cause marred flowers and broken stems. Staking not generally required; plants are trouble free.	Divide plants in spring; sow seeds of available kinds in spring.
Helleborus, see Rose, Christmas, and Rose, Lenten **Hemerocallis,** see Day lily			
Heucherella *(Heucherella)* Resembling but daintier than the related coralbells, with panicles of small bell-shaped flowers above tufts of leaves in summer. The heucherella is not widely available. H 1-1½ ft.; S 9-12 in.	*H. tiarelloides,* hybrid of *Heuchera brizoides* and *Tiarella cordifolia,* carmine, 1-1½ ft. *H. t. alba,* white, 1½-1¾ ft.	Grow plants in sun or partial shade in well-drained soil fortified with ample peat moss or compost. Cut flower stems almost to ground level after flowering. Leaves often mottled brown when young; do not mistake mottling for disease. Plants do not set seeds.	Divide plants in spring.
Hibiscus, or Giant mallow *(Hibiscus)* A spectacular tall plant with enormous flowers up to 10 in. across with 5 or more petals. Bloom period is mid to late summer. H 4-6 ft.; S 2-4 ft.	Hybrids are mostly derived from *H. moscheutos.* *H.* 'Cotton Candy,' soft pink, 3½ ft. *H.* 'Crimson Wonder,' red, 6 ft. *H.* 'Mallow Marvels,' mixed colors, seed-grown, 3 ft. *H.* 'Ruby Dot,' white with red throat, 3½ ft. *H.* 'Southern Belle, mixed colors, seed-grown, 4-5 ft.	Does best in sun. Incorporate peat moss or compost with soil; plants need plenty of moisture. When seeds are sown indoors in early spring, plants flower same season. Easily grown but difficult to transplant. Spray if Japanese beetles appear.	Divide plants in spring; sow seeds in spring.

Hollyhock
(*Althaea rosea*)

Hosta hybrid

Incarvillea delavayi

Inula royleana

Jacob's ladder
(*Polemonium caeruleum*)

Common and botanical names, general characteristics	Species and varieties	Special requirements and remarks	Propagation *(See p. 234)*
Hollyhock *(Althaea)* Tall spikes of 4- to 6-in., single or double, often ruffled flowers blooming in midsummer. Plants may be short-lived; so often grown as biennials. H 3-8 ft.; S 1½ ft.	*A. rosea,* single, mixed colors, including pink, red, apricot, copper, yellow, and white, 6-8 ft. *A. r.* 'Chater's Double,' red, pink, yellow, white, purple, variegated, 6 ft. *A. r.* 'Majorette,' double, mixed colors, 2 ft. *A. r.* 'Powderpuff,' double, mixed colors, 4-5 ft.	Grow in full sun toward rear of mixed border or as accent plant by fence or wall. Foliage often attacked by Japanese beetles and rust fungus, but both can be controlled by spraying. Tall varieties may need to be staked, but 'Majorette,' only 2 ft. tall, seldom does unless planted in windy location.	Sow seeds in spring or early summer. Some varieties bloom first year from seeds sown outdoors in spring.
Hosta, or Plantain lily *(Hosta)* Grown primarily for handsome varied foliage, although some produce attractive funnel-shaped flowers on long stems in mid to late summer. H 8 in.-1½ ft.; S 1-3 ft.	Many species and hybrids available, but nomenclature is confused at present. Leaves, smooth or deeply ribbed, may be small or large, green or blue-green, solid color or edged in white or creamy yellow, plain or wavy edged. Flowers are white or shades of lilac, often fragrant. Catalogs of specialists offer tantalizing assortment.	Grow in shade or partial shade. Mix a generous amount of compost or peat moss with soil that should be moderately rich. Remove faded flower stalks. Self-sown seedlings usually inferior. Water in dry weather. Control slugs to prevent holes in leaves, which detract greatly from their appearance.	Divide plants in spring or early fall. Seldom grown from seeds, as many kinds do not produce seeds.
Incarvillea *(Incarvillea)* Two-lipped tubular flowers bloom in late spring or early summer in clusters held well above deeply cut leaves. H 1½-2 ft.; S 1 ft.	*I. delavayi,* rose-red with yellow throat, 1½-2 ft. *I. grandiflora brevipes,* crimson, 1½ ft.	Grow in well-drained soil; water standing in soil over winter can be fatal. In cold climates mulch in late fall, or lift and store roots covered with soil in cool place; do not allow to dry out to stage where roots shrivel.	Divide fleshy roots in fall (often difficult). Sow seeds in spring; takes 2-3 yr. to bloom.
Inula *(Inula)* Flowers resemble 4- or 5-in. sunflower but with narrower and more graceful petals. Coarse leaves. H 2 ft.; S 1-1½ ft.	*I. ensifolia,* yellow, 16 in. *I. orientalis,* yellow, 15 in. *I. royleana,* yellow, 10 in.; leaves, 2 ft. or more.	Set out plants in spring in sunny location and in moisture-retentive soil (clay acceptable). Divide and replant about every 3 yr. to contain spreading habit. Remove faded flowers.	Divide plants in spring; or sow seeds (when available) in spring. Not widely available.
Iris, see p. 337			
Jacob's ladder *(Polemonium)* Chief assets are attractive, finely divided leaves and small, clear blue, loosely arranged flowers blooming in spring or early summer. H 8 in.-3 ft.; S 1-2 ft.	*P. caeruleum,* blue, 1-3 ft. *P. c. album,* white, 14 in. *P. c.* 'Blue Pearl,' light blue with yellow center, 8-10 in. *P. reptans,* blue, sprawling, 8 in.	Locate where there will be partial shade and soil of average fertility. When grown in full sun, leaves will probably yellow in midsummer, especially if water is scant. The low forms show to best advantage in rock gardens.	Sow seeds in spring. Divide in spring (except for *P. caeruleum* and its hybrids in fall).

Lamium maculatum

English lavender (*Lavandula officinalis*)

Liatris spicata

Ligularia clivorum 'Desdemona'

Lily of the valley (*Convallaria majalis*)

Common and botanical names, general characteristics	Species and varieties	Special requirements and remarks	Propagation *(See p. 234)*
Lamb's ears, see Stachys			
Lamium, or Dead nettle *(Lamium)* Spikes of small hooded flowers bloom in spring for many weeks. Leaves often variegated. Best in wild-flower garden or as ground cover. H 9 in.-2 ft.; S 3 ft. or more.	*L. galeobdolon variegatum,* yellow, 1-1½ ft. *L. garganicum,* red, 1 ft. *L. maculatum,* purple, 9 in.-1 ft. *L. m. album,* white, 1 ft. *L. m.* 'Chequers,' amethyst-violet, 6-8 in.	Plant in shade or partial shade. Most do best in moist soil except *L. garganicum,* which tolerates dry soil. *L. galeobdolon variegatum* grows in alkaline or slightly acid soil. Only occasionally planted in borders because of tendency to spread rapidly.	Divide plants in spring; or take cuttings in summer.
Lavender *(Lavandula)* Of interest in borders for gray-green foliage and spikes of small lavender flowers that open in early summer. Scented flowers are dried and used in sachets. H 1-4 ft.; S 1-1½ ft.	*L. dentata* (French lavender), lavender-purple, 3 ft. *L. officinalis,* or *L. spica* (English lavender), gray-blue, 3-4 ft. *L. o.* 'Hidcote,' deep violet-blue, 1½ ft. *L. o.* 'Munstead Dwarf,' deep lavender, 1 ft. *L. stoechas* (Spanish lavender), dark purple, 1½-3 ft.	Plant in sun and in average well-drained soil, preferably alkaline. Technically a subshrub but grown in perennial gardens, particularly dwarfer forms. Tall kinds often clipped to make low hedge in warm climates. To dry flowers, pick when open, dry in sun or in dry, airy place.	Take cuttings in summer of half-ripened shoots with heel (sliver of main stem). Or sow seeds.
Liatris, or Gayfeather *(Liatris)* Tufted plants with tall spikes of fluffy flowers that bloom above grasslike foliage in late summer. In most kinds, flowers open from top of spike downward. H 2-5 ft.; S 1½ ft.	*L. pycnostachya* (Kansas gayfeather), pinkish lavender, 5 ft. *L. scariosa* (tall gayfeather), purple, 2-3 ft. *L. s.* 'September Glory,' purple, opens all at once, 5 ft. *L. s.* 'White Spire,' white, opens all at once, 5 ft. *L. spicata* (spike gayfeather), purple, 3 ft. *L. s. montana* 'Kobold,' dark purple, compact, 1½-2 ft.	Plant in sun or light shade and in well-drained, moderately fertile soil. Soggy winter soils prove fatal. Tall kinds may require staking. Division may be needed after 4-5 yr. Very adaptable plants. Good cut flower that dries well. Favorite of bees.	Divide tuberous-rooted plants in spring; sow seeds in spring.
Ligularia, or Senecio *(Ligularia)* Bold plant with large roundish leaves; evergreen in South. Spikes of small flowers bloom in midsummer. Good ground cover or container plant. H 1-2½ ft.; S 2 ft. or more.	*L. clivorum* 'Desdemona,' orange-yellow, leaves green with purple tinge, 2-2½ ft.	Plants require plenty of moisture in summer; so incorporate generous amounts of compost or peat moss prior to planting, and water during dry spells. Does best in partial shade. Remove faded flower stalks by cutting back to ground level.	Divide plants in spring.
Lily of the valley *(Convallaria)* Sprays of fragrant, waxy, white or pinkish, bell-shaped flowers bloom in spring; old favorite of gardeners. Best as shady ground cover. Fruit poisonous. H 6-8 in.; S 2 ft. or more.	*C. majalis,* white, 6-8 in. The following are only rarely available: *C. m. flore pleno,* double, white, 6-8 in. *C. m. fortunei* (Fortune's giant), white, 1 ft. *C. m. rosea,* pink, 6-8 in. *C. m. striata,* white, variegated leaves, 6-8 in.	Plant rootstocks (pips) in humus-enriched soil in shaded location. Plants respond to fertilizer by producing more and larger flowers; apply after tops die down. Use about 3 handfuls of organic fertilizer per 10 sq. ft.	Divide into single crowns in early fall; division seldom needed and only after flowering deteriorates.

Lilyturf *(Liriope muscari)*

Linum perenne

Lobelia cardinalis

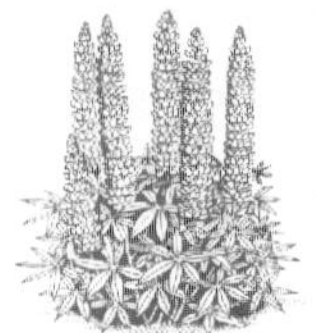
Lupine *(Lupinus* hybrid)

Common and botanical names, general characteristics	Species and varieties	Special requirements and remarks	Propagation *(See p. 234)*
Lilyturf, or Liriope *(Liriope)* Graceful, recurving, grasslike leaves with leathery texture; evergreen in South. Spikes of flowers in midsummer to fall that are good for cutting. Blue-black berries follow flowers. H 1-1½ ft.; S 1-2 ft.	*L. muscari,* dark violet, 1½ ft. *L. m. exiliflora,* light violet, early, 1 ft. *L. m.* 'Majestic,' dark violet, cockscomblike, 20 in. *L. m.* 'Monroe No. 1' ('Monroe White'), white, 1-1½ ft. *L. m.* 'Monroe No. 2' ('Christmas Tree'), violet, 1-1½ ft. *L. m.* 'Silvery Sunproof,' lilac, striped leaves, 1½ ft. *L. m. variegata,* lilac, yellow-edged leaves, 1 ft. *L. spicata,* pale violet to white, 9 in.	Plant in sun in coastal areas, partial shade elsewhere. *L. spicata* (hardiest form), Zone B; others, Zone C. Requires ample moisture but withstands short periods of drought. In cold areas leaves may brown in late winter and should be cut back in spring. Makes good edging or accent plant as well as ground cover.	Divide tufted or rhizomatous plants in early spring before new growth starts. Self-sown seedlings may be inferior. *L. spicata* spreads by underground stems.
Limonium, see Sea lavender			
Linum, or Flax *(Linum)* Dainty 5-petaled flowers are borne in profusion intermittently from early to late summer on fine stems. Blue-green leaves are needlelike except broad in *L. flavum.* H 1-2 ft.; S 1-2 ft.	*L. flavum,* yellow, 1½ ft. *L. narbonnense,* azure blue with white centers, 1½-2 ft. *L. n.* 'Heavenly Blue,' deep blue, 1-1½ ft. *L. perenne,* pale blue, 2 ft. *L. p. album,* white, 2 ft. *L. p.* 'Tetra Red,' red, 1½ ft.	Grow in sun in well-drained soil; winter sogginess can prove fatal. Unobtrusive seedpods, but removal of faded flowers will help to keep plants blooming. Because plants are so dainty, they look best in front of border. Not good for cutting, as flowers last only a day.	Sow seeds in spring. Take basal cuttings in spring; nonflowering stem cuttings in summer. Plants difficult to divide.
Lobelia *(Lobelia)* Spikes of small tubular 2-lipped flowers bloom over long period from midsummer to early fall. Especially good woodland or streamside plant. H 2-4 ft.; S 1-1½ ft.	*L. cardinalis* (cardinal flower), scarlet red, 3-4 ft. *L. c. alba,* white, rare, propagated from cuttings, 3-4 ft. *L. siphilitica* (great blue lobelia), deep blue, 2-3 ft.	Grow in light to medium shade in well-drained, moisture-retentive soil. Mulch in summer to retain moisture. Where snow cover cannot be counted on all winter, mulch after soil has frozen. May be short-lived but often self-sows. Makes long-lasting cut flower. Often listed in wild-flower catalogs.	Divide plants immediately after flowering or in early spring; sow seeds in spring.
Loosestrife, see Lysimachia and Lythrum			
Lupine *(Lupinus)* Towering spikes of pealike flowers bloom in mid to late spring above deeply divided leaves. Dwarf types are recent introductions. H 1½-3 ft.; S 6 in.-1½ ft.	Almost all popular garden lupines have been derived from crosses of *L. polyphyllus* with *L. arboreus,* and recrosses between hybrids. Known as 'Russell Hybrids,' they grow to 3 ft. and come in shades of red, pink, blue, yellow, salmon, and purple; often bicolor. Dwarfs that grow 1½ ft. tall include 'Little Lulu' and 'Minarette.'	Provide well-drained soil that contains plenty of compost or peat moss, and locate plants in full sun. Grows best in cool regions. Remove faded flower stalks unless self-sown seedlings are desired. Soak seeds overnight in water to hasten germination.	Sow seeds in spring; treat as for peas with nitrifying powder. Take basal cuttings in spring.

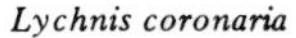
Lychnis coronaria

Lysimachia clethroides

Lythrum 'Morden's Pink'

Mayapple (*Podophyllum peltatum*)

Mertensia virginica

Common and botanical names, general characteristics	Species and varieties	Special requirements and remarks	Propagation *(See p. 234)*
Lychnis, or Campion *(Lychnis)* As a group these have widely divergent flower forms, ranging in shape from upright spikes to rounded heads or loose clusters. Blooms mid to late summer, depending on kind. H 1½-3 ft.; S 6 in.-1 ft.	*L. chalcedonica* (Maltese cross), true red, 2½-3 ft. *L. c. alba,* white, less showy than above, 2½-3 ft. *L. coronaria* (rose campion, mullein pink), red-purple, 2 ft. *L. haageana* (hybrid of *L. fulgens* and *L. coronata sieboldii),* orange-red, 1 ft. *L. viscaria* (German catchfly), reddish purple, 1-1½ ft. *L. v. splendens florepleno,* double, rose-pink, 1-1½ ft.	Position plants in full sun and very well drained soil. Some varieties tend to be short-lived but can be easily replenished from seeds.	Sow seeds in spring. Divide plants in spring.
Lysimachia, or Loosestrife *(Lysimachia)* Showy plants. The two listed are quite different in flower form and bloom at different times. Reasonably good cut flower. H 2½-3 ft.; S 1 ft.	*L. clethroides* (gooseneck loosestrife), white flower spikes curved like a goose's neck in late summer, 3 ft. *L. punctata,* small yellow flowers arranged in tiers around stem bloom in early summer, 2½-3 ft.	Select moist location in sun or partial shade. Average soil satisfactory if it retains moisture. Otherwise, add compost or peat moss, and water during dry spells. May need some support. Plants spread rapidly and can become invasive but are easily eradicated by digging.	Divide plants in spring. Roots are rhizomatous.
Lythrum, or Purple loosestrife *(Lythrum)* Long spires of closely set small flowers bloom over long period from midsummer until early fall. Plants withstand neglect. H 15 in.-6 ft.; S 1-2 ft.	*L.* varieties; parentage probably *L. salicaria* and/or *L. virgatum.* *L.* 'Dropmore Purple,' violet-purple, 3-4 ft. *L.* 'Happy,' dark pink, 15 in.-1½ ft. *L.* 'Morden's Gleam,' bright carmine, 3-4 ft. *L.* 'Morden's Pink,' clear pink, 3-4 ft. *L.* 'Robert,' bright rose-red, 2 ft.	Grow in partial shade or sun and in ordinary soil. Tolerant of wet areas and suitable for wild settings. Hybrids are not as invasive as the species. Plants are generally trouble free and long-lived.	Divide plants in spring.
Mayapple *(Podophyllum)* Broad, toothed leaves. Large nodding saucer-shaped flowers appear in late spring, followed by lemon-shaped fruits, edible when ripe. Poisonous leaves and roots. H 1½ ft.; S 1 ft.	*P. peltatum,* white, 1½ ft.	Provide moist soil where possible, but plants will grow under less than ideal conditions. Does best in shade. Best suited to wild-flower garden or wherever deciduous ground cover is needed. Plants spread rapidly; have thick, fibrous roots.	Divide plants in early fall. Sow seeds in fall.
Meadow rue, see Thalictrum			
Mertensia, or Virginia bluebell *(Mertensia)* Unusual late-spring-flowering plant with pink buds and nodding sapphire-blue bell-shaped flowers above smooth light green leaves. H 1½ ft.; S 1-1½ ft.	*M. virginica,* blue, 1½ ft.	Grow in partial shade in soil well fortified with peat moss or compost. Foliage dies down soon after flowering; so plant where other foliage will cover; mark area with a stake so that plants will not be disturbed later.	Sow seeds as soon as ripe in early summer. Divide plants in early fall.

Monarda didyma 'Adam'

Nepeta faassenii

Oenothera fruticosa youngii

Pea *(Lathyrus latifolius albus)*

Penstemon gloxinioides 'Firebird'

Common and botanical names, general characteristics	Species and varieties	Special requirements and remarks	Propagation *(See p. 234)*
Monarda *(Monarda)* Tubular flowers in crowded clusters bloom in mid to late summer. Square stems, mint-scented foliage. Good cut flower. H 2-3 ft.; S 2 ft.	*M. didyma* 'Adam' (bee balm), ruby-red, 2-3 ft. *M. d.* 'Croftway Pink,' rose-pink, 2-3 ft. *M. d.* 'Mahogany,' wine-red, 2-3 ft. *M. d.* 'Melissa,' soft pink, 2-3 ft. *M. d.* 'Snow Queen,' white, 2-3 ft. *M. fistulosa* (wild bergamot), lavender, white, 3 ft.	For best results grow in full sun, although they will take partial shade. Wild bergamot tolerates drier soil than hybrids, but all benefit from plenty of moisture during summer. Divide every 3 yr. for maximum bloom.	Sow seeds in spring. Divide plants in spring.
Nepeta, or Catmint *(Nepeta)* Somewhat sprawling plants with small gray-green leaves; 5-in. spikes of small lavender flowers bloom in early summer, often into fall. H 9 in.-1 ft.; S 1½ ft.	*N. cataria* (catnip), favorite of cats, is not very ornamental and is best grown in herb garden or inconspicuous corner. *N. faassenii,* a hybrid, pale lavender, 1½ ft.	Grow in full sun and well-drained sandy soil. This is excellent seaside plant. Shear plants back after first bloom to encourage further flowering. Seldom needs support if grown in full sun and not too rich soil.	Divide plants in spring. Take stem cuttings in summer. Sow seeds of *N. cataria; N. faassenii* sets no seeds.
Oenothera *(Oenothera)* Showy single flowers 1½ in. or more across appear in early to mid summer over period of several weeks. Foliage is relatively inconspicuous. For annual oenothera, see p. 303. H 8 in.-2 ft.; S 1-1½ ft.	*O. fruticosa youngii,* or *O. tetragona* (common sundrop), yellow, 2 ft. *O. f. y.* 'Fireworks,' yellow with red buds, 1½ ft. *O. f. y.* 'Highlight,' golden yellow, 1½ ft. *O. f. y.* 'Yellow River,' canary-yellow, 1-1½ ft. *O. missourensis* (Ozark sundrop), yellow, 8 in.-1 ft.	Locate plants in full sun and well-drained light soil. *O. missourensis* is late to appear in spring; mark position so that it will not be disturbed. All tend to spread, and *O. missourensis* may be invasive. Water freely during dry spells.	Divide plants in early spring.
Pea *(Lathyrus)* Climbing or trailing plants with clusters of long-lasting flowers borne from midsummer to early fall. Useful to cover fences or as ground cover. Good cut flower. For annual sweet pea, see p. 306. H 6-9 ft.; S 2 ft.	*L. latifolius albus,* white, 6-9 ft. *L. l. roseus,* rose, 6-9 ft. Generally offered in assorted colors, either as plants or seeds.	Locate in full sun and well-drained soil. Provide some means of support unless plants are grown on slopes or over rocks. Keep faded flowers picked to encourage further flowering. Remove vines from supports after frost kills them and discard. Easily grown plants.	Sow seeds in spring. Soak seeds overnight before sowing to hasten germination.
Penstemon, or Beardtongue *(Penstemon)* Semi-evergreen, often short-lived plants. Spikes of foxglove-shaped flowers appear in mid to late summer. Excellent cut flower. H 1-2 ft.; S 1-2 ft.	*P. barbatus,* pink to red, 1½ ft. *P. b.* 'Pink Beauty,' shell-pink, 2 ft. *P. b.* 'Prairie Fire,' orange-red, 1½ ft. *P. gloxinioides* 'Firebird,' red, somewhat tender, 1½-2 ft. *P. newberryi,* light purple-blue, 1 ft.	Full sun and well-drained soil are essential for all penstemons. Some varieties are not hardy; so check locally. Remove faded flower stems, and plants may bloom again. An interesting plant, and many fine hybrids are constantly being developed and made available.	Sow seeds in spring. Divide in spring. Take softwood stem cuttings in summer.

Chinese peony
(Paeonia lactiflora hybrid)

Phlox paniculata hybrid

Phygelius capensis

Physostegia virginiana

Plume poppy
(Macleaya cordata)

Common and botanical names, general characteristics	Species and varieties	Special requirements and remarks	Propagation *(See p. 234)*
Peony *(Paeonia)* Long-lived plants with large flowers, ranging from single to double, that appear in late spring; often fragrant. Attractive leaves all season. Good cut flower. H 2-4 ft.; S 2-4 ft.	*P. lactiflora* hybrids (Chinese, or herbaceous, peony). Here are found most popular peonies, in single, double, and intermediate forms. Colors include white, cream to nearly yellow, pink, salmon-pink, and red. *P. suffruticosa* (tree peony), technically a shrub. Many forms; colors as above, plus yellow. Plants do not die back in winter; only leaves are killed.	Grow in sun and well-drained soil. Tree peonies do best in slightly alkaline soil; other peonies can take slightly acid soil. Cover eyes with soil: 1½ in. for herbaceous, 6 in. for tree. Mulch first winter. Cut back (herbaceous only) to soil level in fall. Spray in spring to control Botrytis fungus.	Divide in late summer, 3-5 eyes per division. Tree type is usually grafted; so division is not practical.
Phlox *(Phlox)* Valuable group for spring or summer bloom. Best show from large heads of *P. paniculata* that bloom once in midsummer and then intermittently until frost. H 5 in.-3½ ft.; S 1-2 ft.	*P. carolina* 'Miss Lingard,' or *P. suffruticosa* 'Miss Lingard,' white, early summer, 2½ ft. *P. divaricata,* blue, mid to late spring, 15 in. *P. paniculata* hybrids, all colors but yellow and orange, midsummer to early fall, 2-3½ ft. *P. stolonifera* 'Blue Ridge,' light blue, late spring, 6 in.	Provide sunny location except for *P. divaricata* and *P. stolonifera,* which need shade. *P. paniculata* needs rich soil, plenty of water in summer, frequent division, spraying to control two-spotted mites and mildew, and removal of spent flowers to prevent self-seeding.	Divide plants in spring. Take tip cuttings in summer, also root cuttings of *P. paniculata.*
Phygelius, or Cape fuchsia *(Phygelius)* Shrubby, somewhat weedy plant in mild climates with pendent tubular flowers in loose clusters from midsummer to early fall.	*P. capensis,* red with yellow throat, 3-4 ft.	Locate plants in sun and rich well-drained soil with ample humus. Cut stems back to near ground level in spring. Prune in summer for neatness. Plants not dependably hardy north of Zone C without protection.	Sow seeds in spring. Divide plants in spring. Take basal cuttings in spring.
Physostegia, or False dragonhead *(Physostegia)* From midsummer to early fall spikes of small tubular flowers appear in profusion. Small, neat leaves. Good cut flower. H 2-3 ft.; S 1½-2 ft.	*P. virginiana,* purplish red, 3 ft. *P. v. alba,* white, 1½-2 ft. *P. v.* 'Bouquet Rose,' 2½-3 ft. *P. v. variegata,* pink, green and white leaves, 2½ ft. *P. v.* 'Vivid,' deep rose-pink, 2 ft.	Grow in sun or partial shade and well-drained but moisture-retentive soil. Divide every 2 or 3 yr., saving only outer portions of clump. Water during dry spells. Called obedient plant because flowers stay put when pushed left or right.	Sow seeds in spring. Divide plants in spring, replanting outer portions, discarding others.
Plume poppy *(Macleaya,* or *Bocconia)* Statuesque plants suitable for large gardens. Tall plumes of tiny flowers appear in midsummer or early fall. Handsome, large, deeply lobed leaves. H 5-8 ft.; S 3-4 ft.	*M. cordata,* creamy white, mid to late summer, 6-8 ft.	Provide plenty of moisture in humus-rich soil. Invasive; control by cutting outside growth yearly. Best grown by itself so that sculptured gray-green leaves can be seen. Flowers and seedpods dry well.	Sow seeds in spring. Divide plants in spring. Root suckers in summer.

Oriental poppy
(*Papaver orientale* hybrid)

Potentilla nepalensis hybrid

Primrose
(*Primula polyanthus* hybrid)

Pulmonaria saccharata

Pyrethrum roseum hybrid

Common and botanical names, general characteristics	**Species and varieties**	**Special requirements and remarks**	**Propagation** *(See p. 234)*
Poppy, Oriental *(Papaver)* Impressive, mostly single flowers, many with black centers, bloom for short period in early summer. Basal foliage, fleshy roots. H 2½-3 ft.; S 1½-2 ft.	*P. orientale* hybrids—only a few of the dozens available listed here. *P. o.* 'Barr's White,' white, purple-black markings. *P. o.* 'Carmine,' cardinal-red, black markings. *P. o.* 'Crimson Pompom,' double, red. *P. o.* 'Pandora,' salmon-pink, red markings. *P. o.* 'Show Girl,' ruffled, white and pink bicolor.	Provide well-drained soil in full sun. Plants may need staking. For cut flower, char basal end of stem in flame; put in water immediately. Foliage dies down soon after flowering, reappears in late summer. New plants usually set out in late summer as roots without leaves.	Divide in early spring. Sow seeds in spring. Take root cuttings in summer.
Potentilla, or Cinquefoil *(Potentilla)* Of value for single flowers that continue to appear all summer. Leaves with 3-5 leaflets. For lower-growing types, see p. 364. Better known are the shrubby potentillas (p. 168) that have similar flowers. H 6 in.-1 ft.; S 1-2 ft.	*P. nepalensis* hybrids. *P. n.* 'Miss Willmott,' bright rosy crimson, 1 ft. *P. recta warrenii,* yellow, 1 ft. *P. tonguei,* yellow, 1 ft.	Plant in sun or very light shade and in soil of average fertility. Water during periods of extreme dryness. Plants tend to sprawl and may need support. Divide every 3 or 4 yr. for best results.	Sow seeds in spring. Divide plants in spring. Take cuttings in summer.
Primrose *(Primula)* Delightful plants valued for spring bloom in wide assortment of colors, patterns, and forms. Clustered flowers are long lasting when cut. H 8 in.-1 ft.; S 1 ft.	A diverse group of plants with varying characteristics. Best known are hybrids of *P. polyanthus* and *P. vulgaris.* Others available include hybrids of *P. auricula, P. beesiana, P. bulleyana, P. cortusoides, P. denticulata, P. japonica, P. sieboldii,* and *P. veris,* or *P. officinalis.*	Locate plants in partial shade and in acid soil fortified with generous amounts of compost or peat moss to help retain moisture. Divide plants when they get crowded, generally every 2 or 3 yr. Primroses grow best where spring temperatures are cool.	Divide plants immediately after flowering in late spring or summer. Sow seeds in spring or fall.
Pulmonaria, or Lungwort *(Pulmonaria)* Dainty drooping clusters of small flowers in mid to late spring. Often valued more for leaves that remain attractive all season. H 8-10 in.; S 1-2 ft.	*P. angustifolia* (blue cowslip), bright blue, 8-10 in. *P. saccharata* (Bethlehem sage), pink turning to blue, white-spotted leaves, 1 ft. *P. s.* 'Mrs. Moon,' deep blue, 9 in. *P. s.* 'Pink Dawn,' rosy pink, 9 in.	Grow in shade where soil will remain moist and cool. Plants spread quite rapidly. They need to be divided only when vigor wanes. Water well after dividing. Makes excellent ground cover or border plant.	Divide plants in late summer.
Pyrethrum, or Painted daisy *(Pyrethrum)* Large single or double flowers on long stems above finely divided leaves bloom for many weeks in late spring and early summer. Excellent long-lasting cut flower. H 2-3½ ft.; S 1½ ft.	*P. roseum,* or *Chrysanthemum coccineum,* hybrids. *P. r.* 'Buckeye,' semi-double, rose-red, flecked white, 2 ft. *P. r.* 'Crimson Giant,' single, red, 3½ ft. *P. r.* 'Helen,' double, light pink, 2½ ft. *P. r.* 'Snowball,' double, white, 2½ ft.	Plants grow best in full sun and in fairly rich moist soil. Not reliably hardy unless soil is well drained. Needs warm weather for best performance. Cut back after flowering to encourage further blooming.	Sow seeds in spring. Divide plants in spring.

Ranunculus acris florepleno

Red-hot poker (*Kniphofia uvaria* hybrid)

Romneya coulteri

Christmas rose (*Helleborus niger*)

Rudbeckia fulgida sullivantii 'Goldsturm'

Common and botanical names, general characteristics	Species and varieties	Special requirements and remarks	Propagation (*See p. 234*)
Ranunculus, or Buttercup (*Ranunculus*) Showy, glistening, waxen double flowers bloom on slender stems in late spring or early summer. H 1½-2 ft.; S 1½ ft.	*R. aconitifolius florepleno,* double, white, 1½ ft. *R. acris florepleno,* double, yellow, 1½-2 ft. *R. repens pleniflorus,* double, yellow, 1-1½ ft.	Grow in sun or partial shade. A moist soil is essential to success with ranunculuses; so mix compost or peat moss with soil before planting and mulch in spring. Plants may need support. Remove faded flowers to encourage further flowering.	Divide plants in spring.
Red-hot poker (*Kniphofia,* or *Tritoma*) Dense spikes of closely set drooping flowers bloom in mid to late summer. Grasslike foliage. Long-lasting flowers attract hummingbirds. H 2-4 ft.; S 2-3 ft.	*K. uvaria* hybrids (may be listed as *K. pfitzeri*). *K. u.* 'Comet,' orange-red, 2½ ft. *K. u.* 'Primrose Beauty,' primrose-yellow, 2-3 ft. *K. u.* 'Royal Standard,' red top shading to cream, 2-3 ft. *K. u.* 'White Giant,' white, 3 ft.	Full sun, rich soil, and excellent drainage are essential. Hardy in northern part of Zone C if mulched over winter. In colder areas dig up roots and store them in boxes of soil in cool place. New plants may not bloom during first year of growth.	Sow seeds in spring. Divide plants in spring.
Romneya (*Romneya*) Spectacular plants have deeply cut gray-green leaves. Towering stems bear fragrant 6-petaled flowers to 9 in. across. Blooms in early to mid summer. H 8 ft.; S 4 ft.	*R. coulteri* (Matilija poppy), glistening white, crinkled petals, center of clustered yellow stamens, 8 ft. *R. c. tricocalyx,* white, 3-6 ft.	Provide sunny location and soil with plenty of peat moss or compost. Water sparingly in summer to restrain growth. Plants are invasive; so best located where they can spread undisturbed. Plants hardy in southern part of Zone C.	Remove and replant suckers in spring or fall. Take root cuttings in spring or summer.
Rose, Christmas, and Lenten (*Helleborus*) Lustrous evergreen leaves. Stunning, waxy, cup-shaped flowers bloom in late winter or early spring. Leaves and roots of *H. niger* poisonous if eaten. H 1-1½ ft.; S 1½-2 ft.	*H. niger* (Christmas rose), white, early winter, 1 ft. *H. n. altifolius,* white, larger flowers than above, 1 ft. *H. orientalis* (Lenten rose), purple shades, midspring, 1½ ft. *H. o. atrorubens,* chocolate and greenish purple, 1½ ft. *H. o.* 'Millet Hybrids,' white, pink, red, chocolate, some speckled and striped, 1½ ft.	Grow where readily seen when in bloom and where there is winter sun, summer shade. Provide nearly neutral soil (pH 6.5-7). Cover crown with 1 in. of soil. Use plastic- or glass-covered frame, open at bottom or side, to protect flowers from severe weather.	Sow fresh seeds in early summer. Late-sown seeds need freezing to break dormancy. Divide plants in late summer.
Rudbeckia, or Coneflower (*Rudbeckia*) Showy, single or double, daisylike flowers bloom over long period in mid to late summer. 'Goldsturm' blooms are particularly weather resistant. Good cut flower. For annual rudbeckia, see p. 305. H 2½-7 ft.; S 2-4 ft.	*R. fulgida sullivantii* 'Goldsturm,' deep yellow, black conelike center, 2½ ft. *R. laciniata hortensia* (golden glow), double, yellow, 7 ft. *R. l.* 'Golde Quelle,' double, yellow, 2½ ft.	Grow in sun or partial shade and in well-drained but moisture-retentive soil fortified with liberal amounts of compost or peat moss. Division required every 4-5 yr. Remove faded flowers on 'Goldsturm' to prevent self-sowing if this is not desired.	Sow seeds in spring. Divide plants in spring.

Rue
(*Ruta graveolens*)

Russian sage
(*Perovskia atriplicifolia*)

Salvia haematodes

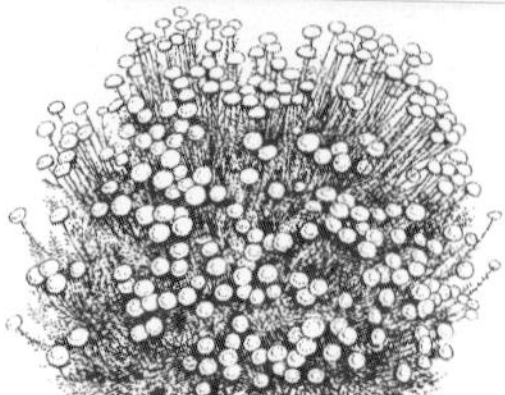
Santolina virens

Caucasian scabiosa
(*Scabiosa caucasica*)

Sea lavender
(*Limonium latifolium*)

Common and botanical names, general characteristics	Species and varieties	Special requirements and remarks	Propagation (*See p. 234*)
Rue (*Ruta*) Shrublike, with aromatic blue-green leaves, evergreen in Zone C. Small flowers and decorative brown seed capsules. H 2-3 ft.; S 1 ft.	*R. graveolens,* greenish yellow, 2-3 ft. *R. g.* 'Blue Beauty,' greenish yellow, 1½-2 ft.	Provide well-drained soil in full sun. Cut plants back in spring. Some gardeners remove flowers to emphasize blue-green leaves. Often grown in herb gardens.	Sow seeds in spring. Take cuttings in summer.
Russian sage (*Perovskia*) From mid to late summer tall spikes of violet-blue flowers are borne above small, silvery gray leaves with a sage scent. H 2½-3 ft.; S 1-2 ft.	*P. atriplicifolia,* lavender-blue, 2½-3 ft.	Set plants in full sun, in soil that is not too rich. Grows best in alkaline soil. Shrublike stems may die back to ground in North, but usually come back from roots. Withstands drought.	Take stem cuttings in summer.
Sage, see Russian sage and Salvia			
Salvia, or Meadow sage (*Salvia*) Slender spikes of small flowers bloom over long period at various times in summer according to variety. Excellent cut flower; good dried. H 1½-4 ft.; S 1½-2 ft.	*S. azurea grandiflora,* or *S. pitcheri,* sky-blue, 3-4 ft. *S. haematodes,* lavender-blue, 3 ft. *S. sclarea* 'May Night,' violet-blue, 1½-2 ft. *S. superba* 'East Friesland,' or 'Ostfriesland,' deep blue, 3-3½ ft. (may be erroneously listed as *S. nemorosa*).	Set plants in sunny location. Easily grown in average soil but will perform best when soil contains ample humus. Plants may need to be staked. Remove faded blooms to promote further flowering.	Sow seeds in spring. Divide plants in spring.
Santolina, or Lavender cotton (*Santolina*) Really a shrub, but because often grown as low edging plant it is included here. Small flowers and aromatic gray or green foliage. H 6 in.-2 ft.; S 1½-3 ft.	*S. chamaecyparissus,* or *S. incana,* silver-gray foliage can be trimmed to 6 in. or left to grow to 2½ ft. *S. c. nana,* silver-gray foliage, 8-10 in. *S. virens,* or *S. viridis,* emerald-green foliage, 1½ ft.	Locate in sun and in any average soil that does not remain very wet. If desired, trim to control size. In northern part of Zone C plants must be wintered in greenhouse.	Take cuttings in summer.
Scabiosa, or Pincushion flower (*Scabiosa*) Globular heads of flowers with protruding stamens give plant its common name. They flower from early summer into fall. H 2½ ft.; S 1 ft.	*S. caucasica* (Caucasian scabiosa), blue, 2½ ft. *S. c. alba,* white, 2½ ft. *S. c.* 'Blue Snowflake,' amethyst-blue, 2½ ft. *S. c.* 'Isaac House Hybrids,' lavender-blue shades, 2½ ft. *S. c.* 'Miss Willmott,' white, 2½ ft. *S. columbaria,* blue, pink, and white varieties, 2½ ft.	Set out plants in sunny location where soil (preferably alkaline) can be kept moist in summer but extremely well drained in winter. Keep flowers cut to prolong bloom; divide as needed to maintain vigor. May require staking.	Divide plants in spring. Sow seeds in summer.
Sea lavender, or Hardy statice (*Limonium*) Valued for its fine sprays of small flowers in mid to late summer. Semi-evergreen leathery leaves. H 1½-2 ft.; S 2-3 ft.	*L. latifolium,* bright lavender, 1½-2 ft. *L. l.* 'Collier's Pink,' pink, 1½ ft. *L. l.* 'Violetta,' deep violet-blue, 1½ ft.	For best results grow in full sun and sandy soil; excellent seaside plant. Best left undisturbed for years. Plants have very long roots; so provide deep planting hole.	Sow seeds in spring. Divide woody roots in spring.

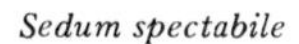
Sedum spectabile

Sidalcea malvaeflora

True Solomon's seal (*Polygonatum commutatum*)

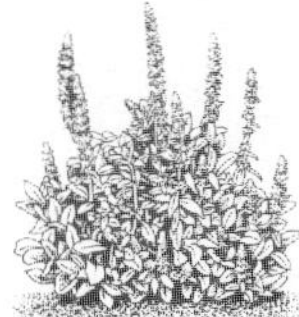
Stachys lanata

Stokesia laevis

Common and botanical names, general characteristics	Species and varieties	Special requirements and remarks	Propagation (*See p. 234*)
Sedum, or Stonecrop (*Sedum*) Fleshy-leaved plants with large clusters of small flowers in late summer or early fall. Attractive even when not in bloom. H 15 in.; S 12-15 in.	*S. spectabile* (showy stonecrop), rosy pink, 15 in. *S. s.* 'Brilliant,' carmine, 15 in. *S. s.* 'Meteor,' wine-red, 15 in. *S. s.* 'Star Dust,' ivory-white, blue-green leaves, 15 in. *S. telephium* 'Autumn Joy,' rust-brown, 15 in. *S. t.* 'Indian Chief,' copper-red, 15 in.	Grows easily in full sun and in any well-drained garden soil. Wet soils, especially in winter, will cause rot at the crown. Plants are very tolerant of drought and generally pest free. Division necessary only to maintain good flowering.	Divide in spring. Even small rootless pieces take root quickly.
Sidalcea (*Sidalcea*) Slender spikes with 5-petaled flowers resembling small hollyhocks appear mid to late summer. Lower leaves differ in appearance from upper leaves. H 1½-3 ft.; S 1½ ft.	*S. malvaeflora* and other species have been crossed to form hybrids commonly offered as miniature hollyhocks. Varieties such as 'Stark's Hybrids' often sold in mixed-seed packets of assorted colors, including white, lavender, or pink.	Locate in sun and in well-drained but moisture-retentive soil. Cut back after first flowering period to encourage later bloom. Less showy than hollyhocks; rarely has rust fungus that attacks hollyhocks. Hardy in southern part of Zone B.	Divide plants in spring. Seeds are occasionally available; sow in spring.
Snakeroot, black, see Bugbane			
Solomon's seal (*Polygonatum*) Attractive blue-green leaves on arching stems with small flowers that hang from stalks in late spring. Greatest asset is foliage. H 1½-4 ft.; S 2-3 ft.	*P. biflorum* (small Solomon's seal), white, 1½-3 ft. *P. commutatum* (true Solomon's seal), white, 3½-4 ft.	Locate in partial shade, preferably in rich, moisture-retentive soil. Plants multiply by creeping rhizomes but are not rapidly invasive. Flowers fall naturally, need not be removed to maintain neatness. Ideal plant for woodland garden.	Divide plants in very early spring or late summer.
Stachys, or Betony (*Stachys*) Two species listed are quite different in appearance and use. The first is grown more for its gray leaves, the other for its flowers. H 1-2 ft.; S 1½-2 ft.	*S. lanata,* or *S. olympica* (lamb's ears), thick, gray, hairy leaves that form low mat, inconsequential flowers, midsummer to fall, 1 ft. *S. macrantha,* or *S. grandiflora,* or *Betonica grandiflora* (big betony), wrinkled, hairy leaves, spikes of showy, purple mintlike flowers in early summer, 1½-2 ft.	Grow in sun and provide very well drained soil of average fertility. *S. macrantha* will tolerate partial shade and is good cut flower. *S. lanata* can be invasive, especially in rich soil, but is still one of more valuable gray-leaved perennials.	Divide plants in spring.
Stokesia, or Stokes' aster (*Stokesia*) Cornflowerlike flowers appear in mid to late summer on slender stems. Foliage is evergreen in mild areas. Good cut flower. The only species in this genus. H 1-1½ ft.; S 1 ft.	*S. laevis,* or *S. cyanea,* hybrids are generally available. *S. l.* 'Blue Danube,' deep blue, 1-1½ ft. *S. l.* 'Blue Moon,' silvery blue to lilac, 1-1½ ft. *S. l.* 'Blue Star,' light blue, 1-1½ ft. *S. l.* 'Silver Moon,' white, 1-1½ ft.	Well-drained soil in winter is essential to survival. Grow in full sun and divide plants when they appear crowded—generally not until the third or fourth year.	Sow seeds in spring. Divide plants in spring. Make root cuttings in summer.

Thalictrum aquilegifolium

Thermopsis caroliniana

Tradescantia virginiana 'Snowcap'

Snow trillium (*Trillium grandiflorum*)

Valerian (*Valeriana officinalis*)

Common and botanical names, general characteristics	Species and varieties	Special requirements and remarks	Propagation *(See p. 234)*
Sunflower, see Helianthus and Heliopsis			
Thalictrum, or Meadow rue *(Thalictrum)* Attractive gray-green or blue-green leaves that resemble maidenhair fern. Loose sprays of tiny flowers in late spring or summer. H 2-4 ft.; S 1½-2 ft.	*T. aquilegifolium,* cream, early summer, 2-3 ft. *T. a. roseum,* rose, early summer, 2-3 ft. *T. dipterocarpum,* rose-purple, late summer, 3-4 ft. *T. rochebrunianum,* pale purple, midsummer, 3-4 ft. *T. speciosissimum,* or *T. glaucum* (dusty meadow rue), yellow, midsummer, 3-4 ft.	Grow in sun or partial shade and in well-drained but moisture-retentive soil. May be difficult to transplant. Plants gradually increase in size but are not invasive. Rabbit proof. Easily grown plants with airy appearance found in few other plants.	Sow seeds as soon as ripe or in spring. Divide plants in spring.
Thermopsis, or False lupine *(Thermopsis)* Spikes of lupinelike flowers tower above attractive pealike foliage in early to mid summer. Foliage remains effective after flowering. H 2-4 ft.; S 2-3 ft.	*T. caroliniana,* sulfur-yellow, 5 ft. *T. montana,* yellow, 2 ft.	Grow in sun or partial shade and average garden soil. Avoid very rich soil. Transplanting difficult because deep rooted. Plants may need staking. Generally trouble free.	Divide (difficult) in spring. Sow seeds in late summer. Inoculate with nitrifying bacteria as for peas and beans (see p. 571).
Tradescantia, or Spiderwort *(Tradescantia)* Clusters of 3-petaled flowers rise above long narrow leaves from midsummer to early fall. Flowers close on sunny afternoons. H 1½-2½ ft.; S 2-3 ft.	*T. virginiana* 'Iris Prichard,' white, violet flush, 2-2½ ft. *T. v.* 'J. C. Weguelin,' porcelain-blue, 2-2½ ft. *T. v.* 'Pauline,' rose-mauve, 2-2½ ft. *T. v.* 'Purple Dome,' rose-purple, 2-2½ ft. *T. v.* 'Red Cloud,' rose-red, 1½ ft. *T. v.* 'Snowcap,' pure white, 2-2½ ft.	Locate in partial shade or sun and in moisture-retentive soil. Plant tends to be invasive and difficult to eradicate; so may best be grown in isolated areas, although effective in border if its spreading tendencies are curbed. Easily grown.	Divide plants in spring. Occasionally grown from seeds or cuttings.
Trillium *(Trillium)* Choice spring-blooming wild flower with showy petals and sepals mostly in white or shades of pink or red above a whorl of 3 leaves. H 6 in.-1½ ft.; S 1 ft.	Many species offered, usually by wild-flower specialists. *T. grandiflorum* (snow trillium), white, one of showiest, 1 ft. Others available include *T. chloropetalum, T. erectum, T. nivale, T. ovatum, T. recurvatum, T. sessile,* and *T. undulatum.*	Grow in partial shade and in moisture-retentive soil well mixed with compost or peat moss. Soil should be acid; some species apparently require greater acidity than others. Plants go dormant in summer and leaves disappear.	Sow seeds when ripe in early summer. Divide thick-rooted plants in early fall, but only if more plants are desired, since best left undisturbed.
Valerian *(Valeriana)* Tall straight stems bear loose clusters of fragrant flowers in mid to late summer above finely divided leaves. Effective cut flower. H 4 ft.; S 2 ft.	*V. officinalis* (garden heliotrope), white, lavender, or pink, 4 ft., often sold by herb growers. See also the true heliotrope, an annual, p. 298. Another plant, the perennial centranthus, p. 244, is often sold under the common name valerian.	Grow in sun or partial shade and in average soil. Tolerates fairly moist soil. Plants spread by underground runners and tend to be invasive and somewhat weedy.	Sow seeds in spring. Divide plants in spring.

Verbascum hybridum 'Pink Domino'

Verbena rigida

Veronica spicata alba

Viola cornuta hybrid

Yucca filamentosa

Common and botanical names, general characteristics	Species and varieties	Special requirements and remarks	Propagation *(See p. 234)*
Verbascum, or Mullein *(Verbascum)* The 5-petaled flowers are borne on tall spikes above basal rosettes of silver-gray or green leaves in mid to late summer. H 2-4 ft.; S 1-1½ ft.	*V. hybridum* 'Cotswold Gem,' amber, purple center, 3-4 ft. *V. h.* 'Pink Domino,' rose-pink, maroon center, 4 ft. *V. nigrum,* yellow, purple center, 2-3 ft. *V. phoeniceum* (purple mullein), violet to purple, 2½-3 ft.	Grow in sun and in average well-drained soil, preferably alkaline. Remove faded flowers and side spikes may develop. Cutting also encourages new basal rosettes of leaves, and these may help plant to live longer. May self-sow. Often behaves like biennial (see p. 290). *V. nigrum* said to be longer-lived.	Sow seeds in spring. Divide plants in spring.
Verbena, or Vervain *(Verbena)* Clusters of small flowers over long period in summer and small, very divided leaves. Useful as ground cover or in front of border. H 3 in.-1 ft.; S 1-2 ft.	*V. bipinnatifida* (Dakota verbena), light purple, 3 in. *V. rigida,* or *V. venosa,* purplish to sky-blue, 1 ft.	Grow in sun and average soil that is well drained. Roots of *V. rigida* are tuberous and can be dug up in fall and stored like dahlias over winter in frost-free place. Not widely available, but both seeds and plants are sometimes sold.	Sow seeds in spring. Usually blooms first year. Take cuttings in summer.
Veronica, or Speedwell *(Veronica)* Widely grown for spikes of closely set, small flowers from mid to late summer. Neat, often attractive foliage. Good cut flower. H 15 in.-2 ft.; S 1-1½ ft.	*V. incana,* lilac-blue, silver-gray foliage, 1-1½ ft. *V. latifolia* 'Crater Lake Blue,' gentian-blue, 1½ ft. *V. longifolia subsessilis,* royal blue, 2 ft. *V.* 'Minuet,' pink, 1 ft. *V. spicata alba,* white, 15 in.	Locate in full sun or partial shade and in well-drained soil. Water in dry weather. Stake as needed. Divide only when plants no longer bloom satisfactorily. Easily grown plants that provide color over fairly long period, especially if faded spikes are removed.	Divide plants in spring. Sow seeds of available kinds in spring or early summer. Take cuttings in spring.
Viola, or Violet *(Viola)* Fragrant flowers are borne in profusion; mostly solid colors. Rich green, oval or heart-shaped leaves. Useful for bedding, borders, rock gardens, or as ground cover. H 6-8 in.; S 9 in.-1 ft.	*V. cornuta* hybrids (tufted pansy) often grown as annuals, 6-8 in.: 'Avalanche,' white; 'Jersey Gem,' purple; 'Yellow Perfection,' yellow; 'Chantryland,' apricot; 'Arkwright Ruby,' crimson. *V. odorata* hybrids (sweet violet), 6 in.: 'White Czar,' white; 'The Czar,' blue; 'Royal Robe,' deep purple. For annual pansy, see p. 303.	Grow in full sun or partial shade and in soil that has been well mixed with plenty of compost or peat moss. Water in dry weather. Keep flowers picked to prolong bloom, which is heaviest in spring but continues intermittently until fall.	Sow seeds in spring or late summer. Divide plants or take basal cuttings in spring.
Yucca *(Yucca)* Basal evergreen swordlike leaves, above which towering spikes of long-lasting, often fragrant, close-set flowers to 2 in. across rise in midsummer. H 3-6 ft.; S 3-4 ft.	*Y. filamentosa* (Adam's needle), creamy white, 3-6 ft. *Y. flaccida* 'Ivory Tower,' creamy white, 5-6 ft. For larger species, *Y. aloifolia* and *Y. gloriosa,* see p. 187.	Locate in sun and in well-drained soil. Tolerates drought. Aphids may attack flowers; control with malathion. Generally grown from plants set out in spring. 'Ivory Tower' least hardy. Makes striking accent plant.	Separate rooted offshoots from base of plant in spring. Take root cuttings in spring.

Chrysanthemums

Native to China and revered by the Japanese, chrysanthemums are among the most popular plants in temperate zones around the world.

Chrysanthemums are unequaled in the garden for their late-summer and fall blooms. They flower for three to eight weeks with blossoms that range from tiny buttons to immense globes measuring 8 or more inches across.

Aside from their beauty in the garden, chrysanthemums are a hobbyist's delight and can be grown as show specimens either outdoors or in the greenhouse. Hybridists have developed thousands of varieties, many of which vary greatly from their common ancestors. They can be induced to blossom in any season, particularly in greenhouses.

In general, chrysanthemums are short-day plants, their blossoming periods triggered by the shortening days of late summer. It is then that the plants' energies switch from vegetative growth to the production of flowers, which usually appear about six weeks after the buds. Some varieties require up to 12 weeks of relatively short days before they bloom. Catalogs often provide approximate flowering times.

For the gardener who wishes to control the blooming process, several methods are available. Special shading and lighting techniques can induce blooming at just about any time. But it is important to know the response time (the elapsed time from when the buds first set until the flowers come into bloom) for each variety.

Low-growing, bushy chrysanthemum plants are in the six- to seven-week response group. These varieties are found mostly in flower classes 1 to 5, as shown below. A few are in Classes 12 and 13.

The 8-, 9-, and 10-week response groups include all the flower forms. The varieties in the 11- and 12-week group are usually greenhouse grown, but even these will bloom outdoors in some climates. If the temperature drops much below 32° F, however, the buds and flowers will be damaged unless precautions are taken. A plastic cover placed over a plant will often suffice; an open shelter will keep temperatures 4–6 degrees higher than outside.

The popular term "hardy chrysanthemums," used to describe the low, bushy types, is somewhat misleading. The roots of all perennial chrysanthemums are capable of withstanding temperatures slightly below freezing. It is alternate freezing and thawing that causes most winterkill by lifting these shallow-rooted plants out of the ground.

One way to prevent this is to dig up the plants after they have bloomed and to store them in a cold frame. Another is to store the plants on the ground along the north side of a building and cover them with straw. If the plants are in very well drained soil, they may be left and covered with 2–4 inches of loose mulch after the ground freezes.

The basic requirements for success with chrysanthemums are the same whether you grow them for the garden or for shows, although for shows you may want to alter natural growth patterns to produce fewer but larger blooms. The required techniques are explained on the following pages.

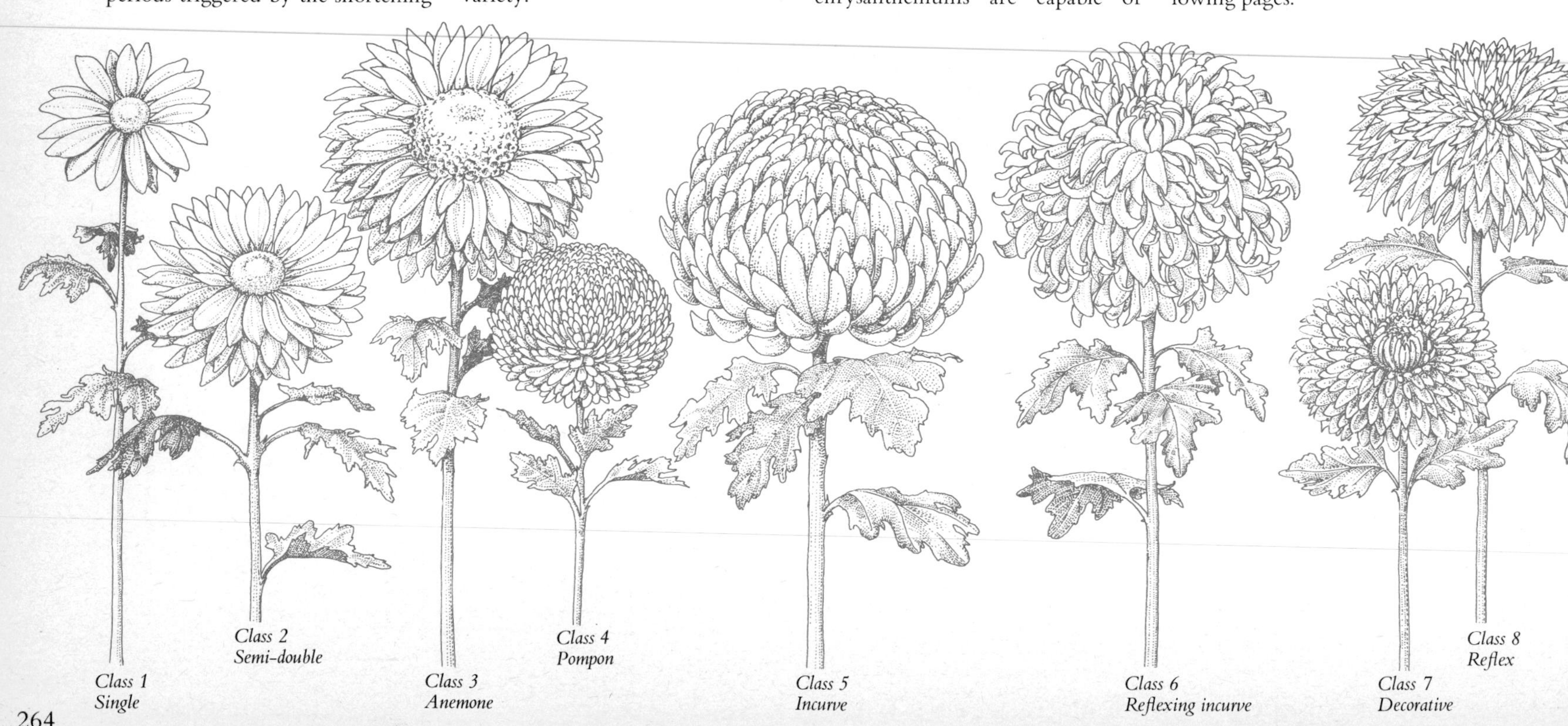

Class 1 *Single* · *Class 2* *Semi-double* · *Class 3* *Anemone* · *Class 4* *Pompon* · *Class 5* *Incurve* · *Class 6* *Reflexing incurve* · *Class 7* *Decorative* · *Class 8* *Reflex*

Variables of Latitude and Climate

Since length of day is the primary factor that determines the time of year a chrysanthemum will bloom, each response group blossoms slightly earlier in northern latitudes than it does when grown farther south.

Other factors also enter in. Thus, because of various environmental considerations, chrysanthemums of any given variety may bloom up to 10 days later around New York City than they do in the San Francisco Bay area. Because of temperature differences, chrysanthemum plants grown at high elevations or in inland areas bloom later than do those along the coast.

Bloom dates for the varieties listed in the accompanying tables are average for Zone C (see map on p. 9). To determine more exact dates in other areas, it is best to check with local growers or hobbyists.

Propagating New Plants

A friend may offer you chrysanthemums from his garden, or you can purchase some from a nursery. If you are given a chrysanthemum plant that has survived over the winter, it can be separated into pieces, each consisting of a single new, leafy stem with the fleshy stolon (creeping stem) connected to it. This is called a Dutch cutting. With care it can grow into a mature plant, but there may be problems.

The new growths, for example, appear in March or April, and by mid-May they may be quite tall (8–10 inches) and difficult to transplant. And if the stolon is planted any deeper than it was before it was divided, it may rot before new roots can develop.

In general, softwood cuttings (explained on the next page) will give better results.

Purchasing Plants by Mail

Snow may still be on the ground when the first chrysanthemum catalogs arrive. It is then that the gardener's imagination takes flight as he envisions the colorful flowers in the catalog transposed to his own garden. Caution is advisable at this point, for too many varieties will lessen the overall effect when the plants flower. Also, it may cost less to order three plants of one variety than one each of three types.

Some plants do better in one climate than in another. For example, types grown in Britain are suitable for our Pacific Northwest, but some may produce more open flowers when grown elsewhere. And deep-hued types tend to fade in the strong sun of the American South.

The sooner you receive your order from a nursery, the more time you will have to take cuttings from them and to increase the number of plants in your garden. The plants are shipped with their roots carefully packed in material that maintains their moisture. Even if they should appear dry upon arrival, the plants will probably recover if they stand overnight in water. Next, transfer them to containers or, weather permitting, to permanent locations.

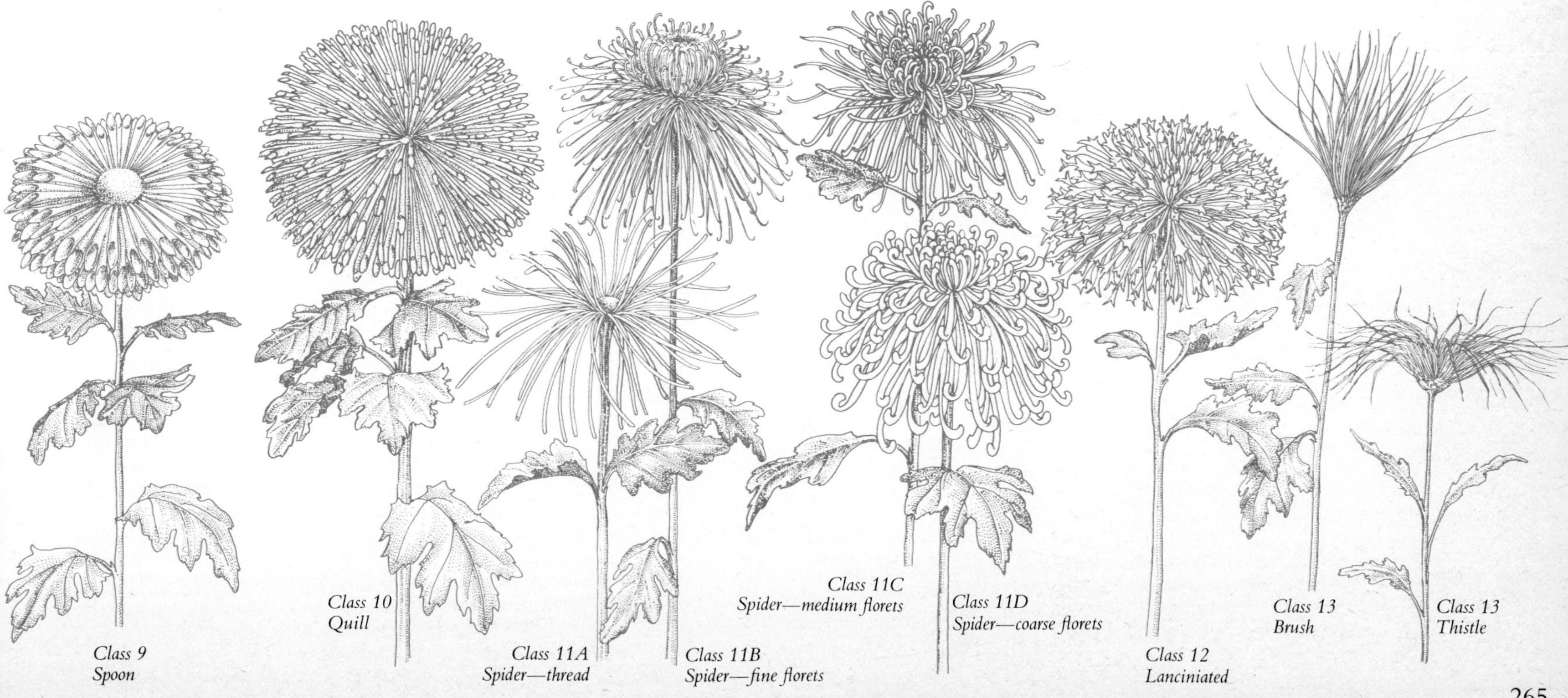

Class 9 Spoon

Class 10 Quill

Class 11A Spider—thread

Class 11B Spider—fine florets

Class 11C Spider—medium florets

Class 11D Spider—coarse florets

Class 12 Lanciniated

Class 13 Brush

Class 13 Thistle

Making Softwood Cuttings

Because new basal growth around an old chrysanthemum clump is pliable, the term "softwood" is used. An individual stem can be removed from this basal growth to make a cutting, as shown below. May and June are the best months for taking these softwood cuttings.

Since chrysanthemum stolons spread out underground, trace each growth back to its parent before removing it, in order to avoid mix-ups with other plants. Also, work with one variety at a time to keep from mixing varieties. Prepare each cutting as depicted in the illustrations.

When planted in a rooting medium in a flat, a softwood cutting will root in 10 days to 2 weeks during late spring. Builder's sand or mixtures containing peat moss, perlite, and vermiculite are recommended rooting mediums; the proportions are not critical as long as the mixture is kept moist but not soggy.

The medium should be spread to a depth of 3 inches in a flat that is not too big to permit easy handling. Discarded grape boxes, available at supermarkets, are ideal.

It is a good idea to protect the cuttings from infestation by dipping them in a combination insecticide and fungicide before planting them. For extrafast rooting, dip the bottom ends of the cuttings in a rooting hormone powder.

As each row is planted, label it with the name of the variety and the date the cuttings were made.

The rooting process will be accelerated if heat is supplied to the bottoms of the flats. The cuttings should be kept in a partially shaded area. Check the rooting medium often to make sure that it does not dry out.

Do not be deceived if the cuttings appear to wilt during midday heat. By the next morning they may well be standing erect. After the roots begin to form, this temporary daily wilting becomes less pronounced.

A week after the cuttings have been set out, carefully lift one and examine it for roots. When the roots are half an inch long, remove the cuttings from the rooting medium, and plant them in the ground.

The plants removed from the rooting mix are like rooted cuttings bought from a nursery. Their subsequent treatment is the same and is described under the headings below.

1. *Remove a new 2 ½- to 3-in. growth from the base of the old clump.*

2. *Carefully pinch off the lower leaves; do not strip skin from the stem.*

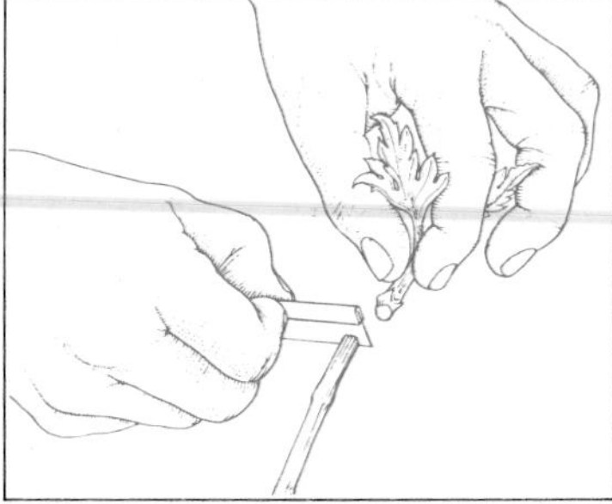

3. *Using a razor blade, sever the plant stem just below a leaf joint.*

4. *Make holes 1 in. deep, 2 in. apart, in a rooting medium. Insert cuttings.*

5. *Place cuttings in a bottom-heated propagator or in a cold frame.*

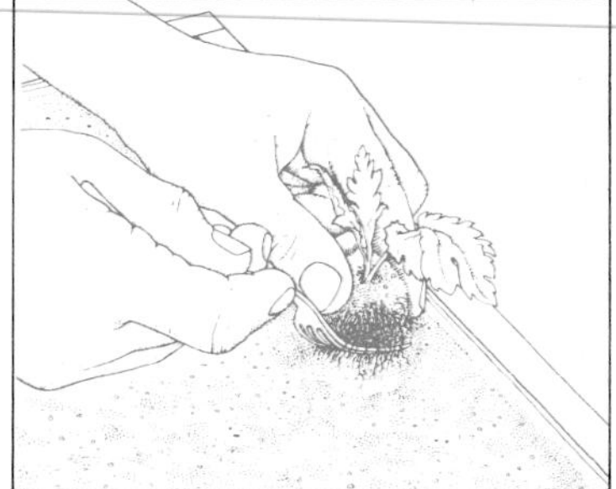

6. *Transplant rooted cuttings to pots or boxes, or directly into the ground.*

Growing Chrysanthemums in Flats

The same type of container used to root cuttings can be employed to grow plants until it is time to place them in the garden. When you set plants in flats, you give them an opportunity to establish their roots in soil while eliminating problems that develop when soil is too wet or too dry—conditions prevalent in many gardens in the spring. When in the flats the plants will do best in a loose, nutritious growing medium—either a commercial potting mix or one combining equal parts of rich soil (or compost), peat moss, and builder's sand (or perlite).

For potting chrysanthemum cuttings, use 3-inch-deep pots made of clay, plastic, or peat. The first two kinds of pots are reusable, but peat pots are designed to be placed in the soil with their plants. If the soil is kept moist, the plant's roots will penetrate the peat, and the pot will disintegrate.

Generally, most chrysanthemums should be kept in pots for two or three weeks before being planted in their permanent locations. Though starting chrysanthemums in pots requires more work than placing them directly in the garden, the extra effort usually pays off by producing plants that are stronger than those exposed to the vagaries of the elements at an earlier age.

Planting in the Garden

Rooted cuttings can be planted directly in the garden. Bear in mind, however, that they will need a great deal of care to keep them from drying out in the sun and to protect them from the ravages of insects, beating rains, and strong winds. Also, it is best to provide some form of temporary shade until the plants have become firmly established.

Growing the Six- to Eight-Week Response Groups

Preparing Beds for Chrysanthemum Plants

Once established, chrysanthemums need a predominantly sunny exposure, an evenly sustained food supply, and plenty of space around them to develop properly. Their roots require a soil that is loose and drains well after a heavy rain. A soil that is too soggy during either the growing season or the winter resting period will adversely affect growth and subsequent survival.

The difficulties imposed by compacted clay soil and poor drainage can often be overcome by planting chrysanthemums in raised beds. Such beds can be made by using a 6- to 8-inch-high wood frame or a 4-inch-high cinder-block enclosure.

A growing medium of peat moss and leaf mold combined with a sandy or clayey soil is ideal for supplying the organic material and slightly acid conditions under which chrysanthemum plants thrive. A soil in the 6–7 pH range is best. (For an explanation of pH and information on how to test your soil, see p. 594.)

Though chrysanthemums can be planted at any time in May or June, the bloom date will be approximately the same for all plants in a particular response group, whether they are planted early or late. Early planting, therefore, offers no significant advantage. On the contrary, it may result in plants taller than the gardener desires.

Planting Out and Spacing

Left to themselves, chrysanthemum plants can spread several feet in all directions from the main stem within three or four years. By controlling growth, the gardener can direct some of this tremendous plant energy into producing fewer but bigger and better flowers.

The early bloomers are normally grown for mass effect, although some can be induced to yield terminal sprays and flowers that are large enough to enter in a flower show. When they are grown for maximum bloom, the chrysanthemum plants should be spaced 18 inches apart. To get the largest possible blooms with upward- or downward-curving petals, they should be restricted to only two or three blooms per plant. Such plants are best grown in rows that are a foot apart, with each plant 8–12 inches from its neighbor next in line.

If you plan to have a number of rows, plant them in groups of four, with at least 3 feet separating each group. This will give you room to cultivate two rows from each side without being cramped.

Plants that were started in clay or plastic pots should be moistened before planting. Then you can remove them easily by tapping the rim of the pot while holding the plant upside down (see illustration at right).

All plants should be placed in a hole no deeper than the ball of soil that was removed from the pot. After the root ball is planted, the ground should be tamped down.

HOW TO REMOVE AND REPOT

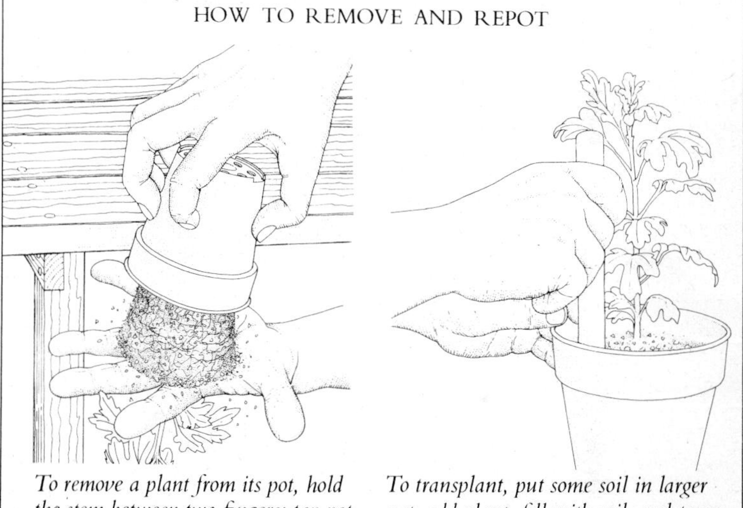

To remove a plant from its pot, hold the stem between two fingers; tap pot.

To transplant, put some soil in larger pot, add plant, fill with soil, and tamp.

Making Instant Borders

The shallow roots of chrysanthemums give them a distinct advantage over many other plants. They can be dug up with a spading fork and moved to a new location (as shown on p. 268 at lower right), where they will generally thrive if watered well during the first few days.

For the gardener this ability of chrysanthemums to flourish after being replanted opens up an exciting area of landscape design. Chrysanthemum plants can be grown all summer in a sunny location and then moved to a border position, which may be in partial shade. Once the blooms have shown color, they will open in the shade and last longer there than if in full sun.

Plan your chrysanthemum borders carefully before transplanting; you may wish to draw a sketch of the kind of border you want. Think in terms of proper spacing to accommodate both the robust and the delicately shaped varieties. Also, take advantage of the different heights available.

In autumn many garden centers sell chrysanthemums in bloom. Either these come in pots or their root balls are wrapped in burlap. These plants can be used to fill in bare spots in your garden.

If these chrysanthemums have been grown naturally, they can spend the winter in the garden or a cold frame and be propagated for the next year. If, however, they are late bloomers that have been forced by shading and lighting techniques to bloom earlier than they normally would have, they will revert to their natural patterns during the next growing season. Any cuttings taken from them will produce plants that will blossom at the appropriate time for their response group.

Mulching Plants to Control Weeds

Chrysanthemum plants are shallow rooted and do best when the root area is covered with a mulch to keep down weeds and conserve moisture. Many organic materials, such as peat moss, partially composted leaves, and cocoa-bean hulls or other locally available humus, can be used. A combination of leaves with an overlay of no more than an inch of peat moss is both adequate and attractive. Remember that peat moss becomes compacted and can prevent moisture from seeping through to the roots.

Pinching, or Stopping

One of the least understood techniques of chrysanthemum growing is called pinching by Americans and stopping by the British. Both terms simply mean cutting or breaking off the top half inch of growth. This stops upward growth and forces the plant to produce side shoots, called breaks, directly below the point of the pinch. All plants should be pinched when they are 6–8 inches high (see illustration at right).

Three breaks are usually formed after each pinch. Each break can itself be pinched after it has grown about 6 inches, and it may even be possible to pinch it once more. However, no pinching should be attempted after the plant is within 90 days of its normal bloom time.

Some varieties tend to be self-branching; so pinching must be coordinated with the chrysanthemum's natural break development to produce a well-branched, compact plant. Such a plant will have hundreds of small blooms. If, however, the plants are included in Classes 3, 4, 6, 7, 10, 11, 12, or 13, they are usually grown to produce a few large flowers. For show purposes three blooms per plant are enough, and all but the strongest breaks that result from pinching should be removed. The illustration below shows the results of pinching.

HOW TO PINCH

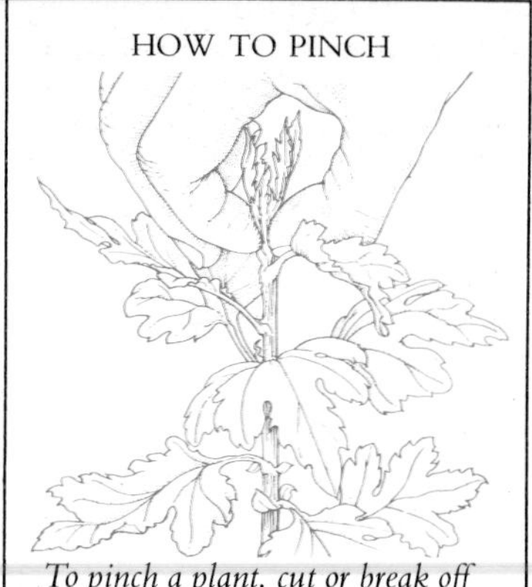

To pinch a plant, cut or break off shoot above topmost full leaves.

HOW PINCHING AFFECTS FLOWERING

Pinched plant. *For larger, earlier flowers, pinch out the main stem and most of the side branches.*

Natural form. *A chrysanthemum plant that has not been pinched back produces many small blooms.*

Supporting Chrysanthemum Plants

Ingenious gardeners have developed a variety of methods for supporting chrysanthemums. Plants with only a few blooms are generally supported by a steel or bamboo stake for each branch, as illustrated here at right. Plastic- or paper-covered wire ties are used to fasten the stems of the plants to the stakes.

Another way to support chrysanthemum plants is to use metal hoops with three or four wire legs. These hoops are sold in most garden centers and are often used to support peonies. They are long lasting and convenient to store because they can be folded flat. Such hoops work reasonably well if the plants grow no taller than 3 feet.

If an entire bed is planted with chrysanthemums, a checkerboard of strings can be stretched between supporting wires to form squares about 8–10 inches across. The first row of strings can be positioned when the plants are about 1 foot high. As the plants grow, additional strings can be added, so that each plant is enclosed in its own square, several tiers high.

A bamboo or steel stake is necessary to support plants grown for large blooms.

Care During the Summer Months

Feeding. Many fertilizers, ranging from 5–10–5 dry formulas to 20–20–20 liquid solutions, are suitable for chrysanthemum plants. In addition, slow-release fertilizers, incorporated in the soil at the time of planting, will nourish the soil for several months. Too much fertilizer promotes foliage at the expense of flowers; so diluted feeding once a week is usually best. The most practical way to obtain a diluted solution of liquid fertilizer is to mix it at one-half the strength recommended on the label.

Watering. In dry spells a thorough weekly watering is required. Together with a good mulch to reduce surface evaporation, this will help grow superior plants. In summer overhead watering is acceptable; but in early autumn this method may spread mildew. Chrysanthemums seldom need watering after the blooms show color.

LATE-FLOWERING VARIETIES

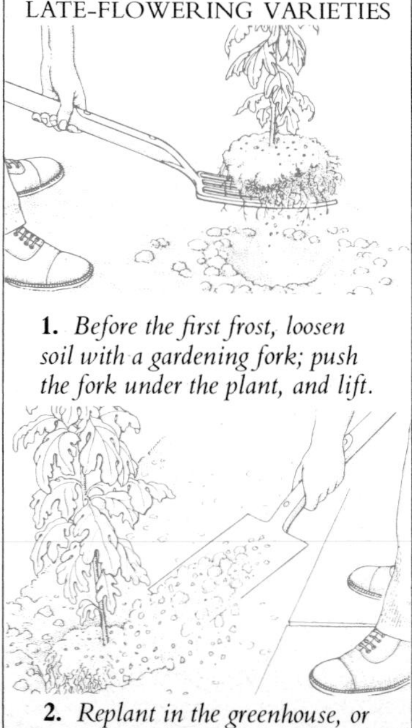

1. *Before the first frost, loosen soil with a gardening fork; push the fork under the plant, and lift.*

2. *Replant in the greenhouse, or in protected border, tub, or box.*

Growing the 9- to 12-Week Response Groups

Bolder in form and often with larger flowers and longer stems than the chrysanthemum plants in the shorter response groups, these late bloomers are highly prized and require the best of care. These are the plants proudly displayed on flower-show tables, and their growers go to great lengths to nurture them to the absolute peak of their bloom potential. They are usually grown in those gardens where protection from frost can be provided or in pots that can be moved to sheltered areas.

Two especially popular classes for exhibition are the incurves and the spiders. The incurves are illustrated on page 264 as Classes 5 and 6. The spiders are shown on page 265 as Class 11. The incurves can produce the largest of all chrysanthemum flowers, and the spiders are considered to be the most unusual and interesting. But many other classes are grown for display in flower shows.

In addition, growers often train chrysanthemum plants in bonsai, cascade, or specimen forms.

The bonsai chrysanthemums are trained by pruning and using wire to shape the stems in the same way as tree and shrub bonsai (p. 200). The plants at flowering time are generally about 10 inches high and 12–13 inches wide.

Cascades are trained on a U-shaped frame of wire about 4 feet long bent at a 45-degree angle. As the plant grows, pinch out side shoots to encourage the growth of the main stem. Gradually bend the frame to the horizontal and finally to the vertical so that flowers form a cascade.

Specimen plants for special display are often grown to cover a wire form made in the shape of a figure, such as a peacock, a globe, or an upright triangular shape similar to that of a Christmas tree.

Growing in the open ground. Late bloomers need all the care that is lavished on the earlier bloomers, and then some. Provide maximum practical spacing between plants, and restrict each plant of the large-bloom type to two stems. Bush types are trained to produce from three to six sprays in accordance with National Chrysanthemum Society standards. Many growers install a frame of pipe or redwood around this type of chrysanthemum; when needed, the frame can support a frost cover or a black shading cloth. An example is illustrated on page 271.

Growing in pots. Many growers of the late bloomers prefer to concentrate on a small number of plants and to cultivate them in pots—sometimes kept above the ground, sometimes below. If the pots are aboveground, they should be supported to keep them from blowing over. Pots give the grower greater control because they can be turned to prevent blooms from leaning to one side or another, and during rainy spells they can be carried to a sheltered area. If pots are belowground, they can easily be lifted out for moving.

Normally, each potted plant is transplanted twice as it grows to maturity—first from its 2- to 3-inch pot to a 4-inch model and finally to a 7- or 8-inch pot. However, a plant can be transplanted directly from a 2- to 3-inch pot to a 7- or 8-inch pot if care is taken to prevent the larger pot from becoming waterlogged. A mulch of peat moss in the large pot deters weeds and conserves moisture. Many flower shows accept only potted plants for display, and these, of course, must be grown for the full season in pots.

Aboveground potting. British gardeners will frequently grow chrysanthemums in pots set on rows of tiles or bricks and use a double wire for support. This technique is illustrated below left. Though this method discourages soil-borne insect infestation, watering may become something of a problem, particularly in hot, dry weather. Since a 4-foot chrysanthemum requires a large amount of water, close attention must be paid to its watering needs when it is potted in this manner.

Plunge pit. The plunge pit is a variation of aboveground potting in which pots are buried up to their rims in moist sand or soil. Watering is less of a problem, particularly if clay pots are used. The clay lets some moisture through the wall of the pot. Plastic, however, does not. But if heavy rains bring an overabundance of water, the plants may have difficulty absorbing the moisture.

ABOVEGROUND POTTING IN SUMMER

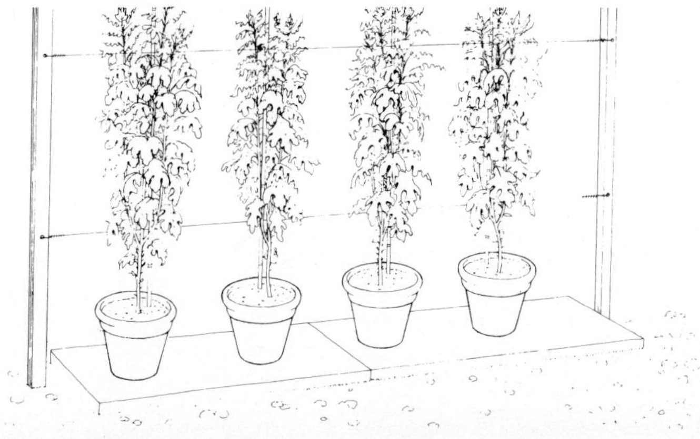

Late-flowering chrysanthemums can spend the summer outdoors. Place the pots on tiles or bricks in a sunny location. To prevent the pots from being blown over, attach the supporting stakes to horizontal wires.

Making a Time Pinch to Produce Large Blooms

The 9- to 12-week response group varieties are pinched in the same way as the earlier bloomers except that a final pinch—called the time pinch—is made toward the end of the growing season in order to generate the largest possible blossoms. There is a period of 90 to 110 days before the bloom date when a final pinch will produce a terminal bud cluster on stems of adequate length to qualify the chrysanthemums as entries in competitive shows. If the last pinch is made late in the growing season, a terminal bud cluster will form. (The word "terminal" here means the last flowering effort in the sequence.) Had there been no pinching, the plant would branch by itself to produce many blooms on short stems.

The grower who looks forward to winning show honors is primarily interested in concentrating the energies of the plant on producing large blooms. Ideally, these flowers will form a superb terminal spray in which a central crown bloom is surrounded by smaller satellite blossoms. In addition, top show honors require that the terminal bloom be set on an underpinning of chrysanthemum leaves. British show growers often give primary consideration to the chrysanthemum flower in making awards. American judges, however, will withhold up to 10 points of a possible 100 if the terminal bloom lacks a sufficient number of leaves directly beneath it.

What then determines success or

failure in producing a prizewinning show chrysanthemum? After the final pinch has been made, the rest is largely up to the inherent qualities of the plant itself as well as the weather. Both play as great a role as the grower in producing award-winning blooms.

Still, if a grower seriously desires top recognition for his chrysanthemums, he must follow certain steps. As a general rule plants grown to produce sprays should be pinched 90 days before the expected bloom date. Those designed for large blooms to be entered in competition should be time-pinched 100 days before the plant is expected to flower.

The time pinch usually generates three lateral growths, or breaks, just as other pinches do. If show entries are the goal, only two breaks should be allowed to grow, and these will yield two large blooms per plant. For sprays, all three breaks created by the time pinch can be retained.

After the plants have become well established, and throughout the growing season, lateral growth will occur at the junction of each leaf below the terminal bud. These shoots must be removed as soon as they are about half an inch long. If they are allowed to remain, they will rob the terminal bud of needed strength.

Their removal is a simple operation: just use your thumb to rub off the unwanted bud stems. This must be done on a regular basis when the buds are young. If buds are permitted to grow, removal of them will leave ugly scars on the plant stem.

In September a change occurs in the terminal growth of each stem: a central bud appears, surrounded by side buds. For plants that are intended to have one large bloom per stem, the central buds should be retained and the others removed.

Remove side buds as early as possible, but not until they have grown distinct stems that can be rubbed off without disturbing the center bud.

In the case of prospective sprays, the central bud and all side buds should be left to develop untouched. The central bud will become the primary bloom, and it will be surrounded by smaller blossoms.

WHEN FLOWER BUDS APPEAR

1. *Flower buds grow in groups—a central bud surrounded by side buds.*

2. *If you want only one large bloom per stem, pinch out the side buds.*

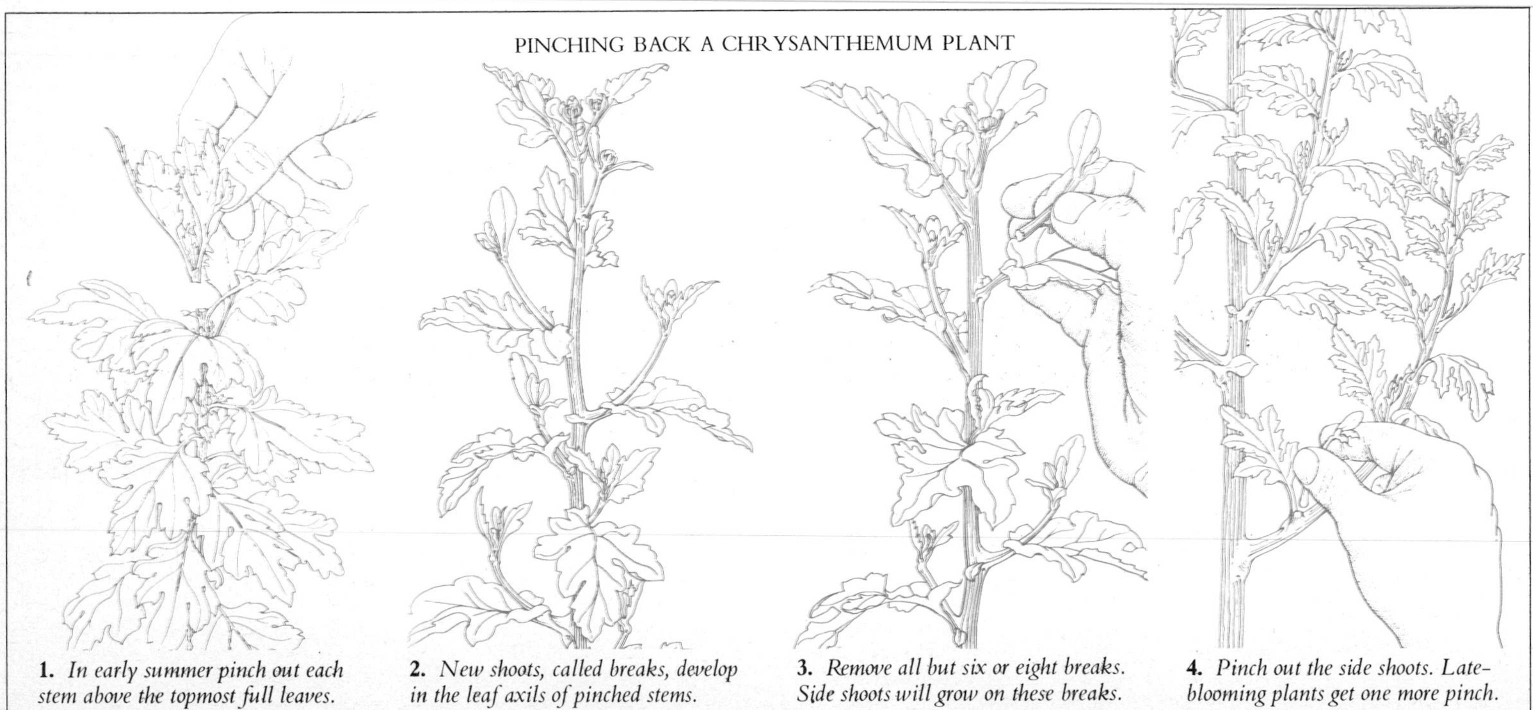

PINCHING BACK A CHRYSANTHEMUM PLANT

1. *In early summer pinch out each stem above the topmost full leaves.*

2. *New shoots, called breaks, develop in the leaf axils of pinched stems.*

3. *Remove all but six or eight breaks. Side shoots will grow on these breaks.*

4. *Pinch out the side shoots. Late-blooming plants get one more pinch.*

Summer Care for Outstanding Flowers

To win top awards at shows, the chrysanthemum grower must give his plants considerably more attention than if he were interested only in home display. Because show entries must have straight stems and dark foliage, and be free of insect damage, daily checking is required, and corrective measures must be taken before trouble occurs.

New terminal growth of stems is soft, but as it ages it becomes hard, and once hardened, its configuration cannot be changed. Therefore, the stems of prospective show plants must be supported during their growth to keep them straight. Long steel or bamboo stakes are recommended, and wires encased in paper or plastic can be twisted around the plant, attaching it to the stakes. Two supports usually suffice for a single stem, but the wires should be moved up the stakes to keep pace with the stem's growth.

The development of good foliage requires ample feedings. Both inorganic fertilizers, such as a 20-20-20 formula, and organic materials, such as fish emulsion, should be used. Diluted weekly feedings will bring better results than concentrated but infrequent feedings. Too much nitrogen can harm chrysanthemum plants, resulting in coarse leaves that curl at the edges.

Many growers find that chelated iron and trace-element compounds are excellent dietary supplements. Should the color of a plant's leaves appear too light, try sprinkling magnesium sulfate—1 pound per 100 square feet of soil—in the area around the plant.

Prevention, rather than cure, is the key word in disease control. There are many insecticides and fungicides that can control insects and guard against disease. Malathion and dicofol are compounds capable of killing most insects that attack chrysanthemum plants. These compounds are contained in various commercial garden sprays. To control mildew and leaf spot, try the compound Benomyl, used alone or with an insecticide. Such chemicals can be applied with a hand-pumped tank-type sprayer. Be sure the sprayer has a gun and nozzle adequate to give thorough coverage on the top and bottom of all leaves.

Young chrysanthemum plants set out in the garden are often damaged by slugs, cutworms, and birds. Pellets of metaldehyde bait can be placed around the plants to control slugs, and cardboard collars encircling the plant bottoms will help to discourage cutworms.

To avoid damage by birds, which sometimes tear at chrysanthemum leaves, try frightening them away with strips of cloth tied along wires stretched above the plants.

Greenhouse Cultivation

Because chrysanthemums need all the sun they can get for part of their life cycles, it is best to grow them in the garden as long as possible.

The plunge-pit method described on page 269 is ideal for late-blooming types. Because the plants are buried in pots, they can be moved into a greenhouse before a frost.

Before the potted plants are taken indoors, they should be well sprayed with an all-purpose insecticide that includes fungicide, such as Benomyl, to guard against powdery mildew. Put the pot on its side, and tilt it against three bricks so that you can easily spray both sides of the leaves.

Good ventilation in the greenhouse is important. Water should be applied directly to the soil in the pots, not sprayed on the foliage. Feeding should be discontinued as soon as the flowers show color.

Making a Frame for Shading and Frost Cover

Many of the chrysanthemum varieties bloom after the first frost, which often comes too late for autumn shows. Growers can force early blooming by using the black-cloth shading method.

A frame of galvanized pipe or redwood two-by-fours is needed to support the shading cloth. The frame should be high enough to keep the cloth from touching the plants and should provide a roof slope so that rain will run off.

The cloth itself should be dense enough to screen out almost all light. Attach it to the frame in such a way that it can easily be installed and removed daily. Position the cloth on the north end of the structure so that it can be pulled to the south end late in the day and back to provide full sun the following morning.

Since chrysanthemums remain at a peak bloom for a long period, a plant that is scheduled to bloom on October 15, for example, can be entered in shows as much as a week before or after that date. Because each response group requires a designated number of short-day weeks, subtract that number from October 15 to decide when to begin the shading process. If different response groups are grown together, pick an average date. This will usually be around August 6. Shade should be applied each afternoon at a time that will ensure 12 hours of darkness. Shading should continue until bud clusters are visible on the terminals.

Chrysanthemum plants can withstand temperatures as low as 28° F. But when the temperature drops below freezing, moisture may damage the petals. A frost cover will prevent this kind of injury. The shading frame can be used to support the frost cover, which should be made of a 6-mil vinyl material.

Make sure that the cover contains openings, to prevent heat buildup. Also, a fan can be placed within the frame to circulate air on warm days. A 500- to 1,000-watt heater will prevent damage on a cold night.

A frame like this one can support a frost cover or a shading cloth, which blocks out light and forces early bloom.

For Flowers Out of Season

With a greenhouse you can schedule chrysanthemums to bloom throughout the winter. Take softwood cuttings from the lateral growths of garden-grown plants after the growths have reached 4 or 5 inches in length. Root them as described on page 266.

When the day length in August reaches the critical point that triggers the change from vegetative to flower growth, the new cuttings will not yet be mature enough to generate blossoms. To avoid premature bud set in the cuttings, shine artificial light on them shortly after they have been rooted. The light period should last from 10 P.M. to 2 A.M. These extra four hours of light will prevent flowering. A 75-watt incandescent lamp shining from 3 feet above the plants is sufficient to cover a 4-foot length of bench or ground bed. The lights can be switched on and off automatically by a timing device.

In a small greenhouse with limited headroom, it is probably better to plant in the ground rather than on a bench. The distance between plants should be at least 6 inches. Directions for feeding, spraying, and controlling lateral growth are the same for greenhouse plants as for plants that are grown in the garden.

Whenever lighting is stopped, the chrysanthemums will immediately switch to bloom production, a process that takes 8 to 12 weeks. The greenhouse blooms will be somewhat smaller and less colorful than those grown in the normal chrysanthemum season because the winter sun is less powerful. After the first bloom, side growth will continue to produce blossoms as late as May.

WINTER CARE FOR CHRYSANTHEMUM PLANTS

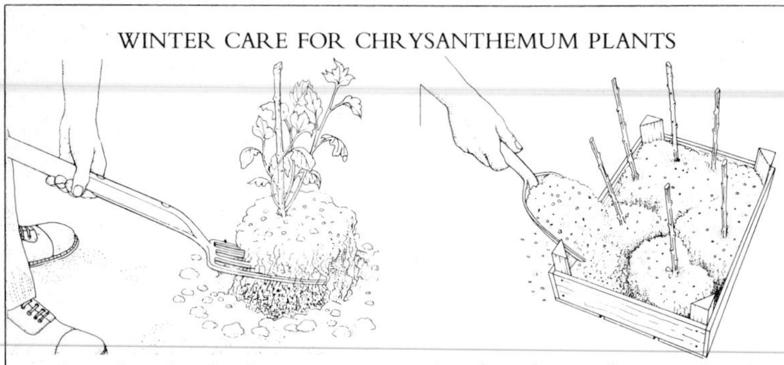

1. *Several weeks after flowering, cut back the stems to 9 in. Insert a spading fork under the roots; then lift the plant. Cut off leafy growths.*

2. *Place plants in boxes, pack with compost, and water lightly. Store in a cold frame until conditions are appropriate for renewed growth.*

Using Chrysanthemums and Growing Them Well

Chrysanthemums are ideal as hardy garden plants. The ease with which they can be moved to make instant borders eliminates problems caused by spacing or height differences. And as show plants, chrysanthemums have few peers.

When you enter chrysanthemums in a show, check the schedule carefully to make sure that your entries are placed in the proper class. Groom your show flowers carefully. If you enter a competition for three-bloom or spray classes, be sure the blossoms have a uniform configuration.

In beds where chrysanthemums have been grown for many years, nematodes or verticillium wilt disease may be present. This may necessitate soil fumigation with a product containing the chemical metam-sodium.

Soil that has a high clay content presents problems for the chrysanthemum grower. Avoid digging in damp weather. Mixing the soil with builder's sand, cinders, or perlite will make the earth more friable. If your soil breaks up easily when turned over in the spring, its clay content is probably not too high.

Slightly acid soil (pH 6–7) is best for chrysanthemums. If the soil has a pH of 5–6, the excess acidity can be corrected by adding ground limestone. If the pH is 7–8, the soil is too alkaline, and peat moss or sulfur in one of their various forms should be worked in. See page 594 for more information on changing pH levels of the soil.

What Can Go Wrong With Chrysanthemums

The chart below describes the commonest problems that are likely to occur in the growing of chrysanthemum plants. Symptoms and signs of common plant disorders appear in the first column; their cause is stated in column two; measures to control the problem are in column three. If plants show symptoms that are not described below, turn to the section on plant disorders on page 600. Look up chemicals on page 635 to find trade names.

Symptoms and signs	Cause	Control
Sinuous whitish lines in leaf tissue.	Leaf miners	Remove mined leaves. Spray with Diazinon.
Distorted buds and flowers. Leaves crippled or with small holes.	Four-lined, harlequin, or tarnished plant bugs	Spray with Diazinon, malathion, or nicotine.
Leaves flecked with brown. Webs at end of new growths.	Two-spotted mites (red spider mites)	Spray with dicofol, malathion, or tetradifon.
Young shoots eaten off, especially on stolons.	Slugs (if slimy trails present) or caterpillars	Spread methiocarb or pellets of metaldehyde for slugs. For caterpillars use carbaryl.
V-shaped or triangular patches between leaf veins.	Foliar nematodes (eelworms)	Burn damaged leaves. Spray with Diazinon or dichlorvos.
Plants yellowed and often stunted. Leaves and shoots wilt during warm, sunny weather. Thin stems; small, pale leaves.	Root knot nematodes or symphilids in soil	Drench soil with Diazinon or dichlorvos. Before planting, treat bed with dazomet or metam-sodium; follow instructions on label.
	Lack of water	Check for dryness.
	Starvation or chlorosis	Check feeding program; add several tablespoons of magnesium sulfate.
Petals (ray flowers) show brown spots. Flowers deformed.	Ascochyta ray blight (fungus)	Spray with Captan, ferbam, or maneb.
Powdery gray or brown masses on buds and petals.	Botrytis, or gray mold (fungus)	Ventilate on warm days. Spray with chlorothalonil or dichloran.
Whitish coating over leaves and shoots, which may be deformed.	Powdery mildew (fungus)	Spray with Benomyl, cycloheximide, or dinocap.
Brown or black spots on leaves.	Rust disease or septoria leaf spot (fungus)	Apply Benomyl, ferbam, maneb, or zineb.
General wilting of entire plant. Leaves turn brown at base of plant and die progressively upward. Dead brown leaves hang on for a long time.	Verticillium wilt or Seidewitz disease (fungus)	Destroy infected leaves and stems. Apply Benomyl at rate of 1 lb. to 1,000 sq. ft. of bed area. Mix with water; apply to infected plants with watering can.

Chrysanthemums for All Purposes

This selection of popular varieties is arranged by flower color. Each color grouping is subdivided according to response time, as explained on page 264. The NCS class is the flower form designated by the National Chrysanthemum Society, as illustrated on pages 264–265. Blooming dates are approximate. In the South they may be a little earlier than those given here; in the North and at high elevations, somewhat later.

Names	Response groups	NCS classes	Bloom dates	Remarks
White	**6–8 wk.**			
'Autumn Bride'	6	9	Sept. 15	Quilled anemone
'Avalanche'	7	7	Sept. 20	Weather resistant
'Baby Tears'	6	4	Sept. 10	White button cushion
'Betsy Ross'	6	7	Sept. 10	4-in. creamy blooms
'Chapel Bells'	6	7	Sept. 15	Wide petaled
'Daisy White'	6	1	Sept. 15	Medium cushion
'Drifted Snow'	8	7	Oct. 5	Snowy white
'Early Snow'	6	7	Sept. 5	Semi-cushion
'Ermine'	7	7	Oct. 1	Creamy center
'French Vanilla'	7	7	Sept. 20	Grand sprays
'Good Humor'	6	4	Sept. 15	Ball-shaped blooms
'Newport'	6	7	Sept. 10	Large mound cushion
'Powder River'	6	7	Sept. 15	Large bloom cushion
'Raggedy Ann'	7	12	Oct. 1	Carnation flowered
White	**9–12 wk.**			
'Bicentennial'	11	5	Nov. 1	Large exhibition
'Cloudbank'	10	3	Oct. 25	Fine terminal sprays
'Donlope's White'	11	11C	Nov. 5	Show winner
'John Hughes'	11	6	Nov. 1	Perfect ball form
'Lamont'	11	9	Nov. 5	Good pot plant
'Matterhorn'	12	5	Nov. 10	Perfect globe
'May Shoesmith'	12	5	Nov. 12	Completely globular
'Nightingale'	11	11C	Nov. 5	Unique green spider
'Nob Hill'	11	5	Nov. 1	Good pot plant
'Ping Pong'	11	4	Nov. 1	Excellent sprays
'Thunderhead'	11	5	Nov. 5	Incurving pure white
'Ugetsu'	12	3	Nov. 15	Best as cascade
Lavender and purple	**6–8 wk.**			
'Alert Purple'	7	7	Oct. 1	Silvery purple
'Geisha Girl'	7	11B	Sept. 28	Quilled petal spider
'Grandchild'	7	4	Sept. 25	Lavender-red eye
'Gypsy Wine'	6	4	Sept. 15	Waxen shapely globes
'Lovely Lass'	7	7	Oct. 1	Low, orchid-lavender
'Mango'	8	3	Oct. 10	Variant of 'Ann Ladygo'
'Purple Waters'	7	4	Sept. 22	Long stemmed

Names	Response groups	NCS classes	Bloom dates	Remarks
'Royal Flush'	6	7	Sept. 15	Plum-cerise sprays
'Small Wonder'	7	4	Sept. 25	Button pompon
'Tinker Bell'	7	4	Oct. 1	Strong and compact
'Twinkle'	7	7	Oct. 1	Cyclamen-purple
Lavender and purple	**9–12 wk.**			
'Grape Festival'	11	5	Nov. 5	Sturdy grower
'Playmate'	11	6	Nov. 1	Deep purple
'Potomac'	10	1	Oct. 25	Best wide petaled
'Pretty Polly'	9	7	Oct. 10	Silver reverse
'Purple Glow'	11	5	Nov. 5	Silver reverse
'Shin Otome'	11	3	Nov. 1	Large cascade
Pink	**6–8 wk.**			
'Ann Ladygo'	8	3	Oct. 10	Low growing
'Bessie Bates'	7	7	Sept. 28	Incurving
'Cameo'	6	7	Sept. 15	Deep pink cushion
'Cherish'	7	7	Sept. 28	Dahlia-type flowers
'Fall Charm'	6	7	Sept. 15	Gold center
'Grandchild Rose'	6	7	Sept. 15	Variant of 'Grandchild'
'Lindy'	6	7	Sept. 15	Slightly quilled
'Spinning Wheel'	7	3	Sept. 15	Spoon tips
'Stardom'	7	1	Oct. 1	Good pot plant
'Tenderness'	7	2	Oct. 1	True pink
'Whirlaway'	6	9	Sept. 15	Spoon cushion
'Yorktown'	6	7	Sept. 10	Clear rose-pink
Pink	**9–12 wk.**			
'Angel Face'	11	3	Nov. 1	Excellent sprays
'Carillon'	11	4	Nov. 4	Best show sprays
'Diamond Wedding'	10	5	Oct. 25	English pot plant
'Epic'	11	3	Nov. 5	Large pink anemone
'Escapade'	10	5	Oct. 28	Fine show flowers
'Fuyo'	11	3	Nov. 1	Bonsai or hanging
'Georgia Hedinger'	9	11C	Oct. 15	Reliable early spider
'Lola'	9	11C	Oct. 15	Best early spider
'Maiko'	12	3	Nov. 10	Good cascade
'Miss Olympia'	11	12	Nov. 5	Short, vigorous
'Novato'	11	9	Nov. 5	1975 award winner
'Otome Pink'	11	7	Nov. 1	Formal decorative
'Pink Champagne'	11	11B	Nov. 5	Full centered
'Seiko Giant'	12	6	Nov. 10	Japanese import
'Southern Queen'	11	5	Nov. 5	Wide florets
'Venoya'	12	3	Nov. 15	Specimen to train

Names	Response groups	NCS classes	Bloom dates	Remarks
Yellow	**6–8 wk.**			
'Bunker Hill'	6	7	Sept. 10	Butterscotch-yellow
'Daisy Yellow'	6	1	Sept. 15	Gold-toned center
'Gold Arrow'	7	5	Sept. 20	Free flowering, large
'Golden Galleon'	7	5	Sept. 28	Best early incurving
'Golden Regards'	7	7	Sept. 20	Variant of 'Best Regards'
'Golden Sunshine'	6	4	Sept. 12	Good pompon sprays
'Jackpot'	8	5	Oct. 10	Clear yellow cushion
'Lee Powell'	7	7	Sept. 20	Long a top favorite
'Lemon Lace'	7	9	Sept. 28	Unique spoon anemone
'Ruby Breithaupt'	8	7	Oct. 5	Gold to cream
'Sea Urchin'	7	10	Sept. 20	Gold to cream
'Spunky'	8	4	Oct. 5	Orange center
'Sunburst Cushion'	8	9	Oct. 5	Spooned tips
'Sunny Thoughts'	8	3	Oct. 3	Spoon anemone
'Yellow Starlet'	7	9	Sept. 25	Variant of 'Starlet'
Yellow	**9–12 wk.**			
'A.T. Bumann'	12	11B	Nov. 8	1972 award winner
'Centennial Fiesta'	11	5	Nov. 1	Sturdy plant
'Connie Mayhew'	10	5	Oct. 28	Excellent incurve
'Garden State'	11	5	Nov. 5	Top show bloom
'Georgia'	10	5	Oct. 28	Good show bloom
'Jackstraw'	11	12	Nov. 5	Best of its type
'Miss Oakland'	11	5	Nov. 1	Giant show winner
'Peter Rowe'	10	5	Oct. 25	Clear yellow
'Primrose Supreme'	11	5	Nov. 1	Large and full
'Statesman'	10	4	Oct. 28	Best button
'Yellow Knight'	11	11C	Nov. 5	Always a winner
'Yellow Margarita'	10	1	Oct. 25	Best yellow single
Orange and bronze	**6–8 wk.**			
'Apache'	8	7	Oct. 5	Deep bronze
'Best Regards'	6	7	Sept. 15	Low, large flowered
'Continental'	6	7	Sept. 5	Low border plant
'Daisy Bronze'	7	1	Sept. 20	Upright bushy plant
'Fall Festival'	6	7	Sept. 15	Good corsage bloom
'Fine Feathers'	7	9	Sept. 25	Fully double spoon
'Jascinth'	6	7	Sept. 15	Pure orange
'Minnautumn'	6	4	Sept. 5	Orange-red
'Pancho'	7	4	Sept. 24	Low mounded pompon
'Starlet'	7	9	Sept. 25	Low and bushy
'Ticonderoga'	7	7	Sept. 20	Weather resistant
'Welcome Sign'	7	9	Oct. 1	Double spoon

Names	Response groups	NCS classes	Bloom dates	Remarks
Orange and bronze	**9–12 wk.**			
'Autumn King'	11	5	Nov. 1	Fawn colored
'Daybreak'	11	3	Nov. 5	Best anemone
'Dignity'	11	5	Nov. 3	Mammoth incurve
'Edwin Painter'	10	2	Oct. 20	Good for disbudding
'Festival'	11	7	Nov. 1	Good pot plant
'Flame Symbol'	11	8	Nov. 5	Best reflex variety
'Gypsy Queen'	11	11C	Nov. 1	Full centered
'Honey'	10	10	Oct. 25	Short grower
'Honey Ball'	10	5	Oct. 20	Ball shaped
'Miss Atlanta'	12	11B	Nov. 10	1968 award winner
'Noble Knight'	11	5	Nov. 1	Red reverse
'Nova Gold'	10	5	Oct. 25	Tightly incurving
'Walnut Queen'	12	11D	Nov. 12	Robust grower
'Welcome News'	11	5	Nov. 1	English show bloom
Red	**6–8 wk.**			
'Bandana'	7	7	Sept. 20	Ruby-red cushion
'Chippewa Red'	7	7	Oct. 1	Deep red old-timer
'Daisy Red'	6	1	Sept. 15	Sturdy
'Daredevil'	7	7	Sept. 24	Deep red and bushy
'Drummer Boy'	6	7	Sept. 15	Bright red cushion
'Fireside Cushion'	8	1	Oct. 12	Tolerates cold
'Red Climax'	6	7	Sept. 15	Ideal for cutting
'Red Headliner'	6	7	Sept. 15	Best ruby-red
'Redheart'	6	7	Sept. 1	Best early short red
'Ruby Mound'	6	7	Sept. 15	Dense low mound
'Scarleteer'	8	7	Oct. 5	Good in pots
'Valley Forge'	7	7	Oct. 1	Maroon to crimson
'Volunteer'	8	8	Oct. 12	Slightly reflexing
Red	**9–12 wk.**			
'Achievement'	10	11C	Oct. 26	1970 award winner
'Akagane'	11	3	Nov. 5	Best as bonsai
'Ethel'	11	4	Nov. 5	Dark red button
'Fireflash'	10	8	Oct. 20	English favorite
'John Riley'	8	8	Oct. 5	Best early reflex
'Liberty Bell'	11	2	Nov. 1	Good sprays
'Matador'	11	5	Nov. 1	Reddish bronze
'Mimi'	11	3	Nov. 1	Good terminal sprays
'Oberlin'	9	10	Oct. 25	Good pot plant
'Red Bonanza'	10	7	Oct. 25	Bronze reverse
'Red Glory'	10	2	Oct. 28	Strong stems
'Red Jetfire'	11	4	Nov. 5	Large sprays

Flowers of the popular giant cactus dahlia can measure 10 in. across.

Dahlias

The brightness of the flowers, their complex shapes, and their rich foliage make a glorious addition to the garden from mid to late summer.

The dahlia comes originally from Mexico. It was known to the Aztecs and recorded by Europeans there in the late 16th century. The Spanish introduced it to Europe in the 18th century. It was, however, a very different plant from the dahlia that we know today

One of the original species, *Dahlia imperialis,* had single lilac-colored or reddish flowers and grew in a tree-like form to a height of 6–18 feet. Smaller species were also discovered, including *D. coccinea,* which had single red flowers. From several of these single-flowered species, the modern plants with their large, complex blooms were developed. The plant was called dahlia in honor of the eminent Swedish botanist Dr. Andreas Dahl.

The dahlia, native to Mexico, is a subtropical plant that needs humus-rich soil, constant watering, and regular feeding. It has tuberous roots, hollow stems, bright green to bronze-green leaves, and flowers ranging from pure white through attractive shades of yellow to the deepest maroon. Some dahlias are bicolored. There are two plant types: bedding dahlias, most commonly grown annually from seeds but also available as tubers; and exhibition, or show, dahlias, which are almost always grown from tubers.

The most popular ones for mixed borders are the bedding dahlias, which grow to about 2 feet tall. Catalogs offer 'Coltness' and 'Unwin' dwarfs 15–25 inches high with double or semi-double flowers about 2 inches across. You can also buy seeds for taller kinds with flowers that include the types oftenest grown for show, such as the formal and informal cactus, decorative, and pompon dahlia. Seed packets are of mixed colors, since the hue of dahlias grown from seeds cannot be predicted. Tubers are available in specific colors as named varieties. If you grow plants from seeds, you can lift and store the tubers of favorite colors for use the following year.

Exhibition dahlias are propagated by taking stem cuttings from growing tubers or by division of the tubers. The color of flowers that have been grown from a tuber will be true to the parent plant.

Dahlias are classified into groups according to flower form and size. More than a dozen are recognized by the American Dahlia Society, dealers, and hybridizers.

Singles may be as much as 4 inches across and have one row of petals and open centers.

Mignons are singles that grow on plants less than 18 inches tall.

Duplexes are like singles, but there are two rows of outer, or ray, petals and an open center.

Orchid-flowering dahlias resemble singles except that the rays curve up and in.

Anemones are similar to singles, but the petals in the center are rolled or tubular.

Collarettes have flowers with yellow centers made up of stamens and a single row of petals around the edge. An inner collar of smaller petals surrounds the stamens, lying between them and the petals. This inner ring of petals is the reason for the name collarette.

Peony dahlias can be 4 inches across; they have open centers with twisted petaloids (sepals or stamens that look like petals) and up to four rows of flat ray petals.

Incurved cacti have fully double flowers with narrow, quilled rays, or outer petals, that curve in at the tips, toward the center of the flower. The blooms of cactus dahlias can be as much as 10 inches wide.

Recurved, or straight, cacti are like the above, but all the rays are straight or recurve outward.

Semi-cacti are similar to cacti, except the petals are broader and quilled for half their length or less.

Formal decorative dahlias have a symmetrical shape and are fully double with no central disk. The petals are broad and rounded at the ends and slightly curved in. The blooms of these dahlias can measure more than 10 inches wide.

Informal decorative dahlias are similar to the above, but, as the name implies, the arrangement of the petals is less regular.

Ball dahlias are rounded but sometimes flattened on top. Petals are blunt or rounded at the tip and arranged spirally. Each petal is rolled for more than half its length. The flowers are more than 4 inches wide.

Miniatures are ball dahlias with flowers that are no more than 4 inches in diameter.

Pompons are ball dahlias that are less than 2 inches across.

The leaf color of dahlias ranges from rich green to deep bronze or greenish red. Variegated foliage occasionally appears on young plants, but leaves revert to solid color at maturity. The shape of the leaves is generally oval, but there are also decorative dahlias that have deeply cut, fernlike foliage.

Exhibition dahlias are best grown alone in a bed where there is plenty of sun. They should not be in the shade of buildings or of overhanging trees. They can, however, be used in a perennial border: the yellow, scarlet, and bronze varieties contrast well with white flowers or those with cool colors. Wherever used, these striking flowers bring a richness, splendor, variety, and warmth of hue to the late-summer garden that few other flower species in North America can equal.

Plant bedding dahlias, either of one color or a variety of colors chosen to blend well together, in groups of three or five along the edge of a border or in a bed by themselves.

Decorative, cactus, semi-cactus, collarette, ball, and pompon dahlias should be planted singly or in groups of three of one variety.

If you are mixing types, groups of three planted in a triangular pattern make the best display.

It is essential to reach the tall kinds for tying, disbudding, fertilizing, and weeding; so leave an access path when planting.

At the end of the season there is usually no urgent need to clear the bed and lift the tubers if the dahlias have been grown for garden display. They can be left in the ground until autumn frosts blacken the leaves.

With exhibition plants, however, there is little point in leaving them in the ground after the tubers have ripened. A spell of cold, wet weather can encourage the growth of fungi and bacteria, and valuable plants can be destroyed.

As soon as the tubers are ripe, lift them. The evidence of ripeness is when the leaves begin to turn yellow, blooms are poorly colored and somewhat daisy eyed, and bud production is slowing down.

Do not lift the tubers before they are ripe, because they must absorb enough nourishment from the leaves to carry them through the winter and to produce strong new growth the next season. In short-season climates this will probably mean leaving them in the ground until after the first heavy frost.

Dahlias grown from seeds form tuberous roots, but most gardeners discard the tubers and plant new seeds the next year.

Single. *One row of petals (two if duplex) encircles a central disk of stamens.*

Orchid. *Outer, or ray, petals curve up and in around the central disk.*

Anemone. *Flat ray petals surround tightly packed, tubular disk petals.*

Collarette. *A collar of small petals is between the ray petals and the yellow disk.*

Peony. *Two to four rows of flat ray petals surround a disk of twisted petaloids.*

Cactus. *Fully double flowers have narrow, pointed ray petals, quilled for more than half their length. There are two types: incurved (left) and recurved, or straight (right).*

Semi-cactus. *Similar to cactus, but petals are broader and quilled for half their length or less.*

Decorative. *The double flowers have no central disk. Petals are broad, rounded at the ends, and slightly curved in. Formal style (left) is symmetrical; informal (right) is irregular.*

Where, When, and How to Plant Dahlias

Sun and Rich Soil for Better Blooms

Dahlias need full sun and a rich, porous soil that retains moisture well but drains easily. Ideal soil pH is neutral to slightly acid.

Locate dahlias in a warm, sunny spot where there is good air circulation. A site with some shade from the afternoon sun will do.

Since dahlias are heavy feeders, in the fall dig into the bed a rich dressing of dried or well-rotted manure, compost, or other organic material. Sprinkle on a topdressing of 4 ounces of bone meal or 2 ounces of superphosphate for each square yard. To allow frost and air to penetrate and break down the added materials, do not smooth down the ground. If the soil is not rich, apply a complete fertilizer (such as 5–10–10), according to package directions, monthly after growth begins.

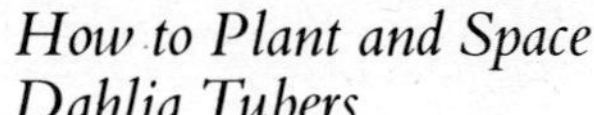

How to Plant and Space Dahlia Tubers

Plant tubers as soon as the danger of frost no longer exists—mid to late spring in most areas. Allow 2–3 feet between tubers for tall dahlias (4–5 feet), 2 feet between for medium plants (3–4 feet), and 15 inches between for shorter ones.

New growth comes from eyes at the base of the previous year's stem. Each stem has several tuberous roots. These can be planted as a clump or divided into single tubers (see p. 282).

In the planting bed insert a 1-inch-square stake long enough to support tall plants. In front of it dig a 6-inch-deep hole. Prepare a mixture of half peat moss and half soil, and incorporate about a handful of bone meal. Fill the hole with this mixture to a level that will bring the tuber's eye to about 2 inches below the surface. Place the tuber in front of the stake with the eye against it. Cover the tuber to ground level with the soil and peat moss mixture. Firm the soil gently over the tuber. Except in extremely arid regions, do not water until new growth begins. Label the stake.

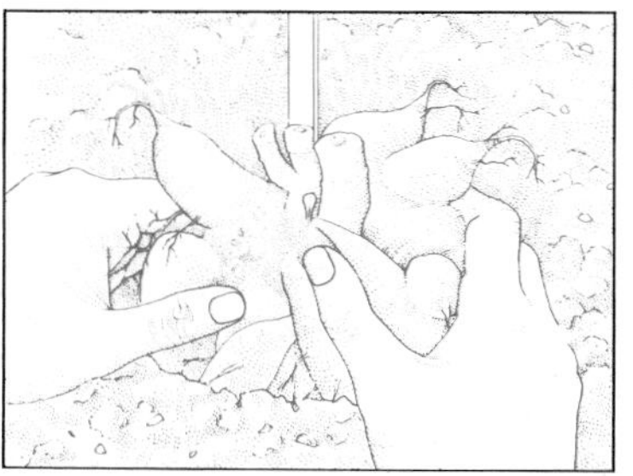

1. *Partly fill hole with enriched soil. Plant tuber with its eye against a stake.*

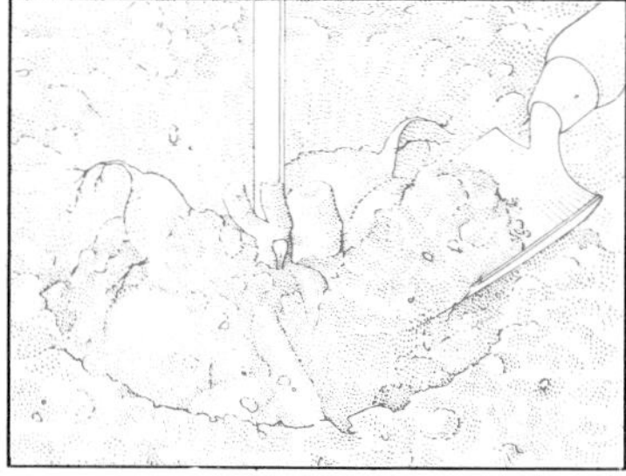

2. *Cover with soil, filling spaces between roots. Eyes should be 2 in. deep.*

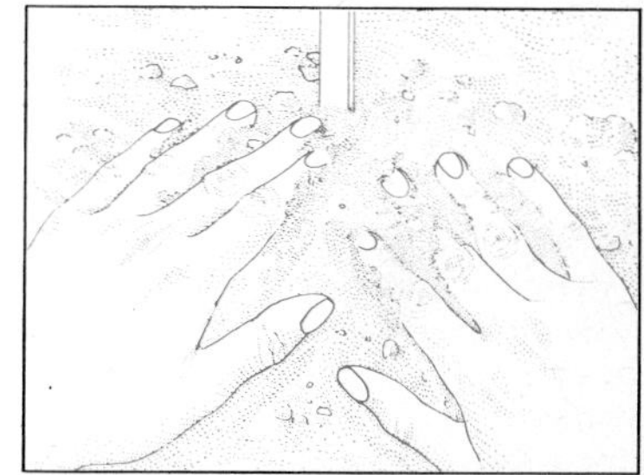

3. *Firm down soil over tuber. Label the stake with variety name.*

Ball. *The spherical flowers have blunt, quilled petals, set in a spiral pattern.*

Pompon. *The flower is a ball type, but less than 2 in. wide. Those 2–4 in. are called miniatures.*

Setting Out Young Pot-Grown Plants

Young plants in pots can be bought from mail-order growers, local nurseries, and garden-supply centers. Mail-order houses generally ship when it is the appropriate time for planting in your area—after the last frost has occurred.

Pot-grown plants are planted in much the same way as tubers (described above). Before you plant, set out stakes; space according to ultimate size. Water the plants lightly. Prepare a mixture of half soil and half peat moss; work a handful of bone meal thoroughly into the mixture so that it is evenly distributed.

Next to the stake dig a hole 2–3 inches deeper than the root ball and wide enough to fit it. Add a few handfuls of the mixture. Remove the plant from the pot with soil ball intact. If the roots appear twined, do not try to get them loose.

Set the ball in the hole with its top 2 inches below soil surface. Make sure the stem is straight and close to the stake. Fill the hole with the soil and peat moss mixture and tamp it down, leaving a shallow depression around the stem in which moisture can collect to give plants a good start. After about two days water well. When the plant begins to show signs of top growth, fill up the depression around the stem with soil, and firm it down level with the surrounding soil.

1. *An hour before planting, water plant lightly. Prepare enriched soil.*

2. *Set in stake, and dig hole beside it. Remove plant from pot.*

3. *Put plant in hole, and fill in with soil mixture, leaving a depression.*

Caring for Dahlias Throughout the Year

Water Thoroughly As the Buds Develop

When potted plants or tubers are first planted, watering represents a danger to them—it can cause the tubers to rot. It does the roots no harm to search for moisture.

For the best results, give dahlias a great deal of moisture as they approach their flowering season. In dry spells the plants should be watered freely, whether or not they are coming into bloom.

When weather is hot and sunny, water every five days or so on heavy clay soils. Lighter soils dry out more quickly, and the plants should be watered about every three days.

It is best to use an automatic sprinkler that throws a fine spray up high enough for the water to fall vertically on the plants. This will ensure that the whole area around the dahlias receives the required thorough soaking.

If, however, you use a can or hose, give about 3 gallons of water to each plant when they are 2–3 feet apart; use less if they are set closer together.

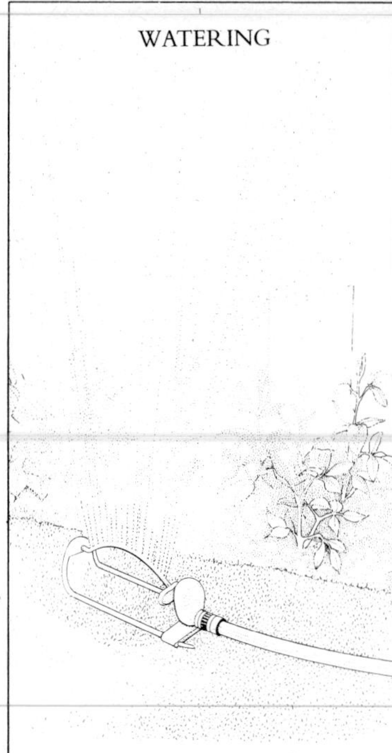

Use a sprinkler so that a fine spray will fall on the plants.

Mulch Plants to Keep Down Weeds

When the plant is about 12 inches high, put a 1-inch layer of mulch around the base but not against the stem. This helps keep down weeds and retain moisture. Use materials such as wood chips, buckwheat hulls, cocoa shells, or clean, dry straw.

If you mulch with grass clippings, do not use grass from a lawn that has been treated with a selective weed killer. Apply in thin layers, and allow each to dry before applying more.

Do not mulch too early. Wait until the plants have grown to a height of 1 foot. The ground should be moist when mulch is applied and well soaked immediately after.

If weeds appear before mulching, remove them by hoeing, which will also keep the soil aerated. Do not disturb more than an inch of soil.

Dampen the ground and apply a 1-in. layer of mulch. Water well.

Remove early weeds with a hoe. Do not hoe more than 1 in. deep.

Add Supports As the Dahlias Grow

Dahlias need support to prevent wind damage.

Two or three weeks after planting, loop string around each stake 4–8 inches above the ground. Tie every plant, taking the string around the stem in a figure eight. Fasten the knot against the stake.

As the plants grow, make further ties higher up the stem. Be sure the lower ties have not become too tight around the main stem.

To prevent damage to the side growths, insert thin canes firmly in the ground—three in a triangular pattern around the main stake and about 9 inches from it—sloping out. Loop soft string around these canes to support the side growths.

1. *Two or three weeks after planting, tie each plant to its stake with soft string.*

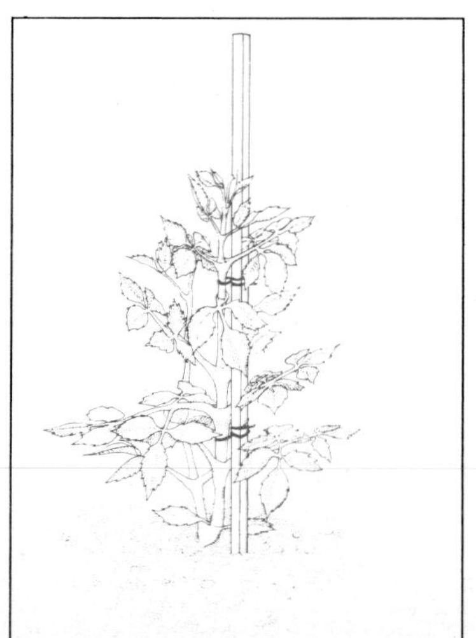

2. *As the plants grow, add more ties. Check that lower ties are not too tight.*

3. *Support side shoots with soft string tied around a triangle of thin stakes.*

Pinching Out and Disbudding the Big Dahlias

Most exhibition or large-flowered dahlias send up strong center shoots but develop little side growth until the center shoots have flower buds.

To encourage side growth and more flowers, pinch out the center shoots two or three weeks after planting. The center shoot is the growing tip of the stem. Usually, this is done in late spring or early summer for tuber-grown plants and somewhat later for pot-grown plants.

In two weeks or so half a dozen side shoots should have developed in the leaf axils. Remove the top pair of shoots to promote growth in the lower side shoots. These will each produce a terminal bud and several side buds.

To encourage big flowers, remove the side buds as soon as they are large enough to be removed without harming the tip buds.

To promote longer-stemmed side shoots and to encourage more growth in the upper part of the dahlias, cut off all the leaves that develop on the main stem a few inches from the ground.

1. *Two or three weeks after planting, pinch out growing point of main stem.*

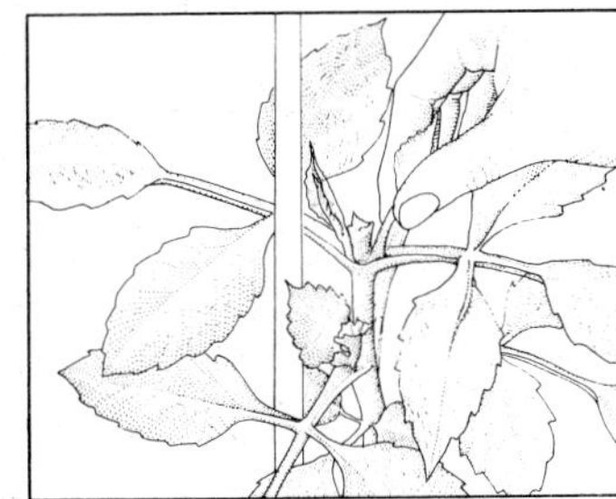

2. *Two weeks later remove the top pair of side shoots from leaf axils.*

3. *For large blooms remove side buds from remaining side shoots later on.*

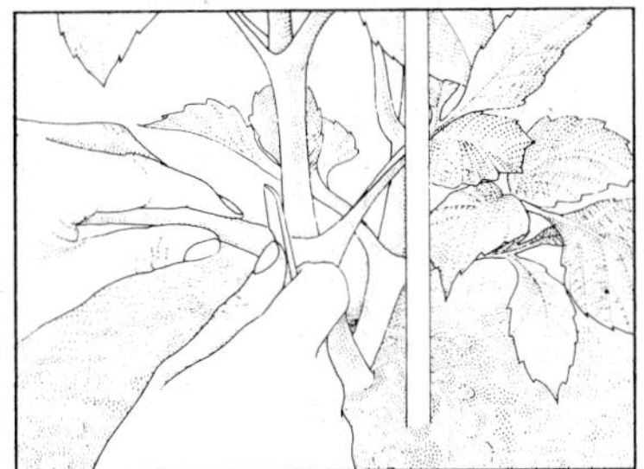

4. *Cut off leaves growing on main stem within a few inches of ground.*

What Can Go Wrong With Dahlias

On the chart below are listed the pests and diseases that can afflict dahlias. If your plants show symptoms not described, consult the section on plant disorders on page 600.

Look up chemicals on page 635 to find trade names.

Symptoms and signs	Cause	Control
Young shoots (particularly ones with flower buds) are stunted or malformed and covered with small, sticky, black or green insects.	Aphids	Spray with carbaryl, Diazinon, malathion, or systemic insecticide, such as dimethoate or oxydemeton-methyl.
Buds, flowers, and new leaves are eaten; tips die. Stems and stalks tunneled; plants later wilt.	Borers (European corn or stalk)	Dust plants weekly with carbaryl, methoxychlor, or rotenone. Lindane excellent in areas where use not restricted.
Petals are eaten; flowers look ragged.	Earwigs	Spray with chlorpyrifos, Diazinon, or trichlorfon. Alternatively, invert 3-in. pot on stake after loosely packing pot with straw; earwigs will crawl up into container. Shake out pot daily over bowl of hot water.
Flower buds and opening flowers are deformed. Leaves develop irregular holes and are spotted, ragged, or malformed.	Plant bugs, or leaf bugs	Spray with carbaryl, Diazinon, malathion, or nicotine.
Leaves are finely mottled, with overall silvery look.	Thrips	Spray or dust with Diazinon, malathion, or methoxychlor.
Leaves and shoots of young plants are eaten. Silvery slime trails may be apparent.	Slugs or snails	Apply slug killer (in liquid or pellet form), such as metaldehyde or methiocarb.
Leaves develop yellow or brown rings or spots and may be distorted. Plants are stunted.	Virus disease	No chemical control. To prevent spread of disease, remove and destroy affected plants immediately. Spray for control of insects that carry virus.
Plants are dwarfed, with thin stems and relatively small yellowish leaves.	Nutrient deficiency	Dahlias are heavy feeders and require moist, fertile soil. Apply dressing of rotted compost or manure; feed with balanced all-purpose fertilizer (5–10–5).

An Extra Feeding for Healthy Growth

Soil that has been well fed before planting will not need much additional fertilizer during the growing season. Mulching with rotted manure or rich compost will help to develop the growth of the plants if the soil is poor or if extraordinary blooms are the objective.

An additional feeding can be given when bedding dahlias show their first buds or after exhibition dahlias have been pinched out for the second time.

For quick results, use a 20–20–20 fast-release liquid fertilizer. For a slower response, scatter a handful of 5–10–10 around the plant.

Too much nitrogen at this time of year will encourage an overabundance of foliage rather than flowers and can reduce the winter storage quality of the tubers as well. After feeding the dahlias with any dry fertilizer, water them well to make sure that the nutrients are carried all the way down to the root area.

It can be helpful to feed the plants every two to three weeks until the end of summer. If you plan to store the tubers, top-dress the soil in late summer or very early fall with a mixture of equal parts of superphosphate and sulfate of potash.

Cutting Flowers for Indoor Display

The best time to cut dahlia blooms is in the evening or early morning, when the air is cool and the stems are full of moisture.

Cut the stems with a sharp knife rather than scissors or pruning shears, which might bruise the stems and reduce their ability to take up water. Make the cut at a 45-degree angle to expose more of the stem. The length of the stem should be in proportion to the size of the flower. Giant blooms will probably need stems about 2 feet long; smaller blooms can be cut proportionately shorter.

Take a container of warm water with you when cutting the blooms. Plunge them into it immediately, and when you take them indoors, transfer them to a bucket of cold water up to the top of the stems. Hold them underwater, and cut another inch off the stems. Leave flowers in a cool place for a few hours before arranging them.

Use a sharp knife to prevent bruising. Cut stems and immediately plunge them into warm water up to the blossoms.

Storing Tubers to Survive the Winter

At the end of the growing season, exhibition dahlias should be lifted and stored for the winter in a frost-free place. The following spring they can be used for stem cuttings, or be divided and replanted.

In some mild parts of the country, where the soil is sandy and the water table is low, tubers can be left in the ground through the winter, but there is always the danger that in a particularly severe winter they will be killed. The damage to the tubers is caused by a combination of cold and damp soil.

Immediately after the first frosts in autumn have blackened the foliage, cut the stems back to about 6 inches above the ground. The roots can be left in the ground for two or three more weeks if light frosts come early in your area, but they should be lifted immediately if there happens to be a hard frost.

With a fork loosen the soil around the tubers, being careful not to damage them, and lift them by pressing back on the handle. Using a blunt-ended stick, gently remove surplus soil from between the tubers. Take care not to break off any of the old stems. Tie labels to the stumps of the stems for easy identification in the spring.

Place the tubers upside down in a dry, airy place for about two weeks to allow the moisture to drain out of the stems. If it collects there, it will cause the necks to rot, and although the tubers may not be damaged, the area of new growth will be lost. The tubers must be completely dry before they are stored for the winter.

Dust the tubers with sulfur to prevent fungous attack, and store them in a cool, dry, frost-free place away from drafts.

Where winter temperatures stay above 15° F, a simple and easy way to store tubers is to place 6 inches of dry leaves or peat moss in the bottom of a 2-foot-deep cold frame. Space out the tubers on the leaves, keeping them 9 inches from the sides of the frame. Cover tubers with another layer of dry leaves or peat moss at least 12 inches deep.

Finally, cover with a piece of burlap or similar material to absorb condensation. The leaves will insulate the roots against heavy frosts. Replace the frame top.

Alternatively, store the tubers in trays of dry sand or peat moss beneath the benches in a cool greenhouse or in a dry cellar or cupboard at 40°–45° F. Never store them in a warm cupboard; they will dry out and shrivel rapidly.

When only a few tubers are to be stored, netting or sealing the roots will provide adequate protection. For netting, first wrap the roots in straw. Place tubers inside garden netting drawn tightly into a hammock shape; hang from the ceiling of a frost-free building until spring. The tubers can also be placed in a box lined with sheets of Styrofoam (sold for insulation) about $\frac{1}{2}$ inch thick.

Alternatively, store tubers by placing them in a heavy-grade, black plastic bag without additional packing material, and seal the bag tightly with wire. This will prevent the roots from dehydrating; however, there is a danger that they will sweat and rot. Keep the tubers in a frost-free shed or, if you have such a space, underneath the basement stairs indoors. In spring new shoots will have developed on the crowns.

It is advisable to inspect the tubers every few weeks during the winter to check for disease or shriveling. Diseased parts can be cut off and the wounds dusted with sulfur. Place shriveled tubers in a bucket of water overnight to plump them up. Allow them to dry thoroughly before returning them to storage.

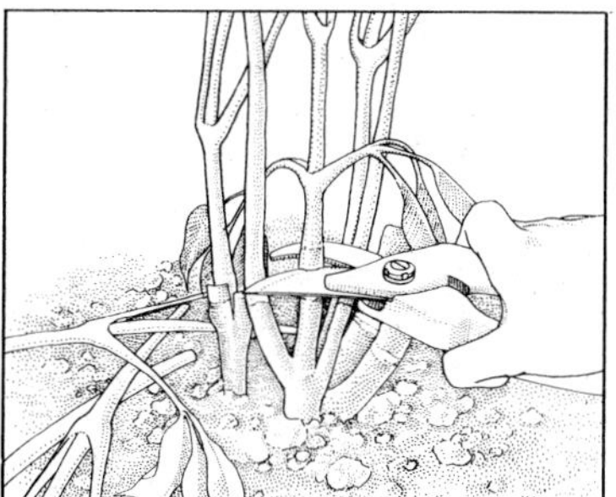

1. *As soon as frost has blackened the foliage, cut stems back to about 6 in.*

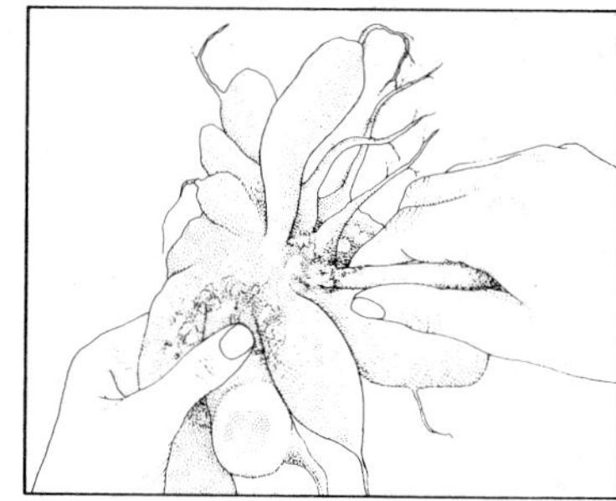

2. *Lift tubers and with a blunt stick remove loose soil from between them.*

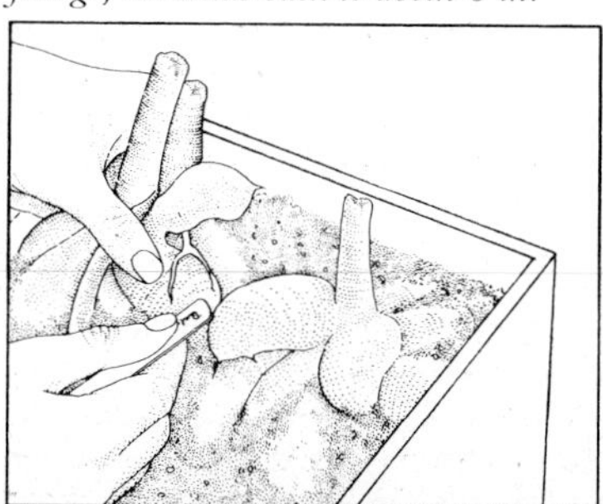

3. *Place tubers on a 6-in. layer of peat moss or dry leaves in a box.*

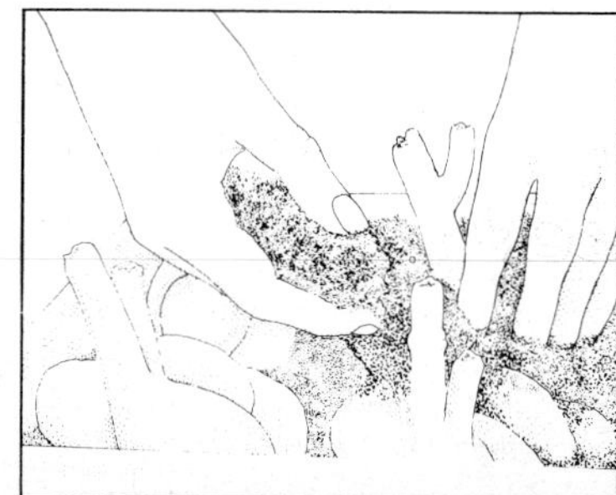

4. *Cover with another layer of peat moss or dry leaves, about 12 in. deep.*

How to Grow New Dahlias From Existing Stock

Taking Cuttings for the Greatest Number of Plants

New plants can be raised from cuttings or by division of tubers in spring. Tubers deteriorate if they are not separated at regular intervals; so replanting the parent clump indefinitely is not recommended. Only exhibition or big dahlias are grown from cuttings or by tuber division. Small bedding types are usually started from seeds each season.

Seeds collected from exhibition plants will not run true to parent color or form, but plants grown from cuttings or division reproduce the parent plants exactly.

In late winter or early spring, take the tubers from storage, clean away any old soil, cut out diseased parts, and dust the wounds with sulfur.

To start new plants from cuttings, place the tubers in a flat or on a layer of loamy soil, peat moss, or compost. Cover them with this material to just below the old stems. Water moderately. Place the flat in a greenhouse or cool (between 60° and 65° F), sunny window; keep the soil moist.

In two or three weeks, when shoots are 3–4 inches long, cut them off a little above their bases with a sharp knife or razor blade. Do not cut out any of the tuber itself, since this will prevent more new shoots from forming.

The first shoots may be hollow. Discard these, since they are hard to root. Subsidiary stems will develop after the first shoots, and these are usually normal and more suitable for propagation.

Trim back shoots to just below the lowest leaf joint. Remove the lowest pair of leaves, taking special care neither to injure the buds that will have developed in the leaf axils nor to leave stem stubs.

For each four shoots fill a 3-inch peat pot with equal parts of peat moss and sand. Make four holes about 1 inch deep around the edge.

Dip the base of each cutting in water and then into hormone rooting powder. Place cuttings in the holes, and firm the mixture around the cuttings. Water the pots, label them, and mark the date.

Place pots in an unheated propagating case in the greenhouse; or tent them with plastic, and set them in a cool, well-lighted window. Keep soil moderately moist. Ventilate to avoid excessive humidity and condensation, which will encourage the growth of fungus. Keep cuttings shaded from direct sun.

After two or three weeks, when cuttings have roots—indicated by the growth of new leaves—put them singly into 3-inch peat pots. Use any sterile potting soil that drains well, and keep it uniformly moist.

After potting, shade the plants for two days. Then until late spring keep them in a well-ventilated greenhouse or in an airy place indoors where there is sun. Then move them to a cold frame for hardening off. The frame need not be closed unless there is danger of frost.

If you have no cold frame, harden off the plants in a warm, sunny, sheltered corner outdoors for one week before planting. In cold climates postpone the hardening-off process until after the last frost.

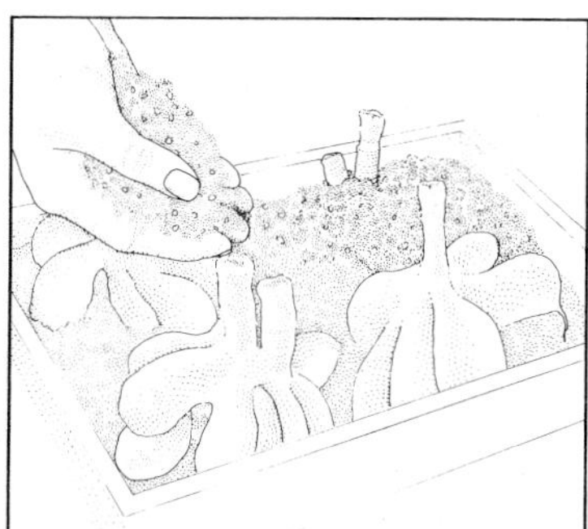

1. *Take tubers from storage, clean, and cover with damp soil or peat moss.*

2. *Keep in a greenhouse or window until shoots are 3–4 in. high; then sever.*

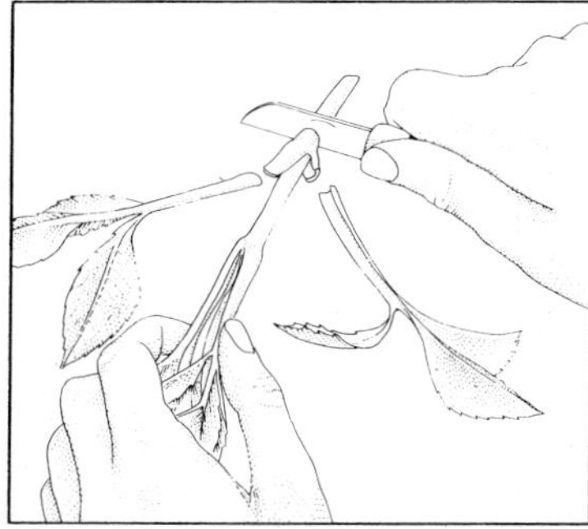

3. *Trim shoots with a sharp knife, and remove the lowest pair of leaves.*

4. *Dip cuttings in rooting powder, and plant in pots of peat moss and sand.*

5. *Water well. Label the pots and set in a cool, well-lighted, protected spot.*

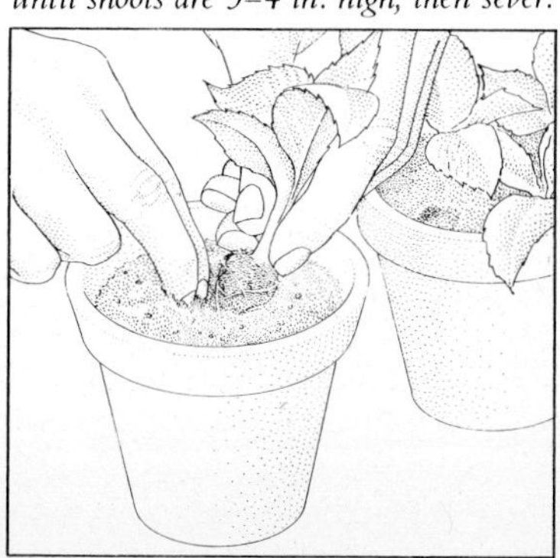

6. *After two or three weeks pot the cuttings individually in 3-in. pots.*

7. *Shade plants for two days; then move to greenhouse or sunny, airy window.*

8. *After the last frost harden off in a cold frame for a week; then plant out.*

Dividing Tubers: The Easy Way to Propagate

Propagating by taking cuttings produces more new plants, but propagating by dividing tubers is easier—so if the need is for only a few new plants, divide the old tubers in mid or late spring.

For each new plant you will need one section of the tuberous root and a piece of the stem with an eye in it. New growth comes from this eye.

Each plant needs only enough tuber to keep the plant growing until new roots form. A single piece of tuber with a single piece of stem attached is best. Too large a section of the tuberous root will delay formation of new roots, and the plant will produce a mass of leafy growth, which will further result in few and inferior blooms.

Before cutting the clump of tubers, examine each stem to locate the eyes. If they prove difficult to locate, place the tubers in damp peat moss or soil, and keep them in a warm place for a few days to give the buds time to develop.

As soon as the eyes or buds are visible, use a sharp knife to cut down through the stem, doing your best not to damage any of the eyes in the process. Dust raw cuts thoroughly with sulfur to prevent rot.

Plant the divisions of the tubers following the techniques described on page 277. The best time for planting in most areas is late spring or early summer—or as soon as all danger of frost is past.

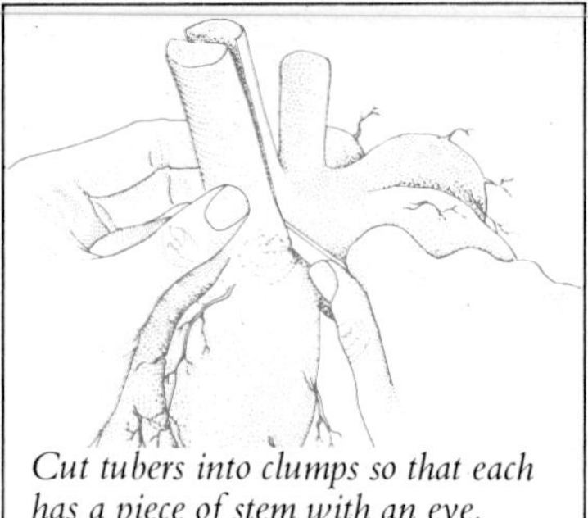

Cut tubers into clumps so that each has a piece of stem with an eye.

Growing Annual Dahlias From Seeds

Seeds are sold for both small bedding dahlias and tall exhibition kinds, but they will not run true in color or form. To start a collection of exhibition dahlias from seeds, plant them one year, and save the tubers of the best plants for the next year.

Start seeds in early spring if an indoor space or a warm greenhouse is available. In a cold frame plant four to six weeks before the safe outdoor planting date.

Prepare pots or flats of sterilized soil or seed-starting mixture, level the surface, and firm it. Water thoroughly. Thinly sprinkle the seeds over the surface, and cover them with about $\frac{1}{4}$ inch of vermiculite. Cover the pots or flats with glass shaded by brown paper or with plastic film. Set in a warm place in a greenhouse or in a dim, warm room to germinate—in 10 to 21 days.

When the seedlings are up, remove the glass or plastic. If you are growing them indoors, set them on a sunny sill. When the seedlings are sturdy, transplant them to individual 3-inch peat pots filled with potting soil. Once established, they can take full light and sun.

If the plants are being grown in a cold frame, harden them there several weeks before setting them out. If there is no cold frame, set them in a dependably warm, sunny spot outdoors for a week before planting.

For instructions on planting potted dahlias outdoors, see page 277.

COLLECTING YOUR OWN SEEDS

1. *When the seed heads of annual dahlias begin to go dry, remove them with 9-in.-long stems.*

2. *Hang heads upside down in a dry place until the heads are dry. Remove seeds and store them.*

1. *In spring sprinkle seeds in 5-in. pot. Lightly cover with vermiculite.*

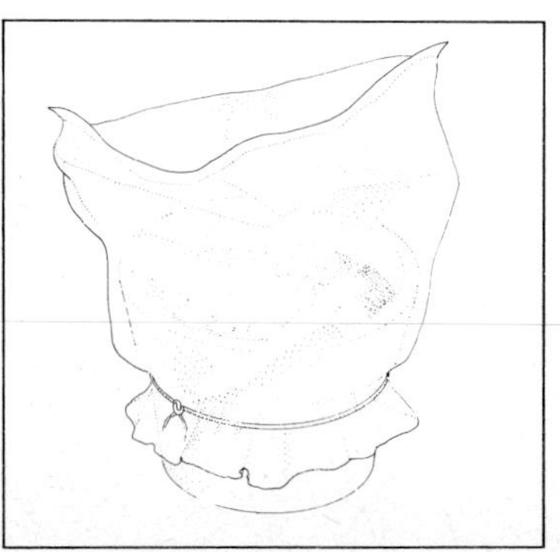

2. *After watering, cover with a plastic bag. Keep warm, out of direct sun.*

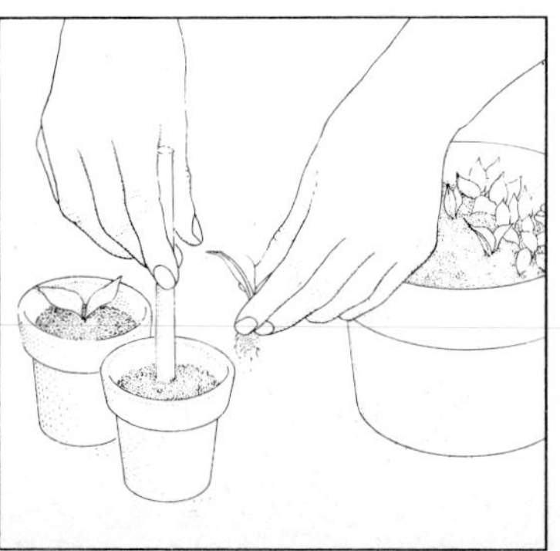

3. *As soon as the seedlings are sturdy, transplant into individual 3-in. pots.*

4. *After the last frost harden off the plants in a cold frame.*

Annuals and Biennials

A garden can be quickly filled with color by using annuals and biennials. These plants flower longer than many others and are ideal for filling gaps in a border.

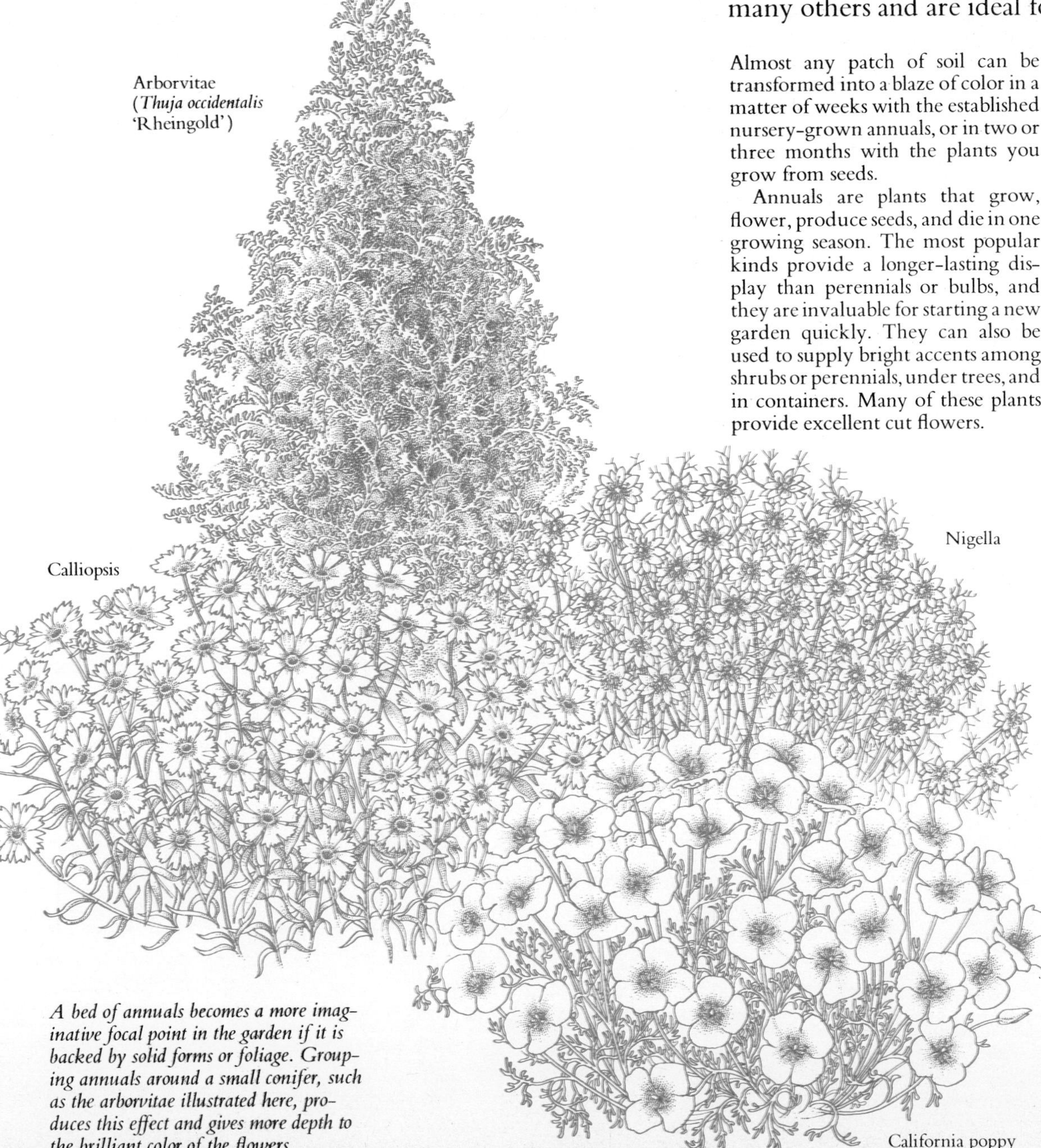

A bed of annuals becomes a more imaginative focal point in the garden if it is backed by solid forms or foliage. Grouping annuals around a small conifer, such as the arborvitae illustrated here, produces this effect and gives more depth to the brilliant color of the flowers.

Almost any patch of soil can be transformed into a blaze of color in a matter of weeks with the established nursery-grown annuals, or in two or three months with the plants you grow from seeds.

Annuals are plants that grow, flower, produce seeds, and die in one growing season. The most popular kinds provide a longer-lasting display than perennials or bulbs, and they are invaluable for starting a new garden quickly. They can also be used to supply bright accents among shrubs or perennials, under trees, and in containers. Many of these plants provide excellent cut flowers.

Most annuals are inexpensive, easy to grow, and available in a broad range of colors and heights.

Plants that are similar in their general effect are biennials, such as sweet Williams. These are started from seeds one year; they flower the next year; and then they die.

In mild climates, however, some of the plants grown as annuals may survive the winter (they actually are tender perennials), and some biennials can be grown as annuals.

Annuals are classified in most books, in some catalogs, and on some seed packets according to the British system, which divides them into two groups—hardy and half-hardy. The hardy annuals, which tolerate cold weather, can be sown earlier than half-hardy annuals. This terminology often proves more confusing than helpful, however, because it does not apply to all areas of the United States. Therefore, it is not being used in this book.

The quickest and easiest way to enjoy flowers in the garden is to purchase young annuals or biennials in plant form in spring (or even fall in warmer climates) and set them directly in the garden. A wide choice of plants is available, but seeds, especially those offered in catalogs, provide an even greater diversity.

Seeds can be given an extraearly start (especially in cold regions) by sowing them in a protected and controlled environment. This is almost a necessity for very fine seeds, such as those of the wax begonia; for seeds that need high temperatures to germinate, such as those of the impatiens; and for those plants that are slow to bloom from seeds, such as the vinca, petunia, and ageratum. Seeds can be started indoors if sufficient light and proper temperature are provided (see p. 287); or outdoors if a cold frame or hotbed that protects them from the elements can be located advantageously.

Seeds can also be sown directly outdoors where they are to flower. This is a popular and practical method for plants that bloom quickly and those that have large seeds (see p. 286).

Biennials, although fewer in number than the annuals or perennials, have some of the showiest flowers. Particularly popular are sweet Williams, Canterbury bells, foxgloves, hollyhocks, and pansies. They are usually sown in the late spring or early summer outdoors in a protected location.

When seedlings are large enough to handle, they can be transplanted in rows to grow until late summer. By then they should be sturdy enough to be transplanted to permanent positions or to spend the winter in a cold frame.

Many annuals and biennials have been garden favorites for centuries. A worthwhile advance in recent years has been the development of the F_1, first generation, and the F_2, second generation, hybrids (the F stands for filial). They are the end result of selecting and inbreeding different parent lines of the same plant to get the most desirable characteristics and then cross-pollinating the plants to combine the best characteristics of each.

Several generations of this kind of breeding are required to produce plants of the desired quality. Some home gardeners may be deterred by the relatively high price of the seeds, especially since seeds saved from such hybrid plants will not produce plants of equal vigor or identical color the next year.

But the first generation of flowers grown from F_1 hybrid seeds will demonstrate such superiority to the less expensive types that they are well worth the added cost. These hybrids offer clearer colors, more vigor, larger size, greater weather and disease resistance, and better, more uniform growth habits than their forebears.

F_2 hybrids are the results of the hybridizers' attempts to improve the quality without the high cost of the F_1 method. This is achieved by self-fertilizing the F_1's. In some cases, for example with pansies, it has worked. Generally, the F_2 hybrids are an improvement on standard seeds, though not so spectacular as the F_1's. Most seed catalogs do not mention the designations, but the difference in the price is usually an indication that the most expensive seeds are F_1 hybrids or a new variety.

Selecting varieties from a catalog or seed rack can be confusing. In an attempt to simplify the choice, an organization known as All-America Seed Selections, founded in 1932, began growing new varieties submitted by hybridizers in official test gardens throughout this country. Those awarded the highest number of points are designated as the All-America Selections, and every seed packet of those varieties is so labeled. The buyer can be assured that these varieties have proved to be superior to other plants under varied climatic and soil conditions.

Among the most recent All-Americas are the geranium 'Showgirl,' a compact, early-blooming, rose-pink plant; the marigold 'Primrose Lady,' with large, light yellow flowers on $2\frac{1}{2}$-foot plants; the marigold 'Yellow Galore,' large flowered, butter-yellow, and $1\frac{1}{2}$ feet tall; and the petunia 'Blushing Maid,' a soft salmon-pink double flower with ruffled petals. Other All-Americas are indicated by an asterisk on the chart beginning on page 291.

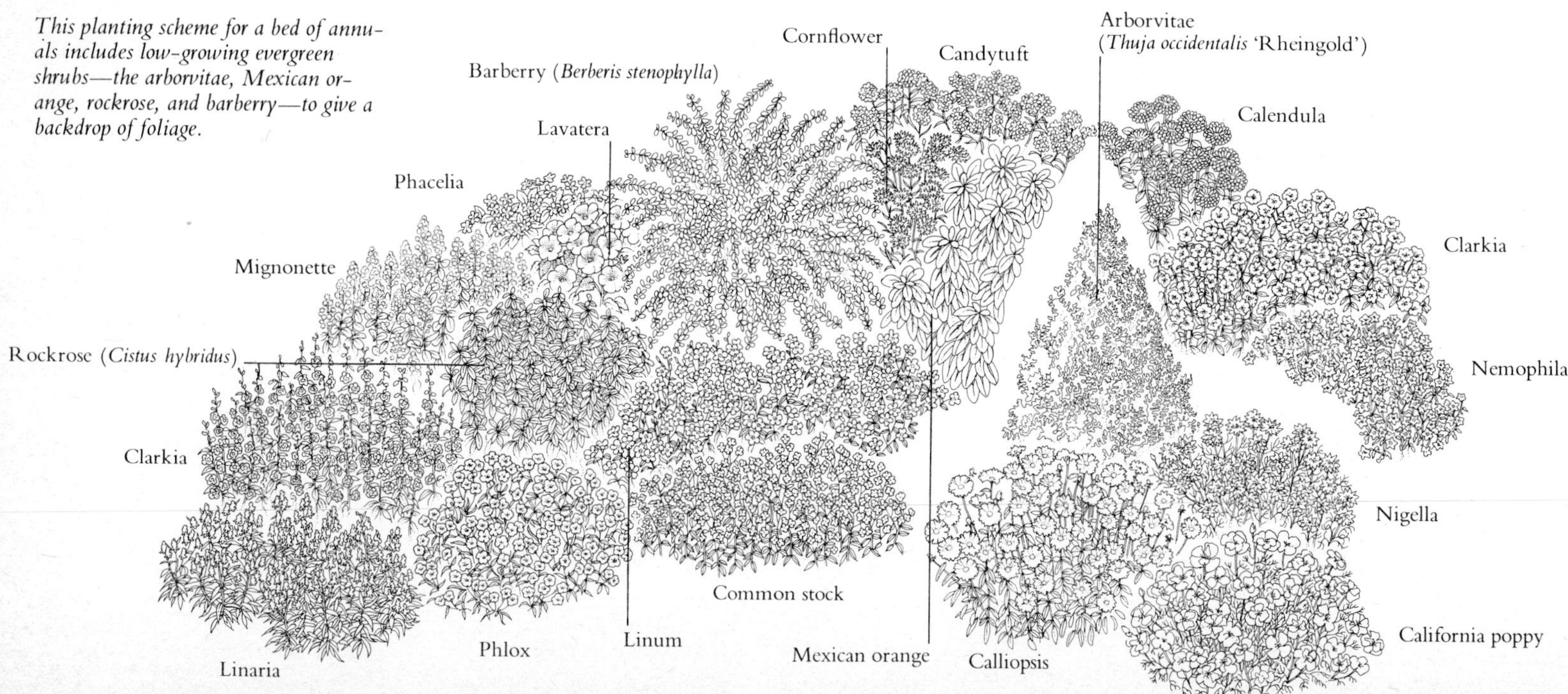

This planting scheme for a bed of annuals includes low-growing evergreen shrubs—the arborvitae, Mexican orange, rockrose, and barberry—to give a backdrop of foliage.

Set Out Bedding Plants for Quick Color

Garden stores offer a wide variety of bedding plants that can be set directly into the garden or planted in pots and boxes. Such plants have usually been grown from seeds that started in a greenhouse and may be from six weeks old to more than three months old. They will flower much earlier than if the seeds had been sown directly outdoors.

Bedding plants are generally sold in small flats containing 6 to 12 plants or in individual plastic or peat pots. It is usually best to avoid buying plants in full bloom, as these often take longer to become established in the garden than younger plants. Always check the color of the leaves. If pale or yellow, these plants may be stunted from insufficient water or fertilizer and may be slow to develop new growth after transplanting.

Determine your needs before buying plants. List the areas to be planted, and note how much sun each area receives. Indicate the number of plants and the colors and heights you want. Use your list as a guide in the garden store. If you are uncertain as to whether a particular plant is suitable for a given area, ask the advice of a store employee. A seed catalog or book can be used to check the information.

Should you be unable to set the plants outside the day you buy them, put them where they will get good light and keep them watered.

For large plantings of assorted annuals, it helps to have a plan on paper to show the approximate location of each grouping. Mark the corresponding areas directly on the soil with a rake handle, and designate each section with a wooden label. Start to plant from the back of the bed, and work toward the front. Kneel on a flat piece of wood while you are planting to avoid compacting the soil.

Run a knife between the plants, and carefully remove each plant with its roots and soil from the flat. Dig a hole with a trowel, and set the plants in at the same depth they were set in the flat. Never leave a plant on top of the soil for more than a few seconds, or the roots may dry out. If seedlings are in compressed peat pots, break the pots gently before planting. Otherwise, roots may be bound inside, and growth will be hindered. Always cover the top of a peat pot with soil to keep water that is needed by the roots from evaporating.

Water plants individually as you work, or thoroughly water the entire bed when finished. In hot, sunny weather, shade may be needed for a day or two to prevent excessive wilting. A pot or basket inverted over each plant works well if some ventilation is provided. Remove the covering in the late afternoon, and replace it again the next day if it is necessary.

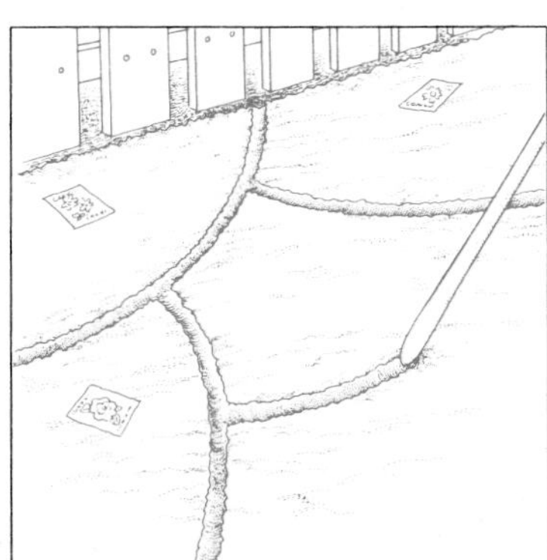

1. *Use a rake handle to mark the area where each variety will be set.*

2. *Before planting out a seedling from a peat pot, tear the pot partly open.*

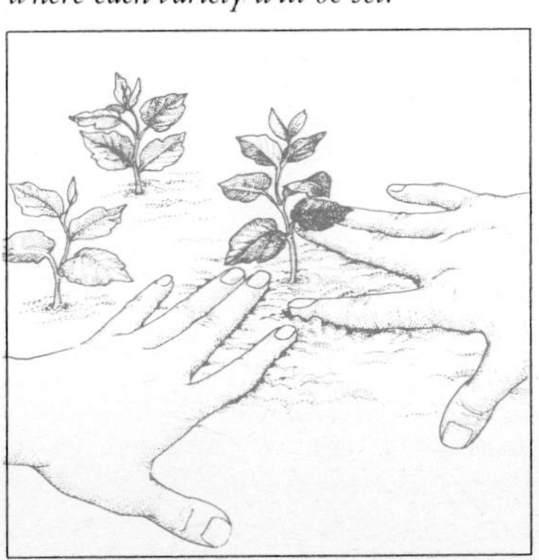

3. *Set the plant at its previous depth; firm the soil with your fingers.*

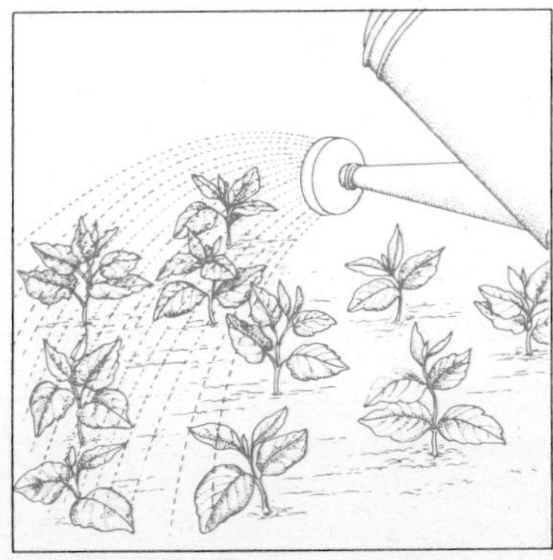

4. *Water the plants immediately in order to settle soil, prevent wilting.*

PLANTING IN CONTAINERS OUTDOORS

1. *Improve the soil by mixing it with one-third by volume of peat moss. This prevents caking.*

2. *Put an inch of pebbles in the bottom of the container for drainage. If the container has no holes, drill some.*

3. *Set the plants in position with the tallest toward the center or rear. Allow enough space for them to grow.*

4. *To prevent water from splashing on foliage and flowers, apply mulch. This also slows drying of soil.*

How to Succeed With Annuals Sown Outdoors

Clearing the Site and Preparing the Soil

Ideally, soil in which annuals are to be grown is best prepared in the fall or at least a few months before sowing seeds. However, if this cannot be done, you should still work in some organic matter before sowing seeds. This will help the seedlings to break through the soil, improve root growth, increase moisture retention, and make cultivation simpler by preventing caking of the soil.

Dig up any weeds and other vegetation, and consign them to the compost pile. Then put down a 1- or 2-inch layer of organic material, such as peat moss, garden compost, or manure (the latter should be well rotted if applied just before sowing). This helps to retain moisture in light sandy soil and breaks up heavy clay soil. Such materials, except for peat moss, also supply some nutrients and help to keep the soil surface from crusting. If lime is needed, it can be added at this time.

Turn the added organic matter into the soil with a spading fork, or use a power tiller to do the job with less effort. If the soil is prepared in the fall, leave it lumpy. In cold climates the soil structure is improved when winter frosts contact a maximum surface, breaking it into a crumbly structure that is preferred by plants.

Slightly moist soil is easier to turn than dry soil, which falls through the spading fork. If the soil is too dry, water a day or so in advance. If rain makes the soil sticky, wait a few days.

If the soil is low in fertility or lacking in humus, a green-manure cover crop can be sown in fall. For example, if annual rye is sown, it can be turned under in spring or any time after it grows to a foot or more in height. This adds humus and nutrients to the soil. Check locally for the recommended cover crops.

In spring (sometimes fall in mild areas) or a few weeks before sowing seeds, loosen the top 6–10 inches of soil with a spading fork or power tiller. The soil should be dry enough so that a handful squeezed into a ball will fall apart readily. If the soil is too wet, and especially if the soil has a high clay content, you are likely to end up with clods that dry as hard as concrete. As you turn the soil over, hit the clods with the back of the spading fork to break them up.

This is a good time to spread a general-purpose organic or inorganic fertilizer evenly over the soil at the specified rate; rake it lightly.

How to Sow Seeds Directly Outdoors

It is a good idea to prepare a planting plan in advance, indicating where each variety is to grow.

Sowing seeds directly where they are to grow eliminates the need for special planting containers, as well as the work involved in transplanting the small seedlings. However, heavy rains can occasionally prove troublesome. Cats and dogs can also be a problem because they love to dig in moist, freshly turned soil.

Most seeds are sold loose in packets, but some are available as pellets, on tapes that can be cut to the desired length, or attached to sticks.

A pellet is made by coating a seed with a decomposable material to increase its size and make spacing easier. The coating also includes plant food and disease-preventive materials to nurture and protect the seedling as soon as it starts to grow.

Seeds on a tape are evenly spaced between two strips of decomposable paper or plastic. Such tape can be cut to a specific length, laid in a furrow, and covered with soil.

A seed stick is a wooden label with a few seeds attached to the base. The label is stuck into the soil so that the seed is planted at the proper depth. Although expensive, seed sticks are practical if only a few plants of a given variety are needed.

As a general rule, most seeds can be sown in the open after the last expected frost. In frost-free regions seeds can be sown much earlier in spring—or in late summer or fall for winter or early-spring bloom.

Water the soil the day before sowing unless it is already moist. If you have not yet added humus, lightly fork a pailful of slightly moist, crumbled peat moss per square yard into the top few inches of soil to keep it from caking. If the ground is too wet, add some dry peat moss.

Mark areas to be planted (as shown below) according to your plan. Within each area seeds can be sown in grooves, or drills, or scattered (broadcast) over the entire section and gently raked into the soil. The advantage of sowing in drills is that it is easier to hoe out weeds between seedlings grown in rows than between those growing at random. Allow ample space between the seeds to minimize thinning out later on.

The distance between rows should be determined by the eventual size of the plants. In general, tall, narrow plants should be spaced in rows that are the width of half their height. For bushy dwarf plants the rows should be the width of their full height. The expected height of a plant is indicated on the seed packet.

Keep the seedbed moist. Use the finest spray from a hose nozzle, and take care not to wash the seeds out or puddle the soil. In sunny weather seedlings may need watering every day. Excessive dryness delays germination and stunts growth.

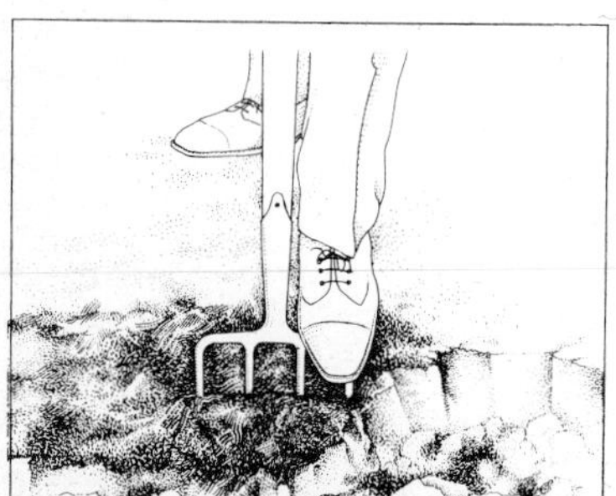

1. *Before sowing seeds, use a fork to incorporate peat moss or compost.*

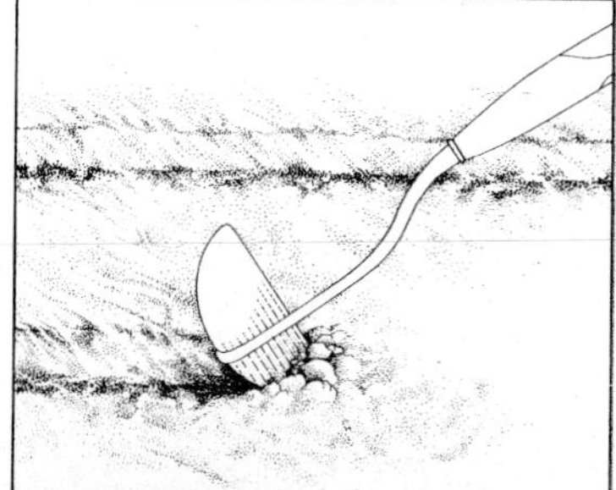

2. *Mark out the rows, $\frac{1}{4}$–$\frac{1}{2}$ in. deep, with the edge of a hoe, or use its handle.*

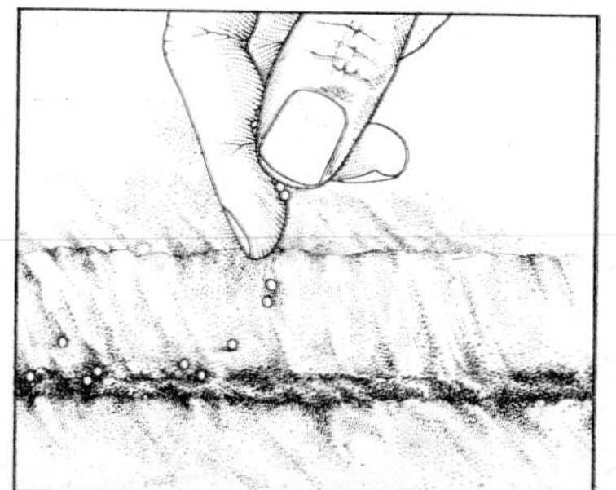

3. *Sow the seeds sparingly to avoid the need for too much thinning later.*

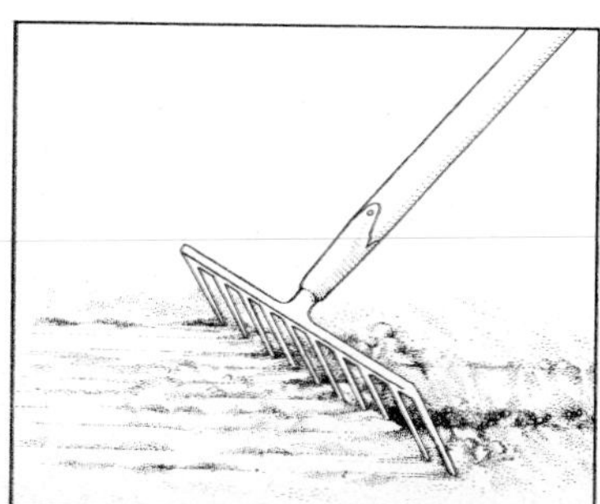

4. *Thinly cover the seeds by drawing a rake lightly along the row.*

Raising Annuals From Seeds Sown Indoors

Sowing Indoors or in a Greenhouse

The requirements for success in starting seeds and growing seedlings indoors are adequate light, a sterilized growing mixture, and the proper temperature. In the home, light is often the limiting factor. Even a window facing south does not have the intensity of a greenhouse's overhead light. However, where natural daylight is nonexistent or insufficient, two 40-watt fluorescent tubes (four are even better) set about 6 inches above the plants will provide adequate light. An indoor temperature of 70°–75° F serves to germinate most seeds, but seedlings grow better at 50°–60° F. Too high a temperature, especially when coupled with insufficient light, results in weak, spindly seedlings that will be difficult to establish when transplanted to the garden.

Sow seeds in flats or pots, or use a presown container. It can be helpful to use a commercial seed-starting mix, which usually consists of peat moss, vermiculite, and/or perlite, with some added nutrients. To mix your own, use equal parts of peat moss, vermiculite, and perlite—none of which require sterilizing. This mixture lacks nutrients, however; so the seedlings will require liquid fertilizer each time they are watered. If sterilized soil is used (see p. 597), feeding will be unnecessary, since soil has adequate nutrients.

Unless you have plenty of room to grow seedlings with adequate spacing, do not start seeds too early, since one pot of seeds can suddenly become many pots of seedlings. For all but the slowest growers, six to eight weeks before the safe outdoor planting date is generally enough time. For really fast growers like French marigolds, four weeks may suffice. The slowest growers, such as wax begonias, impatiens, and vincas, need a three- or four-month advance start to ensure bloom in early summer.

Sow the seeds in rows, particularly when several kinds are grown in one container, or scatter them thinly. Sowing too thickly necessitates transplanting when seedlings are too small to handle easily. Barely cover the seeds with the growing mixture. Very fine seeds, such as those of the wax begonia, need not be covered.

After sowing and covering, gently mist the bed with water. Cover the container with glass or clear plastic; inspect frequently. At the first sign of germination, remove the cover.

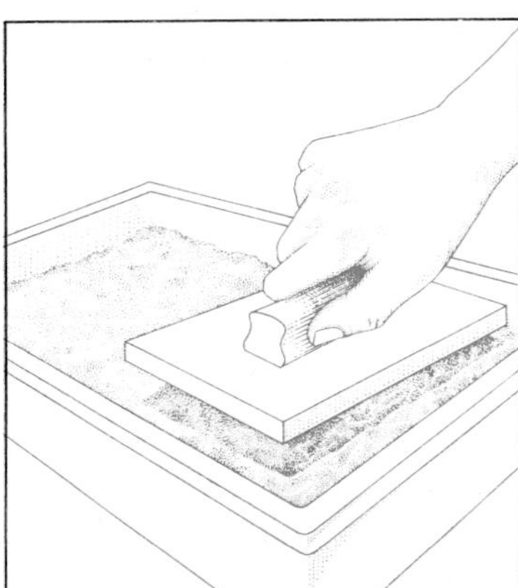

1. *Fill a flat with moist seed-starting medium, level it, and tamp gently.*

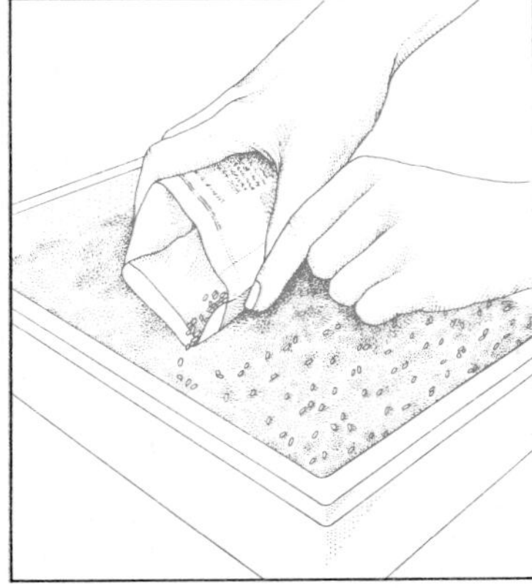

2. *Sprinkle the seeds over the surface or sow in rows. Try to space seeds evenly.*

3. *Cover the seeds with ¼ in. of sifted medium. Fine seeds need no covering.*

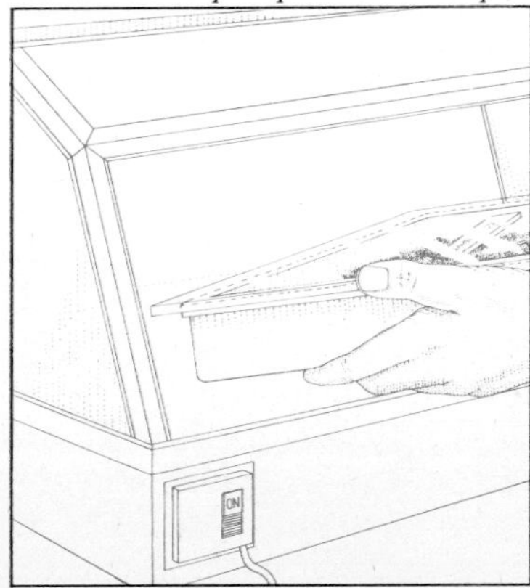

4. *Water the flats and place them in a propagator, or cover with plastic.*

SOWING IN A POT

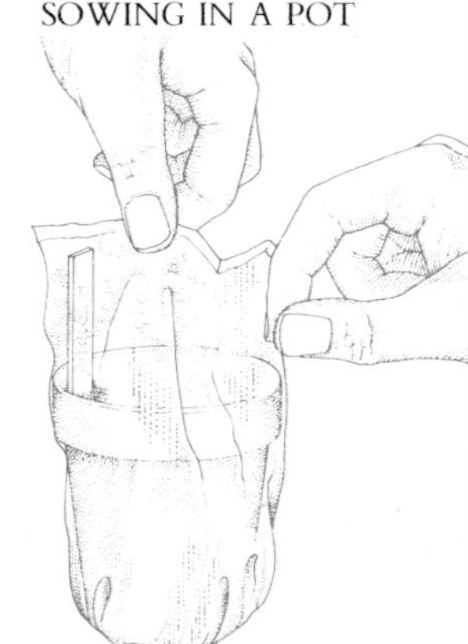

When only a few seeds of a single variety are to be sown, a 2- to 3-in. pot serves as a convenient container. Fill the pot with seed-starting medium to within ¼ in. of the top; level and firm gently. Sprinkle the seeds over the surface, and cover lightly with the same medium. Water with a fine spray, and allow the pot to drain thoroughly before covering. If a clay pot is used, watering can be done by standing the base of the pot in water until the top of the medium is obviously moist. Then enclose the pot in a plastic bag supported by a plant label.

PRESOWN PLANTER

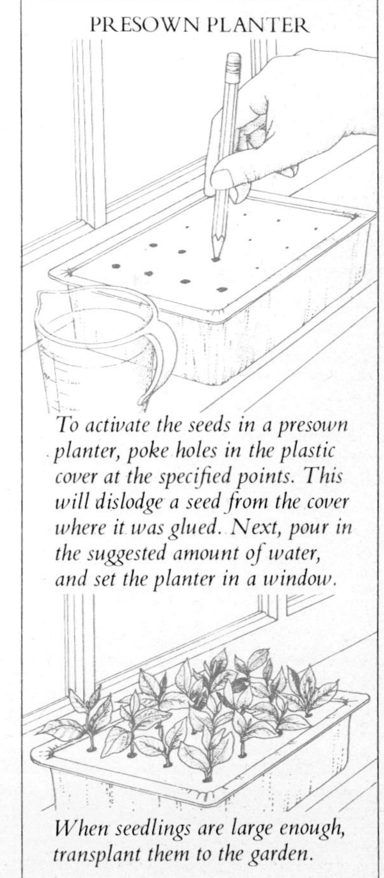

To activate the seeds in a presown planter, poke holes in the plastic cover at the specified points. This will dislodge a seed from the cover where it was glued. Next, pour in the suggested amount of water, and set the planter in a window.

When seedlings are large enough, transplant them to the garden.

Thinning Out and Transplanting Seedlings

When seedlings are too crowded together to grow properly, or when they reach the proper size, transplant them. (Seedlings that remain crowded become weak and spindly.) Seedlings are large enough to be transplanted when they have grown three or four leaves. Larger seedlings can be transplanted, and although they are easier to handle, wilting is apt to be severe, and growth slowed.

Make certain that the soil is moist so that the seedlings can be lifted out easily with some soil clinging to their roots. Avoid pulling them out, as this can damage the fine roots. First, loosen the seedlings with a label stake. After loosening them, hold those to be lifted with one hand; at the same time, use the fingers of your other hand to press the soil down on each side of the seedlings that are to remain, in order to disturb them as little as possible. Water the remaining seedlings to resettle the soil.

The distance to be left between the transplanted seedlings in the new container depends somewhat on the kind of plant being transplanted. Generally, 1–2 inches between seedlings at the first transplanting is adequate. If they should become crowded before they can be set in the garden, they can be transplanted again with more space between them. Where window areas are at a premium, it is often better to space them closely at first and then make a second transplanting later when they begin to crowd.

If you are unable to transplant immediately all the seedlings you have dug out, be sure to protect them from drying out in the meantime. One good way is to put them close together temporarily in a small pot of soil. Even if several days elapse before you can tend to them, they will suffer only a minimal setback.

As the plants grow, avoid any check in their growth by making sure that the soil stays moist. Remove any weeds that appear (few will if the soil is pasteurized).

Before seedlings are set out in the garden, they should be hardened to take outdoor conditions as described at the right. If this is not done, seedlings may suffer a setback, and flowering will be delayed.

When you have surplus seedlings, always keep the strongest ones. Discarded seedlings should not be left lying on the soil, as they often attract fungi or pests—particularly in a greenhouse.

Hardening Off the Young Plants

Whenever seedlings or even mature plants are moved outdoors from the house or greenhouse, they need a short period of acclimatization because light intensity and outdoor temperatures are quite different from indoor conditions. If this is not done, the seedlings will be severely set back, and flowering will be delayed.

A cold frame is the ideal place for this transition. The transplanted containers of seedlings can be set directly into the frame, or seedlings can be planted into the soil within the frame. Careful attention must be paid to watering and ventilating. On cool nights close the frame, but open it again as soon as the sun strikes it in the morning to prevent overheating. After a week or two in the cold frame, seedlings can be moved to their permanent locations outdoors.

When a cold frame is not available, similar acclimatization is accomplished by setting the containers of seedlings outdoors for an increasing amount of sun each day and by taking them in at night whenever the night temperature falls below 50° F. After a week of hardening seedlings can be transplanted.

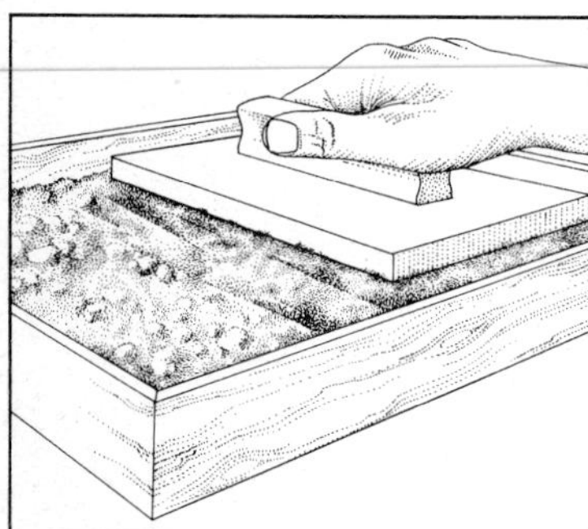

1. *Fill a flat with slightly moist soil; then firm the soil gently and level.*

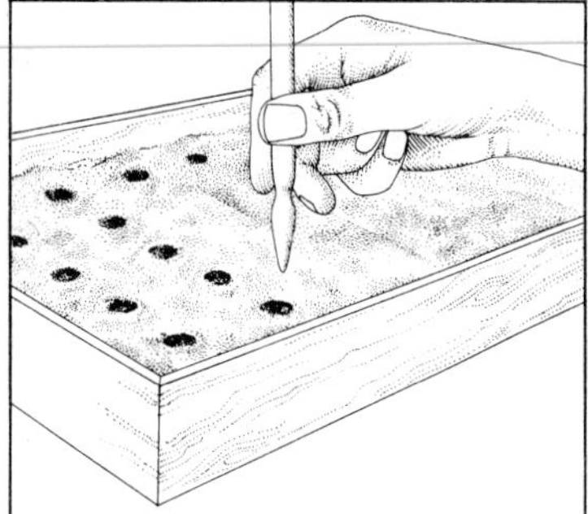

2. *Make rows of planting holes with a dibble or pencil; space 1–2 in. apart.*

3. *Carefully lift out a small clump of seedlings with a plant label.*

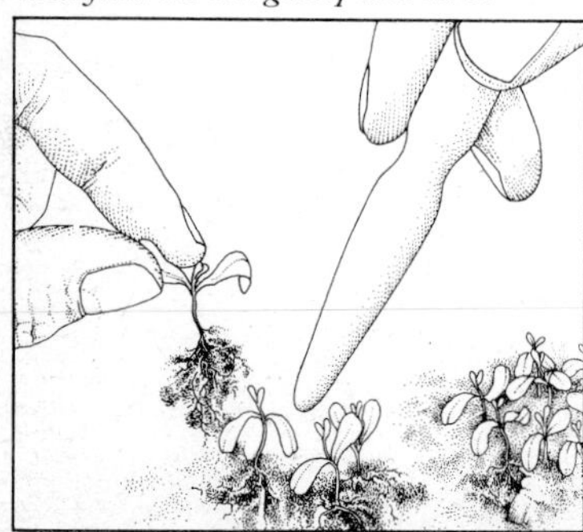

4. *Hold a seedling by a leaf, and gently tease it away from the others.*

5. *Plant one seedling per hole, and firm soil around it with fingers or dibble.*

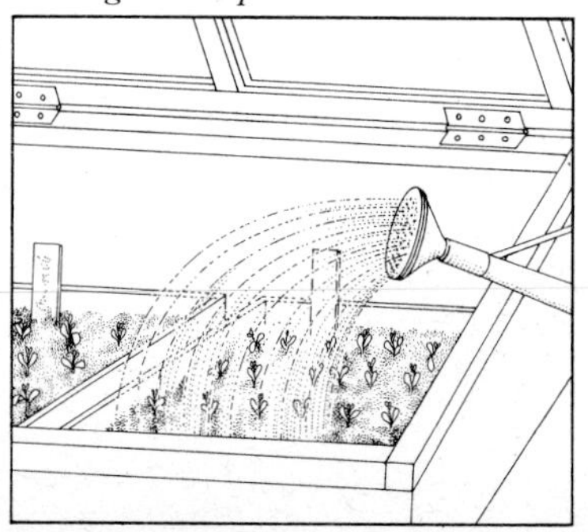

6. *Water the seedlings, and place in a cold frame or window.*

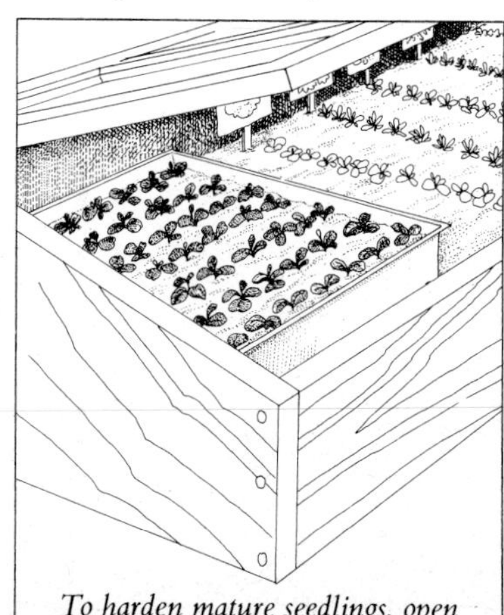

To harden mature seedlings, open the cold frame wider each day.

Caring for Young Seedlings Outdoors

Planting Out Young Seedlings

Once hardened off, the young plants are ready to be set into their permanent places in the garden, provided there is no danger of frost. The latest possible planting date varies from region to region.

Prepare the site in the manner described on page 286.

Transplant only when the soil is moist. With a trowel or your fingers, lift a single plant or a row of plants from the container or directly from rows in the cold frame. (It sometimes helps to separate the plants in a container by running a knife between them.) Separate into individual plants, taking care that each retains as many roots as possible. With a trowel dig a planting hole that is wide enough and deep enough to accommodate the plant's root system.

Insert the plant so that the base of its stem is level with the surface of the soil. Fill the hole and firm the soil with your fingers.

Water after planting to settle the soil around the roots and to minimize wilting. Shade if necessary.

Break away the first row of plants with a trowel or your fingers.

Protecting Seedlings From Dogs, Cats, and Birds

Unfortunately, there is no foolproof way to keep animals out of flower beds. A specially treated rope to repel dogs can be strung around the bed's perimeter, and there are cat-repellent sprays of varying effectiveness. To deter birds, insert low stakes around the perimeter of the bed; tie black thread to one, and loop it crisscross over the bed. Or use netting sold for supporting pea vines.

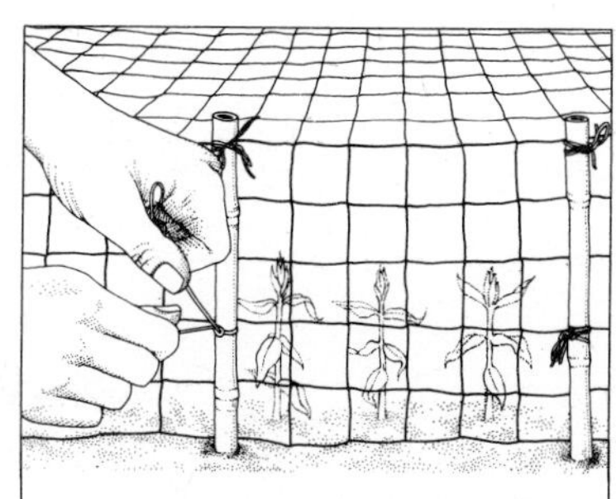

If birds are a nuisance, protect seedlings with netting supported by stakes.

Pinching Seedlings to Encourage Branching

Immediately after planting or shortly thereafter, encourage any plant that is not normally bushy to produce several stems and more blooms by pinching off its growing tip. The easiest way is to use your thumb and forefinger, but shears can be used if you prefer. Pinch just above a set of leaves. Side shoots can be pinched later to make the plant bushier.

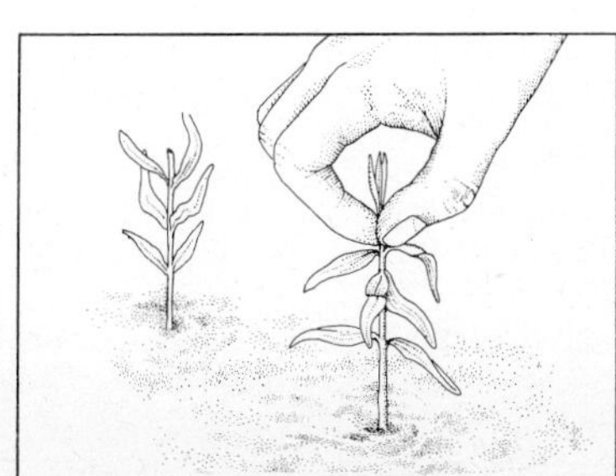

Encourage more stems on any plant not normally bushy by pinching off tip.

The Best Way to Stake Tall Flowers

Some tall annuals need support. When twiggy branches pruned from shrubs are available, put them in position after thinning the seedlings. Place the branches at 1-foot intervals around each group of seedlings, with several more in the center of the group. Such branches should be about two-thirds the ultimate height of the plants so that they will eventually be hidden.

More readily available supports are plastic-covered metal or bamboo stakes. Use green twine, plastic tape, or covered-wire tape to tie each plant to a stake.

Support tall annuals with twiggy branches around groups of seedlings, or tie each one to a stake.

Deadheading to Encourage Further Flowering

"Deadheading" is a descriptive British term for removing faded flowers. If dead blooms are left, the plant's energy goes into producing seeds rather than more flowers. Deadheading is also essential if the appearance of the garden is to be maintained at its best. Cutting fresh blooms for indoor use will reduce the need for deadheading.

If you want to save some seeds for the next season (although they will probably be inferior to commercial seeds), allow one or two blooms to wither on each plant. Then harvest the seeds when ripe and store dry.

Remove faded flowers by snapping them off between finger and thumb, or use pruning shears. This will encourage more blooms and improve the plant's appearance.

Cleaning Up the Garden in the Fall

After the annuals no longer have a pleasing appearance, or whenever the production of flowers ceases, pull them up and consign them to the compost pile. By not postponing this job until the following spring, you will not only have a better-looking garden all winter but you will also have an opportunity to improve the soil before the next planting season.

This is an excellent time to incorporate humus in the form of compost or peat moss, or to apply lime if it is needed. A green-manure crop such as annual ryegrass can also be sown (see p. 595). However, it is usually only practical to do this in gardens where annuals are grown exclusively. Fall is also a convenient and practical time to take a soil sample to test for next season's fertilizer needs.

How to Grow Biennials

Biennials are plants that complete their life cycle in two growing seasons. They produce rosettes of leaves and sometimes stems the first year but do not flower until the second, after which they die.

Some biennials will flower the same year they are sown if given an early start. This can be a disadvantage, however, because the plants will then bloom later than they ordinarily would and at a time when temperatures may be too high for them to last well. This is particularly true of pansies, which produce sturdier plants and flower more prolifically when the weather is cool.

Certain biennials, such as the honesty, tend to behave like perennials because they perpetuate themselves by self-sowing each year.

Also generally included among biennials are some plants that are actually perennials but are usually grown as biennials. This is because, after producing vigorous growth and plenty of blooms in their second year, they deteriorate to such an extent that it is not worth retaining them. Examples include sweet Williams, some forget-me-nots, and wallflowers.

Seeds of biennials can be sown in early to mid summer in Zones A and B; in early to mid fall in Zone C; and in late fall in Zone D.

Sow directly outdoors, as for annuals (see p. 286), in a lightly shaded area. Seeds can be sown in rows or broadcast. (If preferred, sow in a flat or in a large pot.) Water the seeds with a fine sprinkler. To keep them from drying out, it is helpful to cover the seeded area with a piece of burlap topped with a sheet of plastic. After a week inspect daily for germination. Remove the cover as soon as the first seeds sprout; otherwise the seedlings will become spindly or die.

When the seedlings are well developed, lift them carefully and transplant them to a sunny or lightly shaded nursery bed.

If it is more convenient, plants can be raised in an unheated greenhouse or cold frame and then set out into flats or beds (as shown on pp. 287–289). Sow them at the same time as when seeding directly outdoors, and take care not to allow the temperature to rise above 70° F. Some form of shading may be needed.

In cold regions it is essential for biennial plants to be set in their flowering positions in time to become established—six to eight weeks before the first hard frost. This includes those that have been raised in a greenhouse or cold frame.

Before final planting, clear the bed, dig over the soil, and work in well-rotted manure or compost, together with some bone meal or superphosphate at the rate of 3–5 pounds per 100 square feet.

Lift the plants from the site to which they had been transplanted, easing them out with a trowel and leaving as many roots attached as possible. If the soil is dry, water it first to ease the lifting and to minimize the possibility of root damage.

After lifting, put the plants in their permanent positions as soon as possible, before their roots can dry out. Firm the soil around the plants and water it. Wilting is seldom a problem at this time of year because the sun is not intense; if it is, provide shade.

In cold areas plants put out in exposed positions will need winter protection. Lay a few evergreen branches over them after the soil freezes, and then remove them gradually in spring. An alternative is to winter plants in a cold frame.

Although biennials are usually transplanted at least once, they can be sown in their permanent positions and later thinned.

Some so-called biennials, notably sweet Williams and foxgloves, will often survive an extra season if the stems are cut back to the basal rosette of leaves immediately after flowering. In general, however, it is best to sow seeds each year to ensure good plants of the desired colors.

What Can Go Wrong With Annuals and Biennials

Most annuals and biennials are remarkably free of pests. However, if your plants show any symptoms that are not described below, consult the section on plant disorders on page 600. Look up chemicals on page 635 to find trade names.

Symptoms and signs	Cause	Control
Young stems appear distorted. Flowers do not develop properly. Plant is covered with sticky green or black insects.	Aphids	Spray with dimethoate, endosulfan, formothion, malathion, or rotenone.
Leaves and petals have irregular, ragged holes.	Earwigs	Spray or dust with carbaryl, chlorpyrifos, Diazinon, or malathion. Trap earwigs in flowerpots stuffed with straw.
Leaves have silvery spots. Leaves, buds, and flowers may be entangled with webs.	Mites (cyclamen or two-spotted)	Spray or dust with dicofol, endosulfan, or tetradifon; or apply dimethoate or oxydemeton-methyl as foliar spray or soil drench.
Shoots and leaves are stunted and crippled. Leaves, especially younger ones, have spots and sometimes small, ragged holes. Flower buds are deformed or fail to develop.	Plant bugs (four-lined, harlequin, or tarnished)	Spray with Diazinon, malathion, methoxychlor, or nicotine.
Leaves are finely mottled and appear silvery, especially during hot, dry weather. No webbing.	Thrips	Spray or dust with chlorpyrifos, malathion, nicotine, or rotenone.
Young shoots are spun together with fine threads; growing points are eaten out of shoots by small greenish caterpillars.	Tortrix caterpillars	Spray with carbaryl, methoxychlor, rotenone, or trichlorphon; or pick off infested shoots by hand.
Small white flies dart about when plant is touched.	Whiteflies	Spray with malathion, pyrethrum, or resmethrin.
Seedlings (particularly those thickly sown in pots, pans, or boxes under glass) rot at ground level and topple over.	Damping-off (fungus)	Water with Captan, quintozene, or thiram. Best way to prevent disease is by using sterilized medium, sowing thinly, not overwatering, and using protective seed dressing.
Leaves and young shoots are covered with fine white or gray powder; accompanied by stunting or slight crippling of plant.	Mildew (fungus)	Spray with Benomyl, dinocap, sulfur, or thiophanate-methyl.
Plants are stunted, with small or malformed leaves showing yellow mottling or veins. Plants flower poorly.	Virus disease	Destroy plants as soon as symptoms are noticed. Spray to control piercing-sucking insects that carry virus.

Annuals and Biennials to Grow

In the chart that follows are popular and readily available annuals and biennials. Plants are listed according to their best known common names as found in most catalogs and on seed packets. These are followed by the botanical names. If you cannot find a particular plant, check the name you know in the Index.

The height (H) and spread (S) given in the second column indicate the possible range, but the specific height will depend on the variety. Hence it is important to check this point before making a purchase. For example, marigolds range in height from the dwarf 7-inch French varieties, through the intermediates, to the 3-foot-tall African varieties.

Those variety names that are followed by an asterisk, such as anchusa 'Blue Bird,'* are All-America Selections (see p. 284). They are generally superior in growth and bloom.

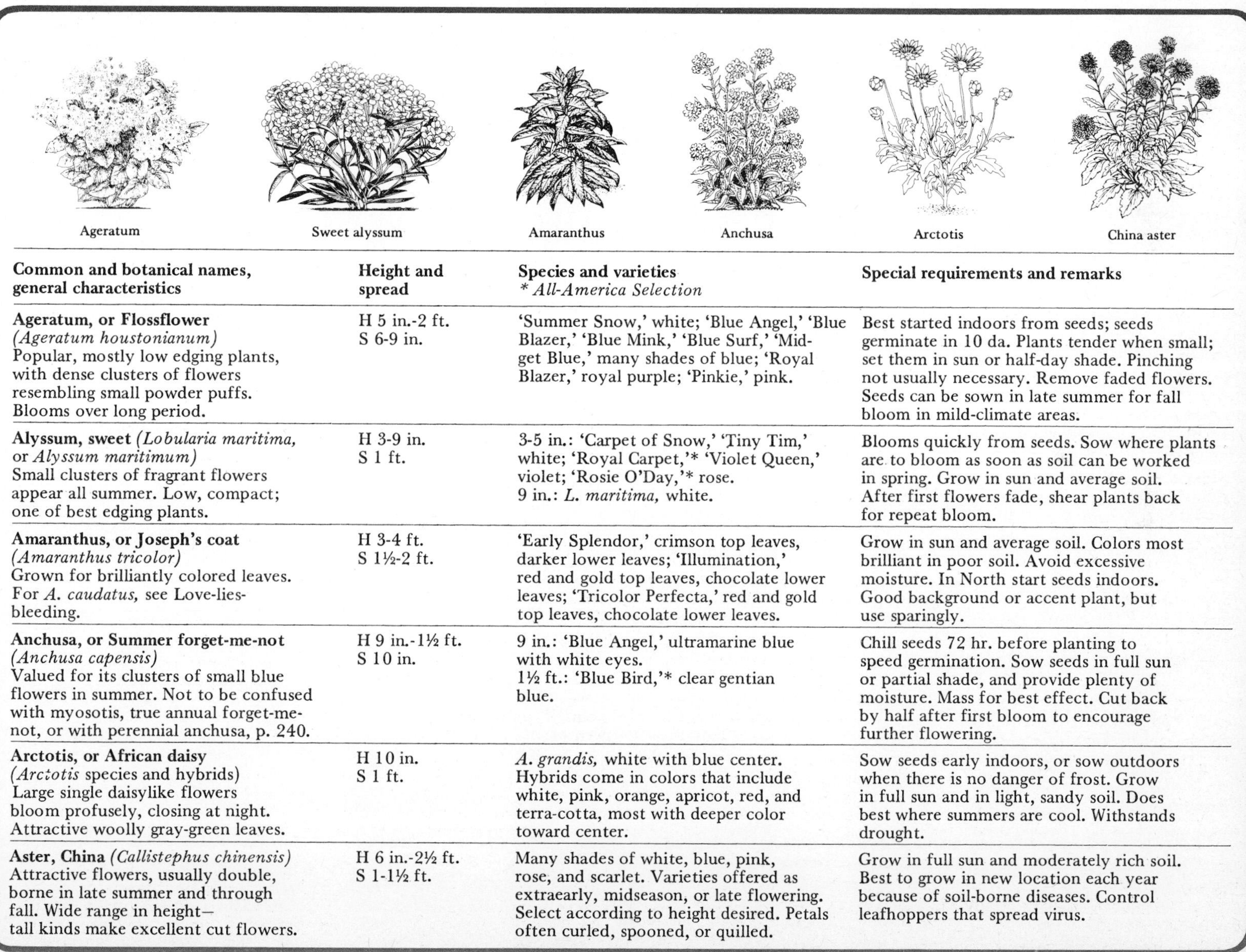

Ageratum — Sweet alyssum — Amaranthus — Anchusa — Arctotis — China aster

Common and botanical names, general characteristics	Height and spread	Species and varieties ** All-America Selection*	Special requirements and remarks
Ageratum, or Flossflower *(Ageratum houstonianum)* Popular, mostly low edging plants, with dense clusters of flowers resembling small powder puffs. Blooms over long period.	H 5 in.-2 ft. S 6-9 in.	'Summer Snow,' white; 'Blue Angel,' 'Blue Blazer,' 'Blue Mink,' 'Blue Surf,' 'Midget Blue,' many shades of blue; 'Royal Blazer,' royal purple; 'Pinkie,' pink.	Best started indoors from seeds; seeds germinate in 10 da. Plants tender when small; set them in sun or half-day shade. Pinching not usually necessary. Remove faded flowers. Seeds can be sown in late summer for fall bloom in mild-climate areas.
Alyssum, sweet *(Lobularia maritima,* or *Alyssum maritimum)* Small clusters of fragrant flowers appear all summer. Low, compact; one of best edging plants.	H 3-9 in. S 1 ft.	3-5 in.: 'Carpet of Snow,' 'Tiny Tim,' white; 'Royal Carpet,'* 'Violet Queen,' violet; 'Rosie O'Day,'* rose. 9 in.: *L. maritima,* white.	Blooms quickly from seeds. Sow where plants are to bloom as soon as soil can be worked in spring. Grow in sun and average soil. After first flowers fade, shear plants back for repeat bloom.
Amaranthus, or Joseph's coat *(Amaranthus tricolor)* Grown for brilliantly colored leaves. For *A. caudatus,* see Love-lies-bleeding.	H 3-4 ft. S 1½-2 ft.	'Early Splendor,' crimson top leaves, darker lower leaves; 'Illumination,' red and gold top leaves, chocolate lower leaves; 'Tricolor Perfecta,' red and gold top leaves, chocolate lower leaves.	Grow in sun and average soil. Colors most brilliant in poor soil. Avoid excessive moisture. In North start seeds indoors. Good background or accent plant, but use sparingly.
Anchusa, or Summer forget-me-not *(Anchusa capensis)* Valued for its clusters of small blue flowers in summer. Not to be confused with myosotis, true annual forget-me-not, or with perennial anchusa, p. 240.	H 9 in.-1½ ft. S 10 in.	9 in.: 'Blue Angel,' ultramarine blue with white eyes. 1½ ft.: 'Blue Bird,'* clear gentian blue.	Chill seeds 72 hr. before planting to speed germination. Sow seeds in full sun or partial shade, and provide plenty of moisture. Mass for best effect. Cut back by half after first bloom to encourage further flowering.
Arctotis, or African daisy *(Arctotis* species and hybrids) Large single daisylike flowers bloom profusely, closing at night. Attractive woolly gray-green leaves.	H 10 in. S 1 ft.	*A. grandis,* white with blue center. Hybrids come in colors that include white, pink, orange, apricot, red, and terra-cotta, most with deeper color toward center.	Sow seeds early indoors, or sow outdoors when there is no danger of frost. Grow in full sun and in light, sandy soil. Does best where summers are cool. Withstands drought.
Aster, China *(Callistephus chinensis)* Attractive flowers, usually double, borne in late summer and through fall. Wide range in height—tall kinds make excellent cut flowers.	H 6 in.-2½ ft. S 1-1½ ft.	Many shades of white, blue, pink, rose, and scarlet. Varieties offered as extraearly, midseason, or late flowering. Select according to height desired. Petals often curled, spooned, or quilled.	Grow in full sun and moderately rich soil. Best to grow in new location each year because of soil-borne diseases. Control leafhoppers that spread virus.

Garden balsam

Ornamental basil

Wax begonia

Bells of Ireland

Blue lace flower

Browallia

Common and botanical names, general characteristics	Height and spread	Species and varieties * *All-America Selection*	Special requirements and remarks
Baby's breath, see Gypsophila **Bachelor's button,** see Cornflower			
Balsam, garden *(Impatiens balsamina)* Waxy, usually double, camellialike flowers borne close to and toward top of stem. Not good for cutting.	H 10 in.-2½ ft. S 1-1½ ft.	Many colors available, including white, purple, pink, salmon, and red, some with white markings on petals. Various heights available.	Sow seeds early indoors or outdoors after there is no danger of frost. Grow in full sun or partial shade, in moist soil. Does not tolerate cold, wet weather.
Basil, ornamental, or sweet *(Ocimum basilicum)* Grown primarily for ornamental leaves that are also used to flavor many foods. White- or purple-tinged flowers are relatively inconspicuous.	H 1-1½ ft. S 1 ft.	*O. basilicum,* green leaves; *O. b.* 'Dark Opal,'* dark purple leaves, variety most often grown as garden ornament.	Start seeds indoors, 6-8 wk. in advance of outdoor planting season. Grow in full sun and light, sandy soil. Pinch to encourage branching. For drying, cut stems when in bloom, and hang upside down in cool, dry place. Can be cut back and potted up in fall for growing indoors.
Begonia, wax *(Begonia semperflorens)* A prolific, long-flowering plant with attractive, waxy green or reddish leaves. Numerous small, usually single flowers drop cleanly. Few plants equal this for summer display.	H 6 in.-1 ft. S 6 in.-15 in.	A wide selection of varieties is available in white, white-tinged pink, and shades of pink and red. Leaves are bright green-copper or purple flushed. Some nurseries offer 'Butterfly,' with very large flowers in white, pink, or red.	Buy plants or start dustlike seeds indoors at least 2 mo. in advance of outdoor planting time. Easily started indoors. Plant in full sun or partial shade and in soil mixed with peat moss or compost. Pot up in fall for growing indoors.
Bells of Ireland *(Molucella laevis)* An unusual plant having long spikes covered with large, pale green, shell-like calyxes, each surrounding a small white flower. Good cut flower; used fresh or dried.	H 2-3 ft. S 9 in.	*M. laevis,* green calyxes surrounding inconspicuous white flowers. This is the only species widely offered.	Seeds are best sown where plants are to grow as seedlings. Difficult to transplant. Sow seeds early but after there is no danger of frost; germination (4 wk.) best in cool weather. Grow in full sun. To dry flowers, remove leaves and hang in cool, dark place.
Blue lace flower *(Trachymene caerulea,* or *Didiscus caerulea)* Heads of tiny sweet-scented flowers up to 3 in. across resemble wild Queen Anne's lace. Borne on long stems above finely divided leaves.	H 2½ ft. S 9 in.	Only blue kind generally available, although occasionally offered in white.	Sow seeds indoors or outdoors where plants are to grow as soon as soil can be worked in spring and after there is no danger of frost. Grow in full sun and light soil. Blooms best in cool weather. Stems weak; stake with twiggy brush.
Browallia *(Browallia* species*)* Trumpet-shaped flowers up to 2 in. across on slender branched stems; small leaves.	H 10 in.-2 ft. S 10 in.	*B. americana,* bluish-purple flowers with pale yellow "eye" in center; *B. speciosa,* dark purple; *B. viscosa alba,* white.	Sow seeds early indoors, or buy plants already started. Grow in partial shade. Provide ample water. Fertilize several times during growing period. Pinch plants when 3 in. tall to force side shoots. Cut back in fall; grow indoors in winter.

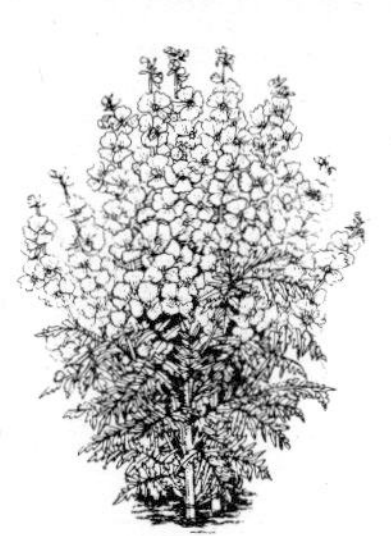
Butterfly flower

Ornamental cabbage

Calendula

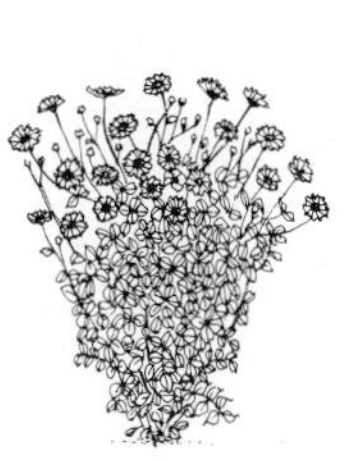
Calliopsis

Candytuft

Canterbury bell

Common and botanical names, general characteristics	**Height and spread**	**Species and varieties** ** All-America Selection*	**Special requirements and remarks**
Burning bush, see Kochia			
Butterfly flower, or Poor man's orchid *(Schizanthus wisetonensis)* Dainty, loosely arranged flowers on stems that rise above lacy foliage. Somewhat resembles orchids, hence one of common names. Often grown in containers.	H 1-1½ ft. S 1 ft.	'Angel Wings' and 'Hit Parade' are two improved compact varieties offered in mixed-seed packets. Flowers are mostly bicolors of white, violet, purple, pink, or crimson.	Sow seeds indoors 6-8 wk. before last spring frost or outdoors when weather warms. Grows best where summers are cool. In Zone D sow in fall for flowers in late winter, early spring. Slow to germinate. Grow in full sun or partial shade and in moist soil.
Cabbage, ornamental, and Kale, ornamental *(Brassica oleracea acephala)* Grown for ornamental leaves, which are tinged with cream, purple, pink, rose, or red, especially toward center of plant.	H 6 in. S 1½ ft.	These two plants, actually strains of a single variety, look very much alike. They are commonly sold interchangeably or in mixed-seed packets.	Can be started indoors or sown directly outdoors. Need full sun. Actually tender biennials that are killed by frost the first year before they can bloom the next. Flowers of no value. Leaves useful in flower arrangements.
Calendula, or Pot marigold *(Calendula officinalis)* Flowers to 4 in. across, single or double. Light green leaves have pungent aroma. Good cut flower. Not to be confused with African or French marigolds.	H 6-20 in. S 6 in.-1 ft.	'Golden Gem,' dwarf, double, yellow; 'Pacific Beauty,' double, yellow, orange, apricot; 'Orange Gem,' double, medium orange; 'Sunny Boy,' dwarf, mixed-seed packets of assorted colors.	Seeds germinate readily outdoors; can be sown in fall or winter in frost-free areas. Tolerates low-fertility soil, in sun or partial shade. Does best in cool weather; double flowers may be semi-double in extreme heat. Self-sows.
Calliopsis *(Coreopsis tinctoria)* Multitudes of daisylike flowers are carried on wiry stems with fine foliage. Easily grown. Good cut flower.	H 8 in.-3 ft. S 1 ft.	8 in.: 'Golden Ray,' yellow with crimson central zone; 'Tiger Star,' crimson, striped and mottled with yellow; mixed-seed packets of bicolors: purple, yellow, red. 3 ft.: mixed-seed packets of bicolors: yellow, orange, red.	Sow seeds early outdoors where plants are to grow. Grow in full sun and in average soil. Cut back after first bloom to encourage further flowering. Low-growing kinds tend to cease flowering in very hot weather.
Candytuft *(Iberis species)* Numerous small flowers in heads (globe flowered) or spikes (hyacinth flowered).	H 8 in.-1½ ft. S 6 in.-1 ft.	*I. amara* (hyacinth flowered): 'Empress,' giant, white; 'Iceberg,' large, white. *I. umbellata* (globe flowered): 'Dwarf Fairy,' white, lavender, purple, pink, rose, and red; 'Red Flash,' red with yellow centers.	Sow seeds early, in a sunny location where plants are to bloom. Does best in cool weather; in frost-free areas, can be sown in fall for bloom in winter. Remove faded blooms to encourage further flowering unless self-sowing is desired. Withstands air pollution.
Canterbury bell *(Campanula medium)* Spikes of large, bell-shaped flowers, single or double. Usually grown as biennial.	H 2-2½ ft. S 10 in.	Mixed-seed packets of white, blue, mauve, pink, or separate colors. *C. m. calycanthema* (cup and saucer) includes two types: in fully double flowers, one bell (or cup) fits closely within the other; in others, cup sits on a saucerlike outer bell.	Buy plants in spring to bloom in early summer, or sow seeds in midsummer to bloom the next year. Grow in full sun and in well-drained, fertile soil. Water freely in dry weather. May need staking.

Carnation

Castor bean

Celosia

Chrysanthemum

Clarkia

Cleome

Common and botanical names, general characteristics	Height and spread	Species and varieties * *All-America Selection*	Special requirements and remarks
Carnation *(Dianthus caryophyllus)* Garden-grown plants bear the familiar, fragrant florists' blossoms, but usually smaller. Wiry stems. Excellent cut flower.	H 1-2 ft. S 1 ft.	White and many shades of purple, pink, yellow, salmon, apricot, and red. Available in seed packets of separate or mixed colors. 'Juliet,'* red, does especially well as annual.	In cold regions grow as annual; start seeds early indoors. In warm areas can be grown as biennial or perennial. Plant in full sun and in well-drained, neutral or slightly alkaline soil. Stake tall varieties.
Castor bean *(Ricinus communis)* Quick-growing plants valued for large, sharply lobed leaves. Good background plant. Flowers insignificant. Seeds poisonous; leaves and seedpods may irritate skin.	H 8-10 ft. S 3 ft.	*R. communis,* green leaves. *R. c. sanguineus,* red leaves. *R. c. zanzibarensis,* extralarge green leaves, sometimes variegated.	Soak seeds 24 hr. before sowing. In colder areas can be started early indoors. Grow in full sun and in fertile, well-drained soil. Protect from strong winds. Usually perennial and shrublike in very mild regions (Zone D).
Celosia, or Cockscomb *(Celosia argentea)* Showy plants with widely differing forms. Flowers of crested cockscomb are stiff, resemble rooster's comb; plumed cockscombs are feathery. Excellent dried flowers.	H 6 in.-3 ft. S 9 in.-1 ft.	*C. a. cristata* (crested): 'Yellow Toreador,' yellow; 'Gladiator,' gold; 'Toreador,'* red; 'Fireglow,'* scarlet. *C. a. plumosa* (plumed): 'Golden Triumph,'* yellow; 'Red Fox,'* deep orange-red; 'Forest Fire,'* red; 'Jewel Box,' bright mixed colors, dwarf.	Sow seeds after soil warms outdoors. Grow in full sun and in fertile soil. Does best in warm weather. Stake tall varieties. Plants usually available. To dry, pick in prime, strip off leaves, and hang upside down in airy, shaded place.
Chrysanthemum, annual *(Chrysanthemum* species and hybrids) Easily grown plants, with mostly single, daisylike flowers and finely divided foliage. Especially good for those who find perennial kinds difficult. Taller kinds good for cut flowers.	H 10 in.-2½ ft. S 9 in.-1 ft.	'Paludosum,' white with gold edge; 'Golden Raindrops,' yellow; 'Golden Gem,' yellow, double. Many perennial types, notably 'Korean,' will bloom first season if sown early; colors include white, yellow, and red.	Grows quickly from seeds started indoors or sown outdoors. Grow in full sun; water in dry weather. Pinch to encourage branching. Plants transplant readily; can be moved at any time, even when in bud or bloom.
Clarkia *(Clarkia elegans, C. pulchella,* and *C. amoena)* Varied group with single or double flowers carried in loose clusters or spikes. Good border plants.	H 1-2 ft. S 6 in.-1 ft.	Offered in mixed-seed packets of assorted colors that include white, lavender, pink, creamy yellow, salmon, and crimson. *C. amoena* (godetia, or satinflower) is bushier than other clarkias.	Grows best in cool weather. Sow seeds early outdoors. Thrives in full sun and average to poor soil that can be relatively dry in summer. Do not grow where humidity is high. In frost-free regions seeds can be sown in fall. Does not transplant readily.
Cleome, or Spider flower *(Cleome spinosa)* Dramatic plants with airy, scented flower heads, each flower with long stamens that give spidery effect; long seedpods have similar appearance. Foliage palmlike.	H 3-4 ft. S 1½-2 ft.	'Helen Campbell,' white; 'Purple Queen,' lilac-purple; 'Pink Queen,' pink; 'Cherry Queen,' cherry-rose; 'Ruby Queen,' ruby-rose; 'Rose Queen,' salmon-pink.	Sow seeds outdoors, preferably where plants are to grow, after weather warms; or buy plants. Locate in full sun or very light shade and in average garden soil. Flowers close in afternoon. Stems have sharp thorns. Self-sows; generally trouble free.

Coleus

Cornflower

Cosmos

Cynoglossum

Dahlia

English daisy

Common and botanical names, general characteristics	Height and spread	Species and varieties ** All-America Selection*	Special requirements and remarks
Coleus *(Coleus blumei)* Luxuriant foliage in many colors and patterns, some leaves edged in contrasting color, some with fringed or narrow leaves. Flowers insignificant.	H 8 in.-3 ft. S 8 in.-1 ft.	'Candidum,' ivory, green edge; 'Chartreuse,' yellow-green; 'Flamenco,' red, edged yellow; 'Volcano,' red; 'Carefree,' low, compact, finely divided leaves, seed packets of assorted or separate colors.	Start seeds indoors. Grow outdoors in partial shade for best colors. Pinch to encourage branching. Plants easily propagated by tip cuttings. Can be grown over winter as house plants. Control aphids and mealybugs with malathion.
Coreopsis, annual, see Calliopsis			
Cornflower, or Bachelor's button *(Centaurea cyanus)* Tall or dwarf plants with myriads of 2-in. flowers and small gray-green leaves. Good cut flower.	H 1-3 ft. S 1 ft.	1 ft.: 'Snowball,'* white; 'Jubilee Gem,' blue. 16 in.: 'Polka Dot Mixed,' white, blue, lavender, pink, and red. 2½-3 ft.: 'Snow Man,' white; 'Blue Boy,' blue; 'Pinkie,' light pink; 'Red Boy,' red.	When planting outdoors sow seeds early where plants are to grow, since they resent transplanting. Seeds can be sown in late fall for earlier bloom. Grow in full sun and in light, preferably neutral soil. Blooms best in cool weather. Often self-sows.
Cosmos *(Cosmos bipinnatus* and *C. sulphureus)* Delightfully airy plants with large single or semi-double daisylike flowers on long, wiry stems. Very fine foliage. Excellent cut flower.	H 1½-4 ft. S 1½-2 ft.	Klondyke type *(C. sulphureus),* semi-double—1½ ft.: 'Dwarf,' yellow; 2-2½ ft.: 'Sunset,'* orange-scarlet; 'Diablo,'* red. Sensation type *(C. bipinnatus),* single—4 ft.: 'Purity,' white; 'Pinkie,' pink; 'Radiance,'* rose; 'Dazzler,' crimson.	Sow seeds outdoors or buy young plants. Grow in full sun and in average soil. (Very rich soils encourage more foliage than flowers.) Tall types may need support. Remove faded flowers for further blooming. Put cut flowers in deep water immediately to prevent wilting.
Cynoglossum, or Chinese forget-me-not *(Cynoglossum amabile)* Clustered, small fragrant flowers and gray-green foliage. Biennial, usually grown as annual.	H 1½-2 ft. S 1 ft.	1½ ft.: 'Firmament,'* sky-blue. 2 ft.: 'Blanche Burpee,' white and various shades of blue; *C. amabile,* blue.	Best sown early outdoors where plants are to flower, in full sun or partial shade. Blooms quickly from seeds. Can also be sown in fall in warmer areas, such as Zone C.
Dahlia *(Dahlia* hybrids) Neat and attractive bushy plants that bear single to double flowers over long period. Shiny green leaves. Makes excellent cut flower. See also p. 275.	H 1-2 ft. S 1½-2 ft.	Mixed-seed packets of assorted colors, including white, pink, yellow, orange, and red. Double and semi-double: 'Border Jewels,' 'Early Bird,' 'Redskin.'* Single: 'Annette,' 'Coltness.' Taller kinds take longer to bloom.	Sow seeds early indoors, later outdoors, or buy young plants. Grow in full sun and in well-fertilized soil. Water during dry spells. Remove faded blooms for further flowering. Tubers can be dug after foliage has been killed by frost; store over winter in cool, dry place.
Daisy, English *(Bellis perennis)* Flowers, usually double, 1-2 in. across, appear in spring and early summer on low, compact plants. Perennial, usually grown as biennial. Often used to edge spring-flowering bulb beds.	H 4-6 in. S 3-6 in.	'Pink Fairy Carpet,' pink; 'Kito,' cherry-rose; 'Carpet Mixture,' mixed-seed packets of assorted colors including white, pink, red.	Plants commonly sold in early spring, along with pansies, but can be started from seeds one year to bloom the next. In Zone D seeds sown in fall will produce plants that bloom in spring. Grow in full sun or partial shade, in moisture-retentive soil. Remove faded flowers.
Daisy, gloriosa, see Rudbeckia			

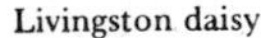

Livingston daisy

Swan River daisy

Dusty miller

Euphorbia marginata

Feverfew

Common and botanical names, general characteristics	Height and spread	Species and varieties * *All-America Selection*	Special requirements and remarks
Daisy, Livingston *(Dorotheanthus bellidiformis,* or *Mesembryanthemum criniflorum)* Succulent with single 2-in. flowers resembling true daisies. Leaves are bright green and fleshy.	H 4 in. S 1 ft.	Mixed-seed packets of assorted colors including buff, pink, rose, primrose, apricot, and crimson. Related to ice plant *(Mesembryanthemum crystallinum,* or *Cryophytum crystallinum)* grown in Calif. for its leaves flecked with silver.	Sow seeds indoors at least 2 mo. prior to safe outdoor planting date, or sow directly outdoors after danger of frost is past. Plants often available. Grow in full sun and well-drained soil. Does best in hot, dry regions of Zone D.
Daisy, Swan River *(Brachycome iberidifolia)* Single 1- to 1½-in. flowers with yellow centers appear on compact plants. Very finely divided leaves.	H 1 ft. S 6 in.	Mixed-seed packets of assorted colors including white, blue, dark violet, and rose.	Sow seeds outdoors after danger of frost is past, or sow indoors 6 wk. in advance of safe outdoor planting date. Locate plants in full sun and in average soil. Plants tend to sprawl; so supports may be needed.
Delphinium, annual, see Larkspur **Dianthus,** see Carnation, Pink, annual, and Sweet William **Didiscus,** see Blue lace flower			
Dusty miller *(Senecio cineraria)* Grown for its deeply cut silvery gray leaves. Plants shrublike and perennial in Zone D, with tiny yellow flowers. Good with colorful annuals.	H 8 in.-2½ ft. S 1-3 ft.	'Diamond,' finely cut white leaves; 'Silverdust,' very finely cut silvery leaves. Other plants sold as dusty miller include *Centaurea cineraria* and *C. gymnocarpa.* All very similar.	In cold regions buy plants, or sow seeds indoors 2 mo. in advance of outdoor planting date. Grow in full sun and ordinary soil. Withstands drought and seaside conditions.
Eschscholzia, see Poppy, California			
Euphorbia *(Euphorbia heterophylla* and *E. marginata)* Both these euphorbias are grown for ornamental leaves and bracts that are attractively colored, give effect similar to flowers, and last over very long summer season. Latex sap of both kinds can cause skin irritation.	H 1½-3 ft. S 1 ft.	*E. heterophylla* (Mexican fire plant, or annual poinsettia), green leaves turn bright red toward top in summer. *E. marginata* (snow-on-the-mountain), green leaves are edged or streaked in white. To 2 ft. high.	Sow seeds of *E. heterophylla* indoors early or outdoors after soil warms; sow *E. marginata* seeds very early outdoors (often self-sows). Grow both in full sun and in sandy soil that is low in nutrients. Sear stem ends in flame or dip in boiling water to prevent loss of sap when using branches as cut flowers.
Feverfew, or Matricaria *(Chrysanthemum parthenium,* or *Matricaria capensis)* Small, double, button-type flowers grow in clusters on tall or short plants. All have pungent scent. Perennial, often grown as annual. Tall kinds good for cut flowers.	H 6 in.-2 ft. S 9 in.	6-10 in.: 'Snowball,' white; 'White Stars,' white, yellow center; 'Golden Ball,' yellow. 2 ft.: 'Ball Double White,' white.	For earliest bloom, sow seeds indoors 6-8 wk. in advance of outdoor planting season. Or sow outdoors for later bloom. Grow in full sun or partial shade.
Forget-me-not, see Anchusa, Cynoglossum, and Myosotis			

Four-o'clock

Foxglove

Gaillardia

Common geranium

Globe amaranth

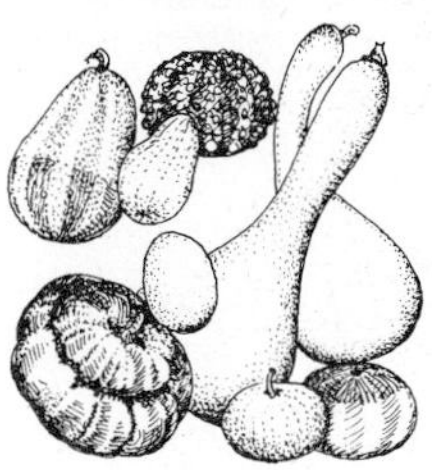
Ornamental gourds

Common and botanical names, general characteristics	Height and spread	Species and varieties * *All-America Selection*	Special requirements and remarks
Four o'clock *(Mirabilis jalapa)* Trumpet-shaped flowers up to 1 in. across open in late afternoon, stay open until next morning. Dense, dark green foliage. Perennial in mild areas.	H 1½-4 ft. S 1-2 ft.	Usually sold in mixed-seed packets containing white, lavender, pink, yellow, and salmon. 'Jingles,' striped flowers; 'Pygmy,' 1½ ft.; 'Petticoat,' gives flower-within-flower effect.	Sow seeds outdoors in full sun and in well-drained soil. Grows quickly. Dig up tubers after frost, store as for dahlia, p. 280. Makes good screen or hedge; withstands air pollution.
Foxglove *(Digitalis purpurea)* Tall spikes of closely set tubular flowers. Large, basal leaves. Generally grown as biennial unless started very early. Leaves poisonous if eaten.	H 3-5 ft. S 1-1½ ft.	In mixed-seed packets of white, purple, pink, rose, and yellow. 'Excelsior' and 'Shirley' have flowers all around stem, with 'Excelsior' more horizontal than pendent; 'Foxy,'* recently developed, blooms in 5 mo.	Sow early indoors for bloom same season or outdoors in late summer for bloom next year. Locate in partial shade in well-drained, moisture-retentive soil. Mulch with very light, airy material after ground freezes.
Gaillardia, or Blanketflower *(Gaillardia amblyodon* and *G. pulchella)* Single or double daisylike flowers, often with contrasting color on tips of petals. Tall and short kinds. Good cut flower.	H 1-2 ft. S 1-1½ ft.	In mixed-seed packets of assorted colors or separate colors including rose, yellow, orange, scarlet, mahogany. 'Lollipop,' double ball-shaped flowers; 'Goblin,' perennial, blooms first year from seeds.	Start seeds early indoors or sow outdoors later. Thrives in heat and sun in almost any soil. Drought tolerant. Remove faded blooms to encourage further flowering. Self-sows.
Geranium, common, or zonal *(Pelargonium hortorum)* Large clusters of flowers above handsome leaves with concentric markings. Good in containers. Widely grown as annual but perennial in Zone D.	H 1-2 ft., except far south, 3-6 ft. S 1 ft.	Many varieties sold as plants. Colors include white, pink, salmon, and red. The following can be grown from seeds to bloom in 5 mo.: 'Show Girl,'* bright pink; 'Nittany Lion,' red; 'Sprinter,' scarlet; 'Carefree,' seed packets of assorted colors or separate colors.	To grow from seeds, sow 2 mo. in advance of outdoor planting date. Grow in full sun and average, well-drained soil of moderate fertility. Plants readily increased from terminal cuttings that can be grown in sunny window indoors over winter in areas where hard frosts occur.
Globe amaranth, or Gomphrena *(Gomphrena globosa)* Small, round, papery flower heads on tall or dwarf plants. Long-lasting cut flower; dries well.	H 9 in.-1½ ft. S 6-8 in.	'Dwarf Buddy,' rich purple; 'Tall Mixed,' mixed-seed packets of assorted colors in shades of white, purple, and red.	Sow seeds early indoors or directly outdoors after soil warms. Germinates in 2 wk. Best grown where summers are hot. To dry, pick when flowers open; hang them upside down in dry location.
Gloriosa daisy, see Rudbeckia **Godetia,** see Clarkia			
Gourds, ornamental (several genera: *Cucumis, Cucurbita, Lagenaria, Luffa,* and others) Tropical vines grown for ornamental fruits in unusual shapes, some with showy flowers. Inedible fruits are dried and used for indoor decoration.	H 8-10 ft. S 12 ft.	Generally offered in mixed-seed packets of several genera or separately by common names descriptive of the fruit's shape: bottle, caveman's club, dolphin, Hercules' club, nest egg, penguin, serpent, spoon, striped pear, Turk's turban, warty.	Sow outdoors after soil warms where plants are to grow. Grow in full sun. Provide fence or trellis; fruits less perfect if they rest on ground. Let ripen on vine; harvest before frost. Do not bruise. Wash with household disinfectant; dry in airy place. Apply floor wax; polish.

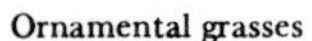

Ornamental grasses

Gypsophila

Heliotrope

Helipterum

Hibiscus

Hollyhock

Common and botanical names, general characteristics	Height and spread	Species and varieties * *All-America Selection*	Special requirements and remarks
Grasses, ornamental (several genera) Primarily grown for variously shaped and colored seed spikes or sprays that are cut and dried for arrangements. Good garden ornaments when well located.	H 1-4 ft. S wide range because seldom planted singly.	Seed packets of mixed or separate kinds: animated oats *(Avena sterilis);* cloud grass *(Agrostis nebulosa);* foxtail millet *(Setaria italica);* hare's-tail *(Lagurus ovatus);* Job's tears *(Coix lacryma).*	Sow seeds outdoors where plants are to grow. Locate in full sun, in average garden soil. Harvest before seed heads open. Store in dry, well-ventilated place until ready to use.
Gypsophila, or Baby's breath *(Gypsophila elegans)* Masses of small, starry flowers lend airy effect to garden when intermixed with more substantial plants. Narrow leaves. Good filler for flower bouquets.	H 15 in.-1½ ft. S 8-10 in.	*G. e. alba grandiflora* 'Covent Garden,' giant flowered, white; *G. e. rosea,* pink. For perennial gypsophila, see baby's breath, p. 241.	Sow outdoors where plants are to grow; thin seedlings if necessary. Needs sun; does best in alkaline soil. Make repeated sowings at 4- to 5-wk. intervals to ensure continued bloom, since plants flower for relatively short time.
Helianthus, see Sunflower, annual			
Heliotrope *(Heliotropium* hybrids) Old-fashioned plants prized for fragrant heads of small flowers. Grown as shrubby perennial in southern parts of Zone D. Good container plant; often grown as standard.	H 15 in.-2 ft., taller in South. S 1-1½ ft.	'Blue Opal,' dark blue; 'Marine,' rich violet.	Sow seeds indoors 2 mo. in advance of outdoor planting date. Wait until weather warms before setting out, since very sensitive to cold. Grow in sun or very light shade, in rich soil, with not too much water. Plants often sold.
Helipterum, or Acroclinium *(Helipterum* species) Attractive, long-lasting flowers resemble double daisies, with stiff, strawlike petals. Prized for drying.	H 15 in.-2 ft. S 6-8 in.	*H. manglesii,* rose-pink flowers; *H. humboldtianum,* yellow flowers, leaves woolly and silvery; *H. roseum,* or *Acroclinium roseum,* mixed-seed packets of white, cream, pink, rose, cerise, salmon, and apricot.	After weather warms, sow seeds where they are to grow, since seedlings are difficult to transplant. To use dried, cut when flowers begin to open and hang upside down in cool, dry, airy place to harden stems.
Hibiscus, or Rose mallow *(Hibiscus moscheutos)* Huge, open bowl-shaped flowers, 10 in. across, on tall, fast-growing plants. Usually grown as perennial, but a recent variety that blooms first year from seeds justifies inclusion as annual.	H 5 ft. S 2 ft.	'Southern Belle,'* in mixed-seed packets of assorted colors or separate colors of white, white bicolor, and pink.	Sow indoors 6 mo. before outdoor planting date; takes 3 wk. to germinate. Grow in sunny window. Transplant to individual pots. When frost danger is past, plant outdoors in sunny location. Water in dry spells. Mulch in cold regions over winter.
Hollyhock *(Althaea rosea)* Spectacular tall spikes of single or double flowers up to 4 in. across, some frilled. Grown largely as biennial, but recent varieties can be grown as annuals.	H 2-6 ft. S 1-1½ ft.	Biennials commonly offered in mixed-seed packets of assorted colors, including white, mauve, pink, rose, yellow, and red. Can also be grown as annuals: 'Majorette,'* double, 2 ft; 'Summer Carnival,'* double, 6 ft.	Sow annual types indoors or later outdoors after frost. Sow biennial types outdoors after frost or in early summer. Grow in full sun. Annual forms may live over winter. Annual hollyhocks seldom troubled by rust fungus as are biennials. To control, spray with zineb.

Honesty

Impatiens

Kochia

Larkspur

Lavatera

Common and botanical names, general characteristics	Height and spread	Species and varieties * *All-America Selection*	Special requirements and remarks
Honesty, or Money plant *(Lunaria annua)* Small, slightly fragrant flowers; coarse leaves. Called money plant because its seedpods have center partitions of white papery disks the size of silver dollars. Good in dried arrangements.	H 2 ft. S 1 ft.	*L. a. alba,* white; *L. annua,* purple. There is a perennial, *L. rediviva,* but this is seldom available.	As annual sow seeds in spring; as biennial sow in summer. Sow outdoors in full sun or partial shade, in any well-drained soil. To dry, gather as soon as seeds start to turn brown; rub off outer part of pod to expose papery disk. Self-sows; can be invasive.
Iberis, see Candytuft **Ice plant,** see Daisy, Livingston			
Impatiens, or Patience plant *(Impatiens wallerana* hybrids) Single or double flowers, mostly in solid colors; waxy, deep green leaves. Superior plant for constant bloom all summer. Little or no care required.	H 6 in.-2 ft. S 1-2 ft.	Available in seed packets of mixed or separate colors that include white, purple, pink, orange, salmon, carmine, and red, some with deeper-colored centers or striped or flecked petals. 6 in.-1 ft.: 'Elfin Series.' 1-2 ft.: 'Imp Series' and many others.	Buy plants or sow seeds indoors 8-10 wk. before safe outdoor planting time, when weather is warm. Grow in partial shade and in soil well mixed with compost or peat moss. Water in dry spells. Not necessary to remove faded flowers. Perennial in frost-free areas. Cuttings root quickly.
Joseph's coat, see Amaranthus **Kale, ornamental,** see Cabbage, ornamental			
Kochia, Burning bush, or Summer cypress *(Kochia scoparia trichophylla)* Grown for feathery green foliage in dense bushy form that turns bright red in fall. Insignificant purple flowers.	H 2-3 ft. S 1½ ft.	'Childsii' is often listed in catalogs, considered improved form.	Sow seeds outdoors when weather warms. Grow in full sun and in average soil. Tolerates very hot weather but will grow anywhere. Can be pruned to shape if desired. Self-sows and may become weedy in mild regions. Good background plant.
Larkspur *(Delphinium ajacis* hybrids, or *Consolida ambigua* hybrids) Single or double blooms densely set along tall, tapering spikes with feathery, finely cut, bright green leaves. Good cut flower that also dries well.	H 14 in.-4 ft. S 1 ft.	Available in seed packets of mixed or separate colors that include shades of white, blue, lavender, pink, salmon, and red. Two types: base branching with long side spikes, and hyacinth flowered with single 14-in. spikes. Catalogs are seldom clear on offerings. *D. chinense,* or *D. grandiflorum,* perennial, also grown as annual or sometimes as biennial north of Zone C.	Sow seeds outdoors in very early spring or in fall. In Zone D make fall sowing in time for seedlings to emerge before cold weather; in Zones A and B sow just before soil freezes so that seeds will not germinate until spring. Flowers best in cool weather. Grow in full sun or partial shade, in average soil. Difficult to transplant.
Lavatera, or Tree mallow *(Lavatera trimestris)* Bushy plants with single, satiny holly-hocklike flowers in mid to late summer. Leaves resemble those on maple tree.	H 2½-3 ft. S 2 ft.	'Loveliness,' deep rose; 'Tanagra,' rose, a tetraploid hybrid (4 times normal number of chromosomes) with flowers up to 3 in. across. White form is sometimes available.	Sow seeds in spring as soon as soil can be worked and where plants are to grow, since they are difficult to transplant. Does best in full sun and average soil. Remove faded flowers for further flowering. May need support.

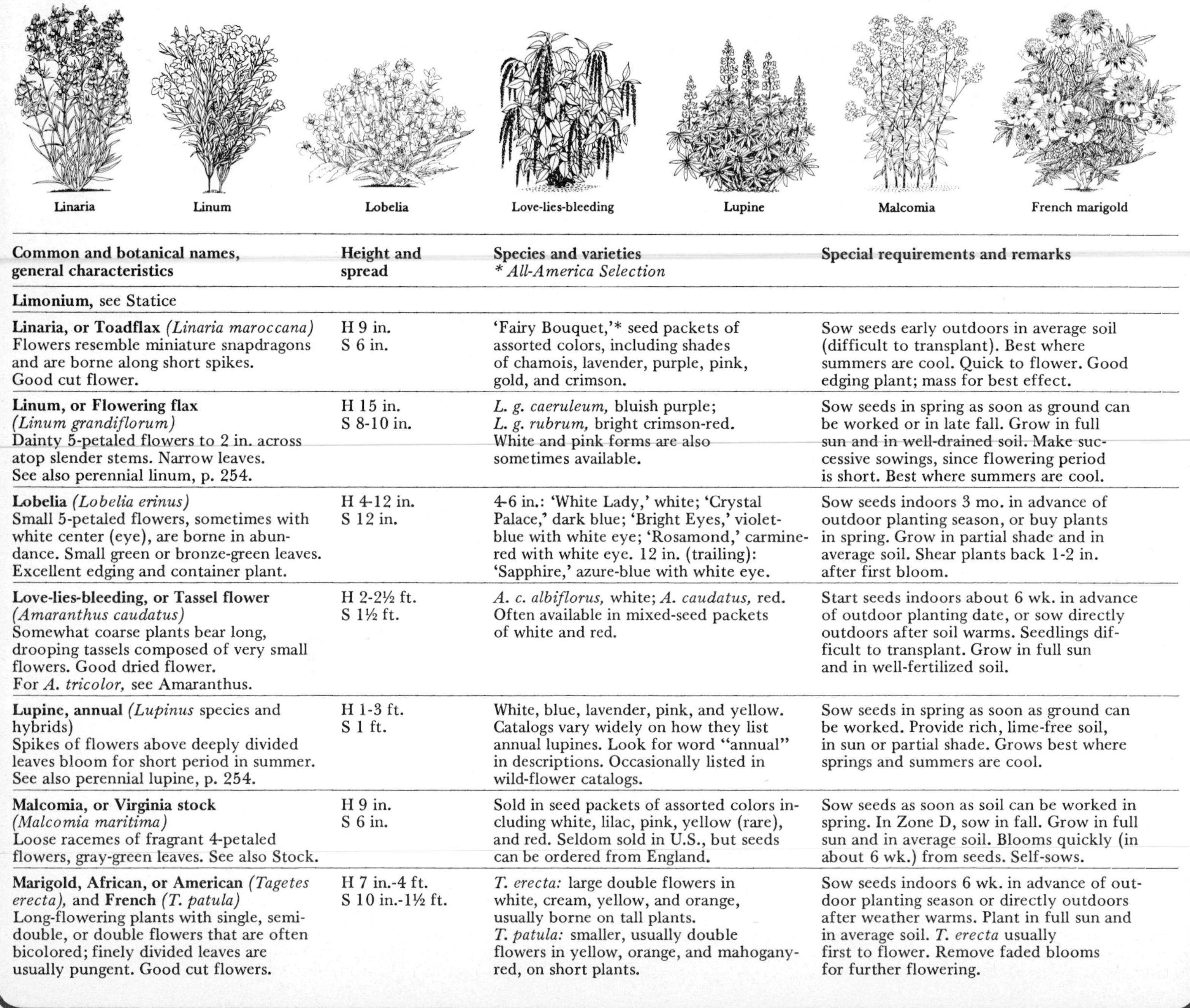

Common and botanical names, general characteristics	Height and spread	Species and varieties ** All-America Selection*	Special requirements and remarks
Limonium, see Statice			
Linaria, or Toadflax *(Linaria maroccana)* Flowers resemble miniature snapdragons and are borne along short spikes. Good cut flower.	H 9 in. S 6 in.	'Fairy Bouquet,'* seed packets of assorted colors, including shades of chamois, lavender, purple, pink, gold, and crimson.	Sow seeds early outdoors in average soil (difficult to transplant). Best where summers are cool. Quick to flower. Good edging plant; mass for best effect.
Linum, or Flowering flax *(Linum grandiflorum)* Dainty 5-petaled flowers to 2 in. across atop slender stems. Narrow leaves. See also perennial linum, p. 254.	H 15 in. S 8-10 in.	*L. g. caeruleum,* bluish purple; *L. g. rubrum,* bright crimson-red. White and pink forms are also sometimes available.	Sow seeds in spring as soon as ground can be worked or in late fall. Grow in full sun and in well-drained soil. Make successive sowings, since flowering period is short. Best where summers are cool.
Lobelia *(Lobelia erinus)* Small 5-petaled flowers, sometimes with white center (eye), are borne in abundance. Small green or bronze-green leaves. Excellent edging and container plant.	H 4-12 in. S 12 in.	4-6 in.: 'White Lady,' white; 'Crystal Palace,' dark blue; 'Bright Eyes,' violet-blue with white eye; 'Rosamond,' carmine-red with white eye. 12 in. (trailing): 'Sapphire,' azure-blue with white eye.	Sow seeds indoors 3 mo. in advance of outdoor planting season, or buy plants in spring. Grow in partial shade and in average soil. Shear plants back 1-2 in. after first bloom.
Love-lies-bleeding, or Tassel flower *(Amaranthus caudatus)* Somewhat coarse plants bear long, drooping tassels composed of very small flowers. Good dried flower. For *A. tricolor,* see Amaranthus.	H 2-2½ ft. S 1½ ft.	*A. c. albiflorus,* white; *A. caudatus,* red. Often available in mixed-seed packets of white and red.	Start seeds indoors about 6 wk. in advance of outdoor planting date, or sow directly outdoors after soil warms. Seedlings difficult to transplant. Grow in full sun and in well-fertilized soil.
Lupine, annual *(Lupinus* species and hybrids) Spikes of flowers above deeply divided leaves bloom for short period in summer. See also perennial lupine, p. 254.	H 1-3 ft. S 1 ft.	White, blue, lavender, pink, and yellow. Catalogs vary widely on how they list annual lupines. Look for word "annual" in descriptions. Occasionally listed in wild-flower catalogs.	Sow seeds in spring as soon as ground can be worked. Provide rich, lime-free soil, in sun or partial shade. Grows best where springs and summers are cool.
Malcomia, or Virginia stock *(Malcomia maritima)* Loose racemes of fragrant 4-petaled flowers, gray-green leaves. See also Stock.	H 9 in. S 6 in.	Sold in seed packets of assorted colors including white, lilac, pink, yellow (rare), and red. Seldom sold in U.S., but seeds can be ordered from England.	Sow seeds as soon as soil can be worked in spring. In Zone D, sow in fall. Grow in full sun and in average soil. Blooms quickly (in about 6 wk.) from seeds. Self-sows.
Marigold, African, or American *(Tagetes erecta),* and **French** *(T. patula)* Long-flowering plants with single, semi-double, or double flowers that are often bicolored; finely divided leaves are usually pungent. Good cut flowers.	H 7 in.-4 ft. S 10 in.-1½ ft.	*T. erecta:* large double flowers in white, cream, yellow, and orange, usually borne on tall plants. *T. patula:* smaller, usually double flowers in yellow, orange, and mahogany-red, on short plants.	Sow seeds indoors 6 wk. in advance of outdoor planting season or directly outdoors after weather warms. Plant in full sun and in average soil. *T. erecta* usually first to flower. Remove faded blooms for further flowering.

Signet marigold

Mignonette

Monkey flower

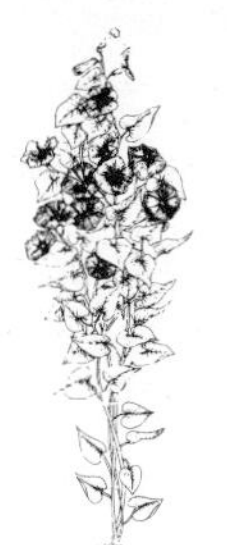
Morning glory

Dwarf morning glory

Common and botanical names, general characteristics	**Height and spread**	**Species and varieties** ** All-America Selection*	**Special requirements and remarks**
Marigold, signet *(Tagetes tenuifolia pumila,* or *T. signata pumila)* Masses of small single flowers on compact plants completely hide lacy foliage. Long blooming. Similar to French marigold, which is more widely available.	H 8 in. S 6 in.	'Lemon Gem,' yellow; 'Golden Gem,' orange.	Sow seeds outdoors after danger of frost is past, or sow indoors 6 wk. before last spring frost. Grow in full sun and in average, well-drained soil. Keep flowers picked for further flowering.
Mathiola, see Stock **Matricaria,** see Feverfew **Mesembryanthemum,** see Daisy, Livingston			
Mignonette *(Reseda odorata)* Grown primarily for fragrance of its yellowish-green flowers. Leaves are coarse, and plants tend to be sprawling. Good cut flower.	H 1 ft. S 9 in.-1 ft.	Available in mixed-seed packets with flowers of varying colors from yellowish green to brownish red. Also as 'Bismark,' red; 'Machet Giant,' pale red, a large-flowered variety.	Sow after danger of frost is past where plants are to grow, since seedlings are difficult to transplant. In frost-free areas can be sown in late fall or early winter. Grow in full sun or partial shade, as filler among showier plants. Grows best in cool weather.
Monkey flower, or Mimulus *(Mimulus luteus* and hybrids) Showy flowers with speckled petals on low, compact plants. Good plant for bloom in partial shade. Tender perennial, but usually grown as annual.	H 1 ft. S 9 in.	Available in mixed-seed packets including various shades of yellow and red with contrasting spots. Large-flowered strain is sometimes available.	Sow seeds indoors 2 mo. in advance of safe outdoor planting date; set outdoors after danger of frost is past in partially shaded location in rich, moist soil. Or sow outdoors for late bloom. Good in pots and hanging baskets.
Morning glory *(Ipomoea purpurea* and *I. tricolor)* Popular vine with single or occasionally double flowers, some edged or striped with white, up to 8 in. across. Older varieties close in afternoon; some newer ones stay open most of day.	H 10 ft. S 1 ft.	'Pearly Gates,'* white; 'Flying Saucers,' white and blue striped; 'Early Call,' blue, rose, or mixed; 'Heavenly Blue,' sky-blue; 'Wedding Bells,' rose-lavender; 'Scarlet O'Hara,'* crimson; 'Japanese Imperial,' mixed colors, huge flowers; 'Tinkerbell's Petticoat,' double. For dwarf forms, see below.	Speed germination by enclosing seeds in wet paper towels for 48 hr. in warm (75°-80° F) place prior to sowing, or nick pointed end of seeds. Start early indoors in pots (resents root disturbance), or sow outdoors where plants are to grow, in full sun and in average soil (not too rich). Provide support.
Morning glory, dwarf *(Convolvulus tricolor)* Fairly large flowers resembling true morning glories are borne on low, bushy, somewhat trailing plants. Flowers stay open all day, unlike older varieties of more familiar vine (see above).	H 9 in.-1½ ft. S 6 in.-9 in.	Seed packets of assorted colors including white, blue, rose, and red. 'Royal Ensign,' royal blue. Offered by only a few seed companies.	Nick or file hard seeds before sowing to hasten germination. Sow after soil has warmed. Plants need full sun, average soil, and warmth to prosper. Can be used in hanging baskets or as edging plant in tubs. Remove faded blooms for further flowering.

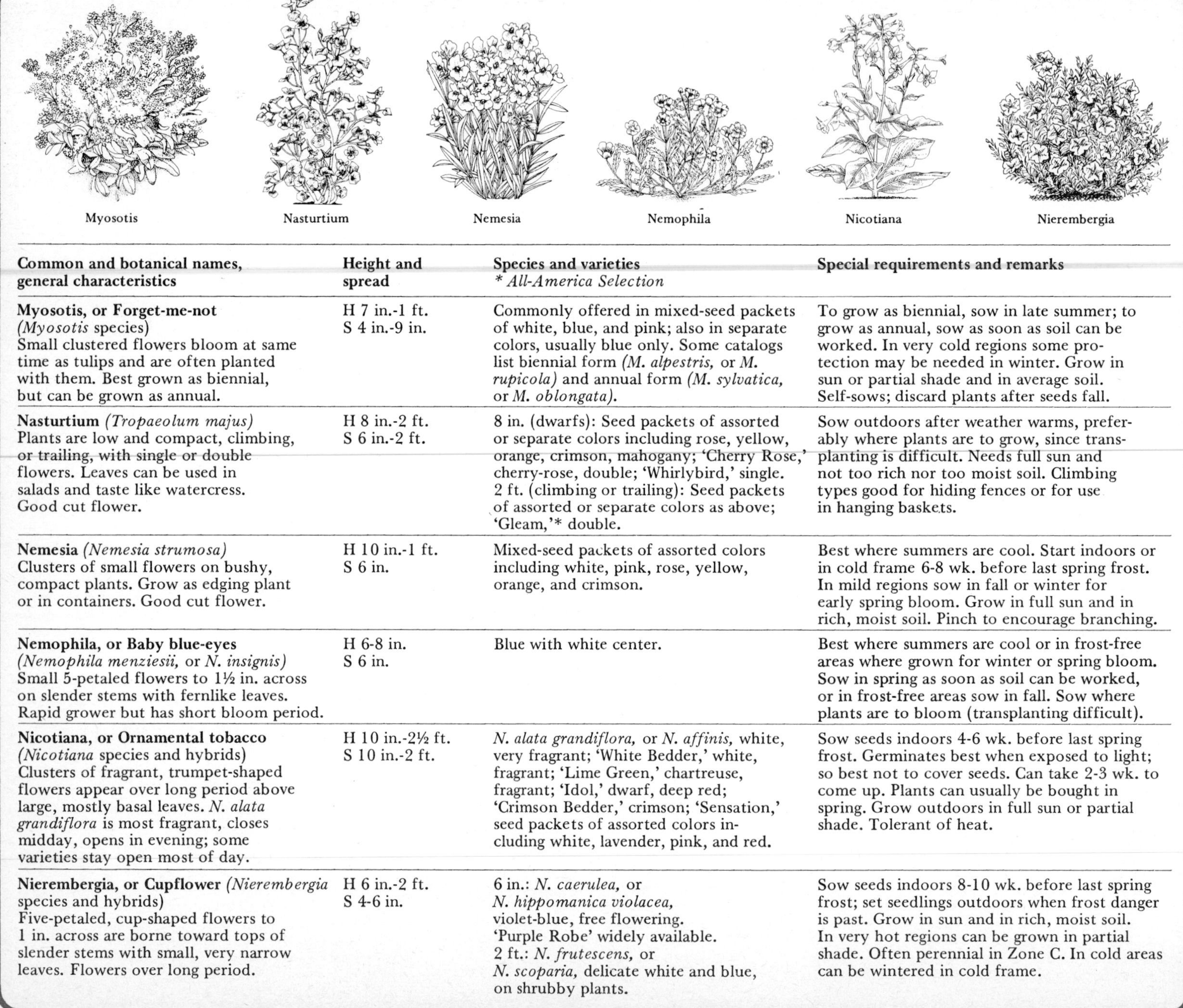

Myosotis Nasturtium Nemesia Nemophila Nicotiana Nierembergia

Common and botanical names, general characteristics	Height and spread	Species and varieties ** All-America Selection*	Special requirements and remarks
Myosotis, or Forget-me-not *(Myosotis* species) Small clustered flowers bloom at same time as tulips and are often planted with them. Best grown as biennial, but can be grown as annual.	H 7 in.-1 ft. S 4 in.-9 in.	Commonly offered in mixed-seed packets of white, blue, and pink; also in separate colors, usually blue only. Some catalogs list biennial form *(M. alpestris,* or *M. rupicola)* and annual form *(M. sylvatica,* or *M. oblongata).*	To grow as biennial, sow in late summer; to grow as annual, sow as soon as soil can be worked. In very cold regions some protection may be needed in winter. Grow in sun or partial shade and in average soil. Self-sows; discard plants after seeds fall.
Nasturtium *(Tropaeolum majus)* Plants are low and compact, climbing, or trailing, with single or double flowers. Leaves can be used in salads and taste like watercress. Good cut flower.	H 8 in.-2 ft. S 6 in.-2 ft.	8 in. (dwarfs): Seed packets of assorted or separate colors including rose, yellow, orange, crimson, mahogany; 'Cherry Rose,' cherry-rose, double; 'Whirlybird,' single. 2 ft. (climbing or trailing): Seed packets of assorted or separate colors as above; 'Gleam,'* double.	Sow outdoors after weather warms, preferably where plants are to grow, since transplanting is difficult. Needs full sun and not too rich nor too moist soil. Climbing types good for hiding fences or for use in hanging baskets.
Nemesia *(Nemesia strumosa)* Clusters of small flowers on bushy, compact plants. Grow as edging plant or in containers. Good cut flower.	H 10 in.-1 ft. S 6 in.	Mixed-seed packets of assorted colors including white, pink, rose, yellow, orange, and crimson.	Best where summers are cool. Start indoors or in cold frame 6-8 wk. before last spring frost. In mild regions sow in fall or winter for early spring bloom. Grow in full sun and in rich, moist soil. Pinch to encourage branching.
Nemophila, or Baby blue-eyes *(Nemophila menziesii,* or *N. insignis)* Small 5-petaled flowers to 1½ in. across on slender stems with fernlike leaves. Rapid grower but has short bloom period.	H 6-8 in. S 6 in.	Blue with white center.	Best where summers are cool or in frost-free areas where grown for winter or spring bloom. Sow in spring as soon as soil can be worked, or in frost-free areas sow in fall. Sow where plants are to bloom (transplanting difficult).
Nicotiana, or Ornamental tobacco *(Nicotiana* species and hybrids) Clusters of fragrant, trumpet-shaped flowers appear over long period above large, mostly basal leaves. *N. alata grandiflora* is most fragrant, closes midday, opens in evening; some varieties stay open most of day.	H 10 in.-2½ ft. S 10 in.-2 ft.	*N. alata grandiflora,* or *N. affinis,* white, very fragrant; 'White Bedder,' white, fragrant; 'Lime Green,' chartreuse, fragrant; 'Idol,' dwarf, deep red; 'Crimson Bedder,' crimson; 'Sensation,' seed packets of assorted colors including white, lavender, pink, and red.	Sow seeds indoors 4-6 wk. before last spring frost. Germinates best when exposed to light; so best not to cover seeds. Can take 2-3 wk. to come up. Plants can usually be bought in spring. Grow outdoors in full sun or partial shade. Tolerant of heat.
Nierembergia, or Cupflower *(Nierembergia* species and hybrids) Five-petaled, cup-shaped flowers to 1 in. across are borne toward tops of slender stems with small, very narrow leaves. Flowers over long period.	H 6 in.-2 ft. S 4-6 in.	6 in.: *N. caerulea,* or *N. hippomanica violacea,* violet-blue, free flowering. 'Purple Robe' widely available. 2 ft.: *N. frutescens,* or *N. scoparia,* delicate white and blue, on shrubby plants.	Sow seeds indoors 8-10 wk. before last spring frost; set seedlings outdoors when frost danger is past. Grow in sun and in rich, moist soil. In very hot regions can be grown in partial shade. Often perennial in Zone C. In cold areas can be wintered in cold frame.

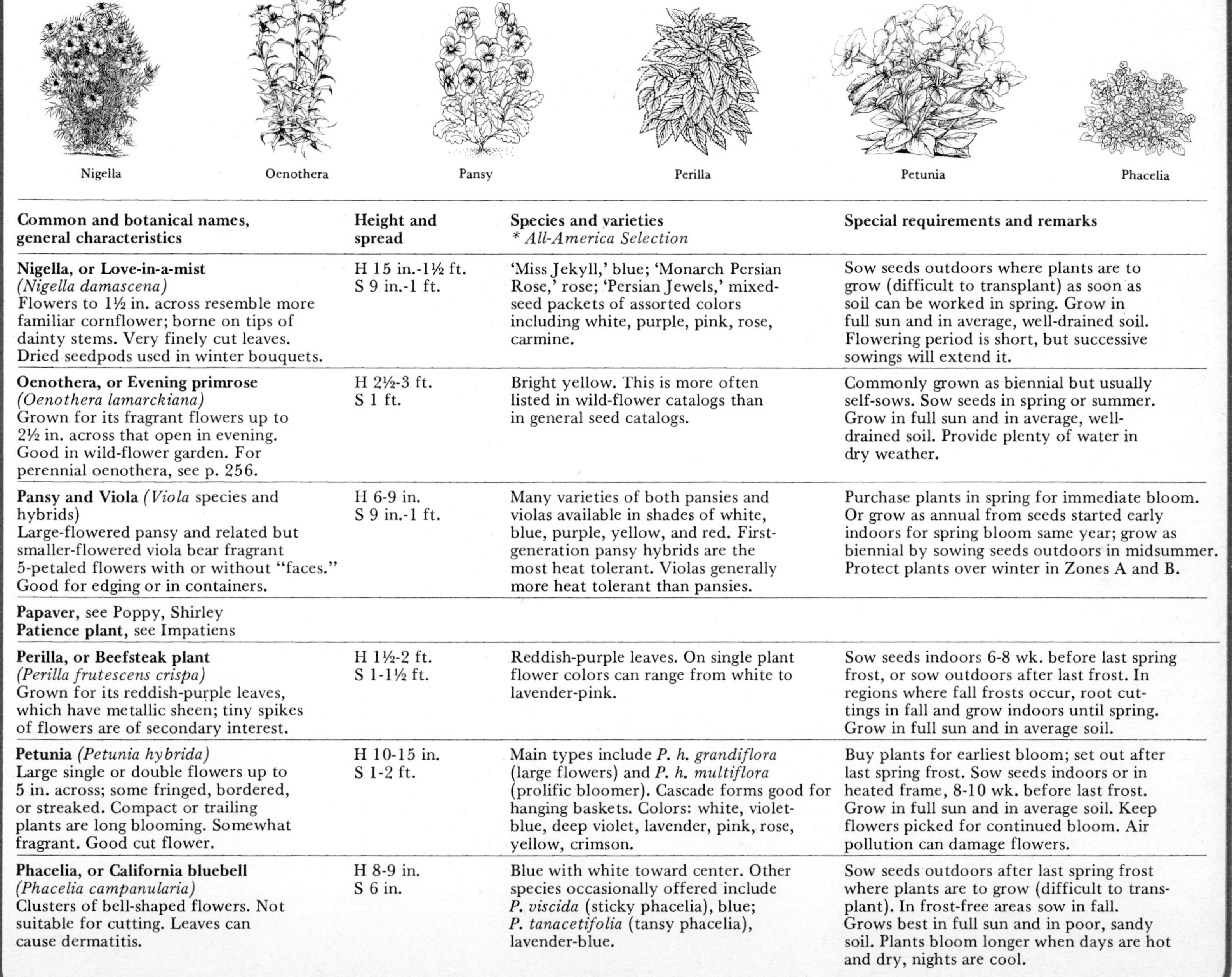

Nigella — Oenothera — Pansy — Perilla — Petunia — Phacelia

Common and botanical names, general characteristics	Height and spread	Species and varieties * *All-America Selection*	Special requirements and remarks
Nigella, or Love-in-a-mist *(Nigella damascena)* Flowers to 1½ in. across resemble more familiar cornflower; borne on tips of dainty stems. Very finely cut leaves. Dried seedpods used in winter bouquets.	H 15 in.-1½ ft. S 9 in.-1 ft.	'Miss Jekyll,' blue; 'Monarch Persian Rose,' rose; 'Persian Jewels,' mixed-seed packets of assorted colors including white, purple, pink, rose, carmine.	Sow seeds outdoors where plants are to grow (difficult to transplant) as soon as soil can be worked in spring. Grow in full sun and in average, well-drained soil. Flowering period is short, but successive sowings will extend it.
Oenothera, or Evening primrose *(Oenothera lamarckiana)* Grown for its fragrant flowers up to 2½ in. across that open in evening. Good in wild-flower garden. For perennial oenothera, see p. 256.	H 2½-3 ft. S 1 ft.	Bright yellow. This is more often listed in wild-flower catalogs than in general seed catalogs.	Commonly grown as biennial but usually self-sows. Sow seeds in spring or summer. Grow in full sun and in average, well-drained soil. Provide plenty of water in dry weather.
Pansy and Viola *(Viola* species and hybrids) Large-flowered pansy and related but smaller-flowered viola bear fragrant 5-petaled flowers with or without "faces." Good for edging or in containers.	H 6-9 in. S 9 in.-1 ft.	Many varieties of both pansies and violas available in shades of white, blue, purple, yellow, and red. First-generation pansy hybrids are the most heat tolerant. Violas generally more heat tolerant than pansies.	Purchase plants in spring for immediate bloom. Or grow as annual from seeds started early indoors for spring bloom same year; grow as biennial by sowing seeds outdoors in midsummer. Protect plants over winter in Zones A and B.
Papaver, see Poppy, Shirley **Patience plant,** see Impatiens			
Perilla, or Beefsteak plant *(Perilla frutescens crispa)* Grown for its reddish-purple leaves, which have metallic sheen; tiny spikes of flowers are of secondary interest.	H 1½-2 ft. S 1-1½ ft.	Reddish-purple leaves. On single plant flower colors can range from white to lavender-pink.	Sow seeds indoors 6-8 wk. before last spring frost, or sow outdoors after last frost. In regions where fall frosts occur, root cuttings in fall and grow indoors until spring. Grow in full sun and in average soil.
Petunia *(Petunia hybrida)* Large single or double flowers up to 5 in. across; some fringed, bordered, or streaked. Compact or trailing plants are long blooming. Somewhat fragrant. Good cut flower.	H 10-15 in. S 1-2 ft.	Main types include *P. h. grandiflora* (large flowers) and *P. h. multiflora* (prolific bloomer). Cascade forms good for hanging baskets. Colors: white, violet-blue, deep violet, lavender, pink, rose, yellow, crimson.	Buy plants for earliest bloom; set out after last spring frost. Sow seeds indoors or in heated frame, 8-10 wk. before last frost. Grow in full sun and in average soil. Keep flowers picked for continued bloom. Air pollution can damage flowers.
Phacelia, or California bluebell *(Phacelia campanularia)* Clusters of bell-shaped flowers. Not suitable for cutting. Leaves can cause dermatitis.	H 8-9 in. S 6 in.	Blue with white toward center. Other species occasionally offered include *P. viscida* (sticky phacelia), blue; *P. tanacetifolia* (tansy phacelia), lavender-blue.	Sow seeds outdoors after last spring frost where plants are to grow (difficult to transplant). In frost-free areas sow in fall. Grows best in full sun and in poor, sandy soil. Plants bloom longer when days are hot and dry, nights are cool.

Phlox

Pink

California poppy

Shirley poppy

Portulaca

Primrose
(Primula malacoides)

Common and botanical names, general characteristics	Height and spread	Species and varieties ** All-America Selection*	Special requirements and remarks
Phlox, annual *(Phlox drummondii)* Dense heads of small 5-petaled flowers, some bicolored or fringed, are borne over long period above neat foliage. Good cut flower.	H 7-15 in. S 9 in.	7 in.: 'Dwarf Beauty,' seed packets of assorted or individual colors including white, blue, pink, salmon, crimson; 'Twinkle,'* fringed petals, seed packets of assorted or individual colors. 15 in.: 'Glamour,'* salmon, white eye.	Quick to flower from seeds sown outdoors after last spring frost. Sow where plants are to bloom (difficult to transplant). Easily grown in full sun and in average soil. Cut plants back after first bloom to encourage further flowering.
Pink, annual, or China pink *(Dianthus chinensis)* Scented, single to double flowers borne in great profusion on stiff stems above neat foliage. Good cut flower.	H 7 in.-1 ft. S 6 in.-1 ft.	8 in.: 'Baby Doll,' single, bicolors of white, pink, red; 'Magic Charms,'* single, serrated, white, pink, red. 1 ft.: 'China Doll,'* semi-double, fringed, white edged in pink, rose, red.	Sow seeds outdoors as soon as soil can be worked or indoors 6-8 wk. earlier. Grow in full sun and in well-drained, slightly alkaline soil. Keep faded blooms picked to encourage further flowering.
Poinsettia, annual, see *Euphorbia heterophylla*			
Poppy, California *(Eschscholzia californica)* Masses of saucer-shaped flowers on low-spreading plants with finely cut leaves. Flowers close at night and reopen next day. Can be perennial in Zone D but usually grown as annual.	H 1 ft. S 6 in.	'Sunset Mixed,' single, cream to dark red; 'Ballerina Yellow,' semi-double or double, yellow; 'Mission Bells,' semi-double or double, in shades of rose, yellow, orange, crimson; many two toned and with ruffled edges.	Sow seeds in early spring where plants are to grow (difficult to transplant). In Zone D sow in fall. Locate in full sun and in average soil. Does well in dry areas. Flowers best in cool weather. When weather is hot, foliage yellows, and plants are best discarded. Usually self-sows.
Poppy, Shirley *(Papaver rhoeas)* Satiny flowers, single or double, on wiry stems above divided leaves. Good cut flower. See also perennial Oriental poppy, p. 258.	H 1½ ft. S 1 ft.	Singles and doubles, often bicolored, in seed packets of assorted colors including pink, yellow, salmon, apricot, red—many shaded and edged with other colors.	Sow seeds outdoors in late fall or as soon as soil can be worked in spring. Difficult to transplant. Grow in full sun and in average soil. In Zone D fall-sown seeds germinate immediately, bloom early.
Portulaca, or Rose moss *(Portulaca grandiflora)* Ground-hugging plant with succulent, narrow leaves and single to double flowers to 2½ in. across. Profuse blooms remain open only when sun shines.	H 5-7 in. S 6 in.-2 ft.	Many varieties offered in singles and doubles. Seed packets of mixed or individual colors including white, lavender, rose, yellow, orange, coral, red.	Sow seeds outdoors where plants are to grow or in cold frame, or start 6-8 wk. earlier indoors. Young seedlings transplant easily. Grows best in sunny, dry places and in not overly rich soil. Blooms quickly; often self-sows.
Primrose *(Primula malacoides, P. obconica,* and *P. polyantha)* Masses of flowers in terminal or tiered clusters above basal foliage. *P. obconica* may cause skin irritation. *P. polyantha* perennial often grown as biennial. For perennial primrose, see p. 258.	H 1-1½ ft. S 9 in.-1 ft.	*P. malacoides* (fairy primrose), white, rose, scarlet; *P. obconica,* white, blue, rose, red; *P. polyantha,* cream-white, yellow, orange are commonest colors.	Purchase plants in fall, and set out for late-winter and spring bloom. Plant in partial shade and in moist, fertile soil. Or start from seeds sown in late summer in seed flats in partial shade; transplant seedlings into garden. *P. malacoides* and *P. obconica* popular in Southwest.

Rudbeckia

Salpiglossis

Salvia

Scabiosa

Snapdragon

Common and botanical names, general characteristics	Height and spread	Species and varieties * *All-America Selection*	Special requirements and remarks
Primrose, evening, see Oenothera			
Rudbeckia, or Gloriosa daisy (*Rudbeckia hirta* varieties) Large single or double daisylike flowers up to 5 in. across, with green or brown centers, long stems. Showy perennial, but often grown as annual. Good cut flower.	H 2-3 ft. S 1-2 ft.	2-2½ ft.: 'Irish Eyes,' single, yellow, green center; 'Orange Bedder,' single, orange. 3 ft.: 'Double Gold,'* double, yellow; 'Pinwheel,' single, gold and mahogany bicolor.	Sow seeds outdoors as soon as soil can be worked in spring, or sow in fall. Grow in full sun or partial shade and in average, well-drained soil or even poor, dry soil. Plants usually survive winter except in parts of Zone A. Self-sows freely. Long blooming and trouble free.
Salpiglossis, or Painted tongue (*Salpiglossis sinuata*) Funnel-shaped flowers up to 2½ in. across with velvety texture, delicately veined petals. Long-lasting cut flower.	H 2-2½ ft. S 1 ft.	Mixed-seed packets of assorted colors: purple, rose, gold, scarlet. 'Splash,' first-generation hybrid, bushy; 'Bolero,' second-generation hybrid, bushy. Both are more rugged than older strains.	Sow seeds indoors 8 wk. before last spring frost, or buy plants in spring. Grow in full sun and in fertile soil. Seedlings grow slowly in early stages. Blooms best before weather turns hot; so early start is important.
Salvia, or Scarlet sage (*Salvia splendens*) Spikes of closely set flowers on bushy plants that bloom over long period. Popular and easily grown plant that is extremely showy. Actually a tender shrub, but grown as annual. Not good for cutting.	H 7 in.-3 ft. S 1 ft.	Wide assortment of varieties in shades of red, some listed as early flowering. Check for height desired. Also offered in white, lavender, purple, rose, salmon. Also often listed: *S. farinacea,* blue; *S. patens,* blue; *S. horminum,* mixed-seed packets of assorted colors.	Sow seeds indoors 4-6 wk. before last spring frost, or sow outdoors when weather warms. Or buy plants in spring. Grow in sun or partial shade and in fertile, well-drained soil. To keep leaves dark green, apply light feedings of liquid fertilizer, but do not overfeed.
Scabiosa, or Pincushion flower (*Scabiosa atropurpurea*) Rounded flower heads up to 3 in. across give pincushion effect because of protruding silvery stamens. Delicate stems and leaves. Long-lasting, fragrant cut flower. For perennial scabiosa, see p. 260.	H 1½-3 ft. S 9 in.	Offered in mixed-seed packets of assorted colors including white, blue, lavender, pink, rose, crimson, maroon; both dwarf and tall varieties.	Sow seeds indoors 4-6 wk. before last spring frost, or sow outdoors when weather warms. Can be sown in fall in southern Zone C. Grow in full sun and in well-drained soil. Taller varieties tend to be floppy, often need staking. Flowers can be dried for bouquets.
Schizanthus, see Butterfly flower			
Snapdragon (*Antirrhinum majus*) Spikes of closely set individual flowers, mostly single, with unusual construction that enables them to be squeezed so that they snap open, hence common name. Tall kinds are excellent for cutting.	H 7 in.-3 ft. S 9 in.-1½ ft.	Many varieties in seed packets of mixed or separate colors: white, lavender, pink, rose, yellow, orange, red. Butterfly type has open-faced flowers with flaring petals. Check height of variety when buying, since there is wide range.	Sow seeds indoors 6-8 wk. before last spring frost; grow at 50° F. Or sow outdoors in cold frame. Or buy plants in spring. In Zone D and southern Zone C, set out plants in fall. Grow in full sun and in fertile soil. Remove faded blooms for further flowering.
Snow-on-the-mountain, see *Euphorbia marginata*			
Spiderflower, see Cleome			

Statice

Stock

Sunflower

Sweet pea

Sweet William

Tithonia

Common and botanical names, general characteristics	Height and spread	Species and varieties * *All-America Selection*	Special requirements and remarks
Statice *(Limonium bonduelii* and *L. sinuatum)* Clusters of little straw-textured flowers are borne on stiff, slender stems above basal leaves. Good seaside plant. Long-lasting flowers used fresh or dried.	H 1-2½ ft. S 1 ft.	*L. bonduelii,* yellow. *L. sinuatum* 'Iceberg,' white; 'Heavenly Blue,' blue; 'Midnight Blue,' dark blue; 'Gold Coast,' yellow; 'American Beauty,' rose; 'Apricot Beauty,' peach and yellow bicolor. Also in mixed-seed packets of assorted colors.	Sow seeds outdoors as soon as soil can be worked. If earlier flowers are desired, sow indoors 8 wk. before last spring frost. Seed packets often contain clusters of flower seed heads; separate before sowing. Grow in full sun and in well-drained, fairly dry soil.
Stock *(Mathiola bicornis* and *M. incana annua)* Fragrant flowers, single or double, are borne in spikes on bushy plant. Good cut flower.	H 1-2½ ft. S 9 in.-1 ft.	*M. bicornis* (evening stock), single, in loose spikes, 12-18 in. high, lilac; *M. i. annua* (ten-week stock), seed packets of assorted or separate colors including white, lilac, purple, pink, rose, yellow; 'Trysomic Seven Week' and 'Dwarf Ten Week' bloom most quickly.	Sow seeds outdoors as soon as soil can be worked, or buy plants. Difficult to start indoors unless 50° F temperature can be maintained. In Zone D sow in fall for late-winter, early-spring bloom. Grow in full sun and in moderately rich, moist soil.
Stock, Virginia, see Malcomia			
Sunflower, annual *(Helianthus* species) Low-growing varieties of sunflower are best for general garden use; tall kinds for background plants. For perennial sunflower, see Helianthus, p. 251.	H 1½-10 ft. S 1-2 ft.	1½-4 ft.: 'Italian White,' single, white to cream; 'Teddy Bear,' double, yellow. 6-10 ft.: 'Giganteus,' large single, yellow; 'Sungold,' double, yellow; 'Red,' single, chestnut-red.	Sow seeds outdoors, preferably where plants are to grow (difficult to transplant). Makes rapid growth; so no need to start early indoors. Grow in full sun and in average to poor soil. Birds eat seeds that follow flowers.
Sweet pea *(Lathyrus odoratus)* Old-fashioned favorite with climbing and nonclimbing forms. Many varieties are fragrant. Good cut flower.	H 8 in.-10 ft. S 3-6 ft.	Many varieties of tall climbers offered in mixed-seed packets or in individual colors: white, blue, lavender, orange-red, salmon, scarlet. Popular dwarf nonclimbers in same colors: 'Bijou' and 'Little Sweetheart.' Intermediate in height are 'Jet Set,' 28 in.; 'Knee-Hi,' 2½ ft.	Sow seeds outdoors as soon as soil can be worked; soak seeds several hours prior to planting, and treat with bacterial inoculant (p. 571). Grow in full sun and in rich soil. Does best in cool weather, but heat-resistant varieties now exist. In Zone D sow in late summer for winter bloom; early winter for spring bloom. Support tall varieties.
Sweet William *(Dianthus barbatus)* Densely packed heads of mildly fragrant, single or double flowers above neat basal foliage. Both annual and biennial varieties available; often perennial in Zone C and into Zone B if there is snow cover.	H 4 in.-1½ ft. S 8-10 in.	Annual: 'Red Monarch,'* red; 'Roundabout,' shades of red, some patterned; 'Wee Willie,' shades of red. Biennial: in mixed-seed packets of assorted colors: white, pink, salmon, crimson, scarlet; some bicolored.	Sow seeds of annual kinds outdoors in early spring as soon as soil can be worked. Sow biennial kinds in spring or summer. Grow in full sun and in average to rich soil. In Zones A and B apply light mulch after soil freezes. Self-sows.
Tithonia, or Mexican sunflower *(Tithonia rotundifolia,* or *T. speciosa)* Large daisylike flowers up to 3 in. across resemble zinnias. Flowers in late summer.	H 4-5 ft. S 2 ft.	'Torch,'* orange-red, yellow center.	Plants take 3-4 mo. to flower from seeds; so best started indoors 6-8 wk. in advance of last spring frost. Grow in full sun and in average soil. Drought and heat resistant.

Torenia

Verbena

Vinca

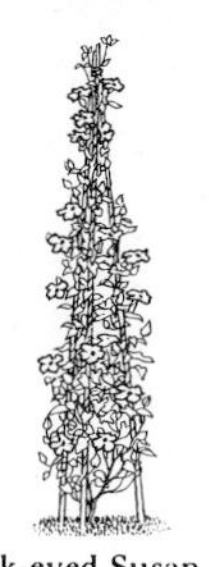
Black-eyed Susan vine *(Thunbergia alata)*

Wallflower

Zinnia

Common and botanical names, general characteristics	Height and spread	Species and varieties ** All-America Selection*	Special requirements and remarks
Tobacco, ornamental, see Nicotiana			
Torenia, or Wishbone flower *(Torenia fournieri compacta)* Bicolored tubular flowers have central yellow blotch. Particularly attractive plant to grow in partial shade.	H 8 in.-1 ft. S 6 in.	*T. f. compacta,* upper 2 petals light lavender, lower petals (lip) deep purple with bright yellow blotch in throat. *T. f. c. alba,* white with yellow throat.	Sow seeds indoors 8-10 wk. before safe outdoor planting date; or set plants out when night temperatures will not drop below 60° F. In cool climates grow in full sun, otherwise partial shade; average soil.
Trachymene, see Blue lace flower			
Verbena *(Verbena* hybrids) Fragrant, small, single to semi-double flowers in large clusters up to 3 in. across. Low, spreading plants. Perennial in Zone D but blooms best as annual.	H 8-10 in. S 1 ft.	Seed packets of assorted or separate colors including white, lavender-blue, rose, salmon-pink, scarlet. 'Amethyst,'* lavender-blue; 'Blaze,'* scarlet.	Sow seeds 12 wk. before last spring frost or buy plants. Grows best in full sun and in average soil. Keep faded flowers picked to encourage more bloom and to keep plants from becoming lanky.
Vinca, or Periwinkle *(Vinca rosea)* Single 5-petaled flowers up to 1 in. across. Shiny green leaves are attractive throughout summer. Perennial in Zone D but blooms best as annual.	H 6-10 in. S 1-2 ft.	'Little Blanche,' white; 'Little Bright Eye,' white with rose-red center; 'Polka Dot,'* white, cherry-red center; 'Little Linda,' deep orchid; 'Little Delicata,' pale pink with red center.	Sow seeds indoors at least 12 wk. in advance of outdoor planting season, or buy plants. Grow in full sun or partial shade and in average soil. Pinch to encourage branching. Withstands city conditions well.
Vines, ornamental (various genera) Besides familiar morning glory (p. 301) and sweet pea (p. 306), there are many annual vines that grow quickly from seeds and provide good flowering cover for fences and trellises.	H 6-10 ft. S 6-10 ft.	*Thunbergia alata* (black-eyed Susan vine), cream, yellow, or orange, with purple throat; *Cobaea scandens* (monastery bells), blue; *Tropaeolum peregrinum* (canary creeper), yellow; *Quamoclit sloteri* (cardinal climber), red.	Sow seeds indoors 8-10 wk. before last spring frost. Grow in full sun and in average soil. All annual vines need some means of support. Canary creeper can only be grown where summers are cool.
Viola, see Pansy			
Wallflower, English *(Cheiranthus cheiri)* Flower spikes consist of fragrant, closely set, 4-petaled flowers up to 1 in. across. Does best in cool coastal areas.	H 15 in.-2 ft. S 8 in.-1 ft.	Listed in various ways in catalogs. *C. cheiri* comes in shades of purple, yellow, orange, red. Siberian wallflower, *Erysimum asperum* (sometimes listed as *C. allionii),* yellow and orange.	To grow as annual, sow seeds 8-10 wk. before last spring frost; to grow as biennial, sow in early summer. Grow in full sun and in nearly neutral soil. In Zone B plants may require winter protection. Often self-sows.
Zinnia *(Zinnia elegans* hybrids) Single or double daisylike flowers with petals often quilled, sometimes bicolored. Wide range of plant sizes. Reliable, easily grown, long blooming. Excellent cut flower.	H 6 in.-1½ ft. S 6 in.-1½ ft.	Wide range of types and colors including white, chartreuse, purple, pink, yellow, orange; study catalogs to select types desired.	Sow seeds indoors 4-6 wk. in advance of outdoor planting time, or sow outdoors after last spring frost. Grows best in warm weather, in full sun, and in well-fertilized soil. Keep faded blooms picked for further flowering. In cool, humid weather can be subject to powdery mildew.

Bulbs, Corms, and Tubers

From the first snowdrop in spring to the last fall-flowering crocus, bulbs, corms, and tubers provide color throughout the year, and most need little attention.

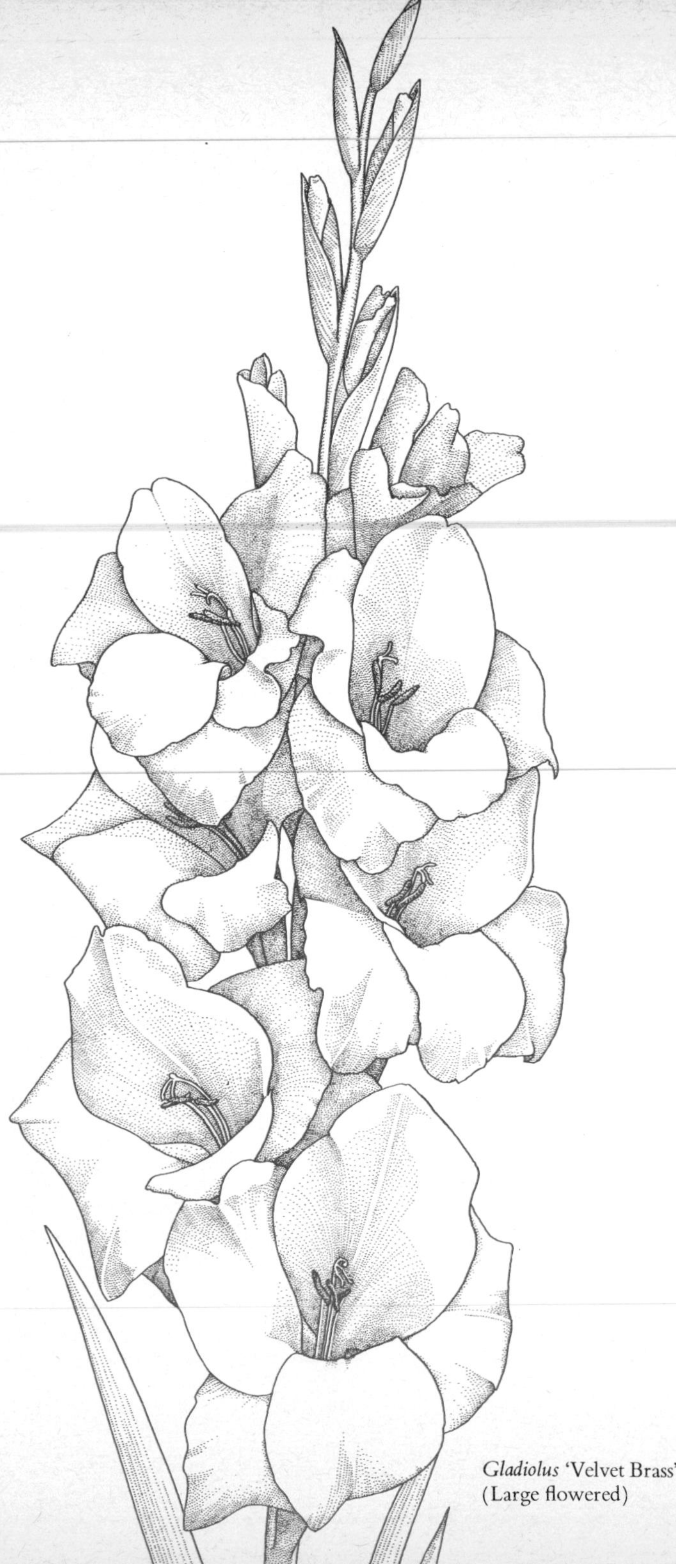

Gladiolus 'Velvet Brass' (Large flowered)

The wide range of bulbs, corms, and tubers available from catalogs and garden centers is a great aid to a colorful garden. On the pages that follow, the group as a whole will be referred to as bulbs or bulbous plants—except where it is necessary to identify the plants specifically as corms or tubers. Once planted, many bulbs will maintain themselves for years, with a minimum of care.

Although the large majority of herbaceous perennials, annuals, and bedding plants flower only during the summer months, the outdoor flowering season for bulbs extends from late winter right through the following fall.

Another advantage of growing bulbs is the ease with which these plants adapt themselves to varied habitats. Most bulbs grow well in average soil and full sun, and a few will do well in partial shade.

In every garden, however small, there is room for bulbs. The spring-flowering bulbs, in particular, flourish in a large number of settings. Where space allows, they can be "naturalized"—planted at random for an informal effect—in lawns and wild-flower gardens. Clumps of bulbs will brighten beds and borders before other perennials reawaken. They bloom beneath trees and shrubs and in perennial borders and fill out nooks of rock gardens and paved areas. In winter they can fill the house with fragrance and color.

The finest displays result if plans for planting and proposed locations of the bulbs are first roughed out on paper. Indicate the kind and quantity that you will need.

Before planting it can be useful to study displays in existing gardens, public and private. Also, do not hesitate to experiment. Although mistakes may occur at first, through experience you will gradually learn which are the best types of groupings, which soils in your lawn or garden are best suited to bulb culture, which colors of flowers harmonize and which clash, where a splash of contrasting color is needed, and so on.

Most specialist bulb suppliers offer species, horticultural varieties, and hybrids. Species are those that grow in the wild. Hybrids and horticultural varieties are obtained by cross-breeding, through pollination, two species or varieties, usually of the same genus, and by selecting spontaneous variants from large plantings. Such improvements are then reproduced in ways other than by seeds so that offspring will be identical.

The popular hybrids often have larger, more vividly colored blooms than the species. Occasionally, new hybrids are sold at high prices for the first few years.

Although some bulbous plants may seem costly, many kinds will reproduce themselves steadily each year without any special attention. A few will, however, eventually need to be lifted and divided in order to continue flowering well.

Bulbs fall into four main categories according to bloom time: late-winter and early-spring flowering, spring flowering, summer flowering, and autumn flowering.

Earliest flowers of the year. The snowdrop (*Galanthus*) is one of the first flowers to make its appearance each year, lifting its delicate white bell-shaped flowers above the ground in mid to late winter. Soon afterward comes the blue glory-of-the-snow, followed by the early crocuses, cyclamens, and scillas.

Another forerunner of spring is the small winter aconite (*Eranthis hyemalis*), with its golden flowers rising above a collar of green leaves.

All these plants associate well with one another, planted in groups beneath deciduous trees or in rock gardens. For an indoor display these winter-flowering bulbs can also be grown in pots and taken indoors after a prescribed period of cold. After flowering plant them out in the garden.

Heralds of spring. March, April, and May are the months when most spring-flowering bulbs appear. First the Dutch crocuses appear, their green-tipped shoots pushing through earth and grass to reveal their goblet-shaped blooms of yellow, lavender, white, mauve, or violet. Some are striped or heavily marked with a contrasting hue, and in bright sunshine they all open wide, revealing deep golden or orange anthers.

The large narcissus group flowers from early to mid spring. Many catalogs list the trumpet-shaped types under their common name of daffodil and those with short-cupped flowers under narcissus; but botanically they all belong to the genus *Narcissus.* They can be left undisturbed for several years in perennial borders or can be naturalized in grass; the smaller types provide an effective display in rock gardens. Many of them are sweetly scented.

Other heralds of spring are the hyacinths and muscaris, the early tulips, and the spring snowflakes (*Leucojum vernum*), with flowers like rounded snowdrops, their white petals tipped with pale green.

Crocuses and narcissi look best naturalized or planted in groups beneath trees or among perennials. But some spring-flowering bulbs, such as tulips, adapt well to formal schemes where one or more beds are devoted to them. In warmer parts of the United States, muscaris and the larger crocuses can be grown in containers on a patio or deck, or placed near a window or glass door so that they are visible from indoors.

Hyacinths are well suited for window boxes; in such locations the heavy aroma of the dense flower spikes can be fully appreciated. For garden planting it is advisable to use moderate-size bulbs—about 5½–6½ inches in circumference—instead of the large bulbs used for indoor flowering. The flower spikes are relatively small but can withstand wind and rain better. Named varieties of hyacinths are available with flowers of white, pink, yellow, salmon, red, and many shades of blue.

The first tulip species, perfect in rock gardens and raised beds, appear in early spring, while the larger-flowered hybrids bloom in mid to late spring. The Darwins and Darwin Hybrids are probably the most popular, with their strong stems, each of which carries the typical cup-shaped flower. They are majestic when grown in clusters and in formal bedding schemes. They can also be grown in rows for cutting. The Darwin Hybrids and Triumphs flower a few weeks before the Darwin and Cottage tulips.

Among the other bulbs that will flower in late spring, less familiar but decidedly worthwhile, are the handsome fritillarias, many of the anemones, the hardy, bright blue Spanish bluebells (*Endymion campanulata*), which naturalize well, the summer snowflake (*Leucojum aestivum*), the delicate camassias, the ranunculuses, and several kinds of ornamental onion (*Allium*).

Vivid summer displays. Ixias and sparaxis brighten warm, sunny borders, followed by the species of gladioli, with their delicate flower spikes.

High summer brings the stately gladiolus hybrids and the shade-tolerant tuberous begonias, as well as dahlias and lilies (see pp. 275–282 and pp. 331–336). These can be grown as accents or in massed displays; tuberous begonias are particularly attractive in containers. Gladioli for cutting can be planted in rows in the vegetable garden.

Many small bulbs, such as Iris reticulata, Anemone blanda, Narcissus triandrus albus, *and muscari (grape hyacinth), are ideal for growing in the rock garden. They can also be used to fill the front of a border where they can easily be seen.*

Every color of the spectrum is represented in the gladiolus hybrids, although there are no really good blues. The trumpet-shaped flowers, in massed array along the strong stems, open from the lower part of the stem upward. The hybrids range in size through the giant-flowered, large-flowered, butterfly, miniature, and primulinus groups. Their display lasts well into early fall.

Color in autumn and winter. In early fall the "autumn crocuses" (*Colchicum*) and fall-flowering crocuses (*Crocus*) follow the late gladioli. Like the spring-flowering crocuses, these are best grown in bold groups beneath deciduous trees, in pockets in a rock garden, or, in the case of colchicums, naturalized among low-growing ground covers, where they make an effective splash of color and can be left undisturbed for many years.

In mild areas autumn also brings *Amaryllis belladonna,* with its massive pink or white trumpet-shaped flowers. Then there are the hardy cyclamens, with their crimson, pink, or white flowers and handsome foliage, and the low sternbergias, whose bright yellow crocus-shaped flowers appear from early to late fall.

In winter, hyacinths, crocuses, tulips, and daffodils, all potted three months or so beforehand for indoor flowering, can brighten dark days. There are also exotic "house plant" bulbs, some of which have been specially treated to produce earlier indoor bloom—the amaryllis is a notable example.

Favorite Flowers From Bulbs and Corms

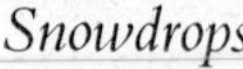

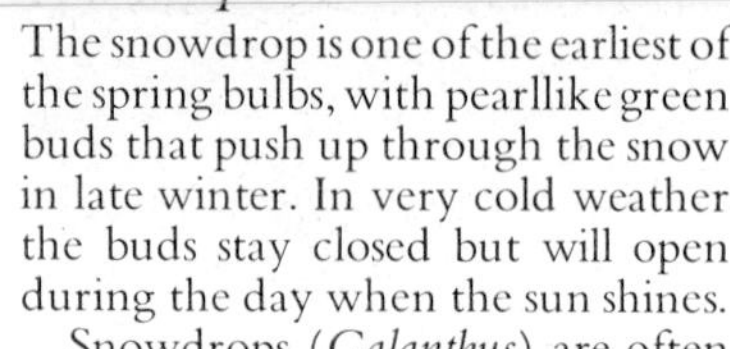

Galanthus nivalis
(Snowdrop)

Crocus 'Remembrance'
(Spring flowering)

Narcissus 'Unsurpassable'
(Trumpet daffodil)

Snowdrops

The snowdrop is one of the earliest of the spring bulbs, with pearllike green buds that push up through the snow in late winter. In very cold weather the buds stay closed but will open during the day when the sun shines.

Snowdrops (*Galanthus*) are often confused with snowflakes (*Leucojum*), which in cold climates flower later. Snowdrops have three long petals and three short ones, whereas the six green-tipped petals of snowflakes are all the same size. Also, two or more flowers are carried on each snowflake stem, compared with the snowdrop's one.

Snowdrops look best in informal woodland settings, in rough grass, under deciduous trees or shrubs, or among low ground covers.

Since snowdrop bulbs dry out quickly, they must be replanted as soon as possible if divided after flowering. If you buy bulbs in fall, these too should be planted immediately. They may not flower prolifically the first year, as they take time to become established; but once recovered, they need little attention. Unlike many bulbs, they prefer a moist heavy soil, with some shade.

Although they are rarely seen indoors, snowdrops can be grown in pots in the same way as crocuses or hyacinths. Keep them comparatively cool. A cold frame is useful until the flower buds are visible. Then they can be brought into a cool room.

Crocuses

Massed crocuses make a brilliant show of color in late winter and early spring, when little else is in flower.

The white, yellow, blue, purple, and bicolored blooms open before the daffodils. They, too, can be naturalized in grass or planted in groups beneath shrubs and trees.

In addition to the spring-flowering crocuses, there are those that flower in autumn and late winter. They all grow from small, flattish corms. The winter and spring crocuses produce their leaves and flowers at the same time, but the autumn-flowering types develop their leaves after their flowers. All are hardy and multiply freely.

The crocus flower, 3–5 inches high, has six petals, which are rounded in the hybrids and named varieties and pointed in the species. In bright sun the petals open out flat, revealing conspicuous golden or orange anthers. The flowers close up at night.

The winter-flowering crocuses, which appear outdoors from midwinter onward depending on the climate, have been developed from *C. chrysanthus* and other species. The 3-inch-high flowers range through shades of yellow, blue, and purple. Many are marked with contrasting stripes or have markings at the base of the petals; the inner color frequently differs from the outer one.

The large-flowered crocuses that bloom in early spring are Dutch varieties of *C. vernus*. The largest of all the crocuses, with flowers measuring 5 inches in height, they come in white, blue, lilac, red-purple, and golden yellow, or they are sometimes striped with different colors.

Fall-flowering crocuses appear from early to late fall. The flowers, which are 4–5 inches high, are pure white, lavender, or violet-blue. They are similar to the larger-flowered colchicums.

Daffodils and Other Narcissi

No garden is complete without clumps of golden yellow, trumpet-flowered daffodils dancing in the spring breezes. Daffodils are among the most reliable, versatile, and hardy of all bulbs. Not only do the bulbs increase each year but their bitter taste repels rodents. Besides, the daffodil is one of the best bulbs for naturalizing in the garden, because it grows well under deciduous trees and in open woodlands.

Most garden varieties of the daffodil are descendants of the wild narcissus. There are now more than 8,000 varieties of narcissi, grouped into a number of divisions according to flower shape and color.

The flower has a central trumpet or cup surrounded by six petals. Daffodils have trumpets that are as long as, or longer than, the surrounding petals.

The trumpet is frilled or flared at the outer edge, and the six overlapping petals are usually pointed at the tips. Colors vary. In some varieties, such as the old favorite 'King Alfred,' both trumpet and petals are clear yellow. In others, petals are a deeper or paler shade than the trumpets. Bicolored daffodils may have yellow or orange trumpets and white petals. Others, like 'Beersheeba,' are all white.

The word "narcissus" is popularly used to describe varieties with a short central cup, even though the large-cupped and trumpet daffodils are also botanically *Narcissus*. Between the large-cupped and the short-cupped narcissi are other varieties with many different cup sizes and great variations in color. Their cups and petals (sometimes contrasting) range from white through cream and yellow to pink, red, and orange. Cups are often ruffled.

The double-flowered varieties have cups that are indistinguishable from the petals. Most are all one color, such as the yellow 'Ingelescombe,' but some of the newer ones are bicolored, like the orange and yellow 'Texas.'

Triandrus and cyclamineus narcissi have pendent, bell-shaped trumpets and backswept petals. Tazetta narcissi (for forcing and mild climates only) carry several blooms on each stem, and poeticus narcissi have frilled, colored centers and conspicuous, nonoverlapping petals. Many are fragrant.

Jonquils (*Narcissus jonquilla* hybrids) are also known for their sweet fragrance. Each stem bears a small cluster of flowers with shallow cream, yellow, or orange cups and contrasting petals.

For further details on daffodils and all the other narcissi, see the chart on page 319.

Hyacinths

In the drab days of winter, the scented blooms of hyacinths bring color and cheer into normally flowerless rooms. Although hyacinths are widely used for indoor forcing, they are very suitable for the garden and for boxes in mild areas.

Some dealers offer specially treated bulbs, which, if planted in autumn, will flower indoors in early winter, instead of from midwinter onward. The technique of forcing bulbs into early flower is described on pages 317–318.

Most hyacinths are derived from a single species—*Hyacinthus orientalis* —and most of the modern varieties have the characteristic large, single-spike flowers. These are known as Dutch hyacinths.

Top-size bulbs with large flower heads are ideal for indoors, but in the garden smaller bulbs with smaller stalks and flower heads withstand the rain and wind better. After several years in the garden, the bulbs and spikes increase in number but are smaller in size.

The sweetly scented flowers are available in white, cream, yellow, salmon, pink, red, light and dark blue, and purple.

The Roman hyacinths (*H. orientalis albulus*) have smaller flower spikes than the Dutch hybrids, and they produce several to each bulb. The individual flowers are more loosely set on the spike than those of the Dutch hyacinths. Much less hardy than their Dutch counterparts, they are often grown indoors, flowering as early as Christmas. The only color is white.

Tulips

More than 300 years ago the tulip was brought from Turkey to other European countries and then to Holland. In the intervening centuries Dutch bulb growers have bred, crossbred, and altered the original varieties to such an extent that it has become necessary to divide them into groups according to their different characteristics.

Tulips, like many other bulbs, produce a dramatic effect with little attention. They almost never fail to flower the first year after planting.

The tulip grows from a pointed, thin-skinned bulb that produces a single erect flower stem (branched on bouquet tulips). One or two large, lance-shaped leaves appear near ground level, and two or three smaller ones grow higher up on the stem. The typical flower is goblet shaped, with six petals, but it varies considerably in overall size and from a short to a long goblet. Some tulip flowers have very pointed petals, and some are double. Still others open flat into star-shaped blooms (*Tulipa kaufmanniana*) or into twisted and fringed shapes (parrot tulips).

The so-called bouquet tulips, which produce five or six flowers per bulb on a branching stem, provide a spectacular garden accent. They are usually planted about 6–8 inches deep, but can be set a foot deep if desired.

Tulips are available in every color but true blue and in many bicolors. They grow best in regions with long winters and should be planted in mid to late fall.

Species, or botanical, tulips, available from mail-order bulb specialists and in the better garden centers, are ideal for rock gardens. They are exquisite, with short, sturdy stems and goblet-shaped flowers of exceptionally brilliant colors.

Gladioli

The name "gladiolus" comes from the Latin word for sword (*gladius*), which describes the shape of the leaves. But the superb flowers are what make the plant so attractive.

The color range is enormous, even greater than that of tulips. Gladioli provide both a brilliant summer display and long-lasting cut flowers.

The individual flowers, on a long, thick stem, all face in the same direction and are set on either side of the stem. The flower spike measures up to 5 feet long and consists of from 16 to 26 trumpet-shaped flowers composed of six petals each; the lower three petals, known as the falls, are slightly reflexed. The flowers are sometimes of one color only, but they are usually bicolored or tricolored, with conspicuous markings in the throat.

Gladioli, which grow from corms, are divided into five different groups, according to the size and shape of the flowers. Some catalogs of specialists use a standardized numerical code to designate the groups.

Two popular groups, the large-flowered and giant-flowered hybrids, are more suitable for garden display than for floral decoration. They produce flower spikes up to 6 feet long, with overlapping flowers 4½–7 inches wide.

Primulinus gladioli have slenderer flower spikes, 15 inches long, with separate 2½- to 3½-inch-wide flowers, arranged in a zigzag pattern. They differ from the typical gladiolus flower in that the upper petal is usually hooded and folded over the anthers and stigma.

Miniature gladioli also have a slightly hooded upper petal, but their flowers are usually smaller (2½ inches or less) than those of the primulinus gladioli. The flowers, which often have frilled or ruffled petals, are set closely together on 15-inch-long spikes.

Butterfly gladioli are similar to the large-flowered varieties in petal and flower arrangement, but the spikes are shorter (less than 18 inches), the edges of the petals are often frilled or ruffled, and the individual flowers are about 3 inches wide. They have the most distinctive throat markings.

Narcissus 'Edward Buxton'
(Small-cupped narcissus)

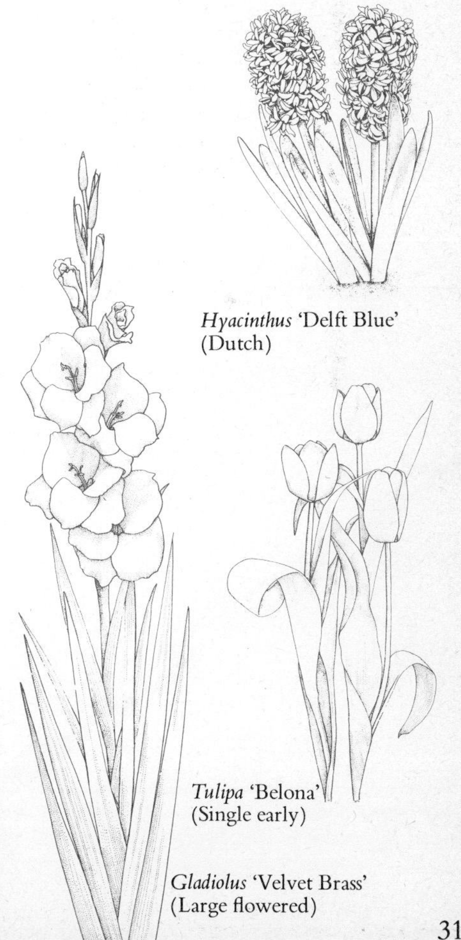

Hyacinthus 'Delft Blue'
(Dutch)

Tulipa 'Belona'
(Single early)

Gladiolus 'Velvet Brass'
(Large flowered)

How to Plant Bulbs and Corms

Choosing the Sites and Preparing the Ground

Given reasonably fertile garden soil, sufficiently well drained to prevent rot, and if they are protected from strong winds, most bulbs will thrive in any part of the garden. They can be grown in beds, borders, and tubs (some kinds in rock gardens), and some of the small ones, such as snowdrops, winter aconites, and crocuses, can be planted beneath shrubs and trees or ground cover. Bulbs that naturalize well in grass, such as crocuses, can be left undisturbed for years.

Most bulbs do best in a sunny location, but a few—cyclamens, endymions, erythroniums, snowdrops, and winter aconites—do well in shaded spots. Some bulbs, including the acidanthera, amaryllis, nerine, and sparaxis, are sensitive to cold weather and are best grown where they can get maximum sun and protection from strong winds, such as at the foot of a south-facing wall.

If you plant spring-flowering bulbs in grass, remember that the area above them must not be mowed until the foliage has fully matured.

Plant spring-flowering bulbs from early to late fall and most summer-flowering bulbs in early spring (mid to late spring for the less hardy ones). Plant autumn-flowering bulbs in late spring to late summer.

Whatever the time of year, the planting site must first be carefully prepared. Spade the ground to a depth of about 10 inches.

Mix well-rotted compost (preferable to peat moss) into the soil (one 2-gallon bucket per square yard), and let it settle for a few days before planting. Also mix bone meal into the planting area at a rate of about 5 pounds per 100 square feet, or add sewage sludge at the same rate. If preferred, mix a small quantity in each planting hole.

Bulbs in Rock Gardens and Between Paved Areas

Many low-growing bulbs—spring, summer, or autumn flowering—easily establish themselves in rock gardens and in small spaces between paving stones on terraces.

Remove any covering of mulch from the site, and dig holes with a trowel to the depths indicated for each kind (pp. 319–330). Plant the bulbs in small groups of at least three or four. After planting, level the soil with the trowel, replace the mulch, and label the site. If the soil is dry, water thoroughly after planting and again when there is little rain.

Good bulbs that provide a welcome show of bright color in the rock garden early in the year include snowdrops (*Galanthus*), the winter-flowering crocuses, glory-of-the-snows (*Chionodoxa luciliae*), winter aconites (*Eranthis hyemalis*), dwarf narcissi, and *Scilla tubergeniana*.

After the spring bulbs there are dwarf alliums to give summer color. These are not as widely available as many other bulbs but are listed in the catalogs of some bulb specialists. These can be followed by sternbergias, colchicums, and the fall and winter crocuses.

Low-growing bulbs look particularly attractive growing through such mat-forming plants as the creeping thyme and *Dianthus*. The green or gray-green foliage provides a striking background for the flowering bulbs when they are in bloom, and then it remains attractive all year, long after the bulb flowers fade.

Where the mat-forming plant is firmly rooted in, loosen it slightly with a hand fork, and then plant the bulbs with a blunt dibble.

If the plant only has a central root—for instance, *Gypsophila repens*—simply roll the matted stems aside, and plant the bulbs beneath them with a narrow trowel.

Planting Bulbs in Groups for Formal Display

Before planting large bulbs for a formal display, place the bulbs over the area, spacing them at regular intervals. With a trowel, dig holes to the recommended depth (the chart on pp. 319–330 gives planting depth and eventual spread, for spacing). For large numbers of bulbs it may be easier to dig out the entire bed to the proper depth before planting. Cover the bulbs with soil, and water thoroughly if it is dry.

When the whole area has been planted, set a label stake in the center for identification, and mark the edges of the planting area in some way in order that other plants will not later be put in there by mistake.

If certain plants, such as forget-me-nots, pansies, or polyanthus primroses, are to be grown between the bulbs to provide additional spring color, space the bulbs a few inches farther apart. Set out the plants before planting the bulbs or in spring as shoots of bulbs show above the ground.

1. *Lay the bulbs over the chosen area, spacing them at regular intervals.*

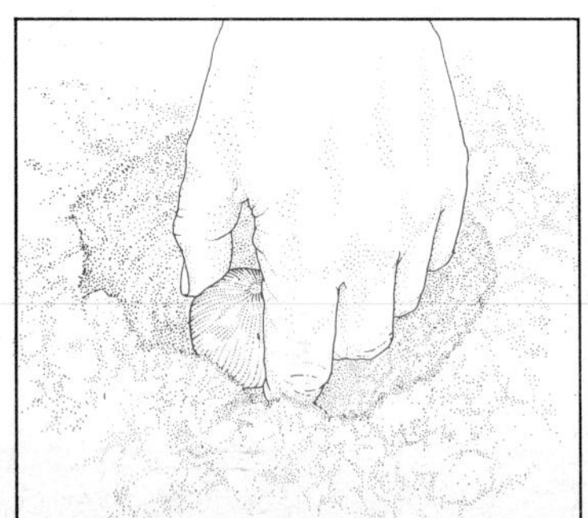

2. *Place each bulb, point uppermost, in a planting hole at least twice its depth.*

3. *Cover the bulbs with soil removed from the planting holes. Label the area.*

Growing Bulbs for Cut Flowers

When picking flowers for indoor decoration, it is advisable to cut as few leaves as possible, so as not to exhaust the bulbs. If cut flowers are of prime importance, grow bulbs in a special area where the garden's future appearance is not critical. Prepare the soil in the normal way, and plant the bulbs slightly closer together than the eventual spread of the plant (see pp. 319–330). Allow $1\frac{1}{2}$–2 feet between the rows.

When you are cutting bulb flowers for arrangements, it is preferable to do so in the early morning or the late evening, using a pair of sharp scissors or a sharp knife. Immediately place the flowers in deep, warm water in a cool, dark place for several hours or overnight. Allowing them to soak up plenty of water will prolong their life when they are placed in the warmth of a living room.

Spring Bulbs in Special Climates

Growing Bulbs and Corms in Grass and Beneath Trees

Daffodils, narcissi, snowdrops, and crocuses look more attractive scattered than placed in formal groups.

Narcissi and crocuses can be naturalized in any convenient lawn area with well-drained soil. A complete fertilizer used for the lawn will be sufficient for the bulbs as well.

Scatter handfuls of the bulbs casually, and plant them where they land. For individual bulbs use a trowel to dig the holes or a special bulb planter, which consists of an open-ended, slightly tapered metal cylinder attached to a long or short handle. The cylinder is forced into the ground to the proper planting depth and then pulled up with a plug of soil and turf. Replace the turf plug after planting the bulb, and water.

When you set out individual groups of bulbs in a lawn area, first cut a figure H in the grass with an edging tool or a spade. Then cut back under each half, and fold the turf back.

Loosen the soil with a garden fork, and dig the planting holes with a trowel. Strive for an informal effect when placing the bulbs in their positions; then cover them with soil, and level it. Roll back the turf, firm it down, and water thoroughly.

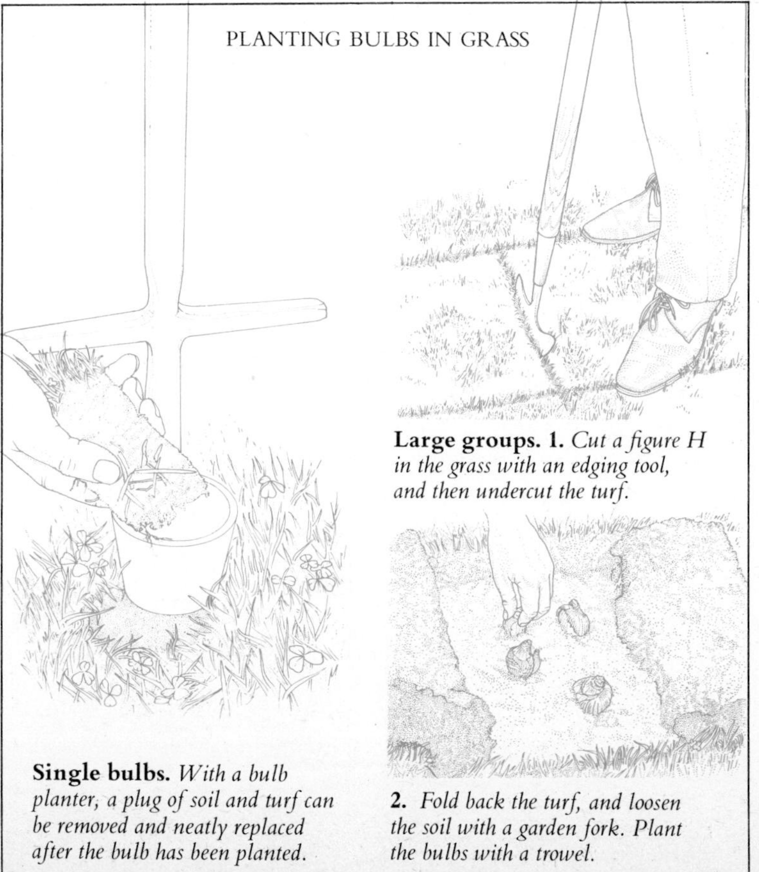

Single bulbs. *With a bulb planter, a plug of soil and turf can be removed and neatly replaced after the bulb has been planted.*

Large groups. 1. *Cut a figure H in the grass with an edging tool, and then undercut the turf.*

2. *Fold back the turf, and loosen the soil with a garden fork. Plant the bulbs with a trowel.*

Many spring-flowering bulbs and corms, if planted and cared for correctly, can be grown in both the coldest and warmest regions of the United States, as well as in the more temperate zones. In the northernmost parts of the country and in high mountain regions such as the Rockies, hardy spring-flowering bulbs should be planted at least three weeks before the ground is expected to freeze, to allow sufficient time for root development. In mountain areas especially, where extremes of temperature between day and night (as well as between sun and shade) are the rule, a partly shaded site and a winter mulch are advisable.

Planting depths in cold climates are the same as they are for more temperate regions. The bulbs, of course, will flower somewhat later, although the sequence of bloom will be the same as it is elsewhere.

In the warmer parts of the South and West, where a winter freeze is either unlikely or nonexistent, spring-flowering bulbs should not be planted until very late fall, since the early- to mid-autumn months are likely to be quite hot.

Dealers in the South and West often have spring-flowering bulbs for sale at the same time as their northern counterparts—in early fall, much too soon for planting. This poses a problem for mild-climate gardeners, but it can be solved if bulbs are bought as soon as available and then stored in a refrigerator, where they can be "precooled" until a safe planting time.

The bulbs can be placed in the bottom of the refrigerator, preferably in a vegetable crisper, in the paper bags in which they were purchased. They should not be allowed to freeze; the best temperature is about 40° F. Keep them there for six to eight weeks or until the ground is cool enough—in late fall or in early winter.

In very warm climates add compost, peat moss, or other organic material to the soil before planting to improve drainage and moisture retention. Plant the bulbs in a lightly shaded site rather than in full sun, and mulch them after shoots appear.

Among the spring-flowering bulbs that do well in warm climates are hyacinths, many of the smaller narcissi, and mid- to late-season tulips, such as Triumphs and Darwins.

Some Pointers on Buying Quality Bulbs and Corms

How can you tell a good bulb or corm? Basically it should be firm, not shriveled, and free of soft spots. Because most of our spring-flowering bulbs come from the Netherlands, where growers exercise strict control over the quality of their exports, they arrive in the United States in good condition. The way they are handled after that, however, can spell the difference between good and bad bulbs. Left in a hot store or subjected to rough handling by customers, they lose quality rapidly. Even when you buy good bulbs, they can deteriorate if you leave them in an airless bag in a hot place.

What about size? The top-size bulbs and corms are the most expensive and generally produce the biggest flowers. The newer varieties will also cost more than the older ones. But the smaller sizes may be perfectly adequate for a good garden display. If you are inexperienced in buying bulbs, purchase a dozen of both sizes and compare the difference.

If you are buying bulbs in considerable numbers, you will find that many mail-order bulb specialists offer a discount for early orders—generally those received by July or August. This may seem early to think about bulbs to be planted in fall, but it is a good way to make sure that you order before the stocks of your favorite varieties are gone.

Care of Bulbs After Planting

General Care of Established Bulbs in Borders and Grass

Most hardy bulbs and corms need relatively little attention during the growing season, and many will thrive for several years.

Remove weeds, by hand or with a hoe, as soon as the bulbs' shoots show clearly. Take care not to damage the shoots, and avoid using weed killers.

Feeding is generally recommended for bulbs that are to be left in the ground for several years. Use a commercial bulb food on these bulbs, raking it lightly into the soil during the spring cultivation.

During prolonged dry spells in spring and summer, thorough watering will improve growth. If the plants are in bloom, water around the base rather than from above. Continue watering in dry spells even after the flowers have faded. The growing cycle does not end until the leaves turn yellow and die.

Unless you cannot avoid lifting bulbs that have finished flowering to make room for other plants, the bulb foliage should be allowed to ripen naturally because it manufactures all the nutrients needed for the plant's future growth. One exception is snowdrops, which if the bulbs are crowded are best transplanted while still growing. After flowering, replant them immediately and water.

Some gardeners tidy the bulb foliage by knotting or otherwise fastening the leaves together. This should be avoided because it reduces the amount of leaf surface exposed to the sun, with a subsequent diminishing of nourishment to the bulbs.

Bulbs grown for cut flowers in summer, such as gladioli, produce larger flowers if fed with a liquid fertilizer every three weeks after the buds form and until they open.

Deadheading. As spring bulbs—daffodils and other narcissi, tulips, and hyacinths—finish flowering, remove their faded blooms. (This is called deadheading.) The bulbs will exhaust themselves if the seeds set.

Tulip flowers can harbor fungous spores (tulip fire) that will be transmitted to the bulbs if not removed at petal fall. Cut off the dead flower heads, as well as 1–2 inches of stem, and leave the remaining stems and leaves on the plant to build up nourishment in the bulbs.

On a hyacinth remove the small flowers that make up the spike by running your hand from below the flower cluster up to the tip. Leave the flower stem, since it will provide nourishment for the bulb.

On a faded gladiolus cut off the flower spike, but leave at least four pairs of leaves.

There are, however, bulbs and corms that multiply freely from self-sown seeds. Snowdrops, scillas, winter aconites, muscaris, chionodoxas, and cyclamens should be deadheaded only if no more plants are wanted.

Supporting tall plants. Few bulbs need supporting if they have been planted deeply enough. In windy, exposed positions, however, the taller varieties of hyacinths, gladioli, acidantheras, and alliums may need to be tied to bamboo canes with raffia or strips of soft cloth.

Gladioli grown in rows for cutting are usually self-supporting. If necessary, however, insert a stake at both ends of each row, and tie strong string tautly between the stakes to the front and rear of the row.

Frost protection. Although certain types of bulbs are usually lifted and stored for the winter, gladioli, ixias, and nerines can be left in the ground in mild areas of the South and West. Protect them with a mulch, however, in frosty weather.

For mulching, some gardeners use a layer of salt hay, straw, or leaves kept in place with evergreen branches. Others prefer peat moss, buckwheat hulls, or pine needles. Gardeners who mulch hardy bulbs in colder areas should do so after the ground freezes.

Lifting, Drying, and Storing Bulbs

Bulbs are lifted from the ground for three main reasons: because room is needed for other plants; because they are not hardy enough to spend the winter outdoors; or because they are crowded and blooming poorly.

Spring-flowering bulbs, such as hyacinths, narcissi, and tulips, ideally should be left until the foliage has ripened. It is easy to recognize when this stage is reached because the leaves will turn yellow. A slight pull should separate them from the bulb if ripening is complete. The foliage is often prematurely removed in an effort to improve the appearance of the garden, but this is poor efficiency because the future performance of the bulbs will be seriously jeopar-

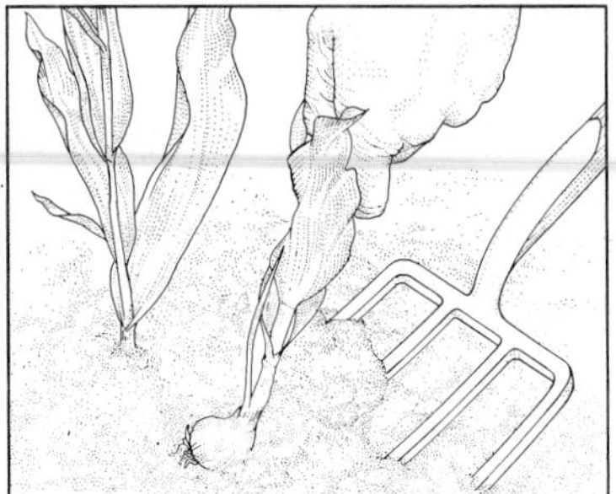

1. *After the flowers fade, lift the bulbs with a fork and remove the soil.*

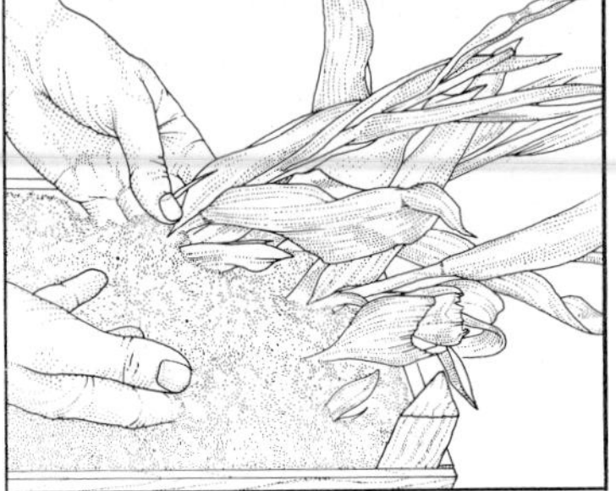

2. *If only a few bulbs are lifted, lay them in deep flats of damp peat moss.*

3. *Set large numbers of bulbs on netting in the trench; cover with soil.*

4. *When all the leaves and stems have shriveled, remove the bulbs.*

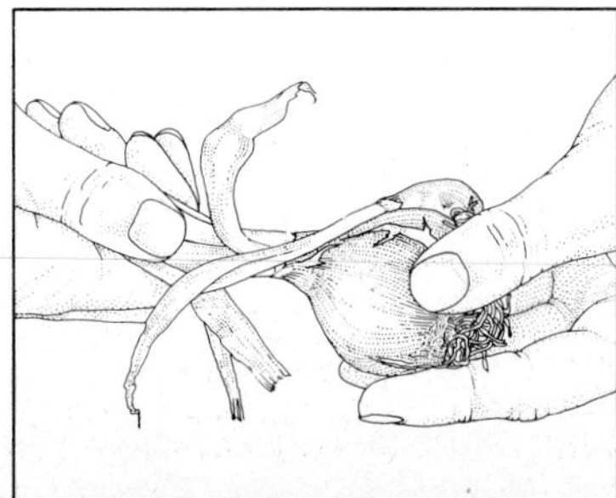

5. *Before storing, remove dead leaves, skins, and roots from each bulb.*

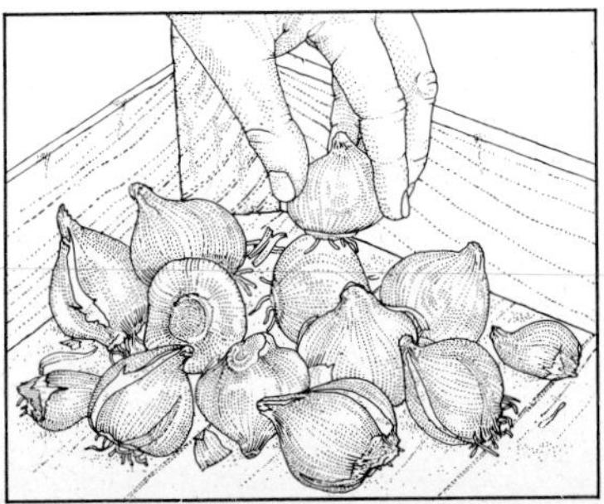

6. *Put bulbs in labeled boxes. Store in a cool, dry place until planting time.*

dized. In some gardens, however, the space may be needed for summer plants. In such cases the bulbs can be dug up and transferred to an unused area to complete their growing.

To transfer, insert a spading fork straight down into the ground, well clear of the plants and deep enough to avoid damaging the bulbs. Carefully lever up the bulbs, complete with soil, leaves, and stems, using extreme care not to break off the leaves. If digging is done when soil is moist, it will adhere to roots. Discard any pulpy or rotting bulbs. Now move the remaining bulbs to a spare, inconspicuous bed in the garden.

Dig a trench about 5–6 inches deep, 12 inches wide, and long enough to take all the lifted bulbs. Lay a piece of fine wire or plastic netting at the bottom of the trench, and place the bulbs on it at a slight angle. They can be set so that they almost touch each other, but at least half the length of the stems and leaves must be above soil level. Let the netting protrude above the trench a little at the ends to make lifting the bulbs easier later on.

Fill the trench halfway with soil, and water thoroughly (repeat during dry spells). After the leaves and stems have withered, they can be removed and discarded, and the bulbs can be taken up for storing. Just pull up the netting at the ends, and lift the bulbs out. Most of the soil will fall through the netting.

If only a few bulbs are lifted before they have finished growing, it is easiest to lay them in deep trays of damp peat moss. Cover the bulbs with more peat moss, and place the trays in a lightly shaded place. Keep the peat moss moist.

When the leaves have ripened fully, remove the bulbs from the trays (or trench). Pull off the dead leaves, roots, and shriveled skins. The bulblets attached to the parent bulb can be used for propagation; otherwise discard them. Place the cleaned bulbs, uncovered, in single layers in labeled flats, and store them in a cool, dry place (safe from rodents) until fall replanting. Do not make the mistake of enclosing the bulbs to exclude air, since they must have air circulation to prevent mold.

If garden space is not a problem, it is best to leave most hardy bulbs in the ground until just after the foliage has ripened; then divide and replant them (p. 316). This is much simpler than the trenching method and is preferred by most gardeners.

In very mild climates gladioli can be left undisturbed in the ground throughout the year. Elsewhere, the corms should be lifted when the leaves begin to turn brown in the fall. Lift them with a spading fork. Cut off the top stems and leaves about an inch above the corm. Place the corms, uncovered, in trays in a cool, airy shed until they are dry, which may be about 7 to 10 days. If necessary, they can be left longer before cleaning.

Break away the shriveled corms, and separate the small cormels that surround the new corm; the number of these depends partly on the variety and partly on cultural practices. The cormels can be discarded or saved for replanting.

Remove the tough outer skins from the large corms, and examine them carefully; destroy any that show signs of lesions or rotting. Dust the remaining corms with lindane to control thrips, with quintozene to prevent dry rot and scab. This is an important step, often overlooked, but it will pay dividends the next year in the performance of the corms. Store the corms in flats or mesh bags in a cool but frost-free place until spring. Make certain that good air circulation is provided. Some gardeners store corms in old nylon stockings.

In cold regions acidantheras and other tender bulbs must be lifted in the fall and dried and stored like gladioli. Label carefully to avoid mistakes when you plant next year.

What Can Go Wrong With Bulbs

If any of your bulbs show symptoms that are not described in the chart below, turn to the identification chart of pests and diseases that starts on page 600. A list of protective chemicals commonly used for control can be found on page 635.

Symptoms and signs	Cause	Control
Stems, leaves, or flower buds are covered with small green or black insects; growth is often malformed.	Aphids (greenflies or blackflies)	Spray with carbaryl, malathion, or systemic insecticide, such as dimethoate or oxydemeton-methyl.
Rust-colored streaks on leaves and flowers, especially those of potted narcissi. Leaves and flowers stunted.	Bulb scales or bulb mites	Destroy severely infested bulbs. Expose dormant bulbs to frost for 2 or 3 nights; or dip in hot water (110°–115° F) for 3 hr. Before planting, dust bulbs with dicofol or endosulfan.
If squeezed gently, bulbs (particularly those of daffodils and other narcissi) feel soft at neck end and base. If planted, bulbs fail to grow.	Narcissus bulb flies or lesser bulb flies	Test bulbs at planting time; discard soft ones. Deter adult flies from laying eggs by raking lindane powder into soil when leaves begin to wilt. Apply chlordane or methoxychlor dust to planting holes. Repeat when spring growth is visible.
Leaves of hyacinths, narcissi, and tulips have pale stripes. Leaves may become distorted and stunted, may eventually die.	Stem or bulb eelworms	Destroy infected bulbs and move healthy ones to new location. No simple control, but sprays of Diazinon, dichlorvos, or oxydemeton-methyl may work.
Flowers and foliage of gladioli have silvery streaks and patches, which eventually turn brown.	Thrips	Dust corms with lindane powder before storing; spray affected plants outdoors with chlorpyrifos, malathion, or methoxychlor.
Soft rot at leaf bases, often causing plants to topple over and die. Corms have round, shrunken craters with distinct, shiny margins.	Bacterial scab	Remove and destroy infected plants. Treat healthy stock with quintozene as for dry rot.
Anemone leaves have patches of whitish powder; leaves may be distorted.	Downy mildew (fungus)	Spray with zineb.
Leaves of gladioli turn yellow and topple over, usually before flowers appear. Corms show black spots or lesions; later, corm shrivels.	Dry rot (fungus)	Remove and destroy infected plants; dust remaining bulbs with quintozene before storing. Replant in new location, raking quintozene into soil first.
Foliage of tulips shows water-soaked specks and streaks, which turn brown. Petals are often spotted. Brown rot may attack stems, which topple over.	Tulip fire, or Botrytis (fungus)	Destroy diseased plants. Dust remaining bulbs with quintozene after lifting from soil. Replant in another location after raking quintozene into soil. Spray leaves with Benomyl.

Increasing Your Stock of Bulbs

Many hardy bulbs and corms increase steadily when they are left in the ground by producing offsets. Eventually, a clump will become congested, producing fewer flowers of poorer quality. Division then becomes necessary. At this stage the offsets can be separated and grown on in nursery rows until they reach flowering size. Some offsets can take as long as seven years to reach maturity, but others, such as some crocuses, lilies, and gladioli, will flower in only two years. The time from offset to bloom also depends on the size of the offset and the general cultural conditions that are provided.

Propagation by seeds is possible, but the seedlings take years to bloom, and the hybrid plants—especially narcissi, hyacinths, gladioli, and tulips—will usually be inferior to, and different from, the parent, unless a controlled cross was made.

HOW TO DIVIDE DAFFODILS

After the foliage has ripened, lever up a clump of daffodils with a garden fork. Ease the soil away from the bulbs, and separate them carefully.

Dividing and Replanting Overgrown Plants

Most bulbs and corms should be lifted and divided every three or four years; those naturalized in grass can be left for many years. When bulbs flourish, they may increase, causing overcrowding and reduced bloom. This is the time to divide.

It is best to dig up an entire clump of bulbs or corms soon after the foliage has withered but while it is still firmly attached to the bulb. After levering the clump out of the ground, brush the soil away. Then separate the bulbs or corms.

Daffodils and other narcissi, tulips, and crocuses can be replanted immediately or dried, cleaned, and stored until fall. But certain bulbs, such as snowdrops and winter aconites, should be divided just after flowering and replanted at once. It is best to replant all bulbs, especially tulips, in a new location.

When you divide and replant, separate small bulbs and corms for propagation purposes, planting only large ones in permanent sites.

Growing Bulblets and Cormels to Blooming Size

Old bulbs and corms that are lifted from the ground will have one or more offsets attached. These are known as bulblets on a bulb and cormels on a corm. They can be used to raise new bulbs or corms identical to the parent variety.

Bulblets are produced on either side of the parent bulb, while cormels appear at the base of the corm as well as alongside it. After the parent bulb or corm has dried, break the offsets away from it with your fingers.

The very small offsets are best discarded, as they will take several years to produce flowers.

Offsets from hardy bulbs and corms can be planted in a spare piece of ground during summer and early autumn. In cold areas offsets from less hardy bulbs or corms should be stored in a frost-free place over the winter and planted the next spring.

In any available area, in sun or partial shade, dig narrow trenches, varying in depth according to the size of the offsets. Large bulblets (about half the size of the parent bulb) should be planted two to three times their own depth; the smaller ones, like crocus cormels, 2 inches deep; tiny cormels, 1 inch deep.

Unless the soil has excellent drainage, put a $\frac{1}{2}$- to 1-inch layer of sand at the bottom of the trench before planting the offsets. The distance between them should be twice their width. Cover them with another inch of sand before filling in with soil. Sand improves drainage and makes lifting easier.

The bulblets and cormels will develop leaves but no flowers the first year. The larger ones usually flower the second year, the smaller ones the third year. They can then be moved to their permanent sites.

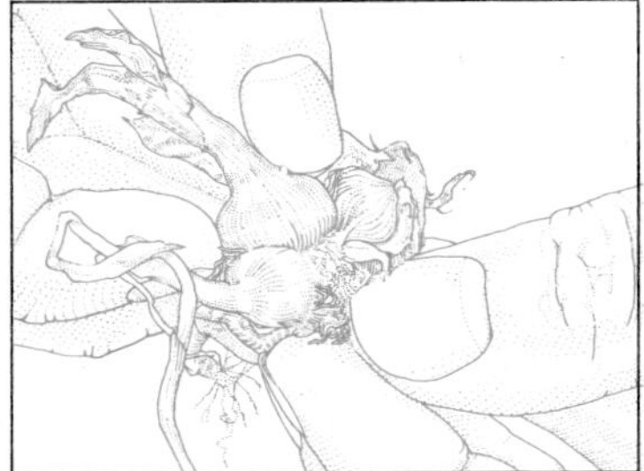

1. *Pull away the cormels or bulblets from the parent bulb.*

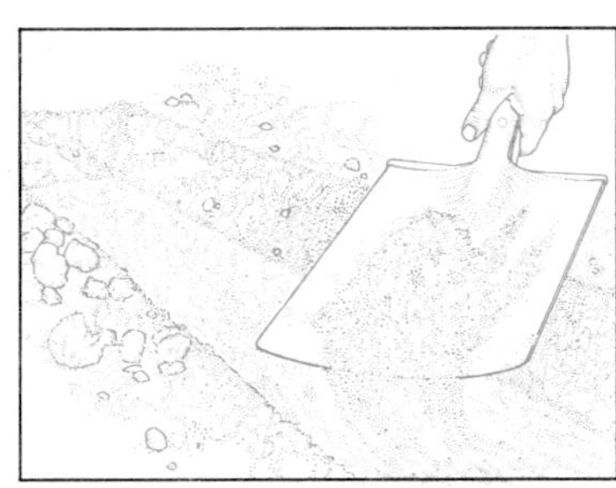

2. *Dig out a narrow trench, and line the base with $\frac{1}{2}$–1 in. of sand.*

3. *Space the cormels or bulblets at a distance of twice their width.*

4. *Put another 1-in. layer of sand in the trench; then fill with soil.*

How to Grow Bulbs for Indoor Flowering

Crocus 'Golden Yellow' (Spring flowering)

Many of the hardy bulbs that bloom outdoors during spring can be had in flower indoors weeks or months earlier. If you pot them in early fall and allow sufficient time in cool conditions for root growth, you can then "force" flowers by placing pots in a warm room.

Among the most popular spring-flowering bulbs for indoor use are hyacinths, crocuses, daffodils and other narcissi, irises, and tulips. Most require storage for 10 to 13 weeks or more at temperatures of 40° F or less before forcing.

Bulb catalogs usually indicate those varieties that respond best indoors. Fragrant, small-flowered *Narcissus tazetta* 'Paperwhite' and 'Soleil d'Or' are especially popular and need no cold treatment. Good trumpet daffodils are 'King Alfred' (yellow), 'Mount Hood' (white), and 'Pink Glory' (white with a soft pink trumpet). Among the tulips the Early Singles, Triumphs, and some Darwin Hybrids and Parrots are easiest to force. Also popular are large-flowered Dutch hyacinths and many crocuses, including *C. chrysanthus* 'Blue Pearl' and the large-flowered *C. vernus* varieties, such as 'Remembrance' and 'Pickwick.'

There are many different potting mixtures available. Some dealers offer ready-to-use planting medium. You can also make your own by mixing equal parts of sifted garden soil, sifted compost, and pulverized peat moss. (Heavy clay soil can be lightened by adding sand and vermiculite.) Generally it is not necessary to add fertilizer to the medium in order to obtain good bloom.

Large bulbs can be planted singly in 3- to 4-inch pots, but they are more effective when several are set close together in bigger pots.

Potting Bulbs for Forcing

When bulbs are potted for indoor flowering, it is best to plant them in pots or bulb containers that have drainage holes so that you will be able to check these holes later for evidence of root growth.

The tazetta narcissi 'Paperwhite' and 'Soleil d'Or' are sometimes grown in water and pebbles in glazed containers without drainage holes. A layer of horticultural charcoal over the bottom keeps the water sweet. If you use a container with drainage holes, cover them with pebbles or shards of clay pots. Then put a layer of moist potting mixture into the pot. The amount used depends on the size of the container and bulbs; when set in place, the tops of the bulbs should be about even with, or slightly above, the top of the pot. Then finish filling the pot. Label all containers, indicating the kind and variety of the bulb and the date.

Gently press the bulbs into place, with the smaller ones almost touching and the larger ones about 1 inch apart. Then carefully place potting soil around them so that they will be held firmly when the roots start to grow. Completely cover the small bulbs. The tips of the larger bulbs, such as daffodils and hyacinths, can protrude above the soil. Level the soil about ½ inch below the pot's rim.

HOW TO OBTAIN A MASSED DISPLAY OF DAFFODILS

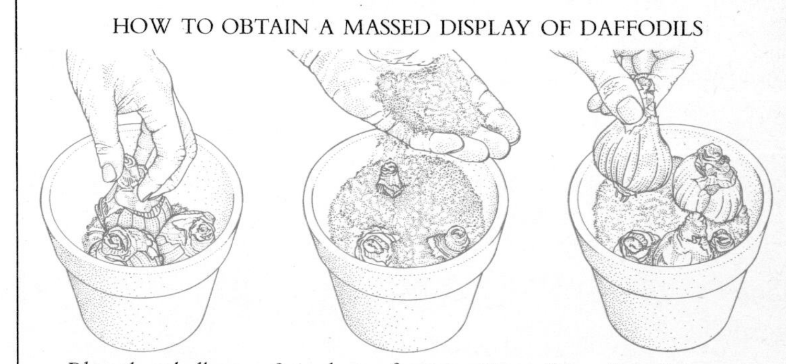

Place three bulbs on a 2-in. layer of moist potting soil in a 5- to 6-in. pot. Cover to the necks; then set three more bulbs between them, and cover again.

Storing Spring-Flowering Bulbs After Potting

A three-month period of cool temperatures and darkness is essential for the proper rooting of bulbs grown for bloom ahead of their normal outdoor flowering time.

A storage area is needed where temperatures remain at 40°–50° F or lower but where bulbs will not freeze. A spare home refrigerator provides these conditions and is especially useful in warm climates. The pots should be kept well watered.

The outdoor method of storage, in a trench or a cold frame, is probably the most reliable, since it duplicates natural conditions. The object is to keep bulbs from freezing and at the same time ensure that the pots can be removed easily to bring them indoors.

Dig a trench at least 6 inches deeper than the deepest pot. Set the bulb-filled pots in the trench. If rodents are a problem, either cover the pots with screening, or dust both pots and trench with a rodenticide. Cover the pots with 3 inches of perlite, sand, or shredded Styrofoam. Over this put a 3- to 6-inch layer of dry leaves, hay, or other mulch, and keep it in place with evergreen boughs. The mulch keeps the ground from freezing solid so that the pots can be removed easily.

When storing pots in a cold frame, bury them in the same manner as in a trench. Put the cold-frame cover on during severe weather or over very cold nights; open it or remove it entirely on warm days.

Where there is space to put a cold frame on the north side of a building, there will probably be little need for opening it.

Another suitable place for storing potted bulbs is a dark area in an unheated garage. The temperature must be warm enough to prevent the bulbs from freezing, yet cool enough for proper root development. An attic is usually too warm.

During extremely cold weather it is advisable to improvise a temporary cover to provide additional protection. An upturned box, a large pail, a basket lined with a thick layer of newspaper, or an insulated picnic hamper will protect a few pots. Such covers should not be left on for more than a few days without providing some ventilation.

If the storage area is open to the outdoors and subject to marauding mice or squirrels, some form of protection for the bulbs will need to be devised. An enclosure made from ½-inch hardware cloth or window screening should be adequate. Make the cover large enough to surround the pots, and allow about 6 inches above the bulbs for air circulation.

All bulbs stored above the ground after potting should be inspected frequently to determine their need for water. This is especially necessary for bulbs in clay pots, which act like a sponge to draw water from the soil. Once the roots have formed, the soil dries out even more rapidly and may even require daily watering. However, care must be taken not to overwater, especially during very cold weather when the bulbs require less water and at the same time are more susceptible to rot.

Bringing Bulb Containers Indoors for Forcing

After the storage period, of 10 to 13 weeks or more, start the forcing process. Move the potted bulbs from their cold beds to a well-lighted, well-ventilated location indoors with a temperature of about 50°–60° F. In this slightly warmer environment the flowers will begin to develop. Remember to keep the bulbs well watered as they grow.

For a succession of flowers, move one container a week into a well-lighted window in a cool room (preferably about 60°–65° F). A good location might be a cool bedroom or an unheated sunroom. If you want to display them in a warm living room, return the pots to a cool room each night. This will prolong the life of the flowers and help preserve their freshness.

Keep the soil moist at all times, but avoid overwatering.

The Aftercare of Forced Bulbs

Once a bulb has been forced, it cannot be so used again. With proper care, however, many bulbs can be saved for outdoor planting.

With bulbs that have been grown in potting soil, remove the dead flower heads, and set the pots in a cool, well-lighted room. Water and fertilize until foliage yellows.

Let the potting soil completely dry out; then remove and clean the bulbs. They can be stored in a cool, dry place until the ground is workable in spring. Then plant them in garden rows for a year before moving them to permanent sites.

Bulbs that have been grown in pots often do not flower outdoors the next year, but they should recover to produce blooms in a few years. Nonhardy narcissi, such as the tazetta 'Paperwhite,' will not survive outdoors in cold climates.

Growing Crocuses in Special Pots

Special glazed clay pots, with holes around the sides, can be bought for growing crocuses. The corms are planted in such a way that the tip of each one, and later on the flower, will protrude through a hole.

Fill such a pot up to the first row of holes with moist potting soil; then plant crocus corms with their necks showing through the holes. Add more soil and set more corms in position. Finally, point the tips of a group of corms through the top opening.

Like other bulb containers, crocus bowls should be kept in a cool, dark place for at least 13 weeks. Then the bowls can be brought into a warmer, well-lighted room.

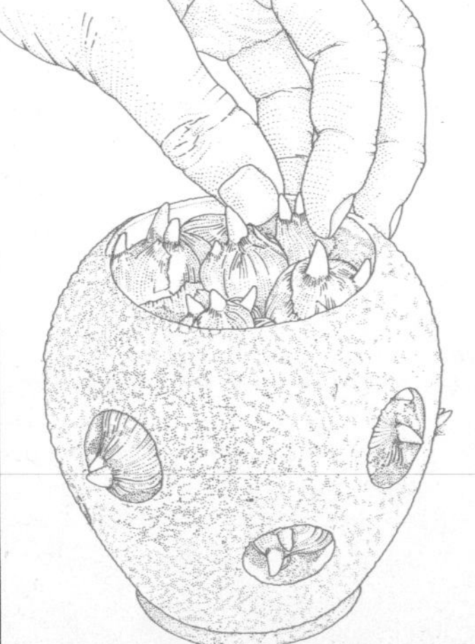

Crocuses can be planted to flower through holes in special pots.

Growing Hyacinths in Glass Jars

Hyacinths are well suited to growing in water. Some garden centers sell hyacinth jars with constricted necks for this purpose.

Fill the jar up to its neck with water, and insert a small lump of charcoal to keep it fresh. Place a hyacinth bulb in the top portion of the jar, root end down and with the water just touching the bulb's base.

Put each jar in a cool, dark place until the roots growing into the water are about 4 inches long and the shoots are showing. Then move the jars to a warmer, well-lighted place. Add water to the jars as the level falls.

After the flowers have faded, discard the bulbs. They will not produce any more flowers.

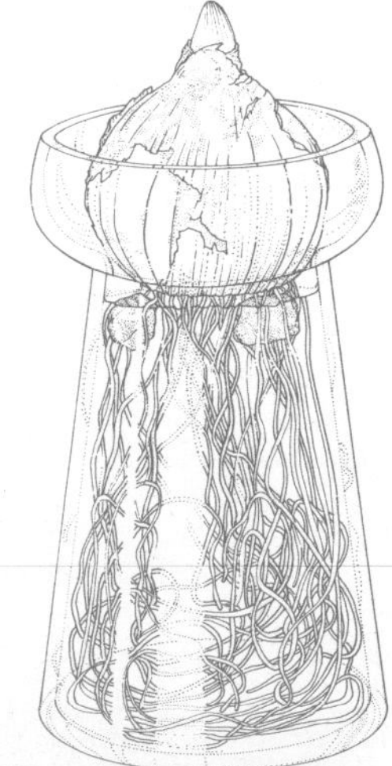

Hyacinth bulbs grow well in water, in glass jars with constricted necks.

Bulbous Plants for All Seasons

All bulbs, corms, and tubers in the chart that follows can be grown outdoors. Some, however, such as the acidanthera, cannot survive a winter in the open and should be lifted after flowering and stored in a frost-free location. The remarks column gives this information when pertinent.

All the botanical names are listed alphabetically. However, where a common name, such as daffodil, is widely used, this name has also been listed in its alphabetical position with a cross-reference to the full entry (e.g., **Daffodil,** see Narcissus). Included here are some of the outstanding species and varieties that are usually widely available.

Flowering times are for moderate climates. They will be later where it is colder and earlier where warmer. There will also be seasonal variations and differences due to microclimates in individual gardens.

Acidanthera bicolor

Allium oreophilum ostrowskianum

Amaryllis belladonna

Anemone coronaria

Botanical and common names	Height and spread	Decorative characteristics and remarks	Planting and propagation
Acidanthera *Acidanthera bicolor*	H 1½-2 ft. S 4-6 in.	Fragrant white flowers with purple centers bloom in late summer. Needs long growing season; so north of Zone C, start corms a month early in pots indoors; then transplant to garden. In all but Zones C and D, lift and store corms over winter.	Plant 3-4 in. deep, after last frost, in sun. Separate cormlets at planting time.
African corn lily, see Ixia			
Allium, or Ornamental onion *Allium aflatunense*	H 2½-3 ft. S 9 in.	Lilac-pink flowers in early summer. Easily grown bulbs. Low growers best in rock gardens; taller kinds may need staking and are best in large groups among other plants. Many kinds dry well for indoor arrangements. Alliums listed grow well from Zone B southward except as noted. *A. aflatunense* is somewhat less hardy.	Plant all alliums at 3 times bulbs' depth, in early to mid fall or as soon as available. Plant in sun and any well-drained soil. Lift and divide in autumn or early spring every 3 or 4 yr. or as needed.
A. albopilosum	H 2½-3 ft. S 1 ft.	Deep lilac flower heads 8-10 in. in diameter appear in early summer. Excellent for drying.	
A. giganteum	H 2½-3 ft. S 1 ft.	Deep lilac flower heads 4-5 in. across from early to mid summer. Good cut flower. Hardy in southern Zone B.	
A. moly	H 1-1½ ft. S 1 ft.	Yellow flowers to 3 in. wide appear in early summer. Hardy in Zone A.	
A. oreophilum ostrowskianum	H 10-12 in. S 3 in.	Rose-pink flowers in early summer. Excellent in rock gardens. Extremely hardy.	
Amaryllis *Amaryllis belladonna*	H 2 ft. S 1 ft.	Fragrant pink blooms in early to mid fall. Leaves appear before flowers and die. Can be grown indoors in pots in cold regions by potting in late summer. Does best in frost-free regions but can be grown in southern part of Zone C. See also *Hippeastrum.*	Plant 6 in. deep in mid to late summer in sun. In cool climates plant deeper and against south-facing wall. Divide bulbs when they become crowded.
Anemone, or Windflower *Anemone blanda*	H 6 in. S 4 in.	White as well as many shades of blue and mauve-pink flowers in late winter to midspring. Plant in small groups. Good in rock gardens. Grow from Zone C southward. Farther north mulch heavily.	*A. blanda:* Plant tuberous roots 2-3 in. deep in early to mid fall, in sun or partial shade. Take offsets or divide tuberous roots in late summer; replant at once. *A. coronaria:* Plant tuberous roots 1½-2 in. deep in sun or partial shade, in late fall far South or early spring in North.
A. coronaria	H 6-12 in. S 4-6 in.	White, lavender, mauve, pink, crimson, and scarlet blooms in early spring or early summer. Excellent cut flower. Nitrogen fertilizer, such as ammonium sulfate, applied as buds appear, helps to lengthen stems. Grows best in Pacific Northwest. Tuberous roots not hardy beyond southern portions of Zone C.	

Botanical and common names	Height and spread	Decorative characteristics and remarks	Planting and propagation
Angel's tears, see Narcissus (DWARF NARCISSUS)			
Autumn crocus, see Colchicum			
Begonia			
Begonia evansiana	H 1½-2 ft. S 1 ft.	White or pink flowers in midsummer to fall. Good flowering plant for shady places. Hardy in southern parts of Zone B and farther north with heavy mulch.	*B. evansiana:* Plant tubers 2 in. deep in spring in partial shade. Remove bulblets from axil of leafstalk. Place in pot on soil surface; cover with glass until young plants form. Set out in spring.
B. tuberhybrida (tuberous begonia)	H 2 ft. S 1 ft.	White, pink, yellow, orange, and red blooms from midsummer to fall. Often sold according to form of flower, such as camellia flowered or carnation flowered. Particularly useful in containers. Tubers must be dug before frost or when flowering slows and stored over winter in peat moss at 40°-50° F. For earliest bloom, start tubers indoors 2-3 mo. prior to outdoor planting time. Keep barely moist in a well-lighted window or greenhouse until top growth appears. Many hybrid strains offered with various flower forms.	*B. tuberhybrida:* Plant tubers 1-2 in. deep in spring in partial shade. Take cuttings of shoots growing from tubers in spring. Plant outside when rooted. Sow seeds in early winter indoors to flower in late summer.
Bluebell, Spanish, see Endymion			
Brodiaea			
Brodiaea coronaria, or *B. grandiflora*	H 18 in. S 3-6 in.	Blue-purple, star-shaped flowers in late spring and early summer. Plant in groups of 5 or 6 in sun. Avoid summer watering. Hardy in southern portions of Zone C.	Plant 3-4 in. deep in fall; mulch heavily in cold regions, or plant in spring if obtainable. Remove offsets from corms at lifting time in early fall; replant.
B. laxa	H 2 ft. S 2-3 ft.	Blue-purple, rarely white, blooms in early spring and early summer. This is most widely offered species. For *B. uniflora,* see Ipheion.	
Buttercup, see Ranunculus			
Caladium			
Caladium bicolor	H 1 ft. S 1 ft.	Valued for attractive leaves in solid colors or patterned with white, green, pink, or red, according to variety. Effective from midsummer until cold weather. Grow in shade or sun. Hardy in southern parts of Zone C. Elsewhere dig in fall; let dry for 1 wk. Store in dry peat moss or perlite at 55°-60° F.	Plant 2 in. deep directly outdoors after temperatures reach 70° F, or start earlier in pots indoors. In spring cut tubers into pieces with one or more eyes each. Dust with fungicide before planting.
Calla, see Zantedeschia			
Camassia, or Camass			
Camassia cusickii	H 2½-3 ft. S 1½-2 ft.	Pale blue flowers in late spring. Grow in sun or partial shade. Good in wild-flower gardens or by pools or bogs. Long-lived bulbs hardy to southern portions of Zone B.	Plant 6 in. deep in early to mid fall in moisture-retentive soil. Remove offsets in fall; replant at once.
C. leichtlinii	H 2-3 ft. S 1½ ft.	White to deep blue flowers in late spring.	

Begonia tuberhybrida

Brodiaea coronaria

Caladium bicolor variety

Camassia cusickii

Botanical and common names	Height and spread	Decorative characteristics and remarks	Planting and propagation
Canna *Canna generalis*	H 1½-4 ft. S 1-1½ ft.	Large flowers on spikes above very large leaves. Colors range from white to shades of pink, yellow, and scarlet. Blooms in midsummer until cold weather. Does best in long, hot summers. Grow in gardens, or in pots or large tubs on terraces. Hardy in northern parts of Zone C. Elsewhere dig up in fall after blackened by frost, dry a few days, store upside down in dry peat moss or vermiculite at 50° 60° F.	Plant rhizomes in spring, after night temperatures stay above 50 -60 F, and cover with 3-4 in. of soil. Or start indoors about a month earlier. Divide rhizomes in spring. 'Seven Dwarfs' strain can be grown from seeds; takes 6 mo. to bloom.
Chincherinchee, see Ornithogalum			
Chionodoxa, or Glory-of-the-snow *Chionodoxa luciliae*	H 6 in. S 4 in.	White, light blue, or pink blooms in midspring. Plant in large groups in rock gardens and at front of borders. Hardy in almost all parts of Zone A.	Plant bulbs 2-3 in. deep in early fall, in open, sunny site. Propagates freely from self-sown seeds. Lift and divide the bulbs when crowded.
Colchicum *Colchicum autumnale* (autumn crocus)	H 6 in. S 9 in.	White or rose-lilac, single or double flowers bloom in early fall. Flowers resemble crocuses and are produced in fall before leaves. Leaves appear in spring, then die. Plant in groups under trees or shrubs. Hardy in Zone B.	Plant corms 3-4 in. deep in late summer, in sun or partial shade. Plant *C. speciosum* 4-6 in. deep. Separate cormlets in midsummer, and replant at once.
C. speciosum	H 6-10 in. S 9-12 in.	White or rose-purple blooms in mid to late fall. Many hybrids between this and *C. autumnale.*	
Crinum *Crinum longifolium*	H 3 ft. S 1½-2 ft.	White or pink blooms in late summer. Hardiest of the crinums and can be grown in sheltered locations as far north as New York City. Widely grown species.	Plant bulbs 6 in. deep or more, in spring or fall in South, spring in North. Remove offsets in early spring; pot singly in 3- to 4-in. pots. Will flower in 3 yr.
C. powellii	H 1½ ft. S 1-1½ ft.	White to pink flowers in late summer. Does best in Zone D but can be grown in pots in Zone C or outdoors against south-facing wall with heavy winter mulch. Pots can be wintered in frost-free place.	
Crocus WINTER-FLOWERING CROCUS	H 3 in. S 3 in.	White, blue, mauve, yellow, or bronze flowers, some striped with contrasting colors, bloom in late winter and early spring. Best in rock gardens, under trees or shrubs, in front of beds or borders, and naturalized in lawns. Large-flowered varieties, such as 'E. A. Bowles,' good for forcing in indoor pots. All hardy in Zone C and often into Zone B.	Plant 3 in. deep in sunny position. Plant in early fall as soon as obtainable. Early planting is especially important for fall-flowering varieties. Lift when leaves turn brown, and remove cormlets. Replant at once; put smallest ones in unused spot until they grow to flowering size.
SPRING-FLOWERING CROCUS	H 4-5 in. S 4 in.	Same colors as winter-flowering varieties but bloom from early to mid spring. Locate as winter-flowering types. Largest flowers are in this most widely planted class.	
AUTUMN-FLOWERING CROCUS	H 4-5 in. S 3-4 in.	White, lilac-blue, lavender, rose, or yellow flowers in midfall. Not recommended for forcing indoors.	

Canna generalis

Chionodoxa luciliae

Colchicum autumnale

Crinum powellii

Spring-flowering crocus

Autumn-flowering crocus

Botanical and common names	Height and spread	Decorative characteristics and remarks	Planting and propagation
Crown imperial, see Fritillaria			
Cyclamen, hardy			
Cyclamen coum	H 3 in. S 6 in.	Pink to carmine, sometimes white flowers bloom midwinter and midspring. Plant in small clusters beneath trees and shrubs or at base of north-facing wall. Mulch in spring. Hardy in Zone C.	Plant 1-2 in. deep, in mid to late summer, in partially shaded site. Cyclamen corms (tuberous roots) do not divide or produce offsets; sow seeds in summer. May take year or more to bloom.
C. europaeum	H 4 in. S 6 in.	Fragrant crimson flowers bloom in late summer, early fall. Hardy in Zone C.	
C. neapolitanum	H 4 in. S 6 in.	Rose to white flowers bloom in late summer.	
Daffodil, see Narcissus			
Endymion, or Wood hyacinth *Endymion hispanicus,* or *Scilla hispanica,* or *S. campanulata* (Spanish bluebell)	H 1 ft. S 6 in.	White, blue, or pink blooms in late spring. Good under trees, shrubs, and in woodland. Can be grown in shade. Good cut flower.	Plant 4 in. deep, in early fall, in full sun or partial shade. Propagation by self-sown seedlings or by division of crowded bulbs after leaves have withered.
Eranthis, or Winter aconite *Eranthis hyemalis*	H 4 in. S 3 in.	Buttercup-yellow flowers bloom in late winter, early spring. Set in groups beneath deciduous trees and shrubs. Combine with galanthus for extended bloom period. Keep well watered in spring. Hardy in all but coldest regions.	Plant tuberous roots 1 in. deep, in late summer or early fall, in sun or partial shade. Lift and divide tubers in late spring; replant at once. Self-sows, except *E. tubergenii,* which is sterile and does not set seed.
Erythronium, or Trout lily *Erythronium* species and varieties	H 6 in. S 4-6 in.	White, purple, pink, rose, or yellow flowers bloom in mid and late spring. Plant in groups in woodland or partially shaded areas. Once established, leave undisturbed; but if necessary, lift and replant after leaves wither. Many species and varieties offered. Hardy in southern portions of Zone B.	Plant corms 2-3 in. deep, in late summer or as soon as available, in partial shade. Provide mulch. Offsets can be removed in summer, planted immediately in unused piece of ground for several years to increase size.
Fritillaria			
Fritillaria imperialis (crown imperial)	H 2-3 ft. S 9-15 in.	Yellow, orange, or red flowers bloom in mid and late spring. Plant in groups in borders. Sometimes difficult to establish, but forms clumps in right site. Divide when crowded. Grows in southernmost parts of Zone B.	Plant bulbs on sides, 8 in. deep, in midfall, in sun or partial shade. Plant *F. meleagris* 4 in. deep. Remove offsets in late summer; grow in cold frame or pots. Seeds sown in summer take 4-6 yr. to bloom.
F. meleagris (guinea-hen flower)	H 1 ft. S 6 in.	Pure white or purple and white flowers bloom in mid and late spring. Treat like *F. imperialis;* can be grown also in short grass. Hardy in Zone A.	

Cyclamen neapolitanum

Endymion hispanicus

Eranthis hyemalis

Erythronium species

Fritillaria imperialis

Botanical and common names	Height and spread	Decorative characteristics and remarks	Planting and propagation
Galanthus, or Snowdrop			
Galanthus elwesii	H 6-10 in. S 4-6 in.	White flowers with green-tipped inner petals appear in late winter, early spring. Plant in groups under trees or shrubs, among low ground covers, and with other small-flowering spring bulbs, such as chionodoxa and eranthis. Sometimes difficult to establish but afterward multiplies freely. Hardy in Zone A.	Plant bulbs 3-4 in. deep, in early fall or immediately after flowering, in area that is partially shaded in summer. Lift and divide after flowering; replant at once.
G. nivalis	H 4-10 in. S 4-6 in.	Flowers are similar to *G. elwesii.* Excellent in rock gardens. 'S. Arnott' is 10 in. tall, large flowered, and fragrant. There is also a double form.	
Galtonia, or Summer hyacinth *Galtonia candicans*	H 3-4 ft. S 9 in.	White flowers tipped with green bloom in mid and late summer. Plant in groups in perennial or shrub borders. Where soil freezes in winter, lift and store as for gladiolus, or mulch heavily.	Plant bulbs 6-8 in. deep in late spring, except in mildest regions, where they can be set out in fall in sunny site. A few offsets are produced; in Zone D remove these in early fall and replant at once.
Gladiolus			
LARGE- AND GIANT-FLOWERED HYBRID	H 3-5 ft. S 4-6 in.	Flowers come in all colors of the spectrum, many bicolored, with attractive markings. Blooming time depends on climate and planting time: summer in cold regions, all months in mild areas. Plant in groups, or in rows for cuttings. Tall types may need staking. In very hot climates, plant late fall to late winter. Dig and store corms over winter in northern parts of Zone C and northward.	Set corms 4-6 in. deep in successive plantings for continuous bloom. In mild regions, plant year round; in cold regions, after frost and into summer. Locate in full sun. Separate cormlets in fall or when foliage yellows; in mild regions, replant; in cold areas, store over winter, plant in spring. Soak cormlets in water for 2 da. before planting, to help speed sprouting.
BUTTERFLY HYBRID	H 2-4 ft. S 4-6 in.	Flowers, smaller than large-flowered hybrids, come in full color range. Seldom needs staking. Well suited to flower arrangements.	
PRIMULINUS AND MINIATURE HYBRID	H 1½-3 ft. S 3-6 in.	Full range of colors; primulinus flowers have hooded upper segments (petals); miniatures have somewhat smaller flowers. Staking not required.	
Gloriosa, or Glory-lily *Gloriosa rothschildiana*	H 3-4 ft. S 1 ft.	Red flowers with yellow-edged petals bloom in early summer, also at other times in mild areas. Attractive vines that can be grown against trellises or in pots with support. Can be left in ground all year in southern part of Zone C and southward; in colder regions dig in fall, store in dry peat moss at 55°-60° F.	Plant tubers horizontally 4 in. deep, in spring. Locate in sun, and provide some support. Separate tubers in spring, and plant at once. Seeds usually take 2-3 yr. to reach flowering size.

Galanthus nivalis

Galtonia candicans

Large-flowered gladiolus

Butterfly gladiolus

Primulinus gladiolus

Gloriosa rothschildiana

Glory-of-the-snow, see Chionodoxa
Grape hyacinth, see Muscari
Guinea-hen flower, see Fritillaria

Hippeastrum hybrid

Hyacinthus orientalis 'Pink Pearl'

Hymenocallis calathina

Ipheion uniflorum

Ixia maculata hybrid

Botanical and common names	Height and spread	Decorative characteristics and remarks	Planting and propagation
Hippeastrum, or Amaryllis	H 2 ft. S 1-1½ ft.	White, pink, salmon, or red flowers, some with striping, bloom in spring outdoors, winter or spring indoors. Flowers usually precede leaves. Hardy in Zone D. Elsewhere grown as house plants. Popular hybrids include 'Apple Blossom' (blush-pink), 'Jeanne d'Arc' (white), 'Belinda' (red). See also Amaryllis.	Plant bulbs outdoors 6-8 in. deep, in midfall, in partial shade. In pots, plant from fall to spring with top third of bulb uncovered. Remove offsets from around bulb in fall and replant. Seeds take 3-4 yr. to flower.
Hyacinth, summer, see Galtonia			
Hyacinthus, or Hyacinth			
LARGE-FLOWERED HYBRID, or DUTCH HYACINTH *Hyacinthus orientalis* hybrids	H 8-9 in. S 6-8 in.	White, blue, mauve, yellow, pink, red, or orange flowers bloom in early to late spring. Plant in groups and near house, where fragrance can be enjoyed. May need staking. Hardy in all zones except the northernmost part of Zone A. Varieties include 'L'Innocence' (white), 'Delft Blue' (blue), 'City of Haarlem' (yellow), 'Pink Pearl' (pink), 'Jan Bos' (crimson).	Plant bulbs 5-6 in. deep, in midfall except in mild climates, where late-fall or early-winter planting is best. Locate in sun or partial shade. Dig up old bulbs when leaves turn yellow; separate and replant.
ROMAN HYACINTH *H. o. albulus*	H 6 in. S 6-9 in.	White flowers, smaller than above, appear in early to late spring. Extremely fragrant. Best for forcing. Not hardy in northern half of Zone B.	
Hymenocallis, or Spider lily, or Ismene *Hymenocallis calathina,* or *H. narcissiflora,* or *Ismene calathina* (Peruvian daffodil)	H 1½-2 ft. S 10-12 in.	White blooms appear in midsummer. Hardy in southern half of Zone C; in colder regions dig in fall and store upside down in vermiculite or peat moss at 65° F. Varieties include 'Advance' and 'Festalis' (white) and 'Sulfur Queen' (yellow).	Plant bulbs 6-8 in. deep, in spring when night temperatures average 60° F, in sun or partial shade. Lift in fall, and separate offsets. In Zone D replant at once; elsewhere, in spring.
Ipheion, or Spring starflower *Ipheion uniflorum,* or *Brodiaea uniflora,* or *Milla uniflora,* or *Triteleia uniflora*	H 6-8 in. S 4 in.	Up-facing white flowers tinged with blue bloom in early spring; have minty scent. Foliage appears in fall. Plant in large groups under shrubs or in rock garden. Hardy in southernmost parts of Zone B and southward.	Plant bulbs 3 in. deep, in early fall, in sun or partial shade. Remove offsets when foliage dies in summer; replant at once. Multiplies rapidly.
Iris, bulbous, see p. 337 **Ismene,** see Hymenocallis			
Ixia, or African corn lily *Ixia maculata*	H 1½ ft. S 4 in.	Hybrids with cream, pink, yellow, orange, or red flowers bloom in late spring, early summer. Soil must be dry in summer for corms to ripen. Grow in groups. Can be grown in pots. Hardy in southern parts of Zone C.	Plant corms 3-4 in. deep in full sun. Plant in early to late fall in southern part of Zone C and southward; in spring, north of Zone C. Remove offsets after foliage dries in summer.
Jonquil, see Narcissus (JONQUILLA)			

Botanical and common names	Height and spread	Decorative characteristics and remarks	Planting and propagation
Leucojum, or Snowflake			
Leucojum aestivum (summer snowflake)	H 1 ft. S 6 in.	White flowers tipped with green, 4-8 per stem, bloom in mid to late spring. Plant in groups in rock gardens or sunny nooks. Hardy in all of Zone A.	Plant bulbs 3-4 in. deep, in early fall, in sun or partial shade. *L. vernum* does best planted in shade. Remove offsets when foliage dies; replant at once.
L. vernum (spring snowflake)	H 6-8 in. S 4 in.	Smaller white flowers, 1 per stem, are tipped with green, bloom early to mid spring. This and summer snowflake do better in mild climates than galanthus, or snowdrop.	
Lycoris			
Lycoris radiata (short-tube lycoris, or spider lily)	H 1½ ft. S 10-12 in.	Deep pink to red blooms in late summer, early fall. Leaves precede flowers, then die; keep fairly dry until flowers appear. Bulbs bloom best when crowded. Makes excellent container plant for late bloom. Hardy in southern half of Zone C.	Plant bulbs 5 in. deep in garden in midsummer; in containers set bulbs with tips exposed. In borderline areas of hardiness, *L. squamigera* should be planted deeper. Grow in partial shade. To propagate, dig after foliage dies (before flowering); remove offsets; replant at once.
L. squamigera (autumn amaryllis, or resurrection lily)	H 2 ft. S 10-12 in.	Fragrant lilac-rose flowers bloom in late summer, early fall. Hardier than *L. radiata.* Can be grown outdoors in southern parts of Zone B.	
Muscari, or Grape hyacinth			
Muscari armeniacum	H 8 in. S 4 in.	Deep blue flowers edged with white appear in mid and late spring. Best in groups at front of borders and rock gardens. One of hardiest bulbs; grows in all of Zone A.	Plant bulbs 3 in. deep, in early to late fall, in sun. Seeds freely where it blooms well. Divide every 3 yr. when leaves yellow; replant immediately, or store until fall.
M. botryoides	H 7 in. S 4 in.	Sky-blue flowers bloom from early to mid spring. White form also available.	
M. comosum	H 1 ft. S 4-6 in.	Upper flowers blue to mauve, sterile; lower flowers olive-colored, fertile. Petals finely cut. Bloom in late spring to early summer.	
Narcissus			
TRUMPET NARCISSUS, or DAFFODIL Trumpet is as long or longer than petals. One flower borne per stem.	H 14-18 in. S 6-8 in.	Flowers are all yellow or white, or with trumpets one color, petals another; bloom in early to late spring. Plant in groups in shrub or perennial borders or under trees. Excellent cut flower. Popular varieties include 'Dutch Master,' 'King Alfred,' 'Unsurpassable' (yellow); 'Beersheba,' 'Mount Hood' (white); 'Spellbinder' (yellow and ivory); and 'Pink Glory' (white and pink).	Plant bulbs about 6 in. deep and 6 in. apart, in mid to late fall, in sun or partial shade. In South, purchase pretreated bulbs that have been given artificial cold period. Lift in early summer after foliage yellows; remove offsets and replant at once or store until early fall.
LARGE-CUPPED NARCISSUS Cup, or corona, is more than one-third length of petals and may be frilled. One flower borne per stem.	H 14-22 in. S 6-8 in.	Trumpets and petals often different colors. Combinations of yellow, pink, and white. Good varieties include 'Gigantic Star' (yellow), 'Easter Morn' (white), 'Flower Record' (yellow and white), 'Mrs. R. O. Backhouse' (pink and white), and 'Duke of Windsor' (white and orange).	

Leucojum vernum

Lycoris squamigera

Muscari botryoides

Trumpet narcissus

Narcissus—continued

	Botanical and common names	Height and spread	Decorative characteristics and remarks	Planting and propagation
	Narcissus—continued			
Small-cupped narcissus	SMALL-CUPPED NARCISSUS Cup, or corona, is not more than one-third length of petals. One flower is borne per stem.	H 14-18 in. S 6 in.	Flowers are all white or combinations of yellow, white, or other colors; bloom from early to late spring. Varieties include 'Edward Buxton' (yellow and orange), 'Verger' (white and red), and 'Chinese White' (white).	See trumpet narcissus, p. 325.
Double-flowered narcissus	DOUBLE-FLOWERED NARCISSUS All types with more than 1 layer of petals. One or more flowers are borne per stem.	H 1-1½ ft. S 6 in.	White, yellow, or bicolored flowers bloom from early to late spring. Varieties include 'Inglescombe' (yellow), 'Texas' (yellow and orange), and 'Mary Copeland' (creamy white and orange-red).	See trumpet narcissus, p. 325.
	TRIANDRUS NARCISSUS Cup is about two-thirds as long as the petals are. One to 6 flowers are borne per stem; may be pendulous.	H 8-16 in. S 6 in.	Varieties include 'Liberty Bells' (yellow), 'Tresamble' (white), and 'Dawn' (white and yellow).	See trumpet narcissus, p. 325.
Cyclamineus narcissus	CYCLAMINEUS NARCISSUS Long pendent cup with petals curving back from it. One flower is borne per stem.	H 8-15 in. S 3-6 in.	White, yellow, or bicolored. Hardy in southern half of Zone B. Varieties include 'February Gold' (yellow), 'Jack Snipe' (white and yellow), and 'February Silver' (white).	See trumpet narcissus, p. 325.
Jonquilla	JONQUILLA, or JONQUIL Cup longer or shorter than petals. Two to 6 fragrant flowers are borne per stem. Tubular leaves.	H 7-14 in. S 4-6 in.	Yellow or bicolored, often with red, pink, or orange cup. Blooms in late spring. Varieties include 'Trevithian' (pale yellow), 'Suzy' (yellow and orange-red), and 'Lintie' (white and pale pink).	See trumpet narcissus, p. 325.
	TAZETTA NARCISSUS (includes poetaz) Four to 8 fragrant short-cupped flowers are borne per stem.	H 14 in. S 6-8 in.	White or yellow, usually with colored cup, single or double. Outdoors, blooms in early to late spring; forced bulbs can bloom from early winter into spring. Except in mildest regions grow tazettas in pots (p. 317); poetaz can be grown as for trumpet narcissus. Tazettas include 'Paper-white' (white) and 'Soleil d'Or' (yellow). Poetaz include 'Geranium' (white and orange-red) and 'Cheerfulness' (yellow, double).	Suitable only for pot culture except in southern part of Zone C and southward. Treat poetaz as for trumpet narcissus. Bulbs grown indoors in pebbles and water should be discarded after blooming.

Botanical and common names	Height and spread	Decorative characteristics and remarks	Planting and propagation
Narcissus—continued POETICUS NARCISSUS Petals white, short cup is contrasting color; fragrant. Usually 1 flower is borne per stem.	H 17-20 in. S 6 in.	White flower has yellow cup edged with red, blooms from mid to late spring. Very fragrant and good cut flower. Excellent in cold climates. Most popular variety is 'Actaea' (white with yellow cup edged with red).	See trumpet narcissus, p. 325.
DWARF NARCISSUS US This is true species, or wild, daffodil. Most are small flowered and short; 1 or more flowers are borne per stem.	H 3-6 in. S 2-3 in.	White or yellow flowers from late winter to mid-spring. Best planted in small groups in rock garden or where readily seen. Some in this group not hardy north of Zone C. Popular are *Narcissus bulbocodium* (yellow) and *N. triandrus albus,* or angel's tears (cream-white).	Plant at least 3 times the depth of bulb, in early to mid fall, in sun or partial shade. Propagate as for daffodils; but also by seeds collected when ripe and sown in early summer. Takes 3-7 yr. to bloom.
Nerine *Nerine bowdenii*	H 2 ft. S 6 in.	Pink flowers bloom in late fall, early winter. After potting grow indoors at 50° F over winter. Do not water until growth commences; then keep moist and fertilize monthly with general-purpose fertilizer. Leaves grow during winter and spring. Gradually dry off and withhold water when leaves start to yellow until growth resumes.	Usually grown in pots except in mildest regions. In pots bury lower half of bulbs; in ground set 4-6 in. deep. Plant in early fall. Lift and divide overgrown clumps after flowering or in spring. Remove and repot offsets from pot plants.
Onion, ornamental, see Allium			
Ornithogalum *Ornithogalum nutans* (nodding star of Bethlehem)	H 1 ft. S 6 in.	White and pale green flowers bloom from mid to late spring. Plant in groups at front of borders, in rock gardens or woodland. Hardy in southern parts of Zone B.	Plant 2-3 in. deep, in midfall, in sun or partial shade. Large bulbs can be set 4-6 in. deep. *O. thyrsoides* is planted 2-3 in. deep, in fall, in mild climates. To grow in pots indoors, barely cover bulb. Lift and remove bulblets after leaves yellow; replant at once.
O. thyrsoides (chincherinchee)	H 1½ ft. S 4 in.	White to cream flowers bloom in late spring, midsummer. Can be grown as pot plant in cool greenhouse (50° F at night) to flower in spring. Also easily grown in window. Cut flowers last well. Hardy in southern parts of Zone C.	
O. umbellatum (star of Bethlehem)	H 9-12 in. S 6 in.	White flowers from late spring to early summer. Multiplies rapidly, may become a nuisance. Hardy in most of Zone A.	
Oxalis *O. adenophylla*	H 3-4 in. S 2-3 in.	Small 1½-in. bell-shaped flowers are lavender-pink, petals veined in deeper shade; bloom in late spring, midsummer. Commonly grown in rock gardens.	Plant tuberous roots 2-3 in. deep and 4-5 in. apart, in midfall. Needs full sun, well-drained soil. Hardy in Zone D. North of this lift in fall; store as gladiolus until planting time.

Poeticus narcissus

Dwarf narcissus

Nerine bowdenii

Ornithogalum thyrsoides

Oxalis adenophylla

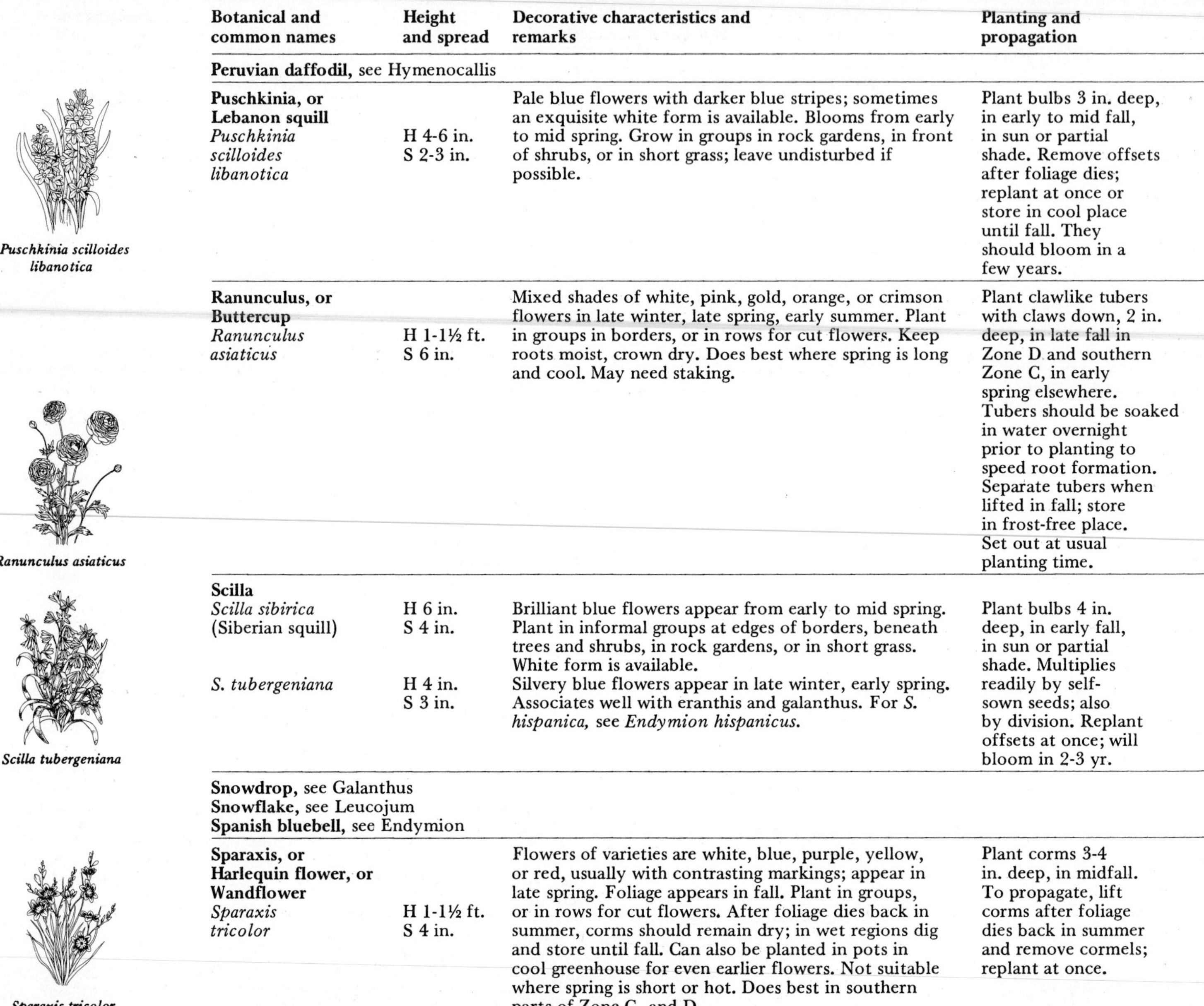

Botanical and common names	Height and spread	Decorative characteristics and remarks	Planting and propagation
Peruvian daffodil, see Hymenocallis			
Puschkinia, or Lebanon squill *Puschkinia scilloides libanotica*	H 4-6 in. S 2-3 in.	Pale blue flowers with darker blue stripes; sometimes an exquisite white form is available. Blooms from early to mid spring. Grow in groups in rock gardens, in front of shrubs, or in short grass; leave undisturbed if possible.	Plant bulbs 3 in. deep, in early to mid fall, in sun or partial shade. Remove offsets after foliage dies; replant at once or store in cool place until fall. They should bloom in a few years.
Ranunculus, or Buttercup *Ranunculus asiaticus*	H 1-1½ ft. S 6 in.	Mixed shades of white, pink, gold, orange, or crimson flowers in late winter, late spring, early summer. Plant in groups in borders, or in rows for cut flowers. Keep roots moist, crown dry. Does best where spring is long and cool. May need staking.	Plant clawlike tubers with claws down, 2 in. deep, in late fall in Zone D and southern Zone C, in early spring elsewhere. Tubers should be soaked in water overnight prior to planting to speed root formation. Separate tubers when lifted in fall; store in frost-free place. Set out at usual planting time.
Scilla *Scilla sibirica* (Siberian squill)	H 6 in. S 4 in.	Brilliant blue flowers appear from early to mid spring. Plant in informal groups at edges of borders, beneath trees and shrubs, in rock gardens, or in short grass. White form is available.	Plant bulbs 4 in. deep, in early fall, in sun or partial shade. Multiplies readily by self-sown seeds; also by division. Replant offsets at once; will bloom in 2-3 yr.
S. tubergeniana	H 4 in. S 3 in.	Silvery blue flowers appear in late winter, early spring. Associates well with eranthis and galanthus. For *S. hispanica,* see *Endymion hispanicus.*	
Snowdrop, see Galanthus **Snowflake,** see Leucojum **Spanish bluebell,** see Endymion			
Sparaxis, or Harlequin flower, or Wandflower *Sparaxis tricolor*	H 1-1½ ft. S 4 in.	Flowers of varieties are white, blue, purple, yellow, or red, usually with contrasting markings; appear in late spring. Foliage appears in fall. Plant in groups, or in rows for cut flowers. After foliage dies back in summer, corms should remain dry; in wet regions dig and store until fall. Can also be planted in pots in cool greenhouse for even earlier flowers. Not suitable where spring is short or hot. Does best in southern parts of Zone C, and D.	Plant corms 3-4 in. deep, in midfall. To propagate, lift corms after foliage dies back in summer and remove cormels; replant at once.
Spider lily, see Hymenocallis and Lycoris **Squill, Lebanon,** see Puschkinia **Squill, Siberian,** see Scilla **Star of Bethlehem,** see Ornithogalum			

Puschkinia scilloides libanotica

Ranunculus asiaticus

Scilla tubergeniana

Sparaxis tricolor

Sternbergia lutea

Tigridia pavonia

Botanical and common names	Height and spread	Decorative characteristics and remarks	Planting and propagation
Sternbergia *Sternbergia lutea*	H 6-9 in. S 4 in.	Shiny yellow flowers, 1½ in. long, appear in early fall, as do leaves, which are narrow and often 1 ft. long. Plant in groups at edge of borders or in rock gardens. Sometimes takes a year to become established and should not be disturbed unless overcrowded. Hardy in Zone C. Give winter mulch where frosts occur.	Plant bulbs 5-6 in. deep, in sunny location where soil is quite dry. Separate offsets in late summer after leaves die down; replant at once.
Summer snowflake, see Leucojum			
Tigridia, or Tigerflower *Tigridia pavonia*	H 1½ ft. S 4 in.	Flowers, in white, yellow, orange, and red with spots of a contrasting color, bloom in mid to late summer. Plant in groups in mixed borders. Can be left in ground in Zone D and warmer parts of Zone C; elsewhere lift after flowering and store bulbs until spring.	Plant bulbs 3-4 in. deep, in spring when night temperatures remain above 60° F. Requires sunny position. To propagate, lift in late summer and remove bulblets; store over winter.
Tuberous begonia, see Begonia			

Single early tulip

Double early tulip

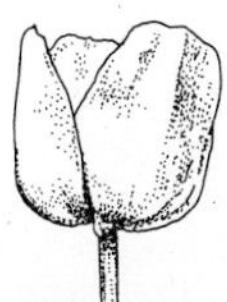

Darwin tulip

Lily-flowered tulip

Botanical and common names	Height and spread	Decorative characteristics and remarks	Planting and propagation
Tulipa, or Tulip			
SINGLE EARLY TULIP Lower growing than late-flowering tulips; flowers open wide, nearly flat.	H 8-14 in. S 4-6 in.	Flowers are white, violet, pink, yellow, red, or bicolored; bloom in midspring. Plant in beds, mixed borders, or in groups in front of shrubs. Do best in Zones A and B; south of this they need precooling. Varieties include 'Christmas Marvel' (pink), 'Bellona' (yellow), and 'Keizerskroon' (red and yellow).	Plant bulbs 6-8 in. deep, in mid to late fall, in sun. Sheltered site is preferable, to protect against variable spring weather. When bulbs become crowded after several years, dig after leaves have withered, and store dry in well-ventilated place until planting time. Smallest bulbs are best planted in an out-of-the-way spot until they are of flowering size, which usually takes several years.
DOUBLE EARLY TULIP Resemble double peonies.	H 12-15 in. S 6 in.	White, pink, yellow, orange, and scarlet flowers appear in midspring. Varieties include 'Peach Blossom' (rose), 'Electra' (red), 'Carlton' (red), and 'Schoonoord' (scarlet).	
MENDEL TULIP Resemble Darwins but bloom 2 wk. earlier.	H 16-26 in. S 6 in.	Large white, pink, yellow, orange, and red blooms in late spring. Varieties include 'Athleet' (white), 'Pink Trophy' (pink), and 'Olga' (violet-red, edged with white).	
TRIUMPH TULIP Angular flowers on sturdy stems of medium height.	H 16-26 in. S 6 in.	White, lavender, pink, yellow, orange, red, and bicolored flowers appear from mid to late spring. Excellent for massed planting; can be forced. Foliage ripens early. Varieties include 'Peerless Pink' (satin-pink), 'Golden Melody' (yellow), and 'Albury' (cherry-red).	
DARWIN TULIP Large, square-shaped flowers on tall, strong stems.	H 2-2½ ft. S 6-8 in.	White, lavender, pink, yellow, orange, or red flowers appear in late spring. The most popular garden tulip for beds and borders. Popular varieties include 'Pink Supreme' (pink), 'Sunkist' (yellow), 'Demeter' (purple), and 'Cordell Hull' (red on white).	See single early tulip (above).
DARWIN HYBRID Largest of all tulips.	H 2-2½ ft. S 6-8 in.	Flowers are cream, yellow, orange, red, and appear in midspring, a week or more before Darwins. Large flowers with strong stems. Varieties include 'Golden Oxford' (yellow) and 'Apeldoorn' (scarlet).	See single early tulip (above).
LILY-FLOWERED TULIP Elongated flowers with pointed petals that bend outward at tips.	H 1½-2 ft. S 6 in.	White, lavender, pink, yellow, red, or bicolored flowers appear from mid to late spring. Very graceful flowers with strong stems. Popular varieties include 'White Triumphator' (white), 'Maytime' (reddish violet, cream edge), 'China Pink' (pink), 'West Point' (yellow), 'Red Shine' (red), and 'Queen of Sheba' (scarlet-brown, edged in yellow).	See single early tulip (above).

Tulipa—continued

	Botanical and common names	Height and spread	Decorative characteristics and remarks	Planting and propagation
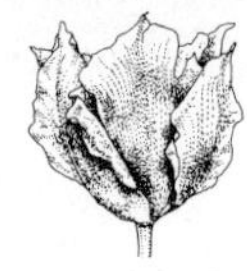 Cottage tulip	**Tulipa**—continued			
	COTTAGE TULIP (SINGLE LATE) Rounded flowers but variable in form.	H 24-28 in. S 6-8 in.	Flowers are white, green, lilac, pink, yellow, orange, red, or bicolored and appear in mid to late spring. Slightly recurved petals and graceful stems. Varieties include 'Rosy Wings' (pink), 'Golden Harvest' (yellow), and 'Renown' (carmine-red).	See single early tulip, p. 329.
 Parrot tulip	PARROT TULIP Large, fringed flowers, often with twisted, bicolored petals.	H 2 ft. S 8 in.	White, lavender, pink, yellow, orange, red, or bicolored flowers with wavy petals appear from mid to late spring. Varieties include 'Flaming Parrot' (red and yellow) and 'Wildfire' (scarlet).	See single early tulip, p. 329.
	DOUBLE LATE TULIP Resemble peonies, and flowers are long lasting.	H 18-22 in. S 6-8 in.	White, pink, yellow, or red flowers appear in late spring. Plant in protected spot, as heavy flowers are easily toppled by wind. Varieties include 'Mount Tacoma' (white), 'Clara Carter' (pink), and 'Golden Lion' (yellow).	See single early tulip, p. 329.
 Kaufmanniana tulip	KAUFMANNIANA HYBRID Flowers open into 6-pointed star.	H 6-10 in. S 5 in.	Some solid-colored flowers but mostly bicolored as red and yellow or red and white appear in early spring. Leaves sometimes mottled. Varieties include 'Goudstuk' (carmine and yellow), 'Praestans Fusilier' (orange-scarlet), and 'Shakespeare' (salmon).	See single early tulip, p. 329.
	FOSTERIANA HYBRID Very large flowers; foliage sometimes mottled.	H 1-1½ ft. S 6 in.	Very large pink, yellow, orange, red, and bicolored flowers appear in midspring. Varieties include 'Purissima' (white), 'Candela' (yellow), and 'Red Emperor' (red).	See single early tulip, p. 329.
 Greigii tulip	GREIGII TULIP Very large flowers; leaves mottled or striped.	H 7-14 in. S 6 in.	Flowers in shades of red, some bicolored with yellow, appear from mid to late spring. Beautiful mottled leaves. Varieties include 'Cape Cod' (apricot edged with yellow), 'Margaret Herbst' (red), and 'Plaisir' (red and yellow).	See single early tulip, p. 329.
	Windflower, see Anemone **Winter aconite,** see Eranthis			
 *Zantedeschia aethiopica*	**Zantedeschia, or Calla**			
	Zantedeschia aethiopica (common calla lily)	H 3 ft. S 1½-2 ft.	White flowers appear from early to mid summer. Keep faded flowers picked, but leave some leaves if rhizomes are to be kept for another year. This species can also be grown as aquatic plant in mild regions. In all but mildest climates (southern parts of Zone D), lift rhizomes after first frost. Dry for a few days; store covered in dry peat moss or vermiculite at 40°-50° F.	In southern parts of Zone D, plant rhizomes horizontally 3-4 in. deep in spring. Elsewhere, start indoors in pots in early spring, and set outdoors after frost danger is past. *Z. elliottiana* is planted 2 in. deep. Does best in mild regions. In cold regions grown mostly in greenhouses. To propagate (except *Z. elliottiana*) divide clumps in fall when they become crowded (mild climates only). Sow seeds in spring. Will flower in 1-2 yr.
	Z. albomaculata (spotted calla)	H 2 ft. S 1½-2 ft.	White flowers with purple appear in early to mid summer. Leaves are spotted with white.	
	Z. elliottiana (golden calla)	H 1½-2 ft. S 1½-2 ft.	Yellow flowers appear from early to mid summer. Can take more sun than the white forms. Dwarf variety is sometimes available.	
	Z. rehmannii (pink, or red, calla)	H 1-1½ ft. S 1½-2 ft.	Pink or red flowers appear from late spring to early summer. Leaves are green or spotted with white. Can take more sun than white forms without flowers burning. Hybrids come in lavender, purple, and orange.	

Lilium davidii

Lilies

Stately lily plants, with their exotic flower forms and their great variety in color and size, add a dramatic accent to the summer garden.

One of the oldest cultivated flowers, the lily has been cherished for at least 3,000 years—in ancient Egypt, Rome, Greece, China, and Japan. For centuries only a few species were known, the most famous being the pure white Madonna lily (*Lilium candidum*)—traditionally a symbol of purity—from the eastern Mediterranean. Another species fairly widespread in Europe was *L. martagon,* with nodding dark-spotted pink-mauve flowers.

Few plants are as versatile as the lily, a genus of mainly hardy bulbs with about 90 species. They vary widely in flower size and form, height, color, flowering period, and the growing conditions they need.

Like many other wild plants, lily species can be difficult to transfer to the cultivated garden. Their requirements are not always understood, and it is sometimes difficult to re-create a suitable situation for them. When transplanted, if they survive at all, these lilies often languish a season or two.

However, wild lilies have caught the fancy of plant breeders, who have produced hybrids from them that are generally far superior to their parents.

For summer color in the garden, the hybrid lilies are a welcome addition. When most spring perennials have bloomed, lilies start to flower and provide continuing interest into late summer. As its many buds open each day, an established clump of lilies will bloom over an extended period. Coming in all colors but blue, and having a wide range of sizes and forms, hybrid lilies can be used in many ways.

After more than half a century of hybridizing by professionals and amateurs around the world, named varieties now exist that are free flowering, robust, and disease resistant. Many outshine their parents in vigor and variety of color and form. The named varieties are propagated vegetatively from the bulbs' scales and are thus identical to the parent.

Some lilies are grown commercially from seeds from selected crosses, making them relatively inexpensive. They vary from one another only slightly, usually in color rather than form. They are sold as strains, such as the Burgundy, the Golden Splendor, and the Imperial strains. They can be grown in a mixed border with evergreens and deciduous shrubs for a color accent, used among perennials, or grown in pots or for cut flowers.

Lilies have a variety of forms. The trumpets, so called for the flaring trumpet shape of their flowers, are exemplified by the Sentinel strain and the Easter lily (*L. longiflorum*). Many lilies are shaped like saucers, which face either upward or outward. 'Enchantment' and 'Connecticut King' face upward; the Imperial strains face outward. The familiar Turk's cap form is represented by *L. tigrinum* and *L. davidii,* as well as most of their hybrids. 'Nutmegger' and the varicolored Harlequin hybrids have that shape too.

There are other variations and combinations that many plant breeders find fascinating to work with in order to produce new lilies. Combining the different forms, colors, and seasons of bloom has become an unending challenge.

Many lilies are fragrant. The Trumpet, Aurelian, and Oriental hybrids are so heavily scented that they can be overpowering in a confined area.

Most of the species cross easily with only a few others. During the past 40 to 50 years, however, significant breakthroughs have been made by breeders working on a small scale in the United States, Canada, New Zealand, and Japan. These have resulted in greater vigor, adaptability, and color range. Improved production methods greatly increased the availability of hybrid lilies to professional and amateur growers.

In a mixed border lilies will make a good show as long as they are not crowded by other plants.

Because they are not particularly attractive when out of bloom, lilies look best when grown with ground covers or low-growing companion plants that do not hinder lily roots.

A planting of lilies—for example, the large Trumpet types, the early-flowering Asiatics, or the later-flowering Oriental hybrids, with low-growing annuals at their base—is a magnificent sight. A clump of lilies in bloom, between or in front of shrub plantings, also creates an attractive picture. For two or more weeks the added color complements the green foliage.

Hybrid lilies have been grouped under headings loosely based on species' origins and flower forms, but there is overlapping.

For instance, the Asiatics, most of whose parents originated in China, are usually lilies bred from *L. tigrinum, L. davidii, L. cernuum,* and others that readily intercross.

The Asiatic hybrids are the most widely varied group in color and form. Some have upright flowers; the blooms of others face outward; and some have backswept petals. An established clump of Asiatics has one of the longest blooming periods of all lilies—from early summer to midsummer. They are the hardiest and most reliable performers. Many breeders consider them to have the greatest hybridizing potential.

American hybrids are derived from native American species. Best known are the Bellingham hybrids. Hybrids developed in America from nonnatives are not included here.

Martagon hybrids are most often used in natural settings at the edges of wooded areas. Among the first of the lilies to bloom, they should not be disturbed after being put into place. They may take two years to reappear after transplanting.

The Backhouse hybrids originated before 1900 in England. They are the offsprings of *L. martagon,* a lily native to European mountains and western Asia to Mongolia, and *L. hansonii,* of Japan, Korea, and Siberia. Although small flowered, they have many blooms and do well in shade. They are not widely available. The newer Paisley strain is similar.

The Trumpet hybrids are the offsprings of four Chinese species: *L. regale, L. sargentiae, L. leucanthum,* and *L. sulphureum.* A clump of white, yellow, or pink Trumpets standing 4–6 feet tall is a spectacular sight in midsummer. They are less hardy than the Asiatics and have fragrant, usually outfacing or occasionally pendent flowers.

The Aurelian hybrids result from crosses of the Trumpets with the Chinese *L. henryi,* which imparts adaptability and additional hardiness. Varying in form from reflexed stars to wide-flaring bowls and trumpets, they often have willowy stems that need support. They bloom from mid to late summer.

The most exotic and difficult hybrids are the Orientals, with magnificent flowers in shades of white, pink, or red on sturdy stems. But they are susceptible to bulb rot and virus disease, and many lily growers settle for one season of colorful bloom and treat them as annuals or biennials. They are derived from *L. auratum* and *L. speciosum.* The Jamboree hybrids are closer to *L. speciosum* and are among the most dependable of the Orientals. They bloom in late summer.

Among the true species, *L. davidii, L. tigrinum, L. henryi, L. regale,* and *L. speciosum* are easy to obtain and among the most reliable.

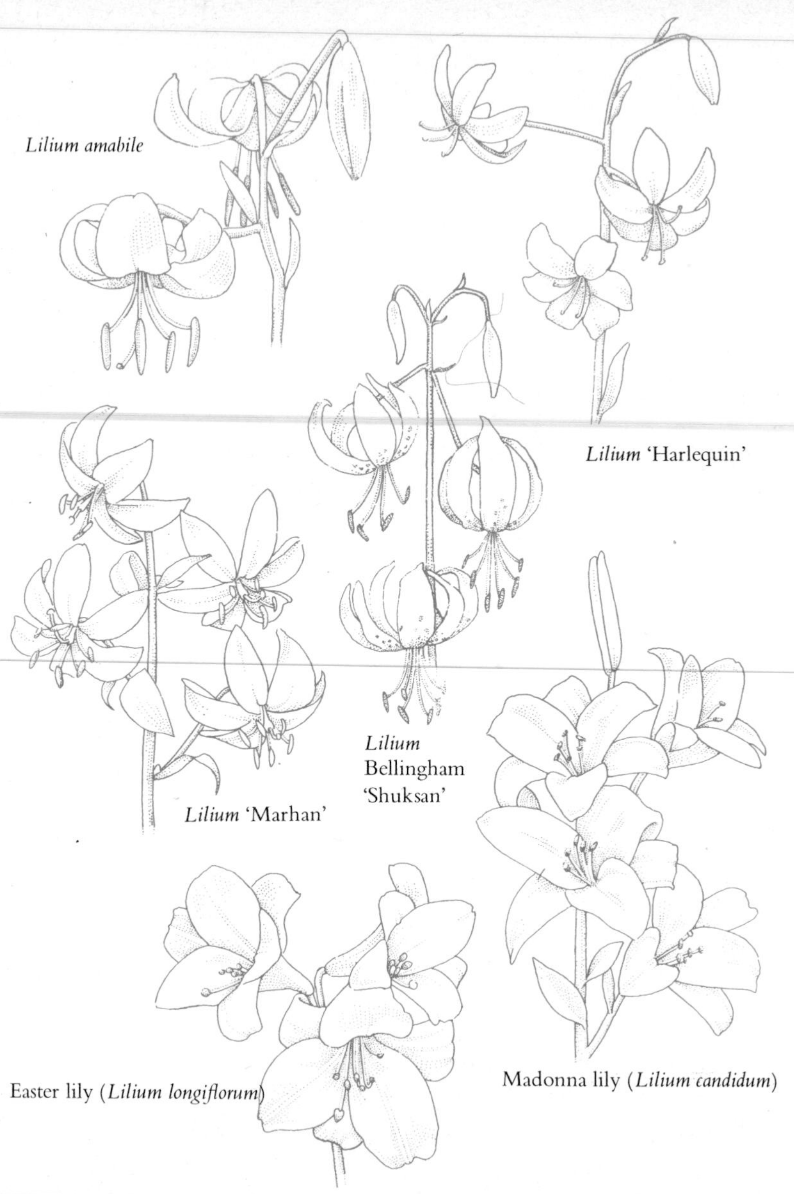

Flower shapes. *Lilies are grouped into categories based on flower shape. Shown are Turk's cap and Trumpet. Turk's cap lilies—all those shown above except the Madonna lily* (Lilium candidum) *and the Easter lily* (L. longiflorum)*—have pendent flowers that are usually about* $1^1/_2$ *in. long, the petals rolled and curved backward at the tips. The flowers of the Trumpet lilies range in form from narrow tubes with flared ends to large bowl-shaped blossoms.*

Planting and Caring for Lilies

Preparing the Soil and Selecting the Bulbs

Lilies will grow in almost any well-drained soil that has a pH slightly on the acid side. An exception is the Madonna lily, which does best in a neutral to slightly alkaline soil. Full sun will provide the most vigorous growth, but lilies also perform well in partial shade.

Soil preparation before planting lilies is important, just as it is with other bulbs. In light soils a generous addition of peat moss or well-composted organic material will improve moisture control. Bear in mind that lily bulbs and roots will be damaged if fresh manure is applied.

In heavy soils, coarse sand or light gravel should be added. Superphosphate, well mixed in, will enrich and condition the soil for several seasons (see pp. 593–595).

The subsoil must also provide good drainage so that water will not accumulate around the bulbs. Where impervious subsoil prevails, raised beds with well-drained soil can be prepared. Planting on a gentle slope serves the same purpose.

Buy only plump, healthy-looking bulbs. They are available in late fall and sometimes in early spring from mail-order nurseries, lily specialists, and some local nurseries. The bulbs should be firm, with closely packed scales and a dense root system. If you do purchase bargain lots of bulbs, which may be bruised or limp, remove the loose outer scales and put the bulbs into plastic bags with slightly moist peat moss, adding a pinch of fungicide such as Benomyl or Captan. Close the bags and store in a cool, dark place for several days until the bulbs are plump. Then remove them from the bags and plant.

Medium-sized bulbs in a given category are best. They reestablish in a new location more dependably than the large bulbs, which may perform well the first year but fail to repeat their initial showing. Also, the medium-sized bulbs are considerably less expensive than the large bulbs.

Lilies for Cut-Flower Arrangements

Lilies make superb cut flowers. The same plant should not be cut in successive years, however, as this tends to weaken the bulb. Each plant can be cut every second or third year. Leave as much stem as possible to nourish the bulb. Leave at least half of the foliage. It is preferable to cut lilies just as the first buds on a stem begin to open so that you will have the enjoyment of seeing most buds opening indoors.

Plunge the fresh-cut stems into warm water and let them stand for several hours before using them in an arrangement. Strip the lower leaves so that none will stand in water. If possible, change the water every day. This will prolong the life of the flowers, and every bud on the stem should eventually open.

CUTTING A LILY

To nurture the bulb, remove only the top one-third to one-half of the stem every two or three years.

When and How to Plant Lily Bulbs

Lilies can be planted any time the ground can be dug, but fall planting is best. Madonna lilies, however, should be planted in late summer so that there will be enough time for them to grow leaves before winter.

If planting is delayed because of bad weather or late arrival of your bulbs, you can protect them through the winter in pots, as described on the next page. If planting will be delayed for only a short period, the bulbs can be held in a cool, dark place in a plastic bag with some slightly moist peat moss.

In cold climates the best procedure, when possible, is to anticipate probable late arrival and prepare the planting holes, mulch heavily to keep the ground from freezing, and plant the bulbs as soon as they arrive.

The planting hole should be three times as deep as the height of the bulb. Most lilies grown in North America are stem rooting and put out a covering of roots on top of the bulb. Others root from the base, as do most bulbs.

When planting, spread the roots and set the bulb so that it will rest with its tip beneath 3 or 4 inches of soil. (Madonna lilies require only 1 inch of soil over the bulb.)

In climates where it does not freeze, dig up the bulbs in fall and provide 8 to 10 weeks of simulated winter in the refrigerator.

1. *Spread the roots of the bulb in a deep hole in well-drained soil.*

2. *Spread soil over the roots, then fill the hole completely.*

Staking, Watering, and Feeding

Lilies that grow more than 3 feet tall may be damaged by strong winds unless they are sturdily staked. Those with arching stems—such as *L. davidii, L. henryi,* and their hybrids—also look better if supported.

Use a sturdy stake for each bulb. When placing it, take care not to drive it through the bulb. As the plant grows, tie the stem to the stake with twist ties or other soft material.

Lilies need a steady supply of moisture, particularly during the growing season. A summer mulch is a good way to conserve moisture. Mulch will also keep the stem roots cool during very hot weather and will help control the weeds. Mulch to a depth of 3 or 4 inches with oak leaves, pine needles, salt hay, or any other loose material that will allow passage of water and air to the soil.

In early spring when the stems are emerging, a complete fertilizer should be applied. Another application when the buds are forming will be beneficial. And after the lily has bloomed, one more feeding will prepare the bulb for the next season.

Growing Lilies in Pots and Other Containers

Lilies make excellent pot plants. They can be grown in pots to full bloom, or they can be started early indoors and set out when the weather warms up. Low-growing, early-blooming varieties, such as the Mid-Century hybrids 'Enchantment' and 'Cinnabar,' are best.

In recent years many new varieties have been developed, having a wide range of colors. Some of these are 'Connecticut King,' 'Connecticut Lemon Glow,' and the Sundrop strain. 'Red Carpet' is a fine, low-growing, spotless red lily that is hardy and easy to force at almost any time of year.

Bulbs available in the fall can be potted and put into a cold frame for two or three months and then brought indoors for forcing. Pre-cooled bulbs are available from some lily dealers; these are ready to be started at any time. If you want good results in midwinter, supplementary light may be needed. Lily bulbs that are purchased in the spring should be potted immediately.

Use a 5-inch pot for a small to medium bulb, an 8- to 10-inch pot for a large bulb. Put drainage material in the bottom and over the hole.

The soil mixture should consist of 1 part coarse sand or perlite, 1 part peat moss, and 1 part good garden soil, well mixed together.

Water well upon planting. Thereafter, keep the soil barely moist until the lily is in active growth (to avoid bulb rot). Daytime temperatures should not exceed 68° F, nor night temperatures fall lower than 40° F.

The plants should be fed every second week until the flowers have completed their blooming cycle. Afterward, plants grown indoors can be planted in the garden or kept in the same pots for another year. In either case, the foliage should be allowed to mature and turn yellow in order to nourish the bulb.

For good results the second season, bulbs should be kept in a protected cold frame over the winter or buried in the ground in a sheltered location.

Lilies can be grown in large containers outdoors. Plant them in the soil recommended for pots, and give them regular garden care.

POTTING TWO TYPES OF LILY

Base rooting. *Half-fill the pot with mixture of sand, peat moss, and loam. Make a mound and place the bulb on top. Fill with the soil mix.*

Stem rooting. *Fill the pot only a quarter full with the same soil mix. Insert the bulb with roots spread, and just cover with soil.*

Deadheading to Stop Seeds From Forming

Pinch off the flowers after they fade. This will prevent seed formation, which tends to weaken the plant.

As the stem dies down naturally, trim off only the dry material and remove it completely from the garden. To prevent the spread of possible disease, do not put these trimmings into the compost pile.

To save seeds from which to grow new bulbs, leave no more than one or two pods on each plant. Hybrid varieties do not come true from seeds, but seeds from the species' plants will produce lilies with only minor variations. Harvest the seedpods as soon as they turn yellow, and let them open indoors; otherwise the seeds will scatter in the wind.

REMOVING OLD FLOWERS

Unless you plan to grow lilies from seed, pinch off flowers as soon as they have faded.

What Can Go Wrong With Lilies

The chart describes the commonest problems that are likely to occur in the growing of lilies. If your plants show symptoms that are not described here, turn to the full-color identification chart of pests and diseases starting on page 600. Look up the relevant chemical on page 635 to find trade names.

Symptoms and signs	Cause	Control
Shoot tips and flower buds are covered with greenish or pinkish insects. Leaf undersides may be sticky. Buds and leaves may be malformed.	Aphids	Spray with carbaryl, Diazinon, endosulfan, or malathion.
Leaves and flowers are chewed.	Beetles or caterpillars	Spray or dust foliage with carbaryl or methoxychlor.
Bulb scales are injured and roots destroyed.	Bulb mites	Destroy severely infested bulbs. Dust bulbs before planting with dicofol, endosulfan, or tetradifon. Or put in hot water (110°–115° F) for 3 hr.
Leaves and shoots eaten; slime trails present.	Slugs or snails	Apply pellets of metaldehyde, methiocarb, or mexacarbate.
Water-soaked areas on leaves turn gray or white. Stems may rot and topple.	Botrytis, or gray mold (fungus)	Spray with Benomyl, dichlobenil, or dichloran (DCNA).
Leaves have pale or yellow striping or mottling.	Virus disease	Destroy plants. Spray against insects that spread disease.

How to Propagate Your Own Lilies

Producing Plants From Scales

The easiest and most widely used method of increasing lilies is to propagate from the scales that make up the bulb. Flowering plants are produced from these scales in two or three years.

A bulb can be scaled at any time. Use only plump, healthy bulbs, because damaged or infected scales either will not produce new bulbs or will make new bulbs that do not grow properly. If the bulb that is used to supply scales has a virus disease, the new bulbs will have it too.

Remove any withered or damaged scales and discard them. Separate the plump, healthy scales by breaking them off as close to the base as possible, taking a bit of the basal plate with the scale. If only a few new bulbs are wanted, take two or three scales. If you want to develop a number of a given variety, a bulb can be scaled completely, leaving only its heart. Some varieties, however, do not produce good bulbs from scales. If you use a valuable lily, try just a few scales the first time. If you are successful with that bulb, it can be scaled again.

Wash the scales thoroughly; let them dry for several hours or overnight. Plant as shown, or place the scales in a plastic bag with enough slightly moist peat moss to keep them separate. Add a pinch of fungicide, such as Benomyl or Captan. Seal the bag and label with the name of the variety and the date.

Put the bag in a warm place, such as a cupboard or closet. Check the bag every week or two to see that the moisture is maintained. If the scales show signs of mildew or other fungus, wash them and rebag.

In 8 to 10 weeks the miniature bulbs, called bulbils, should be formed along the bottom edge of the scale. When the bulbils reach a quarter of an inch or more in diameter, they should be chilled in your refrigerator at about 40° F for six to eight weeks. The original bag with scales can be refrigerated for the cooling period, or the bulbils can be separated and put into a fresh bag with moistened peat moss and fungicide. Check the temperature in various sections of your refrigerator to determine the best location.

The alternate method is to separate the scales and plant them in seed flats as shown below. This can be done if the time of year permits you to put the flats into a cold frame for at least a six-week cooling period before the weather turns warm.

When the scale bulbils begin to show growth, treat them as you would seedlings (p. 336). By the end of the second or third season, the plants will be large enough to bloom.

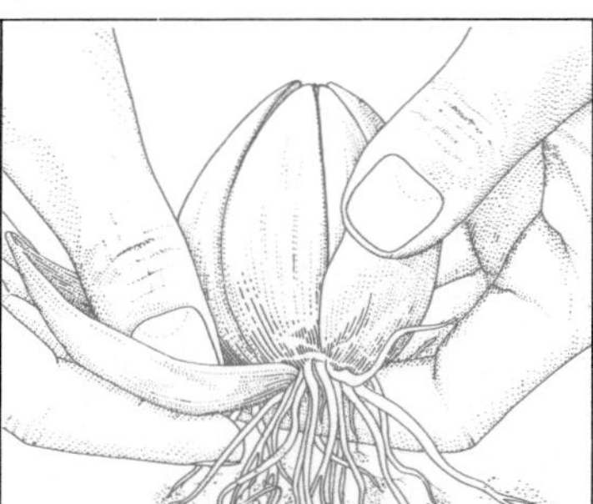

1. *Remove and discard the dried-up outer scales from bulbs.*

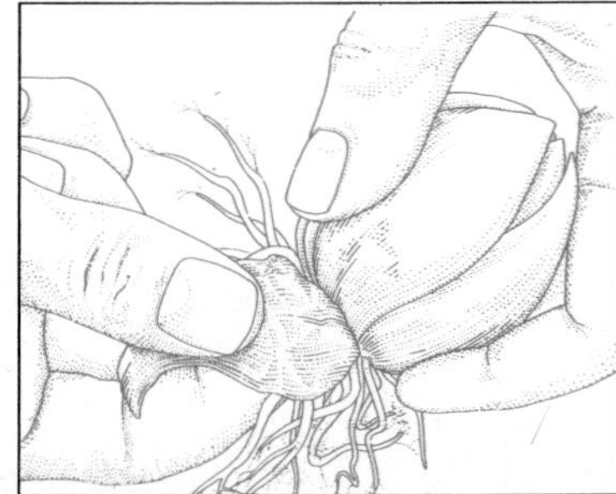

2. *Gently break off the plump scales, taking some basal plate with each.*

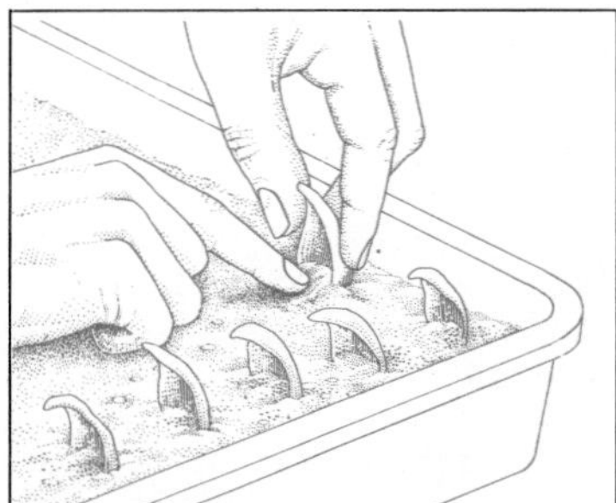

3. *Plant each scale to half its depth and cover container with a plastic bag.*

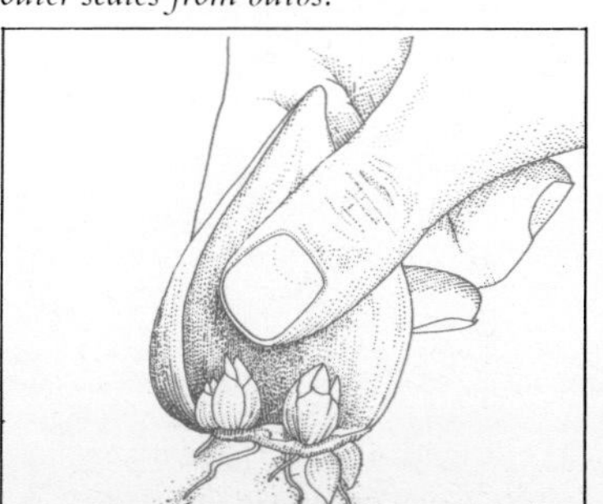

4. *In 10 weeks bulbils should be formed. Refrigerate for six weeks.*

5. *Early in the spring, place each new plant in a $2^1/_2$- to 3-in. pot.*

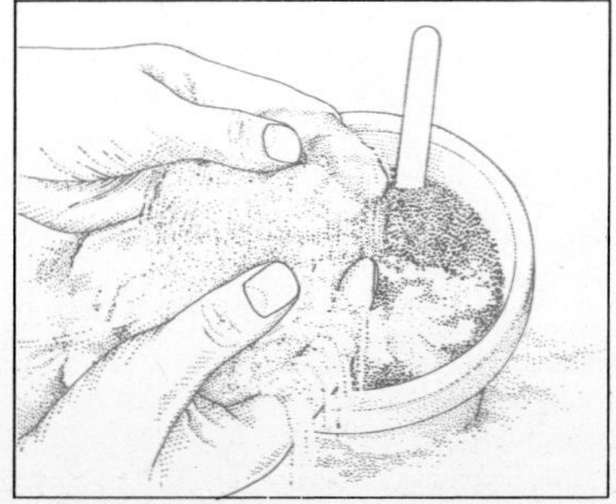

6. *Sink the pots in sand or peat moss outdoors. Cover with 1 in. of sand.*

Lifting and Dividing Lilies

Some lilies self-propagate quickly and need to be divided every third or fourth season. The best time to divide is in early fall when the stems are drying off. Lift the clump carefully with a garden fork or shovel; remove the soil; then wash with a gentle stream of water. Separate the bulbs carefully; replant in fresh soil.

Some of the offsets may be of blooming size. Those that are smaller can be planted in an area of the garden set aside to bring scale and seedling bulbs into bloom. Or let them develop in pots before planting them in the open garden.

A few lilies have rhizomatous bulbs (as illustrated below), which should be divided simply to keep them flowering well. Sever these bulbs with a sharp knife, dust with a fungicide, and replant.

Lilies need a full season to settle into a new location after transplanting and may not perform at their best the first year. Therefore, divide only a few clumps each year.

DIVIDING BULBS

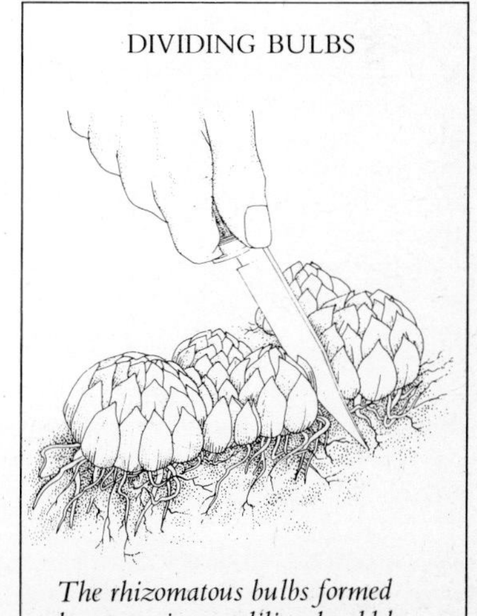

The rhizomatous bulbs formed by some vigorous lilies should be lifted every three or four years and separated with a sharp knife.

Increasing Lilies From Aerial Bulbils

Aerial bulbils are small green or purple-black bulbs that grow in the leaf axils of lilies like the tiger lily and several of its hybrids.

Detach the bulbils from the lily's stem in late summer or fall when they are loose and easy to remove. Plant them about 1 inch deep and 1 inch apart in seed flats. They will do well in a mixture of equal parts of soil, peat moss, and sand.

Grow them through the winter in a cold frame or in a sheltered location under a loose mulch. When the weather warms up in the spring, move the flats into partial shade, and water and feed the bulbils just as you would potted lilies. In fall plant the new lilies in the open garden.

REMOVING AERIAL BULBILS

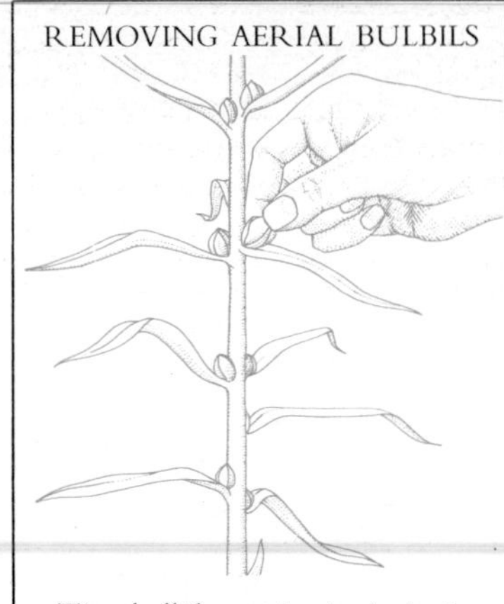

Tiny bulbils growing in the leaf axils of some species can be taken in late summer to propagate new plants.

New Lilies From Bulblets

Many lilies form bulblets on top of the bulb. Some also form bulblets at the base of the mother bulb. If these offsets are small and do not have roots, plant them in the same way as bulbils. Larger bulblets with established roots can be planted directly in the ground.

In late summer remove the soil from around the stem of each plant and carefully detach the bulblets. Those that are less than ½ inch in diameter are best grown in seed flats for a season (as described for bulbils) before you plant them in the garden. The larger ones should be planted directly in the garden. Lightly spread 1–2 inches of soil over them, according to the size of the bulblets.

COLLECTING BULBLETS

Bulblets, which grow among the stem roots or on the base of some lilies, can be detached and planted out in late summer.

Growing Lilies From Seeds

Sowing seeds is a good way to produce a large collection of lilies. Virus disease is not transmitted through the seeds; therefore, you can use this method to produce disease-free lilies for your garden. Such bulbs will also save you considerable money.

Hybrid seeds will not produce plants identical to the parents, but most of the seedlings will be attractive, and there is always the chance that a new lily of superior quality will show up. Flowers first appear the second or third season after sowing, but plants take a year or two more to attain full bloom.

Seeds can be sown immediately after harvesting or in the spring. Young lily seedlings are susceptible to soil-borne fungi and should be grown in a sterile soil (p. 597) during the early stages of development.

Using pots or trays, sow the seeds an inch apart, covering them with about half an inch of soil.

A cool greenhouse (or a windowsill that has some sun for part of the day) is a good location. A temperature range of 55°–75° F is best. Seeds germinate faster at warmer temperatures. A steady supply of moisture and nutrients is essential, as is good drainage.

Seeds can be started at any time of the year indoors, and fluorescent lighting can be used with excellent results. Set the lights 2–3 inches above the flats; then raise the lights or lower the flats as the seedlings grow, always maintaining the same distance. When the seeds have germinated, give them from 14 to 16 hours of light per day.

Lily seeds are of two types: epigeal (which means close to the ground) and hypogeal (which means underground). Some of the former are among the easiest to grow. They germinate quickly and send up a leaf three to six weeks after sowing. Asiatics and most Trumpet types fall into this category.

The hypogeal seeds germinate differently. They do not show aboveground until they have had a warm period of three to four months, followed by two or three months of cool temperatures in the 34°–38° F range. A good example of this type is *L. speciosum.*

When two or three leaves show on the seedlings, they can be transplanted 1–2 inches apart in a larger, deeper container or left to grow the first full season in the original flat.

Seedlings with bulbs more than half an inch in diameter and good roots can be put into the open garden at the end of the first season, or they can be grown in a 3- to 4-inch pot for another year before being set out.

TWO TYPES OF LILY SEED

Both epigeal and hypogeal lily seeds should be sown in the same way, ½ in. deep and 1 in. apart in trays of sterile soil. Keep moist and warm.

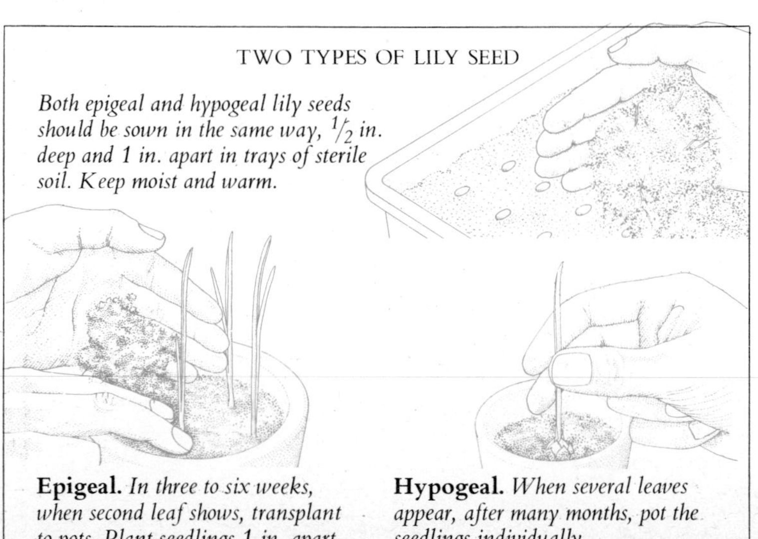

Epigeal. *In three to six weeks, when second leaf shows, transplant to pots. Plant seedlings 1 in. apart.*

Hypogeal. *When several leaves appear, after many months, pot the seedlings individually.*

Irises

From the stately bearded iris—long known as the flag iris—down to the tiny plants that grow from bulbs, these flowers provide a delicate beauty in any garden.

'Galilee,' a pure blue and white tall bearded iris.

Irises are garden plants that were cultivated in Asia long before the birth of Christ.

There are two groups: those that grow from rhizomes (thick underground stems) and those that grow from bulbs.

The rhizomatous types develop pointed, straplike leaves that grow in fans from the ends of the rhizomes and produce stalks that bear one or more flowers. Colors include white, pink, blue, purple-black, gold, and red, as well as many combinations of these hues.

The most popular of these types are the bearded irises, which have fleshy hairs like a beard on the outer petals, or "falls."

Botanically, the rhizomatous types are divided into two categories: Eupogons, which include the popular tall bearded iris, and Arils.

Both Eupogons and Arils are true bearded irises and are grown in the same way. Both include wild species as well as many hybrids developed from them. The more exotic and difficult Arils differ from other bearded irises in flower forms and patterns. Their beards are somewhat narrow but conspicuous, frequently in vivid colors, on flowers that are veined, stippled, and more closely clustered than Eupogon irises. Leaves are short and sickle shaped.

The numerous hybrids of the Eupogons, called bearded irises, are classified further by height, starting with the standard tall forms (at least 28 inches high). These are followed by four classes of median irises in the following descending order of height: border, miniature tall, intermediate, and standard dwarf. The smallest bearded irises, the miniature dwarfs, vary from 3 to 10 inches.

Most Eupogons bloom in mid to late spring or early summer, but some varieties flower in early spring. Reblooming irises, which are varieties of tall bearded forms, may also bloom in fall, depending on the climate.

Aril irises, which range in height from about 5 inches to 18 inches, begin blooming as much as a month earlier than most Eupogons.

Ideally, the taller bearded irises should be planted in their own beds or in groups in front of perennial or shrub borders. The lower-growing types look best in the foreground of beds or borders, or in rock gardens.

Dwarf bearded irises do not tolerate strong competition and are best used only in rock gardens or grouped in front of small plants.

In addition to the bearded irises, there are the equally beautiful Eurasian beardless (Spathula) types. Among them are *Iris dichotoma,* a lavender-flowered August bloomer, and *I. foetidissima,* which has brilliant vermilion seeds that more than make up for its plain gray flowers and the unpleasant odor of its leaves when crushed.

The Apogons, an important section of the beardless group, consist of the following distinct series, or subsections, which vary in height from 4 inches to 5 feet.

The Laevigata series encompasses the Japanese and some American species plus the familiar tall Eurasian yellow flag (*I. pseudacorus*). All are known as water irises because of their preference for growing on the banks of streams and ponds. The American species, *I. versicolor* and *I. virginica,* also are close relatives.

The sun-loving Longipetalae species, *I. longipetala* and *I. missouriensis,* are American natives not often grown in gardens. They share a liking for dampness in the spring but prefer to have drier conditions in summer. The former is distinguished by violet-veined white blooms and nearly evergreen leaves. The latter flowers in white or shades of purple.

The Louisiana irises, which are native to the boggy bayous, will also grow in the northern states with winter protection.

The Siberian irises survive cold weather especially well and are widely grown throughout the United States. They include many hybrids of *I. sibirica* and the Manchurian *I. sanguinea,* or *I. orientalis,* both of which produce flowers in purple, blue, or white.

The Pacific Coast irises, though available in a wide range of colors and easily grown from seed, are seldom seen outside the moist, mild region for which they are named, since they are extremely difficult to transplant in other climates.

Two other excellent Apogons are the spurias, members of a widely varied and much hybridized species, and the miniature kinds, with origins from Japan to Rumania.

Crested irises, or evansias (technically, bearded Apogons), look somewhat like orchids. Their 3- to 10-inch blooms have crests on the falls that resemble a rooster's comb. The broad, glossy leaves are evergreen.

Beardless irises should be planted with the same attention to height as the bearded types, with the tall forms in the background of a bed and the miniatures in the foreground or in rock gardens.

The bulbous irises, which must be grown in full sun, are the only types that are sometimes forced in pots indoors. In the garden they provide a welcome continuity of flowers for borders. They are divided into three subgenera, only two of which—*Scopiris* (the junos) and *Xiphium*—have importance for home gardeners.

The junos (9–15 inches tall) have leaves that give these irises a strong resemblance to tiny corn plants. Their storage roots are fleshy and easily injured. Otherwise they are easy to grow in full sun. All junos bloom in midspring and are crested, except for *I. tubergeniana.*

In the subgenus *Xiphium* (18–24 inches), the well-known Dutch, Spanish, English, and reticulata irises demand little care and offer much.

Dutch irises—noted for their large, long-lasting blooms, which are ideal for indoor arrangements—are the tallest of the bulbous group. They flower in early summer, about two weeks before Spanish irises.

Both Dutch and Spanish irises produce new foliage in the fall, and must be given a protective mulch wherever winters are cold. Their flowers come in white and shades of blue and yellow.

Blooming from early to mid summer, English irises prefer the moist climate of the Pacific Northwest. However, they sometimes bloom in other regions if they are planted where they will have partial shade and somewhat acid soil that is moist but well drained. English irises produce new leaves during the spring only.

Reticulatas are quite distinctive, with their four-sided leaf spikes. They bloom in late winter or early spring, and the flowers of some varieties are sweetly perfumed. They are well suited to the rock garden or any sheltered area in full sun, since their height seldom exceeds 4 inches. Like the little species crocuses, they multiply rapidly and lend themselves well to informal, naturalistic plantings.

In addition to the rich violet *I. reticulata* and its named forms, which vary from red-violet to light blue, other outstanding reticulatas include *I. histrioides major* and *I. bakeriana,* which are native to the Caucasus and Asia Minor, respectively. The former is blue. The latter has blue standards, bluish-purple falls, and dark-speckled yellow and white centers.

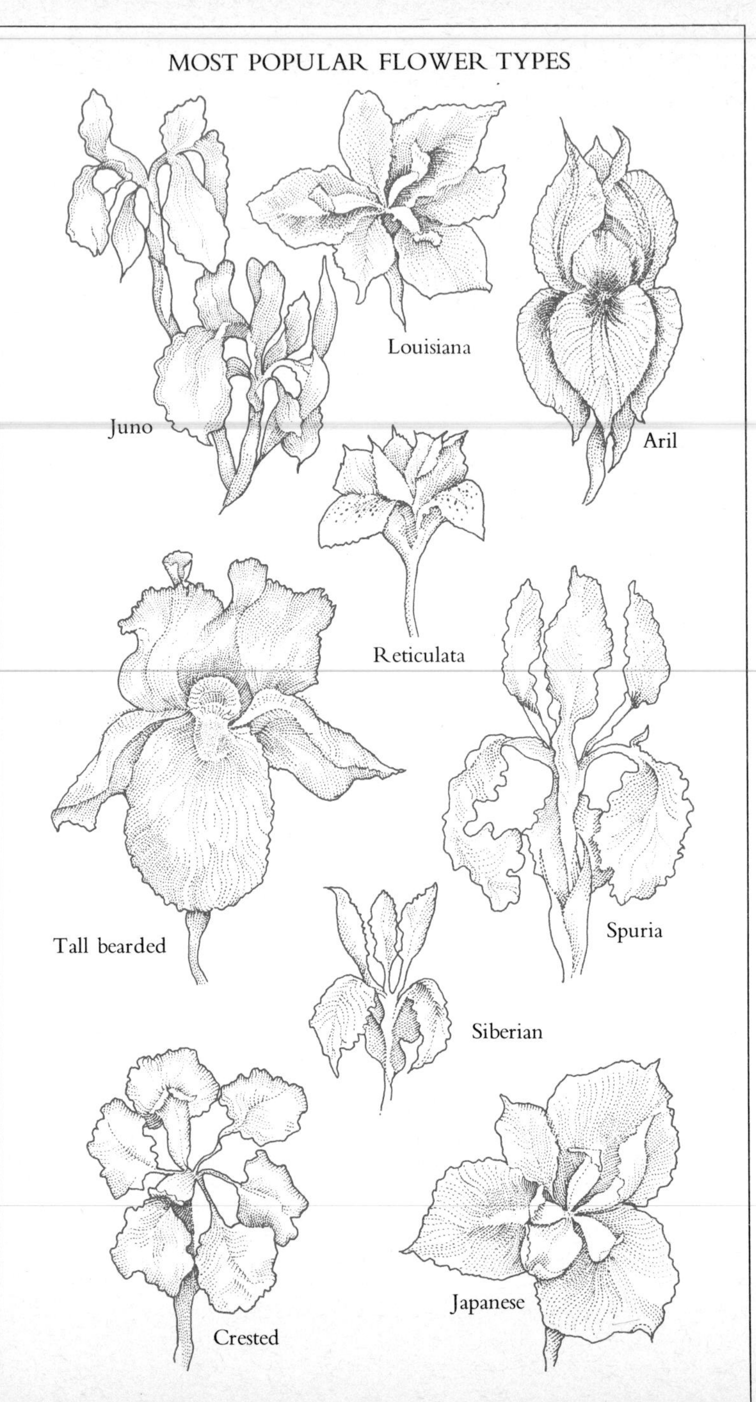

Irises That Grow From Rhizomes

Preparing a Well-Drained, Fertile Soil

Most rhizomatous irises can be planted in the same manner, and all share the need for proper soil preparation if plants are to bloom and multiply through the years.

Good drainage is essential, and a spot in full sun is generally best, although a few varieties prefer a little shade from the hot summer sun.

Almost any soil is suitable for irises, but heavy clay and light sand demand more preparation than loam and clay loam, which are the best mediums for these perennials.

Heavy clay soils can be encouraged to drain better if generous amounts of sharp sand, humus, and peat moss are mixed into them. Conversely, extremely sandy soils will retain moisture longer if humus and peat moss are added.

Before planting, prepare beds by spading a half-inch layer of dried cow manure into the top 10 inches of soil. Dust the surface with 5–10–10 fertilizer, using approximately 10 pounds per 500 square feet.

Add at least 3 inches of humus or peat moss, working it into the subsoil. Then cover the area with the excavated soil. If this topsoil needs sand, humus, or peat moss, mix these additives in before returning it to each bed. Allow beds to settle one to three weeks before planting.

Do not add lime at this time. It will convert some of the nitrogen in the fertilizer to a gas, and some of the nutrients will be lost.

If a soil test indicates a need for lime, apply it with a lawn spreader a few weeks before preparing the beds. Most irises do best in slightly acid to neutral (pH 6.0–7.2 or so) soil. Japanese irises, however, cannot tolerate lime or bone meal. They need acid soil with a pH of 5.0–6.0. Lime greatly improves the physical structure of heavy clay soils, but do not add more than is needed to establish the proper pH.

Planting Bearded Irises Near the Surface

Bearded iris rhizomes should be planted between midsummer and early fall. Where midsummers are extremely dry and hot, early fall planting can help reduce stress on the plants.

Inspect the rhizomes carefully for evidence of damage by borers or rot. With a sharp knife cut away decayed parts and broken roots. Dust all cut surfaces with sulfur, or soak the rhizomes for half an hour in a mixture of folpet and streptomycin to discourage recurring disease.

For best effect, plant three to seven rhizomes of the same variety in a clump. Place the rhizomes no deeper than 1 inch in planting holes, facing all leaf fans in the same direction regardless of whether the clumps form circles or curved lines.

Press the soil firmly around the rhizomes to drive out air pockets, which cause soil to dry out and also impede anchoring. Label clumps.

Watering and Feeding Bearded Irises

Immediately after planting, water the soil thoroughly, using a fine mist to prevent washing the soil away from the rhizomes and exposing them to the sun.

Irises should be watered often for up to three weeks after planting, especially if the weather is dry.

Bearded irises, especially the tall varieties, feed heavily. Apply a 5–10–10 fertilizer in early spring and again about one month after the blooms fade. Put on a handful of fertilizer for each large clump in spring and about half this amount for the second feeding. Scatter the fertilizer near the rhizomes, but not on them, and water it in. Note that the recommended nutrient is relatively low in nitrogen, which promotes leaf growth at the expense of the flowers.

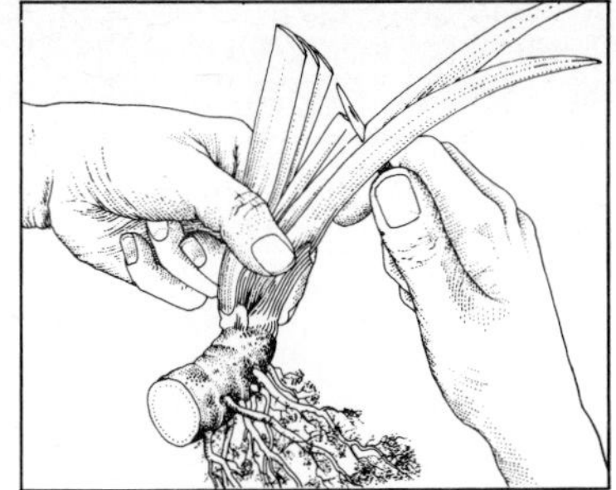

1. *Before planting use a sharp knife to trim the long leaves to a neat fan shape.*

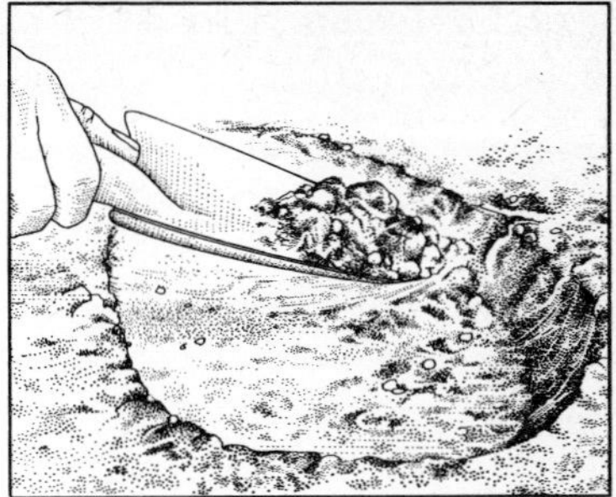

2. *Dig each planting hole so that rhizomes will be set no deeper than 1 in.*

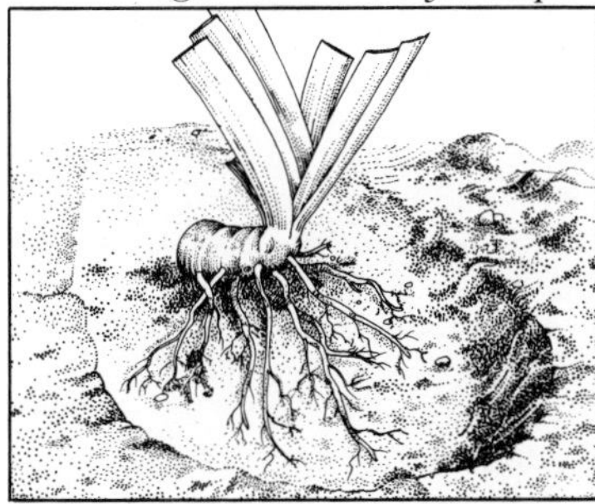

3. *See that all leaf fans face the same way. Spread roots out gently and evenly.*

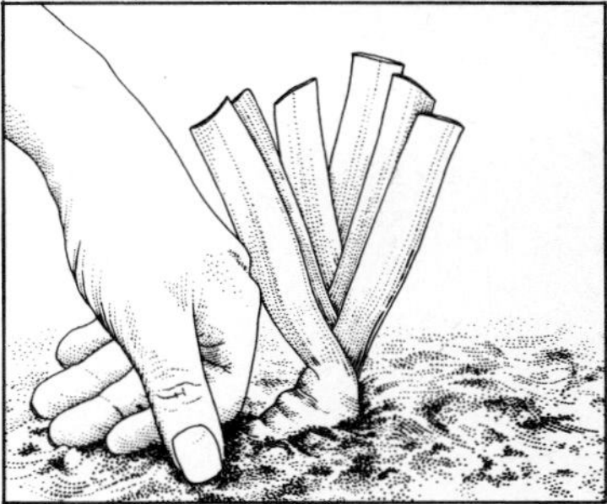

4. *Firm soil around rhizomes to eliminate air pockets and hasten anchoring.*

FROST HAZARD

If frost lifts the rhizomes, do not press them back, since this can damage or break roots and weaken plants. Instead, bank up sand or soil around the rhizomes.

SPRING TRIMMING

Trim foliage in the early spring. This will reduce each plant's exposure to wind, which can loosen or break roots. Destroy dead leaves that may shelter slugs.

Planting Beardless Irises Below the Surface

Before planting beardless irises, take the same precautions regarding borers and rot as you would with bearded types.

In general, beardless irises do best in well-drained soils, although Japanese, Louisiana, and American irises will live in wet soils in southern gardens.

Japanese and American irises can use plenty of humus. They also need more nutrients than other types do. Being acid lovers, they prefer acid fertilizers, such as those that are used for azaleas and rhododendrons.

Begin planting in early fall, except with Pacific Coast irises. These respond better to midspring planting, which takes less energy from the rhizomes. In the South spurias should be planted in mid to late fall, since early fall weather is often too dry.

Rhizomes of all varieties should be planted 15–18 inches apart and about 2 inches deep, with two exceptions: Louisiana irises do best at a depth of $1\frac{1}{2}$ inches, while the long, narrow rhizomes of the crested irises should be covered with no more than a very thin layer of soil.

When planting more than one variety in the same bed, make certain that flower colors will complement each other if bloom dates coincide. Color clashes can be further avoided by planting early and late-flowering types together.

Water new plantings well, and keep them moist until rhizomes are well established.

Apply a mulch to conserve moisture and diminish the unavoidable shock of transplanting. This is especially important with crested irises, which are planted close to the soil surface and are vulnerable to drying out. A mulch is also useful for discouraging the growth of weeds.

Use any mulch that will not wet down and get soggy. However, do not use oat or wheat straw over Japanese iris beds, since wheat rust disease may be transmitted to the plants.

1. *Cut leaves of beardless and crested irises to 9 in. to ease transplanting shock.*

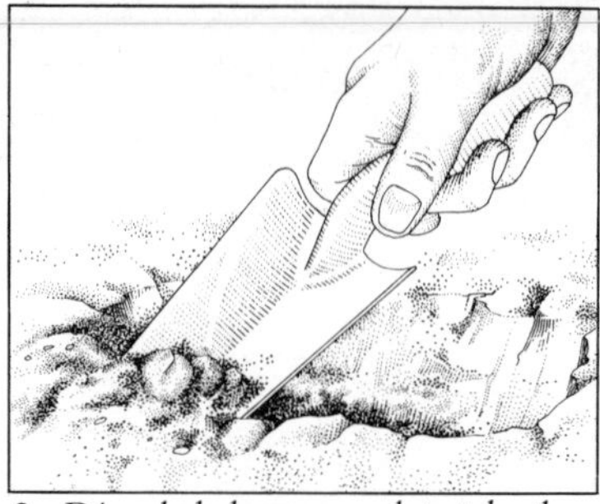

2. *Dig a hole large enough to take the roots at proper depth for each variety.*

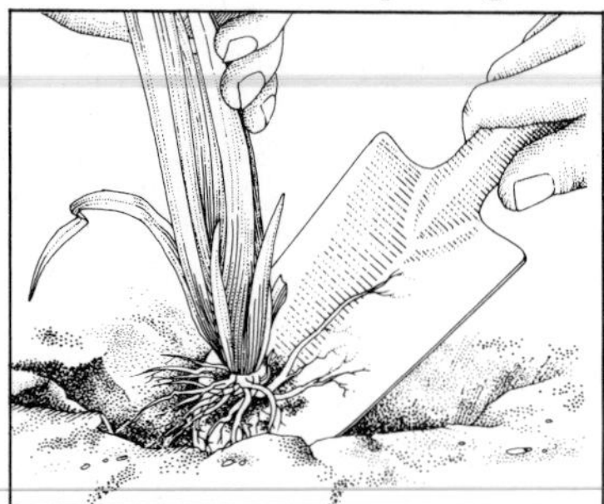

3. *Mix humus into the hole. Spread roots out evenly and cover. Firm the soil.*

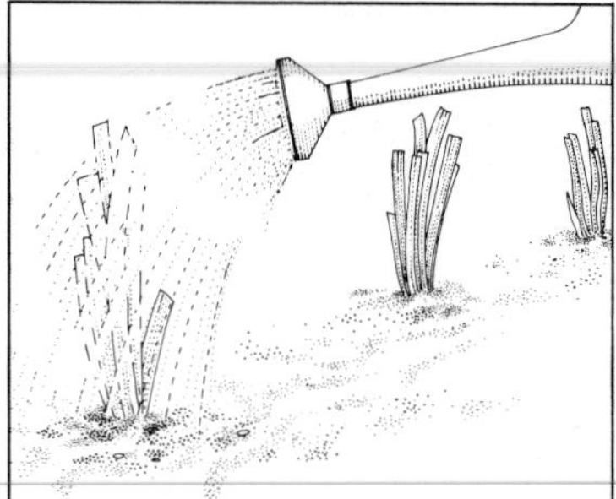

4. *Water well and keep soil moist until plants are established. Label each group.*

Keeping Beardless Irises Vigorous and Healthy

In cold winter areas the leaves of many beardless irises shrivel up and die down to the ground.

Unless slugs or other pests are active, this dead foliage can remain on plants as a means of reducing damage to roots caused by alternate thawing and freezing.

In spring, however, all dead leaves should be removed and destroyed. Do not add them to the compost pile, since they may carry diseases or insect eggs that can pose problems elsewhere in the garden.

Avoid cultivating the soil around the plants, since their roots are near the surface and are easily injured. Remove weeds by hand, or better still, add a thick mulch in early spring. This will discourage weeds and help conserve moisture. It will also prevent soil surface temperatures from becoming too high on hot days.

After blooms fade, break them off. If left on the plants, they will form seeds that use energy needed for the further development of roots, rhizomes, and leaves. Seed heads can also choke the surrounding soil with seedlings.

If spring weather is dry, water the beds thoroughly, keeping in mind that one deep watering is better than several shallow sprinklings.

Apply fertilizer as soon as the surface soil can be worked in spring, and give a second feeding after flowering is over. Read the directions on the container. Avoid overdoses; too much fertilizer can burn the plants.

Do not worry if spurias fail to bloom, or bloom only sparsely, for as long as two years after planting. This kind of iris often takes considerable time to begin producing well.

SPRING MULCHING

Add to mulch scattered by winter winds. This cover helps suppress weeds and retain moisture.

SEEDPOD REMOVAL

Seedpods develop after blooms have faded. Break them off to keep seedlings from choking beds.

Dividing the Rhizomes of Bearded Irises

Clumps of bearded irises should be divided and replanted before they become overcrowded.

A single rhizome will branch many times over the years, developing into a heavy crisscross clump, choked with old leafless rhizomes. If it is not divided, it will exhaust the surrounding soil, and the mass of leaves will exclude sun and air from the roots. This leads to poor flowering or no flowering and also weakens the plants, making them more susceptible to insects and disease.

Dividing is best done at the same time of year that initial plantings should be made. Lift each clump by gently prying it loose from the soil. A spading fork is better for this than a shovel because it is less likely to cut roots and rhizomes.

Use a sharp, strong-bladed knife to trim younger rhizomes into sections that include healthy-looking roots and one or two strong leaf fans. Carefully wash soil off the roots under low pressure from a hose. Discard the old rhizomes from the center sections.

Prepare the leaves as shown and replant the rhizomes (see p. 339).

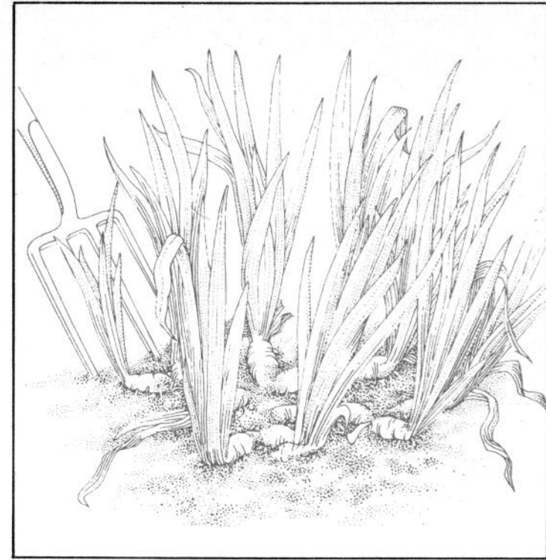

1. *When clumps of bearded irises become crowded, they cease to flower.*

2. *Loosen soil around the clumps. Pry them out with a gentle rocking motion.*

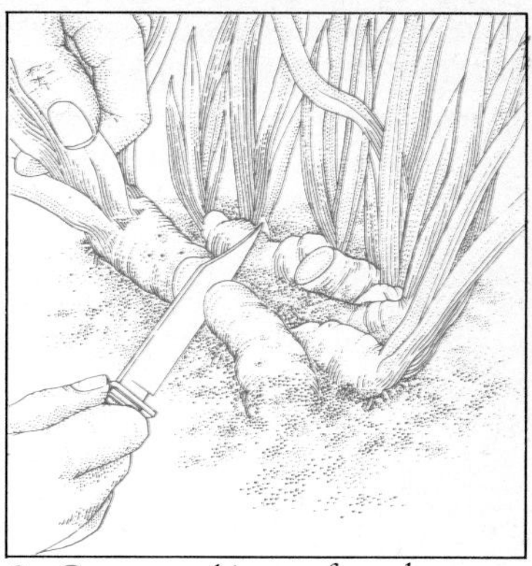

3. *Cut young rhizomes from clump edges. Each should have one or two fans.*

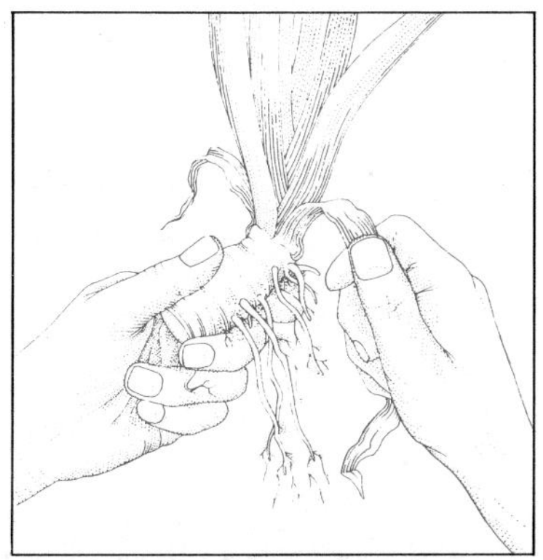

4. *Peel withered leaves from rhizomes, retaining only fresh, healthy foliage.*

5. *Trim foliage to a fan shape. Remove damaged roots. Replant rhizomes.*

6. *Fill in soil around each rhizome; leave tops exposed. Water thoroughly.*

Dividing the Rhizomes of Beardless Irises

Beardless irises also need periodic dividing to maintain their vigor. Sparse growth in the center of large clumps is a sure sign that the soil has been exhausted. Make divisions in the same season in which each variety should originally have been planted.

The rhizomes of certain beardless irises need considerable care because they are very much smaller and thinner than the bearded ones.

Clumps are more easily handled if the foliage is first trimmed back to about 9 inches. All the dead leaves should then be removed from the center of each clump and destroyed.

Loosen the soil around the clumps with a spading fork, and carefully lever them from the soil. Separate them with a spading fork into sections with five to nine shoots.

Trim each section, leaving about six leaf spikes. Then gently wash the soil from each section, and cut away any damaged or rotted roots. Be sure to use a sharp knife.

Do not allow the divisions to dry out. If delays in replanting are unavoidable, put the sections into plastic bags, with the leaves exposed to the air, and place them in a shady, wind-free spot. Replant according to the directions on page 340.

1. *Before lifting beardless irises, cut back foliage and remove it from beds.*

2. *Separate clumps. Cut off damaged roots. Then replant divisions.*

Staking and Cutting Bearded Iris Flower Stems

The few tall bearded-iris varieties that have weak stems should be staked in late spring when the flower spikes first appear. Use 3-foot canes, and loosely secure the flower stems to them with soft string. Lower-growing irises need not be staked.

Some foliage may turn brown or may develop withered tips before flowering. Remove any unsightly leaves, either by peeling them away or by cutting off the brown tips.

After bearded irises have flowered, the parent rhizomes may have produced offset rhizomes with small fans. If so, cut off the flower spikes close to the rhizomes. This will prevent water from collecting in the stems and causing rhizome rot.

If no offset rhizomes have formed, merely cut the spikes back to a point just below where the lowest flowers have bloomed. This will prevent further weakening of already weak rhizomes. It will also promote offsets.

SUPPORTING TALL FLOWERS

In late spring weak-stemmed tall bearded-iris varieties should be staked. Loop soft string around stems and fasten it to stakes.

REMOVING OLD FLOWER STEMS

After flowers have faded, their stems should be removed before seed heads form. If offset rhizomes are present (left), cut stems close to the rhizome to prevent water from collecting and rotting it. If no offsets have developed, cut off stems below the lowest flower (right).

What Can Go Wrong With Irises

Check foliage and rhizomes often for pests or disease. Weeds should be controlled so plants get sufficient light, nutrients, and air circulation. See page 600 for symptoms not listed below, and page 635 for trade names of suggested chemicals.

Symptoms and signs	**Cause**	**Control**
Leaf and flower stems are distorted.	Aphids	Apply Diazinon, endosulfan, or malathion to foliage at weekly intervals.
In midspring, edges of young leaves appear saw-toothed. Later, larvae tunnel into rhizomes.	Iris borers	Apply malathion or methoxychlor to foliage once a week from early spring until plants bloom. Use stiff wire to mash borers inside rhizomes.
Seeds in pods are damaged or destroyed.	Verbena bud moths	Apply carbaryl or methoxychlor at weekly intervals when larvae are active.
In wet weather large irregular spots appear on leaves; thick liquid seeps out. Rhizomes are not attacked.	Bacterial leaf blight	Remove and destroy affected foliage and all debris in beds. Drench plants and surrounding soil with streptomycin.
Rhizomes are pulpy; bloom points are often destroyed. Damage is most likely from early spring through midsummer.	Bacterial soft rot	Cut away soft areas and destroy. Treat cut surfaces with half-strength liquid chlorine bleach. Streptomycin, applied in early spring and during humid weather, may minimize losses.
Dry rot at base of leaves; dead leaf tips. Rot spreads into rhizomes. Thin webs may occur on soil, later becoming brown and seedlike.	Crown (or sclerotium) rot	Cut away and destroy affected parts of rhizomes. Drench surrounding soil with 1 application of quintozene.
In early summer, leaves have oval, yellow blotches. Affected foliage often turns brown and dies.	Leaf spot (fungus)	Remove and destroy dead foliage. Cut off green leaves below lowest blotches. Spray maneb or zineb weekly from spring through summer. Avoid overhead watering.
Pale yellowish-green stripes on foliage. In wet weather petals may be mottled.	Mosaic (virus)	Plant only resistant varieties. Control aphids, which spread this disease, with malathion.
Affects tall bearded irises only. Rhizomes and leaves turn reddish brown. Leaves are stunted and look burned. Scorch is usually associated with nematode damage.	Scorch	No known control. Dig up and destroy affected plants.
Rot is visible in rhizomes and roots. Disease enters through cuts in rhizomes; occurs only in cool weather.	Winter rot (fungus)	Cut away and destroy all affected growth. Soak healthy plants for 15 min. in calomel and water. Protect rhizomes with winter mulch.

How to Breed Your Own Hybrid Irises

Any interested amateur can produce new hybrid irises by cross-pollination, but beginners should limit themselves to plants of the same general type and color. Bearded varieties are the easiest to handle.

As soon as the blooms on the selected plants open, remove a pollen-covered anther from one of them with tweezers. Expose all three stigmas in a flower on a second plant, and wipe the pollen onto the lip or outer edge. Use only dry pollen.

Remove the falls from the second flower to prevent chance insect pollination from taking place.

Label each pollinated bloom, indicating the names of both parent plants and the date of pollination.

When the seedpod starts swelling, remove any leafy bracts on the stem to keep moisture from rotting it. Support each pod with a stake.

After about eight weeks the seedpod will have ripened, changing from green to brown. When it begins to split, the seed is ripe.

Ripened seeds should be planted in a mixture of screened topsoil, peat moss, and sharp sand. A cold frame offers good protection, but seeds can also be planted in beds, provided they can be left undisturbed for up to three years in cases of slow germination. The soil should not be allowed to dry out.

Transplant in late spring when seedlings are 1–2 inches tall, allowing 8–10 inches between tall bearded irises and 3 inches between miniature dwarfs. Space rows at least 15 inches apart. Water and feed with a mild dose of water-soluble fertilizer.

When young plants begin to bloom, examine them closely to evaluate their good and bad points. Look for adequate leaf-fan production. Flower stems should not be too thick or too thin. Stems should support three branches plus a terminal with six to eight flower buds.

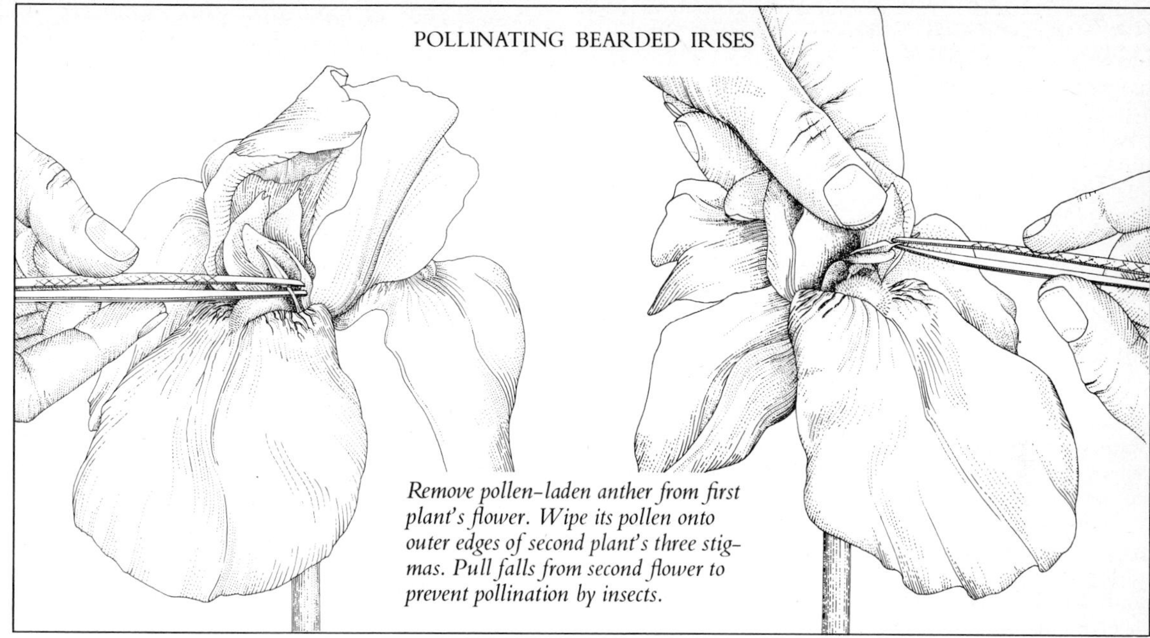

POLLINATING BEARDED IRISES

Remove pollen-laden anther from first plant's flower. Wipe its pollen onto outer edges of second plant's three stigmas. Pull falls from second flower to prevent pollination by insects.

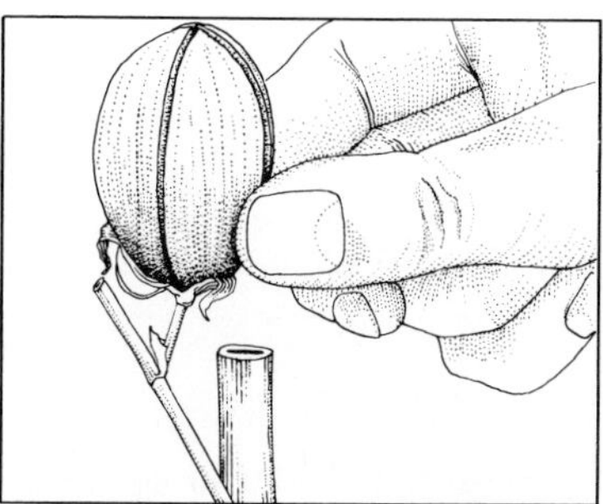

1. *When seedpod starts to swell, pull bracts from stem and fasten to stake.*

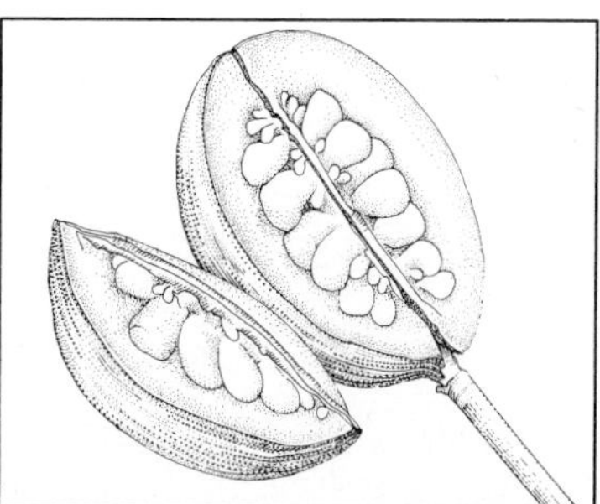

2. *Pod turns brown as it ripens. When it splits open, seeds are ready to plant.*

3. *Fill pots with moistened potting mix. Plant seeds no deeper than ½ in.*

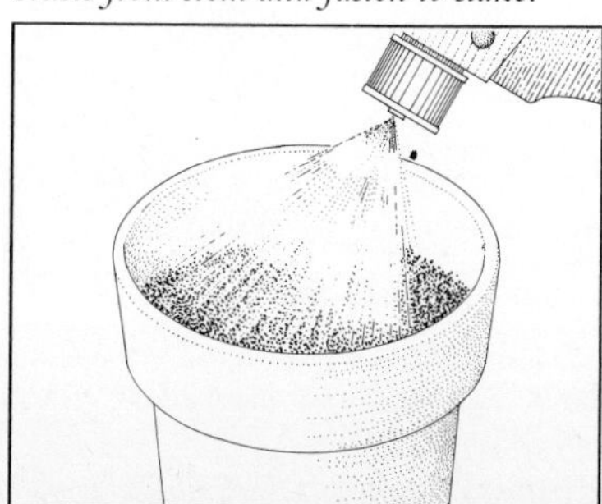

4. *Frequent light waterings are vital, especially while seeds are germinating.*

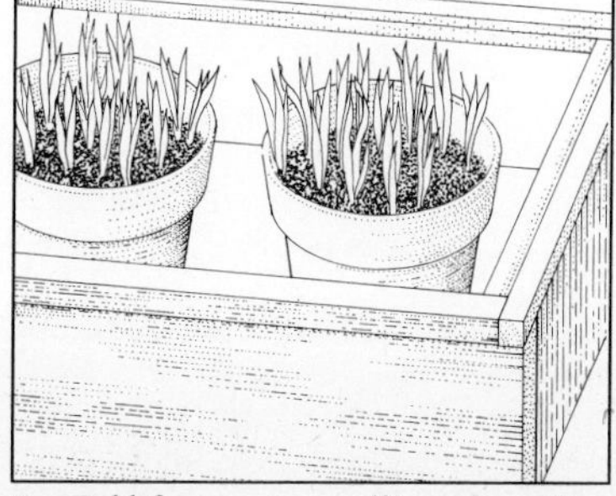

5. *Cold frames give seedlings protection from low temperatures and heavy rains.*

6. *Transplant 2- to 3-in. seedlings in late spring. Fertilize beds. Water well.*

Irises That Grow From Bulbs

Bulbous irises make valuable additions to the garden by providing a continuity of attractive flowers.

The reticulatas often bloom in late winter and last into midspring. They overlap the blooming period of junos, which flower in midspring. The vivid flowers and unique flower form of the reticulatas seldom fail to attract attention.

Dutch, Spanish, and English irises provide color in early and midsummer. This makes them useful at a time when most other bulbs have faded and annuals have only begun to reach their peak.

Flowering periods vary with climates. In southern gardens, for instance, bulbous irises may bloom earlier than indicated here.

Setting and Planting Bulbous Irises

With only minor variations, as noted below, all bulbous irises like a well-drained soil and a spot in full sun where they can soak up plenty of summer heat.

Good drainage is a key factor in growing junos. They generally require raised beds containing nearly neutral (pH 6.5–7.0) soil with a high clay content. Plant them singly or in clumps in early fall at a depth of 2 inches. Allow 6–9 inches between the bulbs. Handle them carefully to avoid breaking off the long, brittle storage roots, from which the vitally essential feeding roots develop during the growing season.

Among the xiphiums, reticulatas should be planted in early to mid fall. Set them 3 inches deep and 3 inches apart in raised beds. Their soil should contain plenty of sharp sand, since poor drainage can be fatal.

Dutch and Spanish irises can be treated alike. Plant them in midfall at a depth of 4 inches where winters are cold; in milder climates plant at about $2\frac{1}{2}$ inches.

Do not expect too much from these bulbs. Even under the most favorable circumstances, they may have to be replaced every two years.

English irises usually have a longer life than their Dutch and Spanish relatives. They need a mildly acid soil and semi-shade. Plant them 6 inches deep in early fall.

Periodic Maintenance of Bulbous Irises

During the growing season watch the iris beds closely for signs of attack by pests and disease. Serious trouble is often easy to stop, assuming that it is identified in time.

Remove any flowers that have faded. After the blooming season has ended for each variety, dust the beds with 5–10–10 fertilizer, and scratch it into the top inch of soil. Give the planting bed a good watering at this time, if rainfall is inadequate, but do not water during the summer months.

Add to the mulch as needed. If weeds penetrate it, pull them out and place on the compost pile.

Allow foliage to ripen undisturbed. Do not remove it until after it has turned brown, or the bulbs will not perform well the following year.

To help screen the ripening foliage, you can sow annual seeds in the bulb beds. Do not do this where bulbs must be divided after their leaves have withered, however.

In the South, Dutch and Spanish irises should be dug up when their foliage has died. Leave them in a shaded, airy spot to dry out for three weeks. They can then be separated, stored in a dry place, and replanted in midfall.

Since the foliage of Dutch and Spanish irises develops in the fall, their bulbs must be mulched for protection in cold regions.

Propagating Bulbous Irises by Division

All bulbous irises can be increased by separation of the offset bulbs. This can be done any time after their foliage has ripened and died.

Carefully remove the bulbs from the ground with a spading fork. Gently shake off the soil, and dry them on the surface for a few weeks. Then divide the clump into single bulbs, discarding any that show signs of rot. Be sure that each separated bulb has a segment of root attached to it.

Replant in the season recommended for each variety. Provide proper drainage, soil type, exposure, and depth of planting.

Large bulbs will flower the following year. Small offsets, however, may need up to two years to reach maturity and begin flowering. Plant offsets in 1-inch-deep rows in a seedbed containing light, well-worked soil. Spread a handful of bone meal evenly over each square yard of this soil and mix it in.

When junos are divided, each bulb should have at least one storage root attached. As with initial planting, do not break off this growth, since bulbs will be weakened and will not flower until new roots have developed. It may take two seasons for them to flower.

Never allow the roots of junos to dry out. Replant them immediately after lifting and dividing.

If the bulbs of Dutch and Spanish irises fail to flower after being divided, discard them and order fresh stock from a grower.

DIVIDING THE THREE IMPORTANT KINDS OF BULBOUS IRISES

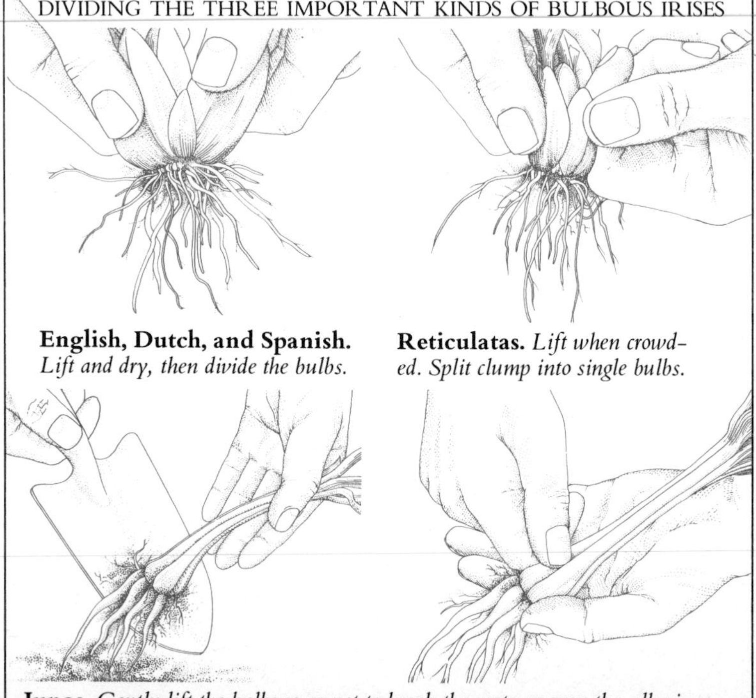

English, Dutch, and Spanish. *Lift and dry, then divide the bulbs.*

Reticulatas. *Lift when crowded. Split clump into single bulbs.*

Junos. *Gently lift the bulbs so as not to break the roots; remove the adhering soil. Divide so that each bulb retains a thick storage root; then replant bulbs.*

Rock Plants

A successful rock garden re-creates the natural rock outcrops on mountain slopes. Select only those plants that thrive in stony terrain.

With their delicate detail and exquisite form, alpines and other rock plants have a particular fascination—the wonder of the miniature.

Since the original habitats of many species are the mountainous and rocky regions of the world, they are for the most part hardy and can tolerate thin, stony soils, and some can sustain drying winds. Provided their natural habitat with good drainage is imitated for them, many rock plants are easy to grow.

Their brilliant colors enhance any garden, and since their size allows them to grow well in troughs or containers, no garden, however small, need be without them. Once planted, they demand little attention, except to be kept clear of weeds.

In their natural habitats most mountain plants are covered by an insulating blanket of snow each year, have a short growing season, and do not suffer from the high temperatures and humid conditions that they may have to endure under cultivation in many regions. Where there is little dependable and sustained snow cover, even if the winters are cold, plants will need the protection of a loose mulch. (Pine boughs are especially good.) This should be applied after the soil freezes.

Rock plants have a place in every garden—cascading over rocks, peeping through paving stones, or growing in old troughs and other containers. Most do best in full sun but tolerate partial shade; all need good drainage.

Some high-altitude plants are best grown in pots in an "alpine house." This is simply a greenhouse with little or no heat. The majority of rock plants, however, grow best in the open and are most commonly used in specially prepared rock gardens. Select a variety of plants in order to have a long show of flowers and interesting foliage effects. Many dwarf bulbs, which can be planted under carpeting plants, provide color in early spring.

Ideally, a rock garden should be on a slope, but a flat site is suitable if adequately drained.

Rock gardens are most practically constructed by using the "outcrop" principle—that is, partially embedding a few large rocks in the soil to give the impression of more rocks beneath the surface. The outcrop system is possible with all types of rock, although rounded stones require more effort as well as deeper setting in the ground to achieve the proper effect.

Other flat sites on which to grow rock plants are paved areas or "alpine lawns." To grow plants between paving, lay the slabs on sand, with gaps between to accommodate aromatic species that give off fragrance when they are walked on. An alpine lawn consists of low-growing rock plants with bulbs growing among them and can be located in the lower parts of your rock garden.

Alpines and rock plants can also be grown in raised beds. In this manner plants with different requirements—lime lovers, lime haters, or sun lovers that require good drainage—can all be grown in separate beds filled with different soil mixtures. A system of raised beds can be constructed from several types of material. The best material is rocks, built up like a retaining wall, with soil between them. Plants can then be positioned to trail down the sides of the beds.

Bricks can also be used to build raised beds. They must be cemented in place, with holes left for drainage. Railroad ties—or the lighter, easier to handle, and easier to saw "landscape ties"—logs, and even boards can also serve as building material.

Cement blocks, too, can be used. However, they are likely to be unattractive unless used with skill.

The height of a raised bed may vary from 6 inches to about 3 feet. The higher beds are best for those who find it difficult to bend or stoop.

Alpines and other rock plants can also be mixed with other plants in the garden. The front of a shrub border, particularly if it is raised or has a stone edging, can be filled with trailing plants and dwarf shrubs.

Many of the taller rock plants associate attractively with taller herbaceous perennials. In fact, many gardens have these plants mixed in a striking medley.

Before attempting to build a rock garden, the gardener should have in mind (if not on paper) a plan of the basic design for the garden he or she wishes to make. To get an idea of the possibilities, it is advisable to visit a rock garden in one of the many botanical gardens throughout the country. Smaller rock gardens, which might be more appropriate to the owner of a small plot, can be seen in some private gardens that are open to the public on special occasions. Information regarding these can usually be obtained from local gardening clubs, horticultural societies, and garden sections of newspapers.

To build a successful, natural-looking rock garden, it is well to remember a few basic principles. No attempt should be made, for example, to copy an actual mountain in a garden; the scale would be quite out of proportion. It is best to try to simulate a natural outcrop of rock; this will be far more effective.

All rock begins as a solid lump in

How to Build a Rock Garden

the earth's crust. Then, due to various strains and stresses, the lump begins to crack—usually not diagonally, but vertically and horizontally. With alternate freezing and thawing, further cracking takes place, and the lump takes on a different shape. The most exposed parts crumble away, and the main bulk of the rock becomes hidden beneath the soil formed by the crumbled rock particles. Only corners of rock remain in view, as outcrops protruding from the soil. If these geological principles are considered during construction, the rock garden will have a natural look.

If there has been some geological upheaval, the rocks will have been tilted; this, too, can be incorporated into the building of a rock garden. However, once an angle has been determined, it should be maintained; any additional rocks should be positioned at about the same angle.

The relationship between height and width is also a factor that should be taken into account. For every foot in height, a rock garden's planting area should be 4–5 feet wide at the base. A 4-foot mound, for example, should measure about 20 feet across at its base.

Once the basic rock garden has been built, other features can be added. Water is always an attractive feature; but if you construct a waterfall, exercise care not to make it look too artificial.

A temptation to avoid in rock-garden construction is to take a mound of soil (the kind perhaps left on the property by a contractor), stud it with a motley assortment of stones (perhaps left in a pile by the same contractor), and try to make a rock garden from the result. No matter how carefully you plant, the effect will remain unnatural. The best solution is to have a bulldozer spread the mound—if it is too large to handle by hand—and then build a rock garden based on the appearance of natural outcrops.

You may be fortunate in having rocks and outcroppings on your property. If you do not, rocks will have to be located in others' fields (and possibly bargained for) or purchased from a garden center or landscape contractor.

Rocks that are all of one type, such as sandstone or limestone, should be used in a given area. Whenever possible, choose the pieces of rock yourself, selecting for uniformity of color and texture. If you order from a supplier, ask for a variety of sizes. Large rocks, although not always easy to move and put in place, are likely to provide the most natural effects, but smaller sizes will be needed too. A number of small rocks can be arranged together to resemble a large outcropping. An area roughly 10 feet by 15 feet will require about $1\frac{1}{2}$–2 tons of rock.

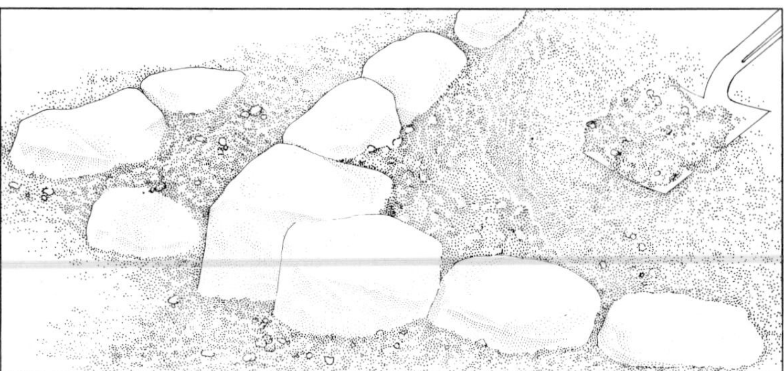

1. *Form an L by placing the largest rock at the corner and making the arms from progressively smaller rocks. Fill spaces with a free-draining soil mixture.*

2. *Additional outcrops can be built either behind or to one side of the first one. Small stones can be laid in a random arrangement on each outcrop.*

3. *Extra tiers can be added as far as space allows, remembering that the rock garden should be four to five times wider than it is high.*

You will also need a supply of $\frac{1}{4}$-inch chips—gravel or crushed stone—to use as a mulch around the plants. Whatever kind of rock mulch you use, the material should blend, rather than contrast, with the surrounding rocks.

The ideal location for a rock garden is a gentle slope protected from strong winds. A sunny site is best for the majority of plants, but dappled sunshine coming through a tree several yards away is acceptable—and even beneficial during very sunny, hot weather. Do not build a rock garden beneath a tree or trees that cast heavy shade, or in other shady areas, unless you plan to grow only woodland plants. (While these plants are not true alpines, most are native to rock-strewn slopes of northern forests that comprise the foothills of mountains.) Too much shade from nearby trees can be reduced by cutting off lower branches and thinning upper growth.

Before a rock garden is built, all perennial weeds must be removed from the site: either dig them out or use weed killers (see p. 648).

If the ground is overrun with honeysuckle or poison ivy, this must be removed. Use several applications of a suitable weed killer if necessary.

If the rock garden is being built on a lawn, remove the sod from the site, and lay it carefully to one side. It can be used as sod elsewhere or can be stacked upside down in the compost heap for later use in potting mixtures or elsewhere in the garden.

Good drainage is essential for a rock garden, since most rock plants will not survive damp conditions. A light soil on a gravelly subsoil will have sufficient natural drainage. But a heavy claylike soil with a subsoil of clay may need artificial drainage if you cannot break through to a porous layer. This is particularly important if the site is flat.

To provide drainage, dig trenches that slope down to a lower level. Make them about 18 inches deep and 3–6 feet apart. Fill the bottom half of each trench with large stones, broken bricks, or rubble. Then place a layer of upturned turf (or several inches of gravel or coarse peat moss) on top to prevent the upper soil from falling between the rubble and blocking the drainage. Finally, fill up with soil.

Sandy soil (or other types of soil that do not require drainage) needs to be dug over only lightly before the rocks are laid.

When the site has been cleared of weeds, and any necessary trenches have been completed, the building of the rock garden can begin.

Start by placing rocks (each weighing as much as 50 pounds) along two sides of the prepared ground to form an L-shaped outcrop. Use the largest rock as the corner, or keystone, of the L. Employ progressively smaller rocks to form the two arms of the L, with the final rocks almost disappearing into the soil. The result should give the appearance of an outcrop of rock protruding from the earth, with a much larger mass of rock below.

A south-facing slope can be made on a north-facing slope by placing rocks on top of one another at the corner of the L to tilt the bed toward the south.

For good drainage place the rocks so that joints line up horizontally and vertically. Do not overlap a joint with the rock above, like bricks in a wall. All rocks have strata lines. Lay the rocks so that these lines run horizontally.

Take care to set the rocks firmly in position. When they have all been properly placed, fill the space between the arms of the L with free-draining soil.

For this purpose, prepare a mixture of 2 parts $\frac{1}{4}$-inch rock chips, 1 part loam, and 1 part peat moss. Shovel this mixture inside the L until it is flush with the tops of the rocks. Then firm it by treading lightly. The mixture will settle; so keep some in reserve for adding later.

After about 10 days (earlier if there has been heavy rain), the soil will have subsided and can be brought to the proper level with the mixture that was held in reserve. Now, rake the surfaces flat.

Finally, apply a mulch layer of $\frac{1}{4}$-inch rock chips, $\frac{1}{2}$–1 inch deep. Rake the chips flat. These chips will reduce loss of moisture from the soil through evaporation, protect the stems of plants from rotting, prevent rain from splashing soil onto the flowers, and keep the soil cool.

When this bed has been completed, further beds can be laid out if the rock garden is to be extended—either behind the first bed or to one side of it.

If the construction is on a slope, the stones should be positioned in such a way as to hold water in place, enabling it to soak into the soil rather than run off the slope.

A waterfall or pool for aquatic plants will enhance a garden's attractiveness. For specific details on how to construct your own water garden, see page 370.

Each builder of a rock garden will have his own ideas as to the kind of effect he wishes to accomplish. To achieve success with his own design, however, he will find it helpful to incorporate two basic principles of rock-garden construction: place joints correctly, and maintain horizontal strata lines.

WAYS OF EXTENDING THE ROCK GARDEN

There are various ways of extending a rock garden. Above, a paved area has been laid in front of the garden, which has been built on a slope. Plants growing between the paving stones make an attractive foreground. A scree can be used instead of the paving (p. 351).

Another attractive way of extending a rock garden is with the use of water—either by making a waterfall or by adding a pool with perhaps fish or aquatic plants. Care must be taken not to make the effect look too artificial or contrived. Details on building a water garden are on page 370.

Planting a Rock Garden

Rock plants do best if set in place in spring or early fall. If they have been pot grown, however, they can also be set out in summer, since they can be transplanted without unduly disturbing the roots. In mild-climate regions rock plants can be set out any time that the ground is workable. Most mail-order nurseries ship at the best planting time for your region.

To remove a plant from its pot, hold it upside down with the stem between two fingers, and gently pull or tear away the pot if it is made of paper or other fiber. If the pot is plastic or clay, tap its rim sharply on a hard surface to dislodge the plant.

With a trowel dig a hole in the soil to the depth of the root ball and insert the plant. Fill the hole with soil, and firm the plant in position with your fingers or the trowel handle. Re-cover the area with stone chips, and water moderately.

Homegrown seedlings, rooted cuttings, or divisions that are ready for transplanting can be put directly into the rock garden. Plant as recommended above, making sure that the planting hole is large enough for the young plant's root system.

Upright shrubs or conifers look best when they are planted at the base of a rock. Prostrate shrubs or conifers, however, are best planted at higher levels; lengthening branches may then cascade over the rocks.

Rosette-forming plants that need to be protected from dampness can be grown in a vertical crevice, where rain will not collect in the rosettes and cause rot. After taking such a plant from its pot and removing the drainage material from its soil ball, check to see whether the plant fits into the crevice. If it does, tease its soil ball into the right shape. Wedge the soil ball into the crevice, and firm in with soil beneath the plant. Finally, fill in the crevice from above the plant with a mixture of soil and stone chips. Ideally, crevice plants should be planted when the rocks are placed in position. This is not always practical, however, and planting may have to be done later.

Large, well-established plants will give a mature effect to a new planting. They can usually be purchased locally or transplanted from a temporary bed or another part of one's rock garden. A good position for large specimens is in the angles between rocks. Dig up the plant during wet weather in autumn or early spring, making sure that a generous ball of soil is taken up with the roots. If necessary, use a crowbar to lift a rock temporarily so that the plant's roots can be wedged beneath it. Firm the soil around the roots. Water all newly set plants.

Before planting, consult the chart of rock plants beginning on page 352 to learn a plant's potential ultimate size and its ideal habitat. Locate fast-growing plants where they will not crowd others.

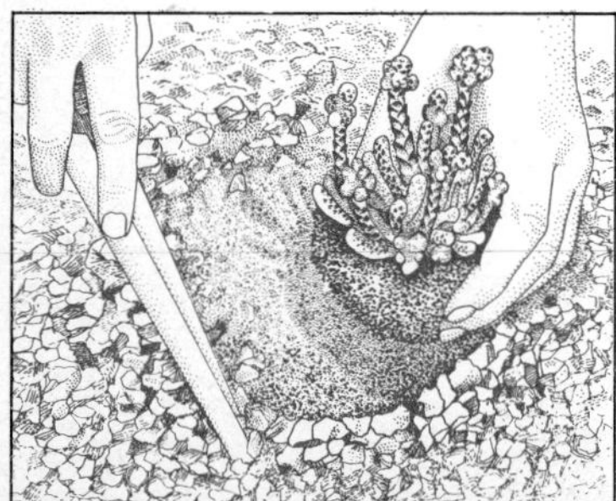

1. *Dig a hole large enough for the entire root ball, and insert the plant.*

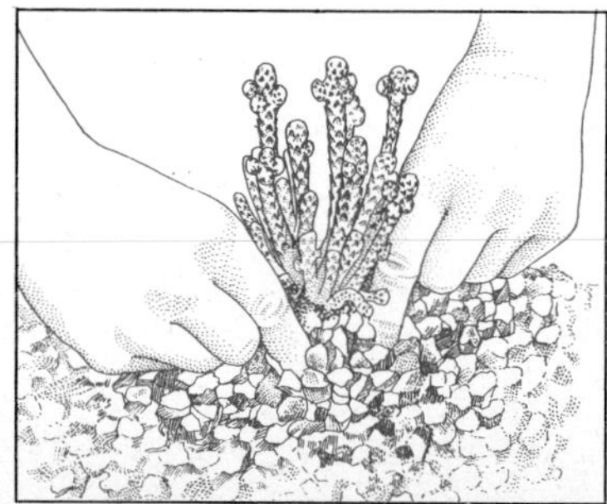

2. *Fill hole with soil. Firm in plant. Cover soil with stone chips, and water.*

FOUR TYPES OF ROCK PLANTS

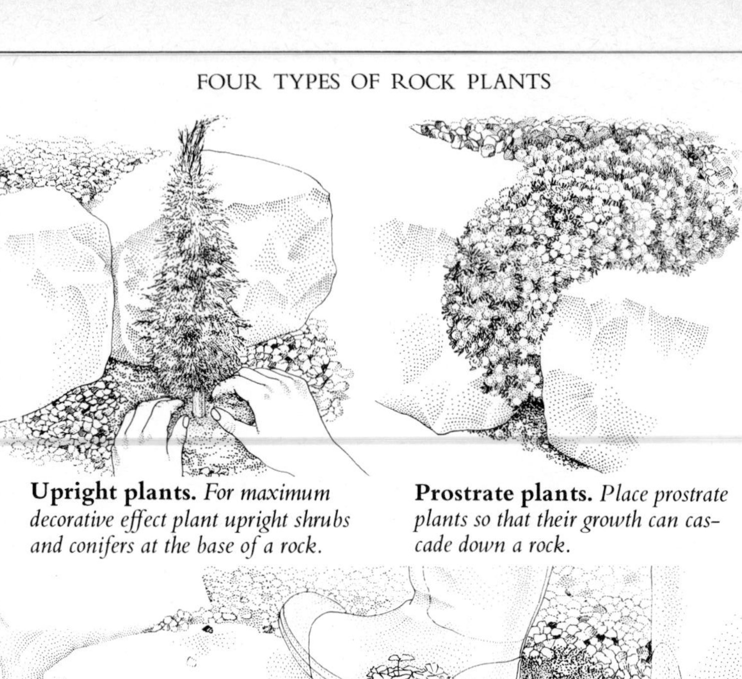

Upright plants. *For maximum decorative effect plant upright shrubs and conifers at the base of a rock.*

Prostrate plants. *Place prostrate plants so that their growth can cascade down a rock.*

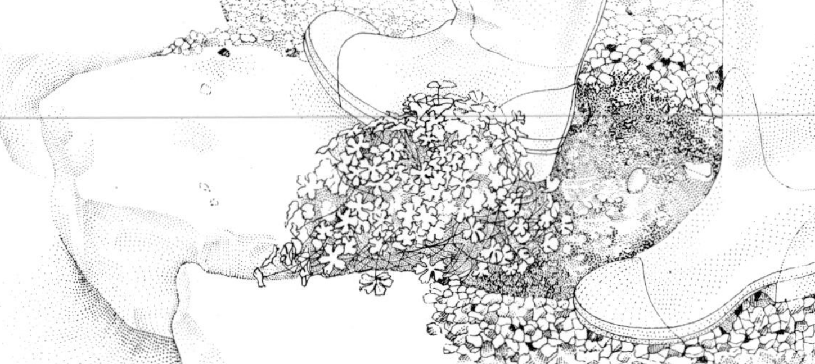

Large specimens. *Large plants, purchased in nurseries or transplanted from other parts of the garden, can be positioned in the angles between rocks. Plant in the usual way; then firm in with your feet.*

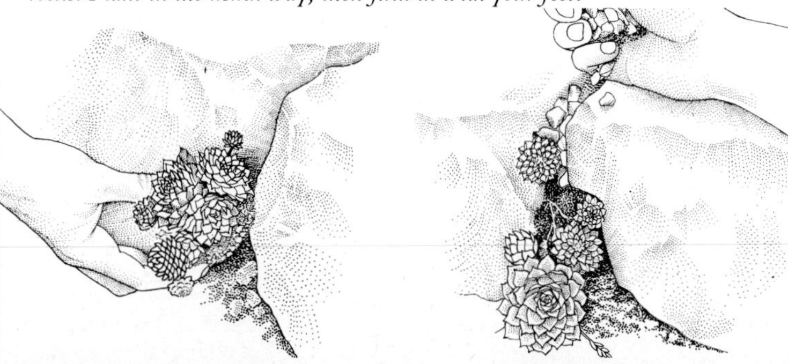

Rosette-forming plants. *Place rosette-forming plants in a vertical crevice. Wedge the soil ball into the crevice. Firm the soil underneath the plant; then fill in from above with soil and stone chips.*

How to Protect Rock Plants and Keep Them Healthy

A layer of stone chips covering the soil will lessen evaporation from a rock garden. So, once rock plants are established in a garden, they are likely to need less frequent watering than many other plants. In time of drought, watering should be done in the cool of the evening. Give the plants a thorough soaking rather than more frequent light waterings.

In spring prepare a bucketful of a mixture composed of equal parts of peat moss, 1/4-inch stone chips, and sieved garden compost or leaf mold, plus a handful of bone meal or superphosphate. Sprinkle a layer of this mixture over the surface of the entire rock garden, working some under the low-growing plants.

Besides conserving moisture, the stone chips discourage slugs. They also keep the stems and foliage of the plants away from wet soil, which could cause rot.

Remove weeds with a hand fork as soon as they appear. Never use a hoe; it can damage bulbs.

A weed killer can be used, but it is better to remove weeds physically from an established rock garden. In such a garden, where plants are often close together, weed-killer spray may be washed onto their roots and may destroy them.

The best way to propagate each kind of rock plant is summarized in the chart beginning on page 352. Full details regarding propagation will be found in each major section of the book dealing with the type of plant to be propagated—shrub, perennial, bulb, and so on.

Some of the less-hardy rock plants and those with gray or woolly leaves may need protection in winter. A glass shelter can easily be constructed (see below).

Drifting leaves often pile up between rocks, forming a soggy blanket. Remove these when necessary.

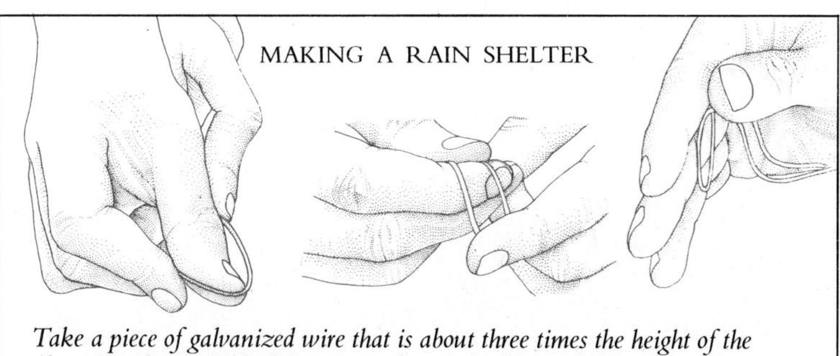

Take a piece of galvanized wire that is about three times the height of the plant. Bend one-third of the wire to form a crook. Bend the crook to form a right angle; then bend it halfway back to make a clip.

Fix wire clips to each corner of a piece of glass. Place the glass over the plant, and push the wires firmly into the ground.

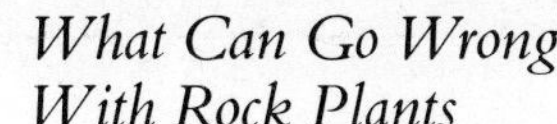

What Can Go Wrong With Rock Plants

To deter snails and slugs, eliminate weeds. Other problems and their appropriate solutions are listed below. If plants show symptoms not described here, see the chart on page 600. Trade names for chemicals appear on page 635.

Symptoms and signs	Cause	Control
Flowering stems or young growth stunted or distorted; covered with small, sticky, greenish, pink, or black insects.	Aphids	Spray with Diazinon, endosulfan, malathion, or systemic insecticide, such as dimethoate or oxydemeton-methyl.
Leaves eaten. No obvious slime trails.	Caterpillars	Spray with carbaryl, malathion, methoxychlor, or rotenone. Or locate and remove caterpillars by hand.
Stems bitten through at ground level or just beneath soil surface.	Cutworms (certain kinds of caterpillars)	Soak soil with Diazinon, malathion, or methoxychlor.
Leaves and young shoots eaten. Slime trails often visible on or around plant.	Slugs or snails	Apply slug pellets or bait of metaldehyde, methiocarb, or mexacarbate.
Fluffy grayish patches atop brown patches when weather is damp.	Gray mold (Botrytis)	Spray with Benomyl, dichlobenil, dichloran, or thiram.
Cushionlike plants with brown patches.	Aging of plants	Propagate living parts.
	Ants' nests cause water to sink too rapidly into lower soil layers	Treat with ant killer, and firm soil around plant. If brown patches are extensive, propagate living parts and discard remainder. Use chlordane dust for ant control.
	Drought conditions	Water regularly during dry spells.

Cutting Back the Soft-Growth Perennials

Prune only if a plant becomes untidy or spreads farther than you would like. Then lift up the mat of foliage, and with pruning shears cut back the lowest branches to the main stem.

Plants that produce a great amount of soft growth, such as aubretias and saponarias, should be cut back quite hard each year after flowering, to encourage the formation of new growth.

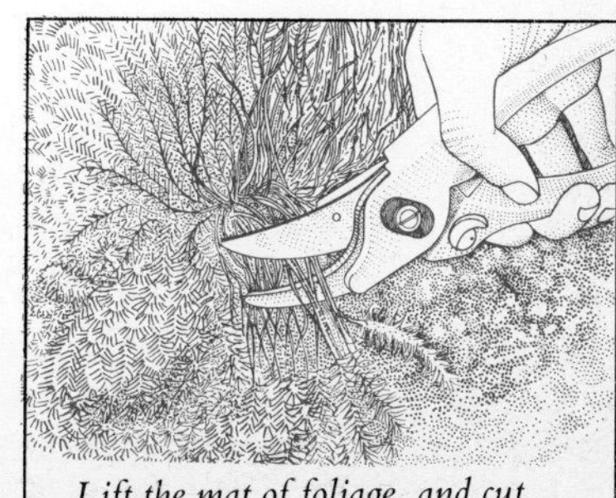

Lift the mat of foliage, and cut back the lower branches.

Growing Rock Plants Without a Rock Garden

Gardens in Troughs and Other Containers

Containers—pots, boxes, troughs—filled with rock plants are attractive additions to a garden. A glazed sink can be camouflaged to look like a stone trough. To do this, combine 2 parts peat moss, 1 part sand, and 1 part cement, and mix with water until a stiff consistency is achieved. For a natural look, leave the mixture rough. Coat the sink with a strong epoxy paint; when it is tacky, apply the "stone coating." Leave a drainage hole at the bottom.

If the container is shallow (3–4 inches deep), cover the drainage hole with stones or fragments of clay pots; if it is deeper, provide 2–4 inches of drainage material.

Fill containers with a mixture of 1 part loam, 1 part peat moss, and 1 part ¼-inch stone chips. Suitable plants can be found in the chart beginning on page 352.

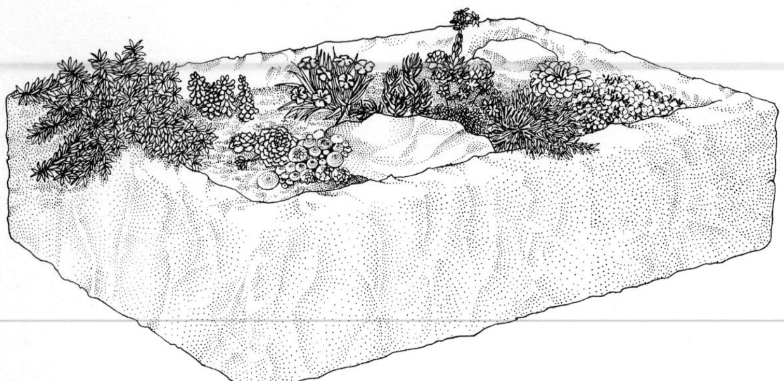

An old glazed sink can be camouflaged with a mixture of peat moss, sand, and cement to make it look like a stone trough. It is then filled with soil and rock plants.

TURNING AN OLD SINK INTO A STONE TROUGH

1. *Mix 2 parts peat moss, 1 part sand, 1 part cement to a stiff consistency with water.*

2. *Coat the sink with a strong adhesive, and let it sit until it is tacky.*

3. *Apply the artificial stone mixture with a trowel; leave the mixture rough. Finally, fill the sink with loam, peat moss, and stone chips.*

Rock Plants in Paths, Patios, and Retaining Walls

To relieve the starkness of a garden path, particularly a straight one, grow rock plants along the edges—or even directly in the path itself.

Rock plants can add interest to a patio. When the patio is being constructed, leave spaces between the paving stones. In the spaces position hardy "carpeting" plants that can withstand trampling upon, such as the mother of thyme. (These plants also emit a pleasant scent.) To provide a varied, three-dimensional look, put one or two taller plants in places such as corners or borders where they are not likely to be trampled on. Dwarf irises, conifers, and shrubs can help achieve this effect.

If the path or terrace is not often walked on in winter, dwarf bulbs such as the crocus and the muscari (grape hyacinth) can be planted to add a splash of bright color in spring.

Plants suitable for growing between paving stones can be found in the chart beginning on page 352.

A retaining wall that is lightly shaded from the midday sun is the ideal place for growing the really vigorous rock plants whose flowers and foliage provide the most striking color effects. With careful planning, the wall can be of interest throughout much of the year.

Some plants will grow well on a wall that is in a shady, perhaps even moist position. Among these are mossy saxifrages and ferns.

For other plants that will grow on retaining walls, see the chart beginning on page 352.

With proper planning, retaining walls, paths, and patios can have plants in flower for many months. Choose plants that can be walked on for use in paths.

Making a Raised Bed With Railroad Ties

A raised bed is ideal for dwarf rhododendrons, heathers, and other plants that flourish in an acid, humus-rich soil. The sides of a raised bed can be made with railroad ties, with the smaller, easier to handle "landscape ties," or even with logs or boards. Although the sides can be as high or as low as desired, a height of about 2 feet is generally convenient. The bed should be in an open position but near some trees that will give it dappled shade during the hot summer months.

If the beds are long enough to require more than one section of whatever material is used for the sides, the joints between the sections can be planted with ferns, ajugas, or other semi-trailing plants.

Fill the beds with equal parts of loam and peat moss. An application of fertilizer can be made each spring. Be sure to water the beds well during droughts.

A raised bed filled with acid, humus-rich soil is useful in alkaline soil regions for growing dwarf rhododendrons, heathers, ferns, and other plants.

1. *Mark the outline. Remove soil to half the depth of the tie. Put in place.*

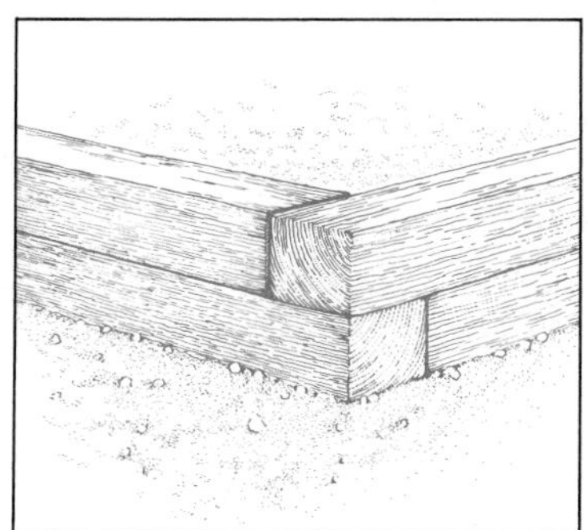

2. *Add the next layers until the desired height of the wall is reached.*

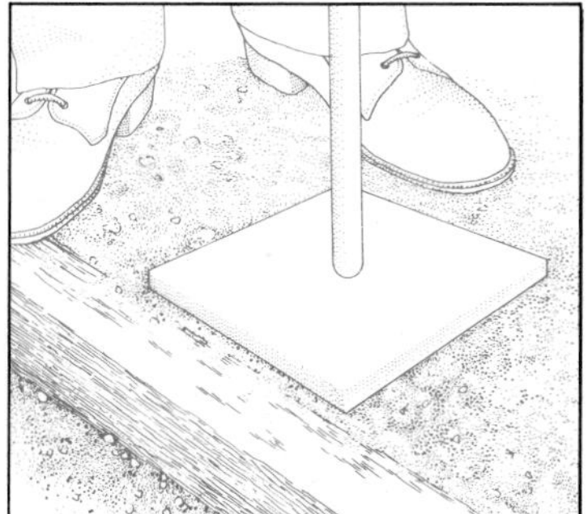

3. *Fill with half peat moss and half soil as each layer is laid. Firm well.*

4. *Ferns and other small plants can be set between tie joints or along bed edges.*

A scree is a deep, well-drained bed made of stone chips and soil.

Screes: Ideal for Rock Plants in Small Gardens

For the small garden, a scree—a bed of stone chips—provides a smaller, more easily constructed setting for rock plants than a full-scale rock garden. Many plants that do not live long in a rock garden do well in a scree because of its excellent drainage.

A slightly inclined site is best for a scree. Ideally, it should face south or west and should be located at the base of a rocky outcropping, as in nature. However, it is more important that the stones provide excellent drainage and sure moisture in spring and summer.

First, dig a hole about 2–3 feet deep. At the bottom of the hole place a 6-inch-deep layer of drainage material, such as rocks, bricks, or rubble. Cover this with a layer of inverted turf sections, if you have some; or use marsh hay, straw, or coarse leaves.

Then fill in the hole with a mixture composed of 2 parts $\frac{1}{4}$-inch stone chips, 1 part leaf mold or peat moss, and 1 part soil. If the soil has a high clay content, add some sand to the mixture to break it up.

Every year, in early spring, apply a $\frac{1}{2}$-inch-deep topdressing of equal parts peat moss (or leaf mold) and coarse sand (or stone chips), plus 2 ounces (about 2 tablespoons) of superphosphate or bone meal per bucketful.

Most of the plants suitable for troughs and sinks do well in a scree.

Suitable plants are listed in the chart beginning on page 352.

PREPARING A SCREE

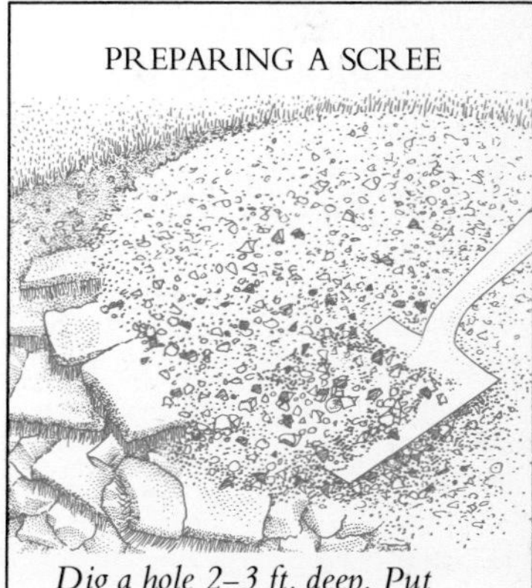

Dig a hole 2–3 ft. deep. Put in a 6-in. layer of drainage material. Cover with coarse compost or leaves. Fill the rest of the hole with stone chips, peat moss, and soil.

Rock Plants for Your Garden

The plants listed in the chart are suitable for growing in rock gardens. Many can also be used between paving blocks and in containers, screes, retaining walls, and alpine lawns. They can also be grown in the foreground of a mixed border if the soil is well drained and gritty.

Many rock plants bloom in spring, but with careful selection it is possible to maintain some plants in flower throughout most of the growing season. To extend the flowering season, plant some early- and late-flowering dwarf bulbs.

The term "rock plant" refers to the natural habitat of the plants discussed here, but the rock plants are shrubs, perennials, or bulbs. For detailed descriptions of how to increase these and other plants not listed here, see the specific information on propagation under the separate headings for shrubs, perennials, and bulbs.

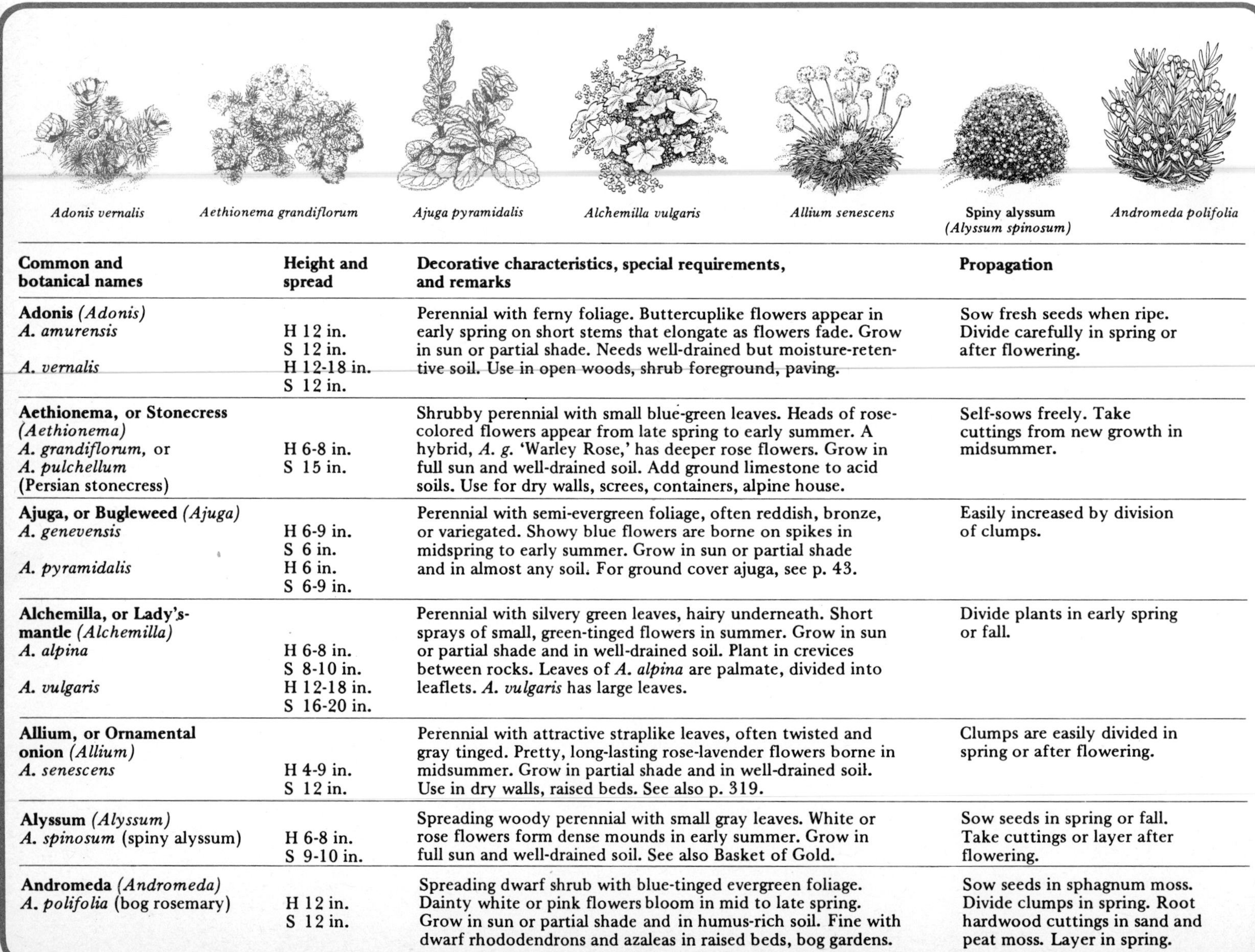

Adonis vernalis — *Aethionema grandiflorum* — *Ajuga pyramidalis* — *Alchemilla vulgaris* — *Allium senescens* — Spiny alyssum (*Alyssum spinosum*) — *Andromeda polifolia*

Common and botanical names	Height and spread	Decorative characteristics, special requirements, and remarks	Propagation
Adonis *(Adonis)* *A. amurensis* *A. vernalis*	 H 12 in. S 12 in. H 12-18 in. S 12 in.	Perennial with ferny foliage. Buttercuplike flowers appear in early spring on short stems that elongate as flowers fade. Grow in sun or partial shade. Needs well-drained but moisture-retentive soil. Use in open woods, shrub foreground, paving.	Sow fresh seeds when ripe. Divide carefully in spring or after flowering.
Aethionema, or Stonecress *(Aethionema)* *A. grandiflorum,* or *A. pulchellum* (Persian stonecress)	 H 6-8 in. S 15 in.	Shrubby perennial with small blue-green leaves. Heads of rose-colored flowers appear from late spring to early summer. A hybrid, *A. g.* 'Warley Rose,' has deeper rose flowers. Grow in full sun and well-drained soil. Add ground limestone to acid soils. Use for dry walls, screes, containers, alpine house.	Self-sows freely. Take cuttings from new growth in midsummer.
Ajuga, or Bugleweed *(Ajuga)* *A. genevensis* *A. pyramidalis*	 H 6-9 in. S 6 in. H 6 in. S 6-9 in.	Perennial with semi-evergreen foliage, often reddish, bronze, or variegated. Showy blue flowers are borne on spikes in midspring to early summer. Grow in sun or partial shade and in almost any soil. For ground cover ajuga, see p. 43.	Easily increased by division of clumps.
Alchemilla, or Lady's-mantle *(Alchemilla)* *A. alpina* *A. vulgaris*	 H 6-8 in. S 8-10 in. H 12-18 in. S 16-20 in.	Perennial with silvery green leaves, hairy underneath. Short sprays of small, green-tinged flowers in summer. Grow in sun or partial shade and in well-drained soil. Plant in crevices between rocks. Leaves of *A. alpina* are palmate, divided into leaflets. *A. vulgaris* has large leaves.	Divide plants in early spring or fall.
Allium, or Ornamental onion *(Allium)* *A. senescens*	 H 4-9 in. S 12 in.	Perennial with attractive straplike leaves, often twisted and gray tinged. Pretty, long-lasting rose-lavender flowers borne in midsummer. Grow in partial shade and in well-drained soil. Use in dry walls, raised beds. See also p. 319.	Clumps are easily divided in spring or after flowering.
Alyssum *(Alyssum)* *A. spinosum* (spiny alyssum)	 H 6-8 in. S 9-10 in.	Spreading woody perennial with small gray leaves. White or rose flowers form dense mounds in early summer. Grow in full sun and well-drained soil. See also Basket of Gold.	Sow seeds in spring or fall. Take cuttings or layer after flowering.
Andromeda *(Andromeda)* *A. polifolia* (bog rosemary)	 H 12 in. S 12 in.	Spreading dwarf shrub with blue-tinged evergreen foliage. Dainty white or pink flowers bloom in mid to late spring. Grow in sun or partial shade and in humus-rich soil. Fine with dwarf rhododendrons and azaleas in raised beds, bog gardens.	Sow seeds in sphagnum moss. Divide clumps in spring. Root hardwood cuttings in sand and peat moss. Layer in spring.

Androsace sarmentosa

Snowdrop anemone (*Anemone sylvestris*)

Anemonella thalictroides

Antennaria dioica

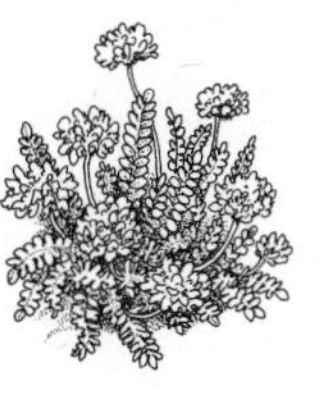
Alps anthyllis (*Anthyllis montana*)

Arabis albida

Trailing arbutus (*Epigaea repens*)

Common and botanical names	Height and spread	Decorative characteristics, special requirements, and remarks	Propagation
Androsace, or Rock jasmine *(Androsace)* *A. sarmentosa* *A. sempervivoides*	 H 4-6 in. S 24 in. H 2-4 in. S 9-12 in.	Perennial rosettes of hairy leaves. Bears umbels of small pink flowers in mid to late spring. Grow in sun or partial shade and in well-drained soil. Mulch with stone chips. Use in dry walls, screes, containers.	Sever rosettes (formed after flowering) from parent plant and root in midsummer; transplant following spring.
Anemone, snowdrop *(Anemone)* *A. sylvestris*	 H 12-18 in. S 15-18 in.	Clump-forming perennial. Fragrant, nodding, 2-in. white flowers appear in late spring. Grow in partial shade and in humus-rich soil. Looks best in groupings in woodlands or in large rock garden.	Divide clumps in early spring or early fall.
Anemonella, or Rue anemone *(Anemonella)* *A. thalictroides*	 H 4-10 in. S 5 in.	Tuberous-rooted perennial with delicate 3-lobed leaflets. Bears single, semi-double, or double white or rose flowers, ½ in. across, in late spring to early summer. Grow in partial shade and in humus-rich soil. Good choice for woodlands or shaded pockets of rock garden.	Gently divide tiny dahlialike tubers after flowering ceases. Foliage dies down in summer.
Antennaria, or Pussytoes *(Antennaria)* *A. dioica*	 H 2-4 in. S 18 in.	Mat-forming perennial with woolly gray leaves, white underneath. Heads of gray flowers, sometimes pink tinged, grow in close clusters in early to mid summer. Grow in full sun and in dry, lean soil. Attractive carpet for small spring bulbs; or use in paving, containers.	Easily divided in spring or fall.
Anthyllis, Alps *(Anthyllis)* *A. montana*	 H 3-6 in. S 10 in.	Mat-forming perennial legume with gray compound leaves. Pink or red cloverlike flower heads open in early summer. Grow in full sun and in well-drained soil. Use in retaining walls, paving, troughs.	Sow seeds or divide in early spring.
Aquilegia, see Columbine			
Arabis, or Rock cress *(Arabis)* *A. albida* (wall rock cress) *A. a. florepleno*	 H 6-10 in. S 24 in. H 1-3 in. S 24 in.	Spreading perennial with soft-textured gray foliage. Racemes of fragrant white flowers appear in mid to late spring. *A. a. florepleno* has long-lasting double flowers. Grow in full sun and in well-drained soil. Cut back after flowering. Use for dry walls, paving, screes.	From see[…] freely if […] flowerin[…] in midsu[…]
Arbutus, trailing, or Mayflower *(Epigaea)* *E. repens*	 H 1-3 in. S 18-24 in.	Mat-forming shrublet with evergreen leaves 3 in. long. Has clusters of fragrant bell-shaped flowers, pink or white, in midspring. Grow in partial to full shade and in acid, humus-rich soil. Mulch over winter; keep newly set plants moist until established. Good plant to use in woodlands or shaded pockets between rocks.	Buy pot-[…] with lea[…] Root cu[…] moss an[…]

Arenaria montana

Armeria maritima

Aster alpinus

Astilbe chinensis pumila

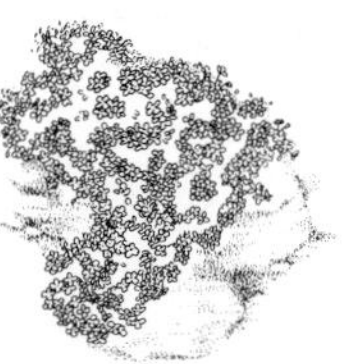
Aubrieta deltoidea

White baneberry (*Actaea pachypoda*)

Basket of gold (*Aurinia saxatilis*)

Common and botanical names	Height and spread	Decorative characteristics, special requirements, and remarks	Propagation
Arenaria, or Sandwort *(Arenaria)* *A. montana* (mountain sandwort)	 H 2-4 in. S 18 in.	Creeping or trailing perennial with small grasslike leaves. Starry white flowers, ½ in. across, in late spring to early summer. Grow in full sun and in well-drained, humus-rich soil. Fine wall plant; also grows in screes and paving.	Seeds offer best success; more difficult are divisions in early fall and cuttings in midsummer.
Armeria, or Thrift *(Armeria)* *A. juniperifolia*, or *A. caespitosa* *A. maritima* (sea-pink, or sea-thrift)	 H 2-3 in. S 6 in. H 6-12 in. S 12 in.	Mound-forming perennial with stiff, grasslike evergreen foliage. Papery-textured flower heads in pink, rose, or white appear from late spring to midsummer. Grow in sun and in well-drained soil. Grow *A. juniperifolia* on top of dry walls, in screes, paving, or containers. *A. maritima* and its varieties are easier to grow.	*A. maritima* by division or fresh seeds. *A. juniperifolia* usually is more difficult; try rooting basal cuttings in peat moss and sand mixture in early summer.
Artemisia, or Silver mound, see *Artemisia schmidtiana,* p. 241			
Aster *(Aster)* *A. alpinus* (rock aster)	 H 8-10 in. S 10-18 in.	Perennial with violet flowers (there are also white, lavender, and pinkish forms) in early summer. Grow in sun and in well-drained soil. Fine plant for large rock gardens, alpine lawns, or between paving stones.	Divide clumps in late summer after flowering.
Astilbe, or False spirea *(Astilbe)* *A. chinensis pumila* *A. simplicifolia*	 H 10 in. S 24 in. H 12 in. S 12 in.	Perennial with attractive clumps or mats of divided fernlike leaves. Leaves of *A. simplicifolia* are glossy and undivided. Showy spikes of pink, rose, or magenta flowers arise from mid to late summer. Grow in full sun or partial shade, in humus-rich soil. Valued as source of late color on top of dry walls, in raised beds, beside pools, or in bog gardens.	Easily divided in spring or early fall. *A. c. pumila* often self-sows.
Aubrieta, or Purple rock cress *(Aubrieta)* *A. deltoidea*	 H 3-6 in. S 18 in.	Mat-forming perennial bears clusters of reddish-purple flowers from midspring to early summer. Grow in sun, but where summers are hot, provide midday shade. Needs well-drained soil. Cut back annually when flowers fade. Good for planting between paving stones and in dry walls.	Sow seeds in spring. Propagate by division, layers, or cuttings in midsummer.
Baneberry, or Actaea *(Actaea)* *A. arguta* *A. pachypoda*, or *A. alba* [illegible]hite baneberry) [illegible]*picata* (black baneberry, [illegible]h-christopher)	 H 18-24 in. S 10-18 in. H 18-24 in. S 10-18 in. H 18-24 in. S 10-18 in.	Perennial forming graceful clumps of fernlike leaves. Racemes of small white flowers open from late spring to early summer. Shiny ½-in. berries follow, handsome but very poisonous—glistening white with dark spot on *A. pachypoda*, red on *A. arguta*, and black on *A. spicata*. Grow in partial shade. Needs humus-rich soil. Attractive plant to grow in woodlands, on rocky slopes, or in raised beds.	Divide clumps in spring or fall. Sow seeds in fall, first separating them from pulp of berry; seeds will germinate the following spring. Established clumps will self-sow.
[illegible]**gold, or Goldentuft** [illegible]*Alyssum)* [illegible]*s*, or	 H 6-8 in. S 12-18 in.	Perennial with gray foliage. Bright yellow flower clusters appear in early spring. Grow in sun and in well-drained soil. Cut back after flowering. Use in dry walls and between paving. *A. s. citrina* has flowers of lighter yellow.	From seeds in spring and summer (self-sows freely). Take cuttings in early summer.

Bearberry
(Arctostaphylos uva-ursi)

Bloodroot
(Sanguinaria canadensis)

Bluets
(Houstonia caerulea)

Kew broom
(Cytisus kewensis)

Bruckenthalia spiculifolia

Bunchberry
(Cornus canadensis)

Buttercup
(Ranunculus gramineus)

Common and botanical names	Height and spread	Decorative characteristics, special requirements, and remarks	Propagation
Bearberry, or Kinnikinnick *(Arctostaphylos)* *A. uva-ursi*	H 1-1½ in. S 15 in.	Trailing shrub with beautiful, glossy evergreen leaves that turn reddish in winter. Small, urn-shaped pink flowers appear in late spring. Long-lasting red berries in fall and winter. Grow in sun or partial shade. Thrives in well-drained, acid, sandy or rocky soil. Useful ground cover for sandy dunes or rock-strewn slopes.	Transplants poorly from wild. Cuttings root easily in peat moss and sand in plastic-enclosed flat. Set out rooted cuttings in spring or summer.
Bloodroot, or Sanguinaria *(Sanguinaria)* *S. canadensis*	H 4-9 in. S 9-12 in.	Perennial with rhizomes and lobed gray leaves. Foliage usually fades by midsummer. Beautiful white flowers (double and longer lasting in *S. c. multiplex*) in early spring. Grow in partial shade and humus-rich soil. Good in woodlands or on shaded slopes.	Rhizomes can be cut apart after flowering, allowing 1 or more eyes per division. Plants self-sow.
Bluets, or Quaker ladies *(Houstonia)* *H. caerulea* (bluets)	H 3-6 in. S 4 in.	Short-lived perennial with mats of fragile foliage. Bears tiny, 4-petaled, starry blue flowers in late spring. *H. serpyllifolia* has deeper blue flowers. Grow in sun or partial shade and in moist soil. Dainty plants to grow for retaining walls, paving, around pools.	Mats are easily divided after flowering. Also easily grown from seeds when available; allow plants to self-sow.
H. serpyllifolia (creeping bluets)	H 1 in. S 3-4 in.		
Broom, see Broom, Kew, and Genista			
Broom, Kew *(Cytisus)* *C. kewensis*	H 10 in. S 24 in.	Trailing shrub with wiry green branches. Bears clusters of creamy white flowers, typical of pea family, in late spring. Needs sun and well-drained, lean soil. For large rock gardens or dry walls.	Take cuttings from nonflowering shoots in late spring or early summer.
Bruckenthalia, or Spike heath *(Bruckenthalia)* *B. spiculifolia*	H 9 in. S 24 in.	Slow-spreading dwarf shrub with needlelike evergreen foliage. Short spikes of small pink bells appear from early to mid summer. Grow in sun or partial shade and in well-drained, acid soil; add peat moss to sandy soil. Mulch with evergreen boughs over winter.	Cut off rooted divisions in spring or early summer and plant in moist, humusy soil. Water well.
Bunchberry *(Cornus)* *C. canadensis*	H 6-9 in. S 12 in.	Mat-forming shrublet with whorls of evergreen or semi-evergreen leaves. Showy white bracts appear around inconspicuous true flowers in late spring to early summer. Handsome bunches of edible red berries in late summer and fall. Grow in partial shade and in acid, humus-rich, moist soil. Use in woodland-type habitats.	Sow seeds in fall to germinate in spring. Plants collected from wild are difficult to establish. Potted plants available at nurseries.
Buttercup, or Ranunculus *(Ranunculus)* *R. alpestris*	H 6 in. S 6 in.	Perennial that forms mats or clumps of divided foliage, gray-green in *R. alpestris* and *R. gramineus.* Yellow flowers (white in *R. alpestris)* are borne in midspring. Grow plant in sun or partial shade, in humus-rich, rocky soil. *(R. alpestris* does better in rich, moist to wet soil, as in bogs or at poolsides.)	Clumps are easily divided in early spring or after flowering season ends.
R. gramineus	H 12 in. S 8-12 in.		
R. montanus	H 6 in. S 12 in.		

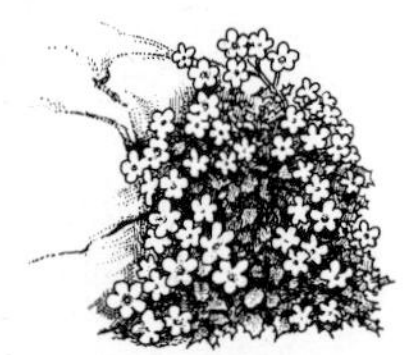

Campanula portenschlagiana

Evergreen candytuft (*Iberis sempervirens*)

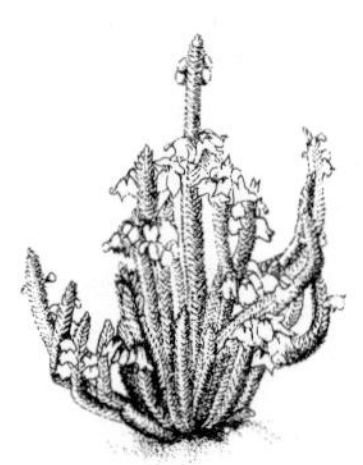
Cassiope tetragona

Cerastium tomentosum

Ceratostigma plumbaginoides

Chrysogonum virginianum

Common and botanical names	Height and spread	Decorative characteristics, special requirements, and remarks	Propagation
Campanula, or Bellflower *(Campanula)* *C. carpatica* (tussock bellflower) *C. cochlearifolia,* or *C. pusilla* *C. elatines* *C. portenschlagiana* (Dalmatian bellflower) *C. poscharskyana* (Serbian bellflower) *C. rotundifolia* (harebell, or bluebells of Scotland)	 H 9-12 in. S 12-15 in. H 4-8 in. S 12 in. H 6-8 in. S 15 in. H 6-9 in. S 10 in. H 4 in. S 24 in. H 8-12 in. S 12 in.	Perennials that may be tufted, clump forming, or trailing in habit. Attractive bell-like or starry flowers in shades of blue or white appear from early to late summer. Most do best in full sun, but *C. rotundifolia,* one of easiest to grow, and *C. portenschlagiana* will tolerate partial shade. All do best in well-drained, gritty soil that retains moisture. Splendid wall plants; use also for screes, paving, in containers, and alpine houses. Many other species exist, some difficult to grow away from their alpine environment.	Sow seeds from spring through fall; some fall-sown seeds will germinate in spring. Seeds are very fine; mix with sand for better distribution. Most plants will self-sow unless fading flowers are cut off. Many kinds can be divided in spring or fall. Take cuttings of nonflowering shoots in late spring or early summer.
Campion, see Lychnis and Silene			
Candytuft *(Iberis)* *I. saxatilis* (rock candytuft) *I. sempervirens* (evergreen, or edging, candytuft)	 H 6 in. S 12 in. H 12 in. S 24 in.	Spreading perennial or subshrub with narrow evergreen leaves. Umbels of long-lasting white flowers first appear in late spring. Grow in full sun, in well-drained soil. Good to use in paving, on retaining walls, or in foreground of shrub and flower borders. *I. sempervirens* 'Autumn Snow' blooms in both spring and fall.	Take cuttings after flowering; transplant following spring. Also by layering and division.
Cassiope *(Cassiope)* *C. lycopodioides* *C. tetragona*	 H 3 in. S 8-12 in. H 10-12 in. S 6-8 in.	Mound-forming dwarf shrub. Small, narrow evergreen leaves on thin stems. Flowers are tiny white bells that develop in mid to late spring. Grow in sun or partial shade, in sandy, well-drained soil improved by peat moss. Difficult to grow except where rock garden is blanketed with snow all winter long.	Take cuttings from nonblooming shoots in mid to late summer; root in sand and peat moss mixture. Also by layering.
Cerastium, or Mouse-ear *(Cerastium)* *C. alpinum lanatum* *C. tomentosum* (snow-in-summer)	 H 4 in. S 8 in. H 6 in. S 4-5 ft.	Mat-forming perennial with woolly gray foliage. Clusters of small white flowers appear in early summer. Grow in full sun, in well-drained soil. *C. tomentosum* is fast-growing creeper that self-sows like a weed. *C. a. lanatum* is more refined. Grow in crevices or screes.	From seeds or division in spring or early fall. Rooted layers can be taken from *C. a. lanatum* in spring or early fall.
Ceratostigma *(Ceratostigma)* *C. plumbaginoides*	 H 6-12 in. S 24 in.	Clump-forming perennial with glossy, semi-evergreen foliage that turns bronze in fall. Bright blue flowers open in late summer. Grow in full sun or partial shade, in average soil. Good wall plant.	Easily divided in late spring or after flowering in fall.
Chrysogonum *(Chrysogonum)* *C. virginianum* (golden star)	 H 8-12 in. S 24 in.	Perennial with coarse, hairy foliage. Yellow, star-shaped flowers from midspring through midsummer. Grow in sun or partial shade, in well-drained soil. Grow in woodlands or among rocks.	Sow seeds in spring. Divide clumps in early spring or early fall.

Clematis alpina

Columbine
(Aquilegia flabellata nana-alba)

Yellow corydalis
(Corydalis lutea)

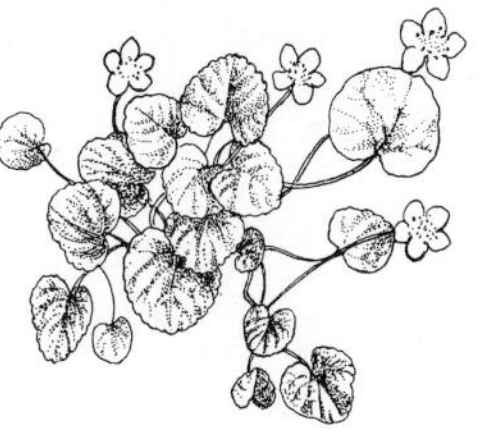
Dalibarda repens

Daphne cneorum

Dianthus alpinus

Common and botanical names	Height and spread	Decorative characteristics, special requirements, and remarks	Propagation
Clematis *(Clematis)* *C. alpina*	H 6 in. S 24 in.	Bushy shrub or vine with violet-blue flowers, 1½ in. long, in late spring. Grow in sun or partial shade, in well-drained, humus-rich soil. Good for large rock gardens; grows over rock faces.	Seeds are slow to germinate; sow them in fall and grow in pots until midspring.
Columbine, or Aquilegia *(Aquilegia)* *A. alpina* *A. caerulea* (Colorado columbine) *A. canadensis* (common American columbine) *A. flabellata nana-alba*	H 12 in. S 12 in. H 2½ ft. S 18 in. H 12-24 in. S 18 in. H 6-12 in. S 12 in.	Perennial with mounds of attractive compound leaves, each leaflet deeply segmented and graceful. Showy flowers with prominent spurs in late spring and early summer. Grow in sun or partial shade; well-drained soil should be lean but contain some peat moss. Good plant for edges of woodlands, alpine lawns, raised beds, or foreground of shrub borders. *A. f. nana-alba,* with white flowers and glaucous leaves, is outstanding, fairly long-lived rock plant. *A. alpina* has blue flowers; *A. caerulea,* blue and white; *A. canadensis,* red and yellow.	Sow seeds in spring or fall; germination may be slow. Most columbines self-sow freely. Some, such as *A. f. nana-alba,* remain true to type.
Corydalis, yellow *(Corydalis)* *C. lutea*	H 8-12 in. S 12 in.	Perennial with fernlike foliage. Short-spurred yellow flowers arise from late spring through summer. Grow in partial to full shade, in well-drained soil. Fine plant for dry walls.	Sow fresh seeds as soon as ripe. Self-sows freely. Transplant only in spring.
Cranesbill, see Geranium			
Dalibarda, or False violet *(Dalibarda)* *D. repens*	H 2-4 in. S 8-12 in.	Creeping perennial with mats of heart-shaped evergreen leaves. Star-shaped white flowers are borne on short stems from early to mid summer. Grow in shade. Requires moist, humus-rich, acid soil. Good plant to grow in shaded crannies.	Divide clumps gently in spring or early summer. Keep roots moist until plants are established.
Daphne *(Daphne)* *D. blagayana* *D. cneorum* (garland flower) *D. retusa*	H 6-12 in. S 6 ft. H 6 in. S 24 in. H 3 ft. S 1½-3 ft.	Small evergreen shrub. Fragrant flower clusters appear in late spring. Grow in sun or partial shade. Well-drained soil should be enriched with leaf mold or peat moss. Useful plant for base of walls, deep soil pockets, raised beds. *D. blagayana* has creamy white flowers on nearly prostrate branches. *D. cneorum* has rose-pink flowers on trailing branches; requires full sun. *D. retusa* bears purple buds followed by pink flowers. Slow grower.	Buy pot-grown plants for best results. Root summer cuttings in peat moss and sand for *D. cneorum* and *D. retusa.* Increase *D. blagayana* and *D. cneorum* by layering.
Dead nettle, see Lamium, p. 253			
Dianthus, or Pink *(Dianthus)* *D. alpinus* (alpine pink) *D. deltoides* (maiden pink) *D. neglectus* (glacier pink)	H 3-5 in. S 6 in. H 4-15 in. S 12-18 in. H 2-6 in. S 6 in.	Carpet- or cushion-forming perennials with grasslike evergreen foliage. Bears showy flowers of rose or pink, often with distinctive "eyes," in late spring to early summer. Grow in full sun. Soil should be well drained and gritty (add limestone to acid soils). Useful for retaining walls, screes, paving, containers. There are many other fine pinks, both species and hybrids, that are useful for rock gardens.	Divide or take cuttings after blooming. Sow seeds in late spring to early summer. Most pinks self-sow, but not all offspring come true.

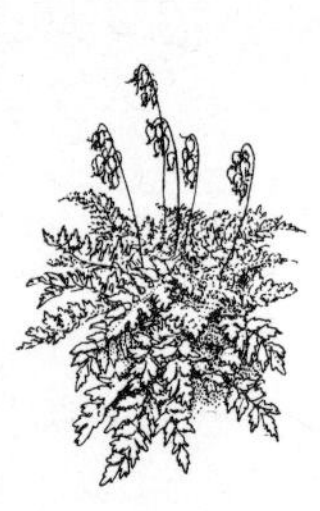

Dicentra eximia

Disporum sessile variegatum

Dodecatheon meadia

Draba aizoides

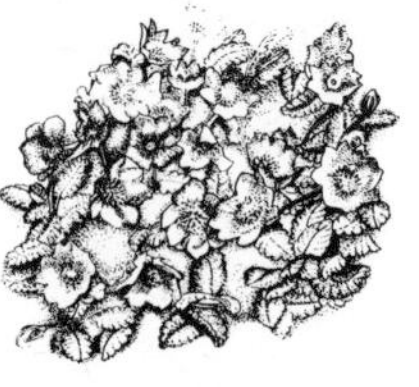

Dryas octopetala

Edelweiss
(Leontopodium alpinum)

Common and botanical names	Height and spread	Decorative characteristics, special requirements, and remarks	Propagation
Dicentra *(Dicentra)* *D. canadensis* (squirrel corn) *D. cucullaria* (Dutchman's breeches) *D. eximia* (fringed bleeding heart)	 H 4-10 in. S 10 in. H 10-12 in. S 12 in. H 12-24 in. S 8-10 in.	Perennial with fernlike foliage. Racemes of dainty heart-shaped flowers appear from mid to late spring. Grow in partial shade, in humus-rich soil. (Add ground limestone to very acid soil.) Good for woodlands, shaded crannies of walls, or rock gardens. *D. canadensis* has short-spurred white flowers. *D. cucullaria* has long-spurred white or pinkish flowers. *D. eximia* has heart-shaped pink flowers borne on spikes. For other perennial dicentras, see p. 247.	Divide clumps by separating tubers after flowering. Seeds are slow to germinate; sow in fall for spring growth.
Disporum, or Fairy bells *(Disporum)* *D. hookeri* *D. lanuginosum* *D. sessile variegatum*	 H 9-16 in. S 24 in. H 12-24 in. S 12-24 in. H 8 in. S 12 in.	Colonizing perennial of graceful habit with lilylike foliage. Cream or greenish bell-shaped flowers appear in late spring. Grow in partial shade, in humus-rich, acid soil. Good plants for woodlands, base of shaded walls, or rock slopes. *D. lanuginosum* is native to eastern U.S.; *D. hookeri,* to western U.S.; *D. s. variegatum,* with showy variegated foliage, to Japan.	Easily divided by separating slender rhizomes in early spring or just after flowering. Sow seeds in late spring.
Dodecatheon, or Shooting star *(Dodecatheon)* *D. dentatum* *D. meadia* *D. pulchellum*	 H 7-10 in. S 10-12 in. H 6-20 in. S 6-10 in. H 6 in. S 5-6 in.	Perennial with foliage in basal rosettes. Graceful flowers of pink, rose, or purple are borne in clusters at end of bare stems in late spring; each flower has reflexed petals and prominent stamens. Foliage disappears after plant blooms. Grow in partial shade, in humus-rich, moisture-retentive soil. Use plant for woodlands or deep soil pockets among rocks.	Divide fleshy roots or take root cuttings after flowering. Seeds germinate quickly, but seedlings grow slowly; will flower in about 3 yr.
Draba *(Draba)* *D. aizoides* *D. fladnizensis* (Arctic draba) *D. sibirica,* or *D. repens*	 H 4 in. S 6-9 in. H 3-4 in. S 6-8 in. H 2-6 in. S 12-24 in.	Mound-forming perennial with rosettes of hairy, often gray foliage. Small white or yellow flowers appear in racemes in mid to late spring. Grow in sun, with some noontime shade. Requires well-drained, gritty soil with added leaf mold. Most drabas are listed as alpines. Grow in screes, paving, alpine house, or in deep soil pockets of rock garden.	Divide by severing rosettes; or top-dress with mixture of leaf mold and gritty soil to induce stem rooting of rosettes, and sever carefully. Also propagate by seeds.
Dryas *(Dryas)* *D. octopetala*	 H 3-4 in. S 24 in.	Creeping shrub with rounded evergreen leaves. White flowers appear in early summer. Grow in sun, in gritty, well-drained soil. Established plants transplant poorly; propagate or buy new plants.	Take hardwood cuttings in early to mid summer. Make layers in spring.
Edelweiss *(Leontopodium)* *L. alpinum*	 H 8 in. S 9 in.	Creeping perennial with woolly gray leaves. Star-shaped white flowers with yellow centers appear in early summer. Grow in full sun. Requires well-drained, gritty or sandy soil. Protect from winter moisture. Grow in walls, paving, screes, or alpine house.	Divide clumps in early spring. Sow seeds in spring in light or sandy soil mixture.

Epimedium grandiflorum

Euphorbia myrsinites

Galax aphylla

Gaylussacia brachycera

Genista pilosa

Gentian (Gentiana acaulis)

Common and botanical names	Height and spread	Decorative characteristics, special requirements, and remarks	Propagation
Epimedium *(Epimedium)*		Spreading perennial with attractive evergreen foliage. Graceful racemes of spurred flowers in shades of white, pink, violet, or yellow, from midspring to early summer. Grow in sun or partial shade and in well-drained, humus-rich soil that retains moisture. Good plant to use for base of walls, woodlands, shrub foregrounds, and rock-strewn slopes. Several varieties and hybrids are available.	Easily divided in early spring, after flowering, or in early fall. Lift clumps and separate underground stems.
E. alpinum	H 6-9 in. S 12 in.		
E. grandiflorum (bishop's hat)	H 9 in. S 24 in.		
E. pinnatum (Persian epimedium)	H 9-12 in. S 10-24 in.		
Euphorbia, or Spurge *(Euphorbia)*		Prostrate perennial with attractive blue-gray foliage on fleshy stems. Sulfur-yellow floral bracts appear in late spring. Grow in full sun and well-drained soil.	From seeds, division, or cuttings in mid to late spring.
E. myrsinites	H 12 in. S 12 in.		
Foamflower, see p. 248 **Forget-me-not,** see Myosotis			
Galax *(Galax)*		Stemless perennial. Heart-shaped, evergreen leaves turn bronze in fall and winter. Bears wands of small white flowers in late spring. Grow in partial shade, in humus-rich, acid soil. Good for woodlands, shaded slopes, or among rocks.	Divide established plants in early spring or fall, separating rhizomatous roots. Growth from seeds is slow.
G. aphylla	H 6-12 in. S 12-24 in.		
Gaylussacia, or Huckleberry *(Gaylussacia)*		Creeping shrub. Handsome, glossy evergreen leaves are bronze in fall. Bell-shaped flowers appear in late spring; edible blue berries in late summer. Grow in sun or partial shade, in humus-rich, acid soil. Slow growing until established. Use for ground cover on slopes, heaths, or rock gardens.	Purchase pot-grown plants from specialists. Divide creeping roots or take cuttings in early summer.
G. brachycera (box huckleberry)	H 18 in. S 24 in.		
Genista, or Broom *(Genista)*		Prostrate shrublets, usually with winged green stems that resemble evergreen foliage. Displays yellow pea-shaped flowers from late spring to early summer. Grow in sun and in deep, well-drained, sandy soil. Does not transplant well; buy container-grown plants or propagate new plants for new locations. Good for hot, dry climates and situations. Useful for banks and slopes, among large rocks, and in retaining walls.	Take cu in early in fall c
G. pilosa	H 4 in. S 2-3 ft.		
G. sagittalis	H 12 in. S 24 in.		
Gentian *(Gentiana)*		Perennials, some with evergreen foliage; handsome, intensely blue flowers. Grow in sun or partial shade. Requires well-drained but moist, humus-rich soil. Good for dry walls, shaded slopes, paving, and alpine houses. *G. acaulis* is evergreen, bears large blue trumpets in late spring; difficult to grow. *G. andrewsii* bears bluish-purple flower clusters in early fall; easy to grow in woodlands and on shaded slopes. *G. scabra* has large, deep blue flowers in mid to late fall; easy for gardens with partial shade. *G. septemfida* bears large, deep blue bells in midsummer.	Divide *andre* cuttin All gr *G. an* *G. se*
G. acaulis	H 3-4 in. S 18 in.		
G. andrewsii (closed, or bottle, gentian)	H 12 in. S 12 in.		
G. scabra	H 12 in. S 12 in.		
G. septemfida	H 9-18 in. S 12 in.		

Geranium sanguineum prostratum

Geum montanum

European wild ginger
(Asarum europaeum)

Goldthread
(Coptis trifolia)

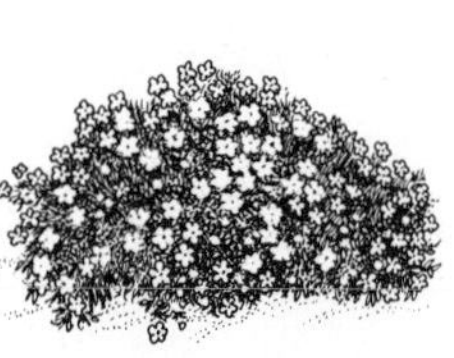

Creeping gypsophila
(Gypsophila repens)

Haberlea rhodopensis

Common and botanical names	Height and spread	Decorative characteristics, special requirements, and remarks	Propagation
Geranium, or Cranesbill *(Geranium)*		Perennial with mounds of attractive, deeply cut leaves. Pretty flowers appear in early summer. Grow in sun or partial shade, and in average rock-garden soil. Useful plants for ground cover, dry walls, paving, containers. *G.* 'Ballerina' has pink flowers. *G. c. subcaulescens* has small scalloped leaves and carmine flowers. *G. dalmaticum* has dark glossy foliage and pink or white flowers. *G. s. prostratum* has pink flowers with rose veining.	Divide clumps of most kinds in early spring or after flowering. Also propagated by root cuttings or seeds.
G. 'Ballerina'	H 6-9 in. S 12 in.		
G. cinereum subcaulescens	H 4-6 in. S 12 in.		
G. dalmaticum	H 3-6 in. S 9-12 in.		
G. sanguineum prostratum, or *G. lancastriense*	H 6-9 in. S 12 in.		
Geum, or Avens *(Geum)*		Perennial with neat mounds of cut leaves. Roselike flowers appear from early to mid summer. Grow in sun or partial shade and in average rock-garden soil. Use for retaining walls, raised beds. *G. borisii* has orange-scarlet flowers; *G. montanum,* golden yellow. *G. reptans,* with ferny, golden foliage, requires some midday shade and moist, cool soil. For perennial *G. heldreichii,* see p. 250.	Clumps are easily divided in early spring, or after flowering in late summer or early fall. Also grows from seeds.
G. borisii	H 10 in. S 12 in.		
G. montanum	H 12 in. S 12 in.		
G. reptans	H 6 in. S 6-8 in.		
Ginger, wild *(Asarum)*		Mat-forming perennial with creeping ginger-flavored rhizomes. Handsome heart-shaped evergreen leaves, often mottled with silver, hide ground-hugging, tubular flowers of brown or maroon, which appear in early spring. Grow in shade and in well-drained, humus-rich soil. Choice but not spectacular for woodlands and shaded rock gardens.	Divide in spring by separating rhizomes and replanting in humus-rich soil. Keep well watered until established.
A. europaeum (European)	H 5 in. S 10 in.		
A. shuttleworthii (mottled)	H 8 in. S 16 in.		
A. virginicum (Virginia)	H 7 in. S 14 in.		
Goldthread *(Coptis)*		Mat-forming stemless perennial with compound, scalloped evergreen leaves. White or yellow buttercuplike flowers are borne in early to mid summer. Grow in partial shade and in moist, humus-rich soil. Flourishes only where winters are cold. Attractive for use in woodlands or among shaded rocks.	Divide in early spring or late summer. Sow fresh seeds in mixture of peat moss and sand; keep moist.
C. trifolia	H 4-6 in. S 12-18 in.		
...sophila, creeping *(...phila)*	H 4-5 in. S 24 in.	Prostrate or trailing perennial with narrow gray-green leaves. Airy sprays of small white flowers appear from early to mid summer. Grow in sun and in well-drained, slightly alkaline soil. Versatile rock plant. *G. r. rosea* has pink flowers on 4-in. stems.	Best increased by seeds.
...lea)	H 3-6 in. S 6-9 in.	Perennial with rosettes of hairy leaves. Bears clusters of lavender flowers in late spring. Grow in shade and in humus-rich, moist soil. Relative of African violet; difficult to grow, but winter hardy. Does best in crevices of north-facing rocks.	Take leaf cuttings with stem as with African violets. Start seeds in mixture of peat moss and sand.

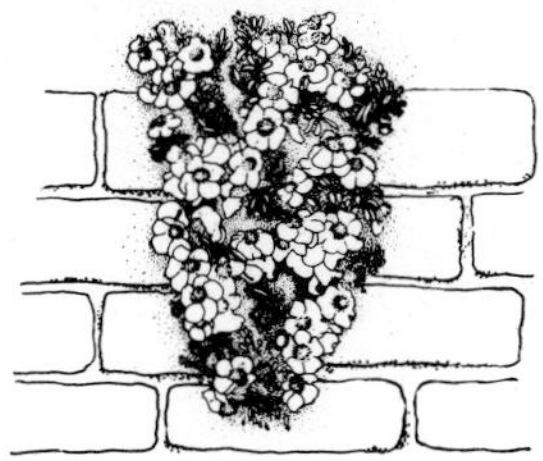
Helianthemum nummularium

Hepatica nobilis

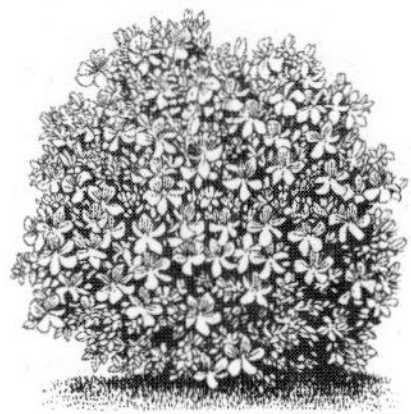
Hypericum polyphyllum

Iris cristata

Common and botanical names	Height and spread	Decorative characteristics, special requirements, and remarks	Propagation
Helianthemum, Sunrose, or Rockrose *(Helianthemum)*		Shrublets with evergreen or semi-evergreen leaves. Roselike flowers abundantly displayed from early to mid summer. Grow in sun and in deep, lean soil. Cut back after flowering. Buy pot-grown plants. Use for ground cover, retaining walls, raised beds, paving. *H. alpestre* has yellow flowers on twiggy plants. *H. lunulatum* has golden flowers. *H. nummularium* has single or double flowers of yellow, pink, or white, many named forms. Needs winter protection in North.	Propagate named varieties by cuttings taken in summer. Start others from cuttings taken in summer or seeds sown in spring.
H. alpestre	H 3-6 in. S 12 in.		
H. lunulatum	H 9-12 in. S 12 in.		
H. nummularium, or *H. chamaecistus*	H 4-12 in. S 24 in.		
Hepatica, or Liverleaf *(Hepatica)*		Perennial with 3-lobed leaves that persist over winter, new leaves appearing after flowers. Pretty violet-blue to near white flowers with showy stamens develop in early spring. Grow in shade and in well-drained, humus-rich soil that does not dry out. Use for woodlands, raised beds, retaining walls, rock-strewn slopes. Species are similar.	Divide clumps in early fall or after flowering. Fresh seeds can be sown in fall for germination in spring. Self-sows.
H. acutiloba	H 6-9 in. S 6-10 in.		
H. nobilis, or *H. triloba*	H 4-9 in. S 9-12 in.		
H. transsilvanica, or *H. angulosa*	H 4-6 in. S 10 in.		
Hosta, or Plantain lily, see pp. 252 and 382			
Houseleek, see Sempervivum			
Hypericum, or Saint-John's-wort *(Hypericum)*		Procumbent shrublets, mostly evergreen in mild climates. Showy golden yellow flowers with prominent stamens appear in early to mid summer. Grow in sun and in well-drained soil. Once planted, avoid disturbing roots. Use for crevices and deep soil pockets in walls and rock gardens; also good for use in paving, screes, and on sunny slopes.	Take cuttings in early summer; root in sand-peat moss mixture. Can also be grown from seeds, when available.
H. coris	H 6-12 in. S 12 in.		
H. olympicum	H 9-12 in. S 12 in.		
H. polyphyllum	H 6 in. S 12 in.		
H. rhodopeum	H 5 in. S 8 in.		
Iris *(Iris)*		Mat-forming perennials with grasslike foliage. Dainty flowers, miniature replicas of large garden irises, are displayed from early spring to early summer. Crested *I. cristata* and beardless *I. verna* have lilac-blue flowers; both grow well in partial shade and in humus-rich soil. *I. gracilipes,* an exquisite Japanese crested species, has 1-in. pinkish flowers with wavy orange crests. Tiny, bearded *I. pumila* blooms in early spring; named varieties are available in wide range of colors. *I. ruthenica,* an Apogon iris, has fragrant white flowers dotted with blue. All grow best in full sun and in rich, well-drained soil. See also "Irises," p. 337.	Divide and transplan[illegible] after flowering. Wat[illegible] until established. Iri[illegible] can be grown from [illegible] plant in fall for spri[illegible] germination.
I. cristata	H 3-4 in. S 12 in.		
I. gracilipes	H 8-10 in. S 8 in.		
I. pumila	H 3 in. S 6-8 in.		
I. ruthenica	H 6-8 in. S 8 in.		
I. verna	H 10 in. S 10 in.		

Jeffersonia dubia

Lewisia cotyledon

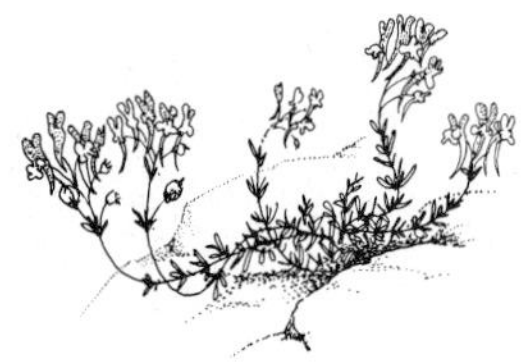

Linaria alpina

Linum perenne alpinum

Lithospermum diffusum

Lychnis alpina

Myosotis alpestris

Common and botanical names	Height and spread	Decorative characteristics, special requirements, and remarks	Propagation
Jeffersonia, or Twinleaf *(Jeffersonia)*		Perennials with distinctive kidney- or heart-shaped leaves in pairs. Pretty anemonelike white flowers (blue in the rare Asiatic *J. dubia)* appear in midspring. Grow in partial shade and in humus-rich soil. Good plant for woodlands, shaded rock gardens.	Divide in early spring after foliage dies down, soon after flowering. Sow fresh seeds in late summer; germination slow.
J. diphylla	H 10 in. S 8 in.		
J. dubia	H 6 in. S 4-5 in.		
Lady's-mantle, see Alchemilla **Lamium,** see p. 253			
Lewisia *(Lewisia)*		Fleshy-rooted perennials with rosettes of succulent leaves. Beautiful wax-textured flowers of pink, apricot, or white are borne in late spring. Grow in sun or partial (midday) shade. Requires well-drained, deep soil (half sharp sand or fine gravel and half loam and leaf-mold mixture) and stone-chip mulch. Difficult to grow outside their western North American habitat. Grow in rock crevices, screes, any site that has spring moisture and dry, cool summers.	Root crown offsets in peat moss and sand after flowering. Will grow from fresh seeds but may not germinate for a year.
L. brachycalyx	H 2-3 in. S 6-9 in.		
L. cotyledon	H 8-10 in. S 6 in.		
L. rediviva (bitter root)	H 4-6 in. S 4-8 in.		
L. tweedyi	H 4-6 in. S 9 in.		
Linaria, or Toadflax *(Linaria)* *L. alpina* (alpine toadflax)	H 3-9 in. S 12 in.	Trailing perennial with blue-green leaves. Small purple and yellow flowers like snapdragons are displayed all summer. Grow in sun or partial shade, in well-drained soil. Use for walls.	Sow seeds in spring. Short-lived but established plants self-sow freely.
Linum, or Flax *(Linum)* *L. perenne alpinum* (alpine flax)	H 4-10 in. S 8 in.	Perennial with narrow gray-blue leaves. Pretty blue flowers are borne in early summer. Grow in sun and in well-drained soil in rock garden. For *L. flavum* and *L. narbonnense,* see p. 254.	Easily increased by fresh seeds; plant in final position as seedlings.
Lithospermum *(Lithospermum)*		Prostrate shrublet with clusters of trumpet-shaped flowers in late spring. Grow in sun and in well-drained, humus-rich soil with limestone chips. Use in dry walls, deep soil pockets. *L. diffusum* has evergreen leaves and deep blue flowers. *L. oleifolium* is deciduous, with whitish, silky leaves and violet flowers.	Root cuttings in summer in peat moss and sand.
L. diffusum	H 8-12 in. S 12-15 in.		
L. oleifolium	H 6 in. S 12 in.		
Lychnis, or Campion *(Lychnis)* *L. alpina*	H 4 in. S 4 in.	Perennials with tufts of narrow leaves. Rose-purple flower heads open in early summer. Grow in sun or partial shade, in average rock-garden soil. Good for screes, paving, containers, alpine houses.	Easy to grow from seeds sown in midsummer.
Mertensia, see p. 255			
[illegible]osotis, or Forget-me-not *([illegible]otis)* *[illegible]tris,* or *M. rupicola*	H 2-6 in. S 4-6 in.	Dainty perennial with short heads of bright blue flowers in early summer. Grow in sun or partial shade, in well-drained, gritty soil that retains moisture. Short-lived plants for use in screes, paving, containers, alpine houses.	Sow seeds in late summer for flowering plants in 2 yr. Also divide by separating foliage rosettes.

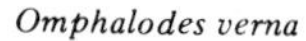
Omphalodes verna

Partridgeberry (*Mitchella repens*)

Pasqueflower (*Anemone pulsatilla*)

Penstemon fruticosus scouleri

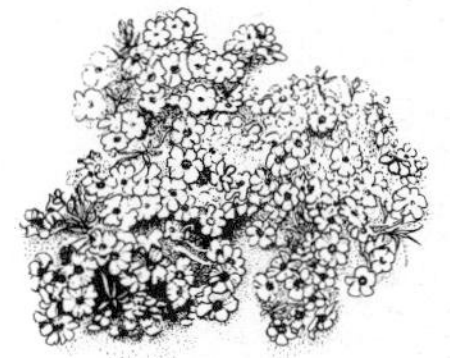
Phlox subulata

Common and botanical names	Height and spread	Decorative characteristics, special requirements, and remarks	Propagation
Nepeta, see p. 256			
Omphalodes *(Omphalodes)* *O. verna*	H 8 in. S 12 in.	Trailing perennial with fine-textured foliage, evergreen in the South. Bright blue flowers, ½ in. across, appear in early spring. Grow in partial shade and in humus-rich soil. Useful plant for ground cover, woodlands, dry walls.	Divide rooted stems in spring or after flowering. Will grow from seeds, but they are rarely offered.
Pansy, see p. 303 **Papaver**, see Poppy			
Partridgeberry, or Twinberry *(Mitchella)* *M. repens*	H 3 in. S 24 in.	Spreading shrublet with small evergreen leaves veined with white. Exquisite tubular white or pink-tinged flowers in late spring are followed by pairs of long-lasting red berries. Grow in shade, in humus-rich soil. Useful ground cover for raised beds, woodlands.	Divide mats after flowering; keep moist until established. Root cuttings in peat moss and sand mixture.
Pasqueflower, or Anemone *(Anemone,* or *Pulsatilla)* *A. pulsatilla,* or *P. vulgaris*	H 8 in. S 12 in.	Perennial with deeply divided leaves, covered with silky hairs. Handsome cup-shaped flowers of white, blue, lavender, purple, or pink appear in spring preceding the leaves. As flowers fade, stems elongate and fuzzy, decorative seed heads form. Grow in sun or partial shade, in humus-rich, well-drained soil. For other anemones, see p. 240.	Sow fresh seeds thinly in late spring; transplant to final position the following spring. Root cuttings can also be made in late spring.
Penstemon, or Beardtongue *(Penstemon)* *P. davidsonii menziesii* *P. fruticosus scouleri* *P. pinifolius* *P. rupicola*	H 4-6 in. S 15-20 in. H 10-18 in. S 19 in. H 8-12 in. S 12 in. H 4-5 in. S 12 in.	Low or prostrate shrublets with evergreen foliage. Showy tubular flowers. Grow in sunny site protected from midday sun. Requires well-drained, gritty soil. Difficult plants; grow in walls, crevices, screes. *P. d. menziesii* has deep blue flowers in early summer; *P. f. scouleri* has purple flowers in early summer; *P. pinifolius* has needlelike leaves, red flowers in midsummer; *P. rupicola* has rose-red flowers during summer.	Take cuttings in summer. Seeds are slow to germinate, sometimes requiring 1 yr. or longer.
Phlox *(Phlox)* *P. bifida* (sand phlox)	H 10 in. S 10-12 in.	Perennial with showy flowers from early to late spring. Forms loose cushion of woody stems; flowers of white to violet-blue in late spring. Grow in full sun and in sandy soil.	Divide *P. pilosa, P. stolonifera,* and *P. subulata* by separating clumps or mats in early spring or after flowering. *P. bifida* is best increased by layering.
P. pilosa	H 10-12 in. S 15 in.	White, pink, or rose-purple flowers borne in small clumps. Grow in partial shade or sun, in average soil.	
P. stolonifera (creeping phlox)	H 8-10 in. S 15-20 in.	Rose-pink to lavender flowers. Grow in partial shade and in humus-rich soil.	
P. subulata (moss pink, or ground pink)	H 3-6 in. S 20 in.	Star-shaped flowers in many shades of pink, rose, red, purple, blue, or white. Evergreen. Grow in full sun and in well-drained soil. For perennial *P. divaricata,* see p. 257.	

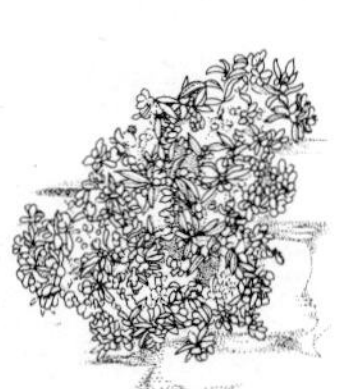
Polygala chamaebuxus

Alpine poppy (*Papaver alpinum*)

Potentilla nitida

Primrose (*Primula auricula*)

Ramonda myconi

Common and botanical names	Height and spread	Decorative characteristics, special requirements, and remarks	Propagation
Pink, see Dianthus			
Polygala, or Milkwort *(Polygala)* *P. chamaebuxus*	H 6-12 in. S 9-12 in.	Spreading shrublet with small evergreen leaves. Pretty, two-toned yellow flowers are produced in early summer. Grow in partial shade and in humus-rich soil. Protect in winter. Useful plant for shrub foregrounds, rocky slopes.	Sow fresh seeds. Take stem or root cuttings in midsummer; root in peat moss and sand mixture.
Poppy *(Papaver)* *P. alpinum* (alpine poppy)	H 4-10 in. S 4-10 in.	Perennial with finely cut foliage. Delicate flowers in wide color range appear in early summer. Grow in sun and in well-drained, gravelly soil with added humus. Mulch with stone chips. Use for retaining walls, paving, screes, or containers.	Scatter seeds in early spring or fall where they are to flower; roots are too fragile to move. Self-sows.
Potentilla, or Cinquefoil *(Potentilla)* *P. alba* (white cinquefoil)	H 8-10 in. S 12-15 in.	Annual or perennial with compound foliage of 3-5 leaflets. Single, 5-petaled flowers. Grow in sun and in well-drained soil. Good for dry walls, paving, screes. *P. alba* has silky leaflets, bears white flowers in early summer. *P. aurea* has yellow flowers in early spring on cushions of dark green foliage. *P. nitida* has pale pink flowers in early summer above mats of silk-textured foliage. *P. tormentillo-formosa* is annual, with trailing stems; apricot flowers in late summer. *P. tridentata* has glossy semi-evergreen foliage, which is red in fall; small white flowers in midsummer.	Divide mats or clumps in early spring or after flowering in late summer. Can also be grown from seeds. Many self-sow.
P. aurea, or *P. verna aurea*	H 6 in. S 6-8 in.		
P. nitida	H 1-3 in. S 12 in.		
P. tormentillo-formosa, or *P. tonguei*	H 8 in. S 24 in.		
P. tridentata (wineleaf cinquefoil)	H 2-12 in. S 12-24 in.		
Primrose *(Primula)* *P. auricula*	H 6-8 in. S 6-10 in.	Perennial with foliage in clumps, rosettes, or tufts. Handsome, bright flowers appear in spring. Grow in partial shade and in fertile, humus-rich soil. Good for woodlands, shrub foregrounds, dry walls, alpine houses, screes. *P. auricula* has richly colored flowers, some fragrant, many with contrasting "eyes." *P. juliae* bears flowers of rose, red, or crimson on tufted dwarf plants; many hybrids. *P. polyantha* has vivid color range of flowers. *P. sieboldii* has white, pink, or rose flowers and soft-textured scalloped leaves. *P. vulgaris* has solitary yellow flowers; many strains and hybrids in shades of blue, pink, red, and white. See also pp. 258 and 382.	Plants require division every 3-4 yr. to maintain vitality. After flowering, lift plants and pull apart, replanting divisions in humus-enriched soil. Sow fresh seeds in midsummer, or sow in fall for spring germination, which may be uneven and slow.
P. juliae	H 3 in. S 6 in.		
	H 10-12 in. S 10-12 in.		
	H 6-9 in. S 9-10 in.		
aulis	H 6-9 in. S 6-15 in.		
da)	H 4-6 in. S 9 in.	Perennial with rosettes of hairy leaves. Clusters of lavender-blue flowers with gold stamens appear in early summer. Grow in shade and in moist, humus-rich soil. Wall crevices. *R. myconi* has hairier leaves; flowers are 5-petaled rather than 4-petaled.	As with African violets, separate multicrowned plants; take leaf-stem cuttings; sow seeds.
	H 4 in. S 6-8 in.		

Box sand myrtle (*Leiophyllum buxifolium*)

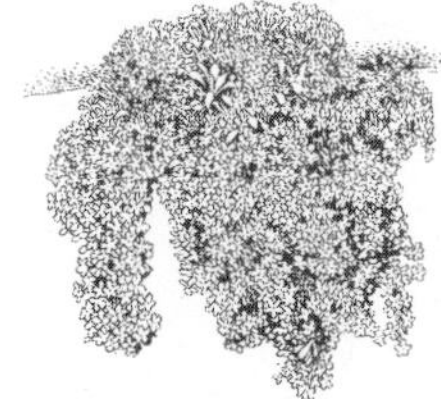
Saponaria ocymoides

Saxifrage (*Saxifraga grisebachii*)

Saxifrage (*Saxifraga umbrosa*)

Sedum sieboldii

Common and botanical names	Height and spread	Decorative characteristics, special requirements, and remarks	Propagation
Rockrose, see Helianthemum **Rue anemone,** see Anemonella **Saint-John's-wort,** see Hypericum			
Sand myrtle *(Leiophyllum)* *L. buxifolium* (box sand myrtle)	H 10-12 in. S 18 in.	Slow-growing shrub with small, shiny evergreen leaves that turn brownish green in autumn. Tight clusters of pink or white flowers are formed in late spring. Grow in sun or partial shade, in sandy loam enriched with peat moss. Good plant for seaside areas, tolerant of salt spray.	Sow seeds under glass in early spring. Take semi-hard-shoot cuttings in mid-summer, or propagate by layering.
Saponaria, or Rock soapwort *(Saponaria)* *S. ocymoides*	H 3 in. S 6-12 in.	Trailing perennial with sprays of small but showy pink flowers in late spring. Grow in sun and in well-drained soil that offers deep, cool haven to taproots. Cut back immediately after flowering. Traditional wall and rock plant; use also for paving, alpine houses.	Sow seeds in spring; transplant seedlings to permanent sites when young. Take cuttings to increase superior forms.
Saxifrage, or Rockfoil *(Saxifraga)* *S. apiculata* *S. cotyledon* *S. grisebachii* *S. longifolia* *S. moschata* *S. sarmentosa,* or *S. stolonifera* (strawberry begonia) *S. umbrosa* (London pride)	H 4 in. S 12-18 in. H 24 in. S 12-15 in. H 6-9 in. S 9-12 in. H 18 in. S 12 in. H 1-3 in. S 12-18 in. H 24 in. S 12-18 in. H 12 in. S 12-18 in.	Creeping cushion- or rosette-forming perennial with silvery or variegated foliage, varying in form from mosslike to succulent. Flowers of white, pink, purple, or yellow appear from late spring to early summer. Grow in sun or partial shade and in well-drained, gritty soil (add leaf mold or peat moss for *S. sarmentosa* and *S. umbrosa).* Versatile plants adaptable to retaining walls, rock cracks and crevices, paving, screes, containers, and alpine houses (especially *S. apiculata* and *S. grisebachii). S. sarmentosa* requires winter protection in North; useful in woodland gardens; may be listed in catalogs as strawberry geranium.	Separate and plant rooted rosettes after flowering; unrooted rosettes can be started earlier in moist sand. Divide some species after flowering, including *S. cotyledon, S. longifolia,* and *S. sarmentosa.* Sow seeds in pots of gritty soil containing some loam mixed with leaf mold or peat moss; flowering plants should be produced in about 3 yr.
Sedum, or Stonecrop *(Sedum)* *S. cauticolum* *S. dasyphyllum* *S. ewersii* *S. sieboldii*	H 3-8 in. S 10-24 in. H 1-2 in. S 12 in. H 4-12 in. S 12-15 in. H 6-9 in. S 12 in.	Spreading perennial with succulent foliage. Easy to grow in sun and in well-drained soil. Useful for walls, paving, ground cover. *S. cauticolum* has grayish foliage; bears rosy red flower clusters in midsummer. *S. dasyphyllum* forms mats of gray-blue foliage; has pink flowers in early summer. *S. ewersii* is neat and shrublike, with gray-green leaves; has pink flowers in late summer. *S. sieboldii* has gray leaves on arching branches; displays pink flowers in late summer and fall.	Division in spring or summer is quickest method of increasing sedums.

Sempervivum arachnoideum

Shortia uniflora

Silene acaulis

Soldanella alpina

Thalictrum kiusianum

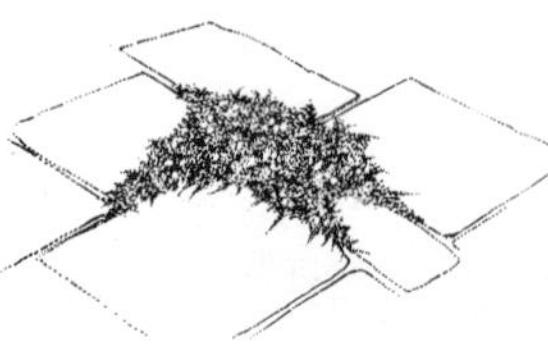

Mother of thyme (*Thymus serpyllum*)

Common and botanical names	Height and spread	Decorative characteristics, special requirements, and remarks	Propagation
Sempervivum, or Houseleek (*Sempervivum*) *S. arachnoideum* (cobweb houseleek) *S. fauconnettii* *S. globiferum* *S. tectorum* (hens and chickens)	H 1-4 in. S 12 in. H 8 in. S 10-12 in. H 6-12 in. S 10 in. H 2-3 in. S 12 in.	Spreading perennial forming small rosettes of succulent foliage. Panicles of star-shaped flowers appear in summer. Grow in sun and in well-drained rock-garden soil. Useful for planting between rock crevices, on ledges, walls, and paving. *S. arachnoideum* is outstanding rock plant, its rosettes connected by gray threads; bears showy rose-red flowers. *S. fauconnettii* has red- and purple-tinged foliage, bright red flowers. *S. globiferum* has pale yellow flowers. *S. tectorum* has gray leaves, pink flowers. Many hybrids and varieties available.	Easily divided by detaching offshoot rosettes when they form. Seeds may or may not produce true to type.
Shortia (*Shortia*) *S. galacifolia* (Oconee bells) *S. uniflora* (Nippon bells)	H 6-8 in. S 1-3 ft. H 6-8 in. S 12-14 in.	Creeping perennial with handsome evergreen foliage. Bell-shaped flowers of white, rose, or pink arise in midspring. Grow in shade, in moist, humus-rich soil. Mulch with oak leaves over winter. Good choice for shady gardens, foreground of shrubs.	Divide after flowering; keep moist until established. Treat sparse-rooted sections as cuttings in moist peat moss and sand.
Silene, or Campion (*Silene*) *S. acaulis* (moss campion) *S. alpestris* (alpine catchfly) *S. schafta*	H 2 in. S 12-18 in. H 6-8 in. S 8 in. H 6-16 in. S 6-10 in.	Fleshy-rooted perennial forming cushions, tufts, or clumps of narrow, pointed leaves. Five-petaled, notched flowers of pink, red, or white are borne in early to late summer. Grow in sun and in deep, well-drained, gritty soil. *S. acaulis* has reddish-purple flowers, does best in tight rock crevices. White-flowered *S. alpestris* and pink-flowered *S. schafta* fairly easy to grow under most rock-garden conditions.	Divide clumps for *S. acaulis, S. alpestris,* and *S. schafta.* Root stem cuttings of *S. acaulis,* in sand and peat moss in summer. Also sow seeds for all species.
Soldanella (*Soldanella*) *S. alpina* *S. montana*	H 3-6 in. S 9 in. H 6 in. S 12 in.	Perennial with kidney-shaped or rounded leathery leaves. Pretty lavender-blue flowers, heavily fringed, appear in early spring. Rare, difficult alpines need light, humus-rich soil with underground moisture. Mulch with stone chips; give winter protection in snowless areas. For alpine houses.	Divide clumps after flowering, or sow fresh seeds as soon as they are ripe.
Stonecrop, see Sedum			
Thalictrum, or Meadow rue (*Thalictrum*) *T. alpinum* *T. kiusianum*	H 6-8 in. S 12-14 in. H 2-8 in. S 10-12 in.	Perennial with graceful ferny foliage. Displays petalless flowers with yellow or rose stamens in midsummer. Grow in partial shade. Provide moist, rocky soil for *T. alpinum;* well-drained, humus-rich soil for *T. kiusianum.* Use for ground cover or in woodlands, raised beds, retaining walls.	Clumps are easily divided in early spring or early fall.
Thyme, mother of (*Thymus*) *T. serpyllum*	H 1-3 in. S 24 in.	Carpeting perennial or shrublet with small aromatic evergreen leaves. Rose-purple flowers bloom from early to late summer. Grow in sun and well-drained soil. Use for paving, dry walls.	Divide clumps, or cut off rooted runners. Plants self-sow freely.

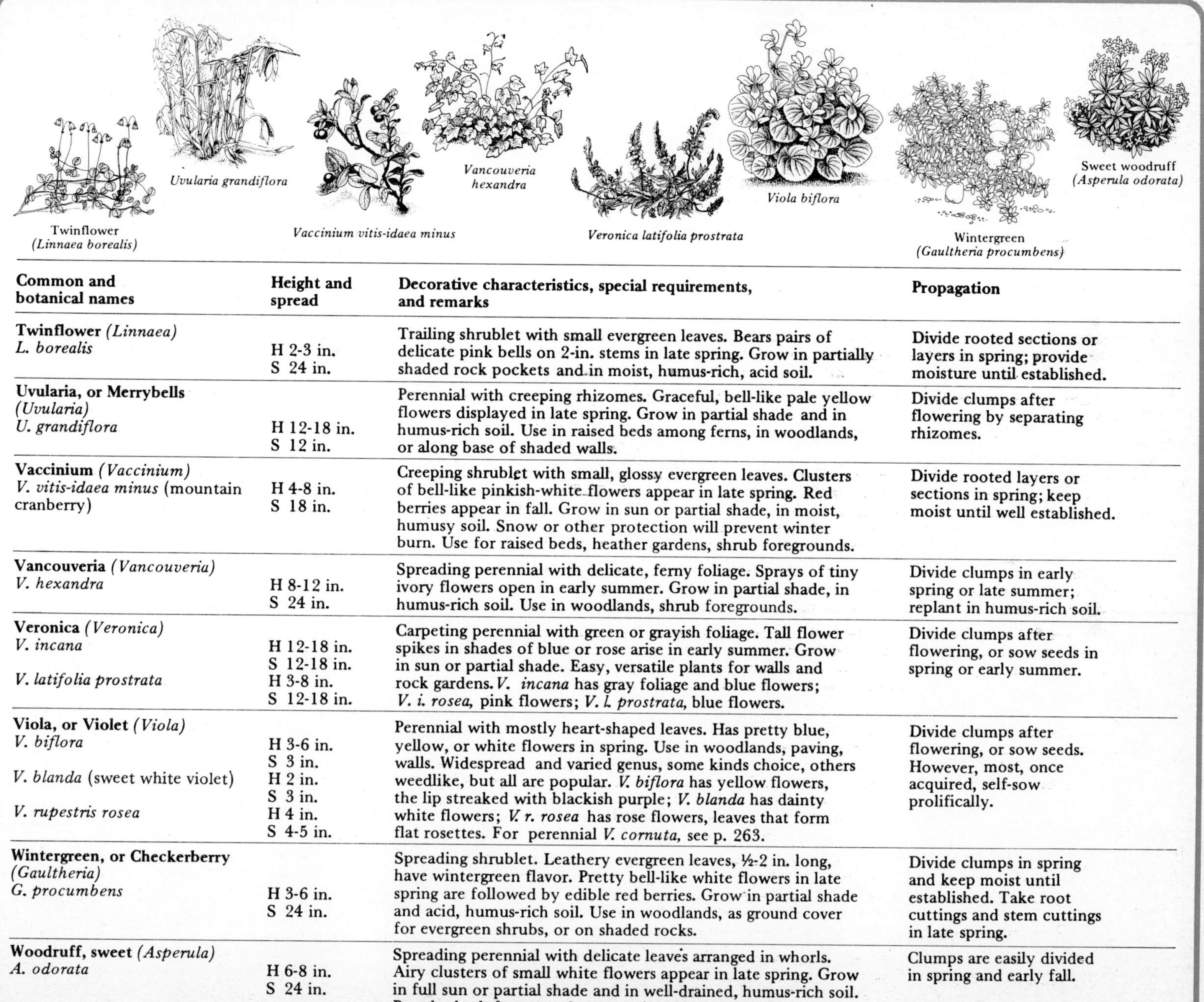

Common and botanical names	Height and spread	Decorative characteristics, special requirements, and remarks	Propagation
Twinflower *(Linnaea)* *L. borealis*	H 2-3 in. S 24 in.	Trailing shrublet with small evergreen leaves. Bears pairs of delicate pink bells on 2-in. stems in late spring. Grow in partially shaded rock pockets and in moist, humus-rich, acid soil.	Divide rooted sections or layers in spring; provide moisture until established.
Uvularia, or Merrybells *(Uvularia)* *U. grandiflora*	H 12-18 in. S 12 in.	Perennial with creeping rhizomes. Graceful, bell-like pale yellow flowers displayed in late spring. Grow in partial shade and in humus-rich soil. Use in raised beds among ferns, in woodlands, or along base of shaded walls.	Divide clumps after flowering by separating rhizomes.
Vaccinium *(Vaccinium)* *V. vitis-idaea minus* (mountain cranberry)	H 4-8 in. S 18 in.	Creeping shrublet with small, glossy evergreen leaves. Clusters of bell-like pinkish-white flowers appear in late spring. Red berries appear in fall. Grow in sun or partial shade, in moist, humusy soil. Snow or other protection will prevent winter burn. Use for raised beds, heather gardens, shrub foregrounds.	Divide rooted layers or sections in spring; keep moist until well established.
Vancouveria *(Vancouveria)* *V. hexandra*	H 8-12 in. S 24 in.	Spreading perennial with delicate, ferny foliage. Sprays of tiny ivory flowers open in early summer. Grow in partial shade, in humus-rich soil. Use in woodlands, shrub foregrounds.	Divide clumps in early spring or late summer; replant in humus-rich soil.
Veronica *(Veronica)* *V. incana* *V. latifolia prostrata*	H 12-18 in. S 12-18 in. H 3-8 in. S 12-18 in.	Carpeting perennial with green or grayish foliage. Tall flower spikes in shades of blue or rose arise in early summer. Grow in sun or partial shade. Easy, versatile plants for walls and rock gardens. *V. incana* has gray foliage and blue flowers; *V. i. rosea,* pink flowers; *V. l. prostrata,* blue flowers.	Divide clumps after flowering, or sow seeds in spring or early summer.
Viola, or Violet *(Viola)* *V. biflora* *V. blanda* (sweet white violet) *V. rupestris rosea*	H 3-6 in. S 3 in. H 2 in. S 3 in. H 4 in. S 4-5 in.	Perennial with mostly heart-shaped leaves. Has pretty blue, yellow, or white flowers in spring. Use in woodlands, paving, walls. Widespread and varied genus, some kinds choice, others weedlike, but all are popular. *V. biflora* has yellow flowers, the lip streaked with blackish purple; *V. blanda* has dainty white flowers; *V. r. rosea* has rose flowers, leaves that form flat rosettes. For perennial *V. cornuta,* see p. 263.	Divide clumps after flowering, or sow seeds. However, most, once acquired, self-sow prolifically.
Wintergreen, or Checkerberry *(Gaultheria)* *G. procumbens*	H 3-6 in. S 24 in.	Spreading shrublet. Leathery evergreen leaves, ½-2 in. long, have wintergreen flavor. Pretty bell-like white flowers in late spring are followed by edible red berries. Grow in partial shade and acid, humus-rich soil. Use in woodlands, as ground cover for evergreen shrubs, or on shaded rocks.	Divide clumps in spring and keep moist until established. Take root cuttings and stem cuttings in late spring.
Woodruff, sweet *(Asperula)* *A. odorata*	H 6-8 in. S 24 in.	Spreading perennial with delicate leaves arranged in whorls. Airy clusters of small white flowers appear in late spring. Grow in full sun or partial shade and in well-drained, humus-rich soil. Popular herb for ground cover, raised beds, dry walls.	Clumps are easily divided in spring and early fall.

Water Plants

The sight and sound of water, the colorful fish and varied plants water can support, and the vitality of the birds that come to drink add welcome life to any garden.

Making a water garden is a fascinating adventure. The smallest garden can have a pool or a waterfall, and even a city terrace or balcony can probably accommodate a container large enough to sustain a water lily, some smaller plants, and two or three fish. Pygmy water lilies can be used for extrasmall spaces, as they will thrive in a container only 2–3 feet across and equally deep.

In a city garden there will often be space to sink a preformed pool of fiberglass into the ground. Then, with the aid of a small submersible pump connected to an electrical outlet, a fountain or waterfall can be created. The same water is used over and over again; so the only running cost is for electricity—a small pump uses about as much energy as one 75-watt light bulb.

Larger gardens, of course, provide greater scope. Water can be used with rocks to form a pool. Or a cascading chain of pools connected by a running stream can be created with the aid of a pump. The same pump can be adapted to make a fountain or a decorative spray in a variety of patterns or even to handle several different features simultaneously.

Concrete pools are rarely built anymore. They tend to develop leaks as the soil settles beneath them and, in cold climates, to crack from

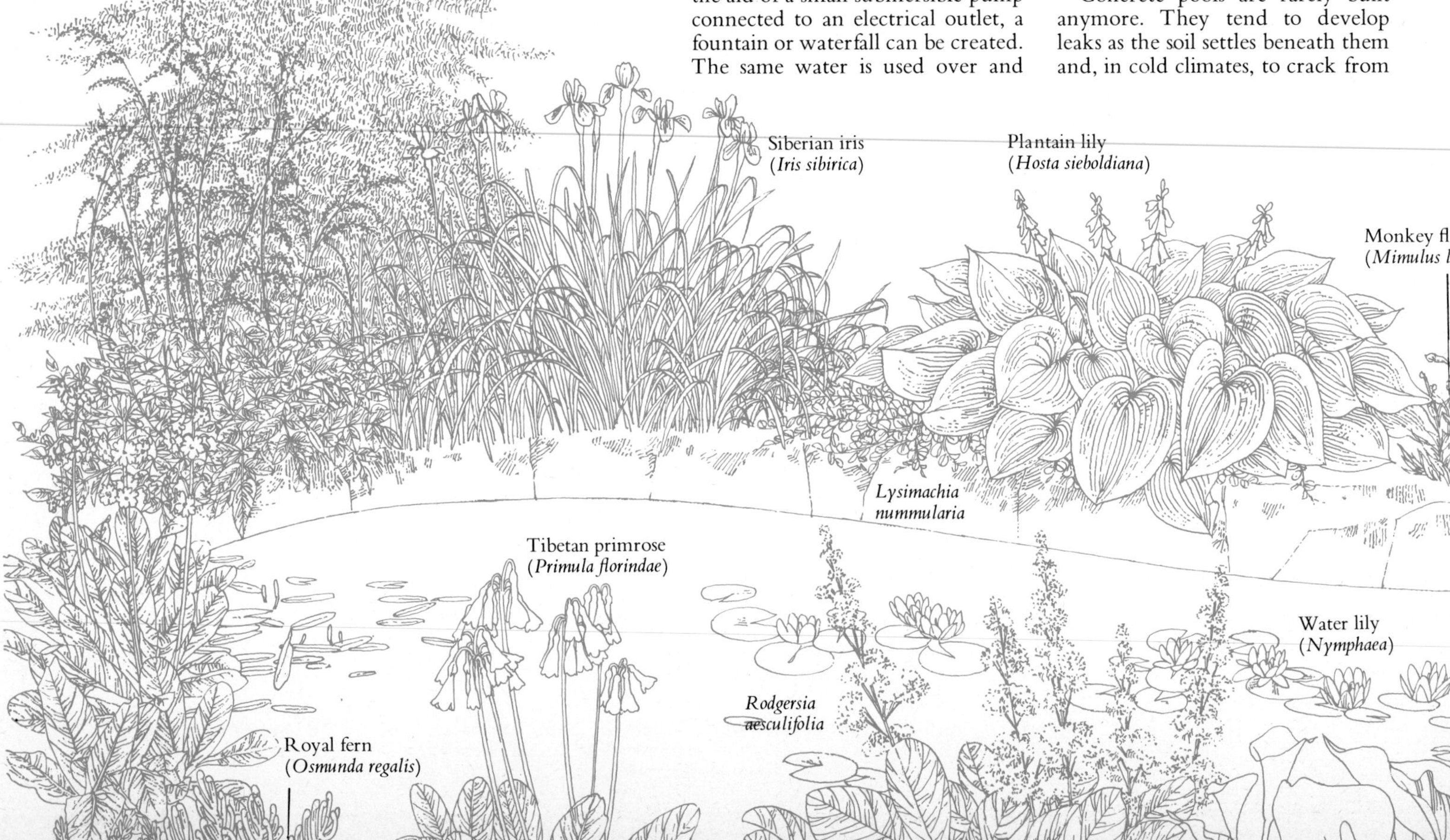

alternate freezing and thawing. Most pools today are built with preformed fiberglass shells or heavy-duty plastic liners, designed specifically for the purpose. Plastic liners are also used to line existing concrete pools that have been damaged. Liner material is available from garden-supply mail-order catalogs and water-garden specialists in sizes suitable for pools of almost any dimension.

One of the great pleasures of water gardening is growing a wide variety of unusual plants. Elegant day-blooming and night-blooming water lilies—the undisputed aristocrats of water plants—can be cultivated in the deep water of a pool. So can the fascinating oxygenating plants, some of which float on the surface of the water and others of which grow completely underwater. Several interesting plants—including one of the most dramatic of all plants, the lotus—thrive in the shallow water around the edges of a pool. And finally, a large group of attractive bog plants do well in the moist soil adjacent to a pool or stream.

All water gardens need plenty of light if the plants are to flower. No more than one-half to two-thirds of the surface of a pool should be covered by lily pads or other plants. The patches of open water will reflect the sky, sparkle in the sunlight, ripple in the wind, and reveal the movement of the fish.

To keep the water in a pool clear, a balance between plant and animal life must be established and maintained. If this is not done, the pool will become murky and foul smelling, and fish will die.

The cause of murky water is algae, microscopic plants that thrive in sunlight and feed on mineral salts in the water. Most of these mineral salts are produced by the breakdown of organic material, such as leaves, twigs, and other debris. It is therefore essential to keep the pool free of leaves and to be quite sure that the soil on the bottom contains no compost or peat moss.

It is, of course, impossible to keep all foreign organic material out of a pool, but the water can be kept clear by growing oxygenating plants. These plants starve out algae by taking up the mineral salts themselves, and they create shady pockets that diminish the sunlight algae need.

In addition to controlling algae, oxygenating plants take in the carbon dioxide given off by animal life in the pool and—as their name implies—release oxygen into the water. Thus, an efficient cycle is established, plants and animals each making use of the other's waste products.

Fish not only enhance the appearance of a water garden but they also keep down the mosquito population by feeding on the larvae. They consume snail eggs, aphids, and caddisworms, and eat a certain amount of algae and submerged vegetable debris. The most satisfactory fish for garden pools are the common goldfish, the comet, the shubunkin, various kinds of fantail, and the golden orfe. These fish are brightly colored, stay near the surface, and can be trained to come for food.

Most dealers in fish also sell snails and tadpoles, which help keep a pool clean by eating algae. Tadpoles eat other debris as well, and they develop into frogs and toads—useful garden occupants that consume incredible numbers of insects.

Planning and Installing a Garden Pool

First, select a sunny, open spot within reach of your garden hose.

Decide on the shape of the pool, and mark the outline with rope. Avoid using narrow necks, dumbbell shapes, and crosses—all of which waste space. You may wish to have a ledge 6–8 inches below the surface for shallow-water plants. If so, place it so that tall plants, such as reeds, will not block the view of the pool.

The next step is to dig the pool and line it with plastic or install a preformed pool. Liners of polyvinyl chloride (PVC) come in 12-mil and 20-mil thicknesses. The heavier material is longer lived. PVC liners do not stand up well where winter temperatures fall much below −10° F. In such areas, the only practical choice may be a preformed pool.

Pools with plastic liners. To determine how much liner you will need, measure the maximum length and width of the pool, and add double the maximum depth to each of these figures. For example, for a pool 12 feet long, 6 feet wide, and 3 feet deep, you would need a piece of liner measuring 18 feet (12 plus 6) by 12 feet (6 plus 6). There is no need to make allowance for ledges or for overlap. The elasticity of the liner will provide sufficient surplus.

Dig a hole of the shape you have marked out, making the sides sloping rather than sharply vertical. If your pool is to include a shallow-water ledge, make sure that its surface is perfectly horizontal.

Span the pool with a plank, and use a spirit level on top of it to see that the ground is level all around the edges. If it is not, build it up with soil from the excavation.

Remove all sharp stones from the hole, and spread an inch of sand over the bottom. If the walls are rough, face them with damp sand.

Unfold the liner carefully in the hole, placing it so that at least 6 inches of material overlaps the edges. Weight this overlap down with bricks or smooth stones.

Run water slowly into the pool, pleating and tucking the liner for a neat finish. When the pool is filled, the water will hold the liner in place, so that the weights can be removed. Check the depth of the ledges; they can be adjusted by adding or removing sand beneath the liner.

Trim off any excess liner with a sharp knife, leaving a 6-inch overlap all around. Lay bricks or stones on the overlap so that they project 1–2 inches over the edges of the pool. When you are finished, no part of the liner should show.

Keep the pool filled. Direct sunlight will overheat the liner material and can cause it to deteriorate in a relatively short time.

Preformed pools. Dig a hole the shape of the pool but a few inches wider. Remove all stones from the base of the hole, pack the soil firmly, and cover with an inch of sand.

Lower the preformed pool into position. Span the pool with a plank, and place a spirit level on it to be sure the pool is level. Fill in the gap around the pool, and tamp the soil down firmly.

MAKING A GARDEN POOL FROM PLASTIC LINER

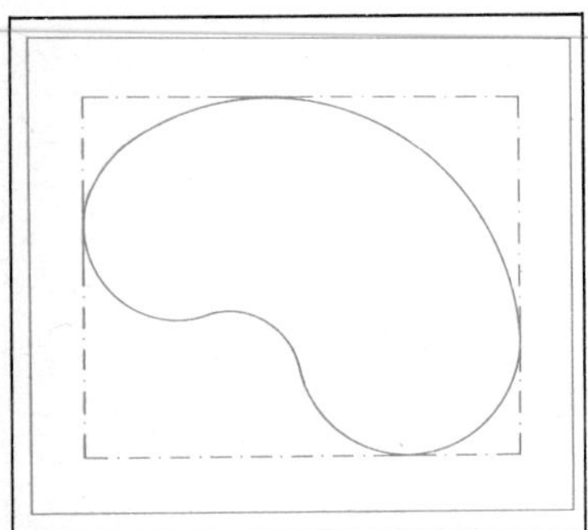

1. *Measure length and width; add double the maximum depth to each figure.*

2. *Dig the hole, making shallow-water shelves. Remove stones and put in sand.*

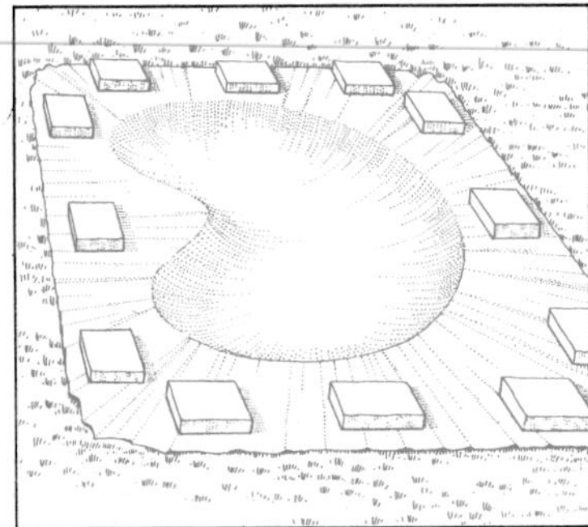

3. *Unfold liner in the hole, and hold it down with bricks or paving blocks.*

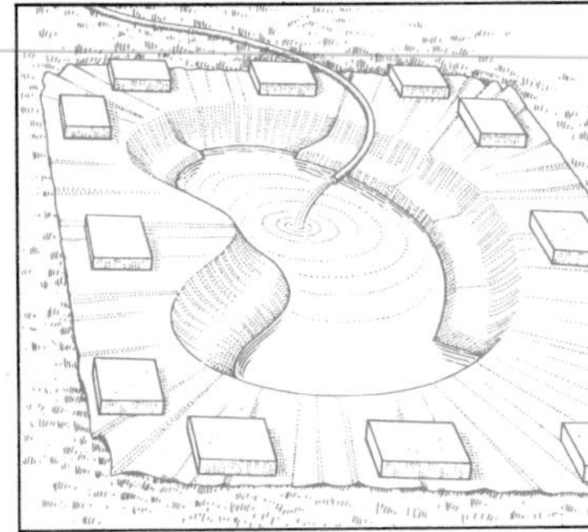

4. *Fill the pool slowly, allowing the liner to adapt to the shape of the hole.*

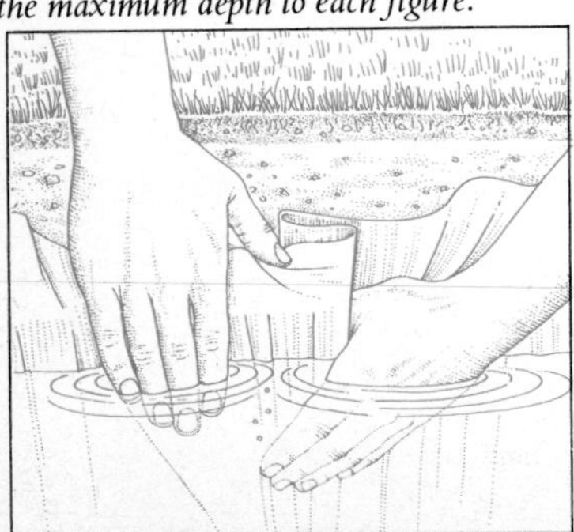

5. *Pleat the liner into shape. Add sand to shallow-water shelves if necessary.*

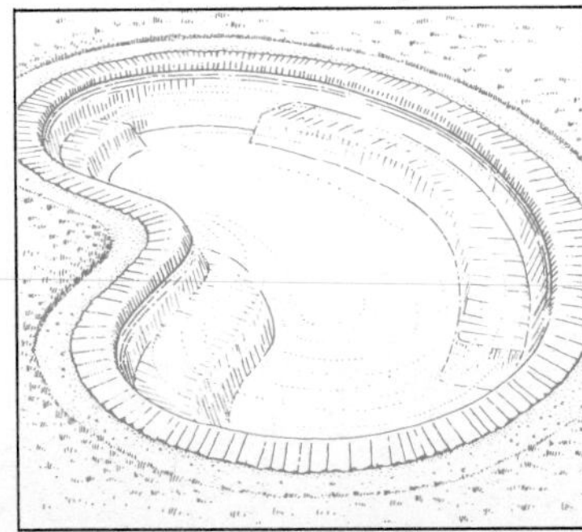

6. *When pool is full, remove weights. Trim liner edges to a 6-inch overlap.*

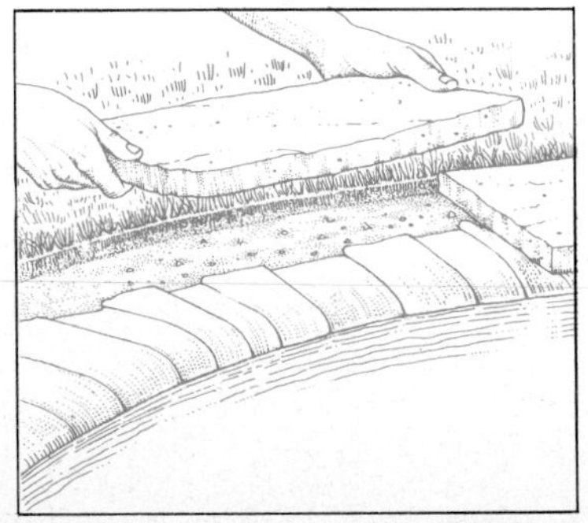

7. *Cover the edges with bricks, stones, or paving blocks, slightly overlapping pool.*

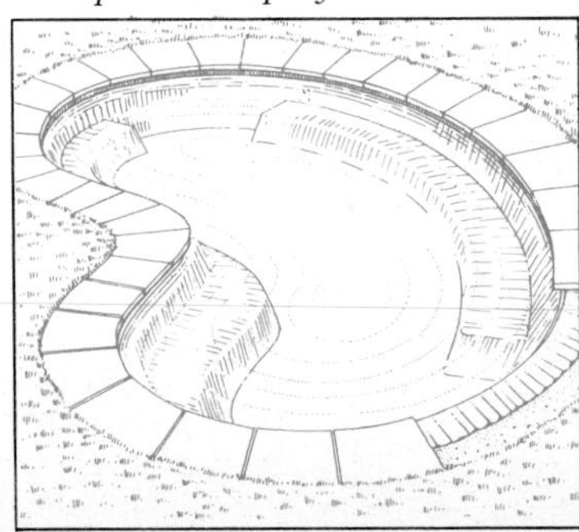

8. *Make sure that no part of the liner is visible when the pool is finished.*

Running Water in the Garden

Recirculating Water for a Fountain

A fountain, waterfall, cascade, or stream creates a lively effect in the garden and improves the oxygen content of the water in a pool.

The running water should be supplied by recirculating the water from the pool itself. Not only would it be wasteful to make a steady draw upon the public water supply but the use of cold tap water would inhibit the growth of plants and might destroy the pool's organic balance.

Two types of pump are available for recirculating water: submersible pumps and surface, or line, pumps. Both are normally powered by standard household electric current.

Submersible pumps sit on the bottom of the pool. They may have attachments mounted on top of them to power fountain jets or sprays, or they may supply waterfalls or streams. Some can be equipped to do both falls and sprays simultaneously.

Surface pumps are concealed near the pool. Water is drawn from the pool and delivered to various outlets through plastic tubing.

The capacity of a recirculating pump is expressed in gallons per hour (GPH) of flow. This figure decreases as the height to which the water is being raised increases. Thus, a pump that delivers about 200 GPH through a $\frac{1}{4}$-inch tube to a height of 1 foot (about the rate of the average kitchen faucet) will pump only 120 GPH to a height of 5 feet, and 78 GPH to a 6-foot waterfall. If the same pump was used to power a fountain, it could provide a steady jet of water up to 4 feet in height, depending on the fountainhead.

By limiting the height of a fountain jet to half the width of the pool, you can avoid splashing water out of the pool. The jet in a pool 4 feet wide, for example, should be no more than 24 inches high.

THE PUMP THAT POWERS THE FOUNTAIN

A fountain can easily be installed in a pool by using a submersible pump fitted with a fountain jet and driven by household electricity.

Building a Waterfall or Cascade

A waterfall is created by pumping water from the main pool to a small pool above it and then allowing the water to run down over a horizontal lip. A cascade is merely a series of small waterfall pools.

CURTAIN OF WATER

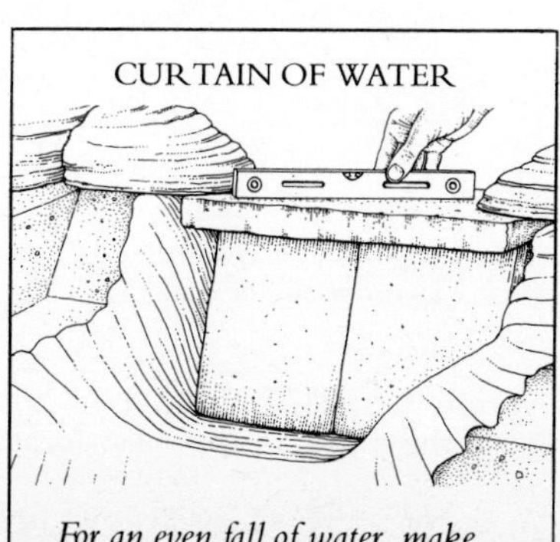

For an even fall of water, make the pouring lip absolutely level.

Preformed shells are available for making waterfall pools or cascades, or you can build your own shell from the same material that you use to line the pool.

For a cascade, cut out a series of steps about 4 inches deep, each of which will be a small pool. Cut shallow pouring lips in the appropriate places. Bury the tube from the pump beneath soil and rocks alongside this watercourse.

Cover the whole watercourse with a sheet of PVC, held in place with large stones along its edges. Use a large, flat rock to hide the vertical sheeting of each small waterfall. Lay a flat stone on the lip of each pool, slightly overhanging the drop, to produce a realistic waterfall effect. Fill in the watercourse with rounded pebbles or pea gravel to add to its natural appearance.

Do not try to grow rooted plants in waterfall pools; the running water will wash away the soil.

CROSS SECTION OF A CASCADE

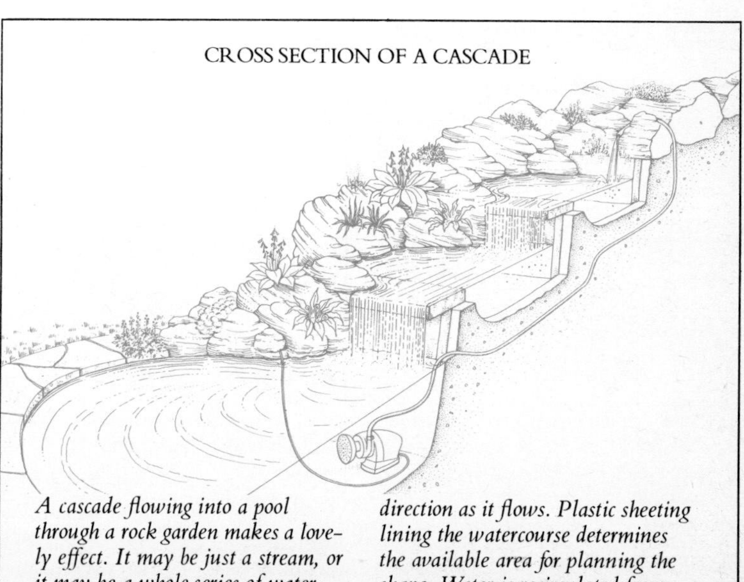

A cascade flowing into a pool through a rock garden makes a lovely effect. It may be just a stream, or it may be a whole series of waterfalls. For the most natural look, plan the cascade so that the water changes direction as it flows. Plastic sheeting lining the watercourse determines the available area for planning the shape. Water is recirculated from the pool to the top of the cascade by an electric pump.

Introducing Water Plants Into a Pool

Planting Water Lilies in Containers

The water lily (*Nymphaea*) is the deep-water flowering plant most often used in pools. There are two types: hardy water lilies with rhizomatous roots, which survive year after year if the roots can be kept from freezing; and tuberous-rooted tropicals, which must be treated as annuals in all but the warmest sections of the United States.

Both types can be bought as established plants in containers. In warm areas you can put them into the pool at any time. In colder areas wait until the water is dependably warm in late spring or early summer.

It is less expensive, however, to buy plants just starting into growth. The best time to plant hardy water lilies in this early stage of development is in midspring—if the weather is reasonably warm—or late spring. Tropicals should not be planted until you can be sure the water in the pool will not fall below 70° F.

Fill the pool at least one week before planting the hardy lilies and two weeks before planting tropicals. This will allow the water to dissipate the chlorine it may contain.

It is a good idea to plant water lilies in containers that can easily be lifted in and out of the pool. You can buy plastic baskets designed specifically for the purpose, or you can drill several $\frac{1}{4}$-inch holes in 12-inch plastic pots to make your own. Wooden boxes or tubs can also be used if several holes are drilled to allow water to circulate. All should be lined with clean, coarse burlap.

For planting soil, take some good, heavy loam from the garden and remove all obvious roots from it. Avoid organic materials, such as peat moss or compost, which will decompose in the water, clouding it, encouraging algae, and harming fish.

Into each bucket of soil, mix either a double handful of sterilized bone meal or a single handful of superphosphate. It is best to let this mixture soak in the pool for a day or two before planting in it. Failing this, moisten the soil with water from the pool. A compressed handful, when tossed in the air, should fall back into your hand without breaking into particles.

Hardy water lilies have sturdy white roots that are used for anchorage and thinner, hairy roots that are for feeding. In mid to late spring new leaf shoots, or growing points, will emerge from the rhizomes. Do not touch these shoots; they are sensitive and easily damaged.

If the nursery has not trimmed the rhizomes, or if they have been damaged in transit, use a sharp knife to cut off dead and broken leaves, and to remove all older brown anchorage roots. Cut back the new white roots to about $3\frac{1}{2}$–4 inches.

Place rhizomes horizontally into a container partly filled with the prepared soil mix. Top up with more moist soil so that the new leaf shoots protrude above the surface. Firm the soil with your fingers, adding more soil if necessary, but do not pack it down too tightly.

The tuberous-rooted tropicals also have thick, fleshy anchorage roots and finer, hairy feeders. Trim these in the same way you would trim the hardy varieties; then plant them vertically, with the roots going straight down; the soil should cover the base of the stems but not the crowns of the plants.

If there are to be fish in the pool, top-dress the container with a thin layer of coarse sand or pea gravel, to keep the fish from disturbing the roots of plants.

When putting hardy lilies into the pool, immerse the container until the soil surface is no more than 2 feet deep. In deeper pools put the container on stacked-up bricks. Lower it to the bottom (by removing bricks) at the rate of a foot per week.

When putting tropicals into the pool, immerse the container no more than a few inches for the first week or two. Then increase the depth to about 6 inches. Although this is the ideal depth, tropicals can survive at depths of up to 12 inches. But if water lilies are to grow that deep, lower them gradually, at the rate of 2–3 inches per week.

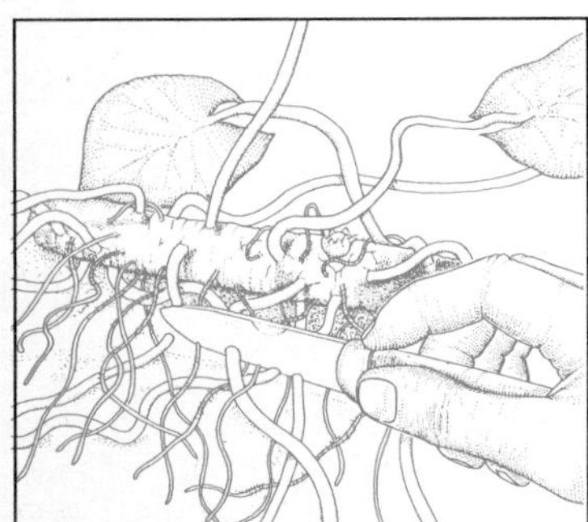

1. *Cut off all old brown roots, and trim new white roots to $3\frac{1}{2}$–4 in. long.*

2. *Plant in burlap-lined containers partly filled with moist, heavy soil.*

3. *Top-dress with coarse sand or pea gravel to protect plants from fish.*

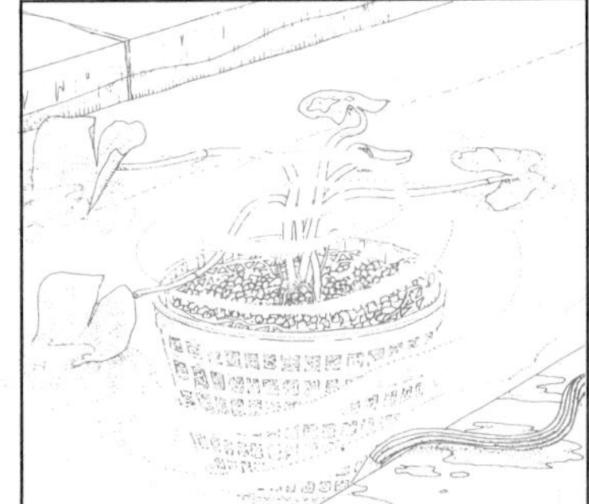

4. *Submerge the container so that the soil surface is just below the water.*

Annual Feedings of Bone Meal for Water Lilies

Water lilies will not last indefinitely in containers without the help of supplementary feeding at least once a year. In their limited environment the roots will soon extract the nourishment from the planting mixture.

The need for fertilizer is indicated by undersized and yellowing leaves, meager blossoms, and a general lack of vigor. Apart from repotting, the best way to improve this condition is to administer special water-plant food, which is available in granules or in tablet form.

You can also make bone-meal pills by mixing a 3-inch flowerpotful of sterilized bone meal with enough clay to bind it firmly. Roll this into two round pills. Lift the container, push the pills into the soil beneath the roots, and return the plant to the pool. For a large water lily, use two pills each spring. One pill should provide sufficient nourishment for a medium-sized water lily.

Edging the Pool With Shallow-Water Plants

A man-made pool looks more natural with some shallow-water plants, such as cattails and water chestnuts, growing around the edges. Pools can be designed with shelves to give these plants the 2–3 inches of water they need over their roots, or the containers holding them can be raised on bricks.

Plants such as the bog arum (*Calla palustris*), with creeping rhizomatous roots, should be planted in containers large enough to accommodate the rootstocks. First, remove dead leaves and old brown roots. Then place the rhizome horizontally on the soil, and use your fingers to pack the soil firmly, but not too tightly, around the roots. Leave the rhizome itself exposed. Cover the surface of the soil with coarse sand or pea gravel, and sink the container just deep enough so that the roots are covered by 2–3 inches of water.

For shallow-water plants with tuberous root systems, such as the pickerel rush (*Pontederia cordata*), begin by removing all dead or discolored leaves. Then trim back any large shoots with a sharp knife. Remove all of the old brown roots, and trim the remaining roots to a length of about 3 inches.

Make a hole in the soil just deep enough to insert the plant, with the roots going straight down and the soil rising to the base of the shoots. Pack the soil firmly around the plant, add coarse sand or pea gravel to the surface, and immerse it to a depth of 2–3 inches.

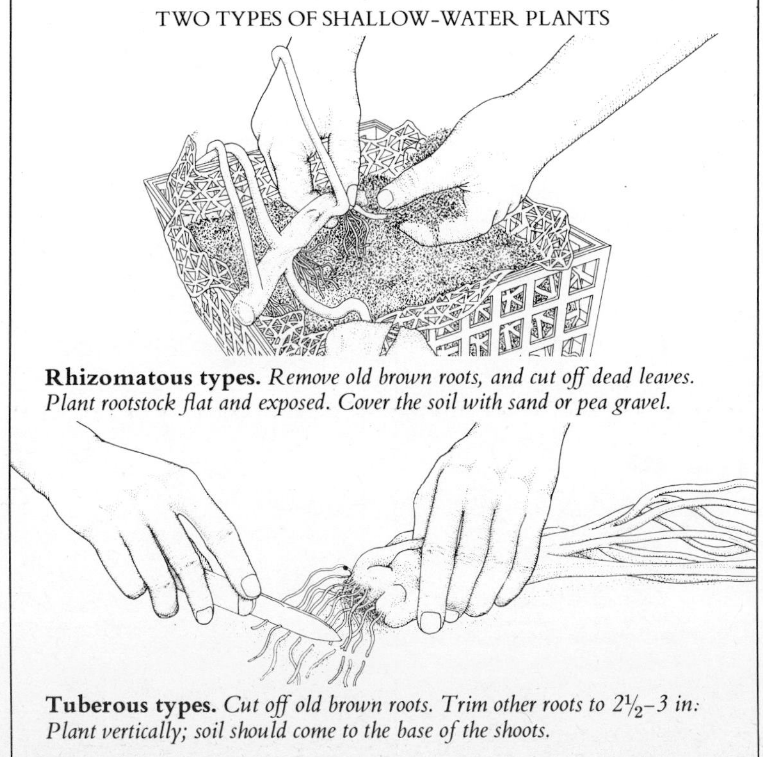

Rhizomatous types. *Remove old brown roots, and cut off dead leaves. Plant rootstock flat and exposed. Cover the soil with sand or pea gravel.*

Tuberous types. *Cut off old brown roots. Trim other roots to $2\frac{1}{2}$–3 in: Plant vertically; soil should come to the base of the shoots.*

Keeping the Balance With Oxygenators

Oxygenating plants are essential in any water garden. They maintain an ecological balance by using up the carbon dioxide produced by fish and other animals and by giving off oxygen that these animals require. They also provide fish with shelter and spawning places; and by competing with algae in the pool for light and nourishment, they help keep the water clear and fresh.

Most of these plants, such as the anacharis (*Elodea canadensis*) and the cabomba (*Cabomba caroliniana*), are sold in the form of bunches of unrooted cuttings. Since their rootstocks are small and develop quickly, they need only be weighted down with lead sinkers, such as those used by fishermen, and dropped into pools with soil-covered bottoms. They can also be planted in soil-filled containers along with water lilies and shallow-water plants. Finally, oxygenating plants can be placed in containers of their own and installed in the pool.

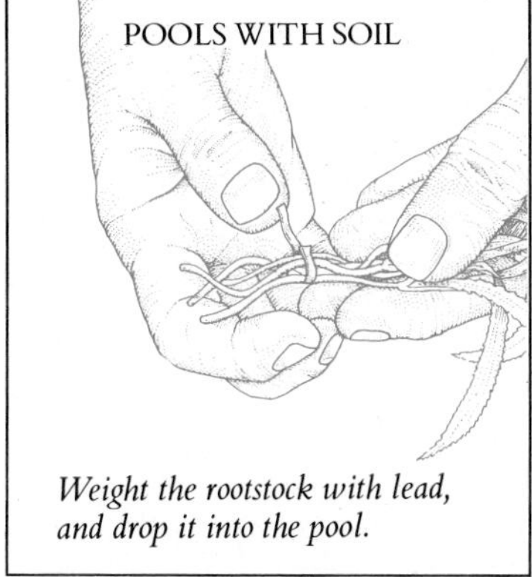

Weight the rootstock with lead, and drop it into the pool.

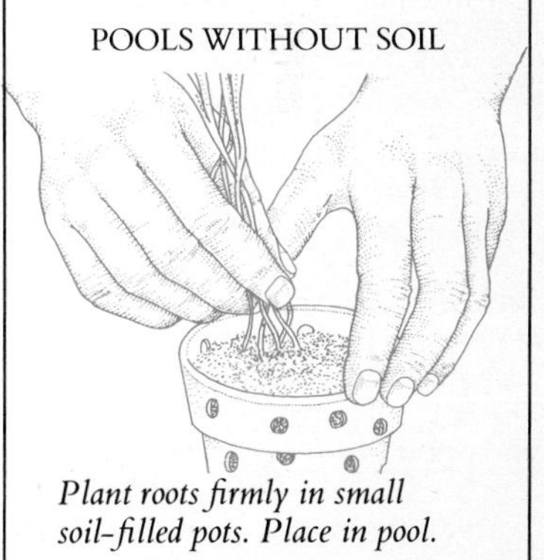

Plant roots firmly in small soil-filled pots. Place in pool.

Floating Plants That Need No Soil

Some plants, such as the water lettuce (*Pistia stratiotes*), float on the surface of the pool. Their trailing roots absorb from the water dissolved nutrients that have come from the soil containers of other plants or the droppings of fish. They are planted simply by putting them into the pool.

Some floating plants, such as the duckweed (*Lemna minor*) and azolla (*Azolla caroliniana*), proliferate so quickly that they may cover the surface of the pool. Simply scoop out extra plants and throw them away.

Water lettuce
(*Pistia stratiotes*)

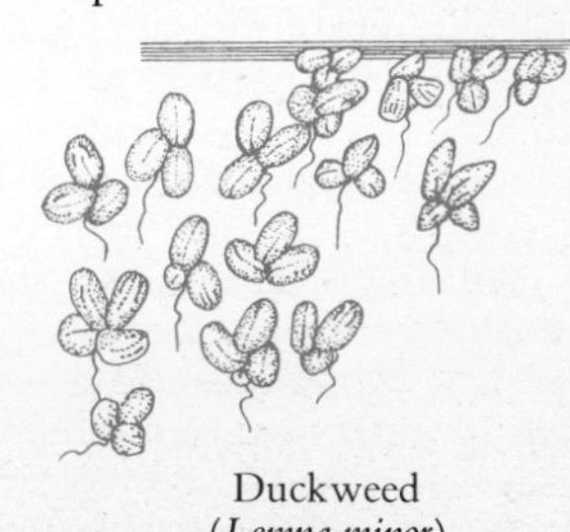

Duckweed
(*Lemna minor*)

Caring for the Garden Pool

Fish and Snails in the Pool

The addition of animal life to a pool helps balance its ecology. Fish and snails exhale carbon dioxide, which is essential to photosynthesis, and plants return the favor by releasing oxygen into the water for the fish to breathe. In addition, fish eat insects and larvae—including mosquito larvae—and snails help keep the pool clean by eating algae and other organic debris.

Do not introduce any animal life into the pool until it has settled—six to eight weeks after planting. Any dealer will advise you on the number and type of fish to use in your pool, taking into account the size of the pool and the local climate.

Fish are usually delivered in oxygenated plastic bags. Submerge the unopened bag in the pool for about 20 minutes so that it reaches pool temperature. Then hold the bag open, and let the fish swim out.

Artificial feeding is seldom necessary for fish living in an outdoor pool. Overfeeding, in fact, is often a problem. In any case, feeding must be stopped altogether from late fall until early spring because the water is too cold to allow the fish to digest food properly.

Feed fish in autumn, before the winter fast, and again in spring. Follow directions on the package.

Protecting Fish and Plants in Winter

The best protection against winter damage to both fish and plants, in all but the coldest climates, is to keep the pool filled with water. As long as the water does not freeze solid, from top to bottom, both goldfish and hardy water plants should survive. If you live in an area where winters are long and severe, it is a good idea to make your pool at least 3 feet deep. In such a pool even a 1-foot-thick ice layer will leave 2 feet of water underneath for the fish.

During autumn prevent leaves from falling into the pool by covering it with fine-mesh screening or plastic netting stretched on a light wooden frame. Use a net or a rake to remove any debris that does get into the pool, or scoop it out with a garden fork covered with wire or plastic netting.

When frost begins, cut the old, dying growth from the shallow-water plants to prevent diseases and to keep pests from wintering among the leaves. Remove all dead leaves from hardy water lilies, and remove and discard all tropicals. The rotting of old vegetation is the main reason for cloudiness in neglected pools.

You can control the thickness of the ice on your pool by insulating the surface. First, lay a covering of narrow wooden planks, leaving some gaps between them so that air can circulate. Spread burlap or plastic netting over this, and then a 3- to 4-inch layer of leaves, straw, or other coarse mulching material. Finally, cover this with another layer of burlap or netting, and stake it down for the winter. In areas where winters are only moderately severe, the surface of a pool thus protected may not freeze at all.

Alternatively, before your pool freezes, float a large rubber ball or a good-sized chunk of wood on the surface. Objects such as these will absorb the pressure of expanding ice, thus protecting the pool itself during the coldest weather. In a large pool several of these objects may be needed.

From time to time throughout the winter, push down on the ball or piece of wood to break the ice and admit oxygen to the shallow layer of air beneath the ice. Do not break the ice with a hammer or other implement; this can injure the fish and do damage to the pool.

What Can Go Wrong With Water Plants

Use no pesticides in a pool that contains fish or other animal life. If your plants show symptoms that are not described below, consult the section on plant disorders beginning on page 600. To find trade names of recommended chemicals, see page 635.

Symptoms and signs	Cause	Control
Young leaves and flowering stems are malformed; flowers are discolored and may fail to open properly.	Aphids	Hose leaves to dislodge insects, or use weighted wire mesh to keep leaves underwater for 24 hr. Apply pyrethrum contact sprays.*
Water lily leaves have ragged holes that often rot around the edges. Grubs may be visible.	Water lily beetles	Destroy affected leaves. Apply Captan or ferbam spray; use carbaryl if no fish are present.
Water is green or cloudy.	Algae	Shade water with floating plants; remove rotting plant matter; introduce more oxygenating plants. If desired, use copper compound (see p. 648).
Leaves of water lilies have brown spots.	Water lily leaf spot	Destroy diseased leaves. Use Captan or ferbam spray.
Water surface has dirty film.	Scum	Remove scum by drawing sheet of newspaper across water surface.
Leaves and flowers near top of plant are small and few. Leaves may be pale.	Starvation	Move plant into larger container with fresh soil, or divide and replant in separate containers.

*Note: *Pesticide sprays should be used on aquatic plants with extreme caution if pool contains fish or if it is used by humans.*

REMOVING INSECT PESTS

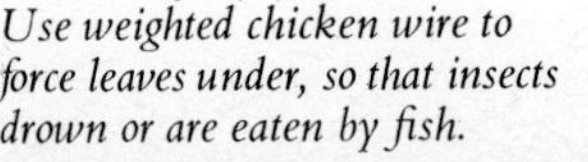

Use weighted chicken wire to force leaves under, so that insects drown or are eaten by fish.

CLEARING FLOATING LEAVES

Cover the tines of a garden fork with netting, or use a rake to scoop out leaves.

Growing Bog Plants Around the Pool

Taking Advantage of a Natural Bog Area

There are a number of so-called bog plants that require a plentiful supply of water but do not actually grow immersed in water. These are ideal for growing around the edge of a pool, since they bridge the gap between the water plants and the rest of the garden.

A bog garden can also be an attractive feature by itself, without a pool. It may be the only choice to occupy an area where water collects to form a natural bog.

As both drought and excess water can be harmful to the various plants that prosper in a bog garden, it may take considerable attention to maintain a precise balance of moisture during wet or dry spells.

Sufficient water is usually present in heavy clay soil. It can be conserved by a topdressing of composted leaves in mid to late spring. If the bog garden is in a low-lying area, however, there is danger that the plants will be totally submerged during periods of heavy rainfall.

Drought is a danger in sandy, well-drained soil. The only solution, short of constructing a special garden bed (see below), is to water the garden often and thoroughly.

Most bog plants are herbaceous perennials. The best time to plant them is in early autumn, while the soil is still warm from the summer.

Make the planting holes wide enough to allow for the roots to be fully spread out. Make the soil finger firm around the roots; if it is wet, however, take care not to compact it too much.

Do not space the plants far apart. Groups of plants of the same type are more striking than the same number of plants dotted about at wide intervals. Where the soil is moist and rich, many bog plants, such as primulas and irises, will add to this cluster effect by self-seeding to make drifts of blossoms in subsequent seasons.

For more detailed planting suggestions, turn to the section on herbaceous perennials, page 227.

AUTUMN PLANTING

Spread the roots of bog plants, and firm the soil around them.

How to Build a Bog Garden

The proper conditions for bog plants can be created, as shown below. Dig a hole 12 inches deep, the width and length you wish, and put an inch of sand on the bottom. Line the hole with heavy-duty plastic sheeting.

Cut holes in the plastic liner all around the sides, about 6 inches up, to drain surplus water. Cover the base of the sheeting with a layer of sod, laid grass side down.

Finally, overfill the hole with about 12 inches of garden soil, mixed with an equal amount of peat moss, to make a raised soil bed. The plastic liner will hold water, and the turf will provide drainage.

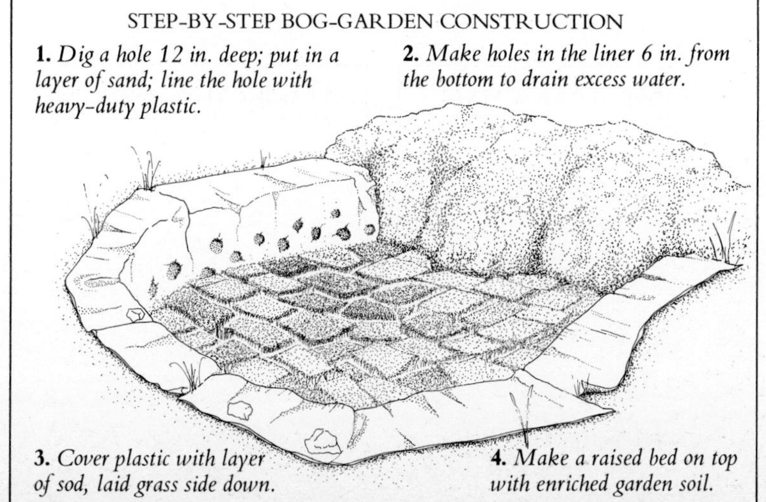

Providing an Adequate Supply of Water

Make sure the soil in your bog garden remains damp at all times. This may require frequent watering in dry weather.

If the bog garden is located downhill from a pool, you can flood it by allowing the pool to overflow as needed. Or you can install a poolside sprinkler system, which will help aerate the pool as well as keep the bog garden moist.

In autumn cut the dead foliage of herbaceous perennials in the bog garden down to the ground. Clean the ground debris, and turn it over lightly with a hand fork. Then apply a 1- to 2-inch mulch of well-rotted compost or of peat moss mixed with dehydrated cow manure. This will nourish the soil and help it retain moisture the following year.

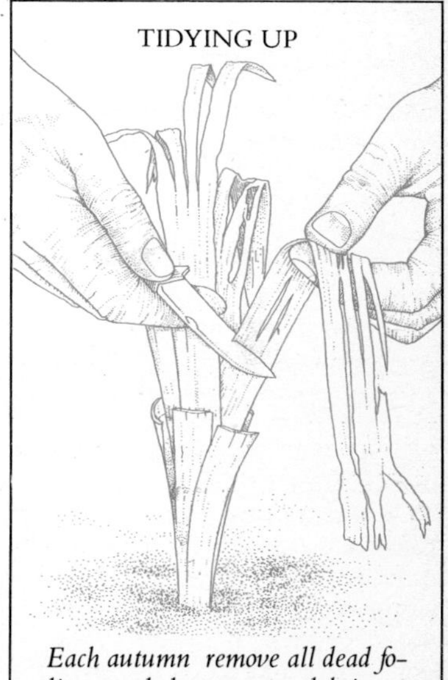

Each autumn remove all dead foliage, and clean up any debris.

Propagation From Rootstocks and Seeds

Most bog-garden plants, including primulas, rodgersias, irises, lobelias, and skunk cabbages, can be easily propagated by division in the spring.

The seeds of the primula and skunk cabbage will germinate readily in a greenhouse or cold frame if they are sown as soon as they are ripe in partially shaded, rich, moist soil. For detailed information on propagation methods, see page 203.

Growing New Water Plants From Old Ones

Dividing Overgrown Old Water Lilies

After four or five years water lilies will have spread and become overcrowded. Those in containers will have become root-bound, the flowers concealed by leaves. Thinning and dividing are necessary and should be done in the spring.

First, remove the roots from their containers and wash them well.

With the tuberous kinds of water lilies, simply tear the rootstocks apart, and replant the sections as required. Before replanting, however, remove broken leaves, cut off old brown anchorage roots, and trim the new white roots to fit the containers. Plant the sections individually as described on page 372.

With water lilies that have rhizomatous roots, cut 6–8 inches from the growing tip and replant the tip. Discard the rest, unless you want to increase your water lily collection.

Growing Water Lilies From Offsets and Eyes

New water lilies can be grown from the eyes found on tuberous rootstocks and from the offset rhizomes found on rhizomatous ones.

When thinning and dividing lilies of the tuberous type, search for the eyes on the roots—young tubers forming on the parent stock—and cut them out with a sharp knife. Fill seed pans or pots with heavy, well-moistened soil. Press the eyes to just below the surface of the soil, and immerse the pan or pot in a container of water. Place this container in a greenhouse or cold frame, and keep it lightly shaded. Within three to four weeks strong young shoots should appear. Replant them in the pool the following spring.

Rhizomatous water lilies have small offset rhizomes springing from the large parent roots. Break these off and pot them individually, pressing each one into the surface of a 3- to 4-inch pot full of rich, moist soil. Keep these pots in a greenhouse or cold frame, immersed in a container of water and partially shaded, until the following spring.

DIVIDING A TUBEROUS ROOT

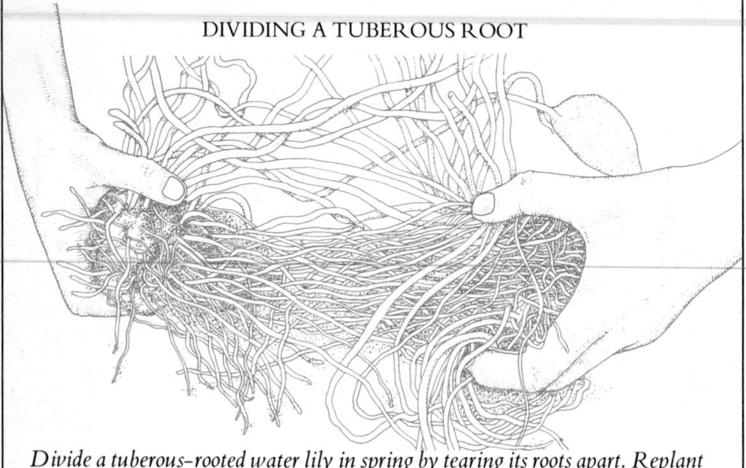

Divide a tuberous-rooted water lily in spring by tearing its roots apart. Replant the number of pieces needed in separate containers.

TAKING EYE CUTTINGS FROM TUBEROUS ROOTS

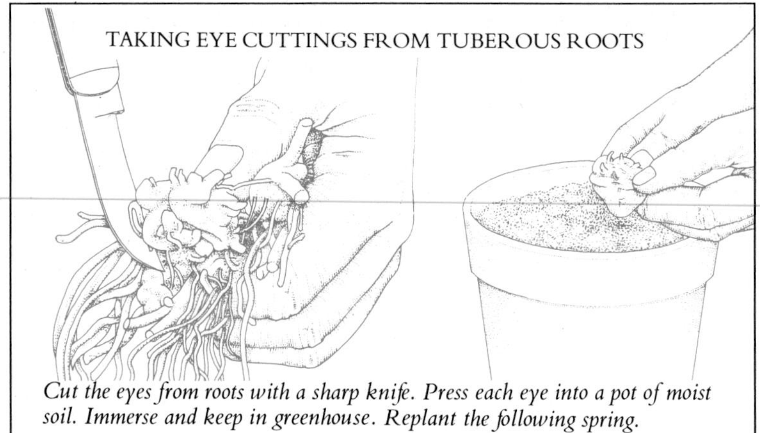

Cut the eyes from roots with a sharp knife. Press each eye into a pot of moist soil. Immerse and keep in greenhouse. Replant the following spring.

DIVIDING RHIZOMATOUS ROOTS

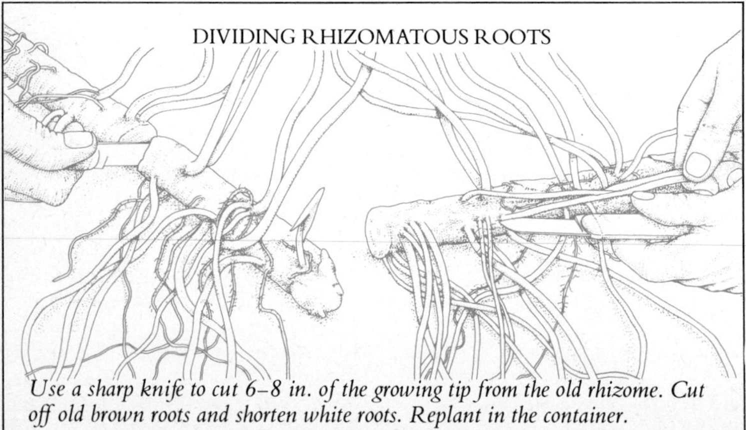

Use a sharp knife to cut 6–8 in. of the growing tip from the old rhizome. Cut off old brown roots and shorten white roots. Replant in the container.

NEW PLANTS FROM OFFSET RHIZOMES

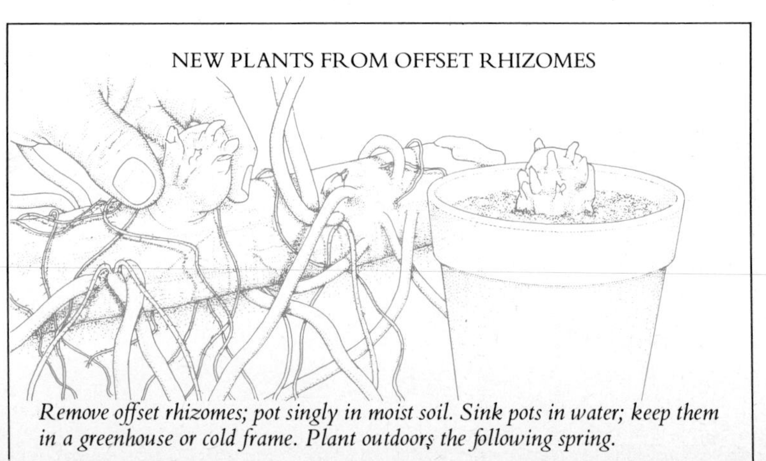

Remove offset rhizomes; pot singly in moist soil. Sink pots in water; keep them in a greenhouse or cold frame. Plant outdoors the following spring.

Dividing Shallow-Water Plants

Rhizomatous shallow-water plants, such as the bog arum (*Calla palustris*), are propagated by dividing the creeping rootstocks. Lift the roots in spring, and cut off a growing tip about 6–8 inches long. Remove all dead leaves and any brown roots, and plant as described on page 373. Even pieces as small as ½ inch long will grow. They will do best in a greenhouse with a temperature of about 60° F until they root. Plant outside in early to mid summer.

Shallow-water plants with fibrous roots growing from a thick, celery-like crown, such as arrowhead (*Sagittaria*) and pickerel rush (*Pontederia cordata*), are propagated simply by pulling the rootstocks apart.

Remove dead leaves and old brown roots. Trim the new white roots to 2½–3 inches, and plant as shown on page 373.

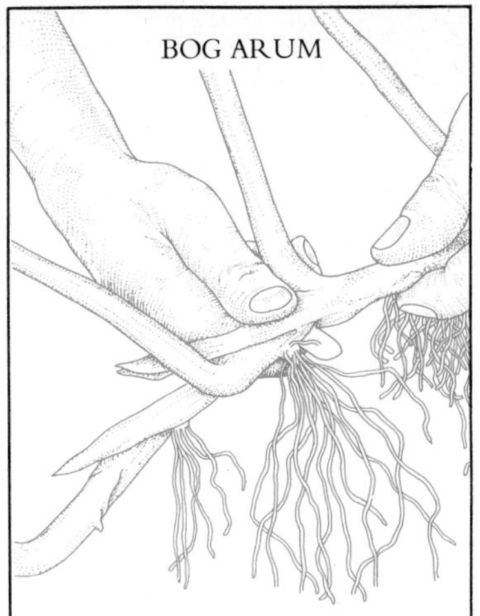

Divide the creeping rootstock of rhizomatous shallow-water plants. Cut off a 6- to 8-in. section of the growing tip, and replant it horizontally in a container of moist soil.

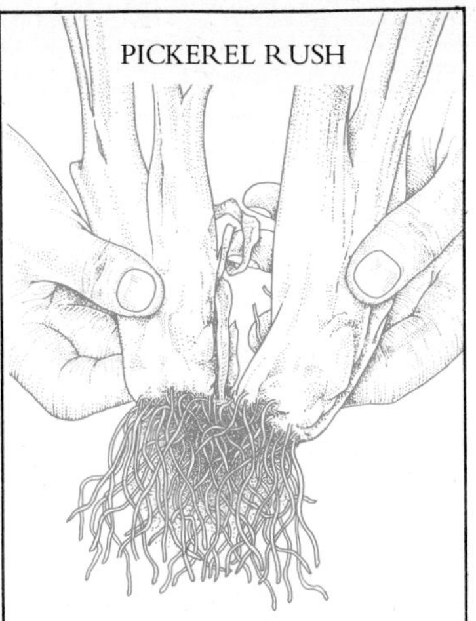

To propagate plants with tuberous or celerylike roots, pull rootstock apart, cut off dead leaves and old roots, and trim new roots to approximately 3 in. Then plant units separately.

Propagating Floaters and Oxygenators

Many hardy floaters can be increased by dividing their rootstocks in autumn. Simply pull them apart, and return the pieces to the pool—or discard them if the pool has become overcrowded. The water chestnut (*Trapa natans*) and duckweed (*Lemna minor*) are two plants that can be treated this way.

Taking soft cuttings in spring and summer is the usual way to increase such oxygenators as the anacharis (*Elodea canadensis*) and curled pondweed (*Potamogeton crispus*).

Cut off growing pieces 3-4 inches long, and plant them in deep, water-retentive containers with 2 inches of soil on the bottom. The containers should be deep enough to allow the cuttings to be covered by 6–9 inches of water. Make sure that the water temperature is kept around 60° F to assist rapid rooting.

Growing Water Plants From Seeds

Though the easiest method of propagating most water plants is by division, some plants, such as the water hawthorn (*Aponogeton distachyus*), can be grown from seeds.

Collect the seeds from the ripe seed heads after they have finished flowering. The best seeds will come from mature pods in late summer. Do not dry the seeds; keep them moist and cold or they will take longer to germinate.

Fill a shallow container with soil, and place the seeds on the surface. Put the container in a pan of water deep enough so that the surface of the soil will be covered by about an inch of water.

The seeds may float at first. This is natural. When all the air inside them has been released, they will lose their buoyancy and sink.

Leave the pan in a partially shaded spot in the greenhouse or cold frame. The seeds should germinate the following spring.

When the first pair of true leaves appears, transplant the seedlings into individual pots or boxes. Keep them standing in water in a cold frame or greenhouse for another year. The following spring, when the pool warms up, transfer the plants into it.

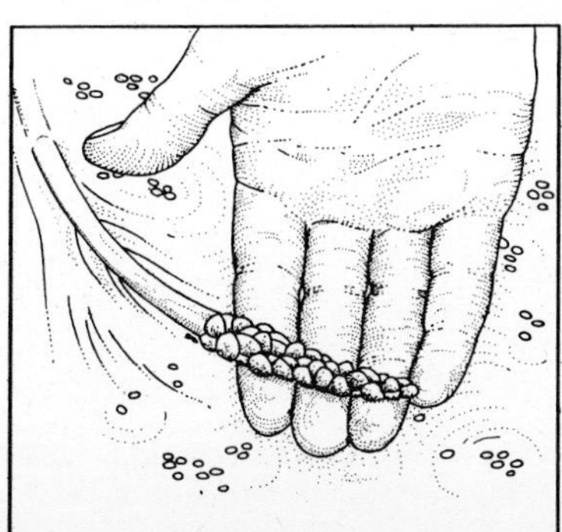

1. *Collect seeds from mature seed heads after flowering. Do not dry seeds.*

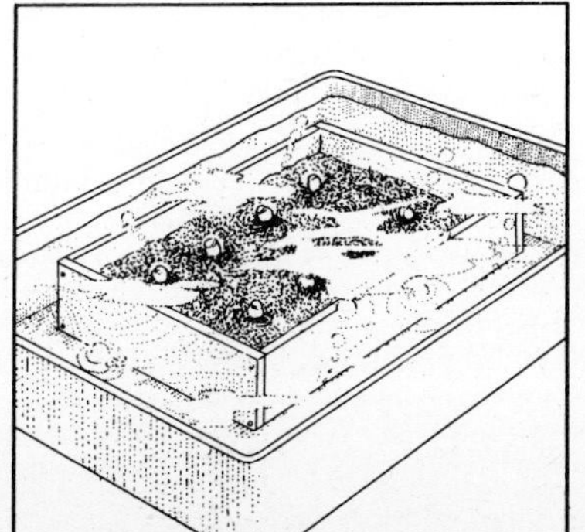

2. *Fill a tray with heavy soil. Put seeds on top. Cover with 1 in. of water.*

3. *When first true leaves appear in two or three weeks, transplant into pots.*

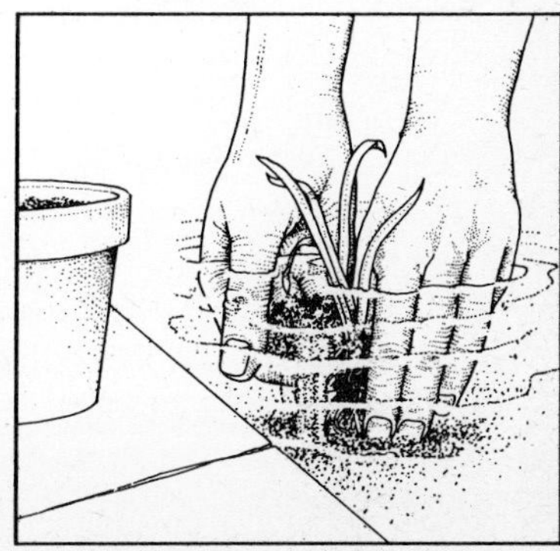

4. *Plant in the spring, after keeping in water in a greenhouse or cold frame.*

Selecting Plants for a Water Garden

A water garden and its environs offer the opportunity to cultivate a variety of fascinating plants, most of which will not grow elsewhere.

The most colorful of these plants are the water lilies, both hardy and tropical. The hardy water lilies will live outdoors the year round, provided the roots are covered sufficiently with water or soil that prevents them from freezing. Their leaves and flowers float on the surface of the water. On sunny days the flowers open in the morning and close in the middle of the afternoon. They are available in all colors except blue.

The tropical lilies, both day and night bloomers, are dependably hardy only in frost-free climates. In colder areas they can be grown as annuals, but they must be replaced each year. Their leaves float, and their fragrant flowers are held well above the surface on stout stems.

Some plants that float on the water and are not rooted in soil tend to propagate rapidly and may have to be thinned. Both the floating plants and the oxygenators are needed to maintain the balance of plant and animal life in the pool.

The plants that grow in shallow water or boggy places provide a visual transition from the plants on the surface of the water to the rest of the garden. Other good transition plants are the ornamental grasses listed on page 383. These require considerable moisture and must have porous, well-drained soil.

The plants in the following charts are grouped by kind: plants for deep water, floating plants, bog plants, and so on. Each group is arranged alphabetically by the best known common names. Botanical names are also given. The headings on the charts are self-explanatory.

DEEP-WATER PLANTS WITH FLOATING LEAVES AND FLOWERS

Floating heart (*Nymphoides peltatum*)

Water hawthorn (*Aponogeton distachyus*)

Hardy water lily (*Nymphaea* 'Formosa')

Tropical day-blooming water lily (*Nymphaea* 'Green Smoke')

Pygmy water lily (*Nymphaea* 'Colorata')

Common and botanical names	Decorative characteristics, special requirements, and remarks	Propagation (*See also p. 376*)
Floating heart (*Nymphoides*)	Heart-shaped green leaves sometimes mottled with yellow.	Division
N. indicum (water snowflake)	Leaves to 8 in. across. Tiny, fuzzy-coated white flowers with yellow centers. Hardy only in warm climates.	
N. peltatum (water fringe)	Leaves about 4 in. across. Bright yellow flowers. Hardy in North as long as rootstock does not freeze.	
Water hawthorn (*Aponogeton*) *A. distachyus*	Green leaves up to 4 in. long. Small white flowers with tiny purple "antlers." Sweet vanilla fragrance. Not winter hardy.	Division or seeds
Water lily (*Nymphaea*) *N.* species and varieties		
HARDY	Flowers float on water surface. Plant 6-12 in. deep.	Division
N. 'Attraction'	Dark red flowers with yellow stamens, to 10 in. across.	
N. 'Chromatella'	Mottled foliage. Clear yellow, cup-shaped flowers.	
N. 'Formosa'	Clear pink flowers. Blooms prolifically.	
N. 'Gladstone'	Large white flowers with yellow centers, 6-8 in. across.	
N. 'Sioux'	Yellow-bronze flowers change to copper-orange as they open.	
TROPICAL DAY BLOOMING	Large flowers rise above water. Plant 4-6 in. deep.	Division, or in some cases, by separating new plants that develop on surface of leaves.
N. 'Director Moore'	Rich purple flowers with yellow centers. Very fragrant.	
N. 'General Pershing'	Large, orchid-pink double flowers open early and close late.	
N. 'Green Smoke'	Large, scalloped green leaves speckled with bronze. Distinctive greenish flowers with smoky blue overcast.	
N. 'Margaret Randig'	Broad-petaled sky-blue flowers. Long growing season.	
N. 'Talisman'	Yellow flowers suffused with pink. Very fragrant. Vigorously viviparous (complete new plants develop on leaf surface).	
N. 'Yellow Dazzler'	Showy, chrome-yellow flowers. Very fragrant. Blooms prolifically.	
TROPICAL NIGHT BLOOMING	Large flowers open at dusk, close following morning.	Division
N. 'Emily Grant Hutchings'	Bright pink, cup-shaped flowers, almost luminous under night lighting. Fragrant and free blooming.	
N. 'H. C. Haarstick'	Coppery foliage. Vivid red flowers to 12 in. across. Fragrant.	
N. 'Missouri'	Creamy white flowers up to 13 in. across, with broad, slightly textured petals. Shows up beautifully in moonlight.	
N. 'Omarana'	Deep orchid-pink, almost lavender flowers with orange-red centers, up to 12 in. across. Very fragrant.	
PYGMY, OR MINIATURE	Needs only 2-3 ft. of water surface.	Division
N. 'Aurora'	Flowers open rosy yellow, turn reddish orange on second day, become deep red by third day. Hardy.	
N. 'Colorata'	Pale violet flowers are 2-3 in. across. Day-blooming tropical.	

OXYGENATING PLANTS

Anacharis (*Elodea canadensis*)
Cabomba caroliniana
Curled pondweed (*Potamogeton crispus*)
Eelgrass (*Vallisneria americana*)
Ludwigia alternifolia
Sagittaria sinensis
Water milfoil (*Myriophyllum spicatum*)

Common and botanical names	Decorative characteristics, special requirements, and remarks	Propagation (*See also p. 377*)
Anacharis (*Elodea*) *E. canadensis*	Whorls of dark green leaves on long, lighter green stems. Grows vigorously, entirely submerged. Plant 12 in. or deeper.	Cuttings
Cabomba (*Cabomba*) *C. caroliniana*	Glossy green leaves, fan shaped and finely divided. Stems red or green. Roots easily, grows entirely submerged.	Cuttings
Curled pondweed (*Potamogeton*) *P. crispus*	Crisped green leaves are densely clustered on long stems. Tiny greenish flowers rise out of water in late spring and summer.	Cuttings
Eelgrass (*Vallisneria*) *V. americana*	Long, ribbonlike green leaves grow directly from roots. Hardy in North, becomes dormant in winter.	Separation of rooted runners
Ludwigia (*Ludwigia*) *L. alternifolia* *L. natans,* or *L. mulertii*	Flat, rounded leaves, green on top, reddish beneath. Erect stems rise above water surface, bear flowers of yellow or white. Does best in water 6-8 in. deep. Leaves coppery on top, bright red beneath. Grow in water 4-6 in. deep.	Cuttings
Sagittaria (*Sagittaria*) *S. sinensis,* or *S. graminea* *S. subulata* (miniature)	Dark green, sword-shaped leaves grow directly from rootstock. Leaves grow to 3 ft. or more. Use in deep pools. Like *S. sinensis* but only 12-14 in. high.	Separation of rooted runners
Water milfoil (*Myriophyllum*) *M. aquaticum,* or *M. brasiliense* (parrot feather) *M. spicatum*	Green feathery leaves like cabomba, but bushier. Bright yellow-green leaves, red tipped in autumn. Pushes out of water a few inches. Dark green leaves in delicate, plumelike whorls. Very hardy.	Cuttings

PLANTS THAT FLOAT FREELY IN THE WATER

Azolla caroliniana
Duckweed (*Lemna minor*)
Water chestnut (*Trapa natans*)
Water fern (*Ceratopteris thalictroides*)
Water hyacinth (*Eichhornia crassipes*)
Water lettuce (*Pistia stratiotes*)

Common and botanical names	Decorative characteristics, special requirements, and remarks	Propagation (*See also p. 377*)
Azolla (*Azolla*) *A. caroliniana*	Tiny plants with crinkly, mosslike green leaves that turn russet-crimson in autumn. Proliferates rapidly. May become a pest in warm weather.	Separation of colonies of individual plants
Duckweed (*Lemna*) *L. minor*	Tiny bright green leaves on many separate floating plants. Goldfish feed on tender young roots. Spreads rapidly by offshoots. May become a pest; scoop out extra plants.	Separation of offshoots
Water chestnut (*Trapa*) *T. natans*	Clusters of small, hollylike green leaves are kept afloat by hollow stems. Small white flowers in summer. Large, spiny seeds are edible, taste similar to true chestnut.	Division or from nutlike seeds
Water fern (*Ceratopteris*) *C. thalictroides*	True ferns, with edible, lettucelike dark green leaves that stand up to 1 ft. above water surface. In North not hardy in winter.	Formation of new plants on edges of fronds
Water hyacinth (*Eichhornia*) *E. crassipes*	Clusters of heart-shaped, glossy green leaves. Showy, blue to purple flowers have yellow centers. Spreads rapidly. A pestiferous weed in warm waterways; cannot be sold across state lines. Will not withstand frost.	Division
Water lettuce (*Pistia*) *P. stratiotes* (shellflower)	Free-floating 6-in. rosettes, resembling pale green heads of lettuce, with velvety coats. Thrives in full sun or shade. Long, feathery roots trail in water, may anchor in wet soil if plant runs aground. Forms colonies of runnerlike offshoots.	Separation of offshoots from parent plant

PLANTS FOR BOGS AND SHALLOW WATER

Common and botanical names	Decorative characteristics, special requirements, and remarks	Propagation *(See also p. 377)*
Arrowhead *(Sagittaria)* *S. latifolia* (giant arrowhead)	Large, arrowhead-shaped leaves rise 2-3 ft. above water. Hardy native plant with large white flowers borne on spikes in mid to late summer. Grow in water 2-6 in. deep.	Division
S. sagittifolia (old world arrowhead)	Foliage sometimes variegated. Flowers smaller than *S. latifolia,* with purple spots at base of petals.	
S. s. florepleno	Double flowers displayed all summer long.	
Arum, bog, or water *(Calla)* *C. palustris* (water dragon)	Heart-shaped, bright green leaves rise 6-9 in. high. Small, creamy white flowers with yellow hearts borne in showy clusters in early and mid summer, followed by bunches of red berries in fall. Grow in bog or shallow water to 6 in. deep. Hardy.	Division
Calla lily *(Zantedeschia)* *Z. aethiopica*	Large, arrowhead-shaped, glossy green leaves grow 2-3 ft. high. Trumpet-shaped flowers appear from late spring to autumn. Bog plant. Can overwinter in mild climates. See also p. 330.	Division, or separation of offsets
Cardinal flower *(Lobelia)* *L. cardinalis*	Narrow, deep-green leaves. Flower spikes of bright cardinal-red are borne in late summer and early fall on sturdy stalks 3-4 ft. high. Grow in bog or shallow water 2-4 in. deep. *L. c. alba* has white flowers; *L. c. rosea* has rose-pink flowers.	Division or cuttings
Cattail, or bulrush *(Typha)*	Flat, sword-shaped leaves rise straight up from water. Brown flower heads are borne on stout, ramrod-stiff stalks. Hardy.	Division; or plant seeds in pots, put in shallow water in spring
T. angustifolia (narrow-leaved, or graceful, cattail)	Leaves very narrow. Flowers appear in mid and late summer on stalks 4-6 ft. high. Grow in shallow water 4-6 in. deep. Plant in containers to check incursive habit.	
T. latifolia (common cattail)	Flower stalks may grow 10 ft. high.	
T. minima (miniature cattail)	Flower heads purple-brown on stalks only 12-18 in. high. Plant in containers 2-6 in. deep.	
Cyperus *(Cyperus)*		Division
C. alternifolius (umbrella palm, or umbrella plant)	Clumps of round stems to 3 ft. high, each topped by umbrellalike tuft of leaves. Not hardy. Grow in containers in shallow water 2-6 in. deep. For winter care as house plant, see p. 418.	
C. a. gracilis (dwarf umbrella)	Dwarf form, to 12 in. high.	
C. isocladus (dwarf papyrus)	Like *C. papyrus* but only about 2 ft. high.	
C. papyrus (papyrus)	Triangular stalks grow 5-8 ft. high, topped by tufts of thread-like leaves. Grow in containers in shallow water 2-6 in. deep. Not hardy in winter; take indoors or discard.	
Fern, osmunda *(Osmunda)*	Hardy bog plant with long, feathery fronds from midspring to first frost. Grow in partial shade and in acid soil. For other ferns suited to boggy areas, see pp. 384-391.	Division or spores
O. cinnamomea (cinnamon, or fiddlehead, fern)	Fronds 2-4 ft. long and 6-8 in. wide, green when young, turning cinnamon colored when spores develop. Fronds emerge from ground in early to mid spring as edible, fiddlehead-shaped sprouts.	
O. claytoniana (interrupted fern)	Fronds 1-2 ft. long and 8-12 in. wide. Requires moist, highly acid soil.	
O. regalis (royal, or flowering, fern)	Dramatically beautiful, with fronds up to 8 ft. long and 12-18 in. across, pale green and much divided. Brownish spore clusters at ends of fronds resemble flowers. Will grow in shallow water, to 4 in. deep. Varieties have reddish or bronze-colored fronds.	
Horsetail *(Equisetum)* *E. hyemale*	Hollow, bamboolike stalks are semi-translucent. Bog plant. Stalks to 4 ft. high. Not winter hardy, but will survive light frost. Spreads rapidly. Divide often, or grow in containers.	Division
E. scirpoides (dwarf horsetail)	Stalks tufted, only 1-2 ft. high.	

Old world arrowhead *(Sagittaria sagittifolia)*

Bog arum *(Calla palustris)*

Calla lily *(Zantedeschia aethiopica)*

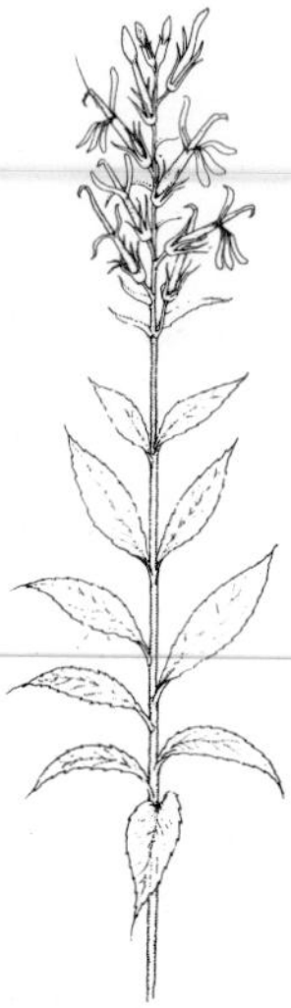

Cardinal flower *(Lobelia cardinalis)*

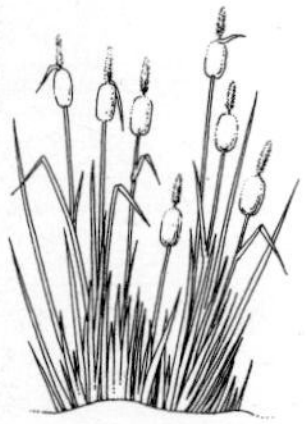

Miniature cattail *(Typha minima)*

Cyperus papyrus

Royal fern *(Osmunda regalis)*

Horsetail *(Equisetum hyemale)*

Japanese iris
(Iris kaempferi)

East Indian lotus
(Nelumbium nelumbo)

Lysimachia nummularia

Marsh marigold
(Caltha palustris monstruosa)

Allegheny monkey flower
(Mimulus ringens)

Common and botanical names	Decorative characteristics, special requirements, and remarks	Propagation *(See also p. 377)*
Iris *(Iris)*		Division or seeds (see p. 343)
I. kaempferi (Japanese iris)	Named varieties have flowers of many colors; bloom in mid to late summer. Root area must be kept well drained in winter.	
I. laevigata	Deep blue flowers in early to mid summer. Varieties available with flowers of white, pink, violet, and shades of blue. Bog plant. Will grow to 2 ft. high in water 2 in. deep.	
I. pseudacorus (yellow flag, or water iris)	Bright golden blooms in late spring and early summer. Will grow 2-3 ft. high in water 2-18 in. deep (will grow higher in deeper water).	
I. sibirica (Siberian iris)	Flowers of white or blue in early summer. Will grow 2-4 ft. high in bog or in water 2-4 in. deep.	
I. versicolor (blue flag, or water iris)	Like *I. pseudacorus,* but has blue or violet flowers. About 2 ft. high. Grow in water 2-12 in. deep.	
Lotus *(Nelumbium,* or *Nelumbo)*	Large round leaves resemble parasols above water. Fragrant, breathtakingly beautiful flowers rise as high as 6-8 ft. on straight stems. Grow in water 6-9 in. deep. Hardy as long as rootstock does not freeze. Not to be confused with the lotus of ancient Egypt *(Nymphaea caerulea* and *N. lotus),* which is actually a water lily, nor with the genus *Lotus.*	Division
N. nelumbo, or *Nelumbo nucifera* (East Indian lotus)	Fragrant pink flowers arise all summer long. Larger than *N. pentapetalum.*	
N. n. album grandiflorum	Deep green leaves. Pure white flowers are delicately scented.	
N. n. album striatum	White flowers are edged with carmine-red.	
N. n. pekinense rubrum	Large, brilliant red flowers. Also available in double form.	
N. n. roseum plenum	Rich, rose-pink, fully double flowers are up to 12 in. across, extremely fragrant.	
N. pentapetalum, or *Nelumbo lutea* (American lotus)	Large bluish-green leaves. Soft yellow flowers, 8-10 in. across, appear all summer long.	
N. p. flavescens	Creamy white flowers, smaller than *N. pentapetalum.*	
Lysimachia *(Lysimachia)*		Division
L. nummularia (moneywort, or creeping Charlie)	Small, round green leaves on creeping vine. Bright yellow flowers appear profusely throughout summer. Grow in bog or in shallow water up to 2 in. deep. Hardy.	
L. n. aurea	Foliage is yellow.	
Marsh marigold, or cowslip *(Caltha)*	Grows in small, rounded clumps, with attractive foliage. Very hardy bog plant.	Division or seeds
C. leptosepala (elkslip)	Rocky Mountain native, 6-12 in. high, with oval green leaves. Bluish-white flowers appear in early and mid summer.	
C. palustris	Heart-shaped green leaves. Covered with golden buttercuplike flowers in midspring to early summer. Dies back mid to late summer. Grows 1-3 ft. high.	
C. p. alba	Flowers are white, long lasting.	
C. p. monstruosa	Golden yellow flowers are double, very large. Prolific.	
Monkey flower *(Mimulus)*	Bushy perennial bog plant. Flowers are odd looking, monkey faced, with 2 distinct lips. Grow in shade or partial shade and in humus-rich soil.	Division or cuttings
M. luteus (golden monkey flower)	Vinelike, 6-12 in. high. Covered all summer long with yellow flowers, spotted with red or purple. Grow in bog or shallow water to 4 in. deep. Not hardy below 0° F.	
M. ringens (Allegheny monkey flower)	Shrublike, to 18 in. high. Purple, soft lavender, or white flowers appear profusely in late summer and early autumn. Grow in bog or shallow water to 6 in. deep. Very hardy.	

PLANTS FOR BOGS AND SHALLOW WATER *(continued)*

Pickerel rush *(Pontederia cordata)*

Plantain lily *(Hosta sieboldiana)*

Tibetan primrose *(Primula florindae)*

Primrose willow *(Jussiaea repens)*

Rodgersia pinnata

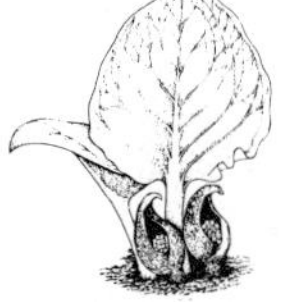

Skunk cabbage *(Symplocarpus foetidus)*

Sweet flag *(Acorus calamus)*

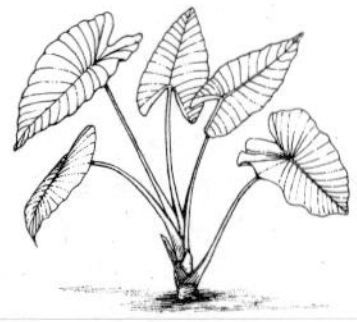

Green taro *(Colocasia esculenta)*

Trollius europaeus

Common and botanical names	Decorative characteristics, special requirements, and remarks	Propagation *(See also p. 377)*
Pickerel rush *(Pontederia)* *P. cordata*	Stalk to about 2 ft. high, bearing spearhead-shaped, shiny olive-green leaves. Azure to violet-blue flower spikes last all summer. Grow in water 2-12 in. deep (start very shallow, increase depth gradually). Very hardy.	Division
Plantain lily *(Hosta)* *H. sieboldiana,* or *H. glauca*	Hardy bog plant with large, stiff, blue-green leaves 12-15 in. long and nearly as wide. Dense clusters of funnel-shaped lavender flowers appear in spring and early summer. Grow in partial shade. See also p. 252.	Division
Primrose *(Primula)* *P. beesiana*	Shade-loving bog plant. Hardy. Grows to 2 ft. high, with oblong green leaves. Stalks of yellow-eyed rose-lilac flowers bloom in early and mid summer.	Division or seeds
P. florindae (Tibetan primrose)	Long, broad, glossy green leaves on reddish stems. Flat clusters of bright yellow flowers appear atop 2- to 3-ft. stems in late summer. Will grow in water 2-3 in. deep.	
P. japonica (Japanese primrose)	Small green leaves. Flowers appear in whorls along 18- to 24-in. stalks, from late spring to midsummer. Available in shades of purple, rose, red, and white.	
Primrose willow *(Jussiaea)* *J. longifolia*	Willowlike foliage. Yellow primroselike flowers borne all summer. Grows 2-3 ft. high, with pointed leaves. Grow in bog or water 2-6 in. deep. Tropical plant; must be treated as annual throughout most of U. S., or overwinter in greenhouse pool or other protected container of water.	Division or seeds
J. repens (primrose creeper)	Fast-spreading vine with small, shiny green leaves on reddish stems. Yellow flowers bloom just above surface of water. Grow in shallow water up to 12 in. deep. Hardy.	
Rodgersia *(Rodgersia)*		Division
R. aesculifolia	Hardy bog plant with large, hairy green leaves. White flowers appear all summer in thick clusters along 1½- to 3-ft. stalks.	
R. pinnata	Stalks 3-4 ft. high, with reddish flowers. Varieties are available in shades of red, pink, rose, and white.	
Skunk cabbage *(Symplocarpus)* *S. foetidus*	Hardy bog plant with large oval leaves that emit unpleasant odor when crushed. Brownish-purple hoods with green mottling, 6-12 in. high, enclose true, club-shaped, blackish flowers. Blooms in very early spring, followed by large, heavy-textured leaves.	Division or seeds
Sweet flag *(Acorus)*		Division
A. calamus	Irislike green leaves rise 2-3 ft. out of water. Small brownish-green flowers bloom in midsummer. Grow in water 2-4 in. deep.	
A. c. variegatus (variegated sweet flag)	Leaves are striped lengthwise with green and creamy white, fragrant when bruised or crushed.	
A. gramineus variegatus (dwarf variegated sweet flag)	Narrow, grasslike foliage striped green and white. Grows 6-12 in. high. Not fragrant.	
Taro, or Elephant's ear *(Colocasia)*	Huge leathery leaves, each on its own 2- to 4-ft. stem, are edible, as are large, tuberous roots. Tropical bog plant, hardy only in Deep South and on West Coast.	Division
C. esculenta (green taro)	Foliage is deep, rich green. Varieties are available with stems of red, purple, and violet.	
C. e. illustris (imperial taro)	Green leaves blotched with dark brown and deep violet.	
Trollius, or Globeflower *(Trollius)* *T. europaeus*	Small palmlike or ferny green leaves. Big, round, buttercuplike flowers of orange and yellow bloom from late spring to midsummer. Grows to 3 ft. high. Many varieties. Hardy bog plant.	Division or seeds

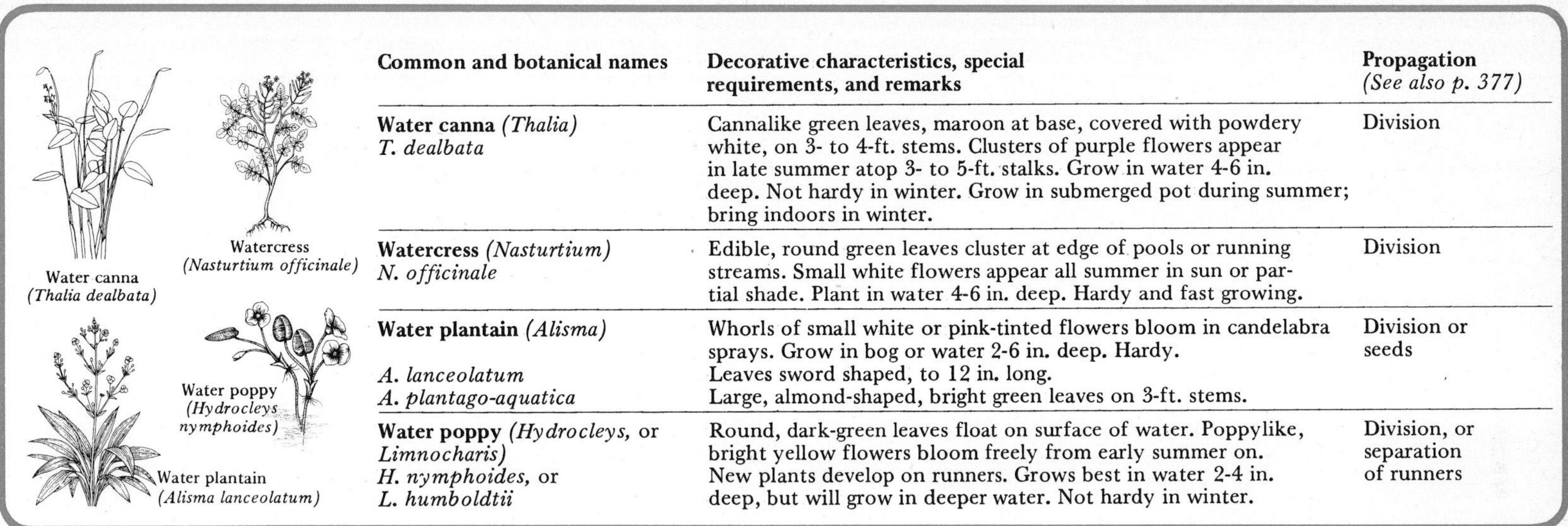

Water canna (*Thalia dealbata*)

Watercress (*Nasturtium officinale*)

Water poppy (*Hydrocleys nymphoides*)

Water plantain (*Alisma lanceolatum*)

Common and botanical names	Decorative characteristics, special requirements, and remarks	Propagation (*See also p. 377*)
Water canna (*Thalia*) *T. dealbata*	Cannalike green leaves, maroon at base, covered with powdery white, on 3- to 4-ft. stems. Clusters of purple flowers appear in late summer atop 3- to 5-ft. stalks. Grow in water 4-6 in. deep. Not hardy in winter. Grow in submerged pot during summer; bring indoors in winter.	Division
Watercress (*Nasturtium*) *N. officinale*	Edible, round green leaves cluster at edge of pools or running streams. Small white flowers appear all summer in sun or partial shade. Plant in water 4-6 in. deep. Hardy and fast growing.	Division
Water plantain (*Alisma*)	Whorls of small white or pink-tinted flowers bloom in candelabra sprays. Grow in bog or water 2-6 in. deep. Hardy.	Division or seeds
A. lanceolatum	Leaves sword shaped, to 12 in. long.	
A. plantago-aquatica	Large, almond-shaped, bright green leaves on 3-ft. stems.	
Water poppy (*Hydrocleys,* or *Limnocharis*) *H. nymphoides,* or *L. humboldtii*	Round, dark-green leaves float on surface of water. Poppylike, bright yellow flowers bloom freely from early summer on. New plants develop on runners. Grows best in water 2-4 in. deep, but will grow in deeper water. Not hardy in winter.	Division, or separation of runners

GRASSES THAT REQUIRE MOISTURE AND GOOD DRAINAGE

Bamboo (*Arundinaria nitida*)

Miscanthus sinensis

Pennisetum ruppelii

Giant reed (*Arundo donax*)

Common and botanical names	Decorative characteristics, special requirements, and remarks	Propagation (*See also p. 377*)
Bamboo (several genera)	Graceful, arching stems with attractive, long, thin leaves.	Division
Arundinaria murieliae	Narrow leaves have yellowish stems. Shrubby clumps have many small branches at each joint of canes. Not hardy in North.	
Arundinaria nitida	Canes 12-20 ft. high. Hardy to Zone C.	
Phyllostachys niger	Arching canes, 8-15 ft. high, are green first year, then turn deep purple-black. Young shoots edible. Incursive in warm climate. Will not survive below 10° F.	
Sasa palmata	Long green leaves with silvery undersides on canes up to 8 ft. high. May be evergreen in mild winters. Spreads by underground runners; must be kept in check. Hardy to southern part of Zone B.	
Miscanthus (*Miscanthus*)	Long, grassy leaves on reedy stems. Flowers in late summer.	Division or seeds
M. sacchariflorus (silver grass)	Stems 6-8 ft. high. Foliage silky and silvery. Flowers are brown spikelets surrounded by long, silky hairs.	
M. sinensis (eulalia grass)	To 10 ft. high, with graceful, 2- to 3-ft.-long leaves. Fanlike, pinkish-white flower plumes in late summer and fall. Hardy.	
M. s. gracillimus (maiden grass)	Miniature form, to 3 ft. high. Narrow leaves have center stripe of white or yellow.	
M. s. zebrinus (zebra grass)	Foliage crossbanded in white or yellow.	
Pennisetum (*Pennisetum*)	Highly ornamental grasses. Not hardy in North.	Division or seeds
P. alopecuroides (Chinese pennisetum)	Narrow, 2-ft. leaves on stems 3-4 ft. high. Plumelike flowers of silvery purple in late summer followed by gaudy seed heads in fall.	
P. ruppelii, or *P. setaceum* (fountain grass)	Very narrow, graceful leaves. Seed heads are 1 ft. long or more, nodding, and very showy, in various shades of purple, coppery orange, red, rose, and pink.	
Reed, giant (*Arundo*) *A. donax*	Long, arching, gray-green leaves on cornstalklike stems 12-15 ft. high. Plumelike reddish or white flowers appear at top of stems in fall. Hardy.	Division or seeds; root stems in water

Ferns

In places with open or partial shade, ferns form delicate patterns of green. And they mix well with other shade-loving plants, such as primroses and columbines.

Ferns, with their arching fronds and cool green colors, are ideal for parts of the garden where there is little sun. They can transform a difficult corner, where few other plants will thrive, into an oasis of delicate foliage.

Ferns are among the most ancient plants on earth, first appearing about 400 million years ago, long before any plants bore flowers.

There are more than 12,000 species of ferns growing throughout the world. The vast majority are found in tropical countries. Of the 360 species that grow naturally in North America, many are concentrated in the North and East, where the higher humidity ensures the moisture necessary for fertilization. Some species from other temperate parts of the world are also available here.

Most of the native ferns can be successfully transplanted into home gardens. A real enthusiast may use ferns alone in a shady border, mixing species of different sizes, shapes of frond, and shades of green. They also make a good foil for shade-loving flowering plants, which thrive in similar conditions as ferns and mix well with them.

Bleeding hearts (*Dicentra spectabilis*) and astilbes blend well with the larger ferns, such as the shield ferns (*Dryopteris*) and the osmundas. Wild flowers, such as wild geraniums and violets, add a touch of color to the ferns' varying shades of green. Columbines and primroses come in a variety of colors and can be interspersed effectively. Some flowering shrubs, such as azaleas, add a mass of color in springtime.

Some of the best foliage plants to grow with ferns are the hostas, some with variegated leaves striped with green and white or yellow. Other types are plain green or blue-green. The pale green and white leaves of the goutweed (*Aegopodium*) also contrast well with the darker green of the ferns, but the goutweed spreads rapidly and may prove too invasive.

To look their best, ferns should be grown far enough apart to prevent the fronds from intermingling. The spaces between the plants or at the front near the border can be filled in with low-growing perennials, such as bergenias or lilies of the valley. The latter are very invasive, however, and should be fenced in with slates, tiles, or corrugated plastic or aluminum edging, sunk into the ground to keep the roots within reasonable bounds.

Torenias and the wax begonias also make good edging plants in a fern garden. And tuberous begonias, hardy begonias (*Begonia evansiana*), with their red stems and leaves, and impatiens scattered throughout the border combine with the ferns to give a very pleasing effect.

Daffodils should be used only with large ferns, which will cover the flowers' untidy leaves after they have finished blooming. When planted among a group of ferns, tall woodland lilies look very elegant, rising above the arching fronds.

Ferns, however, need not be restricted to a shady corner. Some, for example, the hay-scented fern (*Dennstaedtia punctilobula*), grow well in nearly full sun. They can be used to cast interesting shadows on large rocks in sunny places.

Many ferns are evergreen and are invaluable for brightening up a garden in winter. The shield ferns and the polypodies (*Polypodium*) are particularly delightful, especially when their fronds are edged with frost. In a rock garden the evergreen spleenworts (*Asplenium*) remain bright when most other plants have faded.

Ferns of different types can bring the beauty of a natural woodland to a shady or otherwise uninteresting corner of the garden. The taller ferns are arranged as a background, under the shade of the tree. Smaller ferns have been planted among the rough stones in the foreground.

Planting Hardy Ferns

Most ferns will grow in any soil except one where drainage is poor. A few will grow in a bog. They need a position that is shaded from midday sun and protected from wind.

The north side of a house or fence will provide the right kind of shade, protecting the plants from prolonged sunlight but leaving them open to the sky.

Shade cast by trees is also excellent for ferns if it is not too dense. Ferns prefer open shade with patches of sunlight passing over them.

The best time to plant ferns is in autumn or spring. Summer planting is all right as long as the soil is kept moist while the plants become established. If ferns are bought and delivered some time before they can be planted, do not allow their roots to dry out.

Before planting, dig over the planting bed to a depth of 1 foot, and break up the soil. Sprinkle bone meal over the surface at the rate of a scant cupful per square yard. Add a 3-inch layer of leaf mold or garden compost on top of the bone meal, and then fork it all in.

Ferns can be divided into three types: crown forming, those with rhizomatous roots, and rock ferns.

A crown-forming fern is one whose fronds emerge from a stout rhizome in the form of a vase or a crown. The shield ferns (*Dryopteris*) and the ostrich ferns (*Matteuccia*) are examples of this type.

When planting crown-forming ferns, first snap off or cut away any old woody frond bases. This will enable the new roots to emerge more quickly.

Dig a hole to the depth of the fern's root system, place the fern in the hole, and fill with soil so that the crown is flush with the surface, not below. Firm the roots in well by treading with your feet.

Rhizomatous ferns produce fronds along the rhizome without forming a crown. Among them are the hay-scented fern and the polypodies.

To plant, make a shallow depression in the soil with a fork. Place the rhizome in the hole, fill in with soil, and firm down with the fingers.

Rock ferns grow best tucked tightly among rocks, often horizontally. They are ideal for rock gardens or dry-stone walls, especially if lightly shaded. The maidenhair spleenwort (*Asplenium trichomanes*) and the woodsias are examples of rock ferns.

To plant, remove a stone from the wall or rock garden. Place the fern on its side in the resulting gap, and generously cover its roots with leaf mold. Then replace the stone.

PREPARING THE SOIL BEFORE PLANTING

1. *Dig the soil in autumn or spring, and sprinkle bone meal over it.*

2. *Add a 3-in. layer of leaf mold, and fork it into the soil.*

THE THREE PLANTING TECHNIQUES

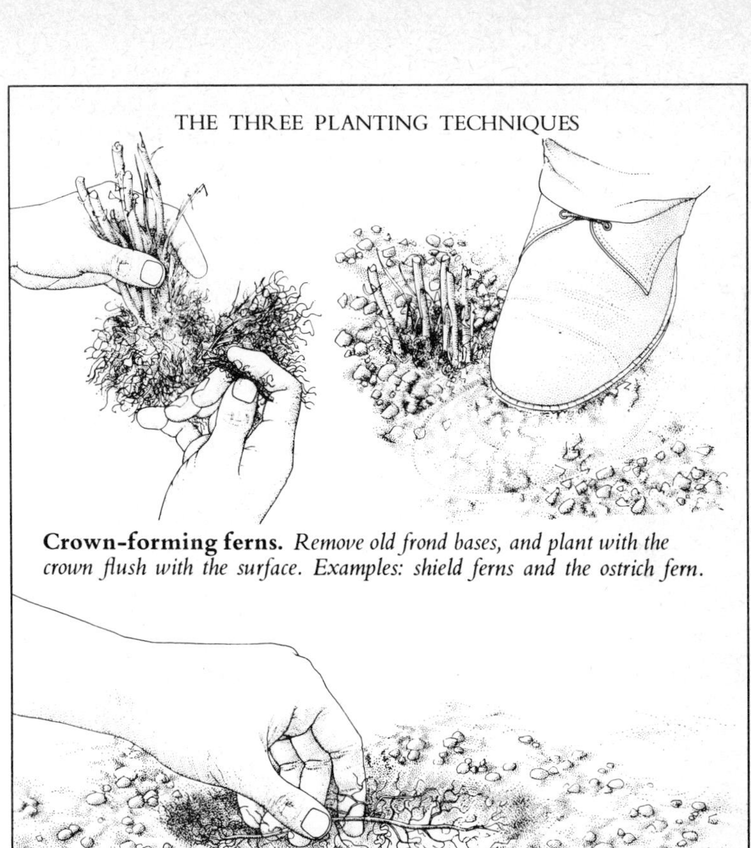

Crown-forming ferns. *Remove old frond bases, and plant with the crown flush with the surface. Examples: shield ferns and the ostrich fern.*

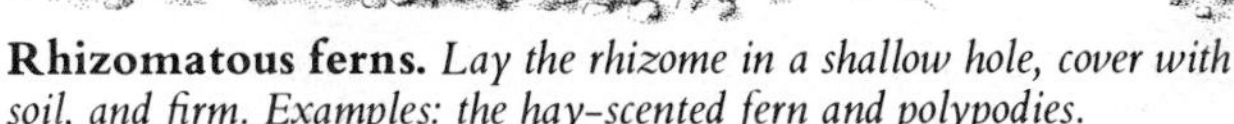

Rhizomatous ferns. *Lay the rhizome in a shallow hole, cover with soil, and firm. Examples: the hay-scented fern and polypodies.*

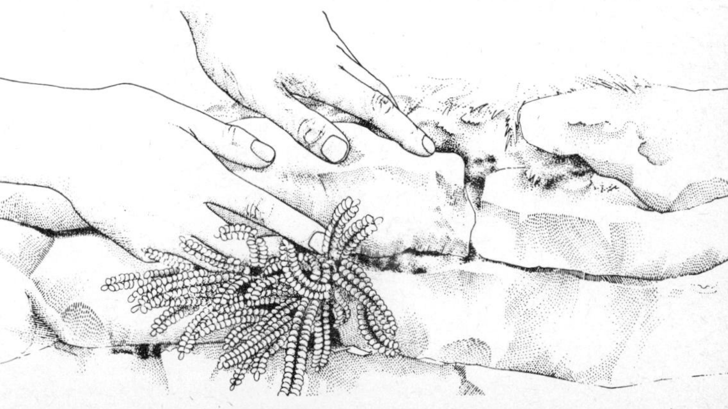

Rock ferns. *Ideal for rock gardens or dry-stone walls. Remove a stone, plant the fern on its side with leaf mold, and replace the stone.*

How to Increase Your Ferns

Mass-producing New Ferns From Spores

To raise large numbers of new ferns rapidly, sow the spores found on the underside of each fertile frond.

Choose only perfect plants, as deformities can be passed on.

Between early summer and early fall cut a frond off a fern, and lay it on half a piece of clean white tissue paper. Fold the other half of the paper over the frond, and put it in a dry place.

A day or two later the spores, which resemble fine dust, will have fallen from their capsules.

Tap the paper to shift the spores into the crease. Then fold the tissue, and carefully place it in an envelope. Label the envelope.

The spores can be sown immediately or the next spring; many species remain viable for several years.

Sowing the spores. Sterilize a seed flat or pan or a 3½- to 4-inch pot, either in a chlorine-based disinfecting solution (1 part disinfectant, 10 parts water) or by pouring boiling water over it.

Put a ½- to ¾-inch-deep layer of gravel or crock fragments in the pan. The pan should have drainage holes.

Sift some potting soil or commercial African violet soil through a ¼-inch-mesh sieve. Put the rough part in the pan first, about 1 inch deep. Then add the fine soil, about ½ inch deep, and firm with the base of a pot.

Put a piece of paper on the soil, and pour boiling water over it into the pan. As the water subsides, add more. Continue this process until the pan is too hot to handle.

As soon as the pan has cooled, remove the paper and place a sheet of glass on top.

When the soil is cold, lift a few spores from the envelope on the tip of a penknife.

Remove the glass from the pan. Gently tap the knife with the forefinger so that the spores are sprinkled evenly over the surface of the soil.

Insert a label stake giving the name of the fern and the date of sowing.

Replace the glass. Put the pan in a shady greenhouse, indoors on a shady windowsill, or under fluorescent lights. Do not remove the glass.

If the soil shows signs of drying out, water it by placing the pan in a bowl filled with a solution of a combination of water-mold inhibitor and general fungicide, such as Banrot, according to the directions on the label. This kills any organisms in the water.

The prothallia. About one or two months later a green film will indicate development of prothallia, the structures that are the intermediate sexual stage in the life cycle of ferns. Three months after sowing, the prothallia should have become small, flat, heart-shaped growths.

Five to six months after sowing, tiny new ferns should be growing from the prothallia. When these are 1–1½ inches high, they will need pricking out into a larger seed tray or flat. A 6- by 8½-inch tray will hold about 35 young ferns.

Place a shallow layer of gravel on the bottom of the tray, covering the drainage holes.

Cover the gravel with sterilized soil (put the soil in a container with drainage holes in the base, and pour boiling water over it). The soil should fill the tray to ½ inch from the rim. Settle the soil by tapping the tray on a firm surface.

Dig out a small clump of ferns from the pan with a penknife and separate them.

Plant each fern in the soil, making sure that the root system is covered. Firm gently.

Stand the tray in a container of water that reaches halfway up its side. When the surface of the soil darkens perceptibly, it has received enough water.

Put the tray in a box, and place a clean sheet of glass over it. An alternative container to the glass-covered box is a clear plastic shoe box or a one-loaf bread box with a clear plastic cover. These boxes are inexpensive and excellent for this purpose as well as for propagating cuttings taken from house plants.

Keep the tray in a cool, shady place—a greenhouse, a windowsill, or under lights. Whenever the soil shows signs of drying out, water moderately from above.

After the young ferns have produced new fronds (probably in about six weeks), they need hardening off. To accomplish this, 10 to 14 days after the new growth appears, gradually raise the cover, inserting progressively thicker wedges be-

GATHERING THE SPORES

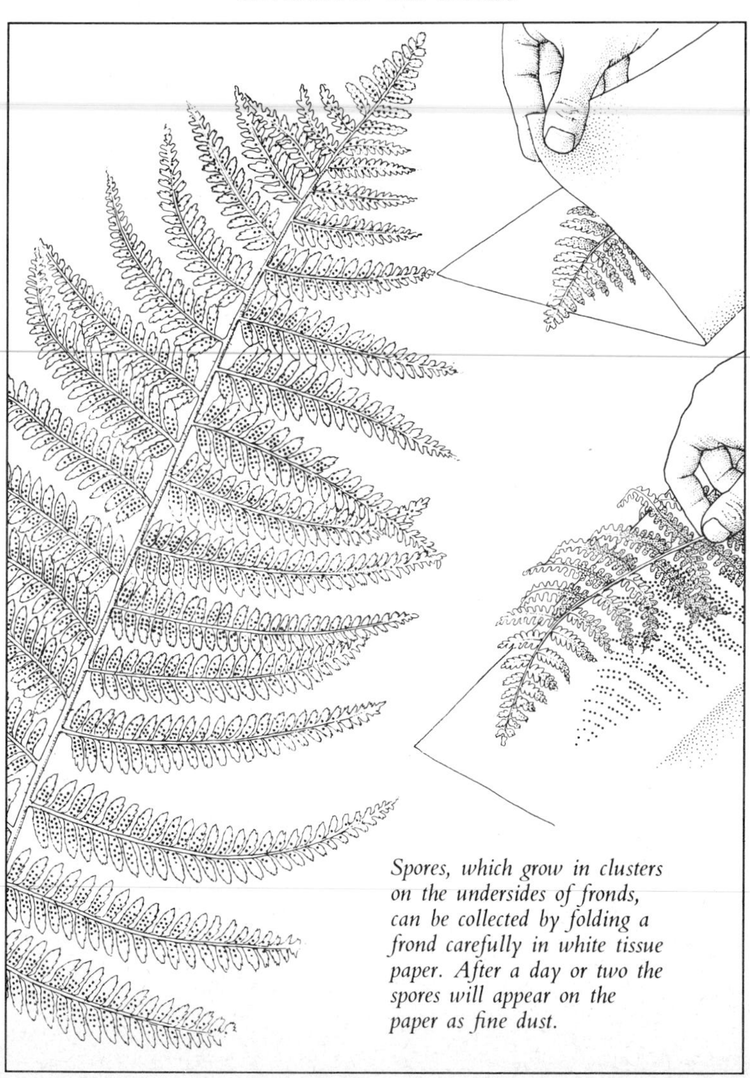

Spores, which grow in clusters on the undersides of fronds, can be collected by folding a frond carefully in white tissue paper. After a day or two the spores will appear on the paper as fine dust.

tween the box and the cover. Two or three weeks later remove the cover altogether. A few days later the plants will be hardened off.

Potting the ferns. The young ferns will now need to be transferred to individual pots.

Fill a $2\frac{1}{2}$-inch pot with a light soil mixture to within $\frac{1}{2}$ inch of the rim. Ease a young fern from the tray with a small trowel, and plant it in the pot. Firm the soil around the plant with your fingers.

Sprinkle a layer of gravel over the soil. This helps to stop the soil from caking when it is watered and keeps the surface cool.

Water thoroughly, and place the pot in a shady greenhouse or indoors on a shady windowsill or under fluorescent lights.

About two months later examine the soil ball for roots. Remove by inverting the pot and tapping the rim on the edge of a table, holding the fern between your fingers.

If the roots have reached the outside of the ball, loosen up the base of the root ball, and plant in a 3-inch pot. Put in a shady place.

When the 3-inch pot is filled with roots, repot into a 4-inch pot, and then into progressively larger pots as the plant continues to grow. Set outdoors when the fern is established and the weather is suitable.

FROM SPORE TO FERN IN 12 STEPS

1. *Sieve soil mixture and place in a seed pan or pot, with the fine soil on top.*

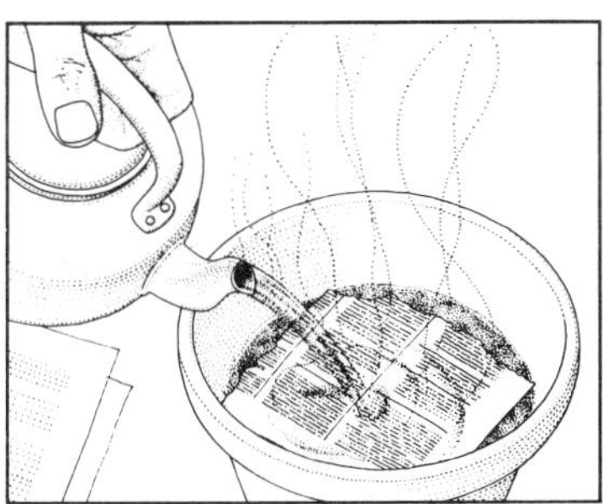

2. *Sterilize soil with boiling water. Paper protects the fine surface.*

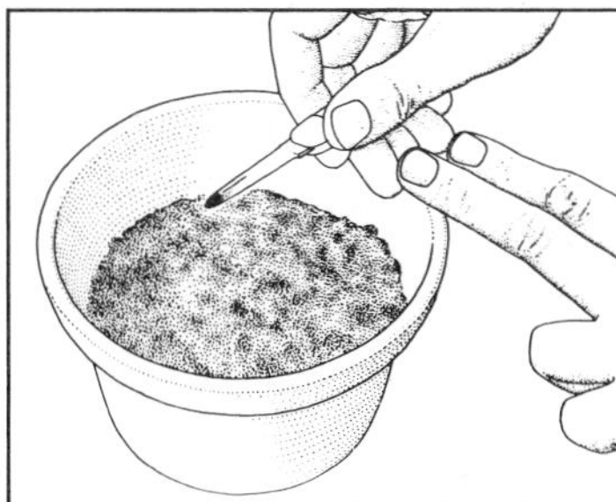

3. *Sprinkle the spores on the soil, and cover with a sheet of glass.*

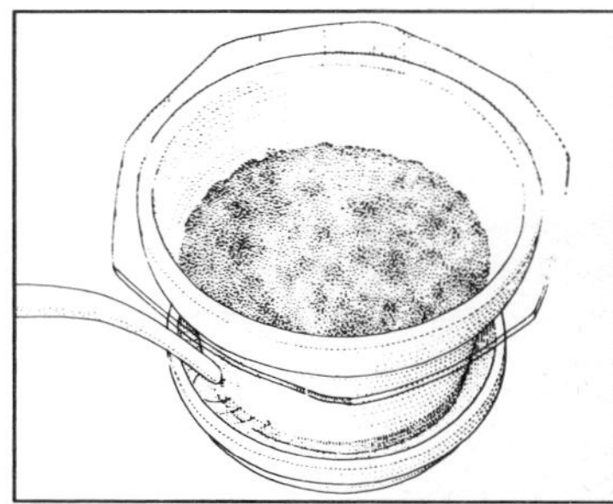

4. *Water dry soil by standing it in a solution of Banrot.*

5. *A month or two later, prothallia (first stages of a fern) will have developed.*

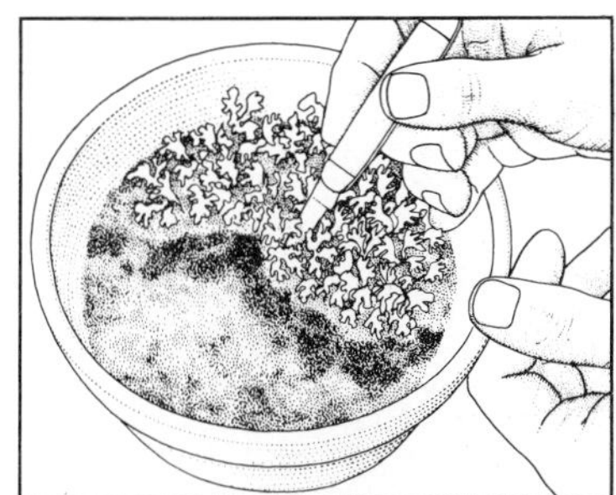

6. *When they are 1–$1\frac{1}{2}$ in. high, the ferns will be too crowded in the pan.*

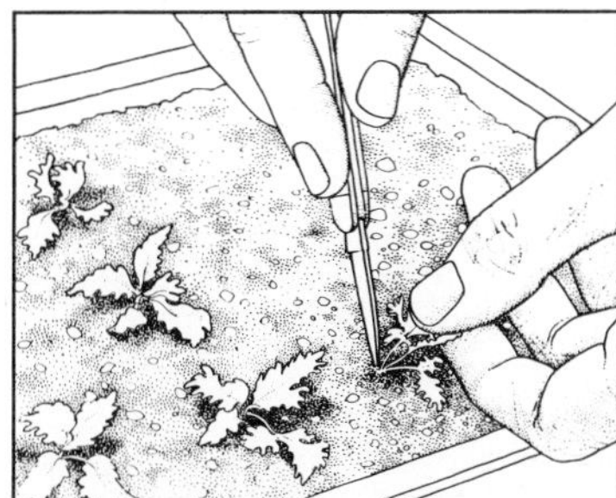

7. *Separate the ferns and plant in a seed tray or flat, firming with the fingers.*

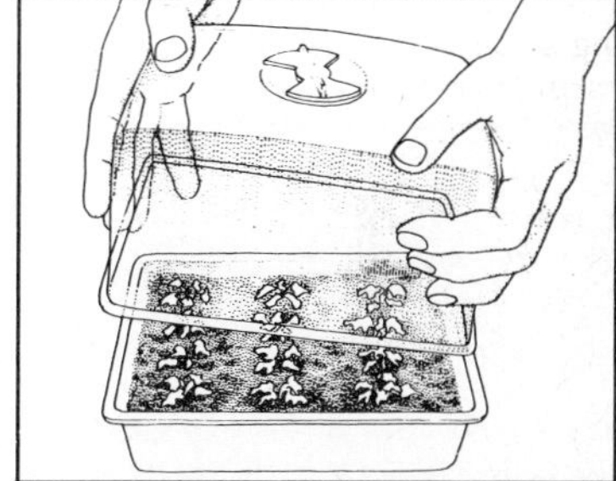

8. *Put on a propagating cover, and keep in a cool, shady place for six weeks.*

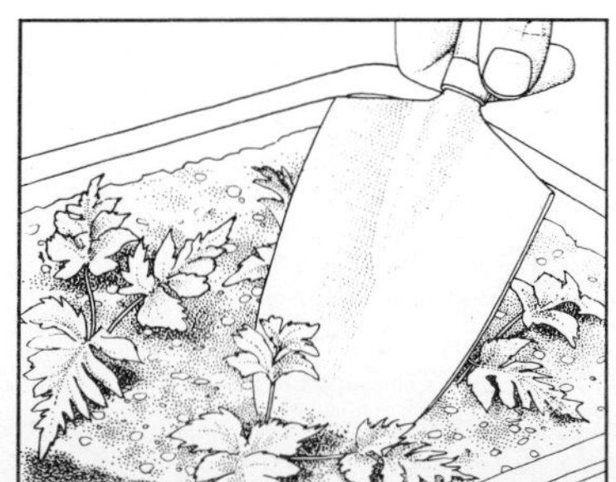

9. *When the ferns grow new fronds, lift from the tray with a small trowel.*

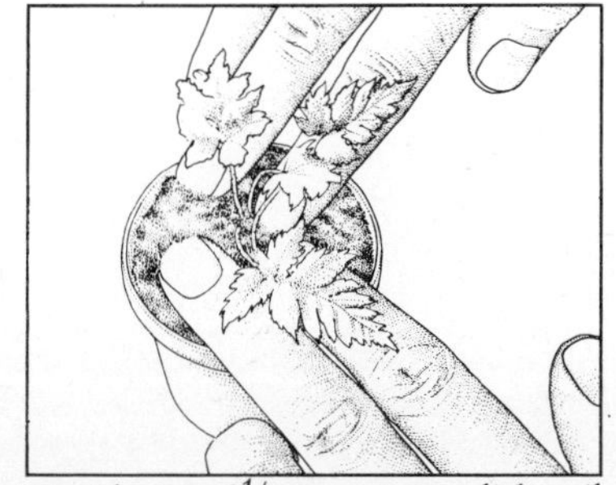

10. *Plant in $2\frac{1}{2}$-in. pots in a light soil mixture. Firm with the fingers.*

11. *Cover the surface with gravel to keep soil from caking when watered.*

12. *Two months later, examine the roots. Move fern to a larger pot if necessary.*

Keeping Ferns Healthy

Division—The Easiest Method of Propagation

The easiest way to propagate the crown-forming ferns, such as shield ferns and ostrich ferns, is by division of the crowns in midspring.

Carefully dig up a clump of ferns with a fork, and cut off the fronds.

With a small clump it may be possible to pull the crowns apart with the hands. If the clump is large, use two garden forks. Push them back to back into the center of the clump. Be careful not to pierce the crowns. Gently push the handles together; then pull them apart until the clump is broken into two parts. It may sometimes be best to make the final division with a sharp knife to minimize possible damage.

Subdivide the two new clumps by the same method to produce several new plants, each with its own root system. Plant these by the method described for crown-forming ferns on page 385.

Rhizomatous ferns can also be propagated by division. In midspring dig up a clump of ferns, and cut off the fronds. With a sharp knife cut the rhizome into sections, each with at least one growing point (the point from which new shoots are emerging). Plant these individual sections by the method described for rhizomatous-rooted ferns on page 385. Each of these will form a new fern.

Watering, Feeding, and General Care

Once ferns are established, they need watering only during hot periods, when the soil may dry out.

After planting, cover the entire surface around the ferns with a 3-inch-deep mulch of garden compost, leaf mold, or peat moss. This will help to conserve moisture during dry spells.

Reapply this mulch each autumn and spring. Also in spring, before spreading the mulch on the bed, scatter bone meal around the plants, using about a cupful per square yard.

Weed ferns by hand, since forking or hoeing can damage the root system, which in established ferns is near the surface of the soil.

Each spring remove dead fronds with a knife or clippers, as near to the crown as possible. This will encourage new shoots to form.

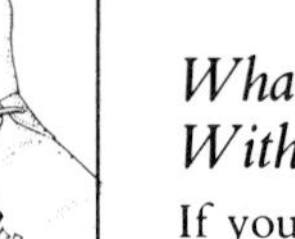

Mulch ferns in spring and fall with leaf mold or peat moss. In spring apply bone meal first.

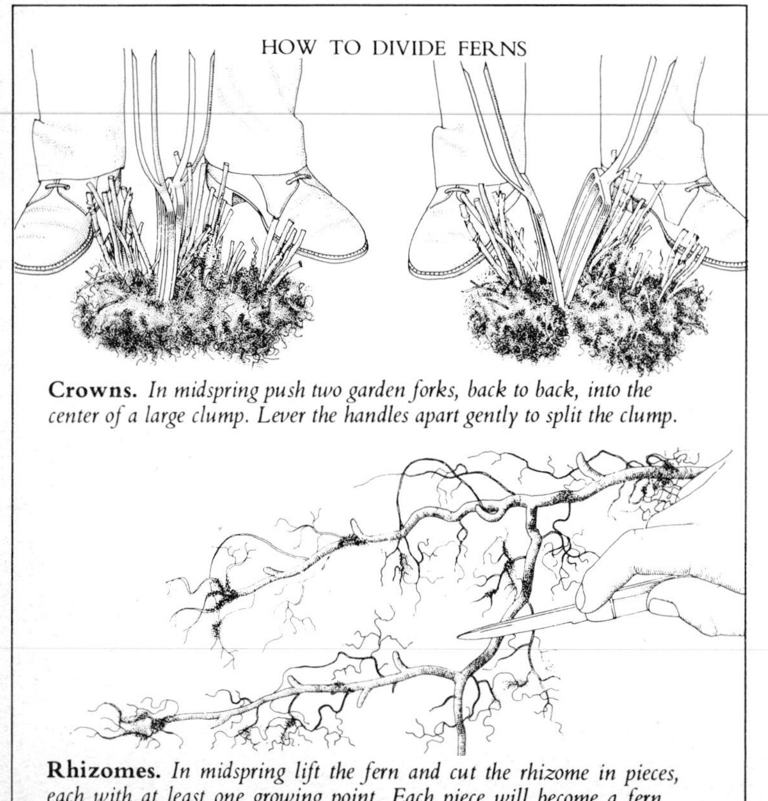

Crowns. *In midspring push two garden forks, back to back, into the center of a large clump. Lever the handles apart gently to split the clump.*

Rhizomes. *In midspring lift the fern and cut the rhizome in pieces, each with at least one growing point. Each piece will become a fern.*

What Can Go Wrong With Ferns

If your plants show symptoms that are not described here, turn to the full-color identification chart that lists pests, diseases, and other plant troubles on page 600. For useful chemicals and their trade names, see page 635.

Symptoms and signs	Cause	Control
Sticky patches, sometimes covered with sooty mold. Fronds may be distorted.	Aphids or plant bugs	Spray with Diazinon, formothion, or malathion for aphids. Use carbaryl, Diazinon, or methoxychlor for plant bugs.
Fronds collapse or wilt during warm or dry spells.	Vine weevil larvae (grubs)	Sprinkle chlordane, lindane, or methoxychlor powder on ground. Or water thoroughly with malathion solution.
Blackish-brown streaks or narrow blotches across fronds. Severe attack causes death of fronds.	Foliar nematodes (eelworms)	No effective control; badly infected plants should be lifted and destroyed. Spraying chlorpyrifos or Diazinon may help. Systemic sprays of dimethoate or oxydemeton-methyl are also useful.
Fronds are eaten off.	Slugs or snails	Sprinkle slug pellets on soil.
Young fronds are chewed around edges.	Wood lice (sow bugs)	Apply carbaryl or Diazinon powder to soil close to fern crowns (not on fronds).

Ferns to Brighten a Shady Place

The following chart provides a wide selection of ferns that can be grown outdoors in North America. Sizes range from the tiny maidenhair spleenwort (*Asplenium trichomanes*), often only 5 inches high, to the royal fern (*Osmunda regalis*), which reaches 6 feet in height.

In subtropical regions of North America where freezing does not occur, there are a great number of ferns available for outdoor planting in various kinds of soil.

The best methods for starting new plants are given for each species in the Propagation column. The term "dimorphic" used in the Remarks column means that fertile and sterile fronds that occur on the same plant are different in form.

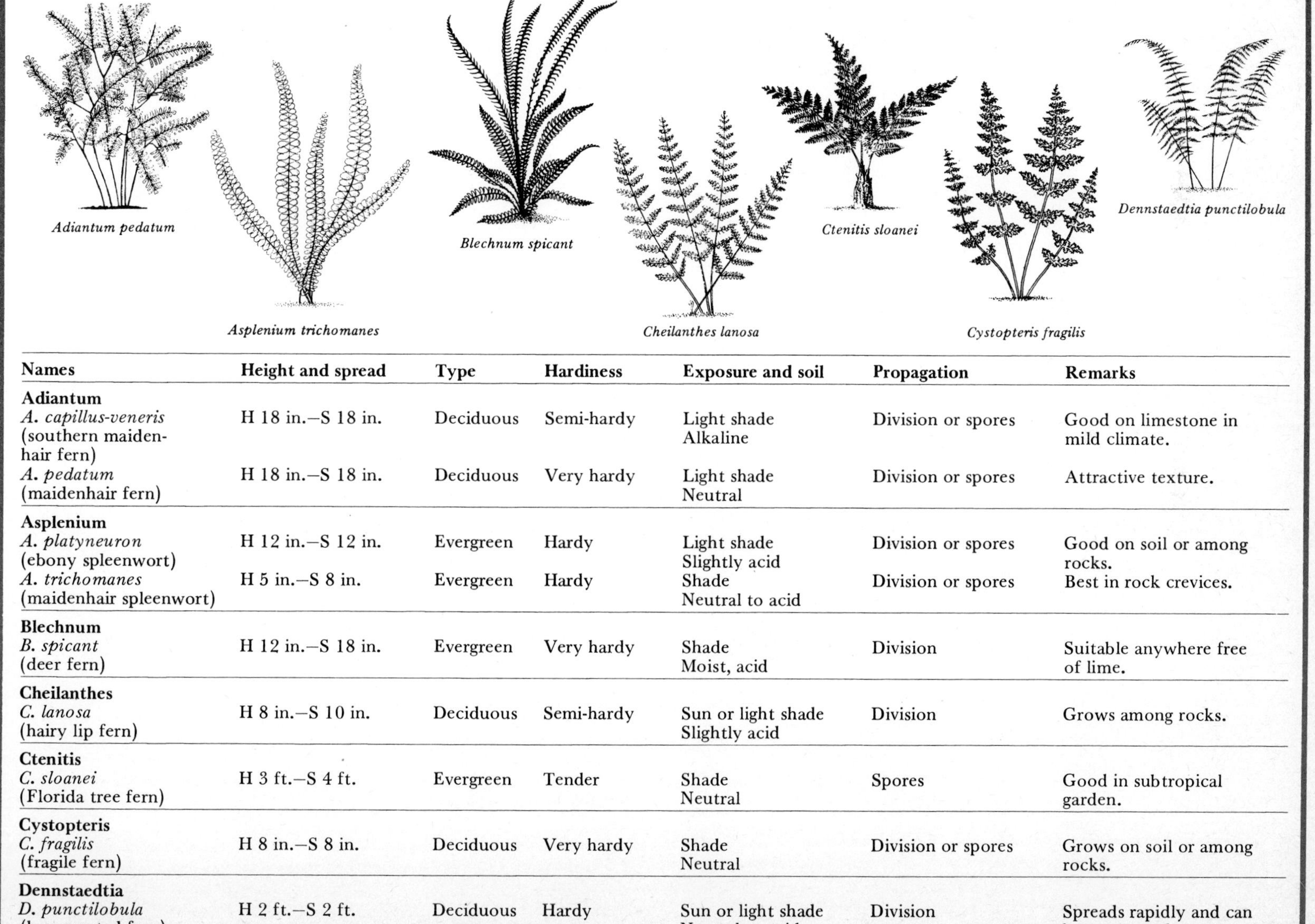

Names	Height and spread	Type	Hardiness	Exposure and soil	Propagation	Remarks
Adiantum						
A. capillus-veneris (southern maiden-hair fern)	H 18 in.–S 18 in.	Deciduous	Semi-hardy	Light shade Alkaline	Division or spores	Good on limestone in mild climate.
A. pedatum (maidenhair fern)	H 18 in.–S 18 in.	Deciduous	Very hardy	Light shade Neutral	Division or spores	Attractive texture.
Asplenium						
A. platyneuron (ebony spleenwort)	H 12 in.–S 12 in.	Evergreen	Hardy	Light shade Slightly acid	Division or spores	Good on soil or among rocks.
A. trichomanes (maidenhair spleenwort)	H 5 in.–S 8 in.	Evergreen	Hardy	Shade Neutral to acid	Division or spores	Best in rock crevices.
Blechnum						
B. spicant (deer fern)	H 12 in.–S 18 in.	Evergreen	Very hardy	Shade Moist, acid	Division	Suitable anywhere free of lime.
Cheilanthes						
C. lanosa (hairy lip fern)	H 8 in.–S 10 in.	Deciduous	Semi-hardy	Sun or light shade Slightly acid	Division	Grows among rocks.
Ctenitis						
C. sloanei (Florida tree fern)	H 3 ft.–S 4 ft.	Evergreen	Tender	Shade Neutral	Spores	Good in subtropical garden.
Cystopteris						
C. fragilis (fragile fern)	H 8 in.–S 8 in.	Deciduous	Very hardy	Shade Neutral	Division or spores	Grows on soil or among rocks.
Dennstaedtia						
D. punctilobula (hay-scented fern)	H 2 ft.–S 2 ft.	Deciduous	Hardy	Sun or light shade Neutral to acid	Division	Spreads rapidly and can become weedy.

Dryopteris cristata

Gymnocarpium dryopteris

Matteuccia struthiopteris

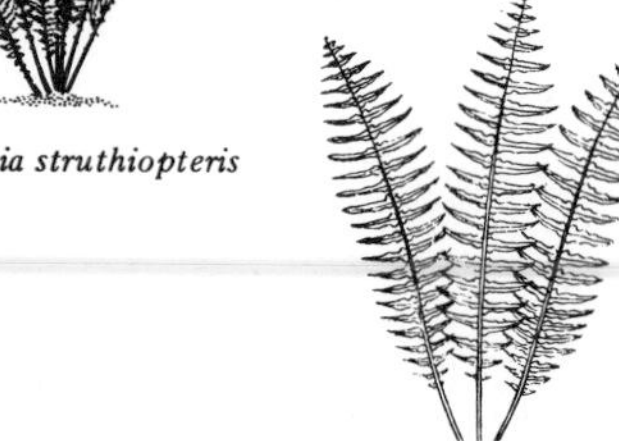

Nephrolepis exaltata

Onoclea sensibilis

Osmunda regalis

Names	Height and spread	Type	Hardiness	Exposure and soil	Propagation	Remarks
Dryopteris						
D. cristata (crested shield fern)	H 2-3 ft.–S 2 ft.	Evergreen	Hardy	Shade Acid, boggy	Division or spores	Leaflets turn horizontally in steplike fashion.
D. goldiana (Goldie's shield fern)	H 4 ft.–S 4 ft.	Evergreen	Hardy	Shade Neutral	Division or spores	Large, impressive plant.
D. intermedia (fancy fern)	H 2 ft.–S 2 ft.	Evergreen	Very hardy	Shade Neutral to acid	Division or spores	Desirable for dark bluish-green leaves.
D. marginalis (marginal shield fern)	H 2-3 ft. S 2½ ft.	Evergreen	Very hardy	Light shade Neutral	Division or spores	Easily established. Grayish-green fronds.
Gymnocarpium						
G. dryopteris (oak fern)	H 9 in.–S 9 in.	Deciduous	Hardy	Shade Acid	Division	One of loveliest American ferns. Suitable for humus-rich garden.
Matteuccia						
M. struthiopteris (ostrich fern)	H 3-5 ft. S 4-8 ft.	Deciduous	Hardy	Light shade Neutral to acid, wet	Division	Good foundation planting. Dimorphic fronds.
Nephrolepis						
N. exaltata (sword fern)	H 2 ft.–S 2 ft.	Evergreen	Tender	Sun or light shade Loose, acid	Division	Grows in ground or on tree trunks in subtropical garden. Many varieties.
Onoclea						
O. sensibilis (sensitive fern)	H 2-3 ft. S 2 ft.	Deciduous	Hardy	Sun or light shade Neutral to acid, wet	Division	Suitable anywhere. Dimorphic fronds. Green fronds shrivel at first frost.
Osmunda						
O. cinnamomea (cinnamon fern)	H 4-6 ft. S 2-3 ft.	Deciduous	Very hardy	Light shade Acid, wet	Division or spores	First fern up in spring. White woolly crosiers.
O. regalis (royal fern)	H 4-6 ft. S 4-8 ft.	Deciduous	Hardy	Light shade Neutral to acid, wet	Division or spores	Golden terminal spore cases resemble blooms.

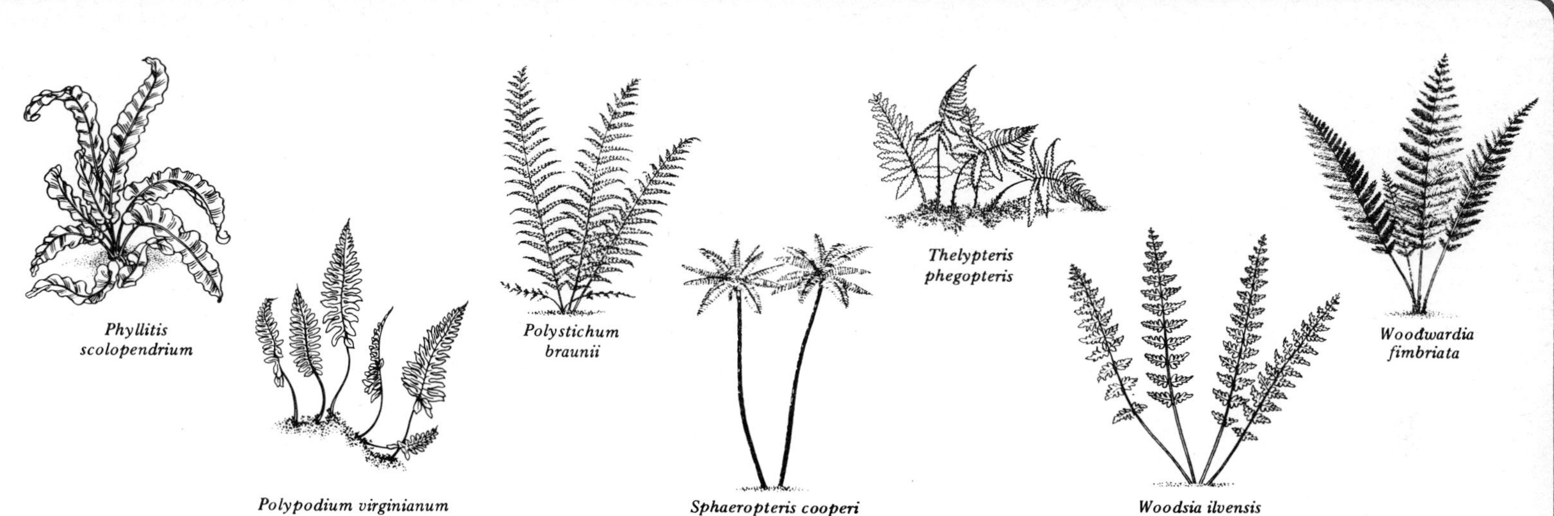

Names	Height and spread	Type	Hardiness	Exposure and soil	Propagation	Remarks
Phyllitis *P. scolopendrium* (hart's-tongue fern)	H 15 in.–S 18 in.	Evergreen	Hardy	Light shade Alkaline	Division or spores	Many crested and frilled varieties.
Polypodium *P. virginianum* (polypody fern)	H 6-8 in.–S 12 in.	Evergreen	Hardy	Light shade Neutral	Division	Grows best on mossy rocks.
Polystichum *P. braunii* (Braun's holly fern)	H 2 ft.–S 2 ft.	Evergreen	Hardy	Shade Acid	Division or spores	Striking glossy, dark green leaves.
P. munitum (western sword fern)	H 3 ft.–S 3-4 ft.	Evergreen	Hardy	Shade Acid	Division or spores	Handsome plant. Grows well in Northwest.
Sphaeropteris *S. cooperi* (Australian tree fern)	H 15 ft.–S 10 ft.	Evergreen	Tender	Light shade Acid	Spores	Fine for tropical garden. Fast growing.
Thelypteris *T. noveboracensis* (New York fern)	H 18-24 in. S 24 in.	Deciduous	Hardy	Light shade Acid	Division	Spreads very rapidly.
T. phegopteris (narrow beech fern)	H 6-12 in. S 12-18 in.	Deciduous	Hardy	Light shade Acid	Division	Excellent for shady rock garden.
Woodsia *W. ilvensis* (rusty woodsia)	H 6 in.–S 8 in.	Deciduous	Hardy	Light shade Neutral	Division or spores	Good in rock garden. Crosiers that appear in spring have silver scales.
Woodwardia *W. areolata* (netted chain fern)	H 2 ft.–S 18 in.	Deciduous	Hardy	Shade Acid, moist	Division	Dimorphic fronds.
W. fimbriata (western chain fern)	H 4-8 ft. S 4-8 ft.	Evergreen	Semi-hardy	Shade Acid	Division or spores	Grows especially well in Northwest.

Gardening Under Cover

House Plants

The secret of growing house plants is to provide the right conditions of light, heat, and humidity. Keep this in mind as you choose plants for each part of the house.

During the past 20 years the interest in growing house plants has increased tremendously. The reasons? In general, houses today provide more favorable conditions for plant growth than they did in the past; the assortment of readily available plants has been added to substantially; and concern for our natural environment has soared.

Many houses, apartments, and offices have large windows that provide the intensity of light necessary for plant growth. Where natural light is inadequate, supplemental artificial light can be provided (see p. 408). The range of indoor plants runs from such easily grown kinds as philodendrons and snake plants to more difficult plants, such as peperomias and false aralias (*Dizygotheca*), and on to a still more challenging group, which includes such plants as anthuriums and certain types of begonias and ferns.

Types of house plants. Broadly speaking, house plants fall into two categories: foliage plants and flowering plants. (Although some foliage plants may produce flowers, they are usually not grown for this purpose.) The chart beginning on page 410 lists some house plants grown primarily for their foliage and others grown primarily for their flowers (or sometimes their colorful fruits).

In general, foliage plants are the easier to grow. Foliage plants are either green leaved or variegated, often with strong, dominating reds or purples. Green-and-white variegated kinds, such as spider plants, are usually as easy to grow as green-leaved plants, but they require more light. Coleuses, which have varied, vibrant leaf markings, are not difficult; neither are the silver-banded, purple-backed wandering Jews. However, two other brilliantly colored foliage plants—crotons and prayer plants—may fail after a few months if their exacting requirements of soil, temperature, and humidity are not met.

Many flowering house plants will continue to bloom indoors year after year under the correct conditions. A few popular ones include African violets, miniature geraniums, and some begonias and orchids. Plants such as cyclamens and poinsettias do not flower as readily year after year, because of their special requirements. For example, the cyclamen needs a cooler temperature than most of us like to live in, and it needs special care after flowering. The poinsettia, although a fairly rugged plant thanks to today's improved hybrids, needs a long period of darkness (14 hours a day) in order to produce the colorful bracts (modified leaves) that surround its flowers.

Some flowering house plants, such as the calceolaria and the cineraria, must be started from seeds each year. Since they require many months under carefully controlled conditions

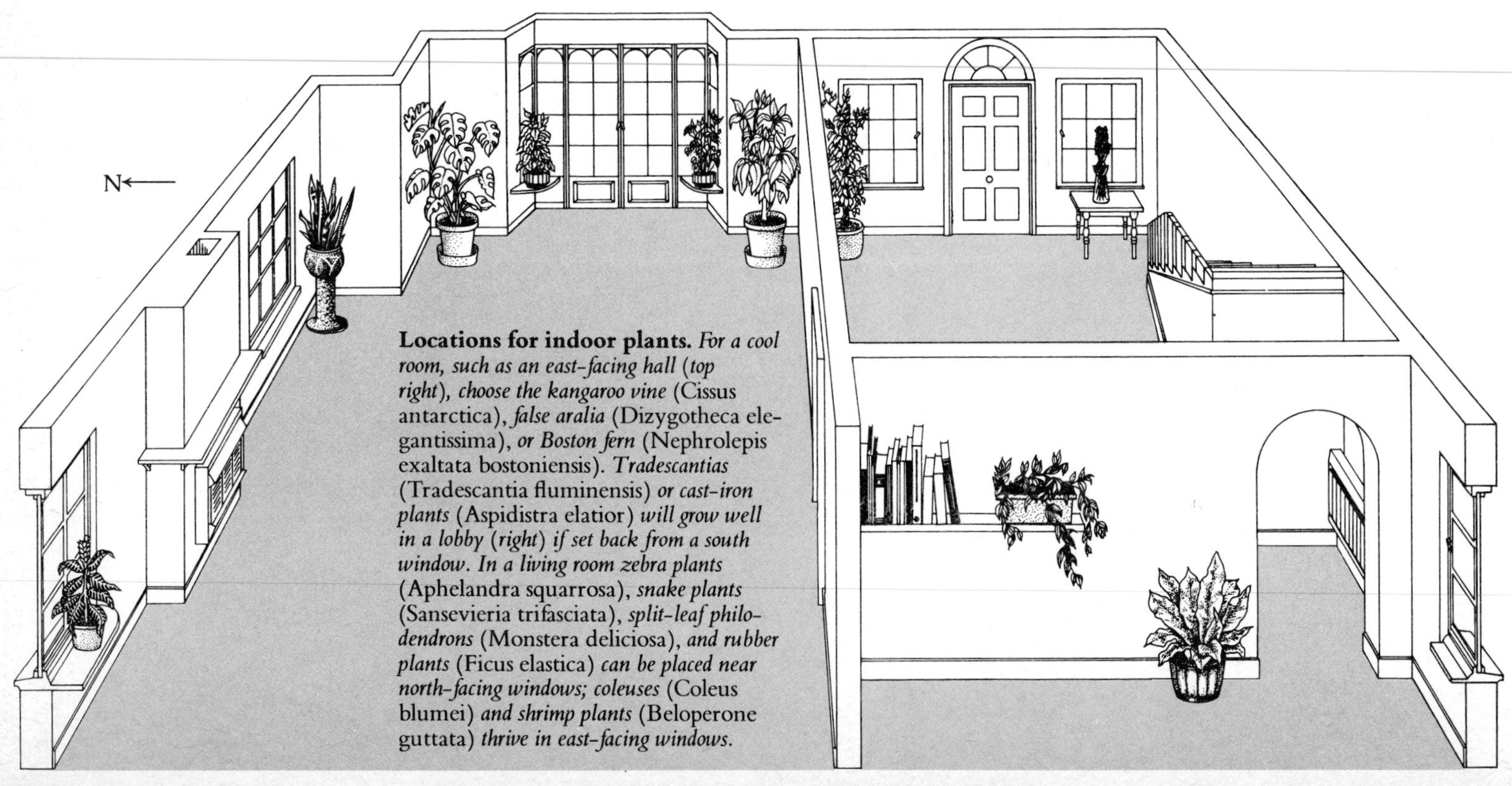

Locations for indoor plants. *For a cool room, such as an east-facing hall (top right), choose the kangaroo vine* (Cissus antarctica), *false aralia* (Dizygotheca elegantissima), *or Boston fern* (Nephrolepis exaltata bostoniensis). *Tradescantias* (Tradescantia fluminensis) *or cast-iron plants* (Aspidistra elatior) *will grow well in a lobby (right) if set back from a south window. In a living room zebra plants* (Aphelandra squarrosa), *snake plants* (Sansevieria trifasciata), *split-leaf philodendrons* (Monstera deliciosa), *and rubber plants* (Ficus elastica) *can be placed near north-facing windows; coleuses* (Coleus blumei) *and shrimp plants* (Beloperone guttata) *thrive in east-facing windows.*

to bring them into bloom, they are usually purchased from a florist when in flower, enjoyed for several weeks, and then discarded.

The azalea, another popular florist's plant, is an exceptionally long bloomer when room temperature is not above 50°–60° F. Azaleas can be placed outdoors for the summer (in a partially shaded location) and brought indoors in autumn to bloom another year.

Bromeliads are a special type of plant, grown as much for their unusual foliage as for their flowers. The silver vase (*Aechmea fasciata*), for example, has a spectacular flower spike that develops in the center of an attractive "vase" formed by the gray-green, silver-banded leaves.

In their natural environments many bromeliads grow on tree branches, where their roots absorb nourishment from the leaf mold and other debris that collect there. Such epiphytes (as these perching plants are called) need a different growing medium from other plants—usually one consisting of equal parts of fir bark, peat moss, perlite, sand, and pea or bird gravel, kept barely moist. To care for these bromeliads, simply pour water into the vase when it becomes dry.

Not all bromeliads are epiphytes. The terrestrial bromeliads, such as the earth star (*Cryptanthus*), grow in the ground and will do well in standard house-plant mix (see p. 397).

Selecting the right plants. Your chances of succeeding with a given plant are increased if you select one whose needs correspond closely to the conditions that you can provide. Also helpful is some understanding of the environmental factors that affect plant growth, such as temperature, humidity, and light.

Fortunately, dwellings are usually kept at temperatures between 65° and 70° F during the daytime, which suits a wide variety of plants. However, some plants, such as cyclamens and camellias, will thrive in chilly 55°–60° F daytime temperatures. Night temperature is important, too, and most plants grow best when there is a 10- to 15-degree drop at night. A greater drop can be harmful to many plants.

Most heated houses and offices have dry air, which is usually harmful to indoor plants, especially tropical and semi-tropical kinds that require high humidity. The humidity can be increased by several methods (see p. 398). Plants that need a higher-than-normal humidity (such as African violets, many orchids, and ferns) do particularly well in moist bathrooms, provided that there is sufficient temperature and light.

Although most plants benefit from freely circulating air, few will tolerate cold drafts or hot air blowing directly on them. Coal fumes or fumes from gas manufactured from coal or oil can be damaging, but plants are not adversely affected by natural-gas fumes.

Well-lighted rooms suit the widest variety of house plants. South- and west-facing windows provide the best light—but only if they are not obstructed by tall buildings, trees, or curtains. East windows can be excellent locations for house plants, and many plants, such as

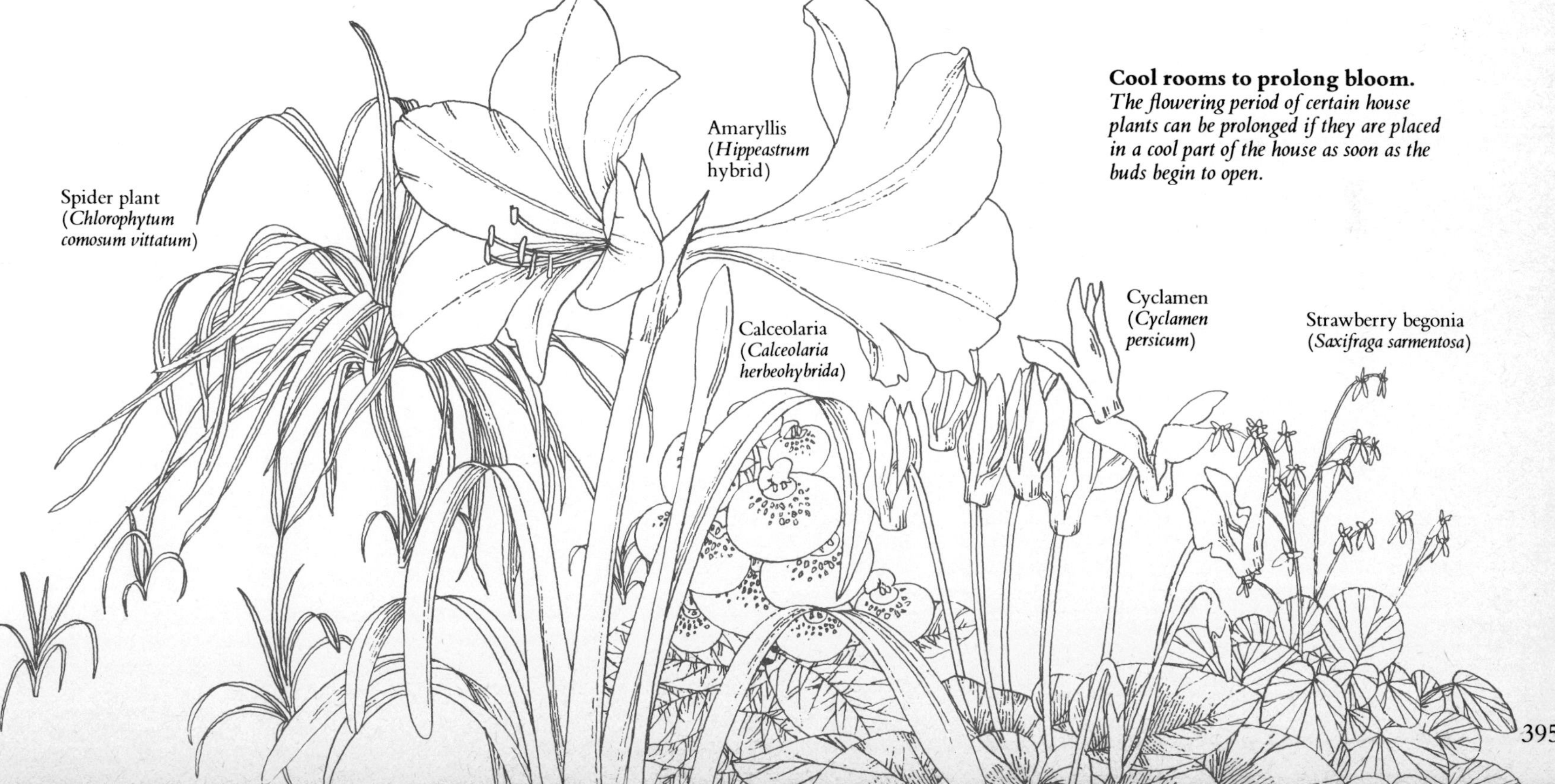

Cool rooms to prolong bloom. *The flowering period of certain house plants can be prolonged if they are placed in a cool part of the house as soon as the buds begin to open.*

rubber plants and aglaonemas, will grow satisfactorily in the lesser light of a north window. Direct sun is generally not too strong for most plants in winter, but as it increases in intensity toward summer, plants may have to be moved farther from the glass or shaded by a net curtain. Too much sun may cause leaves to turn pale green or yellow.

On extremely cold winter nights it is advisable to move plants away from windows. Temperatures on a windowsill may be 20 degrees lower than elsewhere in the room unless the windowsill is protected by insulated glass, a storm window, or a heavy curtain. Cardboard or layers of newspapers, placed between the glass and the plants, can provide temporary protection.

Even for drafty, badly lighted halls, stairs, and landings, there is a considerable choice of house plants. Snake plants, Japanese aralias, fatshederas, cast-iron plants, and several kinds of philodendrons are among those that do well under such seemingly inhospitable conditions.

Where light is totally inadequate, the addition of artificial light makes it possible to grow most plants. To find out how to grow plants under artificial light, see page 408.

Arranging and grouping plants. Many foliage plants are seen to best advantage when several containers are grouped together. When grouping assorted kinds, try to achieve some contrast between leaf size, form, texture, and color for the most attractive effect.

The most practical way to display groups of indoor plants is on trays filled with pebbles and water. The water level should be kept just below the bottoms of the pots; evaporation of the water helps to increase the humidity around the plants. Special trays, usually made of metal or plastic, are available for most standard windowsills; they can be built to fit other locations. Leave enough space between plants so that they get light and air can circulate between them.

Shape is an important factor to be considered when placing house plants. Rubber plants have an erect habit of growth, kangaroo vines are climbers, and both eventually grow to heights of 6 feet or more. Other house plants, such as most pileas and African violets, are small and bushy. Trailing plants, such as the wandering Jews and many forms of English ivy, require little headroom but need plenty of space to display their cascading stems.

Fast-growing climbers are ideal to grow against room dividers and bare walls that are well lighted. Hanging baskets provide an attractive way to display such plants as strawberry begonias (*Saxifraga sarmentosa*) and spider plants, which have runners or offshoots, as well as trailing plants and even some nontrailing plants, such as ferns and impatiens. Usually the baskets are suspended from brackets placed above or around windows or glass walls.

Hanging plants often reveal unexpected dimensions of beauty, perhaps because they are generally observed at or above eye level. One great advantage is that they save shelf space and can easily be moved outdoors in summer to decorate a terrace or patio.

"Dish gardens"—groupings of small plants in a single container of soil—were once a popular means of displaying house plants. Although some florists still sell such arrangements, they are not seen as frequently as they used to be.

Putting together a dish garden requires attention to both horticultural and artistic details; plants grouped together must have the same requirements, and they should complement one another in color and form. With carefully selected plants—and perhaps a few pebbles or pieces of wood—it is possible to emulate the art form of *Saikei* (the making of miniature landscapes) that was perfected by Japanese gardeners.

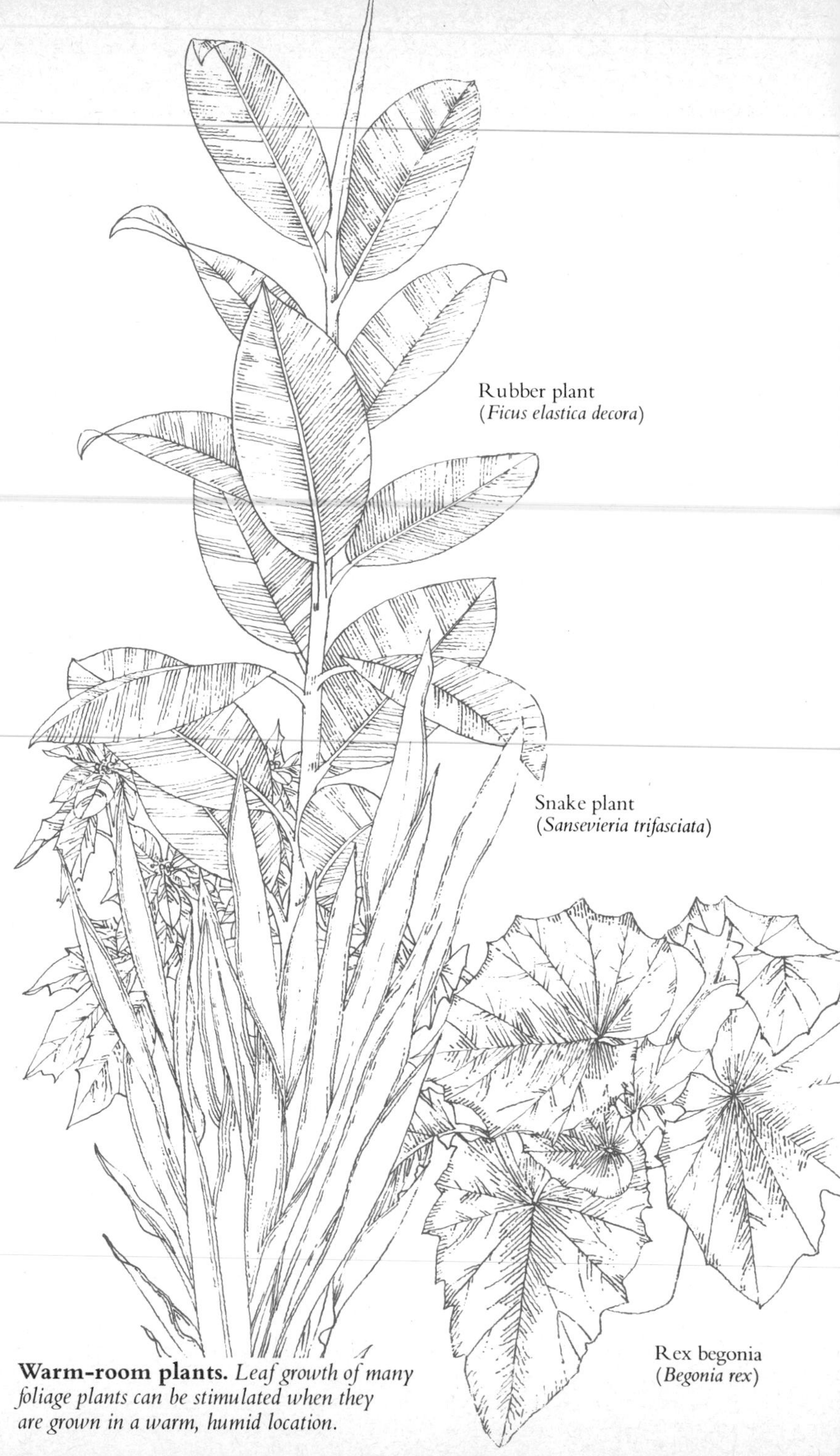

Warm-room plants. *Leaf growth of many foliage plants can be stimulated when they are grown in a warm, humid location.*

How to Get the Best out of House Plants

Potting Plants That Have Outgrown Their Containers

House plants often need repotting when they become pot-bound. You can easily tell when this has happened to a plant: it produces little or no new growth, and it dries out quickly even after frequent watering. The roots of such a plant may protrude from the drainage holes.

Generally, young plants should be repotted into larger pots once a year, usually in spring. Established plants need repotting less frequently; every two or three years should be sufficient. Such plants can usually be repotted in the same container but will require fresh soil. A pot-bound plant should be transplanted only when its soil is slightly moist.

Use only clean pots. If necessary, scrub the pots in a diluted chlorine disinfectant (1 part in 10 parts water). New clay pots should be soaked in water for at least five minutes, or they will absorb some of the moisture from the soil.

When repotting into a clay pot with a large drainage opening, place a crock (a piece of broken clay pot) over the hole, convex side up, to prevent soil leakage. Or use a clamshell or piece of plastic screening, covered with a layer of small crocks. This crocking may not be necessary in plastic pots, which usually have several small drainage holes.

Before repotting, place a 1- to 2-inch layer of soil in the new container. To dislodge the plant, hold the root ball with your fingers (as shown below), and tap the rim of the pot on the edge of a table. Set the root ball on the layer of soil in the new container so that the top of the root ball is $\frac{1}{2}$ inch below the bottom of the pot's rim. With one hand, hold the plant in the center of the pot as you trickle more soil into the space between root ball and pot.

Press the soil down with your fingers; then lightly thump the pot on a firm surface to settle the soil. Fill as necessary with more soil to leave at least $\frac{1}{2}$ inch of space between the top of the soil and the top of the pot. Then water thoroughly.

1. *Invert a pot-bound plant, and shake out the ball of roots and soil.*

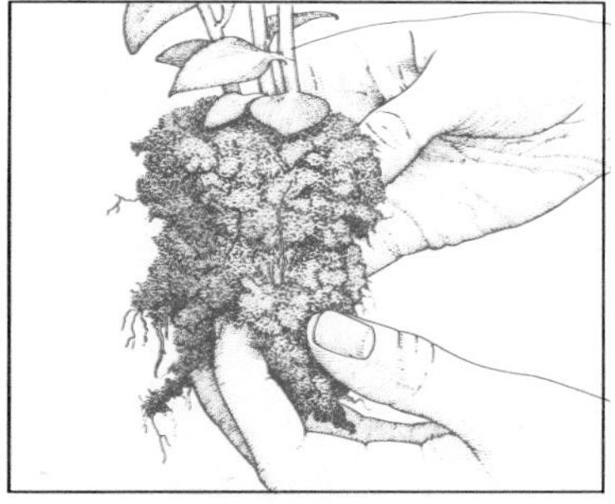

2. *Before putting the plant in a larger pot, ease away some of the old soil.*

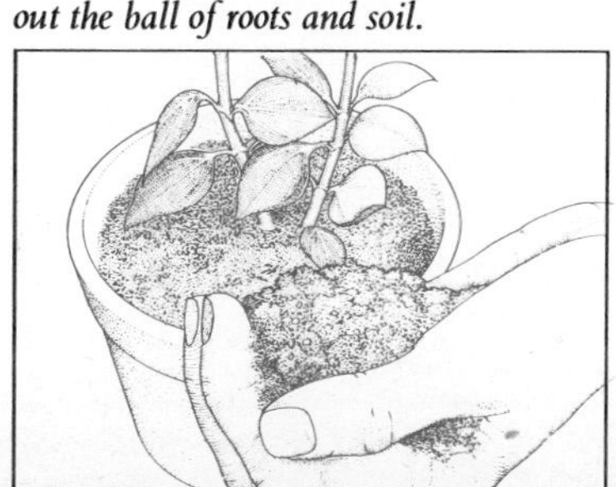

3. *Set the root ball on fresh potting soil, and trickle more soil around it.*

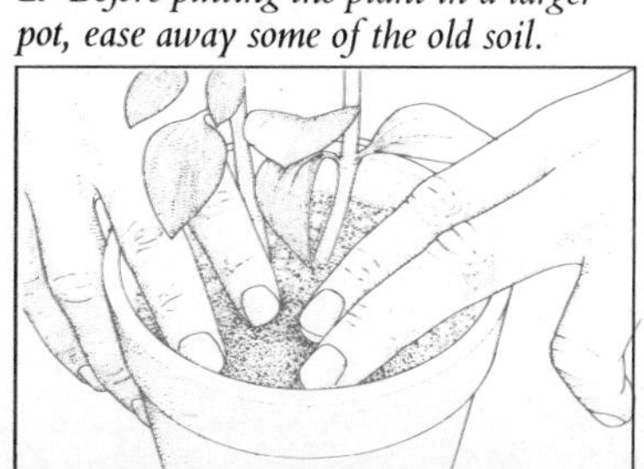

4. *Hold the plant loosely by the stem; firm the soil with your fingers.*

Using the correct soil mixture. The soil in which house plants are grown requires more attention than soil in an outdoor garden. It is most important for house-plant soil—or artificial growing medium, such as peat moss, perlite, or vermiculite—to contain the correct proportions of essential plant nutrients. Ideally, it should be sterilized to ensure freedom from soil-borne pests, diseases, and weeds.

Many gardeners prefer to purchase packaged soil or soilless mixes rather than to prepare and sterilize their own. However, for those who have access to the ingredients and equipment, the following combinations and sterilizing techniques will serve as a guide. The soil mixtures can be made in any quantity.

This general-purpose mixture can be used for most house plants, especially those that have strong root systems.

- 2 parts garden soil
- 1 part peat moss or leaf mold
- 1 part perlite, coarse sand, or bird gravel
- $\frac{1}{4}$ part bone meal or $\frac{1}{8}$ part superphosphate
- $\frac{1}{2}$ part dry cow manure

For plants that need a soil with more organic matter, such as begonias and African violets, use the above mixture with double the amount of peat moss or leaf mold.

For plants that require an acidic soil, such as azaleas, camellias, and gardenias, double the peat moss and dry cow manure, and use superphosphate instead of bone meal.

For desert cacti and succulents, a moist, very porous potting mixture is essential. By volume use 2 parts soil, 2 parts perlite or coarse sand, $\frac{1}{4}$ part bone meal, and $\frac{1}{2}$ part dehydrated cow manure.

Soil purchased in bags frequently contains an overabundance of peat moss, with a small amount of perlite or vermiculite sometimes added. It can be improved or "stretched" by adding 1 part of garden soil to every 3 parts of purchased soil.

An artificial growing medium, or soilless mix, is best purchased, as it is difficult to mix the components sufficiently. Most of these contain some nutrients, but eventually plants growing in them need supplemental feeding—and more frequently than those grown in soil-based mixtures.

Sterilizing Soil

Use one of the methods below.

Formaldehyde drench. To treat soil in a flat 16 inches by 22 inches by 2 inches deep, mix 4 tablespoons of formalin (40 percent formaldehyde) with 6 tablespoons of water. Apply this mix outdoors or in a well-ventilated room. Moisten the soil, sprinkle the solution on it, mix the two well, and cover with plastic for 12 hours. Then air for 24 hours or more before sowing seeds. Wait until all odor disappears before using.

Oven method. Place a 4-inch layer of moist soil in a metal baking pan. Cover the pan tightly with aluminum foil. Insert a candy or meat thermometer in the soil through the foil. Put the pan in the oven at the lowest temperature setting. After the thermometer reads 180°–200° F, leave the pan in the oven for half an hour longer. Then remove the pan from the oven; cool the soil for 24 hours before using.

Pressure cooker. Fill a pressure cooker (canning type) with 2 cups of water; place a rack inside the cooker, and stack shallow pans of soil ($\frac{3}{4}$ inch deep) on the rack. Leave space for steam to circulate. Apply heat. When the pressure in the cooker reaches 10 pounds, maintain it there for 15 minutes before removing the cooker from the stove. When everything has cooled, remove the pans. Wait 24 hours before using the soil.

Watering and Feeding Correctly

More house plants are killed by overwatering than by anything else. The frequency with which a plant should be watered depends on the type of plant, the room temperature, and the time of year. Generally, house plants need more water during the growing or flowering season (late spring and summer) than during the resting period (autumn and winter). However, the dry atmosphere of most heated dwellings may make it necessary to water frequently in winter.

A copious watering once or twice a week is preferable to a light watering every day. Tap water is usually satisfactory, but azalea and gardenia foliage may turn yellow if watered only with hard tap water. Iron chelates, applied to the soil according to the manufacturer's instructions, should correct the yellowing.

Plants can be watered by pouring the water directly on the soil or by subirrigation—standing the pot in a saucer of water for about half an hour and then pouring off the remaining water. African violets are often watered by subirrigation, since leaves may become spotted when splashed with cold water.

A badly dried-out plant can sometimes be revived by thoroughly wetting the root ball. Set the potted plant in a deep container holding a few inches of water. As soon as the top of the soil is saturated, remove the plant.

Fertilizer should be applied during the growing season after plants have been watered. The liquid or powder forms specifically packaged for house plants are easiest to use.

Pot-grown plants that are frequently fertilized can suffer from a buildup of soluble salts, which may injure the roots. Plants so injured may wilt or appear stunted, or foliage may yellow. To remedy these difficulties, reduce the frequency of feeding, and periodically flush the soil by adding a large amount of water and letting it seep out of the drainage holes.

Creating a Moist Growing Atmosphere

Many house plants originated in tropical jungles and rain forests, where the atmosphere is always moist. Although in most cases they can adapt to drier climates, they do better when humidity is increased. Appliances for increasing humidity include humidifiers built into heating units, portable room humidifiers that hold several gallons of water, and cool-vapor humidifiers designed for sickrooms.

However, one of the easiest ways to maintain high humidity around potted plants is to stand the containers on pebbles in water-filled trays or saucers. The water level must remain below the base of the pots, or the roots will rot. Where only a few pots are involved, each one can be set in a larger pot or decorative container, and the space between the two can be filled with peat moss or sphagnum moss. Even though this moss should be kept moist, the plant must also be watered regularly.

Gently spraying, or misting, the foliage of plants with lukewarm water will temporarily raise the humidity. Keep African violets out of the sun until their leaves are dry, to avoid spotting.

Certain plants, especially those with soft or hairy leaves, benefit from an occasional steam treatment. To provide this, stand each pot in a bowl supported by a brick, a clay pot, or some other poor heat conductor. Pour boiling water into the bowl, making sure that leaves are kept clear of the bowl. Remove the plant after water no longer gives off steam.

An occasional steam treatment will benefit plants with soft or hairy leaves.

WATERING HOUSE PLANTS

Bromeliads. *Some plants, such as vriesias, have a central "vase." Keep this filled with water.*

Parched plants. *Stand a dried-out potted plant in a bowl filled with water to the top of the soil.*

TWO METHODS OF INCREASING HUMIDITY

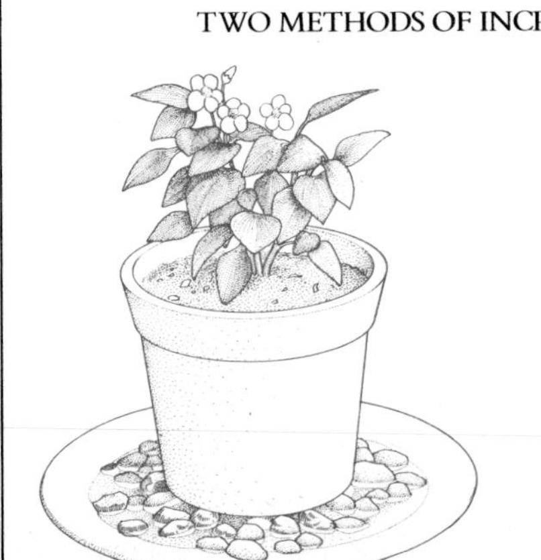

Pebbles. *Set potted plant on pebbles in dish or tray of shallow water.*

Damp peat moss. *Put damp moss between potted plant and larger pot.*

Looking After House Plants During Vacation

Before you go on vacation, arrange with a friend to care for your house plants. If this is not possible, a few precautions will maintain the plants for two or three weeks.

Remove all flowers and flower buds, pinching them off cleanly between thumb and forefinger. This will reduce the amount of water needed by the plants.

Move the plants away from sunny locations. Water the plants well and cover each with a transparent plastic bag. Make certain that the bag does not touch the leaves. Secure the bag around the pot with a rubber band; if the plant is large, the bag can be folded shut around the bottom of the pot. Or pack the plants in deep boxes, surrounding them with crumpled, wet newspapers or soaked peat moss.

A more elaborate method for keeping the soil moist is to set up a capillary system, using wicks or other devices sold for this purpose. Set a large container of water so that its level is above the soil surface in the plant pots. Place the plants around the container. Using one wick per pot, insert one end in the soil, and place the other end in the container of water; keep this end submerged by tying a stone or small weight to it. Water will seep through the wicks into the soil. Very large plants may require more than one wick; so experiment with this scheme before starting your vacation.

Pruning Overgrown Plants and Training Climbers

Most house plants need little or no pruning, but if they become scraggly, shoots can be cut off cleanly just above a leaf joint. Plants that trail naturally can be kept bushier by frequent pinching of the tip growth.

Rubber plants and split-leaf philodendrons that have grown too tall cannot be cut back without encouraging side shoots, which may not be desired. These plants can be started again by cutting off the top 12 inches of the main trunk and inserting this section in a pot of rooting medium (see p. 401). They can also be air-layered (see p. 405). The latter is the safer method; there is less chance of losing the desirable upper portion of the plant, since it is rooted before being detached from the main stem.

Climbing plants, such as ivies and philodendrons, should be trained as soon as they have begun to grow strongly. To do this, insert bamboo canes in the soil, and tie the shoots loosely with plant ties. Shoots can also be tied to trellislike frames, either purchased or made at home. The supports and ties should be as inconspicuous as possible.

Cissus antarctica and some other climbing plants develop aerial roots through which they obtain part of their nourishment. Such climbers are best trained on moss-wrapped poles or on wire frames filled with sphagnum moss, kept moist. Or they can be trained on "totem poles"—slabs of wood without the moss.

THREE WAYS OF KEEPING PLANTS MOIST

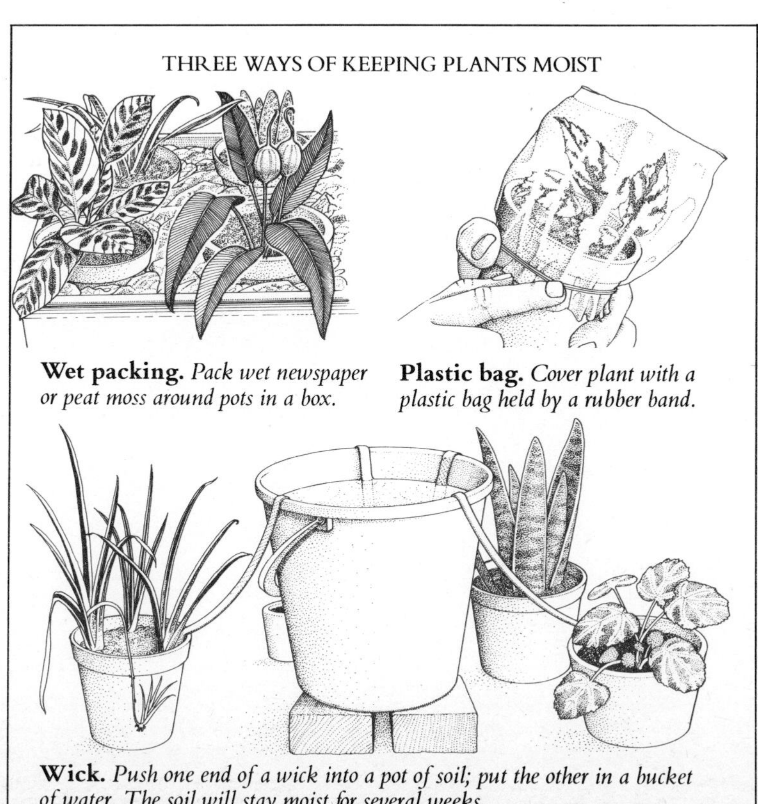

Wet packing. *Pack wet newspaper or peat moss around pots in a box.*

Plastic bag. *Cover plant with a plastic bag held by a rubber band.*

Wick. *Push one end of a wick into a pot of soil; put the other in a bucket of water. The soil will stay moist for several weeks.*

TRAINING HOUSE PLANTS

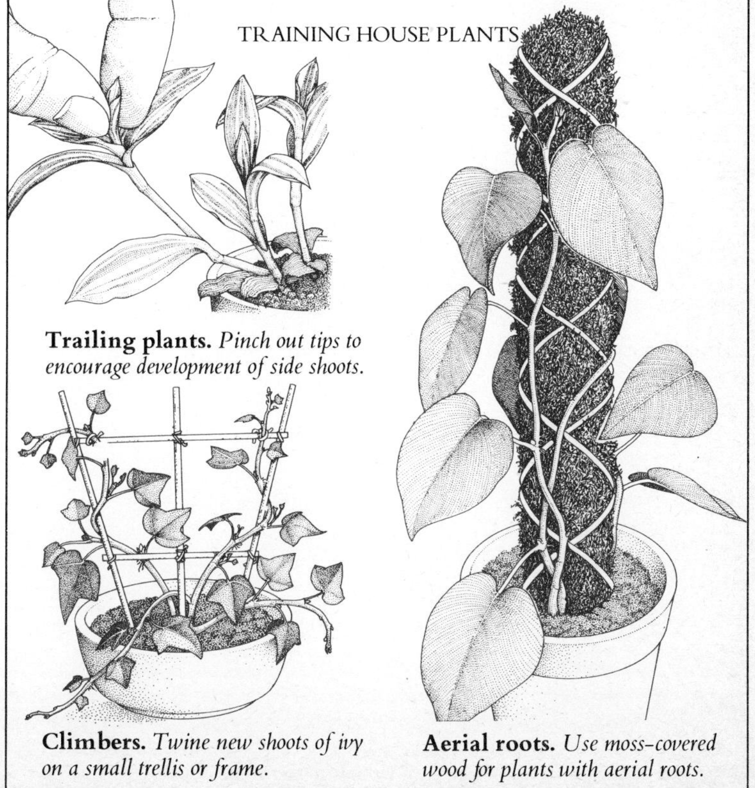

Trailing plants. *Pinch out tips to encourage development of side shoots.*

Climbers. *Twine new shoots of ivy on a small trellis or frame.*

Aerial roots. *Use moss-covered wood for plants with aerial roots.*

How to Grow New House Plants From Old Ones

Some house plants can be propagated by dividing the plant into two or more pieces or by taking tip cuttings that root quickly. Others require more complicated techniques. The main propagation methods are division, tip cuttings from side shoots, plantlets, leaf cuttings, air layering, and offsets. For the best propagation techniques for various house plants, see the chart on page 410.

Many house plants can also be raised from seeds. Seeds of popular plants, such as begonias and impatiens, are often available in nurseries, and some specialized mail-order houses have seeds of less familiar plants, such as false aralias (*Dizygotheca*) and Japanese aralias (*Fatsia*). Most seeds germinate easily, but some plants take several years to reach maturity. Such plants require close attention and care during the early stages.

Seeds can be sown at any time of year in pots, small flats, or boxes filled with shredded sphagnum moss or soilless mix. Or use packaged sterilized soil mixtures or equal parts of peat moss and sand. Wet the medium thoroughly before sowing; then sprinkle fine seeds over the surface; larger seeds can be lightly covered. Slip the container into a plastic bag, and keep it out of direct sunlight at a temperature between 65° and 75° F. When the seeds germinate, remove the plastic bag and gradually increase the light intensity. When two sets of leaves have developed, pot the seedlings singly into $2\frac{1}{2}$- to 3-inch pots (see Using the Correct Soil Mixture, p. 397). Water and fertilize as necessary.

Dividing Multistemmed House Plants

The easiest method of propagation is to divide or split a plant. Only certain types of plants, however, can be propagated in this way. A plant must have at least two (preferably more) stems branching out at or below ground level. Also, every stem must have an independent, well-developed root system.

Plants suitable for division include asparagus ferns, baby's tears, maidenhair ferns, snake plants, and spider plants. See the Propagation column in the chart on page 410 for other suitable plants.

House plants can be divided at any time during the growing period (from late spring to early autumn). To do this, first knock the plant out of its pot. Tease away the soil around the crown and root ball, using your fingers or a small stick. This will expose the rootstock and the points at which the plant can be divided.

Grasp the base of the plant in both hands, and pull it gently but firmly apart. If the crown or rootstock is thick and tough, cut off the largest roots or the underground stems with a sharp knife.

Pot the separated pieces immediately in one of the soil mixtures described on page 397. Water sparingly at first, and keep the pots in a warm, shaded location for two or three weeks.

Certain house plants, especially artillery plants (*Pilea*) and wandering Jews (both *Tradescantia* and *Zebrina*), are often grown commercially from three or more cuttings in the same small pot. As the cuttings grow, they form a single plant, which can later be carefully divided. Pot each piece separately.

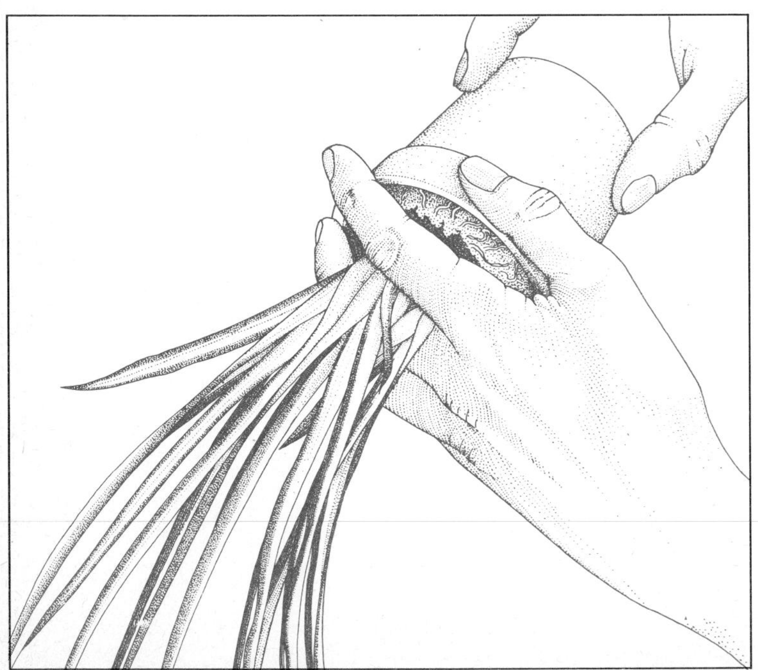

1. *To divide a spider plant, invert pot and place your fingers around stems; knock the pot rim gently against a table edge to dislodge root ball.*

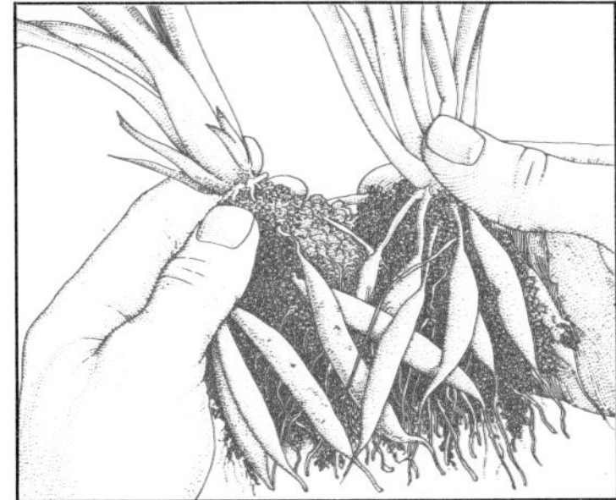

2. *Ease away the soil, and carefully pull the roots of the plant apart.*

3. *With a sharp knife or razor blade, cut apart any tangled roots.*

4. *Set each division into a separate pot filled with general-purpose mixture.*

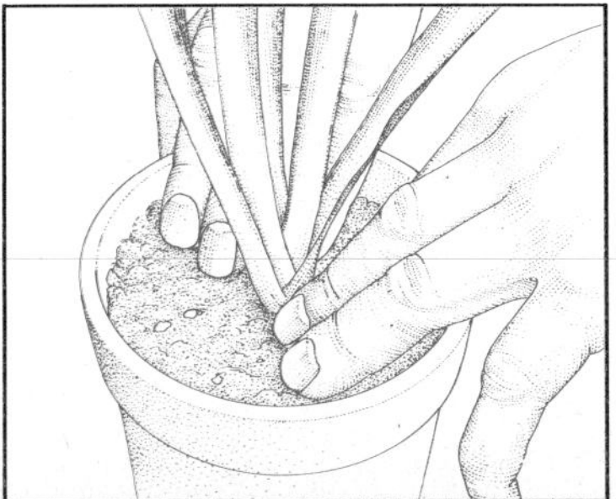

5. *Fill the pot with more soil, and level $\frac{1}{2}$ in. below the top of the pot.*

Taking Tip Cuttings From Nonflowering Stems

Cuttings taken from ivies, impatiens, tradescantias, and certain other house plants are very easy to root. Make these cuttings from the tips of young, nonflowering stems or side shoots in summer. Strip the lower leaves from a 3- to 4-inch cutting, and trim the stem cleanly just below a leaf node. Stand the cutting in a glass of tap water. Roots will appear within 10 to 14 days, and the cutting can then be potted.

With other kinds of house plants, insert the cuttings at once in a rooting medium. Fill a $3\frac{1}{2}$-inch pot to just below the rim with a mixture of equal quantities of peat moss and coarse sand, or with a purchased soilless mix. To make the cuttings, use a sharp knife to cut off the top 3–4 inches of stem or side shoot. Pull off the lower leaves, and make a clean cut across the stem, just below one of the leaf nodes.

With a small stick, make a number of 1- to $1\frac{1}{2}$-inch-deep holes in the mixture (a $3\frac{1}{2}$-inch pot will accommodate four to six cuttings). Make the holes around the edge of the pot. Insert the cuttings so that the stems are supported by the rim. Firm the mixture gently around each cutting. Fill the pot to the rim with water and let it drain.

Cover the pot with a plastic bag, and secure it with a rubber band. Set the pot in a shaded position where a temperature of 65°–75° F can be maintained. Keep the mixture moist.

After three or four weeks the cuttings should have rooted and the tips be showing fresh growth. At this time, remove the plastic bag and carefully invert the pot. Separate the rooted cuttings carefully; then pot them singly in 3- to $3\frac{1}{2}$-inch pots, using the appropriate soil mixture recommended on page 397. Water carefully and keep the plants in a shaded, draft-free location until they have begun to grow well.

HOW TO TAKE TIP CUTTINGS

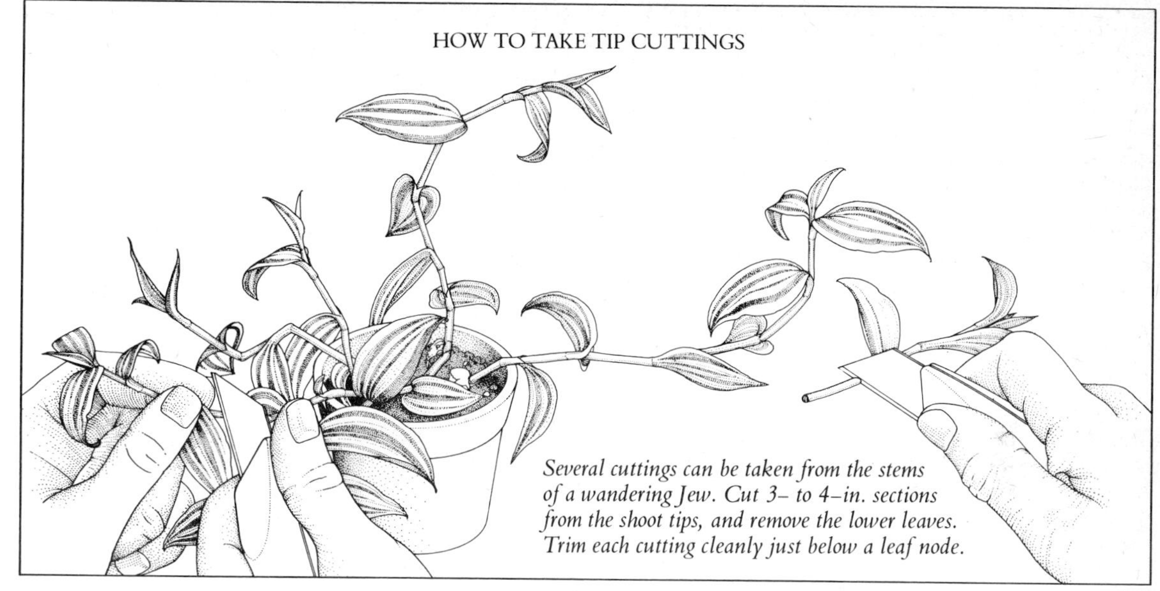

Several cuttings can be taken from the stems of a wandering Jew. Cut 3- to 4-in. sections from the shoot tips, and remove the lower leaves. Trim each cutting cleanly just below a leaf node.

ROOTING TIP CUTTINGS

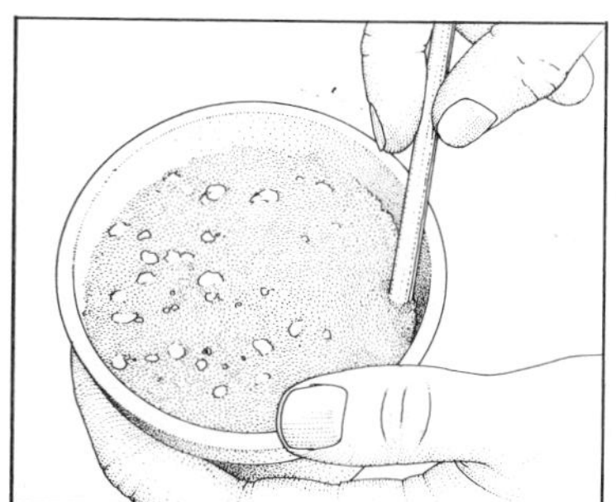

1. *Make four to six planting holes along the edge of a $3\frac{1}{2}$-in. pot.*

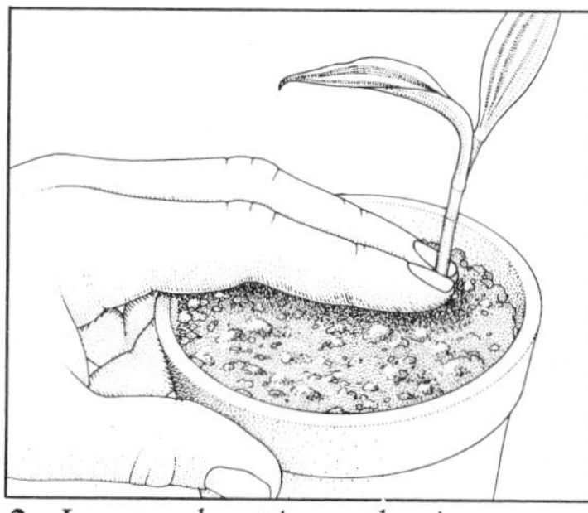

2. *Insert each cutting so that its stem rests against the edge of the pot.*

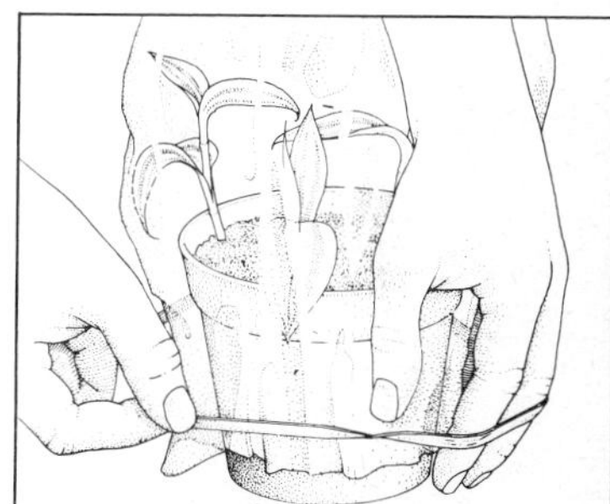

3. *Cover the pot with clear plastic until the cuttings have rooted.*

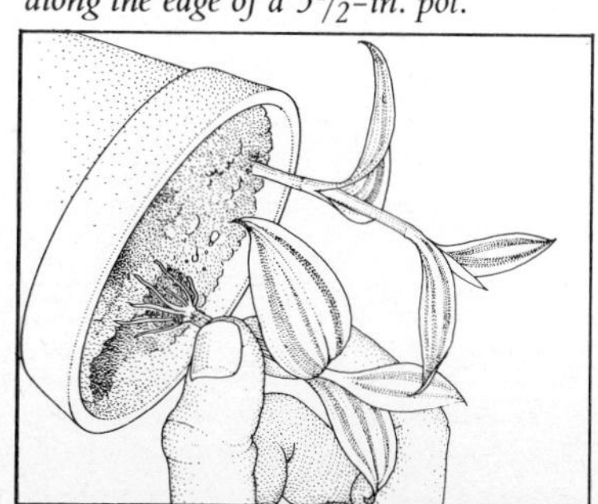

4. *Tip up the pot, and carefully remove the rooted cuttings.*

5. *Put each plant in a 3- to $3\frac{1}{2}$-in. pot filled with general-purpose soil mix.*

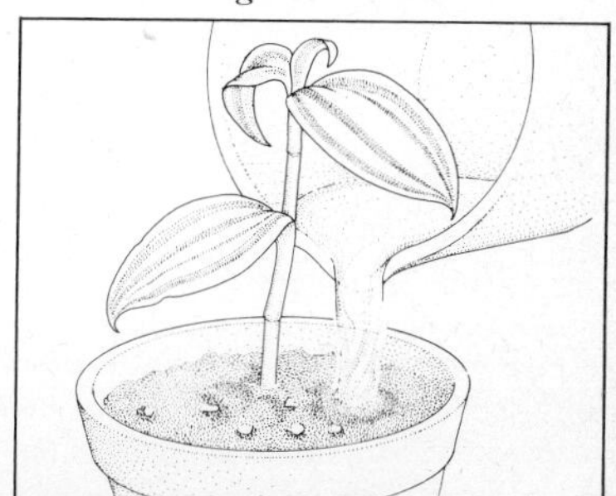

6. *Water the plants; keep them in a shaded place for about a week.*

Removing Rooted Offsets From the Parent Plant

Most bromeliads (such as billbergias and vriesias) as well as other house plants (including amaryllises and aglaonemas) produce offsets, or suckers. These small plants, which develop at the base of the parent plant—either close to it or a short distance away from it—may eventually overcrowd a pot.

Offsets that have grown to about half the height of the parent plant can be easily removed and then potted separately. The best time to undertake this type of propagation is from spring to autumn.

First, place the fingers of one hand around the main stem, and invert the pot with the other hand. If necessary, tap the pot against a table to loosen the root ball.

Now, gently pull the plant from the pot, and crumble away the soil. Hold the root ball, stem and leaves up, in one hand, and pull or cut away the offset, complete with roots. Take care to disturb the roots as little as possible.

Put a layer of moist potting mix (see pp. 395, 397) in a 3- to 4-inch pot, and set the offset on top so that its crown is ½ inch below the rim of the pot. Trickle in more mix; firm the mix with your fingertips. Fill the pot with water to settle mix; allow it to drain.

Tall offsets will need staking for one or two months, until their root systems are well established. Insert a bamboo cane close to each tall offset, and secure cane and offset with ties.

Set each offset in a well-lighted location (but out of direct sunlight) for a couple of weeks. A northwest-facing windowsill is the ideal place. Keep the mix moist during this time.

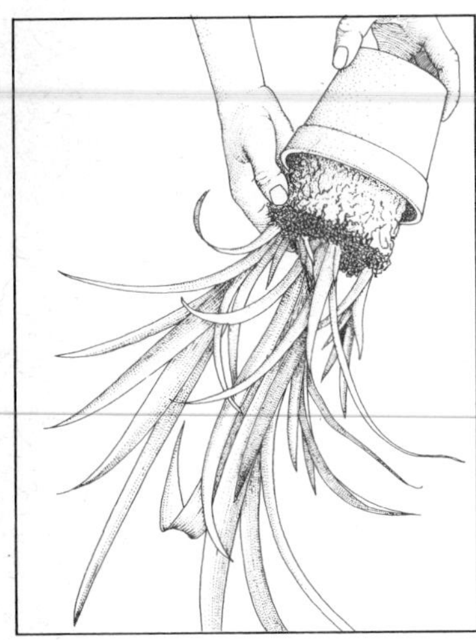

1. *Knock a pot-bound billbergia firmly to loosen its root ball.*

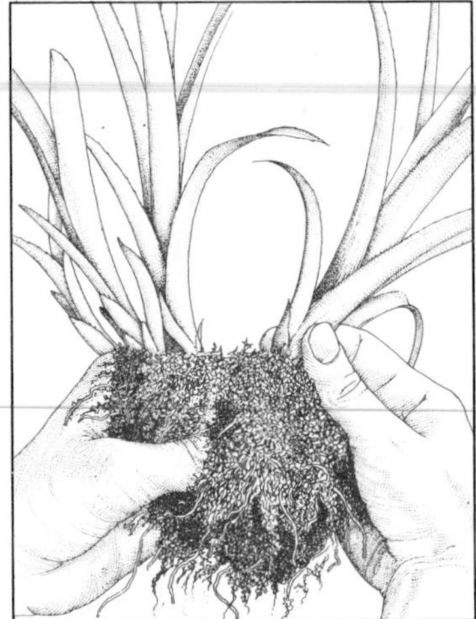

2. *Separate the rooted offset from the parent plant without injuring the roots.*

3. *Insert the offset in a 3- to 4-in. pot of growing medium; firm gently.*

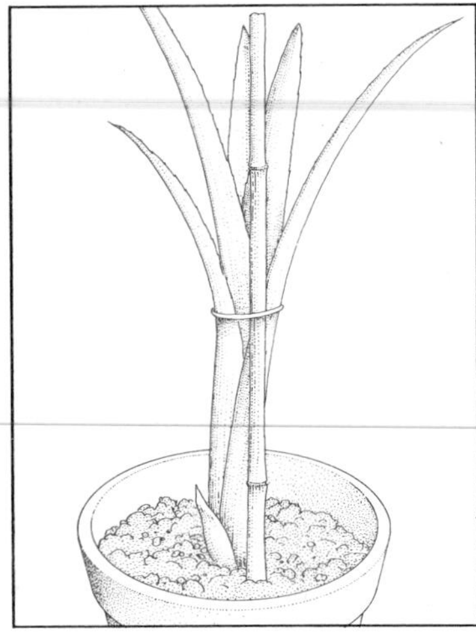

4. *Tie a tall offset to a bamboo stake for a few weeks; keep the mix moist.*

Detaching and Rooting Plants From Runners

Some plants, notably strawberry begonias and spider plants, produce small plants on flowering spikes or runners from the parent plant.

To root the strawberry begonia plantlets, which are produced at the end of threadlike runners, detach the runners from the parent plant. Then cut the runner from the plantlet. Fill a 2½-inch pot with moist potting soil to within ½ inch of the rim. Make a shallow depression in the surface, and set the plantlet in it. Firm the soil mixture around the base of the young plant.

Do not water at this time; but place a plastic bag over the pot, and secure it with a rubber band. Keep the pot out of direct sunlight and at a temperature of 65°–75° F. Be sure that the mixture remains moist. Within about 10 days the plantlet should have rooted. Remove the bag and set the pot in a lighter, cooler place.

Spider plants bear leafy plantlets on tough stalks. To root such a plantlet, place a 2-inch container of moist potting soil under it so that the base of the plantlet is lightly covered with soil. In about three weeks the plantlet should be rooted, at which point the stalk can be severed.

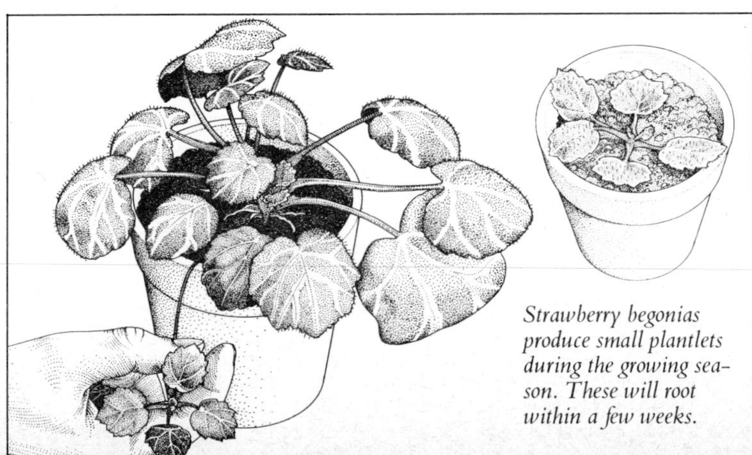

Strawberry begonias produce small plantlets during the growing season. These will root within a few weeks.

Leaf Cuttings From Hairy- or Fleshy-Leaved Plants

Some house plants with thick, hairy, or fleshy leaves—such as African violets, gloxinias, and peperomias—can be propagated by taking leaf cuttings. This can be done whenever the plants are growing strongly (usually early summer to early fall).

To grow new plants, cut two or three healthy leaves, each with a 1- to $1\frac{1}{2}$-inch stalk, from the plant to be propagated. Almost fill a 3-inch pot with perlite, vermiculite, or a mixture of equal quantities of peat moss and coarse sand. With a stick, make a planting hole for each leaf stalk; the hole should be slightly less deep than the stalk is long. Trim the end of each leaf stalk straight across with a sharp knife.

Insert the leaf stalks into the holes. The base of each stalk should touch the bottom of the hole, but the leaf itself should be kept clear of the potting mixture, to prevent rotting. Firm the cuttings gently with your fingertips, taking care not to bruise the slender stalks.

Ideally, the cuttings should be left to root in a heated propagating unit, but a suitable atmosphere can be provided without special equipment. First, fill the pot to the top with water, and let it drain thoroughly. Then, enclose the pot in a plastic bag, securing it with a rubber band. Make sure that the mixture remains moist. If water condenses on the inside of the bag, remove the bag and turn it inside out before putting it back in place.

After three to five weeks roots should have formed and new leaves appeared at the base of the leaf stalk. Invert the pot and carefully separate the rooted cuttings. Place them singly in $2\frac{1}{2}$-inch pots filled with soil mixture (see p. 397). Water the cuttings and keep them in a warm, shaded location for two or three weeks. They can then be moved to a sunnier location.

HOW TO TAKE LEAF CUTTINGS

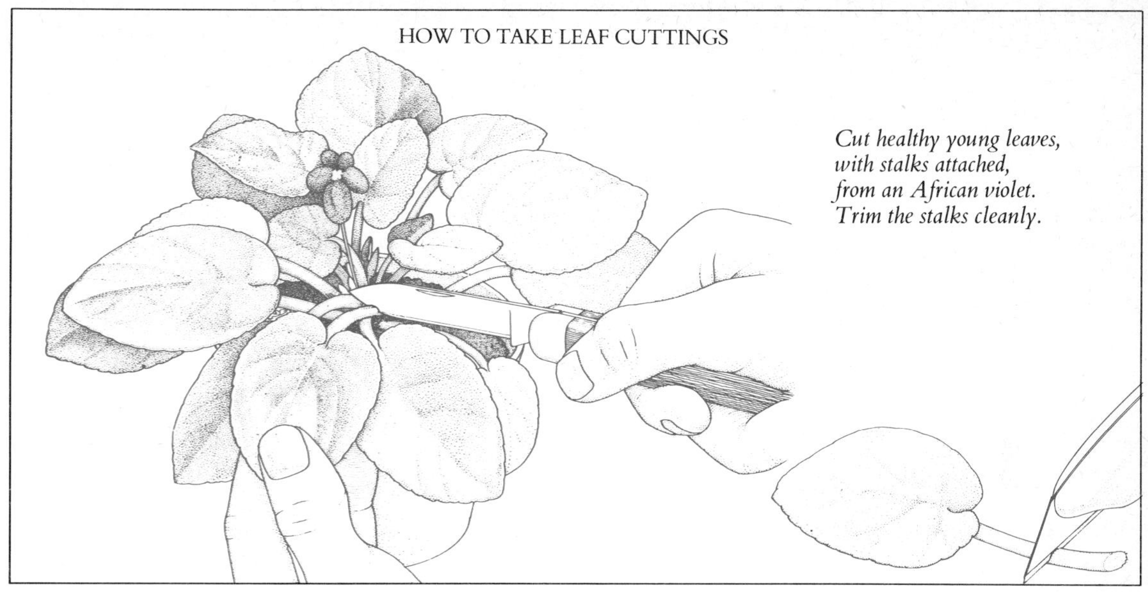

Cut healthy young leaves, with stalks attached, from an African violet. Trim the stalks cleanly.

ROOTING LEAF CUTTINGS FROM AFRICAN VIOLETS

1. *With a stick make a few planting holes in a pot of sand and peat moss.*

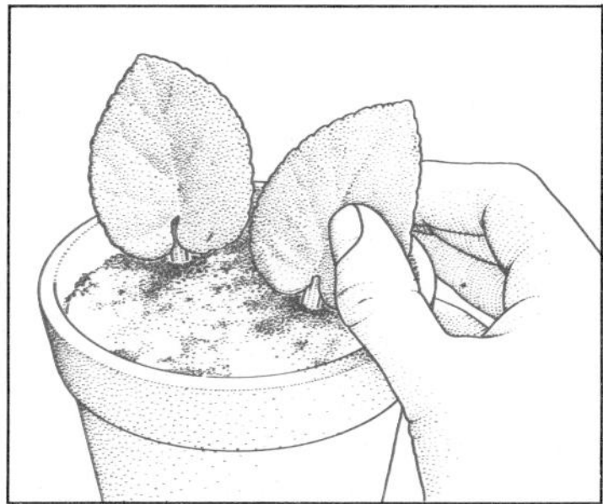

2. *Insert each cutting so that the leaf is just above the rooting medium.*

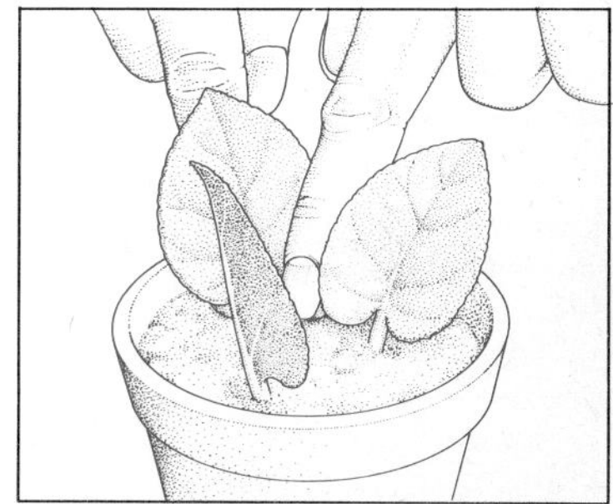

3. *Firm the rooting medium with your fingers, avoiding injury to stems.*

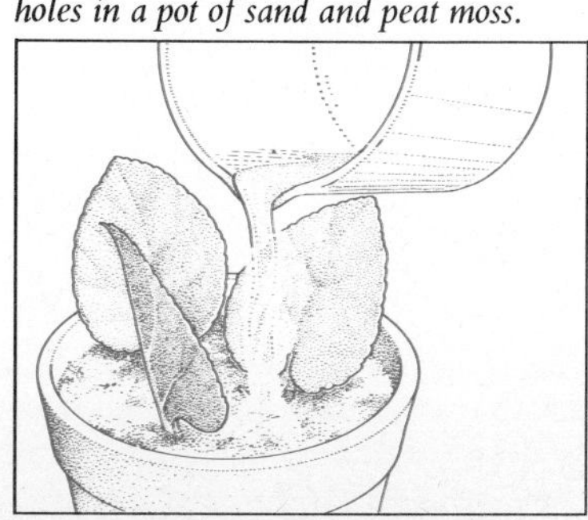

4. *Fill the pot to the top with water, and let it drain completely.*

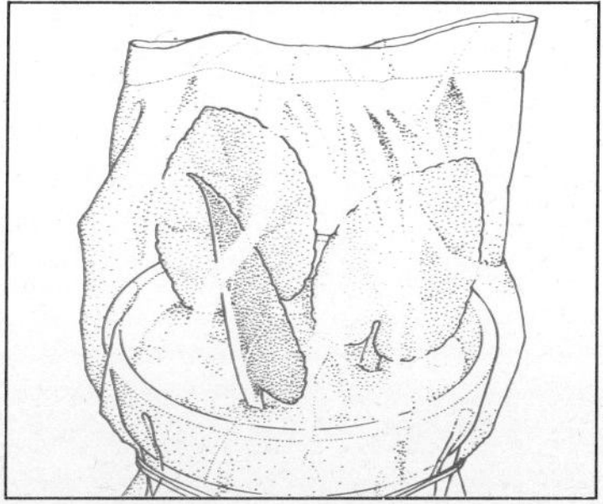

5. *Cover the pot with a clear plastic bag, secured with a rubber band.*

6. *When new leaves have grown, pot each cutting in a humusy soil mix.*

Raising Several New Plants From a Single Leaf

If a plant has large enough leaves, more than one plant can often be grown from a leaf. Rex begonias can be propagated in this way.

At any time of year, detach a mature leaf and trim the stalk to within 1 inch of the leaf base. Using a sharp knife, make several cuts on the underside of the leaf where the main veins meet. Place the leaf, cut side down, in a container of moist vermiculite or a mix of half sand and half peat moss. Weight the leaf down with small stones. Cover the container with clear plastic, and keep it at a temperature of 70° F.

After about four weeks small plants will appear on the cut edges. Remove the plastic and leave the pot in a warm, shaded location for several more weeks. Pot the rooted plantlets individually in $2\frac{1}{2}$-inch pots filled with potting soil (see p. 397).

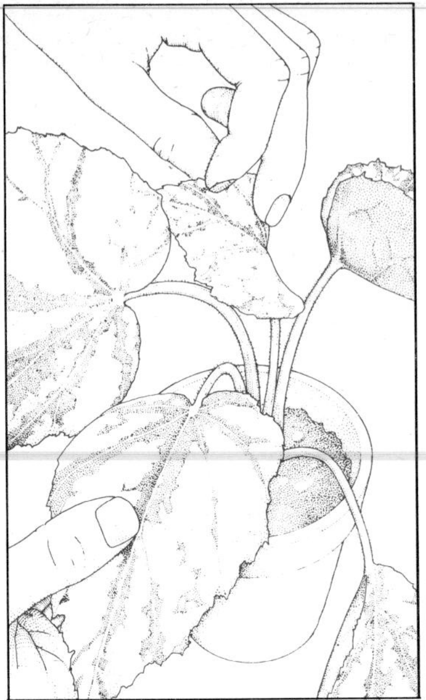

1. *Propagate rex begonias and some other begonias from leaf cuttings.*

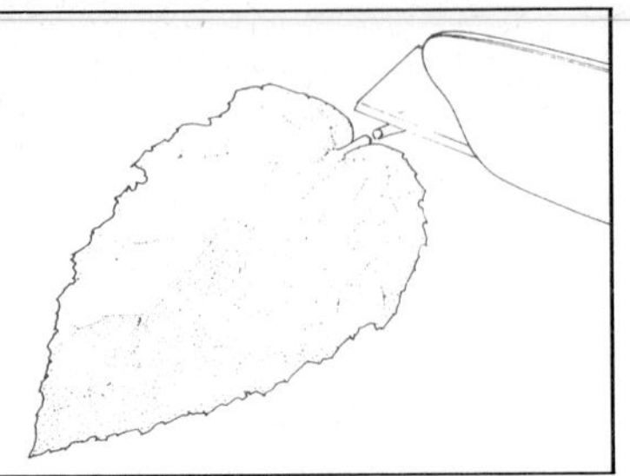

2. *Select a healthy leaf, and trim its stalk to about 1 in. from the leaf base.*

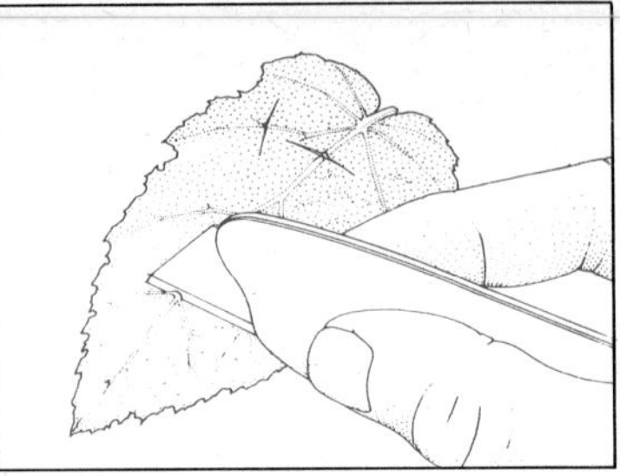

3. *Make cuts where the main veins meet on the underside of the leaf.*

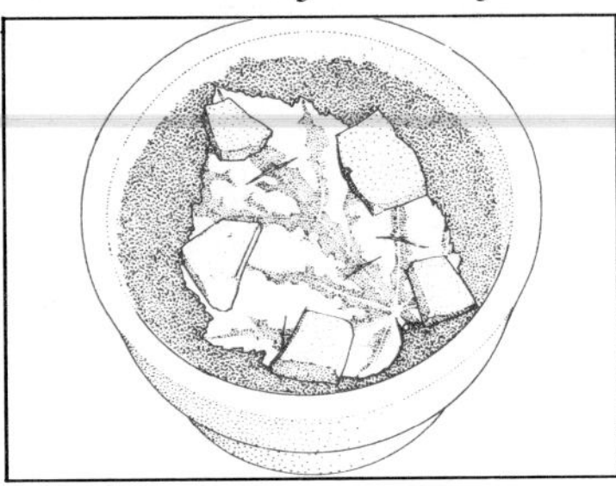

4. *Lay leaf, cut side down, on rooting medium; weight it down with crocks.*

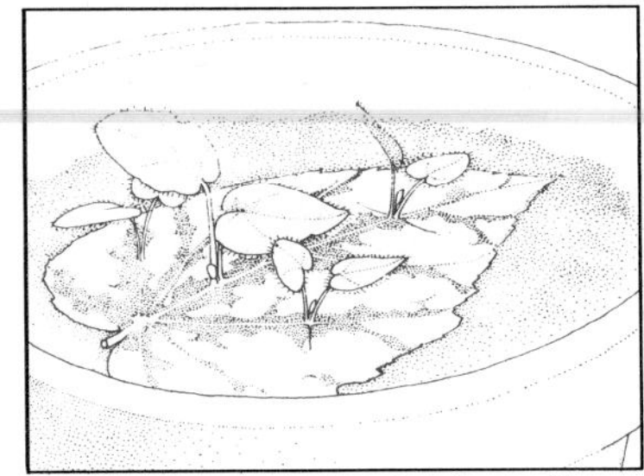

5. *After a few weeks plantlets will appear on the edges of the cuts.*

Increasing Snake Plants From Leaf Sections

The leaves of snake plants can be cut into sections, each of which can produce a new plant.

During spring or summer, cut off a healthy one-year-old leaf close to the base of the plant. Fill a 5-inch pot with moist vermiculite. Using a sharp knife, cut the leaf crosswise into 1-inch-wide sections. Insert the sections into the vermiculite so that they are about half covered. Position each section so that the bottom side is the side that was closest to the roots on the parent plant.

Spray the cuttings with water, and place a plastic bag over the pot. Keep the cuttings in a shaded location at a temperature of about 70° F. When a section begins to produce a leaf—after about six weeks—remove the plastic. Pot the young plants individually in 3-inch containers filled with soil mix (see p. 397).

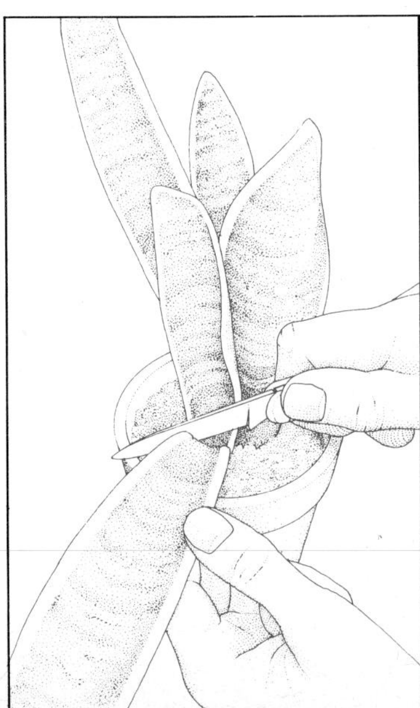

1. *To propagate a snake plant, cut a healthy leaf from the parent plant.*

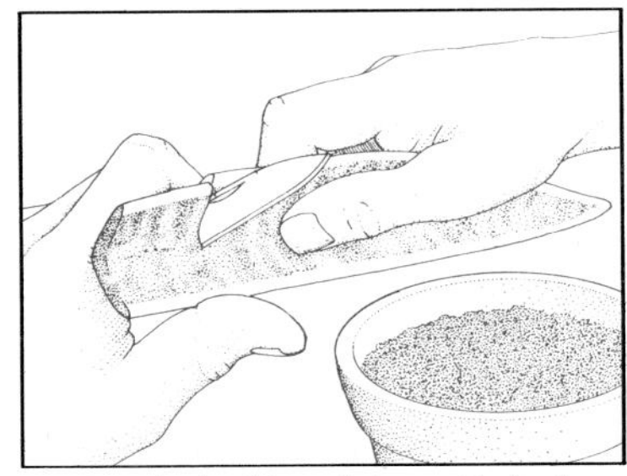

2. *Cut the leaf into 1-in.-wide horizontal sections, using a sharp knife.*

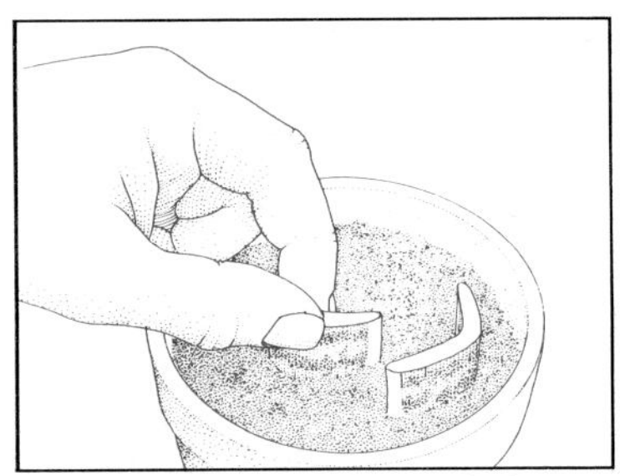

3. *Insert the sections, lower side down, in a moist rooting medium.*

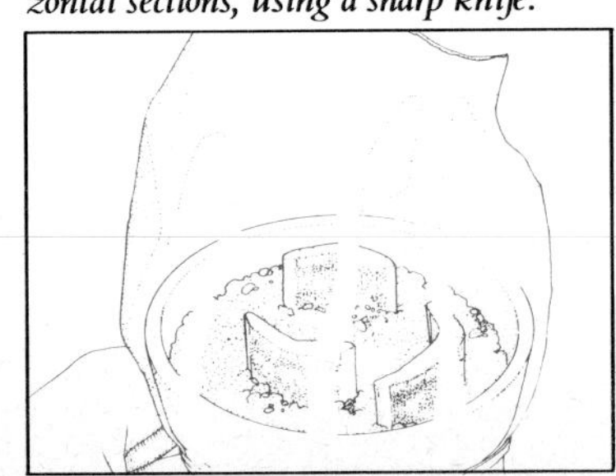

4. *Cover the pot with a plastic bag to provide a humid atmosphere.*

5. *After about six weeks the sections will produce new leaves.*

Propagating Plants by Air Layering

Certain house plants, such as false aralias and rubber plants, may eventually become taller than desired and lose their lower leaves. Rather than discarding such an overgrown plant, air-layer it in spring to produce a new, shorter-stemmed plant.

Using a sharp knife, remove the leaves 6–9 inches below the growing tip, cutting them flush with the stem. Then make an upward-slanting cut about $1\frac{1}{2}$ inches long in the leafless area of the stem, starting just below a leaf node. Tie the stem to a stake above and below the cut.

Prop open the cut with a match, and brush both sides of the opening with a hormone rooting powder. Then remove the match, and wrap clear plastic around the cut. The plastic should be 6–7 inches wide and long enough to cover 3–4 inches below and above the cut. Seal the wrapping with tape below the cut to create a tube, or sleeve, that is open at the top.

Fill the tube with wet sphagnum moss or peat moss, pressing the moss into and around the cut with a small stick. Now seal the top of the tube with tape so that the moss will remain moist. Within 8 to 10 weeks roots should have been produced.

At this time, sever the stem just below the tube, and carefully free the roots from the plastic and moss. Discard the old plant, or let it grow on to produce side shoots.

Pot the new plant in a 3- to 4-inch container filled with potting soil (see p. 397). For the first two or three weeks, until the root system is established, grow the plant at a temperature of 65°–70° F. Syringe the leaves daily with water.

1. *To produce a new rubber plant from an overgrown one, remove several leaves growing 6–9 in. below the top. The stem will be air-layered in this region.*

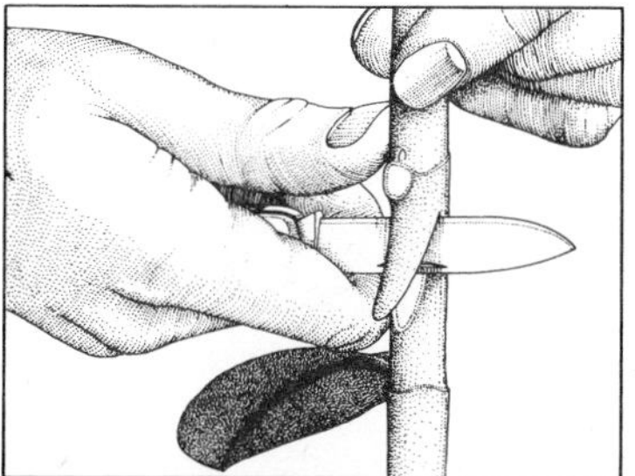

2. *Make a $1\frac{1}{2}$-in.-long upward-slanting cut, starting below a leaf node.*

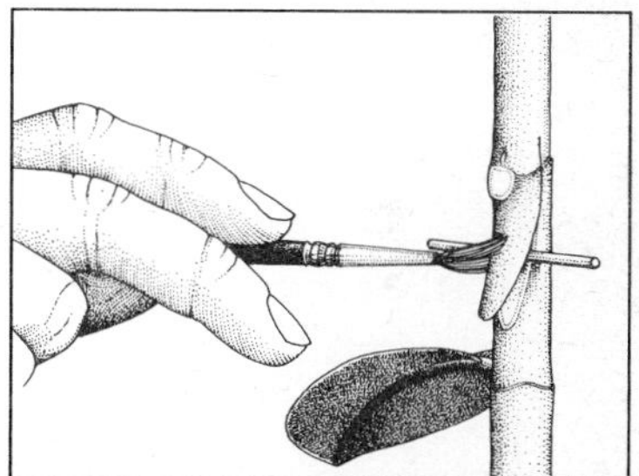

3. *Carefully prop open the cut, and dust with hormone rooting powder.*

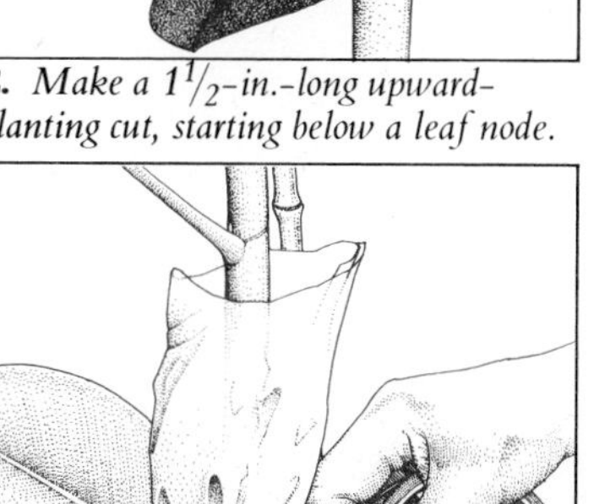

4. *Wrap clear plastic around the cut. Close the bottom with tape.*

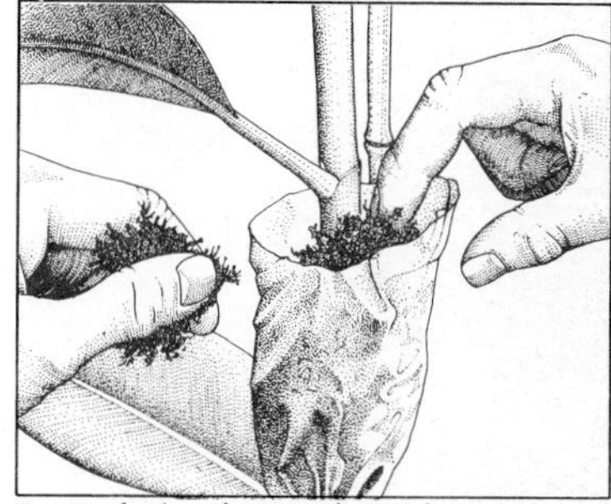

5. *Pack the plastic tube with moist sphagnum moss; seal the top shut.*

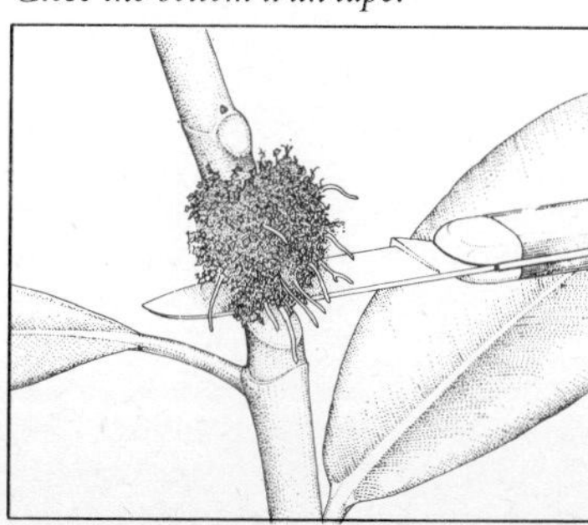

6. *When roots become visible, sever the stem just below them.*

7. *Pot the new plant in a container filled with general-purpose soil mix.*

House Plants From Seeds of Citrus Fruits

Attractive plants can be grown from grapefruit, lemon, and orange seeds. Plant such seeds as soon as they are removed from the fruits.

Fill a 4-inch pot to within $\frac{1}{2}$ inch of the top with a commercial soilless mix or a mixture of one part garden soil and one part peat moss. Water the mixture. Bury four to six seeds $\frac{1}{2}$ inch deep in the mix. Cover the pot with clear plastic, secured with a rubber band. If kept out of direct sunlight and at about 70° F, the seeds should germinate within two or three weeks.

When the seeds have germinated, remove the plastic and gradually expose the pot to more light. After the plants have several sets of leaves, move the plants singly into 3- to 4-inch pots (for potting soils, see p. 397). If pruned occasionally, these plants will grow into bushy, 3- to 4-foot specimens that can be used in bonsai projects (see p. 202).

A seed from a lemon can develop into a fine, glossy-leaved plant.

Growing an Avocado Plant From a Pit

To grow an avocado plant, first insert three matches (or toothpicks) halfway into an avocado pit. Suspend the pit by the matches across a jar of water so that the base of the pit just touches the water.

After two to eight weeks fleshy white roots will appear from the pit's base. Place the rooted pit, half exposed, in a 6- to 8-inch pot of soil mix (see p. 397). Keep in a warm, well-lighted place, and water the soil whenever it is dry. When the stem is about 7 inches tall, cut it back halfway to encourage branching.

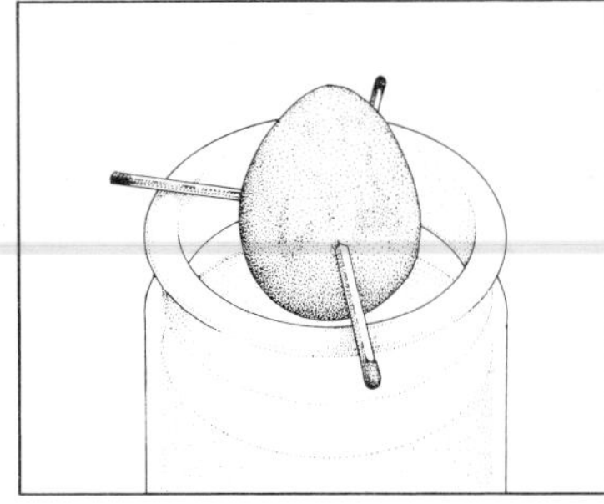

1. *Insert matches or toothpicks into an avocado pit; suspend it over water.*

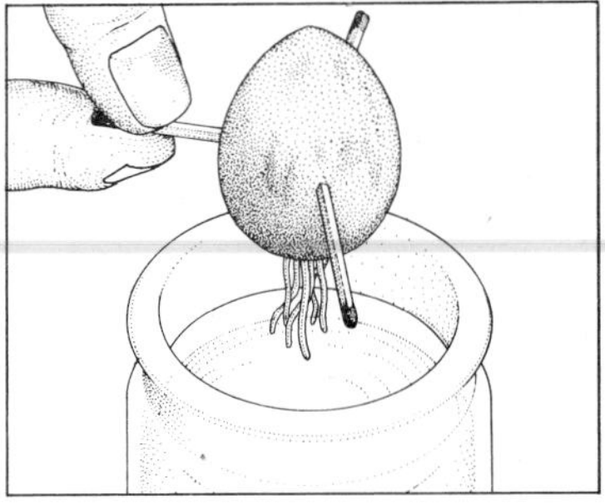

2. *When roots appear, place pit in soil so that it is half covered.*

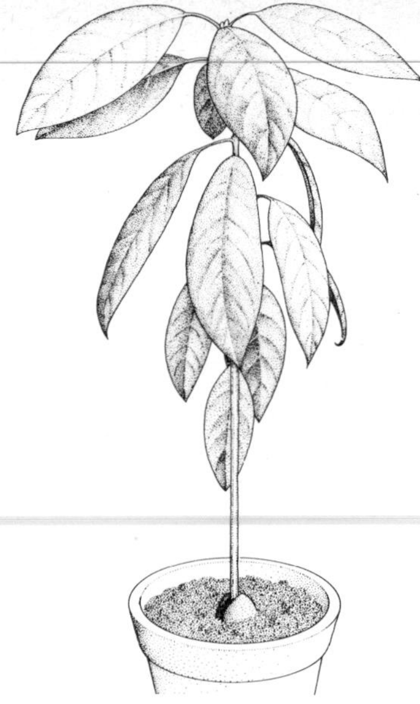

An attractive house plant will grow rapidly from the rooted avocado pit.

Growing a Pineapple Plant From a Fresh Top

Slice the leafy top from a fresh pineapple, together with a thin slice of flesh containing the top row of "pips" on the skin. Dry this top for a day or two.

Fill a 3- to 4-inch pot to within $\frac{3}{4}$ inch of its top with moist potting soil; sprinkle a thin layer of sand on top. Set the pineapple top, leafy side up, on the sand, and sprinkle a little more potting mix over the fleshy portion. Cover the pot with a clear plastic bag, and put it in a shaded place at room temperature.

Roots will generally develop within eight weeks. When the plant shows signs of growth, remove the plastic bag and move the plant to a larger pot.

The plant may grow to 2–3 feet in height and may then be induced to produce fruit. To do this, seal it in a plastic bag with a ripe apple for about five days. (The apple produces a gas that stimulates fruiting.)

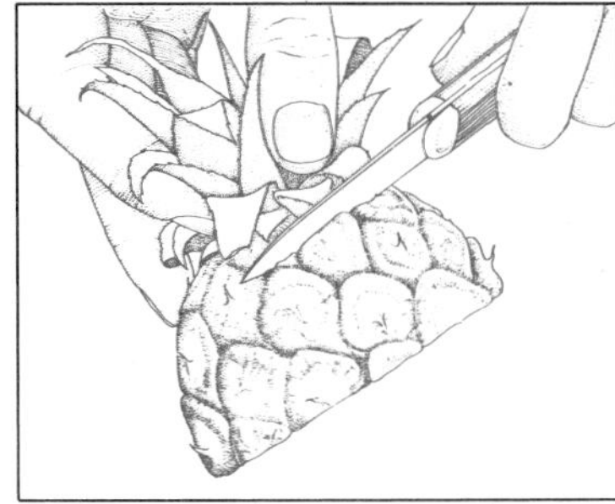

1. *Cut pineapple top so that a thin slice of flesh is attached. Dry the top.*

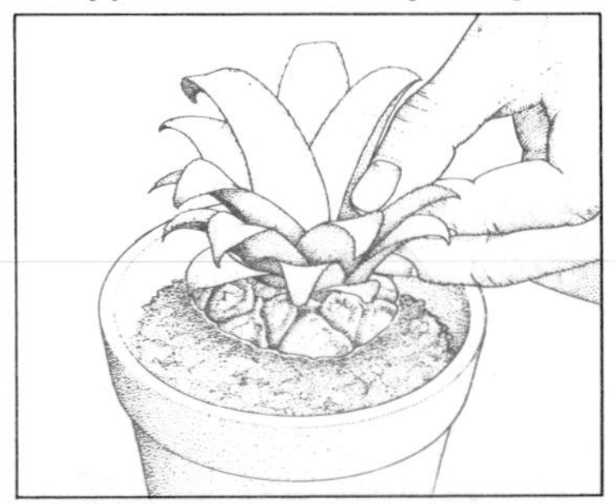

2. *Set top on a layer of sand in a pot of soil. Cover plant with plastic bag.*

This tall, leafy plant was grown from the top of a fresh pineapple.

What Can Go Wrong With House Plants

Most problems are caused by inattention to specific requirements for water and light. But if your plants show symptoms not described below, see the section on plant disorders on page 600. Trade names of chemicals are on page 635.

Symptoms and signs	Cause	Control
Small green, yellow, or brown insects cluster on leaves, buds, and tips of shoots.	Aphids	Dip affected plant in malathion. Or spray with Diazinon, endosulfan, or malathion.
Leaves clump in center of plant. Leaves and buds are curled and twisted; buds do not open properly. (Mites are severe pests of African violets and other house plants.)	Cyclamen or broad mites	Use dips or sprays of chlorobenzilate, dicofol, or endosulfan. Difficult to control.
Larvae (maggots) of small gray flies tunnel into soil, injuring the roots. Plants are sickly and have poor color.	Fungus gnats	Apply soil drench of Diazinon or lindane for maggots. Use aerosol bomb of pyrethrum or rotenone for adult flies.
White powdery insects cluster at nodes, undersides of leaves, and shoot tips.	Mealybugs	Dip in mixture of malathion and detergent. Repeat at 7-da. intervals until insects are controlled.
Round or flat insects on leaves and stems suck juices, causing yellowing and overall poor growth. Leaves have sticky deposits.	Scale insects	Dip plant in malathion mixture, using 2 tsp. per gallon of water. Add $\frac{1}{2}$ tsp. of mild detergent as wetting agent. Or spray with Diazinon or malathion. Repeat 3 or 4 times.
Young seedlings and lower leaves are chewed; roots are also damaged. Tiny hopping insects are visible in soil around plants, especially when plants are watered.	Springtails	Apply soil drench of Diazinon, lindane, or malathion.
Roots and basal plant parts are chewed. Unlike springtails, these tiny white pests have many legs and do not hop.	Symphilids	Apply soil drench of Diazinon, lindane, or malathion.
Tiny yellowish to black insects rasp leaves and stems and suck out juices. Injured parts show silvery streaks and distorted buds and flowers.	Thrips	Dip plant in solution of Diazinon or malathion, or apply as spray.
Leaves have fine webs and silvery spots.	Two-spotted (spider) mites	Dip plant in dicofol, malathion, or tetradifon; sprays are also effective. Repeat as needed.
Foliage is off-color. Has tiny white mothlike insects.	Whiteflies	Spray weekly with resmethrin.

Symptoms and signs	Cause	Control
Water-soaked spots with yellow margins occur on leaves. Entire leaves may wilt, and stems rot.	Bacterial leaf spot	Pick off and destroy infected leaves. Spray with streptomycin.
Gray powdery masses occur on leaves and buds. Black areas appear on leaf tips, twigs, and buds.	Botrytis, or gray mold	Apply spray of chlorothalonil or dichloran.
Leaves show watery spots that become raised and corky.	Edema, or dropsy	Improve light conditions, reduce humidity, and do not overwater.
Upper surfaces of leaves have loose white powdery masses. Leaves may be distorted and blackened.	Powdery mildew (fungus)	Spray with cycloheximide, dinocap, or sulfur.
Plants die back, rot, or wilt.	Root, crown, or stem rot (fungus)	Destroy infected parts. Treat infected soil with steam or with soil fungicide, such as quintozene or Terrazole.
Leaves have brown spots or edges.	Many possible causes	Remove badly affected leaves. Improve cultural conditions as necessary.
Blooms are poor or absent; stems are weak and elongated; leaves are small and pale. Plant is lopsided, with stems and leaves bending to one side.	Light deficiency	Increase light intensity. If necessary, use warm-white fluorescent tubes for flowering plants, daylight fluorescent tubes for foliage plants. Give pot one-quarter turn every other day.
Leaves yellow but stay firm and healthy.	Lime in soil, or tap water used for plants requiring acid conditions	Repot in acidic potting mixture or soilless mix. Use rain water, not tap water.
Stems and leaves grow slowly, even though plant is fed. Soil dries out quickly. Roots grow through drainage holes.	Pot too small	Move plant into larger pot.
Plant wilts.	Air or soil too dry, too much sun or heat, overwatering, or pot too small	Spray leaves frequently, reduce watering, and check drainage. Or move into larger pot.
Buds, flowers, and leaves drop suddenly.	Sudden change in light or temperature conditions, cold draft, or roots too dry	Improve cultural conditions as needed.

Growing Plants Under Artificial Light

The use of artificial lighting makes it possible to grow house plants in dimly lighted apartments and in any interior where natural light is insufficient for healthy growth. Basements, attics, bookcases, hallways, bathrooms, the space beneath kitchen cabinets—all are places where gardens under lights can be established.

Artificial light is a boon to the plant collector who, having filled all available window space, can set up fluorescent fixtures in other areas to accommodate a greater number of plants. African violets, orchids, begonias, miniature geraniums (*Pelargonium*), and bromeliads are some of the plants that grow especially well under fluorescent light.

Home gardeners who enjoy starting their vegetables or flowering plants indoors find artificial lighting much more reliable than natural sunlight in late winter and spring. Tomatoes, eggplants, peppers, petunias, impatiens, ageratums, and wax begonias are only a few of the popular outdoor plants that can be started indoors under light. In fact, most vegetables and flowering plants will respond to this treatment and have a head start on growth.

It is also possible to grow certain vegetables to maturity in winter by using artificial light. Lettuce, radishes, and compact varieties of tomato are among the vegetables that thrive under artificial light.

Sources of artificial light. Even a table lamp with a standard incandescent bulb of 75 watts, turned on for a few hours each evening, will improve the growth of foliage plants beneath it. Ferns, philodendrons, silver pothos (*Scindapsus aureus*), and spathiphyllums are all examples of commonly grown house plants that benefit from this supplemental light treatment. (Some natural light is necessary to provide wavelengths of light that are absent from incandescent emissions.) Keep plants about 1 foot from the light bulb to avoid damage.

One way to avoid the problem of heat generated by ordinary incandescent bulbs—and still keep plants close to the light source—is to use "cool" incandescent bulbs that have been specially designed for plant growth. These bulbs, of which there are several varieties on the market, generally give a floodlit effect and are most useful for lighting tall plants. Because the bulbs can be a fire hazard, they must always be used in ceramic sockets.

By far the most economical and practical artificial illumination for indoor gardens comes from fluorescent tubes. Most widely used is a combination of two or four 40-watt cool white and warm white tubes in various lengths from 20 to 48 inches. Tubes of lower or higher wattage are also available, as are those of different shapes. Some fluorescent tubes have been specially formulated for plant growth and are frequently used for flowering plants, which require wavelengths of light that are not normally emitted by fluorescent tubes used for indoor lighting.

Perhaps the simplest fluorescent lighting arrangement is a tabletop fixture consisting of two 40-watt tubes, each 24 or 48 inches long. The undersurface of the fixture is white and thus reflects the light over as wide an area as possible. By using a pulley system, the fixture can be raised or lowered according to the heights of the plants beneath it and the amount of light the plants require.

The practical home gardener can readily adapt commercial fluorescent fixtures (either hanging or stationary types), while the home craftsman can build wooden frames to improve the utilitarian appearance of some fixtures.

More decorative—and more expensive—units for plant growth are available from some mail-order houses and furniture firms. These range from pole setups for hanging plants, in which the light fixtures are vertical, to carts and stands with several lighted shelves.

Under-fluorescent techniques. All plants grown under artificial illumination have the same requirements as those grown in sunlight: adequate moisture in soil and air, appropriate temperatures, good air circulation, and the correct amounts of nutrients. However, plants grown under lights usually require more water and fertilizer than other indoor plants, which grow more slowly.

Fluorescent lights must be turned on for about 14 to 16 hours a day to simulate the growth-inducing effects of sunlight. Fixtures can be connected to a timer that automatically turns the lights on and off. The tubes must be located no more than 12 inches above flowering plants, but a distance of 4–8 inches can give even better results. And seedlings should be kept to within 3–4 inches of fluorescent tubes. Plants can actually touch fluorescent tubes without being damaged.

THREE TYPES OF ARTIFICIAL LIGHTING

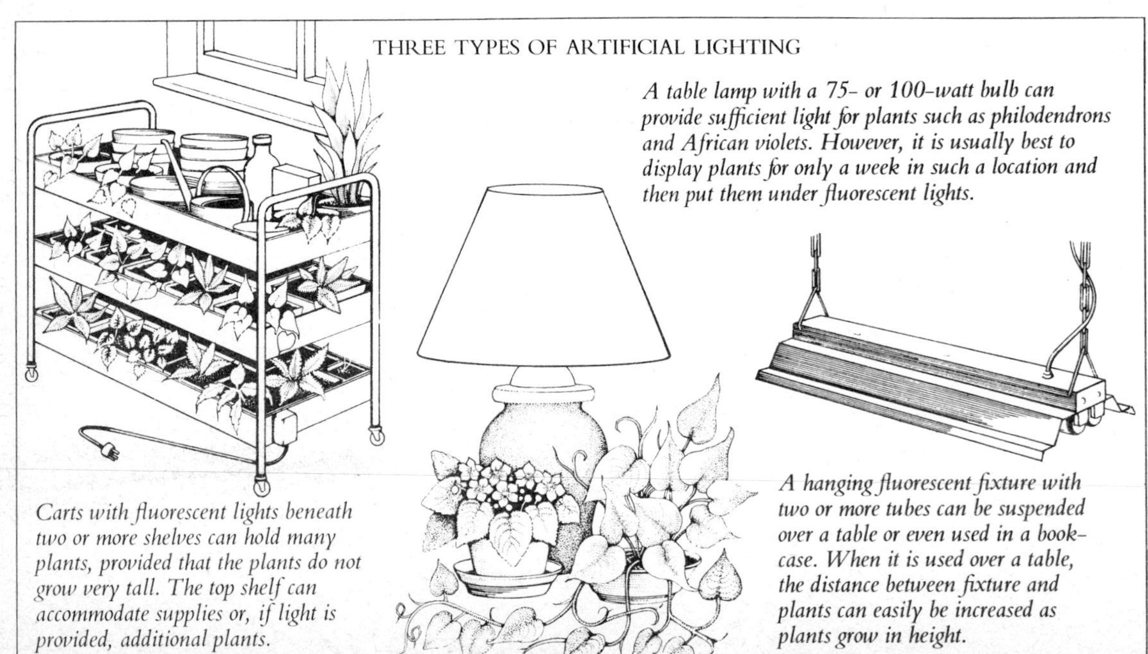

A table lamp with a 75- or 100-watt bulb can provide sufficient light for plants such as philodendrons and African violets. However, it is usually best to display plants for only a week in such a location and then put them under fluorescent lights.

Carts with fluorescent lights beneath two or more shelves can hold many plants, provided that the plants do not grow very tall. The top shelf can accommodate supplies or, if light is provided, additional plants.

A hanging fluorescent fixture with two or more tubes can be suspended over a table or even used in a bookcase. When it is used over a table, the distance between fixture and plants can easily be increased as plants grow in height.

Growing an Indoor Garden in a Bottle

Bottles for indoor gardening—and terrariums in general—are a 20th-century revival of the glass Wardian cases of the Victorian era. Water coolers and wine jugs make suitable containers, but any deep glass receptacle—a fish bowl, a storage jar—can be used, provided it is of clear (not tinted) glass and has an opening large enough to permit the insertion of plants. The container can be kept open or closed.

To set up a garden in a container, first clean and thoroughly dry the container you have chosen. Put a 1-inch layer of gravel on the bottom.

Since aeration of the soil is extremely important, especially in a closed container, the growing medium should be looser and grittier than for potted plants. Use a soilless mixture or soil with a high percentage of peat moss, and add a handful of crushed charcoal lumps to keep the growing medium "sweet" and nontoxic.

Pour in the mix through a paper funnel, and let it settle to a depth of 3–4 inches. Now moisten it, using a small funnel that has been fitted with a slender plastic or rubber tube long enough to reach the top of the growing medium.

Allow the medium to absorb the water; then firm it with a spool wedged onto a dowel or a similar device. Make planting holes by plunging a fork or spoon (tied to a stick) into the mix. Each hole should be just large enough to accommodate the root structure of the plant that will be inserted in it.

Only slow-growing or miniature plants that thrive in moist conditions should be used in bottle gardens (see chart beginning on p. 410). To position a plant, first grip it with long-handled bamboo tongs (sold by house-plant specialists), or bend a piece of wire to fit the root ball. Carefully insert the plants into the planting holes, working from the outer edge inward. Gently firm the medium before positioning each successive plant.

When the last plants are in place, a light sprinkling of water can be applied to remove soil particles from the leaves. The container can then be capped or corked. Place it in a well-lighted location, but out of direct sunlight. To provide even lighting, give the container a quarter turn every few days.

Containers that are left open may require watering every few weeks, depending on the width of the opening (water evaporates slowly from narrow-mouthed containers). To prevent splashing, use a funnel and a slender tube when watering. Closed containers should be opened every two or three months to reduce condensation. A thriving bottle garden may occasionally require the addition of a liquid fertilizer.

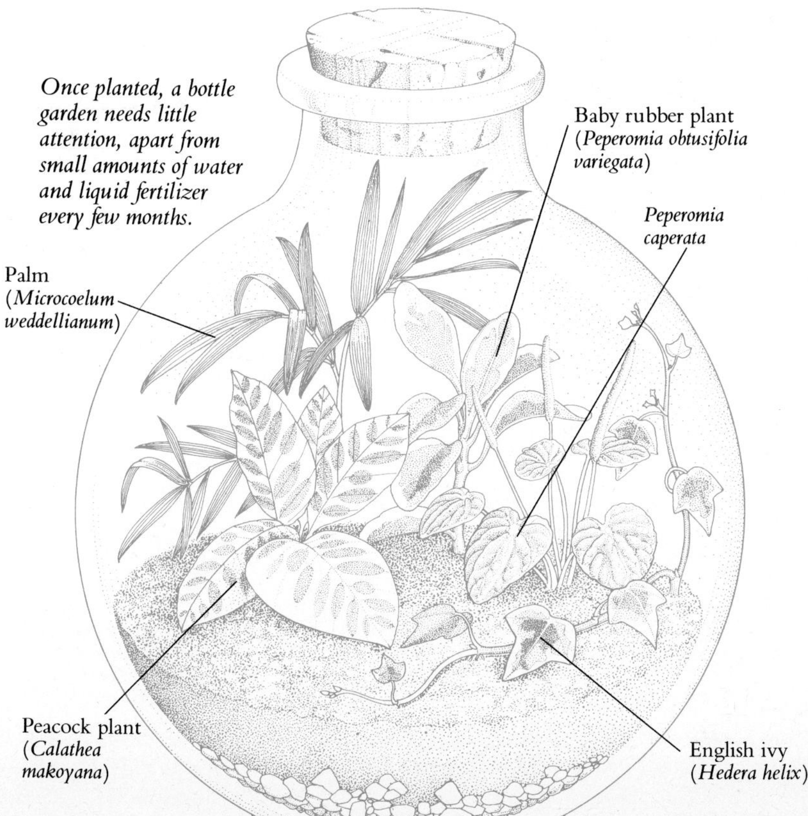

Once planted, a bottle garden needs little attention, apart from small amounts of water and liquid fertilizer every few months.

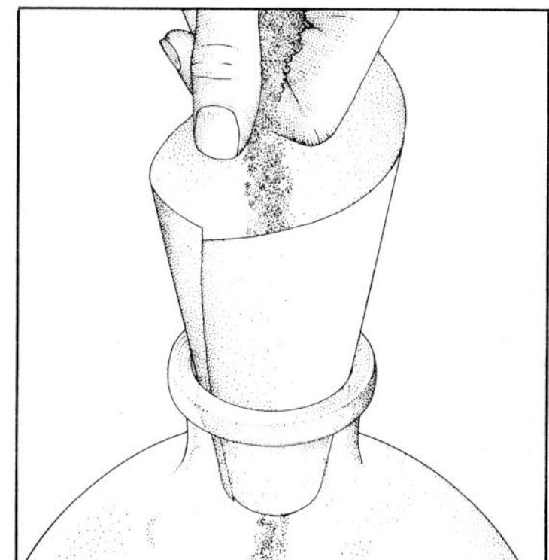

1. *Insert a funnel in the mouth of the bottle, and trickle soil through it.*

2. *With a fork tied to a stick, make planting holes in the moist soil.*

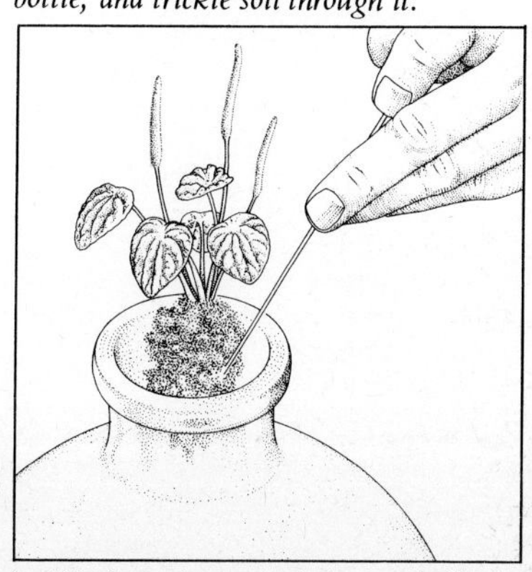

3. *Hook a wire around the root ball, and lower the plant into the bottle.*

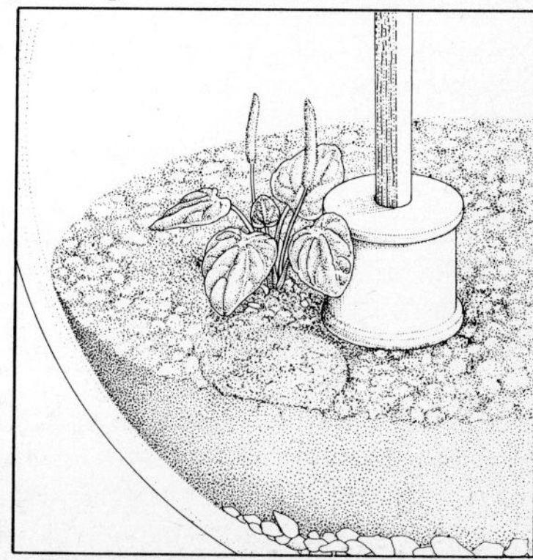

4. *Firm the soil with an empty thread spool wedged on a stick.*

House Plants for Foliage and Flowers

House plants are grouped on the following chart according to whether they are valued primarily for foliage or for flowers. Within each category plants are listed alphabetically by their best known common names.

In the second column the leaves or flowers, and sometimes the fruits, of each plant are described.

The Light column describes each plant's needs in terms of available sunlight. Maximum direct sun can be provided in an unblocked south or east window. "Moderate" means that some sun is needed, as in a west window (or perhaps a south window that is sometimes shaded by a tree). "Diffused" means no direct sun is desirable, but good light is needed, as in a north window. "Minimum" indicates a shade-loving plant. Other requirements, such as temperature, humidity, watering, and feeding, are given in the column on Special Requirements and Remarks.

The best propagation methods are given in the right-hand column.

HOUSE PLANTS GROWN FOR FOLIAGE

Aglaonema modestum

Air plant (*Kalanchoe pinnata*)

Aloe vera

Aluminum plant (*Pilea cadierei*)

False aralia (*Dizygotheca elegantissima*)

Japanese aralia (*Fatsia japonica*)

Common and botanical names, general characteristics	Leaves	Light	Special requirements and remarks	Propagation (*See p. 400*)
Aglaonema, or Chinese evergreen (*Aglaonema modestum*) Durable foliage plant of compact habit. Leaves are clustered on top of single slender cane. H 2 ft.	Lance shaped, leathery, waxy, green. To 8 in. long.	Maximum direct sun best, but tolerates diffused.	Average to high humidity. Keep soil moist, not soggy. Feed every 2 mo. Needs little attention. Grow in water or general-purpose soil mix. Minimum temperature: 60°-65° F.	Divide established plants; or take cuttings.
Air plant (*Kalanchoe pinnata*) Succulent plant with heads of green flowers tinged with purple. Plantlets form on leaf margins. H 1½-3 ft.	Scalloped, fleshy, tinged with red.	Maximum direct sun.	Average humidity. Water only as soil dries. Needs little care. Use general-purpose soil mix with double amount of sand. Minimum temperature: 65° F.	Pot plantlets that form on leaves; also take tip cuttings.
Aloe, or Burn plant (*Aloe vera*) Rosette-forming succulent plant. Leaves contain sap said to heal burns and other skin afflictions. H 2 ft.	Dagger shaped, blue-green, spotted with white when young.	Maximum direct sun.	Tolerant of dry conditions. Allow soil to dry out between waterings. Use desert-cactus soil mix (p. 397). Minimum temperature: 50°-55° F.	Pot up basal offsets.
Aluminum plant (*Pilea cadierei*) Bushy little plant of dainty habit. Also called watermelon pilea. H 10-12 in. Dwarf aluminum plant (*P. c. minima*) is suitable for terrariums and bottle gardens. H 5 in.	Deep veins give quilted effect; silver markings.	Diffused.	Requires high humidity. Keep soil moist, not soggy. Fertilize lightly every 2 mo. Pinch off tip growth. Use general-purpose soil mix. Minimum temperature: 60°-65° F.	Take tip cuttings. For dwarf aluminum plant, divide roots or take cuttings.
Aralia, false, or threadleaf (*Dizygotheca elegantissima*) Graceful, upright shrub often used as floor accent. H 4-8 ft.	Feathery, palmlike, copper colored when young; later turn dark green and become broader.	Moderate or diffused.	Average to high humidity. Keep soil moist, not soggy. Feed monthly spring to fall. Use general-purpose soil mix. Minimum temperature: 65° F.	Air-layer in early spring; or sow fresh seeds.
Aralia, Japanese (*Fatsia japonica*) Handsome, upright plant useful as decorative, bold accent in roomy interiors. H 4-10 ft.	Palmate, shiny, dark green, about 16 in. across.	Moderate or diffused.	Average to high humidity. Keep soil moist, not soggy. Feed sparingly in spring and early summer. Prune in early spring. Use general-purpose soil mix (double amount of peat moss). Minimum temperature: 40° F.	Pot up suckers or offsets from base of plant in spring.

Ming aralia
(*Polyscias fruticosa elegans*)

Arrowhead vine
(*Syngonium podophyllum*)

Artillery plant
(*Pilea microphylla*)

Aucuba japonica variegata

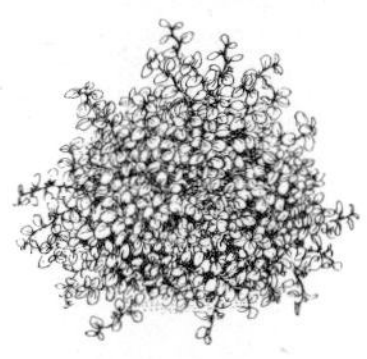
Baby's tears
(*Helxine soleirolii*)

Rex begonia
(*Begonia rex-cultorum*)

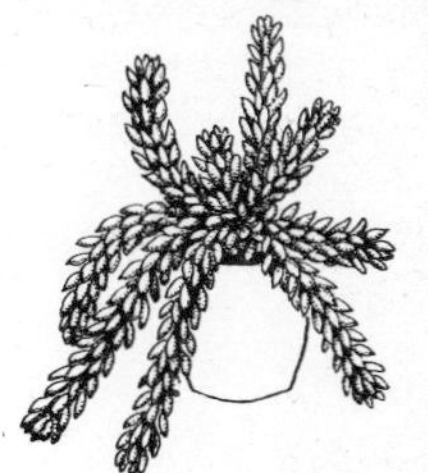
Burro tail
(*Sedum morganianum*)

Common and botanical names, general characteristics	Leaves	Light	Special requirements and remarks	Propagation (*See p. 400*)
Aralia, ming (*Polyscias fruticosa elegans*) Graceful shrub with brown twisted stems and fine-cut foliage. H 3-6 ft.	Lacy, fernlike leaflets are crowded at ends of branches.	Maximum direct sun or moderate.	Average to high humidity. Keep soil moist, not soggy. Feed monthly. Can be pruned as indoor bonsai. Use general-purpose soil mix. Minimum temperature: 65° F.	Take tip or root cuttings in spring. Also propagate by air layering.
Arrowhead vine, or Nephthytis (*Syngonium podophyllum*) Upright or climbing plant with foliage that changes as plant ages. Can be grown against bark or trellis. H 3 ft.	Variegated, arrow shaped when young; later, solid green, fan shaped, to 11 in. long.	Maximum, moderate, or diffused.	Average to high humidity. Keep soil moist, not soggy. Feed monthly spring to fall. Provide support for climbing. Pinch tips for leaf variegation. Use general-purpose soil mix. Minimum temperature: 60° F.	Root cuttings in sand and peat moss or in water. Will grow many months in water.
Artillery plant (*Pilea microphylla*) Low, bushy plant with dainty foliage and inconspicuous flowers that emit bursts of pollen. For edging indoor gardens or use in terrariums. H 4-8 in.	Succulent leaves, about ½ in. across, give fernlike effect.	Moderate or diffused.	High humidity; grow in terrarium or bottle garden, or stand pot on wet pebbles. Keep soil moist, not soggy. Pinch to shape. Use general-purpose soil mix (double amount of peat moss). Minimum temperature: 60° F.	Root cuttings in sand and peat moss or in water.
Aspidistra, see Cast-iron plant				
Aucuba, or Gold-dust plant (*Aucuba japonica variegata*) Evergreen shrub usually grown in tubs as decorative accent. Grow young plants, to 1½ ft. high, in windows. H 3-4 ft.	Oval, waxy textured, bright green sprinkled with yellow spots and splashes.	Diffused or minimum; moderate in winter.	Average to high humidity. Keep soil moist, never soggy. Feed monthly spring to fall. Prune back as needed in early spring. Use general-purpose soil mix (double amount of peat moss). Minimum temperature: 40°-45° F.	Root cuttings in water or in peat moss and sand.
Avocado, see pp. 406 and 510				
Baby's tears (*Helxine soleirolii*) Creeper with tiny leaves, popular in terrariums or in window boxes or under artificial light. H 2-4 in.	Lush, fresh green, abundant.	Moderate or diffused.	High humidity. Keep soil moist, not soggy. Shear to restrict growth in terrariums. Use general-purpose soil mix (double amount of peat moss). Minimum temperature: 50°-55° F.	Divide established plants.
Begonia, rex (*Begonia rex-cultorum*) Rhizomatous plants prized for their richly colored and patterned foliage. White or pink flowers in spring add to their attractiveness. H 1-1½ ft.	Large, heart shaped, sometimes with marginal lobing; dazzling patterns of silver, green, maroon, rose, and red.	Diffused.	High humidity; set pot on moist pebbles in tray. Keep soil reasonably moist, except in mid to late winter when plants rest and need less water. Feed monthly from spring to late summer. Use general-purpose soil mix (double amount of peat moss). Minimum temperature: 60°-65° F.	Divide rhizomes; or root leaf or leaf sections. Plant seeds.
Burro tail (*Sedum morganianum*) Graceful, pendulous succulent with clusters of small pink flowers. Handsome in hanging baskets. H 2-3 ft.	Teardrop shaped, yellow-green with silver-blue bloom.	Maximum direct sun.	Low humidity; too moist atmosphere may cause rot. Allow soil to dry between waterings. Needs little attention. Use desert-cactus soil mix (p. 397). Minimum temperature: 50°-60°F.	Stem cuttings or individual leaves root easily.

HOUSE PLANTS GROWN FOR FOLIAGE *(continued)*

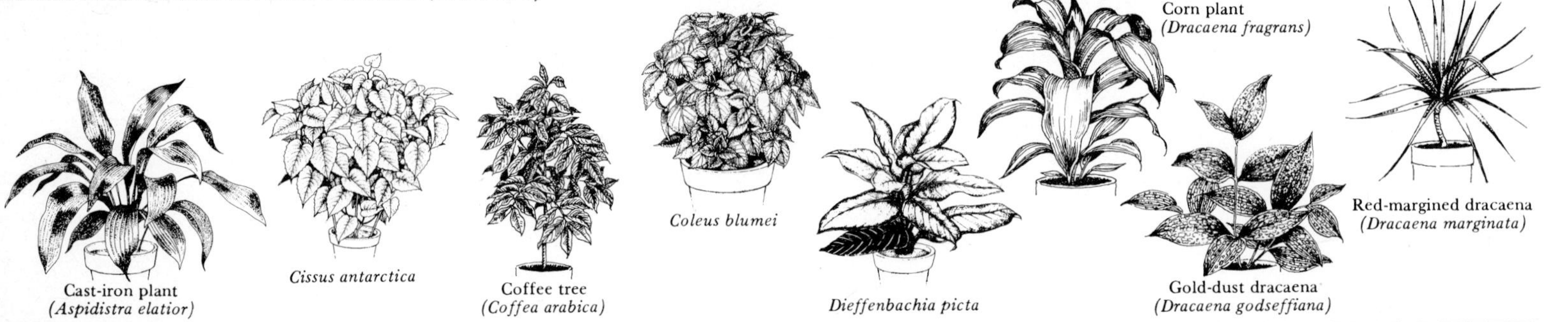

Cast-iron plant *(Aspidistra elatior)*

Cissus antarctica

Coffee tree *(Coffea arabica)*

Coleus blumei

Dieffenbachia picta

Corn plant *(Dracaena fragrans)*

Gold-dust dracaena *(Dracaena godseffiana)*

Red-margined dracaena *(Dracaena marginata)*

Common and botanical names, general characteristics	Leaves	Light	Special requirements and remarks	Propagation *(See p. 400)*
Cast-iron plant *(Aspidistra elatior)* Long-lived plant with tough constitution. Old plants may bear inconspicuous purple flowers near base in summer. *A. e. variegata* has handsome green and white leaves. H 2 ft.	Oblong, leathery, dark green, about 2½ ft. long. There is a variegated form.	Diffused or minimum; moderate in winter.	Average house humidity. Water moderately in winter; keep soil moist but not soggy in summer. Feed monthly in summer. Needs little attention. Use general-purpose soil mix. Minimum temperature: 45° F.	Divide plants in spring.
Chinese evergreen, see Aglaonema				
Cissus, or Kangaroo vine *(Cissus antarctica)* Slow-growing, shrubby vine grown in baskets for handsome foliage. H 3-4 ft. For *C. rhombifolia,* see Ivy, grape.	Large, saw toothed, and leathery; green with metallic tints.	Moderate or diffused.	Average humidity. Allow soil to dry out between waterings. Feed monthly spring to fall. Use general-purpose soil mix. Minimum temperature: 50° F.	Root cuttings.
Coffee tree, or Coffee plant *(Coffea arabica)* Shrubby, upright plant. When 3-4 yr. old, may bear clusters of fragrant white flowers followed by red berries containing coffee beans. H 4 ft.	Wavy margined, fragile textured, glossy green, 3-6 in. long.	Moderate or diffused.	Average to high humidity. Keep soil moist, not soggy. Mist foliage regularly. Fertilize monthly. Pinch new shoots for bushiness. Use general-purpose soil mix (double amount of peat moss). Can be summered on shaded terrace. Minimum temperature: 60° F.	Sow fresh seeds; or take tip cuttings from top growth.
Coleus *(Coleus blumei)* Easily grown plant with multicolored foliage for use in pots or planters. H 8 in.-2 ft.	Oval, often lacy; mottled with purple, pink, yellow, bronze, orange, or red.	Maximum in winter; moderate in summer.	Average to high humidity. Moist, not soggy, soil. Feed twice monthly in spring and summer. Pinch tips to induce bushiness. Use general-purpose soil mix. Minimum temperature: 60° F.	Sow seeds; or take cuttings (both respond well to fluorescent lights).
Dieffenbachia, or Dumb cane *(Dieffenbachia picta)* Imposing plant much used as decorative accent. Leaves poisonous if eaten; sap may irritate skin. H 4 ft.	Glossy, bright green marbled and spotted with ivory, 10 in. long.	Moderate in winter; diffused in summer.	Does best in average to high humidity but can tolerate dry air. Water moderately; soil can dry out between waterings. Feed a few times a year. Use general-purpose soil mix. Minimum temperature: 60°-65° F.	Air-layer; or root side suckers or cane sections in sand.
Dracaena Corn plant *(Dracaena fragrans);* gold-dust dracaena *(D. godseffiana);* red-margined dracaena *(D. marginata)* Shrubby or treelike plants with bold foliage combine well with other plants. Large specimens useful as floor accents. Young plants of *D. godseffiana* fit terrariums and planters. H 2-6 ft.	*D. fragrans:* green, cornstalklike. *D. godseffiana:* glossy, yellow spotted. *D. marginata:* narrow, red margined, in rosettelike crowns.	Moderate or diffused in winter; diffused to minimum in summer.	Does best in high humidity but will tolerate dry atmosphere if foliage is misted regularly. Keep soil moist, not soggy. Feed every 2 mo. Cut back old plants to force new growth. Use general-purpose soil mix (double amount of peat moss). Does best in warm temperatures but will tolerate minimum 60°-65° F at night; can survive 50° F for short periods.	Air-layer; or root stem sections or cuttings.

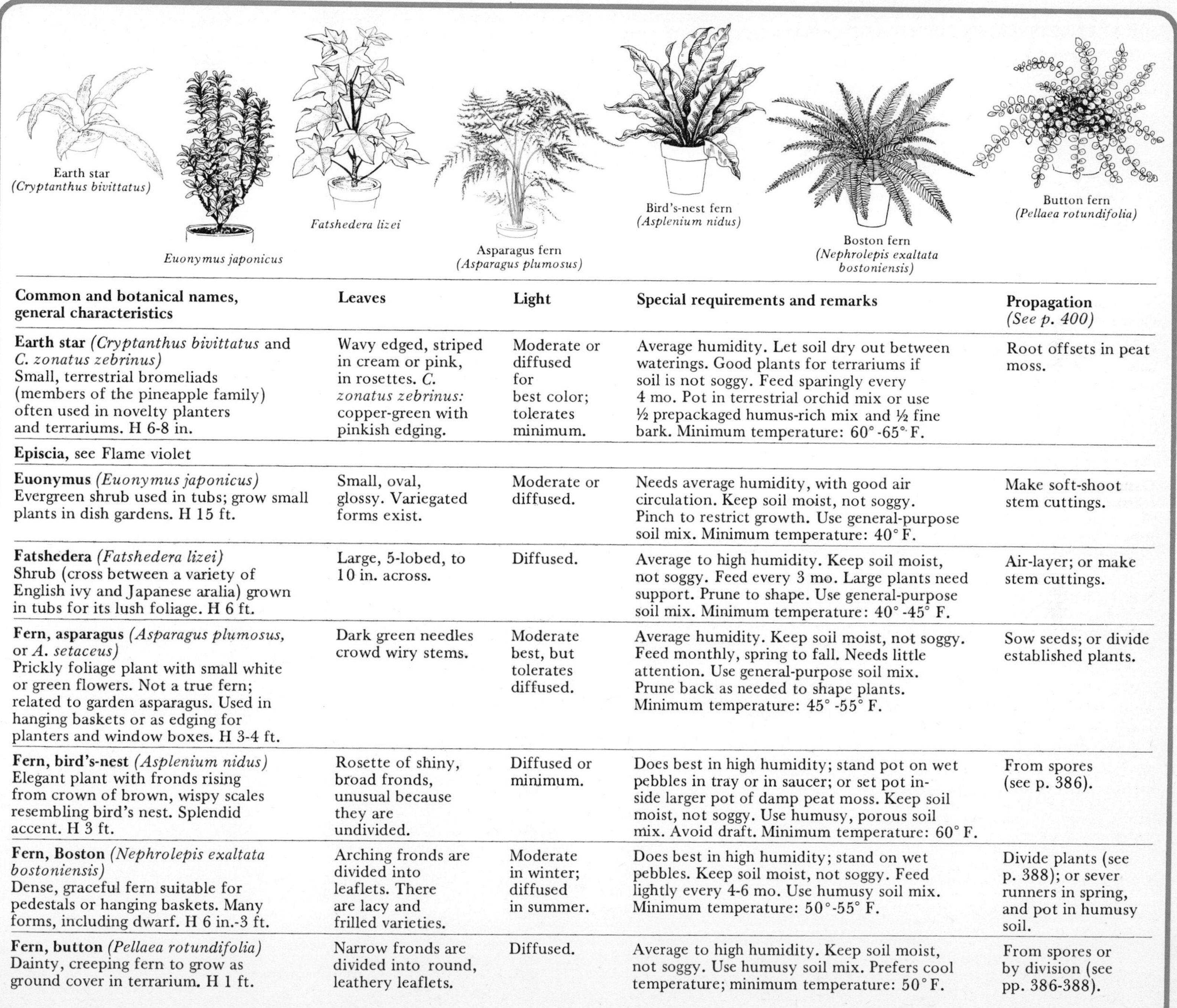

Common and botanical names, general characteristics	Leaves	Light	Special requirements and remarks	Propagation *(See p. 400)*
Earth star *(Cryptanthus bivittatus* and *C. zonatus zebrinus)* Small, terrestrial bromeliads (members of the pineapple family) often used in novelty planters and terrariums. H 6-8 in.	Wavy edged, striped in cream or pink, in rosettes. *C. zonatus zebrinus:* copper-green with pinkish edging.	Moderate or diffused for best color; tolerates minimum.	Average humidity. Let soil dry out between waterings. Good plants for terrariums if soil is not soggy. Feed sparingly every 4 mo. Pot in terrestrial orchid mix or use ½ prepackaged humus-rich mix and ½ fine bark. Minimum temperature: 60°-65° F.	Root offsets in peat moss.
Episcia, see Flame violet				
Euonymus *(Euonymus japonicus)* Evergreen shrub used in tubs; grow small plants in dish gardens. H 15 ft.	Small, oval, glossy. Variegated forms exist.	Moderate or diffused.	Needs average humidity, with good air circulation. Keep soil moist, not soggy. Pinch to restrict growth. Use general-purpose soil mix. Minimum temperature: 40° F.	Make soft-shoot stem cuttings.
Fatshedera *(Fatshedera lizei)* Shrub (cross between a variety of English ivy and Japanese aralia) grown in tubs for its lush foliage. H 6 ft.	Large, 5-lobed, to 10 in. across.	Diffused.	Average to high humidity. Keep soil moist, not soggy. Feed every 3 mo. Large plants need support. Prune to shape. Use general-purpose soil mix. Minimum temperature: 40°-45° F.	Air-layer; or make stem cuttings.
Fern, asparagus *(Asparagus plumosus,* or *A. setaceus)* Prickly foliage plant with small white or green flowers. Not a true fern; related to garden asparagus. Used in hanging baskets or as edging for planters and window boxes. H 3-4 ft.	Dark green needles crowd wiry stems.	Moderate best, but tolerates diffused.	Average humidity. Keep soil moist, not soggy. Feed monthly, spring to fall. Needs little attention. Use general-purpose soil mix. Prune back as needed to shape plants. Minimum temperature: 45°-55° F.	Sow seeds; or divide established plants.
Fern, bird's-nest *(Asplenium nidus)* Elegant plant with fronds rising from crown of brown, wispy scales resembling bird's nest. Splendid accent. H 3 ft.	Rosette of shiny, broad fronds, unusual because they are undivided.	Diffused or minimum.	Does best in high humidity; stand pot on wet pebbles in tray or in saucer; or set pot inside larger pot of damp peat moss. Keep soil moist, not soggy. Use humusy, porous soil mix. Avoid draft. Minimum temperature: 60° F.	From spores (see p. 386).
Fern, Boston *(Nephrolepis exaltata bostoniensis)* Dense, graceful fern suitable for pedestals or hanging baskets. Many forms, including dwarf. H 6 in.-3 ft.	Arching fronds are divided into leaflets. There are lacy and frilled varieties.	Moderate in winter; diffused in summer.	Does best in high humidity; stand on wet pebbles. Keep soil moist, not soggy. Feed lightly every 4-6 mo. Use humusy soil mix. Minimum temperature: 50°-55° F.	Divide plants (see p. 388); or sever runners in spring, and pot in humusy soil.
Fern, button *(Pellaea rotundifolia)* Dainty, creeping fern to grow as ground cover in terrarium. H 1 ft.	Narrow fronds are divided into round, leathery leaflets.	Diffused.	Average to high humidity. Keep soil moist, not soggy. Use humusy soil mix. Prefers cool temperature; minimum temperature: 50° F.	From spores or by division (see pp. 386-388).

HOUSE PLANTS GROWN FOR FOLIAGE *(continued)*

Holly fern
(Cyrtomium falcatum)

Maidenhair fern
(Adiantum raddianum)

Squirrel's-foot fern
(Davallia trichomanoides)

Table fern
(Pteris cretica)

Creeping fig
(Ficus pumila)

Weeping fig
(Ficus benjamina)

Flame violet
(Episcia cupreata)

Miniature holly
(Malpighia coccigera)

Common and botanical names, general characteristics	Leaves	Light	Special requirements and remarks	Propagation (See p. 400)
Fern, holly *(Cyrtomium falcatum)* Small, durable fern often combined with other ferns in dish gardens. H 1 ft.	Fronds divided into pointed, leathery, dark green leaflets.	Diffused or minimum.	Average humidity. Keep soil barely moist. Feed sparingly every month, spring to fall. Use humusy soil. Minimum temperature: 50° F.	Divide plants in spring. Or use spores.
Fern, maidenhair *(Adiantum raddianum)* Popular for its lacy fronds, best displayed in hanging pots. Young plants can grow in terrariums. H 12-16 in.	Delicate, deep green fronds of fan-shaped leaflets on wiry black stems.	Diffused.	Needs high humidity; stand pots on wet pebbles in trays. (See also Bird's-nest fern.) Keep soil moist, not soggy. Use humusy soil. Minimum temperature: 55° F.	Divide plants in early spring.
Fern, squirrel's-foot *(Davallia trichomanoides,* or *D. bullata)* Semi-epiphyte with arching fronds and brown, woolly, creeping rhizomes. Grown in hanging baskets. H 6-18 in.	Broad fronds of feathery, dark green leaflets.	Diffused.	Prefers high humidity, but tolerant of less. Keep soil evenly moist. Use humusy soil mix. Fern-wood pots are good containers, allowing rhizomes to creep over fiber. Best watered by submerging in pail. Minimum temperature: 55° F.	Divide rhizomes. Fasten with wire pins to unmilled, moist sphagnum; keep under glass or plastic.
Fern, table *(Pteris cretica)* Small ferns long popular for use in fern dishes and terrariums. Several named varieties exist. H 6-12 in.	Deeply divided into ribbonlike segments; some varieties are crested or variegated.	Diffused or minimum.	Fairly tolerant of average humidity, but does best in high. Keep soil moist, not soggy. Use humusy soil mix. Feed monthly, spring to fall. Minimum temperature: 55°-60° F.	Divide old plants by carefully cutting crowns. Or use spores.
Ficus, see Fig and Rubber plant				
Fig, creeping *(Ficus pumila,* or *F. repens)* Good vine for hanging baskets, or in planters or terrariums. H 2-6 ft.	Small, heart shaped, dark green; there is a variegated form.	Moderate or diffused.	Average to high humidity. Keep soil moist, not soggy. Use general-purpose soil mix. Stems are self-clinging on walls. Pinch back runners in terrariums. Minimum temperature: 55° F.	Take cuttings or divide plants.
Fig, weeping *(Ficus benjamina)* Evergreen tree or shrub, with pendulous habit that increases with maturity. Provides stylish accent. H 2-5 ft.	Slender, deep green, glistening, and often slightly wavy or twisted; 2-4 in. long.	Moderate or diffused.	Average to high humidity. Keep soil moist, not soggy; let surface dry between waterings. Use general-purpose soil mix. Feed monthly, spring to fall. Minimum temperature: 60° F.	Air-layer.
Flame violet *(Episcia cupreata)* Trailing plant with richly colored foliage and small, showy, yellow or orange-red flowers in summer. Best grown in hanging baskets. H 6-12 in.	Puckered or quilted textures; pink, gray, brown, silver, and other color variegations.	Moderate or diffused.	High humidity. Keep soil moist, not soggy. Use tepid water; do not wet leaves. Use humusy soil mix. Needs warmth. Grow young plants or rooted cuttings in terrarium. Minimum temperature: 65° F.	Take cuttings of trailing stems, which also root where they touch soil. Also take leaf cuttings.
Holly, miniature *(Malpighia coccigera)* Small shrub with evergreen foliage and pretty, small, starlike pink flowers. Suitable for indoor bonsai. H 2 ft.	Small and glossy; mature leaves become spiny.	Maximum direct sun or moderate.	Average humidity. Allow soil surface to dry between waterings. Use general-purpose soil mix. Feed every 3-4 mo. Prune to shape. Minimum temperature: 60° F.	Take cuttings.

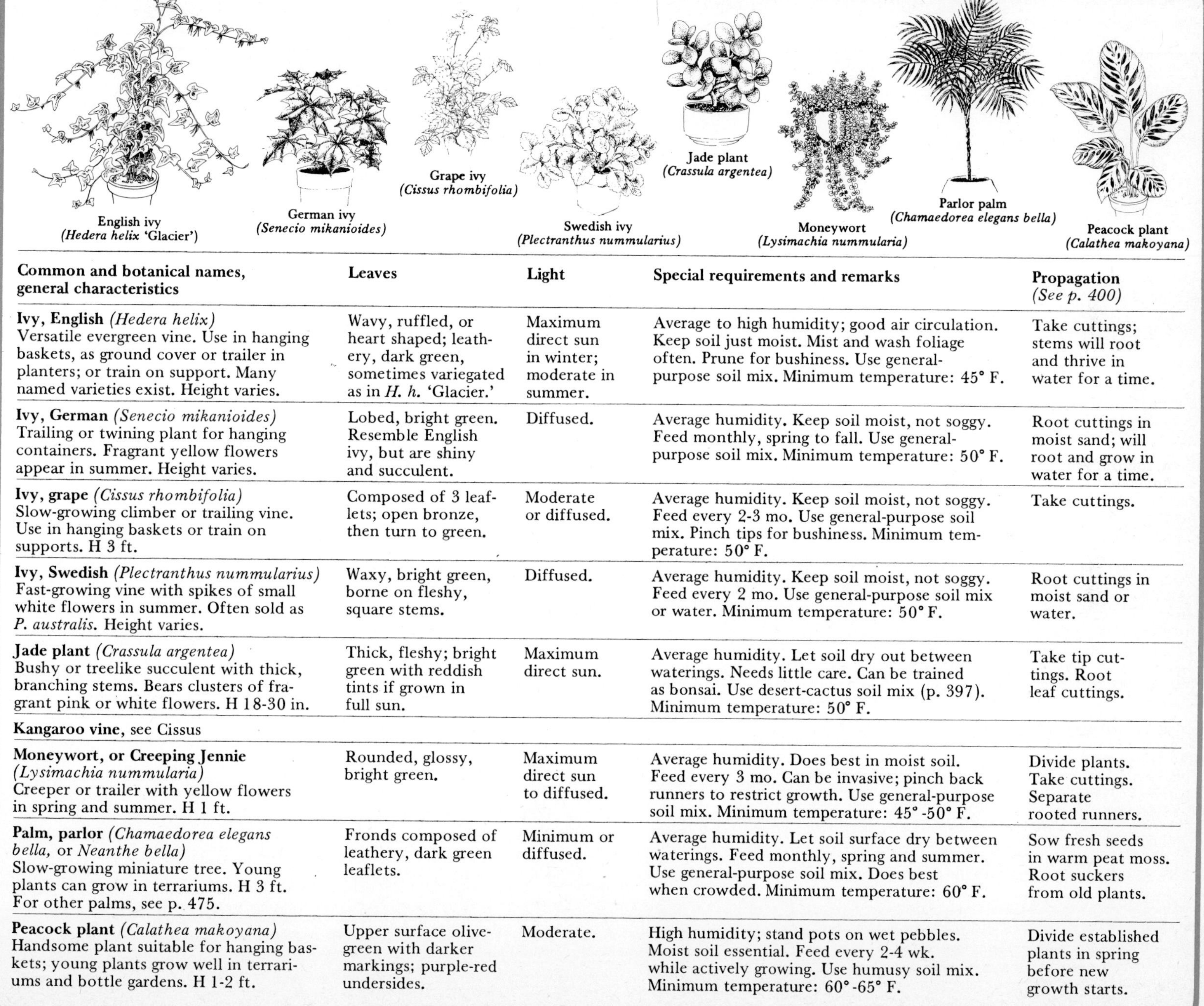

Common and botanical names, general characteristics	Leaves	Light	Special requirements and remarks	Propagation (*See p. 400*)
Ivy, English (*Hedera helix*) Versatile evergreen vine. Use in hanging baskets, as ground cover or trailer in planters; or train on support. Many named varieties exist. Height varies.	Wavy, ruffled, or heart shaped; leathery, dark green, sometimes variegated as in *H. h.* 'Glacier.'	Maximum direct sun in winter; moderate in summer.	Average to high humidity; good air circulation. Keep soil just moist. Mist and wash foliage often. Prune for bushiness. Use general-purpose soil mix. Minimum temperature: 45° F.	Take cuttings; stems will root and thrive in water for a time.
Ivy, German (*Senecio mikanioides*) Trailing or twining plant for hanging containers. Fragrant yellow flowers appear in summer. Height varies.	Lobed, bright green. Resemble English ivy, but are shiny and succulent.	Diffused.	Average humidity. Keep soil moist, not soggy. Feed monthly, spring to fall. Use general-purpose soil mix. Minimum temperature: 50° F.	Root cuttings in moist sand; will root and grow in water for a time.
Ivy, grape (*Cissus rhombifolia*) Slow-growing climber or trailing vine. Use in hanging baskets or train on supports. H 3 ft.	Composed of 3 leaflets; open bronze, then turn to green.	Moderate or diffused.	Average humidity. Keep soil moist, not soggy. Feed every 2-3 mo. Use general-purpose soil mix. Pinch tips for bushiness. Minimum temperature: 50° F.	Take cuttings.
Ivy, Swedish (*Plectranthus nummularius*) Fast-growing vine with spikes of small white flowers in summer. Often sold as *P. australis.* Height varies.	Waxy, bright green, borne on fleshy, square stems.	Diffused.	Average humidity. Keep soil moist, not soggy. Feed every 2 mo. Use general-purpose soil mix or water. Minimum temperature: 50° F.	Root cuttings in moist sand or water.
Jade plant (*Crassula argentea*) Bushy or treelike succulent with thick, branching stems. Bears clusters of fragrant pink or white flowers. H 18-30 in.	Thick, fleshy; bright green with reddish tints if grown in full sun.	Maximum direct sun.	Average humidity. Let soil dry out between waterings. Needs little care. Can be trained as bonsai. Use desert-cactus soil mix (p. 397). Minimum temperature: 50° F.	Take tip cuttings. Root leaf cuttings.
Kangaroo vine, see Cissus				
Moneywort, or Creeping Jennie (*Lysimachia nummularia*) Creeper or trailer with yellow flowers in spring and summer. H 1 ft.	Rounded, glossy, bright green.	Maximum direct sun to diffused.	Average humidity. Does best in moist soil. Feed every 3 mo. Can be invasive; pinch back runners to restrict growth. Use general-purpose soil mix. Minimum temperature: 45°-50° F.	Divide plants. Take cuttings. Separate rooted runners.
Palm, parlor (*Chamaedorea elegans bella,* or *Neanthe bella*) Slow-growing miniature tree. Young plants can grow in terrariums. H 3 ft. For other palms, see p. 475.	Fronds composed of leathery, dark green leaflets.	Minimum or diffused.	Average humidity. Let soil surface dry between waterings. Feed monthly, spring and summer. Use general-purpose soil mix. Does best when crowded. Minimum temperature: 60° F.	Sow fresh seeds in warm peat moss. Root suckers from old plants.
Peacock plant (*Calathea makoyana*) Handsome plant suitable for hanging baskets; young plants grow well in terrariums and bottle gardens. H 1-2 ft.	Upper surface olive-green with darker markings; purple-red undersides.	Moderate.	High humidity; stand pots on wet pebbles. Moist soil essential. Feed every 2-4 wk. while actively growing. Use humusy soil mix. Minimum temperature: 60°-65° F.	Divide established plants in spring before new growth starts.

HOUSE PLANTS GROWN FOR FOLIAGE *(continued)*

Pellionia daveauana

Peperomia caperata 'Emerald Ripple'

Heart-leaf philodendron (*Philodendron scandens oxycardium*)

Tree philodendron (*Philodendron selloum*)

Split-leaf philodendron (*Monstera deliciosa*)

Piggyback plant (*Tolmiea menziesii*)

Creeping pilea (*Pilea depressa*)

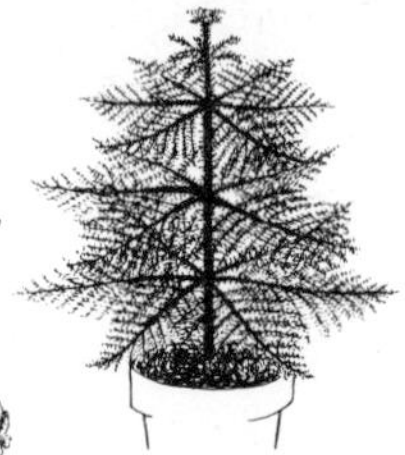

Norfolk Island pine (*Araucaria heterophylla*)

Common and botanical names, general characteristics	Leaves	Light	Special requirements and remarks	Propagation (*See p. 400*)
Pellionia *(Pellionia daveauana)* Creeping plant grown in baskets, as ground cover in planters and terrariums, or against bark. H 3 in.	Fleshy; variegated in brown-purple and green-gray tints.	Diffused; tolerates minimum.	High humidity. Keep soil moist, not soggy. Feed monthly, spring to fall. Pinch tips to control growth. Use general-purpose soil mix. Minimum temperature: 60°-65° F.	Take tip cuttings.
Peperomia Baby rubber plant *(Peperomia obtusifolia); P. caperata* 'Emerald Ripple'; watermelon peperomia *(P. sandersii)* Small, trailing or compact succulents. Attractive foliage. Use in baskets or dish gardens. H 3-8 in.	*P. c.* 'Emerald Ripple': quilted, green with brown tints. *P. obtusifolia:* spoon shaped, waxy. *P. sandersii:* silver veins.	Diffused.	Average humidity. Avoid overwatering; allow soil to dry out between waterings. *P. obtusifolia* can grow in terrarium but will need some pinching. Needs little attention. Use general-purpose soil mix. All peperomias prefer warmth. Minimum temperature: 60° - 65° F.	Divide plants. Or take cuttings.
Philodendron Heart-leaf *(Philodendron scandens oxycardium)*; tree *(P. selloum)* Versatile, durable plants. Heart-leaf philodendron is vine; tree philodendron is self-supporting to 4 ft.	*P. s. oxycardium:* heart shaped, glossy, leathery, 2-4 in. *P. selloum:* dark green, deeply cut, dramatic, 12-18 in.	Diffused; tolerates minimum.	Average to high humidity. Keep soil moist, not soggy. Feed every 3-4 mo. Use general-purpose soil mix (double amount of peat moss). *P. s. oxycardium* will grow in water; needs support for climbing, otherwise it trails. Minimum temperature: 55° F.	Take tip cuttings, or air-layer. Or root stem-joint cuttings in moist peat moss.
Philodendron, split-leaf *(Monstera deliciosa)* Robust tropical vine valued as foliage accent by decorators. H 3-6 ft.	When mature, perforated, glossy, leathery, 8-12 in. long.	Diffused.	Average to high humidity. Keep soil moist, not soggy. Mist leaves. Feed monthly, spring and summer. Give bark support. Use humusy soil mix. Minimum temperature: 60° F.	Take tip cuttings. Air-layer tops of old plants. Root stem sections.
Piggyback plant *(Tolmiea menziesii)* Attractive plant that produces young plants at bases of leaf blades. H 8 in.	Hairy, lobed, toothed, bright green.	Diffused.	Average to high humidity. Keep soil evenly moist. Feed every 2 mo. Use humusy soil mix. Cool temperature best—minimum: 40°-45° F.	Insert leaf-blade bases with plantlets in sand or water.
Pilea, creeping *(Pilea depressa)* Creeping plant with dense foliage habit similar to baby's tears. Good for use in hanging baskets or as ground cover in terrariums. H 4-6 in. For other pileas, see Aluminum plant and Artillery plant.	Oval, glossy, bright green, succulent, about 1 in. long.	Moderate or diffused.	Average to high humidity. Keep soil moist, not soggy. Pinch to shape or restrict growth. Use general-purpose soil mix (double amount of peat moss). Minimum temperature: 60° F.	Divide plants. Or take cuttings. Stems root at nodes where they touch soil.
Pine, Norfolk Island *(Araucaria heterophylla)* Long-lived coniferous evergreen. Fine room accent in pot or tub. H 2-5 ft.	Overlapping, needle-like, crowding tiers of branches.	Diffused; maximum direct sun in winter.	Average humidity. Keep soil moist, not soggy. Feed monthly, spring to fall. Use general-purpose soil mix (double amount of peat moss). Minimum temperature: 50° - 55° F.	Fresh seeds are difficult to obtain; buy young plants.

Pineapple, see p. 406

Podocarpus macrophylla maki

Polka-dot plant (*Hypoestes phyllostachya*)

Golden pothos (*Scindapsus aureus*)

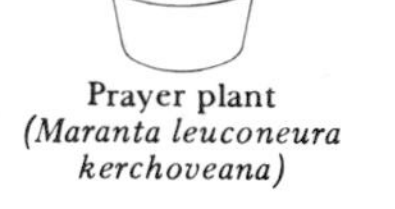

Prayer plant (*Maranta leuconeura kerchoveana*)

Purple heart (*Setcreasea purpurea*)

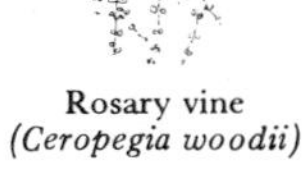

Rosary vine (*Ceropegia woodii*)

Rubber plant (*Ficus elastica decora*)

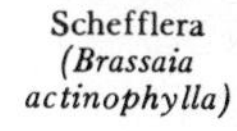

Schefflera (*Brassaia actinophylla*)

Common and botanical names, general characteristics	Leaves	Light	Special requirements and remarks	Propagation (*See p. 400*)
Podocarpus, or Shrubby yew pine (*Podocarpus macrophylla maki*) Evergreen shrub usually grown in tubs; also trained as bonsai. H 6 ft.	Needlelike, dense, dark green.	Diffused; maximum direct sun in winter.	Average humidity. Keep soil moist, not soggy. Feed once or twice in summer. Prune or shear as required. Use general-purpose soil mix. Prefers cool site. Minimum temperature: 50° F.	Root cuttings. Or sow seeds.
Polka-dot plant (*Hypoestes phyllostachya*) Dainty tropical plant, fast growing but short-lived. Does well in artificial light or in windows. H 6-12 in.	Soft, hairy, bright green with rose-pink freckles.	Diffused.	Average to high humidity. Keep soil moist, not soggy. Despite pinching, plants become leggy. Use general-purpose soil mix (double amount of peat moss). Minimum temperature: 65° F.	Cuttings root easily. Grow young plants as replacements for old, leggy plants.
Pothos, golden (*Scindapsus aureus*) Durable vine with variegated foliage. Grow as trailer in hanging pots or as climber. Height varies.	Heart shaped, waxy, with yellow markings. 'Marble Queen' is white and green.	Diffused.	Average humidity. Let soil dry out between waterings. To encourage climbing, provide support. Use general-purpose soil mix. Minimum temperature: 65° F.	Root cuttings in water or moist peat moss.
Prayer plant (*Maranta leuconeura kerchoveana*) Low, spreading plant with leaves that fold upward in evening. Young plants grow well in terrariums. H 6-8 in.	Oval; vivid to pale green with 2 rows of brown blotches, red underneath.	Diffused.	Average to high humidity. Keep soil moist, not soggy. Feed monthly, spring to fall. Use humusy soil mix. Minimum temperature: 65° F.	Divide established clumps in spring.
Purple heart (*Setcreasea purpurea*) Trailing plant with attractive purple stems and foliage; useful for growing in hanging containers. H 6-8 in.	Lance shaped and slender; purple color enhanced by fine hairs.	Maximum direct sun.	Average humidity. Let soil dry out between waterings. Feed every 2 mo. Use general-purpose soil mix. Divide and repot overgrown plants. Minimum temperature: 60°-65° F.	By division. Or root cuttings in water.
Rosary vine (*Ceropegia woodii*) Trailing succulent. Forms many small tubers along stems. H 3 ft.	Small and heart shaped; blue-green marbled with silver.	Moderate.	Average humidity. Water sparingly in winter, moderately spring through fall. Use general-purpose soil mix. Minimum temperature: 55° F.	Take cuttings. Or separate small tubers from stem internodes.
Rubber plant (*Ficus elastica decora*) Rugged, bold foliage plant valued as dramatic room accent. H 5 ft. For baby rubber plant, see Peperomia.	Open bronze, then become glossy green with ivory midribs; up to 1 ft. long.	Maximum direct sun to diffused.	Average humidity. Keep soil moist, not soggy. Feed twice yearly. Wash leaves with mild liquid detergent. Use general-purpose soil mix. Minimum temperature: 65° F.	Air-layer.
Schefflera, or Umbrella tree (*Brassaia actinophylla*) Graceful, fast-growing plant useful as room decoration. H 6 ft.	Long stalked, with 6-8 glossy green leaflets 4-10 in. long.	Moderate or diffused.	Average humidity. Let soil dry out between waterings; then water thoroughly. Use general-purpose soil mix. Repot fast-growing young plants as needed. Tolerant of dryness and warmth in houses. Minimum temperature: 65° F.	Sow fresh seeds. Or take cuttings, or air-layer.

HOUSE PLANTS GROWN FOR FOLIAGE (*continued*)

Snake plant (*Sansevieria trifasciata*)

Spider plant (*Chlorophytum comosum vittatum*)

Strawberry begonia (*Saxifraga sarmentosa*)

Ti plant (*Cordyline terminalis*)

Tradescantia fluminensis

Umbrella palm (*Cyperus alternifolius*)

Velvet plant (*Gynura aurantiaca*)

Wandering Jew (*Zebrina pendula*)

Common and botanical names, general characteristics	Leaves	Light	Special requirements and remarks	Propagation (*See p. 400*)
Snake plant (*Sansevieria trifasciata*) Long-lived, durable plant with racemes of small, fragrant flowers. Endures poor conditions. H 3 ft.	Sword shaped, stiff, leathery; dark green with lighter horizontal bands.	Tolerates maximum direct sun to minimum.	Low to average humidity. Let soil dry out between waterings. Feed a few times from spring to fall. Use general-purpose soil mix. Minimum temperature: 60° F.	Divide rhizomes. Or take leaf cuttings (2-in. sections).
Spider plant (*Chlorophytum comosum vittatum*) Graceful, grassy plant for hanging pots. Spidery plantlets form on wiry stems after flowers fade. H 1 ft.	Ribbonlike, growing in rosettes; green with broad white bands.	Diffused.	Average to high humidity. Keep soil moist, not soggy. Feed every 2 mo. Use general-purpose soil mix. Repot only when overcrowded. Minimum temperature: 50° - 55° F.	Divide fleshy roots. Or remove and root plantlets.
Strawberry begonia (*Saxifraga sarmentosa,* or *S. stolonifera*) Leafy plant that forms plantlets on threadlike runners. Grow in hanging containers. Also known as strawberry geranium and mother-of-thousands. H 6-8 in.	Round, fleshy, hairy; veins marked with gray; undersides reddish.	Maximum direct sun in winter; moderate in summer.	Average humidity. Let soil dry out between waterings. Needs little attention. Use general-purpose soil mix. Does best in cool temperatures; minimum: 40° - 45° F.	Divide established plants. Or root plantlets in moist sand.
Ti plant (*Cordyline terminalis*) Upright tropical plant grown for its colorful foliage. Sometimes sold as *Dracaena terminalis.* H 3 ft.	Sword shaped to paddle shaped; variegated with red tints; 1 ft. long.	Diffused.	High humidity; stand on wet pebbles. Keep soil moist, not soggy. Use general-purpose soil mix; also grows in water. Minimum temperature: 60° F.	Lay leafless 2-in. stem sections horizontally in moist sand.
Tradescantia (*Tradescantia fluminensis*) Trailing, fast-growing fleshy plant for hanging baskets. Also known as wandering Jew and inch plant. H 1 ft.	Blue-green, purple underneath. *T. f. variegata,* silver striped.	Moderate or diffused.	Average humidity. Let soil dry out between waterings. Feed monthly, spring to fall. Pinch tips. Use general-purpose soil mix; will grow in water. Minimum temperature: 55° F.	Root cuttings in mixture of moist peat moss and sand or in water.
Umbrella palm (*Cyperus alternifolius*) Tall bog plant with crown of leaves atop bare green stem. Unusual room accent. Can also grow partly submerged in pools and aquariums. H 1½-3 ft.	Grasslike, radiating from top of each stem like spokes of umbrella.	Maximum direct sun.	Average to high humidity. Moist to wet soil essential; stand pots in saucers constantly filled with water. Fertilize twice monthly, spring to fall. Use general-purpose soil mix. Repot as needed in spring. Minimum temperature: 55° F.	Divide plants. Or cut off leaf rosette with stem portion, and root in water or wet peat moss.
Umbrella tree, see Schefflera				
Velvet plant (*Gynura aurantiaca*) Tropical fleshy plant grown for its mound of unusual foliage. H 2 ft.	Velvety textured, with purple hairs and veins.	Maximum direct sun.	Average to high humidity. Keep soil moist, not soggy. Feed monthly. Use humusy soil mix. Minimum temperature: 65° F.	Take tip cuttings.
Wandering Jew (*Zebrina pendula*) Fast-growing plant for hanging pots. H 8 in. See also Tradescantia.	Variegated green and silver; red-purple underneath.	Diffused.	High humidity. Keep soil moist, not soggy. Feed monthly, spring to fall. Use general-purpose soil mix. Minimum temperature: 55° F.	Root cuttings in moist sand or water.

HOUSE PLANTS GROWN FOR FLOWERS OR FRUITS

African linden (*Sparmannia africana*)

African violet (*Saintpaulia ionantha*)

Amaryllis (*Hippeastrum* hybrid)

Anthurium scherzerianum

Apostle plant (*Neomarica northiana*)

Common and botanical names, general characteristics	Flowers	Light	Special requirements and remarks	Propagation *(See p. 400)*
African linden *(Sparmannia africana)* Fast-growing, multistemmed shrub with coarse, hairy leaves, to 6 in. wide. Tub plant useful as accent; small plants, for window gardens. H 2-10 ft.	Fragrant, white petaled, with yellow and purple stamens; borne from late spring to early summer.	Maximum direct sun; tolerates diffused.	Average to high humidity. Keep soil moist, not soggy. Prune after flowering to control height and keep bushy. Feed monthly, early spring to fall. Use general-purpose soil mix. Minimum temperature: 45° F.	Sow seeds; or take tip cuttings from growth cut back in late spring.
African violet *(Saintpaulia ionantha)* Low, often everblooming plants. Flowers are held above rosette of spoon-shaped leaves. Many hybrids and varieties are available, including miniature and trailing forms. For fluorescent light gardens, windows, plant stands, and terrariums. See also p. 472. H 6 in.	Single (5-petaled) or double, with yellow stamens, 1-1½ in. across, in white, blue, purple, pink, or bicolor combinations.	Diffused.	Average to high humidity; stand pots on trays of wet pebbles. Keep soil moist, not soggy. If washing leaves, use lukewarm water and allow to dry in shade; avoid wetting foliage with cold water. Use general-purpose soil mix (double amount of peat moss). Repot root-bound or multicrowned plants. Minimum temperature: 65° F.	Root leaf cuttings; or divide overcrowded plants, allowing 1 crown per pot; or sow seeds.
Amaryllis *(Hippeastrum* hybrids) Bulbous plant with strap-shaped leaves and large, lilylike flowers. Bulbs can be purchased potted or unpotted; either way, bloom is almost certain in window gardens the first year. See also p. 462. H 1-2½ ft.	Spectacular, trumpet shaped; 3-4 blooms cluster atop thick green stalk from early winter to midspring; colors range from white to shades of pink and red.	Maximum direct sun or moderate.	Average humidity. During active growth, water when soil dries and feed monthly. When foliage dies back in early autumn, stop watering until midwinter or when new bud shows; then resume watering. If needed, support heavy flower stem with bamboo stake. Use general-purpose soil mix. Allow 1-2 in. between pot and bulb, with 1/3 of bulb above surface. Repot every 3-4 yr. Minimum temperature: 55° F.	Separate and pot up bulb offsets; or sow seeds (very slow to develop).
Anthurium *(Anthurium scherzerianum)* Small tropical plant with spear-shaped, leathery leaves and long-lasting flowerlike spathes (large bracts). Fine in large terrarium or bottle garden until plant grows too large. H 1 ft.	Curly spike of tiny true flowers emerges from large bract of salmon or red, sometimes white or pink.	Bright diffused.	High humidity best; stand pots on tray of wet pebbles. Keep soil moist, not soggy. Feed monthly. Use porous but humusy soil mix (equal parts bark chips, peat moss, and sand). Needs warm temperature; minimum: 65° F.	Divide rooted side shoots.
Apostle plant *(Neomarica northiana)* Iris relative with similar flowers and foliage. Old window-garden favorite. Also called walking iris, because young plants form on tips of flower stems that bend down and root. H 1-2 ft.	Irislike. White outer petals; inner ones have brown-yellow bases, violet tips; very fragrant; borne in late winter.	Moderate or diffused.	Average humidity. Keep soil moist, not soggy. Sponge leaves to remove dust. Use general-purpose soil mix (double amount of peat moss). Repot when pot-bound, allowing 1 "fan" of leaves per pot. Minimum temperature: 60° F.	Divide rhizome; or use hairpin to hold down stem plantlet in pot of soil, sever when rooted.

Azalea, see p. 463

HOUSE PLANTS GROWN FOR FLOWERS OR FRUITS *(continued)*

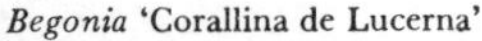

Begonia 'Corallina de Lucerna'

Wax begonia (*Begonia semperflorens*)

Billbergia nutans

Tahitian bridal veil (*Tripogandra multiflora*)

Calamondin (*Citrus madurensis*)

Calceolaria herbeohybrida

Common and botanical names, general characteristics	Flowers	Light	Special requirements and remarks	Propagation (*See p. 400*)
Begonia (*Begonia* species and hybrids) Many fine choices. Old favorite *B.* 'Corallina de Lucerna,' is tall ever-blooming hybrid with silver-spotted leaves. H 3 ft. or more. Wax begonia (*B. semperflorens*) is versatile, also everblooming; glossy foliage varies from light green to red tinged or green and white according to variety. H 5-9 in.	'Corallina de Lucerna' has drooping clusters of large coral flowers. Wax begonia bears multitudes of single or double flowers in white, pink, rose, or red.	Moderate or diffused. Wax begonia needs maximum to moderate for best bloom.	Average to high humidity. Overwatering causes rot; let soil dry out between waterings. Feed monthly. Generally easy to grow. 'Corallina de Lucerna' needs annual spring pruning to restrict height; support canes with bamboo stakes. Cut wax begonias halfway back in spring or summer; divide and repot in general-purpose soil mix (double amount of peat moss). Minimum temperature: 55° F.	Divide plants, or take cuttings. Sow seeds for wax begonia indoors in mid to late winter; grow under fluorescent lights.
Billbergia, or Queen's tears (*Billbergia nutans*) Durable bromeliad. Rosettes of narrow, bronze-tinged leaves, silvery underneath, and graceful flowers. Striking accent for modern interiors. H 2 ft.	Arching stalk arises in winter with rose bracts and clusters of blue-edged green flowers with bright yellow anthers.	Diffused.	Average to high humidity. Allow soil to dry out between waterings. Use general-purpose soil mix (double amount of peat moss) or epiphytic mix (see Silver Vase). Feed every 2 mo. in winter and spring. Minimum temperature: 55°-60° F.	Pot offsets produced after flowering.
Bridal veil, Tahitian (*Tripogandra multiflora*) Trailing plant with small, pointed leaves on wiry stems that are peppered with tiny white flowers. Splendid for hanging pots. H 12 in.	Small, white, everblooming; show up well against glossy foliage.	Maximum direct sun in winter; diffused in summer.	Average to high humidity. Let soil dry out between waterings. Feed every month or two. Pinch back tips for more compact growth. Use general-purpose soil mix. Minimum temperature: 60° F.	Divide old plants. Root tip cuttings in water.
Calamondin (*Citrus madurensis*) Twiggy shrub with glossy foliage, fragrant flowers, and little edible oranges. Easy to grow in pots or tubs, indoors or on patios. H 2-6 ft.	Waxy, white, very fragrant, borne intermittently. For fruit pollinate with paintbrush in winter.	Maximum direct sun; tolerates moderate.	Average humidity. Keep soil moist, not soggy. Feed monthly except in winter. Pinch back new growth for bushiness. Use general-purpose soil mix (double amount of peat moss). Repot when root-bound. Minimum temperature: 55° F.	Take cuttings of semi-hardwood in summer. Also sow seeds.
Calceolaria, or Pocketbook plant (*Calceolaria herbeohybrida*) Short-lived, showy flowering plant with large, bright green leaves. Sold by florists in spring. See also p. 459. H 8-12 in.	Many pouch-shaped 2-in. flowers in shades of yellow, orange, or red, often spotted with crimson or brown.	Diffused.	Average to high humidity. Let soil dry out between waterings, then water thoroughly. Do not wet flowers or foliage. Discard after flowering. Plants last longer in cool (55°-60° F) temperatures; minimum: 40°-45° F.	Virtually impossible to grow from seeds without greenhouse environment; buy young plants.

Camellia, see p. 464
Cape primrose, see p. 464
Cineraria, see p. 459

Cyclamen persicum

Boston yellow daisy (*Chrysanthemum frutescens chrysaster*)

Ivy geranium (*Pelargonium peltatum*)

Gloxinia (*Sinningia speciosa* hybrid)

Goldfish plant (*Hypocyrta nummularia*)

Common and botanical names, general characteristics	Flowers	Light	Special requirements and remarks	Propagation (*See p. 400*)
Cyclamen (*Cyclamen persicum,* or *C. indicum*) Cormous-rooted plant with beautiful flowers above rosette of succulent, heart-shaped blue-green leaves marbled with silver. Popular gift and holiday plant, long lasting in cool rooms. H 6-12 in.	Nodding, 2-3 in. across, with reflexed petals of white, pink, rose, or red; appear from early winter to early spring.	Moderate or diffused.	High humidity. Keep soil moist, not soggy. Feed every 2 wk. while blooming. After leaves die down in late spring, stop watering and place pot on its side. In early fall repot in general-purpose soil mix, with top of corm just above surface. Resume watering. Does best in temperature of 65° F or less; minimum: 50° F.	Sow seeds in late summer to late fall in moist, unmilled sphagnum moss. Maintain cool temperature. Plants should bloom in 12-18 mo.
Daisy, Boston yellow (*Chrysanthemum frutescens chrysaster*) Bushy plant with yellow flowers and divided foliage. For window gardens and summer terraces. H 2-3 ft.	Lemon-yellow; last well when cut; everblooming if given sufficient sun.	Maximum direct sun.	Average humidity. Keep soil moist, not soggy. Feed blooming plants monthly. Discard or cut back overgrown plants. Use general-purpose soil mix. Does best in cool temperatures; minimum: 50° F.	Take cuttings from nonflowering shoots in fall or winter.
Fuchsia, see p. 460 **Gardenia,** see p. 474				
Geranium, ivy (*Pelargonium peltatum*) Trailing plant with bright green deeply lobed leaves and clusters of vivid flowers. Summer house plant for hanging pots or planters on patios or porches. H 1-2 ft.	Single or double; white, lavender, pink, rose, or red; appear from late spring to late fall.	Maximum direct sun.	Average humidity. Let soil dry out between waterings. Feed monthly, spring to fall. Use general-purpose soil mix. Minimum temperature: 45°-50° F.	Take cuttings from old plants in fall; grow over winter in cool window or under lights.
Geranium, zonal, see p. 461				
Gloxinia (*Sinningia speciosa* hybrids) Tuberous-rooted plant with rosette of long-stemmed, hairy, brittle leaves, 5-7 in. long, and richly colored flowers. Spectacular for protected patios and porches. H 8-10 in. Miniature species, *S. pusilla,* is everblooming in terrariums. H 1-4 in.	Large, bell-shaped, velvety; single or double; white, violet, purple, pink, crimson, and bicolors; usually appear in summer and fall—other times under lights.	Moderate or diffused.	Average to high humidity. Keep soil moist, not soggy. Keep water off leaves. Feed monthly while in growth. Plant dormant tuber in 6-in. squatty pot in moist, humusy soil mix; or enclose in moist peat moss in plastic bag until roots form. After leaves yellow, rest tuber for 2-3 mo. Minimum temperature: 60° F.	Root leaf cuttings (as with African violets). Or take stem cuttings from new growth on tuber in spring. Sow seeds.
Goldfish plant (*Hypocyrta nummularia*) Small, fibrous-rooted creeper with oval leaves and odd-shaped flowers. For hanging pots indoors or on protected patios. H 1-2 ft.	Fish-shaped, orange-red, ½-¾ in. long; appear in summer and fall.	Diffused.	High humidity. Keep soil moist, not soggy. Feed monthly, spring to fall. Cut back plants in fall; water occasionally during winter rest period. Use humusy soil mix. Minimum temperature: 65° F.	Enclose tip cuttings in plastic to retain humidity. Also sow seeds.

HOUSE PLANTS GROWN FOR FLOWERS OR FRUITS *(continued)*

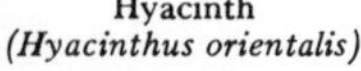

Hyacinth
(Hyacinthus orientalis)

Star jasmine
(Trachelospermum jasminoides)

Moses-in-the-cradle
(Rhoeo spathacea)

Dwarf myrtle
(Myrtus communis microphylla)

Osmanthus fragrans

Oxalis purpurea
'Grand Duchess'

Common and botanical names, general characteristics	Flowers	Light	Special requirements and remarks	Propagation *(See p. 400)*
Hyacinth *(Hyacinthus orientalis)* Spring-flowering bulb that can be brought into bloom indoors from early winter on. H 6-9 in.	Waxy, fragrant, in spikes; white, blue, pink, salmon, red.	Maximum direct sun.	Average humidity. Keep soil moist, not soggy, or grow in water. Buy specially prepared bulbs for forcing, or see p. 317. Minimum temperature: 40° - 45° F.	Take offsets only from bulbs grown outdoors.
Impatiens, see p. 467				
Jasmine, star *(Trachelospermum jasminoides)* Slow-growing, twining vine with glossy green, leathery leaves and fragrant flowers. For windows, hanging pots. Height varies.	Sweet scented, star shaped, white, 1 in. across, in clusters; appear late winter through fall.	Maximum direct sun in winter; diffused in summer.	Average to high humidity. Allow soil to dry out; then water thoroughly. Feed every 2 mo. while flowering. Provide trellis support, or pinch tips to keep bushy. Use general-purpose soil mix (double amount of peat moss). Minimum temperature: 50° F.	Take tip cuttings.
Lily, Easter, see p. 467 **Maple, flowering**, see p. 468				
Moses-in-the-cradle *(Rhoeo spathacea,* or *R. discolor)* Rhizomatous plant with rosettes of stiff, waxy leaves and tiny flowers. Durable basket or pot plant. H 1-2 ft.	Small, white, borne intermittently in boatlike bracts at leaf bases.	Maximum direct sun in winter; diffused in summer.	Average to high humidity. Keep soil moist, not soggy. Feed monthly. Needs little attention. Use general-purpose soil mix. Minimum temperature: 50° - 55° F.	Divide rhizomes. Or take suckers from base.
Myrtle, dwarf *(Myrtus communis microphylla)* Small shrub with tiny, aromatic glossy leaves and fragrant flowers. Fine for indoor bonsai. H 2 ft.	White; appear from spring to midsummer, followed by blue-black berries.	Maximum direct sun.	Average humidity. Keep soil moist, not soggy. Feed every 3-4 mo. from early spring to late fall. Use general-purpose soil mix. Minimum temperature: 40° - 45° F.	Take stem cuttings.
Orchid, see p. 476				
Osmanthus, or Sweet olive *(Osmanthus fragrans)* Slow-growing shrub with leathery leaves and fragrant flowers. Window pot or tub plant to move outdoors to summer terraces. H 2-6 ft.	Small, green-white, in clusters; appear in spring and summer, intermittently in fall and winter.	Maximum direct sun.	Average to high humidity. Keep soil moist, not soggy. Feed monthly. Needs little attention. Use general-purpose soil mix (double amount of peat moss). Does best in cool (65° F) temperatures; minimum temperature: 50° - 55° F.	Take cuttings of semi-hard shoots in late summer; treat with root-inducing hormone.
Oxalis *(Oxalis purpurea* 'Grand Duchess') Spreading bulbous plant with bright green, cloverlike leaflets and pretty flowers that close at night. H 4-8 in.	Bright rose, 2½-3 in. across, borne in winter; white or yellow on some other oxalises.	Maximum direct sun.	Average to high humidity. Let soil dry out between waterings. Feed monthly while in growth. Use general-purpose soil mix. Needs rest after flowering; stop watering until fall. Minimum temperature: 50° F.	Divide bulb offsets while plants are dormant.

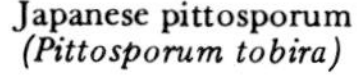

Japanese pittosporum
(Pittosporum tobira)

Dwarf Natal plum
(Carissa grandiflora nana compacta)

Poinsettia
(Euphorbia pulcherrima)

Dwarf pomegranate
(Punica granatum nana)

German primrose
(Primula obconica)

Common and botanical names, general characteristics	**Flowers**	**Light**	**Special requirements and remarks**	**Propagation** *(See p. 400)*
Pittosporum, Japanese *(Pittosporum tobira)* Rugged, long-lived evergreen shrub with 2- to 4-in. glossy green leaves. Popular, dependable tub or pot plant that tolerates difficult conditions. Good indoor bonsai. H 3-6 ft.	Small, creamy, with orange-blossom fragrance; appear in clusters at ends of branches in early spring.	Maximum direct sun; tolerates bright diffused.	Average to high humidity. Let soil dry out between waterings. Wash foliage to remove dust. Needs little attention. Feed twice a year, in early spring and early summer. Prune as necessary to keep spreading habit or to train as indoor bonsai. Use general-purpose soil mix. Does best in cool (65° F) temperature; minimum: 40° - 55° F.	Take stem cuttings in late summer. Also, sow seeds.
Plum, dwarf Natal *(Carissa grandiflora nana compacta)* Spreading shrub with beautiful bright green leaves that are round and leathery. Can be trained as indoor bonsai. H 1-2 ft.	Pretty, very fragrant, white, 1½-2 in. across, appear from spring to fall. For edible red fruits, hand-pollinate flowers with brush.	Maximum direct sun.	Average humidity. Let soil dry out between waterings; then water thoroughly. Wash foliage to remove dust. Feed about 4 times a year. Prune for compactness or to train as bonsai. Use general-purpose soil mix. Needs daytime temperature of 65° F. or higher. Minimum temperature: 55° F.	Take stem cuttings.
Poinsettia *(Euphorbia pulcherrima)* Compact shrub with bright green leaves that contain milky sap. Colorful floral bracts surround true flowers. Florist's plant, best purchased in bloom for Christmas decoration; lasts many months. H 1-4 ft.	Tiny yellow true flowers grow in clusters surrounded by distinctive and long-lasting white, pink, or red bracts.	Maximum direct sun to diffused.	Average humidity. Let soil dry out between waterings. Feed monthly. Use general-purpose soil mix. Discard plant in spring after bracts fade; or repot in spring in larger pot. Cut back to force new growth. Place outdoors in full sun during summer, and water regularly. In midfall bring indoors; give 12-14 hr. daily of steady darkness by covering with black cloth or putting plants in closet until buds form. Minimum temperature: 60° -65° F.	Take cuttings from new growth after plants have been cut back.
Pomegranate, dwarf *(Punica granatum nana)* Slow-growing shrub with bright green leaves, showy flowers, and edible fruits. Attractive in windows and light gardens or as indoor bonsai. H 18 in.	Bell-shaped, 1-in. across, borne mostly in spring and summer; pollinate with soft brush for 1½-in. red fruits.	Maximum direct sun.	Average to high humidity. Keep soil moist, not soggy. Feed monthly, from late spring to early fall. Reduce watering for winter rest period. Pinch back new growth as needed to encourage bushiness. Use general-purpose soil mix. Minimum temperature while resting: 50°F; later: 65° F.	Take stem cuttings in summer.
Primrose, German *(Primula obconica)* Upright, free-flowering plant with coarse, hairy leaves that may cause painful rash. Florist's plant sold in bloom to brighten winter windows. H 1 ft.	Clusters of 2-in. white, lavender, pink, salmon, or red flowers appear mostly from early winter to spring.	Diffused.	High humidity. Keep soil moist, not soggy. No feeding needed because plants should be discarded after flowering. Use general-purpose soil mix (double amount of peat moss). Flowers last longest at cool (65° F) daytime temperatures; minimum: 50° F.	Sow seeds (difficult without cool-greenhouse environment).

HOUSE PLANTS GROWN FOR FLOWERS OR FRUITS *(continued)*

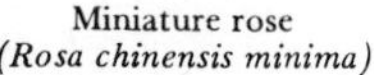

Miniature rose
(Rosa chinensis minima)

Silver vase
(Aechmea fasciata)

Spathiphyllum clevelandii

Veltheimia viridifolia

Zebra plant
(Aphelandra squarrosa)

Common and botanical names, general characteristics	**Flowers**	**Light**	**Special requirements and remarks**	**Propagation** *(See p. 400)*
Rose, miniature *(Rosa chinensis minima)* Small hardy replica of garden rose. Will flower on cool, sunny windowsill or under fluorescent lights in winter, outside in summer. Many named hybrids. H 8-18 in.	Exquisite, 1-1½ in. across, double; white, pink, yellow, red, or blends.	Maximum direct sun.	Average humidity. Keep soil moist, not soggy. Wash foliage for red spider mites. Feed monthly. Remove fading flowers. Prune in spring and fall to shape plants. Use general-purpose soil mix. Not tolerant of extreme heat. Minimum temperature: 50° F.	Take stem cuttings.
Shrimp plant, see p. 470				
Silver vase, or Urn plant *(Aechmea fasciata)* Rosette of leathery green leaves covered by gray scales and silver-white stripes forms cup that holds water. H 2-3 ft.	Tiny, blue; appear on long-lasting pink-bracted spikes from early to late fall.	Moderate or diffused.	Average humidity. Keep center "cup" filled with water; let soil dry out between waterings. Use general-purpose soil mix with added peat moss. Or use epiphytic mixes: osmunda fiber and bark, or equal parts sand, chopped sphagnum moss, and bark. Does best in crowded pot. Minimum temperature: 65° F.	Pot offsets produced after bloom.
Spathiphyllum, or White flag *(Spathiphyllum clevelandii)* Decorative plant with glossy, deeply ribbed leaves and long-lasting flowers. H 12-18 in.	Large white spathe (bract) ages to light green; true flowers form club-shaped cluster in center.	Diffused.	Average to high humidity. Keep soil moist, not soggy. Wash leaves to remove dust. Feed every 2 mo. Use general-purpose soil mix (double amount of peat moss). Minimum temperature: 60°-65° F.	Divide established plants.
Sweet olive, see Osmanthus				
Veltheimia *(Veltheimia viridifolia)* Bulbous plant with rosette of fresh green, wavy leaves. Long-lasting flower spike is dramatic in window gardens. H 1-2 ft. For *V. capensis,* see p. 471.	Dense, conical clusters of drooping, 1- to 1½-in. red and greenish-yellow flowers appear in winter.	Moderate or diffused.	Average humidity. Let soil dry out between waterings. After foliage yellows in late spring, withhold water until fall. Feed monthly while in active growth. Plant bulbs in fall, in general-purpose soil mix. Minimum temperature: 45° F.	Plant offsets from bulbs, with top just above soil surface.
Vriesia, see p. 475 **Wax plant,** see p. 471				
Zebra plant *(Aphelandra squarrosa)* Beautiful tropical plant prized for its glossy, dark green leaves with white veins and for its showy flowers. Makes a handsome accent among indoor plant groupings or for display on protected patio in summer. See also p. 471. H 1-2 ft.	Small, yellow; enclosed in long-lasting bright yellow pyramidal bracts 4-8 in. high, appearing in summer and fall.	Diffused.	High humidity; stand pot in tray of wet pebbles during winter. Keep soil moist, not soggy, from late winter to midfall. Feed every 2 wk. Cut plants back halfway in midfall, and induce rest period until midwinter by reducing water. Use general-purpose soil mix with some added peat moss. Minimum temperature: 60°-65° F.	Take stem cuttings from new growth in spring.

Cacti and Other Succulents

With their bizarre shapes, varied textures, and often vivid blossoms, cacti and other succulents are among the most intriguing of plants.

Plants that store water in their tissues during rainy seasons and draw on it in periods of drought are called succulents. There are two main types: those that store water in their leaves and those that store it in their stems.

Cacti, the largest single family of succulents, are the best-known examples of the stem type, and the various shapes into which their stems develop fascinate gardeners.

In the hot, dry climates of the Southwest, where cacti are native, they are often used for landscaping. A single specimen, such as the organ pipe cactus, makes a dramatic accent, or a grouping may include forms as varied as the globular shape of the barrel cactus, the spiny paddles of the opuntia, and the columnar design of the cereus.

In other parts of the country, any cacti that are grown outdoors in local nurseries will probably survive in that climate. However, they must have full sun and porous soil.

Many people who have neither garden nor greenhouse still collect cacti as a hobby. There are plenty of kinds that flourish on sunny win-

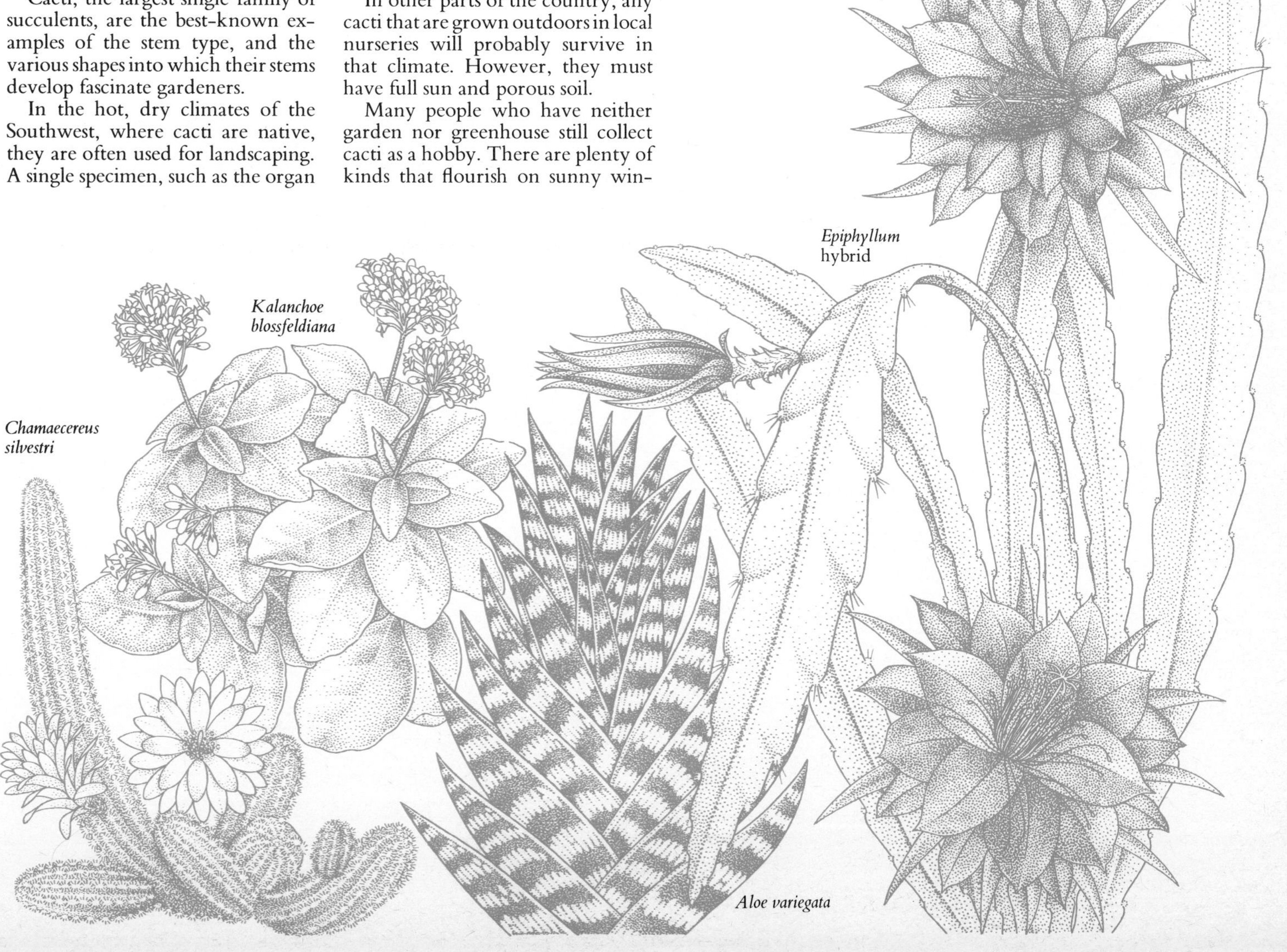

dowsills, where their bizarre contours give an original touch to an indoor display of pot plants.

Some of the most spectacular cacti need long, hot summers, but there are many others that will do well in moderately cool climates.

It is not always easy to differentiate cacti from other stem succulents—they are sometimes very similar in form. Cacti, however, have one reliable distinguishing feature: their areoles, the small, cushionlike structures on their stems from which the spines and flowers are produced.

Cacti are thought of as plants from parched areas, but they rarely grow in regions where the rainfall is less than 10 inches a year—although some survive where only 3–4 inches of rain has been recorded.

Cacti also need nutrients to survive, and although deserts are often considered to be barren, their soil can actually be rich in minerals that originate in weathered rocks.

There are desert cacti that grow in the ground (by far the most numerous) and tree-perching (epiphytic) sorts that grow on trees in the fashion of many orchids and bromeliads.

Desert cacti often receive their year's supply of water in the course of a very short rainy season, during which they grow and flower. Many then need a cool, dry winter rest period. The reason that some do not survive outdoors during northern winters is not only the cold air but also the cold and wet soil.

Cacti also occur in humid forests in Central and South America, where they take root in the debris that collects in the crotches of trees. Usually these forms, which include the popular Christmas cactus and the Easter cactus, have flattened leaflike stems.

The desert cacti vary greatly in form. They may grow as columns more than 40 feet high or as tiny spheres less than an inch in diameter. Whatever their size or shape, their stems are usually covered with either wax or hairs, both of which reduce water loss from evaporation.

The stems of some succulents are "mealy," meaning that they are covered with a white or bluish waxy substance. This is another means by which cacti reduce water loss.

Cactus stems are usually green or blue-green, since they contain chlorophyll and carry out photosynthesis, a process normally performed by leaves. Their root systems include surface roots to catch dew and deep roots to take up groundwater.

Most desert cacti have spines that act as a defense against animals trying to eat them.

Contrary to the popular belief that they flower only every seven years, most cacti bloom annually, given the right conditions. The very large cacti, however, will not flower in a greenhouse, where space does not allow them to achieve mature size.

The typical flowers are bell to trumpet shaped, and they vary in size from $^3/_8$ inch to 8 inches or more across. Most of them open in warm sunshine, but there are some whose flowers are seen only at night.

In general, cactus flowers are showier than those of other succulents. The blooms come in all colors except pure blue, though there are many shades of mauve and violet. Most nocturnal-flowering types are white, and they often have a sweet, lilylike scent. This attracts night-flying moths, which pollinate the flowers. Most cactus flowers last only for a day or two, and nocturnal-flowering plants have an even shorter period of glory: they wait until about midnight before opening and then wilt before morning.

Fruits develop freely if the flowers have been pollinated successfully. They are often brightly colored, as in the case of the mammillarias, many of which will produce fruits without the employment of hand-pollination methods. Most fruits come in various shades of red.

Fruits can take a long time to form. A whole year may elapse after pollination, so that one year's flowers and fruits formed from the previous year's flowers are sometimes seen on the same cactus.

Nearly all of the 2,000 or more species of cacti identified so far are native to dry regions, ranging from the western and southwestern United States to South America and over to the West Indies.

Some cacti, however, are native to moist climates. Among these are the opuntias found in New England and elsewhere, as well as the epiphytic sorts previously mentioned. Also, some succulents that are not true cacti grow in similar climates. These are the stonecrops, or sedums, which grow on rocks, walls, and steep banks or cliffs, where the soil may be very shallow and quick to dry out, even after heavy rains. Their species include *Sedum acre, S. album, S. anglicum, S. reflexum, S. roseum,* and *S. telephium.*

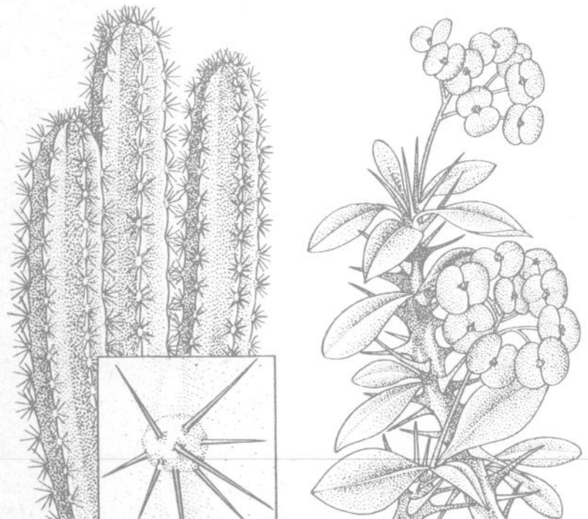

Recognizing a cactus. *Most cacti store water in their stems and have areoles (inset, left) that carry spines and flowers. Most other succulents (right) store water in their leaves.*

Some interesting succulents. *At the front of the strawberry-jar planter hangs the burro-tail sedum; then, clockwise, are* Sedum pulchellum, *sempervivums, and, on top and in front, a collection of echeverias, and at lower right, another sempervivum. In the metal bowl are more sempervivums and a taller* Sedum spectabile.

How to Grow Healthy Cacti

The Care of Cacti in the House

Because of their desert origins, most cacti thrive in bright sunlight.

To grow the widest possible range of cacti, a heated greenhouse with a minimum winter temperature of 40° F is necessary. But many cacti can be grown as house plants in a south- or west-facing window. In summer it is advantageous to put them outdoors in a sunny place.

A few cacti originated in tropical rain forests and require shady growing conditions. If you want plants that are to be kept indoors permanently, these forest cacti, such as epiphyllums, schlumbergeras, and rhipsalidopsis, are good choices. Put them beside an east- or north-facing window.

Central heating causes problems for many desert cacti, which need a cold, dry winter rest in order to flower well. In winter they should be kept in an unheated room, where the temperature remains between 40° and 50° F. Otherwise the high temperature and the consequent need for watering to prevent the plants from shriveling may cause them to grow during the wrong season, which is undesirable. Where temperature permits, they can be kept in a dry cold frame in winter, providing the temperature inside the frame never approaches freezing.

Do not shut the plants between the curtains and the window on winter nights, as this may trap them in a pocket of cold air, which could injure or kill them.

Misshapen growth. *Uneven light has distorted this flat-stemmed opuntia. Rotate plants receiving light from a window to ensure even growth.*

What Can Go Wrong With Cacti

Besides the troubles pinpointed in the table below, cacti are susceptible to several common greenhouse pests: ants, scale insects, thrips, and mealybugs. Spray these pests with a systemic insecticide as soon as they appear, and repeat if necessary.

Root mealybugs are less common pests, but they can be discouraged if the soil is watered thoroughly with a malathion solution.

Symptoms and signs	Cause	Control
Fluffy patches of whitish "cotton."	Mealybugs	Spray with Diazinon or malathion; or wipe over with cotton swab dipped in rubbing alcohol.
Yellowish or brownish mottling.	Red spider mites	Spray with dicofol, malathion, or tetradifon. Use systemic, such as dimethoate or oxydemeton-methyl, as soil drench.
Flat, oval, white or grayish scales on stems.	Scale insects	Same treatment as for mealybugs.
Base becomes soft and wet, followed by collapse of whole or part of plant.	Basal stem rot (fungus)	No control, but firm green tip can be severed and rooted. Do not overwater.
Distinct rings of growth, which become smaller toward top of plant.	Not enough water, plus starvation	Repot or feed during growing season. Water correctly.
Wrinkling and softening; little or no growth.	Not enough water; root rot	Water correctly.
Pale, thin, sappy growth.	Too shaded; too much heat at wrong season	Keep in sunny location and follow correct heating regime.

Growing Cacti Outdoors

The tougher, larger cacti can be summered outdoors in the sun. Take a few cuttings before putting them out in case they grow too big to bring inside.

Choose a south-facing garden bed for the most direct sunlight, and add sand if needed to ensure good drainage. Then put the plants into the bed.

The large opuntias make good background plants. *Opuntia microdasys* takes on an upright branched form and grows 2–3 feet high. The columnar cereus also makes a good background plant.

Smaller plants, such as the 3- to 6-inch-high echeverias and sempervivums, can be planted between the larger ones.

Outdoor cactus gardens blend well with yuccas and perennials that inhabit the same desert areas.

In cold climates cactus gardens should be regarded as summer gardens only, and the plants should be discarded or returned to the greenhouse in autumn. In mild areas, however, they may survive the winter. And in the Southwest, of course, they are hardy outdoors.

Succulents that develop a decorative covering of "meal" on their leaves need protection from the rain so that the meal will not wash off.

In warm climates the sturdier cacti and other succulents can be planted outdoors in a well-drained site facing south to provide an interesting display.

When Plants Need Repotting

Cacti need to be repotted when the mineral salts in their potting soil have been absorbed by the plants or washed away by watering or—in the case of vigorous young specimens—when the roots have filled the pot. Inspect the roots of new plants after you buy them.

Ideally, repotting is carried out in the spring, but it can be done at any time of year. It provides a good opportunity to check the plant's roots for pests, especially root mealybugs.

Disinfect new pots to keep them from spreading pests or diseases.

A moist, very porous potting mixture is essential. By volume use 1 part soil, 1 part perlite, $\frac{1}{4}$ part dehydrated cow manure, and $\frac{1}{8}$ part bone meal.

Tap the pot against a workbench to loosen the soil ball. If tapping fails, push a pencil through the central hole as shown below.

Remove the plant and dislodge the old soil as illustrated below, trying not to disturb the roots.

Take a new pot one size larger than the old one, and if it has a drainage hole, put a piece of broken clay pot over it to keep the soil from washing through. Hold the plant in the center of the pot and pour in the new soil mixture, making sure that it does not rise above the old soil mark on the stem. Spread the mixture around the plant with a spoon.

Tap the pot on a working surface to settle the mixture. Withhold water for a few days to prevent rotting of damaged roots.

Large plants seldom need repotting, but the top layer of soil mixture should be renewed occasionally with fresh soil.

1. *A pencil through the central hole in the pot will loosen the plant.*

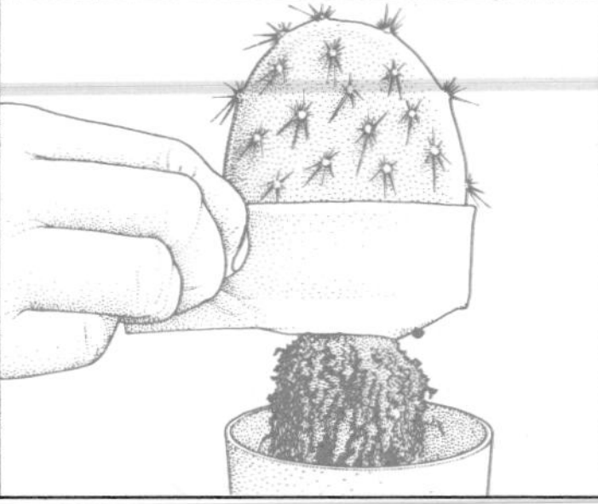

2. *Use a folded newspaper to protect your hands from the spines.*

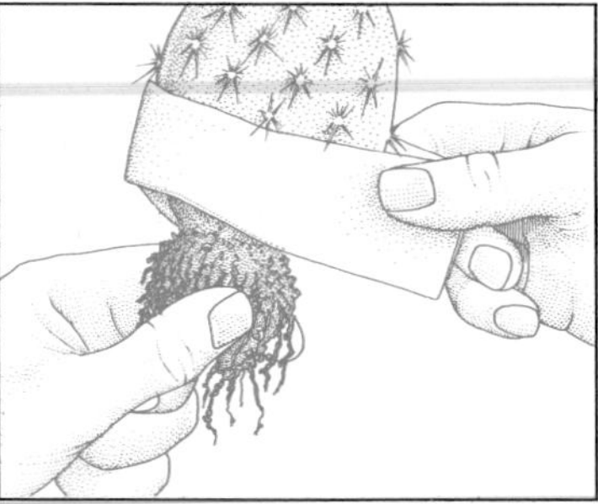

3. *Remove old soil from the base of the plant; shake off any loose soil.*

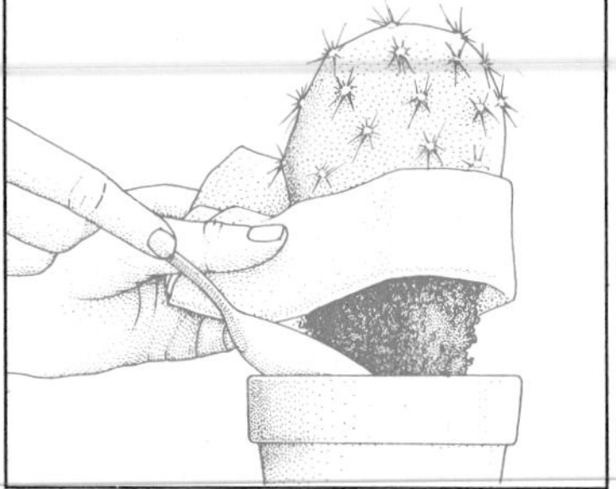

4. *Holding the plant in position, spread new potting soil around it with a spoon.*

When to Water and How to Feed

Cacti should be watered during the growing period whenever the soil is obviously dry. When dormant, they need no water at all or just enough to keep the soil from drying out completely. If they are kept in the house, however, water them oftener. The forest cacti, such as epiphyllums, are an exception; keep these damp in winter. Special watering requirements are described in the chart starting on page 434.

Every two weeks, from the time flower buds begin to develop until the flowers fade, feed the plants with a liquid organic fertilizer at half the strength used for house plants.

WATERING

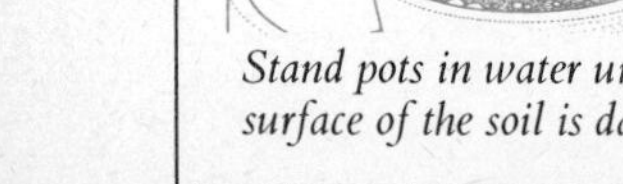

Stand pots in water until the surface of the soil is damp.

FEEDING

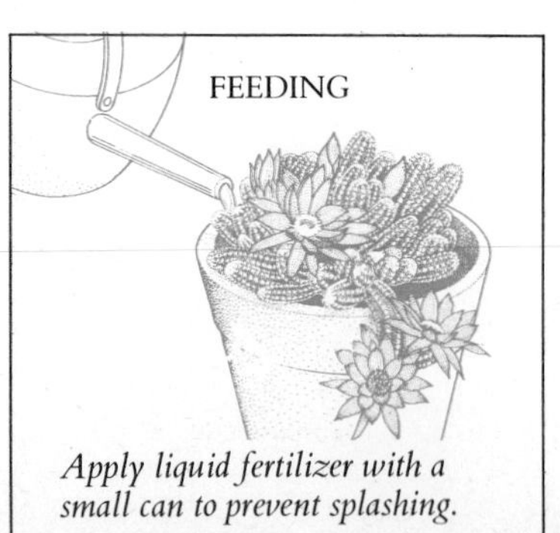

Apply liquid fertilizer with a small can to prevent splashing.

WATERING STONE PLANTS

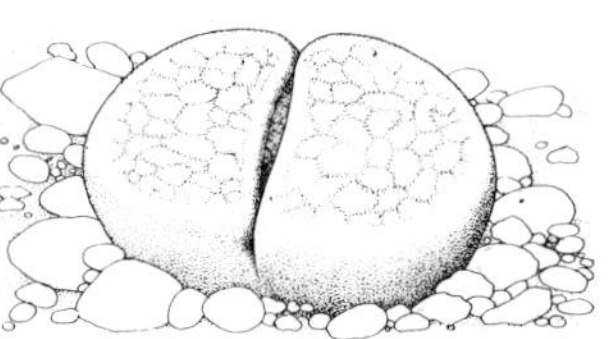

1. *Lithops and pleiospiloses (the stone plants) should not be watered after late autumn.*

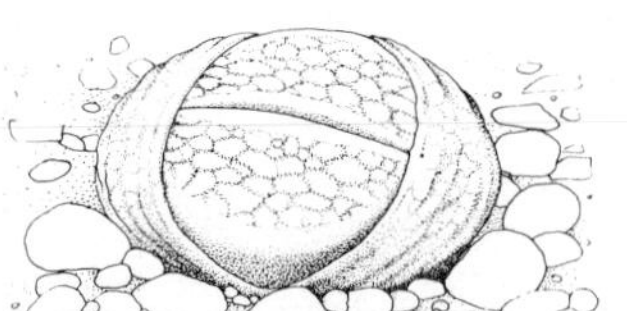

2. *In spring the new plant emerges, but water only after the old leaves have dried.*

The Need to Keep Cacti Clean

To keep plants with shiny stems and pads from becoming dusty in the house, wipe them occasionally with a damp sponge. This helps them to transpire and to absorb sunlight.

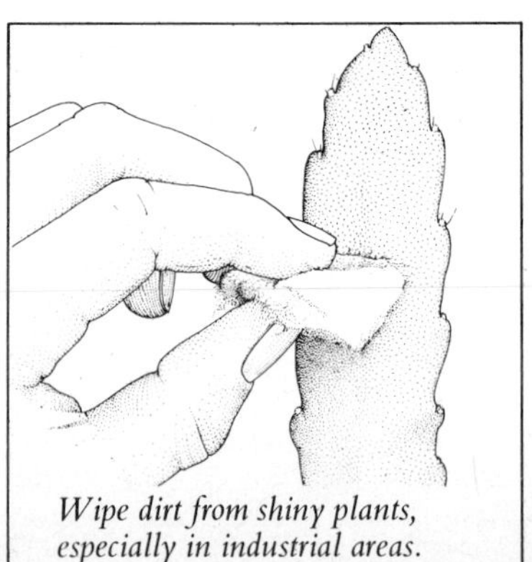

Wipe dirt from shiny plants, especially in industrial areas.

Growing New Plants From Cuttings

Taking cuttings from both stem and leaf is one method of propagating some cacti and other succulents.

A piece of stem is cut off with a sharp knife or razor blade and is rooted in damp sand or potting mixture. If the plant is of a type that has leaves, a leaf can often be removed and made to root.

Some plants produce offsets, or smaller versions of the parent plant, which need only to be cut away and repotted. Some of these offsets are already equipped with their own root systems.

No harm is done to the parent plant by taking cuttings judiciously, and it will continue to grow normally.

Advice on the best method of propagating each type of plant can be found in the chart beginning on page 434.

With the exception of the pereskia, which is not often grown by the home gardener, cuttings of cacti should be left until the cut surface has dried. The time needed ranges from one or two days for the small wounds of opuntias to a week or even longer for the wounds of the large-stemmed cereus.

The drying-off period is advisable to avoid rotting, which is the main danger to these cuttings. For the same reason, cactus cuttings should not be enclosed with propagating covers or plastic, as is often done with other plants in order to aid rooting.

Late spring or early summer, the period of maximum growth of cacti, is the best time to take cuttings, but they can be taken at other times of the year if necessary. For example, when plants drop their leaves or make leggy growth, their tops can be removed and treated as cuttings.

The time that it takes for cuttings to root varies from one kind of plant to another. When new growth begins to appear, you will know that the roots are well established.

How to Take Stem Cuttings of Cacti

To take a stem cutting, remove a section of stem—whether globular, columnar, straplike, or segmented—by cutting it straight across.

Use a sharp knife or a razor blade, except for tough-stemmed plants, such as epiphyllums, which will require cutting with shears.

Slender-stemmed columnar cacti yield enough material for several cuttings from one stem. Make sure you know which is the top and which is the bottom of each section. Growth will be distorted if the cuttings are put into the container with the wrong end up.

With opuntias each cutting should normally be one complete segment or more, cut off at the joint. With short-jointed cacti, such as the Christmas cactus, it is preferable that each cutting consist of two or three segments.

Put all cuttings in a warm, dry place for about three days to allow the wound to dry.

Once the wound has dried, fill a $2\frac{1}{2}$-inch pot to within $\frac{1}{2}$ inch of the top with potting mixture or sand as recommended at the top of the facing page. Insert the cuttings into the mixture just deep enough to keep them in an upright position.

Keep the potting mixture or sand just moist. Overwatering can cause rot, which is usually fatal.

Stem cuttings should root after one to three weeks. The time varies according to the genus.

They should then be moved to individual pots containing potting mixture only—not sand. The pots should be large enough to hold each plant's root system comfortably without crowding.

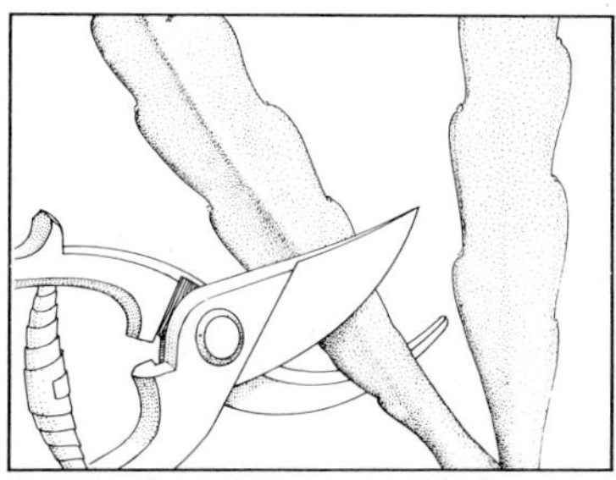

1. *Slice through the stem with shears, a sharp knife, or a razor blade.*

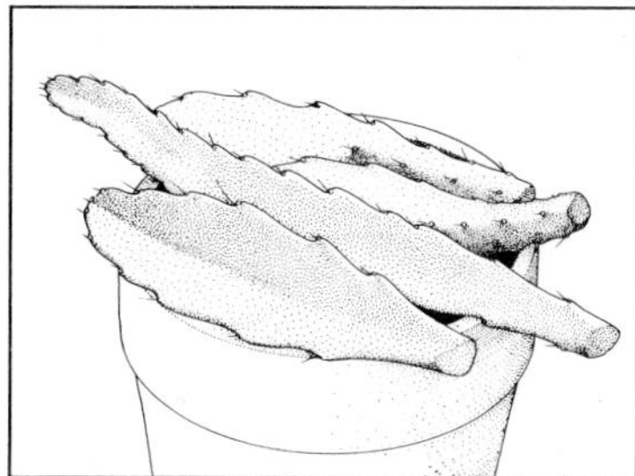

2. *Put cuttings in a warm, dry place until the wound has dried.*

3. *Insert cuttings into potting mix, just deep enough to keep them upright.*

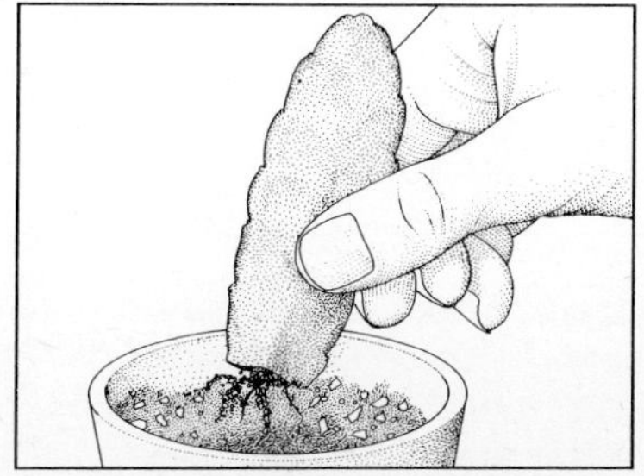

4. *When cuttings show signs of growth, remove them and pot them individually.*

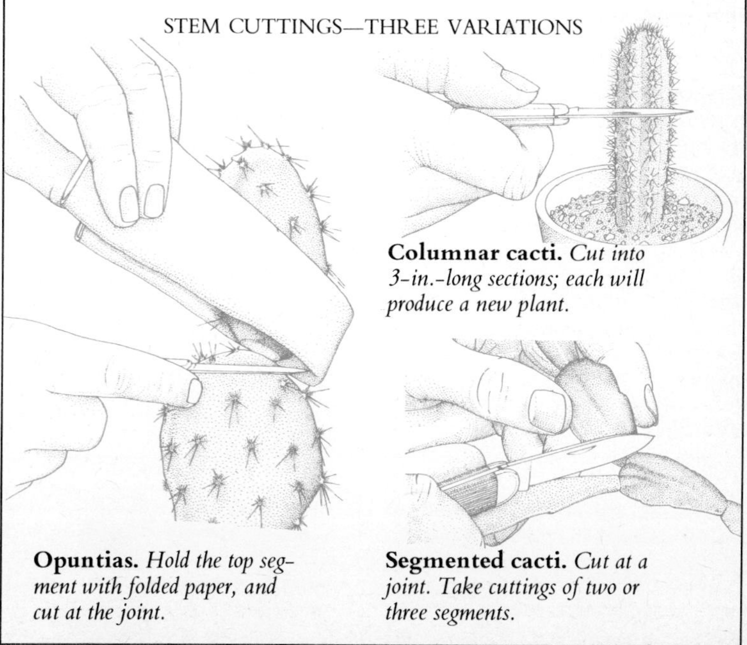

STEM CUTTINGS—THREE VARIATIONS

Opuntias. *Hold the top segment with folded paper, and cut at the joint.*

Columnar cacti. *Cut into 3-in.-long sections; each will produce a new plant.*

Segmented cacti. *Cut at a joint. Take cuttings of two or three segments.*

Taking Cuttings From Leafy Plants

Many succulent plants—such as echeverias, sedums, crassulae, and haworthias—can be reproduced from single leaves. Pull the leaves from the plant with your fingers or tweezers, and allow them to dry for several days. Then insert them into moist sand or potting mixture, just deep enough to ensure that they stay upright. If inserted too deeply, they are quite likely to rot.

Small cylindrical or globular leaf cuttings may simply be laid flat on a moist medium to root.

Cuttings of both types will usually root in six to eight weeks. Rooting is followed by the appearance of a small leaf cluster that develops into a rosette of leaves. When the rosette reaches the height of the parent leaf, move the entire cutting to a 2- to 2½-inch pot containing the soil mixture recommended on page 428. Do not remove the parent leaf until it has completely withered.

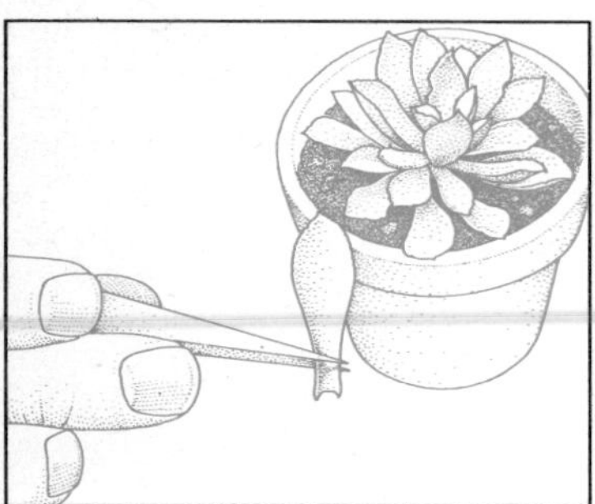

1. *Carefully remove a leaf from the plant with the fingers or tweezers.*

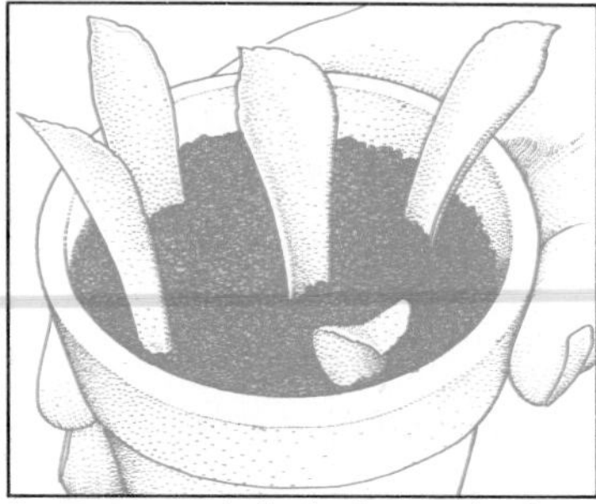

2. *Do not push the leaf in too deeply, but only enough to hold it upright.*

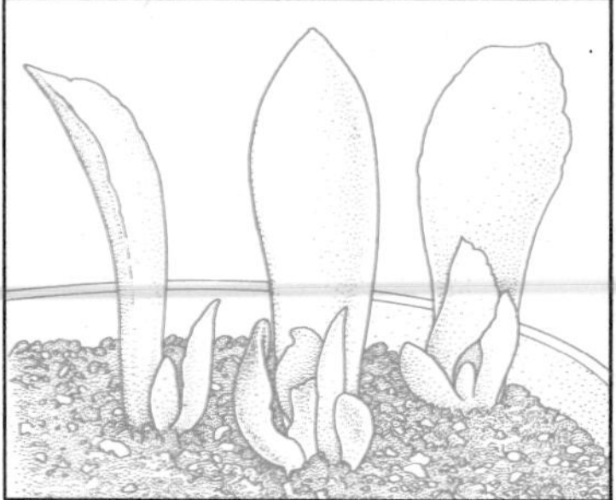

3. *The appearance of shoots beside the leaf shows that the cutting has taken.*

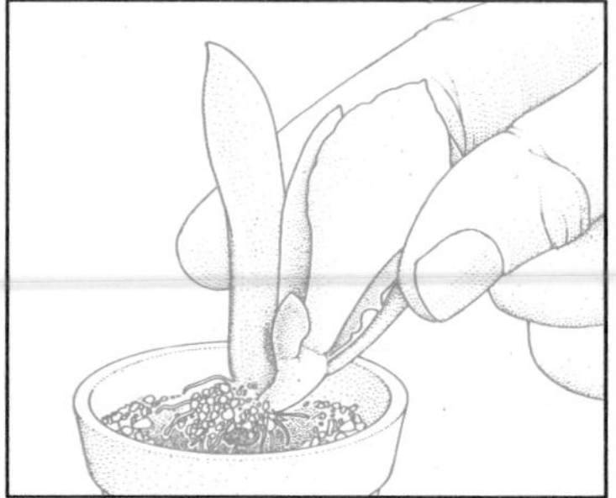

4. *When the rosette reaches leaf height, the cutting is ready for repotting.*

Propagating Cacti From Offsets and Offshoots

Some cacti and other succulents produce young plants that appear around the base and are miniature versions of the parent plant. These offsets usually come from below ground level or low on the stems.

Certain cacti, such as some of the echinopsis and echeveria varieties, produce offsets that have their own root systems. They can be detached and repotted as separate young plants. These offsets should not be detached from the parent until the roots have developed.

Other offsets have no roots. They can be cut away, dried off, pressed slightly into moist sand or potting mixture, and treated in the same way as cuttings.

Sometimes confused with offsets are offshoots—lateral branches sent out by the stumps of plants after cuttings have been taken from them. Offshoots can be treated as cuttings. While the stump continues to grow new offshoots, it can be kept; but once it stops, it should be discarded.

OFFSETS AND OFFSHOOTS

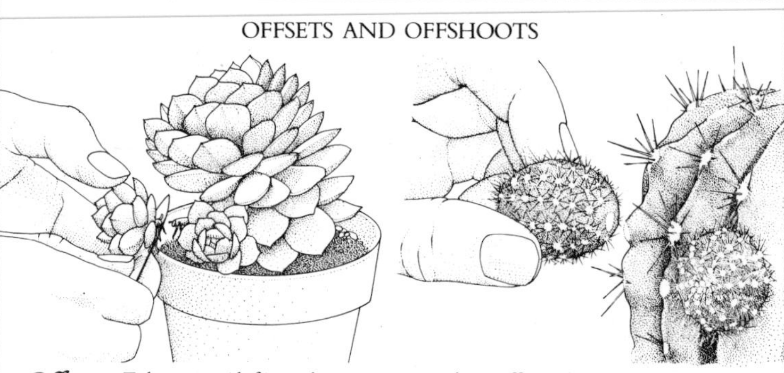

Offsets. *Echeverias (left) and some cacti produce offsets that have their own roots, and these can be potted. Echinopsis offsets (right) appear on the middle part of the stem, not around the base of the plant.*

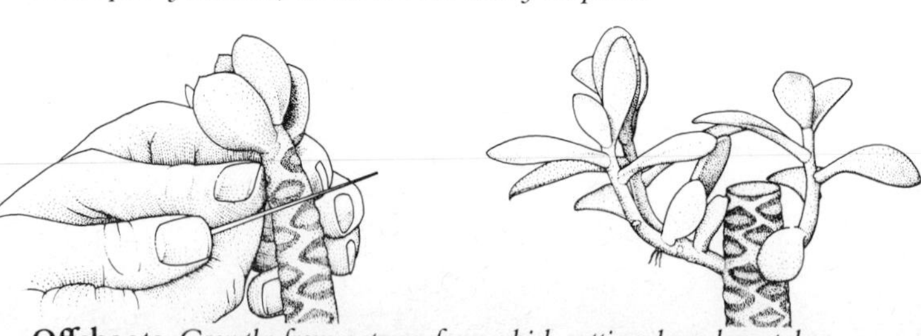

Offshoots. *Growths from a stump from which cuttings have been taken are known as offshoots. They also make good cuttings.*

Propagating Stone Plants by Division

The succulents called stone plants because they resemble clusters of stones can be divided. Loosen the soil around the base of one of the plants, and break it away from its neighbor, making sure that a small, undamaged piece of stem comes with it. The plantlet can be potted immediately. If torn, however, let the plant dry out for a few days; then insert it in sand or potting mixture.

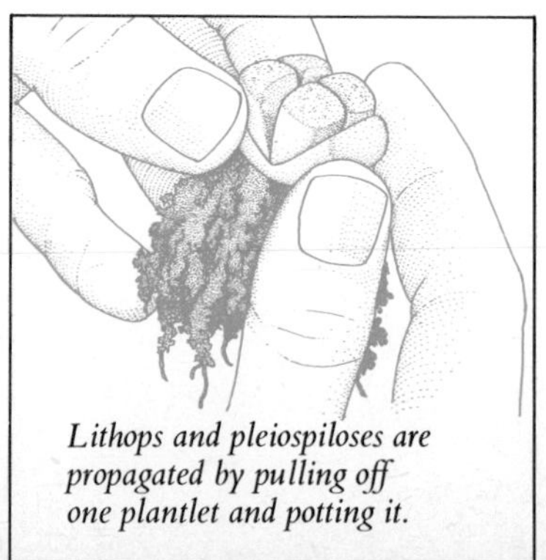

Lithops and pleiospiloses are propagated by pulling off one plantlet and potting it.

Growing Succulents From Seeds

Producing Your Own Seeds

Although nurserymen sell packets of seeds for succulents, it is cheaper and often more practical to produce your own, especially if you wish to grow several specimens of an unusual plant for your collection.

Most species of succulents produce bisexual flowers or male and female flowers on the same plant; very few produce flowers of one sex only on each plant.

Male flowers can always be identified by the tiny grains of yellow pollen they bear.

Those plants that are entirely female cannot produce seeds unless flowers of the opposite sex on another plant of the same species are open at the same time. So it is best to pollinate these types manually. Dab the male flowers with a fine brush to pick up the pollen, and then brush the pollen onto the stigmas of the female flowers.

With most species capsules or berries begin to appear about a week after fertilization. They grow and gradually change color as they ripen.

With the euphorbias a covering of nylon or fine-wire mesh should be placed over the plants at this stage, because the fruits burst open with explosive force, dispersing the seeds.

With most other plants you can remove the ripe fruits with tweezers and put them in a dry, warm place so that they can dry out.

Put the seeds on blotting paper to dry. In a heated room this may take only one day.

When dry, the seeds separate easily and are ready to be sown immediately; or they can be stored in labeled envelopes until you are ready to sow them.

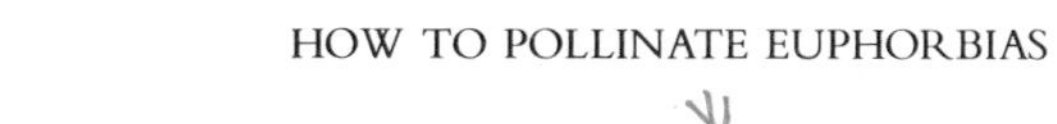

HOW TO POLLINATE EUPHORBIAS

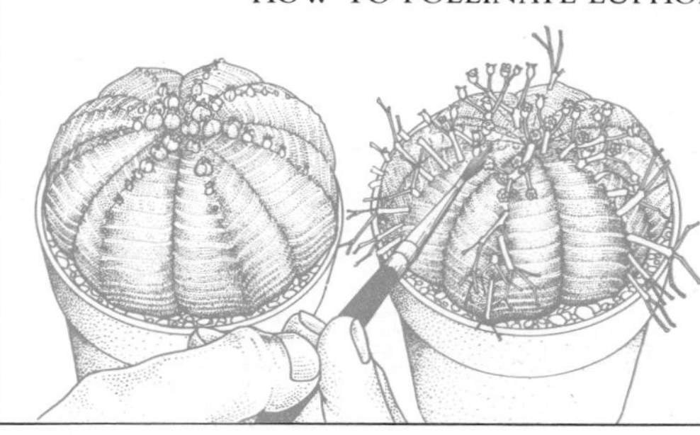

The best way to pollinate is to dab the male flowers with a fine brush to pick up their tiny yellow pollen grains and then dust these onto the female flowers.

HOW TO COLLECT SEEDS

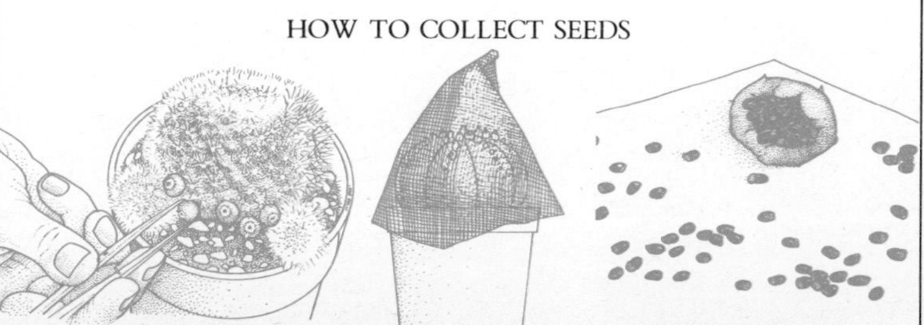

Collect most seedpods with tweezers; but euphorbias eject seeds and need a mesh cover.

Remove seeds and dry on blotting paper.

Sowing the Seeds and Potting the Plants

Thoroughly wash a 3- or 4-inch pot or seed pan, and put a layer of gravel in the bottom. Fill the pot with the soil mixture recommended on page 428. Sift some more of this material over the surface.

Sow the seeds. Do not cover them with the soil. Stand the base of the pot in water until the soil is moist.

Place the pot in a plastic bag or cover it with a piece of glass to keep the soil from drying out. Cacti need a temperature of 70°–80° F in order to germinate.

The seedlings of cacti and other spine-forming sorts will develop spines in a few days to a month. Remove the cover at that time.

When the seedlings are 1/8–1/4 inch in diameter, transplant them into a flat or pot filled with the regular potting mixture.

When the plants are 1½–2 inches across, pot them individually in 2- to 2½-inch pots.

1. *Sift the top layer of potting mix to provide a good rooting medium.*

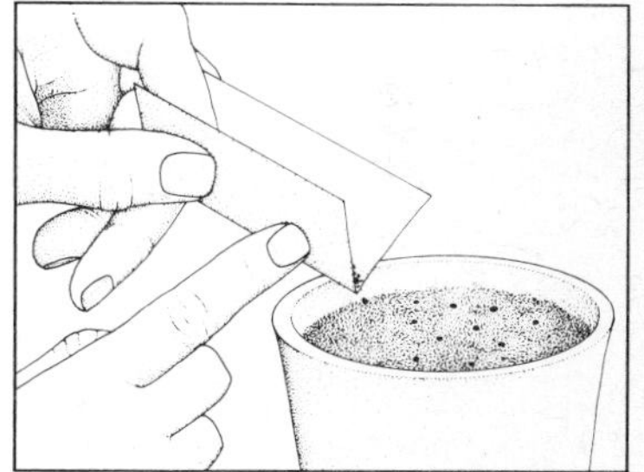

2. *Place the tiny seeds in folded paper, and tap it to spread them evenly.*

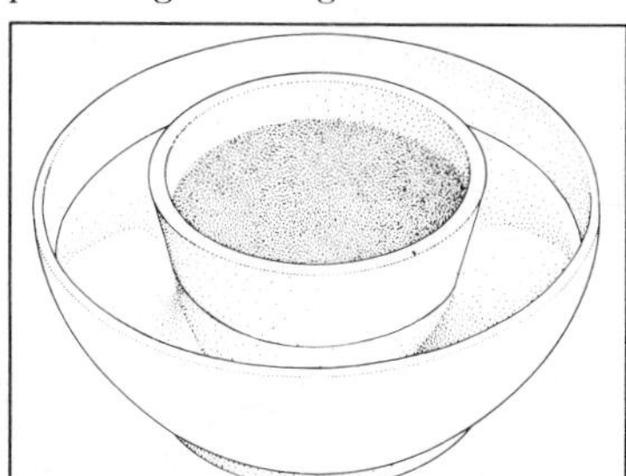

3. *Put the pot in water and leave it until the soil surface is damp.*

4. *When seedlings are 1/8–1/4 in. in diameter, they are ready for a seed tray.*

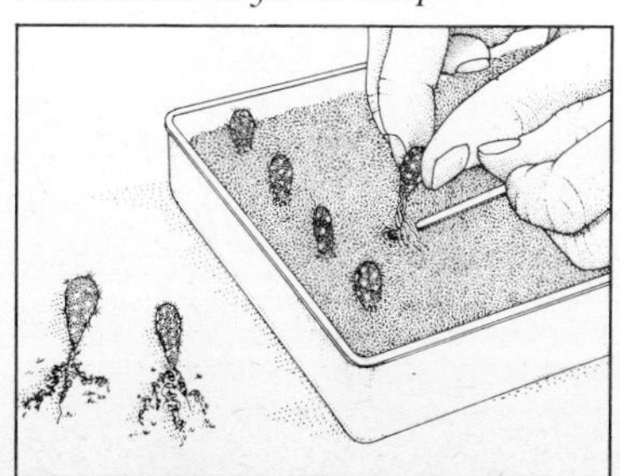

5. *When transplanting, take care to disturb the roots as little as possible.*

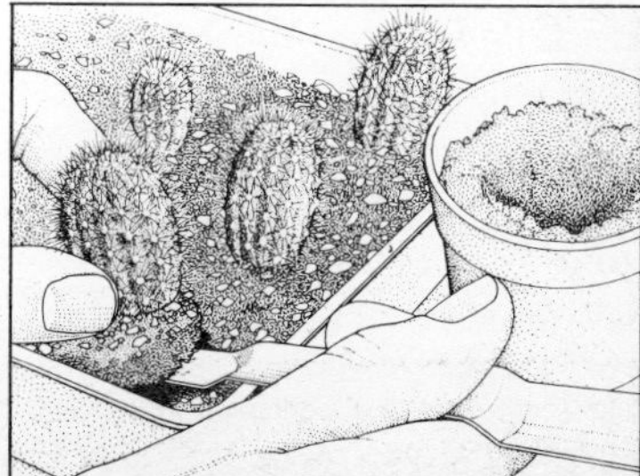

6. *When young plants are 1½–2 in. across, move them to 2- to 2½-in. pots.*

Propagating Cacti by Grafting

Although it is possible to graft other succulent plants in addition to cacti, it is difficult and not often undertaken. In any case, most succulents are propagated more easily by cuttings. All grafted succulents you are likely to see, therefore, are cacti.

Grafting consists of bringing together the upper part of one plant, called the scion, and the rooted part of another, called the stock, so that they form one plant.

The procedure is usually employed for plants that are difficult to grow on their own root systems, for plants that contain no chlorophyll and have been kept alive artificially, or for those that cannot be grown easily from seeds, offsets, or cuttings.

Usually there is no significant difference between grafted cacti and those grown naturally, especially if the rootstock is concealed. But sometimes the union of two species accelerates growth in a way that is not typical of the species.

Though many amateur growers hesitate to graft because it appears to be a drastic treatment, it is a fairly simple process. It is best done sometime between late spring and late summer, in a dry atmosphere with a temperature of 65°–70° F or higher. Any vigorous-growing cactus can be used as rootstock, but it must be about the size of the cactus that is to be grafted.

Usually the aim is to make the graft as unobtrusive as possible. This can be done by hiding the neck of the rootstock with pebbles. But grafting can also result in an unusual shape, as when a trailing cactus is combined with a columnar one to produce a weeping plant.

WHY CACTI ARE GRAFTED

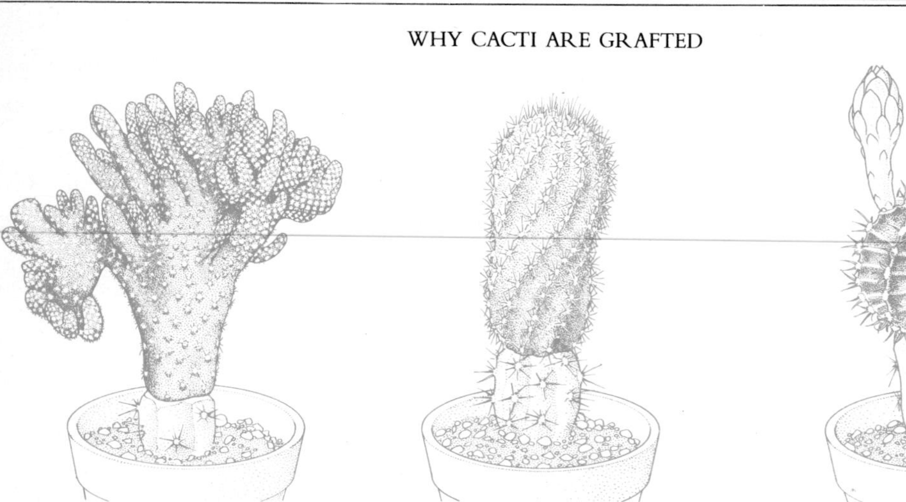

Weak roots. *Some cacti, such as* Opuntia clavaroides, *have weak roots and need a stronger rootstock.*

Propagation. *Cacti that do not grow easily from seeds, cuttings, or offsets are increased by grafting.*

No chlorophyll. *Colored types such as* Gymnocalycium *'Black Cap' need a green rootstock.*

Suitable Species for Rootstocks

Cacti that provide the rootstock for grafting should be easy to grow and propagate. The stock most frequently used for grafting is the trichocereus, a columnar cactus that can be grown easily from seeds. Most species of it are suitable, but those with small spines, such as *Trichocereus spachianus,* are easiest to use.

One-year-old trichocereus seedlings can be used for grafting onto small scions. Cuttings can be rooted and later developed as stocks for larger scions.

The softer-stemmed echinocereus species also make useful rootstocks, especially for sickly, rather dried-up scions. Suitable species are *Echinocereus dubius, E. enneacanthus,* and *E. pentalophus.* They branch freely and root easily; so they can be readily propagated by stem cuttings. Pads of *Opuntia robusta,* about 1–2 inches high, also make good rootstock.

Echinopsis species, such as *Echinopsis eyriesii* and its hybrids, are sometimes useful, as they form offsets prolifically and root easily. They can be used for grafting when they are about $\frac{3}{4}$–1 inch across. A section is cut from the top to correspond to the diameter of the scion, and the graft is made in the usual way.

How to Graft a Columnar Cactus

A vigorous, well-rooted rootstock, of about the same diameter as the plant to be grafted (the scion) is essential.

Cut off the top of the rootstock with a clean, sharp razor blade. The top section can be hardened off and rooted for future use (see p. 429).

Chamfer the edges of the rootstock with a razor blade, as shown on the facing page, to remove any spines and to prevent the surface from becoming concave.

Cut the plant to be grafted in a similar manner. Both surfaces to be joined must be level and smooth.

Press the scion onto the freshly cut stock with a rotary motion, which will remove the air bubbles. Try to match up the central bundle of tissues, which carries sap around the plant. This bundle is in the form of a ring, which varies in diameter from 1 inch in the larger plants to $\frac{1}{4}$–$\frac{1}{2}$ inch in the smaller ones.

Secure rubber bands around the top of the scion and the base of the pot to keep the scion in place. A piece of cotton can be placed on top of the scion to prevent the rubber bands from bruising it.

The grafted plant should be placed in a warm, shady part of the greenhouse or house and watered.

After one or two weeks the scion should be attached to the rootstock. The rubber bands can then be removed carefully. If the graft has not yet taken, the two parts will separate at a touch.

If you want more than one offspring from the original scion, sever it as soon as it begins to grow, leaving $\frac{1}{2}$ inch of scion on the rootstock. Graft the severed portion onto another rootstock.

Offsets will form around the $\frac{1}{2}$ inch of scion remaining on the first rootstock. When they are about $\frac{1}{2}$ inch in diameter, remove and root them or regraft them.

1. *Slice off the top of the rootstock with a clean, sharp knife or razor blade.*

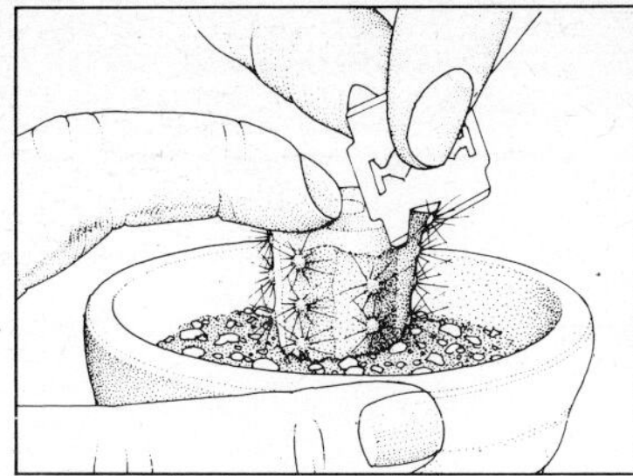

2. *Chamfer the edges with a razor blade, removing the spines.*

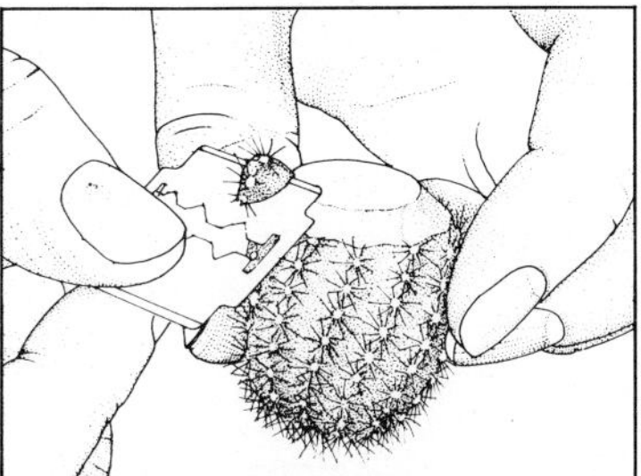

3. *Treat the scion in the same way, so that the edges match up.*

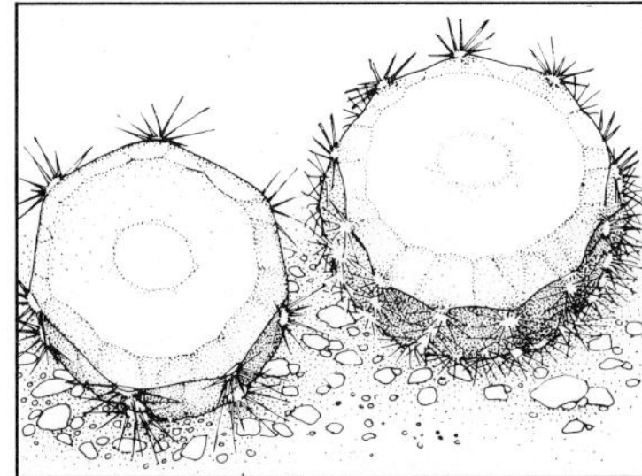

4. *Match up the central bundle of tissues, which carries food from the soil.*

5. *Keep the scion in place with rubber bands; absorbent cotton protects it.*

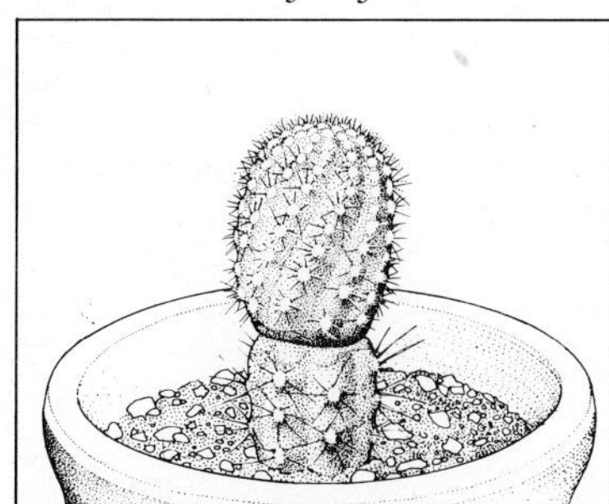

6. *About two weeks later carefully remove the rubber bands.*

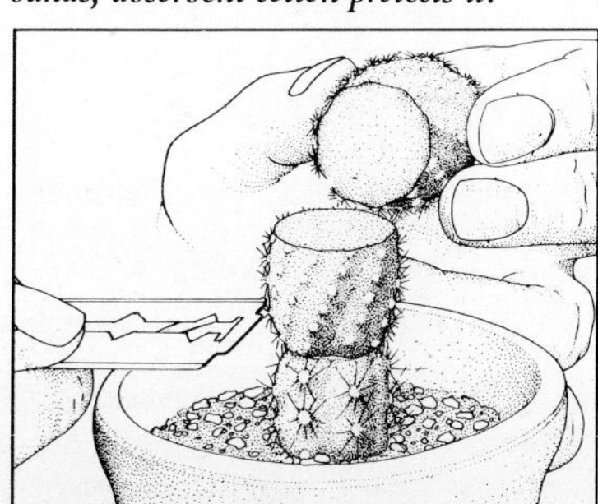

7. *To grow more plants, remove the top of the scion and graft it.*

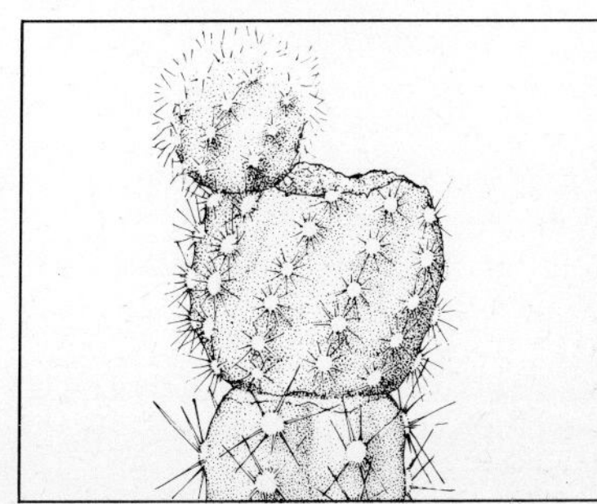

8. *Offsets that form on the portion of scion left can be used for cuttings.*

How to Wedge-Graft a Flat-Stemmed Cactus

Flat-stemmed plants, such as Christmas and Easter cacti, are grafted in a different way from columnar cacti because of their shape. The method is known as a wedge graft.

A useful rootstock is a stout pad of the kind formed by *Opuntia robusta*.

Cut a slit in the top of the pad, using a clean, sharp knife or razor blade. Shape the base of the scion's pad into a wedge, and insert it at once into the slot in the pad of the rootstock. It is important to work quickly in order to prevent drying.

To hold the graft in position, stick an opuntia spine through both the rootstock and the graft.

Keep the plant warm and watered in the normal way. Once the graft has taken (about four to six weeks later), the spine can be pulled out.

This type of grafting is used for multibranched, cascading plants that are difficult to manage.

Christmas cacti and Easter cacti can also be grafted onto pereskia stems to give the strong upright appearance of a "standard," or tree-form, specimen. Grow these at 50° F.

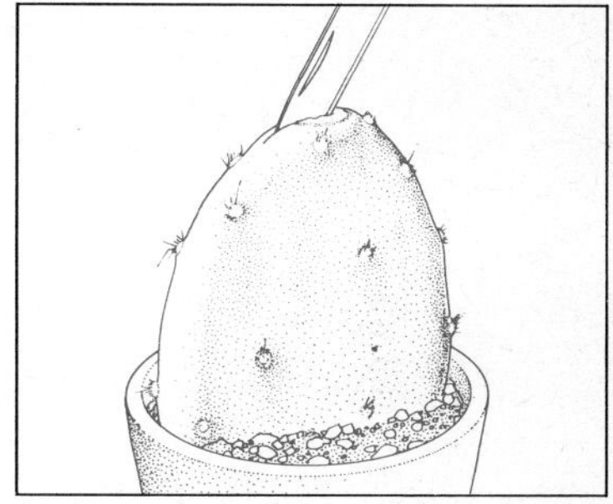

1. *Cut a slot in the top of the pad, using a sharp knife or razor blade.*

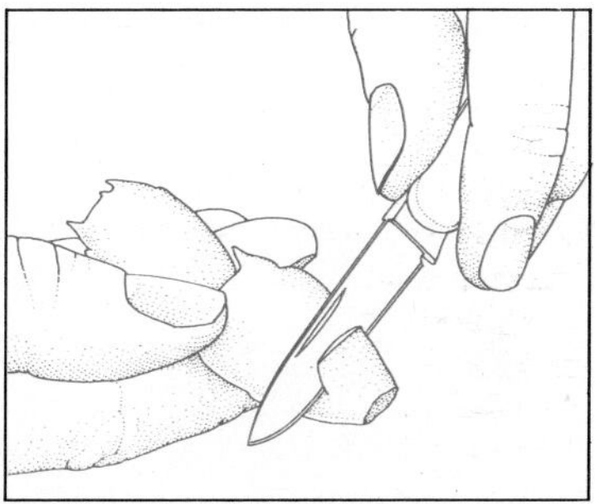

2. *Shape the scion into a wedge and insert it quickly into the slot.*

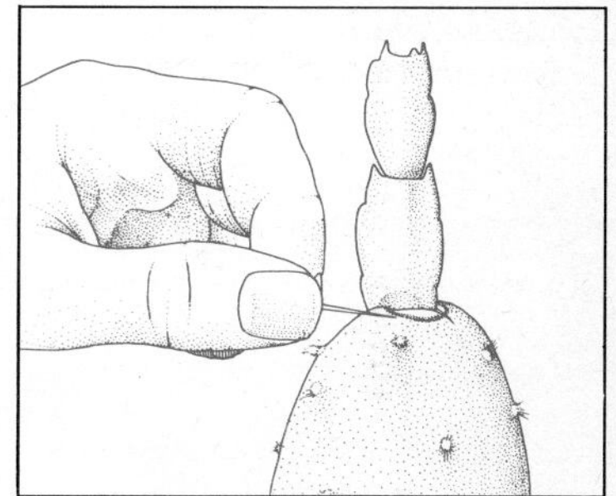

3. *Secure the graft with an opuntia spine; a metal pin will corrode.*

Grafting Seedlings Onto an Opuntia Pad

The cut top of an opuntia pad can also be used to speed the growth of cactus seedlings.

Cut the roots off each seedling in order to form a flat base. Place the seedling bases on the flat opuntia top, and secure each one with a rubber band, as you would for normal grafting, which is shown at left.

When the seedlings are growing well, regraft or pot them.

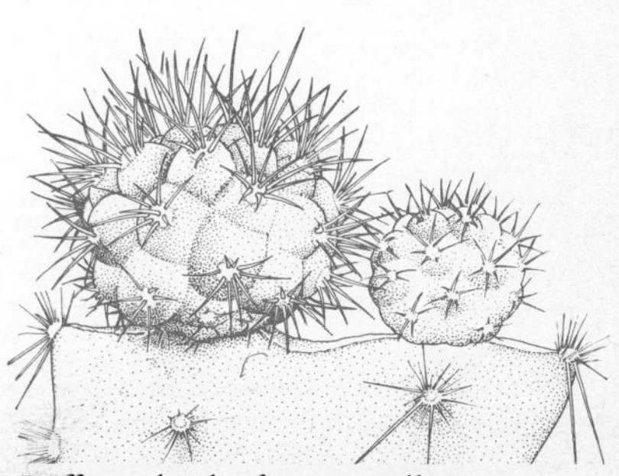

Different kinds of cactus seedlings grafted onto an opuntia pad can be left to grow into an unusual display.

Cacti and Other Succulents to Grow

Plants listed here are characterized (under Remarks) as succulent, desert, or forest cacti.

All the succulents and desert cacti can be grown as house plants if given plenty of sunlight in summer, preferably outdoors. In winter they need to be kept in a cool, dry place with as much light as possible. A temperature slightly above 40° F is ideal, but they can tolerate 10 degrees less, especially if kept dryer.

Forest cacti, which grow on trees as epiphytes (not parasites), can be grown indoors all year round and, except in winter, should be kept out of direct sunlight. Do not allow the soil to dry out.

Flower sizes are given in the chart only when they are exceptional.

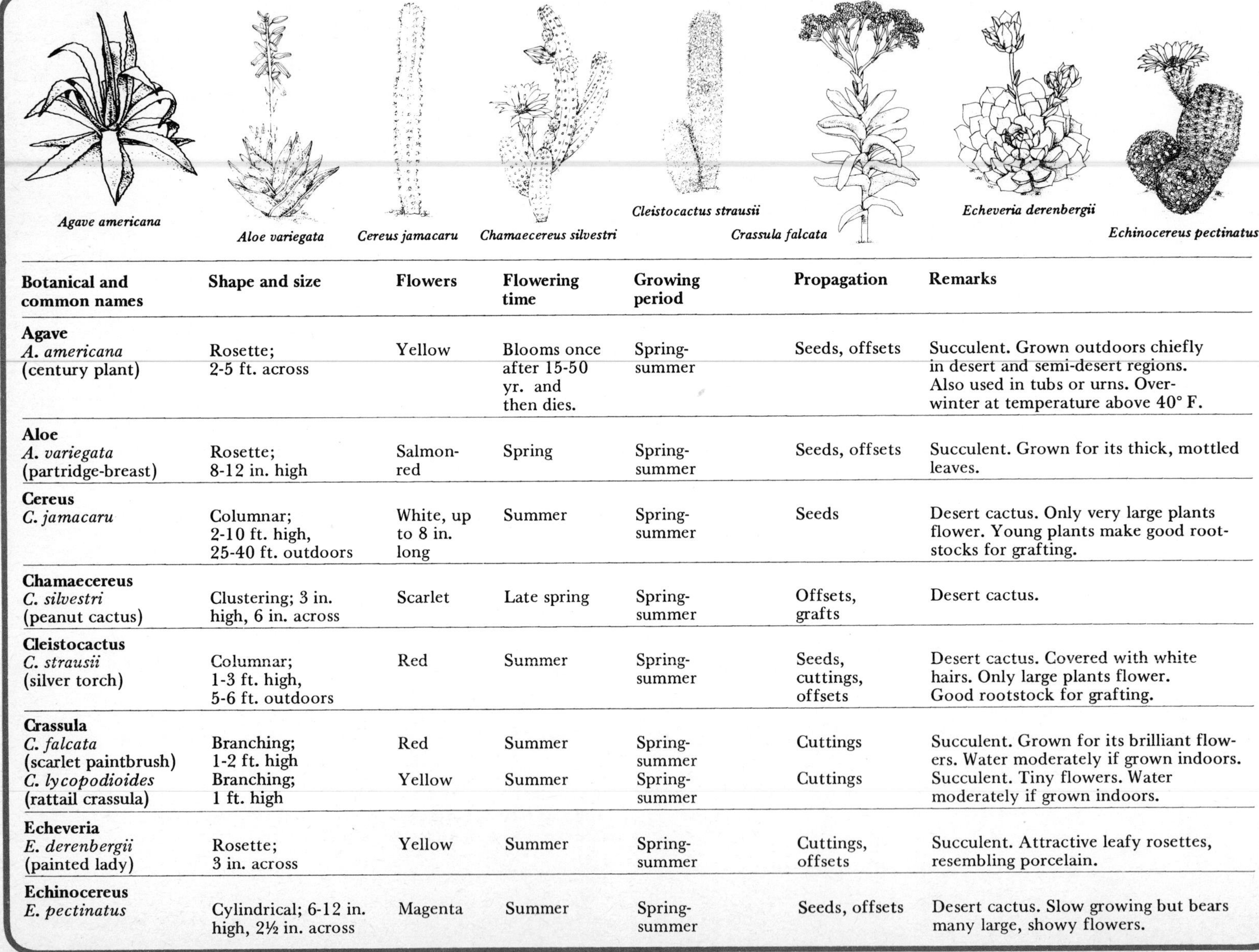

Botanical and common names	Shape and size	Flowers	Flowering time	Growing period	Propagation	Remarks
Agave *A. americana* (century plant)	Rosette; 2-5 ft. across	Yellow	Blooms once after 15-50 yr. and then dies.	Spring-summer	Seeds, offsets	Succulent. Grown outdoors chiefly in desert and semi-desert regions. Also used in tubs or urns. Overwinter at temperature above 40° F.
Aloe *A. variegata* (partridge-breast)	Rosette; 8-12 in. high	Salmon-red	Spring	Spring-summer	Seeds, offsets	Succulent. Grown for its thick, mottled leaves.
Cereus *C. jamacaru*	Columnar; 2-10 ft. high, 25-40 ft. outdoors	White, up to 8 in. long	Summer	Spring-summer	Seeds	Desert cactus. Only very large plants flower. Young plants make good rootstocks for grafting.
Chamaecereus *C. silvestri* (peanut cactus)	Clustering; 3 in. high, 6 in. across	Scarlet	Late spring	Spring-summer	Offsets, grafts	Desert cactus.
Cleistocactus *C. strausii* (silver torch)	Columnar; 1-3 ft. high, 5-6 ft. outdoors	Red	Summer	Spring-summer	Seeds, cuttings, offsets	Desert cactus. Covered with white hairs. Only large plants flower. Good rootstock for grafting.
Crassula *C. falcata* (scarlet paintbrush)	Branching; 1-2 ft. high	Red	Summer	Spring-summer	Cuttings	Succulent. Grown for its brilliant flowers. Water moderately if grown indoors.
C. lycopodioides (rattail crassula)	Branching; 1 ft. high	Yellow	Summer	Spring-summer	Cuttings	Succulent. Tiny flowers. Water moderately if grown indoors.
Echeveria *E. derenbergii* (painted lady)	Rosette; 3 in. across	Yellow	Summer	Spring-summer	Cuttings, offsets	Succulent. Attractive leafy rosettes, resembling porcelain.
Echinocereus *E. pectinatus*	Cylindrical; 6-12 in. high, 2½ in. across	Magenta	Summer	Spring-summer	Seeds, offsets	Desert cactus. Slow growing but bears many large, showy flowers.

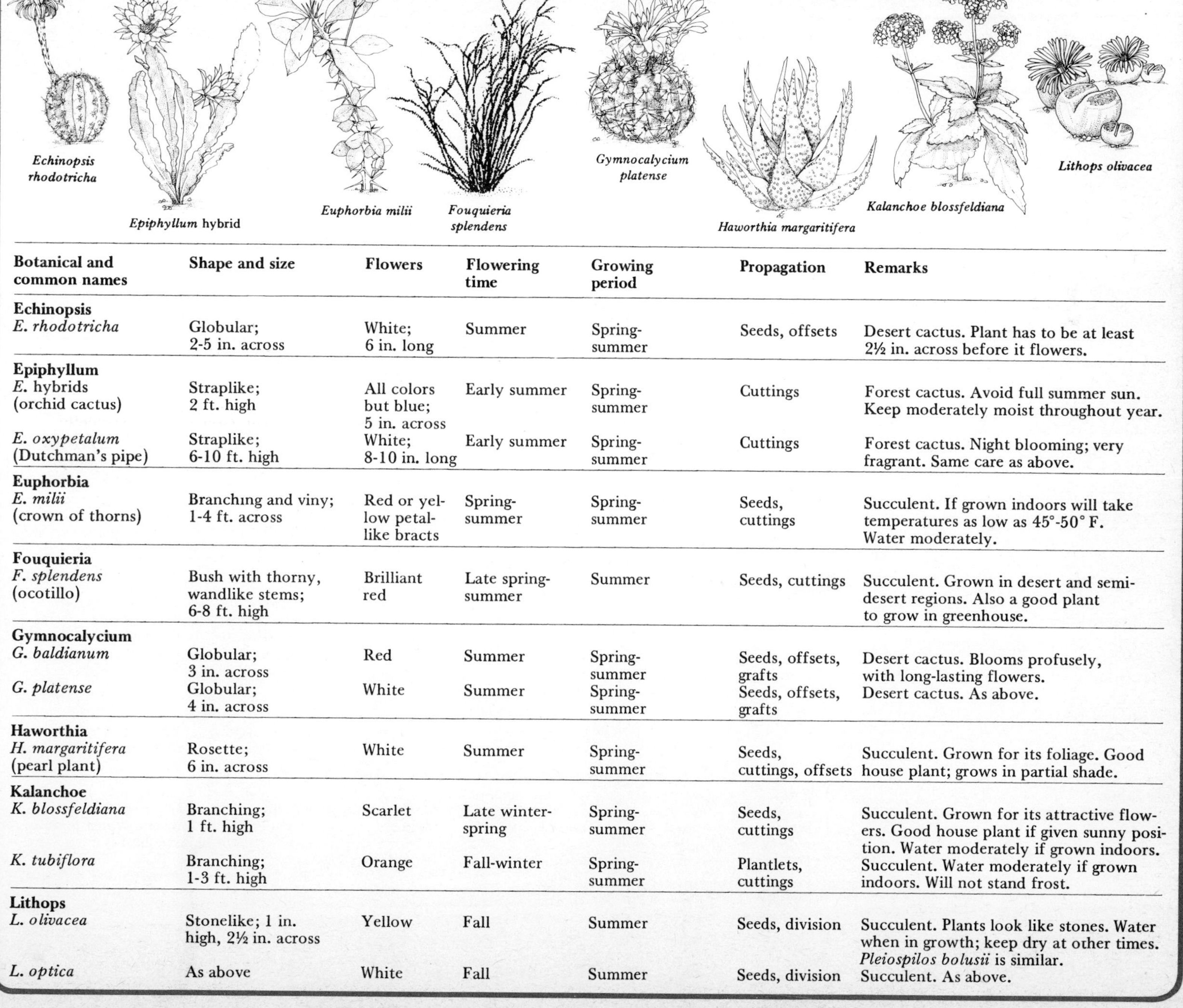

Botanical and common names	Shape and size	Flowers	Flowering time	Growing period	Propagation	Remarks
Echinopsis						
E. rhodotricha	Globular; 2-5 in. across	White; 6 in. long	Summer	Spring-summer	Seeds, offsets	Desert cactus. Plant has to be at least 2½ in. across before it flowers.
Epiphyllum						
E. hybrids (orchid cactus)	Straplike; 2 ft. high	All colors but blue; 5 in. across	Early summer	Spring-summer	Cuttings	Forest cactus. Avoid full summer sun. Keep moderately moist throughout year.
E. oxypetalum (Dutchman's pipe)	Straplike; 6-10 ft. high	White; 8-10 in. long	Early summer	Spring-summer	Cuttings	Forest cactus. Night blooming; very fragrant. Same care as above.
Euphorbia						
E. milii (crown of thorns)	Branching and viny; 1-4 ft. across	Red or yellow petal-like bracts	Spring-summer	Spring-summer	Seeds, cuttings	Succulent. If grown indoors will take temperatures as low as 45°-50° F. Water moderately.
Fouquieria						
F. splendens (ocotillo)	Bush with thorny, wandlike stems; 6-8 ft. high	Brilliant red	Late spring-summer	Summer	Seeds, cuttings	Succulent. Grown in desert and semi-desert regions. Also a good plant to grow in greenhouse.
Gymnocalycium						
G. baldianum	Globular; 3 in. across	Red	Summer	Spring-summer	Seeds, offsets, grafts	Desert cactus. Blooms profusely, with long-lasting flowers.
G. platense	Globular; 4 in. across	White	Summer	Spring-summer	Seeds, offsets, grafts	Desert cactus. As above.
Haworthia						
H. margaritifera (pearl plant)	Rosette; 6 in. across	White	Summer	Spring-summer	Seeds, cuttings, offsets	Succulent. Grown for its foliage. Good house plant; grows in partial shade.
Kalanchoe						
K. blossfeldiana	Branching; 1 ft. high	Scarlet	Late winter-spring	Spring-summer	Seeds, cuttings	Succulent. Grown for its attractive flowers. Good house plant if given sunny position. Water moderately if grown indoors.
K. tubiflora	Branching; 1-3 ft. high	Orange	Fall-winter	Spring-summer	Plantlets, cuttings	Succulent. Water moderately if grown indoors. Will not stand frost.
Lithops						
L. olivacea	Stonelike; 1 in. high, 2½ in. across	Yellow	Fall	Summer	Seeds, division	Succulent. Plants look like stones. Water when in growth; keep dry at other times. *Pleiospilos bolusii* is similar.
L. optica	As above	White	Fall	Summer	Seeds, division	Succulent. As above.

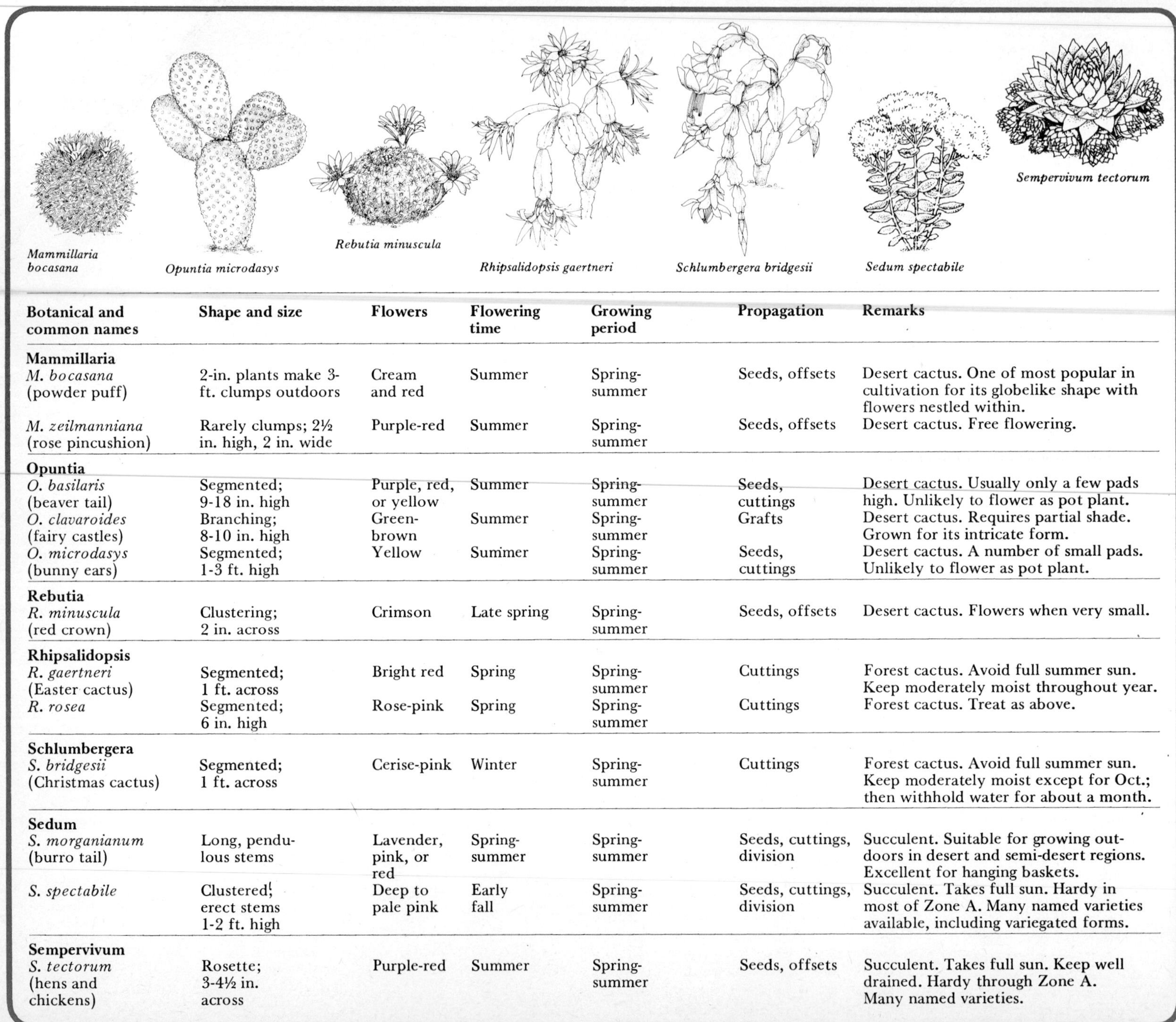

Mammillaria bocasana · *Opuntia microdasys* · *Rebutia minuscula* · *Rhipsalidopsis gaertneri* · *Schlumbergera bridgesii* · *Sedum spectabile* · *Sempervivum tectorum*

Botanical and common names	Shape and size	Flowers	Flowering time	Growing period	Propagation	Remarks
Mammillaria						
M. bocasana (powder puff)	2-in. plants make 3-ft. clumps outdoors	Cream and red	Summer	Spring-summer	Seeds, offsets	Desert cactus. One of most popular in cultivation for its globelike shape with flowers nestled within.
M. zeilmanniana (rose pincushion)	Rarely clumps; 2½ in. high, 2 in. wide	Purple-red	Summer	Spring-summer	Seeds, offsets	Desert cactus. Free flowering.
Opuntia						
O. basilaris (beaver tail)	Segmented; 9-18 in. high	Purple, red, or yellow	Summer	Spring-summer	Seeds, cuttings	Desert cactus. Usually only a few pads high. Unlikely to flower as pot plant.
O. clavaroides (fairy castles)	Branching; 8-10 in. high	Green-brown	Summer	Spring-summer	Grafts	Desert cactus. Requires partial shade. Grown for its intricate form.
O. microdasys (bunny ears)	Segmented; 1-3 ft. high	Yellow	Summer	Spring-summer	Seeds, cuttings	Desert cactus. A number of small pads. Unlikely to flower as pot plant.
Rebutia						
R. minuscula (red crown)	Clustering; 2 in. across	Crimson	Late spring	Spring-summer	Seeds, offsets	Desert cactus. Flowers when very small.
Rhipsalidopsis						
R. gaertneri (Easter cactus)	Segmented; 1 ft. across	Bright red	Spring	Spring-summer	Cuttings	Forest cactus. Avoid full summer sun. Keep moderately moist throughout year.
R. rosea	Segmented; 6 in. high	Rose-pink	Spring	Spring-summer	Cuttings	Forest cactus. Treat as above.
Schlumbergera						
S. bridgesii (Christmas cactus)	Segmented; 1 ft. across	Cerise-pink	Winter	Spring-summer	Cuttings	Forest cactus. Avoid full summer sun. Keep moderately moist except for Oct.; then withhold water for about a month.
Sedum						
S. morganianum (burro tail)	Long, pendulous stems	Lavender, pink, or red	Spring-summer	Spring-summer	Seeds, cuttings, division	Succulent. Suitable for growing outdoors in desert and semi-desert regions. Excellent for hanging baskets.
S. spectabile	Clustered; erect stems 1-2 ft. high	Deep to pale pink	Early fall	Spring-summer	Seeds, cuttings, division	Succulent. Takes full sun. Hardy in most of Zone A. Many named varieties available, including variegated forms.
Sempervivum						
S. tectorum (hens and chickens)	Rosette; 3-4½ in. across	Purple-red	Summer	Spring-summer	Seeds, offsets	Succulent. Takes full sun. Keep well drained. Hardy through Zone A. Many named varieties.

Greenhouse Gardening

Even a small greenhouse affords many new possibilities —from early vegetables to orchids. Available equipment can give complete, automatic control of the environment.

A greenhouse frees a gardener from the tyranny of nature. Here he can raise plants that would suffer from cold, heavy rain, wind, and disease if they were grown in the open. For cold-climate gardeners there is the special enjoyment of having plants in flower in the dead of winter when the outside landscape is buried beneath a blanket of snow.

In a natural setting, moreover, a plant's growth culminates in pollination and seed production; once an insect has pollinated a flower, the bloom begins to fade. In the protected environment of a greenhouse, with its screened ventilators, flowers remain in bloom longer than they would outdoors.

Greenhouses may be either heated or unheated. An unheated greenhouse will not keep out frost, but during the growing season it creates consistently warmer conditions for plants than exist outside. This extra heat speeds the development of plants and helps force shrub branches into flower and fruit ahead of their normal season.

An unheated greenhouse also gives the outdoor gardener a jump on the weather; he can get vegetable and annual seeds germinated, and the seedlings will be ready to set out as soon as the garden soil warms up in the spring. Besides starting plants early, he can bring some into the greenhouse in the fall, thereby extending their season.

This extended growing season begins in spring as the greenhouse glass traps the heat of the sun on clear days. Then in fall the glass retains the warmth that has built up in the soil and brickwork during the summer.

For the ardent gardener who lives in Zone C, where winters have freezing temperatures but more usually range from 35°–45° F, an unheated greenhouse is invaluable. He will find that a wide range of half-hardy shrubs, annuals, and many bulbs, such as lilies and gladioli, can be grown there.

When artificial heat is introduced into a greenhouse, the range of plants that can be grown increases greatly. Tender plants that otherwise would never survive freezing weather can be kept under perfect conditions.

With the installation of automatic equipment for heating, ventilation, shading, and watering, environmental control is almost total.

Before you decide to install a heated greenhouse, however, consider how much you are prepared to spend on fuel—a major expense in greenhouse operation. A guide to the amount of fuel needed to heat greenhouses of various sizes can be found on page 441.

Heated greenhouses are classified according to minimum nighttime temperatures. A "cool" house is kept above 45° F at night, and a "warm" house, above 60° F (daytime temperatures are kept 10–15 degrees higher). Warm houses are now relatively expensive to run because of fuel costs and are therefore not as common as they once were.

A cool house will support a wide range of ornamental plants, including those listed on the chart of greenhouse plants between pages 462 and 471. Also, many vegetables that can be grown in very early spring or late fall in a cold frame will grow in winter in a cool house.

A cool greenhouse is particularly useful for growing flowering plants, from seeds or cuttings early in the year, to be planted in garden beds outdoors at the beginning of summer. Zonal geraniums and calceolarias are two of the most popular of the so-called bedding plants.

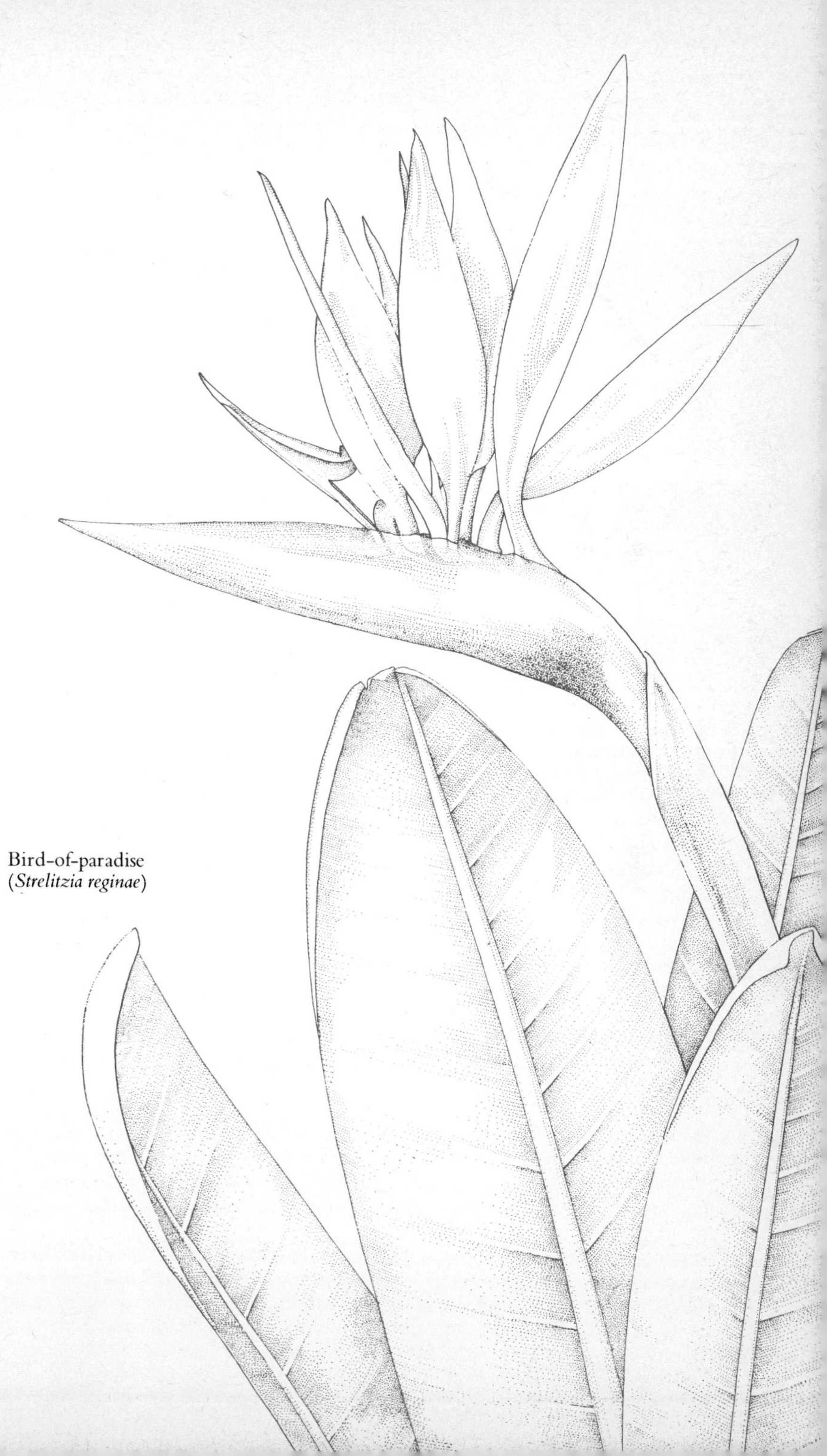

Bird-of-paradise
(*Strelitzia reginae*)

Growing Plants in a Greenhouse—Cool or Warm

The greenhouse shown here can be used as either a cool greenhouse or a warm one, depending on the temperature maintained. The main structure is 20 feet by 10 feet; the building on the left is a potting shed and storage room, and in front of it is a lathhouse, where many types of plants can be kept during summer.

The cool greenhouse. Although the cool greenhouse is designed to sustain plants that need a minimum nighttime temperature of 45° F, it can also maintain a number of species that require more warmth, by reason of various internal microclimates. Along the wall abutting the potting shed, for example, temperatures are higher than along the outside walls.

The large ventilators in the roof allow the air that has been heated by the sun to leave the greenhouse, making room for the steady inflow of fresh, cool air. In summer the vents are left fully open day and night. In spring and fall they are opened in the morning if the day promises to be warm or sunny, and closed in the evening.

If you spend much time away from your greenhouse, you may want to install a special temperature-sensitive device (see p. 443), which opens the ventilators partially when the temperature inside rises above the preset temperature. If the temperature rises higher, the vent is opened fully.

On hot summer days, however, ventilation is not sufficient. To keep the temperature from rising so high that plants are damaged, the glass can be shaded by a rain-resistant shading paint, applied at the start of warm weather and easily brushed off when the weather cools.

Shading is also done with blinds fitted to the outside of the greenhouse, which are drawn down manually when the sun shines.

In the growing area of the greenhouse a selection of flowering plants stands on trays of wet sand, which keeps them constantly moist.

The warm greenhouse. A greenhouse that is furnished with sufficient heating equipment to maintain a minimum winter nighttime temperature of 60° F is called a warm greenhouse; it can accommodate a far greater variety of plants than can a cool house. However, thousands of kinds of plants will grow in greenhouses of either kind. The kinds of plants you are most interested in growing will determine whether you keep the temperature warm or cool. If there is sufficient heating and cooling capacity, the environment can be changed whenever you wish. And, of course, a greenhouse can be partitioned to accommodate plants from both temperate and tropical regions.

Heat can be supplied by oil, gas, or electricity. The cost of utilities in your area, the severity of the weather, and the temperature at which you wish to maintain your greenhouse should determine the heat source you use. In any case, a thermostat can be used to switch the heat on in the greenhouse at the appropriate temperature.

In the new-plant nursery (shown in the greenhouse bench at the top of the illustration) there is a mist propagator that helps in rooting the cuttings that are set in sand. An alternative is a heated, covered propagation bench (shown here flanking the door to the potting shed). This is cheaper but not so effective with cuttings that are difficult to root.

In the left-hand section of the growing area are newly potted rooted cuttings. Later, they will be put into a cold frame to be hardened off (gradually accustomed to outdoor growing conditions) before being transplanted into the garden.

Outside the greenhouse are three cold frames. These are particularly useful in keeping plants dormant until they are taken into the greenhouse for forcing, for preparing cuttings for subsequent propagation, and for hardening off plants.

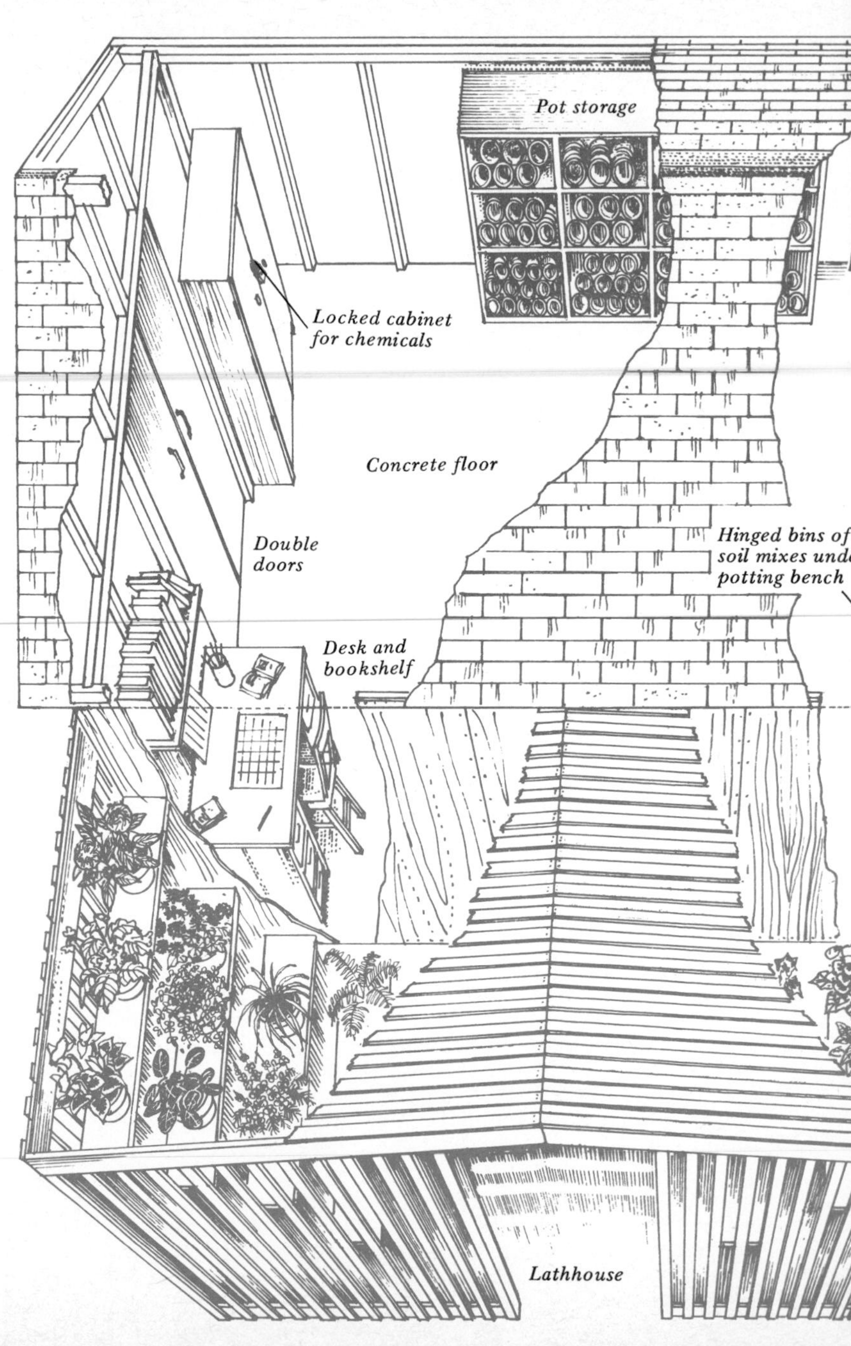

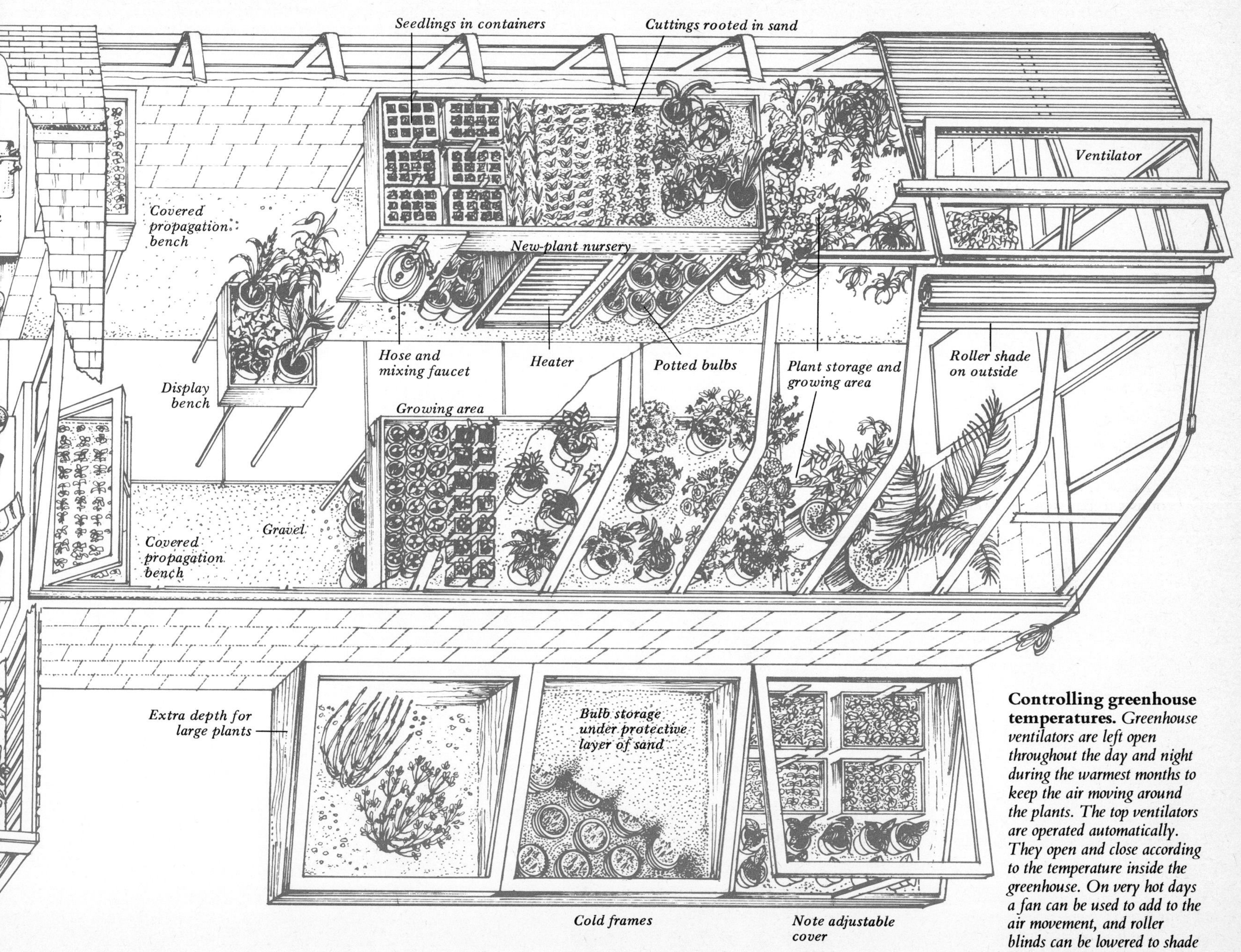

Controlling greenhouse temperatures. *Greenhouse ventilators are left open throughout the day and night during the warmest months to keep the air moving around the plants. The top ventilators are operated automatically. They open and close according to the temperature inside the greenhouse. On very hot days a fan can be used to add to the air movement, and roller blinds can be lowered to shade the greenhouse interior.*

How to Choose a Greenhouse

The first decision when buying a greenhouse is to settle upon a price range with which you can be comfortable. Make this decision only after checking with at least two or three manufacturers of different kinds of greenhouses.

The initial choice is between a plastic house and a glass one. Sunlight readily passes through either glass or plastic panes into the greenhouse, where it heats the surfaces it strikes. Both the light and the heat encourage plant growth. In a glass house the glass acts as a barrier to retain the heat inside the enclosure. Although the plastic panes admit the sun's rays, they do not hold the heat well; so when the sun sets, the greenhouse quickly cools down again.

Plastic houses are usually less expensive—glass costs about 50 percent more than plastic. (Curved-eave glass houses, such as the one illustrated on p. 439, are even more expensive.) On the other hand, glass greenhouses are more durable and weather resistant.

Horticultural grades of fiberglass are available for greenhouses, and these last longer than ordinary plastic sheeting. A recently introduced acrylic plastic is quite similar to glass but is still rather expensive.

It should be noted that plastic is more easily scratched than glass and that the scratches become ingrained with dirt. Condensation can also be a problem: whereas on glass the moisture forms a film, on plastic it collects in droplets, obscuring the light and dripping. This difficulty can be overcome with the efficient use of a fan for ventilation.

Once you have decided on the material for your greenhouse, you can go on to step two: deciding upon design and shape.

Greenhouse Design and Shape

There are two basic shapes for a greenhouse: the lean-to and the even-span roof. The latter shape can be designed with the glass or plastic sides resting on solid walls, or it can have the glass or plastic sides extending down to ground level.

In addition to these conventional shapes, there are various other designs—round, hexagonal, or domed. These can be appropriate for individual situations.

Give thought to the choice of material for the base below the glass. If the architectural setting of your home is traditional, for example, a greenhouse of contemporary design could appear inappropriate. With the variety of greenhouse designs currently available, you can be certain that there is at least one greenhouse that will fit in with your home and surroundings.

Here are some items to bear in mind in selecting a greenhouse:

- The maximum amount of sunlight goes into the greenhouse, and the least is reflected, when the rays strike the glass at a right angle. (Greenhouse sides that are too severely sloped to achieve this end, however, can interfere with the benches and the tall plants inside.)
- A greenhouse with glass sides extending down to ground level is the most versatile type, although the most costly to heat. When benches are installed, it is possible to grow plants below them as well as on top of them. Without benches such a greenhouse is ideal for tall-growing plants that need a great deal of light, such as tomatoes, chrysanthemums, and carnations.
- A lean-to can be more economical to heat than a freestanding greenhouse. If it is set against a brick wall facing south, the wall will act as a heat store, radiating warmth overnight after accumulating it during the day. A common fault of lean-to structures is that the roof does not have enough slope.

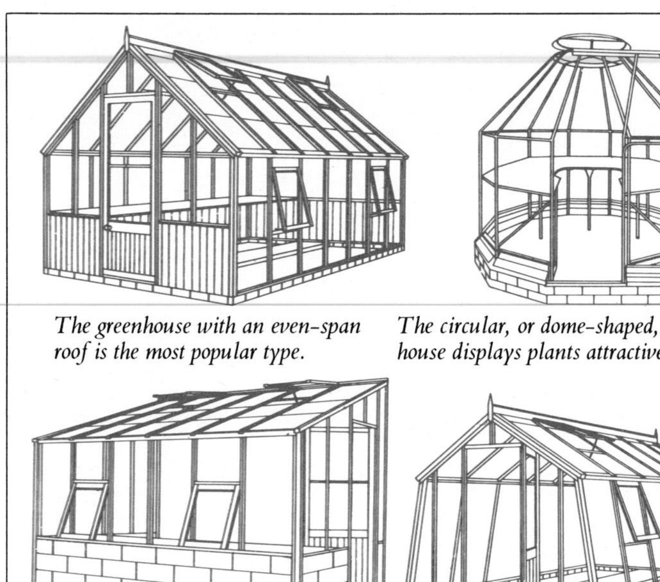

The greenhouse with an even-span roof is the most popular type.

The circular, or dome-shaped, greenhouse displays plants attractively.

The lean-to, erected against a wall, can be the cheapest type to heat.

Glass or plastic walls extending to the foundation admit maximum sun.

Varieties of Greenhouse Frameworks

The framework of a greenhouse should be strong, durable, and attractive.

Aluminum is lightweight and strong, needs no painting, and does not warp or rot. Another of its advantages is that the extrusions form a groove for the glass panes. Strips of plastic are inserted to fill the spaces between metal and glass, thus making the entire assembly weathertight.

Galvanized iron is also strong but needs painting occasionally to prevent rust.

Various woods are used in greenhouse construction. Red cedar and redwood are durable, look attractive, and are relatively inexpensive.

Prefabricated greenhouses are available for erection by the buyer. It is wise to prepare for the installation of these models by building a concrete foundation. Where winters are severe, the foundation should extend below the frost level to prevent heaving. In mild areas the foundation need only extend 6 inches below ground level, with a sheet of galvanized hardware cloth extending from wall to wall, to make the greenhouse vermin proof.

In all cases, lag bolts should be installed so that they protrude from the top of the concrete foundation walls. The bolts are then used to attach the greenhouse structure firmly to the foundation.

Heating a Greenhouse

What to Look for When Buying

Examine as many manufacturers' catalogs as possible before buying a greenhouse. The information will help you make comparisons. Give preference to a greenhouse as large as you can afford, not forgetting maintenance and heating. A greenhouse is so useful and fascinating that space soon becomes filled, and one can quickly regret having bought a small model. If you intend to place benches on both sides of the greenhouse, it is best to choose a model at least 8 feet wide, so that you will have adequate aisle space.

Some of the larger greenhouses contain compartments with connecting doors, so that different temperatures and conditions can be maintained for a variety of plants.

The strength of the framework is always important, but especially in windy areas and if the roof is to be used to support hanging baskets of plants. Wood frames should be examined for knotholes, which can cause weakness. A board base should be strong and thick. The roof should have an adequate slope, so that condensation will run down it.

Sliding doors are an advantage if they are well fitted. They save space, they cannot slam, and they are adjustable for extra ventilation.

The greenhouse should have at least one ventilator on each side of the roof and one on each of the two sides below. Ideally, there should be one roof ventilator and one side ventilator on each side of the house for every 4 feet of glass.

Where to Place a Greenhouse

A greenhouse should be located where it will receive as much light as possible. Try not to place it next to trees; they cast shade, dirty the glass, and can cause damage with falling branches.

Rising ground on the north provides shelter from cold winds.

It is a good idea to have the greenhouse near your house for easy access and to facilitate arrangements for electricity and water.

Position a rectangular greenhouse so that its shorter sides face east and west. The longer sides, where the plants are located, then capture more light in winter; and in summer the greenhouse will probably need shading only on the side that faces toward the south.

Lack of some of the factors mentioned above does not rule out the possibility of success with a greenhouse. For example, even if the only site you can find is in almost constant shade, you can specialize in shade-loving plants.

Hints on Installing a Greenhouse

Prefabricated greenhouses are delivered with full instructions for installation. Even the larger ones can be put up with only one helper; some can be erected single-handed.

Level and firm the ground. If the greenhouse is larger than 8 feet by 6 feet, make a foundation for it. This need not be elaborate, especially if the house is to be mounted on concrete. One way of making a foundation is to dig a trench and fill it with very liquid concrete, which finds its own level by flowing. After this concrete footing has hardened, any base walls supplied with the greenhouse can be set on it. However, a greenhouse with base walls of brick needs a foundation and base built by a professional. Any painting should be done before the glass is installed. Glass is best handled when the weather is dry but not cold.

Fuel Costs and Heat Conservation

The cost of heating your greenhouse will depend upon the volume of fuel consumed, which is largely contingent on the climate in your area. The availability of the various types of fuel will be another factor in your decision on heating.

When a greenhouse is located in the open, the winter sun provides free warmth. A lean-to greenhouse can be positioned against a wall, which will store outside warmth from the house and maintain frost-free conditions overnight in mild winter climates. In windy districts a windbreak of evergreen trees helps to hold down fuel bills.

Many large greenhouses can be divided into compartments to provide different temperatures and conditions. The coolest compartment should be nearest the outside door, and the warmest in the center.

There is increasing interest and progress in the field of solar heating. You can inquire about this at the U.S. Solar Heating and Cooling Information Center, P.O. Box 1607, Rockville, Maryland 20850.

The Amount of Heat That Is Needed

A minimum safe temperature must be maintained at all times. Consequently, the lowest expected nighttime winter temperature must be known, and heating equipment capable of compensating for it must be installed.

The table below assumes an outside temperature of 20° F. It indicates the minimum output of heat (in watts for electrical equipment and in British thermal units per hour for oil and gas) needed to heat a greenhouse of a specific size to 60° F or 45° F. The figures apply to all-glass greenhouses; for houses with brick or concrete base walls, the figures will be lower.

Sample calculation: If you have a greenhouse 6 feet by 10 feet, you will see by the table that a heating unit with an output capable of 4,095 watts or 13,975 Btu per hour is recommended if you want to maintain a minimum greenhouse temperature of 60° F when the outside temperature is 20° F.

This table is only a guide; greenhouse manufacturers should provide calculations for heat needs for your climate and your greenhouse.

Greenhouse size (ft.)	**Desired minimum temperature** (60° F)		(45° F)	
5 × 6	2,340 watts	8,000 Btu/hr.	1,470 watts	5,000 Btu/hr.
6 × 6	2,815 watts	9,600 Btu/hr.	1,750 watts	6,000 Btu/hr.
6 × 8	3,145 watts	11,450 Btu/hr.	2,500 watts	7,100 Btu/hr.
6 × 10	4,095 watts	13,975 Btu/hr.	2,550 watts	8,750 Btu/hr.
6 × 14	4,915 watts	16,800 Btu/hr.	3,100 watts	10,500 Btu/hr.
8 × 8	4,095 watts	13,975 Btu/hr.	2,550 watts	8,750 Btu/hr.
8 × 10	4,575 watts	15,600 Btu/hr.	2,850 watts	9,750 Btu/hr.
8 × 14	5,485 watts	18,650 Btu/hr.	3,400 watts	11,600 Btu/hr.
10 × 10	5,700 watts	14,675 Btu/hr.	3,600 watts	12,250 Btu/hr.
10 × 15	7,385 watts	25,900 Btu/hr.	4,750 watts	16,100 Btu/hr.
10 × 20	8,980 watts	31,450 Btu/hr.	5,800 watts	19,700 Btu/hr.

Gas—The Most Practical Heat

The most efficient and convenient source of heat for the average home greenhouse is gas, either natural or bottled. It is usually trouble free and produces no harmful fumes.

Natural gas is supplied by an underground pipeline; so if your house does not already have an installation, and the greenhouse is not located close to it, the connection may prove costly. Once installed, however, natural-gas heaters are economical to run, for they respond well to thermostatic control. They are excellent for lean-to greenhouses attached to gas-heated houses.

Installations for bottled-gas supplies are situated above the ground and just outside the greenhouse.

Gas heaters frequently incorporate blowers to move the warm, dry air throughout the greenhouse. Depending on the temperature maintained, humidity may have to be provided—by a humidifier or just by hosing down the floors regularly.

For the amateur's greenhouse, the gas heater, which is installed through the wall of the greenhouse and thus vented directly outdoors, is the most popular. It is inexpensive and usually easy to install.

Fin radiators present a large surface to the atmosphere and therefore make efficient use of the heated water they contain. The source for

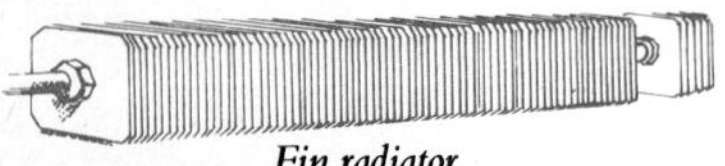

Fin radiator

heating the water can be oil or electricity as well as gas.

Convector heaters, which can be run by gas or electricity, produce a current of warm air without a fan, and are fairly inexpensive and simple to install. Heat distribution is not as good as with fin radiators; so if you use convectors, place one at each end of the greenhouse.

Electric Heaters and Oil Burners

Electric heating systems are excellent and convenient to use, as their clean heat is directed to every greenhouse corner by means of built-in fans. There is the very real problem of cost, which can be prohibitive in the colder regions of the country. In spite of electricity's high cost, it is still practical in Zones C and D.

Portable fan heaters, such as the one shown here, often incorporate a thermostat that controls the fan and the heat output simultaneously. The air circulation that such fan heaters provide is good for the plants.

Always use electrical equipment that has been specifically designed for

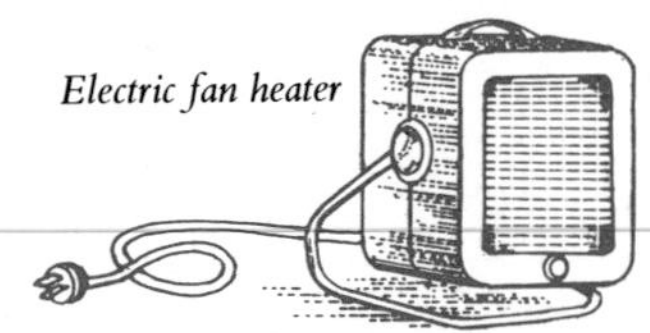

Electric fan heater

greenhouses. Using your household equipment is not satisfactory and can be dangerous.

For economical use of electricity, soil-warming cables are invaluable. Plants will not grow actively during the colder months unless they have a root temperature of 50°–55° F; to maintain this by warming the air with electricity is expensive, but with electrical cables you can warm the soil cheaply and efficiently. The cables themselves are not expensive and are easy to install. They operate on ordinary house current.

On an open bench for winter-flowering pot plants, the cables should be laid on top of a layer of sand about 2 inches deep and then covered with another inch of sand.

In greenhouse areas where tomatoes or other early salad crops are grown, the cables should be buried 9 inches deep in the soil so that they will not be disturbed by cultivation. For details on how to buy and install cables, see page 445.

Compact oil burners are made for greenhouses. The heat they generate can be delivered in either of two forms: as hot water traveling through fin radiation or as warm air that is pushed through ducts with the assistance of blower fans.

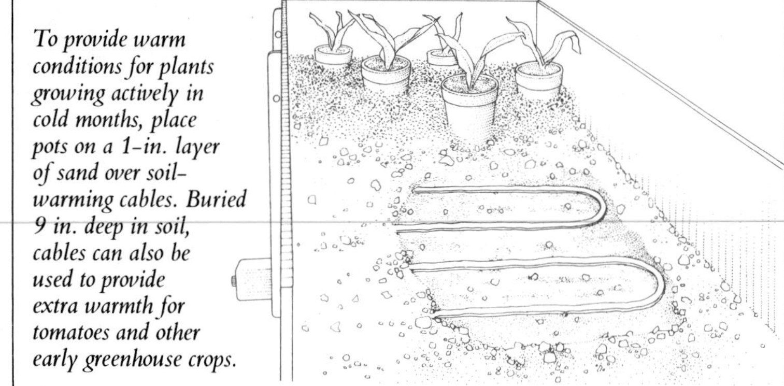

To provide warm conditions for plants growing actively in cold months, place pots on a 1-in. layer of sand over soil-warming cables. Buried 9 in. deep in soil, cables can also be used to provide extra warmth for tomatoes and other early greenhouse crops.

Thermostatic Control of Heating

Most greenhouse heaters are fitted with a thermostat. Electric heating allows highly accurate temperature control; gas is slightly less tractable. Hot-water systems, whatever the source of their heat, are the most difficult to control.

The thermostat should be set so that the minimum temperature does not drop below the prescribed level. A good safeguard for a greenhouse is a temperature alarm device that will ring a bell whenever the inside temperature reaches preset high or low limits. The unit should be battery operated, so that it will be effective during power shortages.

Keeping the Greenhouse Cool and Moist

In the South and even in areas where winter temperatures drop below zero, summer heat can be a real problem in the greenhouse.

Spraying water on the plants is not the answer to keeping them cool, for excessive watering creates fungus problems and, by forcing air out of the soil, may injure the plants. On the other hand, conventional air conditioners, although compact and easy to install, are not desirable either, as they tend to remove humidity from the air and so replace one problem with another.

An effective system for reducing the temperature of the greenhouse while maintaining its moisture is the evaporative cooler. This device consists basically of a fiberglass filter, a perforated water pipe through which water drips from the top to the bottom of the filter, and a fan. The cooler is set on a platform just outside the greenhouse. A short duct connects it to the greenhouse interior, where a thermostat is installed to regulate the cooler's operation.

As soon as the thermostat calls for a heat reduction inside the greenhouse, the fan switches on and blows through the filter, forcing the air, moistened with cold water, into the greenhouse through the duct. When the preset temperature has been reached, the thermostat will automatically turn off the system.

Installing the Essential Equipment

Greenhouse Benches and Shelving

The simplest form of bench is the slatted-wood type. To provide added humidity in summer, cover the bench with plastic sheeting and spread over it a 1-inch layer of moist sand—or you can use special sand trays for the purpose. Potted plants standing on the sand will draw up moisture through their drainage holes by capillary action. The sand can be kept moist either manually or automatically by one of the methods described on page 444. In winter, when high humidity is not wanted, the sand should be cleared away.

In a greenhouse heated by fin radiators, it is sometimes possible to run them beneath that part of the bench used for propagation. Convector heaters can also be put beneath the benches, but you must be careful to avoid overheating. If you use this type of heating, install asbestos or metal sheeting on the bottom of the benches to prevent scorching. For more on propagators, see page 445.

Shelves above the benches provide more room for pots or seed trays and accommodate trailing plants.

Moist sand, over a plastic-lined bench, adds considerable humidity.

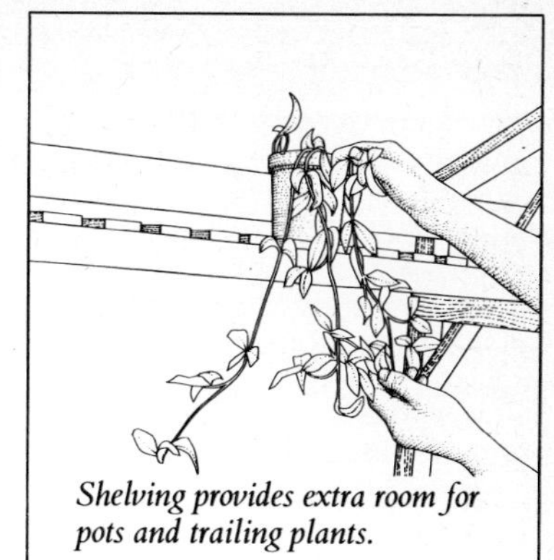

Shelving provides extra room for pots and trailing plants.

Providing Adequate Ventilation

A greenhouse needs at least one ventilator on each side of the roof, and preferably one on each of the side walls below. Otherwise, the house is likely to become too hot in summer. When both the top and side vents are open at the same time, a rapid change of air takes place.

Top vents, and sometimes side vents, can be fitted with automatic electric devices for opening and closing the vents as needed. Nonelectric openers are also available; they operate by means of a compound inside the unit that expands or contracts with changes of temperature and thus motivates a piston system of levers.

An alternative form of automatic ventilation is an electric exhaust fan controlled by a thermostat. The fan is best placed in the apex of the greenhouse roof, at the end opposite the door. As the fan sucks air out of the greenhouse, sufficient fresh air will usually come in under the door and through any other construction gaps. During very hot weather the door or the vents farthest from the fan should be left open to provide maximum interior ventilation.

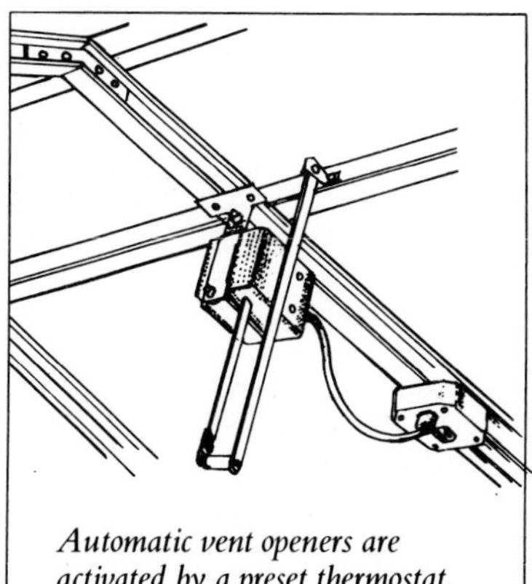

Automatic vent openers are activated by a preset thermostat.

Side vents can be opened by hand or by automatic equipment.

Methods of Shading the Greenhouse

The most efficient way to shade a greenhouse is to install roller blinds, which are usually made of wood or plastic slats or of woven plastic material. These blinds can be lowered on sunny days and rolled back on cloudy ones. They should be fitted to the outside of the roof and set on rails a few inches from the glass.

Blinds are ordinarily used on the greenhouse roof only, although blinds are available for covering the sides as well. A greenhouse whose ends face east and west should be shaded on the south side of its roof; a greenhouse running north to south must be shaded on both sides.

Automatic blinds, operated by photoelectric cells, are also available but are expensive.

An effective and cheaper alternative to blinds is rain-resistant shading paint. A concentrate is diluted in water and brushed or sprayed on the outside of the glass. It is waterproof but can be wiped off.

Rain-resistant shading paint can be applied on the sides as well as on the roof. If a greenhouse runs north-south, paint the south, east, and west sides, plus the roof.

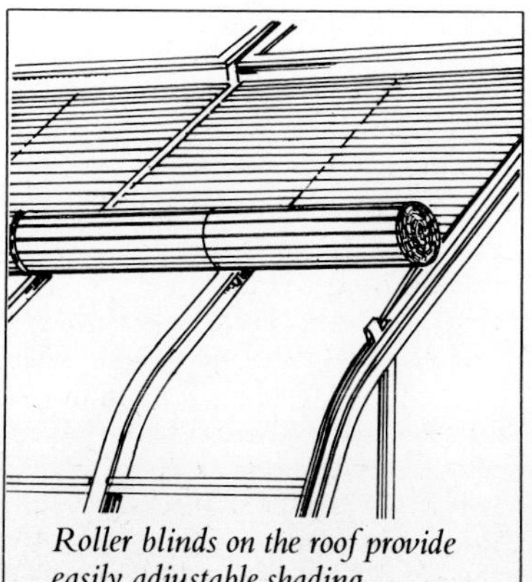

Roller blinds on the roof provide easily adjustable shading.

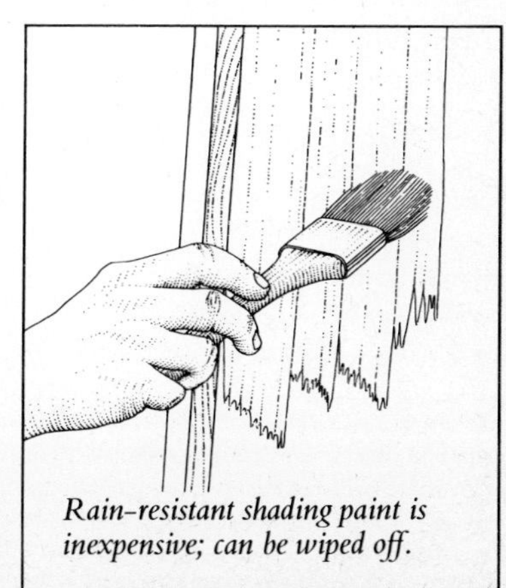

Rain-resistant shading paint is inexpensive; can be wiped off.

A Water Supply in the Greenhouse

Unless a greenhouse is being erected alongside an existing frost-proof garden faucet, a permanent water supply should be installed. Both hot and cold water are desirable, and a mixing faucet will allow you to water plants with tepid water. This installation should be done by a plumber; the expense is justified by the convenience to the gardener and benefit to the plants.

Once a faucet has been provided, greenhouse plants can be watered with a watering can, with a hose, or automatically.

Automatic watering has several advantages. It saves time. It is more reliable than hand watering, and so promotes steady growth of plants. And it enables you to leave the greenhouse unattended for days if suitable equipment is used.

The capillary sand bench is becoming a popular method of automatic watering. Small units are now available. They consist of a plastic tray, a tank or reservoir, and a constant-level float valve.

A layer of sand is placed in the tray according to the supplier's recommendations. Mix the sand with a nontoxic algicide to prevent the growth of algae. An alternative to sand is an absorbent fiberglass mat, sold as building insulation in most hardware stores.

The float valve regulates the level of water in the tray and hence the degree of wetness of the sand.

Use pots with large drainage holes for capillary-bench work. Do not put crocks in when potting.

After potting the plants, press the pots down firmly on the moist sand or absorbent mat, so that the soil makes contact with it through the pot's drainage holes.

Another form of watering is trickle irrigation. This is accomplished by a plastic pipeline with a series of nozzles that drip water into the pots. The frequency and amount of water supplied are controlled by a manually adjustable valve. This method should not be used for plants that need only occasional and minimal watering, such as cacti.

Plastic pipelines can also be used to irrigate sand benches or absorbent matting.

A pipeline with misting jets can be fixed permanently over or under benches to provide overhead watering or damping down.

A modern method of automatic watering is by photoelectric control. A photoelectric cell automatically switches on a water valve when the light reaches a certain intensity. The water then runs for a set period. This method can be used to control capillary benches, trickle irrigation, and overhead irrigation.

If you find it difficult to know when to water plants, a soil-moisture meter (tensiometer) is invaluable. It consists of a dial fixed to a long probe, which is inserted into the soil. The dial is calibrated to give "dry," "moist," and "wet" readings. Some meter dials have numbers on them and come with a guide as to which numbers are best for various plants.

Capillary bench. *The tray of sand is watered by a tank; pots draw moisture from the sand. Moisture meter in pot at right shows when to water.*

Trickle irrigation. *Nozzles on a pipeline drip water onto the soil in the pots. Water flow is controlled by a valve in a water tank.*

Other Useful Fittings for the Greenhouse

There are other fittings that, although not essential, are useful accessories in a greenhouse.

For example, gutters can be fitted to the greenhouse roof to lead rainwater off. This water can be collected in an outdoor or indoor water barrel by means of a downspout and used for watering plants. A supply of rainwater is useful for watering acid-soil plants in hard-water areas. Make sure that an outdoor barrel used for this purpose is covered with a lid, to prevent dirt from entering. The top of the pipe from the roof should be covered with wire mesh to eliminate debris.

A soil thermometer is useful for measuring the temperature of soil heated by cables in a propagator, cold frame, or greenhouse bed. In a propagator soil temperatures must go as high as 64° F to start plants from seeds and cuttings. Cold frames and greenhouse ground beds require a winter soil temperature of 50°–55° F for early salad crops.

Artificial lighting is useful for working during dark winter evenings in a greenhouse. Moisture-proof electric fittings are available and should always be installed by a qualified electrician.

Propagators and Their Uses

A propagator is a box with a transparent cover, which is used for germinating seeds or rooting cuttings. It can be unheated or heated. In addition, many propagators are outfitted with misting units (see p. 454).

An unheated propagator merely provides a sealed humid environment for cuttings or seeds. A heated propagator also provides bottom heat, which makes rooting and germination more certain. Also, many bulbs, corms, rhizomes, and tubers will begin to grow earlier if they are given extra warmth.

Young plants can be kept in a large propagator until they are well established. A large heated unit can also be used as a permanent home for small tropical plants.

There are many different kinds of propagators on the market. Most are heated by electricity, using soil-warming cables.

The simplest units hold one or two seed trays. They can be bought with a heating element fitted into the base, which has only to be plugged into the main electricity supply. The trays rest on a layer of sand or gravel. More elaborate propagators can hold many pots and boxes, and are thermostatically controlled.

You can make your own propagating case. Start with a sheet of fiber cement, such as Transite (available from greenhouse manufacturers), cut to fit the greenhouse bench. Using the sheet as a base and four 9-inch-wide boards as the sides, construct a simple topless box.

The sheet can also be placed directly on the bench supports. If this is done, it should be supported with wooden or metal crosspieces.

Cut three or four drainage holes in the fiber cement, and cover them with pieces of galvanized screening; then install soil-warming cables as directed in the section at the right.

For the top, make a wooden frame and cover it with rigid plastic, or set a glass panel in it.

A large heated propagator can be used to house a collection of small tropical plants, saving the cost of heating the whole greenhouse to a high temperature.

How to Buy and Install Soil-Warming Cables

Cuttings are slow to root and seeds are slow to germinate if the soil temperature falls below 65° F. To heat the soil mixture in a propagator or cold frame by air warmth would be both slow and costly. Moreover, high air temperatures in winter or spring may produce unwanted top growth on the plants being propagated. The simplest answer is the use of soil-warming cables.

Cables are made in lengths to fit any area and to give the desired amount of heat.

To grow early melons or cucumbers in an outside cold frame, for example, 5 watts of electricity per square foot are needed to heat the soil to about 50° F. For seeds and cuttings in a greenhouse propagator, 15 watts per square foot will give a soil temperature of 65° F.

The following table shows the wattage and length of cable needed to heat the soil in a cool greenhouse to a temperature of 65° F.

Area (sq. ft.)	Watts	Cable length (ft.)
Up to 6	75	20
9	112	30
12	150	40
18	225	60
25	300	80
36	450	120
50	600	160

You can buy electric heating cables fitted with a thermostat for controlling the heat. The wire must be fully insulated to reduce risk of damage or shock.

Cables can be connected directly to wall outlets. Or special low-voltage cables can be operated from a transformer—a safer procedure if there is a risk of damage to cables from garden tools.

Remember, for safety's sake, that all major electric work should be done only by a qualified electrician.

Always buy the correct length of flexible cable to fit the area to be heated. Put a 2-inch layer of sand on the base of the propagator. Over this, place the cable, laying it in loops to cover the entire area to be heated. Avoid sharp bends and lay the cable not less than 4 inches nor more than 8 inches apart. The cable must never be allowed to cross itself or any adjacent cables. Cover with an additional inch of sand and 3 inches of moist peat moss.

Cuttings can be planted directly into the peat moss, and pots can be sunk in it so that each base is in contact with the sand.

For air warming alone, or in addition to soil warming, a cable can be fastened to woodwork around the sides of the propagator frame. If the frame has glass sides, the cables can be fastened to a row of wooden stakes that have been pushed into the ground inside the frame.

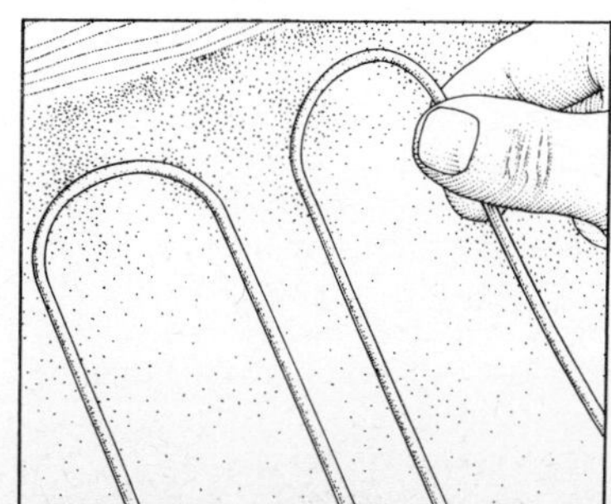

1. *Spread a layer of sand on the bottom of the case, and lay the cable on it.*

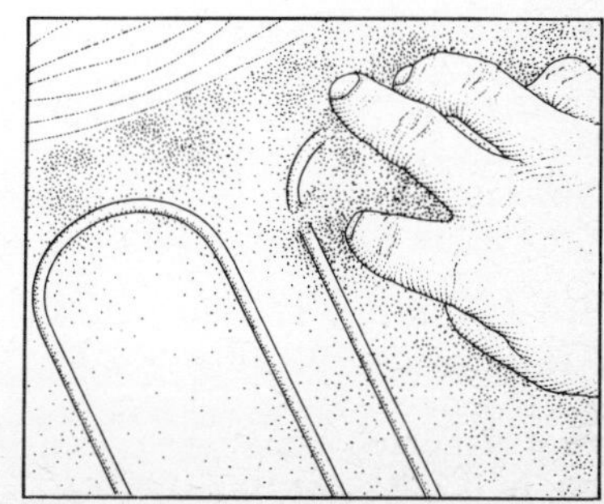

2. *Cover the cable with sand and moist peat moss to distribute the heat.*

Providing the Right Conditions for Plants

Watering, humidity, temperature, shading, and feeding can be controlled in a greenhouse to suit almost any kind of plant.

Watering. Add water slowly until it comes out of the bottom of the pot. Then water again before the soil dries out completely. It is better to be sparing rather than too generous with water, since roots are likely to rot in waterlogged soil.

In fall and winter, when plants are dormant or growing slowly, less frequent watering is required. In spring and summer, when plants are growing actively, they can be watered oftener. When the weather is cool, plants need far less water than when skies are sunny and the temperature is high.

Generally, the best time to water is in the morning. This avoids creating excess moisture at the roots at night, when plants do not use it, and holds down overnight humidity.

Always use clean water. If soft water is required for acid-soil plants, collect rainwater in a barrel with a lid on it to keep out dirt and leaves.

In warm weather, greenhouse plants benefit from overhead spraying with water. This cleans the foliage, enabling it to breathe better.

Humidity and damping down. Humidity is the moisture content of the air. It is increased by spraying plants with water or by damping down—drenching the floor and benches of the greenhouse. (But be sure to keep water off of plants with velvety or hairy foliage.) The presence of a damp surface, such as a capillary bench (see p. 444), will also raise humidity. Humidity is lowered by watering sparingly, by confining water to the area of the plant roots, and by increasing ventilation.

In summer high humidity is beneficial to most plants. It reduces the amount of water that foliage loses through transpiration and that soil loses through evaporation. In a hot, dry summer most of the potted plants will benefit if the greenhouse is damped down at least twice a day, in the morning and evening. However, provided the plants are watered regularly and maximum ventilation is given, all the plants listed in the charts beginning on page 462 should succeed.

In winter, humidity should be held down; ventilate the greenhouse whenever the outside temperature will allow, and water lightly. High humidity in cold weather produces condensation on the glass (which reduces light), increases the possibility of fungous diseases, and increases the danger of waterlogged soil. To keep down humidity during the winter, do not use the capillary watering systems.

Temperature. Control temperature to suit the types of plants grown. In summer temperature is reduced by damping down, ventilation, and shading. Damping down has a cooling effect because heat is dissipated as water evaporates, but this will not happen without ventilation. There should be at least four ventilators (one on each side of the roof and one on each of the greenhouse sides below). In very hot weather the door can be opened as well.

Shading. There are two main reasons for shading a greenhouse. First, many tropical plants originated in forest areas and thrive best in partially shaded sites. Second, few plants, however tropical in origin, require a temperature above 85° F, and for most 75° F is adequate. Temperatures above 90° F can harm many plants. In warm, sunny weather it is difficult in the average small greenhouse to keep temperatures down with ventilation alone; so shading must also be used.

If possible, shading should be graduated from heavy (an overall solid layer of shading paint) to light (dots of spray or wavy stripes of paint with a space between each stripe), to provide different light requirements for different plants. For example, most cacti need either no shade at all or very little shade, whereas most ferns need full shade during the brightest, warmest weather. Slatted blinds can be rolled down completely or partially, depending on the amount of sunlight pouring in. If shading cannot be graduated, shade-loving plants can be grown under the benches or in the shade of climbing plants.

In general, the part of a greenhouse used for propagation will need shading from mid-March to mid-October. For growing potted plants, shading from mid-April to late September is adequate.

As winter ends, plants are often sensitive to a sudden temperature rise caused by sunny spells, which, even in cold weather, can make a greenhouse extremely warm. For this reason, light shading may be necessary in spring.

Feeding. Overfeeding, like overwatering, can often lead to the death of potted plants. A buildup of nutrient salts in the soil can damage plant roots. If the correct potting and seeding mixtures are used, plants will need no further feeding until they have become well established and the pots are filled with roots.

As with watering, feeding must be regulated according to the plants' needs. Fast-growing, heavily productive plants, such as tomatoes, cucumbers, and chrysanthemums, can be fed generously. Slow-growing plants, such as rock plants and many cacti, can be badly damaged by excessive feeding.

Plants absorb nutrients only in solution. For this reason, liquid fertilizers are best, because they act rapidly and effectively. High fertilizer concentrations can damage plants; so never apply more than is recommended on the label.

Unlike plants grown outdoors, a potted greenhouse plant grows each day in a progressively less fertile soil. Nutrients are washed away with daily waterings, and in time the potting mixture becomes little more than an almost sterile material. Therefore, it is important to the plant's survival to feed it every two or three weeks with a complete fertilizer—that is, one containing nitrogen, phosphorus, and potassium in the proper proportions. Most commercial fertilizers of this kind also contain traces of many other elements essential to plant growth.

Foliar fertilizers (applied to and absorbed by the plant's foliage) are available for plants that need a quick boost to growth or whose root action is slow, such as young, newly transplanted plants.

Plants long established in pots can benefit from a dressing of a well-balanced dry fertilizer incorporated into the upper layer of soil and thoroughly watered in.

Before going on vacation. A greenhouse can usually be left untended for a day—although in summer you should be sure to take care of watering and shading each morning if you are not returning until evening. If you are going to be away for a week or more, try to get a friend or neighbor to help. If there is no one available, automatic equipment can be used for watering and for controlling heat and ventilation.

If you prefer not to make the outlay for automatic equipment, carry out the following jobs before going on a summer vacation. Water thoroughly before leaving. Provide humidity by covering the plants with clear plastic sheeting or bags. Or thoroughly damp down the greenhouse, and fill some pans or tubs with water to maintain humidity. Completely shade the greenhouse. Allow plenty of ventilation, but reduce vents on the side of the prevailing wind. Check for pests and diseases, and give routine treatment with systemic pesticides and fungicides if necessary. Remove any flowers and buds about to mature. Do any necessary transplanting or repotting. Gather any fruits or vegetables that are almost ready to ripen.

Keeping Greenhouse and Equipment Clean

Cleanliness is vital to success in greenhouse gardening. It discourages pests and diseases, and it encourages general plant vigor and health. Keep all pots and containers clean. Try to use equipment made of plastic, metal, or glass, which cannot harbor disease organisms.

Wash grime and algae from both sides of the greenhouse glass regularly. Wash down benches and interior structures, using clean water with detergent. Algicides are also available to keep greenhouse floors, benches, and automatic watering systems free from algae.

In an empty greenhouse, where there is no risk of the fumes doing damage to plants, a chlorine-based disinfectant can be added to the water before washing.

A greenhouse should not be used to store garden tools and other equipment, which often harbor pests. Regularly inspect plants and remove dead flowers or decaying foliage. Isolate unhealthy plants outside the greenhouse; or put them in a plastic bag for treatment with an insecticide or a fungicide. Make certain that the plant remains free of pests for a few weeks before removing it from the bag.

Always use sterilized soil mixtures to avoid introducing insects and diseases into the greenhouse and to keep plants free of weeds.

Fumigation is an easy and efficient way to kill pests. It should be done twice a year—in midfall and in early spring. Certain pesticides sold for spraying, such as malathion, can also be used as fumigants.

Fumigation should not be attempted where a lean-to greenhouse is attached to a residence. Keep children and pets away from a fumigated site for at least 24 hours.

Before fumigation, water plants but keep foliage dry. Do not carry out the operation in strong sunlight, on a windy day, or when temperatures are high. Evening is the best time for fumigating, after which the greenhouse should be kept completely shut until morning. Then ventilate it freely. To keep fumes and vapors inside the greenhouse, block any openings with wet burlap or masking tape.

To find out how much fumigant to use, it is necessary to know the cubic capacity of the greenhouse. Multiply its width by its length and then multiply that total by the structure's average height.

If the greenhouse has contained plants badly infected by disease, sterilize the empty building by burning sulfur at the rate of 1 pound per 1,000 cubic feet. The resultant sulfur dioxide is poisonous and will kill all plants; do not inhale it.

The Correct Way to Pot Your Plants

Plastic pots have generally replaced clay ones because they are lightweight, easy to clean, and not so readily broken. Also, since they are nonporous, less watering is needed.

When potted plants are placed on a bed of moist peat moss or sand, however, clay is preferable, since it allows moisture to pass through the pots to the roots. Plants that prefer dry growing conditions also do better in clay pots.

The most popular pot sizes for general greenhouse use are 2 inches (for seedlings), 3½ inches, and 5 inches. (All measurements refer to the inside diameter of the top of the pot.) Large plants, shrubs, and climbers may need correspondingly larger pots. Make sure that all pots have adequate drainage holes.

For short plants, such as rock plants, some succulents, and small bulbs, half-pots or seed pans can be used. They are only half the depth of normal pots. They give a more balanced appearance to short plants and require less potting mixture. Scrub all pots thoroughly before use, to remove any dirt and encrustations.

Thoroughly soak clay pots, especially new ones. Otherwise they will dry out the soil put into them.

Plastic pots with small holes in the bottom need no drainage material. Clay pots up to 5 inches in diameter need no drainage material either, but if you are potting a plant in a clay pot larger than 5 inches, first cover the drainage hole with a few pieces of broken pot or clean pebbles. However, this should not be done if the pots are to be placed on a capillary sand bench.

To pot a plant, put moist potting mixture in the pot, and gently tap it down on the bench. Hold the plant in the pot so that the roots are resting on the soil and the base (top of roots) of the plant comes to about 1 inch below the top rim of the pot.

Position the plant centrally and place more soil around it. Fill the pot with soil to within 1 inch of the rim. Always take care not to damage the roots; a few taps of the pot on the bench will suffice to anchor them firmly. Firm the soil gently with the fingers. Do not pack it down tightly, since this can cause it to become waterlogged.

After potting, water the plant thoroughly. It is usually sufficient to fill the pot to the rim and allow the water to drain through. Do not water again until the soil has become almost dry. If roots have been damaged in the potting process, they can rot in soil that remains too wet.

1. *Place drainage material on the bottom of a clay pot larger than 5 in.*

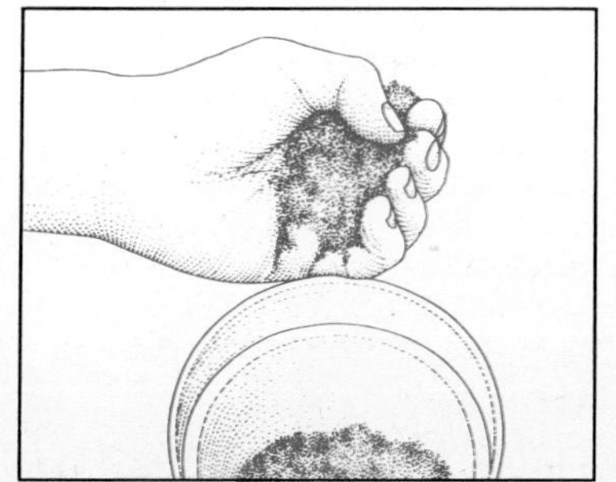

2. *Put moist potting soil into the pot, and tap it down gently.*

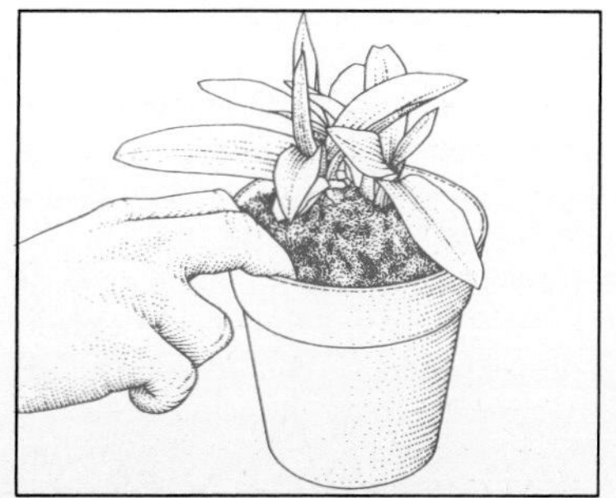

3. *Position the plant centrally, add more soil, and tap the pot to settle.*

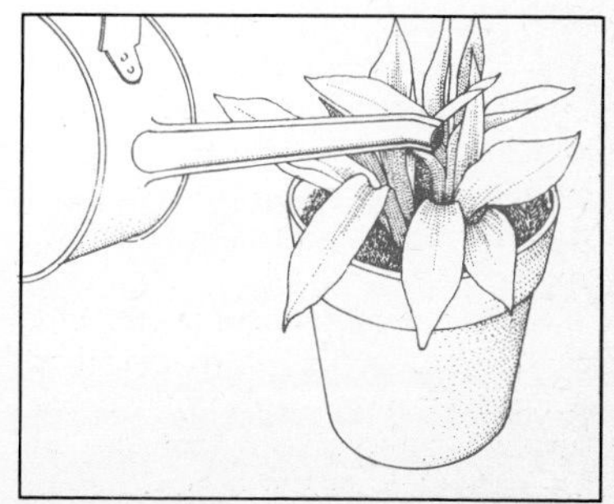

4. *After potting, water by filling the 1-in. space between rim and soil.*

Transplanting Growing Plants

A developing plant should be transplanted into a larger pot each time its roots fill its present pot. When roots appear through the drainage holes, turn the pot upside down, allowing the plant's stem to pass between the fingers. Tap the rim with a stick or tap the pot on the edge of the bench to loosen the root ball; it should then come away cleanly and easily.

The new pot should provide an inch of extra space all around the root ball. Position the plant centrally and fill in around it with potting mixture. Settle the potting mixture by tapping the pot on the bench a few times; then firm down lightly with the fingers. If the gap between pot and root ball is too tight for the fingers, use a potting stick. Leave a 1-inch space at the top for watering.

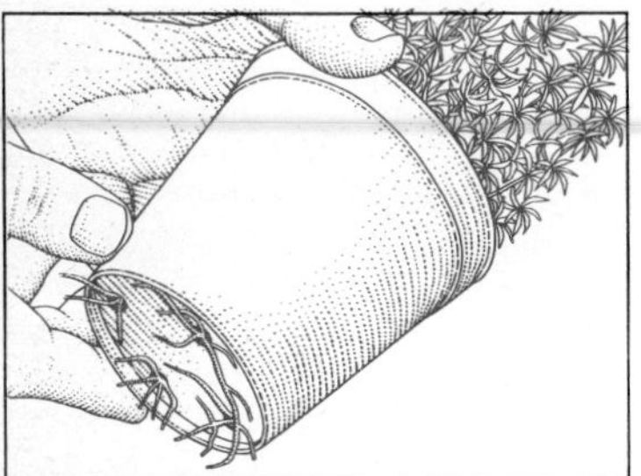

1. *When the roots appear through the drainage holes, it is time to repot.*

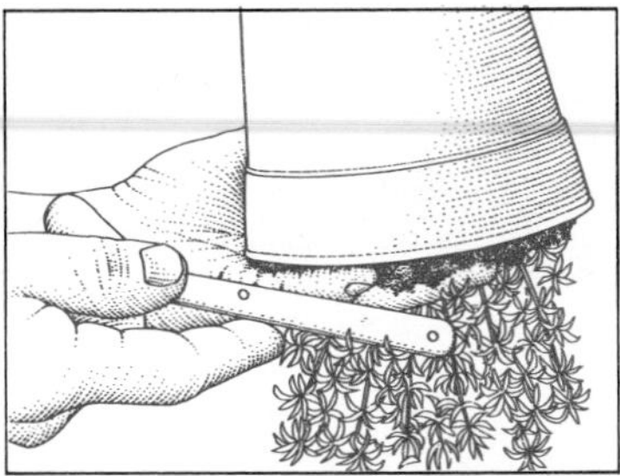

2. *Turn the pot upside down, and tap the rim to release the root ball.*

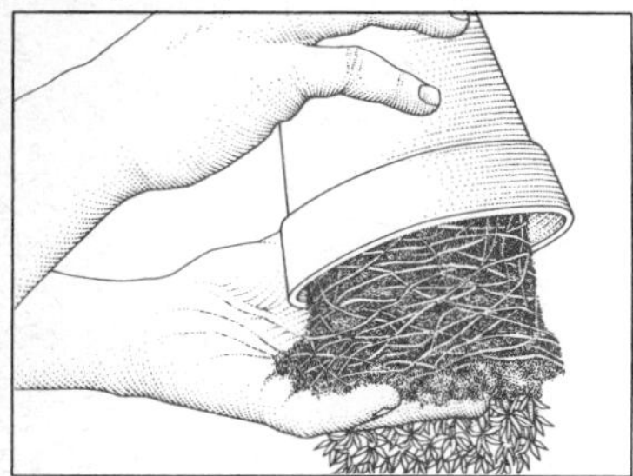

3. *The root ball should come away quite easily if the plant is well rooted.*

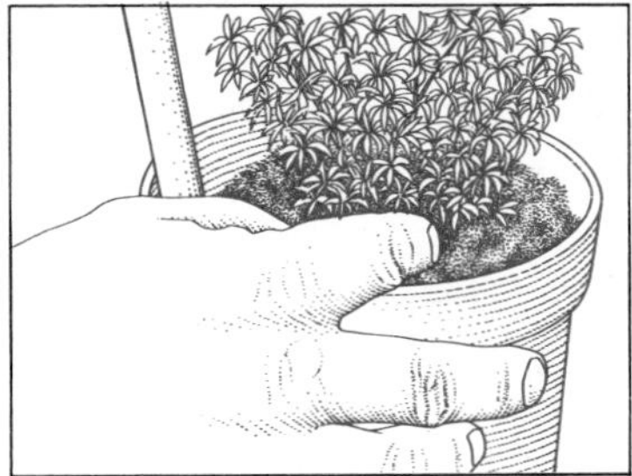

4. *Replant in a pot one size larger in diameter than the old pot.*

How to Pot Large Bulbs

When you are potting extremely large bulbs, such as those of the amaryllis, allow at least one-third of the bulb to protrude above the surface of the potting mixture in a 5- to 6-inch pot. This places the bulb at the right height to provide sufficient room in the pot for root growth. After the bulbs have been potted, they should be left in the greenhouse and watered sparingly until the new roots are well developed.

Amaryllises and nerines can be gently forced to provide early flowers (see p. 317). These two bulbs often make considerable top growth before rooting, which takes place only as the leaves begin to develop. An amaryllis may even flower before making new roots. For this reason, be very careful when you move the plants about, in case too few roots have formed to anchor the plant.

Potting and Seeding Mixtures

Never use ordinary garden soil for growing plants or sowing seeds in containers. Always use good potting and seed mixtures that have been sterilized to destroy pests, diseases, and weed seeds.

Seeding and potting mixtures are widely available. Some are based on soil and some on peat moss, or a mixture of peat moss and sand or perlite. Soil-based mixtures are not difficult to make. If you need a large quantity, making it yourself is cheaper than buying it.

To make small batches of mixes, and also to carry out potting and seed-sowing operations, you will need a potting bench. This consists of a tray with two sides and a back, which can be put on the greenhouse bench. It should have a smooth surface that can be kept clean and reasonably sterile. Sheet aluminum or plastic-covered wood are two good materials.

A seeding mixture is used to provide the ideal conditions for the germination of almost all seeds of popular greenhouse plants. Ideally, the soil referred to in these mixtures is a topsoil of a medium texture, neither too sandy nor with a preponderance of clay. While it is always wise to sterilize soil in order to eliminate the many insects, diseases, and weeds it may harbor, it is not necessary to treat peat moss or lime in any way. A good-quality baled peat moss and clean builder's sand or perlite are essential.

Seeding mixture	**Quarts** (to make a bushel)
Sterilized garden soil	16
Peat moss	8
Coarse builder's sand or perlite	8

To each bushel of seeding mixture add ½ cup of superphosphate and ⅓ cup of ground limestone.

Potting mixture	**Quarts** (to make a bushel)
Sterilized garden soil	19
Peat moss	8
Coarse builder's sand or perlite	5

To each bushel add ¾ cup of a complete fertilizer in granular form and ⅓ cup ground limestone.

There are certain kinds of plants that need special soils for successful growth. If a greenhouse plant has any such special cultural requirement, this is noted in the charts on pages 462–475.

Soilless mixes. It is often difficult to get good-quality soil in sufficient quantities, and sterilizing the soil is a time-consuming process. Consequently, soilless mixes have become popular among greenhouse gardeners. When the appropriate fertilizers have been added, these perfectly textured potting materials are complete and quite easy to use. Their light weight alone makes them a pleasure. Once a plant becomes large, however, what was an asset becomes a liability. Seed germination is good in soilless mixtures, and plants tend to make early growth very quickly. Since the peat moss is lightweight, large plants often become top-heavy. They may topple over, particularly in plastic pots. A large plant, therefore, is probably best grown in a soil-based mixture. Nevertheless, for a great variety of plants, the soilless mixes are practical. Like any other new product or technique, they take some getting used to in terms of watering, fertilizing, and the like.

Soilless potting mixture	
Sphagnum peat moss	1 bu.
Horticultural-grade vermiculite or perlite	1 bu.
Ground limestone	10 tbsp.
Superphosphate (20% powdered)	5 tsp.
5–10–5 fertilizer	15 tsp.

How to Sterilize Ingredients of Soil Mixtures

Only leaf mold and soil need to be sterilized. Never use soils twice, and never sterilize a fully made-up mixture containing fertilizers. The materials to be sterilized must be reasonably dry.

To sterilize leaf mold, pour boiling water on it; then drain.

Soil should be sterilized separately, before being mixed with leaf mold or fertilizer. Various sterilizing chemicals, such as quintozene or Terrazole, are on the market. The best all-round sterilization method for soil, however, is by steam. The soil can be used very soon afterward; there is no risk of damage to plants, pets, or people from fumes; and the method is effective.

Small electric sterilizers can be bought quite cheaply. Some simply use dry heat; others work via the action of steam from boiling water passing through the material that is to be sterilized.

The dry soil is first sifted to free it from lumps, then placed in the bin of the sterilizer, which has a perforated bottom. Water is poured into the boiling compartment of the sterilizer to the level recommended by the manufacturer.

The sterilizing bin is then placed on top of the boiling compartment, and steam is passed through the soil until the temperature at the top reaches 180° F. This should be maintained for about 10 minutes. (Do not let the soil temperature exceed 180° F, or beneficial soil organisms will be killed.) The recommended temperature should be reached within 40 minutes elapsed time.

After sterilizing the soil, tip it out onto a clean surface to cool. It can be used as soon as it cools.

For a simple home method of sterilizing small quantities of soil in the kitchen, see page 597.

STERILIZING SOIL WITH STEAM

Pour sifted soil into sterilizer and pass steam through it until the temperature at the top of the soil reaches 180° F. Maintain heat for 10 minutes.

How to Prepare Your Own Potting Mixture

Do not attempt to make too large an amount of potting mixture at one time—it is too difficult to mix.

Spread out the measured peat moss, sterilized soil, and sand or perlite on the potting bench. (For recommended proportions, see p. 448.)

Put a little of the sand in a bucket.

Measure all fertilizers carefully (weigh them if the mixture is given in ounces), and mix them into the sand in the bucket. Then sprinkle the fertilizer and sand mixture evenly over the surface of the soil, peat moss, and sand. Finally, blend the ingredients together thoroughly so that they are evenly mixed.

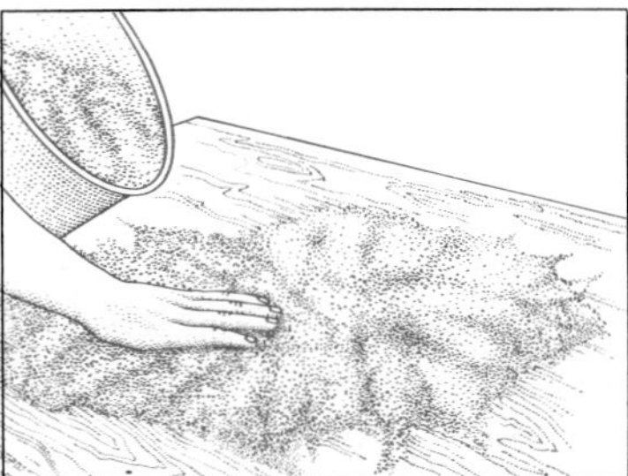

1. *Spread out the measured peat moss, soil, and sand on the potting bench.*

2. *Measure the fertilizers and mix them with a little sand in a bucket.*

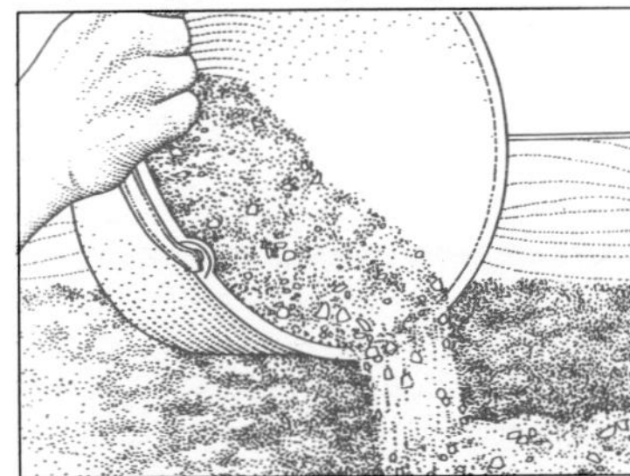

3. *Sprinkle the fertilizer and sand mixture over the basic ingredients.*

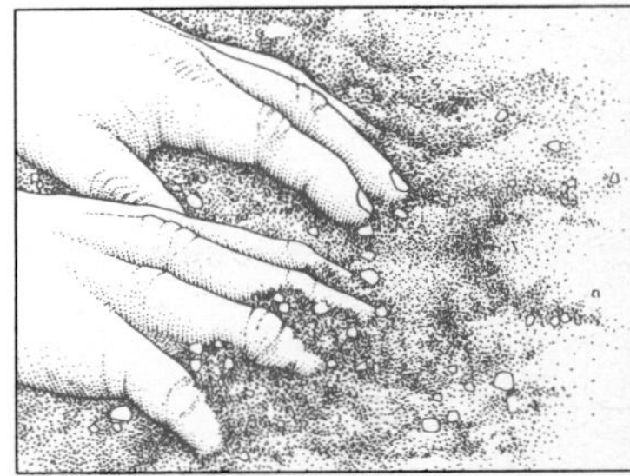

4. *After adding the fertilizer and sand, mix all the ingredients thoroughly.*

Potting Mixtures for Special Purposes

There are a few plants, such as orchids (see p. 481), for which special potting mixtures are needed.

For plants that prefer acid soil, such as azaleas, heaths, and heathers, use the potting mixture described on page 448, but omit the lime. There are prepared soils on the market that are suited to acid-loving plants.

The addition of sterilized leaf mold to the standard formula benefits some plants, such as many lilies, that grow naturally in woodland soils. But in general it is better not to add anything to the standard potting-mixture formulas.

All mixtures should be damp but never waterlogged when used. They should be stored in clean, closed containers and not left open to the air, where they would be exposed to pests, diseases, and weed seeds.

Use a mixture as soon as possible after buying or preparing it. It must not be reused in pots but can be incorporated in the garden to improve the texture of the soil.

A Succession of Plants to Grow Throughout the Year

You can grow a surprisingly varied selection of plants in a single shelter if you see to it that the lighting, heating, and humidity needs of individual plants are met, and if you fit your greenhouse with compartments or accommodate the smaller plants in propagating cases. Even so, you will make things easier for yourself if you avoid combinations of plants with very different requirements, such as cacti and ferns.

It is best to keep members of the following groups of plants in separate sections of the greenhouse: fruits and vines; vegetables and salad crops; plants to be propagated; specialist plants, such as chrysanthemums and alpines; and other ornamentals. If you are growing something to enter in competition at a show or an exhibition, the crop or flowers should probably be given a separate greenhouse. In this way, you can maintain the right conditions, plus pest and disease control, without having to worry about affecting other plants. Try to choose decorative plants to provide year-round interest. The guide to greenhouse plants starting on page 462 offers a wide selection.

Plants grown in succession. In an unheated greenhouse in frost-free areas, a succession of plants with different growing periods can be raised throughout the year. For example, calendula seeds can be sown in late winter for spring bloom. By summer plants can be discarded or planted outdoors. Marigolds and other annuals, started from seeds a few weeks earlier, can take their place to produce flowers all summer. In the fall pots of chrysanthemums, started earlier outdoors, can be moved into the greenhouse to provide late bloom. More chrysanthemum cuttings, planted at monthly intervals, will provide bloom into the spring.

An unheated greenhouse can be used to shelter practically all the favorite outdoor ornamental plants from spring to autumn. Remember, however, that the purpose of the unheated house is to give weather protection only; so always provide maximum ventilation and just enough shading to prevent sun scorch. Special favorites for a greenhouse of this kind are plants that provide flowers for cutting and for flower shows—roses, carnations, sweet peas, dahlias, gladioli, and many other kinds of bulbs.

An unheated greenhouse can also be used in winter to protect otherwise hardy plants that are susceptible to damage by excessive wetness, such as *Lobelia tenuior,* some lily of the Nile varieties, many rock plants, and a few bulbs.

Another use of the unheated greenhouse is to protect early-flowering hardy shrubs grown in pots, such as camellias.

Annuals with alpines. An unheated greenhouse devoted to the needs of alpines—rock plants such as the edelweiss that are native to high mountain regions (see p. 345)—is also excellent for summer-flowering annuals. Many annuals will give remarkable results when grown in pots in an alpine house. After the alpines flower in spring, they can be put outside in cold frames to make room in the greenhouse for annuals.

A cool greenhouse—kept at a minimum of 45°-50° F in winter—is often used for plants such as geraniums and fuchsias. In early spring it can be used to display most of the favorite greenhouse plants, such as calceolarias, cinerarias, primroses, and schizanthuses, grown from the previous autumn's sowings. During this period many different kinds of bulbs can also be brought into the greenhouse for forcing (see p. 317).

In the spring, when summer-flowering plants such as geraniums and fuchsias are coming to life, you can start many summer-flowering bulbs, such as gloxinias, temple bells, achimenes, and lilies.

For a winter display, carnations, African daisies, zonal geraniums, browallias, some fibrous begonias, and even the exotic bird-of-paradise (commonly thought to be suited only to a warm house) are invaluable. Space beneath the benches can be used in winter for forcing rhubarb, endive, and chicory.

In warmer conditions—a minimum wintertime temperature of 60° F—gloxinias, Cape primroses, African violets, columneas, and achimenes grow well together and provide winter blooms as well as additional color at other times of year.

When a greenhouse is kept at an even higher winter temperature—say 65° F in winter—a wide range of attractive subtropical and tropical foliage plants can be grown together.

House-plant shops are excellent sources of greenhouse plants, and most house plants are at their best after being kept under glass for a while. Some will flower and even fruit in a greenhouse, whereas in the home they may provide only decorative foliage.

Many plants need vigorous pruning to keep them compact in a greenhouse. Rampant climbers, such as the passionflower, are among those requiring constant attention.

Foliage plants provide year-round pleasure in the greenhouse and form a background for the display of flowers. All those described in the chart of foliage house plants (see p. 410) are also suitable for growing in a cool greenhouse.

Growing Plants in Hanging Containers

Trailing plants are best displayed in hanging containers, which can be suspended from the greenhouse roof or walls. Some inexpensive, ready-made greenhouses will not take the weight of large baskets, but small pots should be quite safe.

The old-fashioned wire basket for trailing plants can be lined with plastic or sphagnum moss to prevent soil from falling out. Ordinary plastic pots can also be used for hanging: drill holes around the rim of the pot, and pass wires through them.

Before putting trailing plants in baskets, first line the containers with plastic or sphagnum moss. Then fill them with potting mixture, and insert the plants evenly around the edge. In dry weather the soil in hanging containers dries out faster than soil in ordinary pots and needs a daily soaking.

Plants effective in baskets include pendulous begonias, fuchsias, ivy geraniums, and lobelias.

Sometimes bulbs, such as Cape cowslips, are inserted through the mesh of a basket and into the moss. They will grow out in a ball-like mass of bloom.

1. *Line a hanging basket with sphagnum moss to contain the soil.*

2. *Fill the basket with potting mixture, and insert the plants.*

Starting Off Young Plants to Stock the Greenhouse

Seeds: The Cheapest Way for a Mass of Bloom

Growing from seeds is an easy and inexpensive way to stock a greenhouse and fill it with year-round color. Buy seeds from a reputable firm, and sow during the recommended season. Do not sow old seeds; they may have deteriorated.

Use 5-inch pots or seed pans, or small plastic seed trays. Half fill each with slightly moist seeding mixture. Before sowing very fine seeds, sprinkle the surface with a little more seeding mixture that has been rubbed through a fine sieve. Gently level and firm the surface.

Sow the seeds as thinly and evenly as possible by tapping them out of the packet with your forefinger. More even distribution can be attained if very fine seeds are mixed with a little fine sand before sowing. If seeds are known to take six months or more to germinate, incorporate a seed protectant, such as Benomyl, with them to prevent their rotting in the soil.

Many seeds are now available in pelleted form. A coating increases their size and enables you to space them accurately.

After sowing, cover the seeds with a thin layer of seeding mixture. Do not cover excessively, since the seeds need air to germinate, and the emerging seedlings need light and air to develop—ideally, the covering should be as deep as the seeds are thick. Do not cover very fine seeds or those that germinate best if exposed to the light, such as Cape primroses, gloxinias, temple bells, and African violets. Spray the seeding mixture with a fine mist until it is thoroughly moist. Finally, label each seed tray with a waterproof plastic label.

To keep the seeding mixture moist, cover the seed trays with a sheet of glass or plastic. But first cover the tray with a piece of absorbent white paper to prevent condensation from dripping back onto the seeds. The paper allows some light to pass through if seeds need it.

The seeds of most greenhouse plants will germinate well at 65° F. The tenderer the plant, the higher the temperature required. Warm-greenhouse plants may need 65°–75° F. If the temperature in the greenhouse is not high enough—perhaps in early spring—put the seed tray in a heated propagator.

Seeds vary considerably in the time they take to germinate; so never discard seeds that appear to have failed until you have given them time to break and produce roots.

Pricking out. When the first two to four seed leaves have appeared on each seedling, the seedlings are ready to be transplanted, or pricked out.

Transfer the seedlings individually to 2½-inch pots filled with potting mixture, or set them in large seed trays 1–2 inches apart, depending on the size of the seedlings.

As a precaution against damping-off disease, drench the soil with one of the ready-made damping-off chemicals, such as quintozene. If the disease appears after planting, water the plants and the soil with Captan or zineb solution.

After pricking out, the seedlings should be placed in a well-lighted part of the greenhouse but protected from direct sun.

Move greenhouse-plant seedlings into 3½-inch pots when the smaller pots become filled with roots or when seedlings that have been planted in trays touch each other.

Plants for bedding out in the garden need hardening off (see p. 288).

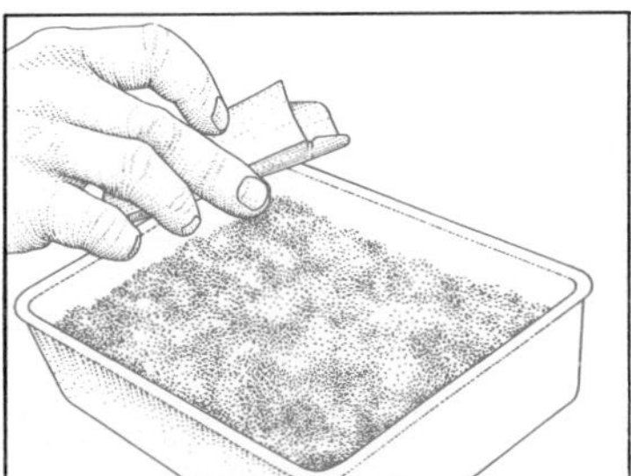

1. *Sow seeds thinly on moist seeding mixture in small trays or pots.*

2. *Cover seeds with more mixture, label tray, and spray with water.*

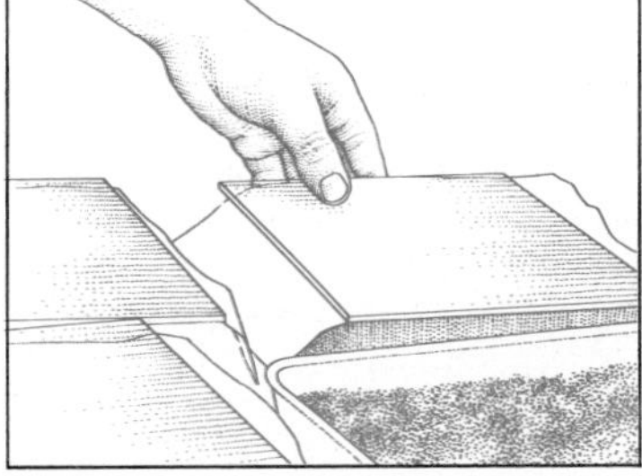

3. *Cover tray with paper, to absorb condensation, then a sheet of glass.*

4. *As soon as leaves appear, move seedlings to pots or flats of potting soil.*

Bulbous Plants for Early Flowers

Many greenhouse plants are grown from bulbs, tubers, corms, and rhizomes. To achieve early results, it is best to start bulbous plants at temperatures 5°–10° F warmer than their normal growing temperature. Examples include achimenes, amaryllises, glory-lilies, temple bells, tuberous begonias, gloxinias, and many of the summer-flowering bulbs and corms that can be given a head start in late winter or early spring. (Exceptions are crocuses, hyacinths, narcissi, and tulips, which are started in temperatures 10°–15° F cooler than normal.)

Bulbs requiring warmth can be put directly into pots and then placed in a warm propagator. However, it is not always easy to determine which end of corms, tubers, and rhizomes should face upward. Hence, they should first be set in moist peat moss in a suitable container and placed in a propagator or on the greenhouse bench. Inspect them every few days until either shoots or roots are visible. Then take them out of the peat moss; pot them, correct end up, in potting soil, and place them in a propagator.

In autumn, after the foliage has begun to fade, allow plants grown from bulbs (also corms and tubers) to go dry. When the plants and soil are quite dry, tip out the contents, and separate the bulbs from the potting soil. Clean any soil from the bulbs, and remove any dead roots. Store the bulbs in dry sand in a dry place at a temperature of 40°–45° F.

Do not tip out and clean plants that have fragile tubers or rhizomes, such as glory-lilies. Such plants are best left in their pots (which should be laid on their sides to avoid accidental watering) in a dry place at 40°–45° F. Then, just before they are due to begin growing again, remove them from their pots and repot in fresh soil mixture. They will probably have multiplied; divide and pot the pieces separately.

How to Increase Your Greenhouse Plants

There are several simple ways of growing new greenhouse plants from existing ones. Some plants respond better to one than another. The easiest techniques of propagation are by stem cuttings and division, both of which produce new plants identical to the parent plant.

Whatever method you use, make sure that you propagate only from completely healthy plants. Never use plants with deformities, yellow or abnormally mottled foliage, or striped or distorted flowers; they may be suffering from virus diseases, and these will be passed on through the cuttings.

Also, if possible, avoid taking cuttings from plants that you feel may have been affected by pests.

Stem Cuttings—An Easy Method

One of the most popular methods of propagating greenhouse plants is to start with stem cuttings. This technique is used for such widely grown plants as fuchsias and regal and zonal geraniums (*Pelargonium*). Stem cuttings can be taken at any time except winter, but spring is best.

Choose a healthy shoot without flowers or flower buds. With a sharp knife, cut off a few inches just below a leaf joint.

Gently pull or cut away the lower leaves and any stipules.

Fill a $2\frac{1}{2}$- or 3-inch pot with equal parts of peat moss and sand or perlite. The mixture should be moist. If the base of each cutting is dipped in hormone rooting powder, rooting will be hastened and made more certain, but this is not essential.

Press the cutting gently into the mixture to just below the lowest leaf. If you are taking more than one cutting, several can be put around the edge of a larger pot.

Cover the pot to keep the cutting in a moist, warm atmosphere, and shade it to prevent loss of moisture through the leaf surfaces. Pots with transparent domes are available for this purpose, or use a piece of clear plastic. Alternatively, ordinary pots or seed trays can be placed in a closed propagating case, or a sheet-plastic tent can be constructed over each pot or tray. To make a tent, bend lengths of wire into the soil, the ends against the rim of the container. Cover with a plastic bag or sheet of polyethylene, and tuck the polyethylene in under the bottom of the container. Keep the pot on a greenhouse shelf, away from strong light.

1. *At any time except winter, cut off a few inches of a healthy shoot without buds or flowers. Cut cleanly immediately below a leaf joint on the stem.*

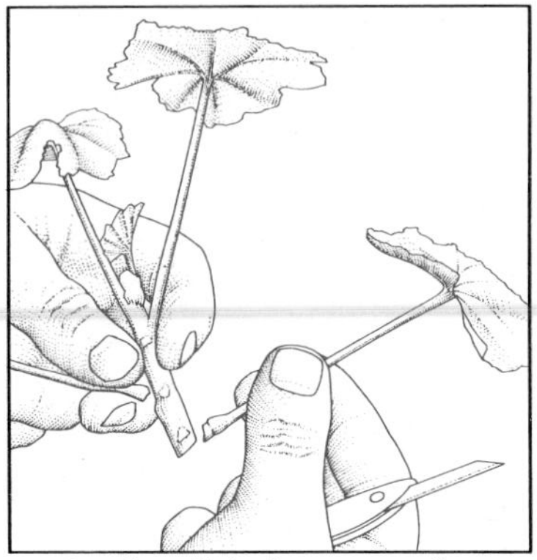

2. *Gently pull the leaves away from the lower part of the cutting.*

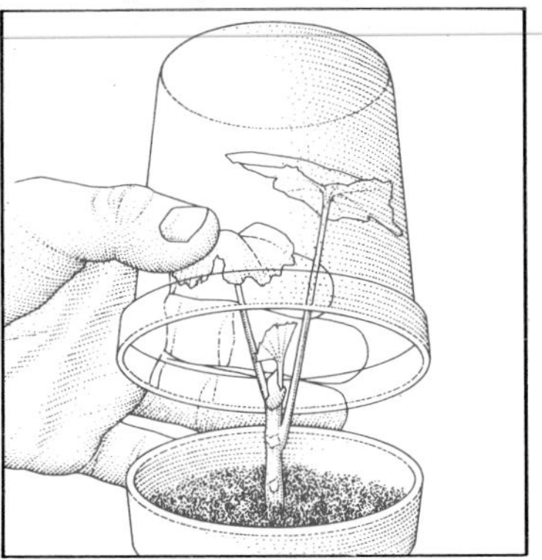

3. *Press the cutting into moist potting mixture, and cover to keep humid.*

Cuttings from many easily grown pot plants can also be rooted in polyethylene bags. Place a little rooting hormone at the bottom of the bag, insert the cuttings in it, seal the top of the bag, and hang it in a warm, well-lighted place—a kitchen is fine.

With all methods except the last, the rooting mixture should be kept moist by spraying occasionally with a fine mist of water.

Bottom heat is essential for the rooting of some warm-greenhouse plants. This heat is most efficiently provided by soil-warming cables that have been installed in a greenhouse propagator (see p. 445).

The formation of top growth is a sign that rooting has occurred. This usually takes three to five weeks. The plants must then be moved into appropriately sized pots of potting mixture (see p. 448).

Most young plants being grown from rooted cuttings should not be exposed to direct sunlight, even if they are sun loving. Only as their roots develop, and then only very gradually, should full sunlight be given to them.

Keep the soil moist but not wet. Waterlogging can prevent formation of roots. Some plants, however, such as *Impatiens sultanii,* will root if you simply put stem cuttings in a glass of clean water.

Leaf Cuttings for Popular Pot Plants

Many widely grown pot plants, such as African violets, Cape primroses, foliage begonias, gloxinias, and snake plants, can be propagated from leaf cuttings in various ways.

One method, often successful with begonias, is to pick a leaf and remove the stalk, and then carefully cut across the veins in several places. Fill a seed tray with coarse builder's sand or equal parts of peat moss and perlite or vermiculite; then, lay the leaves flat on the surface. Weigh them down with pebbles to keep the veins in contact with the soil.

Place a sheet of glass or clear plastic over the tray to retain moisture, and put the covered tray in a warm propagator at a temperature of 65°–70° F. After a few weeks roots should form where the slits were made. Each rooted part will develop a cluster of leaves in six to eight weeks. The parts can then be separated and potted individually in potting mixture. Keep the pots on a greenhouse bench that is shaded from strong sunlight.

For foliage begonias and peperomias, cut the leaves into small triangular sections, with a piece of the stalk at the apex of each. Insert the triangles, apex down, in the potting mixture; cover and treat as above.

The long leaves of plants such as snake plants and Cape primroses can be cut into 2-inch sections. Each section is inserted vertically in the potting mixture, bottom end down.

The best method of propagating African violets and other small-leaved plants is to cut off leaves with ½–1 inch of stem. Insert each stem individually in a 2½-inch pot (or put three stems in a 3½-inch pot) of seeding mixture. Cover the containers with glass or plastic and put in a warm place. Bottom heat of 60°–65° F will produce rooting in 10 to 14 days, and new growth should follow two weeks later.

African violets: taking leaves with stems attached. *Cut off cleanly the required number of leaves, each with ½–1 in. of stem attached. Insert the stems in a pot of seeding mixture so that the base of each leaf just touches the surface. Cover the pot and put it in a warm place.*

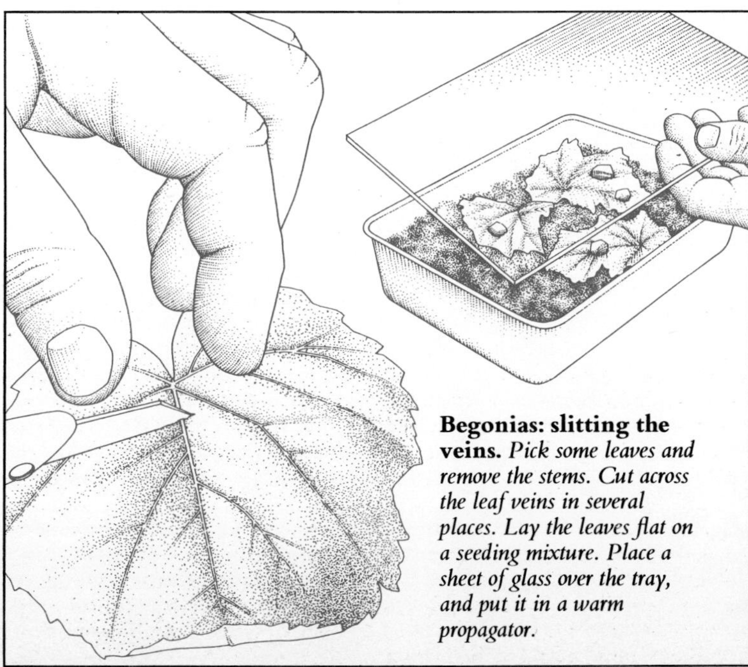

Begonias: slitting the veins. *Pick some leaves and remove the stems. Cut across the leaf veins in several places. Lay the leaves flat on a seeding mixture. Place a sheet of glass over the tray, and put it in a warm propagator.*

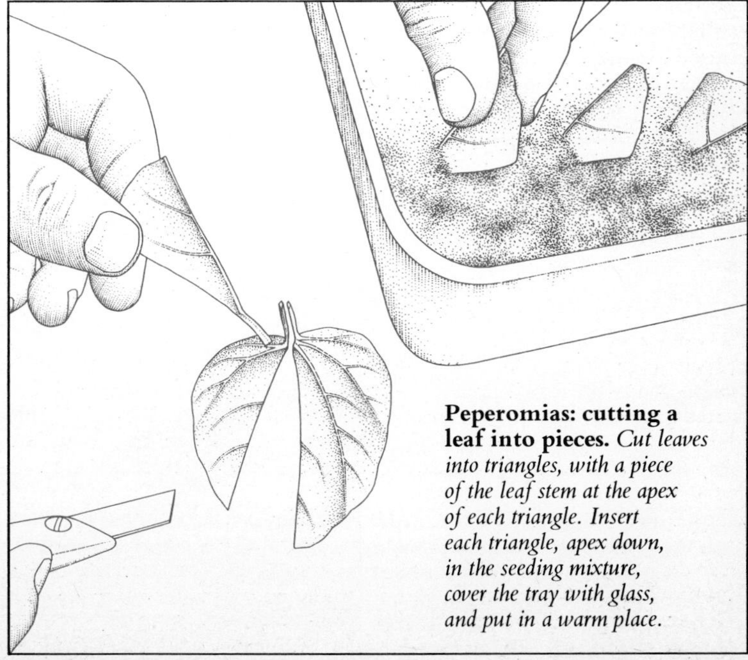

Peperomias: cutting a leaf into pieces. *Cut leaves into triangles, with a piece of the leaf stem at the apex of each triangle. Insert each triangle, apex down, in the seeding mixture, cover the tray with glass, and put in a warm place.*

Increasing Perennial Pot Plants by Division

Division is an easy way of propagating many perennial greenhouse plants. Plants should be divided in early spring, before the new season's growth has begun.

Tap the plant out of its pot along with its soil. If the soil is dry and difficult to dislodge, water it thoroughly first.

Examine the top of the plant to discover where stems or tufts of growth arise. With a very sharp knife, cut firmly down through the plant between the tufts of growth and into the roots. Old or dead roots, or those that have been damaged in the cutting process, should be cut away and discarded.

Pot each segment separately in potting soil. Water the plants moderately, and keep them in shade for a few days. Most flowering plants will bloom the same year.

Many bulbs, including amaryllises, form offsets—small bulbs that sprout from the parent bulb. They can be pulled off when you are repotting and placed individually in 3- to 5-inch pots. Grow the offsets under the same conditions as you did the adult plant. These small bulbs may take two years or longer to reach flowering size.

1. *In early spring cut down through the plant between stems or tufts of growth.*

2. *After removing dead or damaged roots, pot each segment separately.*

Some Other Methods of Increasing Plants

Layering is an effective method of propagating some climbing and trailing plants. Put a mixture of equal parts of peat moss and sand or perlite in a 3- to 4-inch pot near the plant. Bend a branch down so that its stem touches the rooting mixture. Slit the stem at this point, or peel away a tiny piece of the outer skin. Keep the wound in contact with the soil with a staple made from bent wire or with a weight, such as a small stone. When roots have formed, which usually occurs in three or four months, carefully sever the stem from the parent plant.

Greenhouse-grown shrubs that do not root easily from cuttings can often be propagated by air layering. Examples are the gardenia and stephanotis. Air layering is also used to shorten such plants as the rubber plant when they become leggy. The method is described on page 405.

Sometimes seeds can be saved as a means of propagation. There is no use saving seeds from hybrid plants, since they cannot be relied on to yield plants identical to the parent. Seeds of individual species, however, will produce plants that are true to type. Make sure that the seeds are ripe before collecting them, and sow as soon as possible. The technique is explained on page 451.

Some greenhouse plants, such as the strawberry begonia, produce runners with plantlets. These can be pegged down onto soil in the same way as strawberries (see p. 542) in order to produce new rooted plants.

The passionflower can be propagated by detaching the suckers it sends up, each with some roots attached, and planting them.

PRODUCING NEW PLANTS FROM OFFSETS

Some greenhouse bulbs form offsets. Pull these away during repotting, and put each in a pot of the same soil mixture used for the adult plant.

Mist for Quicker and Better Results

Intermittent mist propagation is an expensive but more efficient alternative to keeping cuttings in a closed case or in a plastic bag.

A thin film of moisture can be maintained over all leaf surfaces by means of a water jet automatically controlled by an electronic detector unit. The jet is switched on only when the propagating medium has begun to dry out.

With this method, propagation can be carried out in full sunlight, and the normal processes involved in plant-food formation—known as photosynthesis—can take place.

A mist unit with an enclosure

Bottom heat is usually needed to balance the cooling effect of moisture passing constantly through the rooting mixture and to encourage healing, callus (scab) formation, and rooting of cuttings.

With mist propagation, rooting is more rapid and certain than by other means. Also, there is usually less disease (particularly gray mold) because spores are washed away before they can do any damage.

The only drawback to mist propagation is that cuttings rooted by this method are tenderer than those raised under glass in the ordinary way. They need to be hardened off with great care.

Small misting units with an enclosure to keep the mist within bounds can be bought for slightly more than a heated propagator.

Growing Plants Under Other Forms of Glass

Frames, for Small-Scale Greenhouse Gardening

A garden frame consists of a framework of wood, metal, concrete, or brick covered by hinged, removable, or sliding panes of glass. It can be unheated (then known as a cold frame) or heated.

A frame enables those without a greenhouse to carry out some greenhouse gardening on a small scale. For a gardener with a greenhouse, a frame is an essential adjunct that enables him to "winter over" plants that are in a dormant state until they are needed for forcing or for use in season.

A cold frame is popularly used to harden off plants raised in a greenhouse or on a windowsill before they are planted out in the garden. It can also be used to raise early crops of low-growing vegetables, such as lettuce, radishes, and scallions, thus leaving tomatoes, pole beans, and other tall plants to benefit from the greenhouse's height.

Tender plants, such as calceolarias, cinerarias, cyclamens, and primroses, can be sown in a cold frame in summer and kept there in pots until winter before being transferred to a greenhouse bench.

Cuttings of hardy shrubs and perennials taken in summer can be kept in the frame through the winter before being planted out in spring.

If you provide heat with soil-warming cables, you can broaden the scope of a frame by making it possible to grow even earlier vegetables and to raise a wider range of plants from seeds.

A frame equipped with air-warming cables provides winter protection for many half-hardy plants, such as fuchsias and geraniums, and offers a protected environment for the development of early melons and cucumbers.

Soil-warming and air-warming kits are both available for frames. Have a qualified electrician provide an outdoor electrical outlet. Be sure that a thermostatic control is incorporated in the system (see p. 442).

A portable frame is convenient. (Aluminum alloy framework is lighter and more durable than wood.) It can be moved to sunny or shady locations, depending on the plants being grown or the time of year, and it can be mounted on bricks or concrete blocks to provide extra height.

A row of frames can be placed along one side of a greenhouse that has a brick or concrete base, so that they benefit from its warmth. The frames should be located on the shadier side of the greenhouse to avoid excess heat and sunlight.

To accommodate pot plants the floor of a frame can be covered with gravel. This prevents worms from entering the pots and keeps the potting mixture from becoming soggy.

Cloches, for Vegetables and Cut Flowers

Bell-shaped or tunnellike plant covers, made of glass, paper, or plastic, can be used to great advantage outdoors in combating frost and cold winds. These covers, known as cloches, can be homemade or purchased at garden centers. They speed growth and extend the growing season at beginning and end, particularly in the vegetable garden. Cloches should be placed in position to warm the soil about a week before seeds or plants are put in.

Specific uses of cloches include providing winter protection for hardy crops, such as leeks and carrots; obtaining early yields of strawberries; and growing early cucumbers in relatively cold areas or during cool summers. Several plants grown for cut flowers—such as anemones, violets, or gladioli—can be advanced or protected under cloches.

COLD FRAMES AND CLOCHES

Cold frames are used to grow early vegetables, harden off bedding plants started in the greenhouse, and propagate plants from cuttings and seeds. Heated frames provide even earlier vegetables and widen the range of plants raised from seeds. They can also house tender plants in winter.

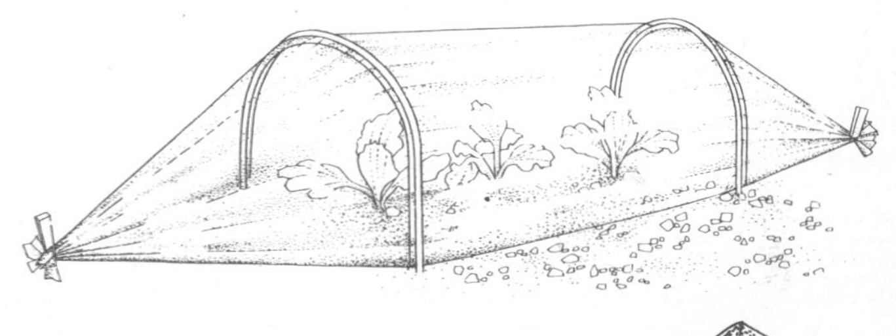

Cloches protect plants, speed up their growth, and extend their growing season at both ends. They can also be used to overwinter hardy crops, to obtain early strawberries, to grow hardy melons and early cucumbers in cold areas, and for propagation. Tunnel- or dome-shaped cloches are easy to make from plastic sheeting supported and secured with double loops of bent wire, one inside the plastic and one outside.

Special Uses for a Greenhouse

Raising Bedding Plants for the Open Garden

Many greenhouse plants can be put out in the open garden to flower during summer. This technique, called summer bedding, can be used for plants needing a minimum greenhouse temperature of 60° F or less. See the chart on page 462.

Using the greenhouse or a frame to raise summer bedding plants from seeds can save a considerable amount of money each year and enable you to experiment with new varieties. Raising greenhouse plants from seeds is described on page 451.

In a greenhouse the seeds of most half-hardy plants can be sown from midwinter to early spring. Fast-growing annuals, such as African marigolds, should not be started until midspring, or they may become spindly by being crowded in boxes until the temperature is suitable for planting them out—in late spring or early summer, depending on the region. The seeds of slow-growing plants, such as wax begonias, should be sown in mid-winter.

Prick out the seedlings into trays or boxes. Plants that are particularly sensitive to root disturbance, such as zinnias and stocks, grow better if seeds are sown directly in individual small pots, then transplanted and kept in large pots until they are ready for planting outdoors.

Some popular bedding plants can be raised from cuttings. Examples are fuchsias, zonal geraniums, and all chrysanthemums except annuals.

All plants for bedding out must be hardened off gradually before they are fully exposed to the weather. First, move plants to a relatively cool portion of the greenhouse. Then, transfer them to closed, unheated frames. Gradually increase the ventilation of the frames until they are left fully open all the time.

Half-hardy bedding plants should not be planted out until all danger of frost has passed.

Growing Climbers and Wall Shrubs

A few climbing vines or wall shrubs trained to grow up to the roof on wires can give your new greenhouse an attractive, well-established look in a fairly short time. Such plants also make use of the upper half of the greenhouse, which is all too often simply wasted space.

Climbing vines and wall shrubs are particularly useful in a lean-to greenhouse, where a bare supporting wall can be effectively covered. They also give shade in the summer, partially covering the greenhouse roof, so that shade-loving plants can be grown below.

Many vines and wall shrubs can be planted permanently in a greenhouse border, where they will flourish for many years, needing little attention apart from an annual topdressing of well-rotted manure or compost and regular cutting back in the autumn.

Ideal for growing in a border are bougainvilleas, flowering maples, glory-bushes, lapagerias, passionflowers, and plumbagos.

Some vines are better suited to growing in pots to contain their growth. And, like jasmine, which flowers in the winter, they benefit from being put outside during the summer months.

Other climbers suitable for pots include the cup-and-saucer vine, dipladenia, glory-lily, and the annual morning glory. Start these plants in 4-inch pots, and repot them as they grow until they are in 8-inch containers, where they will flower. Staking will be necessary.

All the climbers mentioned can be grown in a cool greenhouse where the winter temperature does not drop below 40°–45° F. However, flowering maples, jasmines, lapagerias, and passionflowers can all be grown in a sheltered spot in an unheated greenhouse if it is located in an area where the outside temperature does not drop below 20° F.

Month by Month in a Greenhouse

January

Clean the panes to let in maximum light. Ventilate a cool or cold greenhouse on mild and sunny days. Water sparingly, especially during dull, cold, or foggy weather. Remove dead and dying leaves and flowers before they become a source of disease. Cuttings that are being wintered over, especially those of geraniums, should be regularly checked for leaf removal.

Ventilate a warm greenhouse if the inside temperature exceeds 70° F. Spray the walks and underbench areas with the hose.

Take cuttings of late-flowering chrysanthemums. Cuttings taken in December will be ready for potting at the end of January.

Open the air vents to keep carnations cool on mild and sunny days. Water and feed sparingly. Cuttings can be taken. Pot rooted cuttings taken earlier. Check for aphids and carnation rust; spray if necessary.

Water all orchids only when absolutely necessary. Damp down on sunny days. Paphiopedilums that have finished flowering can be repotted if they are crowded.

February

Ventilate cool and cold greenhouses on sunny and mild days; lightly damp down paths and benches with a fine-spray watering can around midday. Mature plants whose roots have filled the pots dry out quickly and therefore require daily watering.

Ventilate a warm greenhouse if the temperature exceeds 70° F. Also, damp it down lightly.

Move dormant fuchsias to greenhouse benches, and water lightly. Mist plants each day, and as growth commences, increase the frequency of watering. Maintain a minimum temperature of 45°–50° F.

Seeds of half-hardy and tender annuals and perennials, such as tuberous and fibrous begonias, celosias, coleuses, and Cape primroses, can be sown if a minimum temperature of 55°–60° F can be maintained in the greenhouse. Sow schizanthuses in February to provide flowers for late spring and early summer.

Tomatoes for planting out under glass in April should be sown about the middle of February. They will need a temperature near 60° F.

At the end of the month, a batch of achimenes can be started. Place the scaly rhizomes in moist peat moss, about 1 inch apart, at a temperature of 55°–60° F. When the shoots are about 1–2 inches tall, place four or five together in a 5-inch pot, and put the pot on a greenhouse bench, to wait for further plant development to take place.

Passionflowers and plumbagos can be pruned toward the end of February. Cut back all of the previous season's shoots to within 3 inches of their bases.

Pot the chrysanthemum cuttings that were taken in January; keep young plants moist.

Ventilate carnations on mild and sunny days. Water and fertilize them sparingly. Pinch out all but the terminal buds of flowering stems (this is called disbudding). For indoor use cut the flowers as soon as they open. Take more cuttings. Pot those already rooted.

Ventilate orchids during mild or sunny spells. Water sparingly, but make sure that the plants do not dry out and the pseudobulbs do not shrivel. Cymbidiums, dendrobiums, and paphiopedilums that have finished flowering can be repotted.

March

Ventilate, damp down, and water as necessary (see February). Some shading may be needed. Move overwintered annuals and established plants that are pot-bound to larger pots.

Sow seeds of half-hardy and tender annuals and perennials. Prick out seedlings from earlier sowings. Complete the pruning of climbers, such as plumbagos, that was begun in February.

Begonias, achimenes, and other plants with dormant fleshy roots should be started into growth at a temperature of 55°–60° F. Amaryllis bulbs can be started in a slightly cooler temperature. Begin watering when leaves appear.

Prick out tomato seedlings.

Rooted cuttings of late chrysanthemums should be put in a cold frame in midspring. Cover the cold frame if frost is expected.

Repot carnations and pinch out the growing tips. Ventilate freely on warm days.

In long sunny periods shade orchids during the hottest part of the day. Damp down daily except in cold weather. Continue repotting as required.

April

Increase ventilation as the weather grows warmer, and make sure that plants do not dry out. Shade the glass during long sunny spells. Damp down the greenhouse regularly during warm periods.

Complete potting of tuberous begonias and other dormant fleshy roots. Sow seeds of false Jerusalem cherries and campanulas at a minimum temperature of 55°–60° F.

Divide overgrown orchids that have finished flowering. Shade the greenhouse during sunny spells, and damp it down regularly. Water freely; but unless plants are growing vigorously, let them dry out between waterings.

For one of the most spectacular greenhouse color displays, sow cineraria seeds now for flowering next winter. Keep the seedlings as cool as possible, repotting them as they grow. Watch carefully for insects, and spray when necessary. The final potting should be in an 8-inch container. The numerous flower stems will push their way up through the foliage to form a crown of brightly colored, daisylike blossoms.

May

Ventilate freely during the day. Damp down and water the plants daily, and pay special attention to shading young plants. Pinch out the growing tips of young fuchsia, plumbago, and chrysanthemum plants to promote bushy growth. Move plants to larger pots at regular intervals.

Put chrysanthemums into their final pots before the end of the month. Support them with stakes. A week to 10 days later, move the pots to a holding position outdoors.

Ventilate carnations freely. Shade them lightly. Damp down regularly. Move young rooted cuttings to larger pots. Move second-year plants in 6-inch pots to 8-inch pots. Make a second pinching of new growth.

Shade orchids, and damp the walks down often. Water freely.

Ivy geraniums should be well rooted by now, having been started as stem cuttings in early winter. Three or four plants in a 10-inch pot will become a showpiece by early summer, with the trailing stems covered with white, pink, or red flowers against apple-green foliage.

June

Pay particular attention to watering during hot spells, since well-rooted pot plants can dry out in a few hours. Ventilate freely on all warm days, and damp down the paths and benches once or twice daily.

Take softwood cuttings of begonias, coleuses, flowering maples, fuchsias, glory-bushes, and geraniums. Leaf cuttings of Cape primroses and rex begonias can be taken also. As soon as they are well rooted, set them into individual pots.

Give exhibition incurved and single varieties of chrysanthemums a second pinching sometime around the middle of the month.

Wash down unused benches. Replace broken or loose glass. Remove weeds from walks. Control insects.

July/August

Sow seeds of cineraria early in July, and sow seeds of calceolaria from mid-July on in cold frames. Softwood and leaf cuttings can still be taken. Water, ventilate, and damp down as during June.

In August take cuttings of *Campanula isophylla*. Rest amaryllis bulbs by reducing watering.

The stems of late chrysanthemums for exhibition should be reduced to the strongest two or three per plant.

Ventilate carnations freely, and shade lightly on the hottest days. Continue to disbud. Water and fertilize regularly.

Continue to water orchids freely. Begin to expose cymbidiums to full sunlight. Large plants can be placed outdoors in a sheltered location.

September

Continue to ventilate, damp down, and water as during the summer unless the weather turns cold. Reduce feeding toward the end of the month, stopping it entirely for plants that have finished growing. Bring in the young cineraria and calceolaria plants from the cold frames.

Sow seeds of annuals for spring flowering under glass. Begin potting spring-flowering bulbs.

Toward the end of the month, bring late-flowering chrysanthemums into the greenhouse.

Plant tender bulbs such as Cape cowslips in a cool greenhouse.

Water all orchids more sparingly than during preceding months. Give cymbidiums full sunlight.

October

Halt all fertilizing by the end of the month, and remove permanent shading on all but the ferns. Ventilate and damp down on warm days, but prepare to turn on the heat in cool and warm houses in case of frost.

Thin out overgrown climbers.

Ventilate chrysanthemums during the day, but give them a little heat on very frosty nights. Pinch out all but the terminal buds of late-flowering varieties.

Cuttings of carnations can be taken from October until March.

Reduce damping down and watering of orchids. Remove shading by the end of the month. Odontoglossums that have finished flowering can be repotted or divided.

November

Ventilate cool and cold greenhouses on sunny days, but shut the ventilators early in the afternoon. Complete the potting of autumn-sown annuals, like salpiglossises and schizanthuses, for a spring display. Pot rooted cuttings of zonal geraniums, fuchsias, and heliotropes.

Several hardy perennials, such as astilbes and polyanthus primroses, will flower during the late winter in a cool greenhouse if lifted from the garden now. Pot them, but leave them outside until later.

Maintain a minimum temperature of 45° F for carnations; ventilate on mild or sunny days. Disbud flowering stems; feed and water sparingly.

Restrict ventilation of orchids to mild and sunny days.

December

Do any necessary watering and ventilating on mild and sunny days. Clean the glass so that winter sunlight is not further diffused. Remove dead or dying leaves and flowers.

Astilbes and polyanthus primroses (*Primula polyantha*), potted for early flowering, can be brought into a cool greenhouse.

Water stock plants of late chrysanthemums, and increase temperature. Begin taking cuttings toward the end of the month.

Continue to disbud carnations; water and fertilize sparingly. Maintain minimum temperature of 45° F.

Ventilate orchids for a few hours on sunny days only. Water mature plants thoroughly only twice a month until they finish flowering.

What Can Go Wrong With Greenhouse Plants

This chart describes the commonest disorders likely to occur on the plants usually grown in a greenhouse. If any of your plants show symptoms that are not described below, consult the section on plant disorders beginning on page 600. Look up chemicals on page 635 to find trade names.

Symptoms and signs	Cause	Control
Young shoots and leaves are stunted or malformed; covered with greenish, pink, or black insects.	Aphids	Spray with Diazinon, dimethoate, or malathion.
Plant lacks vigor and looks yellowish; may wilt even when soil is moist. When plant is dug up or knocked out of pot, roots will show numerous small, soft insects in white cottony masses.	Mealybugs on roots	Soak root system with Diazinon, malathion, or nicotine.
Stems and leaf axils are infested with small insects covered with white "cotton." Plant may yellow; leaves may drop prematurely.	Mealybugs on stems	Spray with malathion, nicotine, or systemic insecticide, repeating at regular intervals until no insects are visible. If infestation is light, wipe off insects with soft brush or cloth soaked in soapy water; or use cotton swabs and rubbing alcohol.
Leaves are yellow and finely mottled; eventually they shrivel or fall prematurely. In severe attacks shoots become weakened and covered with fine webbing.	Red spider mites	Spray with Diazinon, malathion, or rotenone. Systemic insecticides, such as dimethoate or oxydemeton-methyl, can be used.
Stems and leaves bear small, soft, pale brown insects shaped like shields. Plant vigor may be reduced; leaves may yellow and fall prematurely.	Scale insects	Spray with malathion, nicotine, or systemic insecticide. If infestation is light, wipe off insects with soft brush or cloth soaked in soapy water or mild detergent.
Leaves (occasionally flowers) become brittle and puckered or distorted. Growing points may die.	Tarsonemid mites (cyclamen or broad mites)	Dip plants in chlorobenzilate or dicofol. Or use sprays of chlorobenzilate or dicofol.
Leaves and petals show mottling or bleached areas. Buds and leaves may be distorted.	Thrips	Spray or dust with chlorpyrifos, malathion, nicotine, or rotenone.
Leaves may be mottled with yellow; young shoots lack vigor. When plant is shaken lightly, tiny white insects take wing.	Whiteflies	Spray repeatedly with malathion, pyrethrum, or resmethrin. Fumigate with dichlorvos or nicotine. Whiteflies are especially difficult to eradicate.

Symptoms and signs	Cause	Control
Stems, leaves, flower buds, and flowers show brown dead patches. These become covered with fluffy, grayish-white mold, particularly when weather remains cool and humid.	Botrytis, or gray mold (fungus)	Fumigate with tecnazene smoke; or spray with Benomyl, chlorothalonil, or thiophanate-methyl.
Seedlings, especially those sown thickly in pots or glass-covered pans, rot at ground level and eventually topple over.	Damping-off (fungus)	Water with Captan or quintozene. To prevent occurrence of disease, treat susceptible seeds with protectant (such as Benomyl or Captan) before planting.
Leaves and young shoots have white powdery coating and are often distorted. Powdery areas may take on purplish or reddish hues; leaves may fall prematurely.	Powdery mildew (fungus)	Fumigate with dinocap smoke; or spray with Benomyl, dinocap, or thiophanate-methyl.
Potted rhododendrons and azaleas show mottled yellow leaves and may flower poorly.	Chlorosis or iron chlorosis	Repot in acid compost or peat-based compost lacking lime. Provide with clean rainwater. Spray plants with chelated iron.
Flower buds yellow, wither, and frequently drop prematurely. Growing points may be shriveled; leaves appear somewhat flaccid and lack luster. Plants wilt readily.	Persistent lack of water, which may result from limited space between pot rim and soil level	Affected plants should be watered thoroughly, which can be accomplished by standing pots in bucket of water for several minutes. At subsequent waterings make sure that enough moisture is supplied; some water should trickle from drainage holes. To ensure sufficient space for watering, leave distance equal to at least $\frac{1}{10}$ of pot depth between pot rim and soil.
Plants in pots or containers produce thin growth and lack vigor. Leaves are small and often yellowish. No signs of pests or diseases.	Starvation	Apply liquid fertilizer; foliar feed may also be necessary. If plant is pot-bound, replant in larger pot or divide roots.
Leaves have brown margins and appear scorched or bleached. Plant growth may be checked.	Usually combination of too much heat and lack of shade	If air temperature around plants under glass is greater than 85° F, supply ventilation, shading, or both. (Many cacti and other succulents do well at such high temperatures and should not be shaded or ventilated.) Plants that have suffered excess heat should be shaded and watered sparingly for 3–4 da. If they are pot-bound, apply liquid or foliar feed.

Eight of the Most Popular Greenhouse Plants

Begonias

With their beautiful flowers and foliage, the many begonias (*Begonia* species and hybrids) make excellent greenhouse plants.

Tuberous-rooted begonias. Many large, mostly double-flowered begonias grow from tuberous roots, rather like dahlias. They include the trailing kinds that are popular for growing in hanging baskets.

Start the tubers into growth in damp peat moss (see p. 451) whenever a minimum of 60° F can be maintained. When placing the tubers in the peat moss, make sure that the flat or concave side is at the top, just level with the surface.

Inspect the tubers every three or four days. As leafy shoots appear, pot each tuber into a 3½-inch pot. Use a potting mixture (see p. 448) to which leaf mold has been added in equal parts (50 percent potting mixture and 50 percent leaf mold). As the roots fill these pots, move the plants into final 5- or 7-inch pots.

Begonia stems and foliage are usually brittle; so tie the stems to a bamboo stake at an early stage.

When plants are in their final pots, give liquid feedings monthly.

To obtain deep colors and to keep the greenhouse cool in summer, shade the glass during sunny weather. Blooms of above-average size can be produced by allowing only one shoot to develop from each tuber. Remove the other shoots and use them as cuttings (see p. 452). Remove female flowers (which have a winged capsule behind the bud) as they develop; they will form only single blooms.

Sow tuberous begonia seeds in January in a warm greenhouse or a propagating frame with a temperature of 60°–65° F to get a colorful display the same year. Tubers will form and can be saved.

At the end of the year, when the foliage of tuberous begonias begins to yellow, gradually reduce the amount and frequency of watering until the pots are dry. Turn out the contents of the pots, remove soil adhering to the tubers, and store the tubers for the winter in dry sand or perlite in a dry place at 40°–45° F.

Tuberous-rooted begonias can be put out as summer bedding plants. The winter-flowering Lorraine varieties are grown from cuttings taken in the spring for flowering the following November, at a temperature of approximately 50° F.

Fibrous-rooted begonias. The small-flowered wax begonia (*B. semperflorens*), which is popular for bedding out, is grown from seeds and has fibrous roots.

Fibrous-rooted begonias flower well in 3½-inch pots, but some large-flowered forms do better in 5-inch pots. For the maximum flowering period, sow seeds in early January at a temperature of 65°–75° F. No pinching or staking is necessary. Flowering is prolonged if faded flowers and seedpods are regularly removed.

Foliage begonias. Rex begonias (*B. rex-cultorum*) are grown for their leaves, which are patterned in silver, cream, red, and purple. The iron cross (*B. masoniana*) is another foliage type, with bronze-purple markings.

Give foliage begonias humidity and shade in summer. In winter keep them just moist at a temperature of approximately 60° F. Move them to larger pots in April, and increase them by division at the same time. They can also be increased by leaf cuttings (see p. 453).

Calceolarias

Calceolarias, or pocketbook plants (*Calceolaria herbeohybrida*), have long been favorite greenhouse pot plants. They produce exotic, pouchlike blooms in a wide range of colors and sizes, often with vividly contrasting patterns or spots. Recently introduced F_1 hybrids are particularly easy to grow and fast flowering.

To grow calceolarias as bedding plants, sow seeds in March at 50°–55° F. Plant out in the garden at the end of spring. Discard the plants after they have flowered.

For Christmas and winter flowering sow seeds in May or June. No artificial warmth is required.

For convenience seedlings can first be transferred to seed flats at 2-inch intervals. Keep the flats in cold frames shaded from direct sunlight. See that the plants do not become dry at any stage, and keep a constant watch for aphids.

When the plants are large enough, pot them individually in 5-inch pots; put the more compact types in 3½-inch pots. When buds begin to appear, give the plants regular liquid feeding. The taller varieties will need to be supported with stakes.

Bring the plants into the greenhouse in early fall. Grow them through the winter at about 45° F. Discard plants after flowering.

To prevent wilting caused by sudden temperature rises and strong sunlight, shade plants that flower from late winter to early spring.

During winter ventilate whenever the weather permits to lessen the risk of fungous disease. Since they often blacken calceolarias, fumigants should not be used to control pests. Do not spray the plants when they are in bloom; this can cause rotting.

Cinerarias

The daisylike flowers of cinerarias (*Senecio hybridus*) develop profusely in a cool greenhouse from December to June. They are often richly colored and are sometimes banded with white. Cinerarias are divided into the following groups: large, broad-petaled flowers; broad-petaled flowers; narrow-petaled flowers; and double flowers.

Sow and grow cinerarias as described for calceolarias, with this exception: most kinds will need a final 5-inch pot, and large-flowered forms may require a 7-inch pot. For early and Christmas flowering, seeds

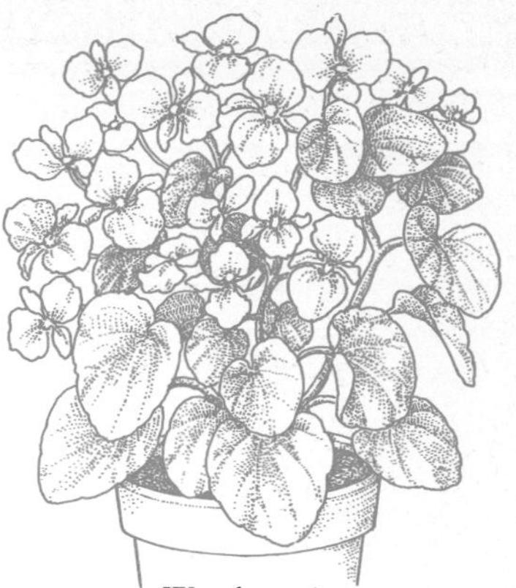

Wax begonia (*Begonia semperflorens*)

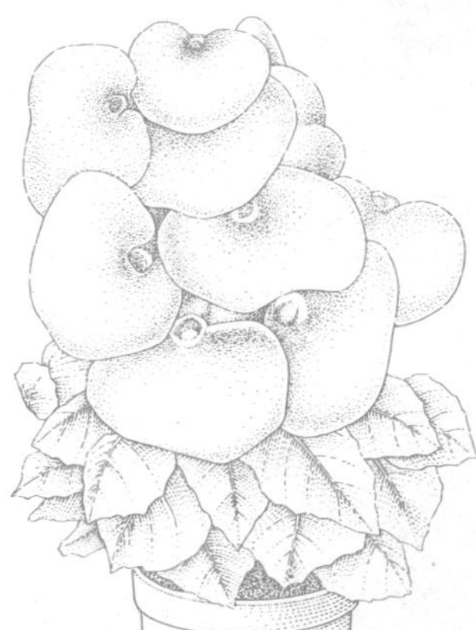

Calceolaria herbeohybrida

Cineraria (*Senecio hybridus*)

Cyclamen persicum

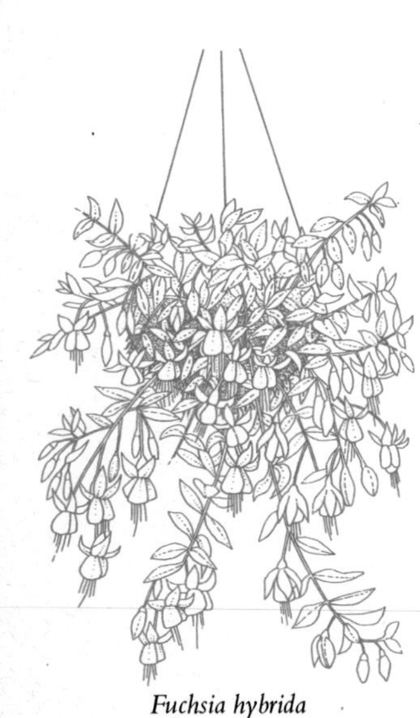
Fuchsia hybrida

should be sown earlier than for calceolarias, in April. Discard the plants after they have flowered.

Cyclamens

Cyclamens (*Cyclamen persicum,* or *C. indicum*) are graceful, sometimes sweetly scented plants. The foliage often bears beautiful silver markings. Miniature varieties and varieties with frilled flowers and double flowers have been introduced.

Cyclamens react to wide differences in temperature, erratic watering, or drafts by wilting and failing to produce flowers.

Repot new tubers in summer, and place the pots in a shady frame. Water lightly until a root system has developed; then begin to water more generously. In late September return the plants to the greenhouse.

A temperature of about 45° F should be maintained for best results. In areas where low autumn temperatures are likely, put the plants in the greenhouse earlier.

Flowering can be expected from winter to spring. Feed and water regularly during late spring and early summer. Later on in the summer rest the plants in a shady cold frame by keeping the soil almost dry. Repot plants the following September, using the same size container and fresh soil.

When moving into a larger pot at any stage, be sure that the top of the tuber, however small, protrudes above the soil. After some years the tuber usually (but not always) begins to produce fewer flowers.

Cyclamens can also be grown from seeds. The seeds are large and can be sown individually. Sow them on the surface of a seeding mixture, and cover them with a ½-inch-deep layer of moist peat moss that has been rubbed through a sieve to remove lumps. The best time for sowing is from August to November. After sowing place the containers in a propagator, and maintain a steady temperature of about 65° F to avoid erratic germination. As the seedlings appear above the peat moss, prick them out promptly into 2½-inch pots of potting mixture (see p. 448). Be sure to soak clay pots in water for at least 15 minutes before using them. This will prevent them from drawing the moisture out of the soil.

Maintain the seedlings in these pots at a temperature of 60°–65° F. Keep the potting mixture moist. When the plants are clearly growing vigorously, lower the temperature to about 55° F. In April move the plants into 5-inch pots. After there is no more danger of frost, transfer them to a shady frame outside.

In September—or earlier if temperatures have descended to 50° F—bring the plants into the greenhouse. Remove any early flower buds to conserve the plants' resources for their major blooming, from December to spring. Give liquid feedings when buds first form.

Fuchsias

Fuchsias (*Fuchsia hybrida*) have many merits. They are relatively easy to grow and have a long flowering season—through summer and autumn. They can be trained to grow into various shapes and are good summer bedding plants. Varieties differ widely: some trail or hang; others are erect; some have variegated foliage; and still others have decorative berries after the flowers.

Buy the plants as rooted cuttings in early spring, and pot them in 2½-inch pots filled with potting mixture (see p. 448). Keep the newly potted plants well shaded for 24 hours to keep evaporation to a minimum, and grow them in a temperature of 50° F. Move the plants to final 5-inch pots in April or May.

Most fuchsias need to be trained into a form. The simplest form is the bush, which is produced by pinching out shoots to induce bushy growth. Rooted cuttings can be stopped (pinched) when they are only a few inches high, so that more shoots will rise from the lower parts of the stem.

The growing tips of trailing plants in hanging baskets should also be pinched out when the leading shoot is just over the basket edge. Large baskets or hanging containers look best if three plants are placed in them at even intervals.

A "standard" is a miniature tree and is a beautiful form to use in displaying fuchsias. In training a standard, do not remove the growing tip immediately. Encourage the plant to grow a single stem by removing all side shoots but retaining the leaves that come directly from the stem. As the stem grows longer, tie it to a cane to ensure upright growth. When the standard is as high as you want it, pinch out the growing tip. Pinch out the side shoots near the top when they are 2 or 3 inches long, to promote branching. Eventually, a bushy head will develop.

During the period of active growth prior to flowering, remove any weak shoots and give liquid feedings. After pinching out, plants should take six to eight weeks to form flowers, so long as they are not pinched again.

Most of the named varieties of greenhouse fuchsias are not hardy and must be kept in a cool greenhouse. Give them just enough water in winter to keep the soil slightly moist. In cool conditions some plants may lose their foliage and become dormant, in which case keep them fairly dry.

In spring, when new growth appears, begin watering and repotting. When the sources of new growth have been identified, cut away all dead shoots. Unwanted new shoots, removed to develop a shape, can be used for cuttings.

During summer fuchsias need a cool, moist atmosphere and ventilation. They should also be slightly shaded. Remove promptly any faded flowers and their seedpods to ensure that the maximum number of flowers is produced.

Geraniums

The commonest geraniums (*Pelargonium*) are the zonals (*P. hortorum*). Recently, some lovely F_1 hybrid strains have been introduced.

Sow zonal geraniums as early in the year as possible, at a temperature of about 60° F, for flowering during summer and autumn. After germination, transfer the seedlings to 3-inch pots, and later move them into 5-inch pots.

To obtain winter flowers, take cuttings (see p. 452) early in the year from last year's plants that you kept in the greenhouse. Pot the rooted cuttings, and encourage bushy growth by pinching the tips when they are a few inches high.

During summer sink the pots in soil outdoors in a sunny position; keep the soil moist. Remove any flower buds, and in autumn move the plants into the greenhouse. Given a minimum winter temperature of 50° F, a dry atmosphere, very little water (water every three days), and as much sunlight as possible, the plants should flower well during the winter months.

The regal, or show, geranium (*P. domesticum*) is the important greenhouse plant, as contrasted with the zonal geranium, which is the outdoor garden species. The former geraniums have a wide color range, but they flower for a much shorter period than zonals. Regals can be bought from a specialist nursery, or cuttings from existing plants can be taken either in early spring or during July and August (see p. 452).

Pinch out the growing tips of young plants at an early stage to promote bushy growth. To avoid straggly specimens, cut back old plants when they show signs of growth in spring.

Ivy geraniums (*P. peltatum*) are mostly trailing plants. They are ideal for hanging baskets but can also be trained on a trellis or along wires on the wall of a lean-to. They have a long flowering period, like zonals, and should be grown in the same way. An early pinching out promotes branching.

The scented-leaved geraniums produce less showy flowers. They include a number of species and varieties named after their leaf scents: nutmeg, lemon, orange, rose, and so forth. The foliage is attractive.

All these geraniums need a moist (but not waterlogged) soil throughout their growing period. In winter most survive best in low humidity and in soil kept rather dry. Excessive cold and damp can cause root rot and basal stem rot. Frost is usually fatal. Ventilate in winter whenever the weather permits.

These geraniums root readily from cuttings taken during spring and summer (see p. 452). Rooted cuttings can be kept growing through the winter with a minimum temperature of about 50° F.

Regal geraniums need some shade when they are grown under glass, but in general geraniums do best in a great amount of light. Shading is necessary only to prevent extremely high temperatures and scorching.

Primroses

The vast primose genus, *Primula,* includes three popular greenhouse plants. The German primrose (*Primula obconica*) is a perennial, notable for seldom lacking blossoms. It will flower in its first year if seeds are sown in January or February. The fairy primrose (*P. malacoides*), which produces dainty circular tiers of flowers in spring, is raised as a biennial. The Chinese primrose (*P. sinensis*), also a biennial, has a thick stem that bears two or three whorls of brightly colored flowers in early spring. *P. obconica* and *P. sinensis* have hairy leaves that can irritate sensitive skins.

Sow seeds of *P. malacoides* and *P. sinensis* from May to August. No supplementary heat is necessary for germination. Sow *P. obconica* seeds from January to June at a temperature of approximately 60° F. In all cases, prick out seedlings into 2½-inch pots. Use the standard potting mixture (see p. 448). These primulas sometimes self-sow, so that all that is necessary is to pot whatever quantity you desire. Move plants into larger pots as required, keeping them well shaded and the potting mixture evenly moist. *P. obconica* needs a final 5- or 6-inch pot; the others need pots 4–5 inches in diameter. Grow them through the winter at a minimum temperature of about 45° F.

Schizanthuses

Schizanthuses (*Schizanthus*), also known as butterfly flowers or poor man's orchids, are dainty annuals that are usually grown as biennials in the greenhouse, flowering in spring from a late-summer sowing. The commonly available giant-flowered hybrids bear masses of richly colored flowers, usually gold veined.

Sow schizanthuses in fall at 50°–60° F. Pinch out the growing tips and side shoots when plants are a few inches high. Three weeks later pinch out the tips again to promote bushy growth. Put in 3-inch pots. In February move into 5- to 7-inch pots.

Schizanthus plants benefit from a liquid feeding every two weeks as they grow. Each plant should be tied to a stake hidden in the foliage.

In winter, schizanthuses can be grown at 45°–50° F, needing only frost-free conditions and all possible light. In summer, shade the plants to prevent scorching.

To grow schizanthuses as annuals, use the dwarf compact varieties described in seed catalogs. 'Dwarf Bouquet' and 'Hit Parade' are especially satisfactory. These can be grown attractively without any pinching and will flower well in 3½-inch pots. If you prefer larger plants, however, they can be pinched once and moved into 5-inch pots. Sow seeds in late summer at about 50° F for bloom in early winter.

Regal geranium
(*Pelargonium domesticum*)

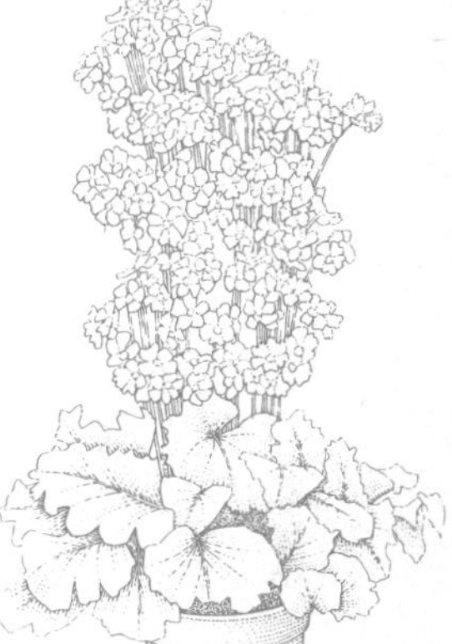

Fairy primrose
(*Primula malacoides*)

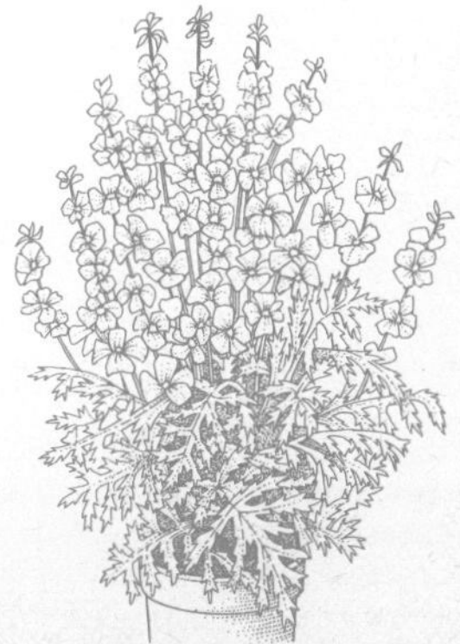

Schizanthus hybrid

Guide to Greenhouse Plants

The following two charts provide a varied selection of plants for the cool and the warm greenhouse. Each of the plants has been listed by its best known common name followed by its botanical name. In the first column its habit of growth, flowers, foliage, fruits, or any other outstanding features are described. Height (H) and spread (S) are also given.

In the second column the flowering times are listed by season.

The third column lists each plant's special requirements for growth, including light, humidity, and other prerequisites. The term "full light" means a full day of direct sun. Unless otherwise specified, temperature requirements are given for minimum nighttime readings in winter.

The last column lists methods of propagation in order of preference; where given simply as "cuttings," stem cuttings are meant (see p. 452).

PLANTS FOR THE COOL GREENHOUSE

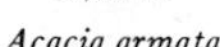
Acacia armata

Achimenes grandiflora

Aeschynanthus speciosus

Amaryllis (*Hippeastrum* hybrid)

Ardisia crispa

Asparagus densiflorus 'Myers'

Common and botanical names, general characteristics	Flowering time	Special requirements and remarks	Propagation
Acacia *(Acacia armata)* Shrub. Thorny branches are covered with soft yellow flowers shaped like powder puffs. Delicate fernlike leaves are soft green. H 4-10 ft.; S 3 ft.	Early spring-midspring	Provide full light, low humidity, and moderate watering from early winter until plant is in full leaf. Then increase watering. Reduce watering after flowering. Prune to control size.	Sow seeds in midspring, first nicking seed coat with knife, then boiling for 30 sec. to hasten germination.
Achimenes *(Achimenes grandiflora)* Tuberous perennial. Tubular flowers in various colors have large lips. Attractive dark green foliage. H 1 ft.; S 1 ft.	Midsummer-midfall	Requires shaded location and high humidity. Reduce watering and allow to rest in cool place from late fall until late winter. Maintain minimum nighttime temperature of 55° F. Good for hanging baskets.	Start tubers in peat moss in early spring. Or root 4- to 5-in. cuttings of new growth in mixture of equal amounts of sand and peat moss; maintain 65° F and high humidity.
Aeschynanthus *(Aeschynanthus speciosus,* or *Trichosporum splendens)* Trailing vines with clusters of tubular yellow and scarlet flowers at ends of branches. Leaves are small, thick, glossy. H 3 in.; S 1-2 ft.	Late spring-early fall	Provide partial shade and high humidity. Potting mixture should have extra peat moss to keep foliage growing. Work 1 tbsp. bone meal lightly into soil every 6 mo.	Root cuttings in mid to late spring, keeping them at 70° F until rooted.
Amaryllis (*Hippeastrum* hybrids) Bulb. Large trumpet-shaped flowers of white, pink, salmon, or red are produced on top of sturdy 18-in. stems prior to growth of straplike dark green leaves. H 1-2 ft.; S 8 in.-1 ft.	Midfall-early summer	Grow in full light to partial shade. Water sparingly when growth starts; increase gradually. After flowering, water until foliage begins to die back; then stop. Pot with top one-third of bulb exposed.	Pot offsets individually in early spring. Seeds sown in late winter will take 1½ yr. to bloom.
Ardisia *(Ardisia crispa)* Evergreen shrub. Small white flowers develop into bright red berries. Deep green leaves with wavy margins have pointed tips. H 3 ft.; S 1½ ft.	Late summer, followed by fruit that remains for 3 mo.	Provide full light, moderate humidity, and plenty of ventilation. Keep well watered and feed once a month. Repot and prune in midspring.	Root heeled softwood cuttings in early spring. Maintain humidity with mist or plastic sheeting. Sow seeds in late summer; keep at 65° F until germination.
Asparagus (*Asparagus densiflorus* 'Myers') Perennial grown for its spires of needlelike evergreen leaves. Small white flowers and red berries do not enhance beauty greatly. Often sold as *A. myersii.* H 2 ft.; S 1½ ft.	All year	Does best in full light and moderate humidity; place on saucer of pebbles, and water if humidity is low. Keep humidity highest during summer.	Divide large plant (8-in. pot) into 6 or 7 plants at any time; place each in 3- to 4-in. pot. Sow seeds in midspring in mixture of equal amounts of peat moss and sand; germinates at 65° F.

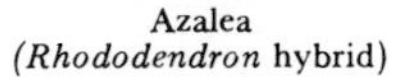

Azalea (*Rhododendron* hybrid)

Bird-of-paradise (*Strelitzia reginae*)

Bougainvillea glabra

Caladium bicolor

Calendula officinalis

Calla lily (*Zantedeschia aethiopica*)

Common and botanical names, general characteristics	Flowering time	Special requirements and remarks	Propagation
Azalea (*Rhododendron indicum* and *R.* hybrids) Shrub. Hybridization between species has produced a wide variety of flower shapes and sizes. Colors include white, pink, orange, salmon, and red, as well as bicolored. H 1-3 ft.; S 1-4 ft.	Late winter-late spring	Needs partial shade and high humidity during growing season. Keep cool (40°-45° F nighttime temperature), and water sparingly from fall to early winter; then increase water and temperature (50°-55° F nighttime) until flowering. Maintain cool nighttime temperature (50° F) while in bloom. Requires acid soil mixture. Prune after flowers fade; rest until midfall.	Take 4- to 5-in. cuttings after flowering; insert in mixture of equal amounts of peat moss and sand.
Bird-of-paradise (*Strelitzia reginae*) Perennial. Bizarre blue and orange flowers resembling bird's heads arise twice a year above narrow fanlike foliage. H 3 ft.; S 2 ft.	Midspring-late spring; late summer-early fall	Provide partial shade and water well during summer. Allow plant to become root-bound in its container; when crowded, repot to next larger size.	Divide overcrowded plants in early spring; cut apart clumps with 6 or more leaves; pot them in separate 7-in. pots.
Black-eyed Susan vine, see Thunbergia			
Bougainvillea (*Bougainvillea glabra*) Clambering vine that produces great numbers of showy purple flowers; also available in white or orange. Foliage consists of bright green 2-in. leaves in abundance. H 2-6 ft.; S 1-3 ft.	Midsummer-midfall	Flowers well in partial shade. Tolerates nighttime temperatures ranging from 50° to 65° F with little difficulty. Clambering stems are covered with thorns; so situate them accordingly.	Root cuttings from early to mid spring in mixture of equal amounts of peat moss and sand. Use bottom heat, and keep soil mix constantly moist.
Caladium (*Caladium bicolor*) Tuberous perennial grown for its large colored leaves. Color varies, with splashings of white, green, pink, and red on 1- to 1½-ft. arrow-shaped leaves. H 9 in.-1½ ft.; S 1-1½ ft.	Midspring-early fall	Grows best in warm, humid shade. Keep well watered in summer. Reduce amount of water and give it less frequently in fall; then store in pots after foliage dies down.	Separate offset tubers when repotting. Start tubers in late winter on bed of moistened peat moss; pot when roots are 1-2 in. long.
Calceolaria, see p. 459			
Calendula, or Pot marigold (*Calendula officinalis*) Annual especially valued for cut flowers. Yellow or orange multipetaled flowers are about 3-4 in. across, supported by thick, hairy stems. Foliage is also hairy, lying quite close to ground. Named hybrids available. H 9 in.; S 9 in.	Late spring-late summer	Grow in full light, moderate to high humidity, cool temperatures. Water only when dry until plants flower; daily watering is then required.	Sow seeds of named hybrids in mid to late winter. Special qualities that hybrids offer, compared with *C. officinalis* species, justify slightly higher price.
Calla lily (*Zantedeschia aethiopica*) Rhizomatous perennial with large flowers of pure white borne on stout stalks. Shiny green leaves are large and arrow shaped. H 1-3 ft.; S 1-2 ft.	Late winter-early summer	Grow in full light, but provide partial shade on hot days. Use large quantities of water when plant is flowering and in active growth; in other seasons, keep soil fairly dry. Needs plenty of room to develop.	Divide rhizomes from midfall to midwinter.

COOL GREENHOUSE *(continued)*

Camellia japonica

Campanula isophylla

Cape cowslip (*Lachenalia aloides*)

Cape primrose (*Streptocarpus hybridus*)

Carnation (*Dianthus caryophyllus*)

False Jerusalem cherry (*Solanum capsicastrum*)

Clivia miniata

Crape myrtle (*Lagerstroemia indica*)

Common and botanical names, general characteristics	Flowering time	Special requirements and remarks	Propagation
Camellia *(Camellia japonica)* Evergreen shrub grown for its beautiful, almost waxlike flowers. White, pink, and red are usual colors. Shiny dark green leaves are somewhat oval. Many named varieties available. H 1-8 ft.; S 1-6 ft.	Midwinter-midspring	Requires full light with some partial shade to prevent scorching. Keep soil evenly moist but never thoroughly wet. Provide warmth (60°-65° F) to start buds and to expand flowers, but keep cool (50° F) at other times.	Root cuttings in mixture of equal amounts of sand and peat moss in late summer.
Campanula, or Bellflower *(Campanula isophylla)* Perennial with trailing stems. Bell-shaped, 1-in. flowers of white or blue-purple; almost equal number of 1-in. leaves. H 2 ft.; S 1 ft.	Early summer-late summer	Provide partial shade and keep well watered. Feed every 2 wk. Plant 3-4 rooted cuttings in single hanging basket, or grow on stakes in separate 6- to 8-in pots.	Root cuttings at any time of year.
Cape cowslip, or Lachenalia *(Lachenalia aloides)* Perennial bulb. Pendent, tubular flowers of yellow or red borne in 10-in. spikes. Strap-shaped leaves arch at base of flower stems. H 6-12 in.; S 4-10 in.	Late winter-late spring	Grow in full light. Water moderately. Provide good ventilation. Repot annually with 3-5 bulbs in each 5- to 7-in. pot.	Insert leaf cuttings upright, 1 in. deep, in damp coarse sand. Shade until rooted. Remove and pot bulblets when repotting each fall.
Cape primrose *(Streptocarpus hybridus)* Perennial. White, blue, purple, or red trumpet-shaped flowers appear almost continuously. Long, rough-textured leaves surround base of flowers. H 9 in.-1 ft.; S 9 in.-1 ft.	Late spring-midfall	Provide partial shade, moderate humidity. Water liberally in summer; reduce watering in winter. Will bloom in 4-in. pots but achieves best display filling 7-in. pots.	Insert leaf cuttings in sand at any time of year; will root in 3 wk. Sow seeds in early spring for flowering plants within 5 mo.
Carnation, or Clove pink *(Dianthus caryophyllus)* Perennial. Showy, fragrant, 3- to 4-in. flowers are carried on wiry stems. Available in white, purple, pink, yellow, and red. H 2½-3 ft.; S 6-8 in.	Early fall-early summer	Needs full sun, moderate humidity, daily watering, cool temperature (45°-65° F). Pinch side growth for single large flower; for bushy plant with smaller blooms, pinch back tip.	Take cuttings in midwinter. Root in mixture of equal amounts of sand and peat moss, with bottom heat. Transplant to 3-in. pots after 4-6 wk.
Cherry, false Jerusalem *(Solanum capsicastrum)* Perennial best grown as annual. Small, cherrylike yellow, orange, or red fruits (poisonous) are very decorative against background of dark green foliage. H 9 in.-1½ ft.; S 6 in.-1 ft.	Midspring	Provide partial shade, cool temperatures, and moderate water until flowering. Then move plants outdoors for pollination (or pollinate with soft brush). Return to greenhouse in fall to let fruits color.	Sow seeds in late winter. Repot seedlings into progressively larger pots as they grow.
Cineraria, see p. 459 **Citrus**, see Orange, Otaheite			
Clivia, or Kaffir lily *(Clivia miniata)* Perennial tub plant. Clusters of orange trumpet-shaped flowers are produced on upright 2-ft. stems amid mass of dark green, straplike leaves. Sometimes sold as Kaffir lily. H 1½-2 ft.; S 1½-2 ft.	Early spring-late spring	Needs slight shade in midsummer; otherwise grow in full light. Water well in summer; reduce frequency of watering in winter. Does best when roots fill container, but needs repotting every few years.	Divide or remove offsets after flowering. Sow seeds in early spring.
Crape myrtle *(Lagerstroemia indica)* Deciduous shrub. Clusters of deep pink flowers almost cover foliage. H 4-8 ft.; S 3-6 ft.	Early summer-late summer	Full light, moderate humidity, and well-ventilated greenhouse will keep crape myrtle blooming. Prune to keep within bounds.	Root cuttings in sand in fall. Dwarf varieties are easily raised from seeds.

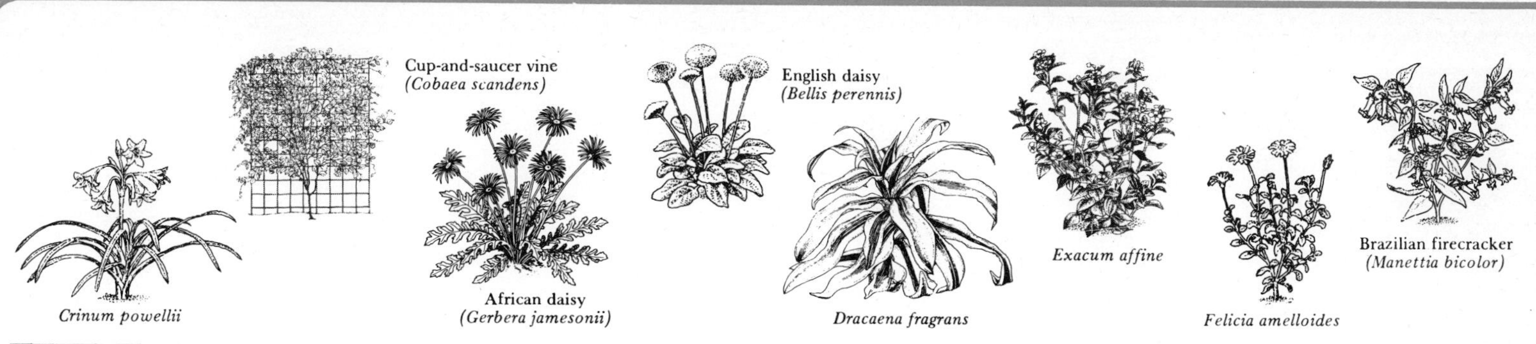

Common and botanical names, general characteristics	Flowering time	Special requirements and remarks	Propagation
Crinum *(Crinum powellii)* Bulb. Soft pink lilylike flowers are produced in clusters atop thick stem arising from basal crown of straplike leaves. H 1½-2 ft; S 1 ft.	Midspring-early fall	Provide some shade and water heavily during summer; add liquid fertilizer to water once a month. Withhold feeding and reduce watering for 5 mo. starting 1 mo. after flowering.	Pot offset bulblets individually when they become crowded in pot.
Crossandra, see Firecracker flower			
Cup-and-saucer vine *(Cobaea scandens)* Climbing vine often grown as annual. Green and violet bell-shaped flowers appear amid plentiful small green leaves. Also sold as Mexican ivy or monastery bells. H 2-6 ft.; S 2 ft.	Early summer-midfall	Provide full light to partial shade. Water well during summer months. Needs wire, string, trellis, or cane to climb upon.	Grows easily from seeds sown in early spring.
Cyclamen, see p. 460			
Daisy, African *(Gerbera jamesonii)* Perennial. Large multipetaled flowers in wide variety of pastel shades. Deeply lobed leaves grow from single crown. H 1½ ft.; S 1-1½ ft.	Midsummer-early spring	Provide full light. Keep soil evenly moist but not wet in summer. Grow cool (45°-50° F) in winter with slightly less moisture. Excellent cut flower.	Sow mixed seeds in late winter to early spring, transplanting progressively to 6-in. pots by early summer. Divide plants in spring.
Daisy, English *(Bellis perennis)* Biennial. Small multipetaled flowers in shades of white, pink, and red above rosette of small tongue-shaped leaves. H 6 in.; S 3-6 in.	Early spring-midspring	Full light in winter will hasten development of flowers. Grow in cool conditions with moderate humidity. Pot each plant individually. Discard plants after flowering.	Sow seeds in mid to late summer. Transplant into flats after leaves reach ½ in.; place in individual pots in midwinter.
Dracaena *(Dracaena fragrans)* Evergreen shrub grown for its foliage. Long strap-shaped leaves emerge in rosettes from slender woody stems. *D. f. massangeana* has broad yellow stripe down center of leaves. H 4-6 ft.; S 1-2 ft.		Grow in partial shade and moderate humidity. Water thoroughly when dry.	Air-layer stems (see p. 93). Or remove basal shoots and pot individually.
Exacum *(Exacum affine)* Annual. Violetlike purple flowers have bright yellow stamens. Small dark green leaves clothe entire length of stems. H 9 in.; S 9 in.	Midsummer-early fall	Grows easily in partial shade and high humidity. Water thoroughly when dry. Use shallow pots for best results.	Sow seeds in early spring.
Felicia, or Blue marguerite *(Felicia amelloides)* Perennial grown as annual. Blue daisylike flowers have yellow centers. Small oval leaves appear below flower heads. H 8-18 in.; S 6-8 in.	Early winter-late winter	Provide partial shade and steady humidity. Pinch growing tips to promote bushiness. Grow 1 plant in 5-in. pot or 3-4 plants in hanging basket.	Root cuttings in early spring. Large plants can be pruned back and grown as perennials for a few years.
Firecracker, Brazilian *(Manettia bicolor)* Climbing vine. Bright orange flowers with yellow tips resemble small firecrackers. Pointed, oval leaves are medium green. H 1-3 ft.; S 6 in.-1 ft.	Early winter-early summer	Needs partial shade to keep foliage from burning. Keep soil evenly moist. Prune regularly to force new growth and better flowering. Provide support for plant to climb.	Root cuttings at 70° F in early spring.

COOL GREENHOUSE *(continued)*

Firecracker flower
(Crossandra infundibuliformis)

Freesia refracta

Globe amaranth
(Gomphrena globosa)

Glory-bower
(Clerodendrum thomsoniae)

Glory-bush
(Tibouchina semidecandra)

Glory-lily
(Gloriosa rothschildiana)

Chinese hibiscus
(Hibiscus rosasinensis)

Common and botanical names, general characteristics	Flowering time	Special requirements and remarks	Propagation
Firecracker flower *(Crossandra infundibuliformis)* Perennial. Scarlet- or apricot-colored flat flowers are borne in showy spikes up to 6 in. long, which resemble bunches of firecrackers. Glossy green leaves. H 1-2 ft.; S 1 ft.-15 in.	All year	Provide partial shade and high humidity in summer, no shade and low humidity in winter. Use humusy soil mix.	Root cuttings in early spring to early summer. Sow seeds in early spring to late summer.
Freesia *(Freesia refracta)* Corm. Small trumpet-shaped flowers exude marvelous perfume; varieties available in white and shades of yellow and orange. Leaves are narrow, upright. H 1-1½ ft.; S 4-6 in.	Early winter-early spring	Give full light, moderate humidity, and good ventilation. Temperatures of 45°-50° F are preferable. Support with bamboo canes. Remove corms from soil in late summer; store until midfall.	Separate offsets and plant 4 in 6-in. pot in midfall.
Fuchsia, see p. 460 **Gazania,** see Treasure flower **Geranium,** see p. 461			
Globe amaranth *(Gomphrena globosa)* Annual. Flowers are 1-in. cloverlike globes in purple, yellow, orange, or red. Dense foliage below flower stems. H 6 in.-1 ft.; S 6-9 in.	Midspring-early fall	Provide full light, moderate humidity, and good ventilation. Cut flowers make attractive dried winter arrangements.	Sow 6 seeds per 5-in. pot. Seeds can be collected when ripe, but for dependable spring sowing it is best to buy fresh seeds.
Glory-bower *(Clerodendrum thomsoniae,* or *C. balfouri)* Clambering vine with eye-catching flowers of white and bright red profusely borne in clumps along wiry stems. Glossy dark green foliage makes good background for blooms. H 3-5 ft.; S 1-1½ ft.	Early summer-early fall	Give full light, plenty of water in early spring; provide partial shade during summer. Feed every 2 wk. Withhold water and allow to rest in winter. Needs 3-ft. stake or supporting trellis.	Root cuttings in midspring.
Glory-bush *(Tibouchina semidecandra)* Shrub producing large, royal purple, pansylike flowers. Attractive leaves have distinct ribs and hairy surface. H 3-4 ft.; S 2-3 ft.	Midsummer-late fall	Provide partial shade and moderate watering. In summer give more light and water more heavily.	Root cuttings in late winter or early spring. Grow at 65° F until late spring when varying temperatures present no problem.
Glory-lily *(Gloriosa rothschildiana)* Tuberous clambering vine. Flowers are yellow and red, with narrow reflexed petals. Leaves are interesting because their tips produce climbing tendrils. H 3-6 ft.; S 1 ft.	Early summer-early fall	Keep slightly shaded and in good humidity. Feed with liquid fertilizer every 2 wk. Dry off in winter and allow to go dormant.	Separate cigar-shaped tubers when repotting in late winter.
Hibiscus, Chinese *(Hibiscus rosasinensis)* Shrub with large (5-10 in.) funnel-shaped flowers in white, pink, rose, and carmine. Attractive foliage. H 3-4 ft.; S 2-3 ft.	Late spring-midfall	Grow in partial shade and in moderate humidity. Water well in summer; reduce watering in winter. Prune in early spring. Large-flowered kinds need 10-in. pot or tub; grow small-flowered ones in 6-in. pot.	Sow seeds in late winter. Root cuttings in spring.

Impatiens sultanii

Jasmine
(Jasminum polyanthum)

Lantana camara

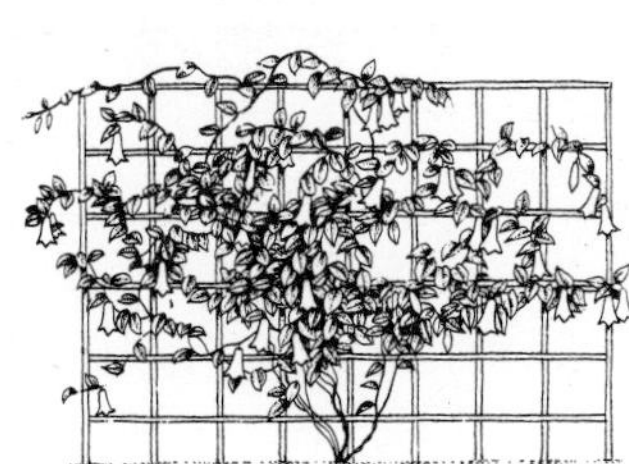
Lapageria rosea

Goldband lily
(Lilium auratum)

Lily of the Nile
(Agapanthus africanus)

Common and botanical names, general characteristics	Flowering time	Special requirements and remarks	Propagation
Hymenocallis, see Spider lily			
Impatiens *(Impatiens sultanii,* or *I. wallerana)* Annual. Flat flowers of white, pink, or red are produced in profusion. H 6 in.-1½ ft.; S 6 in.-1 ft.	Almost continuously	Grow in full light or partial shade with steady but light humidity. Pinch tips to encourage bushiness. Discard leggy plants.	Root cuttings or sow seeds at any time of year.
Jasmine *(Jasminum polyanthum)* Evergreen clambering vine bears masses of sweet-scented tubular white or pinkish flowers. Pointed, oval leaflets grow opposite each other along twining stems. H 3-6 ft.; S 1-2 ft.	Late fall-midspring	Provide partial shade, and water daily during active growth period. Trellis, post, or strings are necessary for vine to ascend.	Root stem cuttings in early spring. Grow new plants in 3-in. pots; repot before plant becomes root-bound until final 10-in. pot is reached.
Jasmine, Madagascar, see Stephanotis **Lachenalia,** see Cape cowslip			
Lantana *(Lantana camara)* Shrub. Clusters of white, pink, yellow, orange, or bicolored flowers borne on stems that may be prickly. Leaves are coarse textured. Many named varieties available. H 6 in.-3 ft.; S 6 in.-1½ ft.	Early summer-early fall	Provide full light and moderate humidity to produce flowers. Can be grown as small flowering plant in 5-in. pot or as miniature tree in 10-in. pot.	Sow seeds in late winter. Root cuttings at 70° F in late summer in mixture of equal amounts of coarse sand and peat moss.
Lapageria, or Chilean bellflower *(Lapageria rosea)* Evergreen vine. Waxy, bell-shaped flowers, usually dark pink, are heavy despite their delicate appearance. Sparse foliage is dark green, leaves are leathery in texture. H 3-6 ft.; S 1-2 ft.	Midsummer-midfall	Grow in partial shade. Water daily during summer and fall; give less water during winter resting period. Train on trellis or bamboo stakes in 6-in. pot when small, moving eventually to 10-in. pot.	Layer stems, keeping sand and peat moss damp (see p. 92). May take up to 2 yr. to root. Seeds are difficult to obtain but can be germinated in late winter at 65° F.
Lily, goldband *(Lilium auratum)* and **Easter lily** *(L. longiflorum eximium)* Bulb. Huge trumpet-shaped flowers top straight stems lined with narrow drooping leaves. White flowers of *L. auratum* are yellow striped and delicately spotted with crimson; *L. l. eximium* is taller, with very large, pure white flowers. H 1½-2½ ft.; S 8 in.-1 ft.	Late winter-midspring	Provide full light, regular thorough watering, and good ventilation during growing season. Allow plant to rest in summer. Repot in midfall in 6-in. pots, or top-dress with 1- to 2-in. layer of leaf mold.	Bulblets can be removed and potted singly, then grown for 2 yr. before flowering. It is best, however, to buy new bulbs each year for quick growth.
Lily of the Nile *(Agapanthus africanus)* Rhizomatous perennial. Huge cluster of small blue trumpets rises on straight stem from dense clump of long, arching, strap-shaped green leaves. H 2½ ft.; S 1 ft.	Early spring-midsummer	Grow in full light and moderate humidity. Plant will increase to fill large pot or tub or will flower despite root-bound conditions. In winter store at 35°-45° F. To force early bloom, gradually increase watering and raise nighttime temperature to 50° F in early winter.	Separate bulblets every few years, since they are forced upward out of pot by excessive crowding.

COOL GREENHOUSE *(continued)*

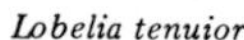

Lobelia tenuior

Flowering maple
(Abutilon megapotamicum)

Monkey flower
(Mimulus luteus)

Nerine flexuosa

Oleander
(Nerium oleander)

Otaheite orange
(Citrus taitensis)

Common and botanical names, general characteristics	Flowering time	Special requirements and remarks	Propagation
Lobelia *(Lobelia tenuior)* Annual. Bright blue flowers literally cover spreading plant, so that only some foliage is visible. H 4-6 in.; S 6-18 in.	Late spring-midfall	Requires shade and high humidity. Pot 3 seedlings in single 5-in. pot or 5 seedlings in 8-in. hanging basket. For more blossoms, shear after flowering.	Sow seeds in early spring; keep at 65° F to germinate.
Lobster claw, see Parrot's-beak **Manettia,** see Firecracker, Brazilian			
Maple, flowering *(Abutilon megapotamicum)* Shrub with slender, pendulous branches bearing green arrowhead-shaped leaves, sometimes variegated with ivory or yellow. Pendent, bell-shaped or lantern-shaped flowers are available in white, pink, yellow, and red. Sometimes sold as weeping Chinese lantern. H 2 ft.; S 1½ ft.	Late spring-midfall	Needs full light during winter; provide partial shade in summer to keep leaves from burning. Maintain moderate humidity. Water when dry. Good plant to grow in hanging baskets.	Sow seeds in early spring for bloom the same year. Root cuttings in fall.
Monkey flower *(Mimulus luteus)* Perennial grown as annual. Bright yellow flowers spotted with purple or red are borne at ends of leaf-covered stems. Variously colored forms and hybrids sometimes sold as *M. hybridus,* or *M. tigrinus.* H 9 in.-1 ft.; S 9 in.-1 ft.	Early summer-early fall	Full light and thorough daily watering will help seedlings flower.	Sow seeds in late winter to early spring. Transplant seedlings, putting 3 in each 5-in. pot.
Nerine *(Nerine flexuosa)* Bulb. Clusters of delicate trumpet-shaped flowers in white or pale pink are borne on stout stalks. Long, narrow leaves appear at base of stalks after flowering. H 2 ft.; S 6-8 in.	Early fall-late fall	Provide partial shade. Begin daily watering at end of summer, and increase amount until flowers appear. Then water moderately until leaves wither in spring. Withhold water during summer rest period. Repot if necessary in early fall.	Separate bulb offsets after flowering, and plant in separate 3-in. pots. Transplant to 5-in. pots in early fall, when large enough to flower.
Oleander *(Nerium oleander)* Evergreen shrub. Clusters of white, pink, or red flowers are borne in profusion at tips of branches. Long, narrow dark green leaves give plant solid appearance. Also sold as rosebay. All parts are poisonous if eaten. H 3-4 ft.; S 2-4 ft.	Early summer-midfall	Full light and high humidity are necessary for heavy flowering. Prune severely in early spring to control growth if desired.	Root cuttings in early summer in damp coarse sand.
Orange, Otaheite *(Citrus taitensis)* Shrub. Decorative orange fruit, borne in early fall through midwinter, is edible; taste is sour, rather like a lime. Waxy pinkish-white flowers are highly fragrant. Green foliage sets off flowers and fruit well. Also sold as Tahiti orange. H 1-3 ft.; S 1-3 ft.	Midspring-early summer	Grow in full light, but give partial shade in midsummer. Keep well watered during active growth. Feed monthly with iron chelates if plant shows signs of chlorosis (see p. 608). Pot in 14-in. tub with slightly acid soil.	Take cuttings in mid to late summer.

Parrot's-beak
(Clianthus puniceus)

Passionflower
(Passiflora caerulea)

Ornamental pepper
(Capsicum annuum)

Madagascar periwinkle
(Vinca rosea)

Plumbago capensis

Rechsteineria
(Sinningia leucotricha)

Common and botanical names, general characteristics	Flowering time	Special requirements and remarks	Propagation
Parrot's-beak *(Clianthus puniceus)* Evergreen clambering vine that produces clusters of distinctive 3-in.-long red flowers, each with one overhanging petal shaped like parrot's beak. Gray-green foliage is sharply divided, almost fern-like. Also called lobster claw. H 3-5 ft.; S 2-4 ft.	Early summer-late fall	Requires full light and good ventilation. Spray with water often during summer to prevent two-spotted mites that thrive in dry atmosphere (see p. 606).	Sow seeds in early spring. Root cuttings in early to late summer.
Passionflower *(Passiflora caerulea)* Evergreen climbing vine. Blue to pure white flowers are intricate in form, stand out boldly against background of star-shaped clusters of deep green leaves. H 4-6 ft.; S 6 in.-1½ ft.	Early summer-midfall	Provide partial shade, high humidity, and minimum nighttime temperature of 50°-55° F. Reduce humidity after flowering. Climbs by attaching tendrils to any nearby support.	Sow seeds in early spring. Root cuttings in midsummer.
Pelargonium, see Geranium, p. 461			
Pepper, ornamental *(Capsicum annuum)* Shrub grown as annual for its long-lasting, edible, and decorative fruits, which are usually bright red, although varieties are available in green, yellow, or black. Abundant star-shaped white flowers are also decorative on some varieties. Foliage is bright green. H 1½ ft.; S 1 ft.	Early summer-late summer	Provide full light and moderate humidity. Maintain steady temperature and avoid drafts to prevent leaf drop. Keep evenly watered. Place plants outdoors to be pollinated when in flower, or pollinate with soft brush when blossoms are fully opened.	Sow seeds in early spring. Transplant seedlings into progressively larger pots as their size increases.
Periwinkle, Madagascar *(Vinca rosea)* Perennial often grown as annual. Fleshy white or rose-pink flower has carmine eye and stands out sharply against background of glossy foliage. Also sold as *Catharanthus roseus.* H 1 ft.; S 1 ft.	Early spring-late fall	Does best in moderate shade and humidity. Water well when flowering. Grow as evergreen perennial; or discard after flowering, and grow new plants annually.	Sow seeds in late winter. Keep at 70° F until germinated. Transplant seedlings into progressively larger pots to eventual size of 5 in.
Plumbago, or Leadwort *(Plumbago capensis)* Clambering vine producing soft blue phloxlike flowers in abundance. Rich green foliage covers lanky stems. H 2-6 ft.; S 1-2 ft.	Midspring-late fall	Full light and steady watering will keep plant flowering. Prune back summer growth in early winter, and reduce watering until early spring.	Take cuttings in midsummer. Sow seeds in late fall.
Pocketbook plant, see Calceolaria, p. 459 **Primula,** see Primrose, p. 461			
Rechsteineria, or Sinningia *(Sinningia leucotricha)* Tuberous perennial often grown as annual. Pendent tubular flowers of brilliant vermilion are produced in clusters directly atop whorls of silvery, velvety leaves 4 in. long. Also sold as Brazilian edelweiss. H 8 in.-1 ft.; S 8 in.-1 ft.	Early summer-late fall	Provide shade, high humidity, and minimum nighttime temperature of 65°-70° F in spring and summer. Reduce watering after flowering. Easily grown as annual in soilless potting mixture. Withhold water and maintain minimum nighttime temperature of 50°-55° F to rest tubers if they are to be carried over winter.	Sow seeds in midwinter and keep them at 70° F.

COOL GREENHOUSE *(continued)*

Shrimp plant (*Beloperone guttata*)

Silk oak (*Grevillea robusta*)

Spider lily (*Hymenocallis harrisiana*)

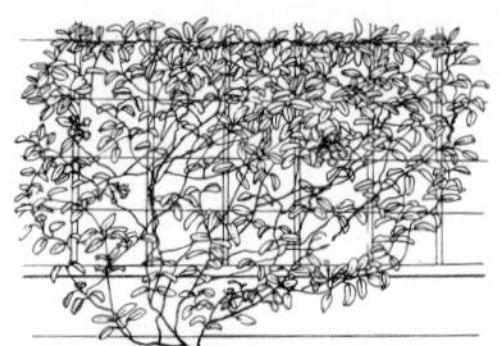
Stephanotis floribunda

Temple bells (*Smithiantha cinnabarina*)

Thunbergia alata

Common and botanical names, general characteristics	Flowering time	Special requirements and remarks	Propagation
Schizanthus, see p. 461			
Shrimp plant *(Beloperone guttata)* Shrub grown as annual for its constant floral display. Shrimp-shaped flower clusters have very showy brownish-pink bracts around small white true flowers. H 1-2 ft.; S 1-2 ft.	All year	Provide full light. Do not let soil dry out at any time. Pinch growing tips off young plants to encourage branching.	Cuttings taken in early spring and inserted in moist sand will root and flower in 3 mo.
Silk oak *(Grevillea robusta)* Tree grown for its graceful fernlike foliage. Deeply cut green leaves, covered with silky gray hairs when young, produce tropical effect. H 2-6 ft.; S 1½-2 ft.		Will tolerate full light to partial shade but must have acid soil to thrive. Pinch out growing tips for bushy appearance.	Sow seeds in late winter to early spring.
Spider lily *(Hymenocallis harrisiana)* Bulb. Greenish-white flowers are dramatic and very fragrant, appearing in clusters of 5-10 spiderlike blossoms atop stout leafless stalk. Green straplike leaves spread upward beneath flowers. H 9 in.-1½ ft.; S 1-1½ ft.	Midspring-late summer	Provide partial shade, moderate humidity, and ample water when growing. Decrease water after flowering, when leaves begin to die down.	Pot offsets individually if plant has become crowded. When repotting parent bulb in midwinter, leave top half of bulb showing.
Stephanotis, or Madagascar jasmine *(Stephanotis floribunda)* Climbing vine with clusters of highly scented, white tubular flowers that are very showy against glossy evergreen leaves. H 3-6 ft.; S 1-2 ft.	Late spring-midfall	Provide partial shade and moderate humidity, and water freely during active growth. Give plants complete fertilizer monthly during summer. Pot in 10- or 12-in. tubs, and provide support for climbing.	Take cuttings in late spring or early summer. Keep at 65°-70° F until rooted.
Streptocarpus, see Cape primrose			
Temple bells *(Smithiantha cinnabarina)* Rhizomatous perennial with clusters of foxglovelike, bell-shaped florets, bright red outside and creamy with red spots inside, which nod on upright stems. Dense foliage of velvety red clusters around bottoms of flower stems, hiding soil surface. H 6-9 in.; S 9-12 in.	All year	Requires some shade and well-watered soil during growth period. Maintain minimum nighttime temperature of 50°-55° F. Can be started into growth at any time of year. After flowering, reduce water for 5-6 mo. of rest.	Divide rhizomes before starting into growth. Plant divisions in boxes of peat moss, kept at 70° F in moderate shade; water amply. Move to individual 3-in. pots of potting mixture after roots and leaves develop, in 3-5 wk.
Thunbergia, or Black-eyed Susan vine *(Thunbergia alata)* Perennial climber often grown as annual. Flattish, funnel-shaped flowers of white, cream, yellow, or orange have dark violet or blackish centers. Green arrowhead-shaped leaves provide attractive background. H 3-4 ft.; S 9 in.-1 ft.	Late spring-early fall	Partial shade will keep flower color from fading. Daily watering will produce growth needed to support heavy flowering. Provide canes, strings, or trellis for plants to climb upon; or place 3-5 seedlings in single hanging basket.	Sow seeds in midspring for flowering plants by midsummer.

Ti plant
(*Cordyline terminalis*)

Torenia fournieri

Treasure flower
(*Gazania rigens*)

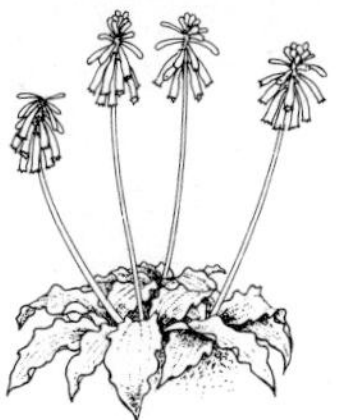
Veltheimia capensis

Wax plant
(*Hoya carnosa*)

Zebra plant
(*Aphelandra squarrosa*)

Common and botanical names, general characteristics	Flowering time	Special requirements and remarks	Propagation
Ti plant (*Cordyline terminalis*) Shrub grown for its rich green or reddish palmlike foliage, each leaf about 1½ ft. long, clustered atop canelike stems. Often sold as *Dracaena terminalis.* Red-leaved varieties sometimes sold as red dracaena. H 3-5 ft.; S 1-2 ft.		Keep plant in shady, moist atmosphere. Water well during summer; water less frequently in winter.	Remove suckers and pot in mid-spring. Or lay 6-in. pieces of stem flat on damp mixture of equal parts of peat moss and sand; keep moist until roots appear at nodes; then cut apart and pot separately.
Tibouchina, see Glory-bush			
Torenia, or Wishbone flower (*Torenia fournieri*) Perennial grown as annual. Bizarre-looking purple and yellow flowers are profusely borne on uppermost part of stems, with narrow, heart-shaped leaves growing below. H 1-1½ ft.; S 9 in.-1 ft.	Midsummer-early fall	Humidity and shade will help produce good growth. Support with sticks is necessary to keep top-heavy flower stems erect. Grow several plants in each 5-in. pot.	Sow seeds in late winter to early spring. Keep them at 65°F until germinated.
Treasure flower, or Gazania (*Gazania rigens*) Perennial grown for large daisylike flowers. Petals are yellow or orange with dark spot near center of each flower. Dark green leaves are long and narrow with white, felt-textured undersides. H 6 in.-1 ft.; S 6 in.-1 ft.	Early summer-early fall	Needs full light and moderate watering when growing. Plants can tolerate temperature of 40°F during winter resting period, but it is easier to discard them and grow new plants each year.	Sow seeds in late winter. Root cuttings in late summer.
Veltheimia (*Veltheimia capensis*) Bulb. Dense clusters of pendent pink flowers grow atop stout stalks. Low-lying leaves are glossy green with wavy edges, grow in rosettes at base of flower stalks. H 1-1½ ft.; S 6-9 in.	Winter-early spring	Needs full light when in active growth. Keep soil dry in summer; water freely from time foliage appears in fall until it dies back in early spring.	Pot offsets individually when repotting bulb every second year; leave top of bulb exposed.
Vinca, see Periwinkle, Madagascar			
Wax plant, or Hoya (*Hoya carnosa*) Climbing vine with waxy round clusters of fragrant white flowers, each a perfect 5-pointed star with red center. Elliptical leaves, equally waxlike, are deep green. H 1-3 ft.; S 8 in.-1 ft.	Midsummer-midfall	Needs full sun and high humidity. Maintain minimum nighttime temperature of 50°-55° F. Water daily during active growing period; slow growth in winter requires less frequent waterings. Provide support for climbing.	Root cuttings in late spring to early summer.
Zebra plant (*Aphelandra squarrosa*) Perennial. Dramatic yellow flowers emerge at each overlapping bract of pyramidal flower head until entire 5-in. head is in bloom. Elliptical 8-in. leaves are equally striking with deep green background boldly accented by chartreuse veining. H 2 ft.; S 1-1½ ft.	Early summer-late fall	Needs shade and warm, moist atmosphere. Place in warm section of cool greenhouse, and maintain minimum nighttime temperature of 50°-55° F. Water abundantly in summer, but very lightly in midwinter.	Root cuttings in early to mid spring. Growing new plants as annuals is usually preferred to growing same plant year after year.

PLANTS FOR THE WARM GREENHOUSE

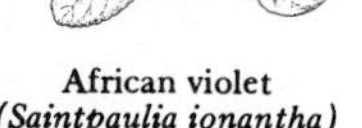
African violet (*Saintpaulia ionantha*)

Aglaonema robelinii

Allamanda cathartica

Amazon lily (*Eucharis grandiflora*)

Anthurium andraeanum

Blood lily (*Haemanthus multiflorus*)

Browallia speciosa

Common and botanical names, general characteristics	Flowering time	Special requirements and remarks	Propagation
African violet (*Saintpaulia ionantha*) Perennial. Plants with single violetlike flowers have been hybridized to include white, blue, and pink blossoms in single and double forms. Velvety foliage is fleshy and provides attractive background for flowers. H 3-5 in.; S 3-6 in.	All year	Provide partial shade, moderate humidity, and steady warmth year round. Keep soil moist, not soggy; water with tepid water, and do not wet leaves. Feed monthly with low-nitrogen fertilizer.	Insert leaf cuttings in damp sand anytime from midspring to early fall; will root in about 3 wk. Sow seeds in spring.
Aglaonema (*Aglaonema robelinii*) Evergreen perennial grown as foliage plant. Large, leathery gray-green leaves are lightly brushed with silver. H 2 ft.; S 2 ft.	All year	Does particularly well in shade. Needs high humidity and minimum temperature of 60° F. Keep soil moist, not soggy. Feed every 6 wk. with complete fertilizer.	Divide at any time of year. Provide humidity and warmth continuously after repotting.
Allamanda (*Allamanda cathartica*) Perennial clambering vine. Flowers are funnel shaped, soft yellow, to 5 in. across, with delicate fragrance. Bright green elliptical leaves are glossy. H 3-15 ft.; S 1-4 ft.	Midsummer-early fall	Needs partial shade and high humidity. Water well during active growth period. Keep almost dry in winter and prune during midwinter dormancy. Support clambering stems with bamboo canes.	Take cuttings in midsummer. Root in mixture of equal parts of sand and peat moss.
Amazon lily, or Eucharis (*Eucharis grandiflora*) Bulb grown for its clusters of delicately fragrant, lilylike, 5-in. white flowers that emerge above large arrowhead-shaped leaves. H 2 ft.; S 1 ft.	Midspring-early summer	Requires partial shade and even moisture, with minimum temperature of 70° F. To promote flowering, reduce watering for 2-3 wk. Plant bulb in deep pot containing mixture of 1 part seeding mixture and 2 parts each of peat moss or leaf mold and sand.	Separate side bulbs having 1 or 2 leaves and pot individually. Plant with tip of bulb level with soil surface.
Anthurium (*Anthurium andraeanum*) Perennial grown for bizarre floral display. Small yellow true flowers are clustered on narrow 2-in. spike that protrudes from center of single, heart-shaped, waxy red bract 2½-3 in. across. Also available in white or pink varieties. Leaves are long, green, leathery. H 2 ft.; S 1 ft.	Midspring-early fall	Grows luxuriously in shade, high humidity, and very warm atmosphere. Plant in mixture of equal parts of general-purpose potting mix and peat moss. Roots should be covered with soil or sphagnum moss when they become exposed.	Sow seeds when they are ripe (about 1 mo. after flowering), or make divisions at any time.
Begonia, see p. 459			
Blood lily (*Haemanthus multiflorus*) Bulb bearing large spherical head of crimson flowers on upright stem that emerges from clump of wavy-edged leaves. H 1½-2 ft.; S 1-1½ ft.	Midspring	Needs full light and moderate humidity. Water thoroughly during active growth; keep almost dry in winter. Allow at least 3 yr. before repotting.	Separate offsets from parent bulb when repotting. Plant with nose of bulb protruding from soil.
Browallia (*Browallia speciosa*) Perennial sometimes grown as annual. Large purple-blue flowers bloom in abundance above leaves of light apple-green. H 1-2 ft.; S 1-1½ ft.	Early summer-early fall	Needs shade in summer to prevent burning; more light in winter. Water well in summer. After blooming ceases, reduce watering until early spring. Good for hanging baskets.	Cuttings root readily in mid and late spring. Sow seeds in early winter for summer flowering.

Brunfelsia calycina

Calathea ornata

Chenille plant (*Acalypha hispida*)

Christmas cactus (*Schlumbergera bridgesii*)

Columnea microphylla

Croton (*Codiaeum variegatum*)

Dipladenia splendens

Common and botanical names, general characteristics	Flowering time	Special requirements and remarks	Propagation
Brunfelsia (*Brunfelsia calycina*) Evergreen shrub grown as pot plant. Brilliant violet flowers with flat 3- to 4-in. petals. Blossoms are set off well by leathery, dark green leaves. H 2-3 ft.; S 1½-2 ft.	Late spring-midsummer	Provide full light, high humidity, and even temperatures. During midsummer period of greatest growth, plant needs shading. Keep almost dry during winter.	Root cuttings in mid to late spring.
Calathea (*Calathea ornata*) Tuberous perennial. Dramatic, large, upright leaves are olive-green above, marked along veins with sharply etched lines of pink or white when young, coppery green when mature; undersides are dull maroon. H 9-18 in.; S 6-12 in.		Grows most vigorously in summer with shade, high humidity, and steady warmth. Reduce water gradually as growth slows in fall. Water moderately in winter.	Divide crowns in midspring. Sow seeds in late spring; seedlings need warmth and humidity until ready for individual pots.
Chenille plant (*Acalypha hispida*) Shrub. Bright green foliage makes good background for pendent flower spikes of bright red (sometimes creamy white or purple), about 8 in. long, and shaped like woolly foxtails. Also sold as *A. sanderi* or *A. sanderana*. H 1-6 ft.; S 1-5 ft.	Early summer-late summer	Needs full light, high humidity, and minimum temperature of 60°-70° F. Grow in standard potting mixture with a little extra leaf mold or peat moss added. Feed every 6 wk.	Root cuttings in late winter.
Christmas cactus (*Schlumbergera bridgesii*) Epiphytic cactus. Fuchsialike, hanging red flowers appear at tips of arching, segmented branches. H 6-18 in.; S 6-18 in.	Early fall-midwinter	Provide partial shade, high humidity, and plenty of water during growth. Allow plant to rest after flowering by reducing water.	Root cuttings in early fall.
Cissus, see Ivy, grape			
Columnea (*Columnea microphylla* and *C.* hybrids) Trailing vine. Showy, pendent red flowers cover long, hanging branches. Small, round, coppery green leaves. Many hybrids available with bolder proportions; flowers in bright shades of pink, yellow, orange, and red. H 1-2½ ft.; S 1-2 ft.	Midfall-midspring	Keep shaded and well watered or misted in summer. Grow in porous, fast-draining soil mixture. Good plant for hanging baskets.	Root cuttings in early to late spring.
Croton (*Codiaeum variegatum*) Evergreen shrub. Glossy leaves of cream, yellow, maroon, red, and every shade between display seemingly endless variegations. H 1-3 ft.; S 1-2 ft.		Provide full light or partial shade, high humidity, and steady warmth. Mist leaves during hottest weather.	Root cuttings in early to late spring.
Dipladenia (*Dipladenia splendens*) Evergreen vine, best grown as annual. Floppy trumpet flowers of soft pink show up well against dark green foliage. H 3-5 ft.; S 1 ft.	Early summer-early fall	Provide shade, and water well in summer. Keep almost dry in winter. Clambering habit makes tying to supports necessary.	Root cuttings in early to mid spring each year. Should flower profusely first year.
Eucharis, see Amazon lily			

Staghorn fern (*Platycerium bifurcatum*)

Fittonia verschaffeltii

Gardenia jasminoides

Grape ivy (*Cissus discolor*)

Ixora coccinea

Jacaranda acutifolia

Jacobinia carnea

Kalanchoe blossfeldiana

Common and botanical names, general characteristics	Flowering time	Special requirements and remarks	Propagation
Fern, staghorn *(Platycerium bifurcatum)* Epiphytic fern of unique form. Green fronds shaped like deer antlers emerge from flat cluster of round brown fronds. H 2 ft.; S 2 ft.		Provide partial shade, high humidity, and steady warmth. Plants best grown on slab of wood or tree fern hung against wall.	Separate new plants whenever they appear. Pot individually in soil until 1 yr. old; then wire to slab of tree fern.
Fittonia, or Mosaic plant *(Fittonia verschaffeltii)* Perennial grown for foliage. Velvety dark green leaf color is accented by network of white, yellow, or red veins. H 3-4 in.; S 6-9 in.		Provide shade, high humidity, and evenly warm temperature. Keep soil moist but not wet.	Take cuttings in midspring; root at 75° F.
Gardenia *(Gardenia jasminoides)* Shrub with sweetly scented white flowers. Glossy leaves cover entire plant. H 2 ft.; S 1½-2 ft.	Early summer-early winter	Full light, high humidity, and steady warmth are essential. Increase watering when growth quickens in summer.	Take softwood cuttings with heels in early spring; root in mixture of equal parts of sand and peat moss at 80° F.
Gynura, see Velvet plant **Helxine**, see Baby's tears, p. 411			
Ivy, grape *(Cissus discolor)* Evergreen climber or trailing vine. Dark green arrow-shaped leaves are marked with silver and pale green, bright purple beneath. H 1-6 ft.; S 1-2 ft.		Needs partial shade, high humidity, and evenly moist (not soggy) soil. Grow in hanging basket, or provide stakes or other supports for climbing in 8-in. pot.	Root cuttings in mid and late spring.
Ixora *(Ixora coccinea)* Evergreen shrub. Displays round heads of star-shaped flowers of bright red or salmon. Light green foliage is dense around flowers. H 2-3 ft.; S 1½-2 ft.	Early summer-midfall	Needs shade and high humidity in summer. Keep drier in winter. Pinch out growing tips to promote bushiness; prune back heavily when necessary.	Take cuttings in early spring; root in damp mixture of equal parts of sand and peat moss, with constant bottom heat of 70° F.
Jacaranda *(Jacaranda acutifolia,* or *J. mimosifolia)* Tree grown as pot plant for its graceful fernlike leaves and clusters of blue-violet flowers. H 2-4 ft.; S 12-15 in.	Late summer	Provide partial shade and moderate humidity. Keep soil well watered but never soggy.	Sow seeds in late winter. Transplant seedlings to 3-in. pots; later transplant to 7- to 10-in. pots.
Jacobinia *(Jacobinia carnea)* Shrub grown as pot plant for its attractive plumes of pink, yellow, or red flowers. Also sold as *Justicia magnifica*. H 2-4 ft.; S 1½-2 ft.	Midfall-early summer	Provide partial shade. Maintain high humidity in summer, keep drier in winter. Pinch out growing tips at beginning of growth in late summer to encourage bushiness.	Take cuttings in early spring; root in mixture of equal parts of sand and peat moss. Maintain even temperature at about 70° F.
Kalanchoe *(Kalanchoe blossfeldiana)* Perennial grown as annual. Bright red tufts of flowers appear on straight stems above compact clusters of succulent leaves. H 4-6 in.; S 4-6 in.	Early fall-late fall	Grow in full light to partial shade. Water daily all summer; reduce watering slightly in fall and winter. Do not let winter temperature fall below 60° F. Does well in soilless potting mixture.	Root cuttings of growth that has finished flowering. Sow seeds in early spring.
Mimosa, see Sensitive plant			

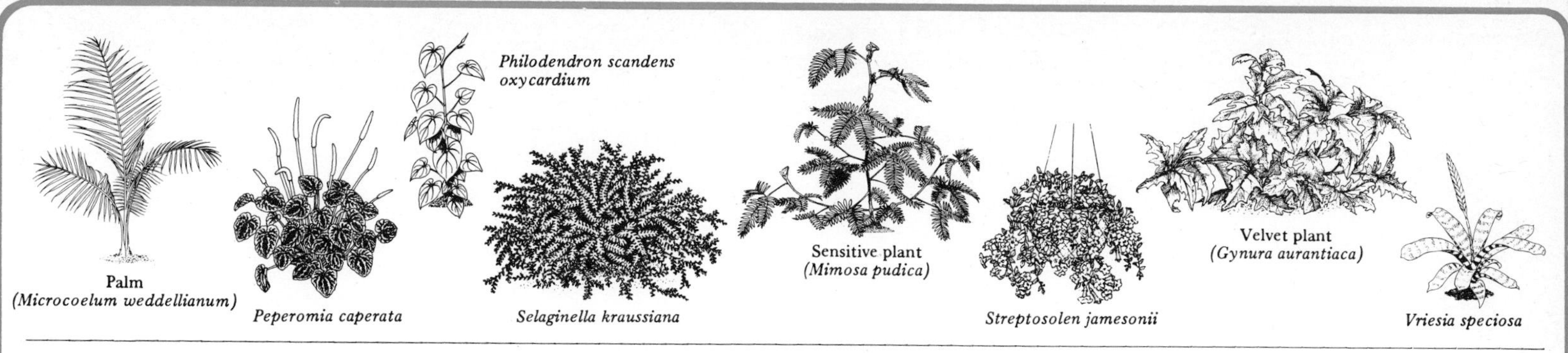

Common and botanical names, general characteristics	Flowering times	Special requirements and remarks	Propagation
Palms *(Microcoelum weddellianum* and *Phoenix canariensis)* Evergreen trees with graceful fronds up to 2 ft. long. *M. weddellianum* also sold as *Cocos weddelliana.* H 1-6 ft.; S 1-3 ft.		Do best in full light but will tolerate partial shade. Need constant high humidity. Water often during summer.	Sow seeds in spring.
Peperomia *(Peperomia caperata)* Perennial with attractive crinkled, heart-shaped leaves. H 3-13 in.; S 3-9 in.		Needs partial shade and moderate humidity. Plant in individual 5-in. pots, or 3 plants in a hanging basket.	Divide in early spring. Take leaf cuttings in midspring and root at 70° F.
Philodendron, heart-leaf *(Philodendron scandens oxycardium)* Evergreen climbing vine with heart-shaped, glossy green leaves. Aerial roots hold to most coarse surfaces. H 1-3 ft.; S 6 in.-1 ft.		Needs moderate shade and watering, with even temperature. Feed monthly. Plant in 6- to 8-in. pots; provide trellis or broad stake for climbing.	Take cuttings in late spring; root at 70°-75° F.
Poinsettia, see p. 423 **Saintpaulia,** see African violet			
Selaginella, or Spike moss *(Selaginella kraussiana)* Perennial grown as pot plant or ground cover for its dense covering of light green leaves. H 3-5 in.; S 5-7 in.		Requires full, constant shade and regular watering; never let soil dry out. Maintain minimum wintertime temperature of 60° F. Even in summer do not expose to direct drafts.	Divide into 1-in. pieces and pot in 3-in. pots. Pieces planted 5 in. apart in border of greenhouse bench will fill in within a year.
Sensitive plant *(Mimosa pudica)* Perennial valued for leaves that fold up when touched. Flowers are small, fluffy, and pink. H 6-18 in.; S 4-12 in.	Midsummer-early fall	Provide partial shade and daily watering. Although plants will survive several years, they are more attractive if started each year from seeds.	Sow seeds in late winter to early spring. Keep flats at 70° F until ready for transplanting to individual 3-in. pots.
Streptosolen *(Streptosolen jamesonii)* Clambering shrub. Trumpet-shaped orange flowers form at tips of branches. Leaves are shiny green. H 6 in.-2 ft.; S 8-18 in.	Early winter-early spring	Needs partial shade, moderate humidity, and thorough daily watering during active growth. Reduce watering after flowering. Good for hanging baskets.	Root cuttings at any time.
Velvet plant, or Gynura *(Gynura aurantiaca)* Perennial. Leaves are bright purple and velvety. Small orange flowers are of secondary importance. H 1-2 ft.; S 1-1½ ft.	Midwinter-early spring.	Give full light in winter, slight shade and moderate humidity in summer. Water daily but keep foliage dry. Pinch back tips to promote bushiness. Discard old leggy plants.	Root cuttings each year in midspring.
Vriesia *(Vriesia speciosa,* or *V. splendens)* Perennial. Stunning flower spike with green, yellow, or red bracts is held upright on stem, above rosettes of equally dramatic green and cream striped leaves. H 1½-2 ft.; S 9 in.-1 ft.	Late spring-early fall	Needs shade and high humidity. Water generously in summer. Grows best in standard potting mixture to which a little extra coarse sand, peat moss, and bone meal have been added.	Remove offshoots in early to mid spring. Pot individually.

Slatted benches are ideal for orchids that need freely circulating air, such as dendrobiums and cattleyas. Solid benches covered with damp gravel are best for orchids that need greater humidity in their growing season, such as cymbidiums and paphiopedilums. To increase the humidity on a slotted bench, hang a platform about 12 in. below it, cover it with gravel, and keep it moist.

Orchids

Many orchids will grow in a small greenhouse—and also in a basement, sun porch, or living room—given proper light, temperature, and humidity.

The ideal small greenhouse for orchids is probably a lean-to type built against the east or south side of your home. It will be more enjoyable if glass doors or windows open into the greenhouse, thus making it an extension of your living area. The more expensive, free-standing greenhouse with a full roof will provide more bench space and is easier to keep ventilated in hot weather.

The size depends on the number of orchids you want to grow and on how much you care to spend. Many small prefabricated greenhouses are available with frames of wood, aluminum, and/or galvanized iron.

Glass is still preferred for strength, light transmission, and long life, although many orchids can be grown under plastic panels. These have the advantage of diffusing light; and being less heavy in weight, they require fewer supporting beams. Before choosing a greenhouse, investigate the types available.

Heat. Every effort should be made to take advantage of the sun's warmth during the day. Still, unless you live in a subtropical or tropical climate, an independent source of heat is necessary. The logical fuel to use is the one that heats your home. Various space heaters are also available.

Temperature. Cool-growing orchids from high elevations need a minimum night temperature of 45°–50 F; warm-house orchids need 65° F. Intermediate orchids do best in a minimum night temperature of 58°–60° F. Day temperatures should be 10–15 degrees higher in winter, considerably more in summer. Among the intermediates are brassias, bulbophyllums, cattleyas, epidendrums, some dendrobiums, laelias, miltonias, and sophronitis.

Conserving heat. You can conserve heat in several ways. Use excess warmth from the furnace by installing a blower near it controlled by a thermostat in the greenhouse (possible only in a greenhouse attached to the home). Line the greenhouse with polyethylene in winter, and insulate the insides of the walls with foil or other material. Windbreaks of hedges, fences, or buildings can also be helpful.

Ventilation. Normally, warm air escapes through sash openings in the greenhouse roof. The most efficient way to ventilate is with automatic thermostat-controlled vent openers. These are especially useful when you must be away all day. They are usually installed on only one side of the greenhouse.

Vents can also be adjusted manually to control temperatures. Open cautiously on cool, windy days. You can use exhaust fans to remove hot air. These are normally installed with a motorized air-intake shutter at one end of the greenhouse.

If you live in a hot, dry climate, evaporative coolers installed in the greenhouse wall provide good conditions for cool-growing orchids.

Humidity. For most orchids 65–70 percent relative humidity is ideal.

An overhead misting on sunny mornings, and again in the afternoon on dry summer days, helps give plants a rain-forest atmosphere. Various humidifiers are also effective in small greenhouses. One that is controlled by a humidistat is an excellent labor-saving device.

Humidity can be increased by using brick rather than concrete walks and by putting gravel under the benches. The floor should be hosed down several times a day in dry weather or when heat is used.

Shading. Special shading is usually necessary from early spring to late fall in the North and for most of the year in the South. It helps to cool the plants and prevents leaf burn.

A white latex paint or a special greenhouse shading compound can be painted or sprayed on the roof and sunny sides. More effective are roll-down shades of aluminum, wooden slats, or heavy plastic, installed a few inches above the glass. The resultant layer of air will help cool the inside. They can be raised in cloudy weather.

Benches. Greenhouse benches are available in various materials. Redwood slats and expanded metal allow for air movement and drainage. Heavy wire mesh on a wooden frame is cheaper but not as rugged. Benches should be about 30 inches high. If possible, consult an experienced grower and visit a few orchid greenhouses before deciding on the kind of bench to install. (Most orchid society members are glad to share information.)

Containers and types. Most orchids grown in greenhouses are epiphytic: they grow on trees or shrubs in their native habitats but are not parasites. Their roots are adapted to cling and to absorb water, food, and air from the atmosphere. Many epiphytes grow well attached to cork bark or tree-fern slabs. You can also hang them from wire mesh. Others do well as pot plants.

Terrestrial orchids grow in the ground in their native habitats. In the home or greenhouse they do well in clay or plastic pots.

Food and water. Since orchids come from many climates and elevations, rules about watering and feeding them vary. Most epiphytes require a good soaking and then should be allowed to dry out before being watered again. This applies to cattleyas, oncidiums, dendrobiums, vandas, and several others. However, never allow paphiopedilums or cymbidiums to become dry.

Plants grown on tree-fern slabs or cork bark require more frequent watering than those in containers. Water early in the day on sunny days. In addition, all will benefit from a good misting on sunny days.

Many orchids need a resting period approximating the dry season of their native habitats—usually in late autumn or early winter, when growth of the pseudobulbs (bulbous enlargements of the stems) is complete. During this time they need cooler temperatures. Some may lose their leaves. Water the plants just enough to keep the pseudobulbs from shriveling.

Plants hanging on tree-fern slabs or bark should be misted daily and submerged in water once or twice a week in sunny weather—even in winter, when artificial heat is used in the greenhouse.

Growing orchids indoors. Many orchids will grow on the sill of a bright window screened from direct sun. The major problem is maintaining humidity. A fairly deep waterproof tray filled with gravel and water can be helpful. Pots may be placed on the gravel, provided they are above the water level. Frequent misting is advisable. On cold nights cardboard or some other form of insulation should be placed between glass and plants.

Many orchids will grow under artificial light—in the basement, on bookshelves, or on specially designed plant carts. For orchids, as with most flowering plants, use no fewer than four 40-watt fluorescent tubes. These should be wide-spectrum plant-growth tubes. Keep the tubes about 6 inches above the tops of the plants, and leave the lights on for 12 to 14 hours each day.

Most orchids can be put outdoors for the summer. This is especially true of cymbidiums, cattleyas, dendrobiums, and vandas. Find a place out of the direct sun—under a tree, in a lathhouse, or against a north wall. Good air circulation, watering, mild feeding, and frequent spraying or misting should produce handsome flowers.

The Week-to-Week Care of Orchids

How Orchids Produce Their Flowers

Besides the epiphytes, which are described on the preceding page, there are other kinds of orchids. These include the lithophytes, which attach themselves to rocks and are grown in much the same way as epiphytes, and the terrestrials, which grow on the ground and require a different growing medium.

Most epiphytic orchids bloom from autumn to late spring, the flowers growing from swollen stems known as pseudobulbs. However, there are a few epiphytic orchids that do not produce pseudobulbs. Vandas, for example, have erect, woody stems with the flowers growing from the leaf axils. Paphiopedilums are tufted plants with thin, almost wiry flower stems that arise directly from the bases of the plants.

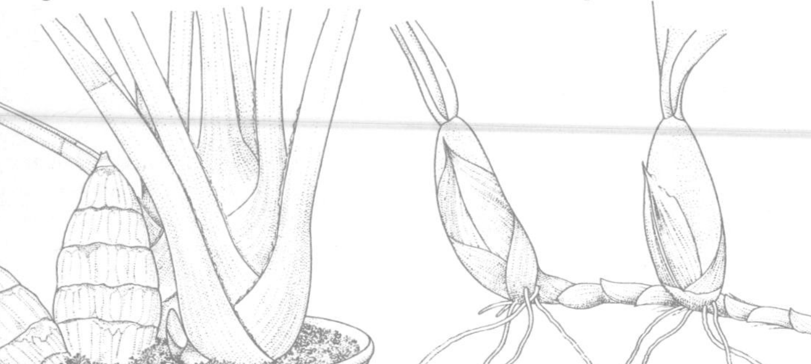

Two types of pseudobulbs. *Cymbidiums (left) have stout pseudobulbs 3–4 in. high, covered with leaves. The old leafless pseudobulbs are called back bulbs. The pseudobulbs of coelogynes (right) grow along a creeping, horizontal rhizome.*

How to Water and Feed Orchid Plants

Orchids should not be watered with very cold or hard (alkaline) water. When possible, keep a tank of rainwater inside the greenhouse where it will stay warm. A 60- to 100-gallon tank would be a good size for an orchid house measuring 8 by 10 feet.

Before washing down the outside of the greenhouse, block the inlet gutter to the tank with a wad of cloth to prevent dirty, lime-containing water from running in.

A tap-water supply to the greenhouse is valuable for filling the tank in dry spells. Even treated water is better than none.

Examine plants once a week to see if the potting mixture is moist, or lift the pot to test its weight. When the mixture has become reasonably dry, water until it is saturated. Do not add any water if it is still wet from the last watering; leave the plant for another week and then check it again.

Hanging plants should be submerged in water until bubbles stop rising from the planting medium.

If you are doubtful about whether the plant is dry enough to water, leave it untouched.

After orchids have been in the same medium for a year, feed them with a liquid fertilizer about once every two weeks during the growing season—late spring to late summer. Water first to prevent the fertilizer from damaging dry roots.

HANGING PLANTS

Submerge until bubbles stop rising from growing medium.

The Resting Period, When Watering Is Rarely Needed

Many orchids require a resting period, usually in late autumn or early winter. During this time they may lose their leaves, leaving only the pseudobulbs, from which new growth will emerge.

When the leaves have fallen or when the pseudobulbs have grown stout and healthy, move the plants to a shelf with better light in a cooler part of the greenhouse. Reduce humidity considerably.

During this period orchids with pseudobulbs need little water unless the potting mixture dries out completely. Then drench thoroughly. Orchids without pseudobulbs may need occasional watering.

When growth begins again, return the plant to its normal place and resume regular watering.

Watering unit for long vacations. *Sink the pots in a tray filled with an equal mixture of coarse sand and peat moss, and insert a hose connected to a tap that has been adjusted to drip very slowly. Keep the greenhouse shaded in summer.*

Caring for Orchids at Vacation Time

Before you go away on summer vacation, soak the plants thoroughly. This watering should last one week.

If your absence is to be longer than a week, keep plants in a capillary watering unit. These units can be bought but are easy to make. Simply fill a plastic flat with a mixture of equal amounts of coarse sand and peat moss, and sink pots in it until they are half submerged. Put a hose in the tray, and allow the water from a tap to trickle into it slowly.

Control temperature by keeping the greenhouse shaded.

Ventilation is the hardest problem. If your greenhouse is not equipped with automatic ventilators, before you leave, open the vents to the average setting that you have been using—and hope the weather holds.

Supporting Top-heavy Orchid Plants

Some orchids, such as cattleyas and dendrobiums, can be top-heavy and need support after potting until they produce strong new roots. Insert a cane at the back of each plant. The cane should be as tall as the eventual height of the plant.

Pass a piece of soft string around two or three of the rear growths, halfway up, and tie it to the cane. Repeat with the other growths.

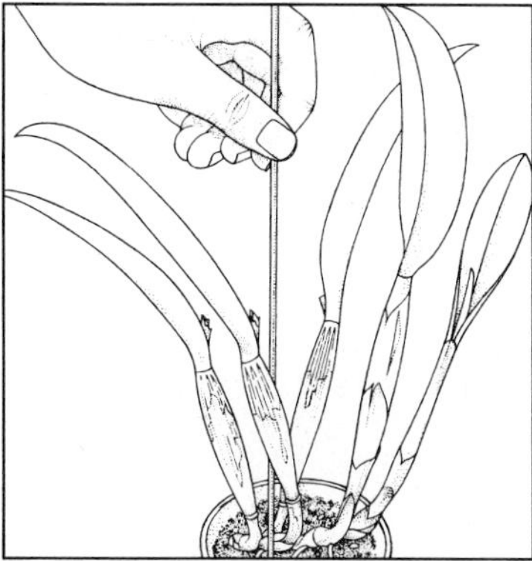

1. *Cattleyas need to be supported after potting, or they may topple over.*

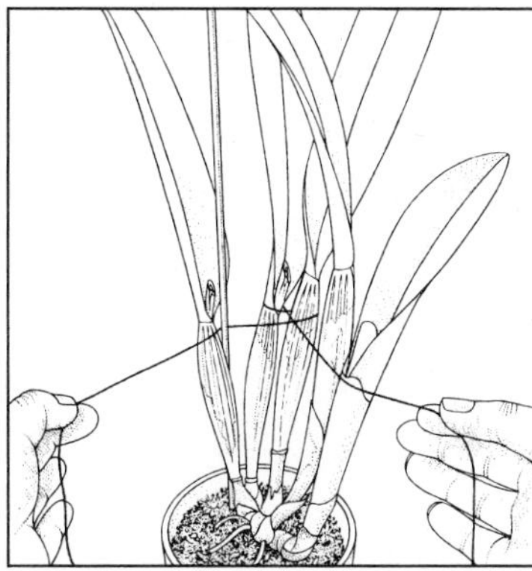

2. *Wind pieces of soft string around the growths, and tie them to a stake.*

Supporting Flowers on Long Stems

Flowers that grow on long stems, such as some paphiopedilums, can be supported by a galvanized-wire prop. Bend the top end of the wire into a loop as shown below.

Support long flower spikes by inserting canes at an angle and attaching the stems to them with twist-ties or pieces of soft twine.

WIRE AND CANE SUPPORTS

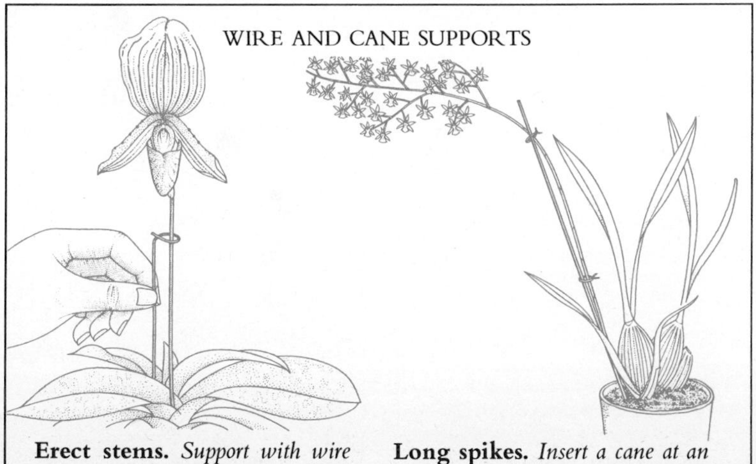

Erect stems. *Support with wire shaped into a loop and bent over.*

Long spikes. *Insert a cane at an angle. Tie the spike to it with twine.*

What Can Go Wrong With Orchids

The chart below describes the commonest problems you are likely to encounter when growing orchids. It is not, however, an exhaustive list, and if your plants show symptoms that are not mentioned here, you will find further information in the section on plant disorders beginning on page 600.

Turn to page 635 for lists of trade names for the chemicals that may be required to solve the problems.

A MALATHION BATH

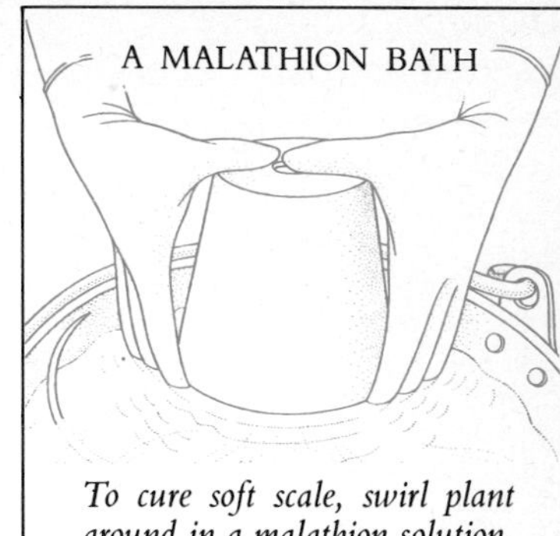

To cure soft scale, swirl plant around in a malathion solution.

Symptoms and signs	Cause	Control
Whitish cottony tufts on leaves and pseudobulbs. Severe attack yellows leaves and weakens plant.	Mealybugs	Remove with soft brush or cotton swab moistened with rubbing alcohol; or spray with malathion.
Yellowish or brownish mottling on leaves, which die prematurely.	Red spider mites or thrips	Spray with chlorpyrifos (for thrips), dicofol, malathion, or tetradifon.
Small, brown, flattened ovoid scales on leaves and pseudobulbs. Severe attack weakens plant.	Soft scale (infestation by scale insects)	Dip entire plant in malathion solution, use systemic insecticide such as dimethoate, or remove scale with alcohol-moistened soft brush or cotton swab.
Young leaves or flower buds are eaten off.	Slugs or snails	Sprinkle slug bait around plants while new growth is forming; use pellets of metaldehyde, methiocarb, or mexacarbate.
Leaves or bulbs begin to rot.	Damping-off disease	Spray with Benomyl or Captan.
Flowers are deformed; leaves have semi-transparent patches.	Virus disease	No control. Destroy plants. Select stock carefully.
Brown speckling on petals and young leaves.	Humidity too high	Provide more ventilation on warm days. Reduce misting.
Yellow leaves, sometimes with brown patches.	Scorch, due to lack of shade, improper ventilation	Make sure greenhouse roof is shaded in late spring and summer. Pay close attention to ventilation.
Small yellowish leaves and pseudobulbs; few or no flowers.	Starvation, or compost too wet	Repot in new compost, dividing plant if necessary. Water carefully.
Flower buds fail to develop properly, usually withering or falling early.	Too cold, or too hot and dry	Make sure appropriate cultural regime is carried out. Use minimum-maximum thermometer to keep check on rising and falling temperatures.

Dividing and Repotting Overgrown Orchids

Splitting a Clump of Pseudobulbs Into Two Plants

Most orchids with pseudobulbs are sympodial: that is, they produce new growth, along with new pseudobulbs, from the base of the plants each year. Such plants will probably need dividing and repotting when they are four to five years old.

Repotting is best done at a time when the plant is beginning to make new root growth. First, take off the old brown leaf bases—if they come away easily in the hand without being tugged. Do not force those that are firmly attached. Then, to remove the plant from its pot, support it and the growing medium with one hand and invert the pot with the other. If necessary, tap the pot rim on the edge of a bench or table to loosen the plant.

Find a natural division in the plant's top growth, and with a large knife cut down through this separation into the root system. (Before cutting into another plant, sterilize the knife by holding it over a flame. A dirty knife will spread any viruses that may be present.)

Pull the plant apart to complete the division. Then, with a pointed stick and your fingers, remove all the old potting mixture from one of the parts, and snip off any dead roots.

Choose a pot or basket that will provide at least 2 inches of space between its front edge and the plant, to allow for new growth. (The back of the plant will rest against the pot.) If you are using an ordinary plant pot, put in crock fragments or gravel to one-fifth of its depth for drainage. This is not necessary in containers made specifically for orchids. Cover the crocks or gravel with growing medium (see next page).

Before putting the newly divided plant in its pot, pack some of the potting medium into its root system. Then insert the plant into the pot with a spiraling motion so that the roots become coiled inside. The back bulbs (old, leafless pseudobulbs) should rest against the rear of the pot, leaving 2 inches at the front.

Fill in around the plant with growing medium to within about 1 inch of the rim of the pot, and firm it down gently but well.

If you use osmunda fiber as the medium, soak it overnight before using it. Then, cut it into small vertical wedges, and pack them firmly around the roots with a stick. This firm packing is required to support the plant. Trim the surface of the fiber with large scissors. If a fir-bark mixture has been used, the plant may need staking until the roots have grown enough to bind the growing medium together.

For orchids without pseudobulbs, such as vandas, repot when needed without disturbing the roots.

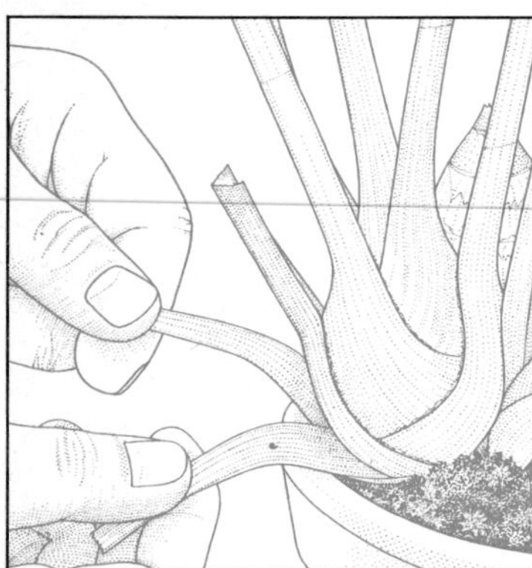

1. *First, in repotting sympodial orchids, remove the old brown leaf bases.*

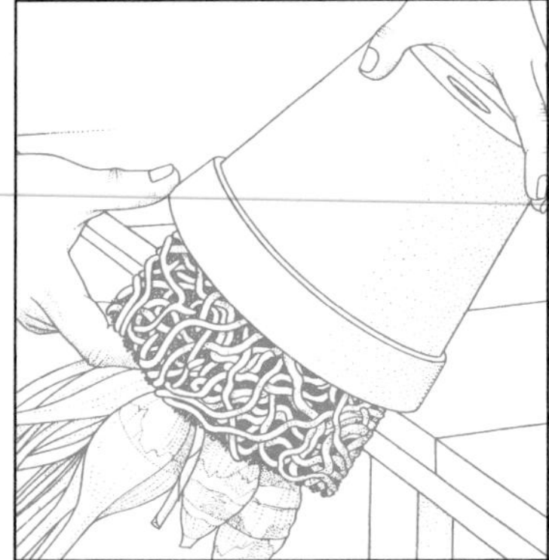

2. *Remove the plant; tap the pot rim on the side of a bench if necessary.*

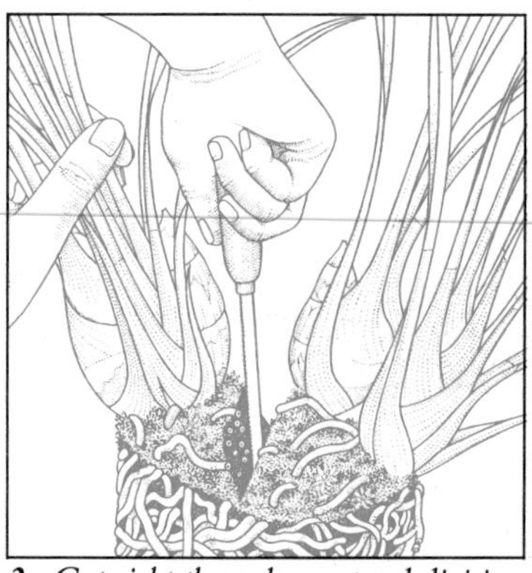

3. *Cut right through a natural division in the plant with a large, sharp knife.*

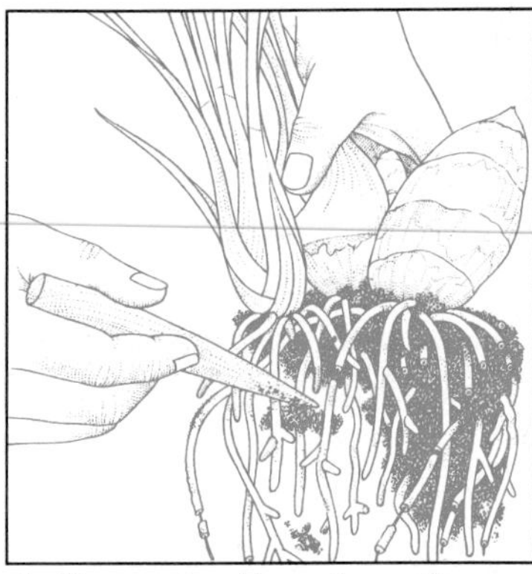

4. *Remove the old growing medium from both parts. Cut away dead roots.*

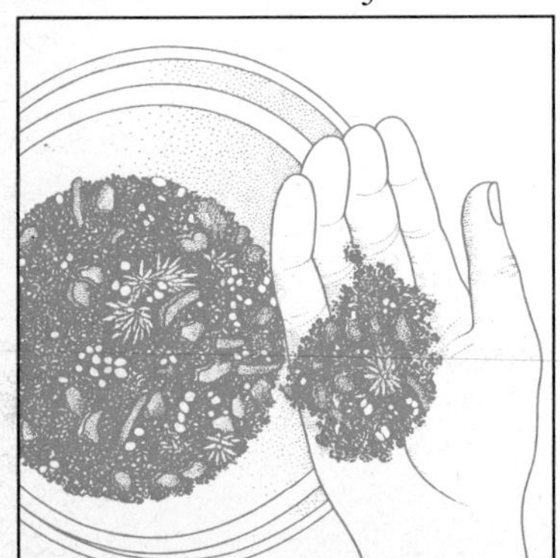

5. *Fill one-fifth of pot with gravel. Add a layer of growing medium.*

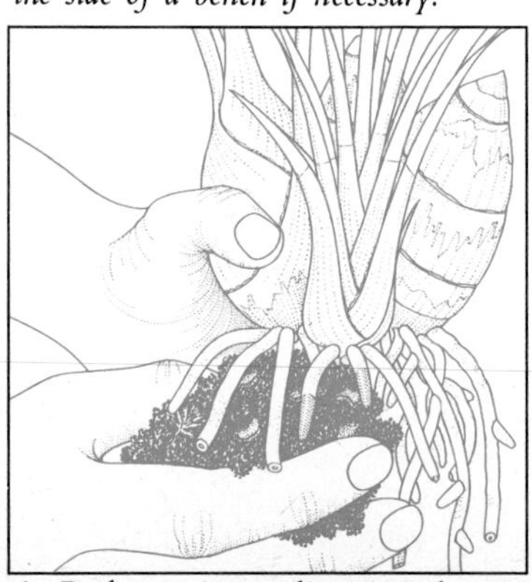

6. *Pack growing medium into the root system of each half of the divided plant.*

7. *Plant with back bulbs against the back of the pot, a 2-in. space in front.*

8. *Pack more of the growing medium around the roots with a stick.*

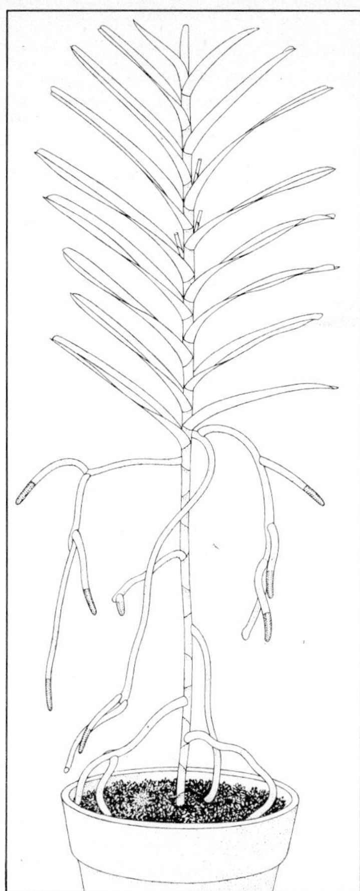

1. *Vanda stems eventually become too tall and must be shortened by half.*

Shortening Vandas and Other Single-Stemmed Plants

Some orchids, such as vandas, are monopodial: they grow vertically on single stems. When they become too tall, they can be divided by cutting the stem in half.

These orchids have aerial roots growing out of their stems. Every year the roots develop laterals, which begin as green points. When these laterals start to grow in the spring, the plant can be cut and repotted.

Fill a 5- to 6-inch pot with crock fragments or gravel to one-third its depth. Add a 1-inch layer of potting mixture and a sprinkling of slow-release general fertilizer.

With clean shears sever the stem beneath a group of aerial roots. Remove any dead leaf bases from the severed section. Twirl this section into the pot as shown. The plant should be centered in the pot.

Fill the pot with growing medium. If you have used osmunda fiber, surface it with a mixture of equal parts of sphagnum moss and osmunda fiber. With a stick, pack the covering mixture tightly into the pot in vertical wedges.

The base of the original stem will later produce lateral shoots. These can be severed and potted separately when roots have formed.

Special Containers and Supports for Orchids

Orchids can be grown in ordinary clay or plastic pots, but the pots must have a good layer of crock fragments or gravel at the bottom to allow for rapid drainage. Special orchid pots or pans are perforated and need no drainage material.

Wooden baskets are suitable for pendulous orchids. Hang such baskets in the greenhouse so that the plants can droop down freely. Alternatively, pendulous orchids can be secured to sections of tree-fern stems or thick pieces of rough bark. The roots should be wrapped lightly in a little tree-fern fiber or sphagnum moss and pinned to the support with galvanized wire staples or plastic-covered wire. The plant can then be suspended so that its stems will trail down naturally.

Upright orchids can be grown in perforated clay pots. Orchids with trailing flowers grow best in hanging wooden baskets or on sections of tree-fern stem.

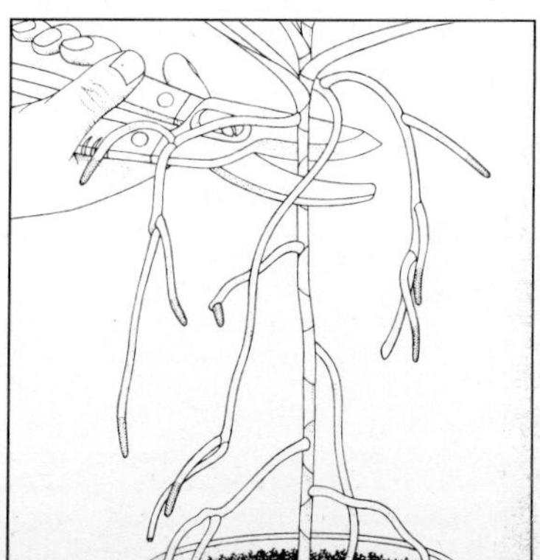

2. *In spring sever the stem below a group of sprouting aerial roots.*

3. *Twirl the roots into a 5- to 6-in. pot, and fill with potting mixture.*

A Choice of Growing Mediums for Orchids

Orchids require a growing medium with excellent porosity and aeration. For years osmunda fiber was usually used for epiphytic orchids, but today it is difficult to obtain.

Orchid specialists offer a growing medium with fir bark as the major ingredient, plus other materials such as peat moss and coarse perlite (or crumbled Styrofoam and bird gravel). Such a potting mixture is easier to use than osmunda, which requires considerable skill. To make your own mixture, use 7 parts fir bark (medium size), 1 part peat moss (German), and 1 part perlite (coarse). Making your own mix is generally less expensive but often not practical for small quantities.

Terrestrial orchids, such as calanthes, require a light soil mixture. Use 1 part soil, 1 part peat moss (German), 1 part fir bark (medium size), and 1 part perlite (coarse).

For paphiopedilums, which do best in alkaline soil, the addition of ground oyster shells is a good idea.

Orchids will grow in these mixtures for four or five years.

How to Grow New Orchids

Bringing Old Bulbs Back to Life

The commonest way to propagate orchids is from back bulbs. These are old pseudobulbs that have lost their leaves. They are given this name because they grow behind the new leafy pseudobulbs.

The best time to remove back bulbs is at the end of the normal resting period, at the same time that an overlarge plant is divided and repotted (see p. 480).

Remove the plant from its pot or basket, and cut off the largest back bulbs with their roots. Leave at least four pseudobulbs—old or new—on the original plant and repot it.

Place a layer of drainage material in the bottom of a 3-inch pot, and half-fill with moist potting mix.

Cushion the base of the back bulb with a little more potting material, and put it in the pot. Fill in with the same medium. Cymbidiums are potted as single back bulbs, cattleyas in groups of three or four. Label the newly potted plant.

Stand the pot in a heated propagating case containing moist sand or peat moss and with a bottom heat of approximately 60° F. Put the case in a warm, shaded part of the greenhouse where you have space to spare.

When shoots begin growing from the base of the bulb, remove it from the propagating case, and place it on a slatted bench—still in its pot. As little time as a month, or as long as a year, may pass before these new shoots appear. Sometimes there will be no new growth at all, and the bulb will yellow and wither away.

Successful new plants will need to be moved into the next-larger-size pot within a year after the new growth appears.

A large cymbidium back bulb, 3–4 inches high, should flower in three or four years.

Buying Community Pots of Seedlings

An interesting and inexpensive way to grow orchids is to buy community pots (a number of seedlings together) from a nursery. However, you will have to wait two to three years before they will flower.

When you get the seedlings, pot them up individually in $1\frac{1}{2}$- to 2-inch pots. Water thoroughly with rainwater, and place the pot in a shaded part of the greenhouse at the temperature recommended for the particular orchid.

Seedlings can also be bought singly, in which case they will probably not need immediate repotting. They should, however, be moved into $2\frac{1}{2}$- to 3-inch pots within six to eight months.

Progression to larger pots depends on the kind of orchid. The following schedule is for a standard cattleya:

After two to four months, check to see if the roots have reached the outside of the root ball. If so, the plant needs to go into a 4-inch pot. Put a few grains of a slow-release general fertilizer on the medium near the pot rim. Water in a shady part of the greenhouse at a temperature recommended for the particular kind of orchid. Keep the growing medium moist but not waterlogged. Put the plant into a 6-inch pot 18 months later or when the roots get crowded. It is then at flowering age.

1. *Just after the resting period, remove plant from its container.*

2. *Cut off the largest back bulbs with roots, leaving four bulbs on the plant.*

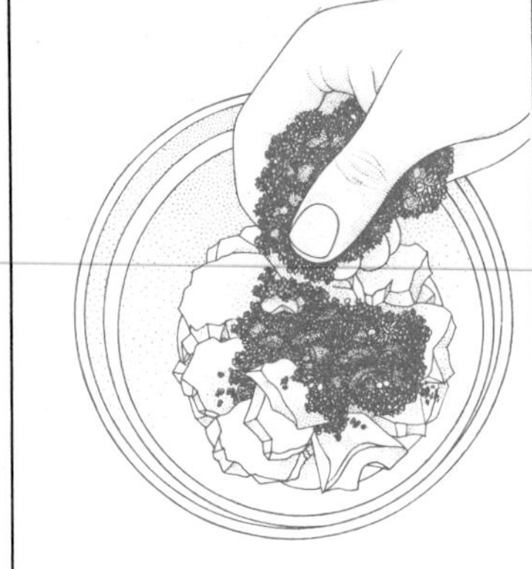

3. *Put some gravel in a 3-in. pot, and half-fill it with the growing medium.*

4. *Cushion the base of the back bulb in the medium, and plant it in the pot.*

5. *Stand the pot on moist sand or peat moss inside a heated propagating case.*

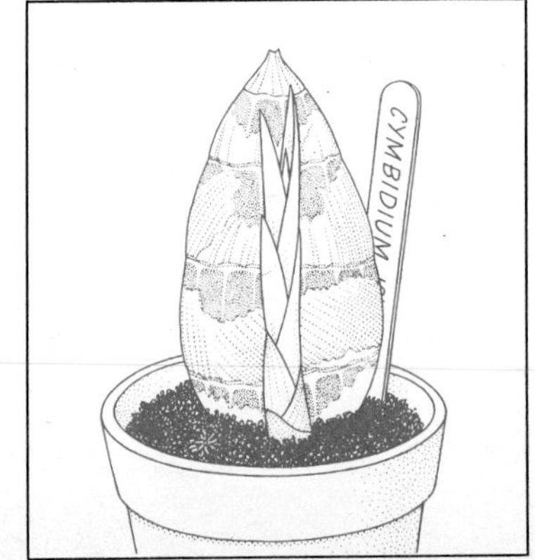

6. *When shoots grow, remove pot from case. Repot when roots become crowded.*

STARTING SEEDLINGS

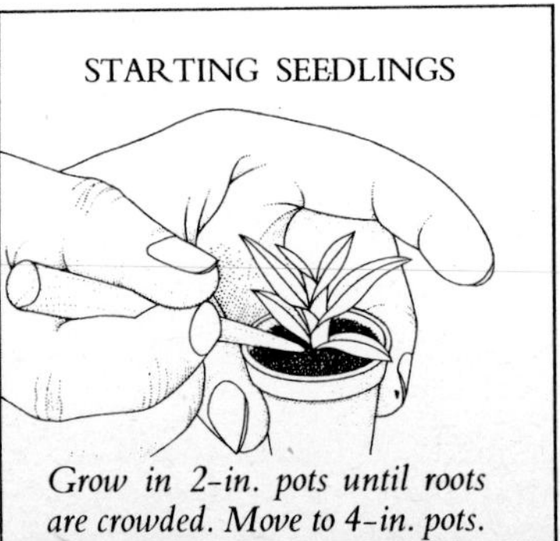

Grow in 2-in. pots until roots are crowded. Move to 4-in. pots.

Orchids for Cool to Warm Greenhouses

The chart that follows provides essential information about some of the most rewarding orchids to grow in the house or greenhouse.

It is divided into two sections: one on cool- to intermediate-growing orchids, which require a minimum night temperature of 45°–50° F; and the other, on intermediate- to warm-growing orchids, which need a minimum night temperature of 65° F. Intermediate orchids will grow best with a minimum night temperature of 58°–60° F. They are listed in alphabetical order by their botanical names.

All orchids can survive summer temperatures of up to 90° F if they have sufficient humidity and if the period of heat is not too prolonged. Winter temperatures can drop 5 degrees below the minimum for up to two weeks without doing significant harm to the plants if they are kept dry during that period.

Warm-growing orchids are more expensive to grow because of the high cost of heating a greenhouse. This expense can be reduced by having a few warm-growing plants in a heated frame in a cool orchid house.

The measurements given in the chart under the heading Height of Plant include the flower spike.

Under Flowers per Stem, "In succession" means that the flowers open progressively along the stem.

Light requirements are classified under Exposure as light, semi-shade, and shade. A light exposure requires a slight stipple of shading compound on the glass of the greenhouse. Semi-shade requires covering all glass exposed directly to the sun. Roll-down shades can also be used to provide the right light requirements.

Those orchids that can be grown in the home (see p. 477) are indicated under Suited to Indoor Culture?

Terrestrial orchids that need soil are so indicated in the Temperature and Remarks column.

COOL TO INTERMEDIATE GREENHOUSE ORCHIDS

Ada aurantiaca — *Anguloa clowesii* — *Bletilla striata* — *Brassia verrucosa* — *Bulbophyllum barbigerum* — *Cochlioda sanguinea* — *Coelogyne cristata*

Botanical and common names	Height of plant	Flower size	Flowers per stem	Longevity of flowers	Flowering time	Resting period	Exposure	Suited to indoor culture?	Temperature and remarks
Ada	9 in.	1¼ in.	10-12	14-21 da.	Winter	None	Semi-shade	Yes	Cool. Showy but small orange-scarlet flowers on vertical 6-in. stems.
Anguloa (cradle orchid)	24 in.	4-6 in.	1	21-28 da.	Nov.-May	Nov.-Jan.	Semi-shade	No	Cool. Keep cool in winter. Very large, free-flowering, showy plant. Do not let water splash young folded leaves.
Bletilla, or Bletia	15-18 in.	1½-2 in.	8-15	21-25 da.	Summer	Winter	Light	No	Cool. Terrestrial. Inexpensive. Easy to grow. Lovely burgundy flowers.
Brassia	18 in.	3-6 in.	7-12	35-40 da.	May-Sept.	Autumn-Jan.	Light	Yes	Intermediate. Large, showy, spidery, spotted flowers.
Bulbophyllum	6-8 in.	1-2 in.	1-7	10-14 da.	All year	Winter	Shade	No	Intermediate. A vast genus. Intriguing flowers of many different forms.
Cochlioda, or Symphyglossum	8-16 in.	1½-3½ in.	10-20	21-28 da.	Dec.-Apr.	Winter	Semi-shade	Yes	Cool. Scarlet and red flowers.
Coelogyne	10-12 in.	1½-4 in.	5-12	10-21 da.	May-Sept.	Winter	Semi-shade	Yes	Cool. White, salmon, or brown flowers, which are often fragrant.

COOL TO INTERMEDIATE GREENHOUSE ORCHIDS *(continued)*

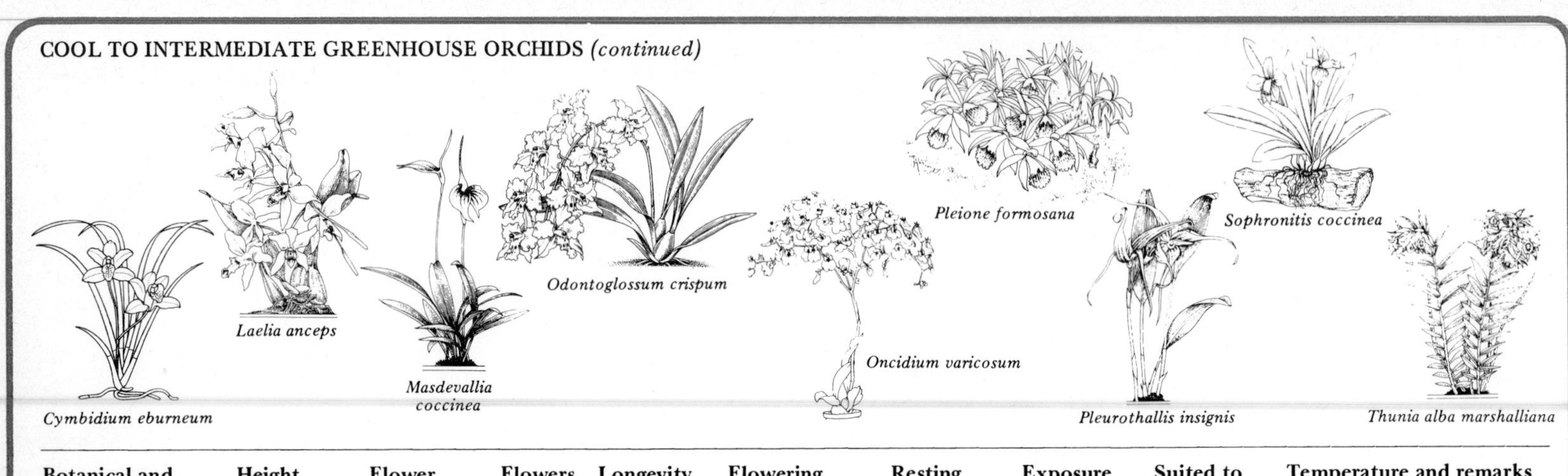

Cymbidium eburneum · *Laelia anceps* · *Masdevallia coccinea* · *Odontoglossum crispum* · *Oncidium varicosum* · *Pleione formosana* · *Pleurothallis insignis* · *Sophronitis coccinea* · *Thunia alba marshalliana*

Botanical and common names	Height of plant	Flower size	Flowers per stem	Longevity of flowers	Flowering time	Resting period	Exposure	Suited to indoor culture?	Temperature and remarks
Cymbidium	48-60 in.	2½-5 in.	12-24	50-60 da.	Dec.-June	Oct.-Feb.	Semi-shade	No	Very cool. Terrestrial. Easy to grow.
Miniature species and hybrids	12-18 in.	1½-4 in.	10-20	50-60 da.	Dec.-June	Oct.-Feb.	Semi-shade	No	Cool. Large and small flowers in many shades.
Laelia	10-36 in.	2-4 in.	1-20	14-21 da.	Autumn	Oct.-Apr.	Light	Yes	Intermediate. Rose to orange flowers.
Masdevallia (tailed orchid)	3-18 in.	1-3 in.	1-5	10-20 da.	Spring-summer	None	Shade	No	Very cool. Does not need sunlight. Requires moisture. Striking floral shapes.
Odontoglossum	10-40 in.	1½-4½ in.	5-35	21-42 da.	Spring	Winter	Semi-shade	No	Very cool. Vast color choice—whites, yellows, and all shades of mauves and reds.
Oncidium	20-40 in.	1-3 in.	10-100	21-42 da.	June-Jan.	Late winter	Light	Yes	Cool. Many have tall branching spikes. Colors mainly yellow and brown.
Pleione	3-5 in.	2½-3 in.	1	10-15 da.	Spring	Oct.-Feb.	Light (or full sun outdoors)	Yes	Cool. Terrestrial. Use rich, peaty soil. One of easiest to grow. Mostly pink flowers.
Pleurothallis	5-15 in.	½-2 in.	1-3	7-21 da.	Winter	None	Shade	Yes	Cool. Small flowers of great interest.
Sophronitis	3-15 in.	2-4 in.	1-3	10-28 da.	Winter-spring	Oct.-Feb.	Semi-shade	Yes	Intermediate. Mostly miniature plants, 3-4 in. high. Scarlets and mauves.
Thunia	20-30 in.	3-3½ in.	3-7	10-20 da.	Spring-summer	Nov.-Mar.	Light	Yes	Cool. Elegant tall-stemmed foliage. White and rose flowers.

INTERMEDIATE TO WARM GREENHOUSE ORCHIDS

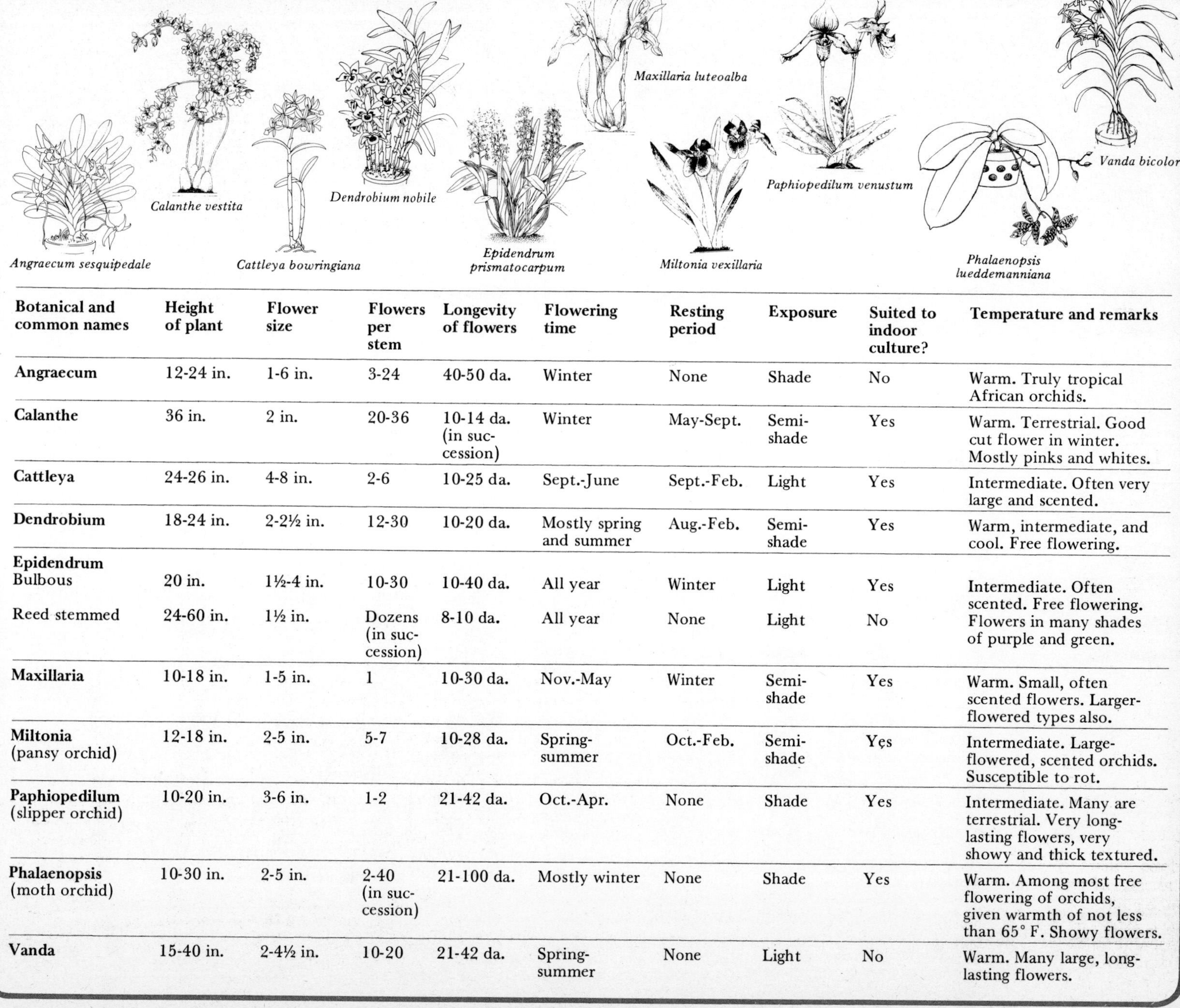

Botanical and common names	Height of plant	Flower size	Flowers per stem	Longevity of flowers	Flowering time	Resting period	Exposure	Suited to indoor culture?	Temperature and remarks
Angraecum	12-24 in.	1-6 in.	3-24	40-50 da.	Winter	None	Shade	No	Warm. Truly tropical African orchids.
Calanthe	36 in.	2 in.	20-36	10-14 da. (in succession)	Winter	May-Sept.	Semi-shade	Yes	Warm. Terrestrial. Good cut flower in winter. Mostly pinks and whites.
Cattleya	24-26 in.	4-8 in.	2-6	10-25 da.	Sept.-June	Sept.-Feb.	Light	Yes	Intermediate. Often very large and scented.
Dendrobium	18-24 in.	2-2½ in.	12-30	10-20 da.	Mostly spring and summer	Aug.-Feb.	Semi-shade	Yes	Warm, intermediate, and cool. Free flowering.
Epidendrum									
Bulbous	20 in.	1½-4 in.	10-30	10-40 da.	All year	Winter	Light	Yes	Intermediate. Often scented. Free flowering. Flowers in many shades of purple and green.
Reed stemmed	24-60 in.	1½ in.	Dozens (in succession)	8-10 da.	All year	None	Light	No	
Maxillaria	10-18 in.	1-5 in.	1	10-30 da.	Nov.-May	Winter	Semi-shade	Yes	Warm. Small, often scented flowers. Larger-flowered types also.
Miltonia (pansy orchid)	12-18 in.	2-5 in.	5-7	10-28 da.	Spring-summer	Oct.-Feb.	Semi-shade	Yes	Intermediate. Large-flowered, scented orchids. Susceptible to rot.
Paphiopedilum (slipper orchid)	10-20 in.	3-6 in.	1-2	21-42 da.	Oct.-Apr.	None	Shade	Yes	Intermediate. Many are terrestrial. Very long-lasting flowers, very showy and thick textured.
Phalaenopsis (moth orchid)	10-30 in.	2-5 in.	2-40 (in succession)	21-100 da.	Mostly winter	None	Shade	Yes	Warm. Among most free flowering of orchids, given warmth of not less than 65° F. Showy flowers.
Vanda	15-40 in.	2-4½ in.	10-20	21-42 da.	Spring-summer	None	Light	No	Warm. Many large, long-lasting flowers.

Growing Plants for Food

Fruits

Even a small garden has room for fruit—not only bushes, canes, and vines but also dwarf trees in restricted form, trained against a wall or fence or grown in an open space.

Most fruits fall into two main categories—small fruits and tree fruits. Among the small fruits are blackberries, blueberries, gooseberries, raspberries, red currants, and strawberries. Tree fruits that are most frequently grown in home gardens include apples, avocados, citrus, figs, cherries, peaches, pears, and plums. Grapes, of course, grow on vines.

Small Fruits

Small fruits are grown in the form of either bushes or canes, except for strawberries, which occur as low-growing bedding plants. Bushes have permanent spreading branches that start at ground level or just above, on a short "leg." They grow about 4 feet high and as wide.

Blueberries, red currants, and gooseberries are grown as bushes. Where space is limited, gooseberries and red currants can be trained flat on a wall or trellis as one-, two-, or three-stemmed espaliers.

Canes are slender shrubs that have stems starting at ground level or just below. They need to be controlled by training to a post or wires and are cut away every year after fruiting to make space for new growth to develop. Raspberries grow as canes, as do blackberries and loganberries. (The latter are a form of blackberry.)

Tree Fruits

The most suitable full-dwarfed tree fruits for the average garden grow in different forms, including cordon, horizontal and fan espalier, and pyramid. They can be grown on M IX or M 26 dwarfing rootstocks (see p. 509). Standard and half-standard trees are used mainly in commercial orchards.

Dwarfed trees. Traditionally the most popular form for apples and pears, these are grafted on a dwarfing or semi-dwarfing rootstock. They have a 24- to 27-inch-high stem, and at this height branches radiate to form the head of the tree. These dwarfed tree forms average 6–10 feet in height and spread. Some interstem trees are also available with an MM 106 root, a 6- to 8-inch M IX dwarfing interstem (a foot aboveground), and a variety such as 'Golden Delicious' on the top.

Cordon espaliers. One of the best tree forms for a small garden, these have a single stem with no major spreading branches. They take up very little space, are easy to manage, and have a high yield for their size. However, cordons involve a higher initial cost, since 6 to 12 are needed to supply a family of four.

Cordons have to be supported on wires; they can be grown upright, but the branches are usually trained horizontally or at an angle of 45 degrees to enable a longer main stem to be grown. The average length is 8–10 feet, and the oblique height is 7 feet. A variation is the U-shaped double cordon, usually grown upright. Apple trees and pear trees are most suitable for training as cordons.

Horizontal espaliers. A single central stem with pairs of opposite horizontal branches is supported by wires. Horizontal espaliers need careful pruning and training. This form is suited to apple and pear trees where space is limited. The average height is 8 feet, the spread 6-10 feet.

Fan espaliers. The branches are trained on supporting wires to form a fan shape. They are usually grown against a wall. All the trees dealt with in this section can be trained as fans. The fan takes considerable wall space and requires careful pruning. The average height is 10 feet, and the average spread will be 10–15 feet.

Dwarf pyramids. These have a central stem with branches that begin about 15 inches from the ground and get progressively shorter toward the top in the shape of a Christmas tree. This basic structure is best suited to apples and pears, but there is a modified form for plums. The average height is 7–10 feet, and the average spread is 3–6 feet.

Pollination

Most flowers will not develop into fruits unless they are fertilized with pollen. The pollen is usually transferred by wind and insects.

Most fruit trees have both male and female organs in the same flower, but not all are self-fertile (fertilized by their own pollen). Some need to be grown with another variety of a similar kind that flowers at the same time, so that cross-pollination can take place.

Before ordering trees, find out about their pollinating needs from a nursery catalog, and then purchase the varieties necessary. If you buy direct from a nursery, the nurseryman can make sure you get the required varieties. Small fruits, except for blueberries, can be fertilized by their own pollen.

Pruning

Fruit pruning is carried out in two main stages. The young tree or bush must be trained to the shape required, and once the framework has been established, it must be pruned annually.

For fruit trees the basic training is generally the same as that given for apples. After that, however, the system varies. As one of its main aims is to regulate the crop and improve the quality of the fruit, pruning depends

on the habit of growth of the tree.

Apples, sweet cherries, and pears bear fruit mostly on wood that is at least two years old. The aim is, therefore, to maintain a balance between old and new wood.

Blackberries, currants, blueberries, figs, loganberries, peaches, raspberries (summer fruiting), and tart cherries bear fruit mostly on one-year-old wood. Grapes bear on the current season's wood and are pruned in spring by removing shoots that have borne fruit. Autumn-fruiting raspberries bear two crops. The summer crop is borne on the same canes that produced the previous fall crop. Prune by removing the fruiting canes after the summer crop.

Plums, red currants, and gooseberries bear on one-year-old or older wood. The aim is to produce plenty of new wood.

For tree crops, pruning is generally done in late fall or late winter. In early fall there is a greater risk of disease entering the wound. Large pruning cuts should be protected with a wound-sealing paint.

Trees grown in a restricted form may need pruning both in summer and later, when dormant.

Raising New Stock

A fruit tree raised from seed varies considerably from its parent. The only certain way of perpetuating a variety is by grafting.

Grafting is best left to an expert nurseryman. A portion of the shoot, which is called the scion, is taken from the variety of tree to be raised and grafted on the rootstock (the root system and part of the stem) of a tree of a different variety. This union between scion and rootstock often shows itself as a bulge in the stem.

The rootstock influences the size, vigor, and fruiting capacity of the tree, and various rootstocks have been standardized and classified, as shown in the diagram on page 509. When buying a fruit tree, tell the nurseryman the form in which you want to grow it, and describe the soil and growing conditions, so that he can provide suitable rootstock.

Small-fruit canes and bushes are grown on their own roots.

Buying Fruit Trees

Fruit trees of various ages can be bought for planting. They can be one or two years old, preferably no older. A one-year-old tree consists of a single stem only. If it has a few side or branched shoots, it is known as a branched one-year-old.

If you buy a year-old tree, you will have to train it yourself. Two-year-old trees are sold partly trained. Do not buy old trees, as they may be slower in reestablishing themselves.

When you buy a tree, ask its age so that you can continue with the correct training. For most trees the age can be worked out simply by noting the pattern of side shoots on the lower branches.

In the first year of a tree's life, only the main stem grows. In the second season the side shoots (branches) grow from the main stem. In the third, side shoots grow from the first branches, and so on.

If, therefore, the lowest branch of a tree has a side shoot that also has a side shoot, you know the tree is four years old. Peach trees are an exception: they usually produce new side shoots from side shoots that have developed during the current year.

Planting Fruit Trees and Bushes

Unless fruit trees have been supplied in containers, plant them between midfall and early spring, the earlier the better. In cold climates plant only in early spring. Trees in containers can be planted at any time the ground can be dug, as long as the roots are established.

Do not plant until the soil is in suitable condition. It must not be frozen or too wet. Ideally, a handful should hold together when squeezed but fall apart when dropped.

On the day of planting, dig a hole wide enough to take the outspread roots and deep enough so that the top roots will be covered with 3–4 inches of soil. Loosen the soil at the bottom of the hole with a fork so that the roots can penetrate as deeply as possible.

Ideally, fruit trees should not be grown in heavy, waterlogged soils; but if you have no option, dig the hole one-third deeper than usual, put some stones at the bottom for drainage, and work in a wheelbarrow load of sandy soil when refilling. However, even this may not help if subsoil is impervious (hard pan).

Place a stake (tall enough to reach the point where the stem begins to branch) as deeply and firmly in the center of the hole as possible. Put 4–6 inches of well-rotted (or dehydrated) manure or compost in the hole. Work this material around thoroughly so that the roots will not come into contact with large pieces.

If the tree's roots are dry, soak them in water for about two hours before planting. Cut out damaged roots with pruning shears, making a sloping cut. Trim off any stumps of deadwood on the top branches flush with the stem; cut back damaged tips.

Plant the tree no deeper than it was in the nursery, indicated by the soil mark around the stem. (You may need a helper to hold the tree.)

Fill in the topsoil first. Shake the tree from time to time to settle the soil around the roots. Once the roots are covered, firm the soil by treading. Then add the rest of the soil, leaving it loose. Level the surface with a fork. Tie the tree to the stake (see p. 47). Do not grow grass around the tree for two or three years.

After planting, the old soil mark should be just visible, and the union between scion and rootstock should be at least 4 inches above soil level.

Apply one or two handfuls of lawn fertilizer in a 1-foot-wide band 3 inches from the trunk.

In areas where rabbits or mice are a nuisance, protect the tree by encircling it with a plastic collar or wire netting to a height of $1\frac{1}{2}$ feet.

Cordons, espaliers, and fans. Before planting, set up supporting wires, attaching them with screw eyes and turnbuckles to a wall or posts. For cordons, stretch wires at 1 foot, 3 feet, 5 feet, and 7 feet above the ground; for horizontal espaliers, every 12–15 inches; for fans, every 9–12 inches, starting at the appropriate height aboveground.

If planting against a wall, set the stem at least 6 inches from the wall to avoid the dry soil in the sheltered area at the base. Lean the stem slightly toward the wall to make it easier to tie to the wires.

The scion on a cordon

Point the stems of cordons toward the north, if possible, to give them the maximum amount of light. Make sure that the scion is uppermost, to prevent it from breaking if the cordon has to be lowered. Plant the last tree in a row at least 8 feet from the end of the posts or wall so that there will be room for lowering.

Other fruits. For planting figs, grapes, raspberries, and strawberries, see the appropriate section. Blackberries, blueberries, gooseberries, loganberries, and red currants are planted like shrubs (see p. 81).

What to Do If You Cannot Plant at Once

If the trees, bushes, or canes arrive at a time when you cannot plant them, temporarily cover their roots with soil in a trench. This protective treatment is called heeling in.

The soil must be neither too dry nor too wet; so a good site for heeling in during wet weather is against the wall of a house where the ground is not soaked. If the site is too dry, it should be watered.

To keep the site moist and to prevent it from freezing, cover it before heeling in: first, with plastic sheeting; then, with dry straw, lawn clippings, or leaves; and finally, with more plastic sheeting. When the trees, bushes, or canes arrive, uncover the heeling-in site, and dig a trench as shown below.

Unfasten the bundle and lay the trees along the sloping side of the trench. Heap soil back to cover roots completely. Make sure that the stems are not covered any higher than the mark indicating the soil level in the nursery. Finally, firm the soil.

If the trees arrive at a time when neither planting nor heeling in is possible, unfasten them, place them in an unheated shed or garage, and cover their roots with moist peat moss or other light mulch. Do not keep them for long in this way, because the roots may dry out.

HEELING IN

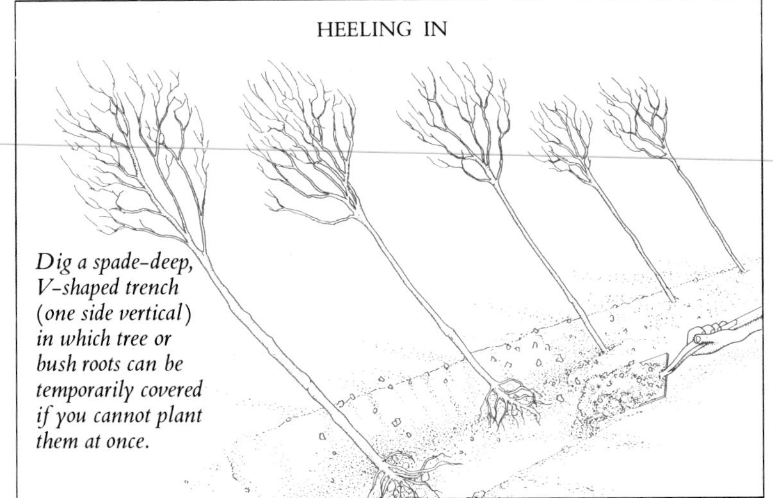

Dig a spade-deep, V-shaped trench (one side vertical) in which tree or bush roots can be temporarily covered if you cannot plant them at once.

The Space a Tree Will Take

The planting distances given in the table to the right are only a guide. Find out the recommended distances when buying trees. The more vigorous the rootstock and the more fertile the soil, the farther apart trees should be planted. Distances given here are mainly for dwarfing or less vigorous rootstocks.

Form of tree	Between trees	Between rows
Dwarf	8–15 ft.	8–15 ft.
Semi-dwarf	10–12 ft.	10–12 ft.
Dwarf pyramid	$3\frac{1}{2}$–4 ft.	7–10 ft.
Espalier		
Cordon	$2\frac{1}{2}$–3 ft.	6–10 ft.
Horizontal	10–15 ft.	8–10 ft.
Fan	15–24 ft.	8–10 ft.

Encouraging a Reluctant Tree to Fruit

If the top growth of a tree is over-vigorous—growing well but producing little or no fruit—one remedy is to reduce its supply of nitrogen by growing grass over the root area. Keep the grass mowed during the growing season so that it will continue to grow and use up the nitrogen in the soil.

Another useful method is to prune the roots of the tree in winter while it is dormant. Inscribe a half-circle, at a distance from the trunk of slightly less than the spread of the branches. Dig a narrow trench along the line deep enough to expose the horizontal roots, and cut through all the roots encountered. The fine roots can be cut with a sharp spade. Use pruning shears to cut through the thick, thonglike roots. When the roots have all been cleanly cut, replace the soil in the trench and tamp it down well. The following winter treat the other half of the tree in the same way.

For apple and pear trees another remedy is bark ringing at blossom time. There is, however, a risk of killing the tree if it is not done properly, as explained below.

About 6 inches below the point where the branches begin, cut off a narrow strip of bark around half of the tree's trunk, and another around the other half, 3 inches below the first strip (so that you do not cut a complete circle around the trunk). The younger and smaller the tree, the narrower should be the strips. On even the largest trees cut strips no more than $\frac{1}{8}$ inch wide.

Use a sharp knife, and cut carefully into the surface bark only. Peel off this layer of bark, and immediately cover the exposed portion with insulating tape. Do not cut too deep. If the cambium layer, just under the bark, is cut all the way around the trunk in a continuous strip, the tree will die.

Protecting Fruit Against Damage and Disease

Fruit buds and growing fruits can be seriously damaged by birds. The only real protection is to cover the trees or bushes with 1-inch nylon mesh or polyethylene netting.

Small fruits and trees grown on supports are most easily protected with temporary cages. Other devices include polyethylene bags, stockings, newspaper cones, or plastic sleeves, put over individual fruits. Less effective are bird-scaring devices, bird-repellent sprays, or cotton or aluminum-foil threads that have been tied among the tree's branches.

Fungi, bacterial and viral diseases, and insects, which can seriously damage or kill trees, are the other main problems in fruit growing.

There are many fungicides and insecticides that can be used to protect fruit, but they should not be used indiscriminately. For home gardeners some spraying is advisable. Sprays should be applied carefully and not when the trees or plants are in bloom because of possible harm to pollinating insects.

Some pests can also develop resistance to chemicals. For instance, there are now red spider mites that are resistant to many sprays commonly used to combat them.

Researchers advocate the use of biological controls to control pests whenever possible, but since the supply is limited, chemical controls are often necessary.

Keep a close watch for pests, and use chemical treatments only when the insects can be seen or, in some cases, if the plant was attacked the previous year. Treat only the infected tree or bush and those nearby.

All-purpose fruit-tree sprays are available in garden stores and are probably the best to use if you have only a few trees to care for.

Good garden hygiene also helps to keep pests and diseases under control. Never leave prunings lying around, and in autumn and winter pick off and destroy old fruit.

To get the maximum possible amount of fruit from your trees, they should be sprayed with the same care and frequency practiced by commercial orchardists. This requires a considerable commitment of time, effort, and expense.

Here, for example, is the annual spray sequence recommended for apples in New Jersey.

When buds show half an inch of green, spray for scales and mites.

At least seven days later but before blossoms open, spray for apple scab and aphids.

When 90 percent of the flower petals fall, spray for scab, curculios, caterpillars, and mites.

Fourteen days later spray again for scab, codling moth, and curculios.

Two weeks later, spray for scab and codling moth.

Twenty-one days later spray for scab, fruit rot, apple maggots, and aphids. Repeat this three times at 3-week intervals.

These recommendations ar
one area. The sprays and the
vary from region to regio
source of up-to-date in
this (and most sim
your county exte

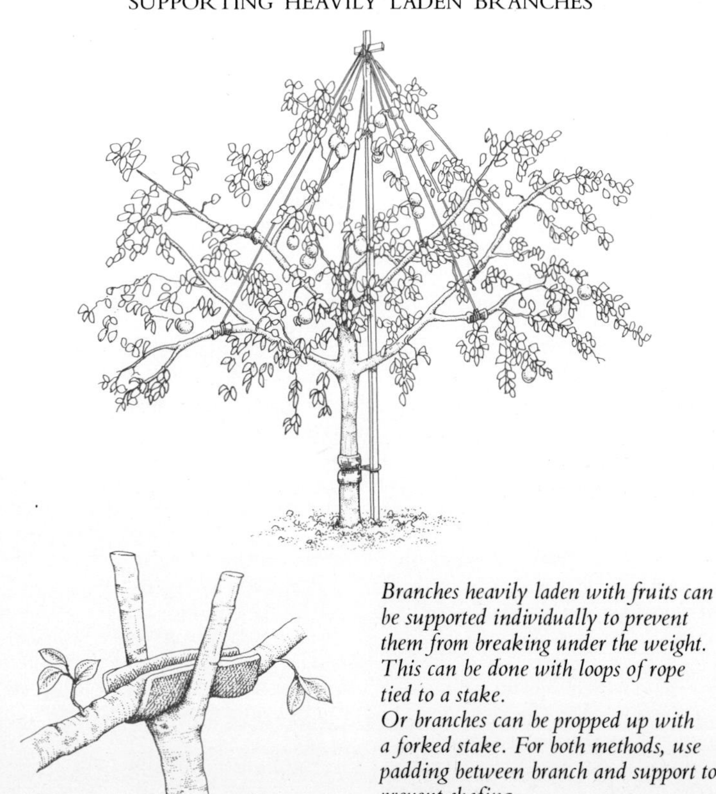

SUPPORTING HEAVILY LADEN BRANCHES

Branches heavily laden with fruits can be supported individually to prevent them from breaking under the weight. This can be done with loops of rope tied to a stake.

Or branches can be propped up with a forked stake. For both methods, use padding between branch and support to prevent chafing.

Apples

Apple 'Golden Delicious'

The apple is one of the most widely grown fruits. Apple trees grow in most soils but do best in well-drained, neutral or slightly alkaline soil that does not dry out in summer.

Apples do not grow well in seaside gardens because salt-laden winds can be damaging. Very few apple trees grow well unless they have a freezing winter. However, a few varieties are now offered for warmer regions.

Most varieties of apple trees need cross-pollinating by another variety that blossoms at the same time (see p. 509). [illegible] ly trees" are [illegible] ree to five [illegible] es growing [illegible] Using these, [illegible] single tree. [illegible] at likes ap- [illegible] ns, 4 espal- [illegible] r 12 cor- [illegible] ple fruit. [illegible] dsummer [illegible] n be kept [illegible] g spring. [illegible] s in au- [illegible] nates, in spring only (see p. 490). The roots of newly planted trees need plenty of water; so make sure that the soil is kept moist.

For the first two or three years, cover the soil in spring with straw or other mulch. Keep mulch 2 feet from the trunk.

In late winter feed trees with a complete fertilizer. This can be repeated in the spring if there is any indication that the trees lack vigor. If a 10–10–10 formulation is used, a sensible average feeding for a mature dwarf tree with a foliage spread of 6 feet is ½–1 pound distributed over the root area. Keep in mind that most of the feeder roots are concentrated away from the trunk toward the outer reaches of the branches.

Sprinkle the fertilizer over the soil, covering an area slightly larger than that overspread by the branches. Let it penetrate naturally. Do not fork it in; this can damage the roots. Remove weeds by shallow hoeing. Trees will need watering during long dry spells.

Thinning a Heavy Crop of Young Apples

The aim of thinning is to allow the remaining apples to grow to full size. Too heavy a crop will crowd the fruits and result in small apples of poor quality.

Start thinning a heavy crop of young apples in late spring or before the natural drop occurs. If this early natural drop seems too heavy, which it may be if the soil is poor or dry, some feeding and mulching as recommended on these pages is in order to prevent further drop.

From each cluster, first remove the central fruit, if it is misshapen, by cutting its stalk with a pair of scissors with pointed blades. Never pull fruit off the tree when thinning, as this can damage the spur. Then cut off any inferior apples, leaving two on each cluster (one if clusters are close). Thin again in midsummer if there is a good crop. For the best fruit, thin dessert apples to 4–6 inches apart, cooking apples to 6–9 inches apart. Leave only one apple on each spur.

In early summer thin fruits to two per cluster.

Harvesting Apples According to Their Season

The best way to test if apples are ready for picking is to lift one up to the horizontal in the palm of your hand and twist it gently. It is ready for picking only if it parts easily from the tree with the stalk remaining on the fruit.

For reaching high fruit use apple pickers—nets on bamboo poles. Push the rigid frame of the net against the stalk. If the apple is ready, it will drop into the net. Because they bruise easily, apples should be harvested with the care you would use in handling eggs. Place ripe apples in a container lined with soft material.

Early apples (ready in early fall) will not keep and are best eaten as soon as they are picked. Midseason and late varieties should be picked in midfall before they are ripe; they mature during storage.

Store midseason varieties (ready for eating from late fall to early winter) separately from late varieties (ready from midwinter onward). This is advisable because the ethylene gases given off by the earlier apples may unduly hasten the ripening of the later ones.

Some late apples will keep until mid or even late spring if they are stored in suitable conditions. After picking the apples, place them in a cool, well-ventilated room or shed to sweat for two or three days. After they have sweated, sort them out for storing, placing to one side any damaged or diseased fruits (even those only slightly affected) or any without a stalk. Those that are suitable can be used immediately.

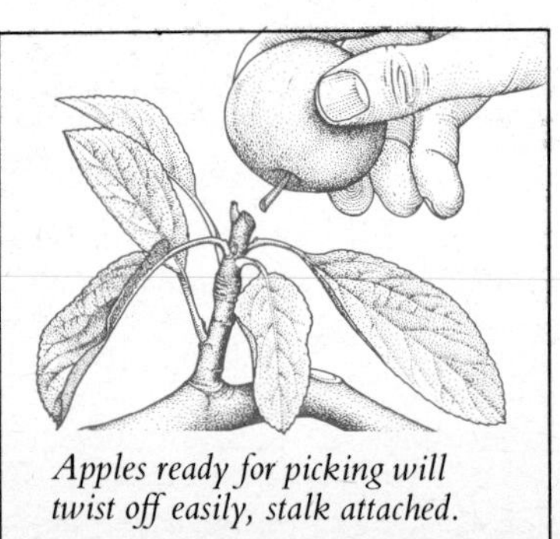

Apples ready for picking will twist off easily, stalk attached.

How to Store Your Apple Crop

The ideal way to store apples is to wrap each one in waxed paper or in a 10-inch square of newspaper. Do not make an airtight seal; just fold one corner of the paper over the fruit, overlap this with the opposite corner, then fold over the other two corners.

Apples can also be stored without wrapping, but there is a danger of excessive moisture loss, as well as spreading of rot.

Store in a dark, humid, cool place, with a temperature of about 35°–40°F. Too much ventilation will cause the fruits to shrivel, but too little may cause them to rot internally. To raise the humidity, damp down the storeroom floor occasionally. Stand wrapped apples, folds underneath, in a single layer on a slatted shelf, or stack them two or three layers deep in a well-ventilated box. Regularly remove any apples that show signs of rotting.

Instead of wrapping apples individually, you can store them in a strong polyethylene bag holding 4–6 pounds. Use small bags for the fruits.

Respiration inside bags slows ripening, but if bags are airtight, apples may rot. Use a nail or pencil point to make six small holes in each 24 square inches of bag.

Do not store more than one variety in each bag, since the ethylene gas from earlier fruits can hasten the ripening of the later ones.

What Can Go Wrong With Apples

The majority of apple pests can be controlled with one dormant spray plus a general-purpose fruit tree spray applied at intervals. The dormant spray goes on just as buds open, followed by a general-purpose spray just before blossoms open, again when petals have fallen, and then at intervals of one, two, four, six, and eight weeks.

Pests can also be controlled individually as suggested on the chart if identification can be made. Look up chemicals and trade names in the section beginning on page 635.

Symptoms and signs	Cause	Control
Leaves curled (sometimes flushed with red); shoots may be distorted. Many sticky insects present.	Aphids (greenfly or several other kinds)	Spray just before blossoming with carbaryl, endosulfan, or malathion. Repeat after blossoming if necessary.
Apples have small skin blemishes. Insides of mature fruits show corky brown streaks; maggots ("worms") visible.	Apple maggots (fly larvae)	Spray with carbaryl or methoxychlor when flies first become active (early to mid summer). To control later broods, spray every 3 wk. until late summer.
Young fruits have small brown holes in skin, often with brown ribbonlike scars leading from them. Unpleasant odor present when fruits are cut open; "worms" visible. Fruits fall prematurely.	Apple sawflies (larvae)	Spray with carbaryl, malathion, or methoxychlor immediately after petal fall.
From midsummer on fruits bear small holes; no associated scar. No noticeable odor when fruits are cut open. White caterpillars feed inside fruits.	Codling moths (larvae)	In early summer spray with carbaryl or methoxychlor. Spray again about 3 wk. later.
Leaves finely mottled, turning yellow or rusty brown.	Two-spotted, or red spider, mites	In early summer spray with chlorobenzilate, dicofol, or tetradifon. Repeat if necessary.
Eggs, deposited on twigs, hatch when flowers are deep pink. Larvae (caterpillars) chew foliage.	Leaf rollers or leaftiers (moth larvae)	Spray with carbaryl or methoxychlor at petal fall and again 7-10 da. later. Repeat at least twice at 7- to 10-da. intervals.

Symptoms and signs	Cause	Control
Curculios puncture and lay eggs in very young fruits. After eggs hatch, larvae (grubs) feed inside apples, causing premature drop.	Plum curculios (weevils)	Spray with carbaryl or methoxychlor at petal fall and again 7–10 da. later. Repeat at least twice more at 7- to 10-da. intervals.
Rough, scaly deposits (white, gray, or brownish) occur on twigs, bark, and fruits. Juices are sucked from trees, causing reduced growth and yellowed leaves.	Scale insects (San Jose, oyster shell, scurfy scale, or others)	Spray with miscible oil before growth begins in spring. Diazinon or malathion can be sprayed as contact control in late spring when new scales ("crawlers") appear.
Leaves and young stems distorted, covered with white powder. Premature leaf fall may occur.	Apple powdery mildew (fungus)	In late spring and early fall spray regularly with cycloheximide, dinocap, or wettable sulfur.
Brown or blackish scabs on fruits, leaves, and shoots. When scabs have coalesced, they may crack and become corky.	Apple scab (fungus)	From the time that bud scales fall onward (until midsummer if necessary), spray with Benomyl, Captan, dodine, ferbam, or maneb. When pruning, cut out and destroy diseased parts.
First symptoms are leaf spots, often called frog eyes because of markings. Fungus may cause complete defoliation. Young stems have slightly sunken areas of dying bark, which become elongated ovals; central tissues crack and flake off. Cankers eventually girdle and kill stem.	Black-rot canker (fungus)	Apply Bordeaux foliar or lime-sulfur spray. Or use folpet or maneb (mix with insecticide if insect pests are also present). Cut out and destroy infected spurs and branches. Paint large cuts with tree-wound paint. If canker is severe, spray with Bordeaux mixture just before leaf fall and at bud burst in spring. Remove old fruits.
In early summer foliage has orange rusty spots, which become dark orange, crusty, and scabby. Fruits may show sunken areas or orange spots; generally unsightly.	Rust (cedar-apple or hawthorn)	If possible, eliminate all red cedars (*Juniperus*) within ½-mi. radius. Cut off overwintering fungous galls on cedars. Spray with a carbamate (ferbam, maneb, or thiram) when flower buds show pink. Repeat at blossom time, again at petal fall, again 10 da. later, and twice more at 10-da. intervals.

Pruning and Training Apple Trees

During the first four years of the life of a fruit tree, the aim of pruning is to develop a strong, regular framework of branches.

After that the aim is twofold: to keep the tree open to light and air and to maintain the right balance between growth and fruitfulness.

Winter pruning (late fall to late winter) promotes growth by directing energy to growth buds at the expense of fruit buds. Summer pruning (from mid to late summer) reduces foliage and promotes the formation of fruit buds.

Fruit buds and growth buds. When pruning a fruit tree, you must be able to distinguish between a fruit bud (which will produce a blossom and then fruit) and a growth bud (which will produce a new shoot). They are illustrated below. Growth buds may develop into fruit buds. A heavy winter pruning promotes growth buds. A summer pruning (after new growth is made) tends to promote fruit buds.

Leaders and laterals. A leader is the leading shoot of a branch. A lateral is a side shoot from a branch.

Spurs and tips. Some varieties produce most of their fruit on short growths known as spurs. These include 'Golden Delicious,' 'McIntosh,' and 'Stayman.' But some varieties also produce fruit on one-year shoots (tips), both terminally and laterally. 'Rome Beauty' and 'Jonathan' fall into this group. We now have so-called spur strains, and these trees make about one-third less growth and are heavily laden with spurs. 'Golden Delicious,' 'Red Delicious,' 'McIntosh,' 'Rome Beauty,' and 'Winesap' are available as spur strains. For backyard apple trees on dwarfing stocks, the spur strains are recommended.

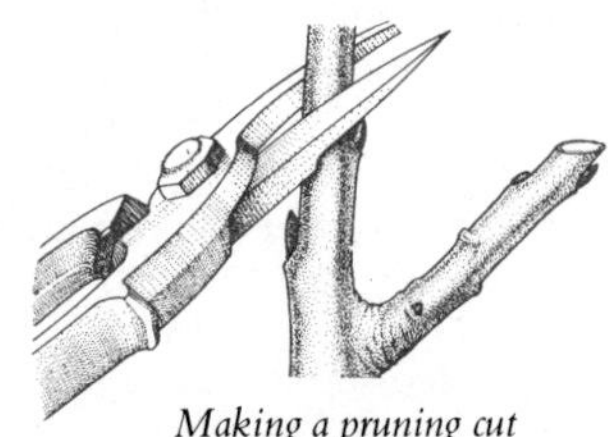

Making a pruning cut

Making a pruning cut. Use sharp shears; otherwise damage may result and disease may enter. Cut just above an outward-pointing bud; do not leave a stump above it, because it will die back and can harbor disease. Cut in the same direction as the bud.

Training. Trees bought from a nursery are usually partly trained and may be up to four years old. Find out the age when you buy so that you can train correctly.

Bearing. A tree should not be allowed to bear more than one or two fruits in the first year after planting. A cordon may fruit within a year after planting; a dwarf tree on a vigorous rootstock may take five years.

The time a tree takes to reach full bearing capacity can vary from 4 to 15 years, depending on the variety of tree, rootstock, and kind of pruning.

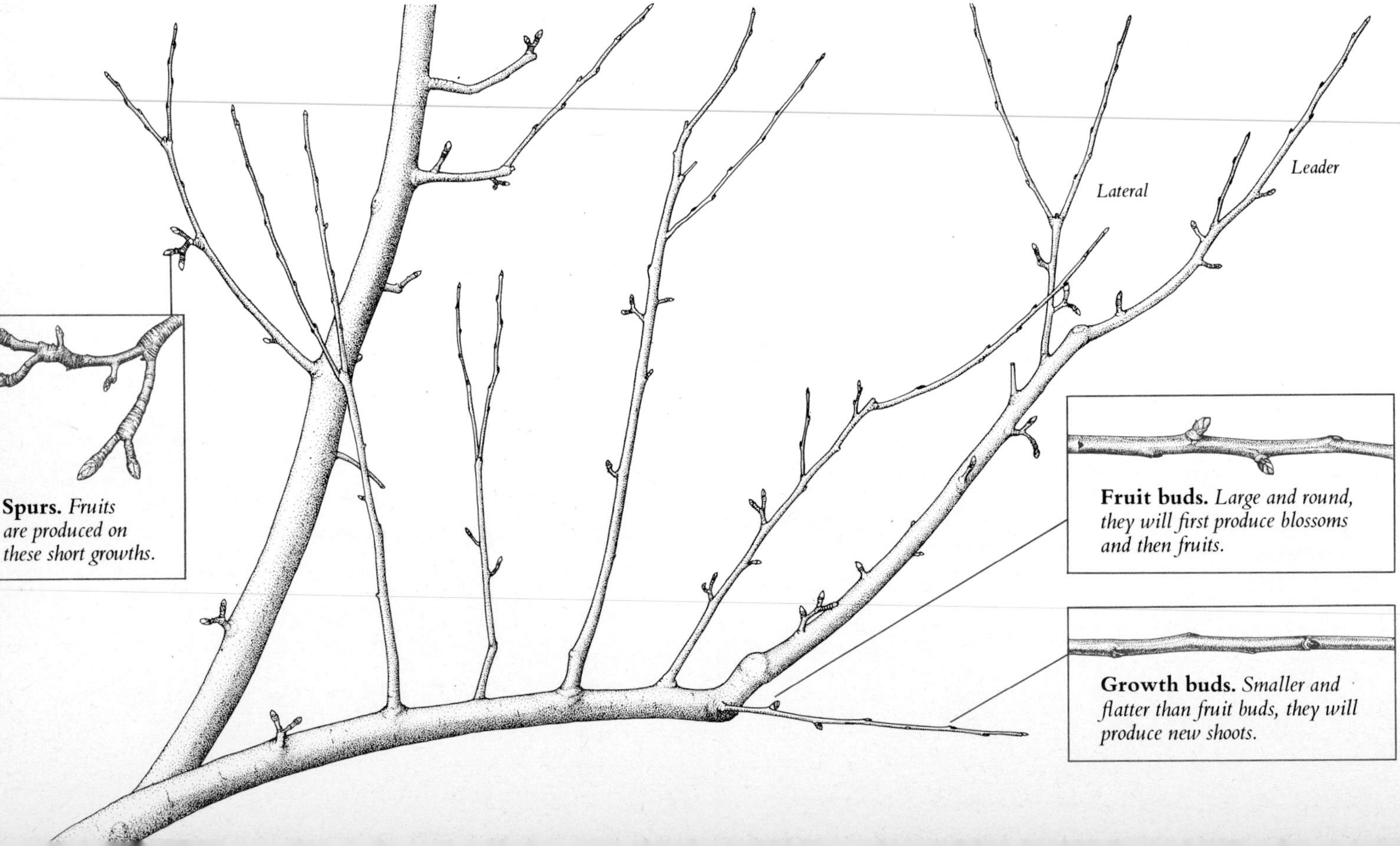

Lateral

Leader

Spurs. *Fruits are produced on these short growths.*

Fruit buds. *Large and round, they will first produce blossoms and then fruits.*

Growth buds. *Smaller and flatter than fruit buds, they will produce new shoots.*

Pruning and Training a Young Dwarf Tree

Training a One-Year-Old Dwarf Tree

Plant dwarf trees 8–15 feet apart, depending on the rootstock (which should be either dwarfing or semi-dwarfing). Check the type and the planting distance with the nurseryman or look in the catalog.

If you buy a one-year-old tree, cut the stem back to an 18- to 24-inch height, just above a bud, after planting in autumn or spring (see p. 490). The buds or small shoots just below the cut will grow out the following summer. There may be only four or five. Choose three or four to form the first branches. They should be evenly spaced around the stem, with none pointing toward the supporting stake. Rub out with your thumb any unwanted buds or shoots.

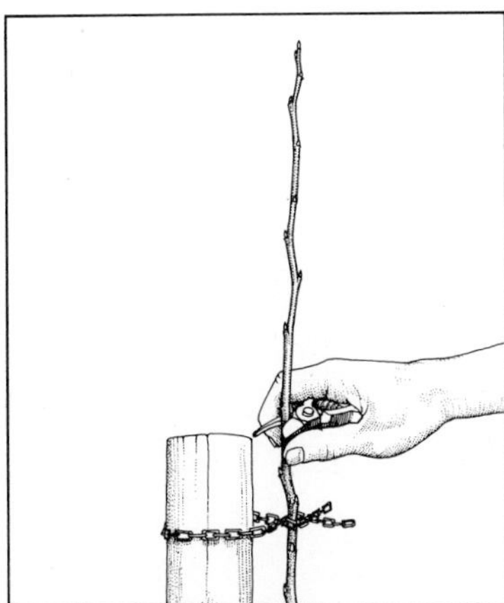

1. *After planting, cut back the main stem above a bud to 18–24 in.*

2. *Leave three or four buds to form branches. Rub out unwanted buds.*

Training a Two-Year-Old Dwarf Tree

In the winter a two-year-old dwarf tree will have the three or four branches that grew in the summer. Cut back each of the branches to an outward-pointing bud; how far back you cut them depends on their vigor.

If the branches are thick and vigorous, cut them back by half. If they are thin and weak, cut them back by two-thirds. Rub out with your thumb any inward-pointing buds just below the cuts.

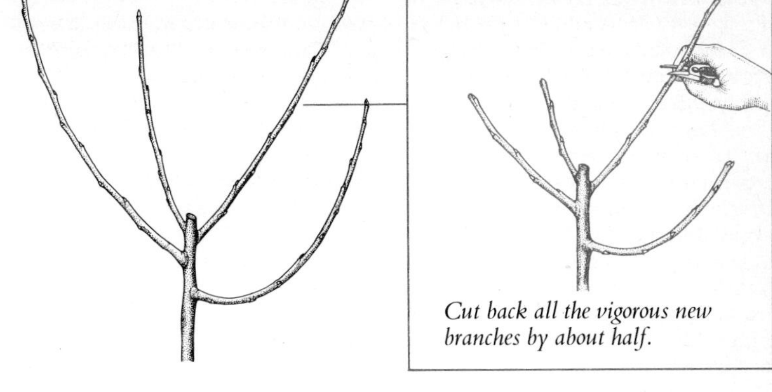

Cut back all the vigorous new branches by about half.

Training a Three-Year-Old Dwarf Tree

By a tree's third winter a number of lateral shoots will have grown out from the branches. Choose some of these laterals to form, with the first branches, the main structure of the tree. They should all point outward, and their tips, after pruning, should be at least 18 inches apart.

Cut all main branches back to an outward-pointing bud, shortening the new growth on each branch by one-third if the branch is growing vigorously or by one-half if it is of average growth. If it is weak, shorten the new growth by two-thirds.

Each of the laterals not chosen to form main branches should be cut back to a point that is four buds from the base of the shoot.

Cut off any side branches on the main stem flush with the stem.

After this third-year pruning, you will have established the basic shape of the tree.

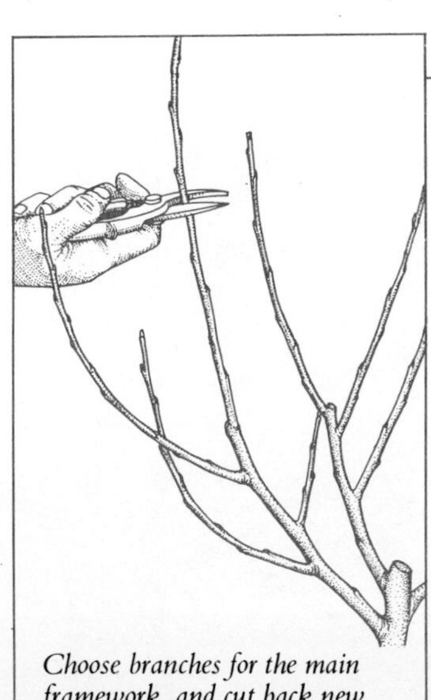

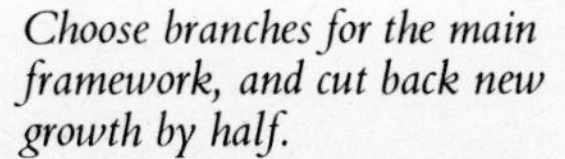

Choose branches for the main framework, and cut back new growth by half.

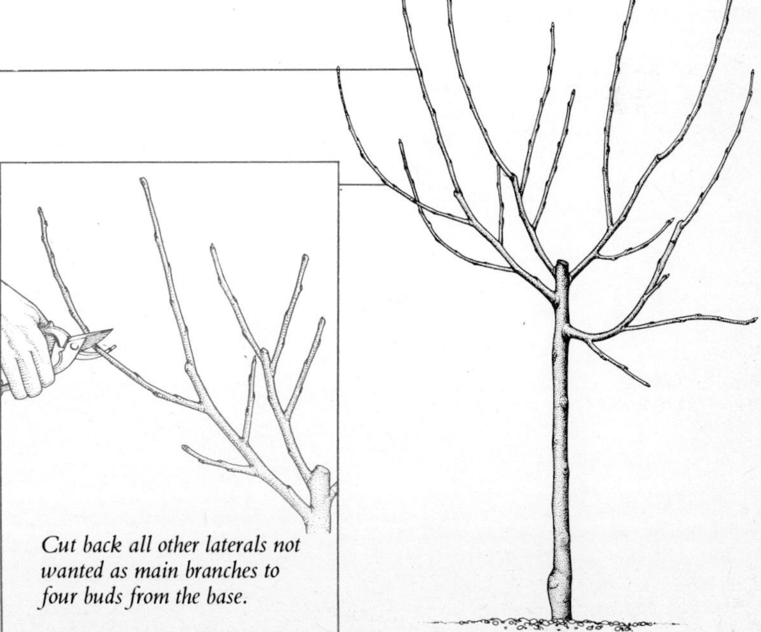

Cut back all other laterals not wanted as main branches to four buds from the base.

Pruning an Established Spur-Forming Dwarf Tree

Established dwarf trees that bear nearly all their fruit on spurs (such as 'Golden Delicious' and 'McIntosh') should be pruned each winter by the method known as the renewal system. The principle of this system is to produce new growth each season to replace some that has already borne fruit. It is based on the three-year cycle of fruiting growth.

During its first summer a growth bud sends out a shoot. During the second summer this shoot produces fruit buds. During the third summer the fruit buds form spurs and bear fruit that same summer and in succeeding summers.

During its second summer a shoot produces not only fruit buds but also new growth from its tip, so that a two-year-old shoot has one-year-old growth extending from it. In the same way, three-year-old growth has both two-year-old and one-year-old growth extending from it.

Under the renewal system several two-year-old and three-year-old shoots are cut back. This prevents overcropping and crowding, improves fruit quality, and makes way for new growth.

There is no rule governing how many shoots to prune and how many to leave. Use your judgment to maintain a balance between growth and fruitfulness. The purpose of pruning is to prevent a tree from becoming overloaded with branches and still allow sufficient new fruit-bearing shoots to form.

Do not prune one-year-old shoots growing out from a main branch. But you cannot avoid cutting away some of the one-year-old extension growth when cutting back two-year-old and three-year-old growth. When choosing shoots for pruning, trace back to older wood from one-year-old tips.

On trees with weak growth, cut selected two-year-old growth back to two fruit buds. On stronger trees leave more buds. Cut back selected three-year-old growth to the lowest fruiting spur. Growth buds on the spur will produce new shoots the following season, and the cycle of growth will start again.

Branch leaders should have their new growth cut by one-third if the branch is growing vigorously, by one-half if it is of average growth, by two-thirds if it is very weak. When branches are fully grown (about 8 feet long), prune them in the same way as shoots.

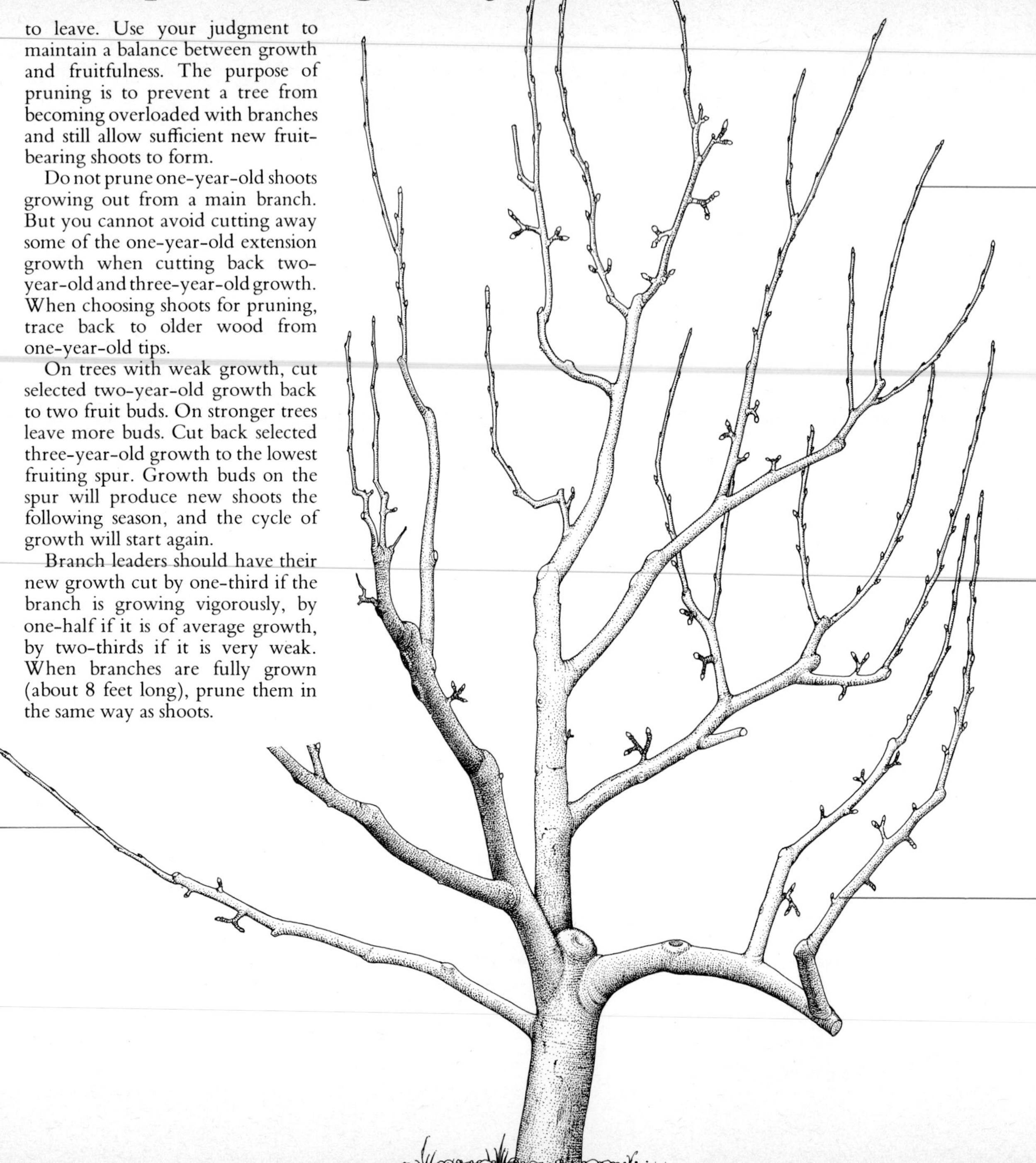

BRANCH LEADERS

Branch leaders of average length should be cut back by half of their new growth. Cut back stronger ones by one-third of new growth and weaker ones by two-thirds.

Pruning an Established Tip-Bearing Dwarf Tree

There are not as many tip-bearing varieties of dwarfs as spur-forming varieties. Tip bearers, which include 'Rome Beauty,' 'Jonathan,' and 'Stayman,' produce many of their fruit buds on the tips of shoots; the rest are produced on spurs. The cycle of growth in these dwarfs is the same as for spur-forming trees, but many one-year-old shoots produce a fruit bud at the tip.

Tip-bearing trees need comparatively little pruning. Once a year, in winter, prune back any shoot without a fruit bud at its tip. Cut just above the highest fruit bud if there is one; otherwise, cut back to four or five growth buds from the base of the shoot.

Shoots that have a fruit bud at the tip should not be pruned unless they are crowded—that is, if the tips are less than 1 foot apart. Thin them out by pruning some tips back to two buds from the base, preferably above a fruit bud if there is one.

Prune branch leaders by removing the fruit bud at the tip, cutting back to a growth bud; this induces the lower growth buds to break and produce more tip-bearing shoots.

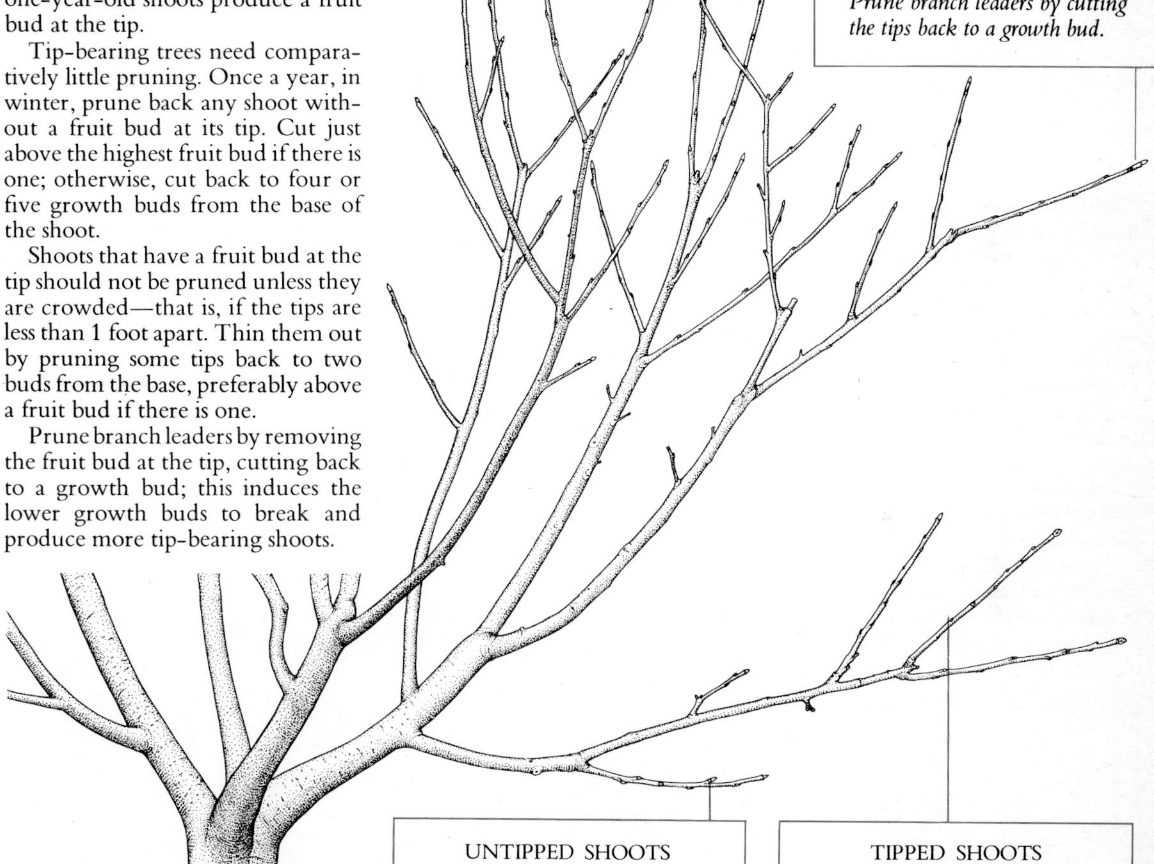

ONE-YEAR-OLD SHOOTS

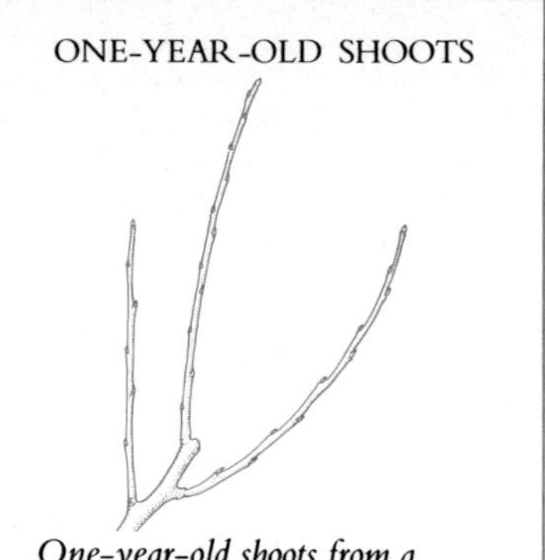

One-year-old shoots from a main branch have only growth buds. Do not prune them.

TWO-YEAR-OLD GROWTH

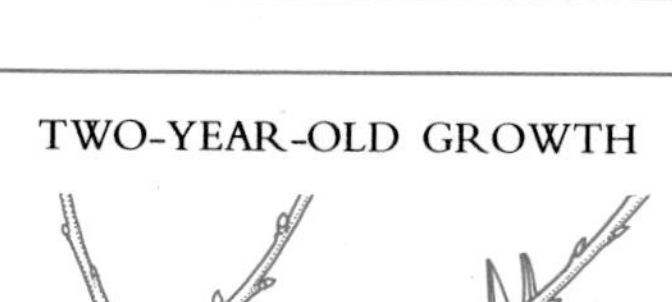

Two-year-old growth has fruit buds. Prune some of them. Cut back to two buds on weak growth; leave more buds on stronger trees.

THREE-YEAR-OLD GROWTH

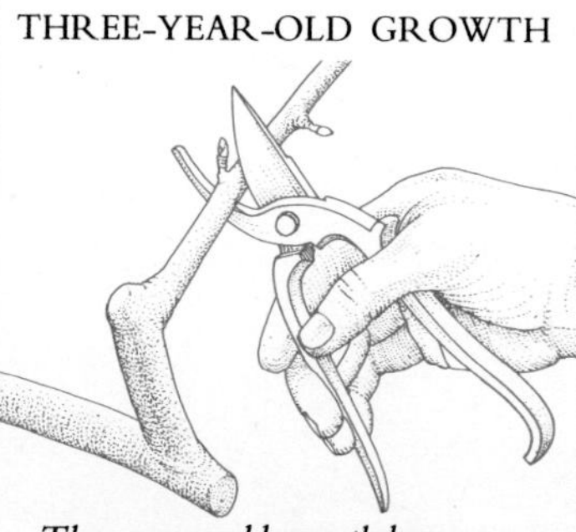

Three-year-old growth has spurs. Prune some growth back to lowest spurs to encourage replacement spurs.

BRANCH LEADERS

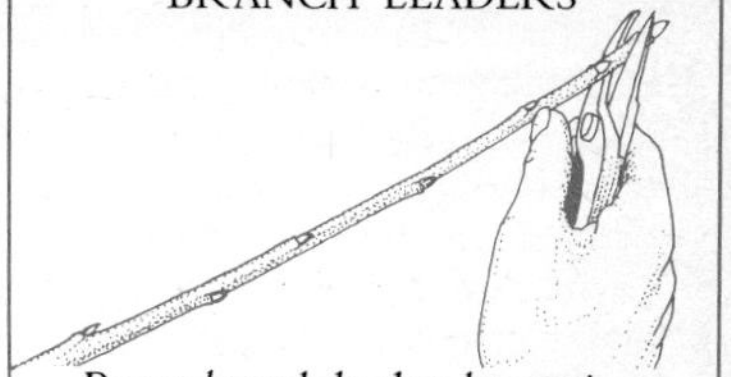

Prune branch leaders by cutting the tips back to a growth bud.

UNTIPPED SHOOTS

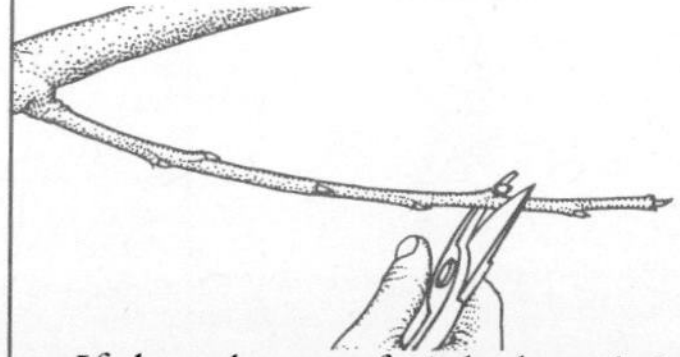

If shoots have no fruit buds at their tips, cut them back to just above the highest fruit bud.

TIPPED SHOOTS

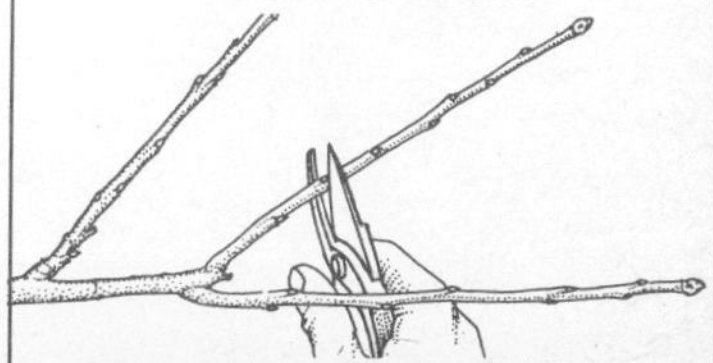

Do not prune shoots with fruit buds at their tips unless overcrowded; then cut back to two buds.

Pruning a Neglected Apple Tree

Unpruned large standard or dwarf apple trees can be restructured in winter. If the tree is making little new growth, all pruning can be done at once; otherwise, space the work over two or three years.

First, remove any dead and diseased branches. Then, let in light and air by removing enough of the large branches, particularly in the center, for those remaining to be 2–3 feet apart in the outer spread where the new growth develops. Cut out any crossed or badly placed branches. On very tall trees shorten the tallest branches back to a lateral.

When removing a whole branch, cut it out as close to the source as possible (see p. 49). Smooth off saw cuts with a sharp knife, and cover the wound with wound-sealing paint.

Thin out any complicated spur systems, reducing some in size and removing others entirely. As a general guide, spurs should be spaced 9–12 inches apart. Spread spur thinning over several seasons, whether the tree's growth is slow or vigorous.

Clear away any weeds and grass around the tree base, and lightly fork the soil in a circle about 8 feet across.

As order is restored, prune each year according to whether the tree is a spur-forming variety or a spur and tip bearer (see pp. 496–497).

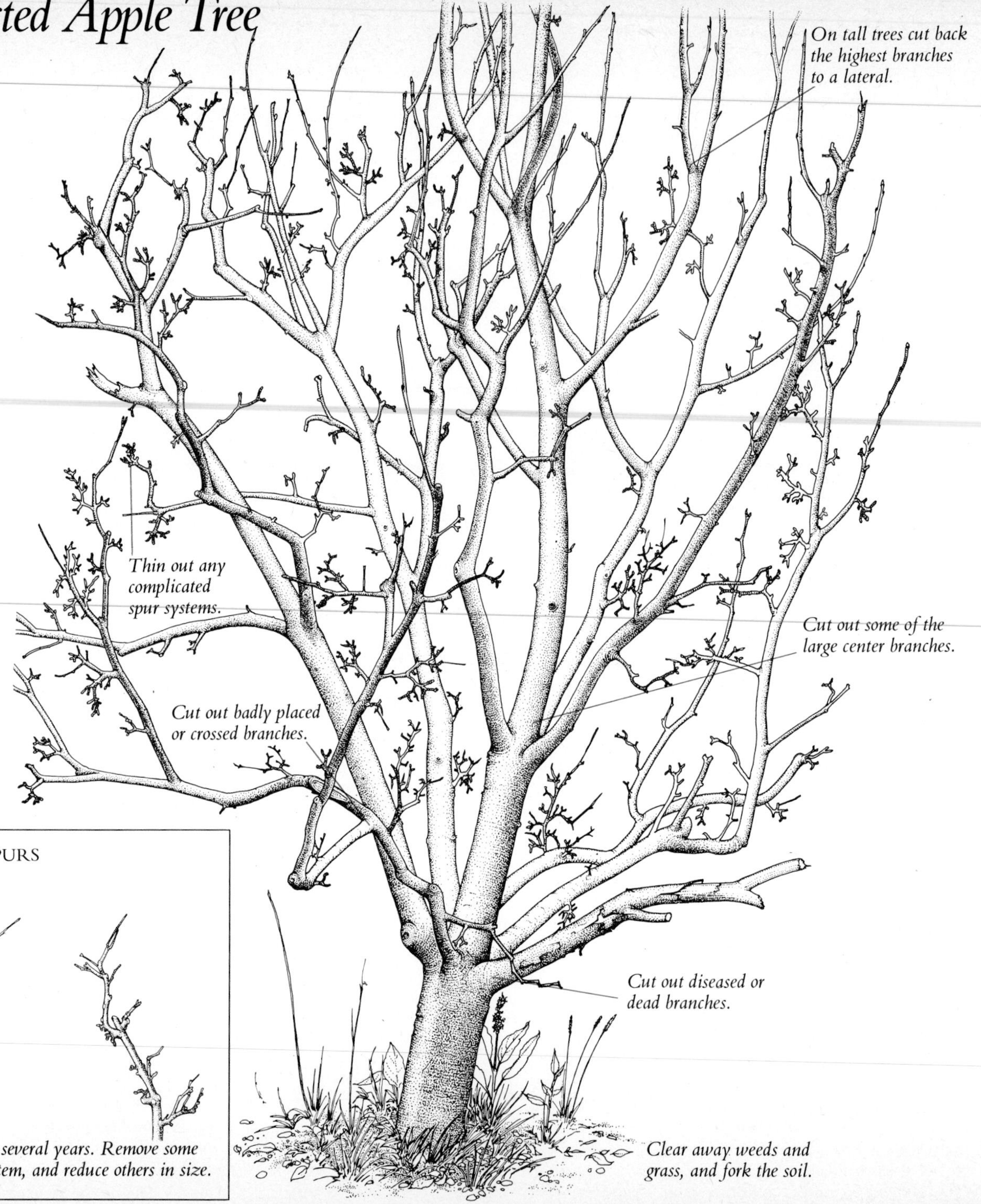

CLEARING SPURS

Thin out complicated spur systems over several years. Remove some entirely, cutting flush with the parent stem, and reduce others in size.

Pruning and Training a Cordon Espalier

Plant cordons $2\frac{1}{2}$ feet apart—3 feet apart on fertile soil (see p. 490). Rows should be at least 6 feet apart.

After planting a tree, whatever its age, wire a bamboo cane, 8–10 feet long, to the horizontal wires, at the same angle as the tree (usually 45 degrees). Tie the stem to the cane with soft string. Remove the cane when the stem of the tree reaches the top wire.

No pruning is necessary at planting time. Prune in the same way each summer as growth becomes mature. This is generally in mid to late summer but may not be until early fall. Mature growth is woody at the base, at least 9 inches long, and has characteristic dark green leaves.

Cut back mature laterals to three leaves from the basal cluster. Cut back the mature side shoots from laterals or spurs to one leaf from the basal cluster. Do not prune the main stem leader.

If you prune in summer, there will probably be secondary growth in the following months. If the summer is reasonably dry and not much new growth occurs, cut all growth back to one bud in the early fall; after a wet summer that produces much secondary growth, you may need to continue pruning into early winter.

If the spurs of mature cordons become overcrowded, thin them out in the winter (see p. 508).

When a cordon grows beyond the top wire, untie it and refasten it at a more acute angle. Do not lower it to less than 35 degrees from the horizontal, however, or it will break. Once it cannot be lowered any farther, trim back new growth at the tip to $\frac{1}{2}$ inch, cutting above a bud. This pruning operation should be done sometime in late spring.

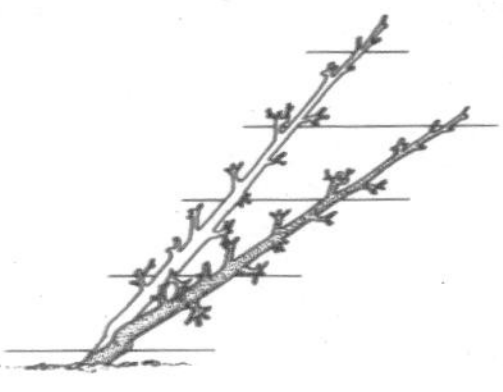

Lowering a cordon

EARLY FALL PRUNING

Cut back all the small secondary growth from the midsummer pruning. Prune it to one bud.

In midsummer prune mature laterals back to three leaves from the basal cluster.

Cut back the mature side shoots growing from laterals or spurs to one leaf from the basal cluster.

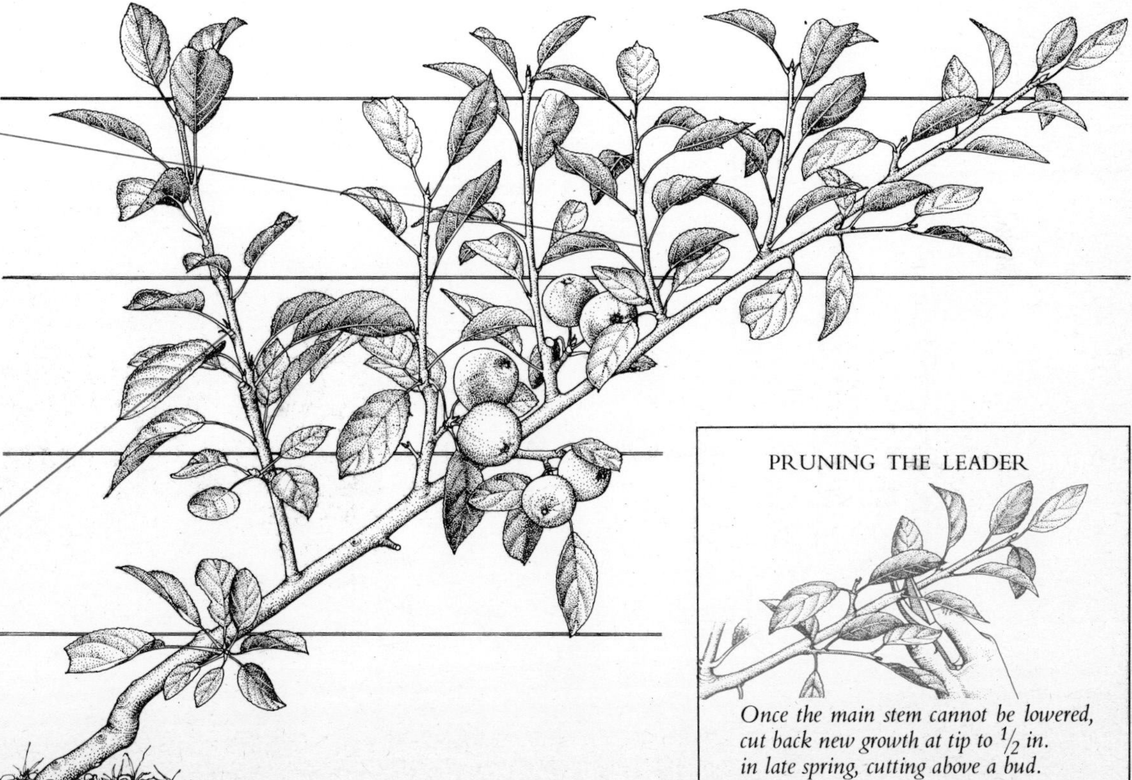

PRUNING THE LEADER

Once the main stem cannot be lowered, cut back new growth at tip to $\frac{1}{2}$ in. in late spring, cutting above a bud.

Pruning and Training a Horizontal Espalier

Training a One-Year-Old Horizontal Espalier

Espaliers should be planted 10–15 feet apart, depending on the rootstock. Ask the nurseryman what the recommended planting distance for that particular rootstock is.

If you buy a young (one-year-old) tree, shorten it immediately after planting. Cut it back to a bud or shoot about 14 inches above the ground—2 inches higher than the first horizontal support wire.

Choose a bud with two other buds or shoots beneath it that are pointing along the line of the wire and are located on opposite sides of the stem. The top bud will produce a shoot to grow upright as the main stem; the two lower buds will produce shoots to form the first tier of opposite horizontal branches. Rub out with your thumb all other buds or shoots.

Notch the bottom bud to stimulate growth. Although the top two buds should grow out strongly, the lowest may not. Use a sharp knife to remove a half-moon of bark from the stem just above the bud.

The following summer, as growth develops, train the three shoots in the required directions by means of bamboo canes. The shoot from the topmost bud is trained upright, the two side shoots diagonally.

Fasten an upright cane to the wires, and use soft string to tie to it the shoot from the topmost bud. Then fasten two more canes to the wires on each side of the first cane—both at an angle of 45 degrees. Tie the shoots from the side buds to the two canes with soft string.

You can train the two side branches to grow equally by adjusting the angles of the two canes. If one branch is growing more vigorously than the other, lower its cane. (Lowering a branch will slow its growth.) At the same time raise the other cane to which the weaker shoot is attached. (Raising a branch will stimulate growth.) Adjust the canes in this way as necessary until growth is matched.

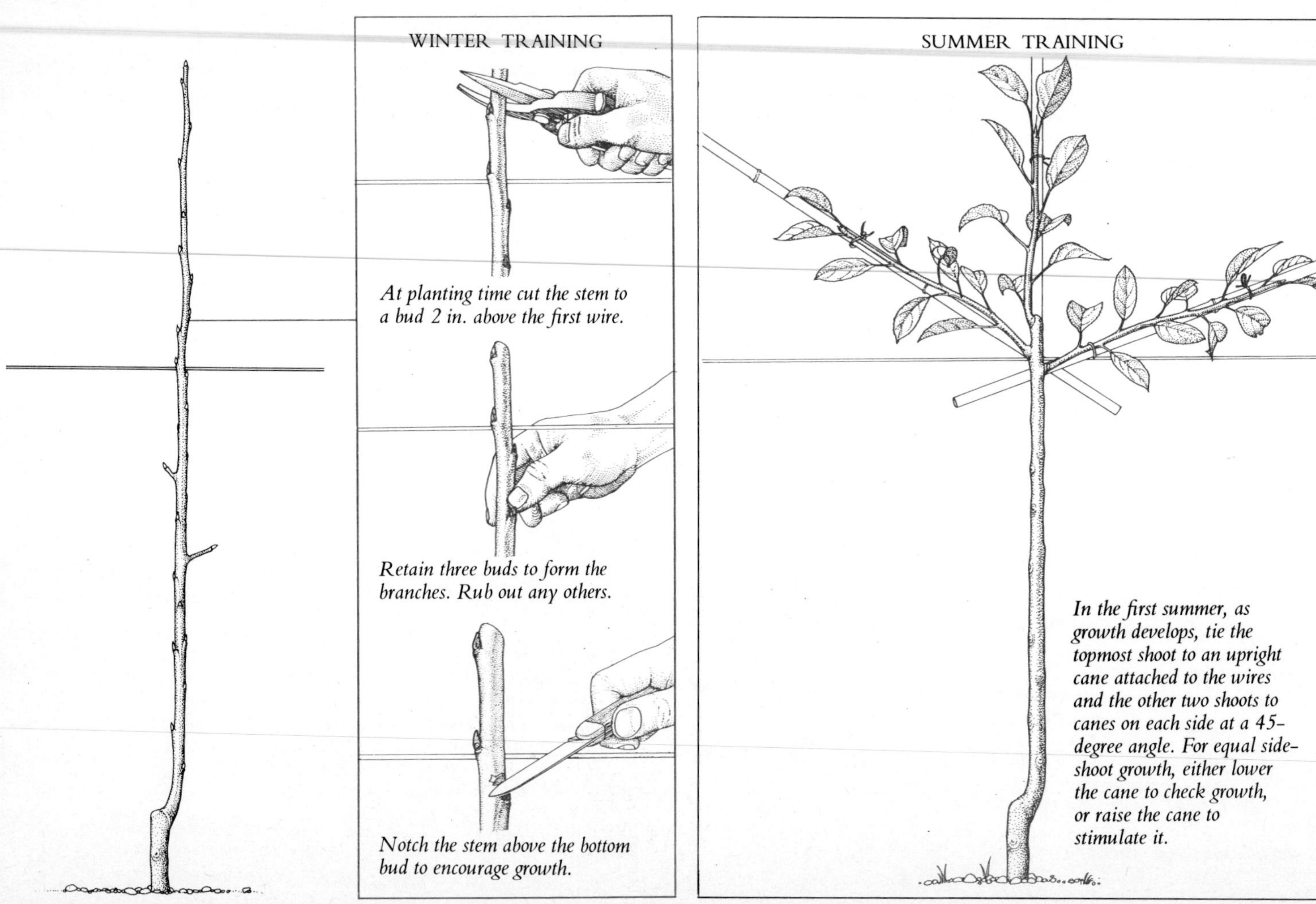

At planting time cut the stem to a bud 2 in. above the first wire.

Retain three buds to form the branches. Rub out any others.

Notch the stem above the bottom bud to encourage growth.

In the first summer, as growth develops, tie the topmost shoot to an upright cane attached to the wires and the other two shoots to canes on each side at a 45-degree angle. For equal side-shoot growth, either lower the cane to check growth, or raise the cane to stimulate it.

Training an Espalier in Its Second and Third Years

During the espalier's second winter lower the two side branches to the horizontal wire on each side of the main stem. Remove the canes and tie the branches to the wire with soft string. This is the age at which many espaliers are bought from nurseries.

Trim back the branch leaders to stimulate the growth of fruiting spurs from them, cutting just past a bud. Strong leaders should be pruned back by less than half, weak ones by more than half. The aim is to make both branches grow to about the same length eventually.

Cut back the main stem to a bud about 2 inches above the second wire. Then select two other buds below it to form a second pair of horizontal branches. Rub out with your thumb all other buds or shoots.

As with the first tier, notch the bottom bud to encourage growth, cutting away a half-moon of bark just above it with a sharp knife.

The following summer fasten canes to the second-tier side shoots at an angle of 45 degrees to the main-stem cane. Train the branches in exactly the same way as the first-tier branches the year before. Tie the extension growth on the first-tier leaders to the wires.

Prune the current season's growth as it becomes mature. This is usually done in midsummer—but in some cases, depending on weather or area, in late summer or early fall.

Mature growth is at least 9 inches long, is woody at the base, and has dark green leaves. Cut back mature laterals to three leaves beyond the basal cluster.

If you have pruned in summer, new secondary growth may spring from the cut wood by fall. Cut it all back to one bud. After a wet summer that has produced considerable secondary growth, you may need to continue pruning into early winter.

In the third winter cut back branch leaders as before, and select buds for the third tier.

In the fourth summer train the third tier, and prune the mature growth, as was done in the third summer. Cut side shoots from spurs or laterals back to one leaf from the basal cluster.

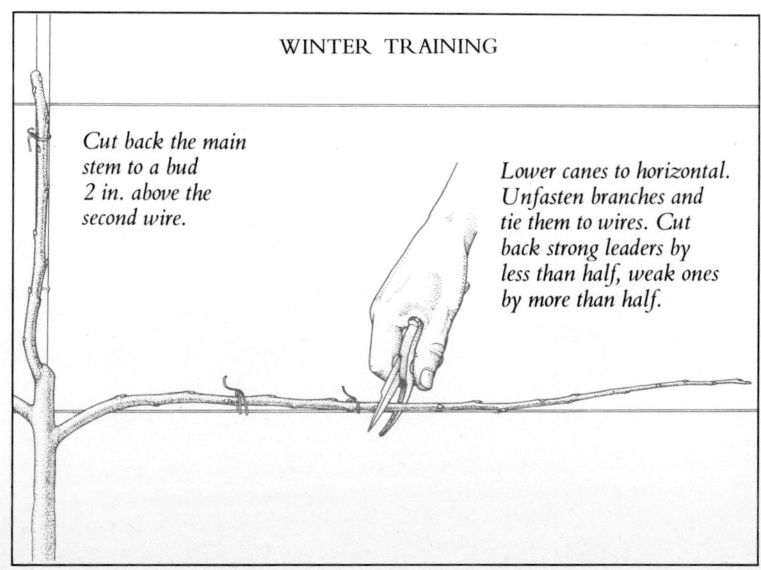

SUMMER PRUNING

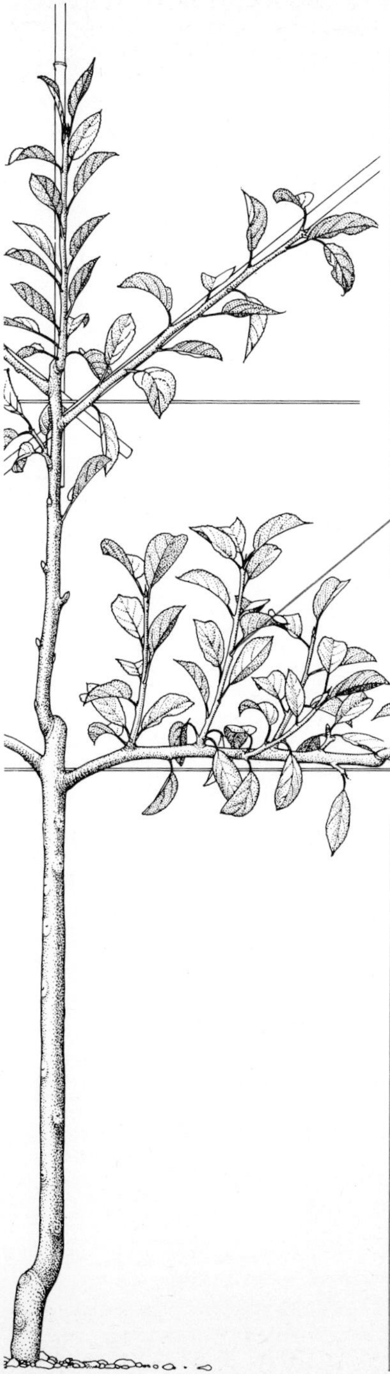

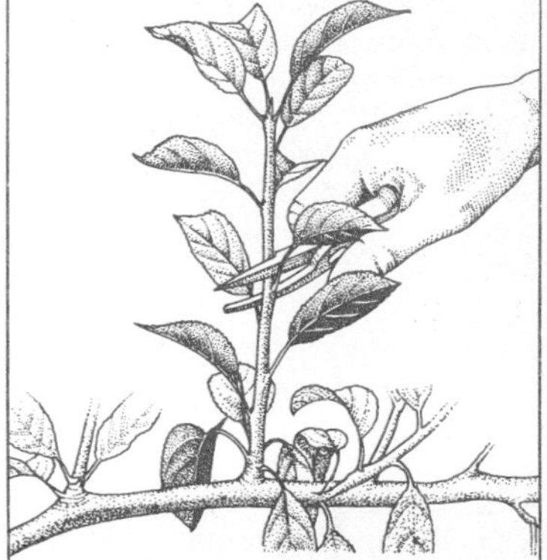

In midsummer cut back mature laterals to three leaves from the basal cluster.

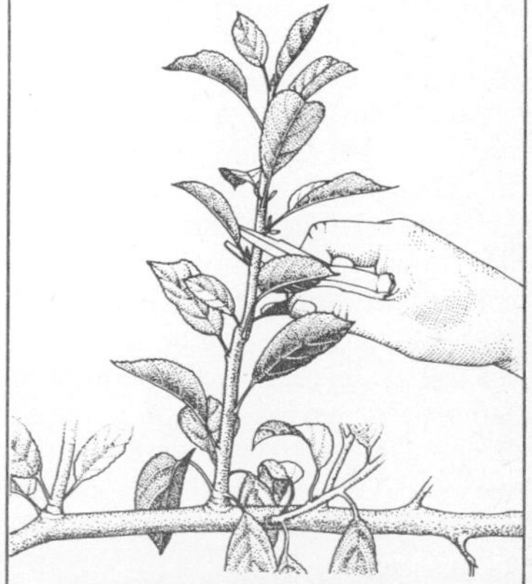

EARLY FALL PRUNING

In early fall cut secondary shoots from the midsummer pruning back to one bud.

Finishing Off the Top Tier of a Horizontal Espalier

The top tier of an espalier is created by pruning in winter. Cut back the main stem to just above two side buds, and rub out unwanted buds below. This effectively stops the main stem from growing upward.

Early in the following summer, when the side buds have put out their shoots, tie them to canes at an angle of 45 degrees. Train the growth of the two branches the same way you handled other tiers in previous summers—raise the cane to stimulate the growth of a weaker branch, or lower it to slow the growth of a stronger branch.

In winter lower the branches to the horizontal, remove the canes, and tie the branches to the wires.

Four or five tiers are usually the maximum to which espaliers are grown, resulting in a tree 6–8 feet high; the usual width is about 12 feet (6-foot branches on each side).

A tree can also be grown to 10 tiers if desired. In this case, for a good crop, the width is usually kept to about 6 feet. Alternatively, trees can be held to one tier in height—about 12–15 inches from the ground.

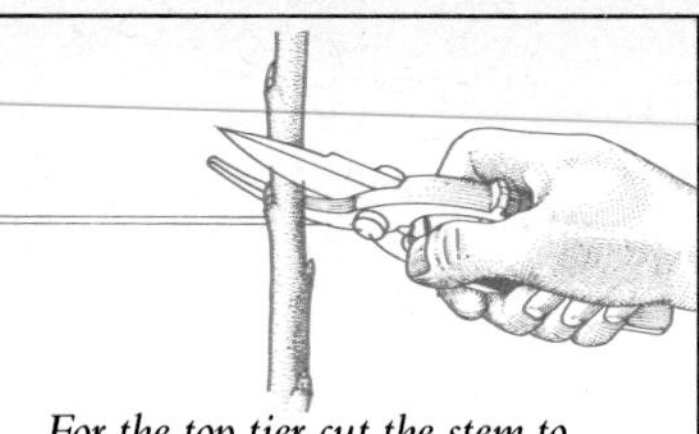

For the top tier cut the stem to leave two side-branch buds only.

Pruning a Fully Trained Horizontal Espalier

Prune the current season's growth each summer as it becomes mature, generally in late summer. Mature growth is more than 9 inches long; its greenish-brown bark has started turning brown at the base, and its leaves are dark green.

Mature laterals growing directly from branches should be cut back to three leaves beyond the basal cluster. Cut back mature side shoots from laterals or spurs to one leaf from the basal cluster.

If new growth is not mature enough in midsummer, it may be ready for pruning in late summer. In the North it may not be ready until early fall.

If you have pruned in the summer, there will probably be secondary growth in the fall. If the summer has been fairly dry and not much secondary growth has occurred, cut the growth back to one bud. After a wet summer that has produced a lot of secondary growth, you may have to keep pruning into early winter.

Apart from that, winter pruning is not usually necessary. Once branch leaders have reached a length of about 6 feet (or have filled the available space), prune them in summer as you would mature laterals.

The fruiting spurs may become overcrowded on mature trees. Thin them out in winter by cutting some flush with the parent stem and by reducing the size of others (p. 508).

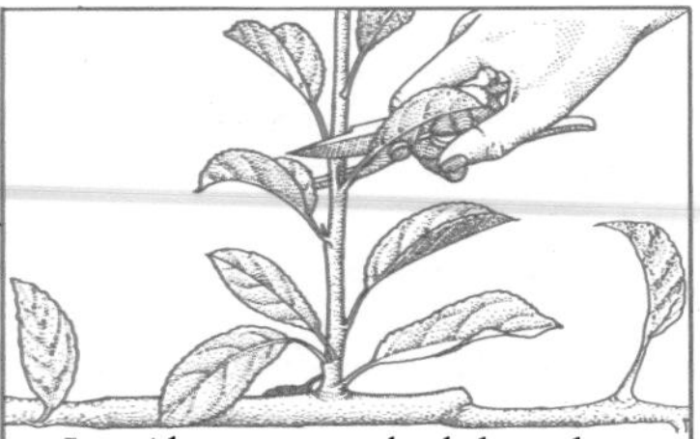

In midsummer cut back laterals to three leaves from the basal cluster.

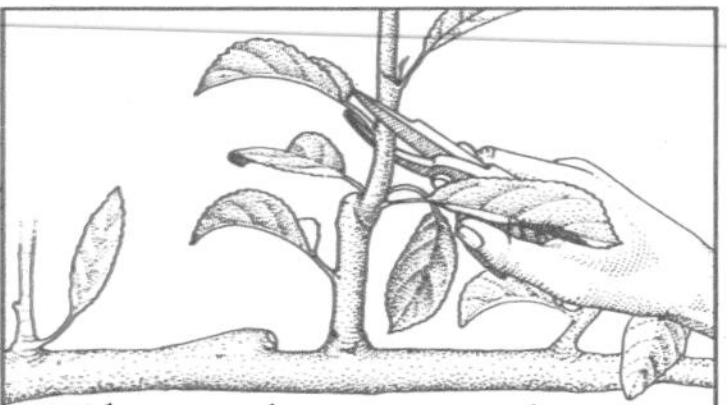

Also in midsummer cut side shoots from laterals to one leaf from the basal cluster.

FALL PRUNING

In fall cut secondary growth back to one bud.

Pruning and Training a Fan Espalier

Training a One-Year-Old Fan-Shaped Tree

Fans should be spaced 15–20 feet apart, depending on the kind of rootstock. Plant the trees in autumn or spring (see p. 490).

If you plant a year-old tree, cut back the stem to about 2 feet from the ground after planting. Cut just above two opposite side buds.

The following summer, when shoots 9–12 inches long have grown from these buds, tie them to canes attached to the supporting wires at an angle of 45 degrees. Rub out any buds or shoots below them.

Regulate the growth of the two branches—the first ribs of the fan—by adjusting the angle of the canes. If one rib is growing more vigorously, lower its cane to slow growth, and raise the other rib cane.

When growth is matched, fix the ribs at an angle of 45 degrees. Remove the canes, and tie the ribs to the wires when stems are woody.

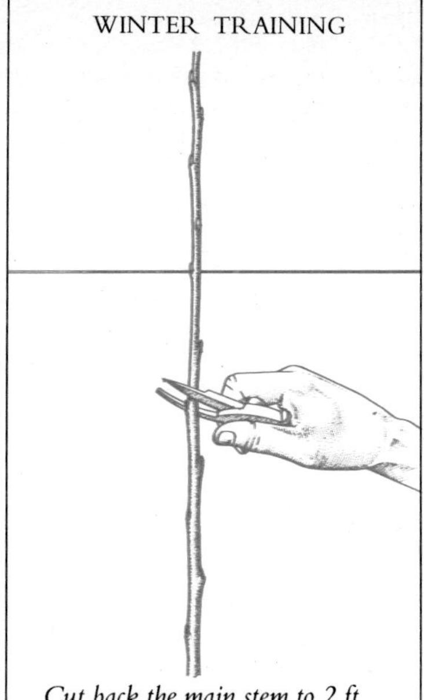

WINTER TRAINING

Cut back the main stem to 2 ft. from the ground, above two buds.

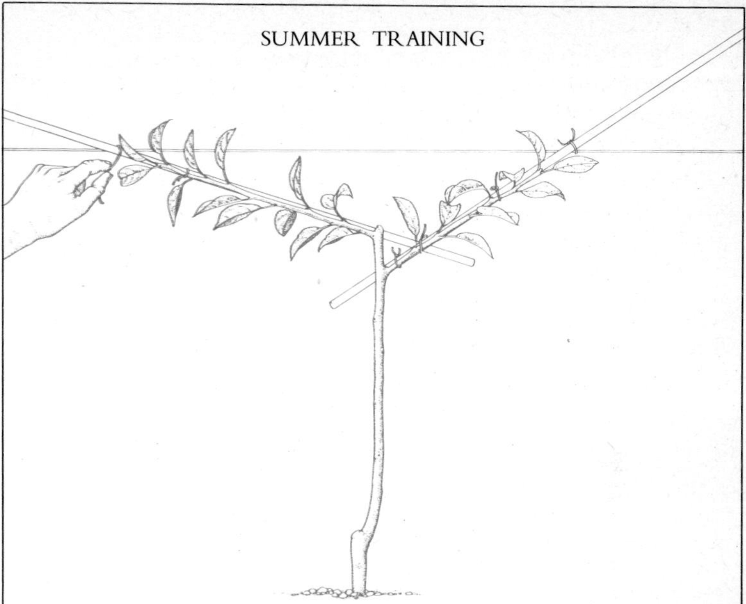

SUMMER TRAINING

When shoots have grown 9–12 in. long, tie them to canes at an angle of 45 degrees. Raise canes to stimulate growth; lower them to slow it.

Training a Two-Year-Old Fan-Shaped Tree

During the second winter prune each of the ribs back to 1–1½ feet. Cut just above a growth bud.

During the second summer tie the extension growth from each end bud to a cane at the same angle as the rib. Then on each rib select two evenly spaced shoots on the upper side and one on the lower side. Rub out all other shoots. As the chosen shoots grow long enough, fasten six more canes to the wires, and train the shoots to them.

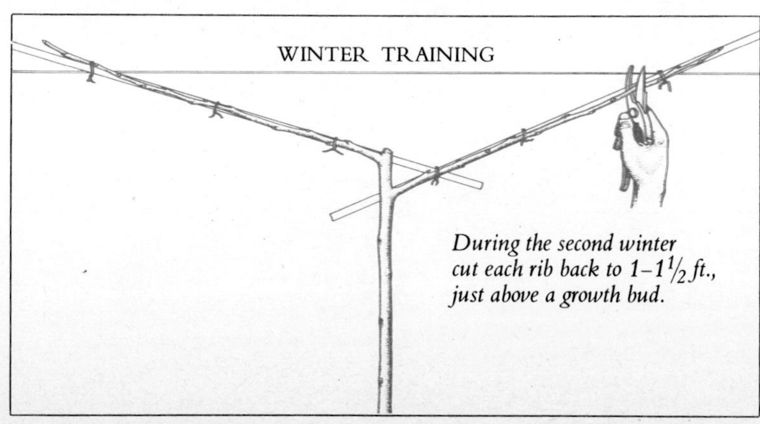

WINTER TRAINING

During the second winter cut each rib back to 1–1½ ft., just above a growth bud.

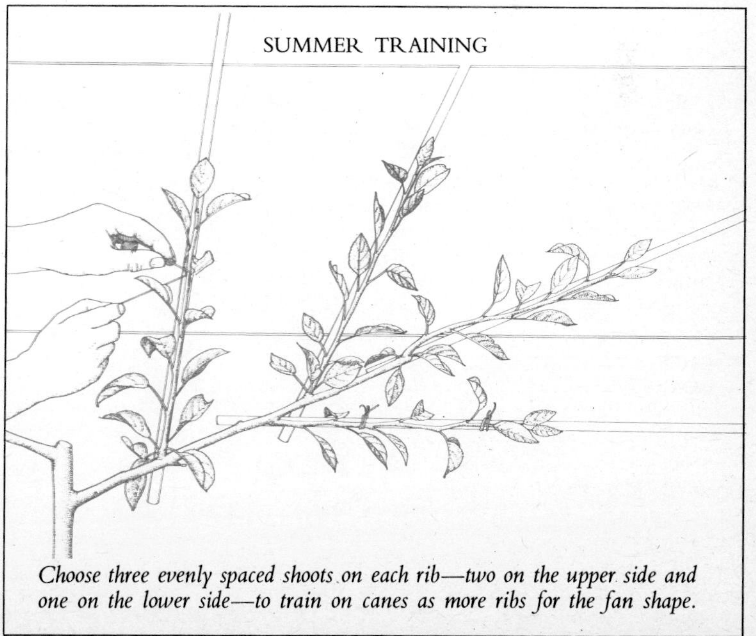

SUMMER TRAINING

Choose three evenly spaced shoots on each rib—two on the upper side and one on the lower side—to train on canes as more ribs for the fan shape.

Training a Three-Year-Old Fan-Shaped Tree

In the third winter prune each of the eight fan ribs back to 2–2½ feet, just above a growth bud.

The following summer tie the growth from the end bud of each rib onto the canes. Choose three evenly spaced shoots from each rib—two on the upper side and one on the lower—for training as additional ribs. Cut mature shoots not wanted as fan ribs back to three leaves from the basal cluster.

Tie the 24 new ribs to the canes when they are long enough. The fan will now have 32 ribs, probably enough to cover the wall. Remove the canes and tie the shoots to the wires when they become woody.

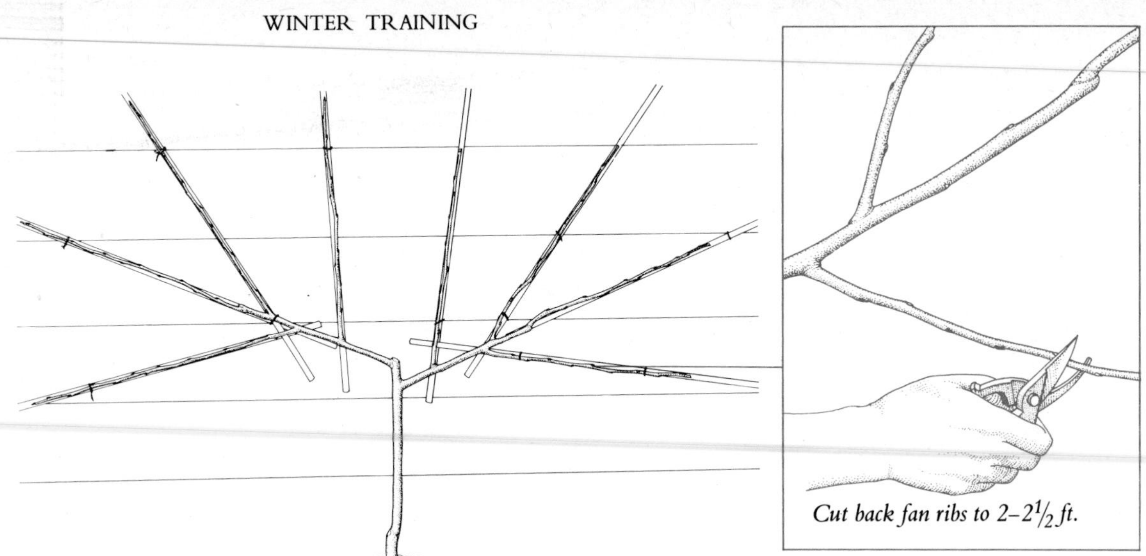

Cut back fan ribs to 2–2½ ft.

SUMMER TRAINING

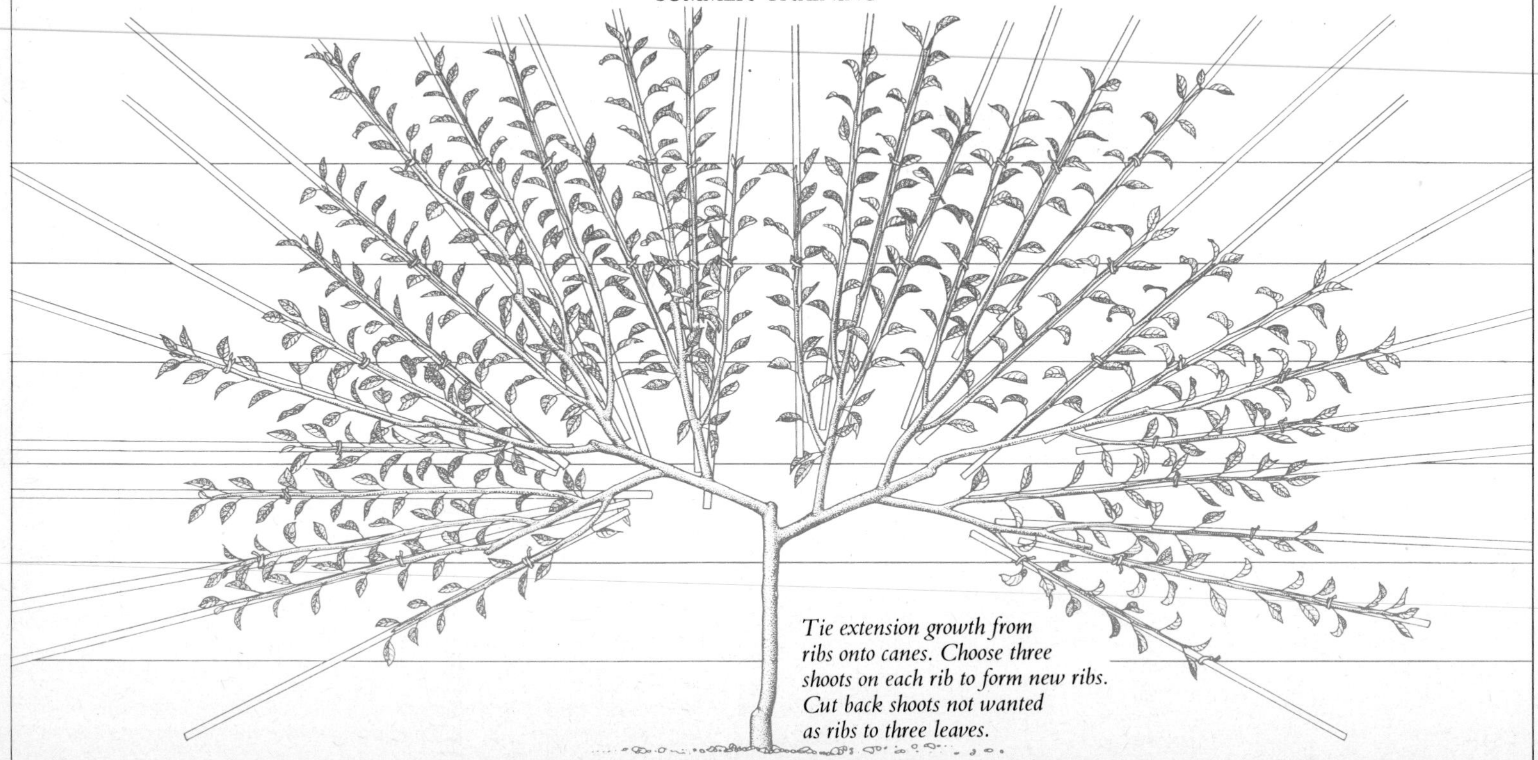

Tie extension growth from ribs onto canes. Choose three shoots on each rib to form new ribs. Cut back shoots not wanted as ribs to three leaves.

Pruning a Fan After It Has Been Trained

Once the tree's fan shape has been established, the only pruning necessary in winter is the thinning out of overcrowded spurs. This will help the tree to produce regular crops and better-quality fruit.

Remove some of the overcrowded spurs entirely, cutting them off flush with the parent stem. Then cut back others to reduce them in size and thin out the cluster of fruit buds (see p. 508).

Prune new growth in summer as it becomes mature, generally starting in midsummer and perhaps continuing for about a month.

Mature growth is at least 9 inches long, has turned woody at the base, and has dark green leaves. Cut back mature new side shoots from ribs to one leaf beyond the basal cluster, unless they are needed as replacements. Tie the replacement shoots to the wires.

New growth that is not mature enough for pruning in midsummer may be ready in late summer. If it is still not mature enough at that time—this may be the case in the North—wait until early fall.

When you prune new growth in summer, secondary growth may develop from the cut wood by fall. After a reasonably dry summer that has not produced much secondary growth, cut it all back to one bud in the fall.

When the summer has been wet and a great deal of secondary growth has occurred, you may need to continue pruning into early winter.

If the ribs of the fan grow beyond the space allotted, cut them back to a strong side branch, and tie it in as a replacement leader.

SUMMER PRUNING

If ribs outgrow the available space, cut them back to a strong side branch, and tie it in as a replacement leader.

In midsummer cut back all mature new side shoots from ribs to one leaf from the basal cluster.

Pruning and Training a Dwarf Pyramid Tree

Training a One-Year-Old Dwarf Pyramid

Dwarf pyramids are usually trained to a height of about 7 feet, with short branches spreading out all around the stem or trunk. When on M IX rootstock, trees should be spaced $3\frac{1}{2}$ feet apart (4 feet on more fertile soils) in rows from 7 to 10 feet apart. Plant them between midfall and early spring (see p. 490).

If you begin with a one-year-old (maiden) tree, cut back the stem to about 20 inches above soil level immediately after planting. Cut just above a bud or side shoot, and then rub out the bud or shoot that is second from the top; otherwise it may produce a second leading shoot.

Select three or four of the buds below the topmost bud to form the tree's first branches. Space them to grow out in different directions. Rub out unwanted buds or shoots.

The topmost bud will grow upward to form the tree's central leader, and the next two buds should form strong branches, but the lowest buds will produce weak branches unless they are stimulated. They therefore need notching; remove a half-moon of bark from above each of these buds.

Training a Young Dwarf Pyramid in Winter

In the second winter cut back the central leader to about 18 inches from the first year's cut. To help produce a straight stem, make the cut just above a bud facing in the opposite direction from the bud chosen during the previous winter.

As in the previous winter, rub out the bud below the top one, and choose three or four buds below it that are well spaced for forming another tier of branches. With a sharp knife carefully notch above the two lower buds as before.

Repeat this training each winter until the main stem has reached a height of about 7 feet.

In the second winter only, cut back the leaders of the first tier of branches to a length of about 9 inches—above a bud on the underside of the limb. After this, cut back branch leaders in summer only.

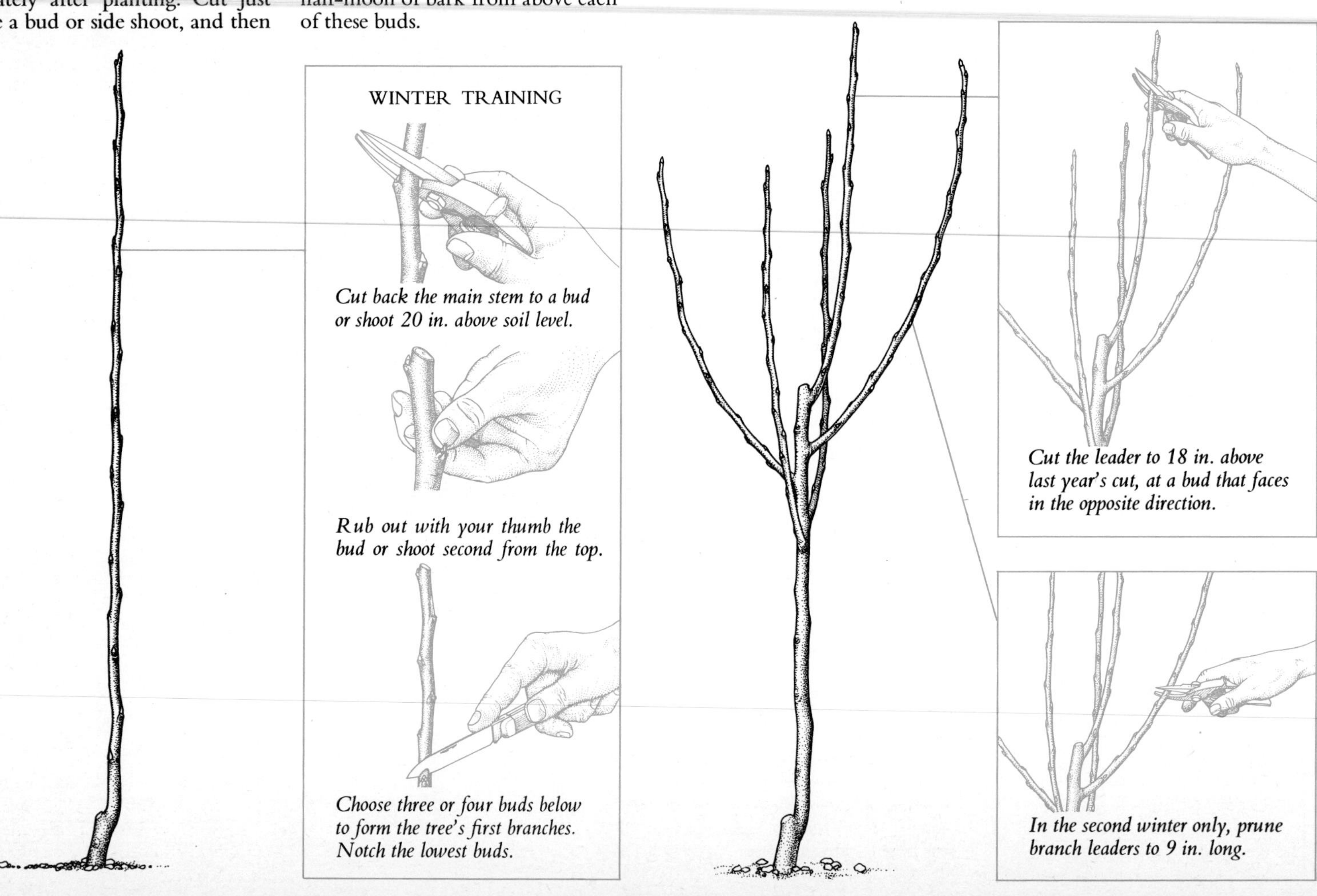

Cut back the main stem to a bud or shoot 20 in. above soil level.

Rub out with your thumb the bud or shoot second from the top.

Choose three or four buds below to form the tree's first branches. Notch the lowest buds.

Cut the leader to 18 in. above last year's cut, at a bud that faces in the opposite direction.

In the second winter only, prune branch leaders to 9 in. long.

Pruning a Young Dwarf Pyramid in Summer

No pruning is needed in the summer after training a one-year-old tree. For older trees prune new growth as it matures, usually starting in midsummer and continuing for perhaps a month.

Growth is mature when it is at least 9 inches long, woody at the base, and has dark green leaves.

Cut back extension growth on branch leaders (but not the central leader) to five or six leaves beyond the basal cluster. Cut above a bud on the underside of the limb.

Cut any of the mature laterals that are growing from the branches back to three leaves from the basal cluster.

If there are any mature side shoots growing from laterals or spurs, cut them back to one leaf from the basal cluster. Until the fourth summer remove new shoots growing from the main stem.

If new growth is not mature enough for pruning in midsummer, it may be ready in late summer. If it is still not mature enough then—this may be the case in the North—wait until early fall.

If you have pruned in summer, you may find that secondary growth has sprung from the pruned shoots by fall. If it has been a rather dry summer and not much secondary growth has occurred, cut it all back to one bud from the parent stem during the fall. After a wet summer that has produced a great amount of such growth, you may have to continue pruning into early winter in order to maintain the pyramidal shape of the tree.

Training a Dwarf Pyramid to Full Height

Continue winter training and summer pruning until the central stem reaches a height of about 7 feet. (This point is likely to be reached when the tree is seven or eight years old.) By this time the tree will have at least six tiers of branches from each winter training.

Then in late spring cut back the central stem by half the previous season's growth. The shape of the dwarf pyramid is now established.

Once the tree reaches about 15 years of age, its upper branches will have grown to the same spread as the lower ones, and the Christmas-tree shape will be lost. All the branches should be kept at a length of about 18 inches.

In midsummer prune new growth on branch leaders—not the central one—to five or six leaves from the basal cluster.

Cut back mature laterals from branches to three leaves from the basal cluster.

FALL PRUNING

In early fall cut secondary growth from the earlier pruning back to one bud.

Cut back mature side shoots growing from laterals to one leaf from the basal cluster.

When the central leader reaches a height of about 7 ft., in late spring, cut it back by about half the previous season's growth.

Pruning an Established Dwarf Pyramid Tree

In late spring cut back the central leader above a bud, leaving only ½ inch of the previous season's growth. When branches reach 18 inches, maintain them at this length.

If branch leaders begin to overlap the branches of neighboring trees, cut back half of the new growth during one spring pruning. Thereafter, cut back to only ½ inch of new growth each spring.

As in previous summers, prune growth as it becomes mature in summer. Cut back mature laterals from branches to three leaves beyond the basal cluster. Cut back mature side shoots from laterals or spurs to one leaf beyond the basal cluster.

If growth is not mature enough for pruning during midsummer, prune in late summer or early fall.

Cut any secondary growth from the summer pruning back to one bud in the fall. After a wet season that has produced a lot of such growth, you may have to continue pruning into early winter.

On older dwarf pyramid trees the fruiting spurs may become overcrowded and need thinning. Do this in winter; remove some entirely, cutting flush with the parent stem, and reduce the size of others.

Thin out overcrowded spurs in winter. Remove some entirely, and reduce others in size.

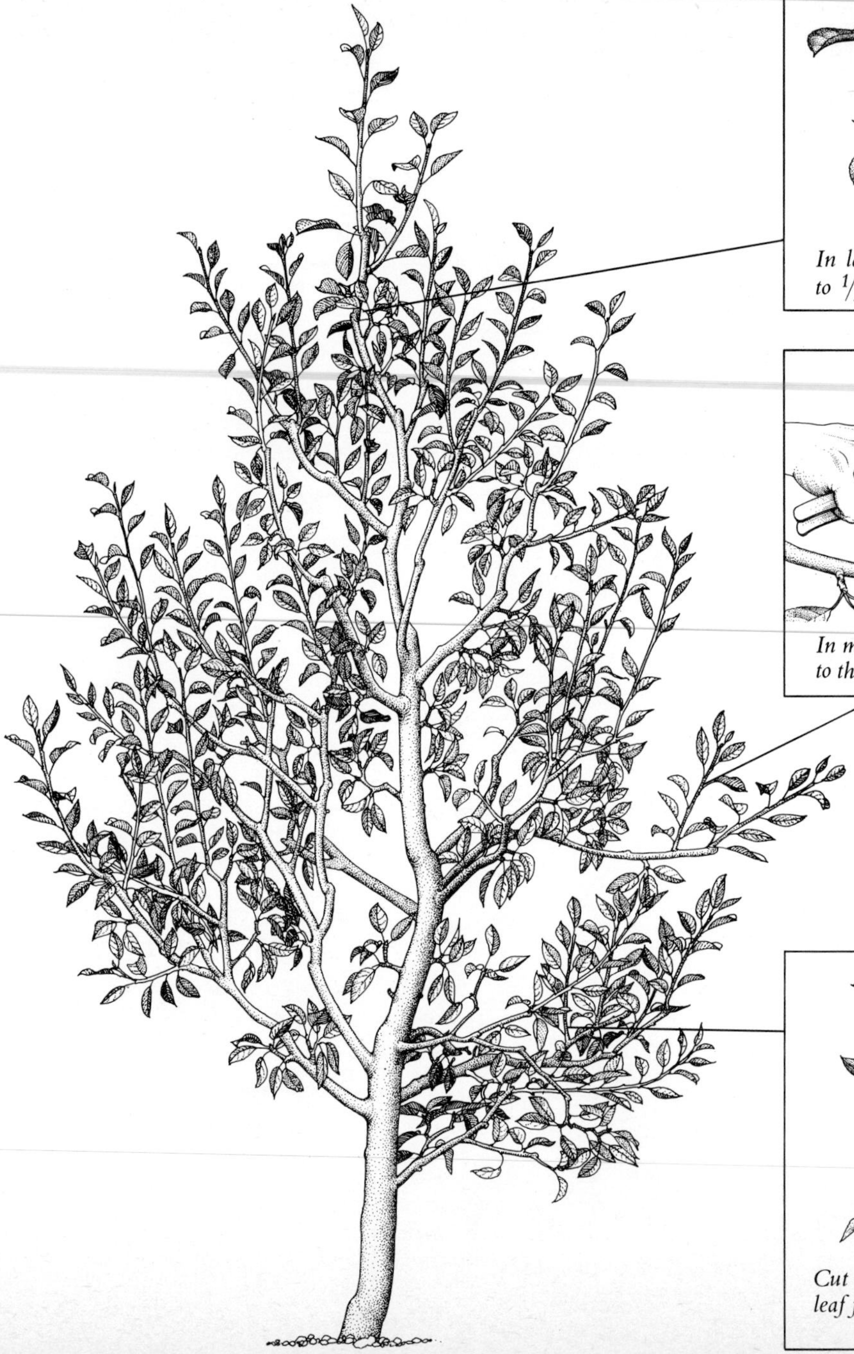

In late spring cut central leader to ½ in. of last year's growth.

In midsummer cut mature laterals to three leaves from basal cluster.

Cut mature side shoots to one leaf from basal cluster.

Varieties of Apples to Grow

The varieties listed should be available at nurseries. They are listed in the order in which they mature.

Pollination group. No apple tree is fully self-fertile; so more than one variety should be grown. Ideally, choose trees from within the same pollination group, although pollination will usually occur between varieties in adjoining groups. The groups relate to flowering time:

1. Early to mid season
2. Midseason
3. Mid to late season

Triploids (marked T) are almost sterile varieties and therefore poor pollinators. They need to be grown with two other varieties from the same group—to pollinate both the triploid and each other.

Picking time. The days from bloom to picking time indicated below are only an average. The exact time varies according to season and locality. All the apples on a tree do not ripen at the same time; and, for the early- and mid-season varieties, more than one picking is needed.

Names	Pollination group	Days from bloom to picking	Color	Remarks
'Gravenstein' (T)	1	90–95	Red striped	Good quality. High acidity. Cooking; 40–60 days' storage.
'Cortland'	2	125–130	Medium red	Good quality. Medium acidity. Dessert and cooking; 90–100 days' storage.
'McIntosh' (S)	1	125–130	Medium red	Good quality. Medium acidity. Dessert and cooking; 60–90 days' storage.
'R. I. Greening' (T)	2	135–145	Yellowish green	Good quality. Medium-high acidity. Cooking; 90–120 days' storage.
'Golden Delicious' (S)	2	140–145	Yellow	High quality. Medium acidity. Dessert and cooking; 90–120 days' storage.
'Jonathan'	2	140–145	Bright red	Good quality. Medium-high acidity. Dessert and cooking; 60–90 days' storage.
'Red Delicious' (S)	2	140–150	Medium red	Popular. Low acidity. Dessert and cooking; 90–100 days' storage.
'Northern Spy'	3	145–155	Red striped	Good quality. Medium acidity. Dessert and cooking; 120–150 days' storage.
'York Imperial'	3	155–165	Light red	Medium-low quality. Medium acidity. Cooking; 120–150 days' storage.
'Rome Beauty' (S)	3	160–165	Medium red	Medium quality. Medium-low acidity. Cooking; 120–150 days' storage.
'Winesap' (T)	2	160–170	Dark red	Medium quality. Medium acidity. Dessert and cooking; 150–210 days' storage.
'Stayman' (T)	2	160–165	Medium red	Good quality. Medium acidity. Dessert and cooking; 120–150 days' storage.

(T) Indicates triploid number of chromosomes and the need for 2 other varieties nearby for cross-pollination. (S) Indicates that spur strains on dwarfing rootstocks are available.

EFFECT OF DWARFING STOCK ON TREE SIZE

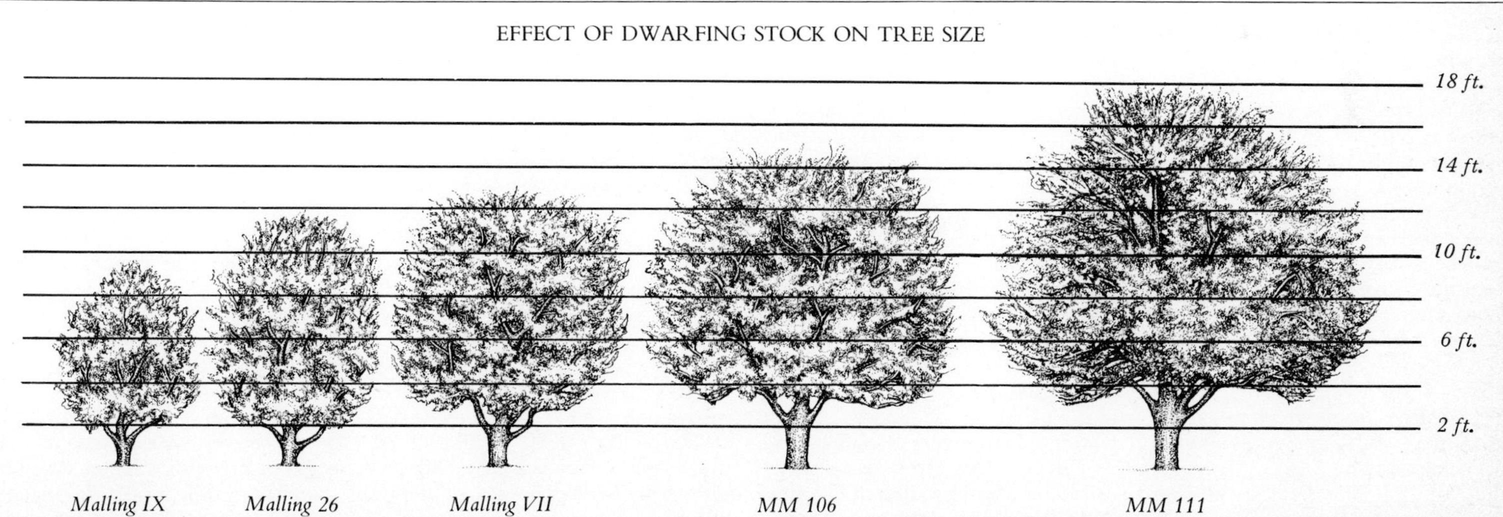

Most home garden apple trees now are sold on full or semi-dwarfing vegetatively propagated rootstocks. These smaller trees are much easier to prune, spray, and harvest. The Malling and Malling-Merten (MM) rootstocks from England, as noted above, will produce trees 6–9 ft. high (Malling IX), as opposed to semi-dwarfs that are from one-half to three-fourths the size of the standard large trees. Spur strains of a given variety reduce the standard-tree size by about one-fourth. And, of course, the fertility of the soil, as well as the amount of fertilizer applied, can make a difference in the ultimate size of a tree.

Avocados

Avocado (*Persea americana*)

Avocado trees are large, broad-leaved evergreens, varying in form from upright to broadly spreading. They make magnificent display plants, resembling in general appearance the evergreen magnolias of the South.

The individual flowers are inconspicuous, but the blooming period itself is impressive because of the profusion of large panicles (long clusters) of flowers borne on the tree over a span of several months. Bloom may begin as early as December and continue into April. This extends the harvest. If early bloom should be damaged by frost, the later bloom will still produce fruit.

The fruits are attractive, varying in color from bright green to a glossy purplish black. They can be round or pear shaped. The popular name for the avocado, "alligator pear," derives from the pear-shaped, coarse-textured varieties.

The fruits range in size from about that of a golf ball to larger than a cantaloupe. The seed may be relatively small but sometimes constitutes almost the entire fruit. Some avocado trees bear a number of seedless fruits that grow to about the size of a human thumb; these are called cukes because of their resemblance to small cucumbers.

The peel, or skin, of the fruit may be smooth and thin, or it may be rough, thick, and woody. It sticks tightly to the flesh of some varieties but slips off easily from others. Most trees bear heavily one year and lightly the next, although a few varieties produce fruit fairly consistently from year to year.

The avocado fruit is low in sugar content; so it is generally used in salads and in sauces, such as the Mexican *guacamole,* rather than in desserts. It is high in calories and its protein content (1–4 percent) is higher than that of most other tree fruits. Avocados are a good source of vitamins A, B_1, C, and G.

Avocado trees are native to tropical and subtropical regions of North and Central America, where three groups, or "races," have developed: the Mexican, Guatemalan, and West Indian. The fruits in these groups vary considerably in their characteristics. Of greatest concern to gardeners in the United States is their relative hardiness.

Most current avocado varieties are hybrids of two or all three races, but only those with some Mexican heritage have any appreciable hardiness to cold. Some pure Mexican types will tolerate temperatures slightly below 20° F, but the West Indian types will be damaged at temperatures below 28°–30° F. The Guatemalan types are generally hardy to temperatures as low as 25° F.

Excessively high temperatures, high humidity, and rainfall also limit the regions where avocados can be grown successfully. The Mexican types are adapted to the cool, dry climate of their native mountains. Their thin peel tends to crack in a hot, humid climate such as Florida's.

How and Where to Plant Avocado Trees

Low temperature is the main factor limiting avocado culture in the continental United States. Commercial production is therefore largely restricted to portions of southern California and southern Florida. The hardier varieties can, however, be grown in home gardens in cooler regions of these states—as well as in parts of Arizona and Texas—if they are planted in warm, protected locations, such as the south side of a building. Before planting, determine the minimum temperatures at the chosen site and select varieties accordingly.

Good drainage is essential. Avocado root rot usually occurs when the trees are grown in poorly drained soil, but it can also be a danger in normally well drained soil if the roots are flooded for a short period. It is best to avoid poorly drained soils altogether; or install drainage ditches or tile drains.

Most avocados are extremely rapid growers. A 3-year-old tree may reach 10 feet in height and a 10-year-old tree 20 feet or more, unless stunted by unfavorable conditions such as poor soil or strong winds. Each tree must be given adequate space to attain its full size because it is difficult to keep it small by pruning. (The distance between trees should be about 25–35 feet.) This vigorous habit of growth can be a benefit because even trees killed back to the ground by frost will produce large tops and fruit within two years.

Avocado trees do best in full sun but will tolerate partial shade. They can be used as a background planting for shrubs or flowers, as a tall hedge, or as a landscape feature. Home gardeners will seldom find it necessary to use pesticides.

Avocado trees may be available as balled and burlapped plants, but most are sold in containers. Planting procedures are similar to those for container-grown citrus (see pp. 517–518), except that the trees should be planted with the graft union below ground level in the cooler regions of Florida and Texas, where hardy varieties are grafted onto tender rootstocks. The soil will protect the underground portion of the trunk of the hardy scion variety as well as the tender rootstock. New shoots arise from the buried portion of the hardy top if frozen to the ground.

California avocado trees are generally produced on hardy rootstocks, but the trunks of all varieties are tender the first year. Protect them by banking them with soil or wrapping them with an insulating material such as burlap. Avocado trees must also be protected from intense sun and wind during their first summer if they are planted on exposed sites. Such protection is usually needed in southern Texas.

Taking Care of Avocado Trees

The soil around young avocado trees should be thoroughly soaked with water every two weeks during the growing season. Allow the soil to dry out somewhat between waterings, to protect the shallow roots from rot. Periodically check the moisture level, especially in clay soils, by digging a foot-deep hole near each tree.

Avocados do not require a precise schedule of fertilization. The same program described for citrus (see p. 518) works well. They do well in both slightly acid and slightly alkaline soils, but chlorosis, or loss of green coloration, may develop in the leaves of trees grown in very alkaline soils. This condition is indicated when the veins of the leaves show up as a dark green network against a pale- or yellow-green background. Chlorosis can usually be corrected with applications of iron chelates to the soil.

The soil around young trees should be kept free of weeds. As the tree grows, the weeds will be shaded out by the lower limbs. Paraquat, a herbicide used to kill weeds around several kinds of fruit trees, should not be applied near the trunks of young avocados.

Little if any pruning is required, other than to keep trees to the desired shape by cutting back occasional limbs. All frost-damaged branches are best removed after new growth matures. However, if large areas of dead bark appear on branches well below the new growth—even if leaf damage is slight—the affected branches should be removed promptly. If damaged limbs are not pruned, they will often break under the stress of heavy crops or wind. However, recovery will be swift following pruning.

Virtually no home-garden avocado trees need be sprayed. Mites may become a problem, but little damage other than leaf drop occurs. Avocado scab fungus can cause ugly lesions on the fruit of some varieties in wet regions, but resistant varieties are available. The blemished fruit is satisfactory for home use.

Because avocado fruits often fall off the tree before ripening fully, they must be harvested when still hard. (They ripen readily off the tree at room temperature and can be safely stored for several weeks.) The fruits should be harvested on the basis of season and size—that is, a given variety attains its mature size during certain months and will ripen satisfactorily off the tree if harvested at the appropriate time. The purplish-black varieties can be harvested at any time after more than half their peel has darkened.

The season of maturity varies considerably. The Mexican varieties crack badly if exposed to hot, humid climatic conditions in summer. But the fruit usually ripens satisfactorily if it is harvested before cracking and placed in a cool, dry room, even if it is not quite mature when it is picked.

Avocados should not be pulled off the tree, as fruit rots if the stem is pulled out. Clip off with the stem attached. A pole with a cloth bag attached to a sharp metal ring or claws is used to remove the fruits from the higher branches of the trees.

Tree Size and Shape

No dwarfing rootstocks are available for avocados; however, varieties differ widely in vigor and habit of growth. Gardeners often select trees for landscape use on the basis of size and shape. This, of course, restricts the choice of fruit characteristics and hardiness. Nurserymen generally carry only commercial varieties; so a gardener who wants a special variety may have to propagate it himself or have it propagated by a nurseryman.

What Can Go Wrong With Avocados

Avocados are essentially trouble free and, in most places, can be grown for years without spraying the tree or treating the soil. Chemicals should be applied only as a last resort. When infestations do occur, the specific materials listed here may be called for. Also consider using biological controls (see p. 635). The best defense against virus is to plant disease-resistant varieties and provide the good drainage in the root area that they must have.

Symptoms and signs	Cause	Control
White powder exudes from small holes in branches.	Ambrosia beetles	Not as dangerous as it may seem. Best defense is to keep trees growing well.
Cottony masses at nodes, on buds, and on undersides of leaves. Plants may show sooty mold fungus.	Mealybugs	Systemics, such as dimethoate and oxydemeton-methyl, are useful. Or use contact sprays of Diazinon or malathion.
Tiny, narrow insects rasp and suck juices from leaves and fruits. Leaves are spotted; fruits are russeted and cracked.	Red-banded thrips	Spray every 10 da. with chlorpyrifos, dichlorvos, or malathion. Systemics, such as dimethoate and oxydemeton-methyl, are also effective.
Leaves are rusty brown or grayish; may drop prematurely. Leaves may be webbed.	Red spider mites	Spray with dicofol or tetradifon for severe infestations; repeat as needed. It is best to spray with 5 tbsp. oil emulsion per gallon of water before damage is severe. (Or use wettable sulfur—1 lb. per 10 gal. of water.)
Encrustations of soft and hard scalelike insects on leaves and twigs.	Scale insects	Spray with 8 tsp. of oil emulsion per gallon of Diazinon or malathion, properly diluted.
Roots and trees suddenly wilt and die.	Avocado root rot (fungus)	Difficult to control. Best possible prevention is to provide better drainage.
Circular black spots on fruits, stems, leaves.	Anthracnose (fungus)	Spray with Benomyl, neutral copper, or dodine.
Small, angular, brownish spots first appear on leaves, then form irregular patches—usually during summer.	Cercospora spot (fungus)	Spray with neutral copper in early May. Spray midseason varieties in early June, late varieties in mid July.
Scabby lesions on fruits.	Scab (fungus)	Spray with Benomyl or neutral copper. For serious problems on scab-susceptible varieties 3 applications may be required. Spray when bloom buds begin to swell, again when fruit begins to set, and finally about 1 mo. later.
Sunken yellow areas on fruits.	Sun blotch (virus)	No control. Destroy infected material. Plant only blotch-free varieties.

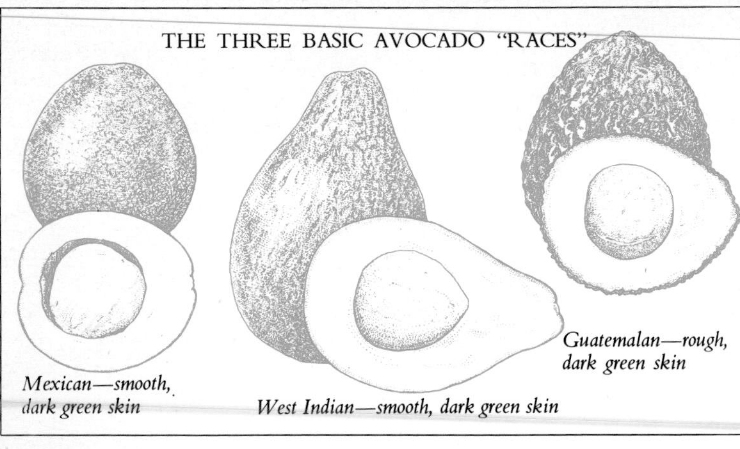

Varieties of Avocados to Grow

The pollination cycle of avocado trees differs according to variety. Those termed type A have flowers that are receptive to pollen in the morning, but their pollen is not shed until afternoon, when flowers are no longer receptive. Other varieties, type B, have the reverse pattern. In theory, therefore, neither type will set fruit if planted alone. However, fluctuating temperatures upset these cycles, thus making all varieties usually self-pollinating.

Names	Hardiness	Season	Remarks
California			
'Bacon'	25°–27° F	Fall	Green, medium. Flower type B.
'Duke'	20°–24° F	Fall	Green, medium. Flower type A.
'Fuerte'	28°–30° F	Winter	Green, medium. Fruit type B.
'Hass'	28°–30° F	Winter	Dark purple, medium. Flower type B.
'Rincon'	28°–30° F	Winter	Green, medium. Flower type A.
'Topa'	20°–24° F	Fall	Dark purple, medium. Flower type A.
'Zutano'	25°–27° F	Fall	Green, medium. Flower type B.
Florida			
'Booth 8'	28°–30° F	Early winter	Green, medium-large. Flower type B.
'Brogdon'	20°–24° F	Late summer	Dark purple, medium. Flower type B.
'Choquette'	28°–30° F	Winter	Green, very large. Flower type A.
'Duke'	20°–24° F	Midsummer	Green, medium. Flower type A.
'Gainesville'	15°–20° F	Midsummer	Green, medium-small. Flower type A.
'Monroe'	28°–30° F	Midwinter	Green, very large. Flower type A.
'Simmonds'	28°–30° F	Late summer	Green, very large. Flower type A.
'Waldin'	28°–30° F	Early fall	Green, large. Flower type A.
Texas			
'Lula'	25°–27° F	Fall, early winter	Green, medium-large. Flower type A.

Blackberries

Blackberry 'Thornless Evergreen'

Boysenberry 'Thornless Logan'

Blackberries can be erect or trailing. Among the trailing types are the loganberry, a red-fruited mutation of wild blackberries, and the boysenberry, a mutation of dewberries (various species of trailing blackberries). All require essentially the same care. The average family will need three to five plants.

Blackberries, loganberries, and boysenberries are used for desserts, jams, and wines. They also adapt themselves well to freezing.

They do best in sun but will take partial shade. Provide a well-drained but moisture-retentive soil, with a pH of about 5.5. Adequate moisture all season is essential.

Rooted canes are best planted in early fall (see p. 81), but they can be put in at any time until early spring if the soil is not frozen. Position erect varieties 5 feet apart in rows 8 feet apart; vigorous, thornless, trailing plants, such as 'Thornless Evergreen,' 8–12 feet apart in rows 10 feet apart; others, 4–6 feet apart in rows 8 feet apart, depending on soil fertility and training system. Immediately after planting, cut the canes back (just above a bud) to 9–15 inches above ground level.

Diseases and insects can be kept to a minimum by using ground that has been cultivated for several years, choosing disease-resistant varieties, buying stock free of nematodes and diseases, removing old canes after harvest, and keeping plants free of weeds and fallen leaves.

The diseases that can attack are verticillium wilt of roots, cane gall, anthracnose (spots on canes, leaves), and orange rust. Troublesome insects include aphids, leafhoppers, mites, fruitworms, scales, leaf rollers, beetles, weevils, cane borers, and white grubs (on the roots). Controls for many of these are given in the chart beginning on page 600. For the necessary control of other disease and insect problems, contact your local county agent for the latest spray recommendations.

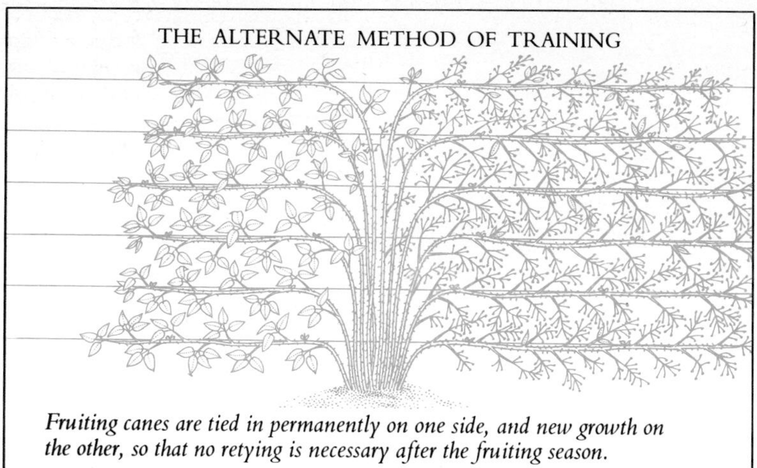

Fruiting canes are tied in permanently on one side, and new growth on the other, so that no retying is necessary after the fruiting season.

Cultivating and Training the Plants

Erect blackberries can be grown without supports, but it is best to use them. For a trellis arrangement, set posts in a row about 15 feet apart, and stretch a wire between them about 30 inches from the ground.

Train trailing blackberries up a post or wires, so that the growing shoots are kept away from the two-year-old shoots, which bear the fruit. This prevents disease from spreading.

For each post use 9–10 feet of 4- by 4-inch timber, leaving 7 feet above the ground. Train the fruiting canes up the post, and tie loosely together to one side the new shoots growing from the ground.

For training canes on wires, use 10- to 12-gauge wire stretched between posts to a height of about 6 feet; place wires 12 inches apart, and fasten to posts with staples.

There are three ways of training the canes. With the fan method the fruiting canes are fanned out on each side, and the new growth is temporarily tied to the top wire. The weaving method is similar, except that the fruiting canes are woven around the wires. With the third method fruiting canes are tied permanently on one side of the wires, new growth on the other side.

Watering and feeding. Water only during dry spells in summer. One to two months before growth starts in spring, apply about 5 pounds of a 10-10-10 fertilizer or a similar mix per 100-foot row. For the first year or two, apply 3–4 ounces of fertilizer in a 12-inch radius at the base of each plant. Mulch with compost to conserve moisture.

A freestanding blackberry vine before pruning in spring (left) and after.

Cutting Out the Old Canes

After the fruit is picked, cut out the fruited canes at ground level. In the case of post training and fan and weaving systems, untie the current year's shoots from their temporary positions, and tie them so as to replace the old, cut-down shoots.

Raising New Blackberry Plants

Trailing blackberries root easily. One way of developing new plants is to layer the tips of shoots (the only method for thornless types). In midsummer bend down a new season's shoot. Where it touches the ground, dig a 6-inch-deep hole with a trowel. Plant the tip of the shoot in the hole. By early fall the tips will have rooted. Sever each new plant from its parent just above a bud. In late fall transfer each new cane to its permanent bed. It will bear fruits in its second or third year.

Another method of propagation (for erect types) is to dig up roots of established plants in early spring, cut them into 3-inch lengths, and bury them in trenches 2 or 3 inches deep.

Varieties of Blackberries to Grow

Always buy plants that are certified to be free from virus. Blackberries—including boysenberries, loganberries, and dewberries—need no cross-pollination, with the exception of 'Flordagrand.' Thornless varieties are easiest to pick.

Names	Season	Usual area	Remarks
Erect			
'Brazos'	Early	Gulf states	Productive. Vigorous.
'Darrow'	Early, long season	Northeast, Central	Productive. Hardy.
'Eldorado'	Early-mid	Not for extreme South	Long-standing, reliable.
'Thornfree'	Late	Pacific Northwest, N.J. to N.C. as far west as Ark.	Thornless.* Semi-upright. Productive. Most cold hardy.
Trailing			
'Boysen'	Late	South, Pacific Coast	Thornless boysenberry.* Soft, large, tart berries.
'Thornless Evergreen'	Very late	Pacific Northwest	Thornless.* Firm, large, sweet berries; big seeds.
'Flordagrand'	Very early	Gulf states	Soft, large, aromatic berries. Needs cross-pollination.**
'Thornless Logan'	Early	Pacific Coast	Thornless loganberry.* Large, flavorful berries.
'Lucretia'	Early	Cooler areas	Dewberry. Hardy if protected against severe winters.
'Young'	Mid	South, Pacific Coast	Thornless.* Large, sweet berries.

* *Winter damage may occur with thornless varieties. Protect where temperatures fall below 0° F.*
** *'Oklawaha' variety is a preferred cross-pollenizer for 'Flordagrand'; very early, similar berries.*

Blueberries

Blueberry 'Bluecrop'

How to Prune Blueberries

Blueberries need no pruning for the first three years after planting. After that, prune each winter. Fruit is borne on the previous year's wood. To promote new shoots that will fruit the following year, cut from one to four of the oldest shoots from each bush. Either cut them back hard to a strong new shoot, or if there are plenty of young basal shoots, cut them down to soil level.

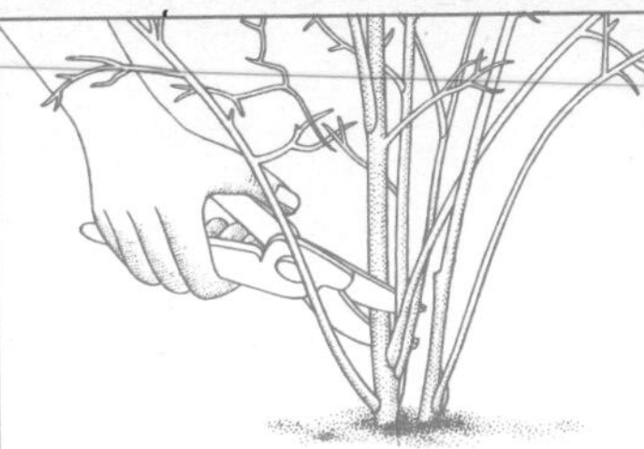

Cut from one to four of the oldest shoots back hard to a strong new shoot or down to soil level.

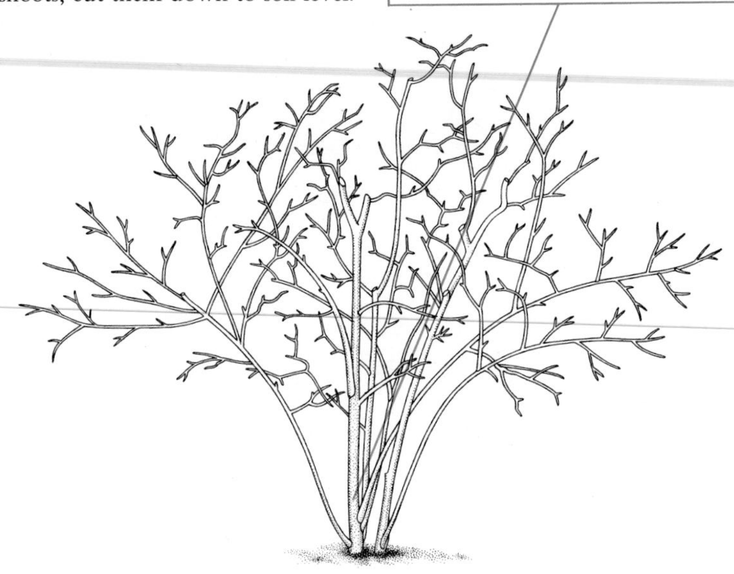

There are many blueberries native to the United States. For the best performance, choose the cultivated forms recommended by your state agricultural experiment station.

The berries, fresh or frozen, are suitable for desserts and jam making, and, of course, make excellent pies.

Blueberries need a moisture-retentive, acid soil—with a pH value between about 5 and 6 (see p. 594). They do best in an open, sunny area, but they can be grown in partial shade. In northern regions the bushes should be given protection from cold winds.

It is useless to try to grow blueberries in alkaline soil. When only alkaline soil is available, blueberries can be grown in containers. Fill the containers with an acid- or a peat-based compost, with no lime added.

From four to six bushes should provide a good supply of blueberries for the average family. The berries are generally ready for picking in mid and late summer. Each of the plants will bear fruit over a period of several weeks.

Blueberries are not completely self-fertile; to ensure a good yield, plant at least two varieties.

Plants can be propagated by layering (see p. 92) in autumn or spring or by taking semi-hard-shoot cuttings in late summer (see p. 88).

Planting and Tending Blueberries

Plant blueberry bushes in fall or spring when soil is favorable. Set the bushes 3–4 feet apart and about 1 inch deeper in the soil than they were in the nursery.

Fertilize as described in the blackberry section, about a month before growth starts (see p. 513). Ammonium sulfate is the best nitrogen source if applied alone, using ½–1 ounce per square yard. In sandy soil repeat the application a month later, after growth starts.

Early each summer mulch with well-rotted manure, garden compost, leaf mold, or peat. Protect plants from birds with netting.

Plants may suffer from chlorosis, which can be caused by too much lime in the soil. Yellow mottling or patches occur on the leaves, growth is poor, and few blueberries are produced. To decrease the pH, dig in acidic material, such as peat moss, and apply sulfur or iron chelates to the soil as directed on the container.

For other symptoms turn to the chart on page 600. Look up the recommended chemicals on page 635.

Varieties of Blueberries to Grow

The season of ripening given below is for most major blueberry areas; ripening will occur later in the North. Ripening time is, however, an estimate only and will vary according to the growing conditions prevailing during the season.

Names	Season	Remarks
'Weymouth'	Early (mid to late summer)	Large, dark blue berries. Usually reliable in bearing. Average quality. Below-average-vigor bush.
'Bluecrop'	Midseason (late summer)	Large, good berries. Average-vigor bush; quite hardy and drought resistant.
'Jersey'	Late (late summer to fall)	Medium berry. Productive. Average quality. Vigorous bush; reliable.

Cherries

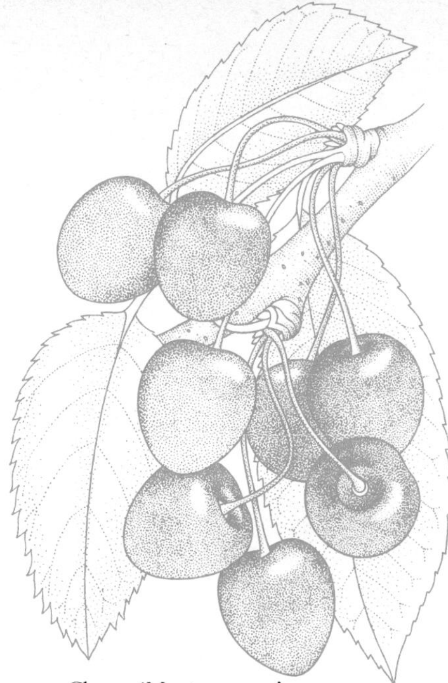
Cherry 'Montmorency'

There are two kinds of cherries: sweet, eaten fresh; and tart, used mainly for cooking, canning, jam making, and pie baking. (The latter cherries are, in fact, often called pie cherries.)

Both need deep, well-drained soil, around pH 6.5. Tart cherries will do better in somewhat poorer soils than sweet cherries.

Sweet cherries are extremely vigorous. Only fan-trained trees are suitable for the average garden, and they take up a great deal of wall space. If plenty of room is available, the trees can be allowed to develop into their natural, large, rounded form. No varieties are completely self-fertile; so at least two varieties must be grown.

Tart cherries are less vigorous, but they are easier to grow than sweet cherries. Grows them as bush trees or as fans. They are self-pollinating; so a single tree will bear fruit.

Two trees of either type will bear enough fruit for an average family.

How to Grow Fan-Trained Sweet Cherries

For sweet cherries there is no suitable dwarfing rootstock as yet. Fan trees will span 15–20 feet. Plant them 18–24 feet apart (see p. 490) against a wall facing either south or west.

A month or two before spring growth starts, apply a 10–10–10 or 10–6–4 fertilizer evenly under the spread of the branches at the rate of about $\frac{3}{4}$ pound for a young tree, 5 pounds for a mature tree, and up to 10 pounds if growth is weak. On alkaline soils in the Northwest, $\frac{1}{2}$ pound of magnesium sulfate may be needed every third year. If only nitrogen is used, apply $\frac{1}{2}$ pound of ammonium sulfate or its equivalent for each year of the tree's age—up to 10 pounds. In late fall mulch with a layer of well-rotted manure or garden compost. Water only during prolonged dry spells in summer.

In early summer drape the entire tree with netting to protect the fruit from birds.

Do not pick sweet cherries until they are completely ripe; then pull them off by hand with an upward twist. The fruit does not keep well; put it in a plastic bag and refrigerate.

Training and pruning. For the first three years after planting a one-year-old, train and prune it like a fan apple (see p. 503), but prune it in early spring before growth begins, not in winter. After the framework is established, treatment differs; sweet cherries have more spurs and fewer laterals, and heavy pruning is not necessary.

In early summer rub out the current year's shoots that are growing directly toward or directly away from the wall. Pinch out the tips of the others in early or middle summer when they have four to six leaves.

When ribs reach the top of the wall, cut back to a weak lateral if there is one. Otherwise, bend the shoot to the horizontal, and tie it to the wire. This tends to slow the rate of growth and encourages new shoots to break out. The shoot can then be cut back to a weak lateral.

In early fall cut back shoots pinched out in summer to three or four flower buds (large, plump ones). Also cut away any deadwood. Make the cuts flush with the parent stem.

On older trees tie new shoots into the fan shape when there is room in early or middle summer. Some may be needed to replace old shoots.

OVERGROWN LEADERS

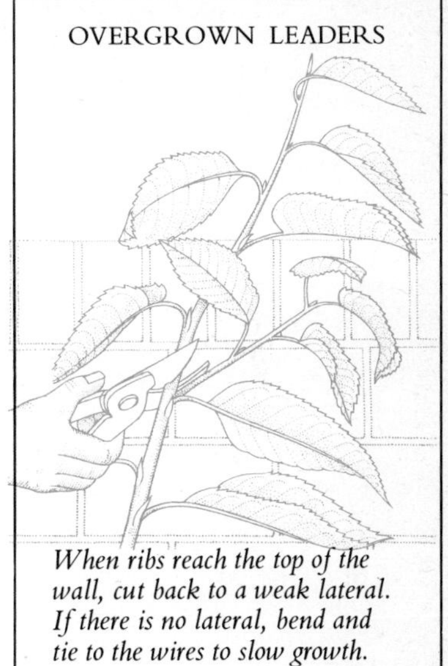

When ribs reach the top of the wall, cut back to a weak lateral. If there is no lateral, bend and tie to the wires to slow growth.

PRUNING AN ESTABLISHED FAN-TRAINED SWEET CHERRY

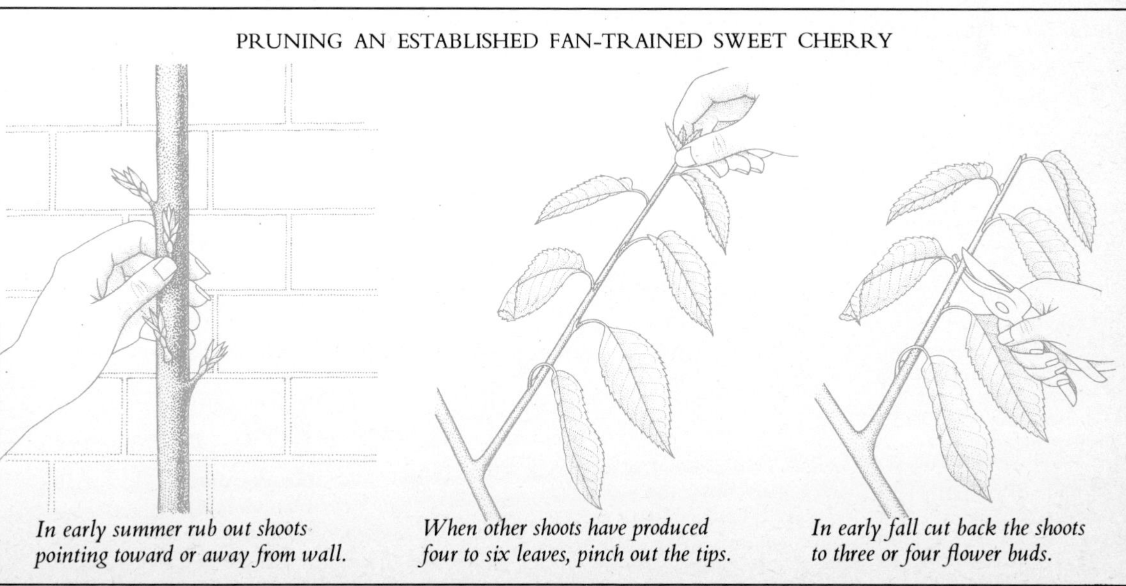

In early summer rub out shoots pointing toward or away from wall.

When other shoots have produced four to six leaves, pinch out the tips.

In early fall cut back the shoots to three or four flower buds.

How to Care for Tart Cherries

Tart cherries can be grown either as bush trees or as fans. (The latter type can be grown against any wall, even one facing north.) Plant both forms of tree 15–18 feet apart (see p. 490). Plant trees upon receiving them.

Weed control by shallow cultivation or mulching is essential around young trees. Later, a cover of closely mowed grass can be used.

Care for tart cherry trees in the same way as sweet cherry trees. Harvesting, however, is different. Cut off the ripe fruit with scissors; otherwise you may break the spurs.

Pruning dwarf trees. For the first three years train and prune dwarf cherry trees like dwarf apples (see p. 495), but prune in spring as growth begins.

Trees bear the most fruit on the previous year's growth. The aim of pruning an established tree is to constantly stimulate new wood.

Once a tree has started to fruit, thin it out to let in light and air, cutting back older shoots to just above one-year-old laterals. Thin out the outer spread occasionally, where new growth develops.

Paint all large pruning cuts on old wood with a wound-sealing paint or water asphalt roof paint.

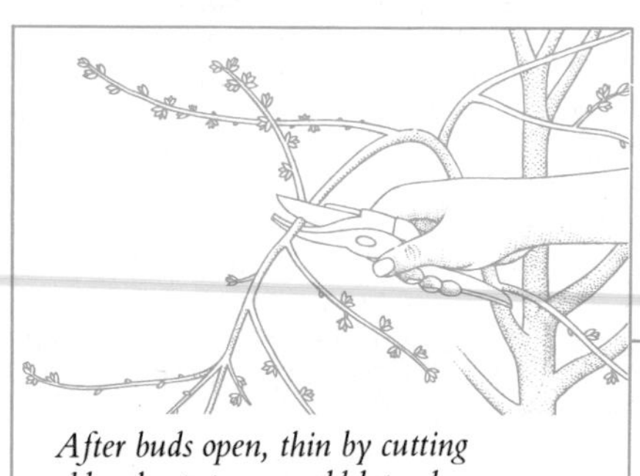

After buds open, thin by cutting older shoots to year-old laterals.

Pruning fan-trained trees. Prune and train fan tart cherries in early spring like fan apples (see p. 503). Thin fans like tart cherry trees.

PRUNING CHERRY TREES

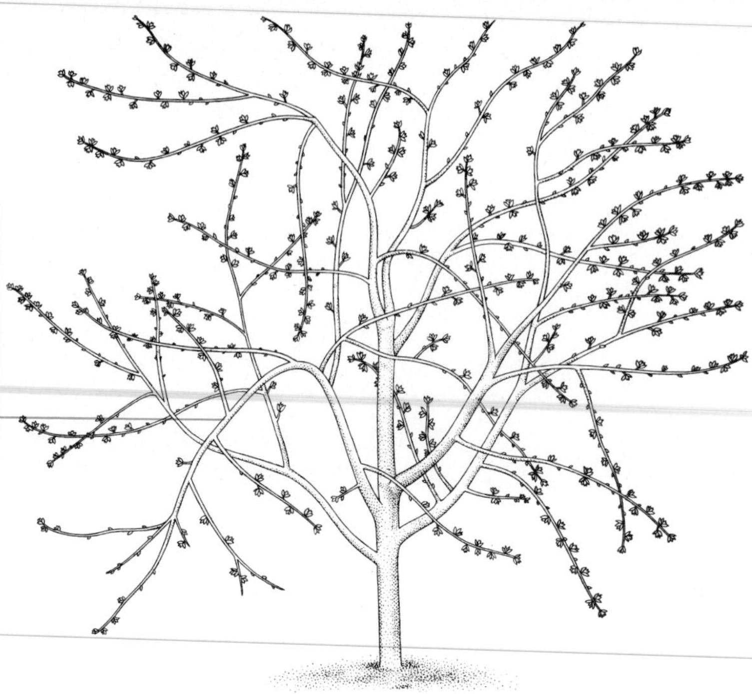

What Can Go Wrong With Sweet and Tart Cherries

The most common problems in cherry growing are aphids and leaf spot. If plants show symptoms that are not described here, turn to the section on pests and diseases on page 600. Look up chemicals on page 635 to find trade names.

Symptoms and signs	Cause	Control
Shoots and leaves distorted, covered with black insects.	Aphids	Immediately after flowering, spray with carbaryl or dimethoate.
Eggs laid in fruits, which show scars. Young insects ("worms") destroy fruits.	Plum curculios (weevils)	Spray with carbaryl at petal fall, and repeat at least 3 times at 7- to 14-da. intervals.
Serious disease of fruits, which are covered with powdery brown spore masses. Also causes twig dieback.	Brown rot (fungus)	Apply first spray at preblossom stage (buds just beginning to open). Repeat 5 or 6 times at 7- to 10-da. intervals. Use Captan, dodine, folpet, or wettable sulfur.
Minute spots, dark blue at first, later reddish brown and black, on flowers, fruits, and leaves.	Cherry leaf spot (fungus)	When petals fall, spray with dodine, folpet, or zineb. Repeat every 7-10 da. except when very dry. Destroy infected leaves.

Varieties of Sweet and Tart Cherries to Grow

Sweet cherries need a partner to cross-pollinate at blossom time; so two trees must be grown. Not all varieties flowering at the same time will pollinate each other. Therefore, at least two different varieties must be grown in close proximity to ensure pollination.

When selecting varieties, follow the catalog recommendations for suitable pollenizers, or check with your county extension agent.

Tart cherries are self-fertile and therefore do not need a pollination partner planted nearby.

Names	Season**	Color
Sweet cherries*		
'Vista'	Early summer	Dark red
'Royal Ann,' also known as 'Napoleon'	Midsummer	Golden, red cheek
'Schmidt'	Midsummer	Black
'Windsor'	Midsummer	Dark red
'Hedelfingen'	Midsummer	Black
Tart cherries		
'Montmorency'	Midsummer	Scarlet

* *Plant more than one variety of sweet cherry to ensure pollination.*
** *Cherries ripen from early to mid summer in most regions.*

Citrus

Although best known for their fruit, citrus trees are handsome, glossy-leaved evergreens that, in warm climates, can be used to great advantage in the landscape.

Some will grow to 30 feet but can be kept smaller by pruning. Others can be considered large shrubs, and there are types that are well adapted to growing in containers.

The many closely related groups of citrus trees include the well-known sweet orange, tangerine (or mandarin), grapefruit, lemon, and lime. Not only are there several varieties of each species, but there are purely ornamental species and more distantly related kinds, such as the deciduous, inedible trifoliate orange (*Poncirus trifoliata*) that can be grown in the United States as far north as Washington, D.C.

The various species have been hybridized with each other and with more distant relatives. Some hybrids of tangerines and grapefruits, known as tangelos, are fine dessert fruits. Citranges are hybrids of trifoliate and sweet oranges. They are resistant to frost and produce juicy, orange-like fruits but are inedible and are used only as rootstocks.

There are red-fleshed, or blood, oranges, red-fleshed grapefruits, and pink-fleshed lemons, as well as those with the commoner yellow and orange flesh. There are also variegated forms of several kinds of citrus in which the fruit peel and leaves are a mixture of green and white.

Citrus trees grow well in a wide range of soils but will not tolerate saline conditions or poor moisture drainage. Citrus is very sensitive to climate. Freezing temperatures ruin the quality of the fruit and, if too low, will kill the tree. This varies with the kind of citrus. Lemons and limes are restricted to the warmest locations, while satsuma mandarins grow well along the Gulf Coast from Florida to Texas, where temperatures can drop to 15°–20° F.

The deepest orange color of both peel and juice is produced in the cooler areas. The thickest peel develops in dry regions and the juiciest fruit under wet, humid conditions. Grapefruit is acid in cool climates and sweet in hot ones. The flesh of blood oranges turns red in cool climates, but in warmer regions it is often mottled or lacking in red.

Lemon and lime trees bloom periodically throughout the year and continue bearing fruit in all seasons. Other citrus trees flower in the spring, but the ripened fruit will stay on the tree for several months.

Three or four mature trees will keep a family of four in citrus fruit much of the year. Few gardens can support four large trees, but even small trees furnish a considerable amount of fruit.

Where and How to Plant

Citrus nursery trees for landscape use are usually grown in containers and are planted as recommended for other evergreen shrubs in containers (p. 83). Plants in containers often become pot-bound because the lateral roots are forced to encircle the root system. These encircling roots should be sheared off or pulled out so that they will grow into the soil after planting. Nursery trees grown in clay or organic soils develop very slowly when planted in sandy soil unless some of the clay soil is washed away from the roots before planting.

Citrus trees grow best in full sunlight. They will, however, tolerate partial shade, and trees can be planted on the south side of buildings, in courtyards, and under tall pine trees, where on cold nights it is warmer than in the open. On the other hand, there are pockets or low areas, even in warm regions, that are too cold for citrus. Such pockets may be as much as 10° F colder than nearby areas on calm, clear nights. In desert areas it is important to plant in places protected from dry winds.

Citrus makes a satisfactory free-standing specimen tree when grown with sufficient space to permit uniform development. It is most frequently used as a background planting rather than as the dominant feature of a front yard.

The size, shape, vigor of growth, and strength of branches of various kinds of citrus trees influence the selection of types to grow and places to plant them. Sweet orange trees grow large, but they are moderately upright and require less space than grapefruit trees, which are large and spreading. Many tangerines and their hybrids produce fruit on the ends of long, brittle branches, resulting in much limb breakage with heavy fruiting; but some varieties are compact and do well as garden trees.

In hot climates lemon trees grow

The limequat (left), a lime-kumquat hybrid, and the calamondin (Citrus madurensis), *a relatively hardy citrus tree, are suited to container culture. Both bear sour fruits. The sweet orange* (C. sinensis, *background*) *may reach 25 ft.*

too fast to be dependably attractive. In cool but frost-free climates, however, they grow slowly and retain their shape. The 'Meyer' is a relatively cold-hardy dwarf lemon.

The 'Tahiti,' 'Bearss,' or 'Persian' lime forms a tree about 15 feet tall, somewhat open and spreading in habit, with coarse-textured foliage. The 'Mexican,' 'Key,' or 'West Indian' lime is upright and compact and has fine-textured foliage. Both of these limes are too tender to survive frost.

The calamondin is upright and grows about 15 feet tall. It makes a beautiful specimen tree and can be useful as an accent by a terrace or to frame a doorway. Limequats, hybrids of kumquats and limes, are shrublike trees for colder areas.

Kumquats are comparatively cold-hardy, shrublike trees about 10 feet tall. The thick, sweet peel of the fruit is used in marmalade.

The sour orange is widely used in formal gardens and along avenues in southern Spain and in other regions with dry climates. Its susceptibility to scab, a fungus that disfigures leaves and fruit, precludes its common use in wet climates. The fruit of the sour orange is used primarily for its peel, which makes excellent marmalade.

Some citrus trees serve well as screens and hedges. These are primarily the low-growing types, such as limequats, kumquats, and even calamondins. However, those that tend toward very vigorous growth can be pruned informally or trimmed to make a hedge or screen planting. The chinotti and bouquet oranges, dwarfish sour-orange variants, do especially well as low hedges. The compact chinotti, with their fine-textured foliage and bright orange fruit, are particularly attractive.

Virtually all citrus tree varieties will bear fruit when grown in containers of various sizes, but some do so more satisfactorily than others. Small-fruited citrus, such as the calamondin, that tend to flower and fruit throughout the year are best. Sometimes called calamondin orange or dwarf orange, the calamondin is neither sweet orange nor dwarf. Stem cuttings develop roots quickly, and the young plants begin to flower and fruit almost immediately, even when only a few inches tall, thus giving rise to the supposition that the tree is a dwarf.

Other citrus well suited for growing in containers are the 'Meyer' lemon, 'Mexican,' 'Key,' or 'West Indian' lime, 'Temple' orange, and kumquat. Sweet orange trees grow well enough in large tubs but do not bear much fruit, and grapefruit trees produce even less.

How to Care for Citrus Trees

Trunks of young trees in desert areas are normally protected from sunscald with wraps designed for this purpose.

In Florida trees are protected from the cold by banking soil about 2 feet high around the trunks in winter. In parts of Texas and the Southwest, special insulating material is often wrapped around the trunks.

The soil from 3 to 6 feet around the trunks of young trees should be kept free of weeds for the first four years. Paraquat or weed oil can safely be used to eliminate weeds if care is taken not to get the chemical on the trunks of young trees. If it should soak in all around the trunk, it could kill the tree. Hand weeding or cutting off the tops with a scuffle hoe is also effective. Mature citrus trees can be grown in lawn grass if extra water and fertilizer are added, but it is best to keep the soil bare beneath the canopy of foliage.

Young trees should be watered once a week during their first year after planting. However, trees in clay soil are often killed by overwatering. To avoid this, allow the soil to dry between waterings. In Florida mature trees do not require irrigation, though their yields are increased by it. Citrus trees require irrigation in Texas and the southwestern United States. One thorough soaking in January may last until March; then water every two to four weeks, depending on how soon the soil dries out. Container-grown plants may need watering daily in hot weather.

Young trees on Florida's infertile sands should have a complete fertilizer, with about 8 percent nitrogen and all minor elements. Minor elements are indicated on the fertilizer container. Assuming the standard February planting, ⅓ pound of fertilizer should be applied for the following five months. Apply less frequently in succeeding years, but increase the amount until, by the 10th year, you apply 7 pounds three times a year. Thereafter, enough general lawn-mix fertilizer to furnish 1 pound of nitrogen is applied twice a year: in late winter and in August. (To determine actual nitrogen content, see p. 594.)

Only nitrogen is needed on the more fertile soils of other regions. The same amount of total nitrogen suffices, but only two or three applications each year are needed on young trees. Ammonium nitrate, urea, and ammonium sulfate are satisfactory sources of nitrogen. Established trees in 18-inch tubs should get about 4 ounces of a complete fertilizer with 8 percent nitrogen every month during the growing season but none during the winter. Overfertilizing can reduce the quality of the fruit and decrease the hardiness of the plant.

Deficiencies in trace elements, revealed by leaves mottled yellow or white, may need correcting. Yellow mottling indicates zinc deficiency. If veins are green and the rest of the leaf is pale, more iron is needed.

Citrus fruits are not thinned to increase fruit size, but it is wise to remove some mandarins before they mature because a heavy crop may break limbs. Thinning can also reduce the tree's tendency to bear only every other year.

Fruit held on the tree long after first maturity gradually improves in quality and keeps better than if picked earlier; it does not improve once harvested.

Selecting Rootstocks

Rootstocks differ in their effect on the yield, quality, resistance to soil pests, and cold tolerance. Citrus on certain rootstocks are severely damaged by viruses. Millions of trees on sour orange rootstock, for example, have been destroyed by the aphid-transmitted *Tristeza* virus, which is harmless if certain other kinds of rootstocks are used.

No true dwarfing rootstocks are available, but dwarfing occurs when trees on some rootstocks are infected with certain strains of viruses.

Most oranges in California, Arizona, and Florida are rooted on specially selected rootstock varieties. Selection depends upon the type and variety of orange as well as the area of the country where the tree is to be grown. Improved rootstocks are constantly being introduced.

In climates where optimum hardiness is important, the best rootstock for citrus is either trifoliate orange (*Poncirus trifoliata*) or sour orange (*Citrus aurantium*).

Where nematodes are a problem, the resistant stock of the 'Milam' lemon (*C. limon* hybrid) is used.

Pruning Citrus

To form a standard single-trunk tree, remove a few of the lower branches. Further pruning is not needed if there is plenty of space for the tree to eventually attain its natural form and size. If necessary, however, trees can be kept smaller.

There are two types of pruning. "Heading back" means shortening a branch. This encourages the development of buds just behind the cut. This response is local. Heading back a branch on one side will force buds on that branch but does little to stimulate growth on other parts of the tree. "Thinning out" means completely removing a branch, regardless of size, at the point where it is attached to another. This does not stimulate growth except where removal of large limbs lets in enough light to force development of dormant buds on interior branches.

The best way to keep a tree at a given size is to keep it thinned out so that it will not get much larger than desired. Thinning out is preferred to heading back. It is better to avoid a sheared look and preserve the attractive natural shape of the tree. Thinning also requires fewer cuts and promotes a more balanced production of fruit.

Neglected trees, which are often left standing when old orchards are used for housing developments, are frequently too large to be in scale with their surroundings. They can be reduced in size and rejuvenated by cutting them back to whatever height is desired. If the tree is sound, a smaller framework can be created by cutting back selected branches as large as 1 or 2 inches in diameter. Prune in early spring before new growth starts but after danger of frost has passed. In one year a vigorous new fruiting top will develop on the framework you have structured in this way.

Whitewashing the tree to prevent sunscald is necessary in desert areas but not in humid places unless pruning is delayed until late spring. Trees cut back more heavily require a longer period of time to fruit and are more susceptible to damage from low temperatures.

The top growth of citrus trees is sometimes killed by frost. When this happens, it is best to wait until leaves of the first flush of spring growth mature before removing damaged large limbs, or further dieback may occur. To remove a limb, make the cut flush with the limb to which it is attached. If the cut is made within a foot or two of the soil, it is advisable to apply a wound-sealing paint. There is no need to treat wounds from cuts that are made higher up on the tree.

Plants in containers should be kept to the desired size largely with thinning-out cuts. Only one light pruning a year is required once the plant is established. The size of the tree is further controlled by confinement in the container.

A container-grown tree can be kept indefinitely if it is removed from the container and repotted in fresh soil when it suffers loss of vigor. Before repotting, the root system should be thinned out and cut back heavily, and the top should be reduced by about one-fourth. Plants grown in 12- to 18-inch tubs will probably need heavy thinning every five to six years to force vigorous new growth.

Various pruning methods maintain a tree's size and form.
1. *Heading back a branch reduces size but stimulates new shoots.*
2. *Thinning out whole branches does not usually stimulate growth.*
3. *Before sawing flush with trunk, undercut large lower branches.*

Varieties of Citrus to Grow

The choice of varieties is by no means limited to those that are included in this chart. But these are all good and are readily available.

'Algerian,' 'Nova,' and 'Minneola' require that pollenizer varieties be planted within 20 yards. 'Temple' and similar seedy mandarin types that bloom at the same time are good to use as pollenizers.

In Florida, 'Algerian,' 'Minneola,' 'Temple,' 'Tahiti,' and satsumas require annual treatment for control of scab.

The season of maturity and the period mature fruit can be held on the tree vary so widely with climate that only generalized comments are made about these characteristics.

Names	Remarks
Calamondins	Very small, bright orange. Very ornamental. Acidic. Relatively frost hardy.
Grapefruits	
'Marsh'	Seedless, white fleshed. High quality.
'Redblush'	Seedless, red fleshed. High quality.
Kumquats	
'Nagami'	Thumb size, oblong, bright orange. Ornamental. Frost hardy. Preserve whole or in marmalade.
Lemons	
'Eureka'	Standard true lemon. Cannot take frost. 'Lisbon' is similar and slightly more frost hardy.
Lemon hybrids	
'Meyer'	Dwarfish tree. Orange-yellow, thin skinned, juicy. Frost hardy. Use virus-free type.
Limes	
'Mexican,' or 'Key,' or 'West Indian'	Few seeds, small, yellow, superior flavor. Cannot take frost.
'Tahiti,' or 'Persian,' or 'Bearss'	Seedless, large, green. Cannot take frost.
Mandarins	
'Algerian'	Small, deep orange, sweet. Bears erratically; early. For desert regions.
Satsuma	Seedless, deep orange. Early. Does best in cool climates. Very frost hardy.
Mandarin hybrids	
'Kinnow'	Seedy, medium, yellowish orange. Bears erratically; midseason.
'Temple'	Seedy, bright orange. Midseason. High quality. Can take relatively little frost.
Oranges	
'Hamlin'	Seedless, pale yellow, juicy. Early. Medium quality.
Navel	Small rudimentary fruit embedded in apex. Coarse flesh, seedless, light to deep orange, excellent flavor. Early.
'Pineapple'	Seedy, red-orange, juicy. Midseason. High quality.
'Valencia'	Seedless, deep orange, juicy. Late season. Best quality and color. Keeps well on tree for months.
Pomelos	
'Chandler' (grapefruitlike)	Red fleshed, sweet even in cool climates. New; available only in Calif.
Tangelos	
'Minneola'	Few seeds, large, bell shaped, deep reddish orange. Best quality of tangelos. Keeps well on tree for 2 mo.
'Nova'	Coarse flesh, medium, reddish-orange skin when fully colored. Best quality.
'Sampson'	Orange-red fleshed, juicy. Good for marmalade. Keeps well on tree for 2 mo.
Tangerines	
'Dancy'	Seedy, small to medium, brightly colored. Bears erratically sometimes; midseason.

What Can Go Wrong With Citrus

Many fungous diseases and insects that attack citrus in the warm, wet climate of Florida are not problems in desert and semi-desert areas. The use of virus-free stock and proper rootstocks has virtually eliminated virus in young trees, but old, virus-infected trees may have scaling bark and be stunted.

Symptoms and signs	Cause	Control
Young leaves and shoot tips are curled.	Aphids	Use malathion only for severe infestation.
White, waxy insects and egg masses on fruit stems and between clustered fruits; sooty mold present.	Mealybugs	Spray malathion, miscible oil,* or oil emulsion before plant is heavily infested. Repeat as needed.
Russeting of fruits. Dull gray or silvered leaves and fruits. Leaves may drop.	Rust mites and red spider mites	Spray with dicofol. Repeat weekly 3–5 times. Be sure to cover all leaf and fruit surfaces.
Encrustations of small insects on fruits, leaves, twigs, or trunks. Sooty mold fungus may be present.	Scale insects	Spray with 60-sec. miscible oil* or oil emulsion; or use carbaryl, malathion, or both. Be sure to spray all infested parts.
Small white insects on leaves fly when leaves are shaken. Sooty mold is present. Leaves yellow.	Whiteflies	Spray with malathion. Use miscible oil* or oil-emulsion spray only if infestation is severe.
Girdled roots and trunk below soil level.	Gophers	Trap and destroy.
Greasy-appearing spots on leaves causing leaf drop.	Greasy spot (fungus)	Spray with Benomyl or 60-sec. miscible oil* in early summer.
Leaves and fruit distorted with scabby, conical lesions.	Scab (fungus)	Spray with Benomyl just before spring growth. Grow resistant varieties.

* Note: *Do not spray with oil when soil is dry or within 3 wk. of sulfur spray.*

Currants

Currant 'Red Lake'

Red currants are the only currant widely available in North America. White currants are rarely seen, and the growth of black currants is prohibited by law due to the fact that they spread white pine blister rust. Red currants do best in the cooler humid regions and are used for desserts, preserves, or wine.

They can be grown as bushes (usually on a 9-inch leg) or cordons —single, double, or triple.

Almost any water-retaining but well-drained soil is suitable, though red currants do best in lighter soils. They will thrive in either sun or partial shade. Because they flower early in the year, take care not to plant in frost pockets.

For a good, regular fruit supply, the average family needs 4 to 6 bushes or 12 to 15 cordons. Harvest time is usually in early summer.

Before planting, dig the bed over, and thoroughly work in a complete fertilizer according to the directions on the package. The plants are especially susceptible to potash deficiency, which causes leaf edges to appear scorched.

Plant in early spring or autumn. Place bushes 5 feet apart; single cordons, 15 inches apart; double, 30 inches apart; and triple, 45 inches apart. Cordon rows should be about 4 feet apart.

Cordons need 2- by 2-inch stakes for each stem. Use stakes 8 feet long with 5–6 feet above ground level. Another method is to grow rows against three or four horizontal wires at 2-foot intervals and tie them to vertical canes fastened to the wires.

In late winter or early spring, feed with a complete fertilizer, ringed a foot away from the plant base. Add a 2-inch mulch of well-rotted manure or garden compost.

Control weeds by mulching or with a paraquat weed killer. Do not hoe. This can cut shallow roots.

Water only during prolonged dry spells. Take out any suckers that spring from the main stem or the roots. If frost lifts young plants, firm them in with your feet. Strong winds may break off shoots. On young bushes stake those shoots that are important to maintain the shape.

Birds are one of the main problems facing a person who grows currants. They will damage buds and strip the plant of fruit. Netting is a good means of protection.

It is best to pick currants as soon as they are fully ripe.

Pruning Bushes and Cordons in Winter

If bird damage is likely, leave winter pruning until the buds begin to swell so that you can prune to an undamaged bud. Red currants bear most of their fruit on spurs that develop on older wood.

Immediately after planting a one-year-old bush, cut each branch back to four buds from the main stem. The cut should be made above an outward-pointing bud.

In the second winter cut out flush with the stem any branches that ruin the overall bush shape. Shorten branch leaders by two-thirds of new growth if growth is weak or by one-half if growth is strong, cutting to an outward-pointing bud. Prune laterals back to one bud from their bases so that they will form spurs.

In the third and fourth years, leave some laterals to grow into branches where there is room, so that the established bush has 8 to 10 main branches on a 6- to 9-inch leg. Cut other laterals back to spurs yearly.

Cut back branch leaders by one-half their new growth in the third winter, regardless of vigor. In the fourth winter remove about one-quarter of new growth. After that, prune back about 1 inch yearly.

Keep the center of the bush open. When the oldest branches become too spreading or unproductive, replace them with strong new shoots.

On cordons cut back laterals to one bud to form spurs. Until the leader is 6 feet high, cut back new growth by 9 inches or two-thirds, whichever is the smaller amount. After the leader reaches 6 feet, remove all new growth each winter—cutting just above a bud.

FIRST WINTER PRUNING

Immediately after planting, cut back branches to four buds.

PRUNING IN THE SECOND WINTER

Shorten new growth on leaders by one-half if growth is strong, by two-thirds if growth is weak.

Cut back laterals to one bud from their bases to form spurs.

Cut out flush with stem any shoots that spoil bush shape.

Pruning Bushes and Cordons in Summer

Bushes and cordons that are two years old or more are pruned similarly every summer. Start pruning in early summer, when new growth starts to turn brown. Cut the laterals back to three or five leaves, just above a leaf joint.

Once a cordon is 6 feet high, cut back new leader growth to four leaves—preparatory to removing it entirely the next winter.

From early summer on, cut back laterals to three or five leaves.

Varieties of Red Currants to Grow

The varieties sold at local nurseries are tried and true in that area. Such varieties are quite likely to perform well in your garden.

If there are no currants available locally, they can be purchased from mail-order sources.

The best-known and most reliable all-round performer is the variety 'Red Lake.' This is a very hardy plant that produces a large crop of dark red fruit of excellent flavor. The fruit is borne on longer trusses than most currants. This makes it easier to pick. It also ripens over a long season. 'Fay' and 'Perfection' are recommended as well.

How to Raise Your Own Currant Bushes

The best way to propagate red currants is from cuttings that are about 15 inches long. In midfall select the straightest shoots from the current year's growth, and cut them off low, just above a bud.

Trim off any softwood at the tip (there should not be more than an inch or so), cutting just above a bud; do not cut if it is brown to the tip. Trim the lower end just below a bud to produce a cutting approximately 15 inches long.

Rub off all but the top four or five buds on the cutting. Buds left on lower down will produce suckers that may prevent the formation of a leg. Dip the lower end of each cutting in hormone rooting powder.

With a spade cut a V-shaped slit 8 inches deep with one side vertical and the other at a 45-degree angle. Sprinkle sand in the bottom for drainage. Set cuttings upright 6 inches apart, leaving 9 inches above soil level. Fill trench and firm well.

Cuttings should have rooted by late fall. Lift them with a fork, and replant them where they are to go.

Set the young plants in the ground 2 inches deeper than they were as cuttings, and immediately after replanting, shorten branches by one-half. Then treat them as you would new plants.

What Can Go Wrong With Red Currants

Aphids and birds are the commonest problems confronted in growing red currants. If plants show symptoms not described here, turn to the section on plant disorders on page 600. Look up chemicals on page 635 to find trade names.

Symptoms and signs	Cause	Control
Leaves are curled or blistered, often with reddish tinge. Shoot tips may be distorted.	Red currant aphids	Spray with 60-sec. miscible oil or oil emulsion in midwinter to kill eggs. Carbaryl, endosulfan, or malathion applied as cover sprays give good control. In spring, just before flowering, apply systemic insecticide, such as dimethoate or oxydemeton-methyl. Repeat after flowering if problem continues.
Leaves are distorted and off-color, with very small silver dots.	Two-spotted mites	Use dicofol or tetradifon spray weekly as needed.
Shoots or large branches die back. Coral-red spots appear on deadwood.	Nectria canker (coral spot fungus)	Cut out and destroy all dead shoots to a point at least 2–4 in. below areas that appear diseased. Feed, mulch, and water plants as necessary to encourage vigor; soil may also require draining. Spray with Bordeaux mixture or lime sulfur solution after pruning.
White powdery masses on plant; later, masses turn brown. Shoots may become distorted.	Powdery mildew (fungus)	Cut off affected shoots in autumn. Spray regularly with Benomyl, dinocap, or thiophanate-methyl.

Figs

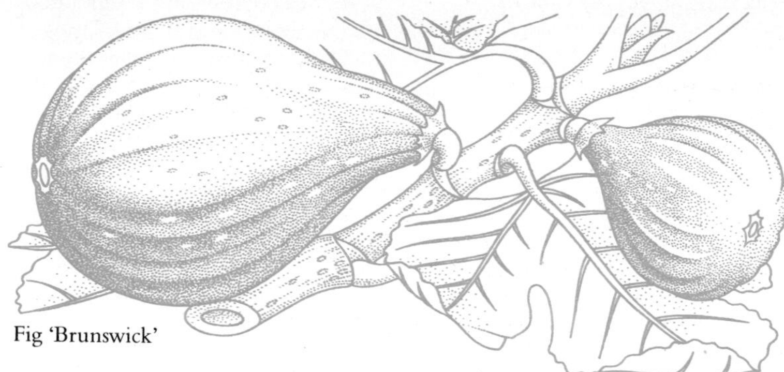

Fig 'Brunswick'

Figs need plenty of sunshine. They do best in the southern half of the country. They can also be grown along the Atlantic Coast as far north as Long Island, New York, but there they must be insulated with straw and wrapped in plastic in winter. This means that only small trees can be grown. They can be grown as fans against a south-facing wall or as bushes in a sunny corner. Figs need well-drained but moisture-retaining soil that is not overly rich. They bear two crops: one in midsummer and another in late fall. One tree should provide enough figs for the average family. Fig varieties include 'Brown Turkey' ('Brunswick'), 'Celeste,' 'Hunt,' 'Kadota,' and 'Magnolia.'

Plant in early spring. Unless roots are restricted, there will be a great amount of soft, unfruitful growth. Dig a hole 3 feet wide and 3 feet deep, and line it with bricks or concrete, leaving drainage holes in the base. Plant the tree in good topsoil.

After planting, mulch with a 1- to 2-inch layer of rotted manure or garden compost. Repeat in mid to late spring. Water well when dry.

Propagate figs by layering (p. 92); or take semi-hard cuttings (p. 88).

Pruning and training. Trees are trained in the same way as fan or dwarf apples (pp. 503, 506) for the first three summers.

In the following years, before midsummer, pinch out side shoots four leaves from their base to encourage new shoots to form. Fruit will develop at leaf axils on the new shoots.

In midsummer select new shoots on fans that will parallel the wall or naturally follow the training canes, and tie them to the canes. Cut the others flush with the parent branch.

On trees cut out a little old wood in midsummer, flush with the parent stem, to let in light and air.

Thinning and harvesting. Take away immature figs larger than peas at the end of the season. The embryo fruits carried in the leaf axils at the tops of new shoots will develop the next spring and ripen in late summer. Pick figs when they are soft to the touch and begin to split.

SUMMER PRUNING OF A FAN

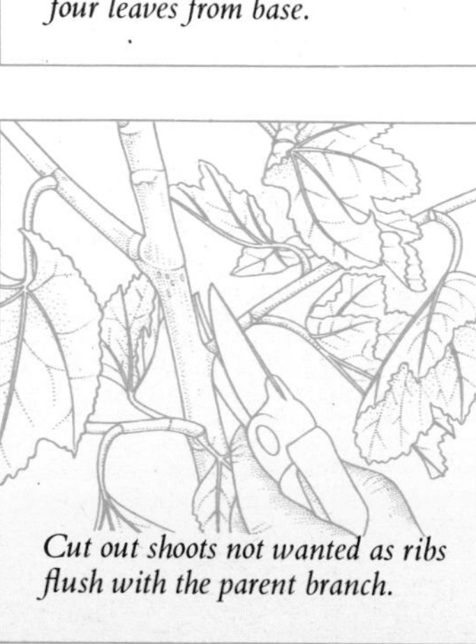

In early summer pinch out shoots four leaves from base.

Cut out shoots not wanted as ribs flush with the parent branch.

What Can Go Wrong With Figs

Mealybugs can be controlled with daily sprayings of chlorpyrifos, Diazinon, or malathion.

Flat or rounded scales on leaves and stems are insects. In late spring spray with malathion, mexacarbate, or 1–1½ percent oil emulsion.

Yellow or rusty leaves, leaf drop, or spotting of fruit may be caused by mites. Spray dicofol, oil emulsion, or tetradifon on new leaves and shoots.

Burned tips or scorched leaves are a symptom of anthracnose. Rosy pustules may develop in browned areas. Destroy infected leaves. Spray plant regularly with copper hydroxide, dodine, or zineb.

Small yellow, red-brown, or black patches on foliage are caused by leaf spot disease. Spray weekly with Captan, ferbam, folpet, or zineb.

Yellow wilted plants may have root-knot nematodes; diseased roots may show knots or tiny lesions. Destroy plants that have knots; plant others in fresh soil or soil fumigated with metam-sodium.

Gooseberries

Gooseberry 'Poorman'

Gooseberries are good for dessert or for making jam. They grow best in the northern half of the country, in any type of well-drained but moisture-retaining soil, and thrive in full sun or partial shade. Do not plant them in frost pockets; frost may prevent fruit formation.

They are grown mainly as bushes. For the average family six to nine bushes should provide enough fruit. Gooseberries are self-fertile. Fruit is available from early summer (for cooking) to mid to late summer and can be green, yellow, red, or white, depending on the variety.

Preferably buy plants two or three years old, and plant them in a mild period between midfall and early spring. If your soil is deep enough, double-dig it (p. 597), and work in plenty of manure or garden compost. Plant bushes 5–6 feet apart. Support them upright with 2- by 2-inch stakes about 5 feet high.

Among the best varieties, 'Poorman' is widely planted in the North; 'Glendale' thrives in eastern mid-America; 'Pixwell,' 'Perry,' and 'Abundance' are favored in North Dakota; 'Welcome,' grown mostly in Minnesota, is nearly thornless; 'Clark' is popular in Ontario and 'Fredonia' in New York.

Tending and Feeding Gooseberries

Each spring apply a mulch of well-rotted compost to prevent the soil from drying out and to keep down weeds. To prevent root damage, do not remove weeds with a hoe or a fork. Pull away any suckers that grow from the stem or roots. Water the bushes only in dry spells during summer.

In late winter give a feed of $\frac{1}{2}$–1 ounce ($\frac{1}{2}$–1 tablespoon) of potassium sulfate to each square yard. Every third year add 2 ounces (2 tablespoons) of superphosphate to each square yard. In early spring apply 1 ounce (1 tablespoon) of ammonium sulfate to each square yard.

In winter firm in any plants lifted by frost. Birds feed on buds in late winter; so protect bushes with netting or cotton threads. At blossom time shield bushes from frost at night with heavy netting, but remove it during the day to allow access to pollinating insects.

Thinning and Harvesting Gooseberries

Start picking gooseberries for cooking when they are the size of large peas. Thin out on each branch so that remaining berries will reach a good size for eating fresh or for using in pies. The thinned fruits should be at least 3 inches apart. Do not pick any fruit for dessert until it is soft and fully ripe.

Pruning a One-Year-Old Gooseberry Bush

Fruit is borne on new wood and on old-wood spurs. Prune during autumn or winter or as late as, but no later than, bud burst if birds are likely to damage the buds.

The aim of pruning is to keep the center of the bush open to light and air. Varieties range from spreading bushes on which branches tend to droop (this can spoil fruit) to very upright bushes. Cut back spreading bushes to an upward- or inward-pointing bud, upright varieties to an outward-pointing bud. For in-between varieties, or if in doubt, prune to an outward-pointing bud.

On a one-year-old bush, choose the best three or four shoots, and cut them back to above a bud to about a quarter of their length. Cut other shoots flush with the stem.

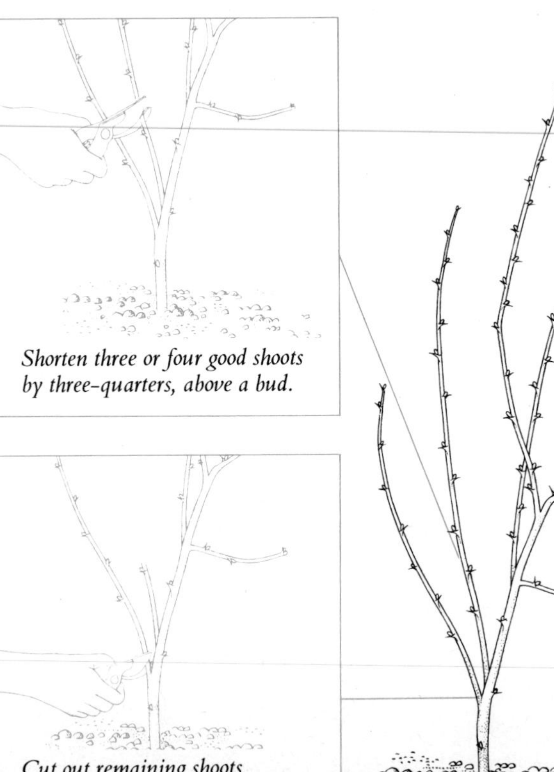

Shorten three or four good shoots by three-quarters, above a bud.

Cut out remaining shoots on the bush, removing them flush with the stem.

Pruning a Two-Year-Old Gooseberry Bush

On a two-year-old bush, choose from six to eight of the strongest shoots. Cut the new growth on these shoots by one-half if they are growing well, or by two-thirds if growth is weak. Cut back other shoots to one bud from their bases.

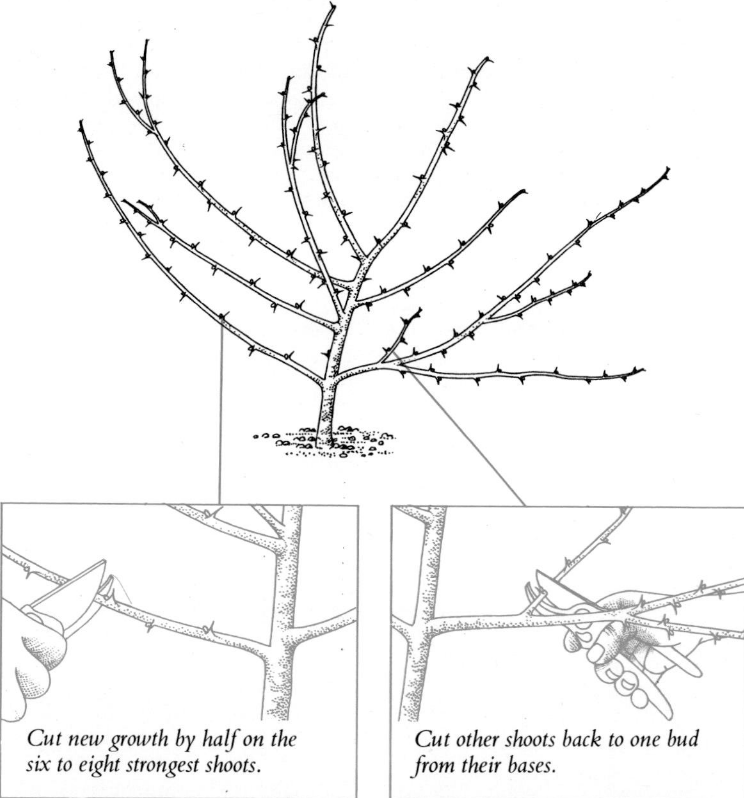

Cut new growth by half on the six to eight strongest shoots.

Cut other shoots back to one bud from their bases.

Pruning an Established Gooseberry Bush

In winter cut back branch leaders of established bushes by half their new growth. To encourage spur formation, prune the strongest side shoots to 3 inches of new growth and the weaker ones to 1 inch. Remove the weakest shoots completely, cutting them flush with the branch.

If a branch has drooped to the ground, choose a new shoot as a replacement, and cut back the drooping branch to the source of the new shoot. Prune the new branch by at least half to ensure sturdy growth. Keep the bush's center open.

In midsummer shorten all of the side shoots to five leaves, cutting just above a leaf joint. Do not prune the branch leaders.

WINTER PRUNING

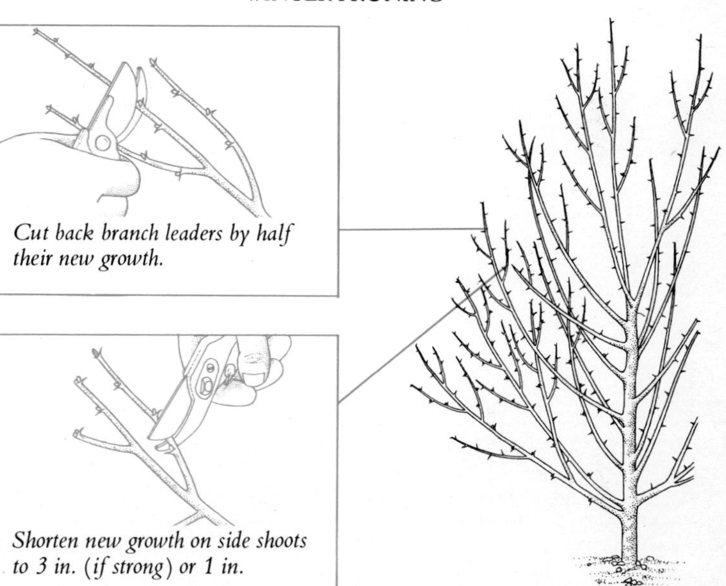

Cut back branch leaders by half their new growth.

Shorten new growth on side shoots to 3 in. (if strong) or 1 in.

What Can Go Wrong With Gooseberries

The most important problems are gooseberry sawfly and gooseberry mildew. If plants show symptoms not described here, turn to the section on plant disorders on page 600. Look up chemicals on page 635 to find trade names.

Symptoms and signs	Cause	Control
Leaves curled or blistered, often with reddish tinge; shoot tips may be distorted.	Aphids	Spray with 60-sec. miscible oil in midwinter to kill eggs. Use carbaryl or malathion as cover sprays. Apply systemics, such as dimethoate, just before flowering. Repeat after flowering if needed.
Leaf tissues are eaten.	Larvae of gooseberry sawfly	When damage is first seen, spray with malathion or rotenone.
Fruits have gray moldy deposits. Leaves often show brownish to black areas. In severe cases twigs die back.	Botrytis (fungus)	Use chlorothalonil or dichloran. Spray before blossoms open; repeat after flowers open and until fruits mature.
White powdery masses on leaves, shoots, fruits; later, masses turn brown, shoots become distorted.	Powdery mildew (fungus)	Cut off affected shoots in autumn. Spray regularly with Benomyl, dinocap, or thiophanate-methyl.

Grapes

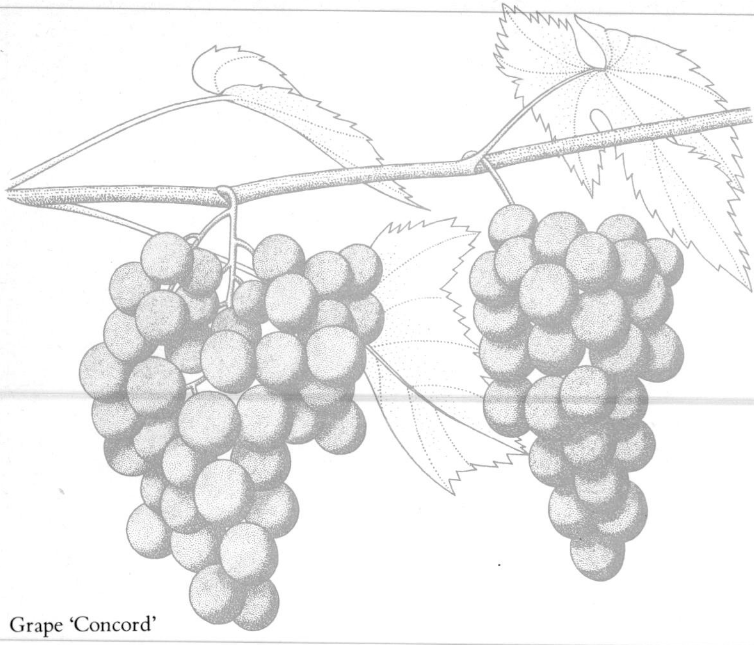
Grape 'Concord'

Grapes can be eaten fresh, dried to make raisins, or converted into juice and wine. With a few exceptions, all grape varieties are cultivated in much the same way. In the United States the European types (*Vitis vinifera*), such as 'Thompson Seedless' and 'Flame Tokay,' are characterized by skins that adhere to the flesh. They are grown mostly in the Southwest and in California. The native American types derived from *V. labrusca* or its hybrids, such as the 'Concord,' have skins that slip free from the flesh. The slip-skin grapes can be grown in many areas but do best east of the Rocky Mountains and north of the Gulf states. Finally, there are the muscadine types (*V. rotundifolia*), which are not noted for their hardiness. These include the 'Southland' variety and are cultivated mostly in the Southeast and the Gulf states.

The main stem of a grapevine is called the trunk. The trunk sends off laterals, which if allowed to grow, develop into arms, spurs, and canes. It is the cane that bears the fruit.

There is perhaps no plant more amenable to training than the grapevine. Depending on your purpose and skill, a single vine can be trained to produce one trunk or two or three. Training to a single trunk saves space, allowing you to grow additional varieties in a given area. If you are growing grapes only for fresh fruit, two single-trunk vines should yield enough for the average family. If juice or wine is your goal, you will need more vines.

Any type of grapevine can be grown on a trellis, a fence, an arbor, or a pergola. European types can also be head trained to grow in the form of small trees, only waist high, supported by individual stakes.

Soils and planting. Good drainage and at least moderately fertile soil are essential for grape cultivation. A fertile loam of medium texture is best. And if the fruit is to have a sugar content high enough for juice or wine and for good eating, the vines must have full sunlight.

Grapevines can be planted in early spring or fall in a hole slightly deeper and wider than their root systems. Plant the vines in rows. The distance between plants in a row should be about 6 feet. Allow about 8 feet between rows for access.

You can start a new vine from a hardwood cutting. Take cuttings in autumn. Prune to 8–12 inches long, with a bud at the top and at the bottom. Plant the cuttings in shallow trenches dug in enriched soil. Dig just deep enough to allow the top bud to show above the surface; place an inch or two of sand in the bottom of the trench. If you buy an already rooted cutting, plant it with the top bud level with the ground; then mound some soil over it, as shown below. The developing shoots will push their way through the mound.

Grapes require a lot of moisture and good drainage, and they use up nutrients quickly. They respond well to mulching early in spring, particularly to the use of well-rotted manure mixed with straw. In humid areas extra nutrients are required. Spread a cupful of fertilizer, such as 10–6–4 or 10–10–10, on the ground in a ring 6 inches wide, a few inches from the base of the vine. In arid areas additional nitrogen compounds, such as ammonium nitrate, may be needed. Apply about ⅓ cup per plant. Consult your county agent for exact feeding instructions.

HEAD TRAINING YOUNG VINES

Plant the rooted cuttings in spring. Next winter prune the best cane to two to four buds. The following winter leave several spurs with two to four buds each.

Training Young European Grapevines

It takes three or four years to train a grapevine. After that it is mature and needs pruning only to improve or maintain grape production.

There are four basic systems for training European grapevines. They can be cane trained to encourage the development of canes. They can be trained as cordons. Or they can be allowed to grow more freely on arbors or pergolas.

Young vines. To encourage a good root system on a rooted cutting, allow the vine to grow one season without pruning. Water well but not excessively, and spray the foliage with a mist of water from time to time, particularly on hot days. During the next dormant season remove all but the strongest cane, and prune it back to two or three buds. When growth resumes, remove all but the best-shaped and strongest single shoot. Tie this loosely to a stake, and permit it to develop side shoots. Remove suckers from the base, and pinch off all of the low-growing lateral

Pruning Mature European Vines

Head-pruned vines. Head pruning is used in growing many wine grapes and a few table varieties, such as 'Flame Tokay.' Vines trained in this way must be cut back extensively every year if they are to flourish and be productive in limited space.

In the winter remove all but three to six of the best canes, leaving those that are evenly placed around the top of the trunk. Cut these back to two to four buds each. Most of the buds will become fruiting spurs the following growing season; some will grow into new canes. Each year select a few new canes that have grown from spurs or that have appeared directly from the trunk, and repeat the pruning process. As the vine gets older, you can gradually allow more spurs to develop.

Cane-pruned vines. Cane pruning, used mainly for raisin grapes and a few wine varieties, also involves heavy annual pruning. Each winter remove canes that have borne fruit. Leave two to four new canes per vine. Prune them back to 6 to 10 buds each. They will bear fruit during the upcoming season. At the same time, prune back two to four other new canes to spurs, as with head-pruned vines. From the several shoots that form at the top of the trunk during the growing season, select the two strongest and tie them to a training wire, facing in opposite directions. These will produce more fruiting canes in years to come.

As each vine ages, you will be able to increase its number of canes to six. If you are training a plant to grow against a wall or over a pergola, the number can be increased to fill any blank spaces. The new canes selected each year should be as close to the trunk as possible so that they will receive the maximum nourishment.

Cordon-pruned vines. Vines that have been trained to form a cordon require considerable attention. Spurs on the arms must be kept 8–10 inches apart, with only two or three buds allowed to grow on each. As the arms increase in girth, they will sag if they are not straightened frequently; strong young shoots must be tied to a wire above the arms.

During the growing season pinch back all overly vigorous growth to permit the weaker shoots to keep pace. Make sure the vines do not overbear. Thin by removing some of the clusters as they appear; if uncrowded, they will yield better bunches of larger grapes.

Arbor-trained vines. Vines that are to grow over an arbor are handled much as cordon-pruned grapes are, except that the trunks are allowed to become longer and the arms, rather than being trained to grow along a horizontal wire, are directed to fill in the spaces on the arbor. After the supporting structure has been covered, a combination of cane and spur pruning is used to maintain the vine's productiveness, as is recommended for growing native American grapes (see p. 528).

Maintain a separation of about 3 feet between the canes that are to develop into arms. When their development is complete, spur-prune for fruit. On arbors and pergolas the horizontal growth will produce most of the grapes.

For training on walls, the multiple-cordon system is the best choice. Space the cordons 3 feet apart, and tie arms to the supports (see Kniffin system, p. 528).

Cane trained. *Prune the vine back each winter to 2 to 4 new canes with 6 to 10 buds on each and several spurs bearing only 2 to 4 buds.*

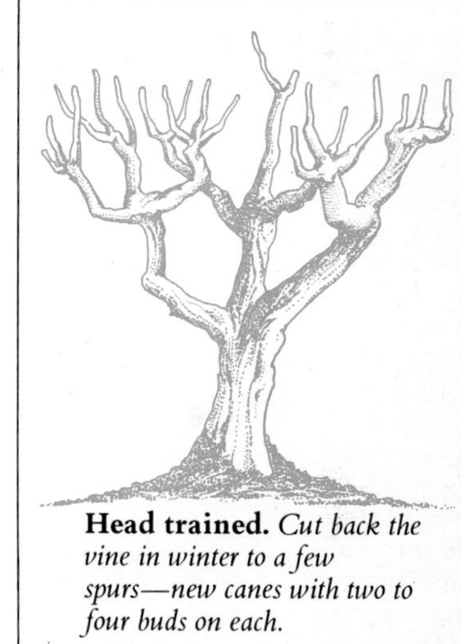

Head trained. *Cut back the vine in winter to a few spurs—new canes with two to four buds on each.*

shoots. If a head- or cane-trained vine is desired, allow the leader to grow about a foot above its supporting stake; then pinch it back.

The second summer. With a cordon-trained vine, early in the second summer prune back all growth except two of the strongest-growing laterals, or work with the leader shoot and one lateral. Tie the chosen shoots along a trellis wire so that they will grow in opposite directions. Let them grow about 18 inches; then pinch back the tips.

For a head-trained vine, cut off the topmost fruit-bearing cane at a node, just above the point where you want the head to form. Be sure to cut completely through the node. By cutting through the node, you effectively destroy the bud. Remove all laterals below the middle of the trunk as well as the weakest laterals above this point. Two to four laterals should be allowed to remain; cut each back to one to four buds. As a general rule, leave one bud on a cane that is as thick as a pencil, two on a cane that is as big around as your little finger, three on a cane the size of your index finger, and leave four buds on a thumb-sized cane.

A cane-pruned vine may have only a single cane with 8 to 10 buds at the end of the second summer. If the cane is weak, cut it back to a spur with only two buds.

The third summer. The next year, on both head- and cane-trained vines, rub off all suckers from the lower half of the trunk.

For cordon-trained vines, trim back the most vigorous shoots to 15–18 inches long. This allows weaker shoots to keep pace with the faster-growing ones. Remove all shoots from the bottom of the arms.

To keep the arms growing straight, tie the strong terminal growths to an upper training wire. If they are allowed to grow without training, they will probably twist around the trellis wire. Remove some clusters early so that they do not crowd together, as this can slow formation of the vine.

By the third season's end the vines will have achieved their permanent shape and should thereafter be treated as mature vines.

How to Prune American Grapes

American grapes, such as the 'Concord' and its hybrids, are trained in much the way as their cane-pruned European cousins. The difference is that they are supported in the manner of the four-arm Kniffin system, as shown below.

Set posts 24–30 feet apart. The top wire (9 gauge galvanized) should be $5\frac{1}{2}$–6 feet from the ground and the lower wire (10 gauge), about 3 feet from the ground. Plant three vines between posts.

The rooted cutting is planted and pruned back so that a single cane bears two buds. During the vine's first summer, pinch back all shoots except the strongest one, which will become the trunk. Tie this shoot to a stake. The next dormant season cut off all new canes except the central one, and with a soft string tie it to the uppermost wire. Tie the lower cane loosely to the bottom wire.

After the second growing season remove all side branches from the trunk except for two at each wire level. Tie these canes to the wires, one to the left and one to the right on each level. These canes will bear fruiting shoots the next summer. If more than four to eight buds, not counting the basal bud, develop on each shoot, remove them.

Shoots will also be produced near the base of these canes. Cut these back to two buds to form the spurs for the next season's growth.

In the years that follow, keep removing old fruited canes each winter so that the new canes of the previous summer can garner the strength to fruit in the next growing season. Cut the new canes back to 6 to 10 buds, depending on their vigor. The spurs, with their two buds apiece, will bear bunches of fruit on their shoots, but most of their strength will go into forming fruiting canes for the next year. All of these steps must be repeated annually.

American grapes can also be trained on arbors, pergolas, and walls, as are the European types. On an arbor extend the trunk to the desired height, and allow well-spaced canes and spurs to grow from it. Prune the vine as described for the Kniffin system.

KNIFFIN TRAINING SYSTEM

In winter cut back to four new canes and tie as shown. Cut back four to six other new canes to two-bud spurs for next year.

ARCH OR PERGOLA

Train vines to cover structure. In winter remove canes that bore fruit. Cut new canes to 6 to 10 buds. Leave spurs for new canes.

Cultivating Muscadine Grapes

Muscadines are grown almost exclusively in home gardens throughout the Southeast and the Gulf states. Though these grapes require little care to survive, they produce better given some attention. Plant them in an area that gets at least a half day of sun. Allow 20 running feet of space per vine on a one- or two-wire trellis, a fence, or an arbor.

This species of grape can be male, female, or bisexual and self-fertile. You will need 1 self-fertile or male vine for every 6 to 10 females. The self-fertile vines, of course, do not need a pollinator. Because bees carry the needed pollen from vine to vine, insecticides should not be used during the blooming period. Before bloom and during ripening, however, use a pesticide containing carbaryl to deal with wasps and other insects. Follow label instructions.

These grapes are grown much as other grapes are. Pruning practices for mature vines (three to four years old) are as follows: During the dormant season all new growth must be cut back to two- to four-bud spurs on the long arms. Clusters of grapes will appear on the third to sixth nodes of that season's new growth. Prune after the first severe freeze, but not later than the beginning of the new year.

Sugar content in the fruit increases when the grapes begin to turn their characteristic color. If you delay the harvest a bit, you will have extra-sweet grapes that will produce excellent wine or juice.

With cordon-trained muscadines prune back all new growth in early winter to 8 to 10 spurs per arm. Fruits will appear on the resultant new canes.

When to Harvest Your Grapes

Tasting is the best test for maturity. If grapes are sweet and flavorful, they are ready to pick. The next best guide is color. Green varieties, such as 'Romulus' and 'Thompson Seedless,' turn whitish or yellowish; black and red varieties take on an added depth of color.

Once grapes have been picked, they will not ripen further. Therefore, wait until your crop is fully mature; then harvest by clipping off the bunches with scissors or a sharp knife. Discard overripe, withered, or diseased grapes.

Grapes that are intended for raisins, such as 'Thompson Seedless,' should be left on the vine somewhat longer than wine or table varieties in order to increase the sugar content. Grapes can be stored for several weeks at a temperature of about 32° F and a humidity of 90 percent.

Tending the Vine While Grapes Are Maturing

You can improve the yield of your vines by giving them a little extra care during the summer, such as thinning the flowers and fruit, pruning extraneous foliage, and girdling the trunk and branches (as explained below).

Grapes can be thinned by three methods: remove flower clusters in spring; remove fruit clusters when they have set; or thin the grapes within a cluster.

Removing some flower clusters as they appear is the simplest way to ensure that those remaining will develop into larger, more compact bunches. More selectively, you can wait for fruit to set before thinning out the smaller clusters.

Thinning grapes within a cluster is tedious, but combined with flower- or fruit-cluster thinning, it enables you to produce excellent bunches of grapes. Shortly after fruit has set, use scissors to remove the lower tip of each bunch and one or more weaker stems within the cluster.

While fruit is developing, leaves shield it from the hot midsummer sun. Later on, too much shade inhibits ripening. In late summer, therefore, pinch foliage-bearing side shoots back to one leaf.

Girdling is a means of interfering with the flow of sugar back to the roots of the vine, thus making more nourishment available to the fruit. To girdle, simply remove a $^{3}/_{16}$-inch-wide band of bark from the trunk, an arm, or a cane. The bark should heal in three to six weeks.

THINNING FRUIT

When grapes start to swell, thin out small fruits from the clusters.

In late summer pinch side shoots back to one leaf from the cane.

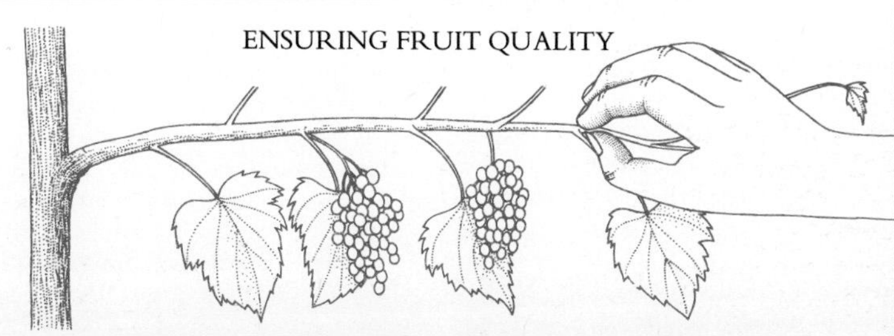

Early each summer pinch canes back to two leaves past a fruit cluster. Leave one bunch per cane the first year; after that, save two or three.

Varieties of Grapes to Grow

Select grapes suitable for your climate and intended use. All are self-pollinating except certain muscadines, which can be male, female, or self-fertile. For muscadines plant 1 self-fertile or male variety for every 6 to 10 females.

Names*	Color	Size: Berry	Size: Cluster	Remarks
American grapes and hybrids				(Grown east of Rockies and north of Gulf states.)
'Campbell's Early'	Blue	Large	Large	Widely planted. Eaten fresh.
'Fredonia'	Black	Med.	Med.	Productive; good for arbors. Hardy.
'Himrod' (seedless)	White	Small	Large	Susceptible to black rot. Eaten fresh.
'Delaware'	Red	Small	Small	For juice, wine; eaten fresh.
'Beta'	Black	Med.	Small	Very hardy. For wine, dessert.
'Niagara'	Yellow-white	Med.	Med.	Popular. Hardy.
'Romulus' (seedless)	Yellow-green	Small	Large	For wine; eaten fresh.
'Buffalo'	Blue-black	Med.	Large	Good home-garden grape.
'Concord'	Blue-black	Med.	Med.	Widely planted. Hardy. For juice, wine.
'Christmas'	Black	Large	Large	Good in arbors. Hardy.
European grapes				(Grown in southwestern U.S. and Calif.)
'Thompson Seedless'	Greenish white	Med.	Large	Cane-prune; early. Popular. Tolerates hot valleys.
'Ribier'	Black	Large	Med.	Cordon-prune. Eaten fresh.
'Scarlet'	Black	Med.	Med.	For juice; eaten fresh.
'Flame Tokay'	Red	Med.	Large	Head-prune. For wine; eaten fresh.
'Muscat Alexandria'	Green	Large	Med.	Head-prune. For raisins; eaten fresh.
'Muscat Hamburg'	Black	Med.	Med.	Head-prune. Highly recommended.
Muscadine grapes				(Grown in southeastern and Gulf states.)
'Carlos'	Bronze	Med.	Large	Very productive. For wine.
'Cowart'	Black	Large	Large	Low acidity. Eaten fresh.
'Higgins'	Bronze to pink	Large	Large	Very productive, one of best. Must be grown with male or self-fertile variety.
'Hunt'	Black	Large	Large	One of oldest. Good all round.
'Southland'	Black	Med.	Med.	Excellent. All uses.

** Each group listed in approximate order of ripening.*

Peaches and Nectarines

What Can Go Wrong With Grapes

Grapes are subject to attack by numerous diseases and insects.

If your plants show symptoms that are not described below, consult the section on plant disorders on page 600. Look up chemicals on page 635 to find trade names.

Symptoms and signs	Cause	Control
Adult beetles come into vineyard when new shoots are 12–15 in. long. Eggs are laid inside shoots about 6 in. from tips. Larvae tunnel inside shoots, destroying them.	Cane girdlers	Spray with methoxychlor in early spring as insects appear. Inspect canes and cut off about 4 in. below girdling area.
Moth larvae feed inside fruits. Grapes are often webbed together. Wormy fruits result.	Grape berry moths	Spray with carbaryl or methoxychlor just after bloom, repeat 10–14 da. later and again in mid or late summer.
Larvae of moths feed on foliage of new shoots, chewing them badly. They may also feed on fruits.	Leaf rollers; leaf tiers	Spray with carbaryl or methoxychlor in early summer. Repeat 2 wk. later.
Adult beetles feed heavily on foliage during day, causing severe skeletonizing of leaves.	Rose chafers, Japanese beetles, and oriental beetles	Same control as for grape berry moths (above).
Fungus attacks leaves in early summer and later appears on fruits that are half grown. Entire grape shrivels to dry, black, raisinlike fruit.	Black rot	Infection occurs during bloom period. Apply Captan, dodine, or zineb just before bloom, after bloom, and every 10–14 da. thereafter up to early fall.
This fungus is one of most destructive of all grape diseases. Fungus first attacks leaves and canes; later it infects young shoots. Dead arm phase results from infection through wounds caused by pruning or winterkill.	Dead arm	Remove infected vine at ground level during winter pruning. Spray with Captan or folpet when new shoots are about 1 in. long and again when they are 5 in. long.
First appears as small yellow spots on tops of leaves. Later, downy white mats appear on lower surfaces. Complete defoliation may occur. Grapes are attacked, harden, and turn off-color.	Downy mildew	Same program as for black rot (above). Varieties such as 'Concord' are resistant to this disease.
Occurs on foliage in early summer and fall, producing white powdery growth on leaves and fruits.	Powdery mildew	Cycloheximide or dinocap sprays should be applied as needed.

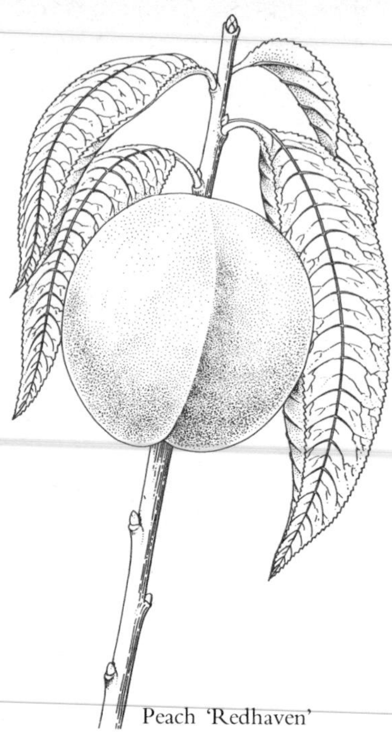

Peach 'Redhaven'

Peaches and nectarines can be grown throughout the United States except in the coldest areas where winter temperatures drop below −10° F.

Trees that are trained as espaliers, as well as the upright dwarf forms, will grow in any location other than a frost pocket or a site exposed to cold winds, but they will, of course, do best in a warm, sunny position. Those that are trained as espaliers have the best chance of success, especially when they are grown against a wall facing south or southwest to catch the sun.

Nectarines are smooth-skinned peaches, and they are becoming increasingly popular in home gardens. Peach and nectarine trees are self-fertile—that is, each flower fertilizes itself—so only one tree is needed to obtain fruit.

One mature tree should provide enough fruit for the average family. Fruit that is grown outdoors will usually be ripe and ready to eat from midsummer on.

How to Care for Peach and Nectarine Trees

Any good, well-drained soil is suitable for peach and nectarine trees. Plant in the same way as other fruit trees (see p. 490).

In late winter apply only nitrogen if you have fertile soil. Use ammonium sulfate at a rate of $\frac{1}{3}$ pound per year of tree age (about 3 pounds maximum). Or for mature trees use a 10–10–10 or 10–6–4 at $\frac{1}{10}$ pound per year of age (7–10 pounds maximum), broadcast over the area of the limb spread. If the soil is acid, apply 5 pounds of lime every other year in humid regions. Peaches need more nitrogen when growing in sod than in cultivated soil. After a few years of fertilizing and mulching, they may need relatively little fertilizer if mulched annually.

Water the soil liberally whenever there is danger that it might dry out.

Nectarines need more frequent watering and a little more fertilizing than peaches while the fruits are swelling. Weed by shallow hoeing, or use a paraquat weed killer.

To ensure a good crop, it pays to assist pollination by lightly dabbing every blossom with a camel's hair paintbrush about every third day. This is best done on warm, dry days at about noon.

When the peaches are the size of marbles, start thinning them out, reducing all clusters to a single fruit. Remove fruits that have no room to develop properly.

When the peaches are the size of Ping-Pong balls, thin them out so that they are spaced 9 inches apart.

Fruit is ready for picking when the flesh around the stalk yields to gentle pressure from the fingers.

Store peaches in a cool place, not touching one another, in containers lined with soft material.

Training and Pruning a Dwarf Peach Tree

Training a One-Year-Old Peach Tree

In spring, when growth buds have appeared on a one-year-old tree planted in very early spring or the previous autumn, cut back the central leader to about 2 feet above the ground. Cut just above a bud.

Leave the top three or four buds or side shoots below the cut to form the first branches.

Remove all the side shoots lower down the stem.

In spring cut back central leader to 2 ft. above the ground.

Leave only the top three or four buds or side shoots on the tree to form branches. Remove the rest lower down the stem.

Pruning the Tree in Succeeding Years

All pruning in the following years is done in late winter. Remove any branch that crosses over another, cutting it off flush with its parent branch. Cut back damaged branches to just above a healthy shoot.

Remove any shoots that are attached to the main stem beneath the lowest branch; cut them off flush with the stem. Any branch that is dying at the tip should be cut back to a good side shoot or outward-pointing branch. If the cut wood shows brown discoloration, it is affected by dieback; so cut it back to healthy wood.

On a well-established tree, cut off any branches that droop to the ground due to heavy fruit bearing. Also remove the older branches as they become unfruitful. This will encourage new wood to develop from the center.

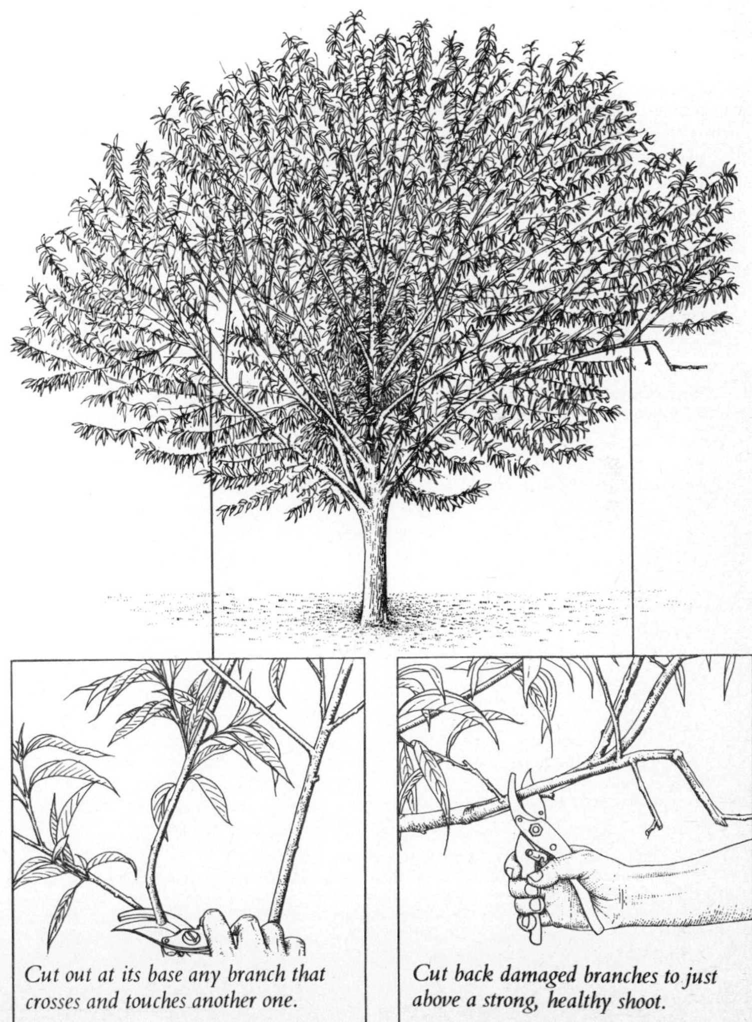

Cut out at its base any branch that crosses and touches another one.

Cut back damaged branches to just above a strong, healthy shoot.

Training and Pruning a Fan-Shaped Peach Tree

Train a young fan peach like a fan apple (p. 503), but prune in early spring as growth begins, not in winter. Unlike apple trees, peach trees produce side shoots off the current year's growth. Pinch out the side shoots one bud from their base.

From the fourth spring after a tree is planted (when it has 24 to 32 ribs), pruning differs, as peaches fruit mainly on the last year's shoots.

When growth starts in the fourth spring, rub or pinch out any buds or shoots that point toward or away from the wall.

From the buds remaining, select some good ones on each side of a rib, at 6-inch intervals, and rub out all others except the bud at the tip.

During the fourth summer these buds will produce laterals that will bear fruit the following summer, and the bud at the tip will grow on as a rib leader. Toward the end of the summer, tie both laterals and leaders to the wires. If a lateral grows to a length of more than 18 inches, pinch off its tip.

The fifth spring let the tips of fruit-bearing laterals grow to help develop fruit. Pinch off side shoots.

In autumn or early winter, after picking fruit, cut back each lateral that has borne fruit.

Repeat this process of removing buds, pinching back, cutting old shoots, and tying in replacements every year. On the extension growth from each rib, choose buds to grow out as new laterals, as in the fourth spring. Treat rib leaders reaching the top wire as laterals.

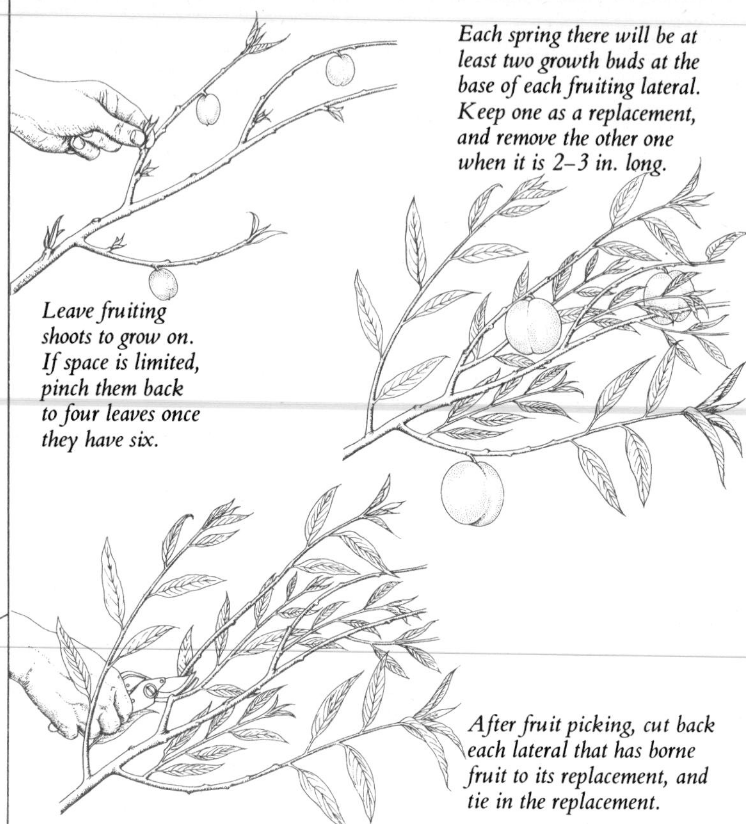

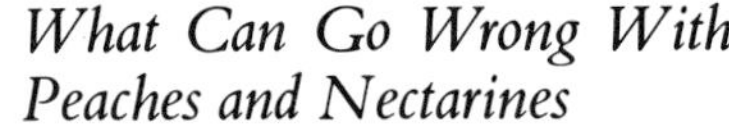

What Can Go Wrong With Peaches and Nectarines

If your peach or nectarine trees show any symptoms or signs that you do not find described below, consult the section on plant disorders that begins on page 600. Look up the recommended chemicals on page 635 to find trade names.

Symptoms and signs	**Cause**	**Control**
Orange-brown gum oozes from base of tree. Borers tunnel under bark, destroying tree.	Peach tree borers	In early spring dig out larvae. Clean wound. For more, see p. 633. In autumn put 3-in. ring of moth crystals 6–8 in. from trunk. Cover ring with soil 10 in. high. In early winter remove soil.
Older leaves gradually turn bronzy yellow and dry out.	Mites	Spray with dicofol, dimethoate, malathion, or tetradifon.
Leaves are eaten or spun together with strands of silk.	Moth larvae	Spray with malathion or trichlorfon as buds open.

Symptoms and signs	Cause	Control
Shoots wilt; fruits exude gummy liquid.	Oriental fruit moths (caterpillars)	After petal fall spray with malathion and methoxychlor: apply 4–5 times every 10-da.
Small green peaches drop prematurely.	Plum curculios (weevils)	Spray with carbaryl or methoxychlor at petal fall and again 7–10 da. later. Repeat twice more at 7- to 10- da. intervals.
Brown powdery masses on fruits. Later, fruits shrivel and form hard "mummies."	Brown rot (fungus)	Spray with Captan, ferbam, folpet, or sulfur at preblossom stage. Repeat when flower shucks split, then weekly for 2 wk.
Large reddish blisters on foliage. Leaves become whitish, then brown, then fall prematurely.	Leaf curl (fungus)	Spray Bordeaux mixture, ferbam, or lime sulfur in early spring; repeat 2 wk. later and again just before leaf fall.
Gummy twigs and bark. Leaves have purplish spots and holes.	Valsa canker (fungus)	Remove cankers; treat area with Dinitrol. Spray foliage with Bordeaux mixture.

Varieties of Peaches and Nectarines to Grow

Peaches and nectarines are self-pollinating; so only one variety need be planted. Each variety's ripening time is based on that of the popular 'Elberta' peach, and the figure given is the number of days before or after this time.

Names Peach (P) Nectarine (N)	Ripens days before (−) or after (+) 'Elberta'	Flesh color	Remarks (*All are freestones except as indicated.*)
'Harbinger' (P)	−60	Yellow	Cling.
'Babcock' (P)	−31	White	Very sweet.
'Redhaven' (P)	−30	Yellow	Dependable.
'Mericrest' (N)	−25	Yellow	Hardy.
'July Elberta,' or 'Burbank' (P)	−16	Yellow	High quality. Stores well.
'Loring' (P)	−11	Yellow	Excellent all round.
'Stark Red-gold' (N)	−3	Yellow	Widely grown. One of best.
'Elberta' (P)	0	Yellow	Widely grown. Ripens in late summer.
'Belle of Georgia' (P)	+3	White	Longtime favorite of its type.
'Rio-Oso-Gem' (P)	+8	Yellow	Widely grown. Firm flesh.
'Summer-crest' (P)	+30	Yellow	Large fruit. Productive.
'Sunred' (N)	Late spring (Fla.)	Yellow	Semi-freestone. Excellent quality.

Pears

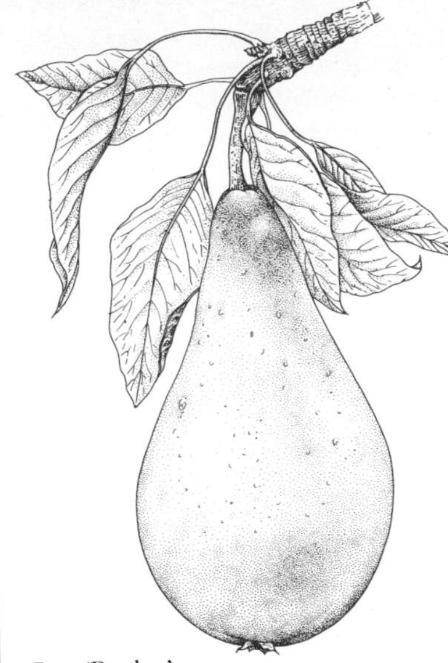

Pear 'Bartlett'

Pears—which can be used for fresh desserts, cooking, or canning—are as easy to grow as apples. But in cold climates, because they blossom earlier, they are more liable to injury by late spring frosts. The trees will do best if planted in a sunny position, sheltered from cold winds.

Being less tolerant than apple trees of dry conditions at their roots, pear trees prefer a deep, loamy soil that will keep its moisture in summer. Like apples, they do not grow well on or near a seacoast because of damage from salt-laden winds.

Pear trees can be trained to the same forms as apple trees. Only one or two varieties are tip bearers. At least two varieties must be grown for cross-pollination. See Varieties of Pears to Grow for more about this important subject. The trees grown on dwarfing rootstocks are preferred by most home gardeners.

As with apples, "family" trees (those with three or more varieties on one rootstock) are available.

An average family should get as many pears as it needs from four dwarf trees (three fans, three espaliers, six dwarf pyramids, or eight cordons).

In humid areas, about two months before buds swell, apply about 10 pounds of a 5–10–5 or 5 pounds of a 10–6–4 fertilizer. In arid regions apply about 2–3 pounds of ammonium sulfate or its equivalent in nitrogen.

There is some natural fall of fruit in early summer, but dry, poor soil can cause an entire crop to drop.

Harvesting the fruit. The time of picking is critical. Pears should not be allowed to ripen fully on the tree. If this happens, they will become soft and mealy inside.

Harvest early varieties by cutting the stalk when the fruit is mature but still hard—before it will twist easily from the stalk by hand. Pick mid-season and late pears as soon as they will part easily from the stalk after a gentle lifting and twisting motion.

After picking, place the pears, not touching, in a single layer on a shelf in a cool room or shed, at a temperature of about 38°–40° F. If possible, the atmosphere should be a little drier than for apples. Inspect pears regularly and remove any fruit that shows signs of rot.

To finish ripening, place the fruits in a warm room at about 65° F for two or three days. If properly stored, they should keep well for several months. Use the small fruits first.

Pruning and training pear trees. Pruning and training are done the same way as for apple trees (see p. 494). Pear trees, however, should be pruned [illegible] severely to avoid forcing the d[illegible] growth susc[illegible]

Pear tree[illegible] spurs more [illegible] more thinn[illegible] should be [illegible] lier than fo[illegible]

If you t[illegible] there is [illegible] dwarf pea[illegible] way as ar[illegible] neglected [illegible]

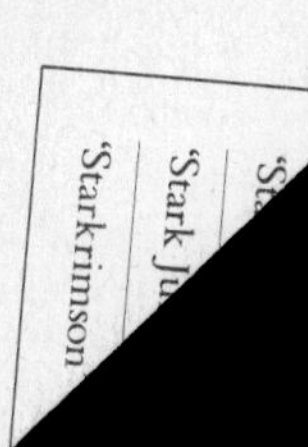

What Can Go Wrong With Pears

Aphids and fire blight are the major problems. If your pear trees show symptoms not described here, turn to the full-color identification section on plant disorders on page 600. Look up chemicals on page 635 to find their trade names.

Symptoms and signs	Cause	Control
Shoots and young leaves are crippled or stunted. Small sticky insects are present.	Aphids	Spray with systemic insecticide (dimethoate or oxydemeton-methyl). Or spray with carbaryl, endosulfan, or malathion.
Numerous tiny dark brown bumps appear on both sides of leaves.	Leaf blister mites	Destroy infected leaves and fruits. Spray with lime sulfur in early spring.
Young fruits become deformed, often elongated or rounded. Later, fruits may crack, decay, and fall.	Pear midges	As a preventative, spray with dimethoate or malathion when petals fall. Destroy all fallen fruits.
Leaf surfaces eaten; later, exposed veins brown and die. Small black caterpillars are visible.	Pear or cherry sawflies	Spray with carbaryl, chlorpyrifos, or malathion when insects are first seen.
Eggs are laid in young fruits. Larvae feed on and destroy fruits.	Plum curculios (weevils)	Spray with carbaryl or methoxychlor at petal fall and 7–10 da. later. Repeat at least twice more at 7- to 10-da. intervals.
Full-sized fruits, on tree or in storage, show pale brown areas with concentric rings of small whitish or yellowish bumps. Sometimes fruits dry up on tree.	Brown rot (fungus)	Destroy all rotten and withered fruits on tree, on ground, and in storage. When pruning, cut out and destroy dead shoots. Spray trees with Captan, folpet, sulfur, or thiophanate-methyl in late summer to reduce rotting of stored fruit.
Cankers develop at base of shoots that have died back; brown, withered leaves hang on.	Fire blight (bacteria)	Contact your county agricultural extension agent, who will suggest suitable treatment or possibly destruction of diseased tree. Antibiotic spray (chlortetracycline or streptomycin) can be helpful.
Twigs or young stems have slightly sunken areas of dead tissue. These areas expand; central tissues eventually crack and flake off. Cankers girdle and kill stem.	Pear canker (fungus)	Cut out or pare off infected parts and destroy. Paint wounds with wound-sealing paint. Improve drainage if waterlogging occurs, as this may aggravate disease.
Brownish or blackish spots appear on leaves and fruits; blisters and cracks develop on shoots in spring.	Pear scab (fungus)	Spray with Benomyl, Captan, thiophanate-methyl, or thiram. Apply spray when flower buds are nearly open, when petals fall, and 3 wk. later.

Varieties of Pears to Grow

All the varieties listed here are considered to be dessert pears because they are sweet and juicy. Except for the variety 'Seckel,' they are all of good size.

Except for the variety 'Duchess,' which is self-pollinating, pears must have a pollination partner in order to set fruit.

To ensure the pollination of the other kinds, three or more varieties should be planted near one another, or three different varieties can be grafted on one rootstock to make, in effect, a self-pollinating tree. Some nurseries offer pears that are grafted on dwarfing rootstock.

Names	Usual area	Remarks
'Anjou,' 'Bosc,' 'Comice,' 'Fame,' 'Tyson'	North Central	Long-standing varieties. 'Anjou' favored by home gardeners.
'Bartlett'	All areas	Highest-quality fruit. Blight susceptible, otherwise easy to grow.
'Duchess'	All areas	Large, good-quality fruit. Self-pollinating, easy to grow. Does well on 'Provence' rootstock.
'Keiffer'	South	Medium-sized, fair-quality fruit but satisfactory if properly stored. Blight-resistant, durable tree.
'Seckel'	All areas	Small, sweet fruit. Blight resistant.
…rking Delicious'	All areas	Good-sized, quality fruit. Easy to grow.
…mbo'	All areas	Most of 'Bartlett' qualities. Very large fruit.
[illegible]	West Coast	Very attractive, highly colored fruit. Blight susceptible, otherwise satisfactory.

Plums, Damsons, and Apricots

Plum 'President'

Plums, damsons, and apricots are all stone-fruit trees of the genus *Prunus;* their culture is essentially the same.

Plums and apricots are eaten fresh or used for canning, cooking, or jams and jellies. Greengages are a particularly flavorful type of plum. Damsons are small, round, and tart.

Prunes are plums with a sugar content high enough that they can be dried without fermentation around the pit. If the fruit is eaten canned or fresh, it is a plum; dried, it is a prune.

All these fruit trees will succeed in most well-drained soils. Plums and greengages flower early and should not be planted in areas where spring frosts are likely.

Gages give best results if they are grown against a wall. Damsons can stand more rain and less sun than plums and greengages can, and they usually flower a little later.

Trees tend to grow too large for the average-size garden unless they are on semi-dwarfing rootstock. The most suitable espaliered forms for home gardens are fans and pyramids. All damsons are self-fertile, but some varieties of plums need to be grown with another variety as a pollenizer.

Two or three trees can provide enough fruit for the average family. Plums ripen from midsummer to fall; damsons, late summer to fall.

In mild regions plant trees in early spring or autumn (p. 490). If the weather is dry, make sure the soil is well watered beforehand. On very acid soils (pH 5 and below), add 1 pound of lime per square yard.

In early spring mulch with a 2-inch layer of straw, well-rotted garden compost, or manure, to keep the soil moist. Repeat this every year. Control weeds by shallow hoeing or with a weed killer.

Pull out suckers as soon as they form—remove enough soil to reveal the root, and tear the suckers from the root. Do not cut them off, or they will increase.

Wasps may suck the juice of the ripening fruit, especially if it is already damaged. If you can find their nest, apply a wasp control. Netting deters birds (see p. 491).

Apricots. This tree does best in the climate of the Pacific Coast; some varieties suitable for the Midwest and East are available. Because they flower early, they need a sheltered site to protect the blooms from frost damage in cold climates.

Apricot trees are best grown as fan trees against a south-facing wall. In milder areas they can be grown as dwarf trees if they are sheltered from cold winds.

One tree should be enough for an average family. The fruiting time is from midsummer to early fall, depending on the variety.

Soil and feeding requirements are the same as those for plums. Trees bear fruit on one-year-old and older wood. Train fan and dwarf trees like apple trees (pp. 503, 506) until the framework is built, but prune in early spring as growth begins. Then prune fans like plum trees, dwarf trees like tart cherries (see p. 516).

Apricots are self-fertile, but they flower when few pollinating insects are about; so artificial pollination is advisable to ensure a good crop. Dab a small, soft paintbrush on the open flowers every two or three days.

Thinning is necessary only if the branches are very heavy with fruit. Wait until the stones are formed (check by cutting a fruit), as there is often a natural drop of fruit just before this. Fruits should be spaced about 5 inches apart on the branch.

Harvest apricots when they are well colored, and easily picked.

Good varieties to grow in the Midwest and East are 'Goldcot' and 'Wilson Delicious'; west of the Rockies, plant 'Blenheim' and 'Tilton.' Apricot trees suffer the same troubles as plum trees do (see pp. 537–538).

Feeding Plum and Damson Trees

In late winter or early spring in humid regions, apply 1–3 pounds of a complete fertilizer, such as a 10–10–10 or 10–6–4 or an equivalent. In arid regions only nitrogen may be needed; it should be applied at a rate of ¼–1 pound of ammonium nitrate for every tree.

Sprinkle the fertilizer evenly over the soil, covering an area a little larger than the spread of the tree's branches. Do not fork it in, as this might damage the roots; allow the fertilizer to work its way into the root area naturally.

Thinning and Harvesting the Crop

Tree branches are often brittle, and if they snap, there is a danger that rot or other diseases will enter and infect the wound.

Start thinning a heavy crop in late spring to take some weight off the branches. Curl a finger around the stalk, and snap off the fruit with your thumbnail, leaving the stalk attached to the tree.

Complete thinning later, after the natural drop of the fruit. Thin dessert plums to 2–3 inches apart; thin cooking plums to 2 inches. This usually means leaving one plum to each cluster.

Pick ripe fruit by the stalk to avoid bruising. The stalk will snap and come away with the fruit.

Allow the plums that you intend to eat raw to ripen on the tree as long as possible. Pick those that will be used for cooking or canning just before they are ripe.

Plums can be kept in good condition for a few weeks if they are picked just before they are ripe, wrapped in paper, and placed in a cool, well-ventilated room or shed. Remove any rotting fruit from time to time, as it may spread disease.

Training and Pruning a Pyramid Plum Tree

Training a One-Year-Old Pyramid Tree

Pyramid plum trees are similar in shape to dwarf pyramid apple trees (p. 506) but slightly taller (about 9 feet) and wider (8–10 feet). Plums are more irregular in outline; they generally grow vigorously, making it difficult to maintain their shape.

After the basic framework has been established, plum trees need less restrictive pruning than apple trees do.

If you decide to train a pyramid from a one-year-old tree, cut the stem back to 5 feet above the ground in early spring after planting. Cut just above a bud. Cut off flush with the stem any young branches lower than 18 inches from the ground.

If the tree is much less than 5 feet high, let it continue growing for another year before training it.

Training a Two-Year-Old Pyramid Tree

On a two-year-old tree cut back the main leader in early spring to about 18 inches from the previous year's cut. Make the cut just above a bud.

Cut back from three to five of the strongest side shoots at the top of the stem to 9 inches, pruning to an outward-pointing bud. Cut back all other side shoots to 6 inches. Since the lower growth is likely to be weaker, it is cut back harder to encourage even growth. All these side shoots will now grow on to form the tree's first main branches.

In spring prune central leader to 18 in. from last year's cut.

Training From Three Years Old to Full Height

Early each spring cut back the central leader to about 18 inches above the previous year's cut and just above a bud. Cut back the branch leaders according to their vigor—by one-third of new growth if they are growing well, by one-half if they are of average growth, or by two-thirds if they are weak.

Cut the strongest laterals from main branches back to 9 inches and the remaining laterals to 6 inches; always make the cut above an outward-pointing bud.

In spring cut back new growth on the branch leaders by half if they are of average growth.

Cut from three to five strong shoots at the top of the stem to 9 in., and all others to 6 in.

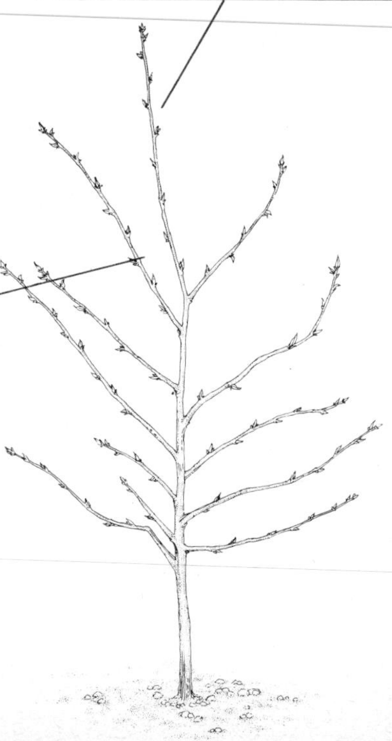

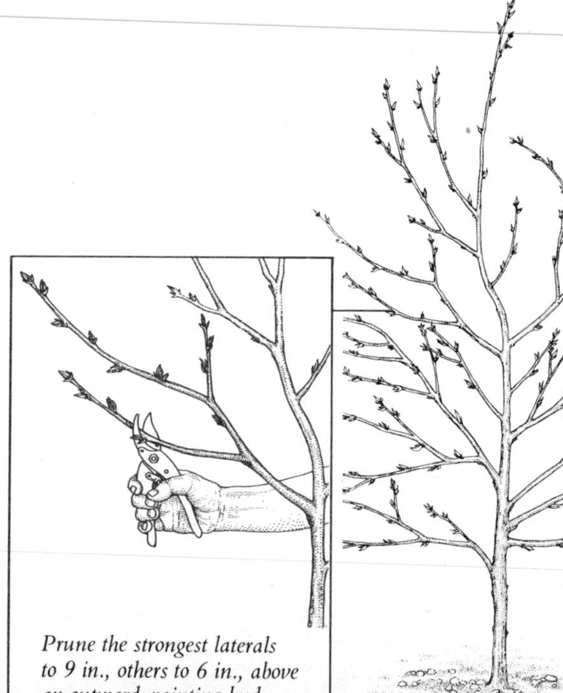

Prune the strongest laterals to 9 in., others to 6 in., above an outward-pointing bud.

Pruning an Established Pyramid Tree

Once the tree has reached about 9 feet (when it is about six years old), keep it at this height by cutting back the central leader to a strong lateral in the summer. You may need to do this every second or third year, depending on growth.

Established trees can be pruned in midsummer, but winter pruning is commoner.

Plum trees bear fruit on the previous season's shoots as well as on spurs on old wood. If the tree is fruiting regularly, prune as little as possible—just pinch vigorous new side shoots back to six or seven leaves from the parent stem.

Thin out overcrowded branches as necessary, cutting flush with the parent stem. Similarly, cut away any deadwood.

If branch leaders grow exceptionally long, cut them back to a strong main lateral. Try to keep branches at a maximum length of 4 or 5 feet.

If the tree grows vigorously but does not fruit regularly, root pruning (see p. 491) may be required to initiate production.

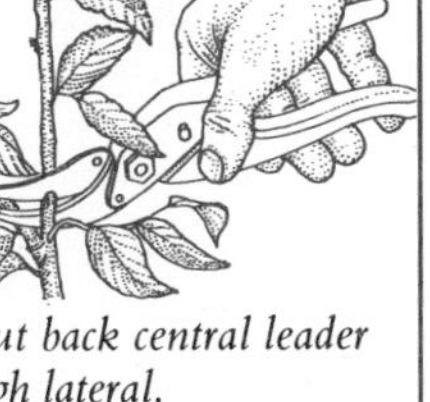

In summer cut back central leader to a 9-ft.-high lateral.

Pinch vigorous new side shoots back to six or seven leaves.

What Can Go Wrong With Plums

The fungous diseases black knot and brown rot are fairly common on plums. If plants show symptoms not described here, turn to the plant-disorder section on page 600. Look up chemicals on page 635 to find trade names.

Symptoms and signs	Cause	Control
Fruits have small skin blemishes; insides may show corky brown streaks. Maggots ("worms") are visible.	Apple maggots (fly larvae)	Spray with carbaryl or methoxychlor when flies first become active (early to mid summer). To control later broods, spray every 3 wk. until late summer.
Leaves have pale or reddish mottling and may fall prematurely.	Fruit tree mites (two-spotted and European red mites)	To kill eggs, spray with dinoseb, miscible oil, or oil emulsion while trees are dormant in winter. Or spray after flowering with dicofol, dimethoate, or malathion.
Leaves and young shoots are twisted and stunted. Tiny, sticky insects are present.	Leaf-curling plum aphids	Spray with carbaryl, dimethoate, endosulfan, or malathion. Apply before trees blossom in early spring and, if necessary, after blossoming.
Leaves are eaten or spun together. Green caterpillars are usually present.	Moth larvae	Spray with malathion, rotenone, or trichlorfon as buds open and leaves develop.
Curculios puncture and lay eggs in very young fruits. Larvae (grubs) feed inside fruits, which drop.	Plum curculios (weevils)	Spray with carbaryl or methoxychlor at petal fall and again 7–10 da. later. Repeat at 7- to 10-da. intervals.
Brown humpbacked insects are visible on twigs and leaves. Scales secrete "honeydew," which drips on leaves and encourages development of fungus.	Scale insects	Apply 60-sec. miscible oil as dormant spray before buds break. About 2–3 wk. later apply Diazinon or malathion.
Brown spots may appear on leaves, eventually becoming holes. Flat cankers develop on stems and smaller branches; branches die back.	Bacterial canker	Cut out infected branches; paint wounds in midsummer. Spray foliage with Bordeaux mixture in midsummer, late summer, and midautumn.
Attacks leaves, twigs, and fruits. Causes development of small spots that range in color from pale green to deep purple or brown. Fruits may crack; twig cankers may develop.	Bacterial leaf spot	Antibiotic sprays of chlortetracycline or streptomycin may help. Applications of Bordeaux mixture at and after leaf fall are beneficial. Prune and destroy badly cankered twigs. Destroy infected leaves.
Fruits have brown powdery masses. Fruits shrivel and form "mummies."	Brown rot (fungus)	Spray with Captan, ferbam, folpet, or sulfur at preblossom stage. Repeat when flower shucks split, then 7–10 da. later, and again 7–10 da. later.

(continued)

Symptoms and signs	Cause	Control
Smoky black knots (galls) on twigs and limbs, which range in size from ½ in. to 1 ft.	Black knot (fungus)	Prune off galls. Make sure to cut at least 4 in. below swellings. Paint cut branches with cycloheximide (diluted according to instructions on label). Apply Captan or zineb at preblossom stage and petal fall. Repeat 10 da. after petal fall and again 7–10 da. later.
Large protuberances at soil line may girdle and kill entire tree.	Crown gall (bacteria)	Root out and destroy infected plants. Disinfect all pruning tools with denatured alcohol or half-strength liquid chlorine bleach. It is sometimes possible to control crown gall with Bacticin, an antibiotic; treat large galls according to manufacturer's instructions.
Narrow strap-shaped leaves are brittle, thick, and coarsely wrinkled.	Prune dwarf (virus)	Plant virus-free stock. Destroy affected plants.
Leaves have yellow rings and spots. Fruits develop surface bumps and may drop from tree.	Ring pox, or ring spot (virus)	No effective control. Infected plant material must be destroyed. Control of insects tends to reduce spread of disease.
May cause reddish spots on leaves and fruits. Later, spots fall from leaves, producing "shot holes." Infected buds die in winter.	Shot-hole leaf spot (fungus)	Spray with Captan or zineb at red-bud stage, again at early bloom, and again at full bloom. In autumn, just after leaf fall, spray with Bordeaux mixture, ferbam, or zineb.
Leaves have silvery sheen. Branches die back after 1 or more yr. When infected branches are cut out, wood shows dark brown staining. Small fungi appear on deadwood.	Silver leaf (fungus)	Cut out affected branches to 6 in. below point where brown stain ceases. Paint all wounds. Feed, mulch, water, and/or drain as necessary to encourage vigor. A foliar feed may hasten recovery.
Stems and sometimes small branches die back. Plant lacks vigor.	Unsatisfactory soil conditions	Improve drainage. Test soil to determine whether addition of lime is necessary.

Varieties of Plums, Damsons, and Prunes to Grow

Although most varieties listed are self-fertile, it is a good idea to plant another tree, as indicated, to ensure pollination. Select pollenizers of the same major type as the tree to be pollinated; thus, a European variety with another European variety.

Varieties that are hardy enough to grow in northern states are so indicated in the Remarks column. Japanese types are most subject to frost damage.

Greengages need a warm, sunny position. If grown in a cold area, they should be planted against a building or garden wall that is oriented toward the south or west.

Names	Color	Remarks
European types		
'Bluefre'	Blue	Prune. Tree bears when young; late season. Hardy tree.
'Burbank Grand Prize'	Blue	Prune. Large fruit; freestone. Early season. 'Bluefre' a good pollenizer.
'Earliblue'	Blue	Prune. Very early ripening. May be slow to produce fruit. Good quality. Hardy tree.
'Giant Damson'	Blue	Damson. Although slightly sour, good for canning.
'Italian'	Blue	Prune. Widely planted. Good fresh and for canning. 'Brook's Giant' good strain where available.
'Pipestone'	Red (gold blush)	Plum. Fine quality. Hardy tree for colder U.S. climates. 'Toka' a good pollenizer.
'President'	Blue	Prune. Late season. Widely planted; fruitful. Fine textured. Cross-pollination advisable.
'Reine Claude'	Yellowish green	Greengage. Good for canning. Some improved strains available.
'Shropshire'	Purple	Damson. Hardy tree. Very good for preserves.
'Toka'	Orange	Plum. Very hardy tree for colder U.S. climates. Rich flavor.
Japanese types		
'Burbank'	Red-purple	Plum. Low tree. Necessary to thin fruit.
'Early Golden'	Yellow (red blush)	Plum. Freestone. Early season. Necessary to thin fruit; several pickings.
'Ozark Premier'	Yellow	Plum. Large, delicious fruit. Hardy tree.
'Redheart'	Red	Plum. Large fruit. Productive. Resistant to bacterial spot. Good pollenizer.
'Santa Rosa'	Red	Plum. A standard variety. Delicious flavor.
'Shiro'	Yellow	Plum. Early season. Productive. 'Burbank' will not pollenize it.
'Starking Delicious'	Red	Plum. Cling. Productive. Resistant to bacterial spot.

Raspberries

Raspberry 'Heritage'

Raspberries can be used for fresh desserts, cooking, or jam making; they can also be frozen. Some varieties bear fruit in midsummer on the previous season's shoots; others fruit in early or mid fall on the current season's shoots. Canes that have produced fruit die and are replaced year by year by new canes that grow from the roots.

There are three types of raspberries grown in this country. The reds, which are the most popular, have erect canes and are propagated by suckers from the roots. The blacks and the purples also grow upright, but they have arched canes that take root at the tips. These are dug up and set for new plants. The purples are hybrids of reds and blacks and are more vigorous. Blacks are grown in the eastern part of the country and in Oregon, while purples are grown in western New York. Yellow varieties are variations of the reds. All kinds of raspberries are self-fertile.

Buy one-year-old canes for planting in late autumn. Raspberries are prone to viral diseases; so get them from a reputable nursery to ensure that they are free of disease. To avoid the risk of spreading viral diseases, it is best not to replenish your stock by raising new plants from those you have; always buy new canes of certified virus-free stock.

Raspberries do best in full sun but will grow in partial shade. Do not plant them in positions exposed to frost or strong winds. They do well in any well-drained but moisture-retaining, slightly acidic soil. Raspberries will also grow in alkaline soil if it is enriched with compost or decayed manure.

The average family should obtain a plentiful fruit supply with 18 to 24 raspberry canes.

Preparing the Bed and Planting the Canes

The best way to grow raspberries is in a row, with the canes trained against wires. First, clear the site of perennial weeds—either dig them up or use a weed killer, such as paraquat.

In late summer or early autumn, prepare the ground by digging a spade-deep trench about $2\frac{1}{2}$ feet wide. Fork well-rotted compost, peat moss, or manure into the bottom at the rate of about two 2-gallon buckets per square yard. At the same time add 2 tablespoons of fertilizer per square yard. Then fill in the trench with soil.

The best time to plant is in the late fall, although it can be done at any time from fall to spring. Dig a shallow trench about 3 inches deep and 6–9 inches wide. Place the young plants upright in it, 18 inches apart and with roots spread out. Cover the roots with 3 inches of soil, and then firm it gently with your feet. Leave 6 feet of space between rows.

Immediately after planting, cut each cane to just above a good bud, 9–12 inches above ground level.

Stable manure, if available, is ideal fertilizer, applied in the fall each year. Approximately a month before growth starts in spring, apply about $\frac{1}{4}$ pound of 5–10–5 per square yard. Allow these fertilizers to be washed into the soil naturally.

In early spring mulch with a 2-inch layer of garden compost, manure, or peat moss, to conserve moisture in the soil. Water well in warm, dry spells.

Control weeds with a paraquat weed killer, or pull them up by hand. Do not hoe between the canes, particularly during the growing period, since this can damage the shallow surface roots.

Protect ripening fruit from birds, preferably with netting.

Supporting the Long, Flexible Shoots

During summer, when the canes are producing fresh growth, sink an 8-foot wooden post 2 feet into the ground at each end of the row. Then stretch two galvanized wires between the posts 3 feet and $5\frac{1}{2}$ feet above the ground; or stretch two parallel wires, 1 foot apart, from crosspieces fixed at right angles to the posts about 4 feet above the ground. Keep the wires parallel with strong S-shaped hooks. For both methods use 12–13 gauge galvanized wire.

The first midsummer after planting, tie canes individually with soft string to the two-wire system. With parallel wires, simply ensure that all canes are inside them.

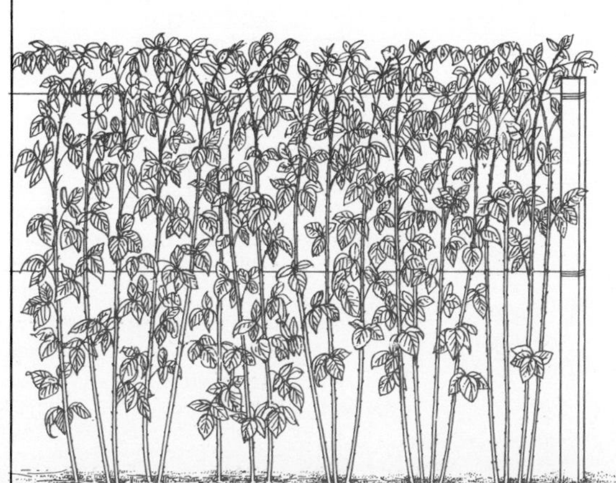
Two-wire system. *Between posts, stretch wires 3 ft. and $5\frac{1}{2}$ ft. above the ground; tie the canes to them.*

Parallel-wire system. *Stretch two parallel wires between 4-ft.-high crosspieces; train canes inside them.*

When to Gather the Ripe Fruit

Do not try for a crop the first summer after planting, as this will reduce the vigor of future canes. Early in the summer after planting, cut off all blossoms or fruits on the young canes. Allow canes to bear in the second year after planting.

Replacing Old Canes With New

Raspberry varieties that bear one midsummer crop are biennial. The canes grow the first summer, fruit the next, then die. In late summer, when summer-fruiting raspberries have been picked, untie canes that have borne fruit, and cut them off just above soil level. Do not cut canes of the current year's growth.

Train eight of the strongest new canes on each plant. Cut out weak new canes at soil level. Also cut out all the canes that spring up between rows in order to reduce crowding.

In late winter cut back each cane growing above the top wire to a bud just a few inches above the wire.

To obtain early-summer *and* fall fruits from everbearing varieties, such as 'Heritage,' prune the canes back to live wood, and thin out the weaker canes in the winter after fruiting in the fall. But, if you also have a summer-bearing one-crop variety, such as 'Sodus,' prune the 'Heritage' type by cutting all canes to ground level in winter. This forfeits the early crop but produces larger and better berries in the fall.

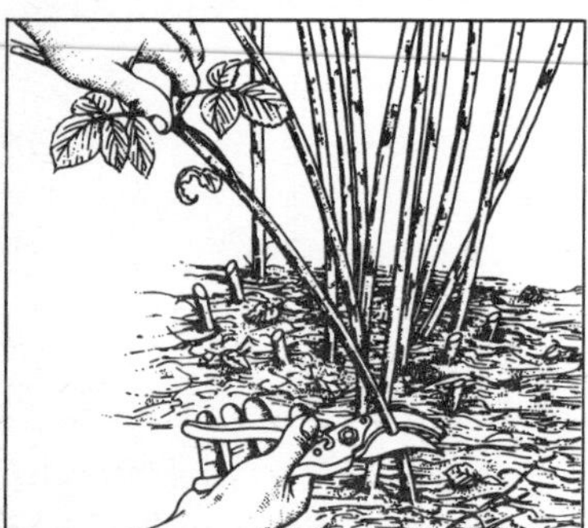

1. *In late summer cut down to soil level all raspberry canes that have borne fruit.*

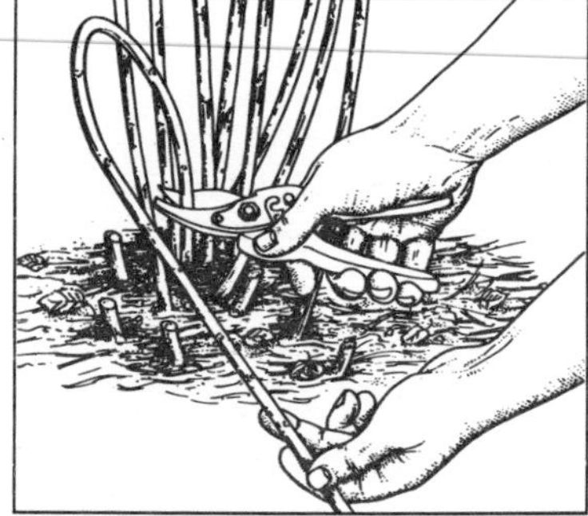

2. *Choose up to eight of the strongest new canes per plant; cut out the rest.*

3. *After supporting the new canes, pull out any suckers springing from roots.*

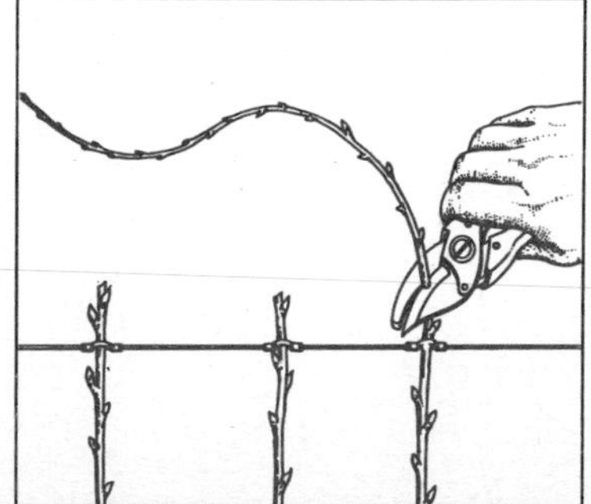

4. *In late winter trim any canes growing beyond the top wire to a bud just above it.*

Varieties of Raspberries and What Can Go Wrong

Select raspberry varieties that are certified to be virus-free.

If raspberry plants have symptoms not included in the table below, see the section on plant disorders on page 600. Trade names of chemicals are on page 635.

Names	Season	Usual area	Remarks
'Bristol'	Mid	East	Black. Large berries.
'Canby'	Mid	Northwest	Red. Thornless canes.
'Fall Gold'	Early and late	East	Yellow. Vigorous hardy.
'Heritage'	Early and late	North Central and Northeast	Red. Productive. Good berries. Vigorous.
'Plum Farmer'	Early	Northwest	Black. Fast ripening; 2–3 pickings. Resists drought.
'Puyallup'	Late	Pacific Northwest	Red. Productive. Quality berries. Freeze or can.
'September'	Early and late	East	Red. Medium-sized berries.
'Sodus'	Mid	Northeast, Western N.Y.	Purple. Large, good-quality berries. Vigorous, hardy.
'Viking'	Early	North Central, East	Red. Thornless canes. Medium-sized, high-quality berries.
'Washington'	Late	Pacific Northwest	Red. Large, high-quality berries. Freeze or can.
'Willamette'	Mid	Pacific Northwest	Red. Good-quality berries. Productive. Vigorous.

Symptoms and signs	Cause	Control
Leaves rolled and/or distorted; sticky insects.	Aphids	Spray with dimethoate.
Adult insects lay eggs at crowns. Eggs hatch and bore into crowns.	Crown borers	In spring cut out infected canes near base. Crush old stubs. Use Diazinon drench on crowns in fall.
Larvae attack fruits, destroying them.	Fruit worms or sawfly larvae	Spray with Diazinon or carbaryl when blossom buds appear and just before blossoms open.
Bugs feed on fruits, causing distortion.	Plant bugs (tarnished, harlequin)	Spray with carbaryl, Diazinon, or malathion.
Foliage distorted, off-color. Fruits poorly.	Two-spotted mites	Spray every 7–10 da. after leaves are fully out.
Fungus enters wound on canes and causes large brown dead areas. Leaves on fruiting canes wilt and wither in summer.	Cane blight	Cut back diseased canes to below-ground. Disinfect knife immediately. Spray with Bordeaux mixture as new canes develop. Ferbam or zineb can be used.
Canes show purple circular spots, which become cankers. Fruits often misshapen.	Cane spot or anthracnose (fungus)	Same as for cane blight except lime sulfur spray can be used also.

Strawberries

Strawberry 'Tioga'

There are two types of strawberries: the kind that produces only one crop each year in early summer; and the everbearing kind that produces one crop in early summer and another one in midfall. Everbearing varieties are generally less hardy.

An average family will need 24 to 36 plants. Buy stock that has been certified free of any viral disease.

Strawberries will grow in fertile, well-drained soil that is somewhat acid, with a pH between 5.5–6. It should contain enough organic matter to retain moisture. Plant in spring or fall in an open, sunny bed, preferably facing south. Avoid planting them in frost pockets.

Preparing the Ground and Planting

For one-crop varieties the best time to plant is in early spring—in mild climates, also in early fall. Plant everbearing varieties in spring.

Double-dig the bed (see p. 597) two or three weeks before planting if the soil is deep enough. Weed and add well-rotted manure or compost to the upper layer—one 2-gallon bucket per square yard for poor soil, half that for good loam.

Dig in well, and lightly fork in a complete fertilizer. Rake to break lumps and level.

Place plants 18 inches apart in rows 30 inches apart. Soak those that are in peat pots for an hour first; plant the pots so that they are just covered with soil. Plant unpotted strawberries in moist soil. Dig a hole 1 or 2 inches deeper than the roots, and put the plant on a mound in the hole with roots spread out.

Position the upper part of the roots (the crown) level with the surface. If it is buried, the crown bud can rot; if its base is exposed, the roots can dry out. Fill in and firm around carefully. Water in dry weather.

Spread roots on a mound so that the crown is level with the surface.

How to Care for Strawberries From Planting to Harvesting

Water regularly in dry weather for the first few weeks after planting. Lack of water at this time can retard growth or kill the plants.

In autumn, to conserve the plants' energy, cut off any runners that have grown. In late winter apply a complete fertilizer according to the directions on the package. If growth is generally poor, spread more complete fertilizer along rows in mid-spring. Avoid letting it touch the foliage. If it does get on the leaves, brush it off immediately. In spring control weeds with shallow hoeing.

In their first season remove the blooms from one-crop strawberries that were planted in late autumn or spring. On everbearing varieties remove flowers in early spring to encourage more and better berries later in the year.

When the developing fruits of the one-crop varieties are heavy enough to almost reach the ground, tuck clean straw beneath the berries and around the plants.

An alternative is to use plastic sheeting to keep the berries off the ground. Be sure the soil is moist before putting it down.

A good way to keep fruit off the ground—particularly useful for plants grown in pots or in a greenhouse—is to use loops made of galvanized wire. Insert them in the soil beside the plants. Hang one stem over each support. Attach carefully —not too tightly—with thin plastic-covered ties.

Water during dry spells, particularly when ripening begins, in order to swell the fruit. But do not overdo it; too much water during the ripening process can encourage a fungus disease known as gray mold. To ensure good flavor, pick strawberries with their stems attached, when the berries are fully ripe all around. Avoid excessive handling, since the fruits bruise easily.

PROTECTING YOUNG PLANTS AND FRUIT

To keep fruits clean and away from soil, use fresh straw or plastic sheeting.

Supports can be made with loops of galvanized wire. Hang one stem over each.

Clearing Out the Strawberry Bed

On one-crop varieties, as soon as all the fruit has been picked, fork the straw well up to the plants, and set fire to it to burn off the leaves. This will not harm the plants but will destroy old, diseased leaves and kill off any pests. New leaves will soon show through and will have plenty of air and light.

If burning in your area is illegal, impractical, or cannot be done immediately after picking, cut down plants with shears to about 3 inches above the crown. Pull off any unwanted runners and old, diseased leaves, and remove plastic sheeting. Rake off litter and destroy it.

Renew strawberry plants every two or three years. After this time they will not crop so heavily, and disease is likelier. New plants can be raised easily from existing plants.

Everbearing varieties will keep on bearing fruit until autumn frosts.

Polyethylene protectors against frost

Cover with clear plastic early in the fall to ensure fruit for picking.

Do not remove leaves from everbearers, as this will destroy new growth, but clear away some of the old leaves. Renew plants after one or two seasons of fruiting.

CUTTING DOWN ONE-CROP STRAWBERRIES

When all fruits are picked, fork straw up to the plant, and set fire to it to burn leaves and kill pests.

Where burning is prohibited, cut plants to 3 in. above the crown. Pull off old leaves and unwanted runners.

Raising New Plants From Runners

Strawberries can be raised from runners. In early summer choose strong, healthy parent plants that have been cropping well. Choose four strong runners from each, and extend them out from the plants.

Runners rooted in pots are easier to transplant. Fill 3-inch pots with good loam, potting compost, or a mixture of the two. On each runner choose the embryo plant—a strong tuft of leaves—nearest to the parent, and with a trowel dig a hole beneath it big enough for the pot.

Sink the pot to its rim in the hole; then pin the runner to the rooting media in the pot. Use a 6-inch piece of galvanized wire bent into a U-shape, as shown below. Do not sever the runner between the parent and the young plant, but pinch off the extra growth just beyond the pot. Keep the rooting media moist.

Pinned-down runners are ready for planting four to six weeks later. In late summer sever the runner connecting each new plant to its parent. Continue to water thoroughly. One week later carefully lift the new plants, and transfer them to their permanent positions. Then tend them in the same way as newly planted strawberries.

1. *In summer extend four runners from a strong, healthy plant.*

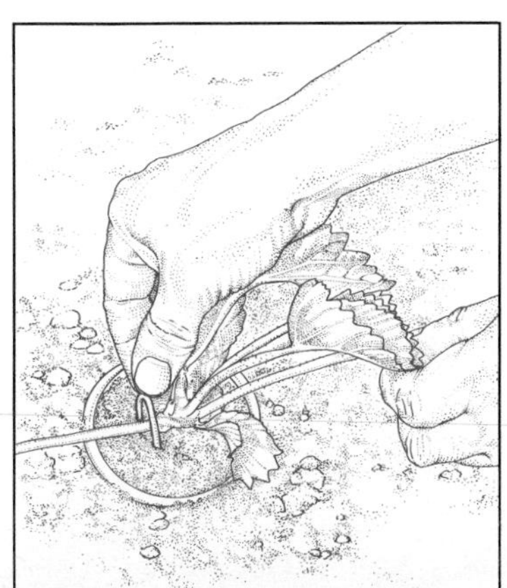

2. *Pin an embryo plant on each runner to a pot of loam buried just beneath it.*

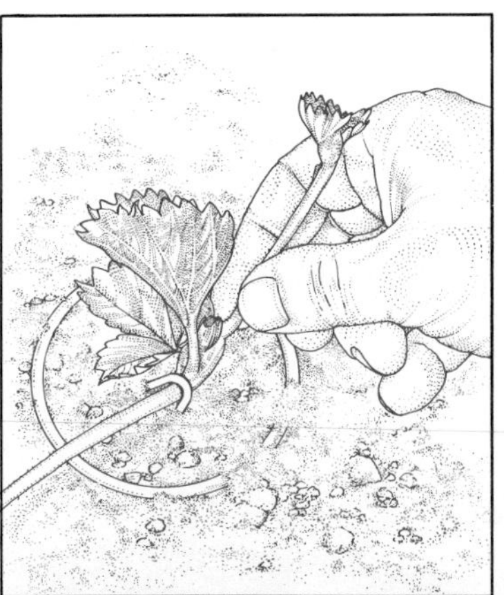

3. *Nip off the runner beyond the new plant, but do not cut it from its parent.*

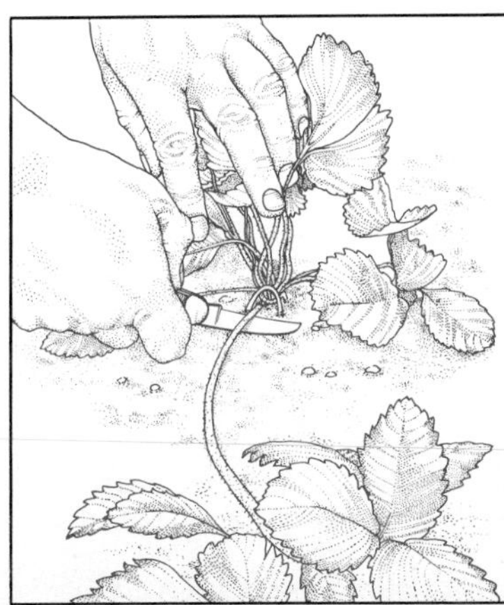

4. *Sever it from its parent four to six weeks later; transplant a week afterward.*

A STRAWBERRY BARREL

Make holes 2 in. wide and about 9 in. apart. Bore six 1-in. holes in the bottom for drainage. Fill barrel with 2 parts good soil, 1 part rotted compost or manure, 1 part coarse sand. Set plants in place as barrel is filled.

A round stairstep strawberry planting bed can be made with aluminum bands, a square one with 1- by 8-in. boards. Soil in the bed should be about 6 in. deep and the planting area itself about 1 ft. wide.

Varieties of Strawberries and What Can Go Wrong

The indicated bearing season will vary with the weather.

If plants show symptoms not indicated in the table at right, see the section on plant pests and diseases on page 600. Trade names of chemicals are on page 635.

Names	Usual area	Season
One crop		
'Blakemore'*	South Central	Early
'Florida 90'	Fla., La., Ga., Texas	Early
'Fresno'	Southwest, Calif.	Mid
'Guardian'	North Central, Northeast	Early
'Midway'*	East Central Coast, North Central	Mid
'Northwest'**	Northwest	Late
'Pocahontas'**	South Central	Mid
'Sparkle'**	North Central, Northeast	Mid-late
'Stark Red Giant'*	North Central	Mid
'Sunrise'*	East Central Coast, North Central	Early
'Surecrop'*	East, North Central, Northeast	Early
'Tioga'*	Gulf states, Southeast, Southwest, Calif.	Mid
'Totem'*	Northwest	Late
Everbearing		
'Ogallala'	Northern areas	
'Ozark Beauty'	Southern areas	

*Freezes well with sugar.
**Excellent quality.

Symptoms and signs	Cause	Control
Chewed flowers and fruits. Leaves chewed, rolled, or tied together.	Caterpillars	Dust plants with carbaryl or methoxychlor.
Distortion of crown, leaves, blossoms, and fruits. Most serious pests in many areas.	Cyclamen mites	Treat infected plants in spring by immersing in hot water (100° F) for 20 min. Spray several times with dicofol, endosulfan, or tetradifon.
Insects feed on fruits and under plants by day.	Earwigs	Use poison bait or dust carbaryl around plants before harvesting.
Leaves are crippled or stunted; turn yellow.	Leaf aphids	Spray with carbaryl, Diazinon, dimethoate, or nicotine.
Insects on roots, leaves, and stems. Plants are pale and lack vigor; small, pale leaves. Fruits are immature and dry.	Root aphids	Dip plants in Diazinon, dimethoate, or malathion before planting. Apply foliar sprays of Diazinon, endosulfan, or malathion.
Small insects feed on foliage and roots.	Root weevils	Apply methoxychlor to soil at planting time. Spray plants with carbaryl or malathion.
Grubs (rootworms) damage roots, adults eat leaves.	Strawberry leaf beetles	Apply chlordane or methoxychlor to soil around plants.
Plants weak, off-color. Mites feed on undersides of buds and new leaves.	Two-spotted mites	Every 7–10 da. throughout season spray with chlorobenzilate, dicofol, or tetradifon.
Fruits rot, become covered with grayish velvety mold.	Gray mold (fungus)	Spray with Benomyl. Repeat 3 times at 14-da. intervals. Destroy diseased fruits. Next year begin spraying as flowers open.
Leaves turn purple and curl upward, exposing undersides.	Powdery mildew (fungus)	Spray just before blossoming with 1½% lime sulfur or dinocap. Repeat every 10–14 da. until 1–2 wk. before picking.
Leaves are small, yellow margined, and in flattened tufts; plants stunted and distorted. Poor crops.	Virus disease	No cure. Dig up and destroy plants. Keep aphids, which spread virus, under control. Purchase virus-free plants.

Vegetables

Homegrown vegetables have a flavor rarely matched by those you buy. And even a small garden can produce enough to be well worthwhile.

There is a truism that more and more people are learning: nothing tastes quite so good as the food you have raised yourself. Gardening has become an avocation for millions—many of whom add beauty to their homes with little more than a few seeds and a spade. In this chapter we advise a somewhat larger investment—growing cabbages requires more thought and effort than growing marigolds does. On the other hand, you cannot eat marigolds.

Before you decide to start a vegetable patch, you need to assure yourself of these basic requirements: an open area with good drainage, plenty of sunlight, and a supply of water. If you have a patch of ground that receives at least six hours of sun daily and is well away from water- and nutrient-greedy trees and shrubs, you have the makings of a successful vegetable garden. Root crops and leafy vegetables will grow with even less sun. As you look for a sunny spot, remember that rocky areas can be cleared, and land that has grown only weeds can be cultivated to produce vegetable harvests.

How large should your garden be? Its limits should be defined by the amount of time you can devote to it and the number of people it will feed. A garden of 300 square feet (15 feet by 20 feet) should provide an adequate supply of your favorite vegetables for a family of four.

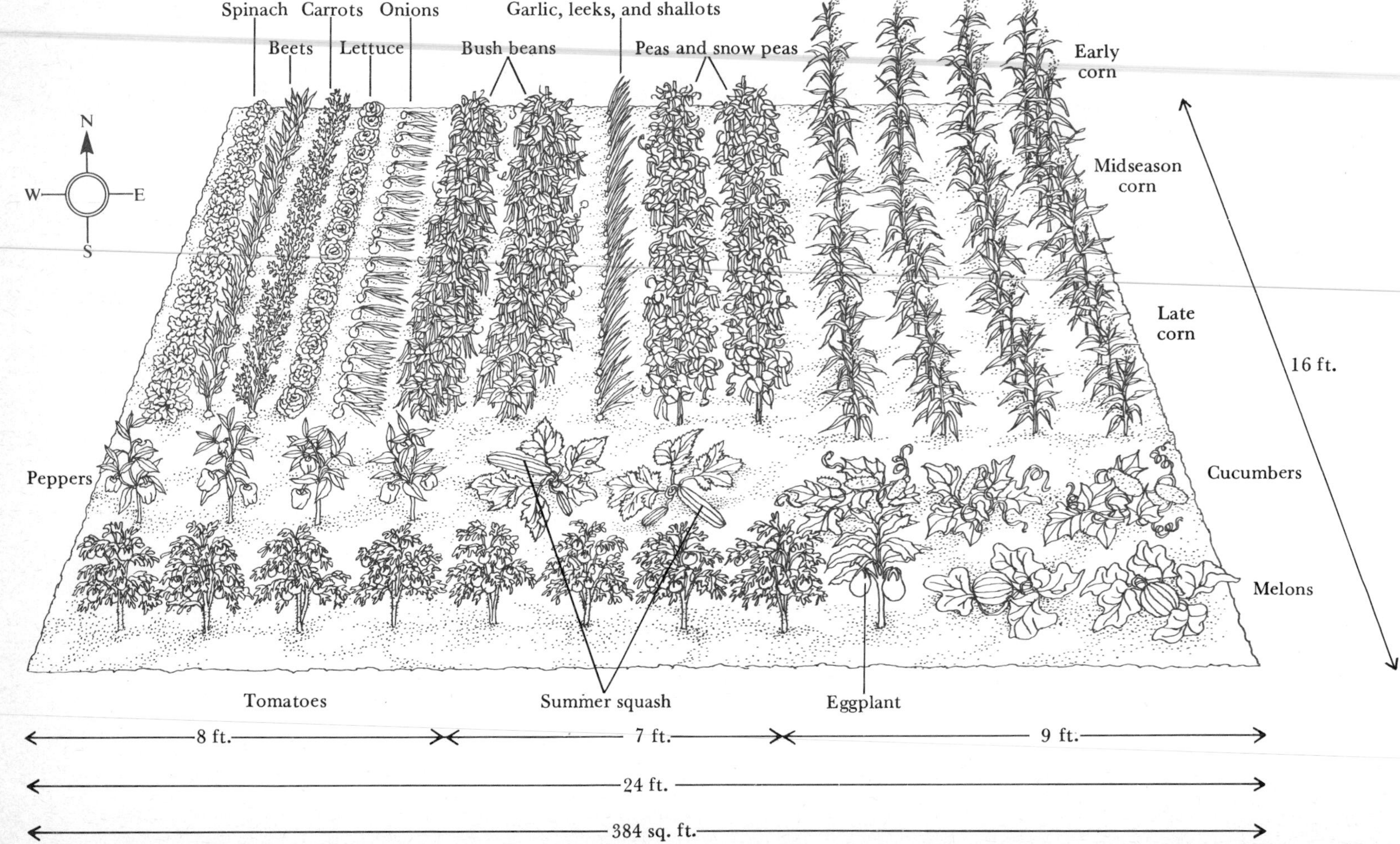

A well-planned vegetable garden, even in as limited a space as that shown above, can provide a full season's vegetables for a family of four. Succession plantings of fast-growing crops will add to the yield. Tall crops, like corn, should be planted so as not to shade smaller plants; sprawling crops, like melons, require ample growing space.

Planning Your Garden for Maximum Yield

Where should you put your garden? Choose the place that gets the most sun throughout the day. Avoid areas near large trees with wide-spreading roots and low areas that might flood or retain too much water. Be sure to stay within a hose length of a water faucet, but try not to plant within 2 feet of the walls of your house. The ground there is usually heavy with lime that has leached out of the foundation, and it may be littered with old nails and other construction debris. Gentle slopes are fine, especially those facing south. But beware of land at the bottom of a hill; it is almost always colder and wetter than the slope itself.

Once you have chosen the location of your garden plot, measure it to find out its exact dimensions. Then, using a large sheet of paper, make a diagram of it on which you can map out where you will plant each crop. You can use a simple scale: 1 inch per foot, for example. Leave space for walkways between groups of rows. In this way you can plan a garden that will produce crops all summer long.

Before you plot your garden, however, there are some important things you should learn about the crops you want to grow.

Size requirements. Each vegetable needs a certain optimum space in which to grow. Do not try to crowd plants into less space than they require. Squashes and melons often sprawl for yards in all directions. Radishes need very little space. Corn grows tall, as do asparagus and pole beans. Their height makes it necessary to plant them where they will not shade other plants. Brussels sprouts and cabbage grow to a hefty size and need plenty of room.

Time to harvest. Leaf lettuce can be picked in a matter of a few weeks, beets in about eight weeks, carrots in less than three months. These and other fast-maturing crops can succeed one another in the same soil: lettuce can be planted several times during the season; carrots or beets can be raised where peas once flourished; early carrots can be followed by fall spinach, lettuce by beans. Such "succession plantings" will give you several harvests from the same patch of soil.

On the other hand, certain crops are planted only once because they need the whole summer to mature. Vegetables such as tomatoes, eggplants, and winter squashes need up to three months to ripen. They also require plenty of nutrients and ample space. Allot them a large, sunny area.

Sunlight. Learn which plants can grow without daylong sunlight: spinach and lettuce will grow well in partially shaded spots or between rows of such taller crops as broccoli or Brussels sprouts.

Interplanting. Many of the fast-maturing vegetables—leaf lettuce, mustard greens, or spinach—may be planted among the seedlings of slow-growing vegetables, such as peppers, eggplants, or tomatoes. The leafy plants will reach maturity long before their neighbors shade them. Radishes are often planted in the rows of slower-growing carrots or parsley. They sprout quickly, thus marking the rows, and can be picked and eaten while the other vegetables are still small.

Perennials. Only three perennials are commonly grown in vegetable gardens: rhubarb, asparagus, and strawberries. If you would like to grow them, remember that they need considerable space. Rhubarb and asparagus will not produce a crop until, at the earliest, two years after planting.

Harvest yields. Some crops have enormous yields. A long row of lettuce planted all at once will produce more salad than you can possibly eat. It is more practical to plant short rows of fast-maturing vegetables and to make succession plantings at two- or three-week intervals.

Learn which vegetables must be eaten right away, which can be frozen or canned, which can be stored in a cellar. If you have storage space, plant more winter squashes, onions, and potatoes. If you have a freezer, grow more Brussels sprouts, carrots, beets, and okra. For home canning, raise extra tomato plants.

Planting times. It is most important when designing your garden to learn when each vegetable should be planted. Peas and spinach require cool spring weather. Tomatoes cannot be put out until it is certain that there will be no more frost. Tender lettuce will "bolt" (produce a stalk) in the heat of midsummer but will thrive in spring and fall.

KEEP YOUR GARDEN GROWING—PLANT FROM SPRING TO FALL

Early spring	**Midspring**	**Early summer**	**Midsummer to fall**
Plant as soon as the ground can be worked:	Plant 2 wk. before the average last frost date:	Plant when soil and sun are warm:	Plant in late June–early July:
PLANTS	**PLANTS**	**PLANTS**	**SEEDS**
Broccoli	Cauliflower	Eggplant	Beet
Cabbage	**SEEDS**	Pepper	Broccoli
SEEDS	Beet	Tomato	Cabbage
Endive	Carrot	**SEEDS**	Carrot
Lettuce	Onion sets	Cucumber	Cauliflower
Onion sets	Parsnip	Lima bean	Lettuce
Pea	Swiss chard	Melon	Radish
Radish	Plant 1 wk. later:	Okra	Plant in early Aug.:
Spinach	**SEEDS**	Pumpkin	**PLANTS**
Turnip	Bean	Squash	Broccoli*
	Corn	Winter potatoes	Cabbage*
	Early potatoes		Cauliflower*
			SEEDS
			Lettuce
			Spinach
			Turnip
			Plant 10 wk. before first killing frost:
			SEEDS
			Beets
			Carrot

*Plants are set out later than seeds are sown because hot weather is not favorable to good growth.

Tools for the Vegetable Gardener

Basic vegetable-gardening tools have not changed for centuries, and if you do any gardening at all, you probably own most of them already. But because vegetable gardens require a great deal more digging and cultivating than flower gardens, it is a good idea to make certain that your tools fit your height, weight, and musculature. Long-handled spades are difficult for short people to use; and if you are tall, doubling over a short hoe will give you a backache. Before you buy a tool, try it for size—it should feel well balanced when you pick it up; the working end should not weigh too much; and the handle should fit your grip comfortably.

Do not buy everything at once, but start with the essentials:

- A square-ended spade and a round-ended shovel, for digging
- A steel rake, for breaking up and smoothing the soil
- A hoe, for weeding, cultivating, and opening seed furrows
- A trowel, for transplanting
- A garden hose and a watering can
- A file or sharpening stone, for keeping the cutting edges of the tools clean and well honed

In addition, you should consider investing in a wheelbarrow—it is almost a necessity if your vegetable patch is situated any distance from your house or storage shed.

A visit to the local garden-supply store will probably convince you of the need for a variety of other tools and equipment: weeders, cultivators, garden forks, tillers, sprayers, stakes, netting, fencing. All have their uses, depending on how much gardening you do and the problems you face. But buy them only when you really need them.

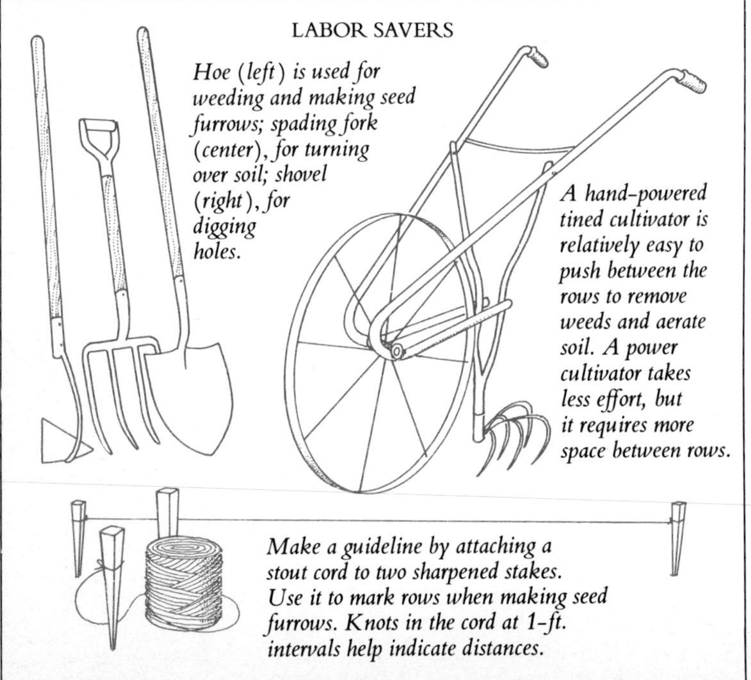

LABOR SAVERS

Hoe (left) is used for weeding and making seed furrows; spading fork (center), for turning over soil; shovel (right), for digging holes.

A hand-powered tined cultivator is relatively easy to push between the rows to remove weeds and aerate soil. A power cultivator takes less effort, but it requires more space between rows.

Make a guideline by attaching a stout cord to two sharpened stakes. Use it to mark rows when making seed furrows. Knots in the cord at 1-ft. intervals help indicate distances.

How to Improve Your Soil

The quality of a tomato, an eggplant, or a crisp green pepper depends first on the variety; it also reflects soil conditions. Vegetables may grow to maturity in poor, uncultivated ground—but they will not produce their best crops. Neither will the soil continue to produce summer after summer if its essential nutrients are diminished or if it is allowed to become dense and hard packed.

What can you do to improve your soil? First, determine the soil texture. If it is heavy and dense, it may contain too much clay; if it is loose and light, it probably has an overabundance of sand. The perfect garden soil is loamy and friable: it is dark and rich in color, and when you work a handful into a ball, it molds easily and keeps its shape but crumbles at a touch. Clay soil forms into a dense ball, which will break up into large, solid clods when you give it a poke. Sandy soil will not hold together at all. Both clay and sandy soils may be deficient in organic matter, which, as it decays, separates and lightens clay particles, while it binds sandy particles together and increases their water-holding capacity. Thus, adding quantities of composted leaves, grass clippings, straw, or manure will eventually change the soil consistency, making it loose enough for seedlings to thrust their way through but dense enough to support their roots. By adding organic matter you will also enrich the soil with nutrients that all plants must have in order to grow and flourish.

The key to soil improvement, then, is the addition of organic matter, and one of the best sources of organic matter is a compost pile (see p. 595). But to begin, almost any soft vegetable matter will do. You can use dried leaves (shredded and bagged with a lawn mower, if you have one), vegetable wastes from the kitchen, hay from a local farmer, or well-rotted manure. All of these help to improve the soil. Add nitrogenous fertilizer to them, to aid in decomposition, and spread to a depth of 2–3 inches. Then dig the additions in by hand or with a rotary tiller if you have access to one.

Soil cultivation is best done in fall when the ground is warm and dry and when you have the winter months ahead to break down the materials into humus. By spring the additions will be blended in, making the soil richer and more friable.

All plants need a proper balance of nutrients—the major three are nitrogen, phosphorus, and potassium. Soils deficient in any one of these elements will not produce healthy plants. One way to ensure proper nutrient balance is to spread on an all-purpose garden fertilizer. Or you can have your soil tested through the office of your county extension agent, in order to learn what deficiencies are present and how to correct them. Many nurseries and garden centers also do soil testing. (For more information on fertilizers and on soil testing, see p. 594.)

The mysteries of pH. If your soil, enriched and fertilized as it is, still does not nurture healthy plants, the reason may be a matter of pH—the term for the degree of acidity or alkalinity of the soil. This is measured on a scale of 1 (totally acid) to 14 (totally alkaline).

Acidity is a common problem, especially in the eastern portion of the United States. Sandy or clay soil, or ground where pines, oaks, or rhododendrons thrive, will probably measure on the lower, acidic end of the pH scale. Vegetables grow best in a soil that has a pH reading of between 6 and 7. If your soil is too acid, the imbalance can be corrected with a dressing of finely ground limestone. Extremely alkaline soil can be treated with peat moss or powdered sulfur. (For a more detailed discussion of pH, see p. 594.)

Know Your Region's Frost Dates

The frost-free states of America's Sun Belt can produce vegetables during most of the year, but in other states winter ends the gardening season. American winters vary enormously in length and severity: a gardener in Minnesota can be sure of only about 100 growing days, while a Georgian may have 300. The length of the growing season is defined by the customary dates of the last frost in spring and the first killing frost in fall. Gardeners use these dates to judge when planting should begin and how long the growing season can be stretched. To find out the frost dates in your area, check with your gardening center or county extension agent. Remember that frost dates are a local phenomenon, dependent on such factors as elevation and proximity to large bodies of water. If you live in a valley or away from the coast, for example, your planting season will be shorter than that of someone in your region who lives on a hill or near the ocean. Set up your planting calendar according to the frost dates in your area. It is also a good idea to watch out for frost warnings so that you can protect plantings.

"As soon as the ground can be worked" is a phrase that you will find printed on many seed packets. Early plantings of vegetables that withstand frost (spinach, onions, and peas, for instance) can begin as soon as the soil has lost its sogginess.

To test whether your soil is workable, squeeze a bit of it into a ball in your hand. If the ball crumbles easily, you can begin gardening. If it holds its shape, the soil is still too moist; wait another few days. Seeds sown in wet soil are likely to rot rather than germinate.

STRETCHING THE SEASONS

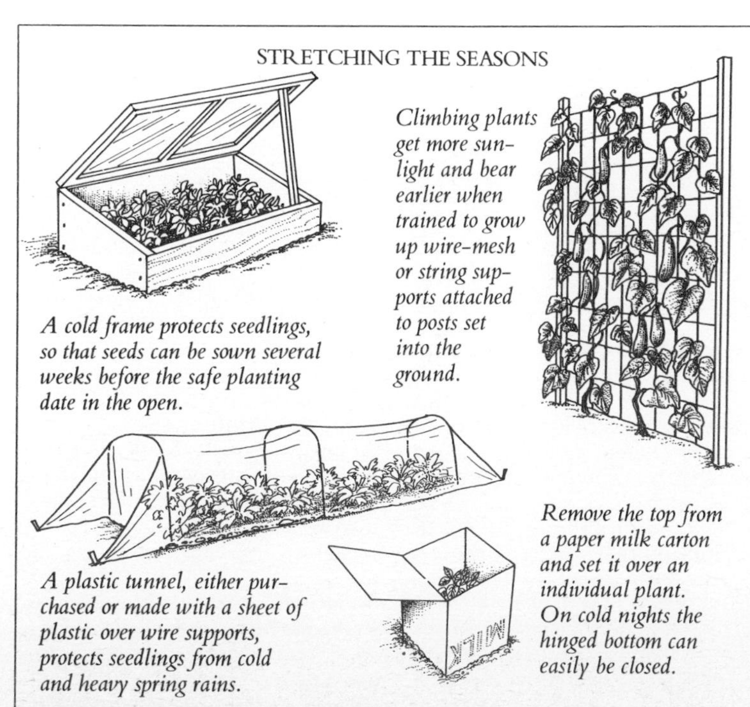

A cold frame protects seedlings, so that seeds can be sown several weeks before the safe planting date in the open.

Climbing plants get more sunlight and bear earlier when trained to grow up wire-mesh or string supports attached to posts set into the ground.

A plastic tunnel, either purchased or made with a sheet of plastic over wire supports, protects seedlings from cold and heavy spring rains.

Remove the top from a paper milk carton and set it over an individual plant. On cold nights the hinged bottom can easily be closed.

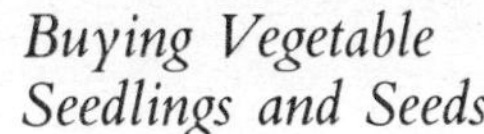

Buying Vegetable Seedlings and Seeds

Some vegetables, including root crops such as carrots and parsnips, must be sown directly into the ground as seeds. Others can be started in flats or pots and then set in the garden as small plants called seedlings.

Buying seedlings. In spring most garden centers are overflowing with flats (usually small boxes with six or eight plants growing in each) and single pots containing seedlings of a variety of vegetables: broccoli, cabbage, lettuce, tomatoes, cucumbers. Such commercially grown plants are convenient. They save time and eliminate the often risky effort of starting seeds indoors at home. For those who lack sunny window space, they are essential.

When you buy seedlings, however, you are limited to a small number of varieties. And if you buy them at a supermarket, you may not be able to get the facts you need—whether a particular tomato plant is a late or an early bearer, for example, or what variety it is. Small growers usually give you this information.

The advantage of single plants in their own pots is that they do not require separating, which might cause root damage. But if you need larger quantities, flats are better because they are cheaper.

Check the plant stems. They should be short and thick; tall, spindly plants probably have weak root systems and may never recover from the jolt of transplanting. Take a close look at the foliage; if it is yellowish or discolored, the plant may be diseased or poorly nourished. A purplish hue on cabbage, broccoli, and cauliflower plants, however, indicates that they have been "hardened off" to make them ready for early planting. (For instructions on setting out seedlings, see p. 549.)

Buying seeds. If you have enough sunny space in your house, or if you have a greenhouse or cold frame, you can grow your own seedlings. (See p. 548.)

How do you choose among the enormous variety of types, colors, shapes, and sizes available for each vegetable? First, obtain a seed catalog. Ask your local garden center to recommend one or more reputable seedsmen who specialize in seeds for your area. Then send a postcard to the company requesting a catalog.

Evaluate each catalog entry according to disease resistance (if it is resistant to the diseases that commonly attack the plant, the catalog will say so), size of plant, yield (heavy yielders will be indicated), and the number of days to harvest. A variety that has won an All-America Award has performed well in trial plots throughout the country—an important indication of quality.

New varieties are often improvements over older varieties. They may be more disease resistant or have a larger yield. The plant may need less room for growth, or its produce may have a better flavor.

In deciding how much seed you should buy, choose the smallest packet. It usually provides adequate seeds for a 25-foot row, and 25 feet will grow up to 20 pounds of beets, 25 pounds of carrots, or 20 pounds of lettuce. Although most seeds will remain viable when kept in a cool, dry place, it is usually safer to buy only as much as you need each year. Catalogs also offer some vegetable seeds in easy-to-handle forms—either "pelleted" (coated with a claylike material to make each seed larger and easier to plant) or secured to a water-soluble tape. The seeds on tapes are spaced at the proper distances; all you have to do is lay the strip in a shallow furrow and cover it with soil. Tapes eliminate the need for thinning; but if some of the seeds fail to germinate, you will have empty spaces in your row. Both pellets and tapes are considerably more expensive than plain seeds.

Planting Seeds

Indoors

You can gain up to 10 weeks extra growing time if you start certain vegetables indoors. Peppers, eggplant, cauliflower, and tomatoes are among the vegetables seldom sown directly in the garden; they are usually started indoors and transplanted. Some basic techniques for indoor seed planting of annual flowers are discussed on page 287. These same techniques can also be used to start vegetables indoors—with the following additional tips.

Potting soils. Do not use plain garden soil. It harbors weed seeds and fungi that can prevent your vegetable seeds from growing properly. Buy sterilized potting soil, or use a mixture of peat moss and sand or vermiculite. Milled sphagnum moss is often recommended for small seeds. Soilless mixtures ("synthetic soils") must be given a liquid fertilizer solution, because they contain no nutrients themselves.

Potting containers. Use flats for all small seeds. Larger seeds can be sown in individual pots of clay, plastic, or peat. Peat pots can be put directly into the ground, where they will decompose; thus, the seedlings suffer less shock from transplanting.

Schedule indoor plantings with an eye to the length of time each vegetable takes to grow and when it can be set out. Peppers, for instance, need 8 to 10 weeks indoors and should be planted outside well after the last frost. Leek seedlings should be set out in early spring, at the age of 12 weeks. Sow cabbage seeds five to seven weeks before setting plants out, cucumbers three to four weeks beforehand.

Most seeds need fairly warm soil to germinate; so keep flats or pots in a warm spot. Cover them until seeds sprout, to keep out light and retain soil moisture. Keep track of expected germinating times. If, for instance, no eggplant sprouts appear by three weeks after sowing, something has gone wrong, and you had better buy a few plants. After the seeds sprout, place them where they will get maximum light.

The "damping off" problem. The conditions of warmth and humidity that encourage seed germination also encourage the growth of fungi that can prevent germination or cause seedlings to collapse in a matter of hours. You can prevent this "damping off" disease by using purchased sterile potting soil, by being careful not to overwater or overfertilize seedlings, and by keeping a watchful eye on your seed trays for signs of too much moisture. If water drops collect on the insides of the plastic or glass coverings, remove them and wipe or shake the water out before replacing them. You can also dust your seeds with a fungicide, such as Benomyl, before sowing them.

Thinning and potting. When seeds have sprouted and young plants have their first set of true leaves, thin out the flat, removing smaller specimens so that the stronger ones will have room to grow. Snip stems with a small scissors; do not pull or you may disturb root systems. Later on, when seedlings are established and the flat is crowded again, prick out the seedlings. Very delicately handling a label stake or fork, use the pointed end to separate the seedlings and transplant them into individual $2\frac{1}{2}$- to 3-inch pots. If they have been growing in synthetic soil, use a mixture of synthetic and potting soil in the new pot to accustom the plant to the heavier quality of garden soil. Water transplants immediately with a weak solution of liquid fertilizer to reduce the shock of transplanting.

Hardening off. Seedlings grown indoors have been treated with tender loving care far beyond anything they will experience in ordinary garden conditions. They must be toughened—that is, conditioned to lower and more variable temperatures and to far less water—before being transplanted. The easiest and safest hardening-off method is to use a cold frame (see p. 288).

When the spring sun begins to warm, and certainly no later than one week before you plan to set out your seedlings, put them inside the frame. If the weather is bright and sunny, protect the tender plants from too much sun by anchoring newspapers over the glass cover. Prop open the lid of the frame a little more each day as the weather warms, making certain that the temperature inside the frame never rises above 70° F. Close the frame at night if temperatures drop below 55° F. If a cold snap occurs, cover the frame with a blanket.

PLANTING SEEDS INDOORS

Weeks to sow indoors before last frost		Weeks to germination	Set out transplants
Broccoli	5–7	1–2	After frost, late summer
Brussels sprouts	4–6	1–2	After frost, late summer
Cabbage	5–8	1–2	After frost, late summer
Cauliflower	5–8	1–2	After frost, late summer
Cucumbers	2–3	1–2	2 wk. after frost
Eggplant	8–9	2–3	Midspring, early summer
Leeks	10–12	2–3	Mid to late spring
Head lettuce	3–5	2–3	After frost
Onions (globe)	6–8	2–3	After frost
Peppers	8–10	1–2	Mid to late spring
Tomatoes	6–8	2–3	Mid to late spring

Outdoors

You have dug up your garden plot, enriched it with organic material, and fertilized it. You have raked out the stones. Now you are ready to plant. Check your garden plan to see that rows run from north to south if this is practical; that tall plants will be on the northern and eastern sides of the plot; and that you have planned to grow early crops (lettuce, peas, spinach) as well as hot-weather vegetables (tomatoes, eggplant, peppers). Remember to design succession plantings: early lettuce followed by late carrots, or radishes followed by beets. Remember, too, that you need not plant entire rows of quick-maturing or very productive plants, such as lettuce or Swiss chard. Plant partial rows and follow up with more plantings later.

Sowing the seeds. Mark your row with stakes at each end, and tie a length of twine between them. Make furrows, barely $\frac{1}{2}$ inch deep for small seeds, perhaps 1 inch deep for the larger ones. Scatter small seeds evenly and close together. Larger seeds can be planted about an inch apart, but for exact distances see the instructions beginning on page 550 on how to raise specific vegetables.

Especially where soil tends to crust over, cover small seeds with a thin layer of an artificial soil mixture, or of soil mixed with sand or fine peat moss. Tamp down over the seeds and water gently. Mark the row with a plant label on which you have written—in indelible ink—the name of the vegetable, the variety, and the planting date.

Seeds must have continuously moist soil around them until they sprout. Check for moisture every day, and if the soil seems too dry, water it lightly. Do not overwater: soggy soil can cause the larger seeds to rot—the soil should be damp, not waterlogged.

Watch for germination. Cold soil and cool weather both impede seed sprouting. Lettuce will germinate in about 10 days in early spring, but in only 4 or 5 days when it is warmer. Carrots and parsnips are slow to sprout; so you should not despair if, after two weeks, nothing has happened. After three weeks, though, you should put in a new row; something has prevented germination. Perhaps the soil was too dry or too cold, the furrow was too deep, or the surface had a crust too hard for seedlings to push through.

Thinning. For beginning gardeners especially, thinning can be a painful process. It seems wasteful to destroy perfectly good seedlings. But it must be done. If unthinned, radishes will not form bulbs. Carrots will not grow or will twist grotesquely. Lettuce will form puny heads.

You should begin thinning when the seedlings are about 1 or 2 inches high. (For the optimum separation between plants, see the discussion of individual vegetables beginning on p. 550.) Do not try to thin out seedlings all at once. A thick row of leaf lettuce can be thinned at first by removing every other plant. You can remove more plants in later thinnings, when the lettuce will be large enough to eat. When thinning a thickly seeded row, pull each plant out carefully, lifting straight up, to avoid disturbing the roots of neighboring plants.

It is possible to transplant well-grown seedlings from a thinned row if you take steps to avoid damaging their roots or stems. Use a small trowel or label stake to dig them up along with a small clump of soil surrounding their roots, and handle them gently. When transplanting small seedlings, move them into soft, fine, moist soil, and shade them with a loose canopy of newspapers or grass clippings.

Setting plants out. When your indoor-grown seedlings have been sufficiently hardened off, wait for a cloudy day to set them out. (Commercially grown seedlings should have been hardened off when you buy them.) Too much heat can wither a plant as quickly as dry soil. If no clouds are imminent, plant the seedlings in the late afternoon, and shade them with newspapers, bushel baskets, or anything that will shield them from the sun's rays but still let in a little air.

When you are ready to set out your plants, dig evenly spaced holes according to the directions for each vegetable. (See discussions of individual vegetables beginning on p. 550.) Fill the holes with water, and let it soak into the soil—this will give the roots of each plant sufficient moisture to make a good beginning.

If you are using peat pots, the plant can be set out in the pot, but be sure to slit its sides in two or three places to allow for root growth. Bury the pot completely in the ground, so that it will remain moist and disintegrate. Plants grown in plastic pots or flats must be handled carefully. Remove or cut out each plant along with the soil that surrounds its roots. When setting these in the holes you have dug, make sure that the garden soil is pushed firmly but gently around the root balls. Leave a slight soil depression around each plant to collect and hold moisture. Then water well.

The vegetables you have carefully planted in soil that you have improved and enriched will thrive if they get plenty of water and lots of sun and if weeds are eliminated. The weeds compete with the vegetables for whatever moisture and nutrients are available and will grow rampant in rich, well-cultivated soil. And if you allow weeds to grow undisturbed at the beginning, when you pull them up later, you may injure the roots of plants you want to keep.

Work out a weeding program, a once- or twice-weekly trip between your garden rows with a hoe. When weeds are small, you can simply scrape them away. But if you dig your hoe more than half an inch or so into the ground, you run the risk of cutting into vegetable roots. Large weeds and those growing within the rows have to be pulled out by hand. Weed pulling is easier if the soil is moist; try to weed after a rainstorm, or schedule weedings for the day after waterings.

Watering. During hot, rainless weather, or whenever the garden soil becomes powdery and dry, you will have to water your garden. Watering is particularly important for young plants with shallow roots. As plants grow larger, their roots thrust deeper into the soil, where moisture remains even when the surface soil is dry. Thorough, deep waterings are far more effective than brief, shallow ones. Mere sprinkling encourages plant roots to stay on the surface where they are susceptible to hoeing damage and to the drying heat of the sun.

A garden hose is a basic watering implement. Adjust the nozzle for a fine spray, prop it on a garden fence or in a forked stick, and let it spray for an hour. Then move it to saturate another portion of your garden. A rotating sprinkler is a great convenience, as is a perforated plastic hose that you lay down along the garden row. Whatever you use, schedule your waterings for the morning or early afternoon, so that leaves can dry off before nightfall. Wet leaves are more susceptible to fungous diseases. Overcast days are better than sunny days, because the water will evaporate less quickly.

Plants need between 1 and $1\frac{1}{2}$ inches of water each week. You can keep track of the amount yours are getting simply by leaving an open container in your garden, marked off in half inches. During dry midsummers especially, be sure to water your garden well once a week.

Mulching. A mulch is a soil cover composed, usually, of organic materials, such as leaves, hay, or grass clippings. Mulch is made in nature every year by the dead leaves, twigs, and plants that fall to the ground and decompose there. Gardeners who use mulch do not have as much weeding to do and find that a layer of mulch around their plants helps to conserve moisture in the soil. It may also help to prevent the spread of various soil-borne diseases to fruit and foliage.

An organic mulch decomposes slowly and is incorporated into the soil. It adds nutrients to the soil, makes it looser and more friable, and provides good living conditions for earthworms, which help aerate the soil, and for many beneficial microorganisms.

Some good mulching materials include hay, especially "spoiled hay," which has already begun to decompose; grass clippings after they have begun to dry and turn gray; shredded or composted leaves; manure mixed with straw; peat moss mixed with sawdust or wood chips (peat moss alone will pack down and dry, and water will not penetrate it). Sawdust, wood chips, and pine needles are also good mulching materials, but they may need an addition of lime, to counteract their acidity, and of nitrogenous fertilizer, to compensate for the nitrogen used by the microorganisms that cause decay. The black plastic strips sold as

Asparagus

mulching material in garden-supply stores will not decompose. They are useful for quick soil protection and for certain plants—melons, for instance—that grow much faster under heat-conserving black plastic.

When seedlings are about 4 inches high, spread a thick layer of mulching material among the plants and between the rows. As summer progresses and the mulch breaks down, add more. Sprinkle mulch with nitrogenous fertilizer to hasten the decomposing process.

If you keep a perpetual cover of mulch on your garden, the soil will take longer to warm up and dry in spring than will unmulched soil. For early planting, therefore, push aside the mulch where you intend to make seed furrows, and wait for the ground to warm up and dry.

Hints for a healthy garden. To protect vegetables from diseases and discourage pest infestations, here are a few simple rules to follow.

- Choose seeds of disease-resistant varieties whenever you can.
- Inspect store-bought plants carefully. Spotty or discolored leaves may be signs of damage, insufficient nutrients, or disease.
- Pull up and throw away any diseased plant. Do not compost it.
- Rotate crops, especially cabbage and its many relatives, to prevent the spread of soil-borne diseases.
- Weed often and dispose of any weeds that harbor plant-eating pests.
- Do not work in your garden immediately after a rainstorm. Wet leaves are more vulnerable to damage and disease, and walking over rain-soaked soil will harden it.
- After harvesting each crop, destroy what remains of the plants. If they were healthy, compost them.

Whatever precautions you take, diseases and pests will occur. In the discussions that follow, you will learn what can go wrong with each vegetable and how to prevent or treat the disorder. See also "Plant Disorders," starting on page 600.

Asparagus is one of the few perennials in the vegetable and fruit garden—the others being rhubarb and strawberries. Like them, asparagus offers the pleasure of a crop to enjoy year after year. A well-cultivated asparagus bed can produce for 20 seasons or more. Bed preparation is much more extensive than for annual vegetables, and the asparagus will not be ready for harvesting until the third year after you plant it. But if you have the time and the space, there are few more rewarding crops, for asparagus is an expensive vegetable to buy at the market. If you decide to grow your own, remember that asparagus retains its delicate flavor when frozen.

Do not try to grow asparagus if you live in an area such as Florida where winters stay fairly warm. Asparagus needs the dormant period that cold winters provide.

Asparagus 'Mary Washington'

How to Grow Asparagus

Gardeners usually start their asparagus beds with roots, not seeds, because a seed-planted bed requires another year's growing time. You can buy roots from a nursery or mail-order house. Allow 25 feet of row for every 12 plants, with rows spaced 4–5 feet apart.

Asparagus can be grown in any well-drained, fertile soil. Test for pH—the soil should be slightly acid but not below pH 6. As soon as the ground can be worked, dig a trench 18 inches wide and 10 inches deep. Add 5–10–5 fertilizer (about 5 pounds per 75 feet of row) to a liberal quantity of organic matter, and mix into the soil you have removed. Fill the trench with this mixture to about 6 inches below ground level. Tamp it down and place the roots on top, crown side up, 2 feet apart. Cover with 2–3 inches of soil. As the plants sprout, add more soil until the trench is full.

To increase the growth rate of asparagus plants, feed them with a 5–10–5 fertilizer two to three months after planting. Each spring and fall fertilize again. Watch for weeds. Hoe them out shallowly to avoid injuring the underground stems. Mulching around the plants will help keep weeds down and moisture in. In fall, when the leaves have been killed by frost, cut off the top growth to ground level and mulch the bed again.

Over the first two years an extensive root system will grow to feed and support the stalks. The second spring after planting, you can pick a few shoots when they are about 7 inches high—but restrict the harvesting to a month at most. From the third year after planting, cut all shoots except the very thin ones. Harvest shoots when they are 5–8 inches tall and buds are still tight; when buds begin to open, the spears are past their prime. Stop harvesting when new stalks start growing thinner. (The harvest season lasts six to eight weeks.) Leave these stalks; they will grow into tall, fernlike branches that will help feed the roots.

Harvest by bending the stalks at ground level until they snap, leaving the white part of the stalk in the ground. If you cannot use them immediately, keep the stalks upright in water until cooking time.

What Can Go Wrong With Asparagus

Rust, once the major cause of failure, can be controlled by buying rust-resistant varieties. If small beetles appear on the stalks, treat with rotenone or some other recommended pesticide. Above all, keep the bed free of weeds.

Varieties of Asparagus to Grow

The most popular and widely available variety is the rust-resistant 'Mary Washington.' Other proven varieties are 'Waltham Washington,' 'U.C. 66,' and 'California 500,' the last two of which are grown primarily on the West Coast.

Beans, Lima

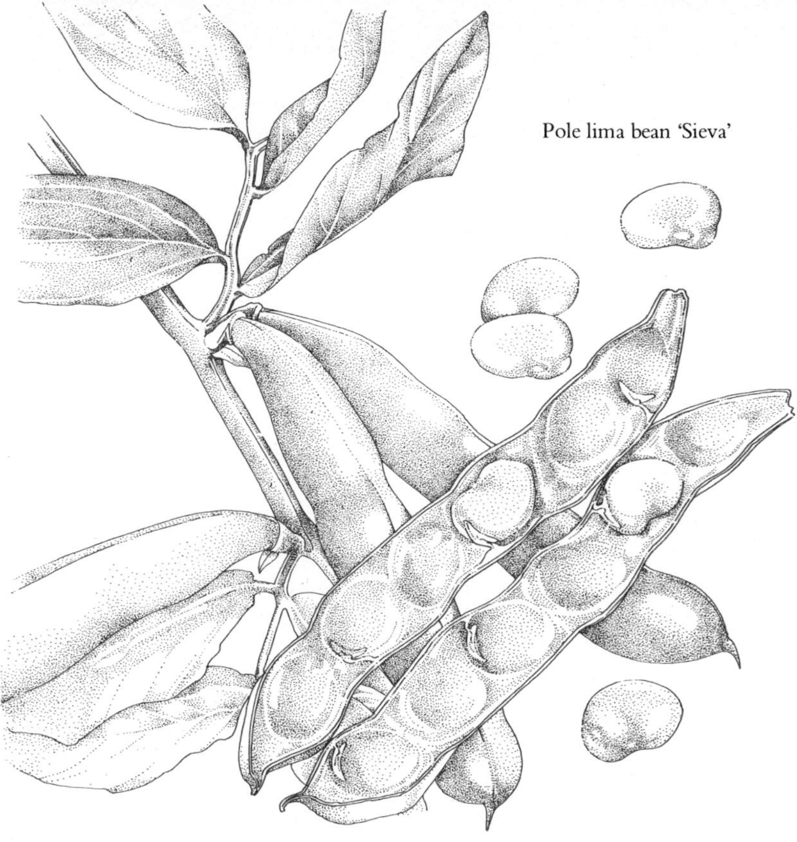

Pole lima bean 'Sieva'

Like all beans, lima beans and baby lima beans (the small-seeded varieties called butter beans) belong to the highly nutritious legume family. Besides being good for you, limas have a delicious nutlike flavor and are relatively easy to grow. However, they do need a long, warm summer to mature and for this reason are grown mainly in warmer regions. (If your climate is not right for limas, you may want to grow fava, or broad, beans, which need a long, cool growing season and have the added advantage of producing well with little care.)

Limas, like the snap beans that are discussed on the following pages, can be grown as either bush plants or pole plants. Pole beans give larger yields in a smaller space than do the bush varieties, but they take somewhat longer to ripen. Pole lima beans mature in about three months—about two weeks after the bush varieties begin to yield.

How to Grow Lima Beans

When preparing the soil for lima beans, fertilize it with a 5–10–10 mixture. Sow the seeds at about the same time that you set out such warmth-loving plants as tomatoes, peppers, and cucumbers.

Plant bush lima seeds 1–1½ inches deep, spacing the seeds 2–3 inches apart, in rows 2 feet apart. Bush beans require only about 4 inches between plants; so unless each seed germinates, thinning is not needed.

The illustration below shows ways to support pole beans, both limas and snap beans. Build the supports before you sow the seeds. Supports for limas should be sturdier than those for snap beans (because lima plants are heavier) and taller (because limas grow up to 8 feet high, compared with 6 feet for snap beans).

If you are growing pole beans along a fence, sow single seeds 3–5 inches apart. Thin seedlings to a spacing of 6–10 inches. To grow plants on poles, stake out the supports 2 feet apart in rows 3 feet apart. Sow about six seeds around each pole, and thin to three or four plants.

Because lima beans are particularly sensitive to mildew and other diseases, cultivate them shallowly and only during dry weather. Water them at soil level (never from above), and always do it in the morning so that the sun will have a chance to dry off moisture that falls on the plants. Mulch to conserve moisture in the soil and to keep weeds down. Fertilize sparingly.

When the pod is round and firm, and the shape of the beans is visible inside, it is time to harvest. Pick steadily as beans ripen, for mature beans on the plant will discourage the growth of new ones.

At season's end you can let the remaining beans dry before picking them. Sterilize them in a very low oven for about an hour, and seal them in jars. Home-dried limas can be stored for several months.

What Can Go Wrong With Lima Beans

If limas blossom in extremely hot weather, they may not set. In the South the lima-bean pod borer may devour the seeds inside the pods. Early plantings are less vulnerable, and cleaning up leaves removes the insects' nesting places.

Varieties of Lima Beans to Grow

For bush-lima-bean plants, select 'Fordhook 242' or 'Baby Fordhook,' which are more resistant to high temperatures at pod-setting time. For pole varieties, take your choice of 'Florida Butter,' 'Sieva,' or that old favorite, 'King of the Garden.'

METHODS OF SUPPORTING BEANS

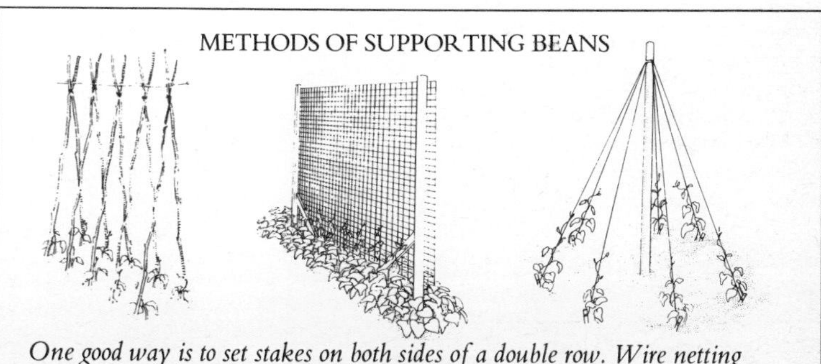

One good way is to set stakes on both sides of a double row. Wire netting can also be used, or a pole with string and pegs made into a tepee shape.

Beans, Snap

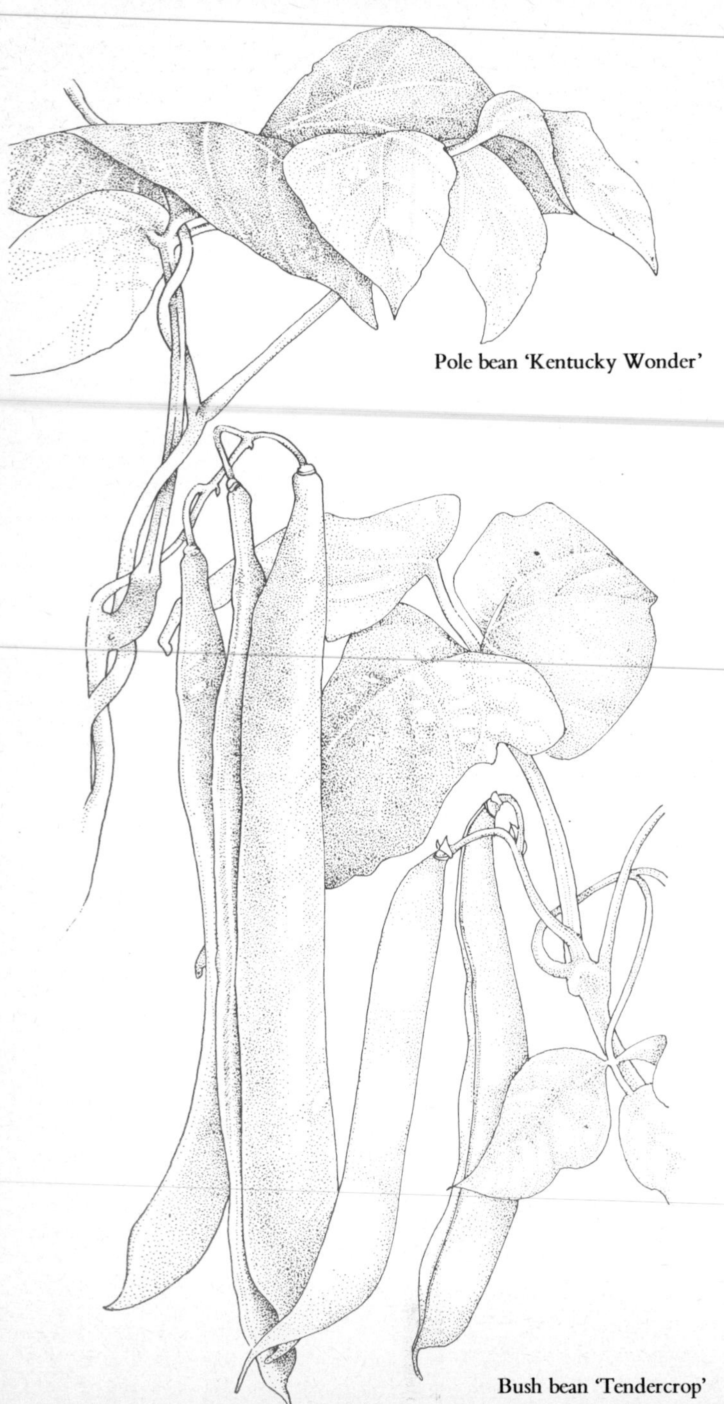

Pole bean 'Kentucky Wonder'

Bush bean 'Tendercrop'

A favorite with vegetable gardeners is the snap bean—easy to grow, prolific, and nutritious. Both the green and yellow (wax) beans that you buy in the market are snap beans and can be grown in any good soil either as bushy plants or as pole beans, climbing vinelike upon a tall support. Bush beans are usually smaller and tenderer than the pole variety, but many people consider pole beans more flavorful. If you have enough space, try both kinds.

Bush-bean plants, which grow to about 1½ feet, mature in about 60 days (or sooner when planted in midsummer) and yield for two or three weeks. Because they mature in such a short time, you can make succession plantings for a constant supply during the summer. Pole-bean plants, which grow to a height of 6 feet or more, take about two weeks longer to mature than bush varieties do, but they bear for a much longer time—about six to eight weeks—and they produce a larger crop. Per square foot of garden plot, pole beans are a more productive crop than bush beans.

How to Grow Snap Beans

Beans, like peas, are legumes, and with all legumes they share the ability to absorb nitrogen from the atmosphere and add it to the soil. Because soil bacteria help in this nitrogen accumulation, you may want to dust your bean seeds with a commercial preparation containing these bacteria—called a soil inoculant—before you plant them.

In preparing your soil, use a 5–10–5 fertilizer at the rate of 3–4 pounds per 100 square feet. Do not apply a fertilizer with a high nitrogen count, or you will grow enormously leafy plants with few beans.

Bean seeds are especially susceptible to fungous infections that cause the seeds to rot. Therefore, the seeds you buy probably have been treated with a fungicide called Captan. This preparation is poisonous if eaten; so be careful not to allow small children to handle the seeds. Some seed companies offer untreated seeds, but in only a few varieties.

Planting bush beans. Make sure that the soil has become thoroughly warm and is no longer soaked from winter rains and snows. Seed catalogs generally recommend soil temperatures of at least 60° F, which is usually attained a week or two before the average date of the last spring frost. If you want to be on the safe side, delay planting until the time of the last expected frost.

Space your rows approximately 2 feet apart, with furrows 1 inch deep. Plant a seed every 2–3 inches. Because bush beans need only about 4 inches of space between plants, thinning will not be necessary unless every seed germinates. Furrows for midsummer sowings should be 2 inches deep, thus putting the seeds closer to the soil moisture. Whether you are sowing in spring or midsummer, however, never cover the seeds with more than an inch of soil. Too much overlay may prevent seedlings from pushing through.

As bush beans have a fairly short harvest period, plan to make succession plantings every three weeks, until about eight weeks before the first fall frost is expected. If possible, do not plant later crops of beans in the same place you grew them earlier in the year.

Cultivating bush beans. When bush-bean plants are 6 inches tall, sprinkle a 5–10–5 fertilizer in a band on either side of the row, being careful to keep the fertilizer from touching the leaves or stems. Keep the soil well moistened, but never water from above—and never touch the plants when the leaves are wet, as this may spread any diseases that the beans may have. Mulch to conserve moisture and to keep down weeds.

Harvesting bush beans. Pick bush beans before they are mature—while they will still snap when you bend them, and before the seeds inside the pod swell visibly. To keep each plant productive for two to three weeks, be sure to remove any pods that have grown large and tough. Ripe beans left on the vine will cause the plant to slow down production.

Be gentle when harvesting. Hold the fruiting stem with one hand while you carefully pull off the bean with the other; otherwise, you may pull away some of the plant as well.

Planting pole beans. Pole-bean plants will produce for much of the summer if you provide sufficient nutrients. Before planting, work in about ½ pound of 5–10–5 fertilizer for each 25 feet of row. Plant pole beans somewhat later than bush beans—when the last frost is due.

You will need to build a solid support system for your pole beans—one that can bear the weight of the plants and hold up in a high wind. (For illustrations of pole-bean supports, see p. 551.) Most gardeners use lumberyard stakes or rough wood poles with the bark left on them to provide a grip for the vines. Set the poles 3 feet apart in rows 3–4 feet apart, and drive them 2 feet into the soil. If you are planting the beans in a corner of the garden, drive three poles into the ground in the shape of a triangle, and tie them securely at the top, tepee fashion.

A tall chicken-wire trellis or solid fence can also be used as a support for pole beans. Be sure that the trellis or fence is on the north side of your garden, where it will cast the least shade. Anchor the trellis solidly in the ground so that it will be able to withstand winds after it has become laden with vines.

Once you have built your support, sow the seeds 1–1½ inches deep. Along a fence or trellis, sow seeds 2 inches apart and thin the seedlings later to 4–6 inches. For pole growing, sow six seeds around each pole. Thin to the four strongest seedlings.

Cultivating pole beans. When the pole-bean plants begin to climb, help them up their support by winding the curly, climbing stem onto its pole or wire fencing. Always wind the stem in the same direction that it curls. Add fertilizer in midseason in a band 6 inches from the plants or in a ring around the poles. As with bush beans, it is important that no fertilizer touch the leaves or stem. Water well at ground level, being careful not to wet the plants. A thick mulch will help keep moisture in the soil and discourage weeds.

Harvesting pole beans. If your plants have received plenty of moisture and food, and if the weather has been warm, you can expect to start harvesting pole beans about 2½ months after planting. Do not pick them when they are small, as you do with the bush varieties. Pole beans should be large and thick when you harvest them for the best flavor.

To ensure a continuous crop, harvest all the pods as soon as they seem mature. The more you pick, the more you will harvest. As with bush beans, pick carefully. Hold the fruiting stems with one hand as you pluck a pod with the other. If you pull off the beans roughly, you risk injuring the vine.

The harvesting season should last until the first frost. If at that time too many beans for immediate use are still on the vine, wait until the pods become dry and beige colored before picking them. Then shell the beans, and heat them for an hour in an oven set at its lowest temperature. This will kill any weevils that may have infested them. Dried pole beans are good for use in soup and stews, and they can be kept stored in sealed jars for several months.

What Can Go Wrong With Snap Beans

In some areas Japanese beetles have become a major pest of snap beans. If there are not too many beetles, knock them off the leaves into a pail of water covered with a film of kerosine or gasoline. This method must be continued every day until there is a significant reduction in the number of beetles. If the beetles are too numerous to knock off, spray the plants with carbaryl, being careful to follow the instructions on the label. You can also take steps to prevent next year's crop from being attacked by Japanese beetles. Ask at your garden center about milky disease spores. This is, in effect, a bacterial soil treatment that introduces a disease harmful only to Japanese beetle grubs, which live in the ground through the winter.

Mexican bean beetles—copper-colored, black-spotted insects that look like ladybugs but are larger and yellower—and their spiny yellow larvae are also major pests of beans. Usually found on the undersides of the leaves, they chew the foliage and eat the beans as well. Several generations may reproduce in one season. To combat these pests, spray with carbaryl or malathion, or dust with rotenone. Check the label to find out when you can safely harvest beans from treated plants.

Aphids attack snap beans, as well as all other vegetables. Wash these pests off with a strong stream of water from the garden hose.

Beans are particularly sensitive to mildews and blights, especially during cool, wet weather. The best preventive measures are to avoid brushing against bean leaves when they are wet and to water during sunny hours so that leaves can dry before evening. If you notice whitish, moldy patches on the leaves, dust with a fungicide powder.

SPRAYING OFF APHIDS

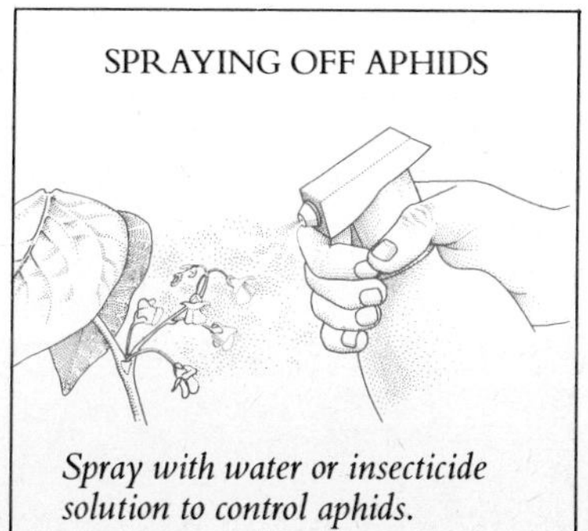

Spray with water or insecticide solution to control aphids.

INCREASING FLOWERING

On maturing plants pinch growing tips to encourage side shoots.

Varieties of Snap Beans to Grow

Bush beans. There are several good bush varieties of snap beans. 'Tendercrop' and 'Bush Blue Lake' are two top-quality green beans. 'Royalty Purple Pod' produces a purple bean that turns dark green when cooked. 'Butterwax' and 'Pencil Pod' are yellow, or wax, beans. 'Bush Romano' grows flat pods.

Pole beans. 'Kentucky Wonder' and the smaller-seeded 'Blue Lake' are two of the most popular green pole beans. 'Romano,' also called Italian pole bean, is a broad, flat bean that matures somewhat earlier than most other pole varieties. 'Burpee Golden' is yellow, and 'Royalty' grows purple beans that turn green when boiled. If you want pole beans for shelling and drying, 'Oregon Giant' is a popular variety.

Beets

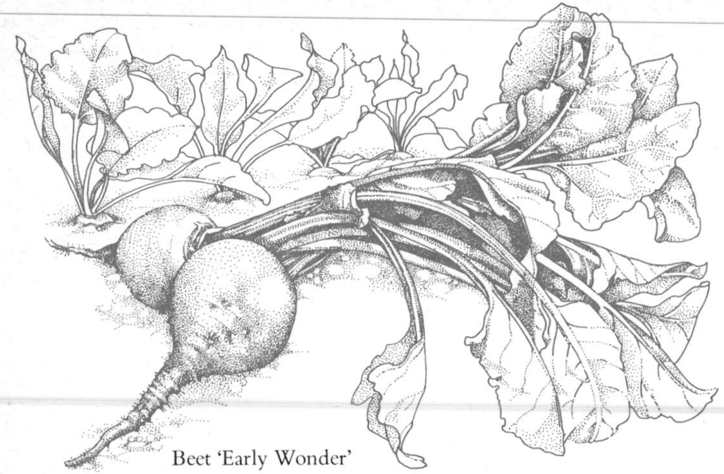

Beet 'Early Wonder'

Beets have a double attraction for vegetable gardeners: they are easy to grow, and practically the whole plant can be eaten. Although they are fairly tolerant of heat, they do best in cool climates, and they can withstand cold weather short of severe freezing. Beets mature quickly (55 to 70 days), take up little room, and require a minimum of care. One caution, however—they will not do well in soil that is extremely acid.

Beets are a root crop whose tops are also edible. When the plants are young and the leaves are tender, beet greens are excellent in salads, and as the plant matures, you can cook the greens as you would spinach. Beet roots are even more versatile. You can cook them fresh from the garden, store them in a cool place for winter use, pickle them, or can them.

How to Grow Beets

To prepare your soil for beets, spade it well, to a depth of about 8 inches, and rake it to remove stones. If your soil is very acid (beets do best in a soil with a pH of 6.0 to 7.5), work in lime at least a week before planting. (For details on liming soil, see p. 594.) Wood ashes, which contain lime and potash, are useful in reducing acidity. Just before sowing, apply a 5–10–5 fertilizer, about ½ pound for 25 feet of row.

Because beets germinate best and grow fastest in cool weather, plant the seeds as soon as the ground can be worked. In areas where summers remain relatively cool, make succession plantings at three-week intervals to ensure a continuous crop throughout the season. If you live where midsummers are long and hot, time your plantings so that the beets mature either before or after the period when daytime temperatures consistently exceed 80° F.

Seed rows for beets should be spaced at least 14 inches apart, and furrows should be ½ inch deep. Sow the seeds, which are actually clusters of three or four seeds within a casing, at 1-inch intervals. The plants will emerge in little clumps, which you should thin to one plant per inch when the seedlings are about 2 inches tall. When they reach 4 inches, thin to four to six plants per foot.

For midsummer plantings make the furrows about an inch deep, to reach the soil moisture, and cover the seeds with leaf mold, vermiculite, or some other material that will not form a crust and will allow water to run through.

Rapid growth and timely harvesting are the key factors in producing tender, juicy beets. Too little water, too few nutrients, or heavy weed infestation slows growth and results in roots that are tough and woody. If you have fertilized your beet rows before planting, you need apply only one more dressing before harvesting. When the seedlings are about 3 inches high, scatter a band of 5–10–5 fertilizer along each side of the row—about 5 ounces for every 10 feet. Then lay down a light mulch of straw, sawdust, or lawn clippings to help conserve soil moisture and keep down weeds. If weeds persist, remove them by hand within each row, and hoe shallowly between the rows to avoid injuring the beets' roots. Water regularly.

You can enjoy the produce of your beet crop early if you harvest the young, tender leaves for salad greens. But be sure to take only a few leaves at a time from each plant. The plant needs some foliage to produce nourishment and maintain growth.

Beet roots mature within 55 to 70 days, depending on the variety. When the root tops begin to push up above the ground, carefully remove the soil from around one of them to check its size. The best harvest size is between 1½ and 2 inches in diameter. Do not let beets grow much larger than this, since they tend to become fibrous as their size increases.

In harvesting, *pull* the roots out of the ground—do not dig them up. As you separate the greens from the root, leave an inch of stem on each root to prevent the root from "bleeding" (losing some of its color) when it is cooked.

Beets usually store well in a cool, dark cellar. To maintain their crispness, bury them in moist sand or peat moss, or put them in plastic bags into which you have cut a few small holes for ventilation.

What Can Go Wrong With Beets

Very early beet sowings may "bolt"—run to seed rather than form edible roots—if temperatures remain below 40° F for several weeks. If this happens, pick the leaves for use as salad greens, and sow the row again. If the beet leaves become stunted or yellowish, and you have already limed the soil, there may be a phosphorus deficiency. In this case, add fertilizer or a dressing of bone meal or superphosphate.

Beets are prey to few pests, especially where winter freeze kills bugs and larvae in the soil. In warm areas beets may be attacked by tiny yellow leaf miners, which can be controlled with malathion or some other recommended pesticide.

If you grow beets exactly where you planted them the year before, leaf spot may develop. This is a fungus that can be destroyed by spraying with a fungicide.

If beet roots develop black areas, it is an indication that the soil may be deficient in boron. You can add this to the soil by mixing ¼ teaspoon of household borax with 12 gallons of water and sprinkling the solution where you plan future beet crops.

Varieties of Beets to Grow

Beets may have red, yellow, or white roots, which may be round or tapering. Recommended red beets are 'Early Wonder,' which matures in about 55 days, and 'Lutz Green Leaf,' grown for its greens and its long-storage quality. 'Cylindra' has a long cylindrical root for easy, uniform slicing. For yellow and white varieties, try 'Burpee's Golden' and 'Burpee's White,' respectively.

Broccoli

Broccoli 'Green Comet'

Broccoli belongs to a large and varied genus, *Brassica,* that includes Brussels sprouts, cabbage, and cauliflower, and that has the ability to grow in cool weather. Not only is broccoli extremely hardy in cold weather but it requires a long, cool season for growth. It will be one of the earliest vegetables you plant in the garden each year, and it will produce its delicate flower heads in late spring and early summer. A second planting made in late summer will be ready for harvest in fall.

How to Grow Broccoli

Broccoli plantings must be timed so that the clusters of small flower buds the plant produces can be harvested while the days remain cool. To accomplish this, it is usually best to start the seeds indoors, especially in areas with short growing seasons. Seed catalogs list the number of days to harvest from the time the seedlings are planted in the garden. In addition to the 60 to 80 days indicated for outdoor growing, you should allow another four to six weeks for starting the seeds indoors. (In warm climates sow seeds directly outdoors as soon as the soil can be worked.)

Start broccoli indoors at least four weeks before the time to set out the seedlings—which you should calculate as two weeks before the date of the last expected frost. If you have a short growing season, six weeks will give you larger plants to set out. Sow the seeds ½ inch deep in flats, sprinkle a thin layer of sterile sphagnum moss or vermiculite on top, and water well. Keep the flats in a dark, cool place until the seeds sprout, or cover them with newspaper. The seedlings should stand about ½–1 inch apart. If necessary, clip out the overly crowded ones with scissors. When the plants are about 1½ inches tall, transplant them into individual pots or into flats where they will have more room. Keep the seedlings in a sunny but cool place in your house; they will not grow well in warm temperatures.

At least two weeks before the time to set out the seedlings (earlier if the weather is not too cold), place them in a cold frame or in a sunny, sheltered spot outdoors, to "harden them off"—get them used to garden temperatures.

In choosing a planting location, remember that broccoli and all its *Brassica* relatives are affected by a number of soil-borne diseases; so be careful not to plant broccoli where any *Brassica* members were grown the year before.

Prepare the soil about two weeks before transplanting time by raking in 1 pound of 5–10–10 fertilizer for every 25 feet of row. Lime the soil now if it is strongly acid and if you did not lime it the previous fall.

About two weeks before the last expected frost, set out your hardened seedlings. Place them 1½–2 feet apart in rows 3 feet apart. Protect the plants against cutworms by surrounding them with paper collars, which you can make by cutting the bottoms out of paper cups. Push each collar 1 inch into the soil. Water well, and mulch the soil thoroughly.

For a fall crop start growing seedlings in late May or in June in a cold frame or in a garden row. Sow the seeds ½ inch deep; cover with a thin layer of soil mixed with sand or peat moss to prevent crusting. Thin the seedlings to stand 1 inch apart. When they reach 5 inches, transplant them into an area where you have harvested a root crop, such as carrots. Before transplanting the seedlings, fertilize the soil.

To raise a good broccoli crop, you need abundant water and rich soil. Ensure moist soil with a thick mulch and deep, slow waterings during dry periods. At least once during the growing season, pull aside the mulch, and apply ½ pound of 10–10–10 fertilizer along every 10 feet of row. Replace the mulch, and water to soak the fertilizer into the soil. If you dig fertilizer in, you may injure the plants' shallow root systems.

A thickened cluster growing at the top of a broccoli stalk will tell you that the plant is nearing maturity. The cluster is the plant's main head and should be harvested before the flowerets begin to open. Slice off the stem 5 or 6 inches below the head. Side shoots should produce smaller clusters for two months or more.

What Can Go Wrong With Broccoli

Clubroot, blackleg, and black rot are serious diseases of broccoli that are best avoided by crop rotation. Weak, yellow plants with swollen, malformed roots indicate clubroot. To combat it, raise the soil pH to about 7.2 by applying hydrated lime, and water transplanted seedlings with a solution of quintozene.

Black lesions on the stem are signs of blackleg, while black rot causes plants to darken and decay. Both diseases affect the seeds. Spray seedlings with maneb or chlorothalonil.

If cabbage worms attack, apply *Bacillus thuringiensis.*

Varieties of Broccoli to Grow

Good early varieties of broccoli include 'Green Comet' and 'Spartan Early.' 'Waltham 29' and 'Calabrese' are recommended for fall crops.

Brussels Sprouts

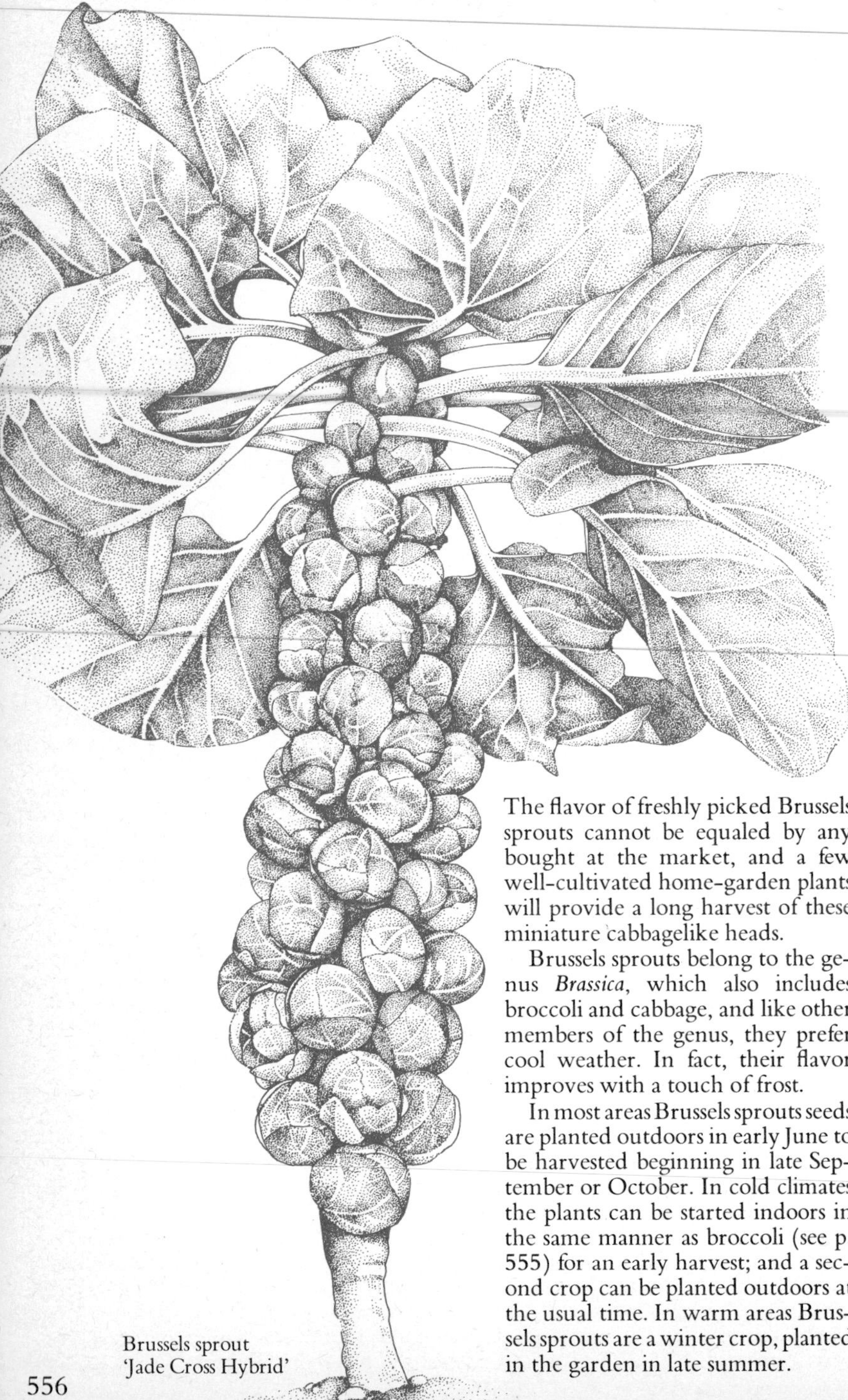

Brussels sprout
'Jade Cross Hybrid'

The flavor of freshly picked Brussels sprouts cannot be equaled by any bought at the market, and a few well-cultivated home-garden plants will provide a long harvest of these miniature cabbagelike heads.

Brussels sprouts belong to the genus *Brassica*, which also includes broccoli and cabbage, and like other members of the genus, they prefer cool weather. In fact, their flavor improves with a touch of frost.

In most areas Brussels sprouts seeds are planted outdoors in early June to be harvested beginning in late September or October. In cold climates the plants can be started indoors in the same manner as broccoli (see p. 555) for an early harvest; and a second crop can be planted outdoors at the usual time. In warm areas Brussels sprouts are a winter crop, planted in the garden in late summer.

How to Grow Brussels Sprouts

Soil preparation for Brussels sprouts is important. First, to avoid the diseases and pests common to *Brassica* relatives, choose a plot of land on which no *Brassica* vegetable was grown the previous year. Two weeks before sowing, dig organic matter—compost, well-rotted manure, or leaf mold—into the soil, and rake in about 1 pound of 5–10–10 fertilizer for every 25 feet of row. If your soil tends to be acid, add a sprinkling of lime.

Sow the seeds in groups of three or four, leaving 2 feet between clusters and 3 feet between rows.

When the seedlings are about 1½ inches tall, clip out all but the strongest plant in each group. Immediately protect these seedlings against cutworms by slipping over each plant a paper cup with its bottom removed. Set the cutworm collars about an inch deep into the soil.

Given rich, well-prepared soil, Brussels sprouts grow splendidly with little more attention. Be sure the plants get plenty of water, especially when they are young. A thick mulch around them will help the soil to retain moisture and will also keep down weeds.

When the first tiny sprouts begin to form around the bottom of the stem (some 10 to 12 weeks after sowing), scatter a 6-inch band of 5–10–10 fertilizer around each plant, and water the fertilizer into the ground.

Because Brussels sprouts grow slowly, their rows make excellent areas for intercropping. If you plant radishes or lettuce between the Brussels sprouts plants, you will harvest these quick-maturing vegetables long before your sprouts grow large enough to shade the area.

Brussels sprouts form all along the main stalk, growing in the spaces between the leafstalks. When the sprouts are hard and firm and at least ½ inch in diameter, they can be harvested. The best harvest size is from ½ inch to 1½ inches.

Properly harvested, one plant can produce for six to eight weeks. The sprouts at the bottom of the stalk will be ready first. To harvest, pull off the lower leaves by snapping them sharply downward. Remove the leaves gradually, from the bottom up, as you progressively harvest the sprouts. With the leaves gone, the sprouts have more room to grow; so take off the leaves slightly in advance of sprout harvesting. Do not remove the top tuft of leaves; if this is removed, the stem will stop growing and sprouts will stop forming.

If you want an early crop, pinch off the growing tip of the plant in September. The sprouts will mature three weeks ahead of schedule—and all at the same time—but the plant will not yield as much as when allowed to produce normally.

What Can Go Wrong With Brussels Sprouts

Avoid clubroot and other soil-borne diseases by not planting Brussels sprouts where they or any *Brassica* relative had been growing the previous year. Treat the soil for clubroot by applying hydrated lime and quintozene (see p. 555.)

If green cabbage worms appear on your plants, spray the plants with *Bacillus thuringiensis*. Cabbage maggots feed on the roots of Brussels sprouts, causing the plants to collapse. Kill the maggots by watering a spray-strength solution of Diazinon into the soil.

Varieties of Brussels Sprouts to Grow

'Jade Cross Hybrid' matures in about 80 days and grows to 22 inches. 'Long Island Improved' matures in 90 days and grows to 20 inches.

Cabbage

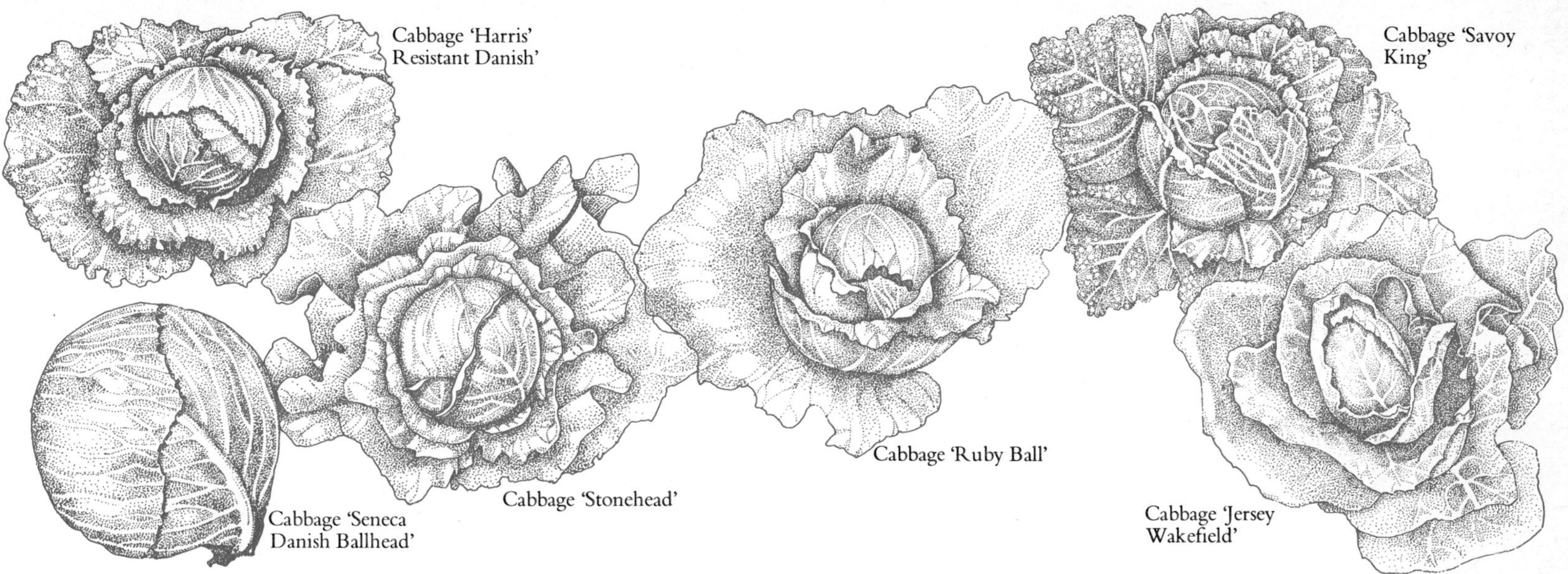

Cabbage is a hardy vegetable that grows well almost anywhere, provided the soil is fertile and not too acid. You can choose among red, savoy, and green varieties, and by planting early, midsummer, and late varieties you can harvest cabbage from summer through fall. But cabbage takes up a considerable amount of space; so if you have a small garden, you should probably limit your crop to a single late variety.

How to Grow Cabbage

To avoid soil-borne diseases, choose a place for cabbage where neither it nor any of its *Brassica* relatives (including broccoli, cauliflower, turnips, and kale) were grown in the previous year. If your soil is strongly acid, lime it as far ahead of planting time as possible—preferably in the fall before your spring planting. Cabbage grows best where the pH factor is from 6.0 to 7.5.

Cabbage matures faster—and will taste better—if it is grown in heavily fertilized soil. Well-rotted manure, if you can obtain it, is the perfect additive because it enriches the soil while improving its texture and its water-holding capacity. Whether or not you use manure, it is generally advisable to work about a pound of 10–10–10 fertilizer into the soil for every 25 feet of row.

Early varieties of cabbage should be sown indoors, five to eight weeks before the last expected spring frost. (For details on starting seeds indoors, see Broccoli, p. 555.) You can also grow early cabbage from seedlings bought at a nursery. Look for young plants that have short, thick stems—an indication of strong, well-started seedlings.

Set out the seedlings two or three weeks before the last expected frost, placing them at least 1 foot apart in rows 2–3 feet apart. Protect each cabbage against cutworms with a collar made from a paper cup with its bottom removed. Set the collar around the stem, 1 inch into the ground.

Sow midsummer cabbage directly outdoors at about the time of the last expected frost. Plant three or four seeds together about $\frac{1}{4}$ inch deep, and space each group of seeds 1 foot apart in rows 2–3 feet apart. When seedlings emerge, thin them to the single strongest one in each group.

Unless your soil is very rich, fertilize cabbage regularly. Once a month scatter a 6-inch-wide band of 10–10–10 fertilizer around each plant, or spread on an organic, high-nitrogen fertilizer.

Cabbages have shallow roots. For this reason it is advisable to mulch the soil around them to keep the moisture in the upper layers. Mulching also discourages weeds from growing; but if some manage to push through the mulch cover, pull them out by hand. If you use a hoe, be careful not to disturb the cabbages' shallow root systems.

Large cabbage heads sometimes split during hot weather. You can avoid this (and slow down growth if too many heads are nearing harvest at one time) by cutting the roots on one side of the plant with a spade.

It is time to harvest when the cabbage feels solid. The length of time to maturity depends on the variety. The range is about 60 to 110 days from the time young plants are set out in the garden, plus 30 to 50 days for starting seedlings indoors. To harvest cabbage, cut the stalk just beneath the head.

What Can Go Wrong With Cabbage

The green cabbage worm is the most serious pest of the cabbage. It chews the tender leaves and may dig into the head. Dust early with *Bacillus thuringiensis* to keep these worms from destroying the whole plant.

Varieties of Cabbage to Grow

Popular early varieties are 'Jersey Wakefield,' 'Stonehead,' and 'Ruby Ball'; midseason, 'King Cole' and 'Savoy King'; and late, 'Seneca Danish Ballhead,' 'Red Danish,' and 'Harris' Resistant Danish.'

Carrots

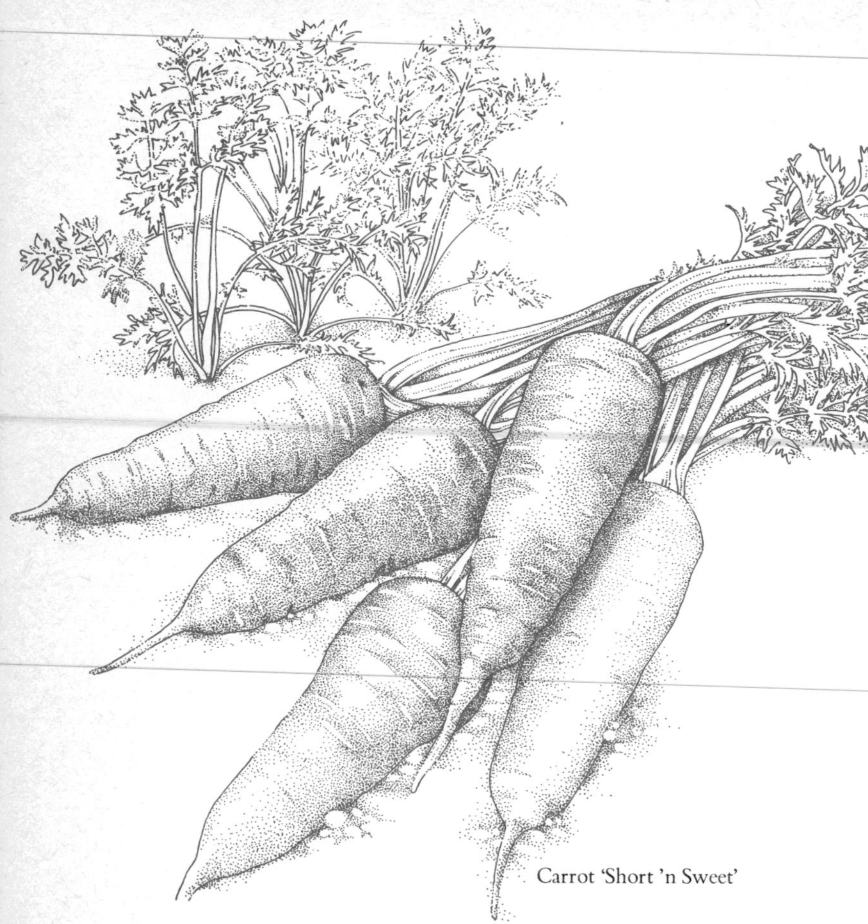

Carrot 'Short 'n Sweet'

The carrot, a domesticated relative of the weed Queen Anne's lace, not only is flavorful, crisp, and rich in vitamin A but is easy to grow and stores well. With judicious planning, you can have a homegrown supply of this healthful vegetable for much of the year.

Because carrots are cold resistant and need a relatively short time to mature (60 to 85 days), you can sow your first crop early and make several succession plantings. Although carrots prefer cool weather, midsummer plantings in all but the hottest areas will produce a good crop if you keep the soil well watered. And where winters are not too severe, a crop planted in September and kept well mulched may produce carrots through Christmas.

Carrots are grown for their roots, which may be short, long, or medium length, tapering or stump shaped. Before you decide which types to plant, determine what kind of soil you have. With a 10- to 12-inch depth of porous, sandy, stone-free soil, you can grow the long, slender varieties, such as 'Imperator' or 'Gold Pak.' In clayey or rocky soils, plant stubbier types, such as 'Danvers Half Long,' which grows to 6 or 7 inches; or 'Short 'n Sweet,' which is round and thick and grows only 4–5 inches long.

How to Grow Carrots

As soon as the ground can be worked, spade the soil to a depth of at least 8 inches, raking it well to remove stones. If you have a heavy clay soil, which discourages carrot growth, be sure to work in quantities of humus or sand.

Mark a row with garden twine, and dig a shallow furrow. Carrot seeds germinate slowly, and the row may be well defined by weeds long before the carrot tops appear. It is a good idea, therefore, to mix a few radish or leaf-lettuce seeds with the carrot seeds. The radishes and lettuce will sprout quickly and will mark the row. Because they will be ready for harvest long before the carrots are, they will not interfere with the growth of the carrots, and you will also be making more efficient use of your garden space.

Sow carrot seeds ¼ inch deep in rows 16–24 inches apart. (For hot-weather plantings, sow the seeds ½ inch deep.) To prevent crusting, cover the seeds with a thin layer of fine compost or sieved soil, firm the soil well, and water. Be sure to keep the soil fairly moist until the seedlings have emerged. Thin them first to stand 1 inch apart; then, as the tops of the carrots grow thicker, thin again to 2–3 inches apart. Plant carrots at about three-week intervals during the season, making your last planting about 40 to 60 days before the first killing frost is expected in the fall.

Carrots require a minimum of care. Once you have spaded and worked the soil and removed any rocks that might impede their downward growth, they require only regular watering and weeding. Mulching will help to retain moisture in the soil and to keep weeds from growing.

Although moist soil is essential for germination, do not make the mistake of keeping the soil soaked as your crop matures. Too much moisture toward the end of the growing period can cause roots to crack.

Apply a light dusting of 5–10–10 fertilizer (about 5 ounces for every 10 feet of row) when the tops are 3–4 inches tall, and again when they reach 6–8 inches. Watch for the appearance of the orange root crowns just at the soil's surface, and keep them covered with soil; sunlight will turn them green.

Carrots mature fully within 60 to 85 days as mentioned, but they may be juicier and tenderer if you pull them earlier. Check each crown, and if it seems sufficiently thick—about ¾ inch in diameter—pull the carrot. There is no need to harvest your crop all at once. Carrots can be left in the ground for a few weeks without growing tough. If late crops are well mulched, you may be able to continue harvesting through a blanket of snow.

What Can Go Wrong With Carrots

The larvae of the carrot rust fly hatch in warm weather and tunnel into carrot roots; to avoid damage, plant early and late crops. The carrot weevil, a small brown beetle, may destroy a crop that it infests. To control it, spray or dust the plants with carbaryl or rotenone.

If carrot roots are misshapen or forked, the cause may be either rocky ground or overcrowding. Spade deeper for your next crop, and thin seedlings earlier.

Varieties of Carrots to Grow

Besides the types mentioned earlier, 'Nantes' and 'Goldinhart' are quality medium-length carrots. 'Little Finger,' which grows to a mere 3½ inches, is considered a gourmet item.

Cauliflower

Cauliflower
'Snow King Hybrid'

Of all the vegetables of the *Brassica* genus (which include broccoli, Brussels sprouts, turnips, kale, and cabbage), cauliflower is the most difficult to grow. It needs cool temperatures, a lot of moisture, and fertile soil. It does not withstand frost as well as its *Brassica* relatives; yet it will not form a head in hot weather. Therefore, although it is often planted as a spring crop, cauliflower is easiest to grow for fall harvesting. Early cauliflower requires 55 to 80 days to mature from the time seedlings are set out. Fall crops are grown outdoors from seed and take about 10 weeks to mature.

The pure white color of cauliflower that you are used to seeing is achieved by blanching—covering the head to shut out the light that would turn the flower buds (called curds) to green. Blanching also preserves the cauliflower's delicate flavor. Although most cauliflower is white, there is a purple variety that does not have to be blanched and is often recommended for home gardeners. It turns green when cooked and tastes somewhat like broccoli.

How to Grow Cauliflower

Soil requirements for cauliflower are much the same as for cabbage. If your soil is strongly acid, give it an application of lime as far ahead of planting time as possible, preferably in the fall. Because a fertile soil is an absolute necessity, work in generous amounts of compost or rotted manure, and apply a pound of 10–10–10 fertilizer for every 25 feet of row.

For spring plantings in most areas, start cauliflower seeds indoors, six to eight weeks before the last expected frost. Sow the seeds in individual pots, three or four seeds to a pot. When the seedlings emerge, snip off all but the single strongest plant. Keep the seedlings in a sunny, cool spot. Two weeks before planting them outside, harden them off in a cold frame. (For more details on starting seeds indoors, see the instructions in Broccoli, p. 555.)

Set out the seedlings at about the time of the last expected frost. Space the plants 16–24 inches apart, in rows 2–3 feet apart. To protect the young plants against cutworms, slip a cutworm collar around each plant. You can make the collars from paper cups with the bottoms removed.

For a fall crop, you can sow seeds directly outdoors in June. Prepare the soil and sow the seeds $\frac{1}{2}$ inch deep, in groups of three or four, spacing the groups 18–24 inches apart. When the seedlings are about 1 inch tall, thin them to the single strongest in each group. To save garden space, sow the seeds in a cold frame or seedbed and transplant the seedlings to the cauliflower row when they are 4–5 inches tall.

Cauliflower grows better in soil that is enriched regularly. Every three or four weeks, scatter a 3-inch band of 10–10–10 fertilizer along each side of the row, being careful not to let it fall on the plants. Water thoroughly to soak the fertilizer into the soil.

Soil enrichment alone, however, will not ensure a good crop. If cauliflower roots are deprived of water for even a short time, the plants will probably not form heads. Be sure that the bed receives a good soaking at least once a week, and mulch the ground with a thick layer of hay or half-rotted compost.

As mentioned earlier, the head must be protected from the sun's rays to grow white. Watch for a small bud to appear at the center of the plant. When the bud is 4–6 inches in diameter, it is time to blanch the head. Draw the lower leaves of the plant loosely over the bud, and fasten them together with a piece of soft twine or a rubber band. Leave enough room inside this leafy bag for the head to grow to full size—about 8–12 inches across.

The cauliflower head is ready to harvest when it is firm and compact. Pick it while the flowerets are still tightly clustered, for it does not keep once it has matured. To harvest, cut the stalk just below the head.

Varieties of Cauliflower to Grow

Recommended early varieties of cauliflower include 'Snow King Hybrid,' which is ready for harvest about 50 days after the plants are set out, and 'Early Snowball,' which averages 60 days. 'Purple Head' matures in 80 to 85 days and can be grown as either an early or a late crop. For late crops, 'Snowball' is a good choice; or you may want to try 'Self-Blanche,' whose leaves grow naturally over the head, eliminating the need for blanching.

What Can Go Wrong With Cauliflower

Cauliflower is susceptible to the same diseases and pests as its *Brassica* relatives. You can avoid the diseases by shifting the location of *Brassica* crops—do not plant cauliflower, Brussels sprouts, cabbage, or turnips in the same soil where any one of these plants grew the year before.

If cabbage worms are a problem, apply *Bacillus thuringiensis.* Wash off aphids with a strong stream of water from the garden hose, or dust plants with Diazinon.

Celery

Celery 'Fordhook'

Because it requires a long, cool growing season (five to six months from seed) and special care in its cultivation, celery is not an easy vegetable to grow. It needs more than the usual quantities of soil nutrients, a particularly well-prepared soil, and an abundant and never-failing supply of moisture. In addition, its tiny seeds are difficult to nurture into seedlings, even under ideal indoor conditions. So if you do raise a crop of this crisp and succulent vegetable, you will have won the right to consider yourself an accomplished horticulturist.

How to Grow Celery

Celery is usually started indoors in flats. Before sowing the seeds, which are small and hard, soak them in water overnight to soften the seed coverings. Use a light soil-and-sand mixture or sterile sphagnum moss as a growing medium, sprinkle the seeds into the flats, and cover with 1/4 inch of sphagnum moss. Keep the soil moist, and be patient—celery seeds take up to three weeks to sprout.

When the seedlings are about an inch tall, transplant them to individual pots. Do not transplant seedlings into the garden until they are at least 3 inches tall—a height they will reach in 10 to 12 weeks after sowing. (You can also buy seedlings from a local garden center, which should have sturdy 6-inch plants available in time for early planting.)

Set out the seedlings two to four weeks before the last expected frost. Count on at least 120 days of outdoor growing time for homegrown seedlings, 115 days for nursery plants. Because celery grows best in cool temperatures, much of that growing time should be in spring, when the weather is moderate. Although celery is planted in early spring in most areas, the seedlings are set out in the fall in the South and in parts of the West Coast, where springs are warm and winters mild.

For years the classical method of planting celery was to dig a trench, set the seedlings at the bottom, and then heap earth around the stems as they grew. The earth helped conserve soil moisture and blanched the celery—that is, kept the stems white and tender by protecting them from the sun's rays. In recent times, however, celery strains have been developed whose sun-greened stalks remain tender and are also more nutritious than blanched stalks. "Self-blanching" varieties, with yellowish stalks, have also been developed. Because blanching is no longer essential, most gardeners now plant celery in ordinary furrows.

But trenching offers advantages even though blanching is not necessary: it protects late crops against frost, makes fertilizing easier, and eliminates the need for weeding. If you decide to use this method, dig a trench 15 inches wide and 10 inches deep, fertilizing it as described below, and filling with topsoil to a depth of 5 inches.

Whether or not you employ the trench method, you must prepare the soil by enriching it with plenty of organic matter—either compost or well-rotted manure—plus 2–3 pounds of 5-10-10 fertilizer per 25 feet of row. Prepare the soil at least two weeks before setting out your plants. Because the fertilizer will burn the seedlings if it comes into contact with them, work it thoroughly into the soil, and water well.

Choose a cloudy day for transplanting. Set the seedlings 6–8 inches apart in rows at least 2 feet apart, and water well. To protect against sun shock, cover the plants for the first few days with some form of shading, such as a newspaper tent.

Because celery is an exceptionally thirsty plant, mulch the soil heavily to conserve moisture and prevent weed growth. Keep the soil rich by pouring around each plant 1 pint of liquid fertilizer, diluted to half strength, every two or three weeks.

If you would like to experiment with blanching but have not trenched your celery, you can still produce white stalks by placing 12-inch-wide boards on either side of the row, holding them upright with stakes driven into the ground. Or blanch each plant separately by wrapping heavy paper around the stalk cluster, leaving the leafy tops exposed to the sun. Begin blanching two weeks before harvest time.

Celery will be ready for harvest about four months from the time they were planted outdoors. But you can begin nibbling at your crop two or three weeks before maturity by cutting off a single stalk from the outside of each plant. To harvest the whole plant, pull or dig it up and cut off the root base. Celery stalks will keep fresh for several weeks in your refrigerator.

What Can Go Wrong With Celery

Fungous diseases, which cause yellow or brown spots on leaves and stalks, are a major problem with celery. You can prevent them by not planting celery in soil where it was previously grown; by not touching the plants when they are wet; and by keeping the bed free of weeds. If spots nevertheless appear, spray or dust the celery plants with copper, maneb, zineb, or ziram. Wash them thoroughly after harvesting.

Varieties of Celery to Grow

'Summer Pascal' (also called 'Waltham Improved') is a popular early green variety. Other recommended green types are 'Fordhook' and 'Giant Pascal.' A good early yellow variety is 'Golden Self-Blanching.'

If you can count on a long, cool summer, you may want to try 'Utah 52-70,' a dark green, thick-stalked celery that will not run to seed—produce a tough, flowering stalk—as readily as most celery varieties do.

Corn

Corn 'Golden Cross Bantam'

There is only one way to truly enjoy the flavor of fresh corn: grow it yourself—for corn loses much of its sweetness within minutes after picking. True corn lovers start water boiling on the stove before they pick, so that they can rush the tender ears straight from the garden into the pot.

The earliest corn matures in about two months, the latest in three. Many gardeners plant early, midseason, and late varieties at the same time to give themselves a longer harvesting season. Some catalogs offer a package of three varieties that will ripen in succession. Another way to reap corn longer is to make succession plantings of an early, fast-maturing variety every 10 days or so until midsummer.

How to Grow Corn

You must have considerable garden space if you are going to grow corn, since each stalk takes up a surprising amount of room and produces only one or two ears. Because corn is wind pollinated, it must be planted in such a way that adjacent stalks can pollinate one another. For this reason, corn is not planted in a single, long row. Instead, several short rows are sown in a block so that pollen from the corn tassels needs to travel only a short distance between plants. Allow space for a block that is at least 6 feet wide by 8 feet long—a total area of 48 square feet. This will allow you to plant four rows of corn 2 feet apart.

Prepare the soil for corn by working into it quantities of rotted manure, compost, or other organic matter. Add 3–4 pounds of 5–10–10 fertilizer for every 50 feet of row, and dig it in 4 or 5 inches below the soil's surface to be sure it does not come into direct contact with the corn seed and cause fertilizer burn.

About two weeks before the last expected frost, sow the seeds 3–4 inches apart and about 1 inch deep. (For summer plantings, sow 2 inches deep, to reach the deeper soil moisture.) Space rows for early corn about 2 feet apart. Later corn, which grows taller, should be planted in rows about 3 feet apart. When the seedlings are about 3 inches tall, thin out the weaker ones, for a final spacing of 1 foot between plants.

Some garden experts recommend planting corn in hills. To do this, sow six seeds along the perimeter of a 12-inch-diameter circle (called a hill, although it is not mounded as melon hills are). Each hill should be 3 feet from neighboring hills. When the seedlings are 3 inches tall, cut off all but the three strongest plants in each circle.

Corn needs plenty of moisture. To retain it (and to hold down weeds), spread on a heavy mulch of rotted straw or hay, or cover the soil with black plastic garden sheeting.

Once corn has sprouted, it grows rapidly and consumes large amounts of soil nutrients; so it is important to fertilize. When stalks are 6–10 inches high, spread a band of 5–10–5 fertilizer on both sides of each row—about $\frac{1}{2}$ pound per 25 row feet. If you have covered the ground with mulch, pull it aside before applying the fertilizer, or use a water-soluble fertilizer that you can pour over the mulch.

Weeds will flourish in the fertilized soil and rob it of nutrients the corn needs. So, weeding is vital, but be careful not to disturb the plants' shallow roots.

Harvest corn while it is young, or it will lose its sweetness, as the sugar turns to starch. Test each ear for ripeness: when an ear feels firm and full and the tips of the silks are dry and dark brown, it is ready to be picked. To remove an ear, pull it downward by hand and twist it off the stalk. Harvest only as much corn as you can eat at one meal. Stored corn rapidly loses its flavor and tenderness. When all the corn has been harvested, cut down the stalks.

1. *Pinch off any side shoots from base of stem when shoots are about 6 in. long.*

2. *Mound soil around stems to encourage rooting for support against wind.*

What Can Go Wrong With Corn

If you find small holes in the base or sides of the ears, the corn has probably been invaded by corn borers—inch-long grubs that feed in the stalks and then attack the ears and sometimes the tassels. Prevent borers by spraying with carbaryl or Diazinon when the stalks are about 18 inches high and the ears are starting to appear. Be sure to cover the leaves surrounding the ears with spray. Respray at five-day intervals at least three times. To protect your next year's crop, destroy old cornstalks and stubble, which can harbor corn borer larvae over the winter.

Crows in your neighborhood may discover your newly sown corn and peck it out of the ground or even pull up corn seedlings as they emerge. A scarecrow may or may not discourage them. You can also try tying old tin cans or aluminum trays together, hanging them so that they rattle in the wind.

Varieties of Corn to Grow

Recommended early varieties include 'Early Sunglow' and 'Early Xtra-Sweet,' which are yellow, and 'Silver Sweet,' a white corn. Good midseason corn includes 'Honey and Cream' (also called 'Butter and Sugar'), a yellow and white type; yellow 'Barbecue'; and white 'Snowcrest.' Popular late varieties are yellow 'Golden Cross Bantam' and white 'Silver Queen Hybrid.'

Cucumbers

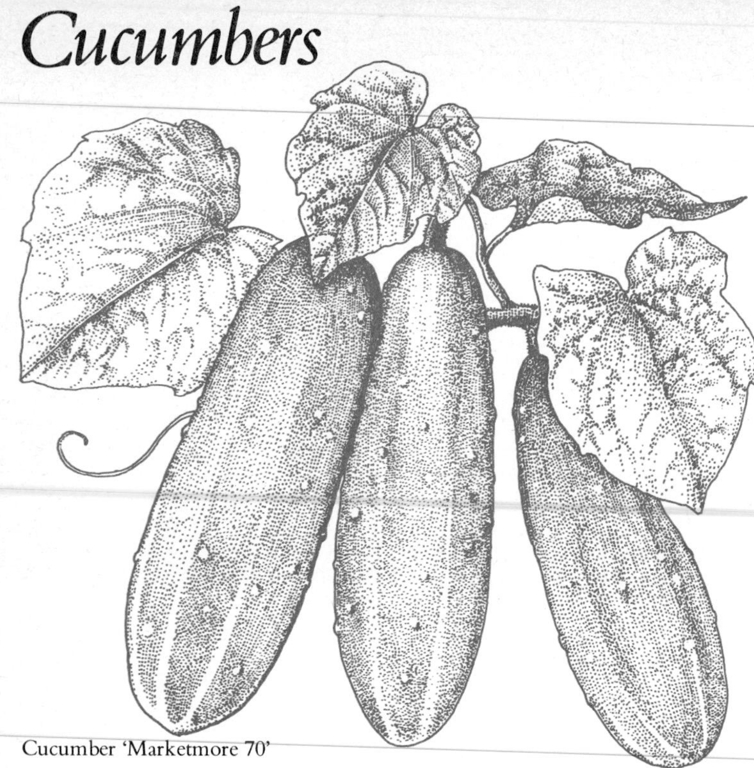
Cucumber 'Marketmore 70'

Cucumbers need a lot of attention, but given the proper care, they are gratifyingly prolific—four or five plants will supply a family of four through the summer. And although the plants require warm weather, they mature so quickly (55 to 60 days) that they can be grown almost everywhere.

Before planting cucumbers, make sure that you have either plenty of garden space to give them or something that they can climb on. A cucumber plant is a vine that, when grown on the ground, will sprawl for over 6 feet in length. If your garden is too small to accommodate such long, trailing vines, however, you can train cucumbers to climb up a fence or a trellis. Besides saving valuable ground space, trellis-trained plants often produce better-formed cucumbers.

In selecting cucumber varieties, you will find a wide choice. There are large, narrow, slicing cucumbers for eating fresh from the garden, and short, fat, pickling types. But note that you can pickle slicing kinds and eat the pickling ones raw.

An important fact to look for in seed descriptions on packages or in catalogs is disease-resistance. Cucumbers are vulnerable to scab, mosaic, and downy and powdery mildew, but horticulturists have bred varieties that are resistant to these diseases. Ask a local nurseryman what will withstand the diseases prevalent in your area.

You will notice that some varieties are described as "gynoecious." Normally, a cucumber vine bears both male and female flowers, with the fruits forming from pollinated females. Gynoecious varieties produce solely or mainly female flowers, so that the vine will bear a larger crop. Such varieties are packaged with a few normal seeds, dyed for identification. These must also be planted to ensure pollination.

How to Grow Cucumbers

Cucumbers can be grown in "hills" (clusters of two or three plants) or in rows. Hills are to many gardeners the traditional way to plant cucumbers, but rows are particularly well suited for growing cucumbers up a fence or trellis. Rows should be spaced 6 feet apart; make hills 1 foot in diameter, spacing the perimeters 6 feet apart.

Soil preparation is particularly important; cucumbers need fertile soil with good drainage. Dig up the earth to a depth of about 1 foot, and work in 1 wheelbarrowful of rotted manure or compost, plus ½ pound of 5–10–5 fertilizer for every 10 feet of row or for every two hills.

In most areas cucumber seeds are sown indoors in individual peat pots two to three weeks before the last expected frost. (Pots are recommended rather than flats because cucumbers will not tolerate the root disturbance that is inevitable when you separate plants grown in flats.) Sow three seeds ½ inch deep in each pot, and when the seedlings are about 1½ inches tall, thin them to the strongest one. If you use gynoecious seeds, label the pots in which you plant the dyed seeds so that you will be sure to set out at least one pollinating plant per 25 feet of row.

Seedlings will be ready for transplanting outdoors in three or four weeks. Space them 1 foot apart in rows, or place two or three seedlings in the center of each hill.

In regions with long growing seasons, sow the seeds directly in the garden at about the time of the last expected frost. Remember to label the pollinating plants so that you do not later thin them out unwittingly. For rows plant seeds ½ inch deep and 4–6 inches apart. When the seedlings are about 1½–2 inches tall, thin them to stand 1 foot apart. For hills plant six to eight seeds per hill, ½ inch deep, and later thin the seedlings to two to three per hill.

Young cucumber plants are often set back by spring rain and cold. You can protect them against the elements by covering them with translucent caps, which are available at most garden centers.

Cucumbers need a lot of moisture; so water the soil frequently, and spread a thick layer of organic mulch or a black plastic mulch to help the soil remain damp. A plastic mulch has the added advantage of warming the soil for early plantings.

If weeds manage to grow despite the mulch, pull them out by hand to avoid injuring the cucumbers' shallow root systems.

Slicing-type cucumbers are fully ripe when they get to be 6–8 inches long; pickling cucumbers, when they are 1½–3 inches long. But either type may be picked before it reaches full size. Strip your vines of mature cucumbers every two or three days, or the plants will stop producing. Pick the cucumbers while they are still dark green; yellow ones are overripe. To pick the fruit off the vine, hold the vine firmly in one hand while you twist off the cucumber with the other hand.

What Can Go Wrong With Cucumbers

Cucumber beetles feed on the plants and spread bacterial wilt. If such beetles are endemic in your area, protect young plants with protective caps. You can use a pesticide to kill the beetles, but be sure to follow label directions carefully.

Varieties of Cucumbers to Grow

Popular slicing varieties include 'Victory Hybrid' (a gynoecious type) and 'Marketmore 70.' Recommended pickling cucumbers are 'Wisconsin SMR 18' and the gynoecious 'Bravo Hybrid.' For a "burpless" type, try 'Burpless Hybrid.'

Eggplant

Eggplant
'Early Beauty Hybrid'

Eggplant, peppers, and tomatoes have much in common. Together, they make the great Mediterranean vegetable stew called ratatouille. All three are related, members of the nightshade family. All need warm, rich soil and a long growing season.

Eggplants are particularly tricky to grow. The seeds must be sown indoors at least eight weeks before the plants are set out, and the seedlings require sunshine and warm, moist soil. Because starting eggplants is such a precarious business, you may want to buy them from a garden center. In selecting seedlings, look for those in individual pots (for minimal root disturbance in transplanting), and check the stems (woody-stemmed plants will not produce as well as those with green, pliable stems).

Eggplants require 100 to 120 days to mature from seeds. The number of days given on seed packets or in catalogs can be misleading, because the days are counted from the time the seedlings are planted outside. Because seedlings should not be transplanted into the garden before daytime temperatures reach 70° F, gardeners in areas where summer arrives late should plant fast-maturing, or early, varieties.

How to Grow Eggplant

If you decide to raise the seedlings yourself, start them eight weeks before the last expected frost. Plant the seeds in pots in which you have placed a layer of vermiculite or sphagnum moss over the potting soil. Sow three seeds in each pot, $\frac{1}{4}$ inch deep, and water thoroughly. Keep the pots in a warm place: a temperature of 75° F is needed for germination, which may take three weeks.

When the seedlings reach $1\frac{1}{2}$–2 inches, clip off the two weakest ones, leaving the best plant in each pot. Reduce the temperature as the seedlings grow, but be especially careful when you harden off the plants—that is, when you expose them to outdoor conditions to prepare them for transplanting into the garden. Temperatures below 50° F will set back eggplant.

When you choose a spot for eggplant in your garden, try to avoid the vicinity of tomatoes or peppers, and, if possible, do not plant in soil where eggplants, tomatoes, peppers, or potatoes previously grew. Because these plants are related, they are all susceptible to the same soil-borne diseases.

To prepare the soil, dig in about 1 bushel of humus, plus $\frac{1}{2}$–1 pound of 5–10–5 fertilizer for every 10 feet of row. Set out the eggplants on an overcast day or in the evening so that the sun will not wilt the tender seedlings. Dig shallow holes about 2 feet apart, in rows 3 feet apart, and fill these with water. When the water has drained out, plant the seedlings, leaving a slight depression around each plant to hold water. Water again as soon as you have planted the seedlings.

To protect eggplants from cutworms, make a collar of stiff paper (or use a paper cup with its bottom removed) and set this around the stem and into the ground an inch or more deep. If the leaves droop or seem wilted, cover the plants for a few days with newspaper tents.

To help your eggplants flourish, keep the ground well watered and weed free. Mulch around the plants to conserve soil moisture and prevent weed growth. Black plastic mulch is preferable because it also warms the soil, but you can use any available mulching material. If weeding becomes necessary, do it by hand.

When the blossoms set and the fruits begin to form, count the number of fruits on each plant. For a healthy crop, each plant should bear no more than six fruits, so pinch off any extra blossoms.

About 80 days from the day you planted the eggplant seedlings in the garden, the fruits will be 5–6 inches long and 4–5 inches in diameter, and will have glossy, dark purple skins. At this point they are ready to pick. Once the sheen on the skin fades, the fruit is past its prime.

Never try to pull the fruit off the plant—you may take some of the stalk with it. Instead, use a sharp knife to sever the stem about an inch below the fruit.

Place the harvested eggplants in a cool place and use them as soon as possible. Eggplants do not store well.

What Can Go Wrong With Eggplant

Verticillium wilt, a soil-borne disease, affects eggplants as well as tomatoes and potatoes. The best prevention is crop rotation: do not plant eggplant where any of these three vegetables have been grown within the last three years.

Colorado potato beetles, flea beetles, and aphids feast on eggplant. Control by spraying or dusting the plants with carbaryl, Diazinon, or methoxychlor. Check the pesticide label for the number of days that should elapse between spraying or dusting and harvesting.

Varieties of Eggplant to Grow

For short growing seasons, 'Early Beauty Hybrid' and 'Black Magic' are recommended; for longer seasons, try 'Mission Bell' and 'Jersey King Hybrid.'

Kale and Collards

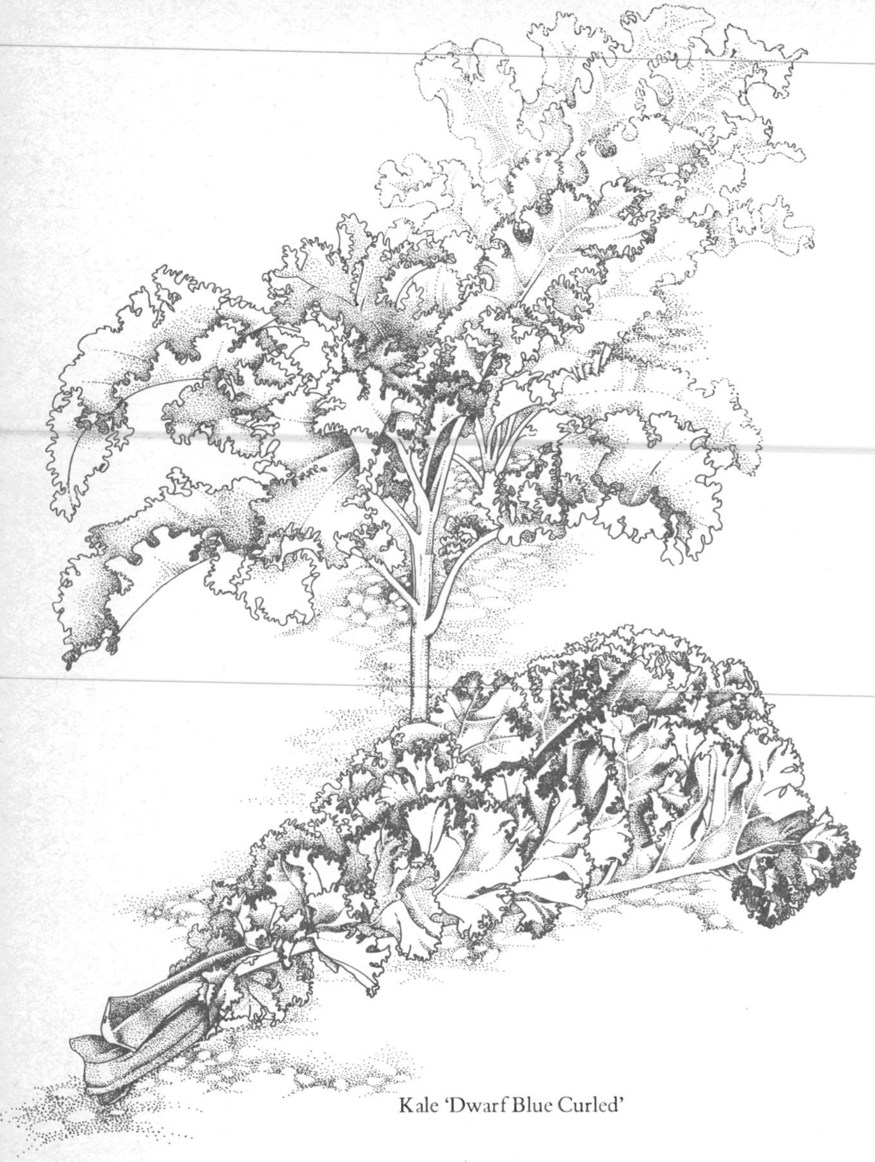

Kale 'Dwarf Blue Curled'

Kale and collards are among the oldest of cultivated vegetables and among the most nutritious; yet many people have never tasted either. Leafy green vegetables related to the cabbage, they can be cooked or, when young and tender, used as salad greens.

Kale and collards are easy to grow and productive, and for gardeners in areas with a short growing season, have the added advantage of improving in cold weather. A touch of frost sharpens their flavor, and kale, especially, thrives well into winter.

Kale grows about 2 feet high and takes 2 months to mature; collards reach about 3 feet in $2\frac{1}{2}$ months.

How to Grow Kale and Collards

Both kale and collards require fertile soil that is not too acid. If acidity is a problem, lime the soil (to a pH of 6.5 or above) well ahead of planting. Enrich it with organic matter, such as well-rotted manure, and work in 1 pound of 10–10–10 fertilizer for every 25 feet of row.

Plant kale and collards outdoors in early spring as soon as the ground can be worked. Sow the seeds an inch apart in 1-inch-deep furrows 2–3 feet apart, and cover with half an inch of soil. The seeds should germinate in 7 to 10 days.

If you have the space, sow a second crop of collards or kale in June—perhaps after you harvest your early peas—for a fall crop. Kale withstands cold better than collards and can be harvested long after other leafy green vegetables have disappeared. In areas where the ground does not freeze, you can sow kale in late summer for harvesting in winter.

When the seedlings are 3 inches high, start thinning them gradually until the plants stand 2 feet apart. (You can use the thinnings for salads.) Because the plants grow fairly tall and have heavy leaves, they should be supported against strong winds. When staking be careful not to injure the shallow, spreading roots: set the stakes along the row during the thinning process, and tie on the plants when they reach about 1 foot in height.

Because kale and collards have roots that grow close to the surface of the soil, be careful in weeding. Hoe no deeper than an inch or so, to avoid cutting the roots. A thick mulch will deter weed growth.

Fertilize these vegetables at least once during the growing season, scattering a band of 10–10–10 fertilizer on each side of the row at the rate of 1 cup per 10 row feet.

You can begin harvesting kale in about a month, when the leaves have turned a rich green. If the leaves become too dark, however, they will be tough and bitter. Do not take too many leaves from a single plant, or it will stop growing. To maintain kale in cold weather, mulch each plant heavily with straw, salt hay, or leaf mulch; or hill earth up around the bottom of the stem for a few inches.

Collards are fully mature two to three months after planting, but you can begin eating them much sooner. You can either harvest the whole young plant or cut off some leaves from the bottom of the stem. But in cutting, be careful not to injure the central growing bud because new leaves are formed only as the stem grows. Cook collards with salt pork, or in a ham-based pea soup; the smoky ham flavor brings out the best in this vegetable.

What Can Go Wrong With Kale and Collards

To avoid diseases of the *Brassica* genus—to which kale, collards, cabbage, broccoli, and Brussels sprouts belong—do not plant kale or collards where any of these plants were grown in the past year or two.

Kale and collards are prey for cabbage worms. If you see these pests, you can control them by spraying the plants with the microbial insecticide *Bacillus thuringiensis*.

Varieties of Kale and Collards to Grow

'Dwarf Blue Curled Vates' and 'Dwarf Siberian' are recommended kale varieties. 'Flowering Kale' is so attractive that it is sometimes grown as an ornamental plant.

Popular collard varieties include 'Georgia,' the standard collard; 'Louisiana Sweet,' with a longer growing season and larger leaves; and 'Vates,' a low-growing, thick-leaved variety.

Lettuce and Endive

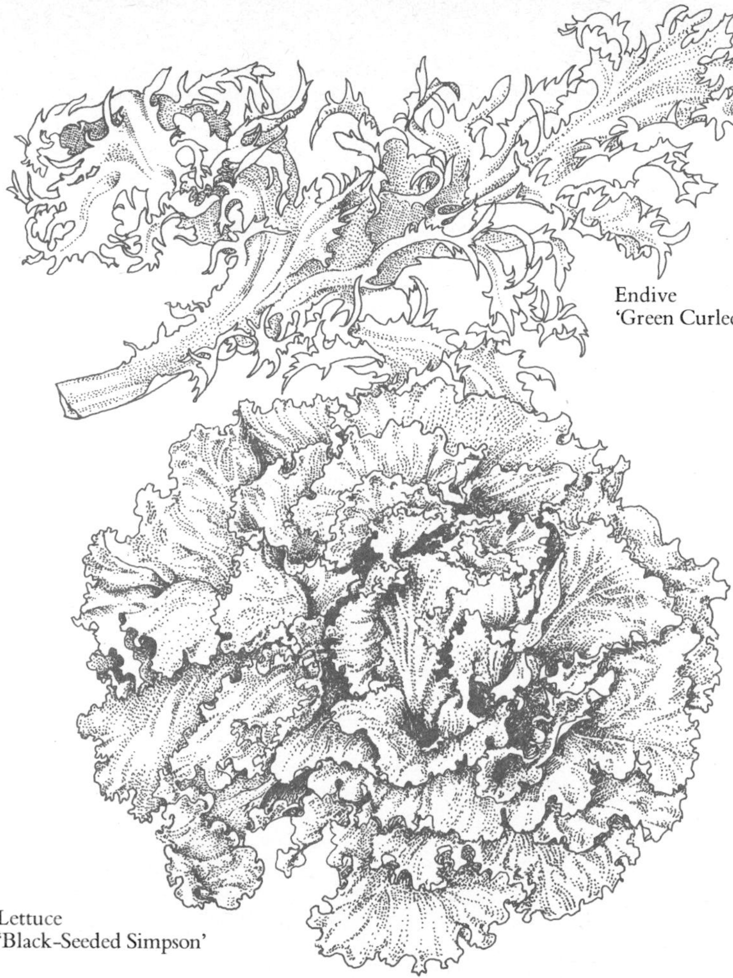

Endive
'Green Curled'

Lettuce
'Black-Seeded Simpson'

There are more kinds of lettuce under the sun than 'Iceberg,' which is often the sole variety that can be bought in grocery stores. Home gardens usually boast a row or two of delicate 'Oak Leaf,' tender 'Buttercrunch,' or any of the numerous other lettuce varieties that can be grown almost everywhere but can rarely be found in stores.

There are four major types of lettuce: true head lettuce (of which 'Iceberg' is the most familiar variety), whose leaves come together to form a tight head, somewhat like a cabbage in shape; butterhead, which also forms a head, but one that is much looser; cos, or romaine, whose tall oval heads may stand almost a foot high; and loose-leaf lettuce, which produces a summer-long harvest of leaves to be cut and replaced by new ones. True head lettuce is seldom grown in home gardens in most parts of the country because of its exacting climatic rquirements. The three other types of lettuce, however, are easy to grow almost anywhere—loose-leaf grows the fastest and produces the largest crops.

Most types of lettuce grow best before midsummer heat. When temperatures reach a fairly consistent 70° F, lettuce has the habit of bolting—sending up a stem that bears flowers and then seeds—and when it bolts, it becomes too tough to eat. Loose-leaf lettuce is the least likely to bolt during hot spells and also takes the least time to mature. So loose-leaf can be planted in late June or July in cool areas where it would be too late to plant the other types of lettuce.

Leaf lettuce matures 6 to 7 weeks after sowing; butterhead, 9 to 10 weeks; cos, 11 to 12 weeks. (The leaves of all types, however, are edible at any stage of growth.) To keep a constant supply of lettuce on your table, make succession sowings, planting a row of about 5 or 6 feet every two weeks. Stop making succession plantings before the hottest weeks and start again after midsummer for fall crops.

You can also plant lettuce between slow-maturing vegetables, such as peppers or cabbage. By the time peppers or cabbage are large enough to need all the surrounding space, you will have harvested the lettuce.

Endive grows like lettuce, looks like lettuce, and is used as salad greens, but it is more tolerant of hot weather, so it will flourish when the temperatures soar too high for lettuce to grow. Endive is also more cold resistant and can be planted for a later harvest than lettuce can.

The two most popular types of endive are the slender, wavy-leaved curly endive and the flatter-leaved escarole. Both have tougher leaves and a sharper flavor than lettuce and need to be blanched (shielded from sunlight) when growing, so that their leaves will become milder and tenderer.

How to Grow Lettuce and Endive

Lettuce and endive grow best in soil that is rich in humus. To prepare the soil, dig in substantial amounts of organic matter, such as compost or rotted manure (about 1 bushel per 25 feet of row), or, lacking this, 1 pound of 10–10–10 fertilizer per 25 feet of row.

Planting and tending lettuce. Loose-leaf lettuce is usually sown directly into the garden as soon as the ground can be worked and is no longer soggy from winter snow and rains. Butterhead and cos can be started indoors in flats about six weeks before the ground can be worked, or they can be sown outdoors at the same time as loose-leaf lettuce.

When sowing seeds in flats, plant them ½ inch deep and about 1 inch apart. Keep the flats in a cool place; lettuce will germinate at 60° F. When the seedlings are 1 inch high, thin them to stand about 2 inches apart, or transplant them into individual pots. Place the seedlings in a cool, sunny spot.

Flat-grown seedlings can be transplanted outside when they reach 2–3 inches in height and the ground can be worked. Give them a week of hardening off—gradual exposure to outside weather conditions—before you transfer them to the garden. When transplanting, place the seedlings 6–8 inches apart, in rows 1–1½ feet apart.

Sow seeds outdoors ½ inch deep, 1 inch apart, and in rows 1–1½ feet apart. When the seedlings are 2 inches high, thin them to stand about 2 inches apart. Thin them again when the plants are almost touching one another. (You can eat these thinnings, or you can transplant them to another row if you are careful not to disturb the roots unduly.) You will probably have to thin the seedlings again to achieve the proper spacing of 6–8 inches between plants.

Although lettuce will grow in crowded rows, the heads will be smaller, and the plants will have a tendency to bolt.

Lettuce needs to be fertilized at least once during the growing season. Spread a band of 10-10-10 fertilizer along both sides of a row at the rate of 5 ounces for every 10 feet of row. If any bits of fertilizer fall on your crop, wash them off immediately to prevent fertilizer burn.

Weed lettuce gently and water it frequently. Because the plants need constant moisture, a light mulch is helpful in retaining it.

Planting and tending endive. You can plant endive directly in the garden. Or if space is a problem, you can sow the seeds in a seedbed, and when the seedlings are 2–3 inches high, transplant them into rows from which you have harvested an earlier crop.

Endive grows best when the seeds are sown in midsummer for a fall harvest. Sow the seeds ½ inch deep, 1 inch apart, in rows 2 feet apart. Thin, as with lettuce, until the plants stand 14–16 inches apart.

Fertilize, weed, and water endive as you do lettuce. In addition, in the final two or three weeks of growth, blanch the heads to mellow the rather harsh natural flavor of the leaves. To blanch, gather the long outer leaves together over the top of the plant and secure them with a rubber band. Another way to blanch is simply to place a wide board directly on the tops of the plants. Because the foliage grows low to the ground, you will not crush it.

Harvesting lettuce and endive. Loose-leaf lettuce is harvested by picking the outer leaves, leaving the center intact to grow new leaves. For butterhead and cos lettuce and endive, cut the entire plant at ground level. Harvest frequently. If you leave lettuce unharvested after the heads reach maturity, they begin to lose their nutritive value as well as their flavor.

What Can Go Wrong With Lettuce and Endive

Lettuce and endive suffer from a few predators. Slugs may be a problem in wet areas. Dispose of them by setting out sunken saucers of stale beer, in which these slimy creatures will drown themselves; or look for them at night with a flashlight, and pick them off by hand. Do not use slug poisons—they are intended for ornamentals and are too lethal to use on vegetables. Aphids can be controlled by spraying the plants with malathion. Leafhoppers may feed on the undersides of leaves and can be controlled with carbaryl. Should pale green worms chew on your lettuce, pick them off by hand, or spray with carbaryl. Always follow insecticide labels exactly.

Varieties of Lettuce and Endive to Grow

Recommended loose-leaf lettuce varieties include 'Oak Leaf,' 'Salad Bowl,' 'Black-Seeded Simpson,' and the red-leaved 'Ruby.' Although these mature in 40 to 45 days, you can start harvesting in a month.

'Dark Green Boston,' 'Buttercrunch,' 'Bibb,' and 'Summer Bibb' (which matures later and is less likely to bolt in hot weather than 'Bibb') are popular butterhead lettuces.

Among cos, or romaine, lettuces, 'Parris Island Cos' and 'Paris White,' which grow about 10 inches high, and 'Dwarf Cos,' which is somewhat smaller, are favored varieties.

'Green Curled' is a popular curly endive variety. 'Florida Deep Heart' and 'Full Heart Batavian' are escaroles that have proved succulent in salads over the years.

Melons

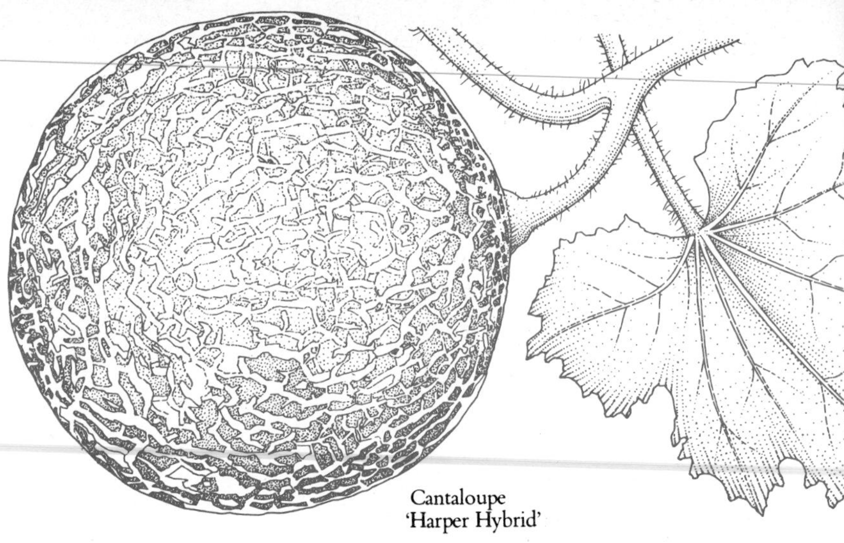

Cantaloupe
'Harper Hybrid'

Although they are fruits, melons are usually grown in the vegetable garden. While they are growing, in fact, it is often difficult to distinguish them from their close relatives, cucumbers and squashes. Like those plants, melons are vines and need a lot of room, warm weather, and plenty of moisture to grow properly.

Melons take a long time to mature, usually from three to four months. For this reason, most varieties of melon—watermelon, honeydew, Crenshaw, Persian, and casaba—are grown in gardens in warm areas. Only the cantaloupe, properly called the muskmelon, matures fast enough—in 75 to 85 days—to be suitable for planting in areas with shorter growing seasons. In recent years, however, horticulturists have developed hybrid varieties of honeydew, Crenshaw melons, and miniature watermelons that mature in 80 to 90 days and so can be grown in many cooler regions.

Melons will not flourish if temperatures fall below 55° F at night and below 80° F during the day. Unless you can count on these temperatures for three months, grow quick-maturing varieties.

Gardeners in areas with short growing seasons have a bagful of tricks for encouraging melon growth. They usually start the melon seeds indoors, in pots, to get the longest possible growing season. In addition, they may plant their melons against a south-facing wall or fence that will reflect the sun's warmth, grow them in cold frames, or set them out in large tubs in warm, sheltered spots. Gardeners often use black plastic mulch on the soil in which the melons grow. Plastic mulch warms the soil with the heat it absorbs, and by acting as insulation also helps keep soil temperatures from dropping at night.

How to Grow Melons

Starting seedlings indoors. To start melons indoors, sow them in pots, three seeds to a pot. Use 3-inch peat pots or large paper cups that you can tear away when the seedlings are set out, because melons will not tolerate root disturbance when you transplant them. Do not use compressed peat cubes, however; they hold too much moisture and may cause the seeds to rot before they germinate.

Sow the seeds about four weeks before the date of the last expected frost, and leave the pots in a warm place: melon seeds need constant soil temperatures of about 70° F in order to germinate.

When the seedlings are about 2 inches high, thin them to the single strongest plant. Set out the seedlings when you can be sure of the required minimum daytime and nighttime temperatures, and preferably before the seedlings have started to grow vinelike tendrils. If melon seedlings are exposed to temperatures below 50° F, they will continue to grow, but they may never bear fruit. Before you transplant melons into the garden, be sure to harden them off—expose them gradually to outdoor conditions.

Planting melons. Melons are usually planted in enriched earth mounds called hills. To prepare a hill, dig a hole 1 foot deep and 2 feet wide, piling the excavated soil to one side. Fill the bottom of the hole with 4–6 inches of compost or well-rotted manure. Return the excavated soil to the hole until it forms a slight mound, about 4 inches high. Space the hills 4–6 feet apart, except for those intended for large watermelons, which should be spaced approximately 10 feet apart.

Cover the mounds with black plastic mulch. If you do not want to use plastic, you can spread on an organic mulch. It will add nutrients to your soil, but it will not trap heat as well as plastic mulch. Let the mounds settle for a few days before planting the seedlings in them.

Seedlings grown in peat pots are transplanted in their containers. Be sure the rims are set well below the ground surface so that the entire pot will remain moist and decompose. Just before setting the plants into the garden, slit the pots down the sides so that the melon roots can grow through the sides more easily. Paper-cup containers should be carefully cut away from the root ball. If you have used clay pots, rap each pot sharply on the bottom to loosen the entire root ball; then slip the plant out as gently as possible, to avoid disturbing the roots.

Make two planting slits in the plastic mulch covering each mound. Plant no more than two seedlings in each mound. Overcrowding will inhibit, rather than increase, yields.

Immediately after transplanting the seedlings, cover each one with a plant protector. You can buy paper protectors at garden centers or from most seed companies. Or you can make your own from half-gallon milk cartons by cutting off their tops and punching a few holes in the sides for ventilation. Plant protectors help retain warmth in the soil and shield the tender seedlings from chill winds and voracious insects. Remove the coverings in a few days when the plants have become established.

Water each hill thoroughly. If you are using a plastic mulch, water the mounds through the slits in the mulch.

Starting melons in warm climates. If you live in a warm-weather region, you can start melons from seeds sown directly into the garden. Prepare the soil as described above; then plant six to eight seeds in each hill. When the seedlings appear, choose the two strongest in each hill and cut off the others. Do not keep more; two plants will amply fill the space provided for them.

Caring for melons. When the melon vine runners are about a foot long, feed the plants with a 5–10–5 fertilizer—about ⅓ cup scattered around each hill. Fertilize again after the first fruits appear. In dry weather, be sure to keep the soil moist with a good soaking through the mulch. If weeds start to grow, pull them by hand, or hoe carefully to a depth of no more than 1 inch to avoid doing injury to the melons' shallow root systems.

If you have not laid down a mulch, when the melons form, lift each one gently and place under it a pad of straw or hay. By pillowing it in this way you will prevent the rotting that may occur when the fruit rests directly on the ground. Like cucumbers, melons can be trained to grow up a trellis or fence. Melons are much heavier than cucumbers, however, and will need support. You can devise a sort of sling from old sheeting; slip a strip of cloth under the melon, and tie each end to the trellis. Or use net bags, such as those onions are sold in. Place a bag over each melon, tying the ends to the trellis. Start training the vines while they are still young—melon vines grow more brittle as they mature. As the vines grow upward, be sure to keep tying the new growth securely to your fence or trellis.

Harvesting melons. Cantaloupes should be picked at the "slip" stage: when you press at the point where the melon joins the stem, the melon will slip off the vine.

Crenshaw and Persian melons are ripe when they give off a sweet, fruity odor, and casabas and honeydews are ripe when they turn yellow.

The surest sign of a ripe watermelon is a hollow sound as you give it a thump. A yellowing of the skin on the side that rests on the ground is another indication that the watermelon is fully ripe.

A word of caution: if melons start to form after midsummer, pick them off the vine. They will not have time to ripen fully and will merely draw nourishment away from the other developing fruits.

What Can Go Wrong With Melons

Striped cucumber beetles attack melon stems, leaves, and fruit, and may spread bacterial wilt, a disease that causes plants to wilt and die. Destroy these pests by spraying with rotenone or methoxychlor.

Wilting leaves may also indicate the presence of squash vine borers, which are hatched from eggs laid at the base of the plant and which tunnel into the stalks. Pick off borers if you see them, and destroy the eggs by spraying around the plant base with methoxychlor.

The major disease of melons, fusarium wilt, can be avoided by planting disease-resistant varieties. If plants show signs of this disease—brown coloration of the stems followed by wilt—destroy them.

White floury powder on the leaves is a sign of powdery mildew, which weakens the plant. Treat by cutting out affected shoots, and spray regularly with Benomyl or dinocap.

Varieties of Melon to Grow

Recommended cantaloupe varieties include the green-fleshed 'Burpee's Fordhook Gem' (82 days to maturity from seed); the orange-fleshed 'Delicious 51' (86 days), which is resistant to fusarium wilt; and the fast-maturing, orange-fleshed 'Harper Hybrid' (74 days).

Popular watermelon varieties include the rosy-fleshed 'You Sweet Thing' (70 days); the crisp, yellow-fleshed 'Yellow Baby Hybrid' (70 days); and the red-fleshed 'Charleston Gray' (85 days), which is resistant to fusarium wilt.

If you want to try one of the long-season melons or their hybrids, choose from: the white-fleshed 'Golden Beauty Casaba' (120 days); green-fleshed 'Honey Dew' (110 days); orange-fleshed 'Persian' (120 days); and pink-fleshed 'Burpee's Early Hybrid Crenshaw' (90 days).

Okra

Okra 'Clemson Spineless'

A relative of the tropical flower hibiscus, okra was brought to the Americas from Africa in the 1600's. Called gumbo, it became a staple of the cuisine of the Deep South. Its sticky consistency makes it a good thickener for "gumbo" soups and stews, and it is also fried or cooked with tomatoes.

Although okra grows best where the summers are long and hot, it will flourish wherever corn grows. By starting its seed indoors and thus getting a jump on summer, northern gardeners can enjoy this vegetable. It can be raised in ordinary garden soil, although like most vegetables, it will do better in rich, loamy ground.

Okra grows up to 5 feet tall and needs a lot of room. (Some people grow it as a hedge or garden border.) Because the plants are sensitive to cold winds, in cool regions they are often planted in a protected area.

The okra plant grows rapidly, producing large, pale yellow flowers, behind which slender, pointed seedpods soon develop. These pods are the edible fruit of okra and are ready to be picked about 60 days after the seeds are sown. Although the pods may grow up to 9 inches long, they are best when they are small—no longer than a finger.

How to Grow Okra

In cool areas—in fact, in any region where frost is common in winter—it is advisable to start okra indoors. Allow the seedlings about a month of indoor growing time.

To speed germination, soak the seeds for 24 hours before planting. Then, sow them in peat pots, two seeds to a pot, and after the seeds sprout, place the pots in a warm, sunny place. When the seedlings are about 1 inch tall, clip off the weaker plant. When nighttime temperatures remain above 55° F, set out the okra plants in their peat pots. Slit the sides of the pots so that the roots can push through easily, and bury the pots well belowground so that they will disintegrate. Space the plants 18 inches apart, in rows 3 feet apart.

In warm regions sow okra seeds directly in the garden. Sow the seeds in clusters of three or four—1 inch deep, 18 inches apart, in rows 3 feet apart. When the seedlings are about 1 inch tall, cut off all but the strongest plant in each one of the clusters.

Feed the plants twice with a 5–10–5 fertilizer—first when the plants are about 10 inches tall, and again when they start to blossom. Sprinkle the fertilizer in a wide band around each plant at the rate of 5 ounces for every 10 feet of row.

Okra needs very little attention beyond regular watering and weeding. A 2- to 3-inch layer of mulch will help keep weeds down and maintain soil moisture. Okra pods are at their peak when they are 2–3 inches long. Once they appear, they grow rapidly and will become tough and stringy in a matter of days; so keep a sharp eye on the pods from the time they start maturing.

To harvest okra, cut off the pods with a sharp knife. Do not leave ripe pods on the plant, because their presence causes the plant to stop production. Harvest daily, and store what you cannot eat in the refrigerator for a few days. If you harvest regularly, your plants should keep producing until the first frost.

What Can Go Wrong With Okra

Okra seldom succumbs to pests or diseases. If borers should infest a crop, spray the ground—where the eggs are laid—with methoxychlor and pick the borers off the plants. Control aphids, Japanese beetles, and corn earworms with Diazinon.

In hot areas, fusarium wilt, a soil disease, can destroy a crop; if it does, protect future crops by sterilizing the soil with metam-sodium.

Varieties of Okra to Grow

Most modern okra varieties are "spineless"—they lack the short, prickly spines that once made it necessary for okra harvesters to wear gloves. 'Clemson Spineless' produces slightly grooved pods that mature at 7–9 inches. 'Spineless Green Velvet' has a 7-inch smooth, round pod. 'Emerald Spineless,' also round-podded, is grown in short-season areas. 'Dwarf Green Long Pod' plants grow 2–2½ feet tall, rather than the usual 4–5 feet. 'Red Okra' produces red pods on a red bush and is both decorative and edible.

Onions and Leeks

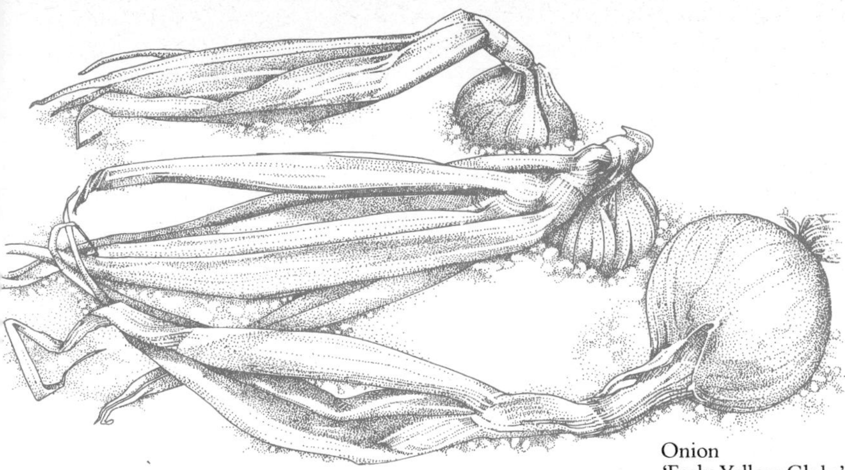
Onion 'Early Yellow Globe'

The common "globe" onion is grown for its bulb, but because the homegrown version is not noticeably superior to the commercially raised product, home gardeners often do not plant them.

On the other hand, scallions, or green onions (the young, green form of the onion), are more flavorful when they come straight from the garden than when they come from the grocery bin—and they also take up less space in the garden than globe onions. Although any onion can be picked at its scallion stage, certain varieties have been bred to be eaten solely as small-bulbed scallions. They are called bunching onions in seed catalogs because they are usually sold at the market in bunches.

The leek is a close relative of the onion. It resembles a giant scallion but has flat, broader leaves and different growing requirements.

The time to maturity for onions and leeks is considerable—three to five months from seed for onions, and about four and a half months for leeks, although scallions can be harvested as early as two months after sowing.

Garlic and chives are also related to onions and leeks, but they are considered herbs and are discussed in the section on herbs which begins on page 582.

1. *When the outer leaves begin to turn yellow, bend over the tops.*

2. *Two weeks later, lift the onions with a fork; spread them out to dry.*

How to Grow Onions and Leeks

Onions and leeks need fertile, carefully worked, moist soil with good drainage. Because they can be replanted for several years in the same spot, it is worth the effort to prepare a good bed for them. Work in 2 pounds or more of well-rotted manure or compost for every 5 feet of row, and apply 1 pound of 5–10–10 fertilizer for every 20 feet of row.

Planting globe onions. Globe onions are hardy, and their seeds can be planted in the garden early in the spring. But home gardeners usually plant onion "sets," or small bulbs, because this shortens the time to maturity by about four to six weeks and is more reliable than starting the plants from seeds. In areas where the ground freezes no more than ½ inch deep, onions can be planted in the fall for spring harvest.

Onion sets are sold by the pound; ½ pound will fill a 25-foot row. The bulbs should be no larger than ½ inch in diameter, or they may run to seed (flower prematurely) before producing edible onions.

Plant onion sets as soon as the ground can be worked. Place them 4 inches apart, 1 inch deep, in rows 12 inches apart. (Garden centers also carry onion seedlings; plant them in the same way as sets.)

If you are starting globe onions from seeds, sow the seeds as soon as the ground can be worked. Sow them about 1 inch apart and about ½ inch deep. When the seedlings are 3–4 inches tall, thin them to stand 2 inches apart. When the seedlings reach 6 inches, thin them to stand 4 inches apart.

Planting scallions (bunching onions). One way to grow scallions is to plant globe-onion seeds close together in clusters—about six to a cluster. Because you restrict their growing space by doing this, the plants will form long, white stems rather than globes. They can be harvested within two to three months.

Another way to raise scallions is from the seeds of specially bred bunching varieties. There are two main types: one is planted in early spring for summer harvest; the other can be sown either in late spring for harvesting in early fall or in fall for harvesting the following spring. In cold areas provide a thick mulch cover for fall planting.

To start scallions from seeds, follow the directions given above for starting globe onions from seeds—but do not thin out the seedlings.

Tending onions and scallions. Globe onions and scallions have shallow root systems, and therefore need frequent watering and careful weeding. To keep the weeds down, hoe shallowly between rows; within the rows pull out the weeds by hand.

The plants will also need additional fertilizer while they are growing. When they are 8–10 inches tall, spread a band of fertilizer along both sides of each row at the rate of ½ pound for every 25 feet of row. To avoid disturbing roots, soak the fertilizer into the soil by watering.

Harvesting onions and scallions. Globe onions are ready for harvest about five months after seeds have been sown or three and a half months after planting out sets or seedlings. The onion tops wither as the bulbs reach maturity, turning yellow and then brown. You can speed up the maturation process—and produce larger bulbs—by bending the tops over when the outer leaves turn yellow. Two weeks later loosen the bulbs by pushing a spading fork beneath them and lifting them slightly. In another two weeks lift out the bulbs with the fork. You can either cut the tops off an inch from the bulb or leave them on for braiding after the onions have dried. Spread the bulbs in a warm, airy place for a few days until they are completely dry. Then braid them and hang them up; or hang them up in mesh bags; or store them loosely in shallow, open boxes. The storage area should be cool and moderately humid.

You can begin harvesting scallions when the bulbs have reached $\frac{1}{4}$–$\frac{1}{2}$ inch in diameter. The only way to determine the size is to pull up a green onion and examine it. Once bunching onions start maturing, pull them up only as you need them—they can be stored for no more than about two weeks. Like onions, scallions should be completely dried before storage.

Planting leeks. Because the leek is grown for its long white bulb end, and the bulb will turn green and grow tough if exposed to sun, leeks are customarily planted in a trench so that the bulbs can be kept covered with earth. To prepare the trench, dig a furrow about 6 inches deep and 9 inches across. If you dig more than one trench, leave 1–2 feet between trenches. Clear the trench bottom of stones and clods, and work about 5 pounds of organic matter and 2 pounds of 5–10–10 fertilizer into every 25 feet of row. Prepare the soil during the fall before planting so that the organic matter and fertilizer will be fully incorporated into the soil by spring planting time.

Because of the time leeks take to mature (130 days), the seeds are sown indoors in most areas, 10 to 12 weeks before the date of the last expected frost. Sow the seeds 1 inch apart and $\frac{1}{8}$ inch deep. When sprouts appear, thin them with clippers so that the remaining plants stand about 2 inches apart. When the seedlings are about 4 inches tall, drop them into holes made 4–6 inches apart in the bottom of the trench, so that only the upper leaves stick partly out. As the leeks grow, heap the soil that you previously excavated for the trench around the lengthening bulbs.

Leek seeds can also be sown directly into the garden as soon as the soil can be worked. Garden-sown leeks may not be fully mature by the fall, but they can be mulched to remain in the soil through the winter, then harvested the next spring.

Plant leek seeds in a seedbed $\frac{1}{2}$ inch deep in rows 6 inches apart, and when the seedlings are 6–8 inches tall, transplant them to a trench (described previously). Cut half the leaf portion of each plant before transplanting; this lessens the shock in moving them.

Tending and harvesting leeks. Cultivate leeks as you do onions, fertilizing them in midseason and watering, rather than raking, the fertilizer into the soil. Weed assiduously and carefully, as with onions.

Leeks can be harvested long before full maturity. To harvest, dig up the plant with a spading fork. Store leeks in soil in your cellar, or leave them heavily mulched in the garden for harvesting. Side shoots can be removed and transplanted to yield another crop.

What Can Go Wrong With Onions and Leeks

Onion maggots feed on onions and leek bulbs. Once they infest a crop, nothing will save it. But you can protect your crop by spraying Diazinon along the rows when the plants are young. Thrips feed on the leaves, causing them to mottle and wither. Spray the plants with malathion to kill the thrips, carefully following the label directions.

Varieties of Onions and Leeks to Grow

Popular varieties of globe onions include 'White Portugal,' 'White Sweet Spanish,' 'Red Burgundy,' and 'Early Yellow Globe.' Among bunching onions, 'Evergreen White Bunching' and 'Hardy White Bunching' are recommended, while the most popular variety of leek is 'Broad London,' also called 'Large American Flag.'

Parsnips

Parsnip 'Hollow Crown'

The parsnip is a root vegetable that takes four months to mature. But because frost enhances its sweet, delicate flavor, it is a favorite with gardeners in areas with short growing seasons. In fact, if the soil is mulched well enough so that it does not freeze, parsnips can be left in the ground and harvested all winter. If the ground does freeze, they can be dug up the following spring.

In regions where winters are mild, parsnips can be planted in the fall for use as a winter crop.

How to Grow Parsnips

Parsnips are raised in much the same way as carrots. The edible root may grow to a depth of 15 inches, and any obstruction will cause it to fork or twist. So the soil where parsnips are to grow must be deeply spaded and raked clear of stones.

The seeds are sown directly into the garden about two weeks before the date of the last expected frost. Sow them thickly, $\frac{1}{2}$ inch deep, in rows 18–30 inches apart. Cover the seeds lightly with soil or with a combination of soil and sand or soil and peat moss; then tamp the soil down firmly. Because parsnip seeds germinate slowly, it is a good idea to sow radish seeds among them. The radishes will come up quickly and mark the row long before the parsnips sprout. When the parsnip seedlings are about an inch high, thin them to stand 2–3 inches apart.

Fertilize the parsnips every six weeks or so during the growing season, using about 5 ounces of a 5–10–10 fertilizer for every 10 feet of row. A mulch cover will help to discourage weeds.

You can begin harvesting parsnips when the tops of the roots are $1\frac{1}{2}$–2 inches in diameter. Dig them up carefully to avoid breaking them. Parsnips left in the ground for spring harvesting should be taken up before the plants begin to sprout new leaves. Stored in a cool place, parsnips remain sweet for weeks.

What Can Go Wrong With Parsnips

Do not plant parsnips near carrots or celery, for the same pests attack all three. The chief pest is the carrot fly, whose maggots bore into the roots. To protect plants, spray Diazinon on the soil after sowing.

Varieties of Parsnips to Grow

Recommended varieties of parsnips include 'Hollow Crown' and 'Harris Model.' 'All-American' is a high-quality parsnip that matures earlier than most of the other parsnips (in about 100 days).

Peas

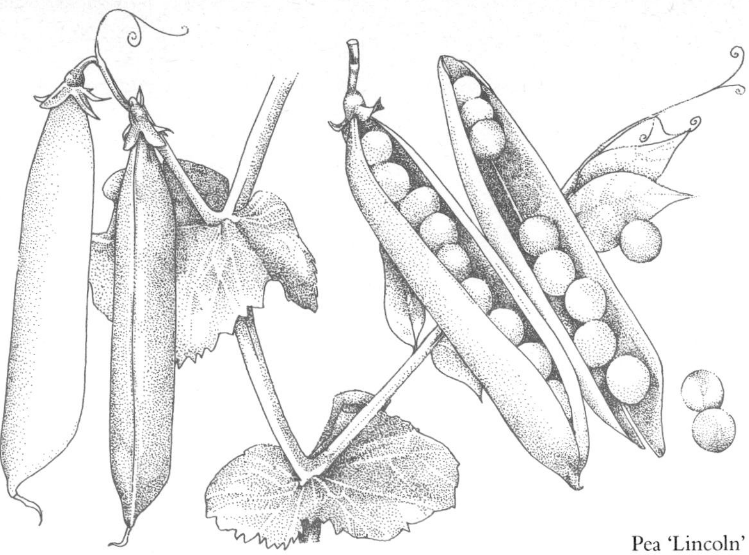

Pea 'Lincoln'

Homegrown peas cooked fresh from the garden are so much better than store-bought ones that a place for them should be found in even the smallest garden. Because peas are a cool-weather crop, planted in early spring, and because they mature quickly—about 55 days for very early peas—you can start another vegetable in their place after they have been harvested.

There are two major pea types: green peas (or English peas) and the edible-pod varieties (called sugar peas or snow peas), which are cooked and eaten with their pods. Although the yield for the edible-pod varieties is smaller, they are well worth growing for their delicate flavor and crisp texture.

Both green peas and edible-pod peas come in tall-vined and dwarf varieties. Dwarf peas usually require no support. The tall varieties need some support on which to climb, but they repay the extra effort with larger harvests.

Peas are extremely susceptible to heat and will stop maturing when the temperature regularly climbs above 70° F. When buying seeds, check the length of time each variety takes to mature. Choose early types if you live in an area with a short, cool spring. If cool weather lasts into summer, buy both an early and a late variety, and plant the two at the same time for a continuous crop.

Most pea seeds are treated with a fungicide that prevents seed rot in cold soil. A few untreated varieties are available, but they are much likelier to fail in a prolonged wet spell. If you buy treated seeds, be sure to keep them away from children and pets.

How to Grow Peas

Dig your pea patch as early in the spring as the ground can be worked. In turning the soil, work in generous amounts of organic material—rotted manure, compost, leaf mold, or old hay. For dwarf peas, dig a flat-bottomed furrow about 2 inches deep, 3–4 inches wide. For tall varieties, which need a trellis for support, make the furrow 10 inches wide, set the support in its center, and plant a row on each side. Tall peas can also be grown up a fence.

If you do not want to bother with a trellis, you can plant a double row of peas, which will support each other as the vines grow. This method works best with moderately tall plants that grow to about 18 inches. The high climbers—2½–3 feet tall—need extra support.

If you use a trellis, set it up before planting. Almost any form of support will serve: chicken wire, the lightweight plastic mesh available at garden centers, or rows of string drawn between two posts. You can also make a rough trellis from several tall, twiggy branches staked close together down the length of the row.

Just before sowing the seeds, cover the bottom of the trench with a small amount (about 2 ounces for every 10 feet of row) of low-nitrogen fertilizer (5–10–10). Mix with soil before sowing the seeds.

Before sowing, you may want to dust the pea seeds with a soil inoculant, a nitrogen-fixing bacterial culture that increases the plants' ability to add nitrogen to the soil. You can buy soil inoculants from a seed-catalog company or at a garden center.

Sow the pea seeds 1 inch apart and 2 inches deep. To prevent birds from eating the seeds, cover the rows with plastic netting or a mesh of string until the peas have sprouted.

When the seedlings reach about 3 inches in height, mound a bit of soil around the stems for support. As plants grow taller, hook their climbing tendrils around the trellis or other support you have provided.

Peas need a good deal of moisture, and mulching the rows is an excellent way both to maintain moisture and hold down weeds. Check the soil occasionally for dryness, and water when necessary. Because peas are especially vulnerable to fungous disease, water the plants at soil level so that the leaves will not get wet.

When the plants are 6–8 inches tall, spread a band of 5–10–10 fertilizer on both sides of each row at the rate of 5 ounces per 10 feet of row. To avoid fertilizer burn, be careful not to spill the fertilizer granules on the leaves.

If your pea vines should start to trail away from their support as they grow taller, tie them against it with long, narrow strips of cloth or with a few pieces of soft twine.

Peas taste best if they are picked while young and tender. One or two days too long on the vine can turn juicy peas into tough specimens. If you harvest regularly, you will be

STAKING TALLER VARIETIES

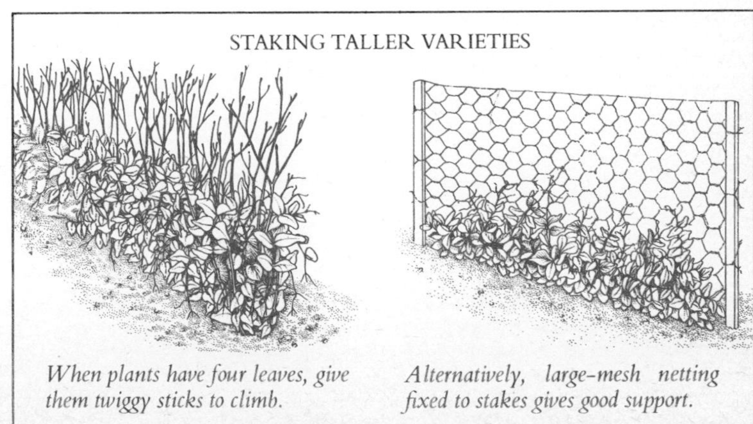

When plants have four leaves, give them twiggy sticks to climb.

Alternatively, large-mesh netting fixed to stakes gives good support.

able to pick the peas when they are just at their prime. Check the lowest pods often, for they mature first.

There is another good reason for harvesting peas regularly: mature pods left on the vine serve as a sort of signal to the plant to halt production.

Green peas should be picked when the pods are well filled but the peas inside are not yet hard. Edible-pod peas are ready to eat when the pods are just beginning to swell. If you wait until the pea shapes showing through the pod are noticeably round, the pods will be too tough to eat. (If you happen to let snow peas remain on the vine too long, all is not lost—you can shell and cook the peas as you would green peas.)

Harvest peas with care, holding the vine with one hand while you pick off the pod with the other. Otherwise you may remove part of the plant along with the pod.

If you are planning a succession crop in your pea patch, bear in mind that peas are heavy feeders and that what they take from the soil should be replaced. When the harvest is over, pull up the plants, and put them in the compost pile if you have one; or dig them directly into the soil. Fertilize the soil again, and add compost to it before you plant another crop in the pea patch.

If, as the end of the harvesting season draws near, there is a superabundance of peas on the vines, you may want to dry those you cannot use immediately. To do this, simply leave the pods on the vine until the peas are completely hard. Then pick and shell them, and dry them for half an hour in an oven set at "low." Store the dried peas in jars. If you plan to keep them over the winter, put the jars in a dry place to prevent mold from forming.

What Can Go Wrong With Peas

Aphids spread pea mosaic, a serious virus disease for which there is no treatment. Therefore, if aphids appear on the stems or undersides of pea leaves, wash them off or spray the plant with malathion. Pea weevils—tiny worms that may be black, white, or brown—can be picked off by hand or eliminated with malathion.

Powdery mildew is a common problem with peas during cold, wet springs. Treat the plants by dusting or spraying with dinocap or sulfur. Root rot may attack the plants at flowering time, turning the leaves yellow and darkening the stems and roots. There is no treatment, but you can avoid the disease the following season by planting peas in well-drained soil, preferably where they have not been grown before.

Varieties of Peas to Grow

Popular dwarf varieties of green peas include 'Little Marvel,' which grows 15–20 inches tall; the smooth-seeded 'Early Alaska' (the earliest variety, maturing in about 55 days); 'Sparkle' (another early variety, maturing in about 60 days), which grows about 15 inches tall; and 'Frosty,' which grows to 24 inches or more.

Among recommended tall types are 'Freezonian,' which grows about 30 inches tall, with 3-inch-long pods; 'Wando,' 30 inches tall, a heavy-yielding variety that will tolerate hot weather; 'Green Arrow,' 30 inches tall, which produces pea-packed pods near the top of the plant, making harvesting easier; and 'Lincoln,' 30 inches tall, which many rank among the tastiest of peas.

Good edible-pod peas are 'Dwarf Gray Sugar,' an early (65 days to maturity) variety that needs no staking; and 'Burpee Sweetpod,' a taller vine that needs support.

Peppers

Pepper 'Ace Hybrid'

There are two kinds of peppers: sweet and hot. Sweet peppers are also called bell peppers (for one of their characteristic shapes) or green peppers, although they turn red or sometimes yellow when fully ripe. Hot peppers also are green at first, turning red or yellow as they mature. Peppers are warmth-loving vegetables, like tomatoes and eggplants, and they are similarly cultivated.

Seed catalogs list a dizzying variety of shapes and sizes for both sweet and hot peppers. Gardeners in areas with short growing seasons find it advisable to choose the early varieties, for even the earliest types need at least two months from the time young plants are set out to the time when peppers are mature enough to be harvested—and this does not include the eight weeks necessary to produce seedlings ready for transplanting outdoors.

How to Grow Peppers

Peppers can be started indoors from seeds about eight weeks before the date of the last expected frost. Sow the seeds in individual pots, placing three seeds, $\frac{1}{4}$ inch deep, in each pot. Keep the containers in a warm location—about 75° F. When seedlings appear, move the pots to a place that is sunny as well as warm. When the plants are about an inch tall, remove all but the strongest one in each container.

Be especially careful in "hardening off" pepper plants—exposing them gradually to outdoor conditions. Too much cold will slow the plants' growth or even kill them.

Pepper seedlings are available at garden centers if you do not want to raise them yourself. Make certain that the plants you buy have short, sturdy stems and deep green leaves.

In planting peppers, avoid areas where you have previously grown tomatoes or eggplants, for all three vegetables are susceptible to similar diseases. Enrich the soil with a 3- to 4-inch layer of organic matter, and work in 1 pound of 5–10–10 fertilizer for every 25 feet of row. Space the rows 2 feet apart.

You can also prepare individual planting areas for the seedlings. Dig holes 6 inches deep and 6 inches in diameter. Put in a 2-inch layer of compost or rotted manure mixed with 1 tablespoon of fertilizer. Then fill the hole with soil. Allow at least 2 feet in all directions between holes. Although it is not absolutely necessary, staking the plants will help keep them from toppling in strong winds. Set the stakes in position before you plant the seedlings.

When all danger of frost is past and daytime temperatures stay above 55° F, it is time to transplant your seedlings. Set them out on a cloudy day or in the evening, so that the sun will not scorch them. Allow 18 inches between seedlings in rows.

After planting, water the soil well, and immediately provide the plants with protection against insects and the elements. Keep cutworms away by placing around each plant a collar made from a paper cup with its bottom removed. Shield the young plants against chilly rains or too much sun by covering them with translucent paper cups which are available at most garden stores.

Peppers are not heavy feeders. If you have provided sufficient fertilizer before planting, you should not need to fertilize the soil again during the growing season.

Pepper plants require a moist soil for fruit formation; so cover the ground surrounding the plants with a mulch, and water regularly in dry weather. If weeds manage to grow through the mulch cover, pull them up carefully by hand.

Sweet peppers can be eaten at any stage of their growth. Full-size green peppers left on the plant will turn bright red and become slightly sweeter. Harvest them as you like or as you need them—but do not leave fully ripe red peppers on the plant. Their presence will reduce its subsequent yield.

When harvesting peppers, always *cut* the fruit off its branch. If you try to pull off the pepper, you may break the branch.

Because peppers mature late in the season, frost may occur before you have harvested all the fruits. If cold weather threatens, protect the plants by covering them with plastic sheeting anchored to the ground with rocks or soil. If the frost is not too severe, this measure may save the plants. Or, if the plants are nearing the end of fruit production, pull them up by the roots and hang them in a cool spot indoors; the peppers on the plant will continue to ripen for a few more days.

Hot peppers should be allowed to achieve full growth and flavor before harvesting. They will keep well if you thread a string through their stems and hang them indoors.

What Can Go Wrong With Peppers

Few pests attack peppers. If aphids appear, wash them away with a stream from the garden hose, or if necessary, spray the plants with Diazinon or malathion. If you see whiteflies, dust the plants with pyrethrum.

Varieties of Peppers to Grow

'Ace Hybrid' is an early sweet pepper. Later types include 'Calwonder,' 'Yolo Wonder,' and 'Bell Boy Hybrid.' Popular among hot peppers are 'Long Red Cayenne' and 'Hungarian Yellow Wax.'

Potatoes

Potato 'Norgold Russet'

It takes quite a bit of garden space—and no small effort—to grow potatoes. But if you have lately sorted through soft, wrinkled potatoes in the market to find a few firm ones, you may be ready to try your hand at a potato patch.

Potatoes will grow almost anywhere if they have fertile, well-drained soil and plenty of sunshine. In most areas two potato crops can be planted: early and late. The former is for summer harvest and use, the latter for fall harvest and storage for winter use. In areas where winters are frost free and summers are very hot, only one crop is planted in fall or early winter.

How to Grow Potatoes

Potatoes are grown from those pieces of the tuber that contain the "eyes," the tiny depressions from which sprouts grow. These "seed" pieces, when planted, will produce leafy vines aboveground and clusters of potatoes below. Do not use store-bought potatoes for seed, since they are often treated with a chemical that inhibits sprouting. You will be much surer of getting a good crop if you order certified disease-free seed potatoes from a seed company or buy them at a farm supply center.

To prepare seed potatoes for planting, cut them into 2-ounce pieces, each about the size of a large walnut. Each piece should contain at least one eye. Cure the seed pieces by spreading them out in a bright, airy place until they dry slightly and their cut surfaces harden. Some gardeners dust the pieces with the fungicide Captan to prevent rot. But Captan is poisonous; so handle it carefully and keep it out of children's reach and away from pets.

Potatoes require acidic soil, tolerating soil with a pH as low as 5.2. Do not plant them in areas that have recently been limed.

An excellent way to prepare the soil for potatoes is to spread a 3- to 5-inch layer of well-rotted manure over the area to be planted; this will serve to enrich the soil and to improve drainage. A 5–10–10 fertilizer should be applied at the rate of 1 pound per 10 feet of row if you have not added manure ($\frac{1}{2}$ pound if you have). Mix the fertilizer thoroughly into the soil; direct contact with concentrations of fertilizer will injure the potato pieces.

As soon as the ground can be worked, plant the seed pieces in furrows 4 inches deep, 3 inches wide, and 3 feet apart. Set the pieces 12 inches apart, with eyes facing upward, and cover with 3 inches of soil.

About three weeks after the seeds are planted, sprouts will push up through the ground. As the vines grow, mound up over them with earth, leaves, straw, or compost to keep the developing tubers covered. Potatoes that are exposed to sunlight turn green and develop a toxic substance called solanine.

It is not necessary to fertilize the plants again during the growing period, but be sure that the soil around them remains loose and free of weeds. To do this, cultivate with a hoe—shallowly because the tubers grow close to the surface.

You can start harvesting tubers at about the time the potato flowers bloom, seven to eight weeks after planting. Push aside the earth at the base of the plant, and carefully pick off some of the small potatoes. These are the highly valued "new" potatoes, which you can boil and eat in their skins. Leave some potatoes to grow to full size.

When the plant foliage begins to wither and die down, the potatoes are full-grown. At this time, dig the tubers from the soil with a spading fork. Although you can leave potatoes in the ground for a time after the foliage has died, you should dig them up before the first heavy frost.

If you want to store potatoes, wash them and put them loosely in a ventilated, covered container to dry for a few hours. (Never expose potatoes directly to sunlight.) Store them in a dark, cool (38°–40° F) place.

What Can Go Wrong With Potatoes

You gain protection against many of the diseases that infect potatoes when you use certified seed potatoes, but potato blight may still be a problem. It first appears as purplish blotches on the leaves, which then turn brown and rot. To prevent blight, spray the potatoes with maneb every 7 to 10 days from the time that the plants reach 6 inches in height.

Another common potato disease is scab. Prevent it by planting scab-resistant varieties, such as 'Norland,' and by keeping the soil acid.

The potato's worst insect enemy is the Colorado potato beetle. Both the adult beetle and its red larvae defoliate and destroy potato plants. Pick off the pests by hand, or dust or spray the plants with methoxychlor. For battling aphids and leafhoppers, which can spread potato virus diseases, Diazinon is effective.

Varieties of Potatoes to Grow

Check with your garden center or county agricultural agent regarding the best varieties of potatoes to grow in your area. Of the early potatoes, 'Irish Cobbler,' 'Norgold Russet,' and 'Norland' do well in most areas. Of the late potatoes, 'Katahdin,' 'Kennebec,' and 'Russet Burbank' are popular.

Potatoes, Sweet

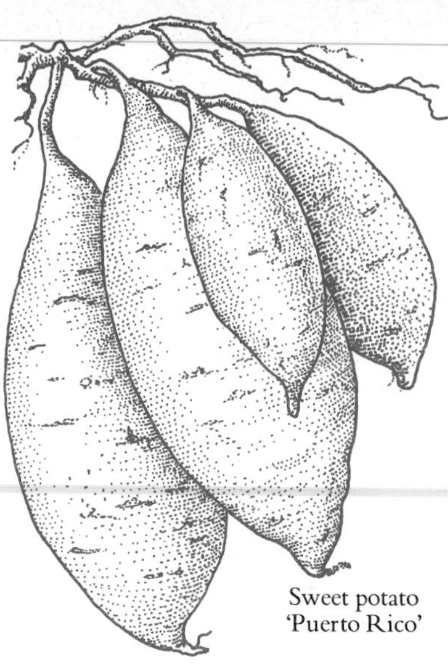

Sweet potato 'Puerto Rico'

Sweet potatoes thrive in the long, hot summers of the South, but they can be raised wherever they will have 150 frost-free days to grow in. Once planted, sweet potatoes produce their nutritious, flavorful roots with little more care.

How to Grow Sweet Potatoes

Sweet potato vines are raised from the sprouts, or slips, that their tubers send out. One potato suspended on toothpicks in a container and half-covered with water will produce several sprouts. Larger quantities can be grown by placing several potatoes on a bed of sand and covering them with a 2-inch layer of moist sand or soil. Keep sprouting tubers at 75° F. Buy slips at a garden center if starting your own is not feasible.

Start the slips a month before warm weather settles in, when nights get no colder than 60° F. During that month the sprouts will grow to 8–10 inches, and each will bear several leaves. Remove the slips for planting by giving them a twist.

Sweet potatoes do best in loose, sandy soil. To prepare the soil, dig in a 5–10–10 fertilizer at the rate of 2 pounds per 25 feet of row. Then push the soil into a foot-wide, flat-topped mound 6 inches high.

Plant the slips 15 inches apart in the center of the mound, and set them 6 inches into the ground, leaving at least two leaves aboveground. Water well.

Sweet potatoes require very little care. A bit of weeding, done carefully so as not to injure the shallow roots, is usually all that is needed.

When the tops of the plants turn black after the first frost, the sweet potatoes are ready to harvest. (In frost-free areas, harvest four months after planting the slips.) In areas with less than four months' growing time, tubers can be dug out before they reach mature size.

Dig sweet potatoes carefully, for their skins bruise easily. Let the tubers dry for several hours, and then spread them in newspaper-lined boxes. Leave them in a dry, warm area for about two weeks; then store in a cool, dry place (50°–55° F).

What Can Go Wrong With Sweet Potatoes

The sweet potato weevil feeds on the leaves of the vine, and its larvae tunnel into the tuber. To ged rid of this pest, keep the ground clear of leaves and other debris. Spray affected plants with methoxychlor, and destroy infested potatoes.

Varieties of Sweet Potatoes to Grow

There are two types of sweet potato: dry-fleshed and moist-fleshed. In cool areas dry-fleshed varieties, such as 'Nemagold,' 'Jersey Orange,' and 'Nugget,' are recommended. 'Centennial' and 'Puerto Rico' are popular moist-fleshed types.

Radishes

Radish 'Champion'

There are two types of radish: the popular bright-red or white fast-maturing summer radish, and the slower-maturing, sharper-flavored winter radish, which has either a black or a white skin.

Children like to grow red radishes because the time between planting and eating them is so short—only three weeks for many varieties. Plant short rows—5 or 6 feet will produce all that the average family can consume during one crop's brief harvesting period. To ensure a supply all season long, however, make succession plantings every week or 10 days—except in midsummer, for radishes will not grow well when temperatures go above 80° F. In most areas a few succession crops can be planted in late summer for harvest before the ground freezes.

Winter radish varieties mature in 60 days or more, and they are planted in midsummer for fall use.

How to Grow Radishes

To prepare the soil for radishes, dig it to a depth of about 6 inches, and work in a 1- or 2-inch layer of compost or well-rotted manure and about 1 cup of 10–10–10 fertilizer for every 5 feet of row.

Sow the radish seeds directly into the garden as soon as the ground can be worked. The seeds are just large enough so that you can space them by hand when planting, and thus avoid much time-consuming thinning later on. In a $\frac{1}{2}$-inch-deep furrow, put down one seed every $\frac{1}{2}$ inch. Tamp the soil firmly over the seeds, and water gently.

You can save garden space by interplanting radishes in rows with slower-growing vegetables, such as carrots and parsnips. The prime requirements for healthy radishes are water (a good soaking at least once a week, and more often during dry spells) and growing space. Overcrowded radish plants will not form the thick roots for which they are grown. No matter how carefully you have sown your seeds, you will probably have to thin the plants to achieve the optimum spacing of 1–2 inches between plants.

Weed often and carefully, remembering that the roots grow close to the soil surface. Loose, cultivated soil encourages root formation.

Depending on the variety, summer radishes mature in about 20 to 30 days, and winter varieties in 60 to 75 days. The seed packet will tell you the best harvesting size for the variety you are growing. If radishes grow too large, they become tough and sharp-flavored. A split or cracked root means the vegetable is overage.

What Can Go Wrong With Radishes

Insects rarely attack the pungent radish. The principal pest is a root maggot, which tunnels into the roots and is often in the soil where cabbage has previously grown. To combat this pest, sprinkle Diazinon granules on top of the rows after planting, according to label directions, and water into the soil. Repeat a week later.

Cabbage worms may also eat radish leaves. Control them with the pesticide *Bacillus thuringiensis.*

Varieties of Radishes to Grow

Popular red summer radishes are 'Cherry Belle' (which matures in 22 days and is $\frac{3}{4}$ inch in diameter), 'Sparkler' (25 days, $1\frac{1}{4}$ inches), 'Champion' (28 days, 2 inches). 'White Icicle' (28 days, 5 inches long) is a mild, white summer radish, best eaten when young.

Recommended winter radishes include 'Round Black Spanish' (55 days, $3\frac{1}{4}$–4 inches in diameter) and 'White Chinese,' also called 'Celestial' (60 days, 6–8 inches long).

INTERPLANTING CARROTS AND RADISHES

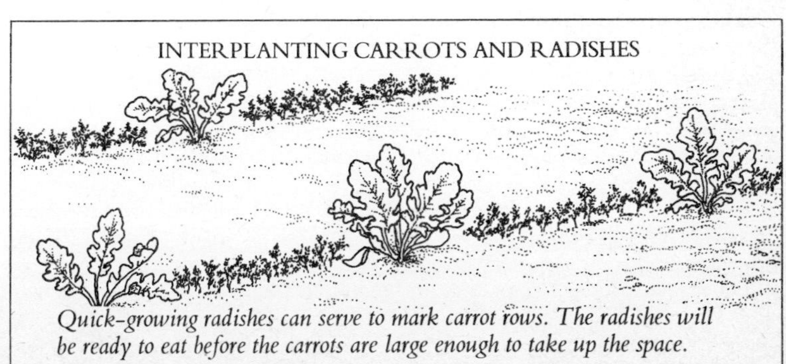

Quick-growing radishes can serve to mark carrot rows. The radishes will be ready to eat before the carrots are large enough to take up the space.

Rhubarb

Rhubarb 'Valentine'

Although rhubarb is generally classified as a vegetable, its long, red, tart-flavored stalks are traditionally used as a fruit—in pies, cobblers, jams, and jellies, or simply stewed and served as a compote. Rhubarb lovers will want to allot space for this vegetable, whose foliage is as attractive as the stems are tasty.

Rhubarb is a long-lived perennial plant, and its cultivation is similar in many respects to that of another prized perennial vegetable, asparagus. Like asparagus, rhubarb is planted in beds that require a lot of preparation, but once the plants are established, they need a minimum of care and will produce for many years. Like asparagus, rhubarb needs a dormant period and grows best in areas where winters are cold enough to freeze the ground to a depth of at least 2 or 3 inches.

Rhubarb, like asparagus, grows well in almost any type of soil, but it is a heavy feeder and should not be planted in poor soil unless you are able to add copious quantities of organic material and fertilizer.

Rhubarb is seldom started from seeds. Instead, it is propagated by planting "crowns"—root divisions that carry the buds from which new plants will grow. Rhubarb crowns can be ordered from seed catalog companies, or you can buy the crowns from your local nursery or garden center.

Because rhubarb is a perennial plant, which inhabits the same piece of ground for many years, it should be given an isolated spot in your vegetable garden—in a corner, for example, or along one side—where it will not interfere with, or be damaged by, your work on annual crops.

How to Grow Rhubarb

Rhubarb plants need well-drained, fertile soil, and the ground has to be worked quite deeply. But rather than having to dig a row or trench, you need only make a hole for planting each crown.

Dig the holes 2 feet deep and 2 feet wide, and space them 3 feet apart in all directions. Fill the bottom of each with a 6-inch layer of compost or manure. Mix the soil you have dug up with an equal amount of compost or manure, and add ⅓ cup of 10–10–10 fertilizer. Fill the hole with the mixture to a depth of 1 foot.

In early spring place one rhubarb crown in each hole so that the top, where the plant buds are located, sits 3–4 inches below the soil surface. Tamp the soil firmly around the roots, and fill each hole with the compost and topsoil mixture until level with the surrounding soil.

When the first growth appears—and every succeeding spring as well—spread half a pound of 10–10–10 fertilizer around the shoots, and scratch it into the soil with a hand cultivator. Maintain a permanent mulch around each plant to help keep the soil moist and to prevent winter frost from setting in too hard around the roots. Remove the mulch before fertilizing, and afterward push it back in place.

Rhubarb plants produce seed stalks which, if allowed to flower, will reduce production of edible stalks. So, cut off seed stalks as soon as you see them.

After several years, rhubarb plants tend to become crowded and the stalks grow noticeably thinner. At this point, dig up the plants and divide their roots. Do this in the spring when the new shoots are just beginning to emerge, or in early fall. Cut the roots into several parts, each of which should have one to three buds. Treat these sections as though they were new crowns, and plant them in another part of your garden. If you plant the crowns in the fall, mulch heavily.

Rhubarb stalks grow to 18 inches or taller. If your plants are of mature size, harvest a few stalks in spring the second year after planting. Beginning the third year, harvest about half the stalks, leaving the thinner ones, which will grow and help to nourish the roots.

Harvest rhubarb by holding the stalk near the base and twisting it off. Do not eat the tops; they are mildly poisonous.

Forcing rhubarb in winter. If you would like to enjoy rhubarb in winter, try this easy forcing method: In the fall, after the tops have died down, dig up a whole plant and place it in a tub 18 inches in diameter, which you have filled with topsoil, compost, and manure. Leave the tub outside for several weeks of freezing weather, and then move it to a dark, cool place. Keep the soil moist. About a month before you plan to harvest, move the tub into a warm area (60° F is best), still in the dark, if possible. The dormant roots will begin to sprout, and you can harvest when the stalks are about 18 inches tall.

What Can Go Wrong With Rhubarb

Rhubarb is relatively free from pests or diseases. The rhubarb curculio—a short, yellow, juice-sucking beetle—thrives in weedy patches, however. Keep the land weed free; pick any curculios off plants.

Varieties of Rhubarb to Grow

'MacDonald' and 'Valentine' are standard red-stemmed rhubarb varieties. 'Victoria' has green, rather than red, stalks. For areas where the winters are relatively mild, 'Cherry' is recommended.

Spinach, Chard, and Mustard Greens

Spinach 'Viking'

Spinach, chard, and mustard greens belong to a group of vegetables loosely referred to as greens because they are grown for their tender, vitamin-rich leaves and stems. (Greens also include kale and collards, discussed on p. 564, and turnip greens, discussed on p. 581.)

Spinach grows well only in cool regions. In warmer areas gardeners often substitute Malabar spinach or New Zealand spinach, which are unrelated to true spinach but taste somewhat like it and are used like it. Chard (or Swiss chard) is a relative of the beet but is grown for its tops only. It is easy to grow and prolific. Mustard greens have a piquant flavor and mature quickly.

Spinach, Swiss chard, and mustard greens have the same soil and nutrient needs: a nonacid soil (with a pH of 6–7.5) enriched with organic matter and high in nitrogen. With the exception of Swiss chard and Malabar and New Zealand spinach, greens are cool-weather crops; in hot weather they will "bolt" (produce seeds and stop growing). Greens are resistant to cold and, if they are given a thick mulch cover, will thrive through a few light frosts.

How to Grow Spinach, Chard, and Mustard Greens

To prepare beds for greens, dig up the soil as soon as the ground can be worked, incorporating up to 1 bushel of rotted manure or compost for every 50 square feet, plus 1–2 pounds of 10–10–10 fertilizer.

Planting and tending spinach. Sow spinach seeds in furrows ½ inch deep, spacing the rows about 15 inches apart. Because spinach matures quickly—in 40 to 50 days—and bolts easily, plant short rows, and make succession sowings every 10 days until daytime temperatures reach a consistent 70° F. Start succession plantings again in late August for harvesting through the fall.

Thin the newly emerged seedlings to stand 3 inches apart. When the leaves of plants touch, pull up every other plant, and use it for salad. The final thinning should leave the plants about 10 inches apart.

When the plants are 6–8 inches high, apply a high-nitrogen fertilizer at the rate of 3 ounces for every 10 feet of row. Weed regularly, and keep the plants thoroughly watered.

Begin culling the outside leaves as soon as they reach edible size. Harvest the entire plant when buds start to form in its center.

Planting and tending Malabar and New Zealand spinach. Malabar spinach is a glossy-leaved vine that does well in extremely hot weather. Trained to grow up a fence or trellis, it takes very little space and produces edible leaves in about 70 days. When all danger of frost is past, sow the seeds ½ inch deep and about 3 inches apart.

New Zealand spinach also does well in warm weather. Sow the seeds in pots indoors, first soaking the seeds overnight. Leave them in a cool place, and when sprouts appear, clip off all but the single strongest seedling in each pot. Set the plants out about two weeks before the last expected frost.

New Zealand spinach can spread 3–4 feet across; so give it plenty of room—18 inches between plants in rows 3 feet apart. About 60 to 70 days after planting outdoors, the leaves nearest the growing tips, and the tips themselves, can be cut off and eaten. The more you cut, the more the plant will grow.

Planting and tending chard. Beginning about 60 days after sowing, Swiss chard will produce greens generously all summer long. Around the time of the last frost, sow the seeds (which are actually clusters of several seeds) in furrows ½ inch deep and 30 inches apart. Space these seedballs about 3 inches apart, and when the seedlings appear, thin the young plants to stand 6 inches apart. When the leaves of plants touch, pull out every other plant; you can eat the plants you remove.

Mulch the ground and fertilize at least once during the season with a 10–10–10 fertilizer—3 or 4 ounces for every 10 feet of row.

To harvest chard, cut off the outer leaves near the base of the plant; new leaves will develop at the center.

Planting and tending mustard greens. Plant mustard greens in prepared soil early in the spring and, in areas with mild winters, in September or October. Sow the seeds 1–1½ inches apart, in furrows ½ inch deep and about 15 inches apart. When seedlings appear, thin them to stand 6 inches apart. Make several succession sowings in the early spring and one or two in late summer. Mustard greens should be harvested in 35 to 40 days, before the plants are full-grown, or they may go to seed.

What Can Go Wrong With Greens

Spinach is often afflicted with a mosaic virus, or blight, that causes the leaves to yellow; to avoid it, buy resistant varieties. If aphids or leaf miners attack, spray the plant with malathion. Leaf miners also sometimes infest chard, although chard and mustard greens are relatively immune to pests and diseases.

Varieties of Greens to Grow

Popular varieties of spring spinach include 'Long-standing Bloomsdale' and 'America,' both crinkly leaved ("savoyed") types, and 'Viking,' a smooth-leaved variety. 'Hybrid No. 7' and 'Winter Bloomsdale' can be planted either in spring or in fall. Look for New Zealand and Malabar under "Spinach" in seed catalogs.

Among Swiss chard varieties, 'Fordhook Giant,' with dark green leaves, and 'Lucullus,' with lighter ones, are popular. 'Rhubarb Chard' has red stalks and green leaves.

Of the mustard varieties, 'Tendergreen' is the fastest growing—about 35 days to harvest. 'Florida Broad Leaf' matures in 40 days and has smooth leaves.

Squash and Pumpkin

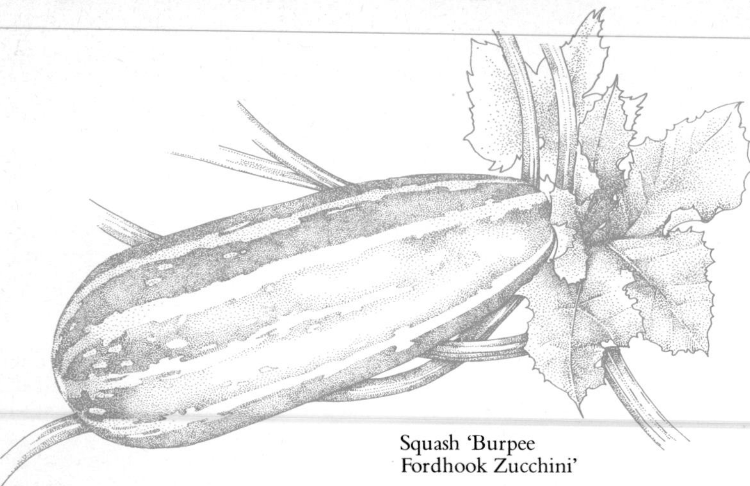

Squash 'Burpee Fordhook Zucchini'

Despite their difference in taste and appearance, the two main types of squash, summer and winter, are closely related botanically and are grown and cultivated in the same way. Along with melons and cucumbers, they belong to the gourd family, all members of which need a lot of room to grow in.

Summer squashes usually grow as sprawling bush plants and are harvested long before they reach maturity, while their skins are still tender and edible. Most winter squashes grow as vines, requiring even more space than summer squashes. They are left on the vine until fully mature; by then, their rinds are tough and generally inedible. Properly stored, winter squashes can be kept throughout the winter.

Pumpkins are simply a kind of squash—some of them growing as bushes, others as vines. Like winter squashes, they are allowed to mature before harvesting.

The varieties of squash seem infinite. Summer squashes include yellow squash, either "crookneck" or "straightneck"; zucchini, or green squash; and the white or pale green scallop squash. Most summer varieties can be picked within 50 to 60 days after planting.

The earliest-maturing winter squashes are acorn and butternut, which are ready to be picked in 75 to 85 days. The turban-shaped buttercup squash matures in about 100 days. Slate-gray or green Hubbard squash, which can grow to enormous size, is ready for harvest in about 110 days. Pumpkins ripen in 100 to 120 days.

All squashes need a rich, loamy soil that will retain moisture, and grow best when nutrients are added in the form of humus or fertilizer.

How to Grow Squash and Pumpkin

Squash is usually planted in mounds of earth called hills. To prepare a hill, dig a hole 12–18 inches deep and about 2 feet in diameter. Fill the bottom of the hole with 4–6 inches of compost or well-rotted manure. Then shovel the excavated soil back into the hole until it forms a mound about 6–8 inches high. Space the hills 4–6 feet apart for bush varieties and 8–10 feet apart for vine plants, including pumpkins.

Squash can be sown outdoors at the same time that tomato and eggplant seedlings are set out—when night temperatures remain above 55° F. Sow six seeds per hill, about 1 inch deep. When the seedlings are approximately 6 inches tall, thin them to the two or three strongest plants in each hill.

Squash seeds can also be sown in pots indoors, about three to four weeks earlier. The seedlings can be set back by transplanting, however, and you must be very careful not to disturb their roots.

If you have provided sufficient compost or manure during soil preparation, you should not have to add fertilizer. But if you are not sure that your squash has enough nutrients, scatter ⅓ cup of 5–10–10 fertilizer around each plant when it has put out a few leaves.

Like other gourd family members, squash needs a lot of moisture. Water the plants slowly and deeply during dry spells, but resist the temptation to soak them constantly.

Mulching is especially beneficial for squash; besides helping the soil retain its moisture and keeping weeds down, a layer of mulch under the vines protects the fruits against insects and keeps them from rotting.

Squash vines can be pruned if you find that they are invading other areas of your garden. At the time that you see small fruits on the vines, cut off the ends of the long runners, making sure that you have left sufficient leaves to nourish the plant.

To harvest squash, cut off the fruits with a knife. A summer squash should be cut when it is still small and when you can easily pierce its skin with a fingernail. Pick elongated squashes when they are 1½–2 inches in diameter; pick scallops when they are 3–4 inches across.

Winter varieties should be left on the vine until their rinds are hard. Cure them in the sun or in a warm, ventilated area for a week or so; then store them in a dry place where the temperature is 55°–60° F.

What Can Go Wrong With Squash and Pumpkin

Squash and pumpkin are subject to the same diseases that attack cucumbers and melons. Striped cucumber beetles can spread a bacterial disease that causes the plants to wilt and die. Destroy the beetles by spraying the plants with methoxychlor or rotenone. Squash vine borers hatch from eggs laid at the plants' base and tunnel into the stalks. The most effective treatment is to spray methoxychlor around the base, but if the borers hatch and tunnel into the plants, cut them out with a knife.

There is no treatment for fusarium wilt, a fungous disease, but it can be prevented by crop rotation or by sterilizing the soil with metam-sodium. If powdery mildew should appear on the leaves, cut off the affected shoots, and spray the plants regularly with Benomyl.

Varieties of Squash and Pumpkin to Grow

Popular summer squashes include 'Burpee Fordhook Zucchini' and 'Cocozelle' (a zucchini type); 'Early Prolific Straightneck'; and 'St. Pat's Scallop Hybrid.' All are bush types.

Recommended winter squash vine varieties include 'Blue Hubbard' (15 pounds); 'Table Queen,' or 'Acorn,' (1–2 pounds); 'Buttercup' (5 pounds); and 'Waltham Butternut' (3–4 pounds). Bush types include 'Gold Nugget' (2 pounds) and 'Bush Ebony,' a 1- to 1½-pound acorn type.

Among pumpkins, 'Small Sugar' grows to a 10-inch diameter and is especially good for pies. 'Big Max' can reach 70 inches in circumference but is better for carving into jack-o' lanterns than for eating. A good bush variety is 'Cinderella,' with fruits about 10 inches across.

Tomatoes

Tomato 'Small Fry Hybrid'

The tomato has for some time been the most popular plant in the home vegetable garden, and seed catalogs devote more space to it than to any other vegetable.

The popularity of this easy-to-grow plant has encouraged seedsmen to develop hundreds of new varieties—in shapes, sizes, and colors that the early Mexican Indians (who grew *tomatl* long before Europeans set foot on their soil) would have difficulty recognizing. More important than the look or taste of the new tomatoes, however, is the fact that a large number of them are hybrid varieties, bred to resist the soil-borne diseases to which tomatoes are particularly vulnerable.

Seed catalog listings always include information about the disease or pest resistance of each variety: the letter V means the tomato is resistant to verticillium wilt; F stands for fusarium wilt resistance; N, for nematode resistance. Both verticillium and fusarium cause wilting of the tomato leaves. Nematodes are microscopic worms that destroy the plant's root system. Buying resistant seeds will not guarantee healthy tomato plants, but it will give your plants a far better chance to grow until harvest time.

Tomato varieties are divided into two broad groups—early and main season. Early tomatoes are usually determinate: that is, they grow to a certain size, produce a crop, and then die. They do not have to be supported. Main-season tomatoes are almost always indeterminate: they will continue to grow and bear indefinitely, until frost kills them. And although they will produce if left to sprawl along the ground, the crop will be more vulnerable to diseases and insects, and it will not ripen as fast as it does when the plants are properly staked and firmly supported.

Because tomatoes are highly sensitive to cold, gardeners in areas with short growing seasons should plant a few early tomatoes, as well as a main crop. In all but the warmest areas of the country, tomatoes are set out as seedlings; and the number of days to maturity given in the catalogs is always counted from the time plants are set out in the garden.

How to Grow Tomatoes

Tomato seeds should be sown indoors about eight weeks before the date of the last expected frost in your area. Sow them $\frac{1}{8}$ inch deep in flats or pots, and when the seedlings are about 1 inch tall, transplant them to individual 3- or 4-inch pots. Keep them moist and in a warm, sunny spot. Be sure to harden them off before transplanting them outdoors.

If you do not want to start your own tomato plants, seedlings are available at garden centers. Ask your nurseryman which types would grow best in your area, and choose sturdy plants in uncrowded flats. Find out, too, whether the tomatoes have been hardened off; if they have not, you will have to do it.

Soil preparation is important for a good tomato crop. The fall before you plant, if possible, dig up your tomato plot, and work it several inches deep, incorporating a 2-inch layer of compost or organic matter into the soil. In early spring rake in a 5–10–10 fertilizer (about 1 pound for 25 feet of row).

If you have not prepared the soil this way, dig a hole for each plant—6 inches deep and 2 feet in diameter for early tomatoes, 3 feet for later ones. In the bottom of each hole place a 2-inch layer of compost or damp peat moss mixed with a handful of fertilizer and some of the topsoil you have dug up.

Supporting tomatoes. If you plan to use a trellis or stakes, set them into the ground before planting. The most popular form of support is a tall stake driven into the ground next to each plant. As the plant grows, the stem is tied loosely to the stake with soft twine or cloth strips. Tall-growing tomato plants will have to be tied several times.

There are other methods of supporting tomatoes: try a 6-foot-high trellis made of chicken wire, running the length of the row; or set in posts at the ends of the row, run a wire between them, then attach each plant to the wire with heavy twine. All these techniques serve the same aims: to support the plants as they grow and to keep the tomatoes off the ground and exposed to the sun so that they will ripen faster.

Smaller, determinate varieties need not be staked, but it is advisable to keep them off the ground. One way to do this is to place a 36-inch-high, 18-inch-diameter wire-mesh cage around each plant after setting it into the ground. Make sure the mesh cage has at least 6-inch openings so that the branches can grow through them. Secure the enclosure with a stout stake driven about 6 inches into the ground.

Another way to keep low-growing tomatoes off the ground is to scatter mulch around each plant (black plastic sheeting serves well, too) while it is still small, to protect the fruits from soil pests.

Planting and tending tomatoes. Set out your tomato seedlings when nighttime temperatures are fairly

PRUNING TOMATOES

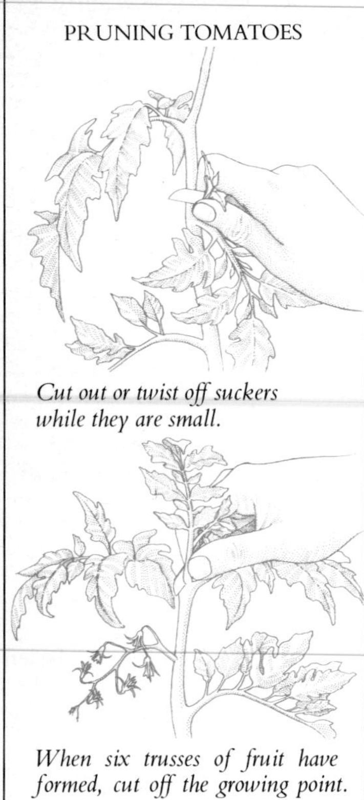

Cut out or twist off suckers while they are small.

When six trusses of fruit have formed, cut off the growing point.

STAKING PLANTS

Tie tomato stems to stakes with soft twine or cloth.

Or twist string from an overhead wire around plants as they grow.

sure to remain above 55° F. Seedlings should be spaced 2 feet apart for early tomatoes and 3 feet apart for main-season types, in rows at least 3 feet apart. Or plant the seedlings in holes prepared as described above.

Set each plant deeply in the ground, burying most of the stem; the stem will produce roots and anchor the plant firmly. Plant tall, lanky seedlings on their sides, placing the entire stem up to the top leaves underground. Immediately after planting, do the following: (1) give the seedlings a boost with 1 cupful of half-strength liquid fertilizer; (2) protect each plant with a cutworm collar, which you can make by removing the bottom from a paper cup, and set the collar into the soil about 1 inch deep; (3) listen for cold-weather warnings, and if a late frost seems imminent, cover the plants at night with newspaper tents.

If you do not enrich the soil before planting, feed tomatoes once a month with about $\frac{1}{3}$ cup of 5–10–5 fertilizer scattered in a 2-foot-wide band around each plant.

Cover the ground with a thick mulch to help keep the soil moist and prevent weed growth.

To keep indeterminate plants from making too much leafy growth, prune them to a single main stem by breaking off side shoots as soon as they appear. You will notice these side "suckers" growing between the main stem and the leaf stem. Cut them out while they are small. And if you see additional suckers growing from the base of the stem, remove them too.

Tomato plants need at least an inch of water per week; so water them well, especially during dry spells. Keep looking for and eliminating sucker growth. And continue tying the staked tomatoes as they grow taller.

Harvesting tomatoes. Given warm weather and abundant rainfall, tomatoes ripen in 60 to 85 days from the time seedlings are set out. When the fruits begin to turn red, check the plants every day, and pick those tomatoes that are fully red (or yellow, if you are growing a yellow variety) and are firm but not hard. Overripe tomatoes will fall off the plant and rot quickly.

A very light frost will usually kill a few leaves, but the plant itself will continue to grow and produce. However, anything more severe than a touch of frost is likely to kill the entire plant. If you hear that frost is coming, protect each plant by draping it in plastic sheeting or old bed sheets; or you can pull up each plant by its roots and hang it upside down in your cellar until the fruit ripens. Neither method is guaranteed to work, and in cool areas an early frost almost always means the end of tomato harvesting.

Unripened tomatoes need not go to waste, however. Pick them and ripen them quickly in a warm place, or wrap them individually in newspaper, and store in a cool, dark place for slower ripening. Also, check your cookbook for ways to use green tomatoes.

What Can Go Wrong With Tomatoes

Tomatoes are prey to many insects and diseases, but if you raise your crop in rich, properly prepared soil (preferably where no tomatoes were grown the year before), you may reduce the damage.

Look for green tomato hornworms in areas where the leaves are tattered, and pick them off by hand. If aphids attack, spray the plants with malathion. Use rotenone to control leaf-chewing flea beetles.

Tomato blight is a fungous disease that first manifests itself in large, dark green wet spots on the leaves. A whitish growth appears on the undersides of leaves and on the petioles and stems. The fungus spreads rapidly and can kill the plant. Prevent it by spraying with maneb every 10 to 14 days from the time that fruits first appear. Blossom-end rot shows itself as a leathery scar or a patch of rot on the blossom end of the fruit. It is usually related to a lack of soil calcium and moisture and can be prevented by liming and watering.

Varieties of Tomatoes to Grow

Recommended early tomatoes include 'Springset,' a determinate variety that takes 67 days to mature from the time seedlings are set out and is resistant to verticillium wilt and fusarium wilt (VF); 'Spring Giant,' determinate, 65 days, VF; 'Campbell 1327,' semi-determinate (grows larger than determinate but does not need staking), 69 days, VF.

Main-season plants generally produce larger fruits than do early tomato plants. Popular varieties, all indeterminate, include 'Beefeater,' 75 days, VFN (N means nematode resistance); 'Better Boy,' 70 days, VFN; 'Big Boy,' 78 days, F; 'Burpee's VF Hybrid,' 72 days, VF; and 'Manalucie,' 85 days, F.

Special varieties include 'Small Fry Hybrid' (a cherry tomato), determinate, 52 days, VFN; 'Roma' (a plum tomato), determinate, 76 days, VF; 'Yellow Pear' (a small yellow variety), indeterminate, 70 days; 'Sunray' (a large yellow-orange tomato), semi-determinate, 72 days, F.

Turnips and Rutabagas

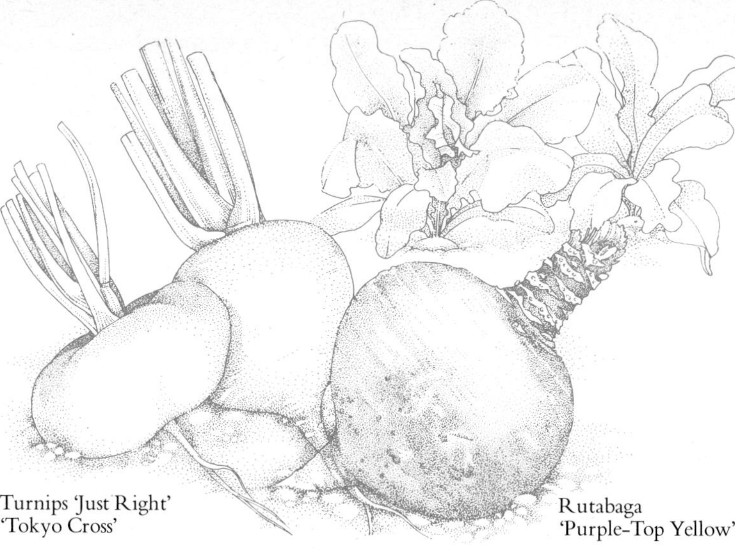

Turnips 'Just Right'
'Tokyo Cross'

Rutabaga
'Purple-Top Yellow'

Turnips are small-rooted vegetables, closely related to the large-rooted rutabagas. Turnip roots taste best when they are about 2 inches in diameter and are good for cooking straight from the garden. Turnips are also grown for their leaves, which are rich in vitamins and minerals. The roots of the rutabaga can reach 5 or 6 inches in diameter and will keep for months in storage.

Both turnips and rutabagas are cool-weather vegetables and are commonly grown as fall crops. Turnips can also be planted in early spring, but they tend to "bolt," or produce seeds, and turn woody during hot weather.

Because they are planted in summer, turnips and rutabagas have the advantage of being suitable as succession crops in the space, for example, where you have finished harvesting spinach, peas, or early potatoes. If you fertilized the soil heavily for the earlier crop, you will need to add very little additional fertilizer. Neither turnips nor rutabagas do well in acid soil, however; so if you find that the pH of your soil is less than 5.5, rake in a scattering of ground limestone as long before planting time as possible.

Depending on the variety, turnips need six to eight weeks to grow to maturity; rutabagas, about three months. Turnips are usually planted in midsummer for harvesting in midfall. There are several turnip varieties that withstand some warm weather and can be planted in early spring. Rutabagas can be planted only once, in early summer.

Turnip varieties that are grown for their greens alone are planted in early spring.

How to Grow Turnips and Rutabagas

To prepare the soil for turnips and rutabagas, dig it up and rake it thoroughly. If the soil has not been fertilized for a previous crop, scatter a handful of a 5–10–5 fertilizer over every 10 feet of row and rake it in.

Sow the seeds in shallow furrows, about ½ inch deep, in rows 1–2 feet apart. To prevent the soil from crusting, which makes it difficult for seedlings to break through, cover the seeds with a mixture of sand and soil.

As soon as the seedlings germinate, thin them to stand about 1 inch apart. A later, second thinning when the plants are 3–4 inches tall should leave turnips standing 4 inches apart, rutabagas 5 inches apart.

Feeding turnips during their growing period is not usually necessary; but if you have not fertilized, or if the plants are not thriving, apply a dressing of 5–10–5 fertilizer on both sides of each row at the rate of about 4 ounces per 10 feet of row.

As with all root crops, turnips and rutabagas must be kept weed free so that their roots can develop normally. A light mulch will help smother weeds as well as retain moisture in the soil. Weeds should be pulled by hand or hoed out carefully to avoid disturbing the tops of the roots, which grow close to the surface and sometimes push through it.

Turnips are at their tenderest when they are 2–3 inches in diameter. If left to grow much beyond this size, they become hard and lose their flavor. Although turnips grow sweeter with a slight touch of frost, they must be harvested before hard frost sets into the ground. Store the turnips that you cannot use right away by burying them in moist sand and keeping them in a cool place.

Turnip leaves, or tops, can be harvested whenever they reach edible size. You can use the tops from thinnings or cut larger leaves from more mature plants. If you want only the tops, harvest all the leaves about a month after planting. But if you want a root harvest as well, cut only a few leaves from each plant.

Rutabagas are ready to eat when they reach a 3-inch diameter, but they can be left to grow until they are much larger. Their flesh coarsens, however, if they grow beyond 5 or 6 inches in diameter. They keep well in storage, placed in moist sand in a cool place. They can also be left, well mulched, in the ground in freezing weather and dug up later.

What Can Go Wrong With Turnips and Rutabagas

The maggots that attack cabbage sometimes infest the roots of turnips and rutabagas. If you discover that maggots are eating the roots, you can try scattering a layer of wood ash on both sides of each row. If, before you plant, you suspect that maggots are infesting the soil, spray Diazinon on the soil after sowing the seeds.

Look for aphids on the undersides of the leaves. If you see them feasting there, blast them off with a hard stream of water. Insecticides, such as malathion, will kill the aphids. If you use one, however, you must delay harvesting according to the instructions on the label.

Striped flea beetles can eat hundreds of tiny holes in leaves. To combat them, dust the leaves two or three times with rotenone.

Varieties of Turnips and Rutabagas to Grow

Popular turnip varieties include 'Purple-Top White Globe,' which has a purplish-red root top and matures in about 55 days; 'Tokyo Cross,' a pure white turnip that matures in about 35 days; 'Just Right,' which is mature in 60 days when grown for its roots, in 30 days when grown for its tops. 'Purple-Top White Globe' and 'Tokyo Cross' are slow to bolt and good for early planting.

Turnips grown primarily for greens include 'Foliage' ('Shogoin'), whose tops mature in 30 days, and 'Seven Top,' ready in 45 days.

Popular rutabagas are the yellow-fleshed 'Purple-Top Yellow' and 'Improved Long Island' and the white-fleshed 'Macomber.' All of these should be ready to harvest in about three months.

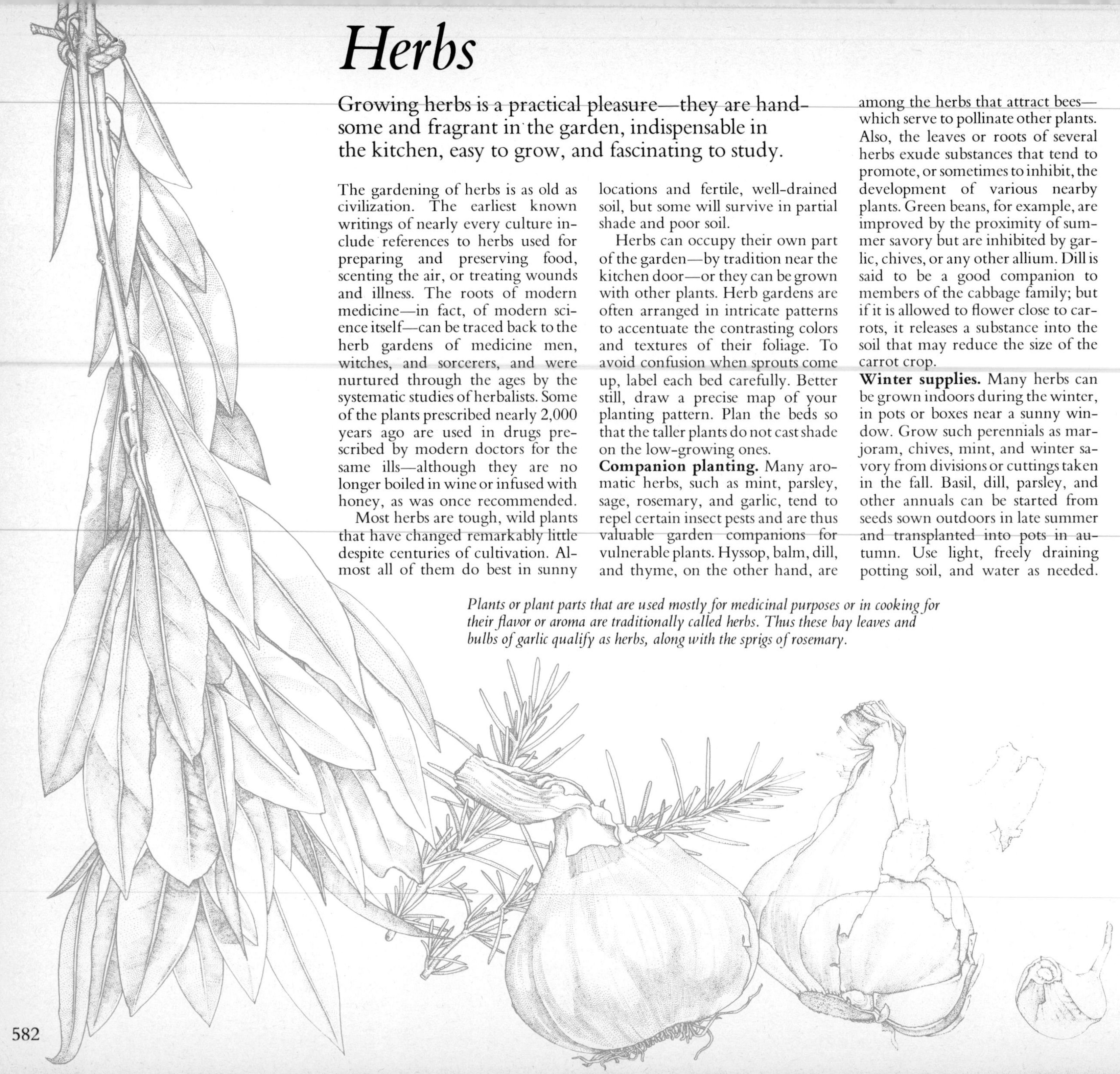

Herbs

Growing herbs is a practical pleasure—they are handsome and fragrant in the garden, indispensable in the kitchen, easy to grow, and fascinating to study.

The gardening of herbs is as old as civilization. The earliest known writings of nearly every culture include references to herbs used for preparing and preserving food, scenting the air, or treating wounds and illness. The roots of modern medicine—in fact, of modern science itself—can be traced back to the herb gardens of medicine men, witches, and sorcerers, and were nurtured through the ages by the systematic studies of herbalists. Some of the plants prescribed nearly 2,000 years ago are used in drugs prescribed by modern doctors for the same ills—although they are no longer boiled in wine or infused with honey, as was once recommended.

Most herbs are tough, wild plants that have changed remarkably little despite centuries of cultivation. Almost all of them do best in sunny locations and fertile, well-drained soil, but some will survive in partial shade and poor soil.

Herbs can occupy their own part of the garden—by tradition near the kitchen door—or they can be grown with other plants. Herb gardens are often arranged in intricate patterns to accentuate the contrasting colors and textures of their foliage. To avoid confusion when sprouts come up, label each bed carefully. Better still, draw a precise map of your planting pattern. Plan the beds so that the taller plants do not cast shade on the low-growing ones.

Companion planting. Many aromatic herbs, such as mint, parsley, sage, rosemary, and garlic, tend to repel certain insect pests and are thus valuable garden companions for vulnerable plants. Hyssop, balm, dill, and thyme, on the other hand, are among the herbs that attract bees—which serve to pollinate other plants. Also, the leaves or roots of several herbs exude substances that tend to promote, or sometimes to inhibit, the development of various nearby plants. Green beans, for example, are improved by the proximity of summer savory but are inhibited by garlic, chives, or any other allium. Dill is said to be a good companion to members of the cabbage family; but if it is allowed to flower close to carrots, it releases a substance into the soil that may reduce the size of the carrot crop.

Winter supplies. Many herbs can be grown indoors during the winter, in pots or boxes near a sunny window. Grow such perennials as marjoram, chives, mint, and winter savory from divisions or cuttings taken in the fall. Basil, dill, parsley, and other annuals can be started from seeds sown outdoors in late summer and transplanted into pots in autumn. Use light, freely draining potting soil, and water as needed.

Plants or plant parts that are used mostly for medicinal purposes or in cooking for their flavor or aroma are traditionally called herbs. Thus these bay leaves and bulbs of garlic qualify as herbs, along with the sprigs of rosemary.

Herbs You Can Grow

Angelica

(*Angelica archangelica*)

Spectacular tall border plant, particularly if allowed to reach its full height and to bear clusters of greenish-white flowers in late spring of its second year. Yellowish-green leaves grow to 2 ft. long. If flower heads are removed, plant will grow on as perennial; if not, it will die back after flowering.

Uses: Cut and candy young stems to decorate cakes and pastry. Blanch midribs of leaves for use in salads, as you would celery. Chopped leaves can replace some of sugar in fruit pies. Brew seeds into sweetish tea.

Type: Biennial or perennial.

Height: 4–7 ft. **Spread:** 3 ft.

Location: Partial shade, in moist, rich soil.

Planting: In early summer sow groups of 3 or 4 seeds 2 ft. apart. When seedlings have 3 or 4 leaves, thin each group to only 1 strong young plant.

Harvesting: Cut young stems in spring of second year, before flowering. Take leaves all summer, seeds when ripe in late summer.

Preserving: Crystallize stems in saturated sugar syrup.

Propagation: Sowing purchased seeds is preferable. Plant self-sows abundantly if allowed to set seed and die back as biennial.

Anise

(*Pimpinella anisum*)

Originated in Middle East, where it is grown today as commercial crop. Small white flowers bloom in midsummer, followed by tiny licorice-flavored fruits called aniseed.

A favorite spice of ancient Romans, who collected it from their colonies in payment of taxes and who ate cakes heavily flavored with aniseed to cure indigestion. Common constituent of cough medicines and of ointments that relieve itching.

Uses: Aniseed adds rich flavor to cookies, cakes, candies, bread, and applesauce. Widely used in Indian curries and stews. Flavors the liqueurs anisette and absinthe. Use fresh leaves in salads.

Type: Hardy annual.

Height: 18 in. **Spread:** 9–12 in.

Location: Warmth and sun, in light, well-drained soil.

Planting: Sow seeds in midspring, ½ in. deep in rows 12–18 in. apart. Thin established seedlings to 9 in.

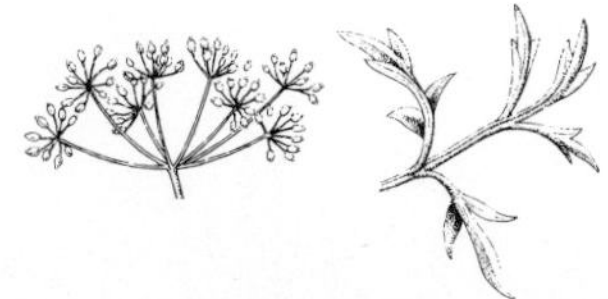

Harvesting: About 1 mo. after flowering, when seeds are ripe but have not fallen, cut flower heads into paper bag. Thresh by hand over sheet of paper.

Preserving: Allow seeds to dry, and store in closed, dry container.

Propagation: From seeds.

Balm

(*Melissa officinalis*)

Often called lemon balm because of fragrance of its light green leaves. Small white or pale yellow flowers appear in late summer and early fall, and are highly attractive to bees—thus the generic name, *Melissa,* from the Greek for "honeybees."

Uses: Leaves lend gentle lemonish flavor to puddings, soups, stuffings, punch, and other summer drinks. Pleasant garnish for fish and shellfish. Brew leaves to make excellent mild tea, which acts as gentle sedative. Like angelica, can replace some of sugar in fruit pies.

Type: Hardy perennial.

Height: 2–4 ft. **Spread:** 12–18 in.

Location: Sun or partial shade, in any soil having good drainage.

Planting: Sow tiny seeds in pan in late spring. Thin established seedlings to 2 in. apart. When they are about 4 in. tall, plant in garden, 1 ft. apart. Set out nursery-grown plants in midspring.

Harvesting: Cut shoots individually as soon as flowers appear, continuing until midfall.

Preserving: Dry or freeze leaves.

Propagation: Divide in spring. Cut root clumps into several pieces, each with 3 or 4 buds, and plant 12 in. apart in rows spaced 18 in. apart.

Basil

(*Ocimum basilicum*)

Perennial in its native tropics; grows as annual in temperate climates. Shiny green leaves, 1–2 in. long, have scent like cloves and are attractive in herb gardens or borders. Repellent to mosquitoes; good companion for tomato plants. White or purplish flower spikes in late summer. Miniature variety, *O. basilicum minimum,* only 1 ft. high, makes good pot plant.

Uses: Leaves have warm, spicy flavor. Use sparingly in tomato soup, sauces, salads, omelets, and with meat, poultry, and fish.

Type: Tender annual.

Height: 1–2 ft. **Spread:** 1 ft.

Location: Sun, in light, rich soil.

Planting: Sow seeds near sunny window or in greenhouse in early spring. Transplant to garden in early summer. Or sow seeds directly in garden in late spring.

Harvesting: For immediate use, take as needed all but 2 or 3 leaves at base of each branch before flowers bloom. Remove flower buds to encourage leaf growth. To obtain larger sections for preserving, cut plants to 6 in. once or twice.

Preserving: Dry or freeze. Leaves can also be kept refrigerated in jars: alternate layers of leaves with salt, and top with olive oil.

Propagation: From seeds.

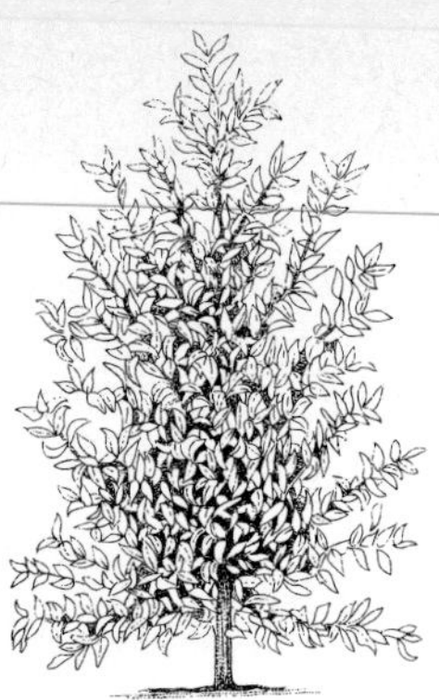

Bay

(*Laurus nobilis*)

This is the laurel tree of ancient Greece, whose leaves were woven into wreaths to honor heroes; do not confuse it with the native American mountain laurel (*Kalmia latifolia*), whose leaves are toxic. On its native Mediterranean shores it grows to 60 ft. tall; in the United States it is often only a shrub (see "Shrubs," pp. 78–187). Where hardy, an attractive lawn or background plant, with dark, glossy foliage. Elsewhere, can be grown in pot or tub and taken indoors in winter; trim 2 or 3 times during growing season.

Uses: Powerful seasoning. Use 1 leaf, whole, in stews, casseroles, or meat sauces. Put leaves in stored grain or flour to repel insects.

Type: Shrub.

Height: 14 ft. **Spread:** 14 ft.

Location: Sun or partial shade, sheltered, in well-drained soil.

Planting: Where hardy, put out young plants in early autumn or midspring.

Harvesting: Pick leaves as needed.

Preserving: Dry in dark. Spread leaves between sheets of absorbent paper, using board on top as press. Or dry quickly in warm oven.

Propagation: Take semi-hard cuttings in late summer (see p. 88).

Borage

(*Borago officinalis*)

Produces pendent, star-shaped flowers of sky-blue, lavender, or pink, with pleasant odor; attractive to bees. Medieval herbals prescribed tea brewed from plant's large, blue-green leaves as source of courage. (One said that syrup concocted from its flowers "purgeth melancholy and quieteth the lunatick person.") Good companion plant for strawberries and in fruit orchards. Repellent to tomato worms.

Uses: Pick young leaves to use in salads for their cool cucumber flavor. Candy flowers for pastry decoration, or float in wine or punch.

Type: Hardy annual.

Height: 1–3 ft. **Spread:** 1 ft.

Location: Full sun or partial shade, in any well-drained soil.

Planting: Sow seeds in late fall or early spring, ½ in. deep in rows 18 in. apart. Thin established seedlings to 12 in. apart.

Harvesting: First leaves can be picked about 6 wk. after seeds germinate. Pick flowers as they appear or just before they open.

Preserving: No satisfactory method for leaves. To candy flowers, dip in beaten egg white, then in sugar, and dry them.

Propagation: From seeds. If flowers are left on, will self-sow.

Burnet

(*Sanguisorba minor*)

Attractive bedding or container plant, also known as salad burnet. Tiny reddish flowers open in thimble-shaped heads from late spring to fall. Remove them to encourage growth of young leaves. Prescribed by early herbalists to stop bleeding and to cure gout.

Uses: Fresh leaves impart mild cucumberlike flavor. Use them whole in fruit cups and iced drinks, or chop into salads, soups, and green vegetables. Mix into cream cheese or melted butter, or use as garnish.

Type: Hardy perennial.

Height: 1–2 ft. **Spread:** 9–12 in.

Location: Full sun, in light, well-drained soil.

Planting: For year-round supply of young leaves, sow seeds outdoors in early spring and again in midsummer and fall where practical. During winter, transplant into pots by south-facing window and keep well watered. Plant ½ in. deep in rows 12 in. apart. Thin established seedlings to 9 in. apart.

Harvesting: Young, tender leaves are best. Cut as needed.

Preserving: No good method.

Propagation: From seeds, or divide in midspring (see p. 235). Self-sows freely if allowed to flower.

Caraway

(*Carum carvi*)

Finely cut leaves and flat, greenish-white flower heads resemble those of carrots. Seeds have been reputed to aid digestion, strengthen vision, improve memory, cure baldness, stop a lover's fickleness, and prevent theft of any objects containing them.

Uses: Seeds add tangy flavor to baked goods. Sprinkle over pork, lamb, or veal before roasting, and on baked apples. Add to cheese dishes, applesauce, and apple pie. To reduce cooking odor of cabbage, place a few seeds in muslin bag, tie, and add to cooking water. Use young leaves in salads and soups; cook old leaves like spinach.

Type: Hardy biennial.

Height: 1–2 ft. **Spread:** 9–12 in.

Location: Full sun, in ordinary well-drained soil.

Planting: Sow seeds in spring or late summer, ¼ in. deep in rows 1 ft. apart. As soon as seedlings are established, thin to 1 ft. apart.

Harvesting: Flowers appear in midsummer of following year. Cut heads as seeds begin to ripen. Pick leaves as needed.

Preserving: Hang seed heads in warm, dry, well-ventilated place to finish ripening; set trays beneath to catch seeds. Store in jars.

Propagation: From seeds.

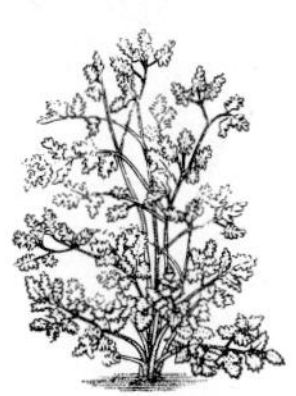

Chervil

(*Anthriscus cerefolium*)

Also known as French parsley. Spreading, fernlike foliage makes it attractive garden plant. To improve leaf production, pinch out flower buds as they appear. Said to give radishes a hotter taste when used as companion plant.
Uses: Fresh leaves are used in French cooking in much the same way as parsley; has slight anise flavor. Chop with equal parts chives, parsley, and tarragon for omelets, soups, and tartar sauce. Shred fresh leaves into potatoes, tuna, or green salads; add to poultry, egg, cheese, and fish dishes. Serve as garnish with red meat and oysters. Include dried leaves in stuffings.
Type: Hardy annual.
Height: 1–2 ft. **Spread:** 9–12 in.
Location: Partial shade, in moist, well-drained soil.
Planting: Sow seeds ¼ in. deep in rows 12 in. apart. Thin established seedlings to 9 in. apart. Sow every 4–6 wk. from early spring to fall for succession of plants. Raise as house plant or in cold frame for winter supply.

Harvesting: Leaves are ready 6–8 wk. after sowing. Cut plant back to ground.
Preserving: Fresh leaves are best, but they can be dried (see p. 591).
Propagation: From seeds only.

Chives

(*Allium schoenoprasum*)

Thin, tubular, grasslike foliage and cloverlike lavender flower heads that bloom in mid to late summer make this an attractive border and edging plant. Bulbs exude substance that makes plants good companions for carrots by discouraging a harmful fungus.
Uses: Leaves have mild onion flavor. Chop them and add to salads, egg and cheese dishes, cream cheese, mashed potatoes, hamburgers, sandwich spreads, and sauces.
Type: Hardy perennial.
Height: 6–10 in. **Spread:** 12 in.
Location: Full sun or slight shade, in rich, well-drained soil.
Planting: Sow seeds in spring or fall, ½ in. deep in rows 12 in. apart. As soon as seedlings are established, thin to 6 in. apart. Or set out nursery-grown plants in early spring, 9–12 in. apart.

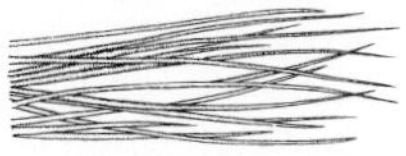

Harvesting: Leaves can be cut 4–6 mo. after sowing; then cut often and close to ground.
Preserving: Leaves lose color in drying. Instead of drying, grow winter supplies indoors by potting a few clumps in fall and keeping them near sunny window. Can also be preserved by deep freezing (see p. 591).
Propagation: Lift and divide clumps every 3 or 4 yr.

Cicely, sweet

(*Myrrhis odorata*)

Delicate fernlike foliage is attractive in borders. Frothy clusters of small white flowers appear midspring to midsummer. Old herbals prescribed mix of wine and cicely roots for bites of snakes and mad dogs; ointment from seeds was thought to ease skin eruptions.
Uses: Use sweetish leaves for aniselike flavor in salads, soups, and stews. Chop them fine to substitute for some of sugar in fruit pies or to sprinkle over strawberries. Seeds are spicy; use them fresh and green in soups and salad dressings. Roots can be eaten raw or boiled, like fennel.
Type: Hardy perennial.
Height: 2–3 ft. **Spread:** 18 in.
Location: Shade or partial shade, in moist, well-drained soil.
Planting: Sow seeds in early autumn for germination the following spring. Plant ½ in. deep in rows 18 in. apart. Thin established seedlings to 12 in. apart. Set out nursery-grown plants in spring.

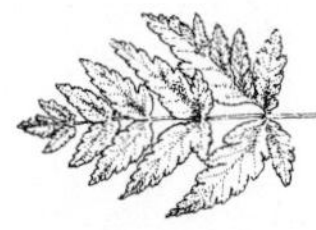

Harvesting: Gather seeds while still green; use fresh. Pick leaves as needed in summer; cut back to ground in autumn.
Preserving: Dry or freeze leaves.
Propagation: From seeds. Or divide roots in fall or spring (see p. 235).

Coriander

(*Coriandrum sativum*)

Ancient spice whose seeds have been found in Egyptian tombs and were used in Rome to preserve meat. Mentioned in *The 1001 Nights* as aphrodisiac and means of summoning spirits. Parsleylike leaves and rosy white flowers are attractive, but their odor is unpleasant until aromatic seeds ripen.
Uses: Grind dry seeds to powder, and dust over veal, pork, or ham before cooking. Sprinkle on cakes, pastries, cookies, or sweet dishes. Use in ground meat, sausage, and stews. Constituent of curry powder. Young leaves taste like dried orange peel and are rich in vitamins A and B_1, calcium, riboflavin, and niacin. Use in salads and soups; serve chopped with avocado pears.
Type: Hardy annual.
Height: 18 in. **Spread:** 6–9 in.
Location: Full sun, in soil with good drainage.
Planting: Sow seeds in early spring, ¼ in. deep in rows 12 in. apart. Thin established seedlings to 6 in. apart.

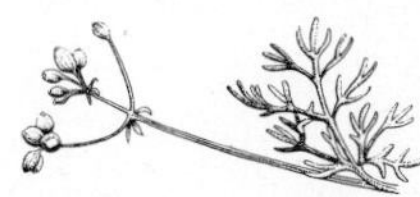

Harvesting: Cut seed heads when ripe. Pick young leaves as needed.
Preserving: Spread seed heads on trays to dry in sun or mild artificial heat. Thresh by hand. Store in jars when completely dry.
Propagation: From seeds.

Costmary

(*Chrysanthemum balsamita*)

Also known as alecost because leaves were once used in brewing ale and beer, and as Bible leaf because the aromatic 6- to 8-in. leaves were used as bookmarks in church by American colonists. Somewhat weedy looking in garden, but leaves have pungent, minty odor. Small, pale yellow flowers bloom in buttonlike heads; pinch them back as soon as they appear in midsummer to encourage leaf growth. Roots are rampant and persistent; they creep freely unless kept in check.

Uses: Leaves taste minty and slightly bitter. Use sparingly in green salads or to flavor iced drinks. Brew leaves fresh or dry to make pleasant tea. Place in drawers and closets for fragrance and to repel moths.

Type: Hardy perennial.

Height: 2–3 ft. **Spread:** 3 ft.

Location: Full sun or partial shade, in rich, well-drained soil.

Planting: Not grown from seeds. Set out nursery-grown plants in early spring, 2 ft. apart.

Harvesting: Pick young leaves as needed. Cut plants back in fall.

Preserving: Dry or freeze leaves.

Propagation: Divide roots in early spring every third year (see p. 235).

Dill

(*Anethum graveolens*)

Light green plumelike foliage stands out against blue-green stems. Yellow umbrella-shaped flower heads, developing in midsummer, attract honeybees. Highly aromatic plant. Good companion plant for cabbage, but root secretions are said to damage carrots.

Uses: Both seeds and leaves have sharp, slightly bitter taste. Use dried or fresh leaves, known as dillweed, to flavor fish, soups, salads, meat, poultry, omelets, and potatoes. Seeds can be used in same way, but remember that they are much stronger. Sprinkle dill on sliced cucumber to make sandwich filling.

Type: Hardy annual.

Height: 2–3 ft. **Spread:** 9–12 in.

Location: Full sun, in moist, well-drained soil.

Planting: Sow seeds in early spring, $\frac{1}{4}$ in. deep in rows 9 in. apart. Thin established seedlings to 9 in. apart.

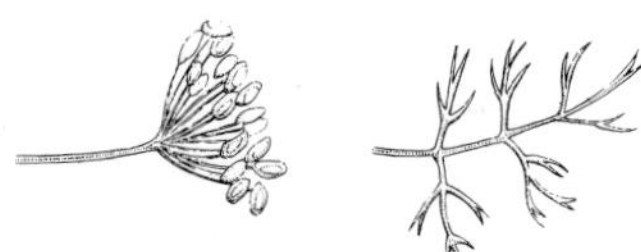

Harvesting: For best flavor pick leaves just as flowers open. Cut stems in dry weather as seeds ripen.

Preserving: Dry leaves slowly at about 100° F. Hang mature flower heads in warm, dry place, with tray beneath to catch seeds. Dry in sun or slightly warm oven.

Propagation: From seeds.

Fennel

(*Foeniculum vulgare*)

Plant resembles dill but is taller and coarser. Some varieties have copper-colored foliage. In ancient times regarded as all-purpose medicine.

Uses: Leaves have sweetish flavor, particularly good in sauces for fish; also useful with pork or veal, in soups, and in salads. Seeds have sharper taste; use sparingly in sauerkraut, spaghetti sauce, chili, hearty soups, and as condiment on baked goods. One variety, Florence fennel (*F. vulgare dulce*), has enlarged leaf base that is cooked and eaten as vegetable called finocchio. Stems of Sicilian fennel (*F. vulgare piperitum*) are blanched and eaten like celery.

Type: Perennial.

Height: 3–4 ft. **Spread:** 2 ft.

Location: Full sun, in ordinary well-drained soil.

Planting: Sow groups of 3 or 4 seeds in midspring, $\frac{1}{4}$ in. deep and 18 in. apart. Thin established seedlings to strongest of each group.

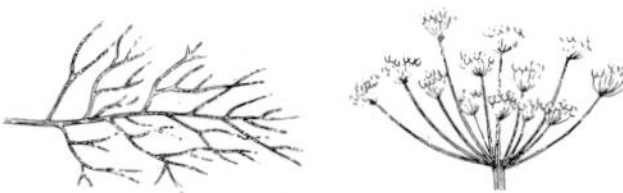

Harvesting: Pick leaves as needed; the best appear just as flowers bloom. To use stems, cut young flower stalks just before blooming. To grow for seeds, cut stems in autumn, and treat flower heads in same way as those of dill.

Preserving: Dry or freeze leaves.

Propagation: From seeds every 2 or 3 yr.

Garlic

(*Allium sativum*)

Among oldest known foods and seasonings. In ancient times reputed to augment physical strength; prescribed at one time or another to treat nearly every human ill. As plant matures, bulb divides into cluster of bulblets, or cloves, covered by papery skin. Cloves are separated for culinary use and propagation of new plants. Has reputation of repelling many pests. Plant among tomatoes and roses and around fruit trees.

Uses: Slice, chop, crush, grate, or grind cloves for pungent seasoning useful with almost any dish—but use with discretion. Salad, for example, can be flavored simply by rubbing a cut clove over inside of serving bowl.

Type: Perennial.

Height: 1–2 ft. **Spread:** 9–12 in.

Location: Full sun, in light soil.

Planting: In early spring plant cloves base down, 1–2 in. deep. Where winter is mild, plant in late fall.

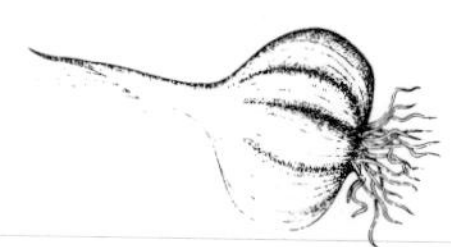

Harvesting: Lift out bulbs when leaves die after plant blooms.

Preserving: Dry bulbs in sun or in dry room. Store in cool, dry place.

Propagation: From separated cloves.

Horseradish
(*Armoracia rusticana*)

Member of cabbage and mustard family, raised for its tough white roots; sometimes found growing wild. Leaves are large and coarse. Roots are voracious and incursive; will invade and choke out other plants if not removed completely every fall. (In any case, young first-year roots are preferable for culinary use.) When planted near potatoes, horseradish discourages fungous diseases. Also said to repel blister beetles, but not potato beetles. Do not interplant; set in corners.

Uses: Shred roots fine to make piquant hot sauce for beef, fish, game, and other dishes.
Type: Perennial.
Height: 2 ft. **Spread:** 12–18 in.
Location: Full sun or partial shade, in deep, moist soil.
Planting: In early spring plant 3-in. root cuttings 1 ft. apart, and barely cover with soil.

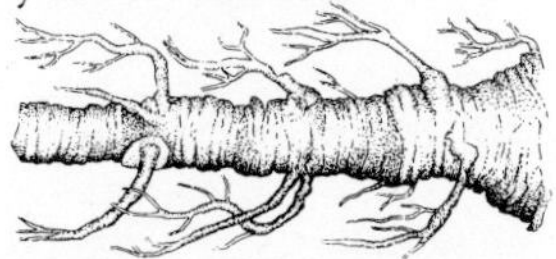

Harvesting: Lift roots in late autumn; be sure to leave no broken pieces.
Preserving: Trim away and discard small side roots. Store cylindrical main roots in sand in dark, cool, dry place.
Propagation: By root cuttings in early spring (see p. 237).

Hyssop
(*Hyssopus officinalis*)

Attractive perennial; evergreen in warm climates. Amenable to trimming; useful as border or low hedge. Glossy dark green foliage has musky odor. Bright blue, pink, or white flower spikes appear from midsummer well into autumn, attracting bees and butterflies. Leaves long used medicinally as purgative and antiseptic.

Uses: Leaves have resinous, bitter flavor, not for everyone's taste. Brew to make invigorating tea, best sweetened with honey. Use sparingly in soups, stews, and salads.
Type: Hardy, partly woody perennial.
Height: 2 ft. **Spread:** 9–12 in.
Location: Full sun, in light, well-drained soil.
Planting: Sow seeds $\frac{1}{4}$ in. deep in seedbed in early spring. As soon as seedlings are established, thin to 3 in. apart. When weather is warm enough, transplant seedlings to garden, 12 in. apart.

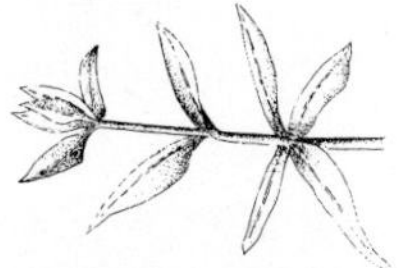

Harvesting: Pick leaves as needed, choosing only youngest for use fresh in salads.
Preserving: Dry or freeze leaves.
Propagation: From seeds, or divide roots in spring (see p. 235). Take tip cuttings in late summer (see p. 236).

Lovage
(*Levisticum officinale*)

Vigorous, nearly shrub-sized perennial that looks, smells, and tastes much like celery but is larger, stronger, and sweeter. Valuable as background planting in garden. Greenish-yellow flowers appear in late summer in flat-topped clusters above foliage. Unless seeds are desired, pinch flowers off as they appear to prevent entire plant from yellowing. Ancient herbalists recommended lovage as cure for ague and intestinal disorders.

Uses: Tender young leaves add rich celerylike flavor to soups, stews, salads, and sauces. Dried seeds, whole or ground, can be used in same way. Blanch stem bases and eat as you would celery.
Type: Hardy perennial.
Height: 3–4 ft. **Spread:** 2–3 ft.
Location: Sun or partial shade, in rich, deep, moist soil.
Planting: Sow seeds in autumn when ripe. Cover lightly with soil. In spring thin seedlings to about 2 ft. apart.

Harvesting: Gather young leaves as needed. Cut seed heads when ripe.
Preserving: Dry or freeze leaves. Treat seeds in same way as dill.
Propagation: From seeds or by root division in spring (see p. 235).

Marjoram, pot
(*Origanum onites*)

Either green stemmed with white flowers or purplish stemmed with pale purple flowers. Valued in gardens for its fragrance. Differs from sweet marjoram in that it is only about half as tall, has larger flowers, and is hardier; nevertheless, it requires warm location in northern areas if it is to flourish.

Uses: Sprinkle chopped leaves fresh or dried over lamb, pork, and veal before roasting. Use to flavor soups, stews, stuffings, egg and cheese dishes, and fish sauces. Flavor is similar to sweet marjoram but is slightly bitter and thymelike.
Type: Perennial.
Height: 1 ft. **Spread:** 1 ft.
Location: Full sun, warm and sheltered, in rich, well-drained soil.
Planting: Sow seeds in autumn or early spring, $\frac{1}{4}$ in. deep in rows 1 ft. apart. Thin established seedlings to 1 ft. apart. Set out nursery-grown plants in spring, 1 ft. apart.

Harvesting: Pick leaves as needed. For drying, cut leaves just before flowers open in midsummer.
Preserving: Dry leaves.
Propagation: Divide plants in midspring (see p. 235). Tip cuttings can be taken in summer (see p. 236).

Marjoram, sweet
(*Origanum majorana*)

The marjoram species most often grown in gardens for fragrance and flavor of its leaves. Also known as knotted marjoram, from form of flower heads. Makes good border planting. Oval, gray-green leaves feel soft and velvety. In ancient Rome they were strewn on floors to sweeten air. Medieval herbalists brewed them into tea to relieve chest congestion.
Uses: Same as for pot marjoram; flavor is much the same but not bitter. Use leaves fresh in salads or dried in sachets.
Type: Tender perennial.
Height: 2 ft. **Spread:** 12–18 in.
Location: Full sun, in rich, well-drained soil.
Planting: Sow seeds in early to mid spring, ¼ in. deep in rows 12 in. apart. Thin established seedlings to 12-in. spacings. In North sow under glass in very early spring; after hardening off, plant out in early summer.

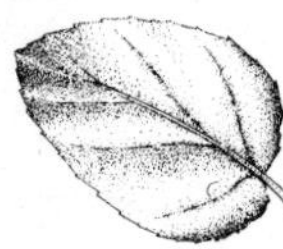

Harvesting: Encourage foliage by removing flowers as they appear. Pick leaves as needed. For drying, cut before flowers open in midsummer.
Preserving: Dry leaves.
Propagation: From seeds. By root division in warm areas, where plant grows as perennial (see p. 235).

Mint
(*Mentha* species)

The most popular mints are apple mint (*M. rotundifolia*), peppermint (*M. piperita*), and spearmint (*M. spicata*). White or purple flower spikes are attractive, but pinch them off to encourage leaves. Mints are repellent to white-cabbage butterflies. Prostrate ground cover pennyroyal (*M. pulegium*) repels ants, thus helping to protect other plants against aphids that ants tend.
Uses: Brew leaves into tea, or use to garnish cold drinks. Spearmint is generally used to make mint sauce or jelly. Sprinkle dried or fresh leaves over lamb before cooking. Used commercially in chewing gum, mouthwash, and candy.
Type: Perennial.
Height: 2–3 ft. **Spread:** 12–18 in.
Location: Partial shade, in rich, moist, well-drained soil.
Planting: In autumn or spring, plant 4- to 6-in. pieces of root 2 in. deep and 12 in. apart. Water well. Check roots' incursive tendency by sinking boards or bricks 1 ft. deep around bed.

Harvesting: Pick leaves as needed. For double crop, cut plant to ground in midsummer.
Preserving: Dry or freeze leaves.
Propagation: Divide roots in autumn or spring.

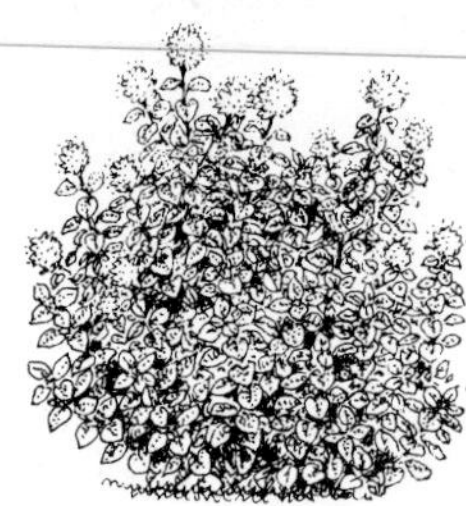

Oregano
(*Origanum vulgare*)

Also called wild marjoram. Plant is similar to sweet marjoram but shrubbier and more spreading; leaves are darker green, with sharper fragrance and flavor. Prescribed by ancient herbalists to aid digestion, stimulate appetite, and act as purgative. Roots tend to be incursive. Small white, pink, or purple flowers are fragrant, but pinch them back to encourage leaf production.
Uses: Dried leaves frequently used in Italian, Spanish, and Mexican cooking—especially in meat and tomato sauces, where they blend well with garlic and hot spices. Use in salads, stews, stuffings, egg and cheese dishes, and with fish.
Type: Hardy perennial.
Height: 2 ft. **Spread:** 18–24 in.
Location: Full sun, in almost any well-drained soil.
Planting: Sow seeds in spring or autumn, ¼ in. deep in rows 18 in. apart. Thin established seedlings to 12 in. apart. Set out nursery-grown plants in midspring, spacing them 12–18 in. apart.

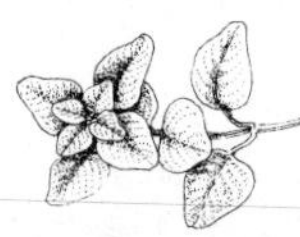

Harvesting: Pick leaves as needed. For drying, cut top 6 in. off stems just before flowers open.
Preserving: Dry leaves.
Propagation: From seeds, or divide in midspring (see p. 235).

Parsley
(*Petroselinum crispum*)

Bright green, crinkly leaves and compact growth habit make this good plant for edging or low borders. Interplant with roses and tomatoes to enhance vigor of both. Used since antiquity to sweeten breath after eating onions, garlic, or red meat and after drinking alcoholic beverages.
Uses: Mix leaves into salads, soups, stews, casseroles, and omelets. Serve fresh as garnish with meat, fish, and onion dishes.
Type: Biennial; grown as annual.
Height: 1 ft. **Spread:** 1 ft.
Location: Sun or partial shade, in rich, moist, deep soil.
Planting: Sow seeds in midspring for summer cutting, midsummer for autumn and winter harvests. Soak seeds overnight and broadcast thinly. Thin established seedlings to 9–10 in. apart.

Harvesting: Cut stems as required—no more than 2 or 3 at a time from any one plant. Pick leaves before flowering in second year; later, they turn bitter.
Preserving: Freeze (see p. 591), or dry by dipping in boiling water and placing on pan in very hot oven for about 1 min.
Propagation: From seeds as annual. Plant will self-sow its second season if allowed to flower.

Rosemary

(*Rosmarinus officinalis*)

Shrublike evergreen valuable as a landscape feature where ground does not freeze solid in winter. Glossy, needlelike leaves have piny scent. Abundant lavender or blue flowers bloom in early summer. Repellent to cabbage butterflies, carrot flies, and mosquitoes.
Uses: Insert a sprig or two into lamb, pork, veal, or poultry before roasting; or toss some onto charcoal over which beef, chicken, or ribs are cooking. Sprinkle chopped leaves over beef or fish before broiling. Use sparingly in soups, stews, sauces, and vegetables. Add to boiling water when cooking rice. Brews into tasty tea.
Type: Tender perennial.
Height: 2–6 ft. **Spread:** 2–6 ft.
Location: Full sun or partial shade, in light, well-drained soil.
Planting: Can be grown from seeds, but buying young plants is generally more satisfactory. Set out young plants in late spring about 2 ft. apart.

Harvesting: Cut sprigs as needed.
Preserving: Dry or freeze leaves.
Propagation: By hardwood cuttings in fall or spring (see p. 87), or semi-hard cuttings of 6-in. shoots in midsummer (see p. 88).

Sage

(*Salvia officinalis*)

Evergreen subshrub, good as low background planting or border, or in its own bed. Narrow gray-green leaves sometimes have white, purple, or yellow variegations. Used as medicinal herb since antiquity, it was prescribed for ailments of blood, brain, heart, liver, and stomach, and as cure for epilepsy and fever, and as preventive of plague. Repellent to white-cabbage butterflies, carrot flies, and ticks. Do not grow sage near annual seedbeds, as it inhibits root production.
Uses: Dried leaves are traditional constituent of poultry stuffing. Use also with lamb, pork, sausage, and in cheese dishes and omelets.
Type: Hardy perennial.
Height: 2 ft. **Spread:** 18 in.
Location: Full sun, in almost any well-drained soil. Fairly drought resistant; avoid overwatering.
Planting: Can be grown from seeds sown in early spring. Set out nursery-grown plants in midspring approximately 1 ft. apart.

Harvesting: Pick leaves as needed. For drying, cut top 5–6 in. of stalks before flowering in early summer; repeat as new growth develops.
Preserving: Dry leaves.
Propagation: Make softwood cuttings in early summer (see p. 90). Divide in spring or early fall every 2nd or 3rd yr. (see p. 235).

Savory, summer

(*Satureja hortensis*)

Small aromatic leaves are shiny green. Tiny lavender or pinkish-white flowers cover plant in midsummer. Attractive to bees; makes flavorsome honey. Interplant with green beans and onions for increased yield and better flavor. Applying bruised savory leaves to skin is folk remedy for discomfort of bee and wasp stings.
Uses: Leaves have peppery, somewhat mintlike flavor. Traditional seasoning with beans. Use in sausages, stuffings, meat pies, soups, stews, bean dishes, rice, and sauces for pork, lamb, veal, and poultry. Add fresh leaves to salads, fish dishes, omelets. Brew into fragrant, tangy tea; or add to vinegar for use in salad dressing.
Type: Annual.
Height: 12–18 in. **Spread:** 6–12 in.
Location: Full sun, in rich, light, well-drained soil.
Planting: Broadcast seeds in early to mid spring, in rows 12 in. apart. Allow about 4 wk. for germination. Thin established seedlings to 6–9 in. apart.

Harvesting: Leaves are most flavorful before flowers form in midsummer. Cut plant partially back for 2nd crop.
Preserving: Dry leaves.
Propagation: From seeds.

Savory, winter

(*Satureja montana*)

Lower, more spreading than summer savory. Glossy, dark green leaves are stiffer, less aromatic, with larger flowers. Makes good low hedge or border. Dwarf form (*S. montana pygmaea*), about 4 in. tall, is ideal for edging.
Uses: Flavor is less delicate than summer savory's and somewhat bitter as well as peppery. Use much the same way in cooking; also, fresh leaves make good dressing for trout. Combine dried leaves with basil to substitute for salt and pepper in salt-free diets. Rub bruised leaves on skin as insect repellent.
Type: Hardy, partly woody perennial.
Height: 6–12 in. **Spread:** 12–18 in.
Location: Full sun, in sandy, well-drained soil.
Planting: Seeds germinate slowly. Sow in fall or early spring, $\frac{1}{4}$ in. deep in rows 1 ft. apart. When seedlings are established, thin to 1 ft. apart. Or set out nursery-grown plants 1 ft. apart in midspring.

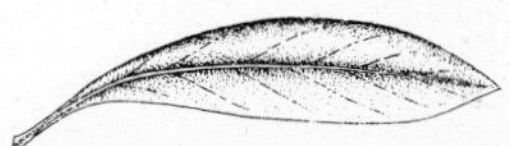

Harvesting: Pick leaves as needed. Cut plants halfway back before flowering for 2nd crop.
Preserving: Dry leaves.
Propagation: Divide established plants in early spring (see p. 94). Take softwood cuttings in late spring (see p. 90). Replace plants every 2 or 3 yr.

Sorrel
(*Rumex* species)

Two species are commonly grown: garden sorrel (*R. acetosa*) and French sorrel (*R. scutatus*). Both are valued for large, light green leaves—heart shaped in French sorrel, spade shaped in garden sorrel. In early to mid summer, both species bear long, reddish-brown flower spikes, popular for dried arrangements.
Uses: Leaves give sharp, acidic taste to stews, soups, and sauces that is more pronounced with French sorrel. Use fresh young leaves sparingly in salads. Cook with spinach, cabbage, or other greens; or cook in place of spinach. Make into puree to serve with fish and meat.
Type: Hardy perennial.
Height: 2 ft. **Spread:** 12–15 in.
Location: Full sun or partial shade, in rich, well-drained, moist soil (slightly drier for French sorrel).
Planting: Sow seeds in early spring, 1/4 in. deep in rows 12 in. apart. When seedlings are 3 in. tall, thin to 12 in. apart. Or set out nursery-grown plants in fall or early spring.

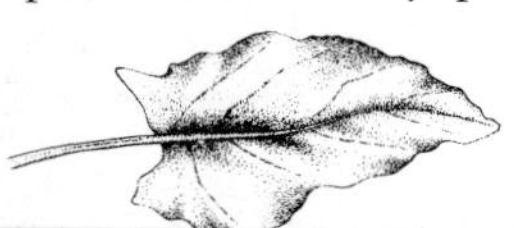

Harvesting: Cut shoots before flowers open. Cut plant to ground after harvest to encourage fall crop.
Preserving: Dry or freeze leaves.
Propagation: Divide roots in early spring (see p. 235), or sow seeds annually.

Tarragon
(*Artemisia dracunculus*)

Has fragrant, shiny, dark green leaves on woody stems. Creeping rhizomatous roots are not completely resistant to severe cold; more likely to be damaged in damp soil than in dry. In cold areas heap coarse sand over plant after top growth has been cut down in autumn to protect against killing frost.
Uses: Chop the anise-flavored leaves for use in soups, salads, egg dishes, stews, and soft cheeses. Excellent with lamb. Serve in melted butter with fish, steak, or vegetables. Constituent of tartar sauce and many chutneys. Makes good flavoring for vinegar when leaves are steeped for 2 or 3 wk.
Type: Hardy perennial.
Height: 2 ft. **Spread:** 15 in.
Location: Full sun, in dry, not too rich, well-drained soil.
Planting: Does not grow true from seeds. Set out nursery-grown plants in early spring, 18 in. apart.

Harvesting: Pick leaves as needed. Cut plant to ground in autumn.
Preserving: Dry or freeze leaves.
Propagation: Divide roots of established plants in early spring (see p. 235).

Thyme, common
(*Thymus vulgaris*)

Shrubby and low growing, with aromatic, gray-green foliage; good as edging plant or low border, or in its own bed. Small, lilac-colored flowers appear in late spring to midsummer; attract bees and make excellent honey. Valued for centuries as medicinal herb, thyme yields an oil—thymol—used today in antiseptics, deodorants, and cough drops. Repellent to the cabbage butterfly.
Uses: Rub chopped leaves (fresh or dried) into beef, lamb, veal, or pork before roasting. Sprinkle over eggs, cheese dishes, vegetables, fish, or poultry. Add to soups, stews, stuffings, and rice. Brew into tea with a little rosemary and mint.
Type: Hardy, partly woody perennial.
Height: 8 in. **Spread:** 9–12 in.
Location: Full sun, in almost any well-drained soil.
Planting: Set out nursery-grown plants in early spring, 6–9 in. apart. Sow seeds in midspring in shallow rows 1 ft. apart. When seedlings are established, thin to 6-in. spacings.

Harvesting: Pick leaves as needed. For drying, cut plants just before flowers open in early summer.
Preserving: Dry leaves.
Propagation: Every 3 or 4 yr. divide established plants in spring (see p. 94).

Thyme, lemon
(*Thymus citriodorus*)

This hybrid between *T. vulgaris* and a procumbent relative, *T. pulegioides,* looks much like common thyme but grows lower and spreads by creeping along ground. Purple flowers attractive to bees.
Uses: Can be used in cooking in same way as common thyme; flavor is less pungent and distinctly lemony, particularly tasty in stuffing for veal and poultry. Mix chopped leaves into custards, puddings, and whipped-cream toppings. Sprinkle lightly over fresh strawberries and other acidic fruits.
Type: Hardy, partly woody perennial.
Height: 6 in. **Spread:** 1 ft.
Location: Full sun, in almost any well-drained soil.
Planting: Cannot be raised from seeds. Set out nursery-grown plants in early to mid spring, 9 in. apart.

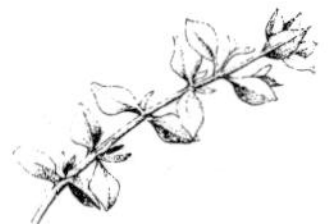

Harvesting: Pick fresh leaves as needed. Cut leaves for drying just before flowers open in early summer.
Preserving: Dry leaves.
Propagation: Divide established plants in spring (see p. 94). Layer in spring by mounding soil on center of each plant, causing branches to produce roots along their length. Each branch can then be severed and planted.

Preserving Herbs for Winter

How to Dry Homegrown Herbs

The leaves of most herbs should be harvested for drying before the flowers open, when the plants are in bud. Gather them on a dry day, early in the morning.

With large-leaved herbs, such as mint, basil, or marjoram, strip the leaves from the stems. Throw away any leaves that have been damaged by pests or are past their prime. Wash the remainder carefully under a cold-water faucet; then spread them out on wire racks, mesh screens, or sheets of newspaper to dry.

Tie whole stems or branches of such small-leaved herbs as rosemary, tarragon, or thyme into small, loose bundles. Wrap the bundles individually in pieces of muslin to keep off dust, and hang them, stems upward, from a wire or clothesline.

Among the best drying places are airy rooms or attics, provided they are dark. Exposure to sunlight destroys the leaf color of drying herbs. For best results, maintain a temperature of 70–75° F until the leaves are crisp and ready to use.

Oven drying. If no suitable room is available for drying herbs, the job can be done in or on the kitchen oven. But exercise care; the object is simply to dehydrate the herbs, not to cook them.

First, wrap the herbs in muslin, and dip them in boiling water for one minute. Then, shake off the moisture, and spread the leaves or branches on wire racks or mesh screening.

Set the oven to maintain a temperature of 110°–130° F with the door open. Put the racks or screens in the oven, and leave them there until the herbs are crisp—probably about an hour.

An alternative is to set the racks of herbs on top of the oven, with the temperature set at 140°–160° F. When this procedure is followed, the herbs will take several hours to dry.

Drying parsley. To dry parsley without losing the distinctive green color requires special treatment.

First, preheat the oven to 400° F. Then, tie sprigs of parsley in loose bunches, and dip them in boiling water for one minute. Shake off the water, and hang the bunches by their stems from the bars of an oven rack. Insert the rack in the oven for one minute; then remove it. Now let the oven cool to 240° F, and reinsert the rack of parsley. Let the parsley dry until crisp.

Crushing and storing. As soon as herb leaves are crisp, crush them gently into flakes with a rolling pin. A notable exception is bay leaves, which should be stored whole or in large pieces.

Do not powder an herb until it is needed in powder form, or the flavor will be lost. When powder is needed, push the bits of leaves through a sieve, or use a mortar and pestle.

Store in airtight containers. If you use glass jars, those containing green leaves should be painted black or stored in the dark—daylight robs herbs of their attractive colors.

Label each jar with the name of its contents and the date of storage. Dried herb leaves seldom keep their flavor for longer than a year.

DRYING LARGE-LEAVED HERBS

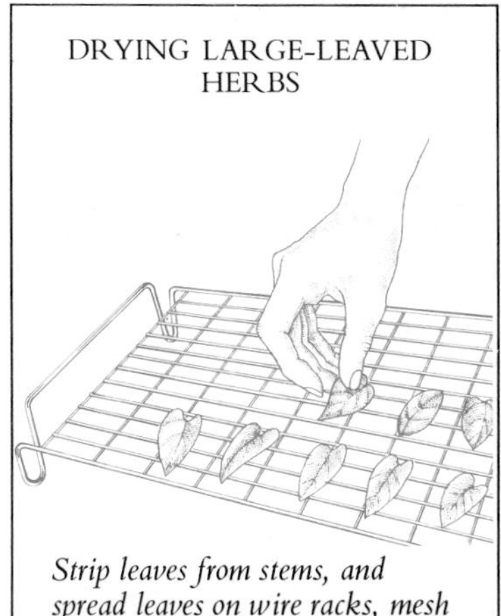

Strip leaves from stems, and spread leaves on wire racks, mesh screening, or newspapers to dry in a dark, airy room.

DRYING SMALL-LEAVED HERBS

Tie branches in loose bundles; then wrap loosely in muslin before hanging them head down in a well-ventilated place.

Preserving Herbs in the Freezer

Many soft-leaved herbs can be preserved by deep freezing. The most satisfactory are balm, basil, chives, fennel, lovage, mint, sorrel, sweet cicely, and tarragon. Young shoots or leaves are preferable; cut them early in the morning, and process them without delay. Do not mix different types of herbs; deal with each kind separately.

First, wash the leaves under a cold-water faucet, and shake off the water. Then, put them into a wire basket of the kind used for deep frying, and plunge the basket into boiling water. (This is called blanching.) Use 1 pint of water for every 2½ ounces of leaves.

Return the water to a boil, and keep it boiling for 30 seconds (1 minute for balm, mint, or sorrel). Then, remove the basket of leaves, and plunge it immediately into ice-cold water. Remove it in one minute. Take out the leaves, shake off the water, and pack them tightly into a plastic bag. Squeeze out as much air as possible and seal the bag. Label the bag with the name of its contents and the date, and put it in the freezer.

When the herb is needed, take a small quantity of leaves from the bag. Let them thaw slowly; use as you would use fresh leaves. Reseal the bag and return it to the freezer.

Freezing parsley. As with drying, parsley requires special treatment when it is frozen. Blanching, which preserves color and flavor, has the drawback of making herbs limp, and limp parsley is not an attractive garnish. Therefore, freeze parsley without blanching, as follows:

Simply wash sprigs in cold water, and shake off the moisture. Then put them in small plastic bags—just enough in each bag to use on one occasion. Seal the bags and put them in the freezer. When parsley is needed, thaw it slowly and use as you would fresh sprigs.

This method has a drawback, too: the parsley's green color will begin to turn yellow in about three months.

CRUSHING FROZEN PARSLEY

If frozen parsley is needed in small pieces, break up frozen and brittle leaves by rubbing the bag gently between your hands before you open it.

What You Should Know About the Soil

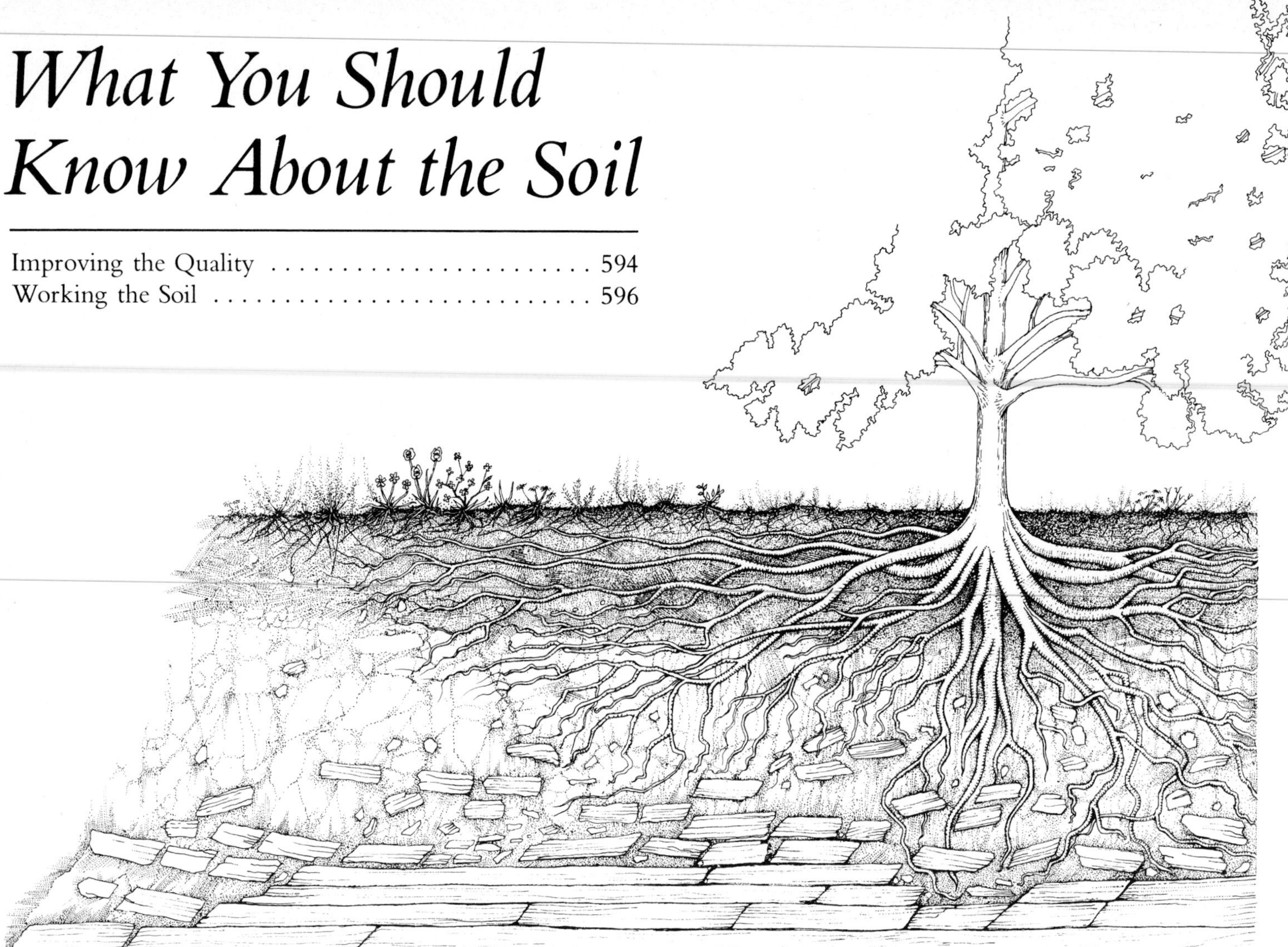

Soil is a complex mixture of diverse ingredients, containing all the nutrients that sustain life on earth. Plants are uniquely adapted to extract these nutrients through their roots and to convert them to forms usable by the plant, and by mankind and other animals. The gardener's job is to keep the soil in the best possible condition and to replace the nutrients that plants have taken up.

Soil has five main components: inorganic particles of rocks and minerals; dead and decaying organic matter, or humus; water; air; and a teeming community of living creatures, ranging from insects, earthworms, and fungi to microscopic bacteria, protozoa, and viruses. The nature of any soil is defined by the quality and proportions of these components.

The nature of soil varies a great deal, not only from place to place but also at different depths in the same location. Dig down 3 feet or more, and you will uncover a series of definite layers, differing in color, texture, and composition. Taken together, these layers constitute what is known as the soil profile.

The upper layer, or topsoil, is generally darker than the deeper layers because it is richer in humus. It is in this layer that life is most abundant, and it is here that most plants develop the roots that take up most of their nutrients. Topsoil may be only an inch or two deep, or it may be a foot or two. It is usually thin on steep slopes and deeper in flat lowlands, where humus and silt are carried by the runoff of rainwater. Although many plants will grow in shallow topsoil, most will need frequent fertilizing and watering to flourish in it.

Beneath the topsoil is the subsoil layer. It is harder to dig and is stickier when wet because of its high clay content, most of which is washed down from the topsoil. Also washed down are oxides of iron and other minerals, often giving subsoil a reddish or orange color. These minerals may collect at a given depth and cement the soil particles into a layer called hardpan, which often blocks the penetration of roots and interferes with drainage.

Beneath the subsoil lies the geologic base, mineral matter that is often—but by no means always—the parent material of the soil above. It may be solid bedrock; or it may be loose and porous to great depths, in which case the roots of trees and some shrubs are likely to reach well down into it.

Texture. The stablest soil component is its framework of rock particles; it is according to the size of these that soil is classified as sand, silt, or clay. Most soil is a mixture of all three. Its texture is defined by the proportions in which they are present. Laboratory analysis will determine the exact composition of any soil, but you can form a rough judgment of texture simply by rubbing a pinch of moist soil lightly between your thumb and forefinger.

Sand feels harsh and gritty, and its grains scarcely hold together. They are the largest soil particles—if they were any larger, they would be called gravel. Sandy, or coarse-textured, soil is easy to work. It came to be called light soil because it could be plowed with only a light team of horses. It drains easily, and with the water that filters through it go many nutrients. To grow most garden plants in light soil, therefore, requires constant replenishment of water, humus, and nutrients.

Silt particles are smaller than sand and larger than clay. They feel smooth and floury between the fingers. Silt packs together with fewer air spaces than sand, which makes for slower drainage, but it does not hold together well, becoming light and powdery when it dries out.

Clay soil was termed "heavy," as opposed to the light, sandy soil, because it took a heavy team to plow it. A particle of clay is at least 1,000 times finer than a grain of coarse sand. Clay particles pack into compact lumps that dry as stony clods. When you rub a bit of moist clay between your thumb and finger, it rolls into a wormlike cylinder. Unlike sand and silt, clay particles actually absorb moisture and nutrients. They swell up in the process, closing pores in the soil, compacting it, and impeding drainage. The soil shrinks again when it dries but remains hard packed, sometimes forming deep cracks on the surface. Though it can be difficult to get plants started in clay soil, once established, most are likely to do well.

Loam is the name given to medium-textured soil containing sand, silt, and clay in such well-balanced proportions that none predominates. The term is a bit vague, including such imprecisions as sandy loam, clay loam, and silty loam, but essentially it means "good soil." It is friable, which is to say that large clods break down easily into smaller particles. A pinch of moist loam rubbed between your fingers will be reduced to a rough smear. Once you have dealt with good loam, you are not likely to mistake it for anything else. It holds moisture well and encourages the organic activity that makes most nutrients available to plant roots. With proper management almost any crop can be grown in loam. Humus and fertilizer must be added regularly, of course, to maintain desirable levels, and liming may be occasionally needed to correct acidity.

Tilth and structure. Tilth refers to the soil's fitness for cultivation. This is largely a matter of structure—that is, the way in which particles of sand, silt, clay, and humus clump together into granules or crumbs.

Dig a spadeful of moist loam, and let it drop onto a hard surface. If it comes apart in porous crumbs that are up to half an inch in diameter, the structure is good. Each crumb will retain moisture; air spaces between them will allow excess water to drain. If soil breaks into blocky clods with flat surfaces and sharp corners, it is too heavily compacted and you have work to do.

Nature's slow, patient method of bringing soil into good tilth is to grow cover crops of grass year after year. The roots of these plants break up compacted soil, the foliage protects the surface from the bombardment of heavy rain, and the grass itself decomposes into humus. Microorganisms in the soil break this organic matter down into usable nutrients. In the process, polysaccharides are produced—useful by-products that serve to bind soil particles into crumbs. For ways to put this method to work in your garden, see green manuring on page 595.

For quicker results, in the fall dig in a 2- to 4-inch-thick layer of dehydrated manure, compost, peat moss, or similar organic material, double digging if the subsoil is extremely heavy (see p. 597). Do this again in the spring, as soon as the soil is not too wet to work.

Also of value are various synthetic conditioners, which perform the same function as microbe-produced polysaccharides. Most are known by the abbreviations of their chemical names—VAMA, CMC, HPAN, IBMA—but they are available under a variety of trade names. They are not substitutes for humus, since they add no nutrients to the soil. But by improving its tilth, they make available more of the nutrients it contains; and by encouraging the workings of its living community, they help to ensure its future productivity.

Humus. Organic material, derived from animals and plants, breaks down in the soil to a dark, gummy substance called humus. Not only is this rich in nutrients but it is the agent by which faulty texture and structure are best remedied. In light soil, humus binds sand particles together; in heavy soil it keeps clay particles apart, allowing room for air and water. Soil containing a great deal of humus is termed "rich," whereas "lean" soil is that which is deficient in humus.

Any bulky organic wastes—animal manure, fallen leaves, grass clippings, sawdust, kitchen scraps—are useful as sources of humus. It is important, however, that these wastes are partly decomposed before they are added to the soil; few nutrients are available to plants until their form has been altered by decomposition. Moreover, the microorganisms that cause decay use up a great deal of nitrogen in the first stages of the process; so the addition of fresh organic waste can cause temporary nitrogen deficiency in the soil. (This is the reason that it is a good idea to mix in a little nitrogen-rich fertilizer to feed the various agents of decay when using sawdust, bark chips, or similar organic material as a summer mulch.)

You can obtain humus-forming materials, such as well-rotted manure, leaf mold, or peat moss, in ready-to-use form from garden-supply centers, or you can process your own by composting (p. 595). Either way, it should be worked well into the soil in large quantities. A good application would be a 6-inch layer of loose organic material worked into the soil to a depth of at least 12 inches.

Improving the Quality

Taking Samples for a Soil Test

To make the best use of the soil in your garden, you should know its properties; before you can improve it, you must know its deficiencies.

Most states maintain agricultural experiment stations, usually as part of the state university, where for a moderate fee you can have samples of your soil analyzed and the results interpreted by experts. They will usually tell you its precise texture and pH value, provide a chemical analysis of its nutrients and mineral content, suggest how it can best be used in its present state, and tell you how it can be improved for the use you wish to make of it.

Soil-test kits are available if you wish to do the job yourself. With the exception of pH-test kits, however, they can be tricky to use, and the results are meaningless without knowledgeable interpretation.

Either way, the reliability of the test depends upon the care with which the soil sample is taken. Avoid contaminating it with cigarette ashes, residue from tools or containers, or any other foreign substance.

It is also important that the small sample you send is representative of an entire area where similar plants, such as roses or vegetables, are to be grown. This means gathering soil from several places and mixing it together to form a composite, from which you need take no more than a pint of soil for analysis. Do not, however, mix together soil from clearly different areas. Have each analyzed separately.

When feasible, take samples in midfall, when the growing season is over. Certain corrective materials, such as superphosphate and flowers of sulfur, take several months to become effective; so they are best applied in fall.

There are special tools for sampling, but the job can easily be done with a sharp spade or trowel. For each sample make a steep vertical cut 6–8 inches deep. From this vertical face take a ½-inch-thick slice to the full depth of the cut. Remove stones and other debris. Mix all the samples from an area thoroughly in a clean container, and take about a pint of soil for analysis.

Put it in a container that will stand the rigors of shipping, such as an ice cream carton or a plastic (not glass) refrigerator jar. Attach to each sample a letter including the following facts: your name and address; the date the sample was taken; the place it was taken (front lawn, garden, etc.); whether fertilizer or lime was used the previous year; what type of crop you plan to grow (grass, shrubs, flowers, vegetables, etc.); and as much information as possible about how the land has been used in the recent past. Enclose the containers and letters in a durable cardboard box. Be sure your name and address are clearly marked on the outside before shipping.

The pH Level: Acid or Alkaline

Acidity and alkalinity are measured on the pH scale, which runs from 0 (pure acid) to 14 (pure lye). From the neutral point, 7, the numbers increase or decrease in geometric progression: thus, pH 5 is 10 times more acid than pH 6; pH 4, 100 times more acid; and so forth.

Slightly acid soil—about pH 6.5 —is best for most plants, but there are exceptions. Rhododendrons, for example, require pH 4–5.5 in order to thrive. Cabbage does best in slightly alkaline soil, about pH 7.5, partly because the clubroot fungus that afflicts it thrives in acidity. Few plants will survive in soil more acid than pH 4 or more alkaline than pH 8.

Acids of various kinds are produced as organic matter decays. Alkali is a property of many inorganic metallic elements. Therefore, most garden soil is somewhat acid and tends to become more so as fertilizers and humus are worked in and various chemicals are leached out.

To increase the alkalinity of the soil, use finely ground limestone, which is available from most garden-supply centers. In fall dig the soil to a depth of 8–12 inches. Spread the lime evenly over the surface, and rake it in. The rate of application depends on the texture of the soil. In sandy loam 50 pounds per 1,000 square feet will raise pH a point; in medium loam use 70 pounds. In heavy soil 80 pounds of limestone is required for the same pH change. The more acid the soil is, the faster additives will work in it; therefore, it takes the same amount of lime to change the pH from 6 to 6.5, for example, as it does from 5 to 5.5.

To increase the acidity of the soil drastically, use flowers of sulfur, which over a period of a few months will turn to sulfuric acid in the soil. This, too, is available from most garden-supply centers. Like limestone, the amount to use depends on the soil texture: in sand 8 pounds per 1,000 square feet will lower pH by about a point; in heavy loam 25 pounds is needed. For the most effective and long-lasting treatment, work the sulfur in to a depth of about 12 inches, along with large amounts of peat moss.

Peat moss is also acidic—50 pounds per 1,000 square feet will lower pH by about a point. It works more gradually than flowers of sulfur, and it has the added advantage of improving the tilth of too light or too heavy soil.

Whether you are raising or lowering pH, there is always the danger of overdoing it. Use only as much corrective material as you are sure you need, based on reliable soil tests.

Supplying Nutrients With Fertilizers

Of the 16 elements known to be necessary to plant growth, 3—carbon, hydrogen, and oxygen—come from the air and water. The rest are taken from the soil. Most of these are called trace elements; they are needed in such minute quantities that they are not likely to be depleted. The others must be replaced to keep the soil productive.

Nitrogen, phosphorus, and potassium are needed in the largest amounts, are used up the fastest, and are therefore the chief ingredients of the so-called all-purpose fertilizers, which are meant to maintain nutrient levels for most plants in average soil. These fertilizers are available in solid form (as powders or granules) and in liquid form. Liquids have the advantage of being easily applied and quickly absorbed. They are generally more expensive, however, and they do not remain in the soil as long as solid fertilizers; so they must be applied oftener, in smaller doses.

When you buy a bag or bottle of commercial fertilizer, you will find at least three numbers on the label (10–6–4, for example). This is the NPK rating. The first number always represents the percentage of nitrogen (N); the second stands for the percentage of phosphorus (P); and the third, the percentage of potassium (K) in the form of potash. If one of these nutrients is missing, a zero indicates its absence. Thus, to apply 1 pound of N, 2 pounds of P, and 1 pound of K requires 10 pounds of a fertilizer rated 10–20–10 or 20 pounds of one rated 5–10–5. The proportions of available nutrients are the same, but the quantity of each nutrient is doubled in the fertilizer with the higher rating—which explains why it is more expensive than the lower-rated one.

All-purpose fertilizers are generally made from inorganic chemical compounds, such as ammonium sulfate for N, superphosphate for P, and sulfate of potash for K. The same nutrients are available from organic sources, but at higher prices. Their advantages are that they do not tend to damage plants if overapplied, as chemicals sometimes do, and they last longer in the soil.

Dried blood and finely ground hoof and horn meal both contain 7–15 percent N. Fish meal and fish emulsion are 5–10 percent N and 2–6 percent P. Finely ground bone meal is 3–5 percent N and 20–35 percent P. Cottonseed meal provides 6–9 percent slow-acting N, 2–3 percent P, and about 2 percent K. Another source of K is thoroughly burned wood ashes, especially those of hardwoods.

Slow-release fertilizers are made either by combining nutrients with chemicals that retard organic breakdown, as with ureaform (a combination of the nitrogenous fertilizer urea and formaldehyde), or by coating particles of fertilizer with a plastic substance through which they slowly escape. They are of particular value with trees, shrubs, and long-lived perennials.

Sometimes in alkaline soil, trace elements, though present, are not broken down into usable forms. Iron deficiency, for example, results in chlorosis, or loss of green color. It can be corrected by applying iron chelates to the soil or the foliage, in the amount recommended by the manufacturer. Manganese deficiency, common in vegetables, can be treated by spraying foliage in spring with a weak solution of manganese sulfate in water.

Foliar feeding can be valuable in other ways as well—not as a substitute for root feeding but as a supplement. Spraying the leaves of shrubs, for example, with a soluble nitrogenous fertilizer can give a boost to growth during dry spells. Plants with poor or diseased root systems can also benefit from sprayings of similarly diluted fertilizer solutions.

Compost and Green Manure: Sources of Humus

Composting is a means of returning to the soil as humus a great amount of organic material that would otherwise be discarded. The best way to make a compost pile is to sandwich vegetable matter between layers of nitrogen-enriched soil. Given adequate air and water, a well-made pile will reduce such potential garbage as leaves, lawn clippings, raw kitchen wastes, coffee grounds, vacuum-cleaner fluff, sawdust, and even well-soaked newspapers to usable humus in a matter of months.

There are limits, however. Do not put woody material on the pile if you want quick results. Also avoid cooked food scraps and anything containing grease, as well as diseased plants, the roots of perennial weeds, and seeds of annual weeds.

If you have room, you can build an open compost pile in a hidden corner of the garden. Start with a 1-foot-thick layer of grass clippings, hay, or leaves laid out in a square shape at least 5 feet to a side—preferably about 7 feet. Tread it down and water well. Sprinkle on a handful of ammonium sulfate (if your soil is alkaline) or sodium nitrate (with acid soil), or add a 1-inch-thick layer of manure. Cover this with a 2-inch layer of soil.

Continue to build the pile gradually, adding vegetable waste as it becomes available. Tread down and water each 8- to 12-inch layer, and cover with enriched soil, until the pile is 5–7 feet high. Make the top of the pile slightly concave to catch rainwater. Cover the finished pile with a 6-inch soil layer. Water well and keep the pile moist but not soggy; in a dry summer it should be watered every two weeks or so.

You can also buy ready-made compost bins in various sizes, or you can make your own from wire mesh or wooden slats as shown below. If one side of the container is removable, it gives easy access to the compost. Never attempt to make compost in a solid trash can or a bin with solid sides because air circulation is vital to the bacteria that break down the vegetable matter.

When the compost is ready to use, it will be black or dark brown, crumbly, and sweet smelling. This should take about three months in summer, longer during winter. Dig it into the soil as you would manure, or spread it thickly around trees, shrubs, and perennials.

Green manuring, or growing a cover crop for the purpose of plowing it under, is another source of humus. Quick-growing crops, such as winter rye, buckwheat, ryegrass, mustard, and rape, are good for this purpose. They should be dug into the soil just before they flower. Solve the problem of temporary nitrogen deficiency after turning these crops over by adding 1 ounce of ammonium sulfate or sodium nitrate per square yard.

Legumes, such as soybeans, vetches, cowpeas, and clovers, have nodules on their roots that house special nitrogen-fixing bacteria. These bacteria take free nitrogen from the air, convert it to forms usable by plants, and hold it. When legumes are used for green manure, added nitrogen is not needed.

BUILDING A COMPOST PILE

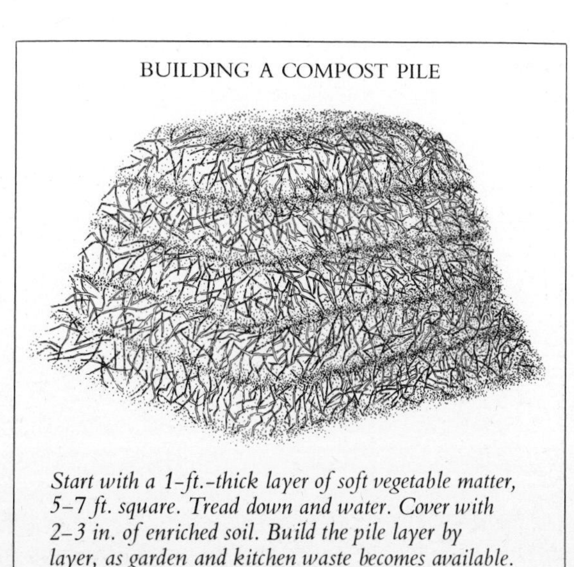

Start with a 1-ft.-thick layer of soft vegetable matter, 5–7 ft. square. Tread down and water. Cover with 2–3 in. of enriched soil. Build the pile layer by layer, as garden and kitchen waste becomes available.

COMPOST CONTAINERS

A removable or hinged front gives easy access. In three-part box compost being used is in left section, decomposing compost is in middle. Right section is being filled by layers.

Working the Soil

Tools for Working the Soil

However small your plot of land, when you set about turning it into a garden you will find that some tools are basic necessities. It is important to have a sharp spade to open the soil, a garden fork to break it up, a shovel to dig holes in it, and a level-head rake to crumble its surface. Then you will need a trowel for small-scale digging, a garden hoe and a scuffle hoe to keep down weeds, and a long-handled and short-handled cultivator to keep the surface loose and friable. You will also need a good long garden hose, equipped with an adjustable nozzle.

If your garden space is larger than a few square yards, a rotary tiller is a good investment; it makes deep cultivation a quick and relatively effortless job. A wheelbarrow is in order, as well as a light roller. Other tools that may come in handy include a crowbar for lifting large rocks, a soil auger for making holes and taking test samples, and a mattock or pick for breaking hard-packed surfaces.

When buying tools, look for the best—cheap tools are always more expensive in the long run. Heft each one to be sure the handle fits your hands comfortably and the tool is well balanced. Look carefully at the way the handle is joined to the working end; this is the weak point. Round handles should be fitted into long metal shanks and riveted firmly in place. All cutting edges should be solid, sharp, and well aligned.

Good tools deserve good care. Clean them off after use. Remove rust spots with a solvent and steel wool. Use a file to smooth out nicks as soon as they occur. Tighten anything that begins to loosen, and occasionally apply a drop of oil to moving parts. At the end of the working season, rub down all metal parts with an oily rag before storing tools for the winter.

Correcting Poor Drainage

Dig a hole about 2 feet deep, and fill it with water. If after 24 hours water still remains, drainage is poor. Even with sandy topsoil, root development will be restricted.

Poor drainage may simply be the result of compacted subsoil or of a hardpan (p. 593). In either case, the problem is fairly easily solved by double digging or using a subsoil plow to break through the hardpan and then working in porous material to lighten the subsoil. If these measures have no effect, it means that the water table is high. You will have to choose between growing only shallow-rooted plants, raising the garden, or lowering the water table.

The water table is the upper surface of a more or less permanent body of water, not unlike an underground lake. It can be only inches beneath the soil surface, as in a marsh, or it can be hundreds of feet deep. Ideally, it should be about 4 feet down, where it can provide a reservoir for the deep roots of trees and shrubs.

In low-lying areas it may be possible to lower the water table by digging trenches across slopes above your garden to divert water as it runs down. Or it may be necessary to install a drainage system.

In the latter case the first step is to decide where excess water will go. It must drain to a point lower than the lowest point of the system. The obvious choices are a nearby pond, stream, ditch, or downward slope. Dig a trench 2–3 feet deep, running downward from the highest point of your garden to such an outlet. On the bottom, place lengths of earthenware or concrete pipe, 4–6 inches in diameter. Leave ⅛-inch gaps between them. Cover with 8–10 inches of coarse gravel or similar material; then replace the soil.

If no simple outlets exist, the alternatives are to connect with a storm drain or to build a dry well, which is a deep, gravel-filled pit. Both jobs are best left in the hands of experts. Consult a reputable landscape architect or building contractor for advice.

How to Dig a Large Area of the Garden

For most purposes it is sufficient to turn the soil to a depth of only 10–12 inches each year. This is best done in fall or early winter. A rotary tiller is the ideal tool for the job, but you can also perform the task with a spade.

First, divide the plot down the middle, and mark the centerline. Dig out a 1-foot-wide trench to the depth of the spade blade, running from one side of the plot to the middle. Put the soil in a pile just outside the plot near the centerline. It will be used later to fill the last trench.

There is a technique to digging, illustrated below, that lightens the strain on your back. Also, avoid overloading each spadeful; it just makes the work more difficult.

If you are adding compost or other humus, spread it evenly over the ground. Hold some aside with the soil for the final trench. Push the humus from the next strip of ground into the trench you have dug, spreading it evenly.

Now, dig the second strip across the half plot, turning each spadeful upside down into the first trench, so that what was on the surface is now about 10 inches deep.

Continue in this way, one strip of soil at a time, to the end of the plot; then work back along the other half. Fill the final trench with the soil from the first one.

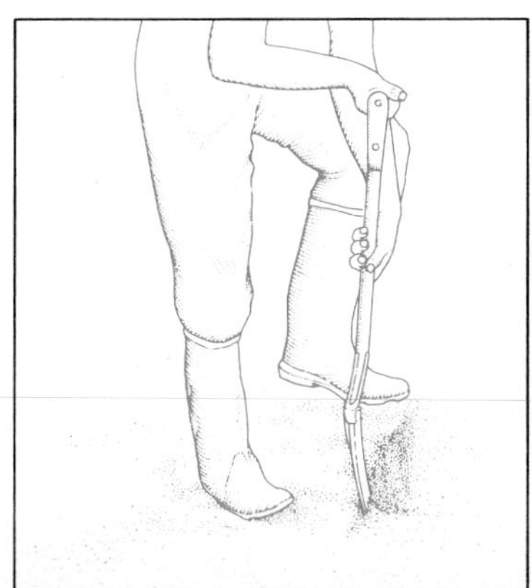

1. *Insert the spade upright, driving it in deeply with the weight of the body.*

2. *Slide one hand down the shaft of the spade, and bend both knees slightly.*

3. *Lift the loaded spade by straightening the legs to take strain off the back.*

Sterilizing and Fumigating Infested Soil

When the same soil is used repeatedly in the greenhouse, cold frame, or even with potted plants, eventually it is almost certain to become infested with nematodes, fungi, and other soil-borne pests and diseases. They can be destroyed by sterilizing the soil with heat or by using chemical soil fumigants.

The simplest and most effective method of heat sterilization is with steam. There are high-pressure units for steaming large amounts of soil at a time, but unless yours is a big greenhouse operation, it is hardly practical to buy one. If, however, a source of steam is available, you can attach a piece of hose to the outlet and insert the end into a flat bushel basket or box of soil. Maintain steam for 45 minutes to 1 hour.

You can accomplish the same end in another way. First, bring ½ pint of water to a boil in a large saucepan. Then put 3–4 quarts of dry soil in the pan, cover tightly, and return to the boil. After 5 to 6 minutes, turn off the heat, but keep tightly covered for another 8 to 10 minutes.

A less thorough method, but probably adequate for most purposes, is to saturate flats of dry soil with two or three applications of boiling water. This can be a messy process, however.

Fumigants, such as formaldehyde and metam-sodium, are sold under a variety of trade names. Most are highly toxic to plants, people, and animals; so they must be used with care. Follow directions and heed all warnings on the labels. All are volatile liquids—they turn quickly to poisonous gas in the soil—so be sure there is adequate ventilation.

After fumigation allow time for the fumes to leave the soil. This will vary with the chemical.

Soil fumigants can also be used to control soil-borne pests and diseases in the garden. Here again, because they can also kill beneficial organisms and because their use presents many hazards, they must be handled with great care.

For further information on soil fumigation, see pages 397 and 449.

Preparing a Bed by Double Digging

Sometimes, to improve drainage or to prepare a bed for certain deep-rooted plants, it is useful to work the soil more deeply than single digging allows. This is done by double digging the soil.

Divide the plot to be dug, and mark the centerline, as with single digging (see opposite page). Dig the first trench 2 feet wide and to the depth of the spade blade, running from the side of the plot to the middle. Pile the soil near the centerline. Spread humus evenly over the ground still to be dug.

Then use a garden fork to thoroughly break up the bottom of the trench. Push in the humus from the top of the next 2-foot strip, and work it in evenly with the fork. Then dig the next 2-foot strip, turning each spadeful of soil upside down into the open trench. Break up the bottom of this trench with the fork, and work in the humus from the next strip. Continue in this manner around the two half plots until the final trench is filled with soil from the first.

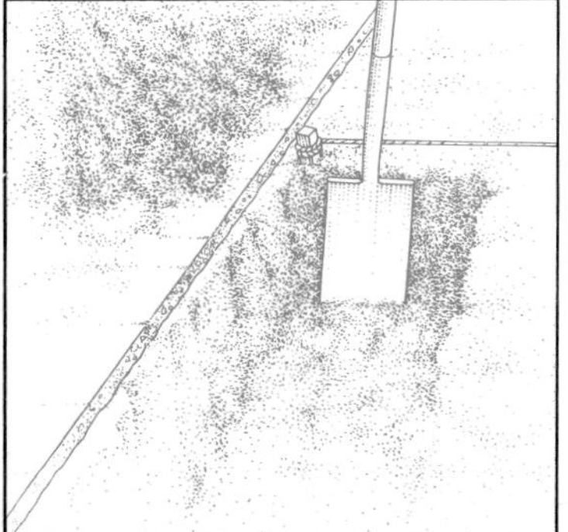

1. *Pile soil from first trench at the end of the plot near the centerline.*

2. *Use a fork to break up the trench bottom, and work in some humus.*

3. *Dig second 2-ft. trench, turning the soil upside down into the first.*

4. *Use the pile of soil from the first trench to fill the final trench.*

Watering: How Much and How Often

Nutrients are useless to plants until they have been dissolved in water. They are equally useless to ordinary land plants if they are in waterlogged soil. The main day-to-day problem facing the gardener, therefore, is likely to be too much or too little water in the soil.

The problem of too little water is easier to solve, provided there is a source from which to augment nature's gift of rain. In general, the time to water is when about half the moisture that the soil is capable of holding has dried out. Determine this point by picking up a handful of topsoil and squeezing it into a ball: if it holds its shape, moisture is probably sufficient; if it crumbles easily, more water is probably needed.

When watering, soak the soil to at least a foot deep. Mere surface sprinkling encourages shallow roots, which are vulnerable to scorching in the hot sun. (Seedlings, however, including young lawn grass, may need as many as two light sprinklings a day until their short roots have grown deeper.)

How often you should water depends on the condition of your soil, the weather, the kinds of plants you are growing, and their location. Vegetables, on the average, need twice as much water as flowers. Newly planted trees and shrubs require frequent watering in dry weather. Plants sheltered by walls or hedges may need watering even after a rainstorm, but they are not likely to dry out as fast as plants in the open. Plants high on a slope will dry out faster then those at the bottom. Plants growing in light, sandy soil need watering oftener than those growing in heavier soil.

Prevent moisture loss by mulching the soil surface. The kind and amount of mulch to use varies with different plants; consult appropriate sections of the book.

Controlling Pests, Diseases, and Weeds

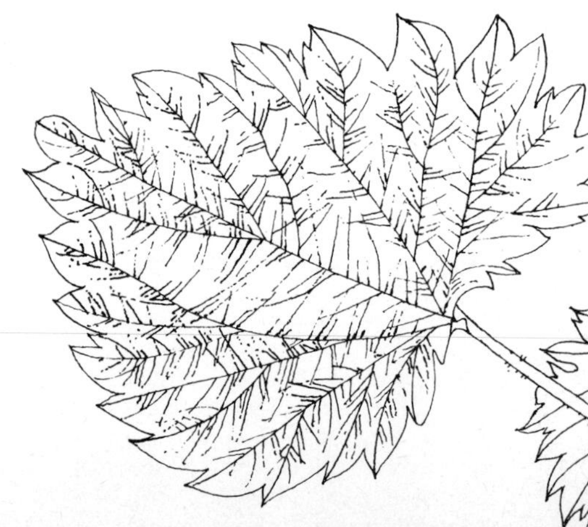

Plant Disorders

Most plant ailments can be treated successfully. First, identify the problem from the pictures and descriptions; then, apply the remedy recommended.

This section will enable you to recognize and control the pests, diseases, and physiological disorders that most commonly strike cultivated plants. Although these problems present a formidable picture when viewed together, only a few are likely to afflict a single garden.

Keep a continuous watch over all your plants to see whether the leaves, stems, or flowers appear in any way unhealthy—distorted or discolored, for example. Take remedial action as quickly as possible. Warning: do not spray when blossoms are open; you may kill the pollinating insects.

Plants that have been regularly attacked in the past by certain pests and diseases should be protected against them in advance. Soils that are known to harbor pests should be cultivated frequently with a fork or hoe, or treated with a soil fumigant (metam-sodium) to control nematodes, weed seeds, fungi, and soil insects. Crop rotation also helps.

Leaves with tattered holes (by plant bugs, or leaf bugs)

Shoots rotting and disfigured (by Botrytis)

Roots attacked (by wireworms)

How to identify plant disorders. On the left is an ailing dahlia. The leaves have tattered holes; the shoots are rotting and covered in places with gray fungous growth; the roots have been damaged by larvae.

The illustrations of symptoms are set out in the following order: leaves, shoots, flower buds, flowers in bloom, fruits, vegetables, root structures, and lawns. The picture may not show the plant affected in your garden, but each caption lists the plants most commonly affected, the symptoms and signs, the danger period, as well as the treatment.

To discover what is wrong with the dahlia's leaves, look through the illustrations under the heading Leaves With Holes (starting on p. 601) until you find the one that most closely resembles the damage. In this instance it is plant-bug damage, as described on page 602, together with the proper control. (This illustration is also shown at the top of the column at right.)

By turning to the section Shoots Discolored, you will find that the shoots of the dahlia may be suffering from gray mold (see p. 617).

When a plant is obviously ailing but no damage is visible aboveground, dig it up. You may find that the dahlia's roots are being attacked by wireworms (see p. 630).

The treatments that are recommended will usually involve a chemical. Consult the list of pesticides, fungicides, and other controls, beginning on page 635, to discover what forms are available and what their trade names are.

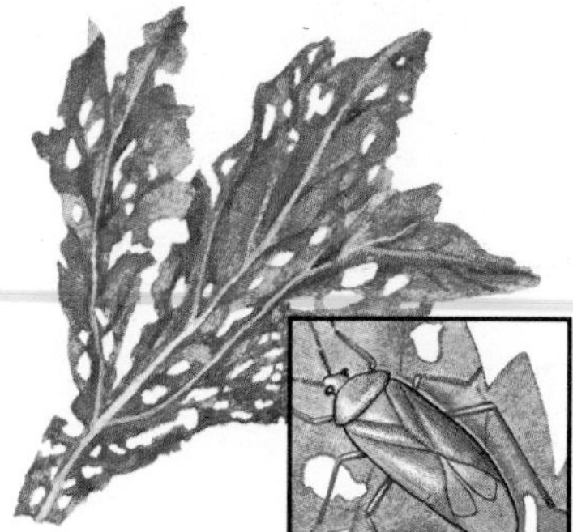

Plant bug, or leaf bug

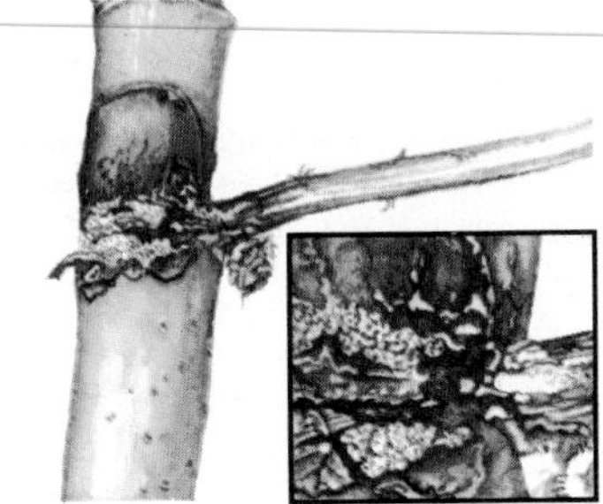

Botrytis, or gray mold

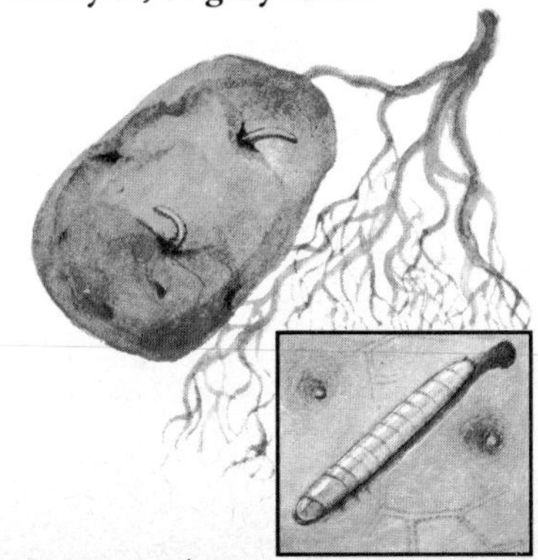

Wireworms

Leaves With Pests Visible

Scale insects
Plants affected: Camellias, citrus, foliage plants, and others.
Symptoms and signs: Flat or rounded scales.
Danger period: Spring, early summer outdoors; any time indoors.
Treatment: On dormant deciduous trees and shrubs, spray 60- to 70-sec. miscible oil or lime sulfur in late winter or early spring. In late spring, spray with dimethoate or malathion, repeating about 3 wk. later; use on greenhouse plants when scale insects are active. Dip house plants in malathion.

Aphids
Plants affected: Nearly all cultivated plants indoors and outdoors.
Symptoms and signs: Colonies of small insects.
Danger period: Spring and early summer outdoors; any time of year indoors.
Treatment: Spray thoroughly with systemic insecticide, such as dimethoate or oxydemeton-methyl, or with nonsystemic insecticides, such as carbaryl, endosulfan, malathion, nicotine, or rotenone. Fumigate greenhouses with dichlorvos or nicotine.

Greenhouse and cabbage whiteflies
Plants affected: Ageratums, azaleas, Brussels sprouts, cabbage, chrysanthemums, cucumbers, fuchsias, gerberas, lantanas, poinsettias, tomatoes.
Symptoms and signs: White insects beneath leaves. Leaves off-color.
Danger period: Late spring to early fall outdoors; all year in heated greenhouse.
Treatment: Spray plants with dimethoate, malathion, or resmethrin. Fumigate greenhouse with dichlorvos. Destroy old plants.

Colorado potato beetles
Plants affected: Eggplants, peppers, tomatoes, white potatoes.
Symptoms and signs: Large pieces of leaves chewed out by larvae (grubs) and adults.
Danger period: Late spring (when adults lay eggs on weeds or other plants) through summer (when larvae and adult beetles feed on leaves).
Treatment: Spray with carbaryl.

Mealybugs
Plants affected: Many indoor plants.
Symptoms and signs: Small pink insects on leaves. Masses of white "cotton" at leaf nodes.
Danger period: Any time.
Treatment: Spray thoroughly with systemic insecticide, such as dimethoate or oxydemeton-methyl, or with nonsystemic insecticide, such as dichlorvos.

Japanese beetles
Plants affected: Grapes, lindens, roses, and many other plants.
Symptoms and signs: Petals frayed and leaves skeletonized. Green beetles may be visible.
Danger period: Early summer to midfall.
Treatment: Spray or dust infested plants with carbaryl or Diazinon. For control of larvae, see Beetle Grubs, p. 634.

Leaves With Holes

Caterpillars (including inchworms, gypsy moth larvae, and tent caterpillars)
Plants affected: Many different plants, especially shrubs and trees.
Symptoms and signs: Irregular pieces eaten from foliage, often leaving large holes.
Danger period: From early spring onward.
Treatment: If possible, remove caterpillars. Or spray thoroughly with carbaryl, malathion, rotenone, or trichlorfon when symptoms appear.

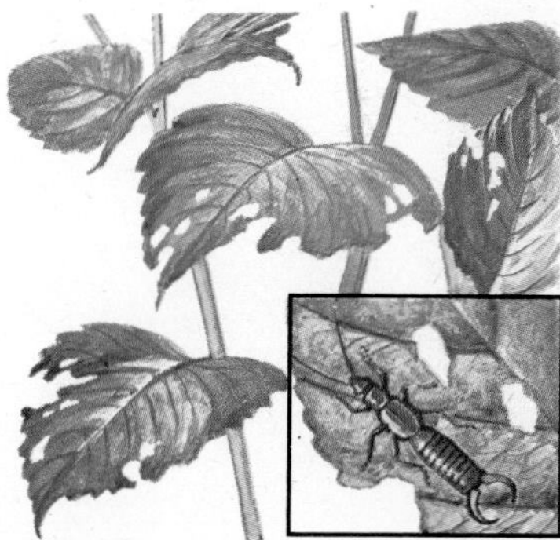

Earwigs
Plants affected: Clematises, dahlias, gladioli, and some other plants.
Symptoms and signs: Irregular, tattered holes in leaves.
Danger period: Late spring to midfall.
Treatment: Spray or dust with carbaryl, Diazinon, or malathion.

Leaftiers and leaf rollers, or tortrix caterpillars
Plants affected: Shrubs, trees, and herbaceous plants, especially apples, chrysanthemums, heleniums, perennial phlox, and various greenhouse and house plants.
Symptoms and signs: Small holes eaten in leaves; later, leaves are drawn together with silk webbing.
Danger period: Late spring to early summer outdoors; any time of year in greenhouse.
Treatment: Spray thoroughly with carbaryl, rotenone, or trichlorfon; or remove caterpillars by hand.

Vine and flower weevils
Plants affected: Camellias, clematises, primroses, rhododendrons, yews, various vines.
Symptoms and signs: Small, irregular notches eaten from leaf edges. Roots chewed by larvae.
Danger period: Spring and summer outdoors; any time of year in greenhouse.
Treatment: Remove accumulations of leaves and other plant debris where weevils rest by day; spray or dust affected plants with chlordane, endosulfan, or methoxychlor.

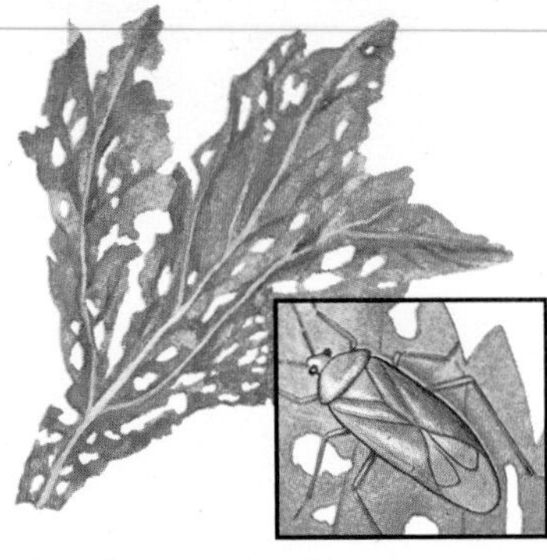

Plant bugs, or leaf bugs (four-lined, harlequin, tarnished)
Plants affected: Apples, beans, buddlejas, currants, dahlias, forsythias, and many other plants.
Symptoms and signs: Tattered holes in young leaves.
Danger period: Midspring to late summer.
Treatment: Good garden hygiene and weed control can reduce damage. Protect susceptible plants by spraying with carbaryl, Diazinon, malathion, or nicotine when symptoms appear.

Shot-hole disease
Plants affected: Cherries, peaches, plums, and other *Prunus* species.
Symptoms and signs: Brown patches on leaves drop out and leave irregularly shaped holes.
Danger period: Growing season.
Treatment: Feed trees annually, mulch, and never allow soil to dry out. Apply foliar fertilizer to small trees. If trouble occurs next year, spray with Captan or dodine every 2 wk. in spring and early summer; or spray with half-strength copper fungicide in summer and full-strength solution at leaf fall.

Rose slugs (sawfly larvae)
Plants affected: Roses.
Symptoms and signs: Irregular areas in leaves eaten partly through, leaving transparent membranes.
Danger period: Early summer to early fall.
Treatment: Spray thoroughly with carbaryl, methoxychlor, or rotenone when symptoms appear.

Bean and pea weevils
Plants affected: Beans, peas.
Symptoms and signs: Leaf edges eaten in scalloped pattern.
Danger period: Early spring to early summer.
Treatment: Apply carbaryl or malathion dust to young plants when symptoms appear. Mature plants are not seriously affected.

Hellebore leaf blotch
Plants affected: Christmas and Lenten roses (*Helleborus*).
Symptoms and signs: Gray or black blotches with concentric rings on leaves, which wither.
Danger period: All year; most troublesome in winter and spring.
Treatment: Remove and destroy diseased parts. Spray plants regularly with Benomyl or with copper fungicide, such as Bordeaux mixture.

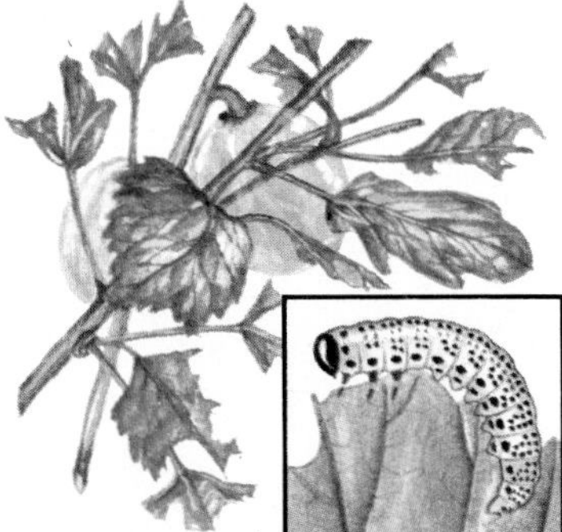

Gooseberry sawflies (larvae)
Plants affected: Gooseberries.
Symptoms and signs: Leaf tissues eaten away, with many leaves reduced to skeleton of veins.
Danger period: Midspring to late summer.
Treatment: Spray thoroughly with carbaryl, malathion, nicotine, or rotenone in midspring or when symptoms first appear.

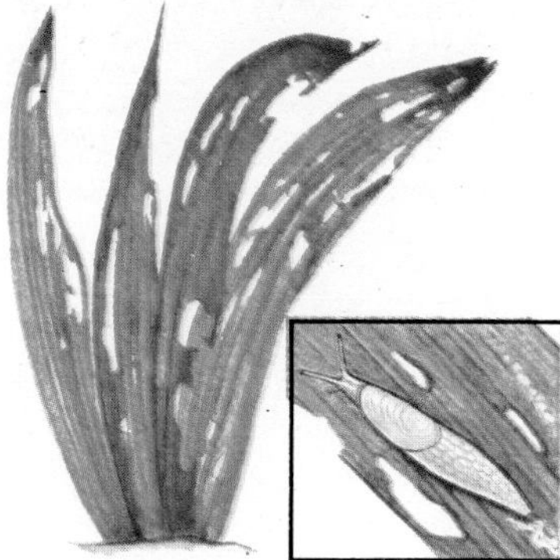

Slugs and snails
Plants affected: Delphiniums, lettuce, lilies, tulips, sweet peas, and many other plants.
Symptoms and signs: Irregular holes in leaves; slime trails visible.
Danger period: Spring to midfall.
Treatment: Cultivate thoroughly, and dispose of decaying plant material. Avoid heavy dressings or organic manures and mulches. Use metaldehyde or methiocarb slug poison baits, or spray with mexacarbate. Beer placed in shallow pans or saucers will drown slugs.

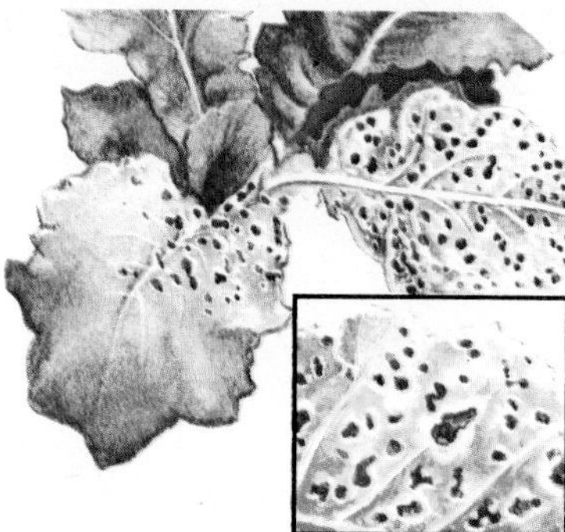

Flea beetles
Plants affected: Cabbage, radishes, tomatoes, turnips, and related plants.
Symptoms and signs: Youngest leaves pitted with tiny holes.
Danger period: Dry spells in late spring.
Treatment: Dust or spray susceptible seedlings with carbaryl, methoxychlor, or rotenone. Good garden hygiene will reduce the risk of attack, and seed treatments will give some protection.

Chocolate spot, or pod spot
Plants affected: Beans.
Symptoms and signs: Small dark brown spots on leaves and stems. Spots may merge.
Danger period: Early to mid winter for overwintered plants. Early to mid summer for spring-sown beans.
Treatment: If disease is known to be severe, spray with copper fungicide soon after leaves appear. Encourage strong growth by applying limestone and high-potassium fertilizer.

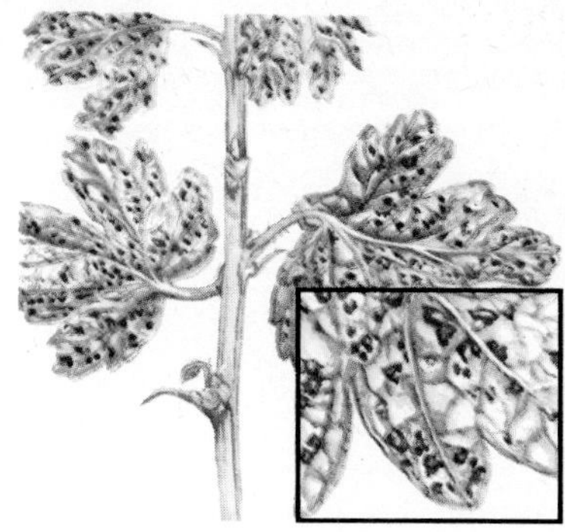

Anthracnose and other dark leaf spots
Plants affected: Many types.
Symptoms and signs: Brown, round or oval spots, often with definite margins and sometimes showing small black pinpoints.
Danger period: Growing season.
Treatment: Remove and destroy leaves of affected plants. Spray them and their immediate neighbors with Benomyl, Captan, dichlofluanid, maneb, thiophanate-methyl, or zineb.

Leaf-cutting ants and bees
Plants affected: Golden chains, lilacs, privets, roses, and a few other ornamental plants.
Symptoms and signs: Semi-circular pieces eaten out of leaf edges.
Danger period: Early to late summer.
Treatment: Spray affected plants with carbaryl, Diazinon, methoxychlor, or propoxur to kill or repel ants and bees.

Water-lily beetles
Plants affected: Water lilies (both species and hybrids).
Symptoms and signs: Surface tissue of leaves eaten away in furrows. Flowers may also be damaged.
Danger period: Early to late summer.
Treatment: Spray or hose plants forcibly with water to knock adult beetles and larvae off leaves so that fish can feed on them.

Willow anthracnose, or leaf spot
Plants affected: Weeping willows.
Symptoms and signs: Small brown spots on leaves.
Danger period: As leaves unfold in spring; sometimes in wet summers.
Treatment: Spray small trees as leaves unfold with fungicide, such as Benomyl, Bordeaux mixture, Captan, copper, dodine, or maneb.

Quince leaf blight
Plants affected: Flowering quinces.
Symptoms and signs: Small red spots later turn brown. Leaves turn brown, fall early.
Danger period: Growing season, but most obvious in late summer.
Treatment: Rake up and destroy diseased leaves. Cut out dead shoots. Spray with ferbam or ziram when leaves unfold. Repeat once or twice during wet weather.

Fungous disease
Plants affected: All types of trees and shrubs, but particularly pears, rhododendrons, and roses.
Symptoms and signs: Small black or purplish-black spots.
Danger period: Growing season.
Treatment: Feed annually, mulch, and water; drain soil if necessary. Apply all-purpose fungicide, such as mancozeb, periodically.

Yellow mottle
Plants affected: Camellias.
Symptoms and signs: Some leaves have white blotches; other leaves turn completely white; can be caused by a virus. Mutation or genetic variegation can also cause these symptoms.
Danger period: Any time after a cutting (scion) from infected plant is used for graft.
Treatment: Destroy badly affected plants. Isolate those with mottle from healthy ones. No infected plant should be used as source of propagating material.

Scab
Plants affected: Apples, flowering crab apples, fire thorns, pears.
Symptoms and signs: Olive-green blotches of fungous growth on leaves, which fall prematurely.
Danger period: Growing season.
Treatment: Spray regularly, starting when young flower buds are visible, and until midsummer if necessary, with Benomyl, Captan, lime sulfur (except on sulfur-sensitive varieties and pears), thiophanate-methyl, or thiram. Start spraying fire thorns when young leaves are half-grown. Rake up and destroy all fallen diseased leaves.

For illustration of scab on fruit, see p. 626.

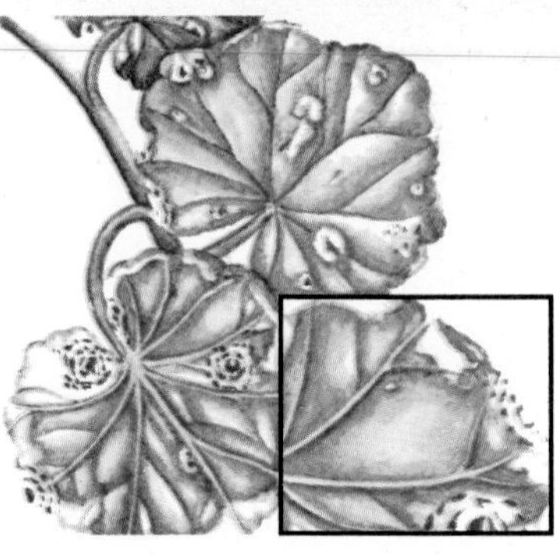

Rusts
Plants affected: Many types, but particularly apples, flowering quinces, hawthorns, red cedars, white pines, asparagus, barberries, beans, carnations, geraniums (*Pelargonium*), hollyhocks, Saint-John's-worts, snapdragons, sweet Williams, wheat.
Symptoms and signs: Brown, orange, or yellow powdery masses of spores develop on affected leaves and stems, and occasionally on flowers and seedpods. Irregularly round galls are found on twigs.
Danger period: Growing season. Late summer for roses; autumn for sweet Williams.
Treatment: Remove and destroy diseased leaves on all types of plants. For plants in greenhouses, reduce humidity by ventilating. Spray geraniums with Benomyl or zineb at weekly intervals; spray other plants with Benomyl, maneb, thiram, or zineb at 10- to 14-da. intervals. These fungicides should also be used outdoors on roses, Saint-John's-worts, and on young sweet Williams before disease becomes troublesome. They can also be tried on hollyhocks. Grow rust-resistant snapdragons. Prune off rusted twigs and galls when found.

Rusts are of 2 types—1 host and 2 host. Two-host rusts have an alternate host; for instance, apple rust attacks red cedars as well as apples. This is true of barberries and wheat, cedars and hawthorns, white pines and currants. For 2-host rusts, it is a good idea to locate and destroy the alternate hosts. This will break the cycle and stop the disease.

Tar spot
Plants affected: Maples.
Symptoms and signs: Large, raised black spots with bright yellow edges.
Danger period: Summer.
Treatment: Rake up and destroy affected leaves. As leaves of small trees unfold, spray them with copper fungicide, such as Bordeaux mixture, or with Captan, ferbam, or zineb.

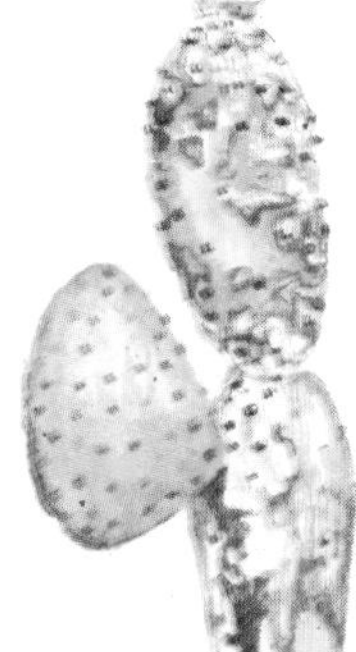
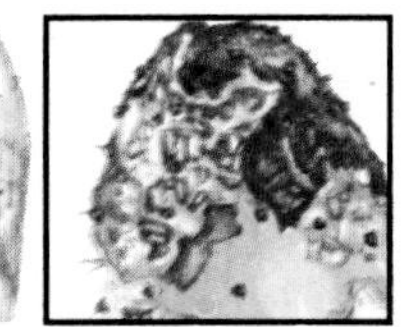

Corky scab
Plants affected: Cacti, especially epiphyllums and opuntias.
Symptoms and signs: Irregular rusty or corky spots that may become sunken.
Danger period: Growing season.
Treatment: Scab is nonpathogenic and is caused by low light and high humidity. Improve cultural conditions. Destroy badly affected plants.

Leaf mold

Plants affected: Tomatoes in greenhouses.
Symptoms and signs: Purple-brown mold on undersides of leaves; on upper surfaces whitish spots appear first and develop into yellow blotches.
Danger period: From early summer onward and sometimes in mid to late spring.
Treatment: Ventilate greenhouse well and spray with copper fungicide, maneb, or zineb. Disinfect greenhouse after severe outbreak. Take care in watering, since spores are spread by splashing water. Grow resistant varieties.

Pear leaf blister mites

Plants affected: Pears, mountain ashes.
Symptoms and signs: Numerous dark brown pustules appear on both sides of leaves.
Danger period: Midspring to late summer.
Treatment: Pick off affected leaves and destroy them, or spray with lime sulfur at beginning of spring. Spray as new leaves open and again a week later with acaricide (mite killer), such as chlorobenzilate, dicofol, or tetradifon.

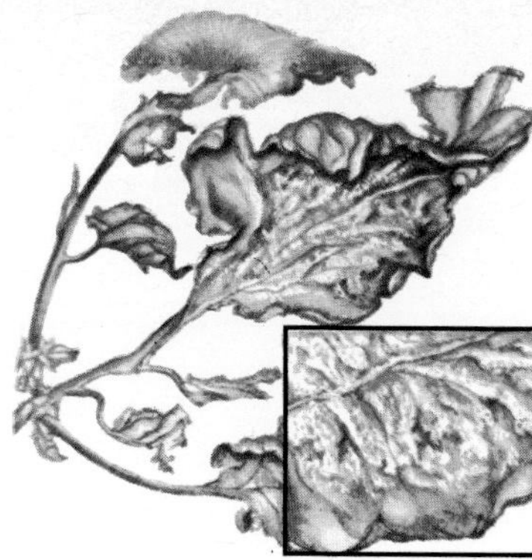

Botrytis, or gray mold

Plants affected: All types, but particularly chrysanthemums, lettuce, and tomatoes in greenhouses, as well as many outdoor crops; also, dogwoods, hydrangeas, lilacs, peonies.
Symptoms and signs: Gray velvety mold on rotting leaves.
Danger period: Growing season.
Treatment: Remove and destroy infected parts. Ventilate greenhouse well; then fumigate with tecnazene smoke, or spray with Benomyl, dichlofluanid, dichloran, thiophanate-methyl, thiram, or zineb.

Rose black spot

Plants affected: Roses.
Symptoms and signs: Distinct black or dark brown spots, either small and diffuse or up to ½ in. across. Leaves soon turn yellow and fall prematurely.
Danger period: Growing season; worst from early summer on.
Treatment: Spray with Benomyl, Captan, dichlofluanid, folpet, maneb, thiophanate-methyl, or zineb, beginning as first leaves unfold and repeating weekly until frost. Rake up and destroy diseased leaves. Encourage vigor in rose bushes by spraying them with foliar fertilizer and by giving good general care through growing season.

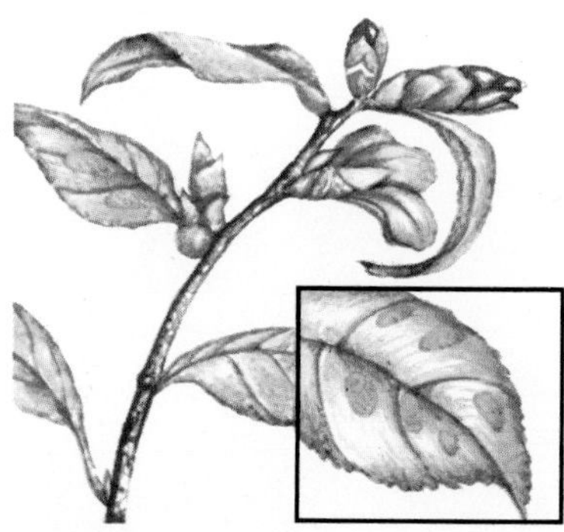

Edema

Plants affected: Mainly camellias, zonal geraniums (*Pelargonium*), and vines; but many other greenhouse plants can have this problem.
Symptoms and signs: Small, water-soaked spots that break out into corky growths.
Danger period: Growing season indoors.
Treatment: Ventilate greenhouse to reduce humidity, and be sure that plants are not waterlogged.

Lace bugs

Plants affected: Mountain laurels, pierises, rhododendrons (including azaleas), and many other deciduous trees and shrubs.
Symptoms and signs: Silvery gray spots on leaves. Hard black spots and tiny lace bugs on undersides.
Danger period: Late spring to early fall.
Treatment: Spray undersides of leaves thoroughly with carbaryl, malathion, nicotine, or rotenone in early summer; repeat about a month later.

Two-spotted, or red spider, mites

Plants affected: Many different greenhouse and house plants, as well as plants growing outdoors in summer. Cucumbers, dahlias, fuchsias, peaches, roses, strawberries, and violets are particularly susceptible.
Symptoms and signs: Very fine, light mottling of upper leaf surfaces, followed by general yellow discoloration and sometimes death. Severely infested plants may be covered with silk webbing.
Danger period: Almost any time of year in greenhouses, early spring to late fall outdoors.
Treatment: Maintain humid atmosphere in greenhouse, spraying plants with water if necessary. Thorough spraying with chlorobenzilate, dicofol, malathion, or tetradifon may check infestations, but mites become resistant to chemicals relatively quickly. Systemics, such as dimethoate or oxydemeton-methyl, are also effective as prevention against mites. As alternative to chemical control, mite predators can be used if available (see p. 635).

White rust

Plants affected: Aubrietas, cabbage, candytufts, honesties, radishes, sweet alyssums.
Symptoms and signs: Blisters or swellings, full of white powdery spores and often glistening, develop on leaves and sometimes on stems.
Danger period: Growing season.
Treatment: Cut off and destroy diseased leaves. Eradicate shepherd's purse, a common weed of the cabbage family that is important overwinter host for white rust fungus.

Cold

Plants affected: Magnolias, morning glories (*Ipomoea*), sweet peas, bedding plants, and others.
Symptoms and signs: Young, soft leaves become white or pale yellow.
Danger period: Seedling stage.
Treatment: None, but applications of foliar fertilizer can help restore green color to foliage.

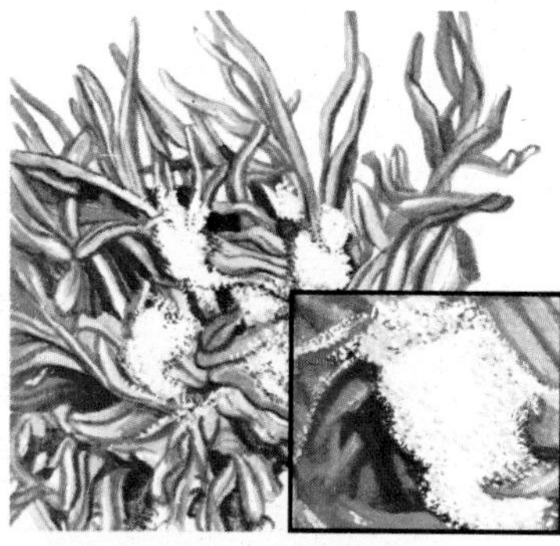

Spittlebugs, or froghoppers

Plants affected: Chrysanthemums, clovers, lavenders, perennial asters, pines, roses, and many other plants.
Symptoms and signs: Frothy masses of "frog spit" covering small pink or green insects.
Danger period: Early to mid summer.
Treatment: Wash off "frog spit" with water from garden hose. Then spray with carbaryl, malathion, or nicotine to kill exposed insects.

Gall aphids

Plants affected: Common and serious on spruces. Can also appear on firs, larches, pines, and other conifers.
Symptoms and signs: Green swelling occurs on new growth in late spring. Colonies of small, dark aphids partially covered by tufts of white woolly wax infest undersides of leaves and leaf axils.
Danger period: Spring, but symptoms may not be noticed until browning appears in summer.
Treatment: Spray thoroughly with carbaryl, Diazinon, or endosulfan. For spruces and Douglas firs, use dormant spray of miscible oil before midspring, and follow with contact spray of carbaryl, endosulfan, or oxydemeton-methyl in late spring. Be sure to spray bark crevices on twig tips and bases of buds. Do not use dormant oil sprays on blue-needled evergreens.

Silver leaf

Plants affected: Cherries, peaches, plums, and other *Prunus* species; apples, lilacs, pears; other trees and shrubs.
Symptoms and signs: Leaves become silvered, and upper surfaces peel off easily. When cross section of affected branch 1 in. or more across is moistened, brown or purple stain appears. Flat, purple fungus eventually develops on deadwood. Affected branches ultimately die back.
Danger period: Early fall to late spring. Symptoms may not appear until some time after infection has taken place.
Treatment: Cut out affected branches to 6 in. below point where stain in wood stops. Paint all wounds with wound-sealing paint. Feed, mulch, water, and/or drain soil as necessary to encourage vigor. Foliar applications of fertilizer may hasten recovery.

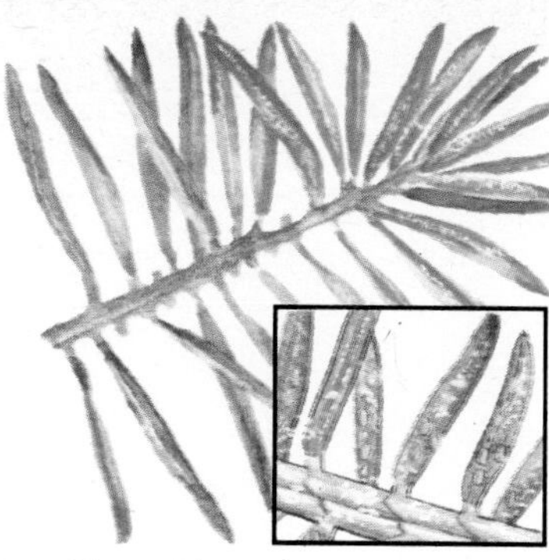

Conifer mites

Plants affected: Cypresses, junipers, pines, spruces, and some other conifers.
Symptoms and signs: Needles of conifers turn bronze and fall prematurely. Needles frequently covered with webbing spun by nearly microscopic mites.
Danger period: Early summer to early fall.
Treatment: Spray thoroughly with acaricide (mite killer), such as dicofol or tetradifon, in early summer; repeat as needed. Systemics, such as dimethoate, are also effective.

Frost damage

Plants affected: Cucumbers, snapdragons, tomatoes, and nearly all tender herbaceous plants.
Symptoms and signs: All leaves on seedlings or young plants are silvered.
Danger period: Seedlings and new-growth stage in spring, mature-plant stage in fall.
Treatment: Protect with plastic sheeting or light blankets.

Leafhoppers

Plants affected: Geraniums (*Pelargonium*), primroses, roses, and other plants, both outdoors and in greenhouses.
Symptoms and signs: Small white spots appear on leaves, caused by hoppers feeding on undersides. Molted insect skins can often be seen on undersides.
Danger period: Midspring to midfall outdoors, but any time of year indoors.
Treatment: Spray thoroughly with carbaryl, Diazinon, or malathion, repeating every 2 wk. if necessary.

Thrips

Plants affected: Gladioli, peas, privets, and many other plants.
Symptoms and signs: Leaves finely mottled, with general silvery appearance. Flowers of gladioli become deformed and discolored.
Danger period: Early summer to early fall, especially during hot, dry weather.
Treatment: Spray or dust with carbaryl, Diazinon, or endosulfan when signs are first seen.

Powdery mildew

Plants affected: Many types, but especially begonias, euonymuses, lilacs, perennial asters, phlox, roses, apples, gooseberries, strawberries, lawn grasses.
Symptoms and signs: White, floury coating on leaves and shoots, and sometimes on flowers. Strawberry leaves turn purple and curl.
Danger period: Growing season.
Treatment: Cut out severely affected shoots on trees and shrubs in early summer and early fall. Spray regularly with Benomyl, dinocap, or thiophanate-methyl. Lime sulfur can be used on some kinds of apples. Benomyl, cycloheximide, dinocap, or sulfur sprays can be used on herbaceous plants and shrubs. In greenhouse fumigate with dinocap smokes, or use one of the above as a spray. For strawberries, immediately before blossom time, dust with sulfur, or spray with dinocap or 1½% lime sulfur. Repeat this at 10- to 14-da. intervals until 1 or 2 wk. before harvest time. Alternatively, at early blossoming stage spray 3 times at 14-da. intervals with Benomyl or thiophanate-methyl. Remove leaves after harvesting or spray again.

Lime-induced chlorosis
Plants affected: Many different types, but particularly ceanothuses, fruit trees, hydrangeas, raspberries; also acid-soil plants, such as camellias and rhododendrons, growing in insufficiently acid soils.
Symptoms and signs: Yellowing between veins.
Danger period: Growing season.
Treatment: Dig in acidifying materials, such as peat moss or sulfur. Apply chelated iron compound or fritted trace elements.

Manganese deficiency
Plants affected: Many types.
Symptoms and signs: Yellowing between veins of older leaves.
Danger period: Growing season.
Treatment: Spray with solution of manganese sulfate (2 tbsp. per $2\frac{1}{2}$ gal. of water) plus a few drops of liquid detergent, or apply chelated iron or fritted trace elements.

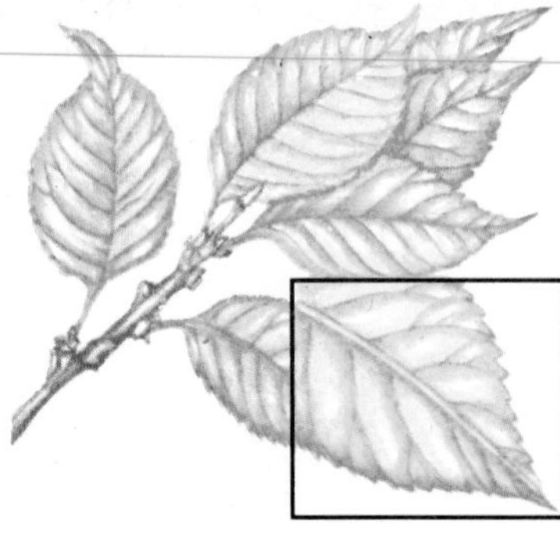

Magnesium deficiency
Plants affected: All types, particularly apples and tomatoes.
Symptoms and signs: Orange bands between veins, which later become brown. Affected leaves may wither.
Danger period: Growing season or after applications of high-potassium fertilizer, which tends to hold magnesium in soil.
Treatment: Spray with solution of magnesium sulfate (Epsom salts): 8 rounded tbsp. to $2\frac{1}{2}$ gal. of water, plus a few drops of liquid detergent.

Scorch
Plants affected: Most types of house and greenhouse plants, beeches, horse chestnuts, maples.
Symptoms and signs: Pale brown spots appear on leaves; entire leaves may become dry and papery.
Danger period: Spring for most trees and shrubs, summer for house plants and greenhouse plants.
Treatment: Shade greenhouse. Make sure that no plant suffers from dry soil (especially trees, during cold, drying spring winds). Spray affected plants with foliar applications of fertilizer.

Virus disease
Plants affected: All types, but particularly daffodils, lilies, raspberries, squash.
Symptoms and signs: Yellow striping (on daffodils and lilies) and blotching or mottling of leaves (on raspberries and squash).
Danger period: Growing season.
Treatment: Dig up and destroy. In the case of small fruits, plant only stocks certified to be free of virus. Spraying insects that carry virus can help prevent it; use carbaryl, Diazinon, or malathion.

Leaf nematodes, or leaf eelworms and bud eelworms
Plants affected: African violets, begonias, chrysanthemums, ferns, peperomias, and some other plants.
Symptoms and signs: Brown or yellow mottling on leaves.
Danger period: Midsummer to early winter outdoors; all year in greenhouses.
Treatment: Keep foliage and stems of plants reasonably dry if possible. Remove and destroy affected leaves and severely affected plants. Apply dimethoate spray or soil drench.

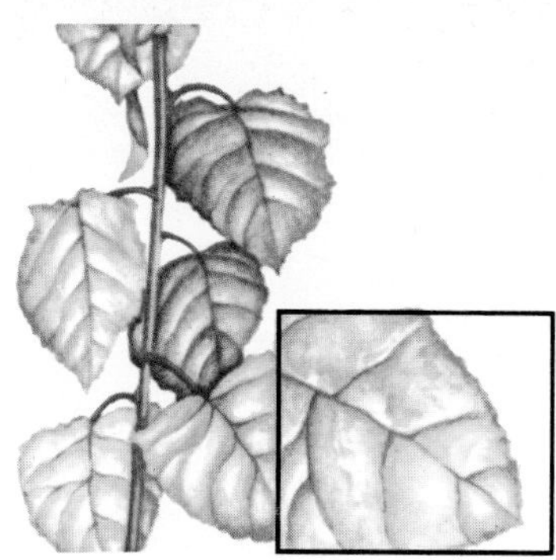

Nitrogen deficiency

Plants affected: All types, but it is commonest on broad-leaved evergreens, fruit trees, and vegetables.
Symptoms and signs: Leaves yellow-green, later becoming yellow, red, or purple. Plants weak.
Danger period: Growing season.
Treatment: Apply nitrogenous fertilizer, such as sulfate of ammonia, on trees and shrubs the following spring. Foliar applications of fertilizer may help during growing season; on vegetables, apply nitrogenous fertilizer as side-dressing.

Nutrient deficiency

Plants affected: All types.
Symptoms and signs: Many leaves turn yellow and may fall prematurely.
Danger period: Growing season.
Treatment: Feed as necessary, mulch, and make sure soil never dries out. Drain if soil is waterlogged. Spray with foliar fertilizer.

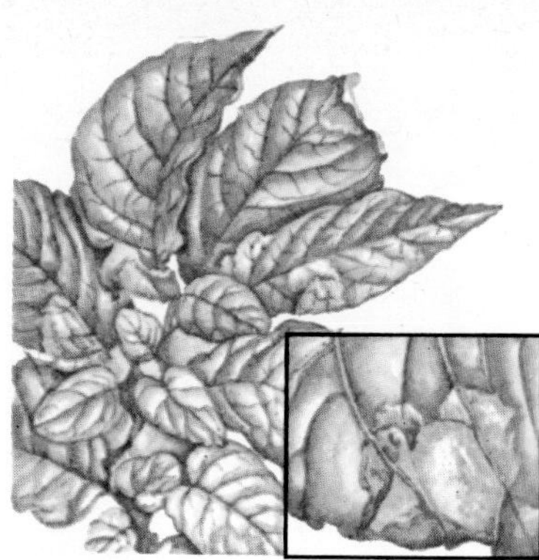

Blight

Plants affected: Potatoes, tomatoes.
Symptoms and signs: Purplish blotches on leaves, with white furry coating on undersides. Leaves quickly turn completely brown and then rot.
Danger period: Midsummer until end of season.
Treatment: Spray at 10- to 14-da. intervals, particularly in wet season, with Bordeaux mixture, copper, maneb, or zineb. Spray potatoes before they flower, tomatoes soon after first fruits set. Remove and destroy top growth as soon as rotting occurs. For illustration of potato tuber affected by blight disease, turn to p. 631; for tomato fruit, see p. 627.

Dutch elm disease

Plants affected: American elms (*Ulmus americana*).
Symptoms and signs: Leaves turn yellow; then they turn brown and hang on dead branches. Brown discoloration of internal wood visible, as well as beetles' "feeding galleries" under bark. Wilting and dying of branches and leaves is caused by fungus, which is spread from tree to tree by elm bark beetles.
Danger period: Late spring to early fall.
Treatment: Destroy dead or badly damaged trees, including stumps; send to local incinerator. Isolate root system to prevent spread of fungus to other trees. Do not store logs for burning in fireplace. In less severe cases, there may be chance of saving tree if you remove diseased branches and apply wound-sealing paint. For prevention it is important to keep trees well watered. Feed in spring and fall to maintain vigor. Prune infected limbs. To control *Scolytus* beetle that carries this disease, apply dormant spray in early spring, using methoxychlor 25% emulsifiable concentrate. Use hydraulic sprayer or mist blower for tall trees. Call in professional tree expert. Plant resistant elm varieties. See also p. 18 and Elm Bark Beetles, p. 615.

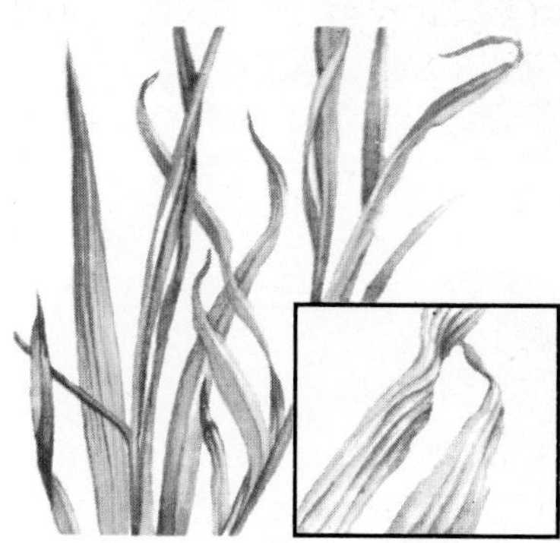

Fusarium yellows

Plants affected: Carnations, freesias, gladioli.
Symptoms and signs: Yellowing of leaves. Affected leaves eventually die.
Danger period: Growing season.
Treatment: Dig up and destroy affected plants. At end of season, dip remaining corms of freesias and gladioli in Benomyl or Captan before storing; plant them in different part of garden the following year. For carnations, sterilize soil with steam or metam-sodium.

Downy mildew

Plants affected: Cabbage, cucumbers, grapes, lettuce, lima beans, onions, wallflowers.
Symptoms and signs: Yellow spots develop on upper leaf surfaces, gray or white furry patches on undersides.
Danger period: Fall and spring.
Treatment: Raise seedlings on new site each year, and spray plants with maneb, zineb, or ziram (carbamate fungicides). Particularly on grapes, spray Bordeaux mixture or low-soluble copper fungicide.

Sooty mold

Plants affected: Many types outdoors and in greenhouses, especially birches, camellias, citrus, lindens, oaks, plums, roses, willows.
Symptoms and signs: Black sooty deposits appear on upper leaf surfaces, and young leaves are sticky.
Danger period: Summer and autumn.
Treatment: Sooty molds develop on plants infested by such pests as aphids, mealybugs, and scale insects. Control pests by spraying with dimethoate or malathion whenever pests are active.

European red mites

Plants affected: Apples, pears, plums, and some related ornamentals.
Symptoms and signs: Older leaves gradually turn bronze-yellow, dry out, and die. Webbing often present.
Danger period: Midspring to late fall.
Treatment: To kill overwintering eggs, spray thoroughly with dinoseb or miscible petroleum oil spray while trees are still dormant. Or spray immediately after flowering with dicofol, dimethoate, malathion, or tetradifon.

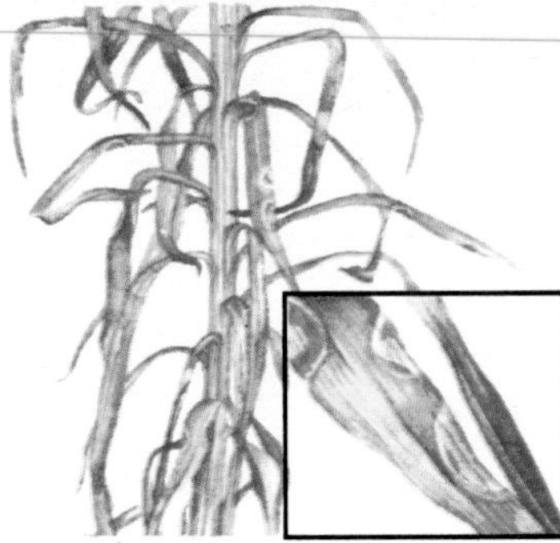

Botrytis, or gray mold

Plants affected: Lilies.
Symptoms and signs: Oval spots, at first water soaked and then brown, eventually spread until entire leaf is affected.
Danger period: Until flowering time.
Treatment: Spray with Benomyl, chlorothalonil, or dichloran as soon as flower buds can be detected, and repeat every 10–14 da.

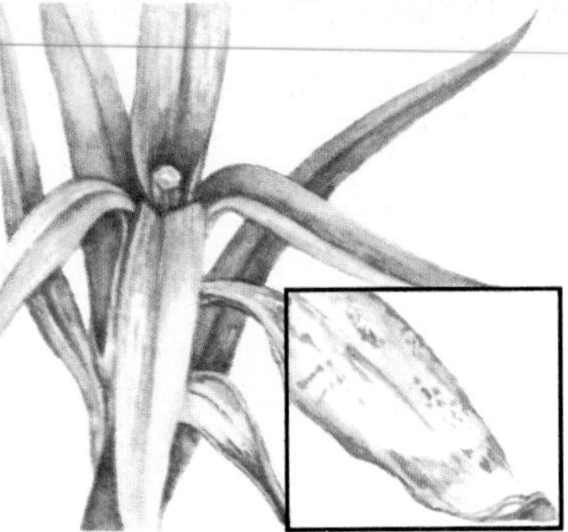

Fusarium wilt

Plants affected: Many types, particularly beans, carnations and other *Dianthus* species, peas, sweet peas, tomatoes.
Symptoms and signs: Leaves become discolored and plants wilt. Stem bases may also be discolored.
Danger period: Growing season.
Treatment: Remove and destroy affected plants. Select resistant varieties when possible. Grow susceptible plants on fresh site each year. Or sterilize soil with formaldehyde, using 1 pt. in 6 gal. of water; apply 5 gal. per square yard.

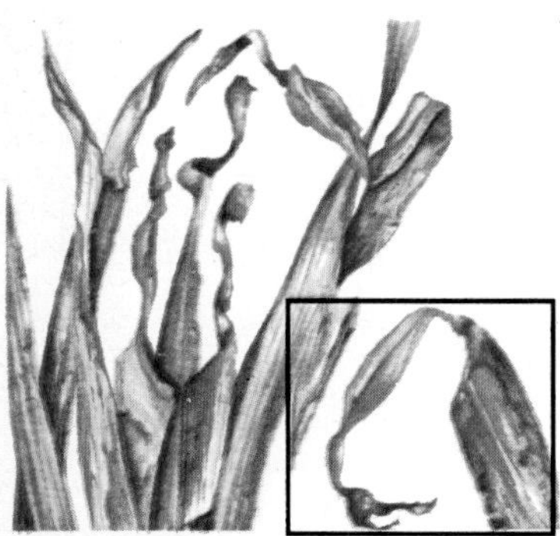

Tip scorch

Plants affected: Amaryllises (*Hippeastrum*), crinums, narcissi.
Symptoms and signs: Scorched or burned appearance at tips of leaves.
Danger period: Spring.
Treatment: Cut off affected leaf tips, and spray with mancozeb, maneb, or zineb to prevent further fungous infection on leaves.

Heather dieback

Plants affected: Scotch heathers.
Symptoms and signs: Dieback of shoots following gray discoloration of foliage. Entire plant may be killed.
Danger period: Any time of year.
Treatment: Dig up and destroy. Do not plant another heather in same position unless soil is first changed completely. Fumigate soil with metam-sodium.

Drought

Plants affected: All types, but symptoms and signs are most obvious on trees.
Symptoms and signs: Many leaves turn orange, sometimes with other tints. Leaves fall prematurely.
Danger period: Growing season.
Treatment: Mulch to conserve moisture, and never allow soil to dry out. Affected plants sometimes benefit from foliar applications of fertilizer.

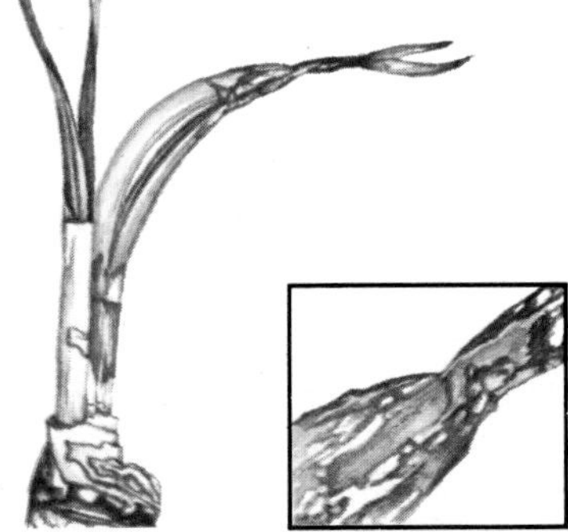

Smolder

Plants affected: Narcissi.
Symptoms and signs: Leaves rotting and covered with gray velvety mold.
Danger period: Spring and during winter storage.
Treatment: Remove and destroy affected plants during growing season when symptoms appear on foliage. Spray rest with zineb at 10-da. intervals, or use Bordeaux mixture. Destroy affected bulbs.

Boxwood leaf miners
Plants affected: Boxwood.
Symptoms and signs: Leaves puffed with yellow blotches. Orange maggots visible if leaves are cut open.
Danger period: Late spring.
Treatment: Spray in late spring when wing pads of pupa turn brown and show through clear areas on undersides of leaves. Use carbaryl, Diazinon, dimethoate, malathion, or oxydemeton-methyl as spray.

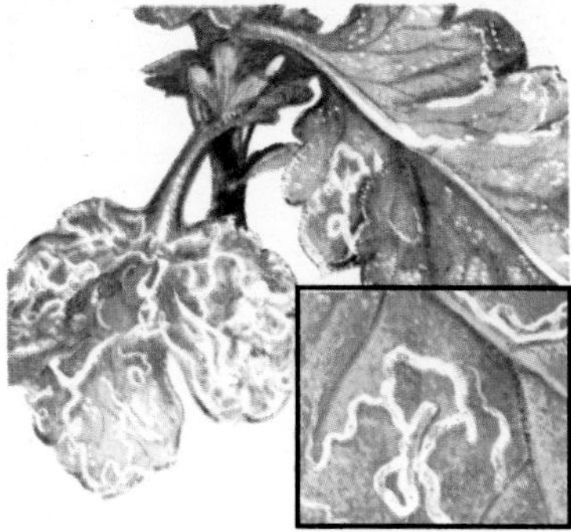

Chrysanthemum leaf miners
Plants affected: Chrysanthemums, cinerarias, columbines, sweet peas.
Symptoms and signs: Narrow, sinuous white mines eaten in leaf tissues; often many mines in 1 leaf.
Danger period: Midsummer to early winter.
Treatment: Remove and burn severely affected leaves. Spray with carbaryl, Diazinon, endosulfan, or nicotine whenever pests are active. Fumigate greenhouses with dichlorvos, nicotine, or resmethrin to kill adult leaf-miner flies.

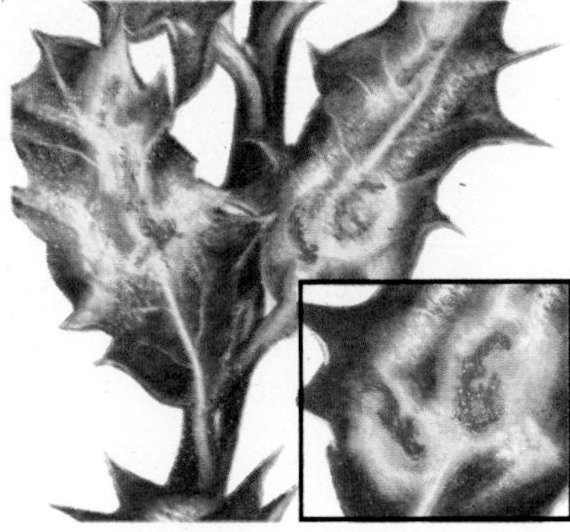

Holly leaf miners
Plants affected: Hollies.
Symptoms and signs: Blotchy yellow snakelike mines in leaves.
Danger period: Late spring to early winter, but symptoms persist throughout year.
Treatment: Remove and destroy affected leaves. Spray with Diazinon, oxydemeton-methyl, or trichlorfon when pests are active in late spring; coat both sides of leaves thoroughly.

Lilac leaf miners
Plants affected: Lilacs, as well as ashes and privets.
Symptoms and signs: Tissues of leaves almost completely eaten out; leaves distorted and rolled. Two generations per year.
Danger period: Early summer to early fall.
Treatment: Pick off and destroy affected leaves. Spray with Diazinon or malathion in late spring, repeating if necessary.

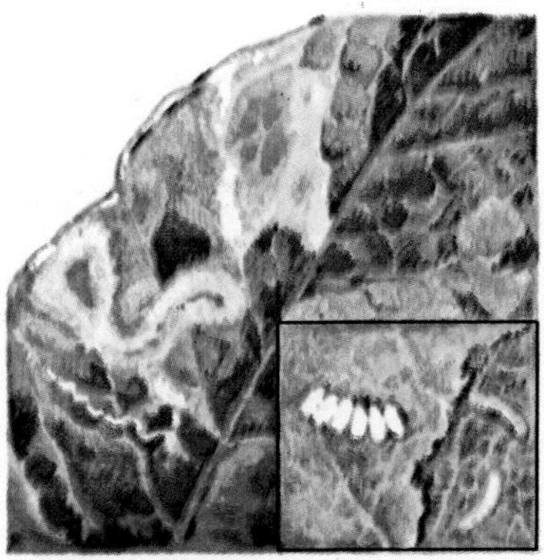

Vegetable leaf miners
Plants affected: Asparagus, beets, corn, eggplant, spinach, Swiss chard.
Symptoms and signs: Leaves show large white puffy blotches or snakelike trails.
Danger period: Spring and early summer.
Treatment: As soon as miners appear, spray or dust with Diazinon or malathion weekly for 4–6 wk. Destroy affected leaves.

Cyclamen and broad mites
Plants affected: African violets, begonias, cyclamens, dahlias, delphiniums, English ivies, ferns, fuchsias, gerberas, and other greenhouse plants.
Symptoms and signs: Leaves distorted in severe infestations, slightly curled at edges, and brittle.
Danger period: Any time of year.
Treatment: Spray with dicofol, endosulfan, or rotenone.

Leaf-curling plum aphids
Plants affected: Damson and other varieties of plums.
Symptoms and signs: Young leaves puckered and curled.
Danger period: Midspring to midsummer.
Treatment: Spray thoroughly with carbaryl or malathion in early spring, before trees blossom, and again after blossoming. Repeat as necessary.

Rose leaf rollers
Plants affected: Bush and climbing roses.
Symptoms and signs: Leaves tightly rolled along their entire length. Holes in leaves and buds.
Danger period: Late spring to midsummer.
Treatment: Remove and destroy affected leaves in late spring. Or spray with carbaryl or a systemic insecticide, such as dimethoate, every 2 wk. in late spring.

Black cherry aphids
Plants affected: Cherries, both ornamental and those grown for fruit.
Symptoms and signs: Leaves at tips of young shoots curled.
Danger period: Late spring to midsummer.
Treatment: Spray thoroughly with carbaryl or malathion in early spring, before trees bloom, and again after blossoming; repeat as necessary.

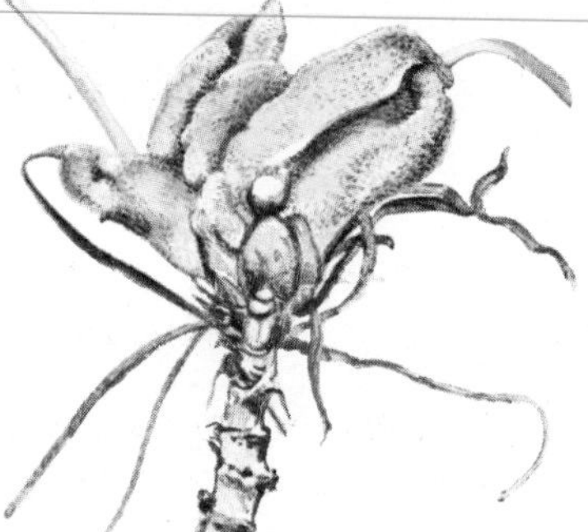

Violet leaf gall midges
Plants affected: *Viola* species.
Symptoms and signs: Young leaves curled upward at edges and greatly thickened. Small galls develop on leaves.
Danger period: Early summer to early winter.
Treatment: Remove and destroy affected leaves as soon as they appear, and dust or spray affected plants with carbaryl, Diazinon, or methoxychlor.

Azalea gall
Plants affected: Small-leaved rhododendrons, including azaleas.
Symptoms and signs: Leaves greatly thickened; at first pale green or pink, then white, finally brown.
Danger period: Any time of year, but symptoms may not appear until months after fungous infection.
Treatment: Cut off and destroy galls before they turn white. Spray with fungicide, such as Bordeaux mixture, copper, ferbam, or zineb.

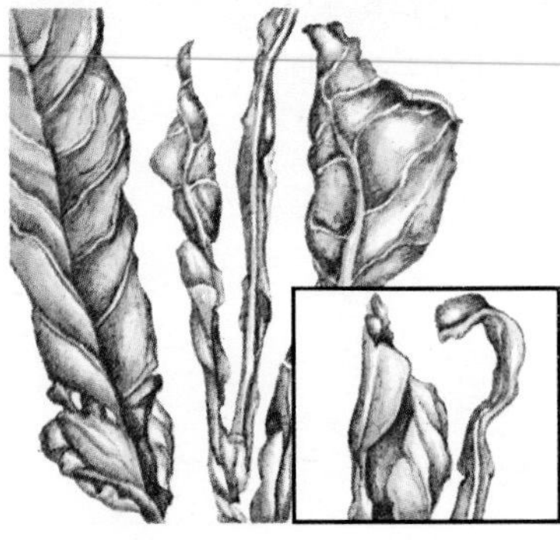

Whiptail
Plants affected: Broccoli, cauliflower.
Symptoms and signs: Leaves ruffled, thin, and straplike.
Danger period: Growing period.
Treatment: Since it is caused by nutrient deficiency and low pH (acid), feed plants, add lime, then water with solution of trace elements containing molybdenum (use according to manufacturer's instructions).

Stem and bulb nematodes, or stem and bulb eelworms
Plants affected: Hyacinths, narcissi, tulips, and some other bulbs.
Symptoms and signs: Leaves stunted and distorted, with small yellow bumps.
Danger period: Midwinter to late spring.
Treatment: Destroy affected plants. Soak bulbs in hot water (110° F) plus formaldehyde ($^{1}/_{4}$ pt. to 6 gal. of water) for 3 hr. Diazinon sprays or dichlorvos fumigation may help.

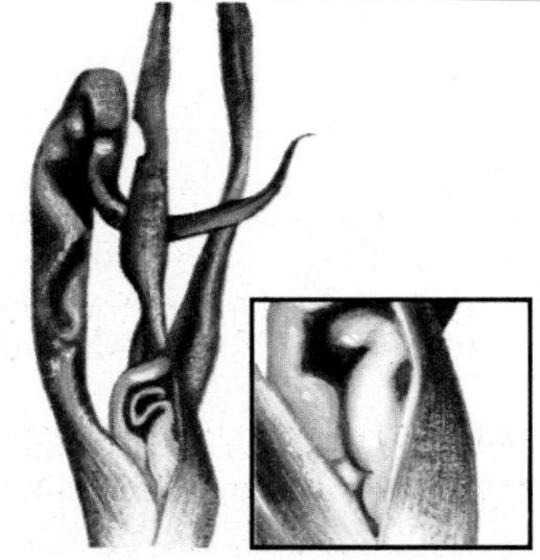

Onion nematodes, or onion eelworms
Plants affected: Onions, as well as chives and garlic.
Symptoms and signs: Leaves swollen and bloated.
Danger period: Early to late summer.
Treatment: Remove and destroy or deeply bury affected plants. Keep to 3-yr. rotation, and grow from seeds rather than from sets if possible.

Phlox nematodes, or phlox eelworms
Plants affected: Perennial phlox.
Symptoms and signs: Leaves become threadlike, wrinkled, swollen, and curled. Younger leaves unusually narrow and die off prematurely.
Danger period: Early spring to early summer.
Treatment: Remove and destroy severely affected plants. Clean stock can be raised by taking root cuttings, but do not replant in infected soil. Systemic pesticides, such as dimethoate, are helpful.

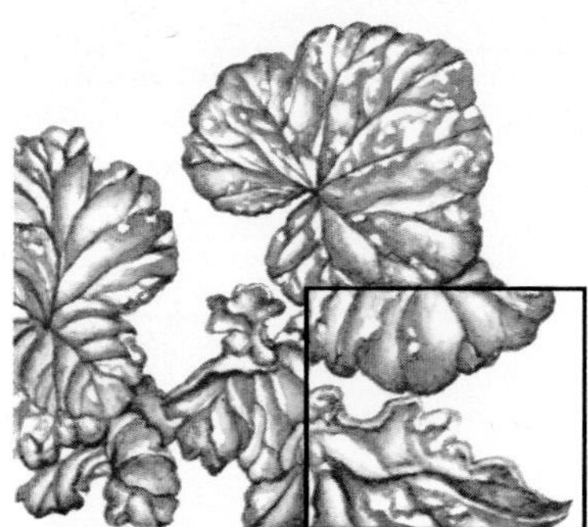

Virus disease
Plants affected: Many types, but particularly geraniums (*Pelargonium*), lilies, squash, and strawberries.
Symptoms and signs: Leaves crinkled, small, and sometimes irregularly shaped.
Danger period: Growing season.
Treatment: Destroy diseased plants. Spray with malathion to control aphids and other insects that carry virus.

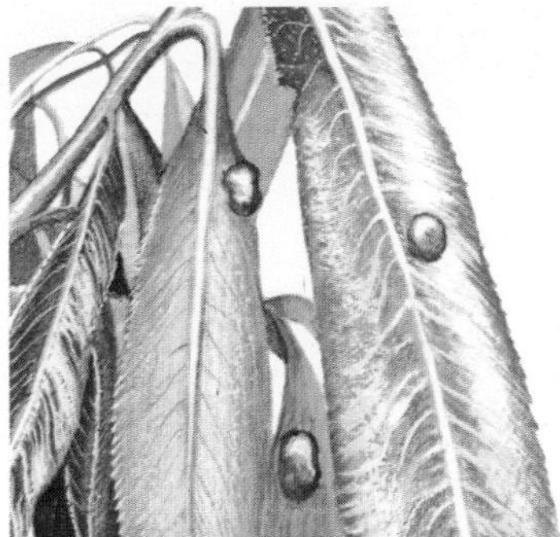

Willow bean gall sawflies
Plants affected: Willows.
Symptoms and signs: Small green, yellow, or red, bean-shaped galls growing out of both sides of leaves.
Danger period: Early to late summer.
Treatment: Though damage is seldom severe, remove and destroy galls if possible. Difficult to control. Call professional tree expert if necessary.

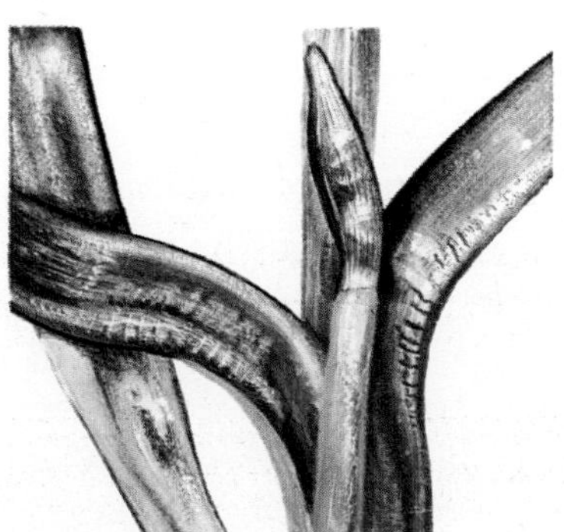

Bulb scale mites
Plants affected: Amaryllises (*Hippeastrum*), narcissi.
Symptoms and signs: Leaves twisted and malformed, with rusty brown or red scars.
Danger period: Midwinter to midspring for narcissi, especially when bulbs are forced. Any time of year for amaryllises in greenhouses.
Treatment: Destroy severely affected plants and bulbs. Expose dormant bulbs to frost for 2 or 3 nights, or immerse them for 1 or 2 hr. in water heated to 110° F. Before planting, spray or dust with dicofol.

Clubroot
Plants affected: Brassicas (broccoli, cabbage, cauliflower), stocks, wallflowers.
Symptoms and signs: Leaves wilted and sometimes discolored from galls on roots.
Danger period: Growing season.
Treatment: Improve drainage if necessary. Apply 14 lb. hydrated lime to every 30 sq. yd. of soil, and put 4% Calomel dust in planting holes. Carry out as long a rotation as possible, or sterilize large area with dazomet.

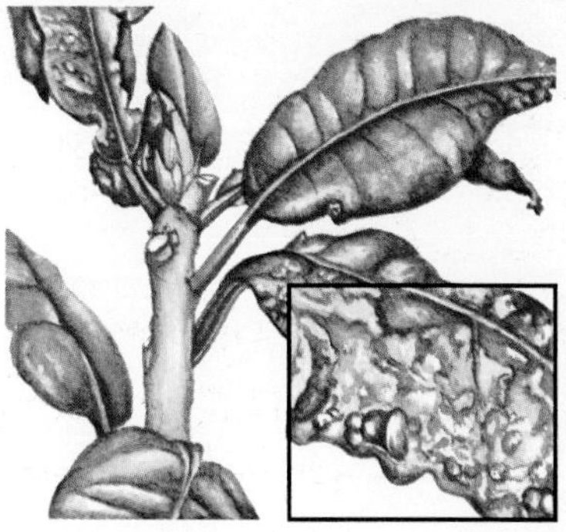

Frost damage
Plants affected: Apples, camellias, chrysanthemums, rhododendrons, and many other plants.
Symptoms and signs: On camellias and rhododendrons, leaves look distorted, particularly at tips. On other plants, leaves pucker; undersides blister and often split and peel.
Danger period: Spring and fall.
Treatment: None. Prevent when possible.

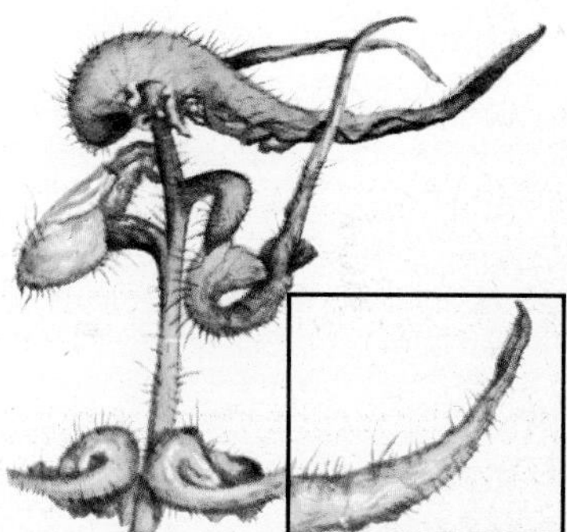

Hormone weed-killer damage
Plants affected: All types, particularly tomatoes and vines.
Symptoms and signs: Leaves narrow, curled, fan-shaped, and frequently cupped. Caused by drift of hormone weed killers, such as Silvex and 2,4-D.
Danger period: Growing season.
Treatment: None once damage has occurred, but plants usually recover. To prevent damage, do not use weed-killer sprays on windy days or weed-killer equipment for any other jobs. Destroy mowings from freshly treated lawn.

Verticillium wilt
Plants affected: Asters (perennial), carnations, chrysanthemums, maples, smoke trees, snapdragons, sumacs, tomatoes. Occurs outdoors and in greenhouses.
Symptoms and signs: Progressive wilting of leaves on several shoots, affected branches eventually dying back. On tomato plants all leaves are affected, but they recover at night.
Danger period: Growing season.
Treatment: On trees and shrubs, cut affected branches back to living tissue, and paint wounds. If trouble persists, dig up plant, destroy it, and grow less susceptible plant in that location. Destroy diseased plants in greenhouse, isolate infected soil from adjacent healthy plants, and sterilize greenhouse at end of season. If necessary to propagate plant affected by verticillium wilt, use tip cuttings with vigorous growth. The likelihood of disease having affected tips of plant is less than on portions of plant nearer roots.

Willow anthracnose
Plants affected: Willows.
Symptoms and signs: Leaves curl, become spotted, and fall prematurely.
Danger period: As leaves unfold in spring, sometimes in wet summer.
Treatment: Destroy any fallen leaves. Spray small trees as leaves unfold with fungicide, such as Captan, Benomyl, Bordeaux mixture, copper, or dodine. Repeat at least twice during summer.

Gall mites
Plants affected: Maples, willows.
Symptoms and signs: Rashes of small, elongated or spherical red galls on upper leaf surfaces.
Danger period: Early summer to midfall.
Treatment: Remove and destroy affected leaves if possible, and spray thoroughly with lime sulfur in early spring. As new leaves appear, spray with dicofol or endosulfan.

Gall wasps
Plants affected: Oaks, some species of roses and willows.
Symptoms and signs: Many different galls, which resemble peas, cherries, silk buttons, or apples growing out of leaves. Sometimes solitary, often numerous.
Danger period: Growing season.
Treatment: Remove and destroy if possible, but gall wasps seldom cause serious damage. Dormant sprays of miscible oil will help.

Red currant blister aphids
Plants affected: Red currants.
Symptoms and signs: Leaves with raised, irregular, red or green blisters.
Danger period: Late spring to early summer.
Treatment: Apply dormant spray of dinoseb or miscible oil in midwinter to kill eggs, and apply systemic insecticide, such as dimethoate, in spring, just before flowering. Repeat after flowering if necessary.

Apple aphids
Plants affected: Apples.
Symptoms and signs: Leaves puckered and distorted, sometimes with curled, thickened red edges.
Danger period: Late spring to midsummer.
Treatment: Spray thoroughly with systemic insecticide, such as dimethoate, just before blossoming and again after blossoming if necessary. Nonsystemic insecticide, such as carbaryl, endosulfan, or malathion, can also be used.

Peach leaf curl
Plants affected: Peaches, nectarines, almonds, including flowering types.
Symptoms and signs: Leaves with large red blisters become white, then brown, and fall prematurely.
Danger period: Before buds open.
Treatment: Spray with fungicide, such as Bordeaux mixture, ferbam, lime sulfur, or zineb, in midwinter, repeating 7–14 da. later and again just before leaf fall. Remove and destroy diseased leaves before they whiten.

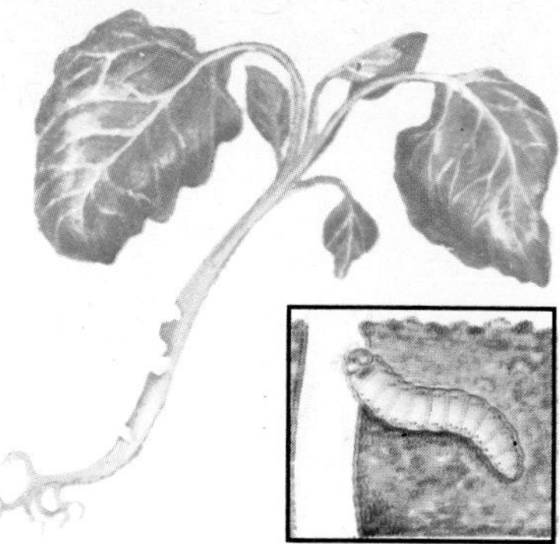

Cutworms
Plants affected: Lettuce, other vegetables, young ornamental annuals.
Symptoms and signs: Shoots eaten through at soil level; fat caterpillars in soil. Daily digging around plants with fingers will usually reveal cutworms, which are gray-brown to black and form a C shape when disturbed.
Danger period: Early spring and late summer.
Treatment: Control weeds, which encourage cutworms, and protect susceptible plants by working small amount of Diazinon or methoxychlor dust into soil. Seed protectants, such as thiram, also give some protection in early stages.

Aphids
Plants affected: Many different types, but especially roses and snap beans.
Symptoms and signs: Colonies of aphids on young shoots.
Danger period: Late spring to midsummer outdoors, almost any time of year in greenhouses.
Treatment: Spray with systemic insecticide, such as dimethoate, or with nonsystemic, such as malathion. See also Aphids, p. 601.

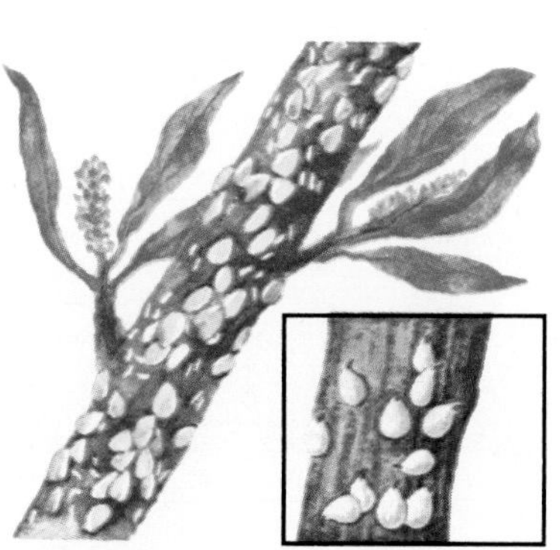

Scale insects
Plants affected: Many different types, both in greenhouses and outdoors, but especially beeches, ceanothuses, cotoneasters, horse chestnuts, magnolias.
Symptoms and signs: Colonies of black, brown, yellow, or white scales on older shoots.
Danger period: Most times of year, but particularly in late spring and summer.
Treatment: Spray with malathion or systemic insecticide, such as oxydemeton-methyl. See also Scale Insects, p. 601.

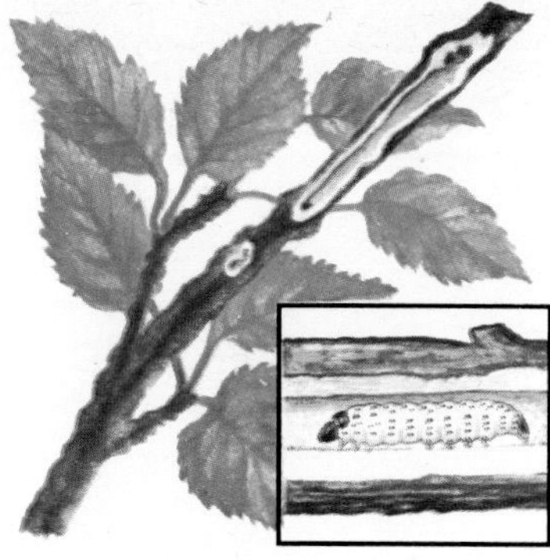

Leopard moths (larvae)
Plants affected: Apples and pears (both fruiting and flowering), ashes, birches, cherries, cotoneasters, hawthorns, and other trees.
Symptoms and signs: Branches tunneled by 3-in. borers (larvae), causing wilting of leaves.
Danger period: Any time of year.
Treatment: Kill caterpillars by spraying endosulfan or lindane on trunks and branches. Or use moth crystals at tree base.

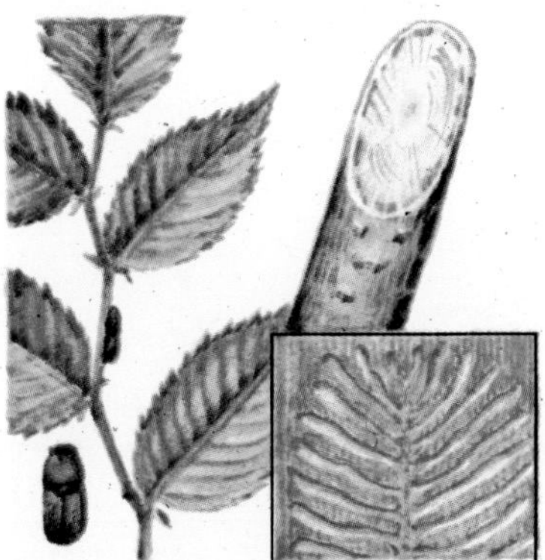

Elm bark beetles
Plants affected: Elms.
Symptoms and signs: Intricate galleries eaten out under bark.
Danger period: Growing season.
Treatment: Remove affected deadwood, including stumps and roots, during winter and send to local incinerator. Spray susceptible dormant trees with 25% emulsifiable concentrate of methoxychlor in early to mid spring. For good coverage, hydraulic sprayer is necessary. See also p. 18 and Dutch Elm Disease, p. 609.

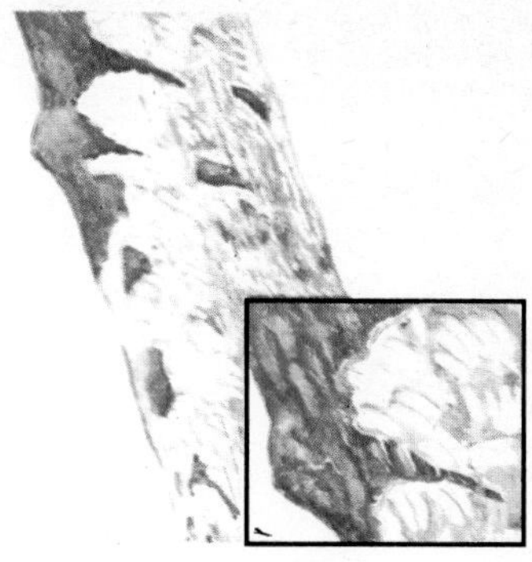

Deer, rabbits, and other animals
Plants affected: Young trees.
Symptoms and signs: Bark stripped from woody shoots at or slightly above soil level or snow line.
Danger period: Winter and early spring.
Treatment: Protect shoots of young trees by winding spiral tree protectors around them or by using small-mesh wire netting.

For deer, spray Thiram 42-S (2 qt. in 1 gal. water) on bark and/or foliage in fall, as well as in growing season. Dried blood has been used successfully to repel deer.

Against rabbits a mixture of tree rosin and denatured alcohol (7 lb. in 1 gal.) can be applied to trunks in fall. Thiram mixture plus a good adhesive can be sprayed on trunks in fall. Commercial preparations are available.

Poison baits of zinc phosphide 1–2% (sold in hardware stores) are good for mouse control. Repellents are also useful for control of these common pests.

Spur blight

Plants affected: Loganberries, raspberries.
Symptoms and signs: Canes bear purple blotches that later become silver, spotted with black. Spurs on these die back.
Danger period: Spring and summer.
Treatment: Cut out old infected canes after fruiting, and remove young thin surplus canes early. Spray with Benomyl, Captan, dichlofluanid, or thiram soon after canes emerge, and repeat 3 or 4 times at 10- to 14-da. intervals. Thiophanate-methyl can also be used; it should be first applied at budbreak and again at 14-da. intervals until end of flowering. Less effective alternative is to spray with copper fungicide at budbreak and again when tips of flowers are just showing white.

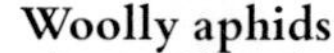

Woolly aphids

Plants affected: Apples, cotoneasters, hawthorns, mountain ashes.
Symptoms and signs: Woody swellings and tufts of white wool on trunks and branches.
Danger period: Midspring to early fall.
Treatment: Where possible, brush spray-strength solution of carbaryl, endosulfan, or malathion onto affected areas when wool first appears, or apply any of these as spray. Systemic insecticide, such as dimethoate, can also be used.

Mealybugs

Plants affected: Greenhouse and house plants, including cacti and other succulents.
Symptoms and signs: Colonies of mealybugs covered with white mealy or waxy wool that is usually concentrated around buds and leaf axils.
Danger period: Most times of year, but particularly late summer and fall.
Treatment: See Mealybugs, p. 601.

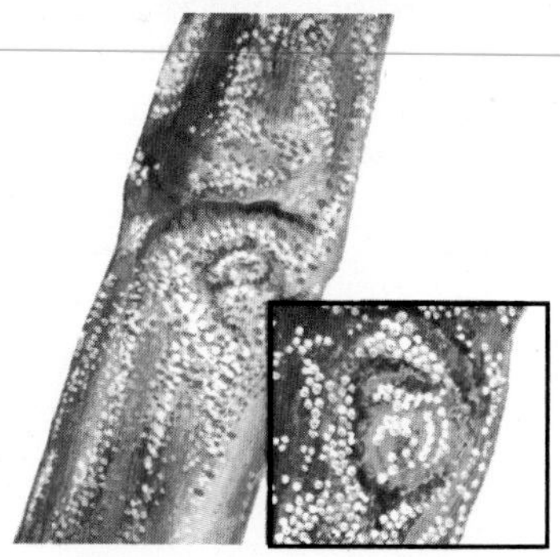

Two-spotted mites and European red mites on fruit trees

Plants affected: Apples, peaches, plums.
Symptoms and signs: Tiny, spherical, red-brown eggs present on shoots, usually near buds.
Danger period: Late fall to midspring.
Treatment: Spray thoroughly with dinoseb or miscible oil while dormant, and apply dicofol, dimethoate, or malathion after blossoming, repeating application about 3 wk. later if needed.

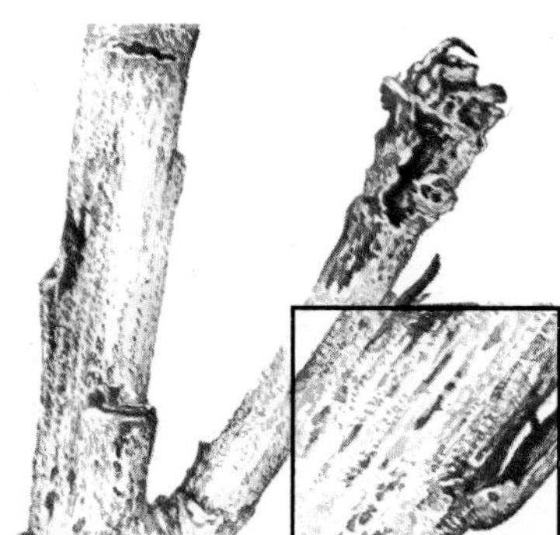

Powdery mildew

Plants affected: Apples, euonymuses, gooseberries, perennial asters, roses, and many other plants.
Symptoms and signs: White powdery coating on shoots.
Danger period: Growing season.
Treatment: Cut off affected shoots at end of season. Spray as for Powdery Mildew on p. 607.

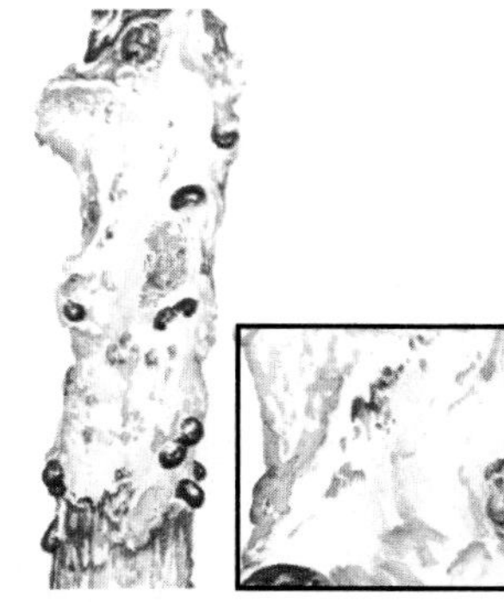

Sclerotinia rot

Plants affected: Many types, but in particular dahlias.
Symptoms and signs: Stems affected by white, fluffy fungous growth with large black areas. Stems decay rapidly and collapse.
Danger period: Spring and summer.
Treatment: Destroy all rotting material.

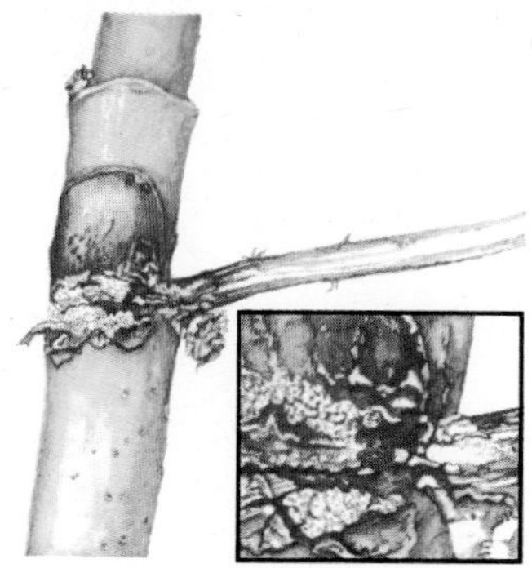

Botrytis, or gray mold
Plants affected: All types, but particularly clarkias, gooseberries, magnolias, roses, zinnias. Also affects cuttings.
Symptoms and signs: Rotting stems covered with gray fungus.
Danger period: Growing season in wet weather.
Treatment: Cut out affected shoots, and spray with Benomyl, Captan, dichloran, thiram, or zineb. For Botrytis on leaves, see p. 605; on lettuce, see p. 622; on peonies, see Peony Blight, p. 623; on flowers in greenhouse, see p. 624; on small fruits, see p. 627; on tomatoes, see p. 628.

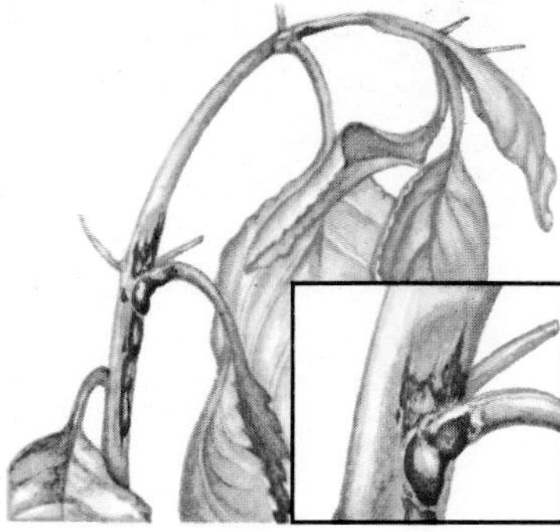

Bacterial canker of stone fruits
Plants affected: Cherries, pears, plums (damsons), flowering *Prunus* species.
Symptoms and signs: Elongated, flattened canker-bearing exudations of gum on shoots that die back; leaves yellow and wither prematurely.
Danger period: Fall and winter, but symptoms do not appear until following spring or summer.
Treatment: Cut out infected branches in summer, and paint all wounds with wound-sealing paint. Spray foliage from late summer to midfall with Bordeaux mixture.

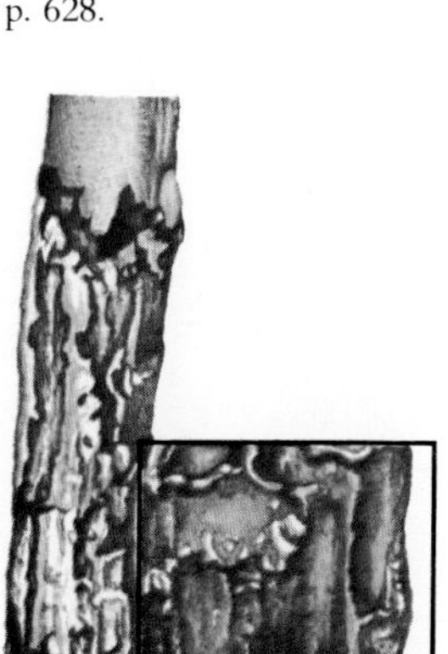

Willow anthracnose
Plants affected: Weeping willows.
Symptoms and signs: Small brown cankers on shoots, which may die back.
Danger period: Growing season.
Treatment: Cut out as many cankered shoots as possible, together with all deadwood. Spray with fungicide (Bordeaux mixture or copper), and repeat at least twice in summer. Or use Benomyl or Captan.

Witches'-broom
Plants affected: Birches, hackberries, *Prunus* species, and many other trees and shrubs.
Symptoms and signs: Several shoots, sometimes bearing blistered foliage, growing from single point and crowded together on infected branches.
Danger period: Throughout life of plant.
Treatment: Cut out affected branch to point 6 in. below broom, and apply wound-sealing paint.

Gumming
Plants affected: Cherries and other *Prunus* species.
Symptoms and signs: Gum exudes on branches and trunks and gradually hardens.
Danger period: Any time of year.
Treatment: Feed, mulch, and water to stop gumming. Gum may have to be removed so that deadwood beneath can be cut out. Apply wound-sealing paint.

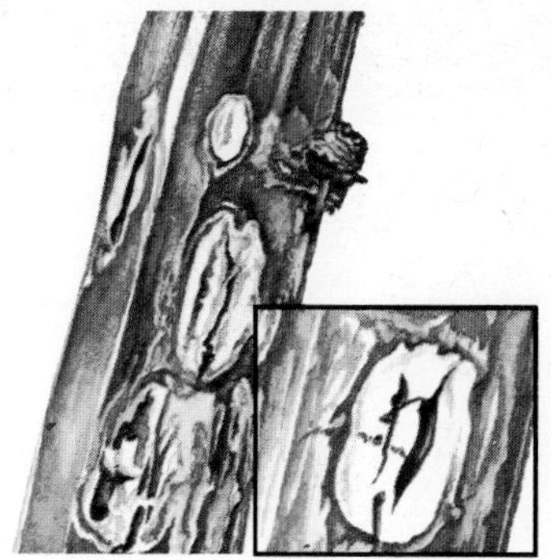

Cane spot
Plants affected: Loganberries, raspberries, and other cane fruits.
Symptoms and signs: Small circular, purple spots enlarge to become elliptic white blotches with purple border, about $\frac{1}{4}$ in. long. These eventually split to form small pits, which give canes rough, cracked appearance. Leaves may also be spotted and fruits distorted.
Danger period: Late spring to midfall.
Treatment: Cut out and destroy badly spotted canes. Spray raspberries with 5% lime sulfur at budbreak and $2\frac{1}{2}$% lime sulfur immediately before blossom time. Alternatively, use copper or thiram at these times, or use Benomyl or thiophanate-methyl at 14-da. intervals from budbreak to end of blossoming. For loganberries, apply copper fungicide or thiram both before blossom time and as soon as fruit has set; or use Benomyl or thiophanate-methyl as for raspberries. Always wash fruits before eating, canning, or freezing.

Rose rust
Plants affected: Roses (in western U.S.).
Symptoms and signs: Early infection, indicated by tiny $\frac{1}{25}$-in. bright orange spots on undersides of leaves and light yellow areas on uppersides. Swellings on stems burst open to reveal bright orange, powdery spores.
Danger period: Spring and summer.
Treatment: Cut out and destroy affected shoots. Spray with fungicide, such as maneb. See also Rusts, p. 604.

Clematis wilt and blight
Plants affected: Clematises.
Symptoms and signs: One or more shoots wilt and die rapidly.
Danger period: Growing season.
Treatment: Cut out affected shoots, even if they are below soil level. As new shoots develop later in season, or following spring, spray them with Benomyl, copper, dodine, or zineb, to help control fungus. Or apply soil drench of metam-sodium around plants or to soil prior to replanting.

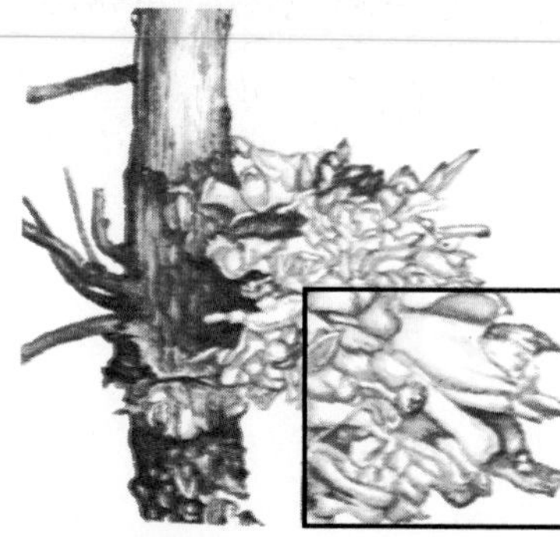

Leafy gall
Plants affected: Many types, but in particular chrysanthemums, dahlias, dianthuses, geraniums (*Pelargonium*), gladioli, strawberries, sweet peas.
Symptoms and signs: Abortive, often flattened shoots with thickened, distorted leaves develop at ground level.
Danger period: During propagation and growing season.
Treatment: Prune infected parts where feasible. Or destroy infected plants. When replanting, grow a nonsusceptible type of plant.

Petunia wilt
Plants affected: Petunias, salpiglossises, zinnias, and other bedding plants.
Symptoms and signs: Plants wilt, often as they are about to flower. Stem bases may be discolored.
Danger period: Growing season.
Treatment: Destroy diseased plants. Rotate bedding plants so that susceptible ones are grown on new site each year. Water planting holes with a solution of copper fungicide; drench plants with it weekly. Quintozene soil drench may help, or sterilize soil.

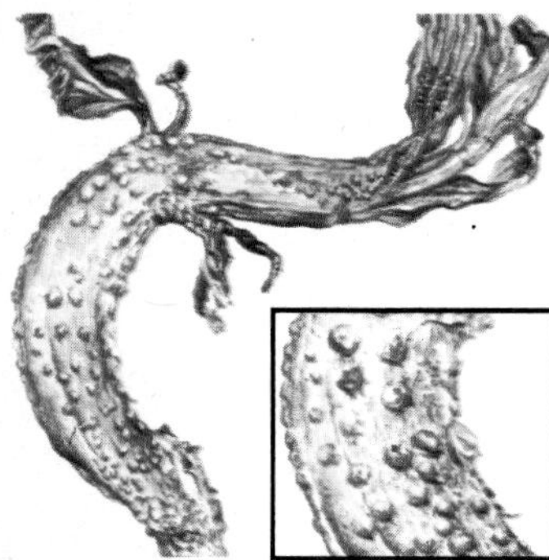

Mint rust
Plants affected: Mints.
Symptoms and signs: Swollen, distorted shoots bear orange-colored spore pustules.
Danger period: Symptoms appear in spring, but affected plants are permanently diseased.
Treatment: Cut out and destroy affected shoots; spray plants with fungicide, such as maneb. Burn over mint bed at end of season where permissible. See also Rusts, p. 604.

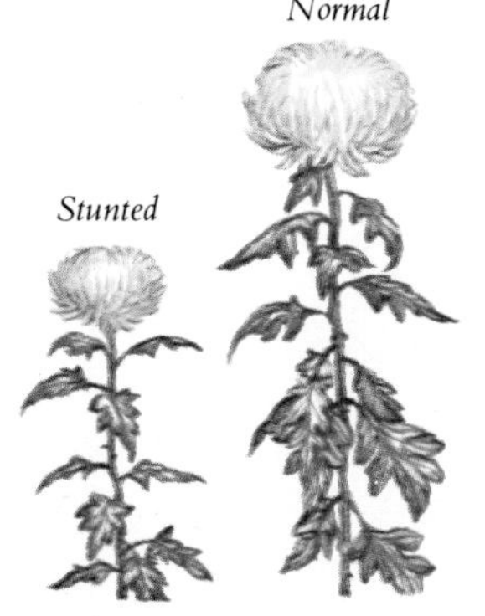

Virus disease
Plants affected: All types, but particularly blackberries, chrysanthemums, dahlias, lilies, strawberries, tomatoes.
Symptoms and signs: Plants are very stunted and may produce discolored leaves and poor flowers. Small fruits may fail to mature.
Danger period: Growing season.
Treatment: Dig up and destroy. Control insects, such as leafhoppers and aphids. They transmit virus to other plants.

Fasciation
Plants affected: Many types, but in particular delphiniums, forsythias, lilies, *Prunus* species.
Symptoms and signs: Shoots are flattened but may branch and bear normal leaves and flowers.
Danger period: Usually spring, but symptoms appear months later.
Treatment: Cut out affected shoots on woody plants to below flattening. No treatment is required for herbaceous plants.

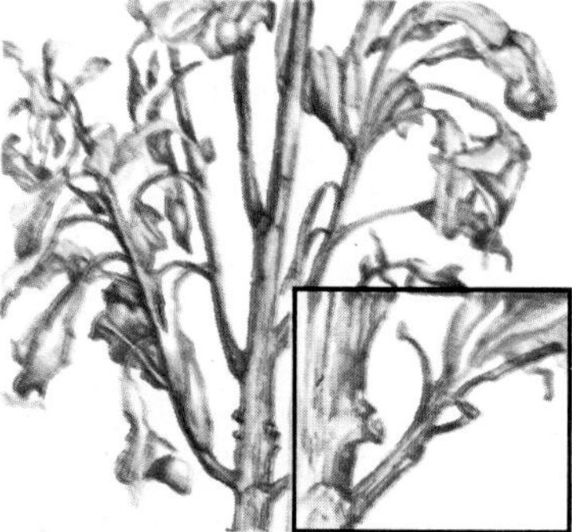

China aster wilt
Plants affected: China asters.
Symptoms and signs: Plant wilts, usually as it is about to flower. Pink fungous growth may be seen on stems just above ground level.
Danger period: Summer.
Treatment: Destroy diseased plants as they appear. Fumigate soil with metam-sodium. Grow resistant varieties on new site.

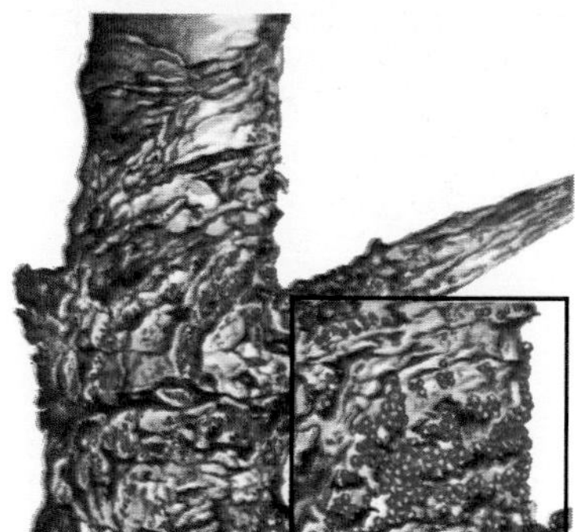

Apple canker

Plants affected: Apples, and less commonly ashes, beeches, mountain ashes, pears, poplars.
Symptoms and signs: Elliptical cankers, with bark shrinking in concentric rings until inner tissues are exposed. Girdling of shoot or branch by canker causes dieback.
Danger period: Any time of year.
Treatment: Cut out and destroy infected spurs and small branches. On larger branches and main trunks, pare away all diseased material (which should be destroyed) until clean wound is left. Coat this with wound-sealing paint. In severe cases spray with Bordeaux mixture just before leaf fall, when half of leaves have fallen, and at budbreak. Benomyl sprays to control scab will also control canker. Improve drainage if waterlogging occurs, since this can aggravate trouble.

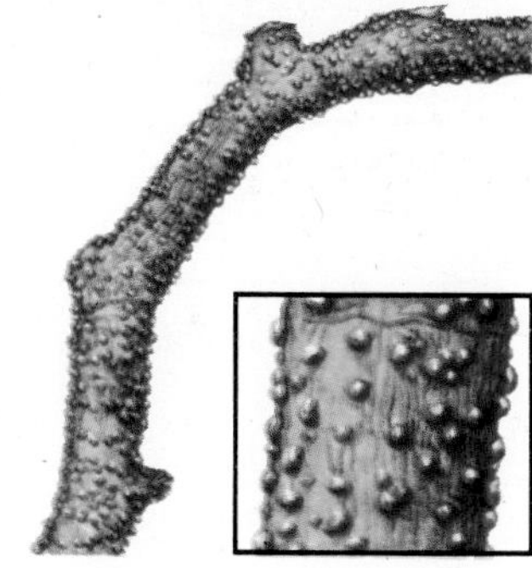

Nectria canker, or coral spot

Plants affected: Many trees and shrubs, particularly figs, magnolias, maples, red currants.
Symptoms and signs: Dieback of shoots or large branches caused by coral-red, spore-filled pustules on deadwood. Entire plant may die.
Danger period: Any time of year.
Treatment: Cut out all dead shoots to point at least 2–4 in. below apparently diseased area, and destroy. Feed, mulch, water, and/or drain soil as necessary to encourage vigor. Follow pruning with copper or zineb spray.

Fire blight

Plants affected: Apples, cotoneasters, hawthorns, mountain ashes, pears, and other related ornamentals.
Symptoms and signs: Shoots die, particularly flowering spurs; leaves wither and cankers develop at their base.
Danger period: Flowering time.
Treatment: Prune and destroy all infected material. Cut at least 4–6 in. below injury. Disinfect pruning shears between each cut with half-strength liquid chlorine bleach. Disease is bacterial; spray with streptomycin.

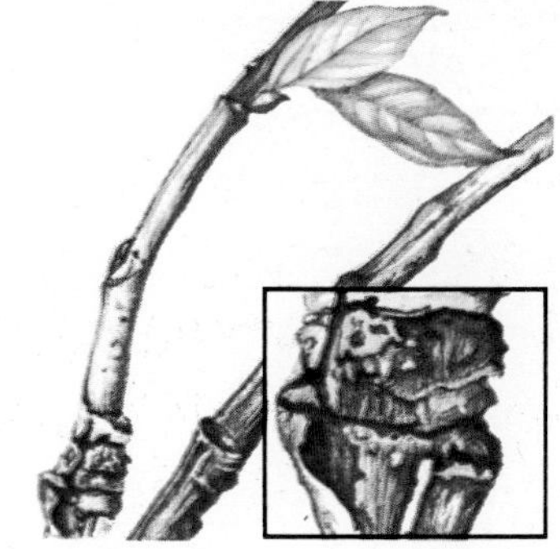

Poplar canker

Plants affected: Poplars.
Symptoms and signs: Unsightly cankers $\frac{1}{4}$–6 in. long erupt on shoots, branches, and sometimes trunk. Dieback of young shoots occurs in early summer.
Danger period: Any time of year.
Treatment: Destroy badly diseased trees. On less severely affected trees cut out and destroy cankered shoots. Paint all wounds with wound-sealing paint.

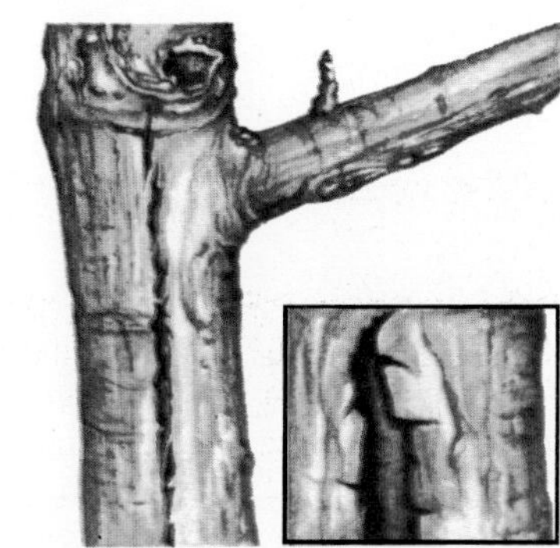

Bark splitting

Plants affected: Many types of trees, including fruit trees.
Symptoms and signs: Bark splits, and cracks open up.
Danger period: Any time of year.
Treatment: Cut out any deadwood, and remove loose bark until clean wound is left. Coat with wound-sealing paint. If tree is then fed, mulched, and watered properly, wound should heal naturally.

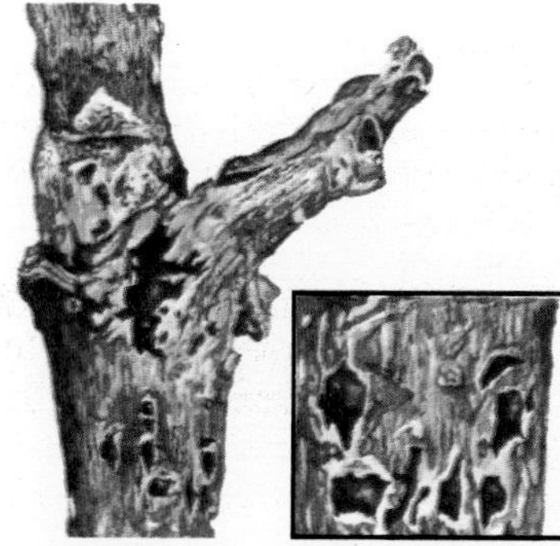

Scab

Plants affected: Apples, pears.
Symptoms and signs: Small blisterlike pimples develop on young shoots, later burst bark and then show as ringlike cracks or scabs.
Danger period: Growing season.
Treatment: Cut out cracked and scabby shoots when pruning. Spray regularly from time flower buds are visible until midsummer with fungicide, such as Benomyl. See also Scab, p. 604.

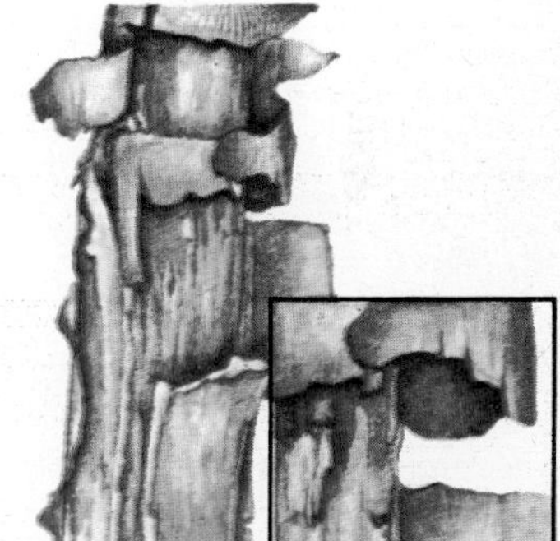

Papery bark

Plants affected: Many types, but particularly apples, mountain ashes, viburnums.
Symptoms and signs: Bark becomes paper-thin and peels off. Dieback follows girdling of shoots.
Danger period: Any time of year.
Treatment: See Faulty Root Action, p. 620. If bark has peeled on shoots not yet dead and that have not been girdled, remove loose bark and apply wound-sealing paint.

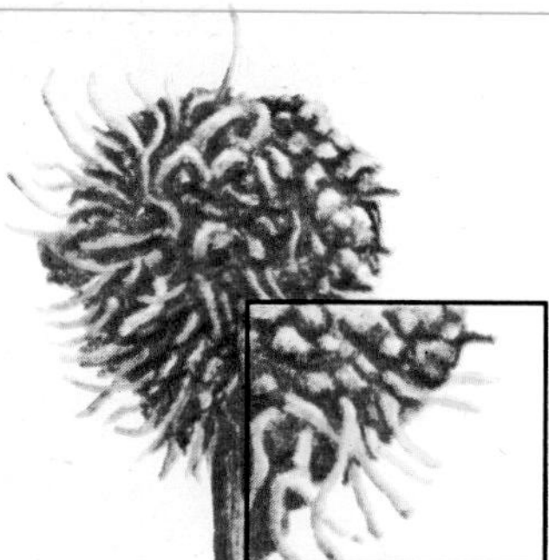

Forsythia gall
Plants affected: Forsythias.
Symptoms and signs: Pea- to tennis-ball-size nodules on stems.
Danger period: When shrubs are at least 5 yr. old, but usually on even older plants.
Treatment: Cut out and destroy affected shoots. Disinfect pruning shears with half-strength chlorine bleach after each cut.

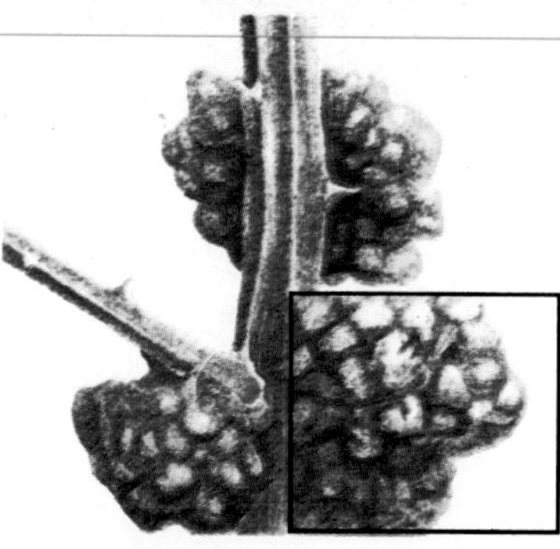

Crown gall
Plants affected: Blackberries, raspberries, roses.
Symptoms and signs: Walnut-size galls, sometimes in chains, develop on aerial shoots or at soil level.
Danger period: Growing season.
Treatment: Cut out shoots bearing galls; or paint Bacticin antibiotic directly on galls. Disinfect tools after each cut. Control on roses is difficult. See also Crown Gall, p. 633.

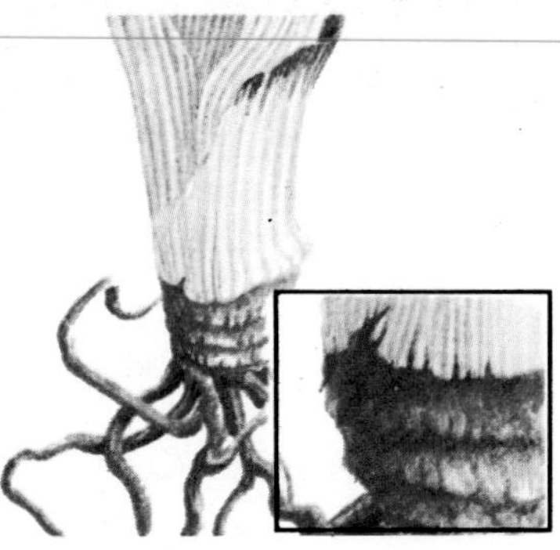

Rhizome rot
Plants affected: Bearded and other rhizomatous irises.
Symptoms and signs: Soft, yellow, foul-smelling rot of rhizome at growing point; leaves collapse.
Danger period: Any time of year, but particularly in wet weather.
Treatment: Improve drainage if necessary, and control slugs and other pests. Destroy badly affected plants; on others cut out rotting parts, and dust with dry Bordeaux mixture or streptomycin.

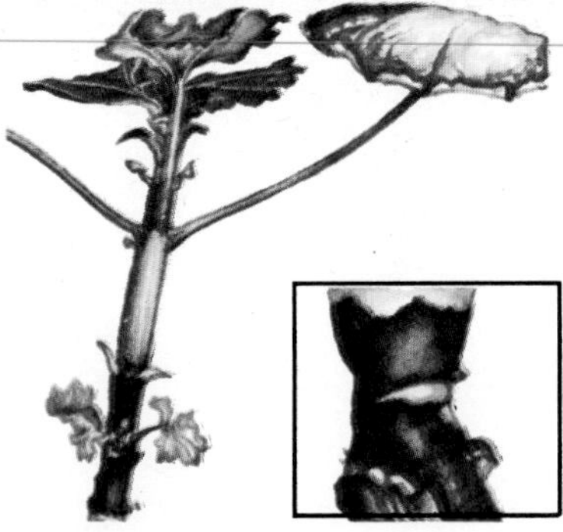

Blackleg
Plants affected: Geraniums (*Pelargonium*), potatoes.
Symptoms and signs: Black rot develops at base of cuttings or at stem base, and affected tissues become soft. Leaves yellow, and entire cutting or stem dies.
Danger period: For geraniums, soon after cuttings are taken; for potatoes, early summer.
Treatment: Destroy badly affected plants. No other treatment is required for potatoes, apart from planting healthy seed tubers. Prevent disease on geraniums by using sterilized soil, maintaining strict greenhouse hygiene, and watering carefully. If valuable cuttings become affected, remove diseased parts with a knife dipped in weak disinfectant (half-strength liquid chlorine bleach), and repot cuttings in clean pots of fresh soil. Chlorothalonil or Terrazole sprays may help if used early enough.

Faulty root action
Plants affected: Trees (particularly fruit trees and poplars) and shrubs.
Symptoms and signs: Shoots bearing discolored leaves turn brown and die back at random.
Danger period: Any time of year.
Treatment: Cut out deadwood until living tissues are reached. Paint wounds with wound-sealing paint. Feed, mulch, water, and/or drain as necessary. Applications of foliar fertilizer may hasten recovery. Determine cause if possible, and correct.

Stem rot
Plants affected: Carnations, clarkias, lobelias, tomatoes; each is affected by different form of this disease.
Symptoms and signs: Rotting of stems, but no very obvious fungous growth is visible on affected areas.
Danger period: Growing season.
Treatment: Where possible, cut out affected parts, and dust or spray with Captan. Alternatively, destroy diseased plants. Prior to planting, treat affected beds with metam-sodium drench or quintozene.

Lilac blight
Plants affected: Lilacs.
Symptoms and signs: Young shoots blacken and wither away (but similar symptoms can be due to frost damage).
Danger period: Spring.
Treatment: Cut affected shoots back to healthy buds, and spray with Benomyl, Bordeaux mixture, or dodine. Spray again next spring, as first leaves unfold.

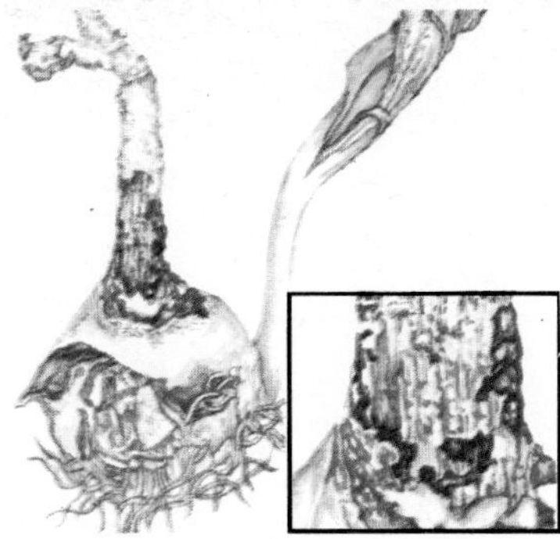

Tulip fire (Botrytis)
Plants affected: Tulips (base of stem).
Symptoms and signs: Shoots rot at ground level and become covered with gray velvety fungus.
Danger period: Spring.
Treatment: See Tulip Fire, p. 629. See also illustration at right. Use chlorothalonil or dichloran early in season as leaves come up. Remove and destroy diseased bulbs.

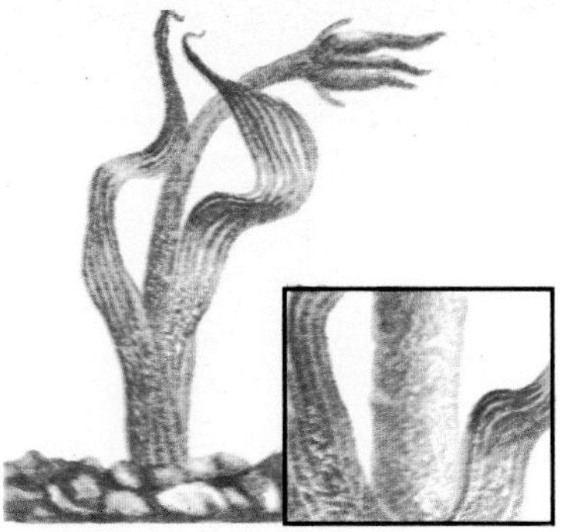

Tulip fire (Botrytis)
Plants affected: Tulips (young shoots).
Symptoms and signs: Young shoots are crippled; they rot aboveground and become covered with gray velvety mold. Flowers become distorted and show streaks.
Danger period: Spring.
Treatment: See Tulip Fire, p. 629. See also illustration at left.

Crown rot
Plants affected: Delphiniums, peonies, rhubarb, and many other herbaceous crown-type perennials.
Symptoms and signs: Rotting of terminal bud, followed by progressive rotting of crown. Leaves are spindly and discolored, and die down early.
Danger period: Growing season.
Treatment: Dig up and destroy. Do not plant this type of plant again in same location. Sterilize soil with metam-sodium drench before planting.

Dry rot
Plants affected: Primarily gladioli, but acidantheras, crocuses, and freesias are also susceptible to infection.
Symptoms and signs: Dry rot of leaf sheaths at soil level makes top growth topple over. Affected tissues are covered with minute black forms, just visible to naked eye.
Danger period: Growing season.
Treatment: See Dry Rot, p. 630.

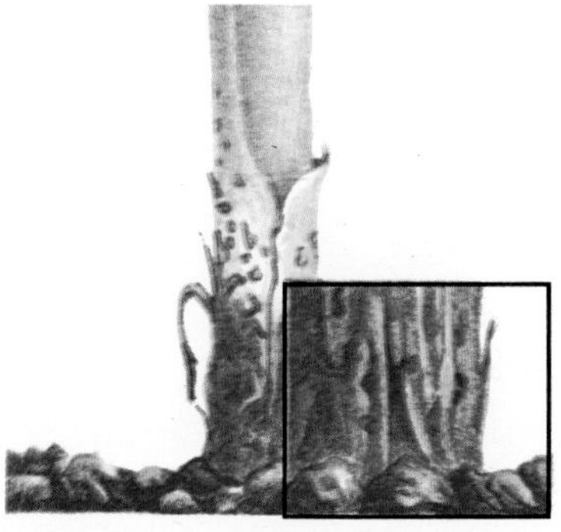

Foot rot
Plants affected: Beans, bedding plants, sweet peas, tomatoes.
Symptoms and signs: Stem bases, which may be discolored, rot. Roots usually die.
Danger period: Growing season.
Treatment: Rotate vegetables and bedding plants, and always use sterile soil for pot plants. Water bedding plants grown in seedboxes with copper, quintozene, or Terrazole when they are put in their planting holes and, if trouble occurs, at weekly intervals.

Peony wilt
Plants affected: Peonies.
Symptoms and signs: Affected shoots collapse at ground level.
Danger period: Growing season.
Treatment: Cut out affected shoots to below ground level, and dust crowns with dry Bordeaux mixture. Spray with Captan, dichlofluanid, thiram, or zineb soon after leaves appear. Use metam-sodium soil drench before planting or before growth begins in spring.

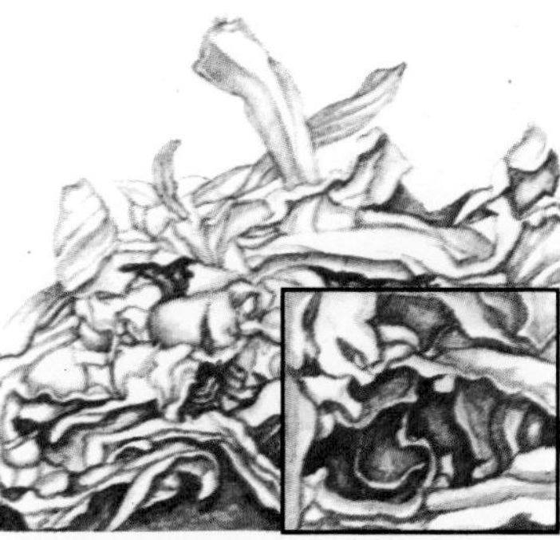

Collar rot
Plants affected: Cinerarias, primroses, and other greenhouse pot plants.
Symptoms and signs: Tissues rot at or just above soil level, and plants collapse.
Danger period: Growing season.
Treatment: Prevent by using sterilized soil and watering carefully. If trouble occurs, remove all affected tissue, and dust infected areas with dry Bordeaux mixture or Captan. Repot plant in lighter soil, and reduce amount of watering.

Pansy wilt
Plants affected: Pansies and other *Viola* species.
Symptoms and signs: Wilted plants with rotten crowns. Plants can be lifted easily.
Danger period: Growing season.
Treatment: Rotate bedding plants so that *Viola* species are not grown in same position every year. Water plants in seedboxes with quintozene or Terrazole. Use in planting holes, and repeat weekly if trouble appears. Lift affected plants, together with all roots, and destroy.

Botrytis, or gray mold, on lettuce
Plants affected: Lettuce.
Symptoms and signs: Wilted plants are rotten at ground level, where tissues are covered with gray velvety mold. Top growth separates easily from roots.
Danger period: Growing season.
Treatment: Dust quintozene into soil before planting outdoors. In greenhouse fumigate with tecnazene; or remove and destroy diseased plants and leaves; spray indoors or outdoors with Benomyl or zineb. Dichloran is specific fungicide for Botrytis control.

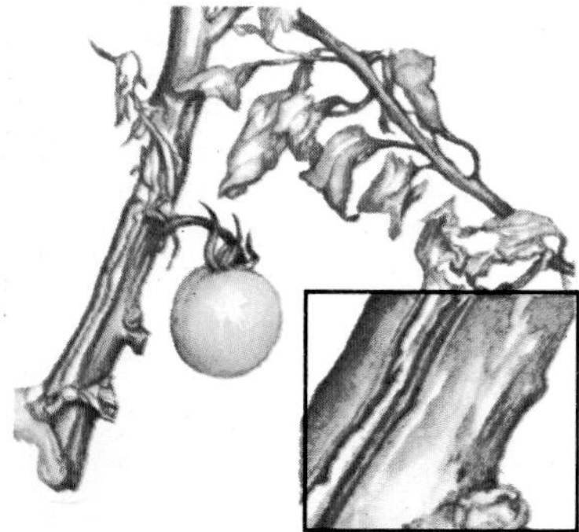

Virus disease
Plants affected: Sweet peas, tomatoes, and many other plants.
Symptoms and signs: Wilting of plants that show streaks on stems and leaf stalks.
Danger period: Growing season.
Treatment: Dig up and destroy affected plants.

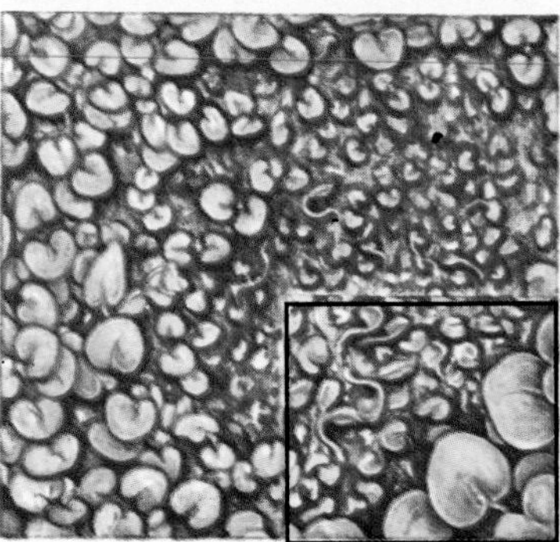

Damping-off
Plants affected: All seedlings can be affected, but lettuce, snapdragons, and zinnias are particularly susceptible.
Symptoms and signs: Seedlings rot and collapse at ground level.
Danger period: As seeds germinate.
Treatment: Prevent by use of sterilized soil and clean pots, and by careful watering. Fungus is carried in soil or on seeds themselves; so to prevent or treat, soil must be sterilized. Small amounts can be treated with steam or hot (180° F) water. Quintozene or Terrazole can be applied to soil or to flats and beds before planting. Seeds can be dusted with protectants, such as Benomyl or thiram, and then planted. If trouble starts, it may be checked by watering with Captan or zineb.

Flower-Bud Disorders

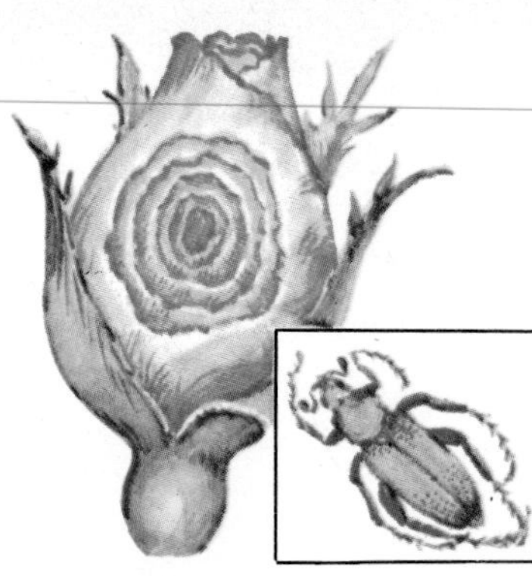

Rose chafers
Plants affected: Peonies, roses, and many other plants.
Symptoms and signs: Petals eaten.
Danger period: Early summer to early fall.
Treatment: Spray with carbaryl, chlorpyrifos, Diazinon, or malathion. If ½-in.-long yellow-tan beetles can be seen, remove and destroy them.

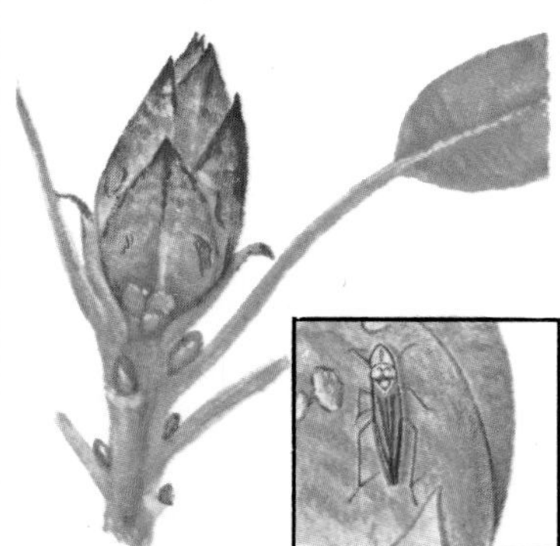

Rhododendron leafhoppers
Plants affected: Rhododendrons.
Symptoms and signs: Buds killed by bud-blast disease, which is spread by leafhoppers.
Danger period: Late summer, when flower buds are developing.
Treatment: Try to prevent disease by spraying plant with carbaryl, Diazinon, or malathion if pests are seen. If disease occurs, remove and destroy infected buds.

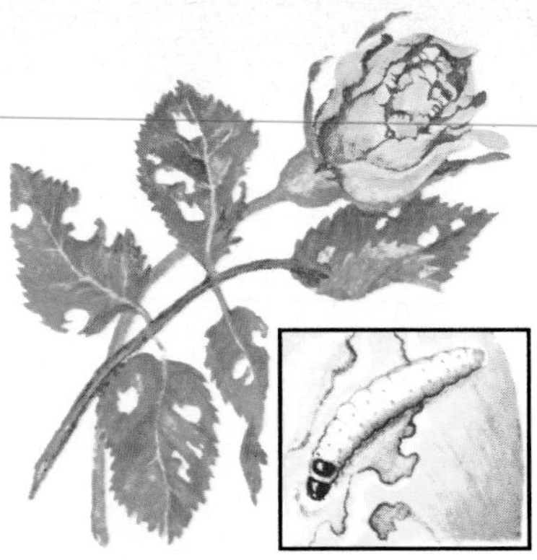

Caterpillars and sawfly larvae ("slugs")
Plants affected: Apples, chrysanthemums, roses, and other plants.
Symptoms and signs: Holes eaten into buds and leaves.
Danger period: Early spring to early summer outdoors, but almost any time of year in greenhouses.
Treatment: Spray with carbaryl, malathion, rotenone, or trichlorfon when pests are present.

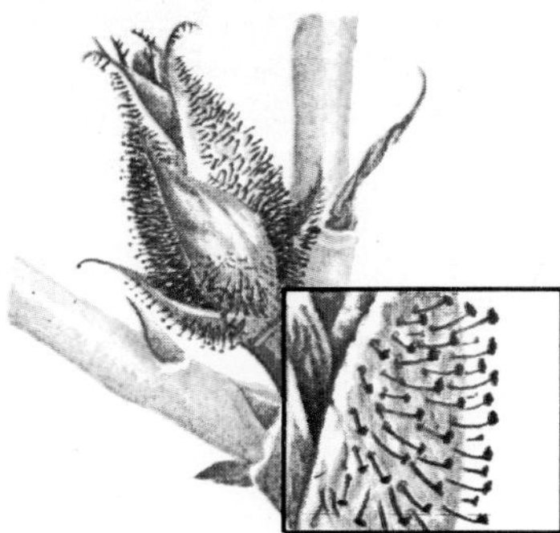

Rhododendron bud blast
Plants affected: Rhododendrons.
Symptoms and signs: Buds die and become covered with black heads of fungous spores.
Danger period: Late summer, when flower buds are beginning to develop—but symptoms are not seen until following spring, when buds fail to open.
Treatment: Cut off and destroy infected buds. Spray with Captan, dodine, or zineb to control fungus. Use Diazinon spray to control rhododendron leafhoppers, which spread disease.

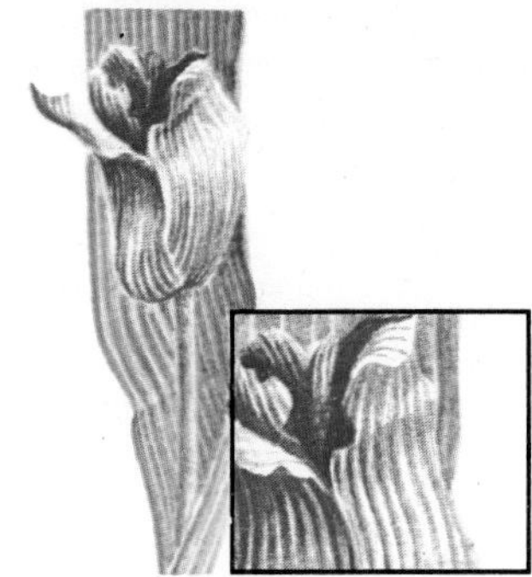

Blindness
Plants affected: Narcissi, tulips, when forced indoors.
Symptoms and signs: Withering of flowers before opening.
Danger period: During storage or growing season.
Treatment: To prevent blindness, store bulbs in cool, dry place. Plant at correct time, and make sure that soil never dries out once growth has started. Do not force bulbs at too high a temperature. Affected bulbs can be replanted.

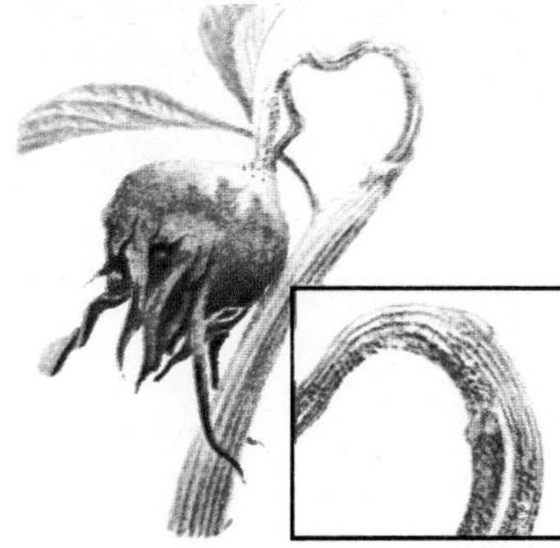

Peony blight, or Botrytis, or gray mold
Plants affected: Peonies.
Symptoms and signs: Flower buds rot and become covered with gray velvety mold.
Danger period: Flowering time.
Treatment: Cut out affected shoots to below ground level, and dust crowns with dry Bordeaux mixture. Spray with Captan, dichlofluanid, dichloran, thiram, or zineb as soon as leaves appear.

Pedicel necrosis
Plants affected: Poppies, pyrethrums, roses.
Symptoms and signs: Discolored patch develops on flower stalk, immediately below rosebuds or slightly lower on herbaceous plants. Stalks collapse at that point. Buds on affected stalks fail to open. Cause is unknown.
Danger period: Flowering time.
Treatment: Mulch, never allow soil to dry out, and feed only at appropriate time with appropriate fertilizers. Dressing of potassium sulfate can also be applied in early spring or late summer. Once disease appears, little can be done apart from cutting out affected flowers—although applications of foliar fertilizer may encourage development of second crop of flowers on roses.

Virus disease
Plants affected: Lilies.
Symptoms and signs: Flower buds are distorted and fail to open properly.
Danger period: Any time of year, but not apparent until flowering.
Treatment: Destroy affected plants. Keep plants well sprayed with carbaryl, Diazinon, or malathion to control insects (aphids, leafhoppers) that spread viruses.

Bud drop
Plants affected: Camellias, gardenias, sweet peas, wisterias.
Symptoms and signs: Buds or partly open flowers fall without opening properly.
Danger period: When flower buds begin to develop, although symptoms will not appear until flowering time.
Treatment: Once bud drop starts, nothing can stop it. Try to prevent trouble by mulching and never allowing soil to dry out. Maintain fairly even temperature for gardenias. Nothing, however, can prevent bud drop of sweet peas and wisterias when it is caused by cold nights.

Caterpillars
Plants affected: Carnations, chrysanthemums, and other plants, outdoors and in greenhouses.
Symptoms and signs: Petals eaten; caterpillars often inside blooms.
Danger period: Any time of year indoors, late spring to midfall outdoors.
Treatment: If relatively few blooms are affected, remove caterpillars by hand. Alternatively, spray with carbaryl or methoxychlor—preferably before plants are in full bloom, since flowers may be marred by spraying.

Earwigs
Plants affected: Chrysanthemums, clematises, dahlias, and some other plants.
Symptoms and signs: Ragged pieces eaten out of petals.
Danger period: Late spring to midfall.
Treatment: Before plants flower, spray or dust them and soil with carbaryl, chlorpyrifos, Diazinon, or malathion. Earwigs can also be trapped in rolls of corrugated cardboard, in old burlap, or in flowerpots stuffed with straw.

Ray blight, or petal blight
Plants affected: Chrysanthemums; occasionally cornflowers and dahlias.
Symptoms and signs: Dark, water-soaked spots spread on petals until flowers rot.
Danger period: Flowering time, particularly in cold, wet summers.
Treatment: Destroy affected flowers. Prevent disease in greenhouses by keeping humidity low. Spray plants with fungicide, such as Benomyl or zineb, just before flowers open. Repeat every 7 da. as necessary.

Virus disease
Plants affected: Chrysanthemums, dahlias, lilies, tulips, *Viola* species, wallflowers, and many other types of herbaceous plants.
Symptoms and signs: Flowers distorted or flower color broken (white streaks, or stripes in lighter or darker shade of background color).
Danger period: Growing season.
Treatment: Destroy affected plants. Many virus diseases are spread by insects and mites; control them with sprays or dusts.

Mycoplasma
Plants affected: Heleniums, *Primula* species, strawberries; occasionally chrysanthemums and narcissi.
Symptoms and signs: Flowers are green, instead of their normal color.
Danger period: Growing season.
Treatment: With heleniums, cut out that part of clump bearing affected blooms. With the others, destroy entire plant.

Plant bugs, or leaf bugs (four-lined, harlequin, tarnished)
Plants affected: Chrysanthemums, dahlias, and many other ornamental annuals and perennials.
Symptoms and signs: Flowers distorted.
Danger period: Early summer to midfall outdoors, but continuing later in greenhouses.
Treatment: Spray with Diazinon, malathion, methoxychlor, or nicotine as soon as first signs of damage appear.

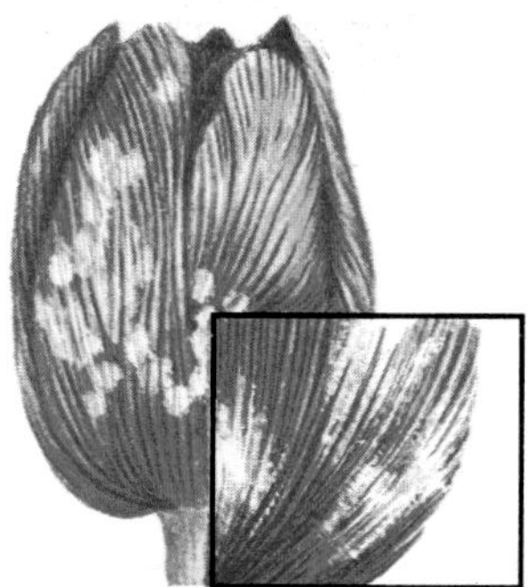

Tulip fire (Botrytis)
Plants affected: Tulips.
Symptoms and signs: Small brown spots on petals. These may rot and become covered with gray velvety mold.
Danger period: Flowering time.
Treatment: See Tulip Fire, p. 629.

Botrytis, or gray mold
Plants affected: Chrysanthemums, cyclamens in greenhouses.
Symptoms and signs: On chrysanthemums, spotting followed by rotting of flowers, which are covered with gray mold. On cyclamens, spotting of petals only.
Danger period: Flowering time.
Treatment: Remove and destroy affected flowers. Reduce humidity. Fumigate with tecnazene smokes, or spray with Benomyl, dichlofluanid, dichloran, or thiophanate-methyl.

Tree-Fruit and Small-Fruit Disorders

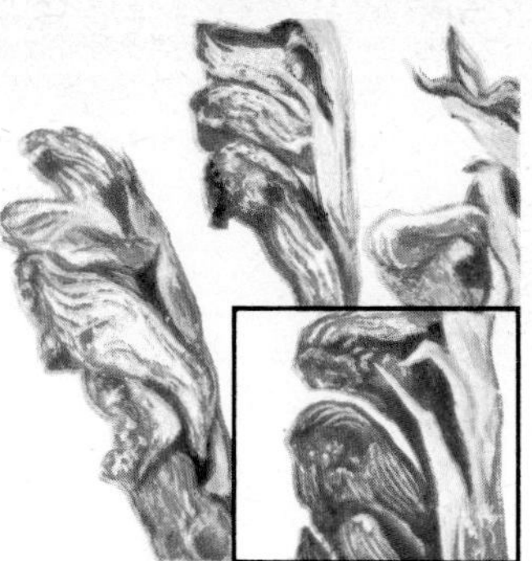

Gladiolus thrips

Plants affected: Gladioli and some related plants.
Symptoms and signs: Silvery flecks appear on petals and leaves. In severe infestations flowers become completely discolored and may die.
Danger period: Early summer to early fall.
Treatment: Dust corms with methoxychlor before storing and again before planting. If symptoms appear, spray affected plants with Diazinon, malathion, or nicotine every week from time leaves break through ground to end of blooming.

Japanese beetles

Plants affected: Roses and other garden flowers, grapes, lindens, and many other plants.
Symptoms and signs: Flowers and leaves are heavily chewed by beetles, leaving petals frayed and leaves skeletonized.
Danger period: Early summer to midfall.
Treatment: For control, see Beetle Grubs, p. 634. Spray or dust infected plants with carbaryl, Diazinon, or methoxychlor.

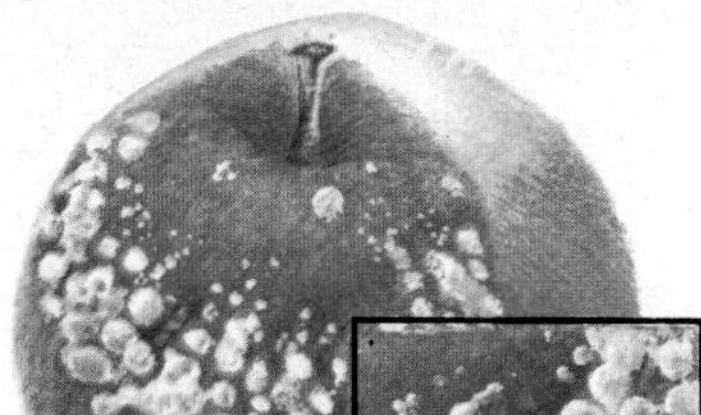

Brown rot

Plants affected: All stone fruits, especially cherries, nectarines, peaches, plums.
Symptoms and signs: Fruit turns brownish white; concentric rings of powdery fungous spores often cover it; fruit withers and shrinks.
Danger period: During storage and in summer.
Treatment: Spray as blossoms open with Captan or dodine. Repeat at petal fall, again at shuck spray. Then 3 sprays 7–10 da. apart as cover sprays. Finally, 2 more sprays—1 just before harvest, 1 after harvest.

Fruit drop

Plants affected: All tree fruits.
Symptoms and signs: Fruit drops prematurely while still very small.
Danger period: During and just after flowering time.
Treatment: See that suitable pollinators, such as bees, are present in garden. Feed, mulch, and water. Do not spray while trees are flowering. Nothing can be done in cold seasons when fruit drop is due to poor pollination. If dropped fruit shows small crescent-shaped scars, cause could be plum curculio (see p. 627).

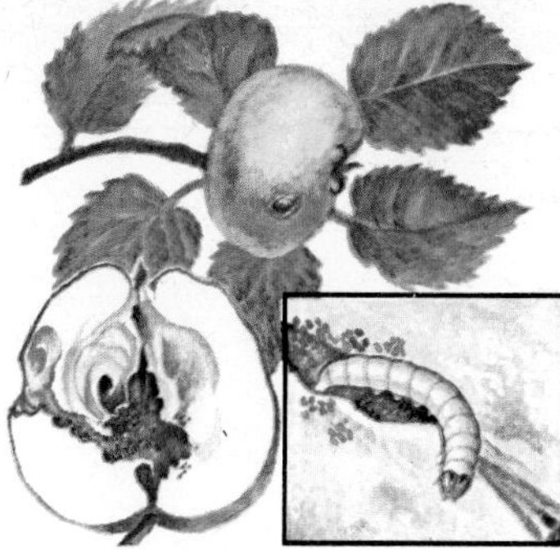

Codling moths

Plants affected: Mainly apples, but also pears.
Symptoms and signs: Caterpillars eat into calyx end of ripening fruit and destroy it.
Danger period: Early to late summer.
Treatment: Spray thoroughly with carbaryl, malathion, or methoxychlor in early summer and twice more at 10-da. intervals to kill young caterpillars before they penetrate fruit.

Apple red bugs and tarnished plant bugs

Plants affected: Mainly apples, but also pears.
Symptoms and signs: Bumps and corky patches on ripening fruit.
Danger period: Midspring to late summer.
Treatment: Spray with dinoseb or miscible oil during dormant period to kill overwintering eggs, and/or spray with Diazinon, methoxychlor, or nicotine just before trees begin to flower.

Bitter pit

Plants affected: Apples.
Symptoms and signs: Slightly sunken brown spots beneath skin and throughout flesh.
Danger period: Growing season, but not apparent until harvesting or in storage.
Treatment: Fertilize and mulch; never allow soil to dry out. In early summer fertilize with spray of calcium nitrate at rate of 8 rounded tbsp. to 5 gal. of water; then repeat 3 times at 3-wk. intervals.

Apple sawflies

Plants affected: Apples.
Symptoms and signs: Caterpillar form of sawfly eats into cores of young fruits, which then drop prematurely. This pest also causes superficial scarring of mature fruits.
Danger period: Late spring to early summer.
Treatment: Spray thoroughly with carbaryl, dimethoate, or methoxychlor immediately after petals fall. Pick up and destroy dropped apples.

Cracking
Plants affected: Apples, pears, plums.
Symptoms and signs: Skin of fruit splits.
Danger period: Growing season.
Treatment: Try to avoid irregular growth by mulching (to conserve moisture) and by never allowing soil to dry out. Overwatering coupled with poor drainage or long, heavy rains can also cause cracking.

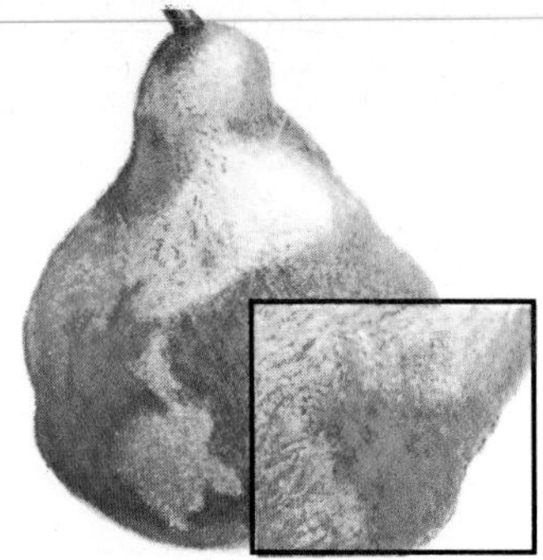

Stony pit
Plants affected: Old pear trees.
Symptoms and signs: Fruit pitted and deformed, with patches of dead, stony cells in flesh that make fruit inedible. Symptoms appear on single branch and over the years gradually spread until all fruit on tree is affected.
Danger period: Growing season.
Treatment: Prune back old wood severely, and feed regularly in spring and fall with 5–10–5 fertilizer.

Faulty root action
Plants affected: Tree fruits and, to a lesser extent, small fruits.
Symptoms and signs: Gradual diminishing of crop over several years, usually accompanied by discolored foliage and perhaps dieback of shoots.
Danger period: Growing season.
Treatment: Apply appropriate fertilizers at correct time. Feed, water, and mulch. Drain if waterlogging occurs. Applications of foliar fertilizer may hasten recovery.

or Poor pollination
Plants affected: Small fruits, tree fruits, tomatoes.
Symptoms and signs: Very little fruit is produced, and that which is formed may be distorted.
Danger period: Flowering time.
Treatment: Since trouble is usually caused by cold weather at flowering time, little can be done for fruit other than to ensure that suitable pollinators for tree fruit are present. For tomatoes, provide good cultural treatment, and spray in dry weather to supply moist atmosphere.

or Virus disease
Plants affected: Small fruits.
Symptoms and signs: Gradual diminishing of crop over several years, usually accompanied by other symptoms, such as stunting of plants and distortion or yellow blotching of leaves.
Danger period: Growing season.
Treatment: Destroy infected plants. Replant on fresh site with stocks certified to be free of virus disease. Spray for insect that carries disease with insecticide recommended.

Raspberry beetles
Plants affected: Raspberries, blackberries, loganberries.
Symptoms and signs: Beetles and larvae feed on ripening fruit.
Danger period: Early to late summer.
Treatment: Spray thoroughly with malathion, methoxychlor, or rotenone when blossom buds appear, again just before blossoms open, and a third time as soon as first fruit begins to turn pink.

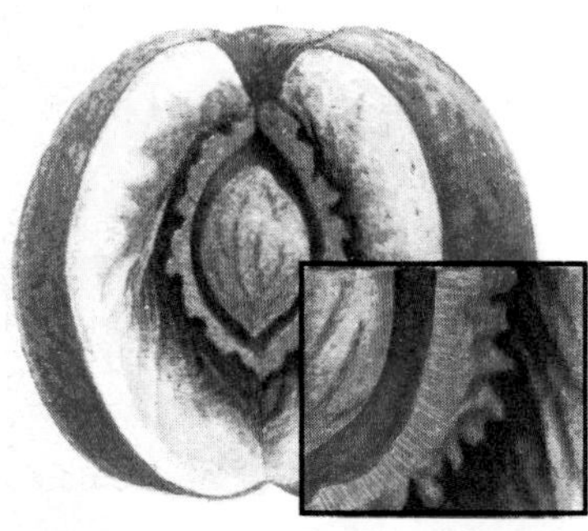

Split stone
Plants affected: Nectarines, peaches.
Symptoms and signs: Kernel rots within stone, which splits and causes fruit to crack at stalk end. Also, cleft in fruit is deeper than normal.
Danger period: Growing season.
Treatment: Fertilize and mulch. Never allow soil to dry out, in order to keep growth even while fruit is swelling.

Scab
Plants affected: Apples, pears (and sometimes fire-thorn berries).
Symptoms and signs: Brown or black scabs on fruit, which may, in severe cases, crack when scabs have merged and become corky.
Danger period: Growing season.
Treatment: See Scab, p. 604.

Powdery mildew
Plants affected: Apples, gooseberries, grapes, strawberries, and many other fruits.
Symptoms and signs: White powder turns brown on gooseberries but may show as loss of color on strawberries. Grapes may split. Apples show powdery leaves.
Danger period: Growing season.
Treatment: Spray as for Powdery Mildew, p. 607

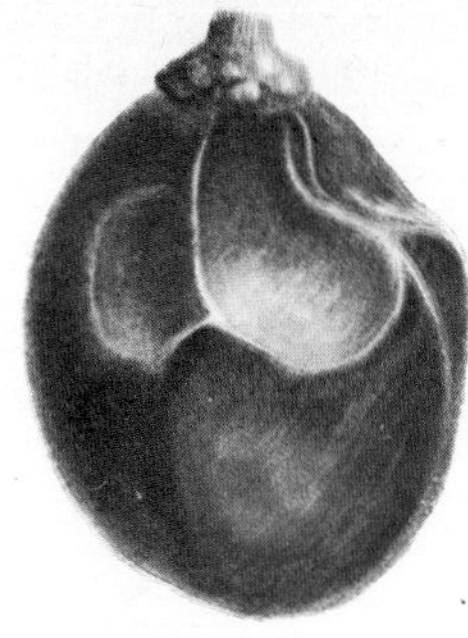

Scald
Plants affected: Grapes, sometimes gooseberries and tree fruits in hot weather.
Symptoms and signs: Discolored sunken patches on fruit.
Danger period: In hot weather.
Treatment: If plants are in greenhouse, shade and ventilate it well. Cut out any affected fruit before it rots.

Plum curculios
Plants affected: Apples, apricots, cherries, peaches, plums.
Symptoms and signs: Crescent- and T-shaped punctures in young fruit, also in cherries at maturity. Larvae feed on developing fruit, destroying it. Small fruit may drop.
Danger period: After petals fall; in some areas again later on.
Treatment: Cultivate around trees to kill larvae and pupae in soil. Destroy fallen fruit. Spray 3–5 times, starting at petal fall, with carbaryl, malathion, or methoxychlor. Allow 7–10 da. between treatments.

Botrytis, or gray mold
Plants affected: All small fruits.
Symptoms and signs: Fruit rots and becomes covered with gray velvety mold.
Danger period: Flowering time, but symptoms do not appear until fruit matures.
Treatment: Spray just as flowers open, repeating 2 or 3 times at 14-da. intervals. Use Benomyl, Captan, chlorothalonil, dichloran, or thiram. Remove diseased fruit. Wash fruit carefully before use.

Shanking
Plants affected: Grapes.
Symptoms and signs: Dark spot develops along stalk of berry and eventually rings it. Berry fails to ripen—it becomes red in case of black varieties and remains green in white varieties.
Danger period: Growing season.
Treatment: Feed, mulch, and never allow soil to dry out. Do not overcrop vine. If trouble occurs, cut out affected berries before they rot.

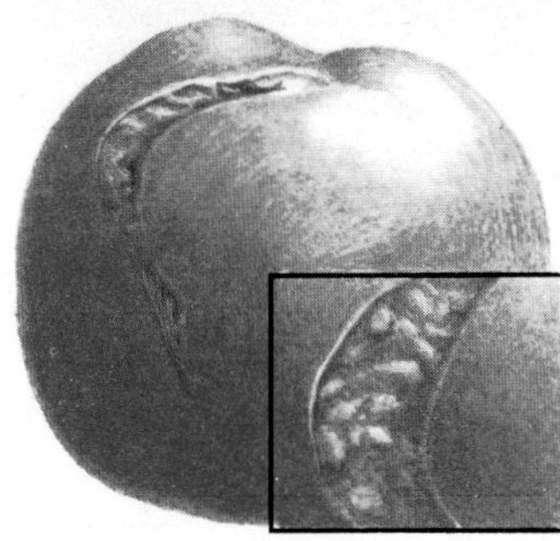

Cracking
Plants affected: Tomatoes.
Symptoms and signs: Skin splits near shoulder, often in form of ring, sometimes vertically.
Danger period: As fruit develops.
Treatment: Try to maintain even growth by never allowing soil to dry out. Avoid giving too much or too little water.

Greenback and blotchy ripening
Plants affected: Tomatoes.
Symptoms and signs: Hard green or yellow patch develops on shoulder of fruit near stalk; similar patches may develop on other parts.
Danger period: As fruit develops.
Treatment: Grow resistant varieties; keep soil moist to maintain even growth of fruit. Shade greenhouse in hot weather. Probably caused by nutrient deficiency; maintain potassium level in soil.

Early blight and late blight
Plants affected: Tomatoes outdoors.
Symptoms and signs: In wet weather dark green water-soaked spots on leaves enlarge, become dark brown to black, with shriveled center. Undersides of leaves, stems, and petioles have whitish growth. Fungus develops rapidly; entire plants are killed overnight.
Danger period: Mid and late summer when weather is very wet.
Treatment: Spray at 10- to 14-da. intervals, from first bloom to early fall, with fungicide, such as maneb.

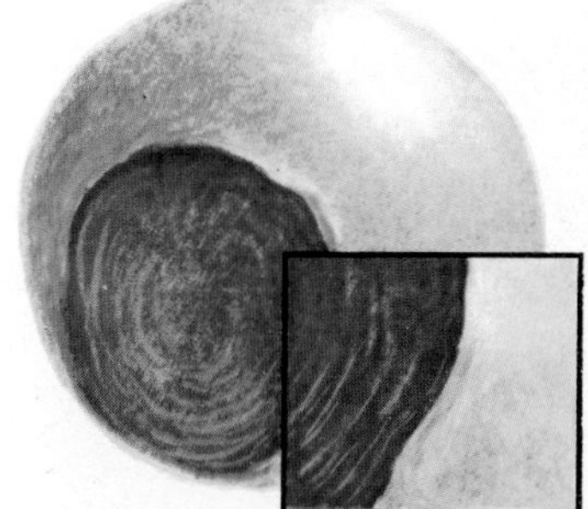

Blossom-end rot
Plants affected: Tomatoes.
Symptoms and signs: Circular brown or black patch at blossom end of fruit, which, despite disease's name, does not usually rot. Nonparasitic disease.
Danger period: As fruit develops.
Treatment: Prevent trouble by never allowing soil to dry out; this maintains even growth. Also, avoid irregular watering. Do not cultivate close to plants.

Tomato wilt (fusarium and verticillium wilt)
Plants affected: Tomatoes.
Symptoms and signs: As first fruit begins to ripen, lower leaves yellow and droop on one side of plant. One shoot often dies first. Fungus enters from soil into roots, goes up stems, and plugs them, so that they wilt.
Danger period: Midsummer to midfall.
Treatment: Use formaldehyde drench on soil 1 wk. before planting or metam-sodium 2 wk. before. Plant wilt-resistant varieties.

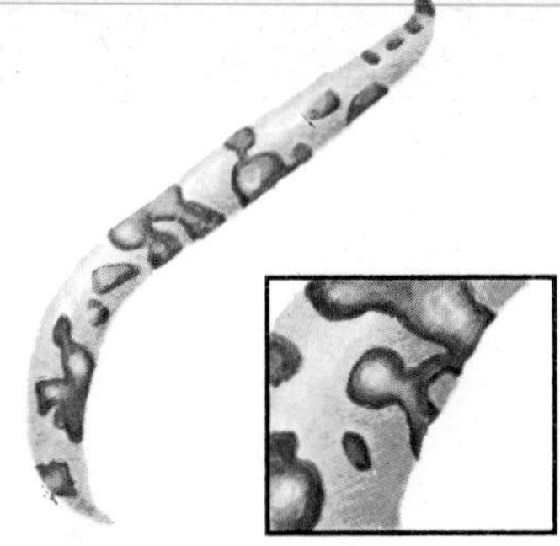

Anthracnose
Plants affected: Many kinds of beans.
Symptoms and signs: Sunken brown-black areas on pods, brown spots on leaves and stems. Leaves may fall.
Danger period: Growing season—particularly cool, wet summers.
Treatment: Destroy diseased plants (avoid touching wet plants, since this spreads disease). Never save beans for seeds; sow new seeds in different site. If disease becomes serious, spray before flowering with Captan, copper hydroxide, or zineb.

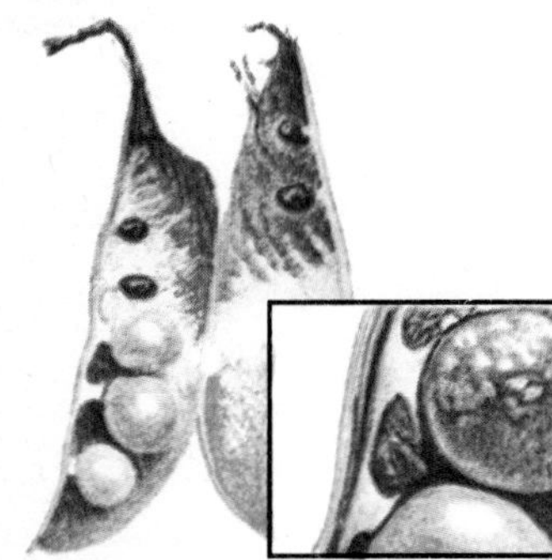

Botrytis, or gray mold
Plants affected: Tomatoes, occasionally bean and pea pods in wet weather.
Symptoms and signs: Gray velvety mold develops on rotting fruit.
Danger period: Growing season.
Treatment: Remove and destroy diseased fruits or pods. Under glass, fumigate with tecnazene; indoors and outdoors, spray with Benomyl, dichlofluanid, dichloran, maneb, thiophanate-methyl, or zineb.

Mexican bean beetles
Plants affected: All kinds of bush and pole beans.
Symptoms and signs: Lacy foliage with spiny bright yellow larvae or black-spotted brown beetles on undersides of leaves. Beans also eaten. Several generations occur per season.
Danger period: Growing season to first hard frost.
Treatment: Spray or dust weekly throughout growing season. Spray with carbaryl, malathion, or methoxychlor, or dust with malathion or rotenone.

Bulb, Corm, Tuber, and Root Disorders

Stem and bulb nematodes, or stem and bulb eelworms
Plants affected: Hyacinths, narcissi, tulips, and some others.
Symptoms and signs: Bulbs discolor internally and eventually rot away. Poor and distorted growth.
Danger period: Dormant bulbs in late summer and autumn; growing plants in spring.
Treatment: Destroy affected plants. Do not replant bulbs in affected areas of soil for at least 3 yr.

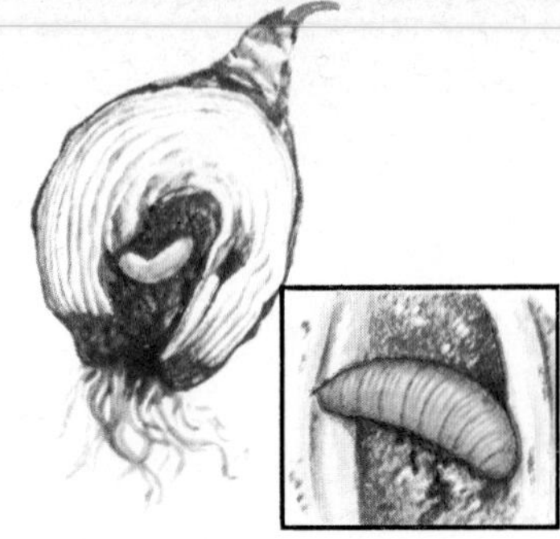

Narcissus bulb flies
Plants affected: Narcissus bulbs.
Symptoms and signs: Bulbs soft and rotten, brownish maggots inside.
Danger period: Between early spring and early summer; symptoms apparent in dormant bulbs in fall or spring.
Treatment: Discard soft bulbs at planting time. Cultivate soil around plants as leaves die, to block holes in soil that would allow flies to get down to bulbs to lay eggs. Dust at this time and at planting time with lindane.

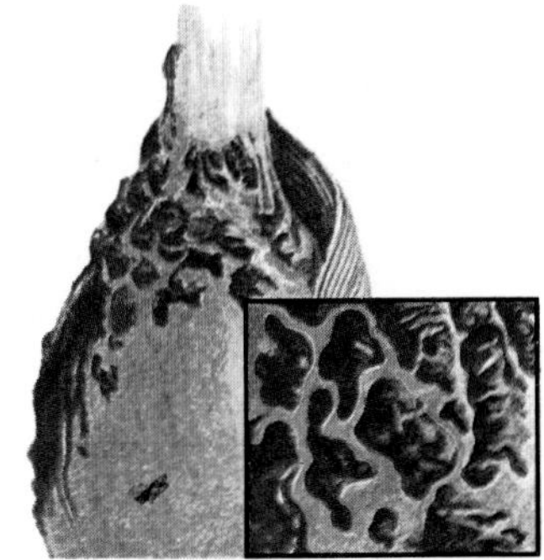

Gray bulb rot (rhizoctonia)
Plants affected: Hyacinths, tulips, and similar plants.
Symptoms and signs: Dry gray rot at neck of bulb, which soon becomes covered with black fungus and disintegrates.
Danger period: Soon after planting.
Treatment: Remove and destroy debris from diseased plants; replace surrounding soil. Before planting bulbs and corms, dust them with quintozene, and rake quintozene into soil.

Basal rot
Plants affected: Many bulbs, such as crocuses, lilies, and narcissi.
Symptoms and signs: Rotting of roots and base of corm or bulb, which, if cut longitudinally, shows dark strands spreading from base or chocolate-brown rot spreading upward through inner scales. Affected corms or bulbs eventually rot completely.
Danger period: Any time, including during storage.
Treatment: Destroy severely affected corms and bulbs. In early stages lily bulbs may be saved by cutting out diseased roots and scales, and by dusting surviving bulbs with quintozene. Quintozene should also be raked into soil before lilies are replanted on fresh site.

Ink disease
Plants affected: Bulbous irises, red-hot pokers.
Symptoms and signs: Black crusts on outer scales of bulb, followed by decay within, leaving small pockets of black powder.
Danger period: Any time of year.
Treatment: Destroy affected bulbs or corms. Destroy foliage at end of season. Replant healthy bulbs or corms in fresh site after dipping them in solution of Benomyl.

Neck rot, or smolder
Plants affected: Narcissi.
Symptoms and signs: Bulbs decay and small, black, flat fungus develops.
Danger period: During storage.
Treatment: Store bulbs in cool, dry place. Destroy affected bulbs. Remove and destroy affected plants during growing season as soon as any symptoms are seen on foliage. Spray the rest with Bordeaux mixture or zineb at 10-da. intervals. See also Smolder, p. 610.

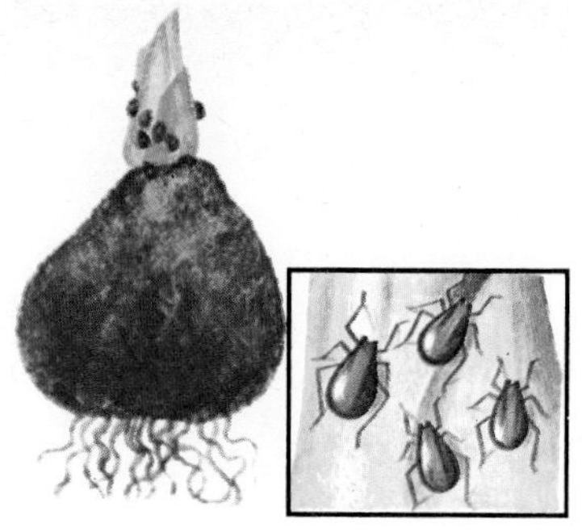

Tulip-bulb aphids
Plants affected: Crocuses, gladioli, irises, tulips.
Symptoms and signs: Colonies of dark green aphids develop on dormant bulbs and corms in storage.
Danger period: Late fall to late winter.
Treatment: Fumigate with dichlorvos or lindane if possible, or dust with lindane. Sprays of endosulfan or lindane can be used instead, but make sure that treated bulbs and corms dry thoroughly afterward.

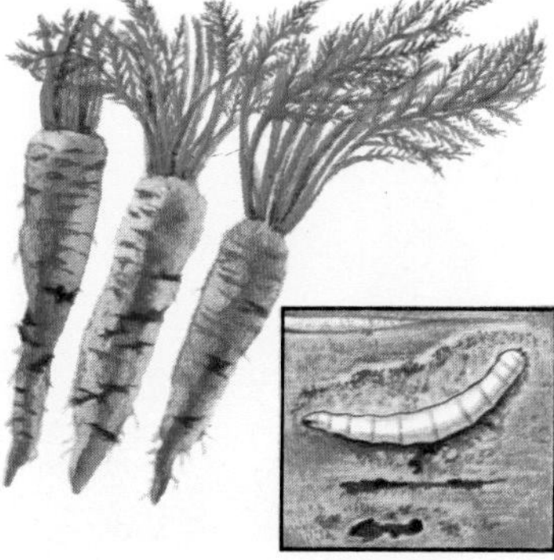

Carrot rust flies
Plants affected: Carrots, celery, parsley, parsnips.
Symptoms and signs: Fly maggots tunnel into roots.
Danger period: Early summer to midfall.
Treatment: In areas where flies are prevalent, sow seeds thinly in late spring (later than normally); use seed protectant. On established plants apply Diazinon or trichlorfon as soil drench along rows 2 or 3 times in late summer and early fall.

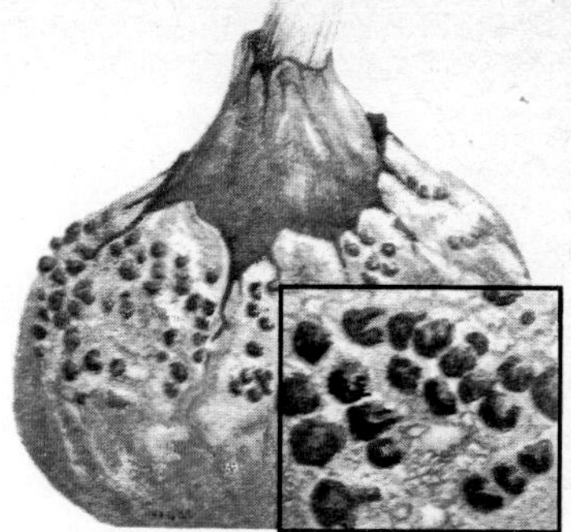

Tulip fire (Botrytis)
Plants affected: Tulips.
Symptoms and signs: Bulbs rot; small black fungus develops.
Danger period: Shortly before or after planting.
Treatment: Destroy rotting bulbs or those bearing fungi. Dust bulbs with quintozene, and rake quintozene into soil before planting. Plant in different site each year if possible, particularly after disease has appeared. Spray with Benomyl, chlorothalonil, dichlofluanid, dichloran, thiophanate-methyl, or zineb when leaves are about 2 in. high; repeat at 10-da. intervals until flowering. Remove and destroy diseased plants as they appear during growing season.

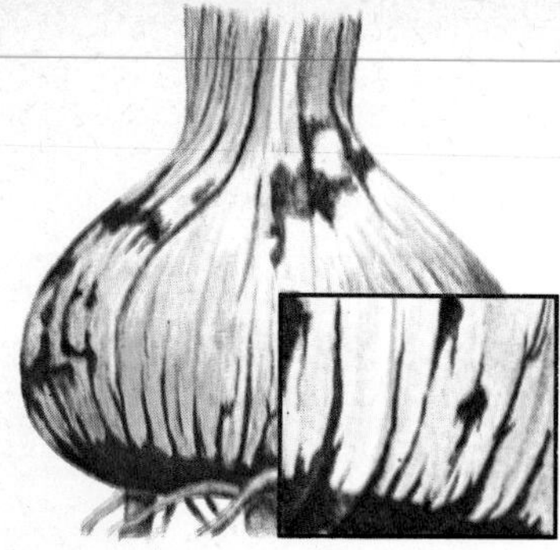

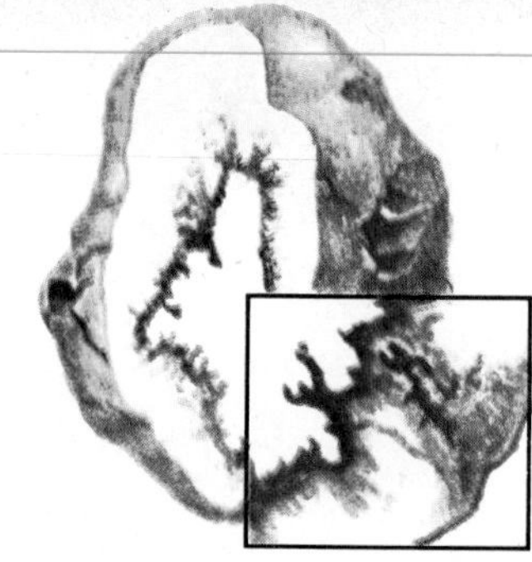

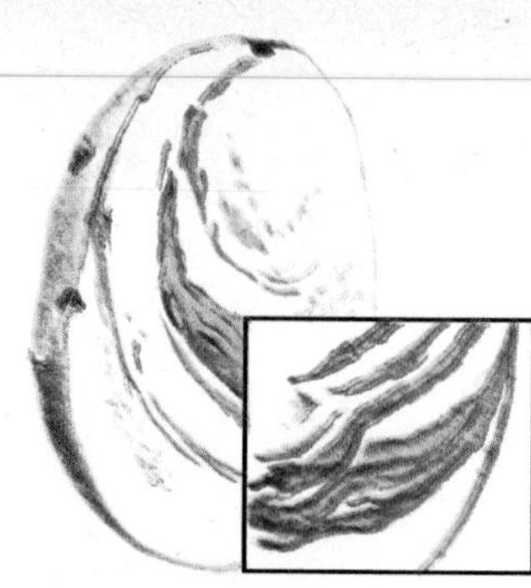

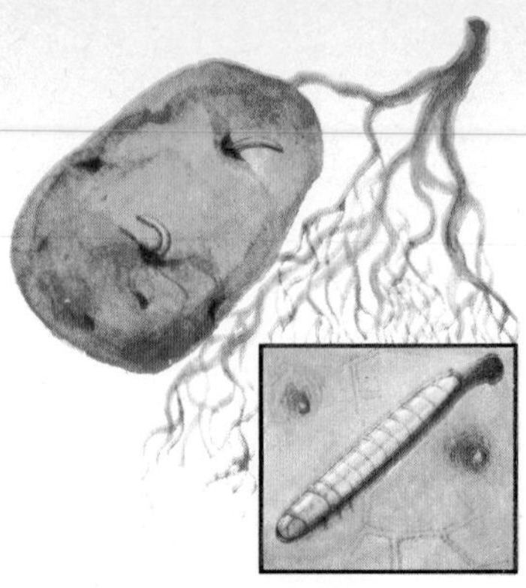

Dry rot
Plants affected: Acidantheras, crocuses, freesias, gladioli, potatoes, and some other tubers.
Symptoms and signs: Many small dark lesions develop on corms or tubers and merge to produce larger black areas before dry rot shrivels corm or tuber completely.
Danger period: During storage.
Treatment: Remove and destroy affected corms or tubers as soon as first symptoms appear. Before storing or replanting healthy ones, dust with quintozene, or dip in solution of Benomyl or Captan. Dry thoroughly before storing. Grow corms or tubers in fresh site each year, and rake quintozene into soil before planting. Also, treat soil with metam-sodium before planting.

Gangrene
Plants affected: Potatoes.
Symptoms and signs: Slight depression on stored tuber, which gradually enlarges until most of tuber is decayed and shrunken.
Danger period: Winter and early spring.
Treatment: Handle tubers carefully; store in airy, frost-free place—not in sacks. Destroy diseased tubers.

Spraing
Plants affected: Potatoes.
Symptoms and signs: Brown arclike marks in flesh of tuber. Might be caused by virus.
Danger period: Growing season.
Treatment: Destroy badly affected tubers, and do not plant potatoes in same site for several years.

Wireworms
Plants affected: Carrots, lettuce, potatoes, tomatoes, and other vegetables; chrysanthemums and other ornamentals.
Symptoms and signs: Underground parts are invaded by larvae.
Danger period: Early spring to early fall.
Treatment: Cultivate infested soil thoroughly and frequently before planting. Control weeds and, if necessary, apply chlordane or lindane to soil around susceptible plants.

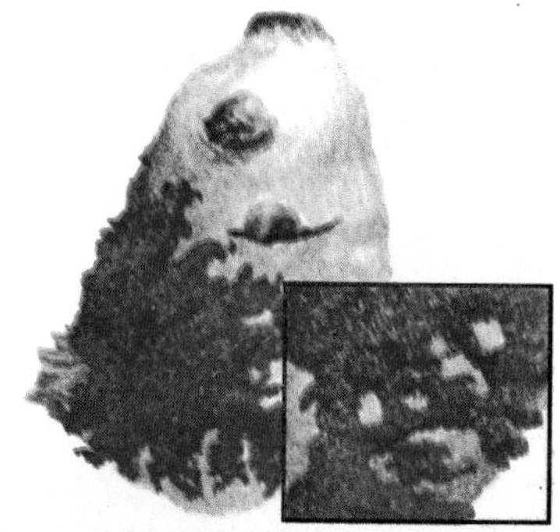

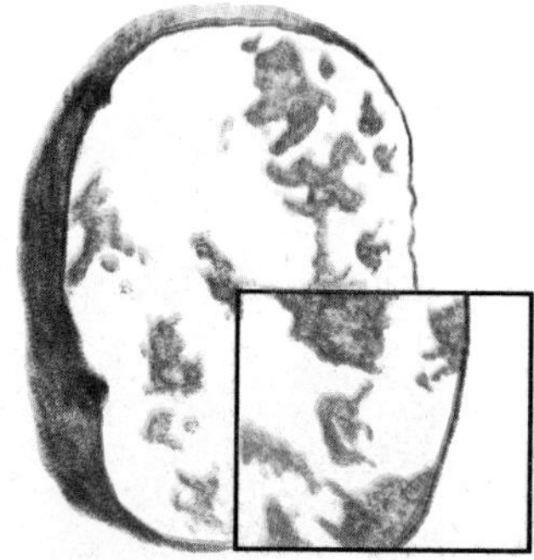

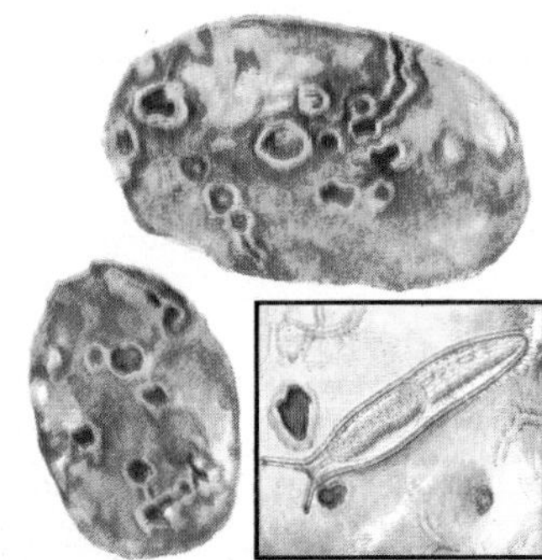

Powdery scab
Plants affected: Potatoes.
Symptoms and signs: Uniform round scabs, raised at first, later bursting open to release powdery mass of spores. Affected tubers may be deformed and have earthy taste.
Danger period: Growing season.
Treatment: Destroy diseased tubers and do not plant potatoes in same site for several years. Provide good drainage; use no lime on soil.

Internal rust spot
Plants affected: Potatoes.
Symptoms and signs: Scattered brown marks inside flesh of tuber.
Danger period: Growing season.
Treatment: Dig in plenty of humus, and try to keep growth even by watering before soil dries out completely.

Slugs
Plants affected: Narcissi, potatoes, tulips, and many other plants.
Symptoms and signs: Irregular holes and tunnels eaten into bulbs, corms, and tubers. Slugs often present; slime residue left on plant.
Danger period: Most of year.
Treatment: Use slug baits based on metaldehyde, methiocarb, or mexacarbate. Lift potatoes as early as possible to minimize damage. Stale beer in shallow dish is useful as slug trap.

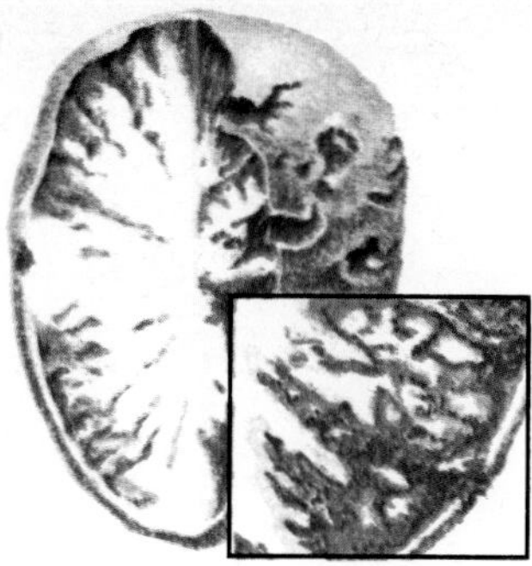

Blight
Plants affected: Potatoes.
Symptoms and signs: Red-brown discoloration appears under skin but shows through as gray patch on surface of potato. Fungous disease spreads inward, and affected areas are often entered by bacteria, which cause evil-smelling soft rot.
Danger period: Midsummer until end of potato-growing season.
Treatment: Destroy diseased tubers; do not put them on compost heap. As soon as plants are 6–8 in. tall, spray with captafol, chlorothalonil, mancozeb, or maneb, and repeat every 7–14 da. until entire crop is harvested.

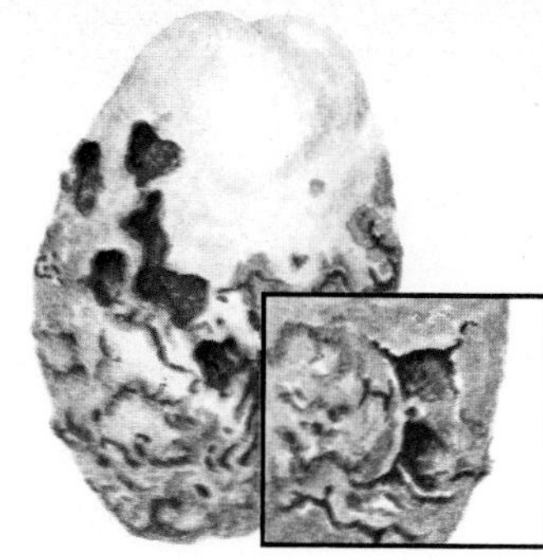

Common scab
Plants affected: Potatoes.
Symptoms and signs: Ragged-edged scabs on tubers.
Danger period: Growing season.
Treatment: Treat soil with metam-sodium or quintozene before planting to kill bacteria. Do not apply lime before planting potatoes. Give soil plenty of humus, and keep growth even by watering before soil dries. If trouble persists, grow resistant varieties, such as 'Norchip,' 'Norland,' or 'Superior.' Destroy debris and infected peelings.

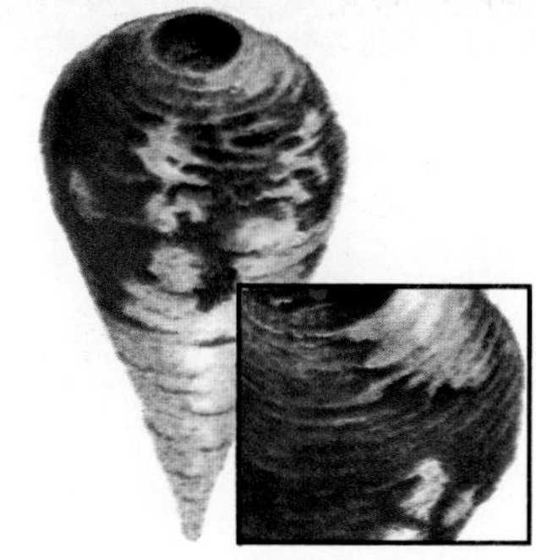

Parsnip canker
Plants affected: Parsnips.
Symptoms and signs: Red-brown or black rotting canker on shoulder of root.
Danger period: Growing season.
Treatment: Grow parsnips in deep, loamy soil, with lime added if necessary. Use balanced fertilizer. Sow seeds early and thin seedlings to about 3 in. apart. Grow resistant varieties or rotate crops if trouble persists. Spray with copper or copper hydroxide. Begin harvesting in midsummer.

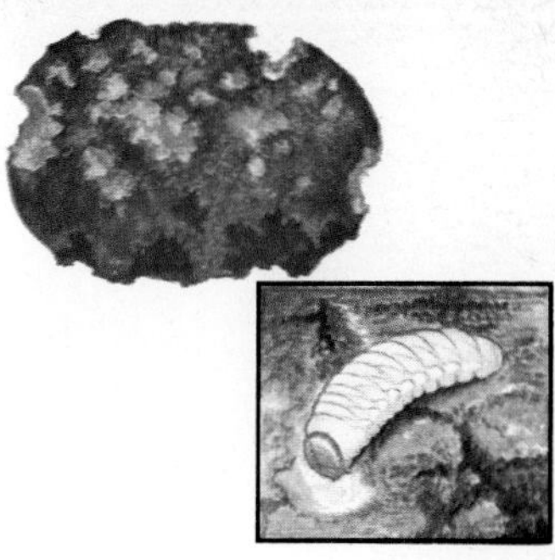

Vine weevils
Plants affected: Tuberous begonias, pot cyclamens, jade plants, primroses, saxifrages, and some other plants. Most damage is done to greenhouse plants, but these pests also appear outdoors.
Symptoms and signs: Small, white, fat, legless grubs that live in soil eat roots, tubers, and corms.
Danger period: Most times of year. Grubs are usually noticed in winter and early spring.
Treatment: Remove and destroy any grubs found when plants are repotted. Infested plants may be treated by working small amount of lindane dust into soil or by applying soil drench of chlordane, endosulfan, or lindane. Paradichlorobenzene (moth crystals) placed among drainage crocks before potting will also protect susceptible plants.

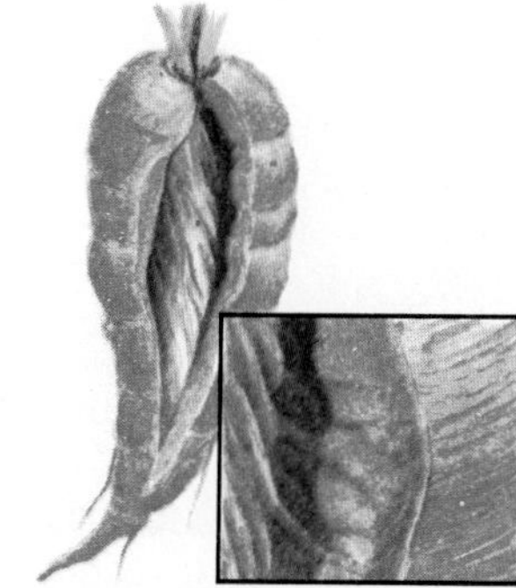

Cracking
Plants affected: All kinds of root vegetables.
Symptoms and signs: Lengthwise splitting.
Danger period: Growing season.
Treatment: Try to avoid irregular growth by watering before soil dries out completely.

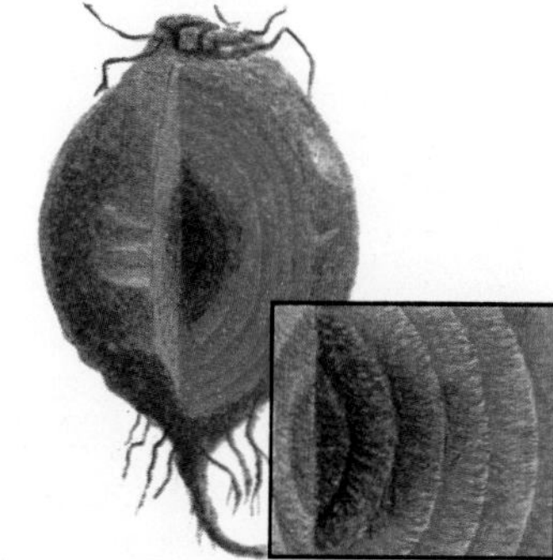

Boron deficiency
Plants affected: Beets, rutabagas, turnips.
Symptoms and signs: Gray or brown patches in flesh of lower half of edible root, or browning—and sometimes eventual blackening—of interior of root.
Danger period: Growing season.
Treatment: Apply 1 rounded tbsp. of borax (mixed with fine sand for easier distribution) to every 20 sq. yd. of soil.

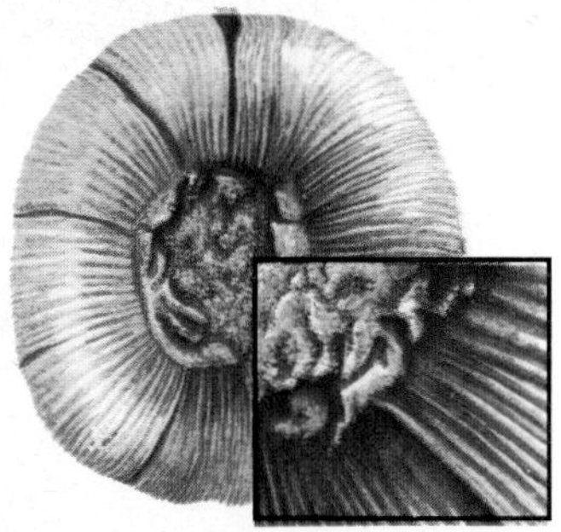

Corm rot
Plants affected: Acidantheras, freesias, gladioli.
Symptoms and signs: Rotting from center outward, corm becomes spongy and dark brown or black.
Danger period: During storage.
Treatment: Store corms in dry atmosphere at 45°–50° F. Before storage dust corms with quintozene, or dip them in solution of Benomyl or Captan. Destroy affected corms.

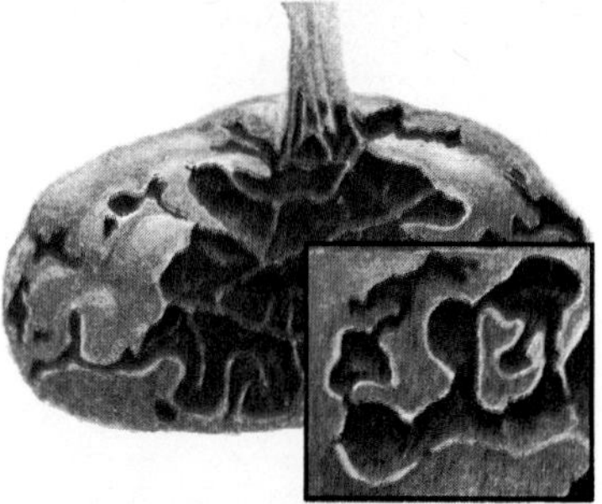

Hard rot (Septoria)
Plants affected: Gladioli, but corms of other kinds can also be affected.
Symptoms and signs: Large, black-brown, clearly outlined, somewhat sunken spots develop on corms, which may become hard and shriveled.
Danger period: Infection occurs during summer, but symptoms show during storage.
Treatment: See Dry Rot, p. 630.

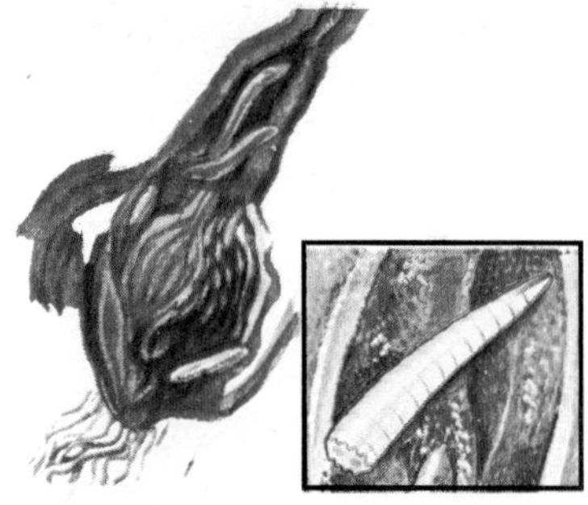

Onion maggots
Plants affected: Leeks and onions.
Symptoms and signs: Bulbs turn mushy. Small maggots are visible feeding on rotting tissue.
Danger period: Late spring to late summer.
Treatment: Dust soil with Calomel before or soon after sowing seeds. Use trichlorfon as soil drench for established plants 2 or 3 times during growth. Or when onions emerge, drench soil with $1\frac{1}{2}$ tsp. 50% Diazinon per gallon of water.

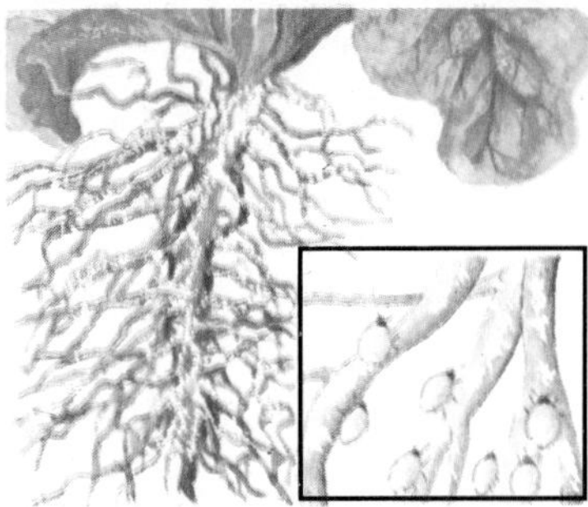

Root aphids and root mealybugs
Plants affected: Cacti and other succulents, primroses, and other pot plants; lettuce; and some outdoor ornamentals.
Symptoms and signs: Colonies of white, wax-covered aphids or mealybugs infest roots.
Danger period: Late summer and fall outdoors; any time of year in greenhouse.
Treatment: Apply soil drench of Diazinon, malathion, or nicotine to roots of affected plants.

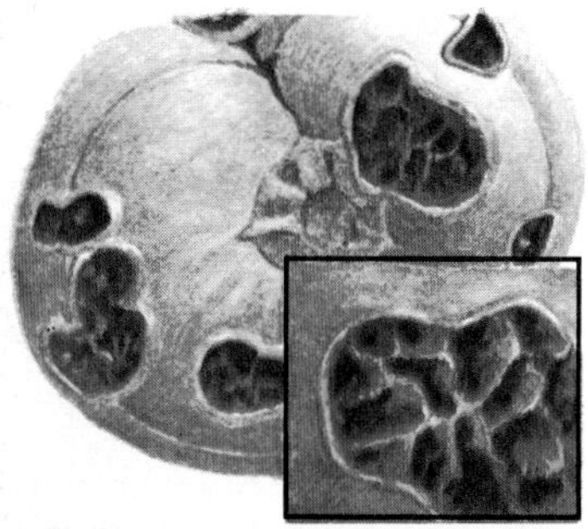

Gladiolus scab
Plants affected: Gladioli.
Symptoms and signs: Round craters develop toward base of corm. Each crater has prominent raised rim and often varnishlike coating.
Danger period: Infection occurs during summer, but symptoms may not show until corms are lifted and put in storage.
Treatment: See Dry Rot, p. 630.

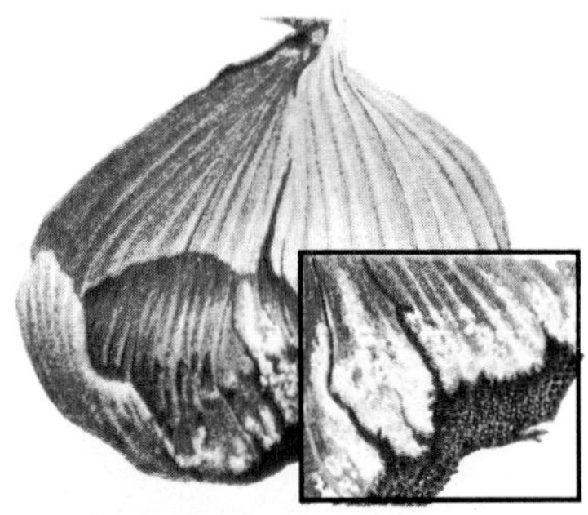

White rot
Plants affected: Onions, especially spring onions; occasionally garlic and leeks.
Symptoms and signs: Base of bulbs and roots are covered with white fungus and rot.
Danger period: Growing season.
Treatment: Grow onions on new site each year if possible; disease contaminates soil for at least 8 yr. Treat planting rows with 4% Calomel dust. Destroy diseased plants.

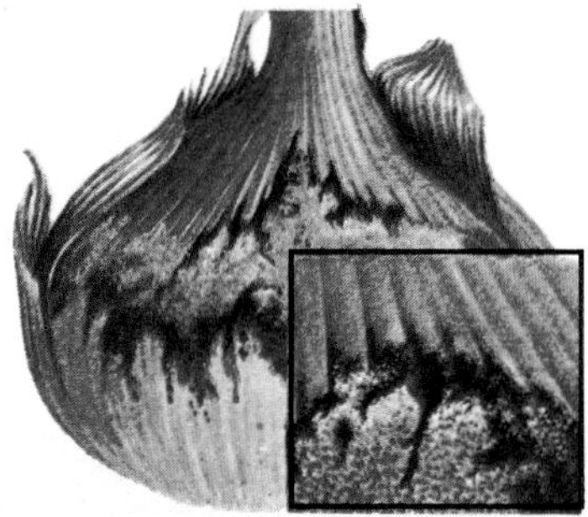

Onion neck rot (Botrytis)
Plants affected: Onions.
Symptoms and signs: Gray velvety mold develops near neck of stored onions, which rot rapidly.
Danger period: Growing season, but symptoms do not show until storage.
Treatment: If possible, buy treated seeds, or treat them with chlorothalonil. Store only well-ripened hard onions; put them in dry, cool, airy place. Destroy diseased onions.

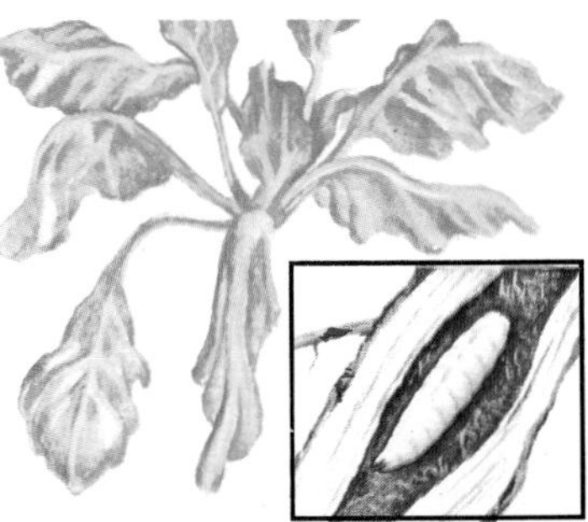

Cabbage maggots
Plants affected: Recently transplanted brassicas, especially Brussels sprouts, cabbages, cauliflower; also wallflowers.
Symptoms and signs: Maggots in soil feed on roots, causing complete collapse of young plants.
Danger period: Midspring to early fall.
Treatment: Protect transplants by applying soil drench of Diazinon or trichlorfon.

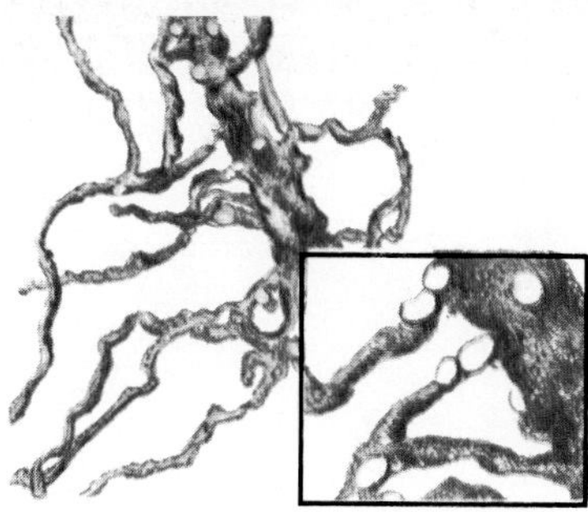

Golden potato cyst nematodes
Plants affected: Potatoes, tomatoes.
Symptoms and signs: Pinhead-size yellow or brown cysts on roots. Plants wilt and die.
Danger period: Midsummer to early fall.
Treatment: If crop is severely affected, wait 5 yr. before replanting. Applications of soil fumigant, such as dazomet or metam-sodium, are expensive and of limited value.

Clubroot
Plants affected: Brussels sprouts, cabbages, cauliflowers, stocks (*Mathiola* and *Malcomia*), and other members of cabbage family.
Symptoms and signs: Roots become swollen and distorted by slime mold. Plants look weak and yellow.
Danger period: Growing season.
Treatment: Improve drainage if necessary. Apply lime to acid soil to increase alkalinity to pH of 7. Put 4% Calomel dust in planting holes. Carry out as long a rotation as possible, or sterilize large area with dazomet.

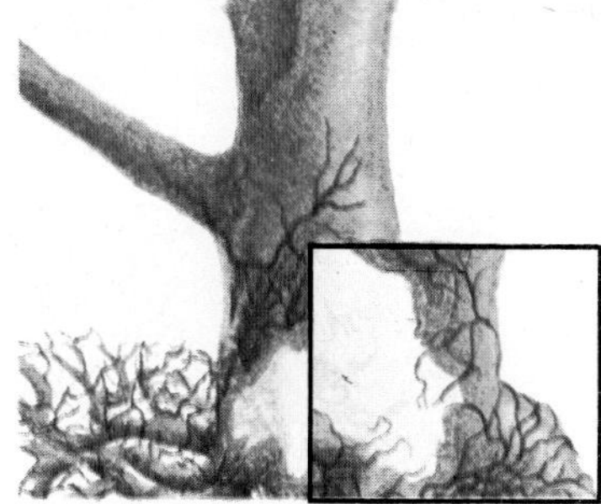

Armillaria root rot, or honey fungus
Plants affected: All kinds of woody plants.
Symptoms and signs: White fan-shaped sheets of fungous growth beneath bark at ground level. Dark threads may appear on roots.
Danger period: Any time of year.
Treatment: Dig up and destroy diseased plants. Sterilize soil, using 1 pt. of formaldehyde (plus some liquid detergent) to 6 gal. of water, applied at 5 gal. per sq. yd. Alternatively, use dazomet or change soil before replanting.

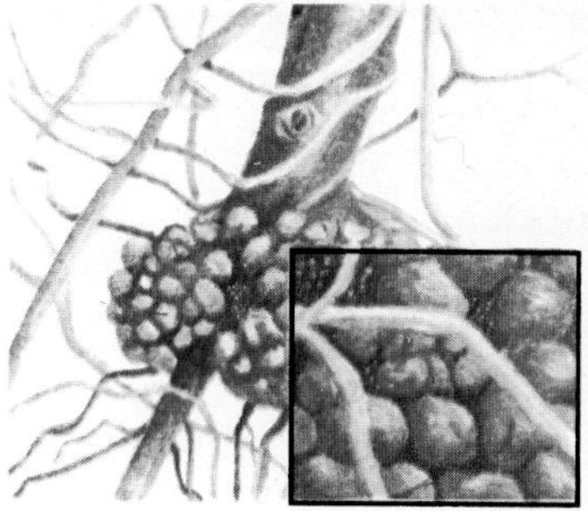

Crown gall
Plants affected: Many plants in rose family.
Symptoms and signs: Walnut- to football-size galls develop on roots and occasionally on stems.
Danger period: Growing season.
Treatment: Avoid injuries to roots. Prevent waterlogging by adequate drainage. Before planting in infected soil, dip roots of new plants in copper fungicide. Antibiotics, such as Bacticin or streptomycin, are useful for reducing infection. Destroy severely diseased plants. Prune and destroy aerial galls.

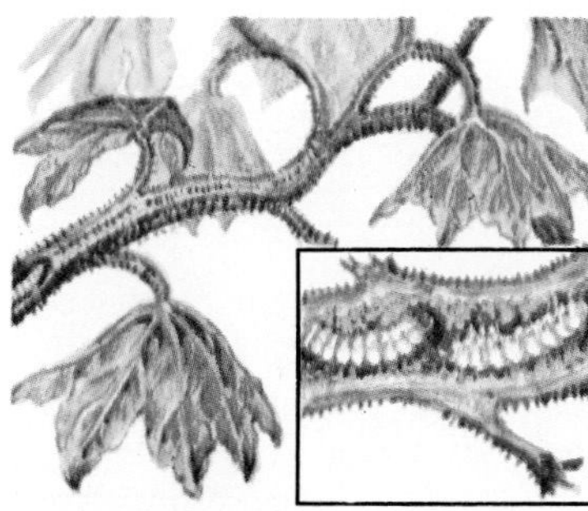

Squash vine borers (larvae)
Plants affected: All squashes, pumpkins, cucumbers, muskmelons.
Symptoms and signs: Wilting of plant; greenish excrement near holes at base of stems. Adult borers—metallic brown moths with red, black, and white markings—may be visible.
Danger period: Late spring and early summer.
Treatment: Spray or dust vines with carbaryl or methoxychlor.

Tree and shrub borers (larvae)
Plants affected: Fruit trees, especially cherries and peaches (see p. 532); also dogwoods, lilacs, rhododendrons.
Symptoms and signs: Stem and tree bases exude jellylike material. Shoots wilt. Branches or entire tree may die.
Danger period: Growing season.
Treatment: Primarily prevention. Spray bark and stems with lindane in late spring and early summer. Repeat 2 times more at 3-wk. intervals. Carbaryl or methoxychlor is also used. Destroy infected parts.

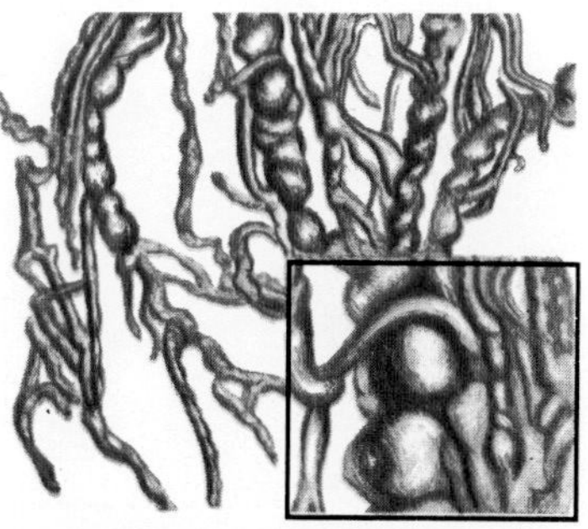

Root-knot nematodes, or root-knot eelworms
Plants affected: Mainly greenhouse plants, especially begonias, coleuses, cucumbers, cyclamens, tomatoes.
Symptoms and signs: Irregular, lumpy galls or swellings on roots. Foliage yellowed, plants stunted.
Danger period: Any time of year.
Treatment: Remove severely infested plants; destroy them to limit possible infection of healthy plants. Treat soil with metam-sodium before planting.

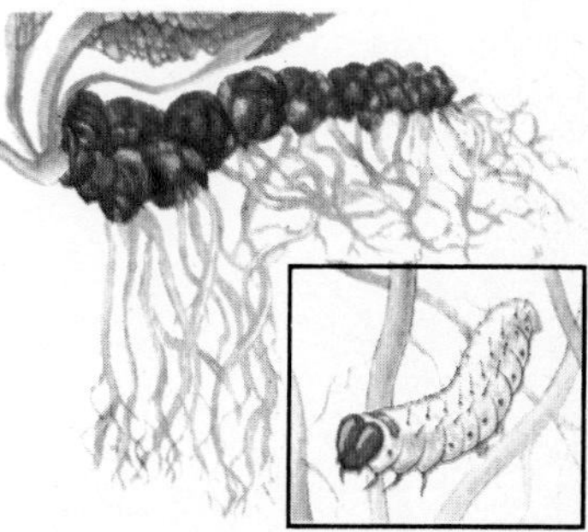

Ghost moth caterpillars
Plants affected: Various herbaceous perennials.
Symptoms and signs: Off-white caterpillars feeding on roots.
Danger period: Anytime.
Treatment: Good weed control and thorough cultivation reduce risk of ghost moth attack. Particularly susceptible plants can be protected by incorporating lindane dust in soil.

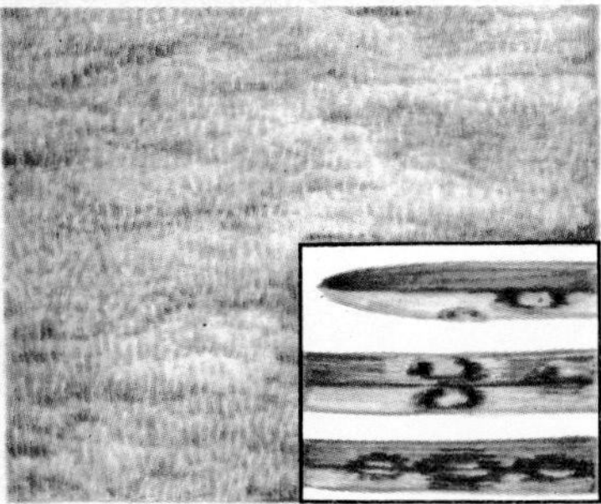

Leaf spot (helminthosporium)
Plants affected: Bent, blue, fescue, and rye grasses.
Symptoms and signs: Small, brown, irregularly oval spots generally appear in pairs on grass blades. Blades shrivel and bend over; stems, crowns, and roots may rot.
Danger period: Early summer to midfall.
Treatment: Use foliar spray of anilazine, chlorothalonil, cycloheximide, or mancozeb. Apply spray every 10–14 da. during period of infection. Avoid giving excess nitrogen in spring.

Pink snow mold
Plants affected: Nearly all types of grasses.
Symptoms and signs: Large dead patches of lawn covered with white fungus, which is most obvious in moist weather and after snow melts.
Danger period: Winter.
Treatment: Apply turf fungicide, such as anilazine, Benomyl, or thiram. Do not apply too much nitrogen fertilizer, especially after late summer.

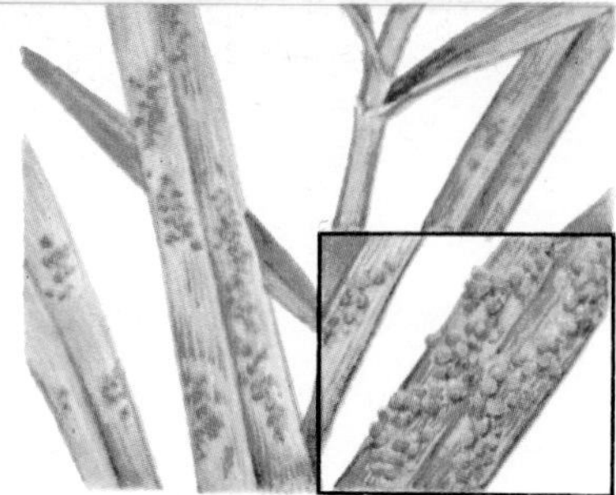

Bluegrass rust
Plants affected: Many kinds of grasses, but primarily 'Merion' Kentucky bluegrass.
Symptoms and signs: Yellow-orange or red-brown powdery spots on leaves.
Danger period: Late summer and early fall (until frost).
Treatment: Apply carbamate fungicide (maneb, thiram, or zineb). Repeat every 10–14 da. and after heavy rains or irrigation. Lawns well fed with nitrogen resist rust. Resistant grass varieties include 'Adelphi,' 'Fylking,' 'Pennstar,' 'Windsor.'

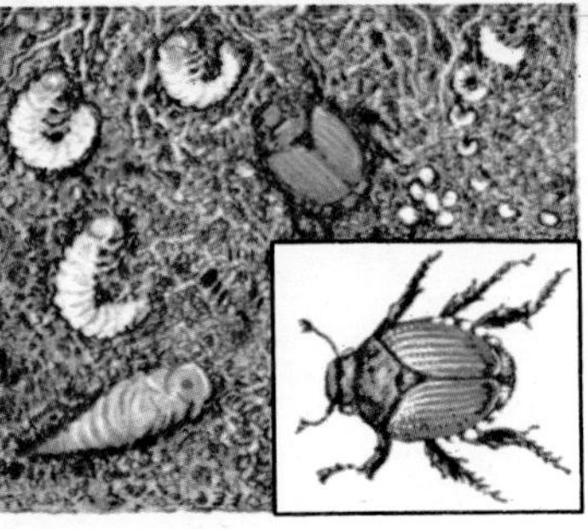

Beetle grubs (larvae)
Plants affected: Primarily roots of lawn grasses, but also roots of corn and many garden perennials.
Symptoms and signs: Turf shows irregular yellow and brown patches that vary in size. Turf can be rolled up like carpet because grubs have severed roots. In such conditions there may be 35 to 60 grubs per square foot of lawn. On other plants grubs chew off roots, causing wilting, drying, and ultimate death of plants. Adult Japanese beetle (see inset) lays eggs in ground that turn into grubs. These beetles do not feed on lawns but do damage many plants aboveground.
Danger period: Spring and fall for most beetles (Japanese, Oriental, Asiatic) and chafers (rose, masked European). For white grubs (May-June beetle larvae), midspring to late fall.
Treatment: Grub proofing is standard method: apply chlordane dust, granules, or spray to lawns in spring, summer, or fall, once every 5 yr. Chlorpyrifos or Diazinon may also be used but must be applied every year. Milky disease spore dust is effective against Japanese beetle grubs only. Apply 1 level tsp. of this dust in spots at 5-ft. intervals with 5 ft. between rows.

Red thread, or Corticium disease
Plants affected: Nearly all types of grasses.
Symptoms and signs: Dead patches of lawn; blades show red fungous growth.
Danger period: After rain in fall.
Treatment: Use turf fungicide, such as anilazine, Benomyl, or thiram, according to manufacturer's instructions. Spike to aerate soil, and apply lawn fertilizer in spring.

Fairy ring
Plants affected: Nearly all types of grasses.
Symptoms and signs: Large brown ring with dark green center on lawn. In late summer, fruiting bodies (mushrooms) appear in outer area of ring.
Danger period: Summer.
Treatment: Apply dolomitic limestone, instead of usual ground limestone, to entire lawn. Mow close to ground where brown ring appears, and apply copper or iron sulfate as drench.

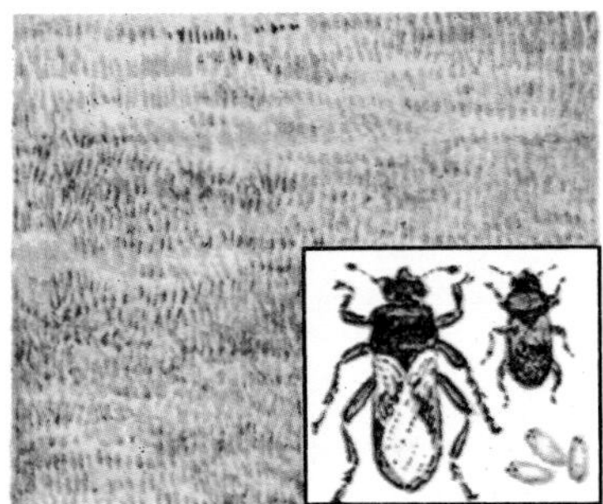

Chinch bugs
Plants affected: Lawn and golf-course turf.
Symptoms and signs: Turf is off-color, yellowing in irregular pattern. Tiny bugs can often be seen hopping.
Danger period: Warm, sunny weather from early summer to midfall.
Treatment: Water lawn first; then spray with ASP-51, carbaryl, chlorpyrifos, or Diazinon. Repeat several times during season to treat successive generations of bugs.

Pesticides and Fungicides for Use in the Garden

The main enemies of any plant are pests (especially insects) and diseases (especially fungi). Most of them can be controlled with pesticides and fungicides. All of these should be used with care.

The continual use of a particular pesticide can encourage the evolution of a resistant strain of the pest or may kill all the pest's natural predators, making it possible for a resistant strain of the pest to multiply.

Natural predators. Research workers are turning increasingly to biological methods of control, using natural parasites or predators to kill pests whenever possible. For example, Japanese beetles can often be controlled with bacteria (milky disease spore dust), which kill only the grubs (larvae) of this beetle.

Ladybugs (ladybird beetles) are natural predators, sold in bulk to be released in gardens to eat insects, such as aphids and mites. Egg cases of praying mantises are sold for placing in the garden. After hatching, the mantises can reduce the insect population—including, however, beneficial species like ladybugs.

Considerable progress is being made with another kind of biological control: synthetic sex attractants, which lure insects to their death. Until these are more readily available, however, alternative chemical controls are required.

The most sensible approach for the amateur gardener is to use approved chemical controls in appropriate situations, in appropriate amounts, and at appropriate times. For example, watch crops known to be susceptible to pests; apply a chemical only when you actually see the pest, and confine treatment to the infested plant and its closest neighbors. Always be sure to follow the manufacturer's instructions.

Terminology. Some of the pesticides and fungicides listed here are described as systemic. This means that the chemical is absorbed through the leaves, stem, or roots into a plant's sap, where it remains for some time, continuing to deter the pest or fungus that it is intended to combat. After using a systemic spray, follow the manufacturer's instructions relative to the time interval prior to harvest.

Chemicals vary in the length of time they remain toxic in soil or water. Those referred to as biodegradable last from a few weeks to a month; those relatively persistent, from one to two years. Persistent chemicals last many years and are gradually being phased out in the United States.

Chemical controls are available in various forms: as dusts, sprays, granules, and baits. Dusts are ready-to-use chemicals that are applied in a duster. Sprays are sold as wettable powders, flowable formulations, emulsifiable concentrates, or oils; each is to be mixed with water before it is applied in a sprayer. A wettable powder should not be used as a dust because it is too strong. In water it forms a suspension that requires frequent shaking to keep the powder from settling. Miscible (mixable) oils are designated by viscosity (rate of flow). A 60-second oil is lighter than a 70-second oil and is thus safer to use on plants.

Granular pesticides are made by combining a toxic substance with a carrier (granule), such as clay or vermiculite. Granular pesticides are applied with a spreader in the same way as lawn fertilizers.

Drenches are made from various spray formulations mixed with water. They are poured around the affected plant or soil area rather than sprayed.

Seed protectants are chemicals that are applied to seeds prior to planting to protect them from certain insects and diseases.

Baits contain a poisonous chemical plus a food substance that attracts certain pests (primarily slugs and snails). They are placed in containers or on the ground near the plants.

Controlling diseases. Fungicides are chemicals used to control fungous diseases. There are three major types available.

A protectant is a preventive substance applied before disease is present. It prevents spores of disease organisms from growing and keeps the plant free of disease until the chemical is washed off or broken down into ineffective substances.

In contrast, a fungistatic substance is applied to plants that are already diseased. As long as the material is active, it prevents further growth of the existing fungi.

Eradicants—chemicals that usually kill the disease organisms—are the third type of fungicide.

In addition to fungicides, antibiotics are sometimes used to kill fungi and bacteria, or to stop their growth. These substances are themselves products of fungi and bacteria.

Many multipurpose mixtures are sold for use in the home garden. Some are formulated for a specific crop or type of plant, such as roses. Such products usually contain an insecticide, an acaricide (mite killer), and a fungicide. When applied properly, they will control a broad range of pests and diseases. A specific chemical, on the other hand, will provide better control if only one kind of pest is known to be troublesome or if a pest or disease is especially difficult to control.

Applying chemicals. Pesticides and fungicides can be combined with other materials to improve their effectiveness. A spreader helps liquids to cover the surface of a leaf. A wetting agent improves contact between a liquid and the plant surface. (Both are particularly useful on waxy-leaved plants.) A sticker, which may also have spreading and wetting properties, causes a liquid or a dust to stay longer on a plant.

Spreaders, wetting agents, and stickers are all available commercially. However, liquid dishwashing detergent, used at the rate of 1 teaspoon per gallon of solution, can serve as a spreader or wetting agent.

There are chemical applicators for every need. Hose-end sprayers are good for lawn, shrub, and general garden use. A hand-pumped trombone sprayer will shoot a spray of liquid to the top of a 30-foot tree. Aerosol sprays are convenient to use on house plants or for occasional spot spraying outdoors. Dusters can have a rotary crank action or push-and-pull cylinders. Compression sprayers that require hand pumping to build pressure come in 1- to 3-gallon capacities; larger sizes are usually motor driven.

The chart that begins on page 636 lists many of the chemicals used in combating garden pests and diseases. In the left column, each substance is listed alphabetically according to its chemical name. The central column indicates the trade names of the chemical and the forms in which it is usually available. The right column indicates the organisms that the chemical is intended to control and, in some cases, provides instructions for its use.

WARNING

Chemical controls are poisonous and should be kept locked up. Never store a pest-control chemical in an unlabeled bottle or in one with a beverage label.

When mixing or applying chemicals, follow the manufacturer's instructions exactly. Most mercury and some arsenic compounds are generally not recommended; they are extremely toxic.

Symptoms of most chemical poisoning include abdominal pain and vomiting. Take an affected person to the nearest hospital immediately. If possible, bring the container or its label, which usually will indicate antidotes or other treatments. Also, check your telephone directory for poison-control centers.

Chemical	Trade names	Description
ANILAZINE	**Sprays:** Dyrene, Kemate	Fungicide used for wide range of turf and vegetable diseases.
ANTIBIOTICS	See Bacticin, chlortetracycline, cycloheximide, oxytetracycline, streptomycin	Antibiotics used to control bacterial diseases.
ASP–51	**Granules:** Aspon 4G **Sprays:** Aspon 6E, Aspon 25	Very effective and relatively safe insecticide to control chinch bugs on lawns.
BACILLUS THURINGIENSIS	**Dusts and Sprays:** Biotrol, Dipel, Thuricide	Biological control for bagworms, cankerworms, gypsy moth and tent caterpillars, loopers. Harmless to humans and animals.
BACTICIN (No common name yet assigned)	**Spray:** Bacticin	Antibiotic primarily used to control bacterial diseases, such as crown gall tumors, especially on cherry, peach, and plum trees.
BENOMYL	**Sprays:** Benlate, Tersan 1991	Fungicide with systemic properties. It is not taken in readily by woody plants; so it must be applied fairly frequently. Used as spray against rose black spot, tomato leaf mold, rusts, apple and pear scab, and cane spot and spur blight on raspberries. Also for gray mold and powdery mildew on ornamental plants, fruits, and vegetables.
BORDEAUX MIXTURE	**Dusts and Sprays:** Bordeaux mixture sold under various trade names	Fungicide mixture of copper sulfate and hydrated lime. This and other pesticides containing lime should not be mixed with current organic pesticides, such as carbaryl, Diazinon, malathion, methoxychlor. Bordeaux mixture should always be used alone. If mixed spray is required, use one of low-soluble coppers. Used for many different plant disorders. Harmful to fish.
CADMIUM SUCCINATE	**Spray:** Cadminate	Fungicide used on lawns for prevention and control of red thread and snow mold.
CALOMEL, or MERCUROUS CHLORIDE	**Dust and Spray:** Calomel	Fungicide used as dust to control clubroot of wallflowers and cabbages, and onion white rot. Spray to control some lawn diseases. Poisonous. Wear protective gloves when handling concentrate.
CAPTAFOL	**Spray:** Difolatan 4F	Fungicide for early and late blight (tomatoes), anthracnose, and many other foliage diseases.

Chemical	Trade names	Description
CAPTAN	**Dust and Spray:** Orthocide Captan	Fungicide to control rose black spot, leaf spot, apple and pear scab, Botrytis, or gray mold, on small fruits, etc. Used as drench to control damping-off and some other soil-borne diseases. Toxic to fish; can irritate human eyes, nose, mouth.
CARBARYL	**Dusts:** Hexavin, Ravyon **Spray:** Sevin	Insecticide to control caterpillars, flea beetles, weevils, and other pests. Do not use near honeybees or when fruit trees are in bloom. Also formulated as worm killer.
CHLORDANE	**Dusts, Granules, and Sprays:** Octachlor, Ortho-Klor, Synklor	Persistent insecticide that should be used only when there is no adequate alternative. Gives good control of ants, earthworms, lawn beetle grubs, and termites when used as spray, as soil drench, and in granular form.
CHLOROBENZILATE	**Sprays:** Acaraben, Akar	Acaricide to control mites.
CHLOROTHALONIL	**Sprays:** Bravo, Daconil 2787	Very safe broad-spectrum fungicide, especially for vegetables. Very effective for Botrytis, or gray mold.
CHLORPYRIFOS	**Granules and Sprays:** Dursban, Lorsban	Broad-spectrum insecticide for lawn pests, as well as for many ornamental-crop pests.
CHLORTETRACYCLINE	**Sprays:** Acronize, Aureomycin	Antibiotic to control bacterial diseases, such as fire blight.
COPPER HYDROXIDE	**Spray:** Kocide	Fungicide for anthracnose, bacterial spot of tomatoes, and blight.
COPPER SULFATE	**Dusts and Sprays:** Basicop, Fixed Copper, Tri-Basic Copper Sulfate	Fungicide that can be used as alternative to Bordeaux mixture. Toxic to livestock and fish.
CYCLOHEXIMIDE	**Sprays:** Acti-dione, Actispray	Specific antibiotic for powdery mildew fungus on lawns, ornamentals, and roses. Effective for soil treatment of pythium damping-off fungus.
DAZOMET	**Spray:** Mylone	Soil fumigant for wireworms, nematodes, and Armillaria root rot.
DIAZINON	**Dusts, Granules, and Sprays:** Gardentox, Sarolex, Spectracide	Relatively persistent insecticide to control aphids, leaf miners, mealybugs, plant bugs, scale insects, springtails, thrips, and two-spotted mites.
DICHLOFLUANID	**Dusts and Sprays:** Elvaron, Euparen	Fungicide used against peony wilt, rose black spot, tulip fire, downy mildew on cauliflower seedlings, Botrytis, or gray mold, on tomatoes and small fruits, and spur blight on raspberries.

Chemical	Trade names	Description
DICHLORAN, or DICLORAN, or DCNA	**Sprays:** Allisan, Botran	Specific fungicide for Botrytis, or gray mold, and storage diseases.
DICHLORVOS, or DDVP	**Fumigants:** No-Pest Strips, Vapona pressure fumigator	Insecticide that is available in impregnated resin strips for use as greenhouse fumigant to control aphids, small caterpillars, fungus gnats, thrips, two-spotted mites, and whiteflies.
DICOFOL	**Spray:** Kelthane	Acaricide to control two-spotted mites and other mites.
DIMETHOATE	**Sprays:** Cygon, DeFend, Rogor, Trimetion	Relatively nonpersistent systemic insecticide. Used as spray or soil drench against aphids, young caterpillars, leafhoppers, mealybugs, scale insects, and two-spotted mites.
DINOCAP	**Dusts and Sprays:** Arathane, Iscothane, Karathane, Mildex	Fungicide to control powdery mildew on ornamental plants, fruits, and vegetables. Dinocap also controls some mites. Toxic to fish; can irritate skin, eyes, nose. Some materials (so marked) are flammable.
DINOSEB	**Sprays:** DN-289, Elgetol	Insecticide and fungicide most commonly used as dormant spray on deciduous fruit and ornamental trees. Controls aphid eggs, plant-bug eggs, and various scales. Gives some control of mite eggs but not as good as miscible oils. Also has fungicidal value for tree cankers and winter stages of fungi.
DODINE	**Sprays:** Carpene, Curitan, Cyprex, Vondodine	Fungicide controlling fungous diseases of fruit—especially scab, cherry leaf spot, brown rot of peaches, apricots, and cherries, and peach leaf curl.
ENDOSULFAN	**Sprays:** Cyclodan, Thifor, Thiodan	Insecticide to control aphids, some mites, woody plant borers, and many other chewing and piercing-sucking insects.
FERBAM	**Sprays:** Fermate, Karbam	Fungicide for leaf disease, rose black spot, rusts, apple scab.
FOLPET	**Dusts and Sprays:** Folpan, Phaltan	Fungicide for many fruit, flower, vegetable, and tree diseases.
FORMALDEHYDE	**Drench:** Formalin 40% solution	General sterilant to control soil-borne fungi. Must not be used near growing plants. Unless otherwise specified, use outdoors at rate of 1 pt. per 6 gal. water, and apply 5 gal. per square yard. Can irritate skin, eyes, nose, and mouth.
IRON SULFATE	**Sprays:** Copperas, Ferrosul, Ferrous Sulfate	Can be used to control certain lawn diseases and undesirable ferns and mosses in lawns.

Chemical	Trade names	Description
LIME SULFUR	**Spray:** Lime sulfur	Used as fungicide to control peach leaf curl, scab on apples and fire thorns, cane spot on raspberries, powdery mildew on fruit. Also used as insecticide spray to control gall mites on maple trees. Do not use on sulfur-sensitive varieties. Wash fruits before use. When controlling insects and fungus, do not mix with organic pesticide, such as carbaryl, Diazinon, malathion, or methoxychlor.
LINDANE	**Dusts, Granules, Smoke bombs, and Sprays:** Gammex, Gammexane	Insecticide that is relatively persistent (especially in soil). Restricted in some states but still labeled for specific pests such as tree borers and bulb aphids, where no other control works.
MALATHION	**Dusts, Granules, and Sprays:** Cythion, Malathion	Very safe nonpersistent insecticide. Used as spray or dust as control for many different insects.
MANCOZEB	**Sprays:** Dithane M-45, Manzate 200	General carbamate fungicide protectant for garden and lawn diseases.
MANEB	**Sprays:** Dithane M-22, Manzate D, Vancide	Carbamate fungicide to control black spot and rust on roses, tulip fire, celery leaf spot, potato and tomato blight, and tomato leaf mold.
MERCURIAL TURF FUNGICIDE	**Spray:** Semesan	Fungicide to control lawn and turf diseases. It is highly poisonous and must be used with care.
METALDEHYDE	**Baits:** Bug-Geta, Slug Kill, Snarol pellets **Spray:** Slugit Liquid	Used only as slug and snail killer, either in spray form or in specially formulated poison baits.
METAM-SODIUM, or METHAM	**Fumigants:** Sistan, Vapam	Soil fumigant. Excellent for control of nematodes, soil-borne diseases, symphilids, and some weed seeds. Apply to soil before lawn or crop is planted; sprinkle water over area as seal after fumigating.
METHIOCARB	**Bait, Dust, and Spray:** Mesurol	Broad-spectrum carbamate insecticide for many insects and mites on fruits, ornamentals, and vegetables. Controls slugs and snails. Toxic to bees; do not spray when blooming.
METHOXYCHLOR	**Aerosols, Dusts, and Sprays:** Marlate, Pratts Methoxychlor, Prentiss Methoxychlor, Alfatox (mixture with Diazinon)	Relatively persistent insecticide with low mammalian toxicity—good substitute for DDT. Used for many leaf chewers on shade and fruit trees.
MEXACARBATE	**Spray:** Zectran	Pesticide to control slugs and snails.

Chemical	Trade names	Description
MILKY DISEASE SPORE DUST	**Dusts:** Doom, Japidemic	Microbial insecticide containing spores of *Bacillus popilliae* mixed with talc. Specifically for grubs of Japanese beetle—to be applied to soil, where grubs ingest it and are killed. Dead grubs release more spores. May take several years to become completely effective but then remains so indefinitely.
NICOTINE	**Fumigants:** Nico-Fume, Plant Products pressure fumigator **Spray:** Black Leaf 40	Nonpersistent but poisonous insecticide, especially as spray concentrate. Used as greenhouse fumigant to control aphids, leafhoppers, plant bugs, and thrips.
OIL EMULSIONS and MISCIBLE OILS	**Sprays:** Gulf 60-sec. spray oil, Pratts 6N spray oil, Sunoco "60" sec. spray oil, Volck "60" sec. miscible oil (some also available as 70-sec. oils)	Sixty-and 70-sec. miscible spray oils and oil emulsions are insecticides used as dormant sprays to control eggs of mites, tent caterpillars, gypsy moths, and other insects. Apply as dormant spray before buds break on deciduous trees and shrubs. Temperature should be above 45° F but not over 70° F. Use as spray to control mealybugs, scale insects, and two-spotted mites on greenhouse and house plants. Reduce application rate in summer and indoors; see directions on label.
OXYDEMETON-METHYL	**Spray:** Metasystox-R	Systemic insecticide that is poisonous. Controls aphids, leafhoppers, two-spotted mites, and many other insect pests.
OXYTETRA-CYCLINE	**Sprays:** Biostat, Terramycin	Antibiotic to control bacterial diseases, such as fire blight.
PROPOXUR	**Dust and Spray:** Baygon	Insecticide to control aphids, lawn insects, two-spotted mites, and whiteflies.
PYRETHRUM	**Aerosol:** Pratts House Plant Bomb **Sprays:** Pratts Red Arrow Spray, Prentiss Pyrethrum Powder	Very safe nonpersistent insecticide. Used as spray or aerosol against aphids, small caterpillars, and whiteflies.
QUINTOZENE, or PCNB	**Dips, Dusts, and Sprays:** Avicol, Terraclor	Fungicide used to control some bulb and corm diseases. Spray to control some lawn diseases.
RESMETHRIN	**Aerosols and Sprays:** Chryson, Synthrin	Safe nonpersistent insecticide. Used against aphids, small caterpillars, whiteflies, and other pests.
ROTENONE	**Dust and Spray:** Usually sold as rotenone dust or spray	Safe nonpersistent insecticide. Used as dust or spray against aphids, small caterpillars, flea beetles, raspberry beetles, thrips, and two-spotted mites. Toxic to fish.
STREPTOMYCIN	**Sprays:** Agrimycin, Agri-Strep, Phytomycin (mixture with oxytetracycline)	Antibiotic fungicide for control of bacterial diseases of plants, fire blight and other blights, bacterial cankers, leaf spots.
SULFUR	**Dusts and Sprays:** Available from many manufacturers	Fungicide to control apple scab and powdery mildews on trees and small fruits but should not be used on sulfur-sensitive varieties. Also controls powdery mildews on many ornamental plants and cucumbers.
TECNAZENE, or TCNB	**Fumigant:** Fusarex	Used as greenhouse fumigant alone to control gray mold on lettuce, tomatoes, and ornamentals. Used in combination with lindane to give additional control of insect pests.
TERRAZOLE	**Spray:** Truban	Fungicide effective for soil treatment against pythium damping-off fungus of seedlings. Can be used as preplant treatment or after germination directly on plants.
TETRADIFON	**Smoke bomb and Spray:** Tedion	Acaricide to control mites.
THIOPHANATE-METHYL	**Sprays:** Cercobin-M, Topsin-M	Fungicide with systemic properties. Controls same diseases as Benomyl.
THIRAM	**Sprays:** Arasan (various formulations according to use; check label), Spotrete, Tersan 75 **Bait and Spray:** Thiram 42-S	Carbamate fungicide used against rusts on ornamental plants; downy mildew on lettuce; pear scab; cane spot and spur blight on raspberries; Botrytis, or gray mold, on ornamentals, fruits, and vegetables; lawn diseases. Also used as seed protectant and animal repellent. Wash fruits before use. Can irritate skin, eyes, nose, and throat.
TRICHLORFON	**Sprays:** Dipterex, Dylox, Neguvon, Tugon	Nonpersistent insecticide. Available as spray against armyworms, caterpillars, cutworms, earwigs, leaf miners, maggots, pine tip moths, plant bugs, and webworms.
WOUND-SEALING PAINT	**Aerosols and Paints:** Pratts Pruning Bomb, Ortho Chevron Tree Wound Paint	Forms protective seal against diseases, pests, and frost on cut surfaces of wood after pruning or injury.
ZINEB	**Dusts and Sprays:** Dithane Z-78, Parzate C, Zineb	Carbamate fungicide to control wide range of diseases on ornamental plants, fruits, and vegetables.
ZIRAM	**Sprays:** Vancide, Z-C Spray, Zerlate, Zitox	Very effective carbamate fungicide for blights of fruits, vegetables, flowers, trees, and shrubs; leaf spots; rusts. Use with caution on roses.

Weeds

Grasslike Leaves

The illustrations in this section show some of the commonest weeds that infest flower beds and lawns.

To help you identify the weeds in your garden, the illustrations are arranged according to the most readily identifiable characteristics: leaf type and habit of growth.

For each weed the common and botanical names are given. The captions indicate whether the weed is an annual or a perennial and how it reproduces. Recommended controls are also included; look up the chemicals and trade names in the chart on page 648.

Color illustrations of some weeds are accompanied by black and white line drawings that show the weeds at their seedling stage. Recognizing a weed at a young stage will help you deal with it as early as possible. If no such drawing is included, this indicates that the seedling has leaves that are similar in general outline to those of the mature plant.

Yellow foxtail (*Setaria glauca*)
Annual. Common in gardens. Spreads by seeds. Control: cultivation or DCPA preemergence.

Wild garlic and wild onion
(*Allium vineale* and *A. canadense*)
Perennial. Spreads by bulbs, bulblets, and seeds. Control: in lawns, 2,4–D spray or 2,4–D-impregnated wax bar.

Bermuda grass (*Cynodon dactylon*)
Perennial. Spreads by seeds and creeping rootstocks. Control: in lawns, spot treatments of dalapon.

Annual bluegrass (*Poa annua*)
Annual or winter annual. Spreads by seeds. Control: preemergence with bensulide; collect seed heads in grass catcher while mowing.

Large crabgrass and smooth crabgrass
(*Digitaria sanguinalis* and *D. ischaemum*)
Annual. Spreads by seeds. Control: in lawns, AMA, DSMA, or MSMA postemergence; elsewhere, bensulide, DCPA, or siduron preemergence.

Goose grass (*Eleusine indica*)
Annual. Often confused with crabgrass. Spreads by seeds. Control: bensulide or DCPA just before emergence.

Quack grass (*Agropyron repens*)
Perennial. Spreads mainly by portions of rhizome. Control: same treatment as for Johnson grass (p. 640).

Grasslike Leaves (continued)

Johnson grass (*Sorghum halepense*)
Perennial. Spreads by seeds and rootstocks. Control: in gardens, apply dalapon and spade 2 wk. later; in lawns, spot treatments of dalapon.

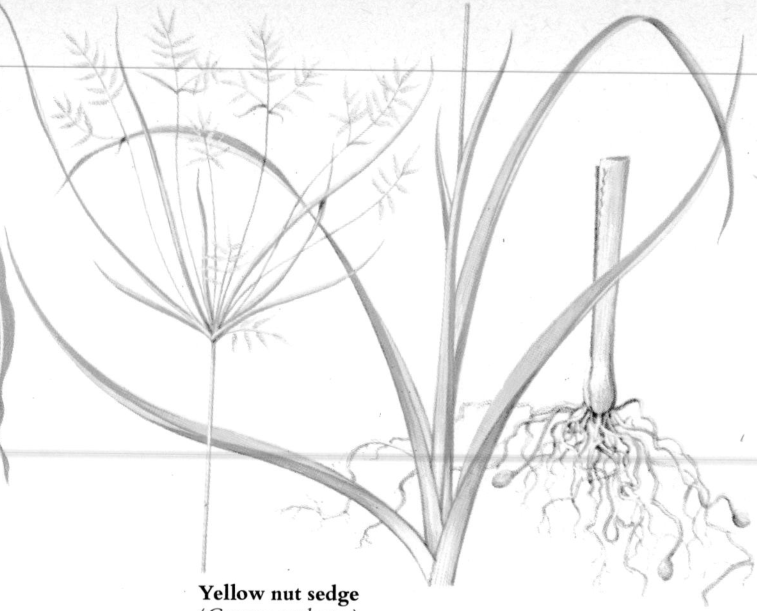

Yellow nut sedge
(*Cyperus esculentus*)
Perennial. Spreads by seeds and nutletlike tubers. Control: in gardens, EPTC added to soil; in lawns, DSMA postemergence.

Common reed
(*Phragmites australis,* or *P. communis*)
Perennial. Found in wet areas. Spreads by seeds and pieces of rhizome. Control: dalapon spray in late spring.

Compound Leaves

Bracken
(*Pteridium aquilinum*)
Perennial. Spreads by spores and rootstocks. Control: Dicamba spray before fronds unfold.

Creeping buttercup
(*Ranunculus repens*)
Perennial. Found in lawns. Spreads by seeds and creeping stems.
Control: 2,4–D plus Dicamba.

Carpetweed
(*Mollugo verticillata*)
Annual. Spreads by seeds. Control: in gardens, diphenamid preemergence; in lawns, Dicamba postemergence.

White clover
(*Trifolium repens*)
Perennial. Spreads by seeds and creeping stems. Control: use mecoprop or Silvex postemergence; feed lawn with nitrogen.

Goutweed
(*Aegopodium podograria*)
Perennial. Spreads by sections of rhizome. Control: repeated treatments of amitrole or 2,4–D plus Silvex.

Pineapple weed
(*Matricaria matricarioides*)
Annual. Spreads by seeds. Control: in lawns, mecoprop; around trees and shrubs, dichlobenil.

Poison ivy
(*Rhus radicans*)
Perennial woody vine. Spreads by seeds and creeping rootstocks. Poisonous. Control: spray foliage with amitrole.

Common ragweed
(*Ambrosia artemisiifolia*)
Annual. Spreads by seeds. Control: in gardens, cultivation; in noncrop areas, 2,4–D.

Common yellow wood sorrel
(*Oxalis stricta*)
Perennial. Spreads by seeds. Control: in lawns, DSMA plus wetting agent, MSMA, or 2,4–D plus Silvex.

Common yarrow
(*Achillea millefolium*)
Perennial. Spreads by seeds and rootstocks. Control: in lawns, 2,4–D.

Field bindweed
(*Convolvulus arvensis*)
Perennial. Spreads by seeds and deep, rootlike rhizomes. Control: spot treatments of 2,4–D amine.

Common chickweed
(*Stellaria media*)
Annual. Spreads by seeds. Control: in lawns, mecoprop or Silvex after weeds have emerged in fall or early spring.

Mouse-ear chickweed
(*Cerastium vulgatum*)
Perennial. Spreads by seeds. Control: Dicamba or repeated applications of mecoprop.

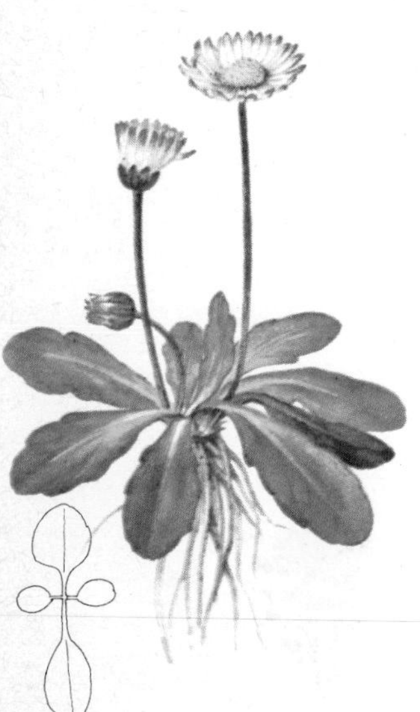

English daisy
(*Bellis perennis*)
Perennial. Spreads by seeds. Control: Dicamba, 2,4–D, or 2,4–D plus mecoprop.

Dandelion
(*Taraxacum officinale*)
Perennial. Spreads by windblown seeds and divisions of deep, fleshy taproot. Control: 2,4–D.

Heal-all
(*Prunella vulgaris*)
Perennial. Spreads by seeds and rootstocks. Control: mecoprop.

Henbit
(*Lamium amplexicaule*)
Annual or biennial. Spreads by seeds and rooting stems. Control: Simazine.

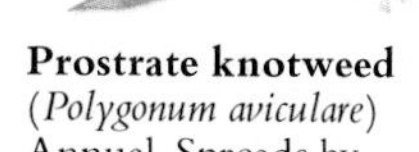

Ground ivy
(*Glechoma hederacea*)
Perennial. Spreads by seeds and creeping stems. Flourishes in damp, shaded areas with rich soil; found in lawns. Control: use 2,4–D plus Dicamba or mecoprop.

Prostrate knotweed
(*Polygonum aviculare*)
Annual. Spreads by seeds. Control: Dicamba or mecoprop.

Liverwort
(several species)
Perennial. Spreads by spores. Control: mulch borders; spray with thiram; or remove weeds by hand.

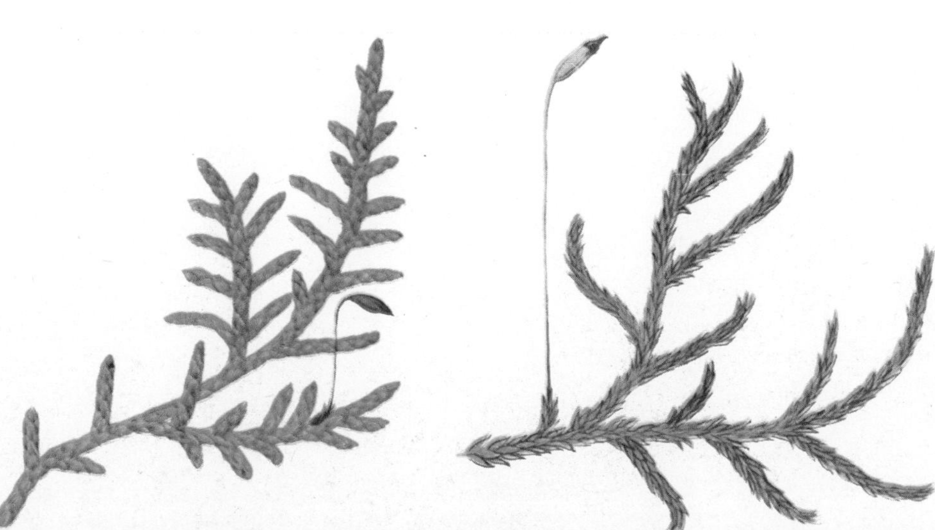

Moss on lawns
(several species)
Perennial. Appearance on lawn usually indicates poor drainage, low fertility, or excessive soil acidity. Spreads by spores. Control: improve drainage, fertilize regularly, and add lime.

Bird's-eye pearlwort
(*Sagina procumbens*)
Perennial. Common in lawns and golf greens. Spreads by seeds. Control: mecoprop; then fertilizer in spring. Do not mow closely.

Broad-leaved plantain
(*Plantago major*)
Perennial. Found in lawns, roadsides, and uncultivated areas. Spreads by seeds. Control: 2,4–D.

Buckhorn plantain
(*Plantago lanceolata*)
Perennial. Also called narrow-leaved plantain. Spreads by seeds. Control: 2,4–D.

> **Common purslane**
(*Portulaca oleracea*)
Annual. Spreads by seeds. Control: in gardens, DCPA or trifluralin preemergence; in lawns, 2,4–D.

Shepherd's purse
(*Capsella bursa-pastoris*)
Annual. Spreads by seeds. Control: in gardens, cultivation; in lawns, 2,4–D.

Red sorrel
(*Rumex acetosella*)
Perennial. Spreads by seeds and creeping roots. Control: 2,4–D plus Dicamba as postemergence spray; feed and add lime.

Creeping speedwell
(*Veronica filiformis*)
Perennial. Spreads by creeping stems. Control: DCPA spray, to be used for this species of *Veronica* only. Control is difficult.

Spotted spurge
(*Euphorbia maculata*)
Annual. Found in lawns, gardens, cultivated fields, and waste places. Spreads by seeds. Control: Dicamba or 2,4–D.

Curled dock
(*Rumex crispus*)
Perennial. Spreads by seeds.
Control: in lawns, spot treatments of 2,4–D; in noncrop areas, amitrole.

Small-flowered galinsoga
(*Galinsoga parviflora*)
Annual. Common in fields and gardens. Spreads by seeds. Control: in fields, Simazine; in gardens, cultivation.

Common groundsel
(*Senecio vulgaris*)
Annual. Spreads by seeds. Control: in gardens, cultivation; in landscaped areas, dichlobenil.

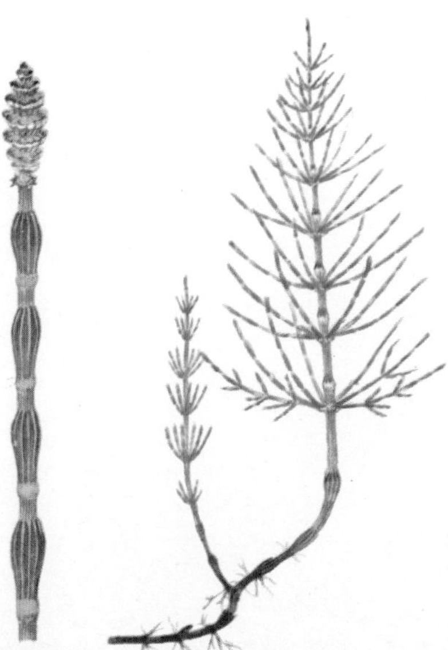

Field horsetail
(*Equisetum arvense*)
Perennial. Spreads by spores and rhizomes. Control: in landscaped areas, dichlobenil; in lawns, spot treatments of 2,4–D.

Japanese knotweed
(*Polygonum cuspidatum*)
Perennial. Spreads by seeds and rhizomes. Control: in noncrop areas, Dicamba; elsewhere, cut back.

Lady's thumb
(*Polygonum persicaria*)
Annual. Spreads by seeds. Control: in gardens, DCPA or diphenamid; in lawns, 2,4–D.

Common lamb's-quarters
(*Chenopodium album*)
Annual. Spreads by seeds. Control: in gardens, DCPA, EPTC, or trifluralin; in lawns, 2,4–D.

Simple Leaves—Upright Plants More Than 6 Inches Tall (continued)

Virginia pepperweed
(*Lepidium virginicum*)
Annual or biennial. Common in fields and in roadsides. Spreads by seeds. Control: in lawns, 2,4–D plus Dicamba.

Redroot pigweed
(*Amaranthus retroflexus*)
Annual. Spreads by seeds. Control: in gardens, diphenamid or other herbicide used preemergence.

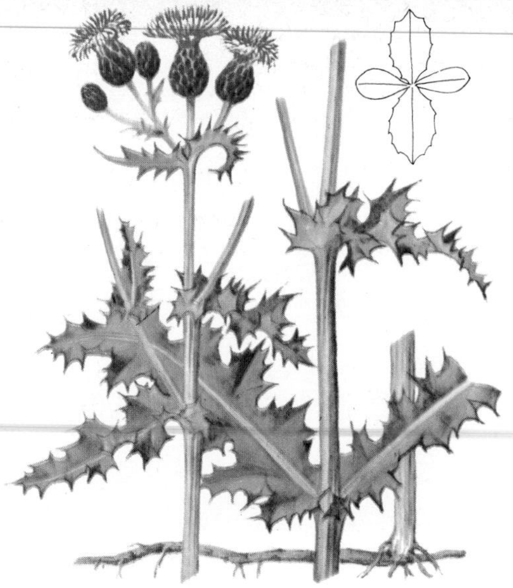

Canada thistle
(*Cirsium arvense*)
Perennial. Spreads by seeds and creeping rootstocks. Control: spot treatments of 2,4–D; repeat if necessary.

Annual sow thistle
(*Sonchus oleraceus*)
Annual. Spreads by seeds. Control: in landscaped areas, dichlobenil; in lawns, 2,4–D.

Waterweeds

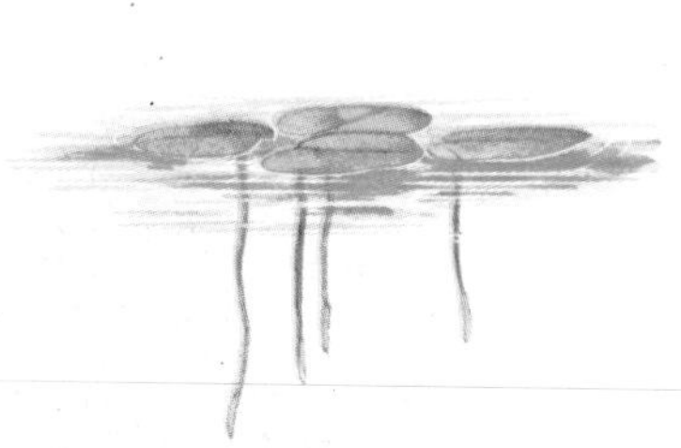

Duckweed (*Lemna minor*)
Floating plants with minute leaves $\frac{1}{16}$–$\frac{3}{16}$ in. across. Multiplies rapidly from new plants on leaf edges or from waterborne seeds. Can be a pest. Control: flush pond; scoop off surface; or use 2,4–D in granular form.

Eurasian water milfoil
(*Myriophyllum spicatum*)
Perennial. Weed is submerged. Spreads by seeds and rooting stems. Control: endothall pellets or 2,4–D in granular form.

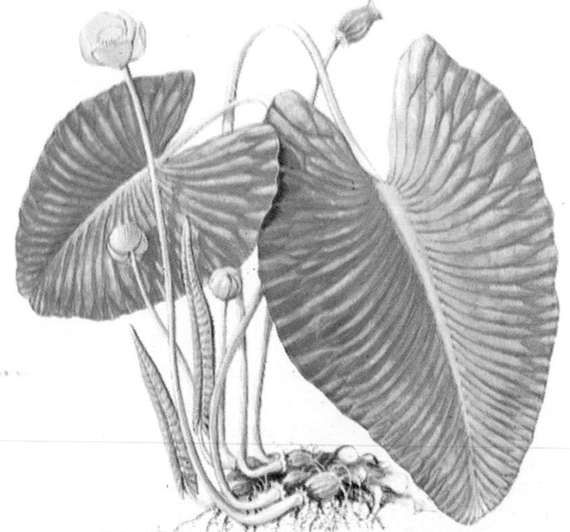

Spatterdock
(*Nuphar luteum* and *N. advena*)
Perennial. Spreads by creeping rhizomes. Control: use 2,4–D in granular form, dichlobenil, or Silvex plus endothall.

Types of Weeds and Their Control

Any plant growing where it is unwanted—a petunia in a cabbage patch, a lettuce in a flower border, a nasturtium in an onion bed—can be considered a weed. In practice, however, the term "weed" is used for any plant that grows rapidly, thrives in a wide range of conditions and soils, competes successfully with surrounding plants, and reproduces itself with ease.

Although weeds often have colorful flowers and can be attractive in a field or on vacant land, they are usually unsightly in a garden. But there are several more practical reasons for removing them from the garden.

Weeds compete with cultivated plants for water, nutrients, and light—to the disadvantage of the cultivated plants. For example, weeds check the early growth of such vegetables as onions and carrots, both of which are extremely slow to germinate and to develop.

Weeds can also be hosts to insects and diseases that attack garden or greenhouse plants. For example, the shepherd's purse harbors flea beetles and cabbage-root flies, both of which infest many types of green vegetables. Weeds can carry over such pests from season to season, thus causing the infestation of any new crops planted nearby.

Two Types of Weeds: Annuals and Perennials

Annuals complete their cycle of growth—from seeds to mature, seed-producing plants—within a few months; then they die. Examples include the prostrate knotweed, common ragweed, goose grass, and common chickweed. Some weeds, such as the henbit, can be either annual or biennial.

Perennial weeds can be herbaceous or woody. Herbaceous weeds are soft-stemmed plants that store food in fleshy roots, tubers, or bulbs, survive the winter in a dormant condition, and resume growth the following spring. These plants usually have deep root systems, which make them difficult to control. Examples are the goutweed, curled dock, and quack grass.

Woody perennial weeds, such as poison ivy, store most of their food in woody stems. Since they do not have extensive root systems, they are comparatively easy to control. For poison ivy, a weed killer, such as amitrole, sprayed on the foliage will usually be effective. However, dead plants remain toxic for about a year.

Keeping Down Weeds by Cultural Methods

Although modern weed killers can control most garden weeds, these powerful chemicals can also harm valuable ornamental plants nearby. A few minutes' work with a hoe or a rake on a dry day, repeated as often as new weeds appear, is a safer way of dealing with weeds growing near ornamentals.

When first cultivating a weedy area, remove as many roots or rhizomes of perennial weeds as possible. Very weedy sites not immediately required for crops can be sown with grass. Close mowing of the grass for two consecutive growing seasons will usually eliminate most perennial weeds; then the area can be planted.

Weed killers will provide only temporary improvement of a weed-infested lawn. Feeding and topdressing are also required to develop the vigor of the grass and to reduce the chance that weeds will reappear. Some weeds, such as red sorrel, can be discouraged from growing in lawns by spreading lime on the soil; this reduces the acidity on which the weed thrives.

How to Control Weeds With Chemicals

Although a weed killer is usually sold under a trade name, the chemical name of the active ingredient must be listed on the label. The method of application, plants on which it can be used safely, and weeds that it can control are also printed on the label.

Weed killers act in various ways. A selective weed killer will affect some kinds of plants but not others—for instance, 2,4-D will kill broad-leaved plants in a lawn. Nonselective chemicals, such as paraquat, kill all or nearly all plants with which they come in contact.

A systemic weed killer, such as 2,4-D, is absorbed by the leaves, transmitted to other parts of the plant, and will eventually kill the entire plant. Nonsystemic chemicals kill by direct contact.

Other terms denote the stage of plant growth at which a given weed killer is effective. Preemergence chemicals, such as DCPA, prevent the emergence of germinating weed seeds for four to six weeks; however, when used at the recommended strength, they will not usually kill established weeds. Preemergence weed killers are safe to use around many desirable plants.

Postemergence weed killers—the most widely used type—are applied directly to the foliage of weeds. These chemicals may be selective or nonselective, and they may kill systemically or by direct contact (occasionally by both means).

Residual weed killers persist in the soil. They should only be used for longtime control and where crops will not be planted until the residue has become ineffective.

Weed killers are sold in several forms. Granules are applied dry with a spreader. The wettable powders, emulsifiable concentrates, soluble powders, and water-soluble concentrates are all mixed with water and applied with a sprayer.

Before buying a weed killer, consult the chart on the next page and the illustrations of weeds, which begin on page 639. This will ensure that you are using the appropriate chemical.

Clearing a neglected area. A wide-spectrum killer, such as amitrole with Simazine, can be used to clear a weed-infested area that has no garden plants or desirable tree or shrub roots.

After the weeds are killed, destroy all dead material. (Never burn poison ivy; the poison can be carried in the smoke.) Then use a residual control to keep the site free of weeds. Weeds that establish themselves between treatments can be killed with a paraquat solution.

WARNING

Weed killers are poisonous. They should always be kept locked up out of children's reach. Never store them in unlabeled containers or ones that appear to hold other substances.

When mixing and applying, follow the manufacturer's instructions exactly. Most mercury and some arsenic compounds are extremely toxic, and their use is generally not recommended.

Symptoms of weed-killer poisoning may include abdominal pain and vomiting. Take the affected person to the nearest hospital immediately. If possible, give the hospital the name of the weed killer; bring along the container or its label, which usually will indicate antidotes and treatment. Consult your telephone directory for poison-control centers.

Weed Killers for Various Situations

Situation	Type of weed	Chemical	Some trade names	Remarks
Bulbs in borders	Established annuals and perennials	paraquat	Paraquat	Leaves no soil residue but is toxic; so handle carefully. Apply when bulb foliage is dead.
	Germinating weeds	DCPA	Dacthal	Cannot reseed grass for 2 mo.
Fruit	Established annuals	paraquat	Paraquat	See paraquat above.
	Germinating weeds, established annuals and perennials	dichlobenil	Casoron	Check label for time between treatment and harvest.
	Grassy weeds	dalapon	Basfapon B, Dowpon	See label for special restrictions.
Garden pools	Green algae	copper-triethanolamine complex	A&V-70, Algaetrol, Cutrine-Plus	Water is safe for fish, swimming, or irrigation.
	Weeds	endothall	Aquathol, Endothal	Handle with care. Follow label directions.
Herbaceous borders and bedding plants	Germinating weeds	DCPA	Dacthal	See DCPA above.
		diphenamid	Dymid, Enide	Apply to moist, weed-free soil surface as spray or granules; safe on foliage.
		trifluralin	Treflan	Incorporate after application to weed-free soil.
Lawn renovation	Most weeds	cacodylic acid	Silvisar 510	Spray area. Reseed when plants die.
		paraquat	Paraquat	See paraquat above.
Lawns, established	Clover, chickweed, pearlwort, etc.	Dicamba	Banvel D	Use only very low rates over tree roots.
		mecoprop	Chipco Turf Herbicide MCPP	Do not use on St. Augustine grass.
		Silvex	Weedone; 2, 4, 5-TP	Below 85° F, apply on moist soil.
	Dandelion, plantain, etc.	2, 4-D	Dacamine, Weedone	Avoid contact with desirable nongrassy plants.
	Both groups above: clover, chickweed, pearlwort, etc.; and dandelion, plantain, etc.	2, 4-D + Dicamba	Super D Weedone	Use at lower rates for southern grasses.
		2, 4-D + Dicamba + Silvex	Weedone 3D	Do not use at temperatures over 85° F; keep away from tree roots.
		2, 4-D + mecoprop	Cleary MCPP; 2, 4-D	Safe on most grasses.
		2, 4-D + Silvex	Weed-B-Gon	Do not use on St. Augustine grass or dichondra.
	Crabgrass postemergence	AMA DSMA MSMA	Super Crab-E-Rad Ansar 8100, Methar Ansar 529, Daconate 6	Apply 3 times 5-15 da. apart; see label for directions on specific formulations. Do not use on St. Augustine or centipede grass.
	Crabgrass preemergence	benefin	Balan	Treat before or as crabgrass germinates. Do not reseed for 45 da.
		bensulide	Betasan	Treat before germination; do not reseed for 4 mo.
		DCPA	Dacthal 2.5 or 5G or 75W	Treat before crabgrass germinates.
		siduron	Tupersan	Treat as for benefin; can sow bluegrass immediately.
	Speedwell (*Veronica filiformis*)	DCPA	Dacthal	Cannot reseed grass for 2 mo.
	Wild onion	2, 4-D on wax bar	Ortho Weed Bar	Will need repeat treatment.
Lawns, newly seeded	Broad-leaved weeds	bromoxynil	Brominal	Avoid contact with desirable nongrassy plants.
	Crabgrass	siduron	Tupersan	See siduron above.
Paths	All types, including perennials	amitrole + Simazine	Amizine	Use only when not planting anything for a year.
	Annuals and germinating weeds	paraquat	Paraquat	See paraquat above.
	Germinating weeds, moss	Simazine	Princep	Residual action depends upon rate; check label.
Tree and shrub borders	Before seedling weeds germinate	DCPA	Dacthal	Apply to moist, weed-free soil surface.
		EPTC	Eptam	Rake into soil immediately after applying.
	Established annuals, perennials	paraquat	Paraquat	Keep off foliage of desirable plants; no soil residue.
	Seedling annuals and established perennials	dichlobenil	Casoron	Apply in very late fall or early spring only; do not use near hemlock and fir.
Uncultivated areas, waste ground	All types: grassy and woody weeds, and others	amitrole + Simazine	Amizine	Do not plant anything for a year.
	Grassy weeds	dalapon	Basfapon B, Dowpon	Persists for 3 mo.
	Woody weeds, poison ivy, suckers from old tree stumps	amitrole	Amizol, Cytrol	Do not use where food crops are to be grown.
		2, 4-D + Silvex	Clover Kill	Persists about 1 mo.
Vegetables	Germinating weeds	DCPA	Dacthal	Apply to moist, weed-free soil surface 3-5 da. after transplanting. Check state recommendations.

Index

Page numbers in **boldface** type indicate main references. All plants are listed by botanical name in *italic* type; common names are in roman type.

A

B

Boldface type indicates main references.

Boldface type indicates main references.

Boldface type indicates main references.

F

Boldface type indicates main references.

G

H

Boldface type indicates main references.

I

Boldface type indicates main references.

M

N

Boldface type indicates main references.

Boldface type indicates main references.

Q

R

Boldface type indicates main references.

S

Boldface type indicates main references.

T

U

V

Boldface type indicates main references.

Credits

Front cover David Trooper. **14** Gottscho-Schleisner, Inc. **15** *left* Guy Burgess; *remainder* Gottlieb Hampfler. **16** Hedrich-Blessing. **17** *left* Architect: Frederich Hobbs, A.I.A./Photo by Hedrich-Blessing; *right* Kent Oppenheimer. **18** Hedrich-Blessing. **19** *left* Gottlieb Hampfler; *remainder* Guy Burgess. **20** Gottscho-Schleisner, Inc. **21** *left* Guy Burgess; *top right* Landscape Architect: Theodore Bruckman/Photo by Hedrich-Blessing; *bottom right* Kent Oppenheimer. **22** *left* Gottscho-Schleisner, Inc.; *right* Kent Oppenheimer. **23** *left* Guy Burgess; *right* Gottlieb Hampfler. **24** *top* Jerry D. Jacka; *bottom* Gottscho-Schleisner, Inc. **25** *left* Shostal Associates; *right* Guy Burgess. **26** Gottlieb Hampfler. **27** *left* Gottlieb Hampfler; *right* Ray Atkeson. **28** *left* Gottlieb Hampfler; *remainder* Gottscho-Schleisner, Inc. **29** *left* Guy Burgess; *remainder* Gottlieb Hampfler. **30** *left and bottom right* Guy Burgess; *remainder* Gottlieb Hampfler. **31** *left* Gottscho-Schleisner, Inc.; *right* Gottlieb Hampfler. **526** *bottom left* Copyright © 1953 by The Regents of the University of California; reprinted by permission of the University of California Press. **Back cover** Gottlieb Hampfler.